ACKNOWLEDGEMENT OF COUNTRY

Hardie Grant acknowledges First Nations People as the Traditional Owners and Custodians of the land, waters and sky. We pay our respects to the Wurundjeri People of the Kulin Nation and the Gadigal People of the Eora Nation, upon whose Country we work, and to their Elders past and present. We also extend that respect to all Aboriginal and Torres Strait Islander People across the continent.

The first edition of *Explore Australia* was published in 1980 as a comprehensive guide for those who wanted to discover the best of Australia by car. Since then, the face of Australia has changed in some significant and smaller ways. Our population has boomed by 11 million; 20 UNESCO World Heritage Sites have been declared; Parliament House was constructed in Canberra; hundreds of national parks have been created and are now protected by state and territory governments; countless bushfires, floods, hurricanes and natural disasters have permanently changed the landscape and devastated communities; the vast network of roads and highways have expanded to further connect the edges and expanses of our nation; and we've witnessed the closing of our borders – international and domestic – as we fight our way through a global pandemic.

Still, this all pales in comparison to the 60,000+ years of First Nations history. We are home to the oldest continuous culture on Earth, and sovereignty has never been ceded. We recognise and acknowledge the ways in which the information and language we present in this book has and continues to prioritise European and colonial history, and with each edition we strive to include more information on First Nations histories and cultures.

As the nation evolves, so too does *Explore Australia*, but at its heart it remains a book about sharing the open road, of unexpected detours, of surprising destinations, of seeing the old with fresh eyes and truly appreciating the beauty of our backyard.

It's a vast land out there, and there's no better time to start exploring. We'll see you on the road!

– The *Explore Australia* team

Disclaimers

While every endeavour has been made to ensure information in this new edition was up to date before printing, opening times are subject to change at very short notice, so please check with the attraction or venue before visiting.

Every attempt has been made to ensure that traditional place names, sacred sites and places of cultural significance are included, along with the proper and accurate record of the many diverse Traditional Owners groups, language groups and Nations. For capital cities and other natural landforms, we have listed the European name first, followed by the traditional name. We have attempted to use trusted sources for all First Nations information included in this book, but understand that much knowledge has been lost and place names and agreed spellings are likely to change over time. The process of truth-telling is ongoing.

Aboriginal and Torres Strait Islander people are advised that this publication contains the names, and may contain images, of deceased people. We apologise for any distress this may inadvertently cause.

Hardie Grant
EXPLORE

Contents

xx
NEW SOUTH WALES & AUSTRALIAN CAPITAL TERRITORY

- 2   Sydney/Warrang at a glance
- 4   Daytrips from Sydney/Warrang
- 8   Canberra/Ngambri/Ngunnawal at a glance
- 10   Regions of New South Wales

200
SOUTH AUSTRALIA

- 202   Adelaide/Tarndanya at a glance
- 204   Daytrips from Adelaide/Tarndanya
- 206   Regions of South Australia

114
VICTORIA

- 116   Melbourne/Naarm at a glance
- 118   Daytrips from Melbourne/Naarm
- 120   Regions of Victoria

- iv   Back in business
- vi   How to use this book
- viii   Explore Australia
- x   First Nations Peoples
- xii   Travel through history
- xiv   Natural wonders
- xvi   Gourmet touring regions
- xviii   Kid-friendly travel

264
WESTERN AUSTRALIA

266 Perth/Boorloo at a glance
268 Daytrips from Perth/Boorloo
270 Regions of Western Australia

328
NORTHERN TERRITORY

330 Darwin/Garramilla at a glance
332 Daytrips from Darwin/Garramilla
334 Regions of Northern Territory

356
QUEENSLAND

358 Brisbane/Meanjin at a glance
360 Daytrips from Brisbane/Meanjin
362 Regions of Queensland

436
TASMANIA

438 Hobart/*nipaluna* at a glance
440 Daytrips from Hobart/*nipaluna*
442 Regions of Tasmania

478 Index

Back in business

This landmark 40th edition of *Explore Australia* celebrates the defining features of the wide brown land as travellers re-embrace open borders and rediscover the wealth of towns and landscapes across the country. Recent years have been rough on Australia – devastating bushfires, a global pandemic, flooding La Niña systems – but through it all, the beauty of the Australian land, the spirit of the people and the life and community in the cities and towns have continued to shine through.

The restrictions placed on our lives by the COVID-19 pandemic well and truly turned the travel focus of Australians onto Australia and redefined how we travel. Many people discovered new places for the first time, travelling far and wide across this continent of contrasts that swings from deserts to rainforests, reefs to rocks, high mountains to salt lakes set below sea level, sometimes just a few hours' drive apart. There's more geographic variety here than arguably any other country on Earth.

Even as international borders reopened after two years of closure, and tourism settled into its new normal, Australian roads remained filled with local travellers. The land and regional towns are once again an invitation to stock up the car, 4WD or caravan and explore. The open road is literally open to everyone once more.

It's an exciting time to be on the road, whether it be for days, weeks or months. Tourism operators are reinvigorated and grateful for the return of livelihoods and the chance to once again show off their patch of Australia. Innovation is key to the new normal and tour operators are offering the likes of cycling tours through wine regions, First Nations cultural experiences and wilderness immersion opportunities. Accommodation providers are catering to all traveller interests, be it off-grid, staying in a tiny house or historic home, activities for kids, or pet-friendly places to stay. Travellers feel a heightened sense of appreciation for the land and the opportunity to freely explore it again. Whether hiking, biking, paddling or driving, travellers are exploring and supporting local – wherever they are. These are some of the positives hidden within the pandemic.

Issues around lack of staff persist across the country though, particularly in tourist regions, so booking ahead for tours, accommodation and dining is still highly recommended, and a little patience with busy staff will be welcomed with a lot of thanks.

Nature has thrown its own customary challenges into the mix. At the time this edition was being researched, La Niña was continuing to wreak havoc on Australia's East Coast, bringing record rainfall to many areas and a rolling series of floods. Recovery in some places will be slow, but towns will always welcome the support of travellers as they rebuild and recuperate.

Such is nature's climate clock that La Niña's high rainfall will eventually swing back into the warmer and drier El Niño, bringing the increased risk of drought and fire in parts of the country once again. These days, it's a weather cycle that turns every three to seven years, and we've all become familiar with the challenges this presents, but whether you want a weekend break or an endless road trip, it's a golden time to be enjoying – and exploring – Australia.

Andrew Bain

Top: Cape Bruny Lighthouse, Bruny Island, Tas **Middle:** Sun setting near Lightning Ridge, NSW **Bottom:** Biking around the Barossa Valley, SA **Opposite:** Many of Australia's beaches are renowned for surfing

How to use this book

In this book you'll find information on 53 key travel regions and more than 700 towns, from well-known regional cities to hidden gems. Each region features an introduction, a 'cheat sheet' overview, top attractions to visit, a list of local festivals, contact details of visitor information centres and the key towns. For each town, we've included an overview of the town and its history, as well as activities and experiences to be found here or nearby.

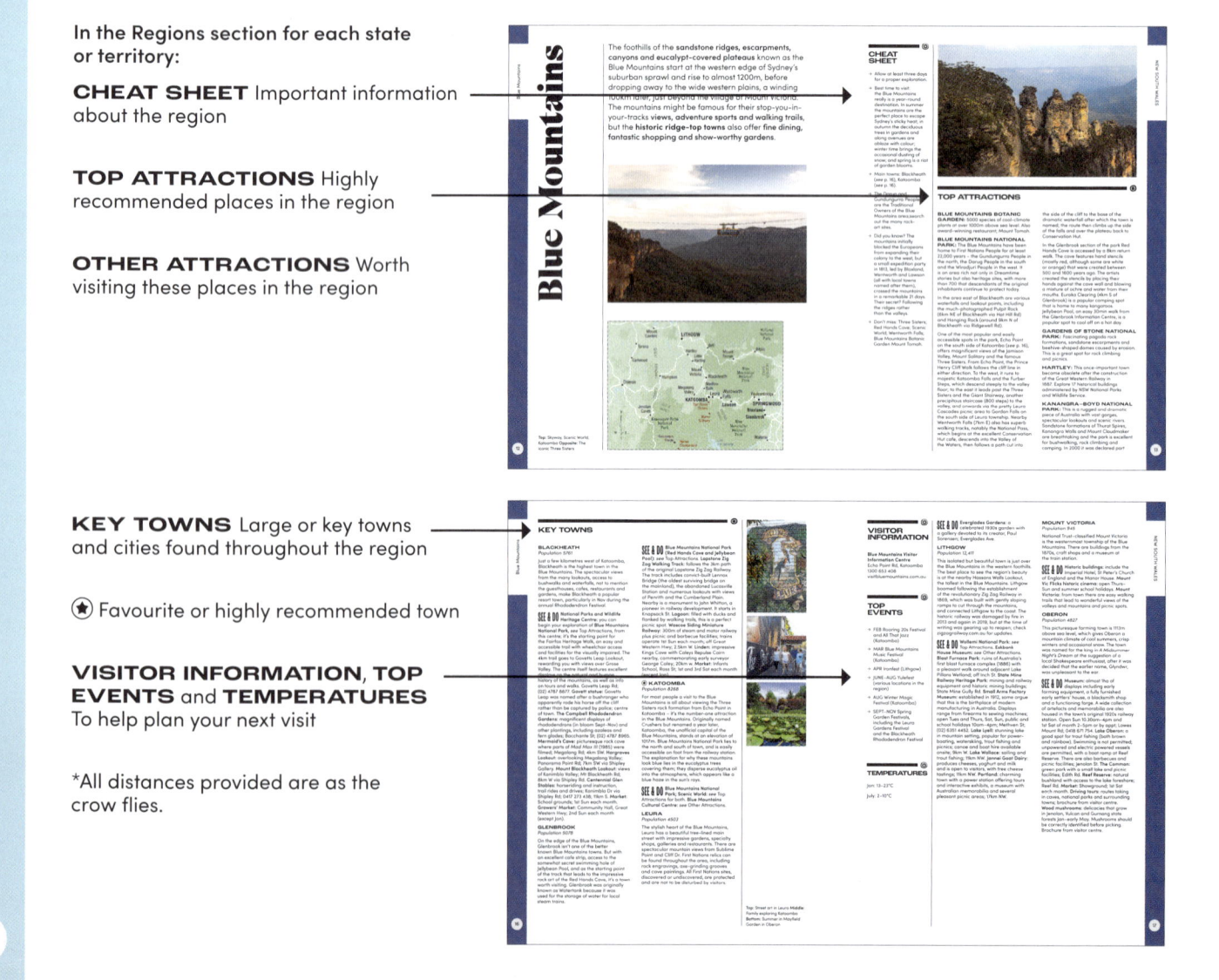

In the Regions section for each state or territory:

CHEAT SHEET Important information about the region

TOP ATTRACTIONS Highly recommended places in the region

OTHER ATTRACTIONS Worth visiting these places in the region

KEY TOWNS Large or key towns and cities found throughout the region

★ Favourite or highly recommended town

VISITOR INFORMATION, TOP EVENTS and **TEMPERATURES**
To help plan your next visit

*All distances provided are as the crow flies.

Dirt road near Hay, NSW

TRAVEL TIPS

FIRST NATIONS
All places across the country have great spiritual and cultural significance for First Nations Peoples. At some of these places, First Nations cultural protocols, such as restricted access, are promoted and visitors are asked to respect the wishes of Traditional Owners. In places where protocols are not promoted, visitors are asked to show respect by not touching or removing anything, and make sure you take all your rubbish with you when you leave.

Some Aboriginal Lands also require permits that need to be applied for well ahead of travel. Check relevant National Parks websites while planning your trip.

NATIONAL PARKS
Each state and territory has a national parks' authority. Check before travel with the relevant authority for any seasonal closures, closed roads, change of access to walking tracks or sites such as waterfalls. Some climbs and longer walks require that you register beforehand with the relevant park authority. Be respectful of flora and wildlife and take rubbish with you. Dogs are not allowed into any national parks. Many national parks require a pass or permit to enter; some are obtained on entry and others must be purchased ahead of time. Always check before you travel.

New South Wales: NSW National Parks and Wildlife Service nationalparks.nsw.gov.au

Australian Capital Territory: Parks and Conservation Service environment.act.gov.au

Victoria: Parks Victoria parks.vic.gov.au

South Australia: National Parks and Wildlife Service South Australia parks.sa.gov.au

Western Australia: Parks and Wildlife Service parks.dpaw.wa.gov.au

Northern Territory: Parks and Wildlife Commission of the Northern Territory nt.gov.au/parks

Queensland: Queensland Parks and Wildlife Service parks.des.qld.gov.au

Tasmania: Tasmania Parks & Wildlife Service parks.tas.gov.au

BEACHES
Australia is renowned for its beaches, many of them isolated stretches of beauty. Surf Life Saving Australia patrols certain beaches at certain times of year and swimming between flags is important as undertows and rips are common. Consult locals to find the safest places to swim and be sure to check the tides. The Surf Life Saving Australia website and app mean you can search by beach and access detailed information (beachsafe.org.au). Beware of marine stingers in tropical coastal waters from October to May.

ROAD CONDITIONS
Australia is vast and driving distances can be long. Road conditions vary from dual-lane national highways to unmade single-track dirt roads. Many regions are remote, especially outback and wilderness areas. Some roads are only accessible by 4WD vehicle. Road closures after rain in certain areas are common, extreme heat can mean seasonal closures within national parks, and black ice can be an issue – especially in Tasmania.

WATER, FUEL AND COMMUNICATION
It is important to carry plenty of drinking water and appropriate supplies whenever you travel. Fuel for vehicles can be limited in remote areas, particularly on weekends or after 5pm, so research and plan ahead and fill up when you can. Phone coverage can be non-existent or patchy in certain regions, so ensure that you're well prepared (consider a PLB: Personal Locator Beacon and also a satellite phone), and that you've informed friends or family of your travel plans. It is also good to carry paper maps, in case your map apps don't work when wi-fi service is sketchy.

BUSHFIRES AND FLOODING
If travelling in summer keep an eye on bushfire and flooding danger warnings as conditions can change very quickly. The Bureau of Meteorology website (bom.gov.au) has weather updates for all parts of Australia, and check news and emergency websites for the latest fire and flood warnings.

WILDLIFE
Australia has an extraordinary array of native wildlife. There are many opportunities to view animals in the wild and some wildlife sanctuaries also offer wildlife rescue services. When you see animals in the wild, keep an appropriate distance, don't feed them and be mindful of their habitats. In some regions you'll notice dead animals on the side of the road; sadly, this is a common sight in many parts of regional and rural Australia and one of the reasons why it is best to avoid driving at night if possible.

CROCODILES
In the northern reaches of the country – the Pilbara and Kimberley in WA, the Top End of the Northern Territory and in tropical north Queensland – saltwater crocodiles can be found in inland waterways and coastal beaches. Obey all warning signs and do not swim or enter the water unless there are signs saying it is safe to do so. *See* p. 340 for more croc safety tips.

Explore Australia

Australia is breathtaking in beauty, daunting in size and rich in diversity! There's so much to explore as you travel the length and breadth of this extraordinary country; Australia is an astonishing 7,692,024sqkm, so you have a lot of land to cover, as well as countless waterways, islands and beaches. You'll need to plan your trip wisely.

The outback may be the place of Australian myth and legend, but most Australians choose to live – and holiday – within reach of a beach. The superb scenery of almost 60,000km of coastline takes in the country's hundreds of offshore islands, and ranges from the sultry mangrove inlets of the far north to the white sweeping sands of the Indian Ocean coast and the rugged cliffs and legendary surf of the continent's south. Going to the beach in Australia can mean an afternoon of bodysurfing in the suburbs, a sojourn in a tropical resort, time out in a fishing community, a dramatic coastal drive, or an exploration of one of several coastal UNESCO World Heritage areas of great beauty and environmental significance.

Bottom: Traditional dwellings at Budj Bim, Vic (photo Wayne Quilliam) **Opposite top:** Margaret River region, WA **Opposite second from top:** Myall Beach rainforest, Daintree National Park, Qld **Opposite second from bottom:** Kangaroos, WA **Opposite bottom:** Snowy Mountains region in autumn, NSW

UNESCO WORLD HERITAGE

Australia has 20 UNESCO World Heritage Sites. Most are areas of natural beauty and hold exceptional conservation value, including Purnululu National Park and The Ningaloo Coast in WA; Uluṟu-Kata Tjuṯa National Park and Kakadu National Park in the NT; Queensland's Great Barrier Reef and K'gari (Fraser Island); and the Tasmanian Wilderness. There are four Australian sites listed exclusively for cultural reasons, the most recent of which is Victoria's Budj Bim Cultural Landscape, which gained the status in 2019 solely for its Aboriginal heritage values. Others in the category include the Sydney Opera House, Melbourne's Royal Exhibition Building, and a group of 11 penal colonies, such as Port Arthur in Tasmania and Fremantle Prison in WA. See the full list at: environment.gov.au/heritage/places/world-heritage-list

First Peoples in Australia have lived on this land for more than 65,000 years, and it abounds with the stories of the land's First Nations Peoples, whose sacred places enrich the landscape.

Australia is home to more than 18,000 flowering plant species, as well as grasses and innumerable fungi and lichens. Among the thousands of unique species still exists nearly seven thousand First Nations foods including plants, nuts, seeds and proteins.

The country's animal life includes the largest diversity of marsupials on Earth, as well as more than 860 bird species (about half of which are only found here), a similar number of reptile species, and more than 200 species of frog. In the water you can also find more than 4600 fish species, and 600 coral species on the Great Barrier Reef alone!

Wherever you go, travel widely and keep your eyes open, as you never know what you'll discover around the next corner.

First Nations People

Australia's First Nations People have the oldest continuous culture of any people in the world – estimated at more than 65,000 years. There are two distinct cultural groupings: the Aboriginal people, who occupied the mainland and Tasmania/*lutruwita*, and the Torres Strait Islanders, from the islands off the tip of Cape York. At the time of European arrival, the estimated 750,000 Aboriginal people comprised around 700 distinct societies. The history of Australia's First Nations People is central to any understanding of what Australia is as a nation. First Nations tourism enables great insight into First Nations culture and might include travelling to a rock-art site, attendance at a dance performance, a visit to a cultural centre or a talk on creation stories to explain the formation of landforms, waterways and bushfoods.

THE OUTBACK, NSW
Lake Mungo is one of Australia's most significant archaeological sites. Burial sites, cooking hearths and campfires, preserved in lunar-like dunes, provide evidence of a period of human occupation dating back at least 50,000 years. Cultural tours operate from Wentworth. Superb rock art is to be found at Mount Grenfell Historic Site (near Cobar), home of the Ngiyambaa People; in Gundabooka National Park, home to the Ngemba and Kurnu Baakandj People near Bourke; and in Mutawintji National Park, Wiljali country, north-east of Broken Hill. (*See* Riverina and Murray p. 96 and Outback NSW p. 106.)

ADELAIDE/TARNDANYA, SA
Adelaide is home to two major centres that promote First Nations culture. The National Aboriginal Cultural Institute, Tandanya houses a permanent collection of art, hosts contemporary art exhibitions and stages performance events. The South Australian Museum cares for one of the largest collection of First Nations cultural materials in the world. The Australian Aboriginal Cultures Gallery features over 3,000 items showing that First Nations People are still living today and rich in cultural heritage. (*See* Adelaide p. 202.)

IKARA-FLINDERS RANGES, SA
These ancient hills are home to the Adnyamathanha People – meaning hills or rock people, a collective term for several language groups. Highlights of this culturally rich and spiritually significant area include Arkaroo Rock (Akurru Adnya), with charcoal and ochre drawings, and Sacred Canyon, with ancient engravings. A number of sites surround the stunning visual centrepiece of Ikara, known as Wilpena Pound. 'Wilpena' derives from an Adnyamathanha word meaning 'cupped hands' or 'bent fingers'. (*See* Ikara-Flinders Ranges and Outback p. 246.)

THE KIMBERLEY, WA
At least 50 per cent of the total Kimberley population comprises of First Nations People. This remote area has one of the country's most important collections of rock art, of which there are two main types: the Gwion Gwion figures (formerly known as Bradshaw) and the Wandjina. At Drysdale River National Park, a painting on the ceiling of a rock shelter, painted by ancestors of the Balanggarra People, has been revealed as the oldest-known rock painting in Australia at 17,300 years old. Many of the big cattle stations allow access to rock-art sites, and a variety of cultural tours operate from the region's community and cultural centres. (*See* The Kimberley p. 322.) Parts of the Kimberley were devastated by floods in January 2023, so check ahead before travelling to this region.

RED CENTRE, NT
The UNESCO World Heritage Uluru–Kata Tjuta National Park is the Traditional Land of the Anangu People, who co-manage the park. There is a range of tours to art sites and other sites of cultural and spiritual significance. To the north, in Alice Springs/Mparntwe, which is Arrernte Country, there are a number of galleries and art centres, including the Araluen Cultural Precinct, home to several sacred sites, as well as seven museums and art galleries focusing on traditional and contemporary First Nations art and performance. (*See* Red Centre p. 348.)

KAKADU, NT
The Bininj People are the Traditional Owners of the northern region of Kakadu National Park and the Mungguy People are the Traditional Owners of the southern regions, and are now joint managers of this UNESCO World Heritage area. The area has more than 5000 rock-art sites, the largest collection in the world. There are numerous ways to explore the magnificent cultural heritage of this area: start at the Bowali Visitor Centre, with its many historic displays and general tour information, and Warradjan Aboriginal Cultural Centre in Cooinda, which features interactive displays. (*See* Kakadu p. 336.)

TROPICAL NORTH, QLD
The distinctive art of the East Cape Peoples in tropical north Queensland survives in the spectacular Quinkan rock-art galleries near Laura and in contemporary community art centres of Cape York Peninsula. (*See* Cairns and Cape York p. 408.)

TASMANIA/LUTRUWITA
The First Nations People of lutruwita/Tasmania are today known as the palawa. On the eve of European invasion, the Aboriginal population, estimated

at between 4000 and 10,000, was divided between nine groups. European settlers incited violence and spread disease. The Black War, as it became known, culminated in the 1830s with the colonial government rounding up the 134 remaining survivors and banishing them to Flinders Island (see Whitemark p. 477). Many of Tasmania's traditional sites, from middens to rock art, lie in protected areas and are not easily accessible. The rich repository of sites played a significant part in UNESCO listing the Tasmanian Wilderness World Heritage Area in 1982 and extending the area in 1989. Kutikina Cave, with evidence of 20,000 years of occupation, can be reached via a rafting tour of the Franklin River. (See Tasmania p. 436.)

TIMELINE OF FIRST NATIONS PEOPLE

Over 65,000 years ago The First People cross from Indonesia to the New Guinea–Australia landmass.

40,000 BCE First Peoples reach Tasmania/ *lutruwita*, via a land bridge.

10,000 BCE Rising sea levels after the last Ice Age isolate First People in Australia from Asia, and those in Tasmania from the mainland.

6000 BCE Distinct groups occupy the entire continent; economies adapt to different environments; religious beliefs and oral traditions derived from the Dreaming indicate complex social organisation; extensive rock art dates from this time.

1770 The Tharawal People of the Botany Bay region make contact with James Cook.

1788 The Eora People are displaced by the establishment of a penal colony at Sydney Cove.

1789 A smallpox epidemic kills about half the First Nations population living in the vicinity of Sydney's penal colony.

1838 A brutal massacre when twelve white people killed 28 Wirrayaraay People at Myall Creek. This is the only time in Australia's history that the white perpetrators are punished by law and are hanged.

1876 Trukanini (pronounced tru kah nee nee; often called Truganini), a Nuenonne woman, who endured horrendous crimes against her people in Tasmania/ *lutruwita*, dies. Despite her wishes to be left buried, her body was exhumed and sent to a museum to be displayed and only returned in the 1970s.

1860–1900 Protection boards are established across Australia; most First Nations People are forced to live on missions or government reserves.

1901 The constitution does not allow federal parliament to legislate for Aboriginal and Torres Strait Islander People to be counted in the census.

1910 Legislation in NSW (the *Aborigines Act* 1910) increases government powers to remove Aboriginal and Torres Strait Islander children from their parents; similar provisions are enacted in other states. This later became known as the Stolen Generations.

1967 In a referendum, Australians vote with a 90 per cent majority to count Aboriginal and Torres Strait Islander People in the census.

1971 Neville Bonner, the first Aboriginal Commonwealth parliamentarian, is elected to the Senate.

1972 Four men set up the Aboriginal Tent Embassy outside Parliament House, Canberra, to address land rights issues, marking a new era of political activism.

1976 Yorta Yorta man Doug Nicholls becomes Governor of South Australia. He is the first non-white person to be a governor of an Australian state.

1992–3 In a decision known as Mabo, named after Eddie Koiki Mabo, the High Court grants the Meriam People of Mer (Murray Island) Native Land Title. **The Native Title Act 1993** rejects the notion of 'terra nullius' ('land belonging to no one') and affirms that Aboriginal and Torres Strait Islander People were in possession of the land before 1788.

1996 In the Wik case, the High Court holds that pastoral leases granted by the Qld government do not extinguish Native Title.

1997 *Bringing Them Home*, the report of a government inquiry into the Stolen Generation, is tabled in federal parliament. The Howard government refuses to make a formal apology.

1998 The first National Sorry Day is held on 26 May to commemorate the landmark Bringing them Home report.

2008 Newly elected Prime Minister Kevin Rudd delivers the long-anticipated 'sorry' speech in federal parliament to Aboriginal and Torres Strait Islander Peoples, particularly the Stolen Generation.

2017 The Uluru Statement from the Heart is established, asking that all Australians walk together by enshrining a First Nations Voice in the Constitution and establishing a Makarrata Commission.

2019 The Uluru–Kata Tjuta National Park Board bans people from climbing Uluru, a sacred site for the Anangu People.

Opposite: Contemporary dancers perform at an international gathering in Darwin/Garramilla (photo Wayne Quilliam)

Travel through history

Australia has a rich history, and travellers can visit and experience many of the most important sites of this history. There have been many challenges and conflicts, especially floods, droughts, bushfires and a pandemic.

Through this turbulent history, the stereotype of the 'Australian spirit' has been forged: easygoing, outdoor-loving people who will barrack for the underdog, stick by their mates, challenge authority, have an adventure, and do it all with a sense of humour that's as dry as the Simpson Desert.

Top: Early morning light on Mutijulu walk, Uluru

MORE THAN 65,000 YEARS AGO
First Peoples arrive in northern Australia.

1629
The Dutch ship *Batavia*, one of several to have explored the Great South Land, is wrecked on the Houtman Abrolhos, Western Australia. See timbers from the wreck at the Western Australian Maritime Museum at Fremantle, and discover more about early maritime explorers.

1700s
Trading occurs between the Yolngu People of north-east Arnhem Land and the Macassans (Sulawesi Indonesians). Conservative estimates indicate trading started in the 1700s (some research indicates it was earlier) and continued until 1907.

1770
Englishman Lieutenant James Cook, aboard the *Endeavour*, sights the east coast, landing several times, including at Botany Bay in Sydney, and the town of Seventeen Seventy, 500km north of Brisbane.

1788
The First Fleet arrives, establishing a settlement at Botany Bay, then at Sydney Cove.

1803
A settlement is established on the Derwent River in Tasmania – the town of Hobart is born.

1824
The Moreton Bay Penal Settlement is established near what will become Brisbane.

1830s
Port Arthur (see p. 448) in Tasmania becomes one of the main penal colonies in Australia.

1851
Gold is discovered in New South Wales and Victoria, leading to mass gold rushes. Relive this history in Victorian towns such as Clunes, Bendigo and Ballarat (see p. 146).

1860–61
Explorers Burke and Wills cross the continent from south to north, but die on the return journey. See the infamous Dig Tree and sites of their deaths along Cooper Creek near Innamincka (see p. 251), in South Australia.

1872
The 3200km Overland Telegraph line between Darwin, Northern Territory, and Port Augusta, South Australia, is completed, allowing fast communication between Australia and the world. The repeater station at Alice Springs has been partially restored (see p. 352).

1880
Australia's best-known bushranger, Ned Kelly, is captured at Glenrowan (see p. 196) in Victoria, and hanged at Melbourne Gaol.

1891
Shearers across Australia go on strike for better pay and conditions. The protests are centred on Barcaldine (see p. 428) in Queensland.

EARLY 1890s
Gold is discovered in remote Western Australian fields, particularly around Kalgoorlie (see p. 305) and Coolgardie, prompting another gold rush.

1901
The six Australian colonies form the Commonwealth of Australia in a grand celebration at the Royal Exhibition Building in Melbourne's Carlton Gardens (see p. 117). The building was listed on the UNESCO World Heritage register in 2004.

1902
Australia gives women the vote. It was only the second country to do so, after New Zealand in 1893.

1908
Land at the foothills of the Australian Alps is chosen as the site of the national capital. It is called Ngambri/Ngunngawal by its Traditional Owners, the Ngunnawal People. It is later named Canberra, meaning 'meeting place' in the Ngunnawal language.

1914–18
World War I: Australia fights against Germany and its allies. Vessels carrying ANZAC soldiers bound for Gallipoli depart from Albany in Western Australia. Learn more of this history at the Australian War Memorial (see p. 8) in Canberra.

1927
Parliament House opens in Canberra. It now houses the Museum of Australian Democracy (see p. 8).

1939–45
World War II: Australia fights in Europe and the Pacific. Darwin is bombed and Sydney is attacked by Japanese submarines. There are still World War II airstrips hidden in the dense jungles and scrub of the Top End (see p. 336).

1949–74
Australia's largest engineering project to date, the Snowy Mountains Hydro-Electric Scheme, is built.

1951
Australia signs the ANZUS Treaty with the US and New Zealand.

1955–63
Large atomic bombs are detonated for testing at Maralinga in western South Australia. Visit the ground zero site at Emu Junction, or the museum at Woomera (see p. 254).

1962
Australia joins the Vietnam War; last combat troops come home in 1973.

1967
In a referendum, Australians vote with a 90 per cent majority to count Aboriginal and Torres Strait Islander People in the census.

1970–1
Moratoriums to end the Vietnam War take place, with the largest in Melbourne on 8 May 1970 with an estimated 100,000 people.

1973
The Whitlam Government legally abolishes the White Australia policy.

1974
Cyclone Tracy devastates Darwin on Christmas Eve.

1975
The Whitlam Government is dismissed by Governor-General Sir John Kerr.

1988
At the bicentenary of settlement, new Parliament House opens in Canberra.

1992
Native Land Title for the Meriam People, Traditional Owners of Mer (Murray Island), is recognised by the High Court on 3 June 1992 after a decade of litigation. This is known as the Mabo judgement, after Eddie Koiki Mabo.

1993
The Native Title Act 1993 is passed, and 'terra nullius' ('land belonging to no one') is overturned.

2000
Olympic Games held in Sydney.

2008
On 13 February, Prime Minister Kevin Rudd apologises for the hurt caused by decades of state-sponsored ill-treatment of Aboriginal and Torres Strait Islander Peoples.

2009
In February, Victoria suffers the most catastrophic bushfire disaster to date in Australian history, with the loss of 173 lives. Saturday 7 February 2009, becomes known as Black Saturday. Towns have now rebuilt, such as Kinglake and Marysville (see p. 125) in Victoria.

2011
In January, three-quarters of Queensland is declared a disaster zone as a result of flooding. Highly affected populated areas include Toowoomba, Brisbane and Ipswich. In February, severe tropical cyclone Yasi devastates Queensland again.

2017
Australia becomes the 26th country to legalise same-sex marriage when Governor-General Sir Peter Cosgrove signs the law-changing bill on 8 December 2017, one month after it received majority support from the Australian people in a national postal survey.

2017
The Uluru Statement from the Heart is established, asking that all Australians walk together by enshrining a First Nations Voice in the Constitution and establishing a Makarrata Commission.

2019
The Uluru–Kata Tjuta National Park Board bans people climbing Uluru, after a long campaign by Traditional Owners, the Anangu People, due to the sacred site's deep cultural significance. Parts of southern Australia suffer one of the worst recorded bushfire seasons in the 2019–20 summer.

2020
The global pandemic of COVID-19 closes Australia's international borders, means state and territory borders close and reopen intermittently, and much of the country endures long lockdowns/stay-at-home orders.

2022
International and state borders reopen following Covid-19 restrictions. Southern Queensland, northern NSW and Victoria experience severe flooding.

2023
The year begins with continued flooding of Murray River towns and in the Kimberley region of WA.

Natural wonders

Australia is renowned for the beauty and diversity of its natural environment. As well as the vast tracts of desert that one would expect on the Earth's oldest, flattest and (apart from Antarctica) driest continent, it is a place of lush forests, wild rivers, ancient mountains, dramatic alpine peaks, glacial lakes and a magnificent coastline. The stunning Great Barrier Reef, the ancient domes of Purnululu National Park in the Kimberley, and the massive monolith of Uluru – all UNESCO World Heritage–listed and among the most recognised natural features in the world – have contributed greatly to Australia's reputation as a major nature-travel destination. Other places, like the remote wilderness of Tasmania and the Flinders Ranges, are valued for their lonely beauty and remarkably unspoiled condition.

THE CONTINENT UP CLOSE

The Australian landscape dates back 290 million years to a time when the continent was submerged under a huge ice cap. Since then, the deep valleys and high mountains of the glaciated environment have been eroded away to a fairly uniform flatness (with some exceptions, spectacular for their shape – the Bungle Bungles and Uluru among them). The loss of high mountains brought a gradual increase in aridity. The formation of rain clouds slowed and vast tracts of desert began to appear where lush forests had once stood. Today approximately 80 per cent of the continent is arid. The figure would probably be more than this except for a dramatic geological episode 80 million years ago – the upthrust of the Great Dividing Range. This feature, stretching from north to south on the east of the continent, is where Australia's tallest peaks, grandest forests and most significant rivers are found.

AUSTRALIAN ALPS, NSW AND VIC

Few people realise that Australia has an alpine area more extensive than the snowfields of Austria and Switzerland combined. Straddling the Great Dividing Range, the Alps are preserved in a series of connecting national parks. A landscape of glacial lakes, mighty rivers and rugged peaks make this one of the world's most spectacular alpine regions. (*See* Kosciuszko and the Snowy Mountains p. 90 and High Country p. 18.)

TWELVE APOSTLES, VIC

These massive limestone obelisks were once part of the cliff-line, but have since become stranded under the constant pressure of sea and wind erosion. Although there are now just eight surviving structures, the Twelve Apostles are regarded as one of Australia's great scenic experiences, and the scenic route that winds along the coast, the Great Ocean Road, is one of the country's best-loved roadtrips. (*See* Great Ocean Road p. 164.)

FLINDERS RANGES, SA

The Traditional Lands of the Adnyamathanha People, who care for many sacred sites throughout the region, the Flinders Ranges is a place of incredible landscapes and rock formations. In 2021, the Flinders Ranges was added to Australia's Tentative List for World Heritage.

PURNULULU NATIONAL PARK, WA

The striped, weathered mounds known as the Bungle Bungles within World Heritage–listed Purnululu National Park rise up out of the remote plains of the Kimberley. Created 350 million years ago, they contain sedimentary layers said to be 1600 million years old. Palm-lined gorges and clear pools intersect the ancient domes. Access to the area is by 4WD or scenic flight. (*See* The Kimberley p. 322.)

ULURU–KATA TJUTA, NT

These rock formations sit above an otherwise flat desert plain at the geographic heart of the continent and are of great spiritual significance to the Traditional Owners, the Anangu. Uluru itself, with a height of 348m and a base circumference of 9.4km, is the largest monolith in the world. Neighbouring Kata Tjuta comprises 36 steep-sided domes that are possibly the eroded remains of a monolith many times the size of Uluru. (*See* Red Centre p. 348.)

GREAT BARRIER REEF, QLD

The world's largest reef is a symbol of the rarity and beauty of Australia's natural environment. Stretching for 2000km along the coast of Queensland, this World Heritage–listed maze of coral reefs and cays supports an astonishing diversity of life, from 2000 species of fish to sea mammals, turtles, seagrasses and molluscs. Although some sections have experienced coral bleaching due to rising ocean temperatures in the past few years, it is still one of the world's great diving destinations. (*See* the Whitsunday Coast p. 400 and Cairns and Cape York p. 408.)

THE DAINTREE, QLD

Part of the Wet Tropics World Heritage Area, the Daintree is a popular place for exploring the dense and tangled primeval rainforests of tropical north Queensland. Phenomenally diverse and spectacularly beautiful, the forests are home to some of the world's most ancient plant species and some of Australia's most brilliant birds and butterflies, as well as saltwater crocodiles. (*See* Cairns and Cape York p. 408.)

TASMANIAN WILDERNESS WORLD HERITAGE AREA

Covering nearly 20 per cent of the total area of the island, the Tasmanian

Wilderness World Heritage Area is one of only three temperate wildernesses remaining in the Southern Hemisphere. It encompasses remote wild rivers, some of the world's oldest trees, and the stunning glaciated landscape of Cradle Mountain–Lake St Clair National Park. (*See* Western Wilderness p. 456.)

AUSTRALIAN FOSSIL MAMMAL SITES

Naracoorte & Riversleigh, SA and Qld, respectively. Two sites that have yielded 20-million-year-old fossils of extinct Australian species. (*See* Naracoorte p. 244 and Mount Isa p. 433.)

Gondwana Rainforests of Australia, Qld Large discontinuous patches of subtropical, warm temperate and Antarctic beech cool temperate rainforest. (*See* p. 370 and p. 408.)

Great Barrier Reef, Qld The world's largest reef, with the most diverse reef fauna. (*See* p. 390, 400 & p. 408)

Greater Blue Mountains Area, NSW A deeply incised plateau with dramatic cliffs and valleys and eucalypt forests. (*See* p. 12.)

Heard and McDonald islands An active volcano (on Heard), glacial landscapes and rare sub-Antarctic flora and fauna.

K'gari, Qld The world's largest sand island, with a complex dune system, freshwater dune lakes and rainforest. (*See* p. 392.)

Kakadu National Park, NT Myriad natural environments and the world's oldest and most extensive rock art. (*See* p. 396.)

Lord Howe Island, NSW Home to a wealth of flora and fauna, with many species unique to this remote volcanic island. (*See* p. 48.)

Macquarie Island, Tas An island composed of oceanic crust and mantle rocks, home to 850,000 penguin pairs.

Purnululu National Park, WA Home of the Bungle Bungle Range, beehive-shaped rock formations that speak of millions of years of geological history. (*See* p. 324.)

Shark Bay, WA Large population of sea mammals, and 3.5-billion-year-old stromatolites representing the oldest life on Earth. (*See* p. 309.)

Tasmanian Wilderness World Heritage Area Forest, rivers, caves, glacial lakes, and 40 Aboriginal cultural sites pointing to at least 30,000 years' occupation. (*See* p. 456.)

Ningaloo Marine Park, WA One of the best places in the world to encounter whale sharks and exceptional underwater scenery in vivid contrast to the arid ranges on shore. (*See* p. 310.)

Uluṟu–Kata Tjuṯa National Park, NT Massive rock formations in the desert, with numerous sacred sites. (*See* p. 350.)

Wet Tropics of Queensland Ancient rainforests containing an almost complete evolutionary record of Earth's plant life. (*See* p. 408.)

Willandra Lakes, NSW Within Mungo National Park, a landscape of ancient lunettes and site of excavations that show a First Peoples presence dating back at least 50,000 years. (*See* p. 97.)

Top: Tasmanian Wilderness World Heritage Area
Opposite: The Twelve Apostles, Vic

Gourmet touring regions

In 1788, the First Fleet carried precious vines in their cargo, which marked the beginning of Australia's now richly successful and highly regarded wine industry. Today there are approximately 2400 wine producers around Australia, spread across 65 designated wine regions. Many wineries have award-winning restaurants as well as tasting rooms – cellar doors – where you can try the wine and purchase a few bottles to take home. Most wine regions are also home to an array of small-scale producers growing everything from truffles to wasabi, and skilled artisans brewing craft beers, distilling fine spirits and transforming grass into cheese, apples into cider and fruit into all sorts of deliciousness.

AUSTRALIA'S UNIQUE TASTES
Everyone likes to joke about Australia's love affair with Vegemite – the thick salty spread made from a yeast extract is an acquired taste – but it's not the only taste you'll find that's unique to Australia. It's possibly the only country in the world that likes to dine out on its coat of arms. You'll find kangaroo and emu on many bush-tucker menus – Parachilna's Prairie Hotel (see p. 248) in the Flinders Ranges or the Sounds of Silence dinner at Ayers Rock Resort (see p. 349) are good spots to try some. Quandong pies, made from a native peach, are worth seeking out in the outback, and if you are on the Kimberley Coast make sure you try some pearl meat. Freshly caught barramundi, particularly if it's crusted with crushed macadamia nuts, is hard to beat in the Top End, and don't be shy if you're offered a crocodile pie; it tastes a lot like chicken.

HUNTER VALLEY, NSW
Australia's oldest and most famous wine region has much more than just wine. Home to around 60 restaurants as well as specialty stores selling handmade gelato, chocolates, cheeses, fine olive oils and smoked fish, it's no wonder the Hunter Valley is a favourite foodie weekend escape for Sydneysiders. Of course, no trip to the Hunter is complete without sampling some of the valley's much-celebrated semillon, chardonnay or shiraz – most of the 150 or so wineries and cellar doors are clustered in and around Pokolbin, Broke and Lovedale. If you only visit one winery in the Hunter, make it Dalwood Estate, the birthplace of Australian shiraz and one of the oldest wineries in the country. (See p. 35.)

YARRA VALLEY, VIC
Winter time is the best season to explore the Yarra Valley. What could be better than curling up in front of a fire with a glass of local red after a day spent on the food and wine trail? The Yarra is one of the best cool-climate wine districts of the world, renowned for its pinot noir, chardonnay and sparkling wines. There are over 70 wineries open and the Yarra Valley Regional Food Trail traces a path between dozens of producers of free-range eggs, honey, fruit, berries, herbs and cheese, game, pasta, preserves, trout, clotted cream, chocolates and ice-cream. Or follow the Cider and Ale Trail that loops through Coldstream to Healesville and Yarra Glen. (See p. 124.)

MORNINGTON PENINSULA, VIC
Leave your diet at home when you tour this boot-shaped peninsula around an hour's drive south of Melbourne. Beyond the beautiful beaches is a lush hinterland where vineyards produce crisp pinot gris and fruity pinot noir, and fertile farmlands yield rich crops of olives, apples and strawberries while cheesemakers and chocolatiers lead you to temptation. Picnic among the vines at Montalto, learn how to make your own bespoke gin in a distillery workshop at Bass and Flinders Distillery or enjoy a refreshing ale at Red Hill Brewery, made from their own hops. (See p. 130.)

BAROSSA VALLEY, SA
Home to some of the oldest shiraz vines in the world, the Barossa has for many years been famous for its rich, full-bodied reds – including the legendary Penfolds Grange and Henschke's Hill of Grace – but the food is just as good, with a strong tradition of wonderful cold meats, sausages, preserved fruits, cheese and delicious breads, thanks to Lutheran settlers who came here in the 1840s. On Saturday mornings the weekly farmers' market is a great place to taste the local produce, and the sellers are the people who grow or make the food. Neighbouring Clare Valley is Australia's best region for riesling, best explored on the Riesling Trail, a 27km sealed walking and cycling path that links the villages of the valley. (See p. 216.)

McLAREN VALE, SA
Just a 40min drive south of Adelaide, the charming rural and coastal scenery and even better food and wine make the Fleurieu Peninsula a much-loved gourmet getaway. All over the peninsula you'll find seriously good wine country (there are more than 70 cellar doors in McLaren Vale alone) and roadside stalls sell local produce in season. Browse the weekly farmers market at Wilunga, enjoy a high-tech tasting or degustation at d'Arenberg Cube, or soak in the views from the cliff-top fine dining Star of Greece kiosk at Port Wilunga. (See p. 210.)

MARGARET RIVER, WA

The Margaret River region is home to some of Australia's finest sauvignon blanc and chardonnay, and plenty of terrific cab sav and shiraz. Caves Road, a 110km scenic drive that stretches from Cape Leeuwin to Cape Naturaliste through the Boranup Karri Forest, is the best way to explore the area. Many wineries feature innovative architecture, extensive formal gardens, art galleries and excellent restaurants. Further south, the area surrounding Mount Barker, Frankland, Porongurup, Denmark and Albany is another premier wine region. (*See* pp. 273–4.)

TAMAR VALLEY, TAS

Beautiful bubbly, aromatic rieslings and elegant pinot noir ... put Tasmania on the top of your foodie bucket list, because there's nothing like Tasmanian food and wine. Almost anywhere you go in Tasmania there is a gourmet experience waiting, and you'll find plenty of organic and boutique food producers making and selling anything from farmhouse cheeses, bush honeys, organic fruit and vegetables to saffron and wasabi. Follow the Tamar Valley Wine Route from Launceston along the banks of kanamaluka/River Tamar to George Town and back via Pipers River. There are 30 or more wineries along the way, but don't miss Christmas Hills Raspberry Farm, Ashgrove Cheese or the House of Anvers chocolate factory. (*See* p. 469.)

BEST FOOD AND WINE FESTIVALS

Taste of Summer, Tas (Jan) Annually in late Dec/early Jan, Hobart celebrates the good life – along with the end of the Sydney to Hobart Yacht Race and New Year's Eve – with a week-long party on the waterfront with food stalls, musicians and performers. thetasteoftasmania.com.au

Melbourne Food and Wine Festival, Vic (March) More than 200 events throughout the city and across the state during March, including the world's longest lunch, international chef dinners, masterclasses, pop-up restaurants, bar crawls and winery tours. melbournefoodandwine.com.au

Orange F.O.O.D Week, NSW (April) Australia's longest-running regional food festival is 10 days in April of foodie fun, including grazing dinners, foraging walks, markets and even the two-day F.O.O.D train trip. orangefoodweek.com.au

Tasting Australia, SA (April) Around 140 events in April: lunches, dinners, famous chefs and tasting classes showcasing the best of South Australia's food and wine across 10 days and 11 regions. tastingaustralia.com.au

Taste Great Southern, WA (May) Eighteen days in April of tastings, markets, wine festivals, workshops and long lunches in various towns across the state's south-west. tastegreatsouthern.com.au

Noosa Food and Wine Festival, Qld (May) Three days in May of fabulous food beside the beach in beautiful Noosa, with barbecues, street carnivals, markets, chef dinners and hinterland food trails. noosafoodandwine.com.au

McLaren Vale Sea and Vines Festival, SA (June) More like a music festival with excellent food and wine, McLaren Vale kicks up its heels over the June long weekend. seaandvines.com.au

The Truffle Festival, ACT (June to Aug) Rug up and head to Canberra for the ultimate foodie feast of black winter truffles. Join a truffle hunt, cooking class or cosy up at a fireside dinner – more than 250 events held over three months from June to August. trufflefestival.com.au

Mudgee Wine and Food Festival, NSW (Sept) Three weeks in Sept of live music, tastings, lunches, dinners and tours with special events at most wineries in the Mudgee district, as well as a wine show and street carnival. mudgeewine.com.au

Margaret River Gourmet Escape, WA (Nov) Join culinary superstars from around the world in a glamorous four-day showcase of local food and wine in Nov, including gourmet beach dinners and celebrity events. gourmetescape.com.au

Bottom: Ubertas Wines, Barossa Valley, SA **Opposite:** Milawa Cheese, Vic

Kid-friendly travel

When it comes to family holidays – the type that are just as much fun for adults as they are for children – Australia is pretty hard to beat. The country's easygoing road-tripping culture means there are family-friendly places to stay in every town. Most holiday parks have fantastic playgrounds and pools and often have prime waterfront positions, and most resorts welcome kids too, with school holiday activities and year-round kids clubs. Australia's a big place, but don't let that deter you from travelling around it or across it with kids, because there is plenty to keep them enthralled as they discover new things along the way.

ROAD-TRIPPING WITH KIDS

Road-tripping with kids can be fun and a time for families to share and discover new experiences. It can also be stressful if someone needs the toilet or to stretch their legs. The trick with little kids is to plan ahead with plenty of rest stops – most towns have playgrounds and parks, public toilets, as well as picnic tables and shade, and it's worth the extra five minutes to detour off the highway.

Get the kids involved in planning your trip – let them pick a couple of things they'd like to see and do along the way. A fun activity is to collect postcards at each town you stop at. Buy a book of stamps before you leave home and the kids can post them off to friends and family on the spot – or stick postcards, maps and brochures that you collect into an old-fashioned travel diary. You can create a treasure list of things to find at each stop, spot wildlife as you drive, or set a mission to find the best vanilla slice or meat pie in regional Australia. If it's a summer trip, try to make at least one stop each day at a playground, council pool or beach, even if it means going a little bit out of your way. It will make the journey seem more like a holiday, less like a commute.

CANBERRA, ACT

You'll find all the big-hitter museums in the nation's capital and kids will love them. Questacon, the National Science and Technology Centre, puts the fun into science; take a tour with an elite athlete and test your athletic skills at the Australian Institute of Sport; learn all about life in space at the Canberra Deep Space Communication Complex; mint your own $1 coin at the Royal Australian Mint; and see the bones on show at the National Dinosaur Museum. Older kids might be interested in Australia's role in wartime and also the country's government, so it's worth visiting both the Australian War Memorial and Parliament House. (See p. 8.)

PHILLIP ISLAND, VIC

An easy daytrip from Melbourne, Phillip Island is jam-packed with family-friendly attractions. Top of the list is the famous Penguin Parade where hundreds of little penguins come out of the sea at dusk. You can see koalas in the treetops at the Koala Conservation Centre, and kids will also love Churchill Island Heritage Farm, where they can watch cows being milked, see sheep being shorn and take a wagon ride. Even hard-to-impress teenagers will get a thrill at Phillip Island Circuit, where you can ride a go-kart or buckle up for a few hot laps with a racing driver. (See p. 132.)

KANGAROO ISLAND, SA

Australia's third-largest island is the ultimate zoo without fences. There are so many wallabies, kangaroos, koalas and echidnas, you're pretty much guaranteed to spot some. You can follow a ranger onto a beach where sea lions sleep at Seal Bay, see fur seals on the rocks at Cape du Couedic, feed pelicans every afternoon at Kingscote and, if you're lucky, even spot a platypus or two. Oh, and the local honey ice-cream is really, really good. (See Fleurieu Peninsula and Kangaroo Island p. 208.)

RED CENTRE, NT

Introduce your kids to the wonder of the Australian desert and the world's oldest living culture at Uluru. Take a camel ride around the rock – or hire a bike – and join a bush tucker and reptile tour with a local guide to try some traditional bush foods and get up close and personal to desert wildlife. Ayers Rock Resort has lots of activities for kids, including family stargazing tours, free storytelling, dance performances and even dot-painting workshops. (See p. 348.)

GOLD COAST, QLD

Australia's version of Disneyland, the theme parks of the Gold Coast – Warner Bros. Movie World, Sea World, Wet'n'Wild, Dreamworld and WhiteWater World – are high on most kids' holiday wishlists, but there are also lots of other things to see and do in south-east Queensland. Feed kangaroos and cuddle koalas at Currumbin Wildlife Sanctuary, which also has the TreeTops Challenge High Ropes Course; head into the hinterland to the Tamborine Rainforest Skywalk; chill out on the beach; or take a whale-watching cruise (June to Oct). (See p. 370.)

THE DINOSAUR TRAIL, QLD

If you've got a dinosaur nut in the family – and who doesn't? – they'll love following the Dinosaur Trail through outback Queensland. Dig for fossils in Richmond, home to the Kronosaurus and Richmond Pliosaur, the best-preserved marine vertebrate skeleton in Australia; see the fossilised tracks of the world's only known dinosaur stampede at Lark Quarry; visit the Age of Dinosaurs Museum in Winton, where volunteers work on excavating dinosaur bones with paleontologists and see where Australia's largest – and newest – dinosaurs have been found in Eromanga. (See Hunting Dinosaurs box p. 435.)

TASMANIA

Tassie is the perfect place for a family roadtrip. Nowhere is very far away from anywhere else, and there's always something fun or interesting to see and do along the way. From chocolate factories, confounding mazes and miniature villages to slippery slides, steam train rides and slightly scary ghost tours, there's plenty in Tasmania to keep kids of all ages happy. Not to mention the waterfall walks, abundance of wildlife, including some wonderful wildlife sanctuaries, and spectacular nature at every turn. (See p. 436.)

Flinders Discovery Centre, Hughenden, Qld
Opposite: Whitehaven Beach, Whitsundays, Qld

10 ATTRACTIONS KIDS WILL LOVE

Australian Reptile Park, NSW Watch spiders and snakes being milked of their venom. (See Gosford, p. 31.)

Koala Hospital, NSW Adopt a wild koala and watch them being fed and nursed back to health at the states only koala hospital. (See Port Macquarie p. 59.)

Puffing Billy, Vic Ride a steam train though the rainforest. (See The Dandenongs p. 123.)

Sovereign Hill, Vic Pan for real gold in an outdoor gold-rush museum; you can keep what you find, too. (See Ballarat p. 151.)

Monarto Safari Park This open-range 1000ha zoo features Australian, African and Asian animals. Jump on a safari bus tour to see the animals up close. (See The Murray p. 238.)

Coober Pedy, SA Visit an opal mine and sleep underground in a dug-out motel. (See p. 250.)

Monkey Mia, WA Feed wild dolphins on the beach. (See Denham p. 313.)

Crocosaurus Cove, NT See crocodiles up close; big kids can dive with crocs in the Cage of Death. (See Darwin, p. 330.)

Cairns Lagoon, Qld Splash about for free in one of the country's best swimming pools. (See p. 413.)

Tasmanian Devil Unzoo, Tas Find out how Tasmanian devils are being conserved and help save them from extinction. (See Eaglehawk Neck/Teralina p. 446.)

New South Wales

HIGHLIGHTS

Spend a day cruising Sydney Harbour, one of the world's most beautiful waterways.

Get back to nature in the World Heritage-listed rainforests of Barrington Tops National Park. *See* p. 43.

Be dazzled by the whitest sand in the world on the beaches of the South Coast. *See* p. 82.

Climb to the top of Australia – summiting Mount Kosciuszko is easier than you think. *See* p. 91.

Chill out in the laidback beachside holiday hotspot of Byron Bay. *See* p. 56.

Go wild with a hike in the Blue Mountains. *See* p. 12.

STATE FLOWER

Waratah
Telopea speciosissima

Freshwater Rockpool, Sydney

The Traditional Owners of the Sydney/Warrang area are the Gadigal People of the Eora Nation.

Sydney/Warrang at a glance

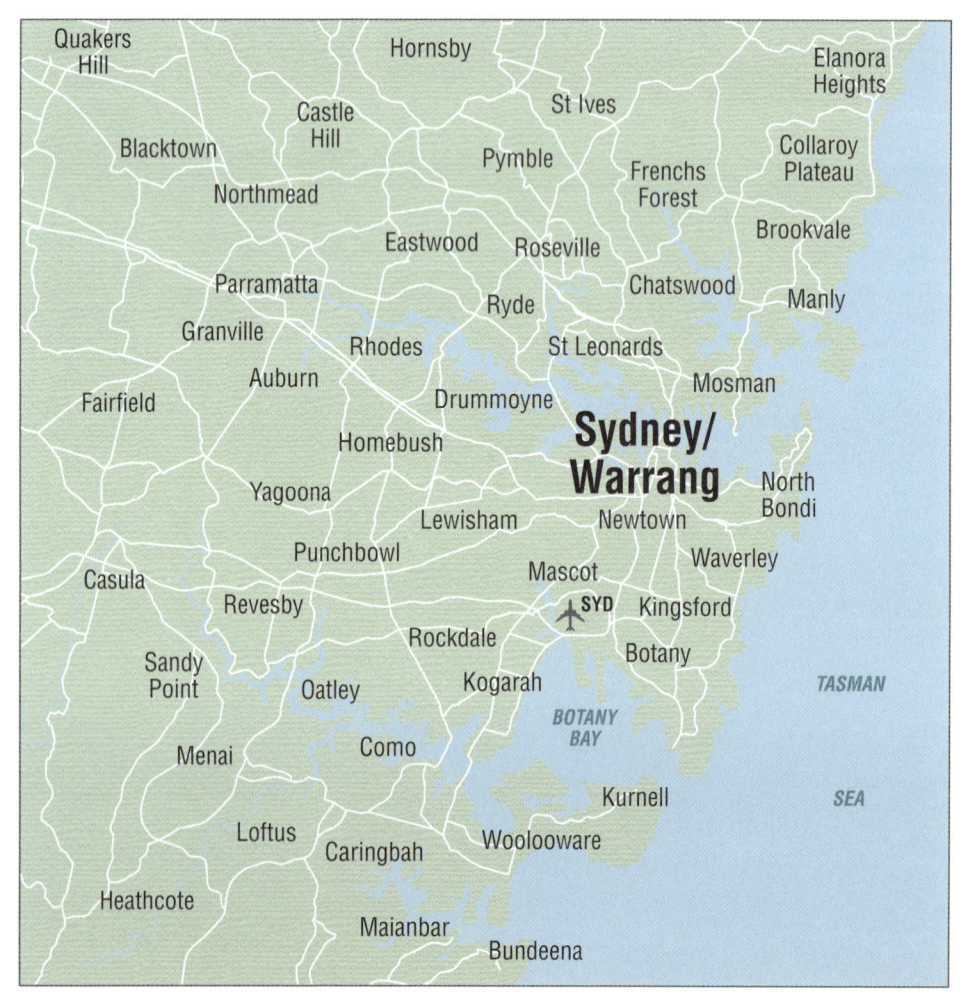

With the expansive waters of Sydney Harbour at its heart, **a string of glorious beaches and national parks**, and an impressive collection of **museums, galleries and historic buildings**, **Australia's largest and oldest city** is always a spectacular place to visit.

Top: Bondi Icebergs pool
Middle: The Harbour Bridge and an iconic ferry **Bottom:** Mardi Gras at Kings Cross
Opposite: The Opera House and the city beyond

IF YOU LIKE …

BEACHES
Bondi Beach
Cronulla Beach
Manly Beach
Palm Beach
Shark Beach, Nielsen Park

EXPERIENCES ON SYDNEY HARBOUR
Captain Cook Harbour Cruise
Cockatoo Island
Fort Denison
Manly Ferry
RiverCat to Parramatta

FESTIVALS AND EVENTS
Sydney Festival, Jan
Sydney Mardi Gras, March
Vivid Sydney, May–June
Good Food Month, Oct
Sculpture by the Sea, Oct–Nov

GALLERIES
Art Gallery of New South Wales (AGNSW)
Brett Whiteley Studio
Museum of Contemporary Art (MCA)
State Library of NSW Exhibition Galleries
Sydney Modern (AGNSW)
White Rabbit Gallery

MUSEUMS
Australian Museum
Australian National Maritime Museum
Chau Chak Wing Museum, Sydney University
Hyde Park Barracks
Museum of Sydney
The Rocks Discovery Museum

VIEWS
Bondi Icebergs
BridgeClimb Sydney
Mrs Macquarie's Chair
South Head, Sydney Harbour National Park
Sydney Tower

WALKS
Bondi to Coogee walk
Harbour Circle walk
Spit Bridge to Manly Scenic Walkway
The Rocks self-guided walking tour
Watsons Bay Walk and South Head Heritage Trail

NEW SOUTH WALES

Daytrips from Sydney/Warrang

BLUE MOUNTAINS
1.5hr from Sydney CBD

It only takes 90min or so heading west – by car or train – to get to the Blue Mountains but, once you're there, surrounded by UNESCO World Heritage–listed wilderness and jaw-dropping views, you'll feel a million miles away. The walking – varying from gentle strolls to challenging hikes – is superb!

The area is also a magnet for those seeking a spot of retail therapy in the galleries, antique stores and boutiques of Leura or Katoomba; and for food lovers, who come up to the mountains for a long leisurely lunch or an afternoon high tea served with style in one of the grand Art Deco hotels in Medlow Bath or Katoomba. In summer the mountains are a welcome cool change from steamy Sydney. The many stately gardens are worth a visit in spring and autumn; in winter you might even see snow. *See* Glenbrook p. 16, Katoomba p. 16.

CABRAMATTA
1hr from Sydney CBD

A daytrip to Cabramatta is like taking a daytrip to Asia. This suburb, on the western fringe of Sydney, is the Asian food and culture capital of the city. It even looks, sounds and smells more like Ho Chi Minh City than other parts of Sydney.

Catch the train from Central Station – it will take around an hour – and spend the day shopping in the food markets and trinket stores, buying excellent value fabrics and other made-in-Asia goodies, slurping pho and other spicy Vietnamese dishes, visiting herbalists, getting a massage and drinking bubble tea. No passport needed.

Top: Sunset over Hunter Valley vineyards **Middle:** Bouddi National Park, Central Coast **Bottom left:** Sea Cliff Bridge, Grand Pacific Drive **Bottom right:** The sweep of Manly Beach

CENTRAL COAST
1.5hr from Sydney CBD

A string of laidback coastal villages flanking blissfully uncrowded beaches makes the Central Coast a favourite weekend destination for Sydneysiders. But at just a 90min drive (or train ride) north of the city, it's also the ideal place for a daytrip.

Gosford is home to some great galleries and the Australian Reptile Park, where you can get an up-close look at Australia's notorious snakes and spiders. Stylish Terrigal has lots of classy waterfront eateries, the Entrance is good for families, and Bouddi National Park in the south offers walking trails and beachside camping. *See* Gosford p. 31, Terrigal p. 31, The Entrance p. 32.

GRAND PACIFIC DRIVE
1hr from Sydney CBD

Victoria's Great Ocean Road might get all the glory, but the Grand Pacific Drive, on the southern outskirts of Sydney between Royal National Park and Wollongong, is every bit as spectacular, with a lot less traffic on most days. A highlight is the thrilling Sea Cliff Bridge, which curves around the cliffs, cantilevered 50m out to sea.

Chill out on one of the beaches along the way, take a dip in a rockpool or stroll through the rainforest. At around 100km each way, it's the perfect length for a one-day road trip. *See* Wollongong p. 27.

THE HAWKESBURY RIVER
1.5hr from Sydney CBD

Ever wondered what Sydney was like 200 years ago? Spend a day driving the back roads to Wisemans Ferry and St Albans and you'll soon have a good idea. This area, about a 90min drive north-west of Sydney, is a rugged landscape with towering sandstone ridges backing onto dense national park bushland. It's punctuated with sleepy villages full of beautiful sandstone buildings and old pubs serving hearty meals.

Everything on the Hawkesbury River moves to a delightfully old-fashioned beat. *See* Wisemans Ferry p. 33.

HUNTER VALLEY
2hr from Sydney CBD

If you're a wine lover, chances are you'll know all about the Hunter Valley's famous wines, particularly its semillon – a unique Hunter white that is regarded as the best of its type. Australia's oldest wine-producing region is a two-hour drive from Sydney, so it's ideal for a daytrip, although the range of accommodation and restaurants makes it the type of place where you'll be tempted to stay overnight.

World-class golf courses, luxury day spas, galleries and gardens make the Hunter Valley a great place to spend the day even if you don't drink. *See* Cessnock p. 38.

NORTHERN BEACHES
1hr from Sydney CBD

'The northern beaches' stretches from Manly (just north of the CBD) to Palm Beach (at the tip of the northern peninsula). The further north you go, the more glitzy it gets; 'Palmy' is a favourite summer holiday playground for visiting celebrities and local socialites. If you're a fan of the TV soap *Home and Away* you'll know Palm Beach as Summer Bay.

You don't have to be rich and famous to enjoy a daytrip here: just catch a bus from the city centre. You'll find plenty of great spots to eat and shop at each coastal 'village' on the way, and the walk around Barrenjoey Head is a delight.

NEWCASTLE
2.5hr from Sydney CBD

Newcastle might be mainland Australia's second oldest city and the second largest city in NSW, but there's nothing second-class about this seriously cool place. Oozing street-smart post-industrial urban chic from every revamped railway yard, work shed, warehouse and laneway, the city overflows with art spaces, cafes, eateries and the work of emerging designers.

Check out Newcastle's convict past, spend some time at one of the city beaches or rockpools, and watch the tankers and tugboats come and go in the working harbour from your perch in a waterfront bar or cafe. *See* Newcastle p. 40.

Top: Cabramatta Freedom Plaza **Second from top:** Newcastle Hunter Valley **Second from bottom:** Kangaroos in the Hunter Valley **Bottom:** Cyclists at Nobbys Beach, Newcastle

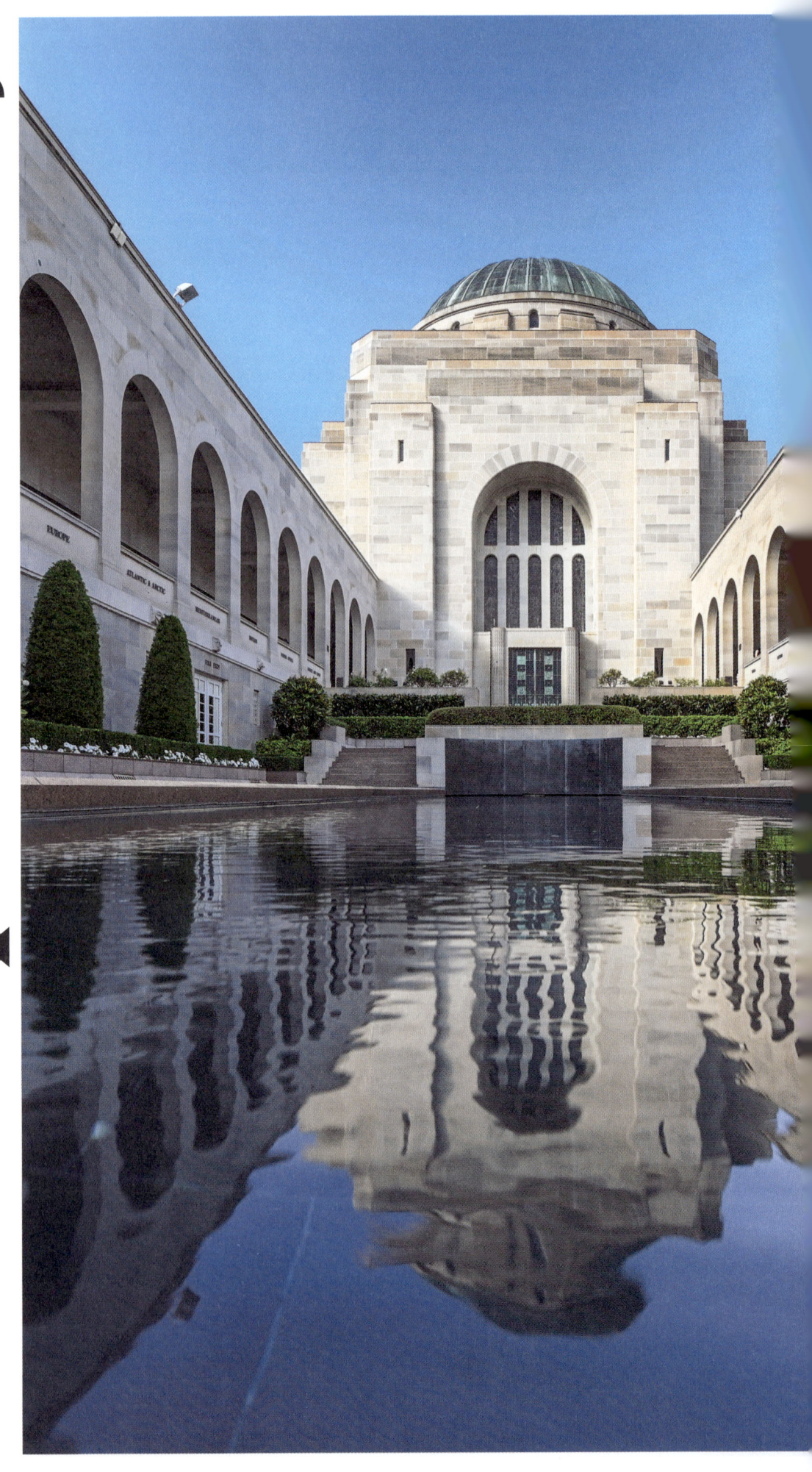

Australian Capital Territory

HIGHLIGHTS

Feed your inner culture vulture at the country's best museums.

Catch the latest blockbuster art exhibition at the National Gallery of Australia.

Watch democracy at work during Question Time at Parliament House.

Walk (or hop) with kangaroos and see ancient rock art in Namadgi National Park.

Watch a classic movie at the National Film and Sound Archive.

Enjoy a glass (or two) of fine wine at one of the many cellar doors in the Canberra wine region. *See* p. 19.

Soak up the beaches and picturesque surrounds of Jervis Bay, part of Jervis Bay Territory which was made so the ACT could have sea access. *See* p. 87

STATE FLOWER

Royal bluebell
Wahlenbergia gloriosa

The poignant Australian War Memorial

The Traditional Owners of Canberra/Ngambri/Ngunngawal area are the Ngunnawal People.

Canberra/Ngambri/Ngunnawal at a glance

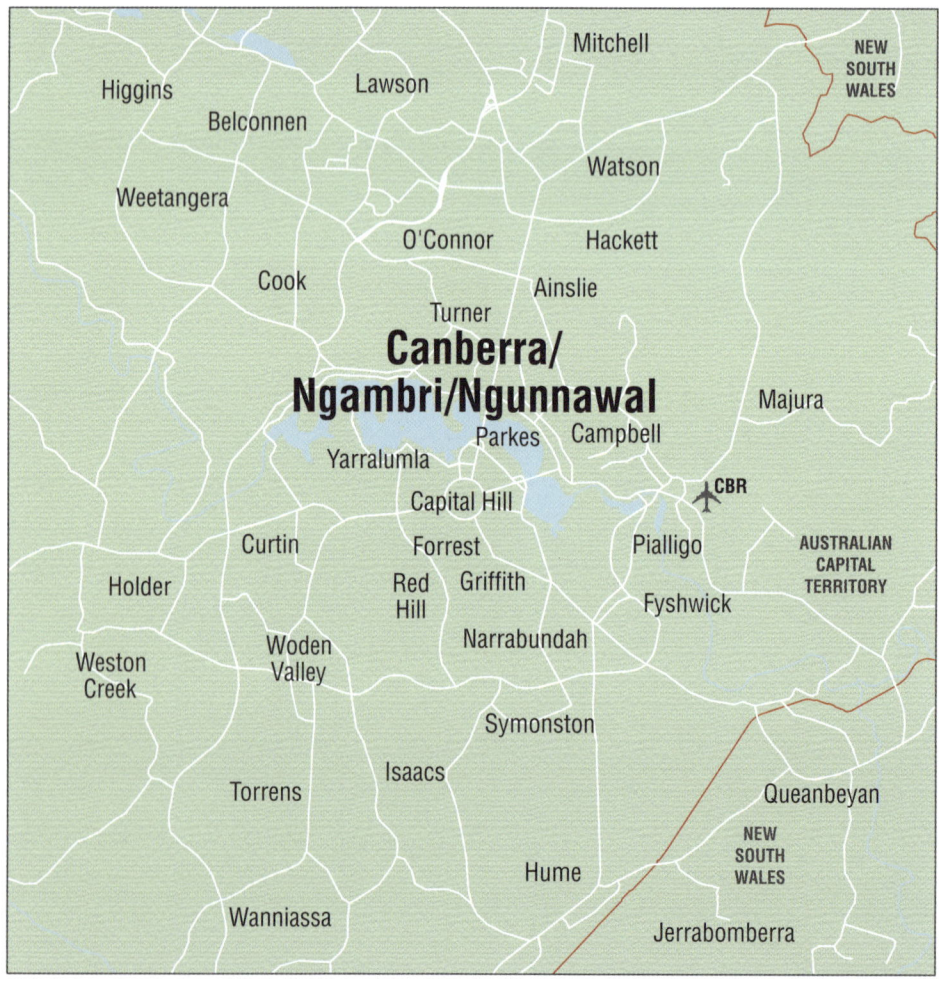

Top: The Aboriginal Memorial at The National Gallery of Australia

Canberra is famous for politics, **monuments and national museums** but it also has plenty of other attractions to pique your interest. From **beautiful gardens** to **dinosaurs and outer space exhibits**, there is plenty to make you see Canberra in an entirely new light.

Top: Lake Burley Griffin **Middle:** Sculpture by John Robinson at The Australian Institute of Sport (AIS) **Bottom:** Old Bus Depot Markets in Kingston

IF YOU LIKE ...

FESTIVALS AND EVENTS
Summernats, Jan
National Multicultural Festival, Feb
Canberra Balloon Spectacular, March
Enlighten, March
National Folk Festival, Easter
Truffle Festival, June–Aug
Floriade, September–Oct

FOODIE FAVOURITES
Grazing Restaurant
Old Bus Depot Markets
Pialligo Estate
Poachers Pantry
The Truffle Farm

FOR KIDS
Cockington Green Gardens
CSIRO Discovery Centre
National Dinosaur Museum
National Zoo and Aquarium
Questacon, the National Science and Technology Centre

GALLERIES
Artworld ADG – Aboriginal Dreamings Gallery
Canberra Glassworks
Canberra Museum and Gallery
National Gallery of Australia
National Portrait Gallery

MUSEUMS
Australian War Memorial
Museum of Australian Democracy at Old Parliament House
National Film and Sound Archive
National Library of Australia
National Museum of Australia

NATIONAL ATTRACTIONS
Australian Institute of Sport
National Archives of Australia
National Capital Exhibition
Parliament House
Royal Australian Mint

PARKS AND GARDENS
Australian National Botanic Gardens
Commonwealth Park
Namadgi National Park
National Arboretum Canberra
Tidbinbilla Nature Reserve

AUSTRALIAN CAPITAL TERRITORY

Regions of New South Wales

**1 BLUE MOUNTAINS
P. 12**

Blackheath
Glenbrook
Katoomba ⭐
Leura
Lithgow
Mount Victoria
Oberon

**2 SOUTHERN HIGHLANDS, CAPITAL COUNTRY AND ILLAWARRA
P. 18**

Berrima
Berry ⭐
Bowral ⭐
Braidwood
Bundanoon
Camden
Campbelltown
Crookwell
Goulburn
Jamberoo
Kiama ⭐
Moss Vale
Picton
Queanbeyan
Robertson
Shellharbour
Wollongong
Yass
Young

**3 CENTRAL COAST AND HAWKESBURY
P. 28**

Gosford
Richmond
Terrigal ⭐
The Entrance
Windsor
Wisemans Ferry
Woy Woy
Wyong

❹ HUNTER VALLEY AND COAST P. 34

Cessnock ✪
Maitland
Merriwa
Murrurundi
Muswellbrook
Nelson Bay
Newcastle ✪
Raymond Terrace
Scone
Singleton

❺ HOLIDAY COAST AND LORD HOWE ISLAND P. 42

Bellingen
Bulahdelah
Coffs Harbour ✪
Dorrigo
Forster–Tuncurry
Gloucester
Kempsey
Laurieton
Lord Howe Island Settlement (Lord Howe Island) ✪
Macksville
Nambucca Heads
Port Macquarie ✪
Stroud
Taree
Urunga
Wauchope
Wingham

❻ TROPICAL NORTH COAST P. 52

Alstonville
Ballina
Byron Bay ✪
Casino
Evans Head
Grafton
Iluka
Kyogle
Lismore
Mullumbimby
Murwillumbah
Nimbin
Tweed Heads
Woolgoolga
Yamba ✪

❼ NEW ENGLAND P. 60

Armidale
Barraba
Bingara
Glen Innes
Gunnedah
Guyra
Inverell
Manilla
Moree
Narrabri
Nundle
Tamworth ✪
Tenterfield
Uralla
Walcha
Warialda
Wee Waa

❽ CENTRAL WEST P. 70

Bathurst
Blayney
Canowindra
Condobolin
Coonabarabran
Coonamble
Cowra
Dubbo
Eugowra
Forbes
Gilgandra
Grenfell
Gulgong
Lake Cargelligo
Mudgee ✪
Nyngan
Orange ✪
Parkes
Rylstone
Wellington

❾ SOUTH COAST P. 82

Batemans Bay ✪
Bega
Bermagui
Bombala
Eden
Huskisson
Jervis Bay ✪
Merimbula
Moruya
Narooma
Nowra
Tathra
Ulladulla

❿ SNOWY MOUNTAINS P. 90

Adaminaby
Adelong
Batlow
Berridale
Cooma
Jindabyne
Khancoban
Thredbo ✪
Tumbarumba
Tumut

⓫ RIVERINA AND MURRAY P. 96

Albury
Balranald
Barham
Cootamundra
Corowa
Culcairn
Deniliquin
Finley
Griffith
Gundagai
Hay
Holbrook
Jerilderie
Leeton
Mulwala
Narrandera
Temora
Tocumwal
Wagga Wagga
Wentworth
West Wyalong

⓬ OUTBACK P. 106

Bourke
Brewarrina
Broken Hill ✪
Cobar
Lightning Ridge
Menindee
Silverton
Tibooburra
Walgett
White Cliffs

Top: Road trip to Thredbo
Middle: The WWII Memorial Clock in Mudgee **Opposite:** Wategos at Byron Bay

NEW SOUTH WALES

11

Blue Mountains

The foothills of the **sandstone ridges, escarpments, canyons and eucalypt-covered plateaus** known as the Blue Mountains start at the western edge of Sydney's suburban sprawl and rise to almost 1200m, before dropping away to the wide western plains, a winding 100km later, just beyond the village of Mount Victoria. The mountains might be famous for their stop-you-in-your-tracks **views, adventure sports and walking trails**, but the **historic ridge-top towns** also offer **fine dining, fantastic shopping and show-worthy gardens.**

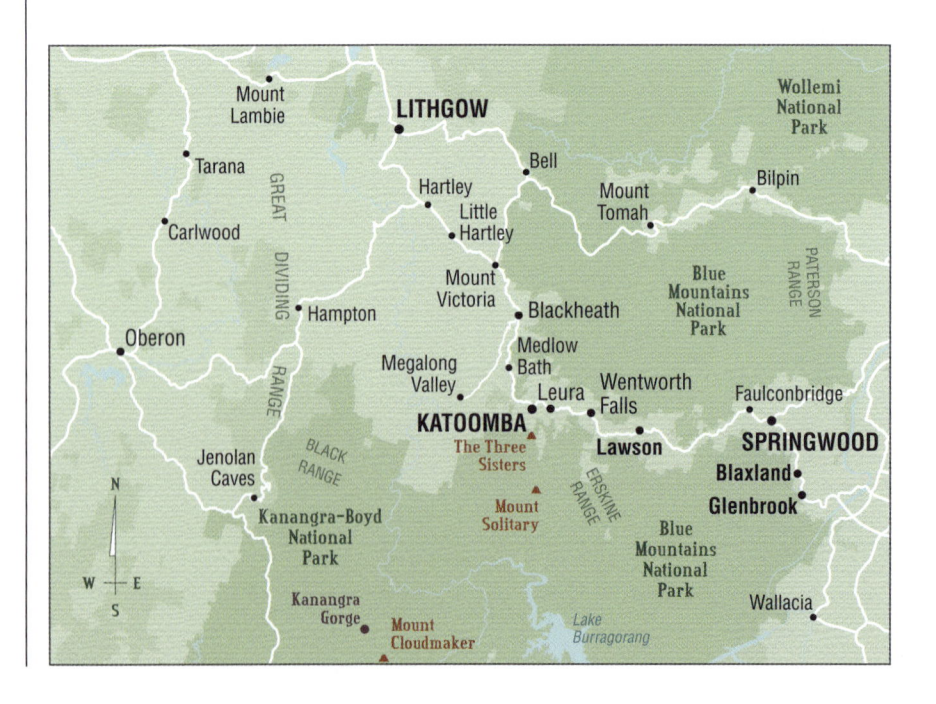

Top: Skyway, Scenic World, Katoomba **Opposite:** The iconic Three Sisters

CHEAT SHEET

→ Allow at least three days for a proper exploration.

→ Best time to visit: the Blue Mountains really is a year-round destination. In summer the mountains are the perfect place to escape Sydney's sticky heat; in autumn the deciduous trees in gardens and along avenues are ablaze with colour; winter time brings the occasional dusting of snow; and spring is a riot of garden blooms.

→ Main towns: Blackheath (*see* p. 16), Katoomba (*see* p. 16).

→ The Darug and Gundungurra Peoples are the Traditional Owners of the Blue Mountains area; search out the many rock-art sites.

→ Did you know? The mountains initially blocked the Europeans from expanding their colony to the west, but a small expedition party in 1813, led by Blaxland, Wentworth and Lawson (all with local towns named after them), crossed the mountains in a remarkable 21 days. Their secret? Following the ridges rather than the valleys.

→ Don't miss: Three Sisters; Red Hands Cave; Scenic World; Wentworth Falls; Blue Mountains Botanic Garden Mount Tomah.

TOP ATTRACTIONS

BLUE MOUNTAINS BOTANIC GARDEN: 5000 species of cool-climate plants at over 1000m above sea level. Also award-winning restaurant; Mount Tomah.

BLUE MOUNTAINS NATIONAL PARK: The Blue Mountains have been home to First Nations People for at least 22,000 years – the Gundungurra People in the north, the Darug People in the south and the Wiradjuri People in the west. It is an area rich not only in Dreamtime stories but also heritage sites, with more than 700 that descendants of the original inhabitants continue to protect today.

In the area east of Blackheath are various waterfalls and lookout points, including the much-photographed Pulpit Rock (6km NE of Blackheath via Hat Hill Rd) and Hanging Rock (around 9km N of Blackheath via Ridgewell Rd).

One of the most popular and easily accessible spots in the park, Echo Point on the south side of Katoomba (*see* p. 16), offers magnificent views of the Jamison Valley, Mount Solitary and the famous Three Sisters. From Echo Point, the Prince Henry Cliff Walk follows the cliff line in either direction. To the west, it runs to majestic Katoomba Falls and the Furber Steps, which descend steeply to the valley floor; to the east it leads past the Three Sisters and the Giant Stairway, another precipitous staircase (800 steps) to the valley, and onwards via the pretty Leura Cascades picnic area to Gordon Falls on the south side of Leura township. Nearby Wentworth Falls (7km E) also has superb walking tracks, notably the National Pass, which begins at the excellent Conservation Hut cafe, descends into the Valley of the Waters, then follows a path cut into the side of the cliff to the base of the dramatic waterfall after which the town is named; the route then climbs up the side of the falls and over the plateau back to Conservation Hut.

In the Glenbrook section of the park Red Hands Cave is accessed by a 8km return walk. The cave features hand stencils (mostly red, although some are white or orange) that were created between 500 and 1600 years ago. The artists created the stencils by placing their hands against the cave wall and blowing a mixture of ochre and water from their mouths. Euroka Clearing (4km S of Glenbrook) is a popular camping spot that is home to many kangaroos. Jellybean Pool, an easy 30min walk from the Glenbrook Information Centre, is a popular spot to cool off on a hot day.

GARDENS OF STONE NATIONAL PARK: Fascinating pagoda rock formations, sandstone escarpments and beehive-shaped domes caused by erosion. This is a great spot for rock climbing and picnics.

HARTLEY: This once-important town became obsolete after the construction of the Great Western Railway in 1887. Explore 17 historical buildings administered by NSW National Parks and Wildlife Service.

KANANGRA–BOYD NATIONAL PARK: This is a rugged and dramatic piece of Australia with vast gorges, spectacular lookouts and scenic rivers. Sandstone formations of Thurat Spires, Kanangra Walls and Mount Cloudmaker are breathtaking and the park is excellent for bushwalking, rock climbing and camping. In 2000 it was declared part of the Greater Blue Mountains World Heritage Area. The **Jenolan Caves** are just outside the park border and are justifiably the country's best known cluster of caves. Of the 300 or so 'rooms', nine are open to the public, by tour only. Tours of the majestic caverns feature flowstone deposits, helictites, columns and lakes. On the south-east edge of the park is **Yerranderie**, a restored silver-mining town with accommodation and walking trails. Inquiries (02) 6336 1972.

NORMAN LINDSAY GALLERY: The former home of artist and writer Norman Lindsay, now a gallery and museum dedicated to his life and work, with a good cafe. Lindsay was the author of *The Magic Pudding* and the subject of the film *Sirens* (1994), which was partly filmed here; open Thurs–Mon 10am–4pm; 14 Norman Lindsay Cres, Faulconbridge; (02) 4751 1067.

SCENIC WORLD: Located near Katoomba Falls, the Three Sisters and Echo Point, Scenic World takes in some of the best scenery in Blue Mountains National Park. Take a ride on the Scenic Railway, which was originally built to transport coal and miners, and is the world's steepest railway, or jump on the Scenic Skyway, a 720m ride in a cable car high above the Jamison Valley. There is also the Scenic Cableway, which descends into the heart of the valley, and plenty of other attractions to explore on foot; (02) 4780 0200, 1300 759 929.

WOLLEMI NATIONAL PARK: This is the largest wilderness area in NSW at 500,000ha, and is a breathtaking display of canyons, cliffs and undisturbed forest. It holds great significance for its Traditional Owners – the Wiradjuri, Darug, Wanaruah and Darkinjung Peoples. There are approximately 120 known sites of significance within the park, including rock engravings, ceremonial grounds and scarred trees. In 1994 the discovery of a new tree species – the Wollemi pine – in a rainforest gully was compared to finding a living dinosaur. Highlights include historic ruins at Newnes, the beaches of the Colo Gorge and the glow worms in a disused rail tunnel. The park also includes Glen Davis, home to more species of birds than anywhere else in the Southern Hemisphere. Mount Wilson, surrounded by the park, is a 19th-century village with large homes and superb gardens, many open to the public. Don't miss the nearby Cathedral of Ferns.

OTHER ATTRACTIONS

ABERCROMBIE RIVER NATIONAL PARK: Low eucalypt forest ideal for bushwalks, with kangaroos, wallaroos and wallabies. Abercrombie River, Retreat River and Silent Creek are havens for platypus and great for fishing, swimming and canoeing.

BLUE MOUNTAINS CULTURAL CENTRE: A changing calendar of exhibitions at the Blue Mountains Art Gallery in Katoomba is just one reason to visit this cultural centre complex – it's also home to a library with free wi-fi, cafe, gift shop and the Blue Mountains World Heritage Interpretive Centre; 30 Parke St, Katoomba; programs (02) 4780 5410.

ESKBANK HOUSE MUSEUM: Built in 1842, this sandstone Georgian mansion houses an extensive collection of Lithgow pottery, memorabilia and photographs. The front four rooms are authentically equipped with Regency and Victorian furniture; open Wed–Sun or by appt; (02) 6351 3557; Bennett St, Lithgow.

EVANS CROWN NATURE RESERVE: Bushwalking area with diverse flora and fauna and granite tors. Crown Rock was an initiation and corroboree site for the Wiradjuri People. It is now popular for abseiling. The reserve is 21km north of Oberon (see p. 17).

EXPLORERS TREE: Stump of a blackbutt tree reportedly carved with the initials of Blaxland, Wentworth and Lawson (there is some question about whether this was done by the explorers themselves or by early tourism operators); off the hwy, 2km west of Katoomba (see p. 16).

SPRINGWOOD: Galleries and craft and antique shops.

Top: View of the Grose Valley **Bottom:** Sunset over the Blue Mountains **Opposite:** The Grand Canyon walk

KEY TOWNS

BLACKHEATH
Population 5761

Just a few kilometres west of Katoomba, Blackheath is the highest town in the Blue Mountains. The spectacular views from the many lookouts, access to bushwalks and waterfalls, not to mention the guesthouses, cafes, restaurants and gardens, make Blackheath a popular resort town, particularly in Nov during the annual Rhododendron Festival.

SEE & DO **National Parks and Wildlife Heritage Centre:** you can begin your exploration of **Blue Mountains National Park**, *see* Top Attractions, from this centre; it's the starting point for the Fairfax Heritage Walk, an easy and accessible trail with wheelchair access and facilities for the visually impaired. The 4km trail goes to Govetts Leap Lookout, rewarding you with views over Grose Valley. The centre itself features excellent displays on the natural and human history of the mountains, as well as info on tours and walks. Govetts Leap Rd; (02) 4787 8877. **Govett statue:** Govetts Leap was named after a bushranger who apparently rode his horse off the cliff rather than be captured by police; centre of town. **The Campbell Rhododendron Gardens:** magnificent displays of rhododendrons (in bloom Sept–Nov) and other plantings, including azaleas and fern glades; Bacchante St; (02) 4787 8965. **Mermaid's Cave:** picturesque rock cave where parts of *Mad Max III* (1985) were filmed; Megalong Rd; 4km SW. **Hargraves Lookout:** overlooking Megalong Valley; Panorama Point Rd; 7km SW via Shipley Gallery. **Mount Blackheath Lookout:** views of Kanimbla Valley; Mt Blackheath Rd; 8km W via Shipley Rd. **Centennial Glen Stables:** horseriding and instruction, trail rides and drives; Kanimbla Dr via Shipley Rd; 0417 273 438; 11km S. **Market:** School grounds; 1st Sun each month. **Growers' Market:** Community Hall, Great Western Hwy; 2nd Sun each month (except Jan).

GLENBROOK
Population 5078

On the edge of the Blue Mountains, Glenbrook isn't one of the better known Blue Mountains towns. But with an excellent cafe strip, access to the somewhat secret swimming hole of Jellybean Pool, and as the starting point of the track that leads to the impressive rock art of the Red Hands Cave, it's a town worth visiting. Glenbrook was originally known as Watertank because it was used for the storage of water for local steam trains.

SEE & DO **Blue Mountains National Park (Red Hands Cave and Jellybean Pool):** *see* Top Attractions. **Lapstone Zig Zag Walking Track:** follows the 3km path of the original Lapstone Zig Zag Railway. The track includes convict-built Lennox Bridge (the oldest surviving bridge on the mainland), the abandoned Lucasville Station and numerous lookouts with views of Penrith and the Cumberland Plain. Nearby is a monument to John Whitton, a pioneer in railway development. It starts in Knapsack St. **Lagoon:** filled with ducks and flanked by walking trails, this is a perfect picnic spot. **Wascoe Siding Miniature Railway:** 300m of steam and motor railway plus picnic and barbecue facilities; trains operate 1st Sun each month; off Great Western Hwy; 2.5km W. **Linden:** impressive Kings Cave with Caleys Repulse Cairn nearby, commemorating early surveyor George Caley; 20km w. **Market:** Infants School, Ross St; 1st and 3rd Sat each month (except Jan).

⭑ KATOOMBA
Population 8268

For most people a visit to the Blue Mountains is all about viewing the Three Sisters rock formation from Echo Point in Katoomba – it's the number-one attraction in the Blue Mountains. Originally named Crushers but renamed a year later, Katoomba, the unofficial capital of the Blue Mountains, stands at an elevation of 1017m. Blue Mountains National Park lies to the north and south of town, and is easily accessible on foot from the railway station. The explanation for why these mountains look blue lies in the eucalyptus trees covering them; they disperse eucalyptus oil into the atmosphere, which appears like a blue haze in the sun's rays.

SEE & DO **Blue Mountains National Park; Scenic World:** *see* Top Attractions for both. **Blue Mountains Cultural Centre:** *see* Other Attractions.

LEURA
Population 4503

The stylish heart of the Blue Mountains, Leura has a beautiful tree-lined main street with impressive gardens, specialty shops, galleries and restaurants. There are spectacular mountain views from Sublime Point and Cliff Dr. First Nations relics can be found throughout the area, including rock engravings, axe-grinding grooves and cave paintings. All First Nations sites, discovered or undiscovered, are protected and are not to be disturbed by visitors.

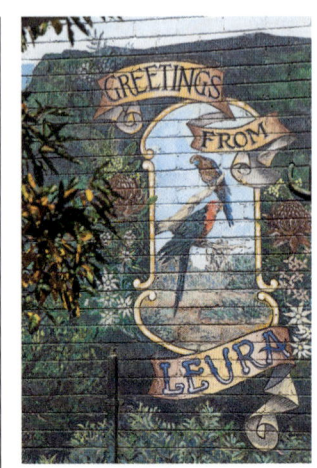

Top: Street art in Leura **Middle:** Family exploring Katoomba **Bottom:** Summer in Mayfield Garden in Oberon

VISITOR INFORMATION

Blue Mountains Visitor Information Centre
Echo Point Rd, Katoomba
1300 653 408
visitbluemountains.com.au

TOP EVENTS

→ FEB Roaring 20s Festival and All That Jazz (Katoomba)

→ MAR Blue Mountains Music Festival (Katoomba)

→ APR Ironfest (Lithgow)

→ JUNE–AUG Yulefest (various locations in the region)

→ AUG Winter Magic Festival (Katoomba)

→ SEPT–NOV Spring Garden Festivals, including the Leura Gardens Festival and the Blackheath Rhododendron Festival

TEMPERATURES

Jan: 13–23°C

July: 2–10°C

SEE & DO Everglades Gardens: a celebrated 1930s garden with a gallery devoted to its creator, Paul Sorensen; Everglades Ave.

LITHGOW
Population 12,411

This isolated but beautiful town is just over the Blue Mountains in the western foothills. The best place to see the region's beauty is at the nearby Hassans Walls Lookout, the tallest in the Blue Mountains. Lithgow boomed following the establishment of the revolutionary Zig Zag Railway in 1869, which was built with gently sloping ramps to cut through the mountains, and connected Lithgow to the coast. The historic railway was damaged by fire in 2013 and again in 2019, but at the time of writing was gearing up to reopen; check zigzagrailway.com.au for updates.

SEE & DO Wollemi National Park: *see* Top Attractions. **Eskbank House Museum:** *see* Other Attractions. **Blast Furnace Park:** ruins of Australia's first blast furnace complex (1886) with a pleasant walk around adjacent Lake Pillans Wetland; off Inch St. **State Mine Railway Heritage Park:** mining and railway equipment and historic mining buildings; State Mine Gully Rd. **Small Arms Factory Museum:** established in 1912, some argue that this is the birthplace of modern manufacturing in Australia. Displays range from firearms to sewing machines; open Tues and Thurs, Sat, Sun, public and school holidays 10am–4pm; Methven St; (02) 6351 4452. **Lake Lyell:** stunning lake in mountain setting, popular for power-boating, waterskiing, trout fishing and picnics; canoe and boat hire available onsite; 9km W. **Lake Wallace:** sailing and trout fishing; 11km NW. **Jannei Goat Dairy:** produces cheeses, yoghurt and milk and is open to visitors, with free cheese tastings; 11km NW. **Portland:** charming town with a power station offering tours and interactive exhibits, a museum with Australian memorabilia and several pleasant picnic areas; 17km NW.

MOUNT VICTORIA
Population 945

National Trust–classified Mount Victoria is the westernmost township of the Blue Mountains. There are buildings from the 1870s, craft shops and a museum at the train station.

SEE & DO Historic buildings: include the Imperial Hotel, St Peter's Church of England and the Manor House. **Mount Vic Flicks historic cinema:** open Thurs–Sun and summer school holidays. **Mount Victoria:** from town there are easy walking trails that lead to wonderful views of the valleys and mountains and picnic spots.

OBERON
Population 48277

This picturesque farming town is 1113m above sea level, which gives Oberon a mountain climate of cool summers, crisp winters and occasional snow. The town was named for the king in *A Midsummer Night's Dream* at the suggestion of a local Shakespeare enthusiast, after it was decided that the earlier name, Glyndwr, was unpleasant to the ear.

SEE & DO Museum: almost 1ha of displays including early farming equipment, a fully furnished early settlers' house, a blacksmith shop and a functioning forge. A wide collection of artefacts and memorabilia are also housed in the town's original 1920s railway station. Open Sun 10.30am–4pm and 1st Sat of month 2–5pm or by appt; Lowes Mount Rd; 0418 671 754. **Lake Oberon:** a good spot for trout fishing (both brown and rainbow). Swimming is not permitted; unpowered and electric powered vessels are permitted, with a boat ramp at Reef Reserve. There are also barbecues and picnic facilities; Jenolan St. **The Common:** green park with a small lake and picnic facilities; Edith Rd. **Reef Reserve:** natural bushland with access to the lake foreshore; Reef Rd. **Market:** Showground; 1st Sat each month. **Driving tours:** routes taking in caves, national parks and surrounding towns; brochure from visitor centre. **Wood mushrooms:** delicacies that grow in Jenolan, Vulcan and Gurnang state forests Jan–early May. Mushrooms should be correctly identified before picking. Brochure from visitor centre.

Southern Highlands, Capital Country and Illawarra

It's not just the **cool-climate gardens**, green farmland and **colonial-era streetscapes** that will remind you of English villages in the pretty towns of the Southern Highlands and tablelands between Sydney and Canberra, but also the climate. Bursting with history at every turn – it was one of the first areas to be settled by Europeans outside of Sydney – the **galleries, boutiques, wineries and guesthouses** make it a popular **weekend getaway** destination, especially in winter when the weather is perfect for **curling up beside a roaring fire with a glass of local wine**. But there's also **beautiful coastline, swim spots and surf breaks** aplenty.

CHEAT SHEET

→ Allow at least three days for a proper exploration.

→ Best time to visit: summer for beaches, spring for gardens, winter for cosy fireside weekends away.

→ Main towns: Berry (see p. 23), Bowral (see p. 23), Goulburn (see p. 25), Wollongong (see p. 27).

→ The Gundungurra, Tharawal and Wiradjuri People are the Traditional Owners of the land in and around the Southern Highlands and tablelands.

→ Don't miss: browsing for antiques in Moss Vale; historic Berrima; springtime gardens; Fitzroy Falls; Kangaroo Valley; the Kiama Blowhole; beaches; Shoalhaven wineries; Wombeyan Caves; summer cherries in Young.

Top: Goulburn's Court House
Opposite: View over Kiama's Blowhole Point

TOP ATTRACTIONS

AUSTRALIAN BOTANIC GARDEN: Australia's largest botanic garden is a striking 400ha garden with 20km of walking trails. Attractions include two ornamental lakes with picnic areas, a nursery, an arboretum, themed gardens, the rare and endangered plants garden and the banksia garden. The botanic garden is a haven for over 160 bird species and mammals such as the wallaroo and swamp wallaby. The human sundial allows visitors to tell the time by standing at its centre and raising their arms. Guided tours are available. Mount Annan Dr, Mount Annan; (02) 4634 7935. It's 3km from Campbelltown (see p. 24).

BIG MERINO: Even though it was only built in 1985, the Big Merino is an instantly recognisable landmark associated with Goulburn (see p. 25) and its thriving merino wool industry. The 15m high and 18m long sculptured sheep has three floors, with a souvenir shop, an educational display on the history of wool in the area, and a lookout. Cnr Hume and Sowerby sts, Goulburn; (02) 4882 8013.

BRADMAN MUSEUM & INTERNATIONAL CRICKET HALL OF FAME: Bowral (see p. 23) was the home town of Sir Donald Bradman and this museum displays a comprehensive history of cricket, including an oak bat from the 1750s. The Don Bradman memorabilia collection includes the bat he used to score 304 at Headingley in 1934. A cinema plays Bradman footage and newsreels. The Bradman Walk through town takes in significant sites including the Don's two family homes. A brochure is available from the museum. Bradman Oval; St Jude St, Bowral; (02) 4862 1247.

BUDDEROO NATIONAL PARK: This park offers views from a plateau across sandstone country, heathlands and rainforest. There are excellent walking trails, including one that is accessible by wheelchair, and there are three lookouts with views of Carrington Falls. The Minnamurra Rainforest Centre is the highlight with an elevated boardwalk through rainforest and a steep paved walkway to Minnamurra Falls. The park can be accessed within a half hour drive from both Jamberoo (see p. 25) and Robertson (see p. 26).

BUNGENDORE: This historic country village is set in a picturesque valley near Lake George and is graced with old stone, brick and timber buildings that have been there since the 19th century. The town square contains charming colonial-style shops selling crafts and antiques, and there are several hobby farms in the area. Several wineries are around Bungendore and have cellar-door tastings and sales. The village is 26km north-east of Queanbeyan (see p. 26).

CANBERRA WINE REGION Canberra has around 35 cellar doors, a few on the boundary of the ACT itself, but the majority are a little further north around Murrumbateman and Lake George. The first vines in this hilly terrain were planted in 1971. Many of the original winemakers had no experience in winemaking and came from government or science jobs in the ACT. Their wine was slow to take off, but there are no such limitations now. The region produces a great range of styles, with many varieties considered excellent. **Clonakilla** makes good shiraz and riesling, but its shiraz viognier is the standout – it is difficult to get hold of, but worth trying at the small cellar door. Helm reaches similar heights with riesling and **Lark Hill** with pinot noir. Follow the signs on Barton Hwy from Yass (*see* p. 27); brochure from Yass visitor centre.

ILLAWARRA FLY TREE TOP ADVENTURES: Visitors can experience the Southern Highlands' native flora and fauna from 25m above ground. The 600m walkway has two cantilevered arms stretching to the forest fall line, with expansive views of Lake Illawarra and the South Pacific Ocean. For those who want to get even higher, a spiralling tower reaches 45m above ground. The environmentally friendly visitor centre has a cafe. Knights Hill Rd (roughly halfway between Robertson and Jamberoo); 1300 362 881.

ILLAWARRA LIGHT RAILWAY MUSEUM: The museum offers tram rides, displays of steam trains and vintage carriages and a miniature railway. The ticket office and kiosk are in an original 1890s rail terminus and the volunteer staff are knowledgeable. Open Tues and Thurs; steam-train rides 2nd Sun each month and Sun during public holiday weekends; Tongarrra Rd. The museum is 8km north-west of Shellharbour (*see* p. 26).

JAMBEROO ACTION PARK: Family fun water park with water slides, speedboats, racing cars and bobsleds; closed during winter; (02) 4236 0114; jamberoo.net.

KIAMA BLOWHOLE: The famous blowhole in the town of Kiama (*see* p. 25) sprays water to heights of 60m and is floodlit at night. Beside the blowhole is a constructed rockpool and a cafe. **Pilots Cottage Historical Museum** has displays on the blowhole, early settlement, the dairy industry and shipping. Blowhole Pt; (02) 4232 2492.

MORTON NATIONAL PARK: The park is the Traditional Land of the Yuin People and there are significant sites here, including Didthul/Balgan (Pigeon House Mountain, *see* p. 85). The park consists mainly of rainforest and eucalypts and is home to myriad native fauna including wallabies, potoroos and bush rats. Belmore Falls plunges into two separate rockpools, which then cascade down to the valley below. The area also features walking tracks and pleasant picnic facilities. At Fitzroy Falls is the National Parks and Wildlife Service visitor centre, which has maps and information about the entire national park and offers guided tours. The falls drop 80m over sandstone cliffs onto black rocks and then another 40m into the valley below. The walking trail around the falls has excellent lookouts. See glow worms at night in the remarkable Glow Worm Glen. Different sections of the national park can be accessed from Bundanoon (*see* p. 24), Nowra (*see* p. 88), Robertson (*see* p. 26) and Ulladulla (*see* p. 89).

NSW RAIL MUSEUM: The museum is open daily and offers steam-train rides on Saturdays and Sundays (except in summer when the diesel trains run). 10 Barbour Rd, Thirlmere; (02) 4683 6800.

ROYAL NATIONAL PARK: Established in 1879, this is the second oldest national park in the world, after Yellowstone in the USA. There is much natural diversity packed into a compact parkland. Highlights include walking and cycling along Lady Carrington Dr through rich forest, swimming at the beach or in the lagoon at Wattamolla, enjoying the Victorian-era park atmosphere at Audley (with causeway, picnic lawns and rowboats) and walking the magnificent 26km Coast Track; (02) 9542 0648. Grand Pacific Dr, a tourist route along the coast, links Royal National Park with Wollongong (*see* p. 27). The 70km drive takes in marvellous scenery and the Sea Cliff Bridge.

SOUTHERN HIGHLANDS WINE REGION: The region around Mittagong, Bowral and Moss Vale is considered the NSW equivalent of South Australia's Adelaide Hills. The elevation is high, ranging from 550m to 880m, and the climate is cool, making it perfect for chardonnay, sauvignon blanc and pinot noir. Other varieties like pinot gris, tempranillo, petit verdot and gewürztraminer are also available.

WOMBEYAN CAVES: Five caves are open to the public including Figtree Cave, widely regarded as the best self-guided cave in NSW. Junction Cave has a colourful underground river; Wollondilly Cave has five main chambers with outstanding formations; Mulwarree Cave is intimate, with delicate formations; and Kooringa Cave is huge and majestic. Wombeyan Gorge is made of marble, providing an unusual swimming experience. There are several campgrounds and walking trails in the area. The caves are 60km east of Crookwell (*see* p. 25).

WOLLONGONG BOTANIC GARDEN: The magnificent gardens encompass 27ha of undulating land and feature a sunken rose garden, a woodland garden, rainforests and flora representing a range of plant communities. Guided walks are available and the all-abilities playground is popular. Various activities include school holiday performances, craft and gardening workshops throughout the year; call for opening hours; Murphys Ave, Keiraville; (02) 4227 7667. The adjacent Gleniffer Brae Manor House is a Gothic-style 1930s house, now home to the Wollongong Conservatorium of Music and used for music recitals; Northfields Ave, Keiraville.

Opposite: Campbelltown Arts Centre

OTHER ATTRACTIONS

AUSTRALIAN MOTORLIFE MUSEUM: Impressive collection of antique cars and memorabilia; open Wed–Sun 9.30am–4.30pm; Darkes Rd, Kembla Grange; (02) 4261 4100. The museum is 10km south-west of Wollongong (see p. 27).

BARREN GROUNDS NATURE RESERVE: This 1750ha heathland plateau on the Illawarra Escarpment protects over 450 species of plant and 150 species of bird, including the rare ground parrot and eastern bristlebird. It has fabulous bushwalking and excellent birdwatching; park details from Fitzroy Falls Visitor Centre (02) 4887 7270.

BELGENNY FARM: The farm includes Belgenny Cottage (1820) and the oldest surviving collection of farm buildings in Australia; (02) 4654 6800. It's 6km south-east of Camden (see p. 24).

BERRIMA COURTHOUSE: In 1841 the courthouse was the scene of Australia's first trial by jury, in which Lucretia Dunkley and Martin Beech were accused of having an affair and tried for murdering Lucretia's much older husband. They were found guilty and hanged. The building now houses displays on the trial and early Berrima, as well as ghost tours. Cnr Wilshire and Argyle sts, Berrima; (02) 4877 1505.

BRAIDWOOD MUSEUM: Built of local granite and originally the Royal Mail Hotel, this museum in the town of Braidwood (see p. 23) houses over 2100 artefacts and 900 photographs. On display are exhibits of First Nations history, goldmining, the armour worn by Mick Jagger in the 1970 movie version of *Ned Kelly*, a machinery shed and a library of local records, newspapers and family histories. Open Fri 11am–2pm; Wallace St, Braidwood; (02) 4842 2310.

BULLI PASS SCENIC RESERVE: A steep scenic drive with stunning coastal views. Bulli Lookout at the top of the escarpment has great views and a walking path leads to Sublime Point Lookout, which enjoys views over Wollongong.

BUNGONIA STATE CONSERVATION AREA: Popular for adventurers with perfect terrain for canyoning, caving and canoeing. Walking trails offer fantastic river and canyon views. One walk passes through the spectacular Bungonia Gorge.

CAMPBELLTOWN ARTS CENTRE: Visitors can see, explore and participate in art at this interactive centre. Exhibitions are diverse and include local, regional, national and international shows of art and craft. Behind the gallery is a sculpture garden established in 2001 as a Centenary of Federation project. New permanent sculptures are added to the garden on a regular basis. Adjacent to the gallery is the Koshigaya-tei Japanese Teahouse and Garden, a bicentennial gift to the people of Campbelltown from its sister city, Koshigaya. The garden is a peaceful area with a waterfall, koi pond and timber bridge, perfect for picnics and tranquil contemplation. 1 Art Gallery Rd, Campbelltown; (02) 4645 4100.

COOMA COTTAGE: The National Trust has restored and now maintains this former home of explorer Hamilton Hume in Yass (see p. 27). He lived with his wife in the riverside house from 1839 until his death in 1873. It operates as a museum with relics and documents telling of Hume's life and explorations. Open 10am–4pm Fri–Sun; 756 Yass Valley Way, Yass; (02) 9258 0126.

MONGA NATIONAL PARK: This park south-east of Braidwood features a boardwalk through rainforest areas dating back to the ancient Gondwana period. Penance Grove, a small pocket of rainforest, is filled with ancient plumwood trees and tree ferns. The park was affected by the 2019-20 bushfires, so check which areas are open before travelling. Maps at visitor centre. Access via Kings Hwy.

NAMADGI NATIONAL PARK: Takes in much of the Brindabella Range, covering almost half of the ACT. It boasts significant Aboriginal rock art and beautiful bushland. Camping and bushwalking are popular. The excellent Namadgi Visitor Centre is just south of Tharwa.

NAN TIEN TEMPLE: The largest Buddhist temple in the Southern Hemisphere with a range of programs available; open Tues–Sun; Berkeley Rd, Berkeley; (02) 4272 0600. It's 5km south-west of Wollongong (see p. 27).

SEVEN MILE BEACH NATIONAL PARK: Surrounded by sand dunes, the lowland forest here is inhabited by birds and small marsupials. It makes a pretty spot for picnics and barbecues, beach fishing and swimming. The national park is 17km south of Kiama (see p. 25).

THE BIG HOLE AND MARBLE ARCH: The Big Hole, in Deua National Park, is thought to have formed when overlying sandstone collapsed into a subterranean limestone cavern creating an impressive chasm 96m deep and 50m wide. Wildlife in the area includes native birds, echidnas, wallabies, wombats and tiger quolls. Marble Arch is a narrow canyon 3–4m wide and 25m deep. It is over 1km in length and bands of marble are visible along its walls. There are caves along the way, but special permission is required to enter some of them. Some are very dark and require a torch, so it's best to check with NSW National Parks and Wildlife Service if you intend to explore; inquiries (02) 4887 7270.

WEE JASPER: This picturesque village, where Banjo Paterson owned a holiday home, is set in a valley at the foot of the Brindabella Ranges. The Goodradigbee River is excellent for trout fishing. Carey's Caves are full of limestone formations and were the site of the 1957 discovery of the spine of a large extinct wombat.

YOUNG HISTORICAL MUSEUM: This museum is recognised as one of the finest in the country. Meticulously maintained photographs and relics tell the story of the town of Young (see p. 27) during the 1800s and 1900s. During the gold rush there were an estimated 20,000 miners in town, 2000 of whom were Chinese. A combination of lawlessness and racism boiled over in the Lambing Flat riots in 1861, which gave rise to the *Chinese Immigration Restriction Act*, the first legislation to herald the infamous White Australia Policy. The full horrific story of the Lambing Flat riots is covered. Campbell St, Young; (02) 6382 2248.

Clonakilla vineyard **Opposite top:** The Famous Berry Donut Van **Opposite bottom:** Recent Acquisitions exhibition at Campbelltown Arts Centre

VISITOR INFORMATION

Southern Highlands Welcome Centre
62–70 Main St, Mittagong
(02) 4871 2888 or
1300 657 559
visitsouthernhighlands.com.au

Southern Gateway Centre
Princes Hwy, Bulli Tops
(02) 4267 5910
visitwollongong.com.au

KEY TOWNS

BERRIMA
Population 813

The perfect weekender spot and an easy drive from both Sydney and Canberra, Berrima is a lovingly preserved 1830s village, nestled in a valley next to the Wingecarribee River. The whole town has been declared a historic precinct by the National Heritage Council, and many of the original Georgian homes and public buildings remain. With cafes and restaurants, pubs, art galleries, shops and a famous lolly shop (famous among children, anyway) this town is well worth a visit.

SEE & DO **Berrima Courthouse:** *see* Other Attractions. **Berrima District Museum:** displays focus on colonial settlement and the struggles of those days; Market Pl; (02) 4877 1130. **Harpers Mansion:** stately Georgian house was built in 1834 and watches over the town of Berrima. Now owned by the National Trust, there's also a maze for the kids; Wilkinson St. **Australian Alpaca Barn:** sales of knitwear and toys; Market Pl. **The Surveyor General:** established in 1834, it's one of Australia's oldest continuously licensed hotels (there are a few contenders for the title of oldest – the devil is in the detail) and is still pumping out the pints and offers food at the Bush Ranger's Bistro; Old Hume Hwy. **Gaol:** Bushranger Paddy Curran was the first man hanged there in 1842 and Lucretia Dunkley was the first and only woman executed there; Argyle St. **Market:** school grounds, Oxley St; 4th Sun each month. **Wineries:** there are numerous in the area with cellar-door tastings including **Joadja Estate**; Joadja Rd; (02) 4878 5236 3km N, and **Southern Highland Wines** in Sutton Forest; (02) 4868 2300, 10km; maps from visitor centre.

★ BERRY
Population 3098

Delightful Berry was established in the early 19th century to support the logging industry; the town is now famous for its trees, with English oaks, elms and beech trees lining the streets of the town. The historic buildings along the lovely main street are perfect for the business of antiquing, which draws visitors to the town – along with the famous bakery, markets and galleries.

SEE & DO **Berry Museum:** records and photographs of early settlement; open Sat 11am–2pm, Sun 11am–3pm, Mon–Sun during school holidays; Queen St; (02) 4464 3097. **Precinct Galleries:** local contemporary art, craft and design; Alexandra St; (02) 4464 3402. **Antique and craft shops:** contact visitor centre for details. **Country Fair Markets:** showground, cnr Alexandra and Victoria sts; 1st Sun each month (except Feb). **Coolangatta Estate:** convict-built cottages, winery (open for tastings) and accommodation on the site of first European settlement in area; 135 Bolong Rd, Shoalhaven Heads; (02) 4448 7131; 11km SE. **Other wineries in area:** open for tastings and sales; map available from visitor centre.

★ BOWRAL
Population 10,764

The commercial centre of the Southern Highlands, Bowral's close proximity to Sydney and its four distinct seasons means it has always been a popular retreat for the wealthy – evident in the magnificent historic mansions and gardens around town. It is known for the extravagant displays of springtime tulips in the town's parks, and foodies delight in the many places to eat and drink. Cricketing legend Sir Donald Bradman is known as 'the boy from Bowral', as he grew up there (although he was born in Cootamundra, *see* p. 100). Bowral has a range of boutique accommodation which means you no longer have to be rich or famous to enjoy a weekend break in this pretty town.

SEE & DO **Bradman Museum & International Cricket Hall of Fame:** *see* Top Attractions. **Ngunungguia:** Guided by artist Ben Quilty, the Southern Highlands first regional art gallery, inside an old dairy, opened in Ocrtober 2021. The name means 'belonging' in the language of the Gundungurra People; Art Gallery Lane; (02) 4861 5348. **The Milk Factory Gallery:** art and design exhibition centre and cafe; Station St. **Bong Bong St:** specialty shopping including books and antiques. **Historic buildings:** mostly in Wingecarribee and Bendooley sts; brochure available from visitor centre. **Produce market:** Bowral Public School, Bendooley St; 2nd Sat each month. **Mittagong:** This small and appealing town has historic cemeteries and buildings. The artificial Lake Alexandra off Queen St is great for birdwatching and walking. There is a market at the Uniting Church hall on the 3rd and 5th Sat each month. 8km NE. **Mount Gibraltar:** bushwalking trails and lookout over Bowral and Mittagong; 2km N. **Box Vale Mine walking track:** begins at the northern end of Welby, passes through old railway tunnel; 12km N. **Nattai National Park:** protects landforms, geological features, catchments and biodiversity in the Sydney Basin. Only low-impact activities are encouraged and there is a 3km exclusion zone around Lake Burragorang; via Hilltop; 19km N.

BRAIDWOOD
Population 1720

Braidwood was once a gold-rush area and has now been declared a historic town by the National Trust. Gold was plentiful here in the 1800s, the largest gold

NEW SOUTH WALES

discovery being a large nugget in 1869. With gold came bushrangers, such as the Clarke Gang and Ben Hall, and Braidwood became one of the most infamous and dangerous towns in the region. The 19th-century buildings have been carefully maintained and restored and are still in use. The town appears to be from a bygone era, which has made Braidwood a perfect setting for movies such as *Ned Kelly* (1970), *The Year My Voice Broke* (1987) and *On Our Selection* (1995). The town is now an artistic hub, with galleries, cafes, antique stores and boutiques.

SEE & DO **Braidwood Museum; Monga National Park; The Big Hole and Marble Arch:** *see* Other Attractions for all. **Galleries and craft and antique shops:** details from visitor centre. **Tallaganda Heritage Trail and scenic drive:** tours of historic buildings such as the Royal Mail Hotel and St Andrew's Church; brochure from visitor centre. **Scenic drives:** rugged countryside; brochure from visitor centre. **Fishing:** good trout fishing, especially in the Mongarlowe and Shoalhaven rivers; details from visitor centre.

BUNDANOON
Population 2869

Surprisingly, the area that's now Bundanoon was originally thought by many convicts to be China. Ex-convict John Wilson was sent to the area in the late 18th century to gather data to prove that it wasn't China, and to convince convicts not to bother escaping from Sydney in that direction. Since then, the town, which celebrates all thing Scottish with the Brigadoon Highland Gathering in April, has settled into being a weekender destination with heritage buildings, a tree-lined avenue and easy access to Morton National Park.

SEE & DO **Craft shops and art galleries:** several featuring local work; contact visitor centre for details. **Drive and walk to several lookouts:** map from visitor centre. **Market:** Memorial Hall, Railway Ave; 1st and 3rd Sun each month. **Exeter:** quaint village with an English feel; 7km N.

CAMDEN
Population 3378

Camden, in a picturesque setting on the Nepean River just south-west of Sydney, was once a hunting ground of the Gundungurra People, who called it Benkennie, meaning 'dry land'. The Camden region was also importantly the intersection of three language groups: the Gundungurra, the Dharawal (Tharawal) and the Darug. European settlement of the area was the accidental result of eight cattle wandering off four months after the First Fleet landed. They were not seen again until 1795 when it was discovered their number had grown to more than 40. The site on which they were found was named Cowpasture Plains, but the name was later changed to Camden. There were skirmishes between settlers and the Gundungurra People, and the Appin Massacre of 14 Aboriginal People took place on the orders of Governor Macquarie in 1816. Notable settlers John and Elizabeth Macarthur, pioneers of the wool industry, established their famous sheep farm here in 1805. They were the first in Australia to grow tobacco, use mechanical irrigation, produce wine of respectable quality and quantity and make brandy. The Macarthurs sent thousands of vines to the Barossa Valley and are thereby credited with helping to start South Australia's wine industry.

SEE & DO **Belgenny Farm:** *see* Other Attractions. **Self-guided walk and scenic drive:** includes historic buildings such as the Macarthur Camden Estate, St John the Evangelist Church and Kirkham Stables; brochure from visitor centre. **Alan Baker Art Gallery:** two ghosts are reputed to roam the rooms inside this historic Victorian gentleman's townhouse, Macaria, built in 1859-60 as a schoolhouse; open Thurs–Sun 11am–4pm; 37 John St; (02) 4645 5191. **Fresh Produce Market:** Camden Town Farm, Exeter St; Sat. **Cobbitty:** historic rural village with market 1st Sat each month Mar–Dec; 11km NW. **The Oaks:** a small town in open countryside featuring the slab-built St Matthew's Church and Wollondilly Heritage Centre, a social history museum; 16km W. **Burragorang Lookout:** views over Lake Burragorang; 24km w. **Yerranderie:** this fascinating old silver-mining town can be reached by normal vehicle in dry conditions, otherwise only by 4WD or plane; 40km W.

CAMPBELLTOWN
Population 16,577

While Campbelltown is now a major centre in Sydney's outer suburbs, it was originally established in 1820 by Governor Macquarie and named after his wife, Elizabeth Campbell. Many of the genteel buildings from Campbelltown's early history remain, including homesteads, the post office and the bank. A famous local legend is that of Fisher's ghost. In 1826 an ex-convict, Frederick Fisher, disappeared. Another ex-convict, George Worrell, claimed that Fisher had left town, leaving him in charge of Fisher's farm. Luckily, a farmer saw the ghost of Fisher pointing at the creek bank where his body was subsequently found. Worrell was tried and hanged for Fisher's murder, and the Festival of Fisher's Ghost is now an annual event held in town – although Fisher has never been spotted at the festival.

SEE & DO **Australian Botanic Garden:** *see* Top Attractions. **Arts Centre:** *see* Other Attractions. **Glenalvon Museum:** display of historic farm equipment and household goods; open 1st Mon, 2nd Sat and 3rd Mon each month 10am–1pm (Feb–mid-Dec), or by appt; 8 Lithgow St; (02) 4625 1822. **Self-guided heritage walks:** take in numerous historic buildings including St Peter's Church (1823), Emily Cottage (1840) and Fisher's Ghost Restaurant, formerly Kendall's Millhouse (1844); brochure from visitor centre.

Top: Blacksmiths Lane in Queanbeyan **Middle:** Bradman Museum and International Cricket Hall of Fame **Bottom:** Kiama blowhole

TOP EVENTS

- JAN Illawarra Folk Festival (Wollongong)
- FEB Australian Blues Music Festival (Goulburn)
- FEB–MAR Festival of Sport (Shellharbour)
- MAR Goulburn Rose Festival (Goulburn), Festival of Steam (Thirlmere)
- APR Autumn Gardens in the Southern Highlands (throughout region), Bundanoon Highland Gathering (Bundanoon), Open Gardens (throughout region), Potato Festival (Crookwell)
- AUG–SEPT Fireside Festival (Murrumbateman Area)
- SEPT–OCT Tulip Time (Bowral and Moss Vale), Open Gardens (throughout region)
- OCT Garden Festival (Berry), Lilac City Festival (Goulburn)
- NOV Bong Bong Races (Bowral), Festival of Fisher's Ghost (Campbelltown), Crookwell Garden Festival (Crookwell), Wings Over Illawarra (Shellharbour), Southern Highlands Food & Wine Festival (Bowral)
- DEC National Cherry Festival (Young)

TEMPERATURES

Jan: 13–25°C

July: 2–12°C

Macarthur Centre for Sustainable Living: showcasing sustainable homes, gardens and lifestyles. To promote sustainable living, the centre is entirely self-sufficient. Regular workshops are also held throughout the year; Mount Annan Dr, Mount Annan; (02) 4647 9828; 3km W. **Steam and Machinery Museum:** history of Australia's working past, including interactive displays; 86 Menangle Rd, Menangle Park; 0417 215 513; 5km SW. **Menangle:** small town featuring a historic homestead (1834) and the Store (1904), an old-style country store with everything from antiques to ice-creams, and the Menangle Railway Bridge (1863), the colony's first iron bridge; 9km SW. **Appin:** historic coalmining town with a monument to Hume and Hovell (who began their 1824 expedition to Port Phillip from this district). Also weekend markets in 10 locations (brochure available from visitor centre); 16km S.

CROOKWELL
Population 2641

Nestled in the Great Dividing Range about 300m above sea level, Crookwell occasionally gets that remarkable weather event for Australian towns – snow! The town is tree-lined and picturesque, with a cool climate and lush gardens, and has historic buildings that hark back to European settler days. The Country Women's Association was formed here in 1922, and Australia's first grid-connected wind farm was opened nearby in 1998. Wombeyan Caves are about 60km away.

SEE & DO **Wombeyan Caves:** see Top Attractions. **Wind Farm:** viewing platform and information board; Goulburn Rd. **Open Gardens weekends:** spring and autumn (dates from visitor centre). **Redground Lookout:** excellent views of surrounding area; 8km NW. **Lake Wyangala and Grabine Lakeside State Park:** upper reaches ideal for waterskiing, picnicking, fishing, bushwalking and camping; cabins for hire; 65km NW. **Bike riding:** the area surrounding Crookwell is popular for bike riding; trail maps from visitor centre. **Historic villages:** associated with goldmining, copper mining and bushrangers, these villages include Tuena, Peelwood, Laggan, Bigga, Binda (all north) and Roslyn (south); maps from visitor centre. **Historic and scenic drives:** explore sites and countryside frequented by bushrangers such as Ben Hall; brochure from visitor centre.

GOULBURN
Population 23,963

Goulburn was Australia's first inland city – declared in letters patent by no less than Queen Victoria – and has a suitable grandeur, with stately historic buildings lining the streets, including the country's oldest brewery. And while some might argue against calling the Big Merino grand, it is certainly big, and celebrates Goulburn's history as a prominent wool-producing region.

SEE & DO **Big Merino:** see Top Attractions. **Regional Art Gallery:** contemporary art with changing exhibitions; 184 Bourke St; (02) 4823 4494. **Historic Waterworks:** displays antique waterworks engines, beside attractive parkland with picnic and barbecue facilities on Marsden Weir. Museum open Sat–Tues; off Fitzroy St. **Rail Heritage Centre:** heritage-listed workshops and museum; open Tues, Thurs and Sat; Braidwood Rd; (02) 4822 1210. **Garroorigang:** historic family home built in 1857 containing much of its original furnishings; open Mon–Sun; 209 Braidwood Rd; 0410 499 374. **War Memorial and Museum:** located on Rocky Hill, erected in 1925 as a tribute to the Goulburn men and women who served during World War I, the lookout offers outstanding views across the city. Museum open Wed, Sat–Sun and holidays, lookout open Mon–Fri; Memorial Dr. **Self-guided tour:** historic buildings include Goulburn Courthouse and St Saviour's Cathedral; brochure from visitor centre. **Lake George:** 25km long lake that regularly fills and empties. It has excellent picnic sites; 40km SW.

JAMBEROO
Population 1910

One of the most picturesque areas of the NSW coast, Jamberoo was once tropical forest. The town is surrounded by nature reserves and national parks, but is situated on the lush green pastures that have made Jamberoo prosperous as a dairy farming region. The surrounding forests are popular with bushwalkers and birdwatchers.

SEE & DO **Budderoo National Park and Jamberoo Action Park:** see Top Attractions for both. **Jamberoo Pub:** charming 1857 building with meals and Sun afternoon entertainment; Allowrie St. **Market:** Kevin Walsh Oval; last Sun each month. **Jerrara Dam:** a picturesque reserve on the banks of a 9ha dam that was once the town's main water supply. Picnic area surrounded by remnant rainforest and freshwater wetland; 4km SE. **Saddleback Lookout:** 180-degree views of the coast and the starting point for Hoddles Trail, a 1hr walk with beautiful views to Barren Grounds escarpment; 7km S.

★ KIAMA
Population 14,761

Kiama is a lovely coastal holiday town that rolls down to meet the Pacific Ocean. Like many of the south coast towns, Kiama would pick up a crown in a town beauty pageant, with its glorious coastal beauty, graceful lighthouse, excellent activities and showstopper attraction in the Kiama Blowhole.

SEE & DO **Kiama Blowhole:** see Top Attractions. **Seven Mile Beach National Park:** see Other Attractions. **Family History Centre:** world-wide collection of records for compiling and tracing family history; Railway Pde; (02) 4233 1122. **Heritage walk:** includes terraced houses in Collins St and Pilots Cottage; brochure from visitor centre. **Specialty and craft shops:** several in town showcasing local work; brochure from visitor centre. **Beaches:** perfect for surfing, swimming and fishing. **Craft market:** Black Beach; 3rd Sun each month. **Farmers' Market:** Surf Beach; Wed afternoons. **Gerringong:** a coastal town with a renowned heritage museum featuring remarkable scale models of the Illawarra coast. Gerringong's name comes from the Wodi Wodi language and is said to mean 'place of peril'. It is unclear where the peril lies, however, because the safe beaches are ideal for surfing, swimming and fishing. Heavy rainfall means the hinterland is lush and green. 10km S. **Little Blowhole:** smaller but more active than the Kiama Blowhole; off Tingira Cres; 2km S. **Bombo Headland:** blue-metal quarrying in the 1880s left an eerie 'moonscape' of basalt walls and columns, which have been used in commercials and video clips; 2.5km N. **Cathedral Rocks:** scenic rocky outcrop best viewed at dawn; Jones Beach; 3km N. **Kingsford Smith Memorial and Lookout:** the site of Charles Kingsford Smith's 1933 take-off in the *Southern Cross* offers panoramic views; 14km S. **Scenic drives:** in all directions to visit beaches, rock formations, cemeteries and craft shops; brochure from visitor centre.

MOSS VALE
Population 8774

The historic town of Moss Vale is the industrial and agricultural heart of the Southern Highlands. It is on the Traditional Land of the Dharawal People. For most of the last century, Moss Vale was a railway town, and it is dominated by the architecture of the Victorian railway station. The annual Tulip Time Festival in mid-September to mid-October is a huge drawcard with both garden lovers and photographers.

SEE & DO **Leighton Gardens:** picturesque area popular for picnics; Main St. **Historical walk:** includes Aurora College (formerly Dominican Convent) and Kalourgan, believed to have been a residence of Mary MacKillop; brochure from visitor centre. **Sutton Forest:** set among green hills, this tiny town is worth a visit for the quirky Everything Store, selling antiques and curios inside the old town post office, c. 1859. **Hillview House:** just north of the forest, was the official residence of NSW governors 1882–1958. 6km SW. **Cecil Hoskins Nature Reserve:** tranquil wetland with over 90 bird species, one-third of which are waterfowl; 3km NE.

PICTON
Population 3847

Located in the foothills of the Southern Highlands, Picton was once a thriving town, but since the re-routing of the Hume Hwy it has become a peaceful and well-preserved village. Originally gazetted as Stonequarry, the town was renamed after Thomas Picton, one of Wellington's generals at the battle of Waterloo.

SEE & DO **George IV Inn:** one of Australia's oldest operating inns, with meals and regular entertainment. Argyle St; (02) 4677 1415. **Botanic Gardens:** quiet rural park with views over the farmland, barbecues and picnic facilities; Regreme Rd. **Self-guided historical walk:** includes the splendid railway viaduct (1862) over Stonequarry Creek, and St Mark's Church (1848). **Thirlmere Lakes National Park:** protects five reed-fringed freshwater lakes that are home to waterbirds and other wildlife. This is a great place for swimming, picnicking and canoeing, and there is a scenic walk around the lakes; 10km SW. **Jarvisfield Homestead:** historic 1865 home, now the clubhouse of Antill Park Golf Club; Remembrance Dr; 2km N. **Sydney Skydivers:** catering for beginners and experienced skydivers with video-viewing facilities and a pleasant picnic and barbecue area; (02) 9791 9155; 5km E.

QUEANBEYAN
Population 37,511

The leafy green city of Queanbeyan is often mistakenly considered part of Canberra. And while this growing city sprawls into the ACT, Queanbeyan is technically part of NSW. Queanbeyan takes its name from a squat that ex-convict Timothy Beard inhabited near the Molonglo River. He called it 'Quinbean' after an Aboriginal word believed to mean 'clear waters'.

SEE & DO **Bungendore:** *see* Top Attractions. **History Museum:** documented history of the city in restored police sergeant's residence; open by appt; Farrer Pl; (02) 6297 2730. **Printing Museum:** includes memorabilia from the first newspaper in Queanbeyan; open Sat–Sun 2–4pm; Farrer Pl. **Queanbeyan Art Society Inc:** exhibits local art and craft; Trinculo Pl. **Self-guided town walks:** include Byrne's Mill (1883) and St Benedict's Convent, built in the 1800s for the Sisters of the Good Samaritan; now home to an art and bead gallery and cafe; brochure available from visitor centre. **Molonglo Gorge:** 3km walking trail provides views of Molonglo River; 2km N. **Googong Dam:** fishing, bushwalking and picnicking; 10km S.

London Bridge Woolshed and Shearers' Quarters: visual history of turn-of-the-century farming and settlement life. Take the easy 1km walk to a remarkable limestone arch; 24km S. **Captains Flat:** tiny mining town, remnants of historic buildings, heritage trail; 45km S.

ROBERTSON
Population 1476

One of the many charming towns in the Southern Highlands, Robertson sits high atop the Macquarie Pass, and you can sometimes catch spectacular views all the way to the Pacific Ocean from spots in town. But it's the view of Robertson's Big Potato that often captivates visitors, mainly because it doesn't really look like a potato at all. You could be mistaken for thinking it a rock or a large brown cylinder, or as the locals like call it, a big poo. The Big Potato celebrates the region's success as the largest spud-growing district in NSW. The bucolic surrounds were also used as the setting for the film *Babe* (1996) and you can access both Budderoo National Park and Morton National Park from here.

SEE & DO **Budderoo National Park; Illawarra Fly Tree Top Adventures; Morton National Park:** *see* Top Attractions for all. **Cockatoo Run Heritage Railway:** steam train (when available) to Port Kembla; Robertson Railway Station; for running times call 1300 653 801. **Art and craft shops:** several in town featuring local work; details from visitor centre. **Market:** Robertson School of Arts; 2nd Sun each month. **Robertson Rainforest:** 5ha portion of what was the 2500ha Yarrawah Brush. It is home to abundant birdlife and features an attractive bushwalk; 2km S. **Burrawang:** 19th-century village with an excellent historic pub; 6km W. **Macquarie Pass National Park:** preserved section of the Illawarra Escarpment with bushwalks through eucalypt forest and picnic facilities; 10km E. **Mannings Lookout:** beautiful views over Kangaroo Valley; 16km SW.

SHELLHARBOUR
Population 76,271

Shellharbour was a thriving port in the 1830s when development could not keep up with demand. The first shops did not appear until the 1850s and the courthouse and gaol were erected in 1877. Prior to this the local constable had to tie felons to a tree. Today the town is an attractive holiday resort close to Lake Illawarra and one of the oldest settlements on the South Coast.

SEE & DO **Illawarra Light Railway Museum:** *see* Top Attractions. **City Museum:** shows area's history through photographs, maps and sketches; 76 Cygnet Ave. **Historic walk:** take in the historical buildings of the town, beginning at the Steampacket Inn, parts of which date back to 1856. Contact visitor centre for more information. **Snorkelling and scuba diving:** at Bushrangers Bay; details from visitor centre or Shellharbour Scuba Centre; (02) 4296 4266. **Lake Illawarra:** This large tidal estuary was once a valuable source of food for the Wadi Wadi People. It is home to waterbirds such as black swans, pelicans and royal spoonbills, and has picnic and barbecue areas. The lake is excellent for boating, swimming, waterskiing, windsurfing, fishing and prawning. 7km N. **Blackbutt Forest Reserve:** remnant of coastal plain forest in urban area. Walking trails offer views of Lake Illawarra and Illawarra Escarpment; 2km W. **Killalea Recreation Park:** foreshore picnic area with an ideal beach for surfing, diving, snorkelling and fishing; 3km S. **Bass Point Aquatic and Marine Reserve:** top spot for scuba diving, snorkelling, fishing and surfing, with a nice picnic area on the shore; 5km SE. **Crooked River Wines:** specialty is Chardonnay White Port, with a gorgeous restaurant onsite; 20km S.

WOLLONGONG
Population 280,153

Known for its heavy industry, Wollongong also enjoys some of the best coastal scenery and beaches in the state, superbly positioned with mountains to the west and ocean to the east. It has the facilities and sophistication missing in many smaller towns and has been awarded the title of 'Australia's most liveable regional city'.

SEE & DO **Wollongong Botanic Garden:** *see* Top Attractions. **Australian Motorlife Museum; Nan Tien Temple:** *see* Other Attractions for both. **Flagstaff Point:** 180-degree views of the ocean and historic lighthouse (1872); Endeavour Dr. **Illawarra Museum:** highlights include handicraft room and Victorian parlour; open Wed, Sat–Sun 12–3pm; Market St; (02) 4228 7770. **Art Gallery:** collection of 19th- and 20th-century art including First Nations art; cnr Burelli and Kembla sts; Tues–Fri 10am–5pm, Sat–Sun 12–4pm; (02) 4227 8500. **Mall:** soaring steel arches and water displays; Crown St. **Illawarra Brewery:** locally brewed beers; Crown St; (02) 4220 2854. **Wollongong Harbour:** home to a large fishing fleet and Breakwater Lighthouse. **Surfing beaches and rockpools:** to the north and south, with excellent surfing and swimming conditions. **Foreshore parks:** several with superb coastal views and picnic facilities. **Market:** Crown St; every Fri. **Illawarra Escarpment:** forms the western backdrop to the city and has lookouts at Stanwell Tops, Sublime Point, Mount Keira and Mount Kembla. **Science Space:** immersive science museum and planetarium with hands-on displays and activities for all ages; Thurs–Tues open 10am–4pm; Squires Way, Fairy Meadow; (02) 4286 5000; 2km N. **Lake Illawarra:** stretching from the South Pacific Ocean to the foothills of the Illawarra Range, the lake offers good prawning, fishing and sailing. Boat hire is available; 5km S. **Port Kembla:** close-up view of local industry and the steelworks at Australia's Industry World with tours most Friday mornings; bookings (02) 4275 7023. **Mount Kembla:** site of horrific 1902 mining disaster. Also here are several historic buildings and a museum featuring a colonial-era kitchen, a blacksmith's shop and a reconstruction of the Mount Kembla disaster. The 96 Candles Ceremony is held each winter in memory of those who died; 10km W. **Symbio Wildlife Park:** koalas, eagles, monkeys, wombats, reptiles and Sumatran tigers; Lawrence Hargrave Dr, Helensburgh; (02) 4294 1244; 32km N. **Lawrence Hargrave Memorial and Lookout:** on Bald Hill, this was the site of aviator Hargrave's first attempt at flight in the early 1900s. Now popular for hang-gliding; 36km N. **Heathcote National Park:** excellent for bushwalks through rugged bushland, past hidden pools and gorges; (02) 9542 0648; 40km N. **Dolphin Watch Cruises:** *see* Jervis Bay p. 87; 50 Owen St, Huskisson; (02) 4441 6311.

YASS
Population 6759

Like any country town worth its salt, Yass has a famous bushranger to call its own. In this case it is Johnny Gilbert, who managed 630 robberies before he was shot dead at the age of 23. Yass is better known for being the home of the famous explorer Hume (the highway is named after him), who passed through the area with Hovell on their expedition to Port Phillip. You can visit his home, Cooma Cottage, just outside town, or follow the famous expedition on the Hume and Hovell Walking Track, which goes to Albury. The town of Yass is historic, and set in rolling countryside on the Yass River.

SEE & DO **Cooma Cottage:** *see* Other Attractions. **Cemetery:** contains the grave of explorer Hamilton Hume; via Rossi St. **Museum:** historic displays including a war exhibit encompassing the Boer War, World War I and World War II; open Sat–Sun; Comur St. **Railway Museum:** history of the Yass tramway; open Sun 10am–4pm; Crago St. **Self-guided town walk and drive:** highlight is the historic buildings in the main street; brochure from visitor centre. **Community market:** Meehan St; 1st and 3rd Sat each month. **Riverbank Markets:** Comur St; 4th Sun. **Bookham:** village with historic cemetery; 30km W. **Binalong:** historic town with glass-blowing studio and the grave of bushranger Johnny Gilbert; 37km NW. **Burrinjuck Waters State Park:** bushwalking, cruises, watersports and fishing; off Hume Hwy; 54km SW. **Brindabella National Park:** birdwatching, camping and bushwalking in alpine surrounds; 4WD access only; via Wee Jasper; (02) 6122 3100; 61km SW. **Hume and Hovell Walking Track:** 21-day, 426km trek from Albury to Yass; for a kit (including maps), see: humeandhovelltrack.com.au. At the time of writing, around 60km of the track remained closed after the 2019/20 bushfires.

YOUNG
Population 7712

Young is an attractive town in the western foothills of the Great Dividing Range with a fascinating history of goldmining. The Lambing Flat goldfields boomed after a gold discovery was announced in 1860. Today the town is the peaceful centre of a cherry-farming district and hosts the National Cherry Festival in Dec.

SEE & DO **Young Historical Museum:** *see* Other Attractions. **Burrangong Art Gallery:** hosts changing exhibitions from guest and local artists; at visitor centre; Lovell St. **Bluestill Distillery:** tours and tastings; Henry Lawson Way; (02) 6382 2200. **Chinaman's Dam Recreation Area:** scenic walks, playground, picnic and barbecue facilities. Includes Lambing Flat Chinese Tribute Gardens with Pool of Tranquillity; Pitstone Rd; 4km SE. **Murringo:** historic buildings and a leatherworks; 21km E. **Hilltops winery:** surrounding region produces cool-climate wines; cellar-door information at visitor centre. **Cherries and stone fruit:** sales and pick-your-own throughout the area (Nov–Dec, cherries blossom in Sept–Oct). **Boorowa:** settled by Irish ticket-of-leave men in the early 1800s, this town retains its Irish flavour, with Shamrock historic walking trails and the annual Irish Woolfest in Oct. Galleries, art and craft co-op, cafes, bakery and river walks make it an ideal daytrip from Canberra.

Central Coast and Hawkesbury

Just north of Sydney, the Central Coast is the ideal weekend getaway, with **beaches, bushland** and **charming seaside towns** that still retain their village vibe, all within a two-hour drive of the city. To the west, the Hawkesbury is one of the country's oldest European settlements and is crammed full of **convict history** and beautifully preserved **historic buildings**, although its wonderful **water vistas** and **gourmet produce** is just as much reason to visit.

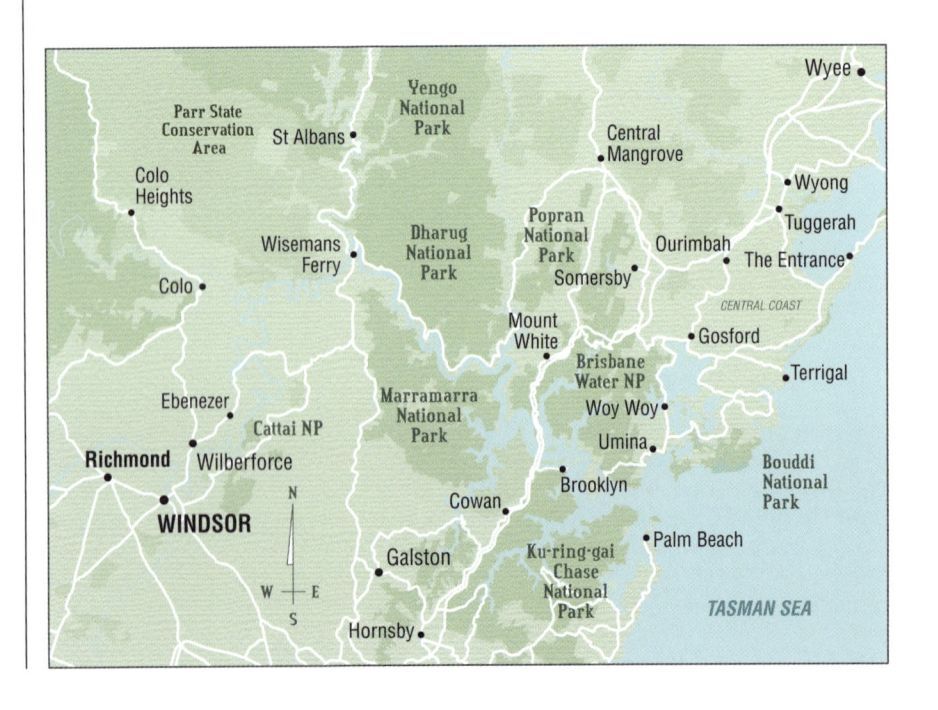

CHEAT SHEET

→ Allow at least two days for a proper exploration.

→ Best time to visit: year-round, although summer is the best beach weather.

→ Main towns: Gosford (*see* p. 31), The Entrance (*see* p. 32), Windsor (*see* p. 32).

→ The Hawkesbury is the Traditional Land of the Darug People, and the Central Coast region is the Traditional Lands of the Awabakal, Darkinjung and Kuring-gai; both areas are rich in Aboriginal sites, including many fabulous rock engravings.

→ Don't miss: Australian Reptile Park; the convict-built Old Great North Road in Dharug National Park; Wisemans Ferry; Bilpin apples; beaches and bushwalks in Bouddi National Park.

Top: Shields Orchards in Bilpin
Opposite: Terrigal Beach at sunrise

TOP ATTRACTIONS

AUSTRALIAN REPTILE PARK: Snakes, spiders and Galapagos tortoises. See shows throughout the day. **Somersby Falls** nearby provide an ideal picnic spot. Pacific Hwy, Somersby; (02) 4340 1022.

BILPIN: This tiny town is known for its apples and apple juice. It was originally named Belpin after Archibald Bell Jnr, who was the first European to cross the mountains from Richmond (Bells Line of Road is also named after him). The fact that he did this with the help of local Aboriginal People, who had been doing it for thousands of years, did not seem to detract from the achievement. Bilpin has many orchards that are part of the Hawkesbury Farm Gate Trail. Brochures are available from the visitor centre. There are markets every Sat. It is 31km north-west of Richmond (*see* p. 31).

BOUDDI NATIONAL PARK: This park near Terrigal (*see* p. 31) ranges from secluded beaches beneath steep cliffs to lush pockets of rainforest, with several signposted bushwalks. There are many sites of cultural significance here, including rock shelters with Aboriginal art. Maitland Bay is at the heart of a 300ha marine park extension to protect marine life, one of the first in NSW, and contains the wreck of the *PS Maitland*. Fishing is allowed in all other areas. Putty Beach is safe for swimming and Maitland Bay is good for snorkelling. Tallow Beach is not patrolled so seek local advice before swimming here.

BRISBANE WATER NATIONAL PARK: This beautiful park of rugged sandstone near Woy Woy (*see* p. 33) offers spring wildflowers, bushwalks and birdlife. Staples Lookout has superb coastal views. Warrah Lookout enjoys a sea of colour in spring when the wildflowers bloom. The Bulgandry engravings on Woy Woy Rd are a highlight.

CATTAI NATIONAL PARK: First Fleet assistant surgeon Thomas Arndell was granted this land and today the park features his 1821 cottage, although the park is on the Traditional Land of the Darug People. There are also grain silos and the ruins of a windmill believed to be the oldest industrial building in the country. The old farm features attractive picnic and barbecue areas and campsites. In a separate section nearby, Mitchell Park offers walking tracks and canoeing on Cattai Creek.

DHARUG NATIONAL PARK: The multicoloured sandstone provides striking scenery on this land. The convict-built Old Great North Road is a great example of early 19th-century roadbuilding. Convicts quarried, dressed and shifted large sandstone blocks to build walls and bridges, but the road was abandoned before it was finished because of poor planning. Signposted walking tracks lead through beautiful bushland and to Traditional Owner's rock engravings. The clear-water tributaries are popular for swimming, fishing and canoeing. You can access the national park from Wisemans Ferry (*see* p. 33).

NEW SOUTH WALES

29

GOSFORD REGIONAL GALLERY AND EDOGAWA COMMEMORATIVE GARDEN: The gallery displays artworks and crafts by local artists and hosts major touring exhibitions; it also has an excellent shop selling local crafts, and an arts centre offering talks and courses. Adjoining the gallery, the Edogawa Commemorative Garden is an exquisite traditional Japanese garden built to commemorate the ongoing relationship between Gosford and its Japanese sister city, Edogawa, near Tokyo. 36 Webb St, East Gosford; (02) 4304 7550.

LAKES: A lake system of 80sqkm, on average less than 2m deep and shark-free. The linked Tuggerah Lake, Budgewoi Lake and Lake Munmorah all empty into the ocean at The Entrance and are fabulous for fishing and prawning (in summer), as well as watersports.

WYRRABALONG NATIONAL PARK: With sections lying north and south of The Entrance, this park conserves the last significant coastal rainforest on the Central Coast. The north forms the Traditional Land of the Awabakal People, and the south the Darkinjung People. Signposted walking tracks lead along rocky cliffs and beaches with lookouts and picnic spots along the way providing stunning coastal views. The national park is just outside The Entrance (see p. 32).

OTHER ATTRACTIONS

BROOKLYN: Access to lower Hawkesbury for houseboating, fishing and river cruises. Historic Riverboat Postman ferry leaves Brooklyn Mon–Fri 10am for cruises and postal deliveries; bookings essential 0400 600 111.

EBENEZER: Picturesque town with Australia's oldest church (1809), colonial graveyard and schoolhouse.

HAWKESBURY REGIONAL MUSEUM: Built as a home in the 1820s, the building became the Daniel O'Connell Inn in 1843. In the late 1800s it was used to print *The Australian*, a weekly newspaper. Today it houses the history of the local area in photographs, documents and artefacts, with special displays on riverboat history and the Richmond Royal Australian Air Force base. Open Wed–Mon 10am–4pm; 8 Baker St Windsor; (02) 4560 4655.

YENGO NATIONAL PARK AND PARR STATE CONSERVATION AREA: Rugged land of gorges, cliffs and rocky outcrops near Wisemans Ferry (see p. 33). Mount Yengo (originally Yango) is an important place for Aboriginal Peoples of South-Eastern Australia as it was from here that the creator spirit, Biamie, left the earth, flattening the top of the mountain with his foot as he went. Discovery walks, talks and 4WD tours are conducted by the National Parks & Wildlife Service; bookings (02) 4784 7301.

Left: Maitland Bay Track in Bouddi National Park **Below:** Brisbane Water, Woy Woy

VISITOR INFORMATION

Hawkesbury Visitor Information Centre
Hawkesbury Valley Way, Richmond
(02) 4560 4620
discoverthehawkesbury.com.au

The Entrance Visitor Information Centre
Memorial Park,
The Entrance
(02) 4343 4213
visitcentralcoast.com.au

TOP EVENTS

- FEB Food and Wine Festival (Terrigal)
- JULY Winter Blues & Jazz Festival (The Entrance)
- OCT Flower Show and Spring Fair (Bilpin)
- OCT ChromeFest (The Entrance)
- NOV Lakes Festival (The Entrance)
- NOV Bridge to Bridge Water Ski Race (Windsor)

TEMPERATURES

Jan: 27–30°C

July: 16–19°C

KEY TOWNS

GOSFORD
Population 178,427

The gateway town to the Central Coast, Gosford is prettily situated next to Brisbane Water National Park, and ticks off access to mountains, lakes, rainforest and beaches, some of which are relatively sheltered. With easy access to Sydney, Gosford is a busy regional centre.

SEE & DO Australian Reptile Park; Brisbane Water National Park; Gosford Regional Gallery and Edogawa Commemorative Garden: *see* Top Attractions for all. **Art galleries and craft and antique shops:** many in town; contact visitor centre for details. **Henry Kendall Cottage:** museum in the poet's sandstone home. Also picnic and barbecue facilities in the grounds; open Wed, Sat, Sun and public holidays 10.30am–2.30pm; 25–27 Henry Kendall St; (02) 4325 2270; 3km SW. **Firescreek Fruit Wines:** open Wed–Sun 10.30am–4.30pm; Holgate; (02) 4365 0768; 10km NE. **Australian Walkabout Wildlife Park:** native forest with 2km of walking trails. Animals extinct in the area have been re-introduced with success thanks to the fence that keeps out feral animals; Darkinjung Rd, Calga; (02) 4375 1100; 16km NW.

RICHMOND
Population 5418

In the early days of British settlement, the colony came close to starving, so 22 settlers were sent to farm the rich plains of the Hawkesbury. This area had already been scouted by the settlers, and Governor Phillip had called a local rise Richmond Hill after Charles Lennox, the 3rd Duke of Richmond. But this area's Traditional Owners are the Darug People, who in 1795 attempted to defend their land at the Battle of Richmond Hill against British troops and armed settlers. You won't find much information about this battle around, but there's now a memorial garden commemorating the battle in North Richmond. These days Richmond is a quiet historic town on the Hawkesbury River with views to the Blue Mountains. It's an easy drive from Sydney, and is considered a satellite town.

SEE & DO Bowman's Cottage: restored c. 1815 cottage, now National Parks & Wildlife office; Windsor St. **Pugh's Lagoon:** pleasant picnic spot with plentiful waterbirds; Old Kurrajong Rd and Windsor St. **Self-guide historical town walks:** features many heritage buildings including St Peter's Church (1841) and adjacent early settler graves; brochure from visitor centre. **RAAF base:** oldest Air Force establishment in Australia, used for civilian flying from 1915; Windsor–Richmond Rd. **Kurrajong:** quaint mountain village that's home to shops, cafes and galleries. Just off Bells Line of Rd; 10km NW. **Bellbird Hill Lookout:** clear views across to Sydney skyline; Kurrajong Heights; 13km NW. **Hawkesbury Lookout:** great views of Sydney over the Cumberland plain; 15km SW. **Avoca Lookout:** stunning views over Grose Valley; 20km W. **Mountain Lagoon:** lovely mountain bushland setting with a range of walking trails leading down to the pristine Colo River; brochure from visitor centre; 40km NW.

★ TERRIGAL
Population 12,730

Terrigal is a scenic and peaceful coastal town well known for its outstanding beaches, which are popular for surfing, swimming and surf-fishing. The Norfolk pines along the beachfront give the town a relaxed feel and the boutique shops and restaurants add a sophisticated touch. In 2011 the decommissioned navy frigate, *HMAS Adelaide*, was scuttled 1.4km offshore and is now a popular diving spot.

SEE & DO Bouddi National Park: *see* Top Attractions. **Marine Discovery Centre:** see fish, corals and a display on the sinking of the *HMAS Adelaide*, as well as touch pools for kids and a cafe overlooking the lagoon; 10am–3pm; 11 Terrigal Dr; (02) 4385 5027. **Rotary Park:** pleasant for picnics and barbecues, backing onto Terrigal Lagoon, a good family swimming spot; Terrigal Dr. **Beach Market:** foreshore; 1st Sat each month. **The Skillion:** headland offering excellent coastal views. **Erina:** pretty town with Distillery Botanica; 4km W. **Ken Duncan Gallery:** one of the largest privately owned photographic collections in Australia; 8km NW. **Several excellent beaches:** Wamberal Beach, a safe family beach with rockpools (3km N), also Avoca Beach (7.5km S) and Shelly Beach (13km N), both popular for surfing.

THE ENTRANCE
Population 4244

This seaside and lakeside town is named for the narrow channel that connects Tuggerah Lake to the Pacific Ocean. Given its proximity to Sydney and Newcastle, it has become a popular aquatic playground for residents of both cities.

SEE & DO **Wyrrabalong National Park:** *see* Top Attractions. **The Waterfront:** town mall with shops, pavement eateries and children's playground. **Markets:** Marine Parade; Sat. **Crabneck Point Lookout:** magnificent coastal views; 6km S. **Nora Head Lighthouse:** attractive automated lighthouse built in 1903 after several ships were wrecked on the coast; 8km N. **Toukley:** unspoiled coastal hamlet with breathtaking scenery. Holds markets each Sun in the shopping centre carpark; 11km N. **Munmorah State Recreation Area:** signposted bushwalking trails with magnificent coastal scenery; 21km N.

WINDSOR
Population 1915

Windsor was the first official town to be announced on the banks of the Hawkesbury River, and was the third settlement on mainland Australia after Sydney Cove and Parramatta. It was an essential farming area for the fledgling colony. Back in those days, the Hawkesbury was highly prized frontier land and the site of battles between settlers and the Traditional Owners, the Darug People. For more insight into this terrible era of settlement, read Kate Grenville's *The Secret River*. There are many historic buildings in town, and it's a popular picnic spot for Sydneysiders, particularly those who come to town for the locally famous fish and chips.

SEE & DO **Hawkesbury Regional Museum:** *see* Other Attractions. **Hawkesbury Regional Gallery:** displays contemporary and traditional works by national and international artists; Wed–Mon; George St. **St Matthew's Church:** designed by convict architect Francis Greenway and built in 1817, St Matthew's is the oldest Anglican church in the country. The adjacent graveyard dates back to 1810 and contains the graves of some of the passengers on the First Fleet; Moses St. **Self-guided tourist walk/drive:** historic sites include the original courthouse and doctor's house; brochure from visitor centre. **Market:** Windsor Mall; Sun.

WISEMANS FERRY
Population 233

Wisemans Ferry is a sleepy town built around what was once an important crossing on the Hawkesbury River. The mainland route from Sydney to Newcastle had always gone via this region, but when people started using the Castle Hill route, former convict Solomon Wiseman, who had been granted a parcel of land and opened an inn, built a ferry in 1827 to take people and cargo across the river. Today the car ferry still crosses at this point.

SEE & DO **Dharug National Park:** *see* Top Attractions. **Yengo National Park and Parr State Conservation Area:** *see* Other Attractions. **Wisemans Ferry Inn:** before it was an inn, this was the home of Solomon Wiseman; he called it Cobham Hall. Wiseman later opened a section of the building as an inn and it is said to be haunted by his wife, whom he allegedly pushed down the front steps to her death. The inn provides food and accommodation. Old Northern Rd; (02) 4566 4301. **Cemetery:** early settlers' graves include that of Peter Hibbs, who travelled on the *HMS Sirius* with Captain Phillip in 1788; Settlers Rd. **Marramarra National Park:** undeveloped park with wetlands and mangroves for canoeing, camping, bushwalking (experienced only) and birdwatching; 28km S.

WOY WOY
Population 11,072

Woy Woy is the largest of the numerous holiday villages clustered around Brisbane Water, a shallow but enormous inlet. Along with nearby Broken Bay, the Hawkesbury River and Pittwater, this aquatic wonderland draws holidaymakers with its mix of surfing, boating, fishing and swimming opportunities. The adjacent national parks encompass breathtaking wilderness and lookouts.

SEE & DO **Brisbane Water National Park:** *see* Top Attractions. **Woy Woy Hotel:** historic 1897 hotel offering meals and accommodation; 33 The Blvd; (02) 4341 1013. **Waterfront reserve:** picnic facilities with Brisbane Water view. **Ettalong Beach:** great swimming beach with seaside markets each Sat and Sun (and Mon on long weekends); 3km S. ***HMAS Parramatta*:** a World War I ship, it ran aground on the Hawkesbury River and the wreck is still there today; 5km S. **Mount Ettalong Lookout:** glorious coastal views; 6km S. **Pearl Beach:** chic holiday spot favoured by affluent Sydneysiders, with magnificent sunsets; 12km S. **Boating, fishing and swimming:** excellent conditions on Brisbane Water, Broken Bay and Hawkesbury River.

WYONG
Population 4530

Wyong is an attractive holiday town surrounded by Tuggerah Lakes and the forests of Watagan, Olney and Ourimbah. After World War II it became a popular area for retirees and it still has a relaxed atmosphere today.

SEE & DO **Olney State Forest:** this native rainforest has several scenic walks. The Pines picnic area has an education shelter and Mandalong and Muirs lookouts have sensational views. 17km NW. **Treetops Adventure:** canopy walkways, rope bridges and flying foxes, plus Networld for smaller kids (and young at heart); Red Hill Forest Rd, Wyong Creek; (02) 4025 1008; 5km W.

Top: Waterskiing on Hawkesbury River **Middle:** The Entrance **Bottom:** Fishing at Wisemans Ferry **Opposite:** Paddleboarding on Terrigal Lagoon

Hunter Valley and Coast

If you like your food and wine, chances are you'll already know all about the gourmet delights on offer in the Hunter Valley, one of **Australia's most well-known wine regions** – and its and oldest producing one. An easy two-hour drive north of Sydney, it's the perfect spot for a **foodie short break**. Just as enticing is nearby Newcastle, famous for being the world's largest coal port but also home to **more artists than any other city in Australia** with the most art galleries per capita, fabulous surf beaches within walking distance of the city centre and lots of **convict history.**

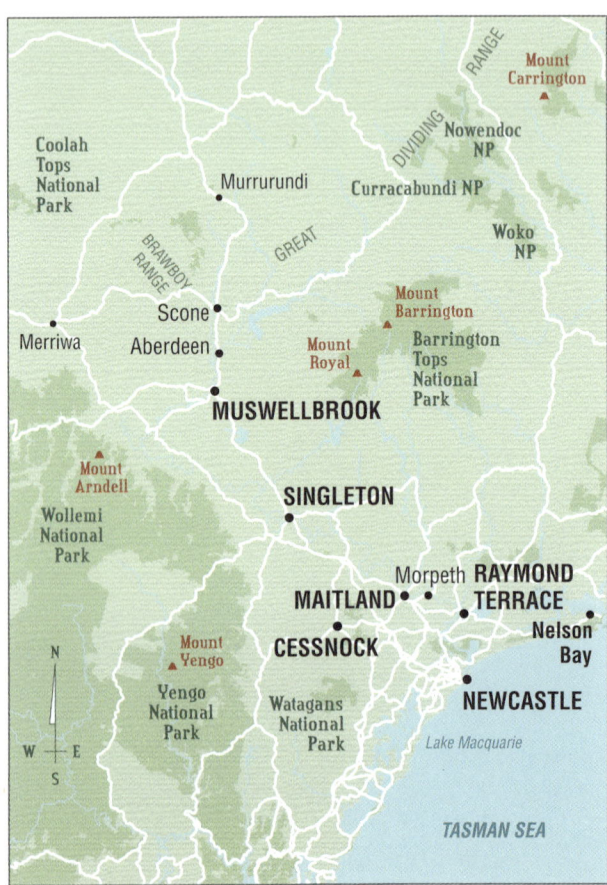

CHEAT SHEET

→ Allow at least two days for a proper exploration.

→ Best time to visit: year-round.

→ Main towns: Cessnock (see p. 38), Nelson Bay (see p. 39), Newcastle (see p. 40).

→ The Wonnarua People are Traditional Owners of the lands in and around the Hunter Valley. The city of Newcastle is on the lands of the Awabakal and Worimi Peoples.

→ Did you know? The Hunter Valley is most famous for its Semillion.

→ Don't miss: Stockton sand dunes; a swim in one of Newcastle's ocean pools; dolphin and koala spotting at Port Stephens; and wine tasting in the Hunter Valley.

Top: Watagans National Park
Opposite: The Hunter Valley is a famous wine region

TOP ATTRACTIONS

COOLAH TOPS NATIONAL PARK: The plateaus at high altitude in this park provide wonderful lookouts over the Liverpool Plains and some beaut waterfalls. Vegetation consists of giant grass trees and tall open forests of snow gums, providing a home for wallabies, gliders, eagles and rare owls. There are superb campsites, walking paths, mountain-biking trails and picnic spots.

FORT SCRATCHLEY: This fascinating fort in Newcastle was built in 1882 amid fears of a Russian attack. Soldiers' barracks and officers' residences were built in 1886. It is one of the few gun installations in Australia to have fired on the Japanese in World War II and it remains in excellent condition. Explore networks of tunnels, gun emplacements and military and maritime museums. Open Wed–Mon 10am–4pm; Nobbys Rd, Newcastle; (02) 4974 1422.

HUNTER VALLEY WINE REGION: Established in 1830 near Singleton, this is Australia's oldest wine region – and one of its most recognised. The area now offers a wealth of vineyards and wineries, with around 120 cellar doors in the lower valley between Singleton, Cessnock and Maitland. Semillon and shiraz are the signature drops, but you will also find beautiful chardonnay and cabernet sauvignon. The terroir of the valley leaves an unmistakable mark in many of the wines, which delights winemakers and drinkers alike. Labels include **McWilliam's Mount Pleasant, Tyrrell's, Lake's Folly, Tulloch Wines, De Bortoli Wines, Drayton's Family Wines** and **Ernest Hill Wines**. Great food and accommodation are also in abundance. If you're interested in attending a two-hour 'wine school', head to **Hermitage Road Cellars & Winery**, Hermitage Rd, Pokolbin; (02) 4998 7777. The upper valley has not captured the public's interest in the same way as its lower counterpart, despite embodying the same hilly scenery fanning out around the towns of Muswellbrook, Aberdeen, Scone and Denman. There are still many fantastic wines to be discovered. See: winecountry.com.au

LAKE MACQUARIE: This enormous saltwater lake is a huge aquatic playground with secluded bays and coves, sandy beaches and well-maintained parks lining its foreshore. Lake cruises leave from Toronto Wharf and Belmont Public Wharf. **Dobell House**, on the shore at Wangi Wangi, was the home of artist Sir William Dobell and has a collection of his work and memorabilia. Open to the public Sat, Sun and public holidays 1–4pm; (02) 4975 4115. The lake is 35km south of Newcastle (see p. 40).

MAITLAND GAOL: The gaol was built in 1844 and served as a maximum security prison for 154 years. The first inmates were convicts, including some children, who were forced to march 6km from the wharf at Morpeth in shackles and chains. The gaol has been home to some of Australia's most notorious and dangerous criminals and is now said to be the most haunted gaol in the country. Audio tours are available or there are guided tours with ex-inmates and ex-officers. John St, East Maitland; bookings (02) 4936 6482.

MORPETH: This riverside village has been classified by the National Trust. Small enough to be explored on foot, it features magnificent old sandstone buildings such as St James' Church (1830s), and antique and craft shops. A self-guided heritage-walk brochure is available from the visitor centre.

NEWCASTLE MUSEUM: A modern museum housed in the old Honeysuckle Railway Workshops. Interactive multimedia exhibits focus on the history of the city, particularly its industrial heritage, and there are travelling exhibitions. A highlight is the free hourly steelmaking simulation. Open Tues–Sun 10am–5pm; 6 Workshop Way, Honeysuckle; (02) 4974 1400.

NEWCASTLE REGIONAL ART GALLERY: Broad collection of Australian art including works by Arthur Streeton, Brett Whiteley, William Dobell, Sidney Nolan and Russell Drysdale, as well as changing exhibitions; open Tues–Sun; Laman St; (02) 4974 5100.

PORT STEPHENS: This is a haven of calm blue waters and sandy beaches, offering excellent boating, fishing and swimming. It is also something of a wildlife haven: over 100 bottlenose dolphins are permanent residents here, migrating whales can be seen in season on a boat cruise, and koalas can be spotted at Tilligerry Habitat.

TOMAREE NATIONAL PARK: This park consists of bushland, sand dunes, heathland, native forest and more than 20km of rocky coastline and beaches. It is part of the Dreaming stories of the Worimi People. There is a signposted walk around the headland and another up to Fort Tomaree Lookout, which offers breathtaking 360-degree views. Yacaaba Lookout across the bay (70km by road) also offers great views. The park is a popular spot for bushwalking, swimming, surfing, snorkelling, fishing and picnicking. The park stretches from Shoal Bay to Anna Bay and is easily accessed from Nelson Bay (*see* p. 39).

WATAGANS NATIONAL PARK: About 33km south-east of the town of Cessnock (*see* p. 38), this park is of great importance to the Awabakal and Darkinjung People and has significant engraving sites and features several lookout points over mountains and valleys. The lookout at Gap Creek Falls reveals rainforest gullies of magnificent red cedar and Illawarra flame trees, and the Monkey Face Lookout takes in the Martinsville Valley below. There are many scenic rainforest walks along the creek, which is ideal for swimming. Some walks lead to picnic and barbecue facilities at Heaton, Hunter and McLean's lookouts and to the serene Boarding House Dam picnic area, which is set among large blackbutt and blue gum trees.

Morpeth Museum **Opposite top:** View of Shoal Bay, Tomaree Head and Mount Yacaaba in Port Stephens **Opposite bottom:** Newcastle Museum

OTHER ATTRACTIONS

ABERDEEN: This small town is famous for its prize-winning beef cattle. The famous Aberdeen Highland Games are held each July. These Scottish festivities include Scottish food and music, highland dancing, caber tossing, a jousting tournament, a strong man competition and a kilted dash.

GROSSMAN HOUSE: National Trust–classified Georgian-style house in Maitland (see p. 38), now a museum with silverware, porcelain and handmade clothing; open 2nd Sun of the month; Church St, Maitland; (02) 4934 8837.

HUNTER WETLANDS CENTRE: 45ha wetlands reserve, 10min from the city centre of Newcastle, with bike trails, playground, treasure hunt, guided eco-tours, canoe hire, picnic areas and cafe; Sandgate Rd, Shortland; (02) 4951 6466.

SKETCHLEY COTTAGE: First built by convicts in 1840, this cottage in the town of Raymond Terrace (see p. 40) was rebuilt after being destroyed by fire in 1857. The cottage and museum displays include early Australian farming equipment, wine casks, furniture, handicrafts and photography. Open 4th Sun each month (except Jan), 10am–4pm; Adelaide St (Old Pacific Hwy), Raymond Terrace.

TANILBA HOUSE: Home to the first European settler in Tanilba Bay, Lieutenant Caswell, Tanilba House was convict-built in 1831. Features of the house include decorative quoins defining the building edge, door and window openings, and high ceilings, archways and large rooms. There is said to be a resident ghost, thought to be an 1830s governess. It is 36km north-east of the town of Raymond Terrace (see p. 40). Open by appt; Admiralty Ave, Tanilba Bay; 0411 148 909.

YENGO NATIONAL PARK: Mount Yengo is of cultural significance to the Darkinjung and Wonnarua People and there are extensive carvings and paintings in the area. The park is a rugged area of steep gorges and rocky ridges with several walking tracks and lookouts. Old Great North Rd, along the south-east boundary, is an intact example of early 19th-century convict roadbuilding. There are picnic and barbecue areas and campsites throughout the park.

NEW SOUTH WALES

KEY TOWNS

⭐ CESSNOCK
Population 23,211

The first port of call for many people visiting the Hunter Valley, Cessnock has a range of cafes, galleries and shops. It welcomes visitors in search of good wine and good food. As the major centre for the Hunter, it has all the essential services you might need; it's also the place to book ballooning, skydiving, gold and wine-tasting tours.

SEE & DO **Hunter Valley Wine Region; Watagans National Park:** see Top Attractions for both. **Hunter Valley Zoo:** hands-on zoo where many animals (native and introduced) can be patted and fed; Thurs–Tues 9am–4pm; 130 Lomas La, Nulkaba; (02) 4990 7714; 7km NW. **Bimbadeen Lookout:** spectacular views over Hunter Valley; 10km E. **Hunter Valley Cheese Factory:** factory tours, tastings and sales; 9am–5.30pm; McGuigan Cellars Complex, McDonalds Rd, Pokolbin; (02) 4998 7744; 13km NW. **Richmond Vale Railway Museum:** rail and mining museum with steam-train rides and John Brown's Richmond Main Colliery, once the largest shaft mine in the Southern Hemisphere; Open 1st, 2nd and 3rd Sun of each month 10am–4pm; Leggetts Dr, Richmond Vale; (02) 4937 5344; 17km NE. **Wollombi:** picturesque village with a wealth of historic sandstone buildings. **Undercliff Winery and Gallery:** Wine tastings with a taster of local art; 49km SW **Baiame Cave:** Open cave with a painted figure, with its arms outstretched, that's believed to be Baiame, who is understood by some First Nations People across NSW and Victoria to be the creator, the 'Father of All', the most important ancestor and law maker; 46km W **Galleries and craft shops:** arts and crafts by local artists; maps from visitor centre.

MAITLAND
Population 89,597

Maitland is a historic town in the Hunter Valley with remarkable old buildings, particularly considering that this town, located on the floodplains next to the Hunter River, has suffered at least 15 major floods since European settlement.

SEE & DO **Matiland gaol:** see Top Attractions. **Grossman House:** see Other Attractions. **Tocal Homestead:** historic Georgian homestead (open Mar–Nov); Tocal Rd, Paterson; 14km N. **Paterson:** signposted scenic drive leads to this charming hamlet on the Paterson River; 16km N.

MERRIWA
Population 1042

This small town beside the Merriwa River in the western Hunter region is known for its majestic early colonial-era buildings. It is the centre of a vast farming district of cattle, sheep, horses, wheat and olive trees. People converge on the town each year on the June long weekend for the Festival of the Fleeces, which includes shearing competitions, yard dog trials and a woolshed dance.

SEE & DO **Colonial Museum:** in stone cottage (1857) with documented history of the region and the belongings of European settlers; Bettington St. **Bottle Museum:** over 5000 bottles of all shapes and sizes; open Mon–Fri; visitor centre. **Self-guided historical walk:** early school buildings, Holy Trinity Anglican Church (1875) and the Fitzroy Hotel (1892); brochure from visitor centre. **Cassilis:** tiny village with historic sandstone buildings including St Columba's Anglican Church (1899) and the courthouse/police station (1858). The main streets have been declared an urban conservation area; 25km NW. **Flags Rd:** old convict-built road leading to Gungal; 25km SW. **Gem-fossicking area:** open to the public; 27km SW. **Goulburn River National Park:** mostly sandstone walking tracks along the Goulburn River, honeycombed with caves; good rafting and access for boats; 35km S.

Patricia Van Lubeck mural *The New One* on Bourke Street, Maitland

VISITOR INFORMATION

Newcastle Visitor Information Centre
Former Civic Railway Station, 430 Hunter St
(02) 4929 2109
visitnewcastle.com.au

Hunter Valley Visitor Centre
455 Wine Country Dr, Pokolbin
(02) 4993 6700
huntervalleyvisitorcentre.com.au
upperhuntercountry.com

Port Stephens Visitor Information Centre
60 Victoria Pde, Nelson Bay
(02) 4980 6900 or
1800 808 900
portstephens.org.au

MURRURUNDI
Population 945

Life moves slowly in Murrurundi (pronounced 'Murrurund-eye'). Set in the lush Pages River Valley at the foot of the Liverpool Ranges, this town is so well preserved the main street has been declared an urban conservation area.

SEE & DO **Paradise Park:** this horseshoe-shaped park lies at the base of a steep hill. Behind the park take a walk through the 'Eye of the Needle', a small gap in the rocks that opens to a path leading to the top of the hill and fantastic views. **Michael Reid Murrurundi:** changing exhibitions of contemporary Australian art in restored convict barracks built around 1840; open Thurs–Sun; cnr Boyd and Mayne sts; (02) 6546 6767. **St Joseph's Catholic Church:** see its 1000-piece Italian marble altar; Polding St. **Self-guided heritage walk:** National Trust–classified sites; brochure from visitor centre. **Wallabadah Rock:** Reaching 959m above sea level, the rock is one of the largest monoliths in the Southern Hemisphere. There are spectacular flowering orchids in Oct. The rock is on private property, with a good view from the road. No public access. 26km NE. **Chilcotts Creek:** diprotodon remains were found here (now in Australian Museum, Sydney); 15km N. **Burning Mountain:** deep coal seam that has been smouldering for at least 5000 years; 20km S.

MUSWELLBROOK
Population 10,901

Muswellbrook (the 'w' is silent) is in the Upper Hunter Valley and prides itself on being 'blue heeler country'. Here cattle farmers developed the blue heeler dog by crossing dingoes with Northumberland blue merles to produce a working dog that thrives in Australia's harsh conditions. The blue heeler is now in demand all over the world. There are several open-cut coalmines in the local area and the Upper Hunter Valley has many fine wineries.

SEE & DO **Art Gallery:** in the restored town hall and School of the Arts building. Its centrepiece is the Max Watters collection, which displays pieces from renowned Australian artists in paintings, drawings, ceramics and sculptures; open Mon–Sat; Bridge St. **Historical town walk:** 4.5km walk featuring St Alban's Church, the police station and the town hall; map from visitor centre. **Bayswater Power Station:** massive electricity source with coal-fired boilers and cooling towers; 16km S. **Sandy Hollow:** picturesque village surrounded by horse studs and vineyards, with Bush Ride in Apr; 36km SW. **Local wineries:** those open for cellar-door tastings include Arrowfield Estate (28km S) and Rosemount Estate (35km SW); brochure from visitor centre.

NELSON BAY
Population 6141

The white beaches and gentle waters of Nelson Bay may not be a secret, but this tourist centre has maintained its charm and is a superb spot for all aquatic activities. It also enjoys close proximity to Tomaree National Park. The attractive bay is the main anchorage of Port Stephens.

SEE & DO **Inner Lighthouse:** this 1872 lighthouse, originally lit with four kerosene lamps, has been restored by the National Trust and is now completely automated. The adjacent museum features a display of the area's early history, souvenirs and a teahouse. The views of Nelson Bay are worth the trek. Nelson Head; (02) 4984 2505. **Port Stephens Community Arts Centre:** oil and watercolour paintings, pottery, china and quilting; off Shoal Bay Rd; (02) 4981 3604. **Self-guided heritage walk:** from Dutchmans Bay to Little Beach; brochure from visitor centre. **Cruises:** dolphin-watching (year-round) and whale-watching (May–Nov); on the harbour and Myall River and to Broughton Island. Also dive charters; bookings at visitor centre. **4WD tours:** along coastal dunes; bookings at visitor centre. **Craft markets:** Neil Carroll Park, Shoal Bay Rd, 1st, 3rd and 5th Sun each month. **Tomaree Markets:** Tomaree Sports Complex, Nelson Bay Rd, Salamander Bay; 2nd and 4th Sun each month. **Medowie Markets:** Bull 'n' Bush Hotel; 2nd Sat each month. **Little Beach:** white beach with native flora reserve behind; 1km E. **Gan Gan Lookout:** spectacular views of Nelson Bay, Lemon Tree Passage, Tomaree National Park and further north to Myall Lakes; Nelson Bay Rd; 2km S. **Shoal Bay:** popular and protected bay with spa resort; 3km NE. **Shell Museum:** diverse display of shells, some rare; 92 Sandy Point Rd, Corlette; (02) 4981 1428; 3km SW. **Toboggan Hill Park:** toboggan runs, minigolf and indoor wall-climbing; Salamander Way; (02) 4984 1022; 5km SW. **Stockton Sand Dunes:** this 32km dune area, the largest moving coastal landmass in the Southern Hemisphere, is popular for sand-boarding and whale-watching; access from James Paterson St, Anna Bay, where 4WD safaris are available (bookings also at visitor centre); 11km SW. **Oakvale Wildlife Park:** 150 species of native and farm animals, with visitor activities and feeding shows; 3 Oakvale Dr, Salt Ash; (02) 4982 6222; 16km SW. **Tomago House:** 1843 sandstone villa with family chapel and 19th-century gardens; ask at visitor centre about open days; 421 Tomago Rd; (02) 4964 8123; 30km SW. **Port Stephens wineries:** several in area, along with Murray's Craft Brewing Co., featuring live music on most weekends and the Easter Blues & Brews Festival; brochure from visitor centre.

⭐ NEWCASTLE
Population 348,539

A compact city with a flourishing arts scene and a string of beautiful surf beaches, Newcastle began as a penal settlement and coal mining town. It soon became an industrial city, known for its steel and port facilities. Since the closure of the steelworks in 1999, Newcastle has developed a reputation as a cool and cosmopolitan seaside city. The harbour is one of the largest working harbours in Australia. This town is bordered by some of the world's finest surfing beaches.

SEE & DO **Fort Scratchley; Newcastle Museum; Regional Art Gallery:** see Top Attractions for all. **Hunter Wetlands Centre:** see Other Attractions. **Queens Wharf:** centrepiece of foreshore redevelopment with restaurants, boutique brewery and observation tower linked by a walkway to Hunter St Mall. **Darby Street:** Newcastle's bohemian enclave has vibrant restaurants and cafes, gift shops, galleries and young designer boutiques. **King Edward Park:** waterfront recreation reserve since 1863 featuring sunken gardens, ocean views, band rotunda (1898), Soldiers Baths (public pool) and Bogey Hole, a hole cut in rocks by convicts; Shortland Espl. **Newcastle Ocean Baths:** public pool with striking Art Deco pavilion; Shortland Esplandade. **Merewether Baths:** largest ocean baths in the Southern Hemisphere; Scenic Dr. **Blackbutt Reserve:** 182ha of bushland with duck ponds, native animal enclosures, walking trails, and picnic and barbecue facilities; New Lambton, off Carnley Ave; (02) 4904 3344. **Self-guided walks:** include Town Walk and Shipwreck Walk; maps from visitor centre. **Cruises:** on the river and harbour; bookings at visitor centre. **City Farmers' Market:** Newcastle Showground; Sun. **Olive Tree Market:** art and design market; Civic Park; 1st Sat every month, plus 3rd Sat Nov and Dec. **Munmorah State Conservation Area:** coastal wilderness with great walking, picnicking, camping, swimming, surfing and fishing; (02) 4972 9000; 30km S. **Swansea:** modern resort town enjoying both lake and ocean exposure. It is popular with anglers and has excellent surf beaches; 24km S. **Surf beaches:** many with world-class breaks and within walking distance from Newcastle city centre, including Newcastle Beach, Merewether and Nobbys; details from visitor centre.

RAYMOND TERRACE
Population 13,453

The charismatic and historic main street of Raymond Terrace was used in the 2010 movie of John Marsden's classic book *Tomorrow, When the War Began* (1993 book). Aside from moonlighting as a movie location, Raymond Terrace is in a great location north-west of Newcastle on the banks of the Hunter and William rivers, in the middle of a koala corridor – thanks to the vast remaining eucalypt forests in the region.

SEE & DO **Sketchley Cottage; Tanilba House:** see Other Attractions for both. **Self-guided historical town walk:** includes the courthouse, built in 1838, and an 1830s Anglican church built of hand-hewn sandstone; map from visitor centre. **Hunter Region Botanic Gardens:** over 2000 native plants and several theme gardens; 2100 Pacific Hwy; (02) 4987 1655; 3km S. **Grahamstown Lake:** beautiful serene lake with picnic facilities; 12km N. **Fighter World:** hands-on displays of old fighter planes, engines and equipment; 49 Medowie Rd, Williamtown; (02) 4965 1810; 16km NE. **Clarence Town:** this historic village was one of the first European settlements in Australia; 27km NW. **Koala Reserve:** boardwalk through koala colony; Hawks Nest; 54km NE.

Top: Mount View vineyard in the Hunter Valley **Middle:** Blue Water Sailing in Shoal Bay **Bottom:** Newcastle's Merewether Ocean Baths **Opposite:** Silo mural by David Lee Pereira

TOP EVENTS

- JAN–MAR Surfest (Newcastle)
- MAR V8 Supercars (Newcastle)
- MAR–APR Harvest Festival (throughout the Hunter Valley region), Hunter Valley Steamfest (Maitland)
- MAY Horse Festival (Scone)
- JUNE Festival of the Fleeces (Merriwa)
- JUL Highland Games (Aberdeen)
- AUG Jazz Festival (Newcastle)
- SEPT End2End Festival (Pokolbin)

TEMPERATURES

Jan: 17–30°C

July: 4–18°C

SCONE
Population 5824

Set among rolling green hills in the Hunter Valley, Scone (rhymes with stone) is a pleasant rural town with tree-lined streets. It is known as the 'horse capital of Australia' and is the world's second-largest thoroughbred and horse-breeding centre. The Scone Horse Festival is held each May.

SEE & DO **Mare and Foal:** life-size sculpture by Gabriel Sterk; Kelly St. **Scone Museum:** large collection of local photographs and household furniture and appliances in an old lock-up (1870); open Wed 9.30am–2.30pm, Sun 2.30–4.30pm; Kingdon St. **Moonan Flat:** This small town sits at the base of the Barrington Tops. It has a beautiful suspension bridge, a small post office and the Victoria Hotel (1856). The hotel was a Cobb & Co. coach stop during the gold-rush era and was reputedly patronised by bushranger Captain Thunderbolt. It is small but friendly, and has accommodation and an adjoining restaurant. 50km NE. **Lake Glenbawn:** watersports, bass fishing, picnic, barbecue and camping facilities and a rural-life museum; 15km E. **Burning Mountain:** deep coal seam that has been smouldering for at least 5000 years. Take the 4.6km track through the bush; 20km N. **Wineries:** several offering cellar-door tastings; brochure from visitor centre. **Tours:** thoroughbred stud and sheep station; bookings at visitor centre. **Trail rides:** throughout area, and mustering opportunities for experienced riders; bookings at visitor centre.

SINGLETON
Population 14,229

In the heart of the Hunter Valley, Singleton was first settled in the 1820s on the banks of the Hunter River, and has some charming historic buildings. It is close to several famous vineyards, as well as national parks and Lake St Clair. Singleton suffered extensive flooding in July 2022, though all of its major attractions remain open.

SEE & DO **James Cook Park:** riverside park with the largest monolithic sundial in the Southern Hemisphere; Ryan Ave. **Historical Museum:** memorabilia in Singleton's first courthouse and gaol from the town's early days; open Tues 10am–1pm, Sat–Sun 12–4pm and public holidays; Burdekin Park, New England Hwy; (02) 6571 1895. **Town walk:** passes a historic Anglican church and lush parklands; brochure from visitor centre. **Market:** showground, Bathurst St; 2nd Sun each month. **Australian Army Infantry Museum:** traces the history of the infantry corps in Australia; open Wed–Sun 9am–4pm; Range Rd; (02) 6571 0497; 5km S. **Wollemi National Park:** the Singleton section features picturesque walking trails, lookouts and campsites; (02) 6372 7199; 15km SW; for further details on the park *see* Lithgow p. 17. **Lake St Clair:** extensive recreational and waterway facilities and a good fishing and camping spot. Nearby lookouts offer magnificent views of Mount Royal Range; 25km N. **Broke:** tiny township with breathtaking national park views and village fair and vintage car display in Sept; 26km S. **Mount Royal National Park:** rainforest with scenic walking tracks and lookouts with 360-degree views from Mount Royal; (02) 6574 5555; 32km N.

Holiday Coast and Lord Howe Island

There's no guessing why the NSW mid-north coast is known as the Holiday Coast. With almost **perfect year-round weather**, a string of unspoiled beaches flanked by World Heritage-listed **rainforests** and lots of friendly **seaside holiday towns**, this stretch of **coastal paradise** between the Myall Lakes and Coffs Harbour and beyond to **Lord Howe Island**, really is the perfect place to kick back and relax. Whether you **swim, snorkel, surf, paddle, cycle, walk** or **drive** – there's no shortage of ways to explore it.

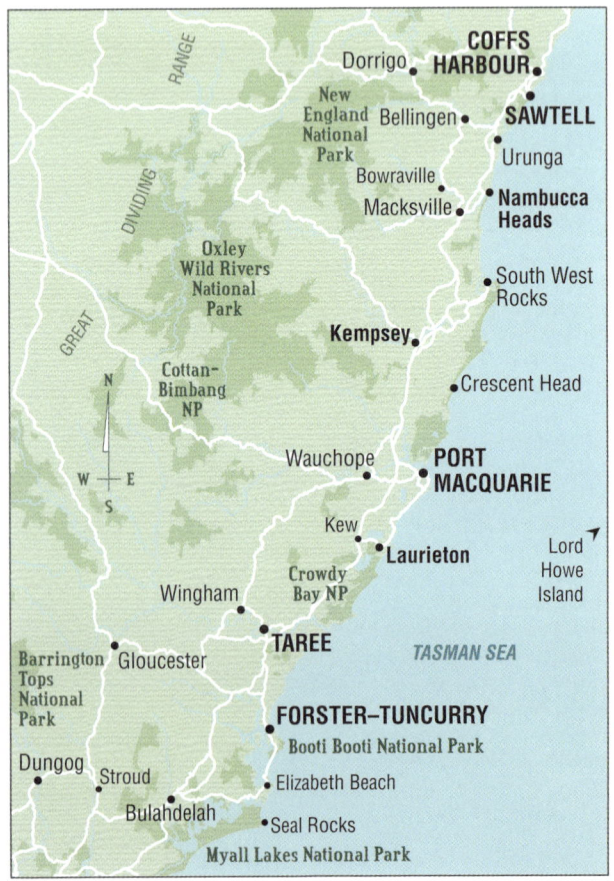

CHEAT SHEET

- Allow at least a week for a proper exploration.

- Best time to visit: year-round, although the coast is very popular in warmer months.

- Main towns: Coffs Harbour (see p. 46), Port Macquarie (see p. 49).

- The Biripi, Dhanggati/Dunghutti, Gumbainggirr and Worimi Peoples are the Traditional Owners of the lands of the mid-north coast.

- Don't miss: the Big Banana; waterfalls and rainforest near Dorrigo; scenic drives and walking trails of the Barrington Tops; art and craft shops in Bellingen; oysters and fresh seafood; Port Macquarie's koala hospital and beaches.

Top: Surfers at Diamond Head Beach, Crowdy Bay **Opposite:** Elizabeth Beach at Booti Booti National Park

TOP ATTRACTIONS

BARRINGTON TOPS NATIONAL PARK: Near to the town of Gloucester (see p. 47), this World Heritage–listed rainforest is on one of the highest points of the Great Dividing Range (1600m). The park is enormous and has a great variety of landscapes, flora and fauna – and even some snow in winter. It is a place of sacred ceremonial sites, ancient campsites and scarred trees and the Traditional Land of the Worimi and Biripi Peoples, and the Wonnarua People. There are some good walking trails, beautiful forest drives, gorges and waterfalls, and breathtaking views from Mount Allyn, 1100m above sea level. The park access road from Gloucester was closed due to weather damage sustained in 2021, so check if it has reopened before travelling; (02) 6538 5300.

BIG BANANA: Large banana-shaped landmark with displays on the banana industry, giant water slides and toboggan rides. Open 9am–4.30pm (5pm in summer); 351 Pacific Hwy, Coffs Harbour; (02) 6652 4355.

BONGIL BONGIL NATIONAL PARK: This glorious park near Urunga (see p. 50) is 10km of unspoiled coastal beaches, pristine estuaries, wetlands, rainforest and magnificent views. It is the Traditional Land of the Gumbaynggir People and was a place for sacred ceremonies and gatherings. The estuaries are perfect for canoeing and birdwatching, with abundant protected birdlife. There's outstanding fishing, surfing and swimming on the beaches, as well as important nesting areas for a variety of wading birds and terns. There are signposted bushwalks and scenic picnic spots.

BOOTI BOOTI NATIONAL PARK: Booti Booti is on the Traditional Land of the Worimi People and there are many sacred sites within the park, including stone quarries and shell middens. The park is near Forster–Tuncurry (see p. 47) and is an ideal spot for water activities. There are beautiful beaches nearby, including Elizabeth, Boomerang and Blueys beaches – all fabulous for surfing and fishing. Elizabeth beach is best for swimming, and is patrolled by lifesavers in season. The lookout tower on Cape Hawke, reached via a steep 400m track, offers 360-degree views over Booti Booti and Wallingat national parks, the foothills of the Barrington Tops, Seal Rocks and Crowdy Bay.

CROWDY BAY NATIONAL PARK: Near Laurieton (see p. 48), this park is on the Traditional Land of the Birpai People. There are shell middens and campsites here – some 6000 years old. The park is known for its prolific birdlife and magnificent ocean beach. Diamond Head is an interesting sculpted rock formation and the hut beneath is where Kylie Tennant wrote *The Man and the Headland*. A headland walking track offers stunning views and the area is also popular for fishing, birdwatching and the abundant wildlife. Campsites are at Diamond Head, Indian Head and Kylies Beach.

DOORAGAN NATIONAL PARK: According to local First Nations legend, Dooragan (North Brother Mountain) was the youngest of three brothers who avenged his brothers' deaths at the hands of a witch by killing the witch and then killing himself. Blackbutt and subtropical forest is home to gliders, bats and koalas. Viewing platforms on North Brother Mountain provide some of the best views anywhere on the NSW coast.

DORRIGO NATIONAL PARK: Near the towns of Dorrigo (see p. 47) and Bellingen (see p. 46), this park takes in World Heritage–listed rainforest and offers plenty for visitors to see and do. Attractions include spectacular waterfalls and a variety of birds such as bowerbirds and lyrebirds. The Rainforest Centre has picnic facilities, a cafe, a video theatre and exhibitions. There is also the Skywalk, a boardwalk offering views over the rainforest canopy, and the Walk with the Birds boardwalk.

ELLENBOROUGH FALLS: At 200m high this is one of the longest single-drop waterfalls in the Southern Hemisphere. There are viewing platforms and a walkway to the bottom of the falls. Bulga Plateau, via Elands.

KOALA HOSPITAL: Koala rehabilitation and adoption centre, the only one of its kind in NSW; open 8am–4pm, feeding at 8am and 3pm; Lord St, Port Macquarie; (02) 6584 1522.

MYALL LAKES NATIONAL PARK: The 'Murmuring Myalls' is near the town of Bulahdelah (see p. 46) and the 10ha of connected lakes and 40km of beaches make this national park one of the most visited in the state. It is the Traditional Land of the Worimi People and Dark Point Aboriginal Place – a rocky headland – has been used for ceremonies and feasts for 4000 years. The park is ideal for all types of watersports – canoe and houseboat hire are available, and Broughton Island, 2km offshore, is a popular spot for diving and fishing. Enjoy the bushwalks and campsites set in the rainforest, heathlands and eucalypt forest.

NATIONAL CARTOON GALLERY: Largest private collection of (mostly political) cartoons in the Southern Hemisphere, housed in a World War II bunker; 1 John Champion Way, Coffs Harbour; (02) 6651 7343.

PORT MACQUARIE HISTORICAL SOCIETY MUSEUM: This award-winning museum has over 20,000 items in its ever-increasing collection. It specialises in letters, photographs and documents covering convict and free settlement and the evolution of Port Macquarie from penal colony to coastal metropolis. The museum is in one of the town's beautifully restored older buildings (c. 1836). Open Mon–Sat 9.30am–4.30pm; 22 Clarence St; (02) 6583 1108.

SOUTH WEST ROCKS: Near to the town of Kempsey (see p. 47), attractions include a pristine white beach and a maritime history display at the restored Boatmans Cottage. The area is excellent for watersports, diving, camping and boating. The nearby Trial Bay Gaol (1886) was a public works prison until 1903 and reopened to hold 'enemy aliens' in World War I. Smoky Cape Lighthouse (built in 1891) in Hat Head National Park offers tours and accommodation and clear views up and down the coast. The Smoky Cape name comes from James Cook seeing fires in 1770 lit by Aboriginal people. Fish Rock Cave, just off the cape, is well known for its excellent diving.

TIMBERTOWN: This re-created 1880s sawmillers' village in the town of Wauchope (see p. 51) demonstrates the struggles and achievements of 19th-century life. It features steam-train rides, replica goldfields, a blacksmith, wood turner, art gallery, farmyard patting pen, bullock demonstrations, whip cracking, boutique winery, old-fashioned lolly shop and saloon bar with bush ballads. Roast meats and damper can be enjoyed in the authentic 1880s hotel. Oxley Hwy, Wauchope; (02) 6586 1940.

WINGHAM BRUSH: The unique brush is part of the last 10ha of subtropical floodplain rainforest in NSW. It is home to 195 species of native plants, including giant Moreton Bay fig trees, a large population of endangered grey-headed flying foxes and 100 bird species. The brush includes a boardwalk, picnic and barbecue facilities and a boat-launching area on the Manning River. Farquhar St, Wingham.

WINGHAM MUSEUM: Housed in an old general store (1880s), this museum has one of the most extensive collections of historical memorabilia on the north coast. It includes displays on local farming, commercial and timber history; and is part of an attractive square bounded by Isabella, Bent, Farquhar and Wynter sts, Wingham; (02) 6553 5823.

OTHER ATTRACTIONS

BINDARRI NATIONAL PARK: Only 20km inland from Coffs Harbour (see p. 46) and not for the unseasoned bushwalker, Bindarri National Park is a largely untouched forest with no facilities – but has amazing views that reward those who make the effort. The headwaters of the Urumbilum River form breathtaking waterfalls in a remote and rugged setting, pockets of old-growth forest are scattered across the plateau and rich rainforest protects the steeper slopes. The name Bindarri is from the Gumbaynggir word 'Bindarray', meaning 'creek system'. While there are no campgrounds, backpack camping is allowed and there are bushwalking trails to follow.

BOWRAVILLE: This unspoiled town in the Nambucca Valley has much to see with a National Trust–classified main street, the Bowraville Folk Museum, Frank Partridge VC Military Museum and craft galleries. There are markets 3rd Sun each month.

COORABAKH NATIONAL PARK: The park, near Taree (see p. 50), is on the Traditional Land of the Ngaamba People and it is believed that the dramatic cliffs were used as navigation aids. The park features the volcanic plug outcrops of Big Nellie, Flat Nellie and Little Nellie. The Lansdowne Escarpment is a line of sandstone cliffs offering spectacular views. From Newbys Lookout you might see sea eagles and wedge-tailed eagles.

DUNGOG: In 1838 this town, nestled in the Williams River valley, was established as a military outpost to prevent bushranging by local villains such as the unforgettably named Captain Thunderbolt. North of Dungog is Chichester Dam, with its blue gum surrounds, and east of the dam is Chichester State Forest. In the foothills of the Barrington Tops, the forest has picnic spots, camping, lookouts and walking trails.

HAT HEAD NATIONAL PARK: On the Traditional Land of the Dhanggati/Dunghutti People and a significant place with ceremonial grounds, burial sites and shell middens. Magnificent dunes and unspoiled beaches, popular for birdwatching, snorkelling, swimming and walking. Korogoro Point is a fabulous spot for whale-watching May–July and Sept–Oct.

MUTTONBIRD ISLAND NATURE RESERVE: Visitors can get a close-up look at the life cycle of one of Australia's most interesting migratory birds. The wedge-tailed shearwaters (muttonbirds) fly thousands of kilometres from South-East Asia each August, with large numbers settling at Muttonbird Island to breed. A walking trail winds through the burrows of the birds (seen Aug–Apr). Muttonbird Island is also a vantage point for whale-watching (June–Nov), and is a great place for fishing and picnics. Access is via a 500m walk along the sea wall from the harbour at Coffs Harbour (see p. 46).

PUB WITH NO BEER: Built in 1896, this is the hotel that was made famous in Slim Dusty's song 'The Pub with No Beer', so named because it would often run out of beer before the next quota arrived. It is still largely in its original form and offers meals. It is 26km south-west from the town of Macksville (see p. 49). Taylors Arm; (02) 6564 2100.

SEAL ROCKS: A fishing village where seals sometimes rest on the offshore rocks. Grey nurse sharks breed in underwater caves and whales pass by (June–Nov). Sugarloaf Point Lighthouse (1875) has a lookout tower, and there are pleasant beaches and camping areas.

WERRIKIMBE NATIONAL PARK: Near Wauchope (see p. 51), magnificent World Heritage–listed wilderness is on the Traditional Land of the Dhanggati/Dunghutti People. The park has rainforests, rivers and wildflowers (best viewed in spring). Also several excellent sites for camping and picnics.

Top: The Port Macquarie Historic Courthouse (1869) **Bottom:** Kayaking on Bellingen River **Opposite:** Dorrigo National Park's Crystal Shower Falls walk

KEY TOWNS

BELLINGEN
Population 3201

It's not hard to see why Bellingen, located on Waterfall Way, is home to a vibrant creative community – the nearby national parks, coast and river running through the centre of town would inspire anyone to put paintbrush or pen to paper. Indeed, Bellingen was the setting for Peter Carey's famous novel *Oscar and Lucinda*. The town was gazetted in the mid-18th century and today it has cafes, galleries, festivals and a range of accommodation options. Bellingen was hard hit by floods in March 2022 when 24 homes were inundated after the town received 200mm of rain in 24 hours.

SEE & DO **Bat Island:** although officially called Bellingen Island, this is bat country; the 3ha island is home to a colony of up to 40,000 grey-headed flying foxes (fruit bats). At dusk the flying foxes set off in search of food, filling the sky in a majestic display. The best time to visit is Sept–Mar; access is via Dowle St (north of the river). **Museum:** discover the early history of town through the extensive photo collection of settler life and transportation; Hyde St; (02) 6655 1259. **Hammond and Wheatley Emporium:** built in 1909 using the then-revolutionary building material of concrete blocks, the emporium has been magnificently restored – including a grand staircase leading to a mezzanine floor – and is now home to boutiques, homewares retailers and jewellery galleries; Hyde St. **Local art and craft:** galleries throughout the town including the Yellow Shed, cnr Hyde and Prince sts, and the Old Butter Factory, Doepel La. **Bellingen Markets:** Market Park, Church St; 3rd Sat each month. **Ralweigh Wines:** tastings available; 36 Queen St, Raleigh; (02) 6655 4388; 11km E. **Walking, cycling, horseriding and canoeing:** along the Bellinger River (a reputed typo in the 19th century led to the river being named this) and in forest areas; information and maps from visitor centre. **Scenic drive:** north-east through wooded valleys and farmlands, across Never Never Creek to Promised Land; map available from visitor centre.

BULAHDELAH
Population 1163

Bulahdelah is a pretty town at the foot of Bulahdelah Mountain (known to locals as Alum Mountain because of the alunite that was mined there). Surrounded by rainforests and the beautiful Myall Lakes National Park, it is a popular destination for bushwalkers and watersports enthusiasts.

SEE & DO **Myall Lakes National Park:** *see* Top Attractions; **Bulahdelah Mountain Park:** a park of contrasts, with meandering walking trails taking in tall forest, rare orchids in spring and the remains of mining machinery. There are picnic and barbecue facilities and a lookout over Bulahdelah and the Myall Lakes. Meade St. **Court House Museum:** displays that describe Bulahdelah's logging past, with cells out the back; open Sat 9am–3pm or by appt; cnr Crawford and Anne sts; (02) 4987 9286. **Bulahdelah State Forest:** with scenic picnic areas and walking trails along old mining trolley lines, and one of the tallest trees in NSW – the 84m flooded gum (*Eucalyptus grandis*); off The Lakes Way; 14km N. **Wootton:** charming small town with a 6km rainforest walk along an old timber railway; 15km N. **Wallingat National Park:** walking trails and picnic facilities. Stop at Whoota Whoota Lookout for sweeping views of forest, coast and lakes; 43km NE.

⭐ COFFS HARBOUR
Population 51,069

Coffs Harbour, a subtropical holiday town on the eponymous Coffs Coast, is known for its banana and blueberry plantations (and the iconic Big Banana) and for its great fishing. The combination of great weather, stunning hinterland forests, sandy beaches and a growing cosmopolitan centre makes it a popular spot for tourists seeking fun and relaxation.

SEE & DO **Big Banana; National Cartoon Gallery:** *see* Top Attractions for both. **Muttonbird Island Nature Reserve:** *see* Other Attractions. **Yarrila Arts and Museum:** varied program of art exhibitions; open 10am–4pm Tues–Sat; Yarilla Place. **International Marina:** departure point for fishing charters, scuba diving and whale-watching trips (June–Nov); Marina Dr; (02) 6651 4222. **North Coast Regional Botanic Gardens:** rainforest, mangrove boardwalks, herbarium and diverse birdlife; Hardacre St; (02) 6648 4188. **Dolphin Marine Conservation Park:** performing dolphins and seals with research and nursery facilities; open 9am–4pm; Orlando St; (02) 6659 1900. **Self-guided walks:** include Jetty Walk and Coffs Creek Walk; maps from visitor centre. **Growers' market:** Harbour Dr; Thurs. **Market:** jetty, Harbour Dr; Sun. **Uptown Market:** Castle St; Sun. **Clog Barn:** Dutch village with clog-making; Pacific Hwy; (02) 6652 4633; 2km N. **Bruxner Park Flora Reserve:** dense tropical jungle area of vines, ferns and orchids with bushwalking trails, picnic area and the Forest Sky Pier at Sealy Lookout where, on a clear day, you can see almost 100km to the south; Bruxner Park Rd, Korora; (02) 6652 8900; 9km NW. **Butterfly House:** enclosed subtropical garden with live native and exotic butterflies, plus a new dinosaur forest with six roaring, moving life-sized dinosaurs.; open Mon–Sun 10am–3pm (closed Mon during school terms);

Top: Feeding wallabies at Billabong Zoo **Middle:** Galahs near One Mile Beach in Forster **Bottom:** Belligen's town centre

VISITOR INFORMATION

Manning Valley Visitor Information Centre
21 Manning River Dr,
Taree North
(02) 6592 5444 or
1800 182 733
barringtoncoast.com.au

Greater Port Macquarie Visitor Information Centre
The Glasshouse,
cnr Clarence and Hay sts,
Port Macquarie
(02) 6581 8000 or
1300 303 155
portmacquarieinfo.com.au
coffscoast.com.au
macleayvalleycoast.com.au

Lord Howe Island
lordhoweisland.info

5 Strouds Rd, Bonville; (02) 6653 4766; 9km S. **Bonville Golf Resort:** North Bonville Rd, Bonville; (02) 6653 4002; 13km SW. **Adventure tours:** include whitewater rafting, canoeing, reef-fishing, diving, horseriding through rainforest, surf rafting, skydiving, helicopter flights, go-karting and surf schools; see visitor centre for brochures and bookings.

DORRIGO
Population 1046

Drive west from Coffs Harbour along the Waterwall Way to reach Dorrigo, an attractive and friendly town nestled in the Great Dividing Range. Surrounded by awe-inspiring wilderness, including Dorrigo National Park, the town has access to the incredible views, bushwalks, waterfalls, birdwatching and lush World Heritage–listed rainforests that make this area so remarkable. It also has excellent visitor facilities.

SEE & DO **Dorrigo National Park:** see Top Attractions. **Historical museum:** memorabilia, documents and photographs detailing the history of Dorrigo and surrounding national parks; Cudgery St. **Market:** showground, Armidale Rd; 1st Sat each month. **Dangar Falls:** viewing platform over beautiful 30m waterfall; 2km N. **Griffiths Lookout:** sweeping views of the mountains; 6km S. **Guy Fawkes River National Park:** rugged and scenic surrounds with limited facilities, but worth the effort for experienced bushwalkers. Ebor Falls has cliff-top viewing platforms and there are also good canoeing and fishing opportunities; 40km W.

FORSTER–TUNCURRY
Population 20,554

Located in the Great Lakes district and with beautiful coastline, Forster and the twin town of Tuncurry are connected by a concrete bridge across Wallis Lake – forming one large holiday town. The area has an excellent reputation for its fishing and seafood, particularly its oysters.

SEE & DO **Booti Booti National Park:** see Top Attractions. **Forster Arts and Crafts Centre:** the largest working craft centre in NSW; Breese Pde; (02) 6554 6900. **Pebbly Beach Bicentennial Walk:** gentle and scenic 2km walk to Bennetts Head, beginning at baths off North St, Forster. **Wallis Lake Fishermen's Co-op:** fresh oysters and cooked lake and ocean fish; Ray St, Tuncurry; (02) 6554 6402. **Dolphin-spotting and lake cruises:** bookings at visitor centre. Dolphins can also be seen from Tuncurry Breakwall and Bennetts Head. **Forster town markets:** Town Park; 2nd Sun each month. **Forster farmers' market:** Forster Visitor Centre, Little St; 3rd Sat each month. **Tuncurry markets:** John Wright Park; 4th Sat each month. **The Green Cathedral:** open-air church with pews and altar, sheltered by cabbage palm canopy; Tiona, on the shores of Wallis Lake; 13km S. **Smiths Lake:** sheltered lake for safe swimming; 30km S. **Tours of Great Lakes area:** kayak, 4WD, nature and eco-tours including bushwalks; brochures available at visitor centre.

GLOUCESTER
Population 2469

Gloucester is the closest town to the magical rainforest in Barrington Tops, and is surrounded by a wealth of national parks and conservation areas. In a valley with the Bucketts Mountains watching over, Gloucester makes the perfect base for adventurous types, particularly as there are nearby wineries where you can toast to having conquered the trail or having seen a Tasmanian devil as part of the Devil Ark program.

SEE & DO **Barrington Tops National Park:** see Top Attractions. **Minimbah Aboriginal Native Gardens:** bush tucker gardens; Gloucester District Park. **Museum:** colonial-era household relics, toys, and gemstones and rocks; open Tues and Thurs 10.30am–1.30pm; Church St; (02) 6558 9989. **Town heritage walk:** brochure from visitor centre. **Walking trails:** through nearby parks; brochure from visitor centre. **Copeland State Conservation Area:** easily accessible dry rainforest, well known for its gold production in the 1870s and large stands of red cedar. Walking trails that utilise the old wagon and logging tracks are open to the public; 17km W. **The Bucketts Walk:** 90min return with great views of town; Bucketts Rd; 2km W. **Lookouts:** amazing views of the national park, town and surrounding hills at Kia-ora Lookout (4km N), Mograni Lookout (5km E) and Berrico Trig Station (14km W). **Goldtown:** former site of the Mountain Maid Goldmine (1876), now mostly covered with rainforest. Also a historical museum, gold panning and underground mine tours; 16km W.

KEMPSEY
Population 11,073

On the Macleay River just off the Pacific Hwy, Kempsey is an attractive town only a short drive inland from the coast in the unspoiled hinterland. The town is the birthplace of two famous Aussies: Slim Dusty was born in Kempsey in 1927 (although he passed away in 2003, he remains one of the country's best loved country singers), and the iconic Akubra hat has been made in town since 1974.

SEE & DO **South West Rocks:** see Top Attractions; **Wigay Aboriginal Cultural Park:** cultural experience, including introduction to bush tucker, learning about the use of plants and throwing a boomerang; Sea St. **Val Melville Centre:** incorporates the Macleay River Historical Society Museum and visitor centre, a settler's cottage, displays on Akubra hats and a working model of a timber mill; an adjacent annexe houses the **Dunghutti Ngaku Aboriginal Art Gallery**, showcasing the work of regional Aboriginal artists; gallery open Tues–Sun 10am–4pm; Pacific Hwy, South Kempsey. **The Slim Dusty Centre:** a museum dedicated to the life and music of the famous singer; 490 Macleay Valley Way. **Historical walks:** carefully restored historic buildings include the courthouse, post office and West Kempsey Hotel; brochure from visitor centre. **Markets:** Riverside Park, 1st Sat each month; South West Rocks, 2nd Sat each month. **Frederickton:** 'Fredo' has beautiful views of river flats, and its award-winning pie shop boasts 148 varieties; 8km NE. **Gladstone:** fishing, antiques and crafts; 15km NE. **Crescent Head:** this seaside holiday town has good surfing and hosts the largest longboard competition in Australia in May; 20km SE. **Bellbrook:** classified by the National Trust as a significant example of a turn-of-the-century hamlet; 50km NW. **Walks and self-guided drives:** nature-reserve walks and historical and scenic drives; details from visitor centre.

LAURIETON
Population 2012

Just north of Crowdy Bay National Park is the holiday town of Laurieton, blessed with incredible natural beauty. The town is ranged around the Camden Haven Inlet with the ocean at its front, and North Brother Mountain – named by James Cook after mountains in his native Yorkshire – at its back.

SEE & DO **Crowdy Bay National Park:** *see* Top Attractions. **Camden Haven Museum:** documents history of the town in old post office; open by appt; Laurie St; bookings (02) 6559 9096. **Armstrong Oysters:** oyster farm on the river, open to the public for fresh oysters; Short St. **Riverwalk Market:** cnr Tunis and Short sts; 3rd Sun each month. **Dunbogan:** this seaside village borders the river and ocean. A fishermen's co-op offers the best fish and chips in the region. River cruises and swimming beach; 2km SE. **Kattang Nature Reserve:** in spring the Flower Bowl Circuit leads through stunning wildflowers. Enjoy good coastal views year-round from sharp cliffs jutting into the ocean; 5km E. **North Haven:** riverside dining, boutique gift shops and patrolled swimming beach; 6km NE. **Queens Lake Picnic Area:** a beautiful reserve with St Peter the Fisherman Church nearby. Kayak access to the river; 6km W. **Kendall:** poets walk, art and craft galleries. Also market on 1st Sun each month at Logans Crossing Rd; 10km W. **Big Fella Gum Tree:** 67m flooded gum tree in Middle Brother State Forest; 18km SW.

⭐ LORD HOWE ISLAND
Population 445

Arriving on the World Heritage-listed tropical volcanic island next to a coral lagoon in the middle of the Tasman Sea, it certainly doesn't feel like you're in NSW anymore, even though you're only 600km east of Port Macquarie (you can fly direct from Sydney, Newcastle and Port Macquarie). Originally spotted by Europeans in 1788 and apparently uninhabited, Lord Howe Island was used for whaling and logging, but the primary industry is now tourism. Fewer than 400 people permanently call the island home, and visitor numbers are capped at 400. Most people roll around the island on pushbikes, all the better to take in the views of the twin mountains, spectacular beaches and famous birdlife.

SEE & DO **Museum and Visitor Centre:** displays and reams of information on the island's history and World Heritage listing. Open Sun–Fri 10am–1pm; Lagoon Rd; 1800 240 937. **The Nursery:** as well as learning about growing the Kentia palm, the biggest-selling indoor palm in the world, see the breeding program for the Lord Howe Island phasmid, an extremely rare stick insect; inquire at visitor centre.

Spectacular Lord Howe Island

TOP EVENTS

- → JAN Camp Creative (Bellingen)
- → MAR Lasiandra Festival (Wauchope)
- → MAY Ironman 70.3 (Port Macquarie); Malibu Longboard Classic (Crescent Head).
- → JUNE Readers & Writers Festival (Bellingen)
- → JULY International Brick and Rolling Pin Throwing Competition (Stroud); Chilli Festival (Sawtell); Camden Haven Festival (Laurieton)
- → SEPT Bellingen Muse (Bellingen)
- → OCT International Buskers and Comedy Festival (Coffs Harbour); Bluegrass Festival (Dorrigo); Slim Dusty Festival (Kempsey)
- → DEC Festival of the Sun (Port Macquarie)

Community Markets: Community Hall; last Sun each month during summer. **Golf:** situated at the base of imposing Mount Lidgbird, Lord Howe Island's golf course is one of Australia's most scenic – its nine holes incorporate lush vegetation and open fairways with superb coastal views. Visitors are welcome to tee off at any time, and you can even participate in the annual Lord Howe Open golf tournament held in Nov; (02) 6563 2179. **Bushwalks:** the island abounds in great bushwalks along stunning coastline, among bird rookeries, through dense subtropical forest, and to the peak of towering mountains. The premier walk is to the top of 875m Mount Gower, a challenging all-day adventure that can only be done with a guide, and involves ropes at some points. Inquire at the visitor centre. **Snorkelling and diving:** Lord Howe Island's coral reefs and drop-offs abound with fish, turtles and other marine life. There are two dive operators and numerous places to hire snorkels on the island. Snorkels and masks are also available at Neds Beach, with an honesty box system.

MACKSVILLE
Population 3023

Macksville is a fishing and oyster-farming town on the banks of the Nambucca River. The town is a short drive from the Pub with No Beer, which was immortalised in Slim Dusty's famous song. The river offers plenty of water-based activities, and there's easy access to the coast and nearby national parks.

SEE & DO **Pub with No Beer:** *see* Other Attractions. **Mary Boulton Pioneer Cottage:** replica of a home from the early 19th century, also farm buildings with horse-drawn vehicles; open 1–4pm Wed and Sat; River St; (02) 6568 2626. **Hotels:** Star Hotel, River St, and Nambucca Hotel, Cooper St, both heritage buildings from late 1800s with many original features; both offer meals and accommodation. **Nambucca MacNuts Factory:** macadamia products at wholesale prices; Yarrawonga St. **Market:** Scout Hall, Partridge St; 2nd and 4th Sat each month. **Mount Yarahappini Lookout:** the highest point in Nambucca Valley with fabulous 360-degree views, in Yarriabini National Park; 10km S. **Scotts Head:** coastal town with good beaches for surfing, swimming, fishing and dolphin-watching; 18km SE. **Local craft:** featured in several shops and galleries in the area; brochure from visitor centre.

NAMBUCCA HEADS
Population 6675

Located at the mouth of the Nambucca River, this is a beautiful coastal holiday town. The stunning long white beaches offer dreamy conditions for fishing, swimming, boating and surfing, and the broad, sheltered river is an ideal spot for waterskiing, kayaking and tranquil cruising.

SEE & DO **V-Wall Breakwater:** also known as the Graffiti Gallery, this rock wall gives visitors the opportunity to paint their own postcards on a rock. Mementos from all over the world are on display, including cartoons, paintings and poetry. Wellington Dr. **Headland Historical Museum:** photographic history of the town and its residents, historic documents, antique farming implements and household tools; open Wed, Sat, Sun 2–4pm; Headland Reserve; (02) 6569 5802 or (02) 6568 9289. **Stringer Art Gallery:** showcases local art and craft; open Wed–Fri 10am–3pm, Sat 9.30am–12pm; Ridge St; (02) 6568 6049. **Mosaic sculpture:** the history of the town portrayed in a mosaic wrapped around a corner of the police station; Bowra St. **Gordon Park Rainforest:** rainforest in the middle of urban development, home to a large flying fox colony; between town centre and Inner Harbour. **Foreshore Walk:** 5km pathway from Pacific Hwy to V-Wall with storyboards on shipbuilding yards and mills. **Valla Beach:** this small but delightful holiday village offers secluded beaches and rainforest surrounds, as well as a tavern, store and headland cafe, and bi-monthly (even-numbered months) community markets on the 1st Sat of the month; the Valla Beach Fair is held each Jan. 10km N.

★ PORT MACQUARIE
Population 47,693

Port Macquarie, one of the oldest towns in NSW, was established in 1821 as a self-sufficient penal settlement. Convicts maintained the fledgling town, doing everything from farming, boatbuilding and blacksmithing to teaching, baking and clerical duties. Today the city is a major holiday resort at the mouth of the Hastings River with historic buildings, nature reserves, excellent surf and fishing beaches and scenic coastal walking tracks.

SEE & DO **Historical Society Museum and Koala Hospital:** *see* Top Attractions for both. **Glasshouse Regional Gallery:** touring art exhibitions; Tues–Fri 10am–5pm, Sat–Sun 10am–4pm; cnr Clarence and Hay sts; (02) 6581 8888. **St Thomas' Church:** third-oldest surviving church in Australia (1824–28), designed by convict architect Thomas Owen; Hay St. **Port Macquarie Historic Courthouse:** built in 1869, it served the community for 117 years; tours of the restored building by appt; open Mon–Sat; cnr Hay and Clarence sts; (02) 6584 1818. **Mid-north Coast Maritime Museum:** shipwreck relics, model ships and early photographs; William St; (02) 6583 1866. **Kooloonbung Creek Nature Reserve:** 50ha of nature reserve with boardwalks and picnic area. Visit the historic cemetery nearby, dating from 1842; Gordon St. **Roto House and Macquarie Nature Reserve:** adjacent to the koala hospital and built in 1890, classified by the National Trust; call for opening times; off Lord St; (02) 6588 5555. **Observatory:** planetarium, telescope and solar system display; call for opening times 0403 683 394; William St. **Billabong Zoo:** wide variety of Australian and exotic wildlife with kangaroo-feeding and koala photo sessions; Billabong Dr; (02) 6585 1060. **Town beach:** patrolled swimming and surfing beach with sheltered coves at one end. **Cruises:** depart daily; bookings at visitor centre. **Scenic walks:** 9km coastal walk from Westport Park in the town centre to Tacking Point Lighthouse; traverses beaches and subtropical rainforest with picnic spots, interpretive signs and viewing platforms along the trail; look out for the dolphins of Hastings River and a variety of birdlife; walk takes 3.5hrs one way; brochure from visitor centre. **Art Society Market Bazaar:** 198 Hastings River Dr; every Sun. **Artists Foreshore Market:** grounds of the Maritime Museum, 2nd Sat each month. **Lake Innes Nature Reserve:** this picturesque reserve is home to koalas, kangaroos and bats, but was once the location of the grand Lake Innes House. Unfortunately, the house was left to decay, and the ruins are all that remain today. Guided tours are available; (02) 6588 5555; 7km SW. **Sea Acres Rainforest Centre:** elevated 1.3km boardwalk through canopy; tours available; Pacific Dr; (02) 6582 3355; 4km S. **Lighthouse Beach:** 16km expanse of white sand with camel rides, dolphin-watching from shore and breathtaking views up and down the coast from the grounds of Tacking Point Lighthouse (1879) at the northern end of the beach (lighthouse not open to public); 10km S. **Lake Cathie:** pronounced *Cat-eye*, a holiday town between surf beach and tidal lake, enjoy swimming and fishing; 16km S. **Wineries:** several in the area offering cellar-door tastings including Innes Lake Vineyard (7km W) and Cassegrain Wines (13km W). **Skydiving, sea plane flights, golf:** brochures at visitor centre.

STROUD
Population 738

This delightful hinterland town seems to be from another era. The absence of tourist facilities combined with its historic buildings gives Stroud an unaffected charm. The annual International Brick and Rolling Pin Throwing Competition in July sees residents competing against towns called Stroud in the United States, England and Canada.

SEE & DO **St John's Anglican Church:** this convict-built church was made with bricks of local clay in 1833 and features beautiful stained-glass windows and original cedar furnishings. The church is noted as the place where bushranger Captain Thunderbolt married Mary Ann Bugg. Cowper St. **Underground silo:** one of 8 brick-lined silos built in 1841 for grain storage, it can no longer be accessed but you can peer into it from above ground; Silo Hill Reserve, off Broadway St. **Self-guided town walk:** covers 32 historic sites including Orchard Cottage (1830s) and St Columbanus Catholic Church (1857), which is still in original condition; brochure from visitor centre.

TAREE
Population 18,110

Taree, situated on the Manning River, has riverside parklands, a portion of the river sectioned off for fishing, and a range of accommodation, cafes and restaurants and farmer's markets. The centre of the Manning River District, Taree has more than its fair share of scenic drives, local produce and is also well known for its handicrafts.

SEE & DO **Coorabakh National Park:** see Other Attractions. **Fotheringham Park and Queen Elizabeth Park:** these parklands are ideal riverside picnic spots from which to watch the boats go by. To mark the bicentenary in 1988, an unusual herb and sculpture garden was established – the herbs are available to locals for cooking. There are also several memorials throughout the parks. Between Pacific Hwy and Manning River. **Craft Centre:** features local work and picnic facilities; Manning River Dr, Taree North; (02) 6551 5766. **Manning Regional Art Gallery:** changing exhibitions always include some local works; 12 Macquarie St; (02) 6592 5455. **Self-guided historical walks:** through eastern and western sections of town; brochure from visitor centre. **Weekly markets:** at various venues in the region; contact visitor centre for details. **Joy-flights and tandem skydiving:** flights over the Manning Valley depart from the airport on the northern outskirts of town; Lansdowne Rd; (02) 6551 7776. **Big Buzz Fun Park:** toboggan run, water slides and go-karts; 33 Lakes Way, Rainbow Flat; (02) 6553 6000; 15km S. **Beaches:** excellent surfing conditions; 16km E. **Hallidays Point:** features a rainforest nature walk; brochure from visitor centre; 25km SE. **Manning River:** 150km of navigable waterways with beaches, good fishing and holiday spots. **Art and craft galleries:** several in the area; brochure from visitor centre. **Nature reserves:** numerous in the area with walking trails and abundant wildlife in rainforest settings; map from visitor centre.

URUNGA
Population 2731

Urunga is a sleepy, attractive town at the junction of the Bellinger and Kalang rivers and is regarded by locals as one of the best fishing spots on the north coast. Because it is bypassed by the Pacific Hwy, the town has remained relatively untouched by tourism. A large percentage of the population are retirees and there are some beautiful walks around the foreshore, including a 1km boardwalk that follows the river to the ocean with fantastic views along its length.

SEE & DO **Bongil Bongil National Park:** see Top Attractions. **Museum:** historic building with photographs, documents and paintings of the local

Top: Town Beach in Port Macquarie **Bottom:** The Cheesemaking Workshop & Deli in Coffs Harbour **Opposite:** Bago Maze at Bago Vineyards near Wauchope

TEMPERATURES

Jan: 18–28°C

July: 6–19°C

area; Morgo St; (02) 6655 6845. **Anchor's Wharf:** riverside restaurant and boat hire. **The Honey Place:** huge concrete replica of an old-style straw beehive with glass beehive display, honey-tasting, gallery and gardens; Pacific Hwy; (02) 6655 6160. **Watersports and fishing:** both on the rivers and beach; brochures from visitor centre. **Hungry Head:** beautiful beach for surfing and swimming; 3km S.

WAUCHOPE
Population 7982

Wauchope (pronounced 'Waw-hope') is the centre of the local dairy and cattle industries, and the gateway to over 40,000ha of national parks and state forests, including the largest red bloodwood tree in the Southern Hemisphere, which has the evocative name Old Bottlebutt, and is found in Burrawan State Forest. Even though the town is now known for its spectacular and leafy surrounds, in the early settlement days the local timber was seen as an invaluable resource.

SEE & DO **Timbertown:** *see* Top Attractions. **Historical town walk:** self-guided walk past historic buildings such as the old courthouse; brochure from visitor centre. **Hastings farmers' markets:** Wauchope showground; 4th Sat each month. **Bago Winery:** cellar-door tastings and sales – and home of Bago Maze, the largest hedge maze in NSW; 8km SW. **Bago Bluff National Park:** signposted bushwalks (various fitness levels) through rugged wilderness; 12km W.

WINGHAM
Population 4556

Heritage-listed Wingham is the oldest town in the Manning Valley. Federation buildings surround the enchanting town common, which was based on a traditional English square. The wonderful Manning River and Wingham Brush bring nature to the centre of town. The Chinese Garden at the town's entrance marks the importance of the early Chinese settlers to the town's heritage. Best-selling Australian author Di Morrissey's book *The Valley* is based on the historic characters and places of the Manning Valley. It is largely set in and around Wingham, where she was born.

SEE & DO **Wingham Brush:** *see* Top Attractions. **Wingham Museum:** housed in an old general store (1880s), this museum has one of the most extensive collections of historical memorabilia on the north coast. Includes displays on local farming, commercial and timber history; part of an attractive square bounded by Isabella, Bent, Farquhar and Wynter sts. **Manning River:** picturesque waterway with several locations for swimming, boating, fishing and waterskiing. **Self-guided historical town walk:** tour of the town's Federation buildings; brochure from museum. **Farmers' market:** Wingham Showground, Gloucester Rd; 1st Sat each month. **Tourist Drive 8:** this enjoyable drive begins in Taree and passes through Wingham, Comboyne and Byabarra before finishing in Wauchope (36km is unsealed; not suitable for motorists towing caravans). The highlight is **Ellenborough Falls** (40km N), *see* Top Attractions. Brochure from visitor centre.

NEW SOUTH WALES

51

Tropical North Coast

If NSW has a beach-holiday capital, it is Byron Bay. Once a sleepy backwater full of alternative lifestylers, Byron Bay is now a magnet for travellers (and celebrities) who flock here for the **surfing, swimming, day spas, yoga, natural therapy centres, cafes and restaurants** and **boho vibe**. The tropical north coast is sprinkled with similarly laidback towns, like Mullumbimby, Brunswick Heads, Lennox Head and Murwillumbah. The **rainforest-smothered hinterland** and its beautiful towns like Bangalow add to the many reasons to visit.

CHEAT SHEET

→ You'll need two or three days to explore the region, but allow yourself a couple of extra days just to chill out on the beach.

→ The best swimming weather is early summer through to Easter, although the climate is delightfully mild all year. The region gets very busy during summer school holidays and long weekends, so book accommodation ahead.

→ Main towns: Ballina (see p. 56), Byron Bay (see p. 56), Grafton (see p. 57), Lismore (see p. 58), Yamba (see p. 59).

→ The people of the Gumbainggir and Bundjalung Nations are the Traditional Owners of the northern coastal area of NSW.

→ Did you know? Protestors Falls in Nightcap National Park is the site of one of the first conservationist protests in Australia – in the 1970s. Today it is World Heritage listed.

→ Don't miss: weekend markets at Byron Bay, Nimbin, Bangalow and the Channon; Nightcap and Border Ranges national parks; sunrise at Cape Byron Lighthouse; Teven Valley Golf Course; Iluka Nature Reserve.

Top: Three Blue Ducks, The Farm, Ewingsdale Opposite: Surfing sub-tropical waters at The Pass, Byron Bay

TOP ATTRACTIONS

BORDER RANGES NATIONAL PARK: World Heritage–listed, this 30,000ha park has walking tracks, camping, swimming, rock climbing and fantastic views of Wollumbin (Mount Warning, sacred to the Bundjalung People, Wollumbin National Park, See Other Attractions) and the Tweed Valley. Sheepstation Creek is an attractive picnic spot. The Tweed Range Scenic Drive (64km) is a breathtaking journey of rainforest, deep gorges and waterfalls. Brochure from visitor centre.

BRUNSWICK HEADS: This town on the Brunswick River estuary is a charming mix of quiet holiday retreat and large commercial fishing town. Despite having some truly beautiful beaches and attracting people who want what Byron used to be, Brunswick Heads has managed to remain remarkably serene and unassuming. Enjoy the excellent seafood, cafes and stores in town.

BUNDJALUNG NATIONAL PARK: Protects ancient rainforest and the Esk River, the largest untouched coastal river system on the north coast. Woody Head has rare rainforest with campground, fishing, bushwalking and swimming. Be sure to stop at Chinamans Beach, a gloriously quiet beach with wild surfing and rockpools to explore.

CAPE BYRON: This headland forms part of the world's oldest caldera – the rim of an enormous extinct volcano (at the centre is Wollumbin/Mount Warning, Wollumbin National Park, See Other Attractions). It is the easternmost point on the Australian mainland and provides breathtaking views up and down the coast. Dolphins can be seen year-round and humpback whales migrate up the coast June–July and back down Sept–Oct. Cape Byron Lighthouse, the 22m structure completed in 1901, houses a visitor centre with displays of the area's cultural and natural history.

GRAFTON REGIONAL GALLERY: Rated as one of the most outstanding regional galleries in Australia, this gallery has permanent exhibitions including the Jacaranda Art Society and Contemporary Australian Drawing collections; open Tues–Sat; Prentice House, 158 Fitzroy St, Grafton; (02) 6642 3177.

ILUKA NATURE RESERVE: This area, nestled on the narrow peninsula where the Clarence River meets the ocean opposite Yamba, was World Heritage listed in 1986. It happens to be the largest remaining coastal rainforest in NSW. It is rich with birdlife and is a beautiful spot for activities such as fishing, swimming, surfing, canoeing, walking and camping.

LENNOX HEAD: The beachside holiday town of Lennox Head is on the shores of Lake Ainsworth, which is often called Coca-Cola Lake or Brown Lake due to the discolouration of the water from the surrounding tea trees – not that that stops the locals from swimming in it! There's a good market held on the 2nd and 5th Sun each month at Williams Reserve, William St. Pat Morton Lookout affords excellent views along the coast, with whale-watching (June–July and Sept–Oct). Below the lookout is the Point, a world-renowned surf beach. The outskirts of town offer scenic rainforest walks.

NIGHTCAP NATIONAL PARK: This lush World Heritage–listed forest (part of the Gondwana Rainforests of Australia) offers signposted bushwalks from easy to very difficult, requiring a map and compass. The dramatic Protestors Falls is the site of the 1979 anti-logging protest that led to the area being gazetted as a national park. Rocky Creek Dam has a platypus-viewing platform and views of Wollumbin (Mount Warning, Wollumbin National Park, see 55).

TWEED REGIONAL ART GALLERY: This gallery displays a variety of paintings, portraits, glasswork, pottery, ceramics and photography. The two main themes are Australian portraits (nationwide subjects in all mediums), and depictions of the local area by regional artists. It is also home to the Margaret Olley Art Centre (MOAC) – a re-creation of the late artist's studio filled with more than 2000 items relocated from her Paddington home studio, as well as exhibitions of her work – and the Doug Moran National Portrait Prize, the richest art prize in Australia. Past winners are on display along with changing exhibitions. Open Wed–Sun; Mistral Rd, Murwillumbah; (02) 6670 2790.

YURAYGIR NATIONAL PARK: Highlights include Wooli for unspoiled surf beaches and Minnie Water for walking trails, secluded beaches, camping and abundant wildlife (especially the very friendly wallabies). Minnie Lagoon is a popular swimming, picnicking and boating spot. The Yamba section offers sand ridges and banksia heath, and is excellent for swimming, fishing and bushwalking. The Woolgoolga section is also excellent for bushwalking, canoeing, fishing, surfing, swimming, picnicking and camping on unspoiled coastline; (02) 6627 0200.

OTHER ATTRACTIONS

BRUNSWICK VALLEY HISTORICAL MUSEUM: The museum covers local history in detail, including timber-getters, dairy farmers and local government. It's in a pleasant park on the banks of Saltwater Creek. Outdoor displays include horse-drawn agricultural equipment and a historic slab cottage. Opening times vary so check with museum; Stuart St, Mullumbimby; (02) 6684 4367.

BYRON BAY WILDLIFE SANCTUARY: Rebranded from the Macadamia Castle, and transformed into a 'bio-ark' filled with native wildlife. And there are still macadamia products to be bought.; (02) 6687 8432. It's 15km north of Ballina (see p. 56).

MACLEAN: This quirky village is known as the 'Scottish town' because of the many Scots who first settled here. Some street signs are in Gaelic as well as English. Highlights in the town include the Scottish Shop, Maclean Museum and a self-guided historical walk with a brochure available from the visitor centre. There is a market on the 2nd Sat each month and a Highland Gathering each Easter. A 24hr ferry service crosses the river to Lawrence.

MINJUNGBAL ABORIGINAL CULTURAL CENTRE: The Aboriginal Heritage Unit of the Australian Museum is dedicated to self-determination and to promoting, protecting and preserving Australia's Aboriginal cultures. The unit runs this museum, which features displays on all aspects of Traditional Owners' life on the north coast. There is also a walk

Top: Anglers at Iluka Beach
Opposite: Cape Byron Lighthouse in Byron Bay

encompassing the ceremonial Bora Ring and a mangrove and rainforest area. Located just over Boyds Bay Bridge in Tweed Heads (see p. 59); open Mon–Thurs 10am–3pm.

NEW ITALY: A monument and remains are all that are left of this settlement that was the result of the ill-fated Marquis de Rays's expedition in 1880. The Marquis tricked 340 Italians into purchasing non-existent property in a Pacific paradise. Disaster struck several times for the emigrants, as they travelled first to Papua New Guinea and then to New Caledonia. Eventually Sir Henry Parkes arranged for their passage to Australia, where the 217 survivors built this village. It's 23km south-west of Evans Head (see p. 57).

RICHMOND RANGE NATIONAL PARK: Protected rainforest perfect for camping, birdwatching, picnics and barbecues, with good bushwalking on a 2km or 6km track.

STORY HOUSE MUSEUM: This quaint museum tells the story of the development of Yamba (see p. 59) from the time it was merely a point of entry to the Clarence River. The collection of photographs and records tells a compelling tale of early development of a typical Australian coastal town. Open 10am–4.30pm Tues–Thurs; 2–4.30pm Sat–Sun; River St, Yamba.

SUMMERLAND FARM: A nursery, working avocado and macadamia farm, garden, crafts, fruit-processing plant and kids' water park – and it serves Devonshire tea! The farm is completely run by people with disabilities; 253 Wardell Rd, Alstonville; (02) 6628 0610.

SUSAN ISLAND: This rainforest recreation reserve on the Clarence River is home to a large fruit-bat colony. Dusk is the best time to visit to watch the bats flying off in search of food (wearing a hat is advisable if visiting at this time); by day the island is a good spot for rainforest walks, barbecues and picnics. You will need to arrange boat access from Grafton.

VICTORIA PARK NATURE RESERVE: Come here to gawk at the pademelons, but stay for the remarkable 68 species of trees. This 17.5ha reserve near Alstonville offers clearly marked walking trails and a spectacular lookout; make sure to keep an eye out for potoroos, water rats and possums. Wardell Rd.

WOLLUMBIN NATIONAL PARK: World Heritage–listed Wollumbin (Mount Warning) is the rhyolite plug of a massive ancient volcano left behind after surrounding basalt eroded away. To the Bundjalung People, Wollumbin is a traditional place of cultural law, initiation and spiritual education, and so in October 2022 the hiking trail to the summit was permanently closed to protect the mountain's cultural values. The rest of the national park was also closed at the time of research, though the majestic Wollumbin can still be admired from surrounding areas and nearby Border Ranges National Park.

YARRAWARRA ABORIGINAL CULTURAL CENTRE: Yarrawarra Cultural Centre is run by Gumbaynggirr People. The focus of this centre is to help Aboriginal and Islander Peoples maintain their heritage while teaching others about it. Visitors are encouraged to browse through the rooms of locally produced art, craft, books and CDs or dine at Pipeclay Cafe. Tours offered through the local area explore middens, ochre quarries and campsites while teaching about bush tucker and natural medicines. Stone and tool workshops and accommodation are also offered. Red Rock Rd; (02) 6640 7104. It's 10km north of Woolgoolga (see p. 59).

KEY TOWNS

ALSTONVILLE
Population 5182

Alstonville, a historic town between Lismore and Ballina, bursts into colour every March when the purple tibouchina trees that line its streets bloom. The quirky antique and gift shops also bring colour to Alstonville, as do the surrounding macadamia and avocado plantations.

SEE & DO **Crawford House Museum:** local history on display; Fri 10am–4pm, Sun 1pm–Sun; 10 Wardell Ave; (02) 6628 1829. **Lumley Park:** walk-through reserve of native plants, a flying-fox colony and open-air historic transport museum; Bruxner Hwy. **Budgen Avenue:** several shops and galleries with local art and craft. **Elizabeth Ann Brown Park:** rainforest park with picnic facilities; Main St. **Summerland Farm:** See Other Attractions.

BALLINA
Population 18,532

Ballina's name is believed to come from the Bundjalung word 'bullinah', said to mean 'fish and oysters'. This sets the scene for this delightful holiday town, which is on an island at the mouth of the Richmond River; the seafood is abundant, the sandy beaches are pretty and the weather is warm.

SEE & DO **Byron Bay Wildlife Sanctuary:** see Other Attractions. **Shelly Beach:** you can see dolphins frolicking in the waves year-round – and if it's good enough for them ... This is a beach for the whole family, with rockpools, a wading pool for toddlers and a cafe. If you come between June–July and Sept–Oct you might just catch a glimpse of migrating humpback whales. Off Shelly Beach Rd. **Naval and Maritime Museum:** in 1973, 12 sailors piloted three rafts from Ecuador to Ballina, a feat that has never been repeated. The museum features a restored raft from the Las Balsas Expedition; Regatta Ave; (02) 6681 1002. **Kerry Saxby Walkway:** from behind the visitor centre to the river mouth, with great river and ocean views. **The Big Prawn:** much-loved Ballina icon; River St. **Northern Rivers Community Gallery:** heritage building hosts exhibitions of local arts and crafts; Wed–Fri 10am–4pm, Sat–Sun 9.30am–1pm; 44 Cherry St; (02) 6681 0530. **Shaws Bay:** swimming and picnic area; off Compton Dr. **Pool and water slides:** River St. **Market:** Canal Rd; 3rd Sun each month.

★ BYRON BAY
Population 10,538

Byron Bay's excellent beaches, laidback feel and great weather have made it a long-time favourite destination for surfers, backpackers and alternative lifestylers. People from all walks of life, including celebrities, flock to Byron for whale-watching, surfing, swimming and relaxing. The town centre has an array of restaurants and cafes; surf shops, New Age shops and upmarket boutiques; and galleries with everything from handmade jewellery to timber furniture. Day spas, yoga retreats and natural therapy centres offer pampering.

SEE & DO **Tours and activities:** everything from diving and sea-kayaking to surfing lessons, skydiving and gliding; contact visitor centre for details. **The Farm:** see Byron's farm-to-table philosophy in action in this farm in nearby Ewingsdale, with a flower nursery, organic produce stores, bakery, the Three Blue Ducks restaurant and workshops that cater to both adults and kids; 11 Ewingsdale Rd, Ewingsdale; (02) 9610 8966. **Beach Hotel:** a well-established venue for live music and dining, with a beer garden that has ocean views; cnr Jonson and Bay sts; (02) 6685 6402. **Beaches:** safe swimming at Main Beach (patrolled during summer school holidays and at Easter); and surfing at Clarkes Beach, the Pass and Wategos Beach; child-friendly swimming at secluded Little Wategos; dogs are welcome at Belongil and Brunswick Heads; or go horseriding or beach-fishing at Seven Mile Beach stretching towards Lennox Head. A solar-powered train runs from the town centre to North Beach along a 3km track. **Health and wellbeing:** relax and unwind with a massage at Byron's numerous spas, including the tropical day spa at Buddha Gardens Day Spa, 1 Skinners Shoot Rd, (02) 6680 7844; and The Haven, with massage therapy and float tanks; Suite 3, 107 Jonson St; (02) 6685 8304. **Arts and Industry Estate:** arts precinct 3km from town with artists', jewellers' and sculptors' studios, galleries, cafes and restaurants; Artist Trail guide from visitor centre. **Farmers' market:** Butler St Reserve; Thurs mornings. **Market:** 1st Sun each month. **Julian Rocks Aquatic Reserve:** protects 450 underwater species and is great for diving; 3km S. **Broken Head Nature Reserve:** rainforest, secluded beaches and dolphin-watching; (02) 6627 0200; 9km S. **Bangalow:** rustic village with magnificent scenery, antique shops, arts and crafts, walking tracks and a popular market on the 4th Sun each month; 10km SW.

CASINO
Population 9968

Found off the delightfully named Summerland Way in the north-east of the state, Casino is named for one of the original properties in the area, which was in its turn named after the Italian town of Monte Cassino. Relaxing by the Richmond River, the town is full of historic buildings and magnificent parklands, and is known as the beef capital of Australia.

VISITOR INFORMATION

Byron Visitor Centre
80 Jonson St, Byron Bay
(02) 6680 8558
visitbyronbay.com

Clarence Valley
myclarencevalley.com

Tweed Valley and coast
visitthetweed.com.au

Top: Nimbin Markets **Bottom:** Yamba in the Clarence Valley

TOP EVENTS

- EASTER Bluesfest (Byron Bay); Yachting Regatta (Yamba); Highland Gathering (Maclean)
- MAY Casino Beef Week (Casino); MardiGrass Festival (Nimbin)
- JUNE Lantern Parade (Lismore); Cooly Rocks On 50s & 60s nostalgia festival (Tweed Heads)
- JULY Splendour in the Grass (Byron Bay);
- JULY–AUG Writers Festival (Byron Bay)
- AUG Tweed Valley Banana Festival and Harvest Week (Murwillumbah)
- SEPT Curryfest (Woolgoolga)
- OCT International Film Festival (Byron Bay); Bridge to Bridge Ski Race (Grafton)
- OCT–NOV Jacaranda Festival (Grafton)
- NOV Country Music Festival (Ballina)
- DEC The Falls Music and Art Festival (NYE, Byron Bay)

TEMPERATURES

Jan: 19–30°C

July: 7–20°C

SEE & DO Jabiru Geneebeinga Wetlands: these parklands have picnic facilities and are home to native bird species and wildlife including the jabiru (black-necked stork), egret and black swan. West St. **Folk Museum:** locally significant documents and photographs; open Mon, Wed and Fri 10am–2pm; Walker St. **Casino Miniature Railway and Museum:** ride on a mini diesel or steam train past the golf course and wetlands, and visit the museum; 10am–4pm Sun; Summerland Way. **Self-guided heritage and scenic walks and drives:** include Bicentennial Mural, St Mark's Church of England and Cecil Hotel; maps available from visitor centre. **Fossicking:** gold, labradorite and quartz (both smoky and clear types); permits required, inquire at visitor centre. **Freshwater fishing:** Cookes Weir and Richmond River are popular fishing spots; maps from visitor centre.

EVANS HEAD
Population 2894

This is an old-fashioned holiday village, nestled at the mouth of the Evans River between two national parks with 6km of safe surfing beaches and shallow river beaches. There's an excellent (and large) caravan park on the river with fantastic shade and access.

SEE & DO Goanna Headland: site of great mythical importance to the Bundjalung People and favourite spot of serious surfers. **Airforce Beach:** as well as being a serious surf beach, Airforce Beach also allows 4WD access without a permit, and dogs are allowed leash free for the first 1.3km. **Razorback Lookout:** views up and down the coast. On a clear day, Cape Byron Lighthouse can be seen to the north; Ocean Dr. **Memorial Aerodrome Museum:** displays of historical military and civilian aircraft; open Sat–Sun 10am–4pm; 61 Memorial Dr. **Market:** Club Evans RSL carpark; 4th Sat each month. **Broadwater National Park:** bushwalking, birdwatching, fishing and swimming; 5km N. **Woodburn:** friendly town on the Richmond River with great spots for picnicking, swimming, fishing and boating; flower show in Sept; 11km NW.

GRAFTON
Population 17,155

Although Grafton is just inland from NSW's famous north coast, this town emphatically embraces land-bound nature, with more than 24 parks and 6000 trees. Many of these are jacaranda trees, and come spring they bloom purple, which is celebrated by the town's Jacaranda Festival in late October and early November. With the Clarence River meandering through town – excellent for rafting, fishing and waterskiing – and heritage buildings, this town is a charming spot.

SEE & DO Regional gallery: *see* Top Attractions. **Susan Island:** *See* Other Attractions. **National Trust–classified buildings:** includes Schaeffer House, home of the Clarence River Historical Society, Christ Church Cathedral, and the notorious Grafton Gaol; heritage trail brochure from visitor centre. **Local art and craft shops:** brochure from visitor centre. **Farmers' market:** Christ Church Cathedral carpark, Fitzroy St; every Thurs. **Markets:** Grafton showgrounds, Prince St, 3rd Sat each month. **Nymboida:** This small scenic village is near the Nymboida River. Canoe hire and lessons are on offer. The beautiful rainforest surrounds are excellent for bushwalking, abseiling, trail rides and platypus viewing. 47km SW. **Ulmarra Village:** National Trust–classified turn-of-the-century river port with exceptional galleries, craft shops and studios where you can watch artists at work; 12km NE. **Fishing:** river fishing for saltwater or freshwater fish, depending on time of year and rainfall; details at visitor centre.

ILUKA
Population 1764

Located at the mouth of the Clarence River, Iluka is a relatively uncommercial fishing and holiday village, with long stretches of sandy white beaches and rare and accessible rainforest. Iluka Nature Reserve has the largest remnant of littoral rainforest (trees obtaining water via filtration through coastal sand and nutrients from airborne particles) in NSW.

SEE & DO Iluka Nature Reserve; Bundjalung National Park: *see* Top Attractions for both. **River cruises:** scenic river cruises Wed and Fri, live music cruise Sun; from the Boatshed. **Passenger ferry:** travelling daily to Yamba; from the Boatshed. **Fish Co-op:** fresh catches on sale daily from 9am; adjacent to the Boatshed. **Walking track:** picturesque coastline walk; access via Iluka Bluff to the north and Long St to the south. **Iluka Bluff Beach:** safe swimming beach with good surf and a whale-watching lookout; brochure from visitor centre; 1km N.

KYOGLE
Population 2804

Kyogle, on the Richmond River in the Northern Rivers region, calls itself the 'gateway to the rainforests' because it's within a close drive of some of the oldest rainforests in Australia. If you're looking for magic closer to town, Kyogle is situated at the base of the charmingly named Fairy Mountain.

SEE & DO Captain Cook Memorial Lookout: at the top of Fairy Mountain, this lookout provides stunning views of the town and surrounding countryside; Fairy St. **Botanic Gardens:** combination of formal gardens and revegetated creek environments on the banks of Fawcetts Creek; Summerland Way. **Wiangaree:** rural community with rodeo in Mar; 15km N. **Roseberry Forest**

Park: picturesque picnic spot; 23km N. **Moore Park Nature Reserve:** tiny reserve with the most important example of black bean rainforest in NSW; 26km NW. **Toonumbar Dam:** built from earth and rocks, this offers scenic bushwalking with picnic and barbecue facilities. Nearby Bells Bay is known for its bass fishing and has a campsite; 31km W. **Toonumbar National Park:** the Traditional Country of the Githabul People this park contains two World Heritage–listed rainforests and the volcanic remnants of Edinburgh Castle, Dome Mountain and Mount Lindesay; 35km W. **Scenic forest drive:** via Mount Lindesay (45km NW), offers magnificent views of both the rainforest and the countryside; brochure from visitor centre.

LISMORE
Population 27,916

The land where Lismore sits is on Widjabul Country. It was once part of a large rainforest known as the 'Big Scrub'. It was mainly chopped down in the 19th century, but there are 11 remnants of the rainforest around town, including a section at the Southern Cross University campus. Lismore is in a lush valley on the banks of Wilsons River and is surrounded by national parks. Just inland from Byron Bay, the area is famous for attracting alternative thinkers. In 2022, the city experienced its worst flooding since modern records began. Countless homes and businesses were inundated when Wilsons River peaked at more than 14m.

SEE & DO **Rotary Rainforest Reserve:** there are 6ha of original tropical rainforest in the middle of the city, but this is only a small remnant of the original 'Big Scrub' that stood here before European settlement. Over 3km of paths, including a boardwalk, lead visitors past hoop pines and giant figs, with rare species of labelled rainforest plants. Rotary Dr. **Lismore Museum:** geological specimens, First Nations artefacts and settler clothing, implements, furniture and handiwork; Molesworth St. **Regional Gallery:** permanent collection of paintings, pottery and ceramics with changing exhibitions by local and touring artists; at the time of writing, the gallery was still closed from the floods, so check ahead for opening details; Molesworth St. **Robinson's Lookout:** views south across the river to South Lismore and north to the mountains; Robinson Ave. **Claude Riley Memorial Lookout:** views over Lismore city; New Ballina Rd. **Wilson Nature Reserve:** contains original rainforest with labelled trees; Wyrallah St, East Lismore. **Riverside Walk:** along the banks of Wilsons River from the town centre to Spinks Park, where there are picnic and barbecue facilities. **Koala Care Centre:** looks after injured and orphaned koalas. Guided tours Mon–Fri 10am and 2pm, and Sat 10am; Rifle Range Rd. **Cafe and Culture Trail:** self-guided walk through sites of historical significance and cafes in the town centre. **Heritage walk:** historic buildings and churches; brochure from visitor centre.

Car Boot Markets: Shopping Sq, Uralba St; 1st and 3rd Sun each month. **Organic Markets:** showground, Alexander Pde; Tues. **Boatharbour Reserve:** 17ha of rainforest, wildlife sanctuary, picnic area and walking tracks; 6km E. **Tucki Tucki Nature Reserve:** woodland planted by local residents to protect the diminishing koala population, with a walking track; 15km S. **Rocky Creek Dam:** between Nightcap National Park and Whian Whian State Forest, includes spectacular views of the lake, boardwalks, walking trails, platypus-viewing platform, barbecues and a playground; 18km N.

MULLUMBIMBY
Population 3589

The Bundjalung People are the Traditional Owners of the area of Mullumbimby. The town is at the base of Mount Chincogan in the lush Northern Rivers region. After most of the sought-after red cedars were chopped down by early settlers, the town became a farming community. Along with other towns in the Byron area, Mullumbimby started attracting those seeking an alternative lifestyle in the 1960s – helped by the subtropical landscape and excellent weather – and today this vibe continues with cafes and stores that reflect this relaxed lifestyle. Like so many towns in this region, Mullumbimby suffered near-record floods in 2022.

SEE & DO **Brunswick Valley Historical Museum:** *see* Other Attractions. **Brunswick Valley Heritage Park:** over 200 rainforest plants, including palms, and a 2km park and river walk; Tyagarah St. **Market:** Stuart St; 3rd Sat each month. **Crystal Castle & Shambhala Gardens:** spectacular natural crystal display, peace stupa and rainforest gardens; 7km SW. **Tyagarah Airstrip:** skydiving and paragliding; Pacific Hwy; 13km SW.

MURWILLUMBAH
Population 9812

Murwillumbah is located on the banks of the Tweed River near the Queensland border. It is a centre for sugarcane, banana and cattle farms. In 1907 Murwillumbah was almost completely wiped out by fire. The town was rebuilt and many of those buildings can still be seen on the main street today. The floods of 2022 affected much of the city, with river levels surpassing 50-year-old flood records.

SEE & DO **Tweed Regional Art Gallery:** see Top Attractions. **Tweed Regional Museum:** local history and changing exhibitions; open Tues–Sat 10am–4pm; (02) 6670 2493; cnr Queensland Rd and Bent St. **Market:** Knox Park, 1st and 3rd Sat each month; showground, 4th Sun each month. **Farmers' market:** Queensland Rd, Wed. **Stokers Siding:** historic village at the foot of the Burringbar Ranges; 8km S. **Madura Tea Estates:** tea plantation with tastings and tours by appt; bookings (02) 6670 6000; 12km NE. **Banana Cabana:** garden and shop with over 20 bush-tucker species and exotic fruits; Chillingham; 12km NW. **Mooball:** small town with a cow theme that has painted almost anything that stands still in the style of a black-and-white cow, including buildings, cars and electricity poles; 19km SE.

NIMBIN
Population 500

Nimbin is a haven for people seeking an alternative lifestyle, including those advocating to make cannabis legal. Situated in a beautiful valley, it's a colourful and interesting town. Originally a place of healing and initiation for the Bundjalung People, the Nimbin area was cleared and used for dairy and banana farming. Nimbin hit a depression in the late 1960s when the dairy industry collapsed. It took the 1973 Aquarius Festival to establish Nimbin as the alternative-culture capital of Australia.

SEE & DO **Candle Factory:** produces environmentally friendly candles sold throughout Australia and the world; Butter Factory, Cullen St; (02) 6689 1010. **HEMP Embassy:** promotes the use of hemp to make all sorts of environmentally friendly products; Cullen St; (02) 6689 1842. **Town hall:** features mural of First Nations art; Cullen St. **Local art, craft and psychedelia:** brochure from visitor centre. **Market:** local craft; Nimbin Community Centre, Cullen St; 4th and 5th Sun each month. **Nimbin Rocks:** spectacular remnants of an ancient volcano overlooking the town. This is a sacred initiation site for the Bundjalung people, so viewing is from the road only; Lismore Rd; 3km S. **The Channon:** town featuring an alternative-craft market, 2nd Sun each month; 15km SE.

TWEED HEADS
Population 63,721

Tweed Heads is the state's northernmost town and – along with its twin town Coolangatta over the Queensland border – is a popular holiday destination at the south end of the Gold Coast. The region has long been celebrated for its weather, surf beaches, nightlife and laidback atmosphere.

SEE & DO **Point Danger:** this lookout is on the Queensland–NSW border and overlooks Duranbah Beach, which is popular for surfing. It was named by then Lieutenant James Cook to warn of the dangerous coral reefs that lay under the waves off the coast. The world's first laser-beam lighthouse is located here. Dolphins may be seen off the coast along the cliff-edge walk. There are picnic spots with ocean views. **Tweed Regional Museum (TRM) Tweed Heads:** four original buildings house maritime, heritage and photographic collections; Pioneer Park, Kennedy Dr, Tweed Heads West; Sun–Wed 10am–4pm. **Tweed cruise boats:** cruises visit locations along the Tweed River; River Tce. **Fishing and diving charters and houseboat hire:** guided and self-guided river excursions; bookings at visitor centre. **Watersports Guru:** whale-watching adventures and snorkelling tours to Cook Island marine reserve; bookings 0430 082 890. **Catch a Crab Cruises, Birds Bay Oyster Farm, deep-sea fishing:** these tours depart daily, bookings from visitor centre. **Craft market:** Florence St; Sun. **Beaches:** idyllic white sandy beaches for surfing and swimming, including Fingal (3km S) and Kingscliff (14km S). **Tropical Fruit World:** home to the world's largest variety of tropical fruit with plantation safari, jungle riverboat cruise, fauna park and fruit tastings; 15km S.

WOOLGOOLGA
Population 5797

'Woopi' (as it is affectionately known to locals) is a charming and relaxed seaside town with a significant Sikh population. Punjabi immigrants who were working on the Queensland cane fields headed south for work on banana plantations, and many settled in Woolgoolga. Today Indians make up between a quarter and a half of the town's population, providing a unique cultural mix. The beaches are popular for fishing, surfing and swimming and the annual Curryfest is a colourful – and tasty – street party in Sept.

SEE & DO **Guru Nanak Sikh Temple:** spectacular white temple with gold domes; River St. Behind it you'll find the **Sikh Heritage Museum of Australia**, open Thurs–Sun 10am–4pm. **Woolgoolga Headland:** you'll catch excellent views (sometimes of dolphins!) from this headland. **Art Gallery:** exhibits local works; Turon Pde. **Bollywood Market:** Woolgoolga Beach; 1st and 2nd Sat each month. **Market:** Beach St; 2nd Sat each month. **Wedding Bells State Forest:** subtropical and eucalypt forest with walking trails to Sealy Lookout and Mount Caramba Lookout; 14km NW.

★ YAMBA
Population 6342

Yamba, at the mouth of the Clarence River, is the sort of holiday town that families come back to year after year. It has a classic holiday town feel, with great facilities, even though it's the largest coastal resort in the Clarence Valley. Don't miss getting fish and chips from here – Yamba is a major fishing centre and famous for its prawns, so you can expect your order to be fresh from the sea. Or you could always catch dinner yourself; the town has excellent sea, lake and river fishing. If the town isn't peaceful enough for you, the wild and surprisingly undiscovered Yuraygir National Park, is nearby.

SEE & DO **Yuraygir National Park:** see Top Attractions. **Story House Museum:** see Other Attractions. **Clarence River Lighthouse:** coastal views from the base; via Pilot St. **Boat Harbour Marina:** departure point for daily ferry service to Iluka, river cruises, deep-sea fishing charters and whale-watching trips. Also houseboat hire; off Yamba Rd. **Whiting Beach:** sandy river beach ideal for children. **Coastal beaches:** several in town with excellent swimming and surfing conditions, including Angourie, a National Surfing Reserve celebrated for its right-hand point break; map from visitor centre. **River Market:** Ford Park; 4th Sun each month. **Farmers & Producers Market:** Whiting Beach car park; Wed mornings. **Lake Wooloweyah:** fishing and prawning; 4km S. **The Blue Pool:** deep freshwater pool 50m from the ocean, popular for swimming; 5km S.

Opposite: Yamba Main Beach

New England

When poet Dorothea Mackellar wrote about her love of **ragged mountain ranges** and **sweeping plains**, she was thinking of the landscape of the Northern Tablelands, inspired by the country surrounding her brother's property in Gunnedah. New England and the Northern Tablelands have something for everyone. Tap your toes in the **country music capital of Tamworth**, live the high life in **gracious Armidale**, unearth **gemstones** in Inverell, immerse yourself in the **misty rainforests** in the national parks and marvel at the most impressive waterfalls on the aptly-named **Waterfall Way**.

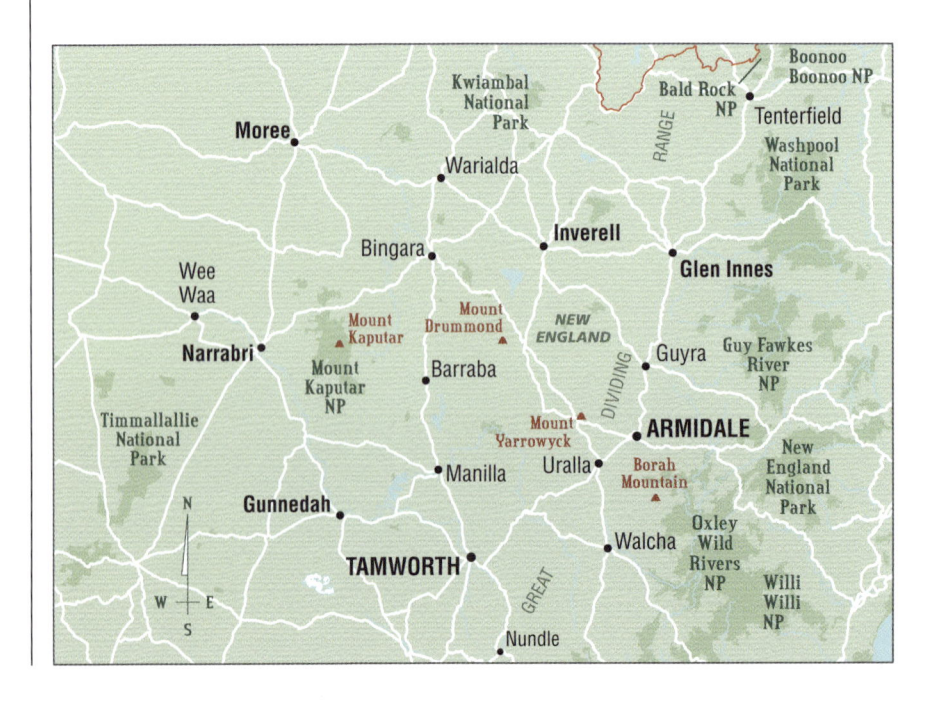

CHEAT SHEET

→ Allow at least a week for a proper exploration.

→ Best time to visit: autumn cloaks the tablelands in a mantle of colour and it's a great place to escape the heat in summer.

→ Main towns: Armidale (see p. 64), Gunnedah (see p. 65), Moree (see p. 66), Tamworth (see p. 67).

→ The Northern Tablelands are the Traditional Lands of the Bigambul, Bundjalung, Gumbainggir, Kamilaroi, Nganyaywana, and Ngarabul Peoples.

→ Did you know? Out of all the world's sapphires, 70 per cent come from Australia, and almost 70 per cent of those come from the Inverell area. Ask at the visitor information centre for tips on where to fossick.

→ Don't miss: hot artesian baths in Moree; wine tasting in Armidale; country music in Tamworth; the Standing Stones in Glen Innes; cool temperate rainforest in Washpool and New England national parks; bushwalking; fossicking; waterfalls; gorges; and the view from Point Lookout.

Top: Historic streetscape, Armidale **Opposite:** 40 metre high mural on Barraba silos by Fintan Magee

TOP ATTRACTIONS

AUSTRALIAN COUNTRY MUSIC HALL OF FAME: From the air, this building is guitar-shaped, and it features various displays including one that cleverly documents the history of country music through lyrics, as well as a display on the Country Music Awards and a theatrette playing films and documentaries. Open Tues–Sun 10am–4pm; 561 Peel St, Tamworth; 0408 660 749.

BALD ROCK NATIONAL PARK: There are excellent 360-degree views from the summit of Bald Rock, the largest granite monolith in Australia. The park is full of canyons and stone arches, and kangaroos abound. Interestingly, Bald Rock was considered 'neutral ground' and a trade route for the Jukambal, Bundgalung and Kamilleroi People.

BIG GOLDEN GUITAR TOURIST CENTRE The 12m golden guitar is a giant replica of the country music award and an Australian icon. Inside the complex is the Gallery of Stars Wax Museum, which features wax models of Australian country music legends alongside current stars. Opposite is the outdoor Country Music Roll of Renown, which is said to be Australia's highest honour in country music. There are special tributes to, among others, Tex Morton, Smoky Dawson and Slim Dusty. 2 Ringers Rd, Tamworth; (02) 6765 2688.

CATHEDRAL ROCK NATIONAL PARK: Just off the Waterfall Way near the village of Ebor, the giant boulders, sculpted rock, distinctive granite hills and wedge-tailed eagles make this park popular among photographers. Walks include a 3hr circuit to the summit of Cathedral Rock for 360-degree views of the tableland.

CENTENNIAL PARKLANDS: In the town of Glen Innes (see p. 65), this Celtic monument of 'Australian Standing Stones' was built with 40 giant granite monoliths in recognition of the contribution made in Australia by people of Celtic origin. A full explanation of the stones can be read at Crofters Cottage, which also sells Celtic food and gifts. St Martin's Lookout provides superb views. Meade St, Glen Innes.

GIBRALTAR RANGE NATIONAL PARK AND WASHPOOL NATIONAL PARK: Around 70km north-east of the town of Glen Innes (see p. 65), these adjoining parks were World Heritage listed in 1986 because of their ancient and isolated remnants of rainforest and their great variety of plant and animal species. Gibraltar Range is known for its scenic creeks and cascades and its unusual granite formations, the Needles and Anvil Rock. Gibraltar Range also contains over 100km of excellent walking trails. Washpool has the largest remaining stand of coachwood trees in the world and a unique array of eucalypt woods and rainforest. It has some of the least disturbed forest in NSW.

HANGING ROCK: Just west of Nundle (see p. 67), the area is popular for mineral fossicking, with good samples of scheelite and an excellent site for gold panning on the Peel River. Sheba Dams Reserve is home to numerous birds and animals. Activities include picnicking, bushwalking, camping and fishing, with regular stockings of trout and salmon.

MCCROSSIN'S MILL: This restored three-storey granite-and-brick flour mill (1870) in Uralla (see p. 68) is now a museum of local history. The ground floor and gardens are used for functions, but the upper levels have fascinating exhibitions, including the Wool Industry, Gold Mining (featuring a replica Chinese joss house) and an Aboriginal diorama. The Thunderbolt exhibition contains a set of nine paintings depicting the events leading up to bushranger Captain Thunderbolt's death, painted by Phillip Pomroy. Inquiries (02) 6778 3022; Salisbury St, Uralla.

MOREE ARTESIAN AQUATIC CENTRE: These spas were discovered accidentally when European settlers were searching for reliable irrigation water. A bore was sunk into the Great Artesian Basin and the water that emerged was 41°C. The complex also has an outdoor heated pool and an array of leisure activities. Cnr Anne and Gosport sts, Moree.

MOUNT KAPUTAR NATIONAL PARK: This is the Traditional Land of the Kamilaroi People, with rock carvings and sacred sites and part of Dreaming stories. This park is excellent for hiking, rising as high as 1200m, and is the site of the now-extinct Nandewar Volcano. The diverse vegetation ranges from semi-arid woodland to wet sclerophyll forest and alpine growth. Wildlife is abundant, especially bats, birds and quolls. Note that this national park was affected by bushfire in 2019/20 so check ahead with NSW National Parks and Wildlife Service.

NEW ENGLAND REGIONAL ART MUSEUM: This bustling regional museum has an impressive selection of Australian artists in the Howard Hinton and Chandler Coventry collections, including Arthur Streeton, Tom Roberts, Margaret Preston and John Coburn. The museum draws big numbers, with more than 40,000 visitors each year strolling through its eight gallery spaces, audiovisual theatre, artist studio and cafe. There is also a separate Museum of Printing (open Tues 10am–2pm and Sun 1–4pm) featuring the F.T. Wimble & Co collection. Open Tues–Sun 10am–4pm; 106–114 Kentucky St, Armidale; (02) 6772 5255.

NEW ENGLAND WINE REGION Most of the vineyards in this cool, elevated area on the western slopes of the Great Dividing Range are clustered around Glen Innes, Inverell and Tenterfield, with a few also around Tamworth. Semillon, cabernet sauvignon, pinot noir and chardonnay are some of the region's best wines. Maps with wineries with cellar doors are available from the Tenterfield (see p. 68) information centre.

OXLEY WILD RIVERS NATIONAL PARK: This dramatically wild national park encompasses a high plateau, deep gorges and protects World Heritage–listed rainforest, as well as numerous waterfalls, including Dangars Falls, a 120m waterfall over a gorge; and Wollomombi Falls, which at 220m is the highest waterfall in the state. The Walcha section of the park features Apsley Falls where seven platforms and a bridge provide access to both sides of the gorge and waterfall. Tia Falls has beautiful rainforest scenery. Campsites at Riverside and Youdales Hut are accessible by 4WD.

PAUL WILD OBSERVATORY (CSIRO AUSTRALIA TELESCOPE): Here you'll find an impressive line of five 22m diameter antennas all facing the sky. They are connected on a rail track and are moved around to get full coverage. A sixth antenna lies 3km away, and all are sometimes connected with telescopes at Coonabarabran and Parkes. The visitor centre features a video, displays and an opportunity to view the telescope. Open Mon–Sun; it's 25km west of Narrabri (see p. 67).

PIONEER VILLAGE This collection of homes and buildings in Inverell (see p. 66) dates from 1840 but was moved from its original site to form a 'village of yesteryear'. Attractions include Grove homestead, Paddy's Pub and Mount Drummond Woolshed. Gooda Cottage has an impressive collection of gems and minerals. Tea and damper are served by prior arrangement. Closed Mon except in school holidays; Tingha Rd, Inverell; (02) 6722 1717.

SAUMAREZ HOMESTEAD: National Trust–owned Edwardian mansion offering tours; Sat–Sun and public holidays 10am–5pm. Gardens and farm open Mon–Sun (closed mid-June to end Sept); Saumarez Rd, Armidale; (02) 6772 3616.

SIR HENRY PARKES SCHOOL OF ARTS: Sir Henry Parkes made his Federation speech in this National Trust–classified building constructed in 1876. Today it stands as a monument to Parkes. Memorabilia includes a life-size portrait by Julian Ashton and Parkes's scrimshaw walking stick made of whale ivory and baleen. Guided tours available. Cnr Manners and Rouse sts, Tenterfield.

OTHER ATTRACTIONS

BOONOO BOONOO NATIONAL PARK: Pronounced 'bunna bunoo' this national park's name comes from an Jukambal word believed to mean 'poor country for game', but today the park has kangaroos, wallabies and quolls. Several bushwalks include an easy 30min stroll to the spectacular 210m Boonoo Boonoo Falls. Pleasant swimming area above the falls. Just 27km from Tenterfield (see p. 68); (02) 6736 4298.

CHAFFEY DAM: Enjoy good swimming, fishing, sailing and picnicking. Dulegal Arboretum, an attractive garden of native trees and shrubs, is on the foreshore.

COPETON DAM STATE RECREATION AREA: Perfect for boating, waterskiing, swimming, fishing, bushwalking and rock climbing. It also has adventure playgrounds, water slides, and picnic and barbecue facilities. Kangaroos graze on the golf course at dusk; inquiries (02) 6723 6269.

CRANKY ROCK NATURE RESERVE: It is rumoured that during the gold rush a 'cranky' Chinese man, after being challenged about a wrongdoing, jumped to his death from the highest of the balancing granite boulders. Today you'll find picnic spots, camping, fossicking, wildflowers and wildlife. A suspension bridge leads to an observation deck above Reedy Creek for breathtaking views. It's 8km east of Warialda (see p. 69).

DALMORTON TUNNEL: Hand-carved (but not by convicts, despite the local legends) road tunnel halfway between Glen Innes and Grafton; Old Grafton Rd.

KWIAMBAL NATIONAL PARK: The name of this national park comes from the Kwiambal People and there are sacred sites still here. The Macintyre River flows through gorges and plunge pools to Macintyre Falls and then leads into the Severn River. The park is rich with protected woodlands of white cypress pine, box and ironbark. Bat nurseries can be viewed with a torch in the remarkable Ashford Caves, which until the 1960s were mined for guano (bat droppings) to be used as fertiliser on local farms. The park makes a serene site for swimming, bushwalking and camping and there is also mountain biking. Encounters with kangaroos, emus and koalas are common.

MANN RIVER NATURE RESERVE: A popular camping spot for its fantastic swimming holes. You can find it 40km north-east of Glen Innes (see p. 65).

MOTHER OF DUCKS LAGOON: This reserve is a rare high-country wetland and home to hundreds of waterbirds. The migratory Japanese snipe is known to stop here, and it is a nesting site for swans. There is a viewing platform with an identification board covering dozens of different birds. McKie Pde, Guyra.

MOUNT YARROWYCK NATURE RESERVE: This dry eucalypt reserve, about a 30min drive from Armidale, has plentiful wildlife including kangaroos, wallaroos and wallabies, and is ideal for bushwalking and picnics. The highlight is the 3km Aboriginal cultural walk – about halfway along the trail is a large overhang of granite boulders under which is a set of red-ochre paintings of circles and bird tracks.

NUNDLE WOOLLEN MILL: This famous wool mill offers a fascinating insight into one of the country's longest-standing industries. View the inner workings of the mill from the observation deck or take the factory tour. Retail store also onsite; Oakenville St, Nundle.

TENTERFIELD SADDLER: Handmade saddles at the place that inspired the eponymous song by Peter Allen. Still open for business, it is classified by the National Trust of Australia, and its customers have included Banjo Paterson; open Tues–Sun 9am–1pm Tues-Sun; High St, Tenterfield.

TORRINGTON: Gem fossicking, bushwalks and unusual rock formations. It's 66km north-west of Glen Innes (see p. 65).

WARRABAH NATIONAL PARK: At this peaceful riverside retreat you'll find enormous granite boulders sitting above still valley pools and rapids suitable for experienced kayakers. Activities include swimming and fishing in the Namoi and Manilla rivers and rock climbing on the cliffs. You can access it from Manilla (see p. 66), Tamworth (see p. 67) or Uralla (see p. 68).

Opposite top: Sir Henry Parkes Memorial School of Arts in Tenterfield **Opposite bottom:** Troy Cassar-Daley's handprint at the Australian Country Music Hall of Fame in Tamworth

KEY TOWNS

ARMIDALE
Population 21,312

With its heritage buildings and birch, poplar and ash trees, Armidale feels like an English village – which is apt considering it's the largest town in the New England district. But the surrounding area is distinctly Australian, with multiple national parks boasting dramatic gorges, wild rivers and forests. The early wealth of the town led to a rash of bushrangers terrorising it, including the famous Captain Thunderbolt. Visit in autumn when the seasonal trees put on a spectacular colour display.

SEE & DO **New England Regional Art Museum:** see Top Attractions. **Saumarez Homestead:** see Other Attractions. **Armidale Heritage Tour:** this 2.5hr tour takes in some of the National Trust–listed buildings in town, including the Railway Museum, St Peter's Anglican Cathedral and the University of New England; departs Mon–Sat 10am from the visitor centre; runs on donations, book at (02) 6770 3888. **Aboriginal Cultural Centre and Keeping Place:** includes museum, cultural tours, bush-tucker walks and cafe; Mon–Fri 9am–4pm, Sat 10am–2pm; 128 Kentucky St; (02) 6771 3606. **Armidale Folk Museum:** National Trust–classified building with a comprehensive collection of historic artefacts from the region, including toys and buggies; 11am–2pm; cnr Faulkner and Rusden sts; (02) 6770 3836. **Bicentennial Railway Museum:** railway memorabilia; Mon–Fri 11am–12.30pm; Brown St; (02) 6770 3836. **Self-guided heritage walk and drive:** pick up a map from the visitor centre and guide yourself on a 3km walk or 25km drive around the historical points in town and the surrounding area. **Farmers' market:** 2nd Sun of each month, Saumarez Homestead. **University of New England:** the centrepiece of Australia's oldest regional university is spectacular settler mansion Booloominbah Homestead. There's also an Antiquities Museum, Zoology Museum and kangaroo and deer park; Handel St; (02) 6773 3333; 5km NW. **Dumaresq Dam:** walking trails, boating, swimming and trout fishing (Oct–June); Dumaresq Dam Rd; 15km NE. **Hillgrove:** former mining town with Rural Life and History Museum featuring goldmining equipment (open Fri–Mon 10am–2pm, honesty box with gold-coin donation) and self-guided walk through old town site; brochure at visitor centre; 31km E.

BARRABA
Population 1035

The tree-lined streets of Barraba lie in the valley of the Manilla River. Surrounded by the Nandewar Ranges, Horton Valley and undulating tablelands, Barraba is a quiet and idyllic town. The area was once busy with mining and, although some mines still operate, the main industries today centre on sheep and wool.

SEE & DO **Heritage Walk:** the walk takes in a heritage-listed organ and historic buildings such as the courthouse, church, clock tower and the visitor centre itself. The Commercial Hotel on Queen St was once a Cobb & Co. changing station. **The Playhouse:** accommodation as well as a theatre and exhibition space; Queen St; (02) 6782 1109. **Market:** Queen St; 2nd Sat each month. **Adams Lookout:** panoramic views of the town and countryside; 5km NE. **Millie Park Vineyard:** organic wine cellar-door tastings and sales; 5km N. **Glen Riddle Recreation Reserve:** on Manilla River north of Split Rock Dam, for boating, fishing and picnicking; 15km SE. **Ironbark Creek:** gold and mineral fossicking, with ruins of old village; 18km E. **Horton River Falls:** 83m waterfall, swimming and bushwalking; 38km W. **Birdwatching trails:** the 165 species in the area include the rare regent honeyeater; guides are available from the visitor centre.

BINGARA
Population 1028

Nestled on the Gwydir River, Bingara boomed in the 19th century when gold and diamonds were discovered; visit a working goldmine near the town to try your luck. Many of the historic buildings from the gold-rush period have been restored, including the local theatre.

SEE & DO **Orange Tree Memorial:** orange trees along Finch St and Gwydir Oval stand as a memorial to those who have fallen in war. During the Orange Festival, Bingara's children pick the fruit and present it to hospital patients and the elderly. **All Nations Goldmine:** a stamper battery is the only visible remnant; Hill St. **Historical Museum:** slab building (1860) displays gems and minerals and 19th-century furniture and photographs; Maitland St. **Roxy Theatre and Greek Museum:** this Art Deco theatre, built in 1936, closed for business in 1958, but was restored and reopened in 2004 as a cinema, multipurpose community space and cafe; the complex is also home to a museum commemorating the role Greek immigrants played in the cafe culture of country towns; tours available, ask at the visitor centre; Maitland St. **Wade Horses:** trail rides and Jackaroo Jillaroo school; 0488 380 641. **Gwydir River:** walking track along the bank and reportedly the best Murray cod fishing in NSW. **Self-guided historic/scenic town walk and drive:** contact visitor centre for maps. **Three Creeks Goldmine:** working mine open to the public for gold panning, crystal fossicking and bushwalking; 24km S. **Myall Creek Memorial:** monument to

Top: Oxley Scenic Lookout in Tamworth **Middle:** Mural at the McCrossin's Mill Museum in Uralla **Bottom:** Cotton farming at the Newport Cotton Farm in Moree

VISITOR INFORMATION

Armidale Visitors Centre
82 Marsh St
(02) 6770 3888
armidaletourism.com.au

Narrabri Shire Visitor Information Centre
117 Tibbereena St, Narrabri
(02) 6799 6760
visitnarrabri.com.au

the many Wirrayaraay men, women and children killed in the massacre of 1838, but the death toll is unconfirmed. The white perpetrators were hanged for the crime, the only time this has happened in Australia's history; Delungra–Bingara Rd; 27km NE. **Rocky Creek glacial area:** unusual conglomerate rock formations; 37km SW. **Sawn Rocks:** pipe-shaped volcanic rock formations; 70km SW. **Birdwatching and fossicking:** maps available from visitor centre.

GLEN INNES
Population 8931

The locals call the highlands of New England 'Celtic Country', and Glen Innes, at an elevation of 1135m, was originally settled by a Scot in the mid-18th century. This heritage is celebrated every year at the Australian Celtic Festival, which happens at Glen Innes's standing stones in Centennial Parklands. There's even a castle on a local station. Just like in Scotland, there are four unique seasons, and the town's parks are particularly striking in autumn. Although the name is Scottish, the bushrangers who terrorised the area in the 19th century were uniquely Australian, and included the infamous Captain Thunderbolt. There's also an intriguing local legend explaining why the area is often called the 'land of the beardies'. Ask one of the locals!

SEE & DO **Centennial Parklands:** *see* Top Attractions; **Mann River Nature Reserve, Torrington** and **Dalmorton tunnel:** *see* Other Attractions for all. **Land of the Beardies History House:** folk museum in the town's first hospital building; it has a reconstructed slab hut, period room settings and relics; cnr Ferguson St and West Ave; (02) 6732 1035. **Self-guided walks:** past historic public buildings, especially on Grey St; brochure from visitor centre. **Market:** Grey St; 2nd Sat each month. **Stonehenge:** unusual balancing rock formations; 18km S. **Emmaville:** the Australian beginnings of St John Ambulance and Medical Benefits occurred here. Includes a mining museum and restored courthouse; 39km NW. **Deepwater:** good fishing for trout, perch and cod with regular fishing safaris; bookings at visitor centre; 40km N. **Horse treks:** accommodation at historic pubs; bookings at visitor centre.

GUNNEDAH
Population 8338

At the heart of the Namoi Valley, Gunnedah is instantly recognisable by the grain silos that tower over the town. The area is abundant with native wildlife, and Gunnedah claims to be the koala capital of the world, with one of the largest koala populations in the country – they are often seen wandering around town. A large centre, Gunnedah still manages to keep a laidback atmosphere and has been home to famous Australians, including Dorothea Mackellar, Breaker Morant and Miranda Kerr.

SEE & DO **Anzac Park:** the Water Tower Museum here, housed in the town's main water tower, has a mural and display of early explorers, memorabilia from several wars and schools, and a First Nations history display (open Sat 10am–2pm and most Mon). Dorothea Mackellar, the renowned Australian poet responsible for '*My Country*', has a memorial statue in the park. Memorabilia of her life and of the annual national school poetry competition in her name, as well as the watercolour series 'My Country' by Jean Isherwood, can be viewed at the Mackellar Centre in the park; centre open Tues–Thurs 10am–4pm; South St. **Rural Museum:** early agricultural machinery and the largest privately owned firearm collection in the country; Mullaley Rd. **Red Chief Memorial:** the first memorial to an Aboriginal historical identity, warrior Cumbo Gunnerah, of the Gunn-e-dar people of the Kamilaroi tribe, who lived in the 1700s; State Office building, Abbott St. **Creative Arts Centre:** changing program of art exhibitions; open Fri–Sun 10am–4pm; Chandos St. **Plains of Plenty:** local craft and produce; South St. **Eighth Division Memorial Avenue:** with 45 flowering gums, each with a plaque in memory of men who served in the 8th Division in World War II; Memorial Ave. **Breaker Morant Drive:** a plaque tells the story of Henry Morant, known as 'the breaker' because of his skill with horses. A 500m path shows sites where he jumped horses; Kitchener Park. **Poets Drive:** celebration of Australian poetry, the Poets Drive is a self-guided drive tour inspired by Gunnedah's iconic landmarks and local heroes. **Bindea Walking Track:** memorials, koala and kangaroo sites, lookouts and Porcupine Reserve; brochure from visitor centre. **Market:** Wolseley Park, Conadilly St; 3rd Sat each month. **Lake Keepit** This lake is great for watersports, fishing and boating, and there is a children's pool. 34km NE. **Porcupine Lookout:** views over town and surrounding agricultural area; 3km SE. **150° East Time Meridian:** the basis of Eastern Standard Time, crossing the Oxley Hwy; 28km W.

GUYRA
Population 2077

Guyra, the highest town on the New England tablelands at an altitude of 1320m, looks like a traditional Australian country town, except for one thing – there's often snow in winter. There's easy access to local national parks from town, such as Cathedral Rock National Park, as well as great fishing in local streams.

SEE & DO **Mother Of Ducks Lagoon:** *see* Other Attractions. **Costa Tomatoes:** largest tomato-growing greenhouse in the Southern Hemisphere. It has boosted Guyra's population and economy enormously; Elm St. **Historical Society Museum:** themed room displaying town memorabilia and the story of the Guyra ghost; open Sat 10am–2pm or by appt; Bradley St; bookings (02) 6779 2132.

Poetry Hall of Fame: poetry library, books sales, cafe and performance space; Bradley St; 0423 478 656. **Burgess Garage Car Museum:** historic cars and automotive memorabilia and second-hand books; check at visitors centre for opening times; Bradley St. **Railway station:** large display of antique machinery; Bradley St. **Farmers' and Craft Market:** Sat at Poetry Hall of Fame (see above). **Thunderbolt's Cave:** picturesque and secluded cave, rumoured to be where the bushranger Captain Thunderbolt hid from police; 10km S. **Chandler's Peak:** spectacular views of the tablelands from an altitude of 1471m; 20km E.

INVERELL
Population 9654

This town on the Macintyre River at the centre of the New England tablelands is known as the 'Sapphire City'. It is also rich in other mineral deposits, including zircons, industrial diamonds and tin. The country here has lush farming land and excellent weather conditions with warm sunny days and cool nights. A Scottish immigrant gave Inverell its name, which means 'meeting place of the swans' in Gaelic.

SEE & DO **Pioneer Village:** see Top Attractions. **Art Gallery:** paintings, pottery and craft; Evans St. **Gem Centre:** see local stones being processed; Byron St. **National Transport Museum:** over 200 vehicles on display with an impressive collection of rarities; Taylor Ave. **Town Stroll:** includes sites such as the National Trust–classified courthouse and the CBC Bank building with stables at the rear; brochure from visitor centre. **Art, craft and wood-turning:** work by local artists; brochure from visitor centre. **Market:** Campbell Park; 1st (except Jan) and 3rd Sun each month. **McIlveen Park Lookout:** excellent views of town and surrounding pastures and nature reserve; 2km W. **Lake Inverell Reserve:** 100ha of unique aquatic sanctuary for birds and wildlife. Also an excellent site for picnics, bushwalking, birdwatching and fishing; 3km E. **Goonoowigall Bushland Reserve:** rough granite country rich with birdlife and marsupials, it offers superb birdwatching, remains of a Chinese settlement, bushwalking trails and picnic areas; 5km S. **Copeton Waters State Park:** perfect for boating, waterskiing, swimming, fishing, bushwalking and rock climbing. It also has adventure playgrounds, water slides, and picnic and barbecue facilities. Kangaroos graze on the golf course at dusk; inquiries (02) 6723 6269; 17km S. **Green Valley Farm:** working sheep property with zoo, accommodation, extensive gardens, playground and picnic and barbecue facilities. The highlight is Smith's Museum, with a rare collection of gems and minerals, local First Nations artefacts, antiques and period clothing; inquiries (02) 6723 3370; 36km SE. **Pindari Dam:** fishing, swimming, camping and picnic and barbecue facilities; 58km N. **Warm-weather wineries:** cellar-door tastings; brochure from visitor centre. **Fossicking sites:** great spots for searching for tin, sapphires, quartz or even diamonds; maps at visitor centre.

MANILLA
Population 2014

This town is located at the junction of the Manilla and Namoi rivers. Originally the land of the Kamilaroi People but settlers used the area for farming and large stations were established in the 19th century. The bushranger Captain Thunderbolt was almost caught while drunk near town. Located between Lake Keepit and Split Rock Dam, Manilla is perfect for myriad activities and is popular spot for gliding: national and international paragliding competitions are held here Nov–Apr.

SEE & DO **Warabah National Park:** see Other Attractions. **Heritage Museum:** incorporates Royce Cottage Collection and exhibits early settler items, such as clothing and furniture, and a bakery. Also has displays on platypus, which are often found in the area. **Manilla St:** antique and coffee shops. **Manilla Paragliding:** offers tandem flights; a two-day introduction, and a nine-day 'live-in' licensing course with equipment supplied; Mount Borah; (02) 6785 6545; 12km N. **Split Rock Dam:** watersports, boating, camping and fishing for species such as Murray cod and golden perch; turn-off 15km N. **Manilla Ski Gardens:** area at the northern end of Lake Keepit with waterskiing, fishing and swimming; 20km SW.

MOREE
Population 7070

Sitting at the junction of the Mehi and Gwydir rivers on rich black-soil plains, Moree's land is so fertile a local once claimed, 'You could put a matchstick in the ground overnight and get a walking-stick in the morning'. It's no surprise then that Moree is the centre of a prosperous farming region. The local artesian spas are a major drawcard for visitors. Moree suffered major flooding in October 2022, with almost 400 homes and business inundated, so check ahead for any lingering closures.

SEE & DO **Moree Artesian Aquatic Centre:** see Top Attractions. **Bank Art Museum (BAMM):** contemporary First Nations art and artefacts and changing exhibitions; Frome St. **The Big Plane:** DC3 transport plane with tours available at Amaroo Tavern; Amaroo Dr. **Dhiiyaan Indigenous Centre:** located in the town's library, this was the first genealogy centre where First Nations People could access historical family information and photographs; cnr Balo and Albert sts. **Barry Roberts Historical Walk:** the self-guided tour includes the courthouse and the Moree Lands Office; brochure from visitor centre. **Market:** Jellicoe Park; 1st Sun each month (except Jan). **Trewalla Pecan**

Top: The Big Golden Guitar in Tamworth **Bottom:** Tamworth Regional Gallery

TOP EVENTS

- → JAN County Music Festival (Tamworth), Lamb and Potato Festival (Guyra)
- → MAR Autumn Festival (Armidale), Minerama gem show (Glen Innes), Week of Speed (Gunnedah)
- → MAR–APR Oracles of the Bush poetry festival (Tenterfield)
- → APR–MAY Australian Celtic Festival (Glen Innes)
- → JUN Orange Festival (Bingara)
- → JULY Hats off to Country Festival (Tamworth)
- → AUG AgQuip field days (Gunnedah)
- → OCT Sapphire City Festival (Inverell)
- → NOV Land of the Beardies Festival (Glen Innes)

Farm: the largest orchard in the Southern Hemisphere yielding 95 per cent of Australia's pecans; tour bookings at visitor centre; 35km E. **Cotton gins:** inspections during harvest (Apr–July); details at visitor centre. **Birdwatching:** several excellent sites in the area; brochure from visitor centre.

NARRABRI
Population 5499

Major Thomas Mitchell led an expedition that led to the establishment of the town of Narrabri, after he heard tales told by a recaptured convict of roaming the Liverpool Plains for three years. Traditionally the lands of the Kamilaroi People, the name Narrabri derives from the word for 'a place having forked waters', and Narrabri Creek runs through town. In 1864 a flood destroyed the fledgling town, although it recovered quickly and became the regional centre – as the two remaining courthouses from this era attest. The town has a foodie culture, cafes and restaurants, museums and other attractions. It has been proudly home to a large number of sportspeople that have represented NSW and Australia.

SEE & DO **Paul Wild Observatory (CSIRO Australia Telescope); Mount Kaputar National Park:** see Top Attractions for both. **Old Gaol and Museum:** historic museum with local artefacts; Barwan St. **Riverside park:** pleasant surroundings next to the Namoi River with barbecue and picnic facilities; Tibbereena St. **Self-guided town walk:** historic buildings including the original courthouse (1865) and police residence (1879); brochure from visitor centre. **Yarrie Lake:** birdwatching, waterskiing and windsurfing; 32km W. **Scenic drive:** includes Mount Kaputar National Park, see Top Attractions, and cotton fields; brochure from visitor centre.

NUNDLE
Population 314

A thriving gold town in the 1850s, Nundle drew prospectors from California, Jamaica, China and Europe. Today the town is a quiet place nestled between the Great Dividing Range and the Peel River, but traces of gold can still be found and it is known as 'the town in the hills of gold'. The Peel River has great fishing, with yellow-belly, trout and catfish being common catches.

SEE & DO **Hanging Rock:** see Top Attractions. **Woollen Mill and Chaffey Dam:** see Other Attractions. **Courthouse Museum:** built in 1880, now housing a history of Nundle and the gold-rush era; open Sat 10am–2pm, 12.30pm–4.30pm Sun; Jenkins St. **Peel Inn:** 1860s pub with meals and accommodation; Jenkins St. **Mount Misery Gold Mine:** walk back in time through a re-created goldmine evoking life on the Nundle goldfields 150 years ago; Gill St. **Fossicker's Way tour:** through scenic New England countryside; brochure from visitor centre.

★ TAMWORTH
Population 33,885

There's a big Golden Guitar just outside Tamworth, which lets you know that you're entering the country music capital of Australia. Thousands of fans descend upon the town every January for the Country Music Festival. It's easy to see why this mountainous farming land inspires singing! Tamworth is the centre for the surrounding farms and small towns, and has a bustling food scene and interesting museums.

SEE & DO **Australian Country Music Hall of Fame and Big Golden Guitar Tourist centre:** see Top Attractions for both. **Hands of Fame Park:** Country Music Hands of Fame Cornerstone features handprints of over 200 country music stars; cnr Kable Ave and Brisbane St. **Calala Cottage Museum:** National Trust–classified home of Tamworth's first mayor, with antique household items and original shepherd's slab hut; open Thurs–Fri 2–4pm, Sat–Sun 1–4pm; 142 Denson St; (02) 6765 7492. **Regional Gallery:** houses more than 700 works including some by Hans Heysen and Will Ashton, and the National Textile Collection; open Tues–Sun; 466 Peel St; (02) 6767 5248. **Powerhouse Motorcycle Museum:** collection of immaculate motorbikes from the 1950s through to the 1980s; 250 Armidale Rd; (02) 6766 7000. **Tamworth Marsupial Park:** sanctuary for kangaroos and other marsupials, with picnic and barbecue facilities; off Brisbane St; (02) 6767 5555. **Oxley Lookout:** views of the city and beautiful Peel Valley. It is also the starting point for the Kamilaroi walking track (6.2km); brochure from visitor centre; top of White St. **Powerstation Museum:** traces Tamworth's history as the first city in the Southern Hemisphere to have electric street lighting (installed in 1888); open Wed–Sat 9am–1pm; Peel St; (02) 6766 8324. **Anzac Park:** attractive picnic and barbecue spot with playground; bordered by Brisbane, Napier, Fitzroy and Upper sts. **Bicentennial Park:** fountains, granite sculptures and period lighting; Kable Ave. **Regional Botanic Gardens:** 28ha of native flora and exotic displays; top of Piper St. **Line dancing:** various venues; lessons offered; brochure from visitor centre; (02) 6767 5482. **Historic town walks:** two available, 90min each, visiting churches, theatres and hotels; brochure from visitor centre. **Art and craft:** several shops and galleries; brochure from visitor centre. **Farmers' market:** Bicentennial Park; every Sat. **Peel Street Cottage Fair and Regional Produce Markets:** Peel St Blvd; 3rd Sun each month. **Oxley anchor:** the original anchor from John Oxley's ship marks the point where he crossed the Peel River on his expedition to the coast; 9km NW. **Birdwatching routes:** great birdwatching walks and drives in and around Tamworth; brochure from visitor centre.

TENTERFIELD
Population 2826

Tenterfield is a town of four seasons with many deciduous trees making it particularly beautiful in autumn. It is perhaps best known from Peter Allen's song 'Tenterfield Saddler', which he wrote about his grandfather George Woolnough. But Tenterfield is also the self-proclaimed 'birthplace of the nation', as it is where Sir Henry Parkes delivered his famous Federation speech in 1889.

SEE & DO **Bald Rock National Park**; **New England Wine Region**; **Sir Henry Parkes School of Arts:** *see* Top Attractions for all. **Tenterfield Saddler and Boonoo Boonoo National Park:** *see* Other Attractions for both. **Centenary Cottage:** 1871 home with local history collection; open Fri–Mon; Logan St. **Railway Museum:** railway memorabilia in a restored station; open Wed–Sun; Railway Ave. **Stannum House:** stately mansion built in 1888 for John Holmes Reid, a tin-mining magnate. Now a guest house and restaurant; Rouse St. **Self-guided historical town walk:** includes early residential buildings in Logan St, St Stephens Presbyterian (now Anglican) Church where Banjo Paterson married Alice Walker in 1903 and the grand National Trust–classified post office; brochure from visitor centre. **Railway Market:** railway station; 1st Sat every 2nd month. **Mount McKenzie Granite Drive:** 30km circuit from Molesworth St in town including Ghost Gully and Bluff Rock, an unusual granite outcrop; 10km S. **Thunderbolt's Hideout:** reputed haunt of bushranger Captain Thunderbolt; 11km NE. **Drake:** old goldmining town now popular for fossicking and fishing; 31km NE.

URALLA
Population 2385

While bushranger Captain Thunderbolt gave himself a somewhat romantic name, his deeds were anything but as he robbed various establishments across the gold-rich New England area. He was shot and killed by a policeman at Kentucky Creek near Uralla, after he'd had one too many drinks. There's now a statue of Thunderbolt on the highway in town and a festival in his name every year. Uralla's name comes from the Anaiwan word for 'ceremonial place'. Uralla is at its most striking when the European deciduous trees change colour in autumn.

SEE & DO **Mccrossin's Mill:** *see* Top Attractions. **Mount Yarrowyck Nature Reserve:** *see* Other Attractions. **Thunderbolt statue:** 'gentleman' bushranger Fred Ward's statue dominates the corner of Bridge St and Thunderbolt's Way. **Thunderbolt's grave:** he was hunted by police for over 6 years before being shot dead at nearby Kentucky Creek in 1870. His grave is clearly identified among some other magnificent Victorian monumental masonry headstones; Old Uralla Cemetery, John St. **New England Brass and Iron Lace Foundry:** founded in 1872, it is the oldest of its kind still operating in Australia. Open for tours by appt: contact the visitors centre; East St. **Self-guided heritage walk:** easy 2km walk that includes 30 historic buildings, most built in the late 1800s; brochure from visitor centre.

Spectacular colours, New England Highway

TEMPERATURES

Jan: 14–27°C

July: 1–13°C

Dangars Lagoon: scenic bird sanctuary and hide; 5km SE. **Gold fossicking:** gold and small precious stones can still be found; map and equipment hire from visitor centre; 5km SW. **Thunderbolt's Rock:** used by the bushranger as a lookout. Climb with care; 6km S. **Tourist Drive 19:** signposted drive includes historic Gostwyck Church (11km SE) and Dangars Falls and Gorge (40km S); brochure from visitor centre.

WALCHA
Population 1369

Walcha (pronounced 'Wolka') is an attractive service town for the local farming regions on the eastern slopes of the Great Dividing Range. Modern sculptures are featured throughout the town and the beautiful Apsley Falls is a must-see for visitors.

SEE & DO **Open Air Gallery of Sculptures:** more than 50 sculptures dotted around town, the works include street furniture created by local, national and international artisans; brochure from visitor centre or download the Walcha Sculpture Soundtrail app. **WGoA (Walcha Gallery of Art):** changing program of exhibitions; 0408 775 891; Derby St. **Pioneer Cottage and Museum:** includes a blacksmith's shop and the first Tiger Moth used for crop dusting in Australia; Derby St. **Fishing:** trout season is Oct–June; pick up a brochure from the visitor centre.

WARIALDA
Population 1130

What do Cranky Rock Nature Reserve, Ceramic Break Sculpture Park and Bikini Tree have in common? They are all attractions around Warialda, a lush and historic town in northern NSW, and a town with a gift for intriguing names. The origin of Warialda's name itself is uncertain but is thought to mean 'place of wild honey' and is presumed to be in the language of the original inhabitants, the Weraerai People.

SEE & DO **Cranky Rock Nature Reserve:** see Other Attractions. **Carinda House:** historic home, now a craft shop featuring local work; Stephen St. **Pioneer Cemetery:** historic graves from as early as the 1850s in a bushland setting; Queen and Stephen sts. **Heritage Centre:** includes Well's Family Gem and Mineral collection; Hope St. **Koorilgur Nature Walk:** 3.6km stroll through areas of wildflowers and birdlife; self-guided brochure from visitor centre. **Self-guided historic walk:** see historic town buildings in Stephen and Hope sts; brochure from visitor centre.

WEE WAA
Population 1571

Wee Waa is a dynamic rural community near the Namoi River and also the base for the Namoi Cotton Cooperative, the largest grower-owned organisation in the country. Cotton has only been grown here since the 1960s, but the town claims to be the 'cotton capital of Australia'. It is believed that 'Wee Waa' comes from the Kamilaroi language and means 'fire for roasting'.

SEE & DO **Namoi Echo Museum:** browse the displays of machinery, artefacts and documents pertaining to the history of the Wee Waa district. Open at various times Thurs–Sat; Rose St; 0427 668 932. **Guided Cotton Gin and Farm Tour:** First the tour visits a local cotton farm to view the picking and pressing of cotton into modules ready for transporting to the cotton gin. At the gin the cotton is transformed from modules into bales and then goes to the classing department for sorting. Runs Mar–Aug; bookings (02) 6799 6760. **Yarrie Lake:** boating, swimming and birdwatching; 24km S. **Burren Junction:** hot artesian bore baths (more than 100 years old) in a pleasant location surrounded by tamarind trees; 51km W.

HIDDEN TREASURES

Here are some of the best spots to fossick for gold, sapphires and other precious stones in the New England region.

NUNDLE
Originally a gold-rush town, tiny Nundle (near Tamworth) has several fossicking sites around the town area, mainly on the flats of the Peel River. Gold panning is popular at Bowling Alley Point, at the nearby village of Woolomin and at Chaffey Dam. You can see remnants of the early mining days in the hills and there are still some working goldmines in the mountains above the town, towards Hanging Rock.

BARRABA
Situated on a geological fault line known as the Peel fault, the area around Barraba (around 90km north of Tamworth) is rich in fossicking sites. Once a rich gold, copper and asbestos mining centre, there is still a diatomite mine (used in the making of kitty litter, among other things) on the northern outskirts of town. Try your luck fossicking around Ironbark Creek, about 18km east of town. Look for gold, pyrites, malachite, jasper and red, brown and yellow quartz.

INVERELL
Seventy per cent of the world's sapphires come from Australia, and almost 70 per cent of those come from the Inverell area.

Central West

Beyond the sandstone curtain of the Blue Mountains, the slopes and plains of the Central West are **classic small town Australia**. There's so much to see and do in this region, with **fascinating museums** and **a famous open-range zoo, beautiful gardens** and several **food and wine** regions. Other highlights include decorated **limestone caves, gold rush and bush ranging history, links to the space race, sightings of Elvis** and millions of stars in **Australia's first Dark Sky Park at Warrumbungle National Park**.

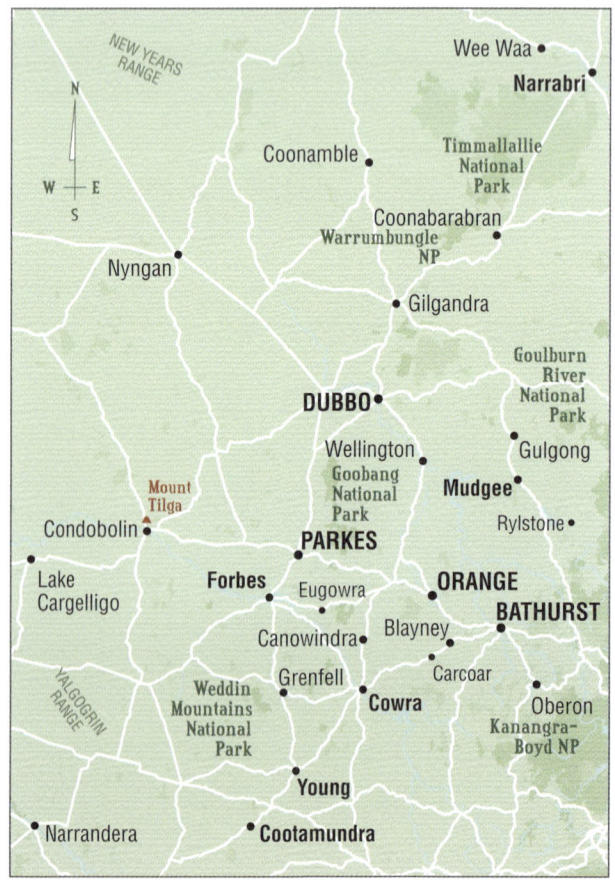

CHEAT SHEET

- → Allow at least a week for a proper exploration.
- → Best time to visit: autumn and spring are delightful; Bathurst and Orange sometimes get snow in winter.
- → Main towns: Bathurst (see p. 76), Dubbo (see p. 78), Orange (see p. 80).
- → The Wailwan and Wiradyuri are the Traditional Owners of most of the central west, one of the largest Aboriginal areas in NSW.
- → Don't miss: a lap of Mount Panorama; The Dish in Parkes; Japanese garden in Cowra; cherries, cool climate wine and fine dining in Orange and Mudgee; Dubbo's Taronga Western Plains Zoo; the Age of Fishes fossil museum in Canowindra; stargazing in the Warrumbungles; and going underground in Wellington.

Top: Cowra's beautiful Japanese Garden **Opposite:** The town of Mudgee

TOP ATTRACTIONS

AGE OF FISHES MUSEUM: Long before dinosaurs walked the Earth, bizarre fish populated local rivers, including fish with armoured shells, fish with lungs and fish with jaws like crocodiles. This museum in Canowindra (see p. 77) displays many of the fossils from the Devonian era found during 1956 and 1993 digs, along with information about the digs. 134 Gaskill St, Canowindra; (02) 6344 1008.

CARCOAR: A National Trust–classified town on the banks of the Belubula River near Blayney (see p. 76), Carcoar is worth a visit at any time of the year, but particularly on Australia Day when the town re-enacts the early days of bushrangers and troopers fighting around town. As one of the first towns west of the Blue Mountains, Carcoar incurred lots of trouble from bushrangers and convicts, such as when Johnny Gilbert and John O'Meally attempted Australia's first daylight bank robbery in 1863 at the Commercial Bank (still standing) on Belubula St. The hold-up was unsuccessful and the robbers fled when a teller fired a shot into the ceiling.

COWRA JAPANESE GARDEN: Opened in 1979, the garden incorporates a cultural centre, traditional teahouse, bonsai house and pottery. The garden itself represents the landscape of Japan, with mountain, river and sea re-created. From its north side, Sakura Ave, lined with cherry trees that blossom in spring, leads to the site of the POW camp and to the Australian and Japanese cemeteries. Off Binni Creek Rd, Cowra; (02) 6341 2233.

COWRA WINE REGION: Though just next door to Orange, the Cowra region has a warmer climate, and the vines are exposed to warm winds that blow across the plains from Central Australia. These conditions best suit chardonnay, the area's main wine. The vineyards surround the towns of Cowra and Canowindra and are side by side with grazing properties in low river valleys.

CSIRO RADIO TELESCOPE: Commissioned in 1961, the telescope in Parkes is the largest and oldest of the eight antennae making up the Australian Telescope National Facility. It has been used for globally important work such as identifying the first quasar in 1963, mapping the Milky Way, and tracking the NASA *Apollo* moon missions. It was most famously instrumental in transmitting images of Neil Armstrong's first steps on the moon to the world. The story of the events on the ground at Parkes is portrayed in the film *The Dish* (2000). The visitor centre explains the uses of the telescope and has 3D displays. 585 Telescope Rd, Parkes; (02) 6861 1777.

HENRY LAWSON CENTRE: Housed in Gulgong's Salvation Army Hall, which was built in 1922 (the year Lawson died), the centre has the largest collection of Lawson memorabilia outside Sydney's Mitchell Library. It includes original manuscripts, artefacts, photographs, paintings and an extensive collection of rare first editions. *A Walk Through Lawson's Life* is an exhibition that uses Lawson's words to illustrate the poverty, family disintegration, deafness and alcoholism that shaped his life, as well as the causes he was passionate about such as republicanism, unionism and votes for women. Mayne St, Gulgong; (02) 6374 2049.

HENRY PARKES CENTRE: Four museums occupy this precinct: the Kings Castle Elvis exhibit, the Parkes Motor Museum, the Henry Parkes Museum and the Antique Machinery collection. Highlights include memorabilia from the gold rush, the fascinating 1000-volume personal library of Sir Henry Parkes and the largest collection of Elvis Presley artefacts in the Southern Hemisphere. Newell Hwy, North Parkes; (02) 6862 6000.

HILL END HISTORIC SITE: This former goldfield 80km north-west of Bathurst (see p. 76) has many original buildings. The area has inspired artists including Russell Drysdale, Donald Friend, John Olsen and Brett Whiteley. Start your visit at the Heritage Centre in the old Rural Fire Service Shed, which has interactive historical displays and artefacts from the gold-rush days; (02) 6337 8206.

MILLTHORPE: National Trust–classified village with quaint shopfronts, art and craft shops, historic churches and a museum with blacksmith's shop and old-style kitchen. Also visit the Golden Memories Museum for displays of life in the 19th century. Millthorpe is 11km north-west of Blayney (see p. 76).

MOUNT PANORAMA AND THE NATIONAL MOTOR RACING MUSEUM: Motor racing started on this circuit in Bathurst in 1938 and the first endurance race, the Armstrong 500, took place in 1963. The 6.2km scenic circuit is a public road that visitors can drive on outside race meetings. The National Motor Racing Museum at the circuit displays cars, bikes, trophies and memorabilia relating to the track's history; 400 Panorama Ave; (02) 6332 1872. McPhillamy Park, at the top of Mount Panorama, provides camping and magnificent views across the city to the Blue Mountains.

MUDGEE WINE REGION: Mudgee lies just over the Great Dividing Range from the famous Hunter Valley, but here the sun is brighter, the nights are colder, and there is less rainfall (what a difference a mountain range can make). These conditions are ideal for the region's specialty cabernet sauvignon, with shiraz a close second. Winemaking here began in 1858, kick-started by three German families. Self-guided drives brochure from the Mudgee visitor centre.

OLD DUBBO GAOL: Closed as a penal institution in 1966, Old Dubbo Gaol now offers a glimpse of convict life. See the original gallows (where 8 men were hanged for murder) and solitary-confinement cells, or walk along the watchtower. An animatronic robot tells historical tales. There are also holograms and theatrical enactments. 90 Macquarie St, Dubbo; (02) 6801 4460.

ORANGE WINE REGION: Orange is a cool-climate area with snow common in winter, thanks to its high altitude above 600m. The result is elegant chardonnay, cabernet sauvignon and shiraz. Philip Shaw, owner of **Philip Shaw Wines**, also believes that Orange has the potential to produce Australia's best merlot. Look out for the beautiful chardonnay by **Ross Hill**, one of the country's first certified carbon neutral wineries. Other popular cellar doors include **De Salis**, **Stockman's Ridge**, **Orange Mountain**, **Highland Heritage**, **Borrodell** and **Printhie**. There are also several cosy wine bars in Orange to enjoy the local product.

The National Motor Racing Museum, Bathurst **Opposite:** Warrumbungle National Park is a Dark Sky Park

PIONEERS MUSEUM: This fascinating museum illustrates every era of Gulgong's history. Exhibits include a replica of a classroom from the 1880s, period clothing and rare antique crockery; cnr Herbert and Bayly sts, Gulgong.

TARONGA WESTERN PLAINS ZOO: Australia's first open-range zoo, with over 700 animals from five continents, is set on more than 300ha of bushland near Dubbo. The zoo is renowned for its breeding programs (especially with endangered species), conservation programs and education facilities and exhibits. There are talks by the keepers and early morning walks, as well as accommodation at Zoofari Lodge. Visitors can use their own cars, hire bikes or walk along the tracks. The Tracker Riley Cycleway covers the 5km from Dubbo and maps are available from the visitor centre. Obley Rd, Dubbo; (02) 6881 1400.

WARRUMBUNGLE NATIONAL PARK: Australia's first internationally recognised Dark Sky Park – a lack of light pollution produces excellent star gazing opportunities – the park also features forested ridges, rocky spires and deep gorges coupled with very good camping and visitor facilities, making this one of the state's most popular parks. Highlights include the Breadknife, a 90m high rock wall, and the Grand High Tops walking trail, which provides fabulous views of ancient volcanic remains. The national park can be accessed from Coonabarabran (see p. 77) or Coonamble (see p. 77).

WEDDIN MOUNTAINS NATIONAL PARK: The park is a rugged crescent of cliffs and gullies providing superb bushwalking, camping and picnicking spots. Two of the bushwalking highlights are Ben Hall's Cave, where the bushranger hid from the police, and Seaton's Farm, a historic depression era homestead set on beautiful parkland. The bush is also rich with fauna including wedge-tailed eagles, honeyeaters and wallabies. The town of Grenfell (see p. 79) sits at the base of the Weddin Mountains.

WELLINGTON CAVES: These fascinating limestone caves 9km south of the town of Wellington (see p. 81) include Cathedral Cave, with a giant stalagmite, and Gaden Cave, with rare cave coral. For thousands of years the caves have acted as natural animal traps, and fossils of a diprotodon and a giant kangaroo have been found here. There are guided tours through the old phosphate mine (wheelchair-accessible). Nearby are an aviary, an opal shop, Japanese gardens, picnic facilities, kiosk and the bottle house, a structure made from over 9000 wine bottles.

OTHER ATTRACTIONS

ABERCROMBIE CAVES: Cave system in a 220ha reserve that features the largest natural limestone arch in the Southern Hemisphere; various tours are available; the caves are 50km south-east of Blayney (see p. 76), contact Blayney visitor centre for details.

ABERCROMBIE HOUSE: Impressive 1870s baronial-style, Gothic mansion; guided tours 11.15am Sat–Sun, self-guided tours Wed–Sun (opening times vary); Ophir Rd; (02) 6331 4929; 6km north-west of Bathurst (see p. 76).

AUSTRALIA'S WORLD PEACE BELL: Each country has only one peace bell and it is normally located in the nation's capital, but Cowra (see p. 77) was awarded Australia's Peace Bell owing to local efforts for peace. The bell is a replica of the United Nations World Peace Bell in New York City and was made by melting down coins donated from 103 member countries of the United Nations. It is rung each year during the Festival of International Understanding. Darling St, Cowra.

COO-EE HERITAGE CENTRE: This architecturally designed, rammed-earth centre is home to three museums – one recounting the eponymous Coo-ee March of 1915, which started in Gilgandra as a way to recruit citizens into World War I – and the Gilgandra Art Gallery, with a cafe and deck overlooking the Castlereagh River. The Joy Trudgett Gallery features a vast collection of shells, fossils and First Nations artefacts. It's in the Coo-ee Memorial Park, Newell Hwy, Gilgrandra (see p.79).

DUNDULLIMAL HOMESTEAD: This restored 1840s squatter's slab-style homestead is the oldest building in Dubbo open to the public; open Tues–Fri 11am–3pm; Obley Rd, Dubbo; (02) 6884 9984.

GOULBURN RIVER NATIONAL PARK: The park follows approximately 90km of the Goulburn River with sandy riverbanks making easy walking trails and beautiful camping sites. Rare and threatened plants abound here, as do wombats, eastern grey kangaroos, emus and birds. Highlights include the Drip (50m curtains of water dripping through the rocks alongside the Goulburn River), sandstone cliffs honeycombed with caves, and over 300 significant First Nations sites. The national park is 30km north-west from Gulgong (see p. 80).

LAKE CANOBOLAS RESERVE: Recreation area with trout fishing, diving pontoons, children's playground, and picnic and barbecue facilities. It's 9km south-west of Orange (see p. 80).

MACQUARIE MARSHES: This mosaic of semi-permanent wetlands includes two major areas: the south marsh and the north marsh. The wetlands expand and contract, depending on recent rainfall, and provide a waterbird sanctuary and breeding ground. It is thought that the Macquarie Marshes contributed to the early myth of an inland sea, which led explorers – most notably Charles Sturt – on many ill-fated journeys. Access is limited; NSW National Parks & Wildlife Service takes visitors on tours of the marshes on their annual Open Day, usually the first weekend in Oct (a long weekend in the ACT, NSW, Queensland and SA). Marsh Meanders offers a range of activities including kayaking and bushwalking. Both tours are seasonally dependent on water levels. Inquiries (02) 6824 2070. The wetlands are 64km north of Nyngan (see p. 80).

MISS TRAILL'S HOUSE: Ida Traill (1889–1976) was a fourth-generation descendant of a family who settled in Bathurst in 1818. She lived in this house from 1931 until her death in 1976. The home was originally built for Reverend Thomas Sharpe in 1845, making it one of the oldest houses in Bathurst. Ida Traill bequeathed the building and its varied collection of artefacts to the National Trust to make sure they would be preserved. The 19th-century cottage garden is particularly charming in spring. Open Sun and public holidays 12–3.30pm; 321 Russell St, Bathurst; (02) 6332 4232.

MUNGHORN GAP NATURE RESERVE: More than 160 bird species have been identified here, including the rare regent honeyeater. The Castle Rock walking trail runs for 8km and offers stunning views from sandstone outcrops. Camping, barbecue and picnic facilities are available. The nature reserve is 34km north-east of Mudgee.

NANGAR NATIONAL PARK: The horseshoe-shaped red cliffs of the Nangar–Murga Range stand out against the central west's plains. Nangar National Park's flowering shrubs and timbered hills provide an important wildlife refuge among mostly cleared land. Rocky slopes and pretty creeks make it a scenic site for bushwalks and popular for rock climbing. The park does not have facilities, so you're advised to take water and provisions with you and to give friends or family your itinerary. The park is 10km east of Eugowra (see p. 78).

OPHIR GOLDFIELDS: This was the site of the first discovery of payable gold in Australia (1851). The 1850s saw an influx of immigrants from Britain, Germany and China, all hoping to strike it rich. Features today include a fossicking centre, picnic area, walking trails to historic tunnels and gold panning. There is still plenty of gold to be found in the area; the gold medals at the 2000 Sydney Olympic Games were made of Ophir gold. The goldfields are 17km north-east of Orange (see p. 80).

PILLIGA FOREST: The Gamilaroi/Kamilaroi and Wailwan Peoples are the Traditional Owners of this forest, which is rich in food and medicinal resources and has many traditional sites. It has 450,000ha of white cypress and ironbark trees, with plains of dense heath and scrub. It is an excellent habitat for now-endangered koalas, which can be spotted from signposted viewing areas. There are also scenic forest drives and walking trails. You can get maps and road condition information from Pilliga Forest Discovery Centre, Wellington St, Baradine; (02) 6843 4011.

PRISONER OF WAR CAMP SITE: In 1944 the largest Prisoner of War breakout in modern military history occurred at Cowra (see p. 77). The camp site includes the original foundations and a replica guardtower, as well as photo displays and signage; audio tours available. Sakura Ave, Cowra; (02) 6342 4333.

SCULPTURES IN THE SCRUB: Award-winning sculptures by various artists in Timmallallie National Park that tell stories of Aboriginal culture. The sculptures overlook Dandry Gorge and there's a walking track and picnic spots; via Baradine, which is 45km north-west of Coonabarabran (see p. 77).

SIDING SPRING OBSERVATORY: Australia's largest optical telescope, with a hands-on exhibition, science shop and cafe. No night viewing but open during the day; Thurs–Sun 10am–2pm; Timor Rd; (02) 6842 6255. It's 27km west of Coonabarabran (see p. 77).

SOFALA: Australia's oldest surviving goldmining village and the setting for scenes from the films *The Cars That Ate Paris* (1974) and *Sirens* (1994). It's 45km north of Bathurst (see p. 76).

WESTERN PLAINS CULTURAL CENTRE: This centre in Dubbo (see p. 78) includes the Dubbo Regional Gallery, Dubbo Regional Museum and the Community Arts Centre. It exhibits local and national visual arts, heritage and social history. It specialises in the theme of Animals in Art, collecting works in a broad range of media and styles by artists from all areas. The museum, housed in the original Dubbo High School building, features a permanent space devoted to the story of Dubbo entitled *People Places Possessions: Dubbo Stories* and a temporary exhibition space. 10am–4pm; 76 Wingewarra St, Dubbo; (02) 6801 4444.

WILLANDRA NATIONAL PARK: Once one-eighth of a huge merino sheep station, the 20,000ha park 163km west of Lake Cargelligo (see p. 80), features a restored homestead (offering accommodation), stables, a shearing complex and men's quarters. The buildings house a display of pastoral and natural history of the area. Plains, wetlands and Willandra Creek make up the rest of the park, with a walking track that is best at dawn or dusk to see the myriad waterbirds, kangaroos and emus. The creek is popular for canoeing and fishing.

Top: Age of Fishes Museum in Canowindra **Opposite top:** Meerkats at the Taronga Western Plains Zoo **Opposite middle:** Cowra Japanese Garden & Cultural Centre Australia **Opposite bottom:** Wellington Caves and Phosphate Mines

KEY TOWNS

BATHURST
Population 36,230

Bathurst was the first town established after the European crossing of the Great Dividing Range into the area traditionally home to the Wiradjuri People. Gold was discovered in Bathurst in the 1850s, and the town boomed – and the resulting Georgian and Victorian architecture still lines the streets of the town. Bathurst is also home to the Mount Panorama racing circuit, and is the birthplace of postwar-era prime minister Ben Chifley.

SEE & DO Hill End Historic Site; Mount Panorama and The National Motor Racing Museum: *see* Top Attractions for both. Abercrombie House; Miss Traill's House; Sofala: *see* Other Attractions for all. **Historic Museum:** features notable local First Nations and early settler artefacts in the east wing of the Neoclassical Bathurst Courthouse; open Tues–Fri 10am–4pm, Sat–Sun 11am–2pm; Russell St; (02) 6330 8455. **Australian Fossil and Mineral Museum:** exhibits close to 2000 fossil and mineral specimens, including rare and unique displays and 3 dinosaur skeletons, housed in the 1876 public school building; open Mon–Sat 10am–4pm, Sun 10am–2pm; 224 Howick St; (02) 6331 5511. **Regional Art Gallery:** focuses on Australian art after 1955, with frequently changing exhibitions; open Tues–Sat 10am–5pm, Sun 11am–2pm; 70 Keppel St; (02) 6333 6555. **Chifley Home:** home of former prime minister Ben Chifley and his wife, Elizabeth, with original furnishings and family collections; guided tours 10am and 12pm; 10 Busby St; (02) 6332 1444. **Ash's Speedway Museum:** speedway memorabilia from around the world; Sat–Sun 10am–4pm; 2/10 Bradwardine Rd. **Machattie Park:** Victorian-era park in the heart of the city, with a begonia house full of blooms (Feb–Apr); Keppel, William and George sts. **Self-guided heritage trails:** pick up brochures from the visitor centre and follow the trails to a range of historic sites including the Bathurst Gaol, courthouse and historic homes. **Macquarie Riverside Markets:** Lions Berry Park; 1st Sat each month. **Farmers' market:** Bathurst showground, Kendall Ave; 4th Sat Jan–Nov (3rd Sat in Dec). **Wallaby Rocks:** wall of rock rising from the Turon River, and a popular spot for kangaroos and wallabies. Also an ideal swimming and picnic spot; 48km N. **Rockley:** one of the district's oldest settlements, this was the site of major gold and copper discoveries and still retains substantial historic buildings; 35km S.

BLAYNEY
Population 2997

While Blayney is predominantly a farming town, the National Trust–classified buildings and avenues of deciduous trees give the town excellent street value. Stop for a drink at the pub, which was originally a changing station for Cobb & Co. coaches, as you explore this part of the central tablelands.

SEE & DO Carcoar; Millthorpe, *see* Top Attractions for both. **Abercrombie Caves:** *see* Other Attractions. **Heritage Park:** small wetland area, barbecue facilities and tennis courts; Adelaide St. **Local craft shops:** contact visitor centre for details. **Self-guided heritage walk:** includes churches and the courthouse; brochure from visitor centre. **Carcoar Dam:** watersports and camping with picnic and barbecue facilities; 12km SW. **Newbridge:** historic buildings and craft shops; 20km E.

VISITOR INFORMATION

Coonabarabran Visitor Information Centre
John St
1800 242 881
warrumbungle.nsw.gov.au

Mudgee Visitor Centre
84 Market St
(02) 6372 1020 or
1800 816 304
visitmudgeeregion.com.au

Orange Visitor Information Centre
151 Byng St
(02) 6393 8225 or
1800 069 466
orange360.com.au

Central NSW
visitcentralnsw.com.au

CANOWINDRA
Population 1451

Found in the Lachlan Valley, Canowindra is a fascinating old-style country town: the main street is heritage listed, 3500 fish fossils over 360 million years old were discovered in town in 1956, and it claims to be the hot-air balloon capital of the state. It also has a unique history with bushrangers. Ben Hall and his gang struck the town twice in 1863. Canowindra means 'home' in the Wiradjuri language. The town has sandstone mountains to the west and the old volcano, Mount Canobolas, to the north-east.

SEE & DO **Age of Fishes Museum:** see Top Attractions. **Historical museum:** local history displays and agricultural equipment; open Sat–Sun or by appt; Gaskill St. **Hot-air balloon rides:** over picturesque Lachlan Valley (Mar–Nov, weather permitting); details at visitor centre. **Historical tourist drive and riverbank self-guided walks:** include historic buildings of Gaskill St; brochure available from visitor centre. **Wineries and vineyards:** cellar-door tastings and tours; maps from visitor centre.

CONDOBOLIN
Population 2579

A resting place for drovers in the early 19th century, Condobolin grew into a town in the 1880s following the discovery of copper and gold. Now an agricultural centre, it has interesting historic buildings. A lookout on Reservoir Hill gives views over the town, which is at the junction of two rivers and surrounded by red-soil plains.

SEE & DO **Utes in the Paddock:** a quirky open-air art gallery featuring decorated Holden utes; The Gipps Way. **Mount Tilga:** said to be the geographical centre of NSW; 8km N. **Gum Bend Lake:** a good spot for fishing and watersports; 5km W. **Peak Hill:** you can wander the open-cut tracks and lookouts of this old gold mine; Mingelo St; 48km N.

COONABARABRAN
Population 2387

You'll have stars in your eyes at Coonabarabran, which is known as the 'Astronomy Capital of Australia' because it has some of the clearest skies in the country and is home to the famous Siding Spring Observatory and a CSIRO telescope. Don't miss the Solar System Drive (there are different routes; start at Pluto in one of five towns), which is a to-scale model of the solar system – just 38 million times smaller! – with the observatory used as the sun. The other star at Coonabarabran is Warrumbungle National Park, with the town nestled in the foothills of the Warrumbungle Mountain Range. And if you have a budding paleontologist with you, there's something for them at the Information Centre too (see opposite)!

SEE & DO **Warrumbungle National Park:** see Top Attractions. **Siding Spring Observatory:** see Other Attractions. **Information Centre:** The Australian Museum worked with Warrumbungle Shire Council to produce the unique Diprotodon and Megafauna Exhibition found at this visitor centre. The diprotodon is the largest marsupial that ever lived on Earth and the skeleton on show was found in a creek bed 40km east of town in 1979. Newell Hwy. **Crystal Kingdom:** unique collection of minerals, including zeolite crystals and fossils, from the Warrumbungle Range; open 8am–5pm; Newell Hwy; (02) 6842 1927. **Goanna Tracks Motocross and Enduro Complex:** a range of tough motocross courses; Kurrajong Rd; 18km NW. **Pilliga Pottery:** terracotta pottery, showrooms and tearooms in an attractive bushland setting; pottery workshops, horseriding and guided birdwatching tours; Dandry Rd; (02) 6842 2239; 34km NW. **Sandstone caves:** formed by natural erosion of sandstone, these impressive caves are not signposted, so visitors are advised to seek directions from the visitor centre; 35km N. **Local wineries:** open for tastings and cellar-door sales; contact visitor centre for details.

COONAMBLE
Population 2353

Grab your Akubra and make sure to visit the farming town of Coonamble during its famous rodeo/campdraft in July, which is reputedly the largest in the Southern Hemisphere. On the Great Inland Way, which is an alternate route between Queensland and the southern states, the town has the fortune of being located between the Macquarie Marshes and Warrumbungle National Park. While many of the historic buildings were destroyed in a fire in 1929, there are some charming Art Deco buildings on Main St and a surprising wealth of street art and public sculpture, including an impressive mural featuring galahs on the water tower.

SEE & DO **Warrumbungle National Park:** see Top Attractions. **Macquarie Marshes:** see Other Attractions. **Museum Under the Bridge:** housed in the old police station, the museum outlines Coonamble's rich Aboriginal and pastoral history. Behind the museum are an authentic Cobb & Co. coach and stables. Open by appt; (02) 6827 1923; Aberford St. **Warrana Creek Weir:** swimming, boating and fishing; southern outskirts of town. **Self-guided town walk:** takes in historic sites; brochure from visitor centre.

COWRA
Population 8254

There are clues that the charming town of Cowra, nestled in the Lachlan Valley, has a history that belies its quiet appearance, from the gorgeous Japanese cherry blossoms to the ruins of a prisoner-of-war (POW) camp. In 1944, 1000 Japanese POWs being held in Cowra staged a mass breakout and over 300 prisoners escaped

Top: Mount Arthur Reserve near Wellington **Bottom:** Parkes Elvis Festival **Opposite:** Cattle grazing near Cowra

(all were eventually recaptured) in what is now known as the Cowra Breakout. The town was also used as a processing centre for the thousands of postwar immigrants from Europe.

SEE & DO **Japanese Garden:** see Top Attractions. **Australia's World Peace Bell; Prisoner Of War Camp Site:** see Other Attractions. **Olympic Park:** information centre with a fascinating POW hologram display and theatre. Also here is Cowra Rose Garden, which has over 1000 rose bushes in more than 100 varieties; Mid Western Hwy. **Cowra-Italy Friendship Monument:** in recognition of Italians who died in World War II. Italian POWs interned at Cowra formed a strong friendship with the town; Kendal St. **Regional Art Gallery:** permanent collection includes artworks made by Italian POWs during WWII, as well as a program of changing exhibitions throughout the year; Tues–Sat 10am–4pm, Sun 2–4pm, 77 Darling St; (02) 6340 2190. **Lachlan Valley Railway Museum:** displays and train rides; 3 Campbell St; (02) 6342 4999. **Indigenous Art Murals:** by local artist Kym Freeman, telling the history of the Wiradjuri People. The murals are on the pylons of the bridge over the Lachlan River. **Cowra Heritage Walk:** Federation, colonial and Victorian buildings including the town's first hotel and oldest home; map from visitor centre. **Community market:** showgrounds; 3rd Sat each month. **Darby Falls Observatory:** one of the largest telescopes accessible to the public; call for opening times; Darby Falls Rd; (02) 6345 1900; 25km SE. **Conimbla National Park:** known for its wildflowers, rock ledges, waterfalls and bushwalks; 27km W. **Lake Wyangala and Grabine Lakeside State Park:** ideal for watersports and fishing; 40km SE. **Self-guided drives:** through countryside, including a wine-lovers' drive; brochure from visitor centre.

DUBBO
Population 38,783

Dubbo is one of the only towns in regional Australia where you can find lions, giraffes and zebras – all courtesy of the famous Taronga Western Plains Zoo. While the zoo is undoubtedly the town's biggest attraction, there's much more to Dubbo, including the historic Dundullimal Homestead, the Old Dubbo Gaol and Western Plains Cultural Centre. The town is a thriving regional centre on the banks of the Macquarie River, with a good coffee culture.

SEE & DO **Taronga Western Plains Zoo:** see Top Attractions. **Western Plains Cultural Centre; Dundullimal Homestead:** see Other Attractions for both. **Shoyoen Sister City Garden:** Japanese garden designed and built with the support of Dubbo's Japanese sister city, Minokamo; Elizabeth Park, off Coronation Dr. **Farmers' market:** Macquarie Lions Park, 1st and 3rd Sat each month. **Observatory:** explore the skies via Schmidt Cassegrain telescopes. Open nightly, subject to weather, bookings essential; Camp Rd; 0408 425 940; 5.5km S. **Royal Flying Doctor Visitor Experience:** displays and talks cover the history of the RFDS and its Dubbo base; open Tues–Sat 1–4pm; Judy Jakins Drive, Dubbo City Airport; 1800 847 487; 8km NW. **Terramungamine Rock Grooves:** the 150 rock grooves were created by the Tubbagah People of the Wiradjuri nation; Burraway Rd via Brocklehurst; 10km N. **Narromine:** agricultural centre well known for gliding and an outstanding aviation museum; the Narromine AusFly Air Show is held here biannually in Sept or Oct; 45km E. **Heritage drives:** brochures from visitor centre. **Wineries:** several in region offering cellar-door tastings; brochure from visitor centre.

EUGOWRA
Population 601

Eugowra, situated in the Lachlan Valley, is famous as the location of the Gold Escort Robbery, where a local bushranger gang stole thousands of pounds (millions of dollars in today's money) from a coach carrying money from the goldfields. The small town is also the gateway to Nangar National Park.

SEE & DO **Nangar National Park:** see Other Attractions. **Museum and Bushranger Centre:** displays on early settler life, a pistol used in the Gold Escort Robbery, gemstones, early farm equipment, wagons and First Nations artefacts; open Fri–Sun; (02) 6859 2820. **Local craft shops:** brochure from visitor centre. **Self-guided bushranging tour:** maps from visitor centre. **Escort Rock:** where bushranger Frank Gardiner and gang (including Ben Hall) hid before ambushing the Forbes gold escort. A plaque on the road gives details; 3km E.

FORBES
Population 6837

When John Oxley passed through in 1817, he was so unimpressed by the area's clay soil, poor timber and swamps that he claimed 'it is impossible to imagine a worse country' – although he'd have to argue with explorers who said much the same thing about the outback. Today Forbes is a pleasant spot bisected by Lake Forbes, a large lagoon in the middle of town. The discovery of gold caused the town to be built and the legends of old bushrangers keep it buzzing today. Forbes was hit by flooding in October 2022, though most of the inundation was outside of the township.

SEE & DO **Mcfeeters Motor Museum:** more than 60 veteran and vintage cars on display; open 9am–4.30pm; Newell Hwy and Oxford St; (02) 6852 3001. **Historical Museum:** features relics associated with bushranger Ben Hall, a vintage colonial kitchen and antique farm machinery; open 2–4pm; Cross St; (02) 6851 6600. **Cemetery:** graves of Ben Hall, Kate Foster (Ned Kelly's sister), Rebecca Shields (Captain Cook's niece) and French author Paul Wenz; Bogan

TOP EVENTS

- JAN Folk Festival (Gulgong); Elvis Festival (Parkes)
- FEB Banjo Paterson Australian Poetry Festival (Orange)
- MAR Festival of International Understanding (Cowra); The Wellington Boot horse race (Wellington)
- APR F.O.O.D Week festival (Orange)
- JUNE Rodeo and Campdraft (Coonamble); Henry Lawson Festivals (Grenfell and Gulgong)
- JUNE–JULY Winter Festival (Bathurst)
- JULY Small Farm Field Days (Mudgee)
- SEPT Wine and Food Month (Mudgee)
- SEPT–OCT Sakura Matsuri cherry blossom festival (Cowra)
- OCT V8 Supercars (Bathurst); Dark Sky Awakens Festival (Coonabarabran); Wine Festival (Orange)
- NOV Streetfeast (Rylstone)

TEMPERATURES

Jan: 31–37°C

July: 14–16°C

Bottom: The Australian Fossil and Mineral Museum Opposite top: Cotton field in Condobolin Opposite middle: Town of Canowindra Opposite bottom: Siding Springs Observatory in Coonabarabran

Gate Rd. **King George V Park:** memorial where 'German Harry' discovered gold in 1861, and a pleasant spot for picnics and barbecues; Lawler St. **Dowling St Park:** memorial marks the spot where John Oxley first passed through in 1817; Dowling St. **Lake Forbes:** picnic spots, barbecue facilities, fishing, and a walking and cycling track; off Gordon Duff Dr. **Historical town walk:** includes the post office (1862) and the town hall (1861) where Nellie Melba performed in 1909; map from visitor centre. **Local art and craft:** brochure from visitor centre. **Somewhere Down the Lachlan Sculpture Trail:** 100km long outdoor sculpture trail begins in the town centre and follows the river to Condobolin. See somewheredownthelachlan.com for details or pick up a brochure at the visitors centre. **Gum Swamp Sanctuary:** birdlife and other fauna, best seen at sunrise or sunset; 4km S. **Banderra Estate:** French winemaker with cellar-door tastings; off Orange Rd; 5km E. **Ben Hall's Place:** marks the site where the bushranger was shot dead by policemen; 8km W. **Jemalong Weir:** with parklands by the Lachlan River, good spot for fishing and picnicking; 24km S.

GILGANDRA
Population 2417

A historic town at the junction of three highways, 'Gil' is the centre for the surrounding wool and farming country. The 1915 Coo-ee March, in which 35 men, given no support from the army, marched the 500km to Sydney to enlist for World War I, left from here. Along the way they recruited over 200 men, announcing their arrival with a call of 'coo-ee!' The march sparked seven other such marches from country towns.

SEE & DO Coo-Ee Heritage Centre: see Other Attractions. **Rural Museum:** vast collection of agricultural artefacts including antique farm machinery and early model tractors on display; Newell Hwy. **Hitchen House Museum:** the home of the Hitchen brothers, who initiated the Coo-ee March. The museum has memorabilia from both world wars and the Vietnam War; Miller St. **Orana Cactus World:** almost 1000 different cacti on display, collected over 40 years; open most weekends and by appt; Newell Hwy; bookings (02) 6847 0566. **Gilgandra Flora Reserve:** 8.5ha of bushland, perfect for picnics and barbecues. Most plants flower in spring, making the park particularly spectacular Sept–Nov; 14km NE. **Emu Logic:** emu farm producing oil, leather and meat; guided tours; Tooraweenah; 40km NW. **Warren:** a popular spot on the Macquarie River with anglers. For a stroll along the riverbank take the River Red Gum Walk, for birdwatching go to Tiger Bay Wildlife Reserve, and for a day of picnicking and swimming visit Warren Weir. The racecourse is known as the 'Randwick of the west' and hosts some fantastic race days; 85km W.

GRENFELL
Population 2022

Grenfell embraces its most famous son, Henry Lawson, by holding a festival in his honour every year, which is often attended by writers of note. The town itself maintains its Lawson-era grandeur, with the opulent buildings constructed during the gold rush still lining the main street. At the foot of the Weddin Mountains, Grenfell is named after Gold Commissioner John Granville Grenfell, who was shot by bushrangers while driving a carriage full of gold.

SEE & DO Weddin Mountains National Park: see Top Attractions. **Henry Lawson Obelisk:** memorial on the site of the house where the poet is believed to have been born; next to Lawson Park on the road to Young. **Museum:** local relics (and their stories) from world wars, the gold rush, Henry Lawson and bushrangers; open Sat–Sun 2–4pm; Camp St. **Chrysler Car Museum:** private collection of Chryslers from the 1930s through to the present day; open by appt; 46 Main St; (02) 6343 2084. **O'Brien's Reef Lookout:** views of the town on a gold-discovery site with walkway and picnic facilities; access from O'Brien St. **Weddin Bird Trails:** unique Grenfell birdlife; maps from visitors centre. **Historic buildings:** walk and drive tours; brochures from visitor centre. **Company Dam Nature Reserve:** excellent bushwalking area; 1km NW. **Site of Ben Hall's farmhouse and stockyards:** memorial; Sandy Creek Rd, off Mid Western Hwy; 25km W.

GULGONG
Population 2057

The name Gulgong means 'deep waterhole' in the Wiradjuri language. The area where the town is situated did not

attract European interest until gold was discovered in 1866, but by 1872 there were 20,000 people living in the area. By the end of the decade 15 tonnes of gold had been unearthed, the prospectors had left and almost all of the Wiradjuri People were gone. Today the town stands visually almost unchanged from the 19th century. The narrow, winding streets follow the paths of the original bullock tracks past iron-lace verandahs, horse troughs and hitching rails.

SEE & DO **Henry Lawson Centre; Pioneers museum:** see Top Attractions for both. **Goulburn River National Park:** see Other Attractions. **Red Hill:** site of the town's original gold strike, featuring restored stamper mill, poppet head and memorial to Henry Lawson; off White St. **Mayne Street Symbols:** inscribed in the pavement by a local artist, to depict the 'language of the road' used by diggers to advise their mates who may have followed them from other goldfields. **Town trail:** self-guided walking tour of historic buildings such as Prince of Wales Opera House and Ten Dollar Town Motel; brochure from visitor centre. **Ulan:** Ulan Coal Mine has viewing areas overlooking a large open-cut mine. Also here is **Hands on the Rock**, a prime example of Aboriginal rock art; 22km NE. **Talbragar Fossil Fish Beds:** one of the few Jurassic-period fossil deposits in Australia; 35km NE. **Wineries:** cellar-door tastings; see Mudgee Wine Region, p. 72.

LAKE CARGELLIGO
Population 1169

An unexpected lake in the midst of the wide, brown Riverina plains, Lake Cargelligo is the name of both the lake and the town on its banks. Unsurprisingly, the town's activities revolve around the water with fishing and regular lake festivals. Bring your binoculars because the lake is known for its birdlife.

SEE & DO **Lake Cargelligo:** the lake dominates the town and is popular for fishing (silver perch, golden perch and redfin), boating, sailing, waterskiing and swimming. It is also appealing to birdwatchers, being home to many bird species including the rare glossy black cockatoo. There is a historic walkway and bicycle track. **Wagon rides and working horse demonstrations:** can be arranged by appt on (02) 6898 1384. **Information centre:** houses a large gem collection and carved stone butterflies; Foster St. **Kejole Koori Studio:** First Nations art, jewellery and didgeridoos; Grace St. **Lake Brewster:** 1500ha birdwatcher's paradise with fishing and picnic area. No guns, dogs or boats; 41km W. **Nombinnie Nature Reserve:** birdwatching, bushwalking and abundant spring wildflowers (Sept–Dec); 45km N. **Hillston:** main street lined with palms, thanks to its situation on top of a large artesian basin. Hillston Lake is popular for watersports and picnics, and a swinging bridge provides access to a nature reserve and walking trail; 93km SW.

★ MUDGEE
Population 11,563

Mudgee derives its name from the Wiradjuri word 'moothi', meaning 'nest in the hills'. The name is apt because the town is situated among green and blue hills in the Cudgegong River Valley. Mudgee is graced with wide streets and historic Victorian buildings and is the centre of the Mudgee Wine Region, one of the largest winegrowing regions in Australia. Local produce features heavily in town and includes fresh silver perch, yabbies, venison, lamb, asparagus, summer berries, peaches and hazelnuts. In 2022, Mudgee was named Australia's 'top tourist town' for the second consecutive year at Australia's Top Tourism Awards.

SEE & DO **Mudgee Wine Region:** see Top Attractions. **Munghorn Gap Nature Reserve:** see Other Attractions. **Colonial Inn Museum:** local history in photographs, documents, machinery, dolls and agricultural implements; open Mon–Fri 10am–3pm, Sat 2–5pm, Sun 10am–5pm; 126 Market St; (02) 6372 7395. **Honey Haven:** honey, jam and mustard tastings, and bees under glass; Church St; (02) 6372 4478. **Lawson Park:** home to possums, water rats and tortoises. Includes a playground, barbecues and duck pond; Short St. **Art and Crafts Mudgee:** local art and craft cooperative at the historic railway station; cnr Inglis and Church sts; (02) 6372 2822. **Brewing Company:** enjoy some pale ale at this homegrown brewery; Church St; (02) 6372 6726. **Roth's Wine Bar:** oldest wine bar in NSW, has displays on the region's winegrowing history and a wide selection of local wines; Market St; (02) 6372 1222. **Observatory:** astronomical wonders of the NSW sky; day and night sessions available; Old Grattai Rd; (02) 6373 3431. **Town trail:** self-guided walk taking in National Trust buildings including St John's Church of England (1860) and the Regent Theatre; brochure available from visitor centre. **Markets:** St John's Anglican Church, 1st Sat each month; Lawson Park, 2nd Sat each month. **Farmers' market:** Robertson Park; 3rd Sat each month. **Windermere Dam:** watersports, trout fishing and camping facilities; 24km SE. **Hargraves:** old goldmining town where Kerr's Hundredweight nugget was discovered in 1851, yielding 1272oz of gold. Ask at general store for gold-panning tours; 39km SW.

NYNGAN
Population 1761

Nyngan is a pleasant country town on the Bogan River on the edge of the outback. It was largely unknown to the rest of the country until 1990, when the worst floods of the century struck here, doing damage worth $50 million. A helicopter was called in to airlift 2000 people – almost the whole town – to safety. Today the town is at the centre of a sheep, wheat and wool district.

SEE & DO **Macquarie Marshes:** see Other Attractions. **Museum:** local memorabilia, photographs, an audio room with local stories, Remembrance Room, doll room, an 1800s kitchen and remnants from the 1990 flood; at railway station, Railway Sq. **Mid-State Shearing Shed:** informative displays of the continuing importance of shearing to the region, with work of local artists in murals; Mitchell Hwy. **The Big Bogan:** quirky 'big thing' of a stereotypical bogan; Pangee St. **Historical town drive and Levee Tour:** includes historic buildings in Cobar and Pangee sts, the Bicentennial Mural Wall and the heritage-listed railway overbridge with a lookout over town. The levee was built after the 1990 floods; brochure from visitor centre. **Bogan River:** the local spot for kayaking, fishing and birdwatching. **Cairn:** marking the geographic centre of NSW. It is on private property but visible from the road; 72km S.

★ ORANGE
Population 40,127

This is the Traditional Land of the Wiradjuri People, who thrived on the plentiful bush tucker resulting from the fertile volcanic soil and the abundant kangaroos and wallabies. The town of Orange was named by explorer Sir Thomas Mitchell after the Dutch Prince of Orange – they had fought together in a war in Spain. Today the prosperous 'colour city' at the edge of Mount Canobolas enjoys a reputation for excellent food, wine, parks and gardens. It is also known for its goldmining history and as the birthplace of renowned Australian poet A.B. (Banjo) Paterson.

SEE & DO **Orange Wine Region:** see Top Attractions. **Lake Canobolas Reserve** and **Ophir Goldfields:** see Other Attractions for both. **Civic Square:** this is Orange's cultural hub and also the first stop for visitors, with the visitor centre, the City Library, the Civic Theatre and the swish new Regional Gallery, which reopened with a $5.5 million extension in December 2021. Its collection includes more than 1500 Australian artworks from the last 100 years. Cnr Byng and Peisley sts. **Cook Park:** colourful in any season with a begonia house (flowers Feb–May), duck pond, fernery, native bird aviary, Cook Park Guildry (for arts and crafts) and a picnic area; Summer St. **Botanic Gardens:** 17ha parklands with an impressive exotic and native plant collection and a signposted walk through billabongs, rose gardens, orchards and woodlands; Hill St. **Banjo Paterson Memorial Park:** remains of Narambla Homestead, A.B. (Banjo) Paterson's birthplace, and a memorial obelisk; Ophir Rd. **Self-guided historical walk:** 90min stroll past historic homes and buildings; brochure from visitor centre. **Farmers' market:** showgrounds; 2nd Sat each month. **Gosling Creek Reserve:** cycle paths, barbecues and play equipment; 3km SE. **Lucknow:** old goldmining town and site of Australia's second gold discovery, now with historic bluestone buildings and craft shops; 10km SE. **Borenore Caves:** undeveloped caves with evidence of fossils. Outside are walking trails, and picnic and barbecue facilities. Torch required if entering the caves; brochure from visitor centre; 22km W. **Cadia Mines:** largest goldmine and coppermine in NSW; check with visitor centre for open days and tours; 25km SE. **Mitchell's Monument:** site of Sir Thomas Mitchell's base camp; 33km W. **Molong:** charming rural town with craft shops and Coach House Gallery; 35km NW. Grave of Yuranigh, Mitchell's Aboriginal guide, lies 2km E of Molong.

PARKES
Population 9832

Parkes is famously home to a huge CSIRO telescope, which played a part in sharing images of Neil Armstrong walking on the moon to the world, as immortalised in the classic 2000 film *The Dish*. Although originally a tent city called Bushman, the town boomed when gold was found in 1862, and was renamed after a visit from NSW Colonial Secretary Henry Parkes in 1873. The town now embraces a different kind of gold with its Elvis festival every Jan.

SEE & DO **Henry Parkes Centre; CSIRO Radio Telescope:** *see* Top Attractions for both. **Memorial Hill:** excellent views of the town and surrounds; Bushman St, North Parkes. **Kelly Reserve:** playground, and picnic and barbecue facilities in bush setting; Newell Hwy, North Parkes. **Bushmans Hill Reserve:** take the walking trail to the lookout, passing mining relics and a memorial to those who lost their lives in local mines; Newell Hwy, North Parkes. **Self-guided historical town walk and drive:** highlights include the police station (1875), post office (c. 1880) and Balmoral, one of the town's oldest homes, noted for its iron lace, Italian marble and stained-glass windows; brochure from visitor centre.

RYLSTONE
Population 624

Stone by name, stone by nature – the town of Rylstone, on the western side of the Blue Mountains, has heritage-listed stone buildings, including the courthouse and post office. If you don't feel like leaving town, the Cudgegong River is great for a spot of fishing. The town is a gateway to Wollemi National Park (*see* p. 14), land so old it feels like it could be Jurassic Park.

SEE & DO **Jack Tindale Park:** this park is a pleasant green reserve, perfect for swimming, picnics and barbecues. Platypus are sometimes spotted in the water here and in the river below the showground. Cox St. **Self-guided historic walk:** includes the Bridge View Inn (restaurant, formerly a bank) and the post office; brochure from visitor centre. **Art and craft outlets:** several featuring local work; details at visitor centre. **Kandos:** industrial town known for its cement. It features the Bicentennial Industrial Museum (open Sat–Sun) and holds the Kandos Street Machine and Hot Rod Show each Jan; 3km S. **Fern Tree Gully:** tree ferns in subtropical forest with walking trails and lookouts; 16km N. **Dunn's Swamp:** camping, fishing, bushwalking; 18km E. **Windermere Dam:** watersports, fishing, camping, picnic and barbecue facilities; also home of fishing competition each Easter; 19km W. **Glen Davis:** this fascinating shale-oil ghost town is at the eastern end of the Capertee Valley. The valley is almost 30km across and is surrounded by sheer sandstone cliffs, which makes it the largest enclosed valley in the Southern Hemisphere; 56km SE. **Wineries:** several in the area; brochure from visitor centre.

WELLINGTON
Population 4581

Wellington is a typical Australian country town with a wide main street, numerous monuments to significant local people and attractive parklands. Sitting at the foot of Mount Arthur, it is best known for the nearby Wellington Caves.

SEE & DO **Wellington Caves:** *see* Top Attractions. **Museum:** the history of Wellington is told with photographs and artefacts; in the old police station; open Mon–Fri 1.30–4.30pm, other times by appt; (02) 6845 2325. **Cameron Park:** known for its rose gardens and suspension bridge over the Bell River, it also has picnic and barbecue facilities; Nanima Cres. **Self-guided town walk:** taking in historic buildings including hotels and churches; brochure from visitor centre. **Market:** Cameron Park; 4th Sat each month. **Mount Arthur Reserve:** walks to the lookout at the summit of Mount Binjang; maps from visitor centre; 3km W. **Lake Burrendong State Park:** watersports, fishing, campsites and cabins, and spectacular lake views from the main wall. Burrendong Arboretum is a beautiful spot for birdwatching and features several pleasant walking tracks. Also excellent camping, picnic and barbecue sites at Mookerawa Waters Park; 32km SE. **Stuart Town:** small gold-rush town formerly known as Ironbark, made famous by Banjo Paterson's poem 'The Man from Ironbark'; 38km SE. **Wineries:** several in the area offering cellar-door tastings and sales; brochure from visitor centre.

Top: Radio telescope, Parkes Observatory

South Coast

The far south coast of NSW between Jervis Bay and the Victorian border – **a string of national parks and wonderfully undeveloped beaches combined with a maze of beautiful waterways** – is one long summer playground, although the **scenery, wildlife, family-friendly attractions** and farm-fresh cheeses and other produce make it a great place to spend time year-round. Pack a picnic blanket, fishing rod and walking shoes, because a holiday in this part of the world is all about getting back to nature and enjoying the great outdoors.

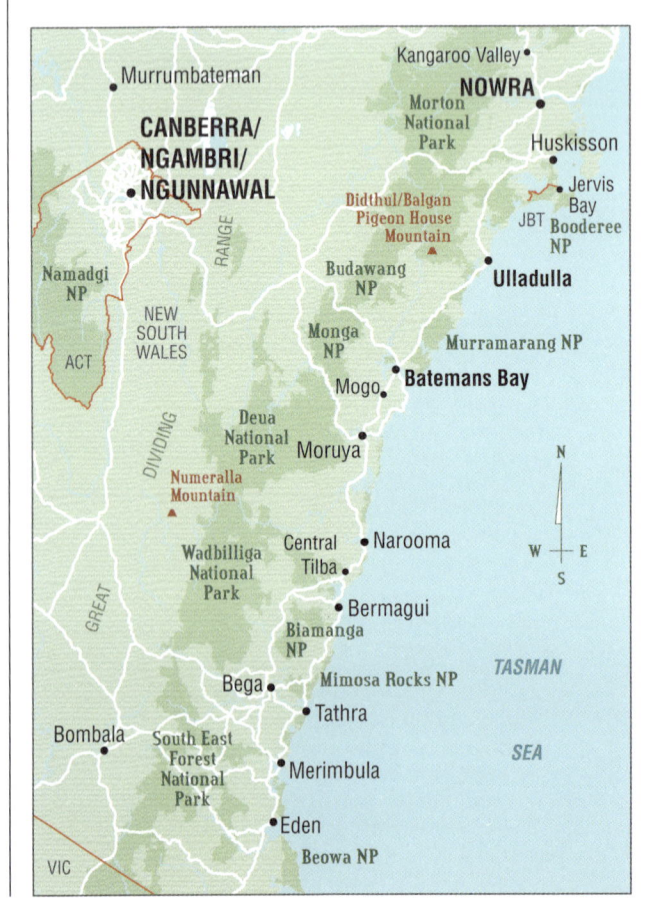

CHEAT SHEET

- You could drive this stretch in less than a day, but that would be no fun at all – four or five days gives you plenty of time to enjoy the good life along the way.

- Best time to visit: best swimming weather is early summer through to mid-autumn. The region is popular during summer school holidays, so plan ahead.

- Main towns: Batemans Bay (see p. 86), Bega (see p. 86), Eden (see p. 87), Merimbula (see p. 87), Narooma (see p. 88), Ulladulla (see p. 89).

- The south coast is Yuin and Wodi Wodi Country. Booderee National Park is the Traditional Land of the people of Wreck Bay, and Booderee Botanic Gardens is the only Indigenous-owned botanic gardens in Australia. A self-guided trail with lots of interpretive boards explains how the Koori people used the plants for food and medicine.

- Did you know? Seek out the story of Old Tom at the Eden Killer Whale Museum. As leader of a pack of killer whales (orcas), he would round up the baleen whales in the harbour and herd them towards the whalers waiting with harpoons, in exchange for whale scraps.

- Don't miss: Hyams Beach; Mogo Zoo; Eden Killer Whale Museum; Montague Island; Green Cape Lighthouse; Central Tilba.

Top: Wasps Head at Murramarang National Park **Opposite:** Blue Pool in Bermagui

TOP ATTRACTIONS

BEOWA NATIONAL PARK: Formerly known as Ben Boyd National Park, this reserve was renamed in September 2022 because of the name's connections to the slave trade. The new name, Beowa, means 'orca' in the local Thaua language. This park's scenery includes rugged stretches of coastline, unique rock formations, heaths and banksia forest. The area is great for fishing, swimming, wreck diving, bushwalking and camping. Boyd's Tower at Red Point was originally built for whale-spotting. **Green Cape Lighthouse** (1883) is the first cast-concrete lighthouse in Australia, the second-tallest in NSW, standing at 29m, and the southernmost lighthouse in NSW; tours by appt; bookings on (02) 6495 5555. The Pinnacles are an unusual earth formation with red gravel atop white-sand cliffs. The national park is near Eden (see p. 87).

BOODEREE NATIONAL PARK: This park used to be known as Jervis Bay National Park and was renamed by the Wreck Bay Aboriginal Community, who also own the park. Booderee is home to some spectacular beaches, including Murrays Beach. There's a range of water-based activities available at this national park, including swimming, snorkelling and whale-watching, as well as some spectacular bushwalks. Booderee Botanic Gardens is part of the national park, and is the only Indigenous-owned botanic gardens in Australia and has a large selection of native plants; Caves Beach Rd; (02) 4443 0977.

BUNDANON: The former home and studio of artist Arthur Boyd opened as a spectacular, partly subterranean art gallery in 2022. The state-of-the-art gallery features 4000 artworks from the Boyd collection, and an architecturally designed 160m-long bridge featuring accommodation for guests. The museum is 19km west of Nowra (see p. 88). Open Wed–Sun 10am-5pm; (02) 4422 2100

CENTRAL TILBA: Classified as an 'unusual mountain village' by the National Trust, Central Tilba was founded in 1895 and has many quality art and craft shops. It also has several old buildings worth a visit. The ABC Cheese Factory is open daily, and you can watch cheesemaking and milk bottling. Tilba Tilba (a further 2km south) features **Foxglove and Co.**, an historic cottage surrounded by a beautiful 3.5ha garden.

FLEET AIR ARM MUSEUM: Australia's largest aviation museum has displays and aircraft including airships, seaplanes, biplanes and helicopters. The exhibitions tell the stories of Australian naval aviation and the Royal Australian Navy's Fleet Air Arm. (02) 4424 1920. The museum is 8km south-west of Nowra (see p. 88).

HYAMS BEACH: This famous beach in Jervis Bay (see p. 87) has dazzling white sand and stunning turquoise water. While the sheltered outlook makes this a great place to swim, the beach is unpatrolled.

JERVIS BAY MARITIME MUSEUM: The Jervis Bay Maritime Museum features the *Lady Denman*, a wooden Sydney ferry that was built in 1910 and retired in 1979, which is the centrepiece of this heritage complex. It is home to the regional visitor centre. In the grounds is a First Nations arts and craft centre. The museum is open 10am–4pm; 11 Dent St, Huskisson; (02) 4441 5675.

KANGAROO VALLEY: This town of historic buildings has the National Trust–classified Friendly Inn, the Pioneer Settlement Reserve (a reconstruction of an 1880s dairy farm) and Hampden Bridge, which was built in 1898 and is the oldest suspension bridge in Australia. The valley was impacted by the 2020 bushfires, although there are signs of regrowth in the forests. The scenic route leading from the highlands to the coast (from Moss Vale to Nowra) takes in 80m high Fitzroy Falls, crosses Hampden Bridge and passes through the historic township. Canoeing and kayaking safaris to Kangaroo River and Shoalhaven Gorge can be booked at the visitor centre. There is also beautiful rural scenery along Nowra Rd. The valley is 23km north-west of Nowra (see p. 88).

KILLER WHALE MUSEUM: This museum in Eden (see p. 87) has fascinating displays on the history of the local whaling industry, including the skeleton of 'Old Tom' the killer whale that herded baleen whales in exchange for scraps from whalers; Imlay St, Eden; (02) 6496 2094.

MERIMBULA AQUARIUM: Twenty-seven tanks present a wide range of sea life and an oceanarium showcases large ocean fish including sharks. Fish feeding time is 11.30am Mon, Wed and Fri (Mon–Fri during school holidays). There's an excellent seafood restaurant onsite. Open 10am–5pm; Merimbula Wharf, Lake St, Merimbula; (02) 6495 4446.

MIMOSA ROCKS NATIONAL PARK: This beautifully rugged coastal park features secluded campsites, surf beaches, caves, offshore rock stacks, lagoons, patches of rainforest and incredible volcanic sculptures. It is excellent for snorkelling, surfing, bushwalking, birdwatching and foreshore fossicking. The name of the park comes from the paddle steamer *Mimosa*, which was wrecked on volcanic rock in 1863 – you will see a pyramid-shaped rock on the Mimosa Rocks walking track and beneath it is the wreck. The park is the Country of the Yuin People and connected to Dreaming stories. On the Mimosa Rocks walking track you cross the largest Aboriginal midden in the park. (02) 4476 2888. The park is 17km north of the town of Tathra (see p. 89).

MOGO: It's a common enough story in Australia – gold was discovered in the creek, and the town of Mogo was born. Sadly, the area was impacted by the 2020 bushfires, and the popular Original Gold Rush Colony, a re-created 19th-century goldmining town, was destroyed. But Mogo is so much more than just the sum of its past. It has a lively community of artists, and the antique and collectibles stores, art galleries and specialty shops in town might have you discovering a take-home curio. Nearby is a zoo that raises endangered species such as tigers, white lions, snow leopards and red pandas; 9am–5pm; 22 Tomakin Rd, Mogo; (02) 4474 4930.

For native animals, **Mogo State Forest** is home to lorikeets, kookaburras, rosellas and cockatoos and is a great spot for birdwatching and bushwalking. Enjoy the sclerophyll forest on the 1.3km Mogo Bushwalk. Mogo is 8km south of Batemans Bay (see p. 86).

MONTAGUE ISLAND NATURE RESERVE: This isolated island, with access only by guided tours (bookings at Narooma visitor centre), is a major shearwater breeding site and home to little penguins and Australian and New Zealand fur seals. Whales can be viewed off the coast Sept–Nov. The tour includes historic buildings such as the **Montague Lighthouse**, which was first lit in 1881 but is now fully automated. Accommodation in the lighthouse keeper's quarters is available. Guides also explain the history of the island (known as Barunguba) as a fertile hunting ground for the Walbanga and Djiringanj People.

MURRAMARANG NATIONAL PARK: An undisturbed coastline with kangaroos and popular beachfront camping areas. Murramarang Aboriginal Area features a signposted walk through 12,000-year-old sites and the largest midden on the south coast.

PLATYPUS RESERVE: Bombala (see p. 87) has one of the densest populations of platypus in NSW. They can be seen here in their natural environment from the Platypus Reserve Viewing Platform. The best times for viewing are at dawn and dusk. The reserve is off Monaro Hwy on the road to Delegate.

OTHER ATTRACTIONS

BEGA CHEESE HERITAGE CENTRE: Things get a bit cheesy at this restored factory with cheese-tasting and displays of cheesemaking equipment; Lagoon St, Bega; (02) 6491 7762.

BIAMANGA NATIONAL PARK: Jointly managed by the National Parks and Wildlife Service and the Yuin People, Biamanga National Park protects sacred cultural sites, as well as pristine coastal foothills and a dramatic, ancient volcanic landscape. The park is ideal for swimming and picnicking, with rockpools and natural water slides aplenty. The park suffered significant damage in the 2020 bushfires and, at the time of writing, the Biamanga National Park Cultural Area and Mumbulla Creek Falls Cultural picnic area remained closed, so check ahead before visiting.

BIRDLAND ANIMAL PARK: A hands-on experience with more than 80 species of native wildlife; open from 9.30am; 55 Beach Rd, Batemans Bay; (02) 4472 5364.

BOURNDA NATIONAL PARK: Picturesque conservation area for great camping and bushwalking. Wallagoot Lake has a wetland area with birdwatching, fishing, prawning, swimming, watersports and boat hire; (02) 6495 5000.

BOYDTOWN: Former rival settlement to Eden (see p. 87) on the shores of Twofold Bay with convict-built Seahorse Inn (still licensed), sheltered beach and good fishing. It's 9km south of Eden.

COOMEE NULUNGA CULTURAL TRAIL: This 30min signposted walk along the headland in Ulladulla (see p. 89) was created by the Ulladulla Local Aboriginal Land Council. Along the path are hand-painted and hand-carved information posts incorporating names of local plants and animals. Dawn and dusk are the best times to experience the wildlife along the walk, but visitors are advised to stay on the path for the good of the local fauna and for their own protection (from snakes). Starts Deering St, opposite Lighthouse Oval carpark, Ulladulla.

DAVIDSON WHALING STATION HISTORIC SITE: Provides unique insight into the lives of 19th-century whalers; Kiah Inlet; 30km SE of Eden.

DEUA NATIONAL PARK: The park is a wilderness of rugged mountain ranges, plateaus, gentle and wild rivers and a magnificent limestone belt, which makes the area popular for canyoning and caving. The rivers are a base for most water activities, including swimming, fishing and canoeing. There are scenic walks and 4WD tracks to explore. It is 20km west of the town of Moruya (see p. 88).

DIDTHUL/BALGAN/PIGEON HOUSE MOUNTAIN: The Ulladulla section of Morton National Park features this eye-catching mountain, which the local Yuin People named 'Didthul', meaning 'woman's breast'. (James Cook thought it looked like a square dovehouse with a dome on top, and called it 'Pigeon House'.) The mountain is a Yuin women's Dreaming area. A 5km return walk to the summit (for the reasonably fit) provides 360-degree views taking in the ocean, the Budawang Mountains and the Clyde River Valley.

EUROBODALLA NATIVE BOTANIC GARDENS: 42ha of native plants, walking tracks, nursery and picnic area; open Wed–Fri 9am–4pm, Sat–Sun, school and public holidays 10am–4pm; Princes Hwy; (02) 4471 2544. The garden is 5km south of Batemans Bay (see p. 86).

MEROOGAL: Said to be the most intact 19th-century home in NSW, this 1885 property in Nowra (see p. 88) was passed down through four generations of women. Furniture, household objects, diaries, letters, scrapbooks, photographs and even clothes have been saved so visitors can see relics from each generation of its occupation. Open Sat 10am–4pm; cnr Worrigee and West sts, Nowra; (02) 4421 8150.

PIONEERS' MUSEUM: Step inside Bega's history in this former hotel (built in 1858), which contains treasures from the town's past, including machinery, clothing, furniture and photographs; open Mon, Wed and Fri 10am–4pm, Sat 10am–2pm; 87 Bega St, Bega; (02) 6492 1453.

WAGONGA PRINCESS: This environmentally friendly, electronically powered boat is a converted Huon pine ferry offering scenic cruises from Narooma most days, taking in mangroves, forests and birdlife. The tour includes Devonshire tea. Commentary and tales (both tall and true) of local history, flora and fauna are provided by a third-generation local. Bookings (02) 4476 2665.

WALLAGA LAKE: The largest lake in southern NSW is a paradise for those wanting to boat, fish, swim, picnic, waterski, bushwalk or just sit back and watch the wildlife. **Gulaga National Park** is on the west side of the lake. The lake is 8km north of of Bermagui (see p. 86).

Opposite: Eden Killer Whale Museum tells of times past

KEY TOWNS

⊛ BATEMANS BAY
Population 12,263

Glittering blue water, pristine white beaches, quiet coves, excellent seafood – once you visit Batemans Bay, at the mouth of the Clyde River, you may never want to leave. Although the surrounding national parks and hinterland still bear the scars of the 2020 bushfires, the forests are regenerating and it won't be long until the region regains its natural beauty.

SEE & DO **Mogo:** *see* Top Attractions. **Birdland Animal Park; Eurobodalla Native Botanic Gardens:** *see* Other Attractions for both. **River cruises:** daily cruises at 11.30am on the *Merinda* to historic Nelligen, depart from the wharf behind the Boatshed; 1 Clyde St; (02) 4472 4052. **Houseboat hire and fishing charters:** bookings at visitor centre. **Marine Rescue Market:** Corrigans Reserve, Beach Rd; 1st Sun each month. **Rotary Market:** Corrigans Reserve, Beach Rd; 3rd Sun each month. **Nelligen:** an important Clyde River port in the 19th century, when goods were shipped from here to Sydney or sent into the hinterland; the town also has a 'bushranger tree' that is linked with bushrangers, the Clarke Gang; nowadays, holidaymakers use the historic town as a base for waterskiing, fishing and houseboat vacations; 10km NW. **Malua Bay:** excellent surfing; 14km SE. **Durras Lake:** fishing, kayaking and swimming; 16km NE. **Tomakin:** coastal holiday village by the Tomaga River with miles of pristine family-friendly beaches and forested hinterland; 15km S.

BEGA
Population 4368

Bega was originally settled by dairy farmers, and a good thing too, because the town is now famous for its cheese. But there's more to attract visitors to Bega than just dairy products. This historic town was fortuitously settled between the Snowy Mountains and the beaches of the east coast – so you can ski and swim on the same day, if you'd like.

SEE & DO **Bega Cheese Heritage Centre; Pioneers' Museum:** *see* Other Attractions for both. **Regional Gallery:** showcasing local and regional art and home to the biennial Shirley Hannan National Portrait Award, one of the richest in the country; open Tues–Fri 10am–4pm, Sat 9am–12pm; Zingel Pl; (02) 6499 2202. **Produce market:** every Fri morning in Littleton Gardens. **Lookouts:** excellent views at Bega Valley Lookout (3km N) and Dr George Lookout (8km NE). **Candelo:** charming and peaceful village with a market on 1st Sun each month; 24km SW. **Brogo Dam:** haven for native birdlife such as sea eagles and azure kingfishers. Also popular for bass fishing, swimming, picnicking, boating and canoeing; 31km NW.

BERMAGUI
Population 1798

As with all good sleepy villages, Bermagui has a mysterious past that involves five missing men ... A geologist, Lamont Young, was investigating Bermagui's new goldfields in 1880, when he decided to go further north to continue his research. Young and his assistant accepted a ride on a small boat with three other men, but the boat was found stranded a few days later with five bags of clothing, Young's books and papers, and a bullet in the starboard side. No trace of the men was ever found. Aside from mysteries, you'll also find excellent angling and water-based activities at Bermagui.

SEE & DO **Wallaga Lake:** *see* Other Attractions. **Bermagui Fisherman's Wharf:** you can buy fresh seafood from the wharf or stay for shopping, a casual coffee, restaurants, a wine bar and even a gallery; harbourside. **Blue Pool:** a large natural rockpool next to the pounding surf is a must-visit swimming spot; off Pacific Dr. **Camel Rock:** this rock formation was named by Bass and Flinders. **Horseshoe Bay Beach and Bruce Steer Pool:** safe swimming spots for children. **Surf beaches:** Beares, Mooreheads, Cuttagee, Camel Rock and Haywards beaches; map from visitor centre. **Gamefishing, deep-sea fishing and reef-fishing:** charter information at visitor centre and harbourside. **Craft market:** Dickinson Park; last Sun each

VISITOR INFORMATION

Merimbula Visitor Information Centre
2 Beach St, Merimbula
(02) 6495 1129 or
1800 150 457

Sapphire Coast
sapphirecoast.com.au

Shoalhaven
shoalhaven.com

Eurobodalla
eurobodalla.com.au

Bottom: The Montague Island Lightstation **Opposite top:** Killer Whale Museum in Eden **Opposite bottom:** The Clyde River Bridge in Batemans Bay

month. **Montreal Goldfield:** calling itself Australia's only seaside goldfield, local historians reveal the lives and stories behind the goldfield on tours leaving at 2pm Tues–Thurs, Sat–Sun; 7km N. **Coastal walks:** along the coast to the lake and nearby towns. **Cobargo:** this historic working village was devasted by the 2020 bushfires, but the town is rebuilding – even the entire main street is being rebuilt. A country market is held every Sat with pop up stalls along the main street; 20km W.

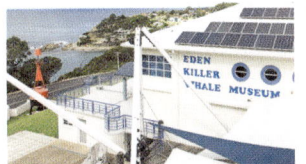

BOMBALA
Population 1136

The heritage buildings in Bombala give it a sense of almost being untouched by time, such as early settler huts, the local bank and even a Russian Orthodox monastery. Situated on the Bombala River between the Snowy Mountains and the coast, Bombala is about halfway between Sydney and Melbourne, and for this reason was one of the places proposed for the nation's capital. The Bombala River is reputed to have the biggest population of platypus in NSW; you can spend some happy hours trying to spot one of these elusive animals. The town is the centre for the surrounding wool, lavender, beef cattle and timber industries.

SEE & DO **Platypus Reserve:** *see* Top Attractions. **Railway Park:** the local railway station was opened in 1921, and is now part of a precinct housing the historic engine shed (open by appt) and a museum of local artefacts and farm implements. A convent building has been turned into a lavender emporium and visitor centre. Monaro Hwy. **Endeavour Reserve:** features a 2km return walking track to a lookout with views over town; Caveat St. **Bicentennial Park:** wetlands and a pleasant river walk; Mahratta St. **Self-guided historic walk:** 1hr walk includes courthouse (1882) and School of Art (1871); brochure available from visitor centre. **Cathcart:** charming township with historical town walk; brochure from visitor centre; 14km NE. **Myanba Gorge:** walks through old-growth eucalypt forest with spectacular views of waterfalls, granite boulders and Towamba Valley; South East Forest National Park; 20km SE. **Delegate:** scenic town with Early Settlers Hut, believed to be the first dwelling on the Monaro plains, also has Platypus Walk and River Walk (brochures from visitor centre); 36km SW. **Scenic drive:** gold fossicking en route to Bendoc Mines in Victoria; 57km SW. **Fly fishing and trout fishing:** maps from visitor centre. **Mountain biking:** there are many trails in nearby state forest areas; maps from visitor centre.

EDEN
Population 3227

If any place can get away with being called Eden, it's this hilly and idyllic town on the Sapphire Coast's Twofold Bay, which is the Southern Hemisphere's third-largest harbour. There are national parks to the north and south, a state forest to the west, and the ocean to the east. The town was founded by whalers, but thankfully some whales survived and humpback whale-watching (May–Nov) is popular these days. This sleepy town is an excellent holiday destination.

SEE & DO **Beowa National Park; Killer Whale Museum:** *see* Top Attractions for both. **Boydtown:** *see* Other Attractions. **Aslings Beach:** surf beach with rockpools and platforms for whale-watching (Oct–Nov); Aslings Beach Rd. **Snug Cove:** working fishing port with plenty of restaurants and cafes. **Market:** Chandos St; 3rd Sat each month. **Nadgee Nature Reserve:** walking track, access via Wonboyn Lake; 35km SE. **Wonboyn Lake:** scenic area with good fishing and 4WD tracks; 40km S.

HUSKISSON
Population 825

Huskisson is a holiday resort on Jervis Bay. It was named after British politician William Huskisson, secretary for the colonies and leader of the House of Commons, who was killed by a train in 1830 while talking to the Duke of Wellington at a railway opening. The idyllic bay is renowned for its white sand and clear water, and there are usually several pods of dolphins living in the bay, making the area ideal for cruises and diving.

SEE & DO **Jervis Bay Maritime Museum:** *see* Top Attractions. **Market:** 1st Sat each month. **Sussex Inlet:** coastal hamlet with fishing carnival in July; 34km SW.

★ JERVIS BAY
Population 310

The waters of Jervis Bay Marine Park have many superlatives justifiably attached, and Jervis Bay, which is more of a locality than a particular town – if you are driving follow the signs to Huskisson – is happily sandwiched between these waters and Booderee National Park. This tiny town is not technically in NSW; it's part of Jervis Bay Territory, which was created to give the ACT access to the sea. It's home to the *HMAS Creswell* Navy Base.

SEE & DO **Hyams Beach; Booderee Botanic Gardens:** *see* Top Attractions for both. **Marine Park:** the clear waters, reefs and deep-water cliffs with caves offer superb diving. Bookings are taken at the visitor centre for dolphin- and whale-watching cruises.

MERIMBULA
Population 8220

Merimbula is the biggest town on the charmingly and accurately named Sapphire Coast. Ranged around Merimbula Lake, and with the Black Lake north of town, the name Merimbula is believed to come from a local Aboriginal language word meaning 'two lakes'. With five beaches – including the 6km Main Beach – in town, this is a popular holiday spot. Middens found in the area indicate that oysters were gathered here by Yuin-Monaro People well before the arrival of Europeans. The town began as a private village belonging to the Twofold Bay Pastoral Association, which opened it as a port in 1855.

SEE & DO **Merimbula Aquarium:** see Top Attractions. **Old School Museum:** town history displayed in excellent collection of photos, documents and memorabilia; open Tues, Thurs, Sun 1.30–4pm; Main St; (02) 6495 9231. **Scenic flights:** view the Sapphire Coast from the air. Bookings through Merimbula Air Services; (02) 6495 1074. **Seaside Markets:** Ford Oval; 3rd Sun each month. **Pambula:** This historic sister village of Merimbula has excellent fishing on the Pambula River and a market on the 2nd Sun each month. Pambula Beach has a scenic walking track and lookout, with kangaroos and wallabies gathering on the foreshore at dawn and dusk. 7km SW. **Magic Mountain:** rollercoaster, water slides, giant carpet slide, toboggan, minigolf and picnic area; open 10am–4pm (summer and Easter holidays), Wed–Sun (Feb–Mar and July school holidays), Sat–Sun (May–June); Sapphire Coast Dr; (02) 6495 2299; 5km N. **Potoroo Palace:** native animal sanctuary in peaceful bushland setting; Princes Hwy, Yellowpinch; (02) 6494 9053; 5km E. **Whale-watching:** Oct–Nov; boat cruises and boat hire; bookings at visitor centre.

MORUYA
Population 2762

Moruya's local granite was used to build the pylons of the Sydney Harbour Bridge, and is also used for some of the local buildings. This town, on the banks of the beautiful Moruya River, was once the centre of the local goldfields, although the business of the town these days is centred around dairy and oyster farming.

SEE & DO **Deua National Park:** see Other Attractions. **Museum:** depicts gold discovery at Mogo and the district history of shipping, dairying and goldmining; town centre. **South Head:** beautiful views across the river mouth. **Market:** Main St; Sat. **Broulee:** great surfing and swimming; 12km NE. **Bodalla:** the All Saints Church, built from local granite, is of historical significance; 24km S. **Nerrigundah:** former goldmining town with a monument to Miles O'Grady, who was killed in battle with the Clarke bushranging gang; 44km SW.

NAROOMA
Population 3395

Narooma is a tranquil fishing town at the mouth of Wagonga Inlet, well known for its natural beauty. The beaches and waterways continue to draw people due to the excellent boating, aquatic sports and big-game fishing. Fresh local seafood is a specialty in many of the restaurants.

SEE & DO **Montague Island Nature Reserve:** see Top Attractions. **Wagonga Princess:** see Other Attractions. **Walking tracks:** several walking tracks incorporate places such as the Mill Bay Boardwalk, Australia Rock and lookout and numerous foreshore paths; maps from visitor centre. **Whale-watching cruises:** humpback and killer whales can be seen migrating, often with calves, Sept–Nov; bookings at visitor centre. **Scuba-diving cruises:** to shipwrecks; bookings at visitor centre. **Mystery Bay:** popular spot with strange-looking stones, snorkelling, camping and access to Eurobodalla National Park; 17km S.

NOWRA
Population 9956

Nowra is the principal town in the Shoalhaven district and is popular with tourists for its attractive river and water activities. The former home and studio of artist Arthur Boyd, Bundanon, is here and opened as a spectacular new gallery in December 2021. Local cafes feature regional produce and Nowra is the gateway to the Shoalhaven Coast Wine Region. Nearby is the beautiful Kangaroo Valley with its water-based activities.

SEE & DO **Bundanon; Fleet Air Arm Museum; Kangaroo Valley:** see Top Attractions for all. **Meroogal:** see Other Attractions. **Museum:** old police station exhibiting the history of the town in records, photographs, household items and tools; cnr Plunkett and Kinghorne sts; call for opening hours (02) 4446 0297. **Shoalhaven River:** fishing, waterskiing, canoeing and sailing. **Shoalhaven River Cruises:** departing from Nowra Wharf, Riverview Rd; at the time of writing, the cruises were still in recess due to the pandemic, so call ahead to check on departures 0429 981 007. **Hanging Rock:** 46m above the river with scenic views; off Junction St. **Shoalhaven Zoo and Adventure World:** native animals, reptiles and birds, regular animal shows and feeding times; Rockhill Rd; (02) 4421 3949. **Scenic walks:** includes Bens Walk along the river and Bomaderry Creek Bushland Walk from Bomaderry; brochures from visitor centre. **Cambewarra Lookout:** views of the Shoalhaven River, Kangaroo Valley and the ocean; 12km NW. **Greenwell Point:** fresh fish and oyster sales; 14km E. **Culburra:** the beaches here and at nearby Lake Wollumboola are good for surfing, swimming, prawning and fishing; 21km SE. **Beaches:** many beautiful beaches in the vicinity for swimming and surfing; maps at visitor centre.

TOP EVENTS

- JAN Blue Water Fishing Classic (Bermagui)
- FEB Triathlon Festival (Jervis Bay)
- EASTER Blessing of the Fleet (Ulladulla); Four Winds Festival (Bermagui); White Sands Carnival (Huskisson); Tilba Festival (Central Tilba)
- MAY Oyster Festival (Narooma); Blues & Roots Festival (Moruya)
- JUNE Jazz Festival (Merimbula), Scarecrow Festival (Milton)
- SEP Escape ARTfest (Milton)
- OCT-NOV Whale Festival (Eden)
- NOV Historic Engine Shed Engine Rally (even numbered years, Bombala), Husky Running Festival (Huskisson)

TEMPERATURES

Jan: 16–26°C

July: 4–17°C

Merimbula's Bar Beach
Opposite top: Bar Rock Lookout in Narooma **Opposite bottom:** Wray Street Oyster Shed in Batemans Bay

TATHRA
Population 1523

Tathra is an idyllic family holiday location with a 3km surf beach. A bushfire in March 2018 destroyed many homes and buildings, but the town recovered quickly and started accepting visitors almost immediately afterwards. Tathra started as a small jetty that served as a shipping outlet for a group of local farmers, and is now the only surviving sea wharf of its age and type on the east coast. The region is abundant with prawns from Nov–May.

SEE & DO **Mimosa Rocks National Park:** *see* Top Attractions. **Sea Wharf:** deterioration of the 1860s wharf led to a demolition order in 1973. Only strenuous local action and the intervention of the National Trust saved the wharf. It has always been a popular fishing platform and there is also a seafood cafe. Above the wharf is the Wharf Museum, which traces the history of the wharf and steam shipping in the area and has replicas of early vessels. Fur seals and little penguins can often be seen. **Tathra Beach:** 3km patrolled beach (various sections) and excellent for fishing. **Fishing spots:** several good spots for salmon and tailor. **Kianinny Bay:** known fossil site with steep cliffs and rugged rocks; diving and deep-sea fishing charters available. The 9km Kangarutha track follows the coast with jaw-dropping scenery; 1km S. **Mogareeka Inlet:** safe swimming ideal for small children; northern end of Tathra Beach; 2km N.

ULLADULLA
Population 14,396

This fishing town, built around a safe harbour, is surrounded by beautiful lakes, lagoons and white sandy beaches. It is a popular holiday destination, especially for surfing and fishing, and enjoys mild weather year-round. Visitors flock here each Easter Sunday for the Blessing of the Fleet ceremony.

SEE & DO **Coomie Nulunga Cultural Trail; Didthul/Balgan/Pigeon House Mountain:** *see* Other Attractions for both. **Funland:** large indoor family fun park; Princes Hwy; (02) 4454 3220. **Warden Head:** lighthouse views and walking tracks; Deering St. **South Pacific Heathland Reserve:** walks among native plants and birdlife; Dowling St. **Wildflower Reserve:** 12ha with walking trails and over 100 plant types including waratah and Christmas bush. Best in spring; Warden St. **Marine Rescue Markets:** harbour wharf; 2nd Sun each month. **Mollymook:** excellent surfing and beach fishing; 2km N. **Narrawallee Beach:** popular surf beach; nearby Narrawallee Inlet has calm, shallow water ideal for children; 4km N. **Lakes:** good swimming, fishing and waterskiing at Burrill Lake (5km SW) and Lake Conjola (23km NW). **Milton:** historic town with art galleries and outdoor cafes. Village markets are held on the highway, 1st Sat each month; 7km NW. **Pointer Gap Lookout:** beautiful coastal views; 20km NW.

Snowy Mountains

Alpine New South Wales – aka the Snowy Mountains – stretches from the ACT to the Victorian border along the spine of the Great Dividing Range. Most of the area, which includes **some of the country's most fragile alpine environments,** is protected by Kosciuszko National Park. The star attraction is the 2228m **Mount Kosciuszko** – even though it is Australia's highest peak, it's surprisingly easy to climb as long as you don't mind a four-hour return walk (you can ride a chairlift almost to the top). In winter the area is a magnet for lovers of **snow sports**; in summer, **fishing, bushwalking and mountain biking rule.** But the good news is you don't have to be an adventurer to see the region, as you can explore a lot of it by car.

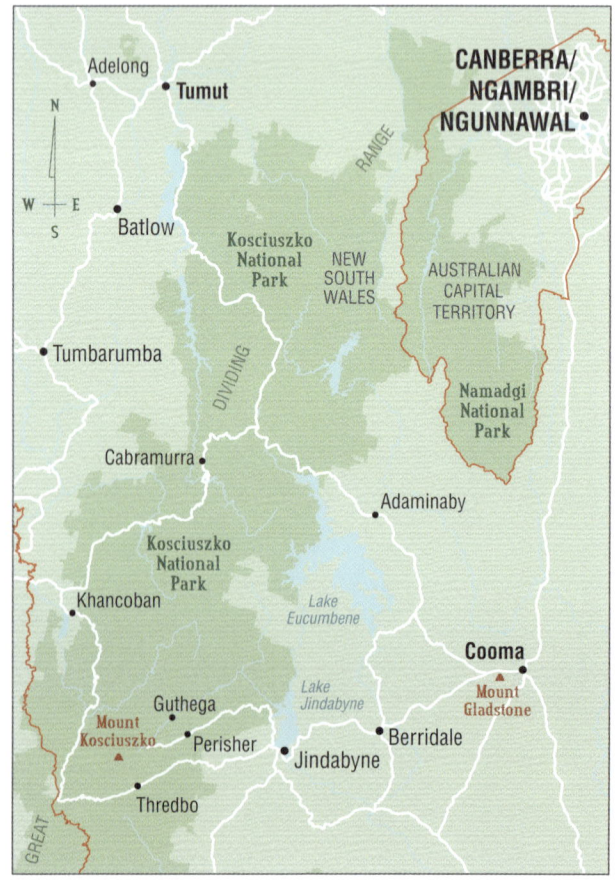

Top: Horse riding, Jindabyne
Opposite: Skiing at Kosciuszko National Park

CHEAT SHEET

→ Allow at least four-five days to explore the region, longer if you are a keen bushwalker.

→ Best time to visit: late spring and early summer for spectacular wildflowers, although autumn is a lovely time to visit the northern towns – Tumut's Falling Leaf Festival is in April.

→ Main towns: Cooma (see p. 94), Jindabyne (see p. 94), Thredbo (see p. 95).

→ The Ngarigo People are the Traditional Owners of the majority of the region now known as the Snowy Mountains.

→ Need to know: most roads are steep, winding and narrow and not recommended for large caravans, whatever the time of year. Perfect for motorcycles though! The road from Khancoban to Cabramurra and many of the minor roads in Kosciuszko National Park are closed because of snow in winter. Snow chains must be carried in 2WD vehicles in the Snowy Mountains between 1 June and 10 Oct; they are recommended for 4WDs. The Snowies were badly affected by the 2019-20 bushfires, but the landscape is regenerating.

→ Did you know? Tom Groggin Station, between Thredbo and Khancoban, was the home of Tom Riley; according to local legend he was the original 'The Man from Snowy River' immortalised in Banjo Paterson's famous poem.

→ Don't miss: Lake Jindabyne; a ride on the Kosciuszko Express chairlift at Thredbo; Yarrangobilly Caves; Scammells Lookout; Paddys River Falls.

TOP ATTRACTIONS

ALPINE WAY: A 111km road through mountains from Thredbo to Khancoban, provides superb scenic touring in summer; chains frequently required in winter.

KOSCIUSZKO NATIONAL PARK: All of NSW's ski fields are within Kosciuszko National Park; the focal point is **Mount Kosciuszko**, Australia's highest mountain. The summit can be reached easily via the Kosciuszko Express Chairlift (operating all year round), which drops you at the beginning of a 13km return walk. There is a mountain of natural delights in the park, but the **Yarrangobilly Caves** are a highlight. The string of 70 limestone caves was formed from the shells and skeletons of sea animals around 40 million years ago. Six caves are open to the public, featuring underground pools, 'frozen' waterfalls, a bizarre web of limestone formations and a naturally formed thermal pool offering year-round swimming. For guided and self-guided tours, call (02) 6454 9597; more details from visitor centre in Jindabyne (see p. 94).

LAKE EUCUMBENE: It's the largest of the Snowy Mountains' artificial lakes, with a large fishing bounty to match. The abundance of rainbow trout, brown trout and Atlantic salmon draws anglers to town, especially in Nov for the Snowy Mountains Trout Festival. Fishing boats can be hired at Old Adaminaby, and for fly-fishing tours contact the visitor centre. Access via Old Adaminaby.

LAKE JINDABYNE: Well stocked with rainbow trout and ideal for boating, waterskiing and other watersports. When the water level is low, remains of the original submerged town can be seen; western edge of Jindabyne.

PERISHER: The largest ski resort in Australia. With an impressive 1250ha of skiing area, Perisher caters for all levels of skier and snowboarder. State-of-the-art equipment includes many high-quality snow guns and Australia's first 8-seater chairlifts. The resort consists of slopes, accommodation, restaurants, bars and all the facilities and equipment hire needed to enjoy winter sports at Perisher and the nearby skiing areas of Smiggin Holes, Mount Blue Cow and Guthega. (02) 6459 4495.

SELWYN SNOW RESORT: Although destroyed by fires in the summer of 2020, this family-oriented ski resort has been rebuilt and is due to reopen in 2023. With 10 lifts spread over 45ha, Selwyn Snow Resort is ideally suited to beginner skiers, snowboarders and tobogganers. Kings Cross Rd, Mount Selwyn; (02) 6454 9000.

THREDBO SKI FIELDS: Thredbo has 480ha of skiing terrain and the longest ski runs in Australia (up to 5.9km) with a vertical drop of 672m. Night skiing is a feature in July and Aug. There are slopes for beginners to advanced skiers and snowboarders, with lessons and equipment hire available. Thredbo Snowsports School offers off-piste skiing, freeheeling (telemark skiing), cross-country and snowshoeing lessons and excursions; Friday Dr; bookings (02) 6459 4044.

OTHER ATTRACTIONS

ADELONG FALLS RESERVE AND GOLD MILL RUINS: The ruins of Richie's Gold Battery, one of the foremost gold-processing and quartz-crushing facilities in the country, are on the banks of Adelong Creek. See the ruins of its reefer machine, including water wheels and a red-brick chimney. Three clearly signposted walks explore the falls and other ruins in the reserve. It's 1km north of Adelong (see p. 93).

BLOWERING DAM: This enormous dam is an excellent centre for watersports and fishing for rainbow trout, brown trout and perch. There is a great lookout over the dam wall, and the Blowering Cliffs make for a pleasant 5km walk in Kosciuszko National Park along granite cliffs. The dam is 13km south of Tumut (see p. 95).

PADDY'S RIVER FALLS: The waterfall cascades over a 60m drop in a beautiful bush setting with a scenic walking track and picnic area. A concreted walkway is at the bottom and lookouts are at the top. It's 16km south of Tumbarumba (see p. 95).

SNOWY HYDRO DISCOVERY CENTRE: This centre in Cooma (see p. 94) has interactive displays, photographs, models and films on the scheme. A memorial next door commemorates the 121 people who died while working on it; Monaro Hwy, Cooma; inquiries 1800 623 776.

THE BIG TROUT: There's a good story behind the fibreglass rainbow trout (the world's largest!) that stands at the entrance to Adaminaby (see p. 93). It was erected after a local angler, attempting to drink a gallon of Guinness while fishing, was pulled into the water by a large trout and almost drowned. Legend has it that the man then managed to finish the Guinness, but the trout got away – hence the tribute to the 'one that got away'. Lions Club Park, Adaminaby.

TUROSS FALLS: Part of Wadbilliga National Park, the stunning Tuross Falls are a drop of 35m. A picturesque 2km walk from the camping area at Cascades leads visitors to the lookout platform, which affords views of the falls and the Tuross River Gorge. The trail was closed due to bushfire damage, so check to see if it has reopened before travelling. The falls are 47km east of Cooma (see p. 94).

Paddy's River Falls

VISITOR INFORMATION

Snowy Region Visitor Centre
Kosciuszko Rd, Jindabyne
(02) 6450 5600
snowymountains.com.au

KEY TOWNS

ADAMINABY
Population 257

The small town of Adaminaby is nestled in the Snowy Mountains on the Snowy Mountains Hwy. Around 100 of the town's buildings were moved to the current town site in the 1950s when the original town and surrounding valley were flooded to create Lake Eucumbene as part of the Snowy Mountains Hydro-Electric Scheme. But that has led to excellent fishing (the lake is regularly restocked with trout). The town is also popular with skiers in winter; it's around 45km from Selwyn Snow Resort.

SEE & DO **Kosciuszko National Park; Lake Eucumbene; Sewlyn Snow Resort:** see Top Attractions for all. **The Big Trout:** see Other Attractions. **Snowy Scheme Museum:** the Snowy Mountains Hydro-Electric Scheme reshaped the mountains (and literally moved a couple of towns, including Adaminaby). This facility houses equipment and machinery, photographs, memorabilia and stories from the construction; Sat–Sun 10am–2pm; 5199 Snowy Mountains Hwy; (02) 6454 1643. **Historic buildings:** several buildings, including two churches that were moved from Adaminaby's original site; details from visitor centre. **Reynella Rides:** make like Banjo Paterson and horseride across the high country with this experienced outfit. There are homestead rides on the 1200ha sheep and cattle property, or excellent multi-day safaris in Kosciuszko National Park; 669 Kingston Rd; (02) 6454 2386; 5km E. **Old Adaminaby Racetrack:** featured in the film *Phar Lap* (1984); on the road to Rosedale, Cooma side of town. **Power stations:** tours and interactive displays; details from visitor centre.

ADELONG
Population 856

Just off the Hume Hwy near Tumut is one of the many towns in Australia that gold built. Adelong was founded in the mid-19th century when gold was discovered and a tent city went up basically overnight. One of the early successful prospectors was William Williams. Legend has it that Williams bought a mining claim for £40,000, only to sell it later the same day for £75,000. The town thrived off the back of its goldfield, but by World War I, with over a million ounces of gold extracted, there was little left. Much of the population left for more golden pastures, leaving Adelong the charming heritage village it is today.

SEE & DO **Adelong Falls Reserve and Gold Mill Ruins:** see Other Attractions. **Historic buildings:** take a stroll through Adelong's streets to discover banks, hotels and churches from the gold-rush era. **Adelong Alive Museum:** scale model of the gold mill and machinery; open 11am–1pm Sat or by appt; Tumut St; (02) 6946 2417.

BATLOW
Population 1022

During the 19th-century gold rush, prospectors converged on nearby Reedy Creek, which sparked a demand for fresh produce to feed the miners. The resulting orchards and farms became the charming settlement of Batlow. Set in the low-lying mountains of the state's south-west slopes, Batlow is a picturesque town still surrounded by orchards of delicious apples, pears, berries, cherries and stone fruit; the annual Ciderfest is in May.

SEE & DO **Weemala Lookout:** breathtaking views of town and the Snowy Mountains; H.V. Smith Dr. **Hume and Hovell Lookout:** great views over Blowering Valley, where the explorers rested in 1824, and Blowering Reservoir; 6km E. **Hume and Hovell Walking Track:** access to short sections of the 426km track, via Tumut Rd; maps available from visitor centre; 9km S.

BERRIDALE
Population 1030

This charming and historic small town is a great midway point between Cooma and the snowfields. Visit in autumn to experience the changing colours of the 100-year-old poplars along the main street; in winter for access to the snowfields; or in spring or summer to see the spectacular local scenery unveiled. The scenery sometimes looks similar to the Scottish Highlands, which inspired one of the original settlers to name the town after his home village in Scotland.

SEE & DO **Community Art Gallery:** work from local artists, with commission going to local charities; open Sat 11am–3pm, Sun 10am–4pm; 12 Myack St. **Historic buildings:** St Mary's (1860), Mary St; Berridale School (1883), Oliver St; Berridale Inn (1863), Exchange Sq; Berridale Store (1863), Exchange Sq. **Boulders:** unique granite boulders near the main road were formed from crystallised magma 400 million years ago. **Snowy Vineyard Estate:** wine tastings, restaurant and microbrewery with the cellar door open Wed–Sun 12pm–5pm; Werralong Rd; 1300 766 608; 3km N. **Dalgety:** small town once touted as a possible national capital city, featuring historic Buckley's Crossing Hotel, which marks the spot where cattle used to cross the Snowy River; 18km S.

NEW SOUTH WALES

COOMA
Population 6447

Cooma feels like a holiday town, even though it's a bustling regional centre for the Snowy Mountains region. Travellers often stop in Cooma on their way to the snow (in winter) or for dry-weather adventure activities in the warmer months. While Cooma started out like many Australian towns, as a farming community that boomed once gold was discovered, it became unexpectedly cosmopolitan when thousands of postwar immigrants flocked to the area to work on the Snowy Mountains Hydro-Electric Scheme. Stop here to check tyres and stock up on petrol and provisions before heading into the alpine country.

SEE & DO **Snowy Hydro Discovery Centre; Tuross Falls:** see Other Attractions for both. **Centennial Park:** originally a swamp, Centennial Park was established in 1890. During World War II, slit trenches were dug here in case of air attacks. The Avenue of Flags was constructed in 1959 to commemorate the 10th anniversary of the Snowy Mountains Hydro-Electric Scheme with one flag for each of the 27 nationalities of the workers. The Time Walk depicts the district's history in 40 ceramic mosaics laid below the flags. There is also a sculpture of Banjo Paterson's famous 'The Man from Snowy River'; Sharp St. **Corrective Services NSW Museum:** features unique displays of over 200 years of history, from convicts through to the modern prison system, in the old Cooma Gaol; open 9am–3pm Mon–Sat; 1 Vagg St; (02) 6452 5974. **Southern Cloud Park:** features Southern Cloud Memorial, a display of remains of the aircraft *Southern Cloud*, which crashed in the region in 1931 and was found in 1958. **Bike path:** picturesque path following Cooma Creek between Lambie St and Church Rd. **Lambie Town self-guided walk:** designed in 1985, with over 5km of easy walking. The tour incorporates three National Trust heritage areas including Lambie St, lined with huge oaks, pines and elms, and St Paul's Church, constructed with local alpine ash and granite and with striking stained-glass windows; brochure available from visitor centre. **Market:** Centennial Park; 3rd Sun each month. **Kosciuszko Memorial:** donated in 1988 by the Polish government commemorating Tadeusz Kosciuszko, a champion of the underprivileged, after whom Australia's highest mountain is named; 2.5km N. **Mount Gladstone Lookout:** impressive views, mountain-bike trails and Austrian teahouse; 6.5km W. **Adventure sports:** abseiling, kayaking, horseriding and more; guided tours available, contact visitor centre.

JINDABYNE
Population 2233

Jindabyne town was established in the 1840s, but the old town site was flooded in the 1960s when Lake Jindabyne was created as part of the Snowy Mountains Hydro-Electric Scheme, an epic project that took 100,000 people 25 years to complete. Only a few houses were moved to the new town site up the hill; the other buildings were left at the old town site. When the water level is low, you can see remains of the original town in the lake. Adjacent to the south-eastern section of Kosciuszko National Park and located just below the snowline, Jindabyne is an access point to the snow resorts, as well as for summer adventure activities.

SEE & DO **Kosciuszko National Park; Perisher:** see Top Attractions for both. **Walkway and cycleway:** around Lake Jindabyne's foreshore (see Top Attractions), from Banjo Paterson Park on Kosciuszko Rd to Snowline Caravan Park and from the Tyrolean Village to the dam wall. **Winter shuttle bus service:** several operators depart from various spots in town to Bullocks Flat and Thredbo; contact visitor centre for more information. **Snowy Valley Lookout:** stunning views of Lake Jindabyne; 8km N. **Gaden Trout Hatchery:** daily tours and barbecues along Thredbo River; 224 Gaden Rd; (02) 6451 3400; 10km NW. **Wildbrumby Schnapps Distillery:** boutique schnapps made from seasonal fruits, with cafe and cellar door; Wollondibby Rd; (02) 6457 1447; 11km W. **Sawpit Creek:** site of the Kosciuszko Education Centre and the starting point of the Palliabo walking track (at picnic area); Kosciuszko Rd; 14km NW. **Bullocks Flat:** terminal for Skitube, a European-style alpine train to Perisher ski resort; operates daily during ski season; 20km SW. **Wallace Craigie Lookout:** views of Snowy River Valley; 40km SW. **Charlotte Pass:** highest ski resort in Australia with challenging slopes for experienced skiers; magnificent 24km walking track past Blue Lake in summer; (02) 6457 1555; 45km W. **Scenic walks:** varying lengths; brochures from visitor centre.

KHANCOBAN
Population 246

Next to a lake on the south-western face of Kosciuszko National Park, with a spectacular mountain backdrop, it's an understatement to say that Khancoban is well situated. It's a small town, but people come here to fish in the majestic surrounds (and well-stocked lake). It's also the start of the Alpine Way, which weaves through the Snowy Mountains to Thredbo (the Alpine Way ends there). Khancoban is only 13km from the border with Victoria.

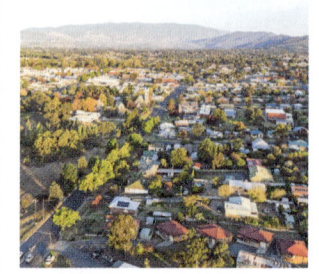

TOP EVENTS

- → JAN Blues Festival (Thredbo)
- → FEB Flowing Festival (dragon boat races, Jindabyne); Snowies Mountain Bike Festival (Thredbo)
- → MAR Multicultural Festival (Cooma)
- → APR–MAY Falling Leaf Festival (Tumut)
- → AUG Top to Bottom Ski Race (Thredbo)
- → OCT–NOV Snowy Mountains Trout Festival (across the region)

TEMPERATURES

Jan: 8–22°C

July: -3–6°C

Opposite top: Town of Tumut
Opposite middle: The Tumut River Walk Opposite bottom: 10 metre high Big Trout by Andy Lomnici

SEE & DO **Kosciuszko National Park:** see Top Attractions. **Pondage:** this 3km long pondage offers plenty of water-based recreational activities, from fishing to boating, as well as plenty of amenities; open year-round. **National Parks and Wildlife Information Centre:** has displays on both the history and natural beauty of the region; 9am–4pm Mon–Sun; 2 Scammel St; (02) 6070 8400.

★ THREDBO
Population 400

Thredbo is a mountain village in Kosciuszko National Park and a unique year-round resort, with some of Australia's best skiing and winter sports in the colder months and angling, bushwalking and mountain-biking in summer.

SEE & DO **Kosciuszko National Park; Ski Fields:** see Top Attractions for both. **Bobsled:** 700m luge-style track; adjacent to ski lifts; open 10am–4pm, closed in winter. **Leisure Centre:** quality sporting facilities used by athletes for high-altitude training, with pool, squash courts, gym and climbing wall; northern end of the village; (02) 6459 4138. **Thredbo River:** excellent trout fishing. **Village walks:** include the Meadows Nature Walk through tea trees and the Thredbo Village Walk for diversity of alpine architecture; brochure from visitor centre. **Mountain-biking:** several tracks including the Village Bike Track; all bike and equipment hire available from Thredbo MTB; 9am–5pm Nov–May; Valley Terminal, (02) 6457 6282. **Pilot Lookout:** magnificent view dominated by the Pilot (1828m) and the Cobberas (1883m) in Victoria; 10km SE. **Skitube:** access to Perisher and Mount Blue Cow ski fields via this European-style train from Bullocks Flat. This winter-only service passes through Australia's largest train tunnel; 15km NE. **Mount Kosciuszko:** Australia's highest mountain, with access via chairlift from Thredbo and 13km walk; contact visitor centre for more details.

TUMBARUMBA
Population 1505

This former goldmining town in the foothills of the Snowy Mountains remains seemingly untouched by the modern world, with old-style charm and well-preserved buildings. This has been helped by the fact that Tumbarumba has been bypassed by major road and rail routes. It experiences four distinct seasons and enjoys European-style vistas of snow-capped mountains, forested hills, rolling green pastures and a crystal-clear creek. Tumbarumba's name comes from the Wiradjuri language and is thought to mean 'sounding ground'. This refers to the suggestion that there are places in the region where the ground sounds hollow.

SEE & DO **Paddy's River Falls:** see Other Attractions. **Bicentennial Botanic Gardens:** mix of native and exotic trees, especially striking in autumn; Prince St. **Artists on Parade Gallery:** run by local artists, exhibitions change regularly; The Parade; (02) 6948 3600. **Museum and Information Centre:** includes working model of a water-powered timber mill; Bridge St; (02) 6948 3333. **Henry Angel Trackhead:** starting point for a 12km section of the Hume and Hovell Walking Track along Burra Creek. It includes waterfalls and the place where Hume and Hovell first saw the Snowy Mountains. **Tumbarumba to Rosewood Rail Trail:** NSW's first rail trail is an easy 21km bike ride past vineyards and beautiful rural scenes. Begins at the old Tumbarumba railway station. Tooma Rd; 7km SE. **Pioneer Women's Hut:** domestic and rural museum focusing on women's stories; open Wed, Sat–Sun; Wagga Rd; (02) 6948 2635; 8km NW. **Tooma:** historic town with old hotel (c. 1880); 34km SE. **Wineries:** several with cellar doors.

TUMUT
Population 6518

Tumut (pronounced 'Tyoomut') is in a fertile valley, surrounded by spectacular mountain scenery. Tumut was the seasonal meeting place for the Ngunawal, Walgalu and Wiradjuri Peoples. Each summer they would journey to the mountains where bogong moths were a prized delicacy. Poplar and willow trees planted by early settlers make summer and autumn particularly striking. The Tumut area is popular for fly fishing, hiking and mountain biking.

SEE & DO **Blowering Dam:** see Other Attractions. **Old Butter Factory Tourist Complex:** visitor centre, souvenirs, books and craft; Snowy Mountains Hwy; (02) 6947 7025. **Millet Broom Factory:** visitors can see Australia's last original millet broom factory in action; open Mon–Fri; Snowy Mountains Hwy; (02) 6947 2804. **Art Society Inc. Art Gallery and Studio:** specialises in work by local artists; open Thurs–Mon 10am–3pm; cnr Tumut Plains Rd and Snowy Mountains Hwy; (02) 6947 6785. **Museum:** large collection of farm and domestic items and an excellent display of Miles Franklin memorabilia (the author was born in nearby Talbingo); ask at visitor centre for opening times; cnr Capper and Merrivale sts; (02) 6947 9899. **River walk:** along Tumut River; from Elm Dr. **Historic and tree-identifying walks:** include Alex Stockwell Memorial Gardens with European trees and a World War I memorial. **Air Escape:** powered hang-gliding; airport, off Snowy Mountains Hwy; 0418 278 012; 6km E. **Tumut Valley Violets:** largest African violet farm in Australia with more than 1000 varieties; Tumut Plains Rd; (02) 6947 2432; 7km S. **Talbingo Dam and Reservoir:** Snowy Mountains Scheme dam in steep, wooded country; 40km S. **Tumut 3 Power Station:** this power station and six huge pipelines can be seen from the carpark; 45km S.

Riverina and Murray

The Murray, Murrumbidgee and other mighty rivers that flow across the south-west of NSW are the lifeblood of the region – **Australia's food bowl** – watering crops, vineyards and orchards, providing recreation, and much needed drinking supplies. In the past, these rivers were also transport corridors, and many of the towns boast **gracious streetscapes** and **impressive architecture** that belie their modern-day size. You might be a long way from the ocean, but many of these inland towns have **beautiful sandy beaches** and the fishing is fabulous.

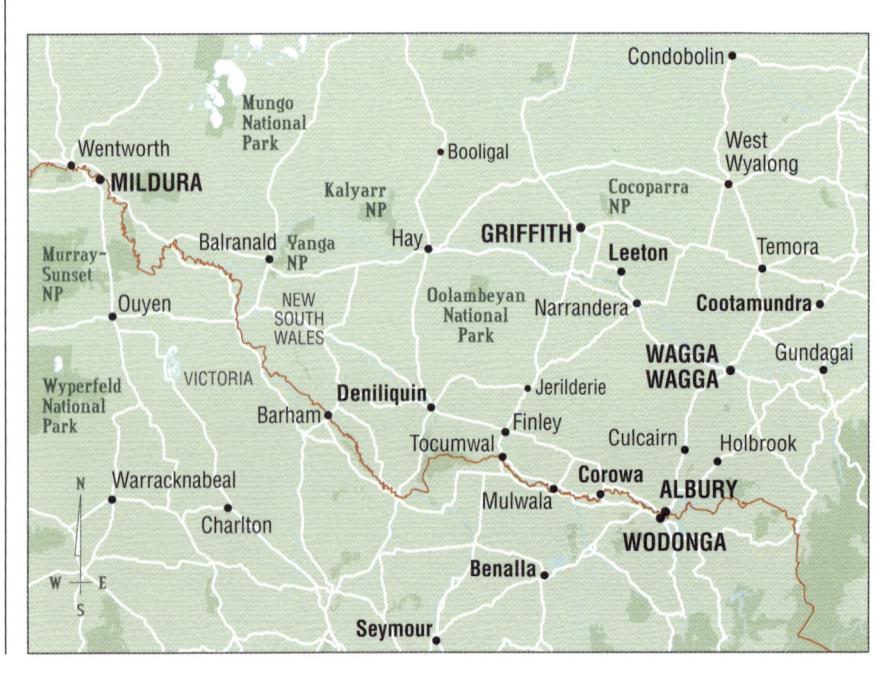

CHEAT SHEET

→ Allow at least three or four days for a proper exploration.

→ Best time to visit: year-round depending on your adventure activity of choice.

→ Main towns: Albury (see p. 100), Griffith (see p. 102), Hay (see p. 102), Wagga Wagga (see p. 105).

→ The Murray and Riverina is the Traditional Lands of the Baraba Baraba, Barindjii, Kureinji, Madi Madi, Nari Nari, Wadi Wadi, Waveroo, Wemba Wemba, Wiradjuri, Yitha Yitha and Yorta Yorta. World Heritage-listed Willandra Lakes, in Mungo National Park, is home to the oldest human remains ever found.

→ Don't miss: Bonegilla Migrant Experience; MAMA; National Art Glass Collection in Wagga; cooling off at river beaches; Mungo National Park; the Dog on the Tuckerbox at Gundagai; the beached submarine at Holbrook.

Top: Farmland near Gundagai **Opposite:** Mungo National Park

TOP ATTRACTIONS

LAKE MULWALA: This artificial lake was formed by the 1939 damming of the Murray River at Yarrawonga Weir and is now home to myriad birdlife. The eastern end has river red gums up to 600 years old. The lake is popular for yachting, sailboarding, canoeing, swimming and fishing (especially for Murray cod). The Mulwala Water Ski Club is one of the largest in the world with 6000 members; it offers lessons and equipment hire for skiing, wakeboarding and tube rides. Day and evening cruises can be booked at the visitor centre in Mulwala (see p. 104).

MUNGO NATIONAL PARK: The Traditional Owners of this remarkable area are the Mutthi Mutthi, Paakantyi and Ngyiampaa People. The dry lakes of the Willandra Lakes World Heritage Area display astounding evidence of the last Ice Age, including Mungo Man, a full male skeleton estimated to be around 40,000 years old. The highlight of the park is the 33km crescent-shaped dune on the eastern edge of Lake Mungo, called the Walls of China, which you can visit on a 70km self-guided drive through the park. There is also the 10km Zanci Pastoral Loop, which you can drive or cycle, starting from the Mungo Visitor Centre and finishing at the site of the old Zanci homestead. The visitor centre delves into the heritage of the Willandra Lakes, and has a replica of the diprotodon, a massive wombat-like marsupial; Arumpo Rd; (03) 5021 8900 or 1300 361 967. Accommodation in the park includes the old Mungo Shearers' Quarters and a campground.

MUSEUM OF THE RIVERINA: The museum is divided into two locations in Wagga Wagga (see p. 105), one at the historic Council Chambers (Baylis St) and the other at the Botanic Gardens (Lord Baden Powell Dr). The chambers museum has a regular program of travelling exhibitions; inquiries on (02) 6926 9655. The museum at the botanic gardens focuses on the people, places and events that have been important to Wagga Wagga and incorporates the Sporting Hall of Fame, which features local stars such as former Australian cricket captain Mark Taylor. Both sites open Tues–Sat 10am–4pm, Sun 10am–2pm.

OLD WENTWORTH GAOL: The first Australian-designed gaol by colonial architect James Barnett. The bricks were made onsite from local clay, and bluestone was transported from Victoria. Construction took from 1879 to 1891. Closed as a gaol in 1927, the building is in remarkably good condition. Beverley St, Wentworth; (03) 5027 3337.

OTWAY SUBMARINE: The inland town of Holbrook (see p. 103) boasts a 30m submarine, once under the command of Norman Holbrook but decommissioned in 1995. The town was given the fin of the submarine by the Royal Australian Navy, and was busily trying to raise funds to purchase the full piece of history, when a gift of $100,000 from Commander Holbrook's widow made the purchase possible. Mrs Holbrook was the guest of honour at the unveiling in 1996. The Submarine Museum next door features submariner memorabilia, including a control room with working periscope, and Commander Holbrook Room. Hume Hwy, Holbrook.

RIVERINA FOOD AND WINE REGION: The Riverina is one of the most diverse and productive agricultural regions in the country and can lay claim to being the 'food bowl' of Australia. Numerous wineries, gourmet food producers and fine restaurants can be visited – contact the Wagga Wagga visitor centre for details.

RURAL MUSEUM: This award-winning museum in Temora (see p. 104) has some seriously impressive displays on rural life, including Don Bradman's first home, a hardwood slab cottage (which has been moved to the grounds from Cootamundra), Willo's Wiradjuri Keeping Place, one-room public school, bush church, country dance hall, shearing shed, printing works, flour mill and historic machinery on display. There is also an impressive rock and mineral collection with an emphasis on the local gold industry. Junee Rd, Temora; (02) 6977 5923.

THE DOG ON THE TUCKERBOX: Originally mentioned in the poem 'Bill the Bullocky' by Bowyang Yorke, this monument to pioneer teamsters and their dogs is recognised throughout the nation as an Australian icon. It was celebrated in the song 'Where the Dog Sits on the Tuckerbox' by Jack O'Hagan (the songwriter responsible for 'Along the Road to Gundagai'). The dog was unveiled in 1932 by Prime Minister Joseph Lyons. The statue is 8km north of Gundagai (see p. 102).

WAGGA WAGGA ART GALLERY: Offers an extensive and changing exhibition program, as well as Australia's largest collection of studio glass in the **National Art Glass Gallery**; open Tues–Sat 10am–4pm, Sun 10am–2pm; cnr Baylis and Morrow sts, Wagga; (02) 6926 9660.

OTHER ATTRACTIONS

AVIATION MUSEUM: This museum in Temora (see p. 104) claims to be the world's finest collection of flying historic aircraft. The museum is home to the country's only two flying Spitfires, the oldest Tiger Moth still flying in Australia, a World War II Hudson, the only flying Gloster Meteor F8 in the world and many more. The museum holds regular flying weekends throughout the year; Tom Moon Ave, Temora; (02) 6977 1088.

BOOLIGAL: Located in an area known as the 'devil's claypan', this hot and dusty sheep and cattle town is mentioned in Banjo Paterson's poem 'Hay and Hell and Booligal'. The poem says that a visit to Booligal is a fate worse than hell; topics of complaint include heat, flies, dust, rabbits, mosquitoes and snakes. Booligal is still off the beaten tourist track but has a relaxed and friendly atmosphere and there is an interesting memorial to John Oxley, the first European to explore the area, in the shape of a giant theodolite (surveyor's tool). Halfway from Hay to Booligal, look out for the lonely ruins of One Tree Hotel.

BRADMAN'S BIRTHPLACE: A restored cottage in Cootamundra (see p. 100) where 'the greatest batsman the world has ever known', Donald Bradman, was born. Contains memorabilia from cricket and his life in the Cootamundra district; Adams St, Cootamundra.

COCOPARRA NATIONAL PARK: Original Riverina forest full of wattles, orchids and ironbarks, the park is spectacular in spring, when the wildflowers bloom. It's ideal for bushwalking, camping, birdwatching and picnicking, and the rugged terrain and vivid colours also make it popular with photographers. The park is 25km north-east of Griffith (see p. 102).

DUNERA MUSEUM: Housed in Hay's magnificent restored railway station, the centre documents the World War II internment in Hay of over 3000 prisoners of war. The first internees, known as the 'Dunera boys', were Jewish intellectuals who had fled Germany and Austria. The camp established a garrison band and a newspaper, and printed camp money. The Dunera boys even ran their own 'university', teaching subjects such as atomic research and classical Greek. Hay Railway Station, 421 Murray St, Hay; (02) 6993 4045.

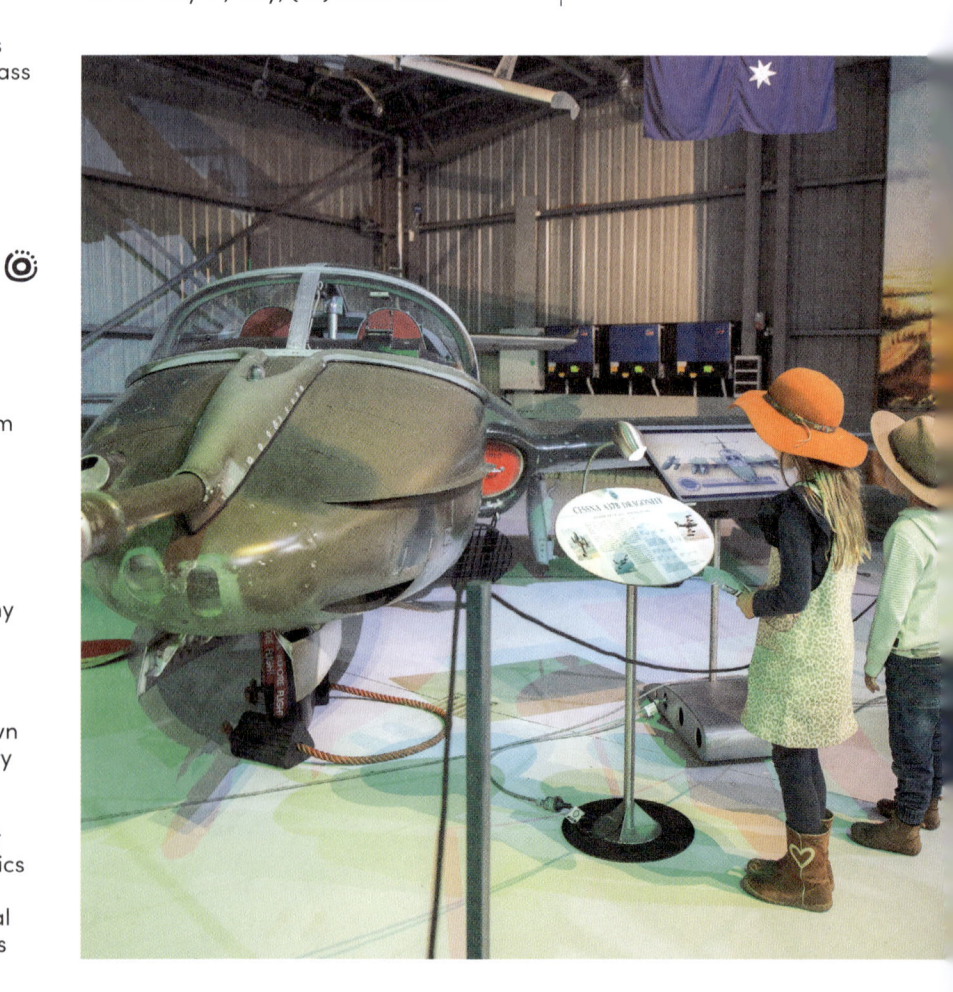

FEDERATION MUSEUM: This museum focuses on the reasons behind Federation and the town of Corowa's (see p. 101) involvement in it. Also on display are local First Nations artefacts, Tommy McRae sketches, horse-drawn vehicles and saddlery, and antique agricultural implements; Queen St, Corowa.

HERMITS CAVE AND SIR DUDLEY DE CHAIR'S LOOKOUT: Hermits Cave is located in Griffith (see p. 102) down a path below the lookout. The cave is named because it was home to Valerio Ricetti, an Italian miner from Broken Hill, from 1929 to 1940. After being jilted, he left his home and job and became a hermit in this cave, landscaping the area around it. After many years of solitude he fell and broke his leg, and when he was hospitalised he was recognised by people who had known him in Broken Hill. In later years he became ill and local citizens collected money to send him back home to Italy, where he died three months after arriving. Scenic Dr, Griffith.

KOONDROOK STATE FOREST: This 31,000ha native bushland forest is perfect for birdwatchers and nature enthusiasts with over 100 bird species, also kangaroos, emus and wild pigs. Forest drives through the park are well signposted. You can access it 12km north-east of Barham (see p. 100).

MARBLE MASTERPIECE: In an amazing display of patience and determination, local Gundagai sculptor Frank Rusconi, who was also responsible for the Dog on the Tuckerbox statue, worked to create a cathedral in miniature. He built it in his spare time over 28 years, hand-turning and polishing the 20,948 individual pieces required to build it. Visitor centre, Sheridan St, Gundagai; (02) 6944 0250.

MURRAY ART MUSEUM ALBURY (MAMA): This museum in Albury (see p. 100) has an extensive permanent collection and touring exhibitions; Dean St, Albury; (02) 6043 5800.

PEPPIN HERITAGE CENTRE: This museum in Deniliquin (see p. 101) is dedicated to George Hall Peppin and his sons' development of the merino sheep industry. Dissatisfied with the quality and yield of the wool from merino sheep, they developed a new breed, the peppin, that was better adapted to the harsh Australian conditions. Peppin sheep now predominate among flocks in New Zealand, South Africa and South America. The museum is housed in the National Trust–classified Old George Street Public School (1879), which still has an intact classroom on display. George St, Deniliquin.

PERRY SANDHILLS: These magnificent orange dunes are estimated to have originated during the last Ice Age, around 40,000 years ago. Skeletal remains of megafauna (kangaroos, wombats, emus and lions) have been found here. In World War II the area was used as a bombing range, but recently it has been used in film and television. Sand-board hire available; 0437 060 637. Off Silver City Hwy. The sandhills are 5km north-west of Wentworth (see p. 105).

PIONEER PARK MUSEUM: The 11ha of bushland in Griffith (see p. 102) features 40 replica and restored buildings, early 20th-century memorabilia and re-created Bagtown Village. It includes the **Italian Museum** with exhibits on the lives of the early Italian immigrants to Griffith and collections of memorabilia and stories from local families; Remembrance Dr, Griffith.

SHEAR OUTBACK: Located in the town of Hay (see p. 102), this centre includes interactive experiences and shearing demonstrations with sheepdogs, the historic Murray Downs Woolshed and exhibitions; Sturt Hwy, Hay; (02) 6993 4000.

TOCUMWAL BLOWHOLE AND THE ROCKS: This area is sacred to the Ulupna and Bangaragn People, who named it Tocumwal meaning 'deep hole'. The Rocks change colour according to weather conditions, and the Blowhole is 25m deep. Adjacent to it is a working granite quarry. Rocks Rd. The blowhole is 8.5km of north-east of Tocumwal (see p. 104).

Top: Calabria Family Wines in Griffith **Opposite:** Aviation Museum at Temora

NEW SOUTH WALES

99

KEY TOWNS

ALBURY
Population 56,093

Situated alongside the Murray River in the foothills of the Great Dividing Range, Albury has a long and varied story. Home to the Wiradjuri People, the town site was 'discovered' in 1824 by explorers Hume and Hovell, who carved their comments into the trunks of two trees. Hovell's tree still stands in Hovell Tree Park. Originally the border town between Victoria and NSW, Albury was the centre of postwar immigration to Australia. Today it is a key border town with its sister town in Victoria, Wodonga (*see* p. 199). It has a vibrant community and all the shops and services you'd expect from a regional centre.

SEE & DO **Murray Art Museum Albury (MAMA):** see Other Attractions. **Library Museum:** exhibits include a display on one of Australia's largest postwar immigrant centres, which was at nearby Bonegilla. Cnr Kiewa and Swift sts; (02) 6023 8333. **Botanic Gardens:** array of native and exotic plants, signposted rainforest and heritage walks, children's garden; cnr Wodonga Pl and Dean St. **Riverside parklands:** Hovell Tree, Noreuil and Australia parks offer walks, swimming and picnic areas; Wodonga Pl. **Monument Hill:** site of the city's war memorial, with fine views of the CBD; Memorial Dr. **Wonga Wetlands:** rehabilitated wetlands along the Murray River, home to the black cormorant, short walking trails and bird hides; Riverina Hwy; (02) 6043 5820. **Wagirra Trail and Yindyamarra Sculpture Walk:** scenic walking trail along the Murray River featuring numerous sculptures. **Farmers' market:** Hovell Tree Park and Lincoln Causeway; Sat. **Rotary Community Market:** Wilson St carpark; Sun. **Lake Hume:** watersports, camping and spectacular dam wall; 14km E. **Jindera Pioneer Museum:** originally a German settlement featuring a general store, a slab hut and a wattle-and-daub cottage; 14km NW.

BALRANALD
Population 1063

Situated on saltbush and mallee plains this old paddlesteamer port on the Murrumbidgee River is a classic example of a frontier heritage town. A popular spot with anglers, the Murray, Wakool, Edward and Lachlan rivers are all within easy reach.

SEE & DO **Heritage Park:** investigate the old gaol, the Murray pine schoolhouse, local history displays and a historical museum. There are also picnic and barbecue facilities. Market St. **Art gallery:** exhibitions by local artists, housed in 1880s Masonic Lodge; Mayall St. **Weir:** barbecues, picnic tables, fishing. **Memorial Drive:** great views. **Frog sculptures:** there are 14 throughout town celebrating the large numbers of the endangered Southern Bell Frog that live in and around the town; you'll hear plenty of frog song after dark between October and March. **Self-guided town walk:** historically significant buildings in the town; maps available from visitor centre. **Moulamein:** the oldest town in the Riverina, Moulamein has fascinating historic structures to explore, including its restored courthouse (1845) and Old Wharf (1850s). There are picnic areas by the Edward River and Lake Moulamein. 99km SE. **Yanga National Park:** historic homestead and woolshed, fishing and watersports; 7km SE. **Homebush Hotel:** built in 1878 as a Cobb & Co. station, the hotel now provides meals and accommodation; (03) 5020 6803; 25km N. **Kyalite:** home to Australia's largest commercial pistachio nut farm and popular with campers and anglers; 36km S. **Redbank Weir:** barbecues and picnics; Homebush–Oxley Rd; 58km N.

BARHAM
Population 1569

Connected by an industrial bridge across the Murray River, Barham and its Victorian twin town, Koondrook, are true river towns and are great for anglers, with Murray cod, golden perch, catfish and yabbies in abundance. Barham is known as the southern gateway to Golden Rivers country and is surrounded by river flats and red hills.

SEE & DO **Koondrook State Forest:** *see* Other Attractions. **Lakes Complex:** the complex is popular with locals and visitors alike. It has four artificial lakes stocked with fish and yabbies, grasslands with hundreds of native plants, a walking track and barbecue facilities. Murray St. **Koondrook:** old sawmilling town and river port with historic buildings and tramway; 5km SW. **Murrabit:** largest country markets in the region; 1st Sat each month; Murrabit Rd; 24km NW.

COOTAMUNDRA
Population 5732

Famously the birthplace of cricketing legend Sir Donald Bradman, Cootamundra has a museum in the Don's honour in his childhood home. The town itself is a prosperous rural centre on the railway line between Sydney and Melbourne. The glorious Cootamundra wattle (*Acacia baileyana*) blooms in the area every July and Aug and the town celebrates with a wattle festival.

SEE & DO **Bradman's birthplace:** *see* Other Attractions. **Pioneer Park:** there's a 1.3km walking trail in this natural bushland reserve on the northern outskirts of town that leads to the top of Mount Slippery; it's worth hiking up for the panoramic views. Make sure to bring a

VISITOR INFORMATION

Albury Visitor Information Centre
Railway Pl, cnr Smollett and Young sts
1300 252 879
visitalburywodonga.com

Hay Visitor Information Centre
407 Moppett St
(02) 6993 4045
visithay.com.au

Wagga Wagga Visitor Information Centre
183 Tarcutta St
(02) 6926 9621 or
1300 100 122
visitwagga.com

The Murray
visitthemurray.com.au

Opposite top: Corowa Whiskey & Chocolate **Opposite bottom:** Victory Memorial Garden in Wagga Wagga

picnic, as there are excellent picnic sites. Backbrawlin St. **Arts Centre:** community arts space with exhibitions, workshops, art sales and a theatre; Wallendoon St. **Captains Walk:** bronze sculptures of Australia's past cricket captains; Jubilee Park, Wallendoon St. **Heritage Centre:** local memorabilia including an Olympic cauldron and war relics; railway station, Hovell St. **Self-guided 'Two Foot Tour':** includes Sir Donald Bradman's birthplace and the town's historic buildings; brochure from visitor centre. **Local craft:** at visitor centre and at Art and Craft Centre; Hovell St. **Markets:** Wallendbeen, 1st Sun each month. **Murrumburrah:** This small rural community has the Harden-Murrumburrah Historical Museum, which is open Sat–Sun and features historic artefacts, including kitchenwares, and an old chemist shop exhibit. Also in town are local craft shops and some outstanding picnic spots; 35km NE. **Migurra Reserve:** bushland walking trail with birdwatching and 5 species of wattles; 15km SW. **The Milestones:** cast-concrete sculptures representing the importance of wheat to the area; 19km NE. **Bethungra:** dam ideal for canoeing and sailing. The rail spiral is an unusual engineering feat; 23km SW. **Cellar doors:** in the Harden area; winery brochure from visitor centre.

COROWA
Population 5595

Corowa has been known for its goldmining, winemaking and timber milling, and as the 'birthplace of Federation'. Traders in the 19th century had to pay taxes in both NSW and Victoria when taking goods over the border, which caused much agitation. It was argued that free trade would benefit everyone and the Border Federation League was formed in Corowa, which led to the 1893 Corowa Federation Conference. In 1895 the proposals put forth at the conference were acted upon and on 1 January 1901 the Commonwealth of Australia was born. In 1889 Tom Roberts completed his iconic painting *Shearing the Rams* at a sheep station near the town.

SEE & DO **Federation Museum:** see Other Attractions. **Self-guided historical town walk:** includes Sanger St, Corowa's historic main street, with its century-old buildings; guide available for groups; brochure from visitor centre. **Corowa Whisky and Chocolate:** old mill where you can make your own chocolate freckle, there's also a shop and cafe; Steel St; (02) 6033 1311. **Art Space:** permanent collection and exhibitions; 100 Edward St. **Market:** Bangerang Park; 1st Sun each month (except Feb). **Savernake Station:** offers eco-heritage tours of its 400ha woodland, including 120 bird species, woodshed and shearers' quarters (1912), cooks' museum (1930) and store; inquiries (02) 6035 9415; 50km NW.

CULCAIRN
Population 1112

This lush town with National Trust-classified buildings, located between Albury and Wagga Wagga, was not always so peaceful; it was terrorised by the bushranger Dan 'Mad Dog' Morgan between 1862 and 1865. He made his hideout at some granite outcrops near town, and you can climb to the top for a panoramic view of the surrounding countryside.

SEE & DO **Station House:** beautifully restored museum (1883) reflects the importance of the railway; just across railway line. **Billabong Creek:** good fishing, one of the longest creeks in the Southern Hemisphere. **National Trust-classified buildings:** these include historic Culcairn Hotel (1891), still operating; Railway Pde and Olympic Way. **Henty:** This historic pastoral town has the Headlie Taylor Header Memorial, a tribute to the mechanical header harvester that revolutionised the grain industry. The nearby Sergeant Smith Memorial Stone marks the spot where Morgan fatally wounded a police officer, and the adjacent Doodle Cooma Swamp is 2000ha of breeding area for waterbirds. 24km N. **John McLean's grave:** McLean was shot by Mad Dog Morgan; 3km E. **Round Hill Station:** where Morgan committed his first hold-up in the area; Holbrook Rd; 15km E. **Walla Walla:** old schoolhouse (1875) and the largest Lutheran church in NSW (1924); 18km SW. **Morgan's Lookout:** granite outcrop on otherwise flat land, allegedly used by Morgan to look for approaching victims and police; 18km NW.

DENILIQUIN
Population 6431

Deniliquin is most famous for being the 'ute capital of the world', and it has the Guinness World Record for the most utes gathered in one place; every year at the Deni Ute Muster in October the town attempts to break its own record. The town lies on the Edward River, a tributary of the Murray River, and has some excellent river beaches and kayaking spots as well as offering excellent fishing, waterskiing and wakeboarding areas. The town is surrounded by sheep and cattle farms, and also has a thriving rice industry, courtesy of the area's irrigation system.

SEE & DO **Peppin Heritage Centre:** see Other Attractions. **Historical Society Museum:** has local history displays in the former Police Inspector's Residence on Macauley St; Tues and Sat 10am–2pm. **Island Sanctuary:** see kangaroos and birdlife, and the burial site of 'Old Jack', a member of the Melville gang – bushrangers who were in Deniliquin in 1851; off Cressy St footbridge. **Ute on a Pole:** confirms Deniliquin's status as 'ute capital of the world'; near National Bridge. **Waring Gardens:** originally a chain of lagoons; Cressy St. **Long Paddock River Walk:** old stock route, includes interpretive panels; from Heritage Centre to Island Sanctuary. **Self-guided walks:** historical and nature walks taking in National Trust–classified buildings and town gardens; brochure from visitor centre. **Farmers' market:** George St; 2nd Sat each month. **Irrigation works:** at Lawsons Syphon (7km E) and Stevens Weir (25km W). **Bird Observatory Tower:** excellent vantage point for birdwatching; Mathoura; 34km S.

FINLEY
Population 1864

This Riverina town, on the Newell Highway and close to the Victorian border, is a tidy and peaceful spot. It is the centre of the Berriquin Irrigation Area. The main street spans Mulwala Canal, which is the largest irrigation channel in Australia.

SEE & DO **Mary Lawson Wayside Rest:** features a log cabin that is an authentic replica of a pioneer home. It houses the Finley and District Historical Museum with displays of antique pumping equipment and machinery. Newell Hwy. **Finley Lake:** popular boating, sailboarding and picnic area; Newell Hwy. **Livestock Exchange:** experience a cattle sale; Fri mornings. **Berrigan:** charming historic town known for its connections to horseracing; 22km E.

GRIFFITH
Population 20,799

Like Canberra, Griffith was designed by Walter Burley Griffin and is similarly graceful and leafy. Another one of NSW's sites described by early explorers as uninhabitable, the town is now a veritable food and wine bowl, producing everything from oranges to rice – all enabled by the Murrumbidgee Irrigation Scheme, as well as the farming success of early Italian immigrants. Griffith has a significant Italian heritage – it even had one of the first pizzerias in Australia!

SEE & DO **Cocoparra National Park; Hermits Cave and Sir Dudley De Chair's Lookout; Pioneer Park Museum:** see Other Attractions for all. **Regional Art Gallery:** exhibition program of international and Australian artists that changes monthly; Banna Ave. **City Park:** features an extensive playground with one of the largest rope-climbing structures in the country, water play area and flying fox as well as an edible garden called the Food Forest. **Market:** Griffith showground; each Sun morning. **Altina Wildlife Park:** range of exotic and native wildlife, on the banks of the Murrumbidgee River, horserides and cart rides; tours and entry by appointment only 0412 060 342; 35km S. **Catania Fruit Salad Farm:** horticultural farm with tours at 1.30pm Mon–Sun; Cox Rd, Hanwood; (02) 6963 0219; 8km S. **Lake Wyangan:** good spot for variety of watersports and picnicking; 10km NW. **Wineries:** several wineries in the Riverina district, including **McWilliams** and **De Bortoli** (De Bortoli's Noble One, a golden botrytis dessert wine, is world famous), are open for cellar-door tastings; map from visitor centre.

GUNDAGAI
Population 1970

The tiny town of Gundagai on the Murrumbidgee River at the foot of Mount Parnassus inspired Banjo Paterson, C.J. Dennis and Henry Lawson. The statue of the Dog on the Tuckerbox, just off the Hume Hwy, immortalises the story of the loyal dog guarding his master's tuckerbox. The story and the statue have themselves inspired songs and poems. The town was also the site in 1852 of Australia's worst flood disaster when 89 of the 250 townspeople died. The count could have been worse but for a local Aboriginal man, Yarri, who paddled his bark canoe throughout the night to rescue stranded victims. Gundagai was moved to higher ground soon after, and there are monuments celebrating Yarri's efforts. Today the town has a wine region and new boutique accommodation.

SEE & DO **The Dog on the Tuckerbox:** see Top Attractions. **Marble Masterpiece:** see Other Attractions. **Old Gundagai Gaol:** historic, well-preserved gaol dating from 1859; self-guided audio tours available (pick up player, headphones and key from visitor centre); cnr First Ave and Byron St; (02) 6944 0250. **Gabriel Photographic Gallery:** outstanding collection of photographs, letters and possessions illustrating Gundagai's unique history; Sheridan St; (02) 6944 1722. **Historical Museum:** relics include Phar Lap's saddle, Frank Rusconi's tools, and artefacts from the horse-and-buggy era; open 9am–3pm; Homer St; (02) 6944 1995. **Lookouts:** excellent views of the town and surrounding green valleys from the Mount Parnassus Lookout in Hanley St and the Rotary Lookout in Luke St; South Gundagai. **Historical town walk:** includes the National Trust–classified Prince Alfred Bridge and St John's Anglican Church; brochure from visitor centre.

HAY
Population 2208

Hay is located in the heart of the Riverina, and has incredible flat plains surrounding it. The saltbush flats afford amazing views across the land, especially at sunrise and sunset. In late 2022 the Murrumbidgee River flooded and the flat plains turned into what looked like a sea.

SEE & DO **Dunera Museum; Shear Outback:** see Other Attractions for both. **Witcombe Fountain:** ornate drinking fountain presented to the people of Hay by mayor John Witcombe in 1883; Lachlan St. **Coach House:** features an 1886 Cobb & Co. coach that travelled the Deniliquin–Hay–Wilcannia route until 1901; Lachlan St. **Gaol Museum:** contains memorabilia and photographs of the

TOP EVENTS

- → JAN Federation Festival (Corowa)
- → MAR Bidgee Classic Fishing Competition (Leeton); John O'Brien Bush Festival (Narrandera)
- → MAR-APR Gold Cup Racing Carnival (Albury), Food and Wine Festival (Wagga)
- → EASTER Deni Fest (Deniliquin); Sunrice Festival (even numbered years Leeton)
- → APR Booligal Sheep Races (near Hay)
- → AUG Wattle Time Fair (Cootamundra); National Cavy Show and Camellia Show (both Narrandera)
- → SEPT-OCT Ute Muster (Deniliquin)

TEMPERATURES

Jan: 17–33°C

July: 3–13°C

Opposite top: Waring Gardens in Deniliquin **Opposite bottom:** Captains Walk in Cootamundra

town, and displays about the building's history from 1878 as a gaol, maternity hospital, hospital for the insane and POW compound; Church St; (02) 6993 4045. **War Memorial High School Museum:** built in recognition of those who served in World War I, the museum displays war memorabilia and an honour roll. The building still operates as a school, so call for opening times; Pine St; (02) 6993 1408. **Water Tower Art:** moving tributes to five locals who served in World War II; Brunker and Pine sts. **Bishop's Lodge:** restored 1888 iron house, now a museum and gallery with a remarkable collection of heritage roses. Opening times vary, call before visiting; cnr Roset St and Sturt Hwy; (02) 6993 1727. **Hay Wetlands:** spectacular in spring, the wetlands, which include a breeding island and tree plantation, are a nesting ground for over 60 inland bird species; north-western edge of town; brochure from visitor centre. **Hay Park:** pleasant picnic spot with a nature walk along the banks of the river; off Brunker St. **Murrumbidgee River:** excellent sandy river beaches and calm water, perfect for waterskiing, canoeing, swimming and picnics. You can also enjoy excellent freshwater fishing for Murray cod, yellow-belly perch and redfin (licence required, available from outlets in town, including visitor centre). **Heritage walk and scenic drive:** walk includes city structures built for the harsh outback, such as the beautifully restored courthouse (1892) on Moppett St and the shire office (1877) on Lachlan St. The drive takes in the parklands, river and surrounding saltbush plains; brochure from visitor centre. **Weir:** on the Murrumbidgee River; excellent for picnics, barbecues and Murray cod fishing; 12km W. **Sunset viewing area:** the vast plains provide amazingly broad and spectacular sunsets; Booligal Rd; 16km N. **Maude Weir:** surprisingly green and lush oasis, ideal for picnics and barbecues; 53km W. **Goonawarra Nature Reserve:** there are no visitor facilities, but the floodplains, with their river red gum forests and black box woodlands, are still worth a visit – there are waterfowl in the billabongs, plenty of Murray cod in the Lachlan River and kangaroos and emus on the plains; 59km N. **Oxley:** tiny town with river red gums and prolific wildlife (best seen at dusk); 87km NW.

HOLBROOK
Population 1251

Holbrook is one of the many towns that the Hume Hwy now bypasses but it's worth a stop for the decommissioned submarine that sits in a park in the middle of town. The town cycled through multiple names in its early days, and made the change from Germanton to Holbrook in World War I. It was named after British Commander Norman Holbrook, a war hero who had been awarded the Victoria Cross and the French Legion of Honour – he was once captain of the town's submarine.

SEE & DO Otway Submarine: *see* Top Attractions. **Bronze statue:** Commander Holbrook and his submarine, a scale model of the one in which Holbrook won the VC in World War I; Holbrook Park, Hume Hwy. **Woolpack Inn Museum:** 22 rooms furnished in turn-of-the-century style, horse-drawn vehicles and farm equipment surrounded by lovely gardens; Albury St. **Ten Mile Creek Gardens:** attractive gardens, excellent for picnics. Also features a miniature railway, operating on the 2nd and 4th Sun each month, and every Sat during holidays; behind museum. **National Museum of Australian Pottery:** extensive range of 19th- and early 20th-century domestic pottery, and photographs; closed Wed and during Aug; Albury St. **Ian Geddes Walk:** through tranquil bushland, following Ten Mile Creek; begins behind Grimwood's Craft Shop; Hume Hwy. **Airfield:** ultralight flights over town and surrounds available; 3km N.

JERILDERIE
Population 922

Jerilderie is the location of one of the infamous Kelly Gang's crimes. In 1879 Jerilderie was attacked by the Kelly Gang, who captured the local policemen, held the townspeople hostage for two days, cut the telegraph wires and robbed the bank. This raid cemented Ned Kelly's legend, as he handed over the famous Jerilderie Letter, justifying his actions and voicing his disrespect for police, whom he called 'a parcel of big ugly fat-necked wombat-headed, big-bellied, magpie-legged, narrow-hipped, splay-footed sons of Irish bailiffs or English landlords'. You can even allegedly see the safe that Kelly robbed in town today. Now more known for being a merino stud region, the town is also the start of an 800km outback highway, the Kidman Way.

SEE & DO Luke Park: features Steel Wings, one of the largest windmills in the Southern Hemisphere. The park is situated on the bank of Lake Jerilderie, which is popular for all watersports, especially waterskiing. **Mini Heritage Steam Rail:** runs along charming Billabong Creek, which also features the 1.8km Horgans Walk; entry behind the old Willows Museum in Powell St; 2nd Sun each month. **Ned Kelly Heritage Trail:** retraces the gang's visit; brochure from visitor centre. **Coleambally:** officially opened in 1968, Coleambally is one of NSW's newest towns and is at the centre of the Coleambally Irrigation Area. It features the Wineglass Water Tower and a dragline excavator used in the irrigation scheme. The excavator is still in working order and can be viewed in the Lions Park at the town's entrance. The area is a haven for birdlife and kangaroos. 62km N.

LEETON
Population 7437

Like nearby Griffith, Leeton was designed in 1914 by Walter Burley Griffin, the American architect who designed Canberra in a similar graceful style. As this town is from a later era than many country towns, its historic buildings are more Art Deco than colonial – the Roxy Theatre, built in 1930, still shows films. Thanks to the Murrumbidgee Irrigation Area, the once dry plains are now fertile, and Leeton has 102ha of public parks and reserves and thriving primary industries.

SEE & DO **Visitor centre:** a beautifully restored building with photographic displays, local artwork and a heritage garden; Yanco Ave. **Museum and Gallery:** showcases the towns water story, as well as travelling art exhibitions; Mon–Sat 10am–3pm; Chelmsford Pl. **Mick's Bakehouse:** home of award-winning pies; Pine Ave. **Art Deco streetscape:** includes Roxy Theatre and historic Hydro Motor Inn. **Yanco:** this town is the site where Sir Samuel McCaughey developed the irrigation scheme that led to the establishment of the Murrumbidgee Irrigation Area. Attractions in town include McCaughey Park, the Powerhouse Museum and a miniature train that runs on market days. Village Markets are held at Yanco Hall on the last Sun each month. 8km S. **Fivebough Wetlands:** 400ha home to over 150 species of waterbird with interpretive centre, walking trails and viewing hides; 2km N. **Brobenah Airfield:** gliding and hot-air ballooning; 9km N. **McCaughey's Mansion:** 1899 mansion with stained-glass windows and attractive gardens, originally built to host a visit by the Prince of Wales it's now an agricultural high school, but drive-through inspections welcome. Yanco Agricultural Institute nearby is open to the public and provides farmer-training facilities, research and advisory services; 11km S. **Murrumbidgee State Forest:** scenic drives; brochure from visitor centre; 12km S. **Whitton Historical Museum:** housed in old courthouse and gaol with photographs, documents and early farming equipment; 23km W. **Gogeldrie Weir:** pleasant spot for fishing, picnics and camping; 23km SW. **Wineries:** cellar-door tastings and tours at **Toorak** and **Lillypilly Estate**; brochure at visitor centre.

Opposite: Griffith Pioneer Park Museum

MULWALA
Population 2557

Mulwala and Yarrawonga (in Victoria, *see* p. 189) are twin towns sitting astride the Murray River. Mulwala prides itself on being an 'inland aquatic paradise', with plenty of water-based activities for visitors to enjoy. It is surrounded by forests and vineyards.

SEE & DO **Lake Mulwala:** *see* Top Attractions. **Pioneer Museum:** historic farming exhibits, photographs and local artefacts; open Wed, Sat–Sun; Melbourne St. **Antique and op shops:** you're sure to find some unique gems; Benalla Rd, Meville St, Beek St. **Tunzafun Amusement Park:** minigolf, mini-train and dodgem cars; Melbourne St. **Savenake Station Woolshed:** 1930s-style woolshed in working order producing merino wool; open by appt; bookings (02) 6035 9415; 28km N.

NARRANDERA
Population 3783

This historic town on the Murrumbidgee River in the Riverina district is an urban conservation area with several National Trust–classified buildings. It has been home to two Australian writers: local magistrate Thomas Alexander Browne, who used the nom de plume Rolf Boldrewood to write early Australian novels such as *Robbery under Arms*, and Father Patrick Hartigan, parish priest of St Mel's Catholic Church, who was better known as the poet John O'Brien.

SEE & DO **Parkside Cottage Museum:** displays include the scarlet Macarthur Opera Cloak, made from the first bale of merino wool the Macarthur family sent to England in 1816, along with various other random and interesting displays, from a valuable collection of shells to a snow shoe and ski from Scott's Antarctic expedition; Thurs–Sat 10am–4pm; cnr Cadell and Twynam Sts; (02) 6959 1372. **Lake Talbot:** boating, waterskiing, fishing and canoeing. Also scenic walking trails around the lake; Lake Dr. **Lake Talbot Water Park:** water slides, swimming and barbecue facilities; aquatic facilities open Oct–Mar; Lake Dr. **Park and Tiger Moth Memorial:** beautiful park that houses the restored DN82 Tiger Moth commemorating the World War II pilots who trained in the district; Cadell St. **Two-foot town heritage tour:** sights include the Royal Mail Hotel (1868) and the former police station (c. 1870); brochure from the visitor centre. **Bundidgerry Walking Track:** track passes through the koala regeneration reserve; best viewing time is at dawn; brochure from visitor centre. **Blue Arrow scenic drive:** historic sites, cemetery and lake; brochure from visitor centre. **John Lake Centre:** fisheries visitor centre with live exhibits, audiovisual presentations and guided tours; open Mon–Fri; 6km SE. **Berembed Weir:** picnicking, fishing and boating; 40km SE.

TEMORA
Population 4016

In 1879 gold was discovered in the area and in 1880 the town site was chosen. By 1881 the Temora district was producing half of the state's gold. Of course this could not be maintained, and the population of around 20,000 dwindled quickly. What remains is a quiet rural Riverina town with several historic buildings. It is also a harness-racing centre with numerous studs in the district.

SEE & DO **Rural Museum:** *see* Top Attractions. **Aviation Museum:** *see* Other Attractions. **Heritage walk and drives:** include Edwardian and Federation buildings around town; brochure from visitor centre. **Lake Centenary:** boating, swimming and picnicking; 4km N. **Ingalba State Forest:** 10,000ha of state forest featuring flora and fauna native to the area; 10km W. **Ariah Park:** town known as 'Wowsers, Bowsers and Peppercorn Trees', with beautiful historic streetscape lined with peppercorn trees; 35km W.

TOCUMWAL
Population 2587

Life's a river beach at Tocumwal, on the northern bank of the Murray River, with 26 river beaches from which to swim, kayak or fish. There's also a giant Murray cod at a riverside park, so you can take a picture with a giant fish, whether you had luck throwing a line in or not. This popular holiday spot was not always so laidback – it was the location of the RAAF's largest training base in World War II.

SEE & DO **Blowhole and The Rocks:** *see* Other Attractions. **Foreshore Park:** peaceful green park shaded by tall gum trees and featuring a large fibreglass Murray cod; Deniliquin Rd. **Railway Heritage Museum:** railway memorabilia and photos; by appt; Deniliquin Rd; (03) 5874 3425. **Historic Aerodrome Museum:** displays cover the remarkable history of the local World War II aerodrome; Tocumwal Bowling Club, Adams St; (03) 5874 2253. **River cruises, walks, drives and bike tracks:** self-guided and guided tours of town and the river; brochures from visitor centre. **Art and craft shops:** several in town featuring local work; brochure from visitor centre. **Aerodrome:** the largest RAAF base in Australia during World War II, now home to Sport Aviation, which offers glider joy-flights and learn-to-glide packages; 5km NE. **Beaches:** there are 26 attractive river beaches in the vicinity, some with picnic areas; map from visitor centre. **Wineries:** there are several wineries in the area; brochure from visitor centre. **Farm gate trail:** itinerary takes in gourmet producers and wineries; brochure from visitor centre.

WAGGA WAGGA
Population 49,686

A cosmopolitan regional centre, Wagga Wagga, meaning 'dance and celebrations' in the Wiradjuri language, is the largest inland city in NSW and is regarded as the hub of the Riverina. In 1864 it received international attention when a man arrived claiming to be Roger Tichborne, a baronet who was believed drowned when his ship disappeared off South America. While Tichborne's mother believed him, the trustees of the estate were not so sure. What followed is believed to be the longest court case in England's history. The man was found to be Arthur Orton, a butcher. He was sentenced to 14 years for perjury. Mark Twain found this story so fascinating that he insisted on visiting Wagga Wagga when he toured Australia in the 1890s.

SEE & DO **Museum of the Riverina; Art Gallery:** *see* Top Attractions for both. **Botanic Gardens:** themed gardens, mini-zoo, free-flight aviary, picnic and barbecue facilities, miniature railway on 1st and 3rd Sun each month; Willans Hill; 1300 100 122. **Lake Albert:** watersports, fishing, bushwalking and birdwatching; Lake Albert Rd. **Charles Sturt University Winery:** offers cellar-door tastings of premium wines; McKeown Dr; (02) 6933 2435. **Rail Heritage Station Museum:** more than 500 artefacts relating to local rail history; open Mon–Sat 11am–2pm. **Bikeways:** along Lake Albert, Wollundry Lagoon, Flowerdale Lagoon and the Murrumbidgee River. **Producers' market:** Showground; Thurs afternoon. **RAAF Wagga Aviation Heritage Centre:** showcases Australia's air force history; open Sat–Thurs 10am–4pm; Sturt Hwy; (02) 6937 5403; 10km E. **Wollundry Grove Olives:** tour the grove and sample the fruits; Mary Gillmore Rd, Brucedale; 0429 201 773; 16km N. **Cottontails Winery:** tasting area and restaurant with views across Wagga; 562 Pattersons Road; (02) 6928 4554; 17km E. **Livingstone National Park:** excellent walking and birdwatching; (02) 6947 7025; 30km S. **The Rock:** a small town noted for its unusual scenery; walking trails through local reserve lead to the summit of the Rock; 32km SW. **Lockhart:** historic town with National Trust–listed Green St featuring an impressive turn-of-the-century streetscape; also several pleasant walking tracks in the area, and picnic races in Oct; 65km W. **Junee:** this important railhead and commercial centre is located on Olympic Way. It has several historic buildings and museums: Monte Cristo Homestead is a restored colonial mansion reputed to be the most haunted house in Australia; and the Roundhouse Museum in Harold St contains an original workshop, locomotives, a model train and memorabilia. Another highlight is Junee Licorice and Chocolate Factory in the old Junee flour mill; 45–61 Lord St; (02) 6924 3574. The Junee visitor centre is located on 84 Broadway St; (02) 6924 3246; 41km NE.

WENTWORTH
Population 1305

Situated at the confluence of the Murray and Darling rivers, Wentworth was once a busy inland port characterised by paddlesteamers streaming in and out of town. The railway ended Wentworth's port days, and it's now a holiday town with charming historic buildings and access to NSW's outback – the photogenic Perry Sandhills are just out of town.

SEE & DO **Old Wentworth Gaol:** *see* Top Attractions. **Perry Sandhills:** *see* Other Attractions. **Pioneer Museum:** over 3000 historic artefacts including space junk, prehistoric animals and the country's largest collection of paddleboat photos; Beverley St; (03) 5027 3160. **Fotherby Park:** *PS Ruby*, a historic paddlesteamer (1907), and statue of 'The Possum', a man who became a hermit during the Depression and lived in trees for 50 years; Wentworth St. **Junction Park:** viewing platform at confluence of Murray and Darling rivers; playground; Cadell St. **Riverboat Rod's Model Paddle Steamer Display:** 30 handcrafted paddlesteamer replicas; Darling St. **Lock 10:** weir and park for picnics; south-west edge of town. **Historical town walk:** self-guided walk includes the town courthouse (1870s) and Customs House (one of two original customs houses still standing in Australia); brochure from visitor centre. **Australian Inland Botanic Gardens:** the desert blooms with some exotic and colourful plant life. Tractor/train tours of the gardens available; (03) 5023 3612; 28km SE. **Pooncarie:** 'outback oasis' with natural two-tier wharf, weir and riverside campground; 117km N. **Heritage and nature driving tours:** various sites include Mildura and Lake Victoria; brochure from visitor centre. **Houseboat hire:** short- or long-term river holidays; brochure from visitor centre.

WEST WYALONG
Population 2698

John Oxley was the first European explorer to visit West Wyalong. He disliked the region, claiming 'these desolate areas would never again be visited by civilised man'. He was proved wrong when squatters moved in, and the discovery of gold in 1893 meant the town became inundated with settlers. West Wyalong is now in one of the state's most productive agricultural regions.

SEE & DO **Bland District Historical Museum:** displays of goldmining including a scale model of a goldmine and records from mines such as the Black Snake, the Blue Jacket and the Shamrock and Thistle; Neeld St. **Art Trail:** self-guided trail visiting a number of outdoor art sites, monuments, murals and sculptures; map available from visitor centre. **Lake Cowal:** when it is full, this is the largest natural lake in NSW, and a bird and wildlife sanctuary. There are over 180 species of waterbird living in the area, many of which are rare or endangered. The lake is also excellent for fishing. No visitor facilities are provided. Via Clear Ridge; 48km NE. **Ungarie:** home of Australia's biggest football, weighing more than 800 kg and mounted on a five-metre-high pedestal, in honour of famous footballing family the Danihers; 41km NW. **Barmedman:** mineral-salt pool believed to help arthritis and rheumatism; 32km SE. **Weethalle Whistlestop:** Devonshire teas, art and craft, with impressive silo art just down the road; Hay Rd; 65km W.

Outback

The big sky plains of western NSW are a great introduction to the outback. You don't need a 4WD as the main roads are sealed, and it feels much more remote than it really is. Follow the twist and turns of the **Darling River**, marvel at **ancient rock-art sites**, visit modern **outback art studios** in Broken Hill, go **underground** in White Cliffs, unearth exquisite black **opals** in Lightning Ridge and spend time in **legendary frontier towns** like Bourke and Tibooburra.

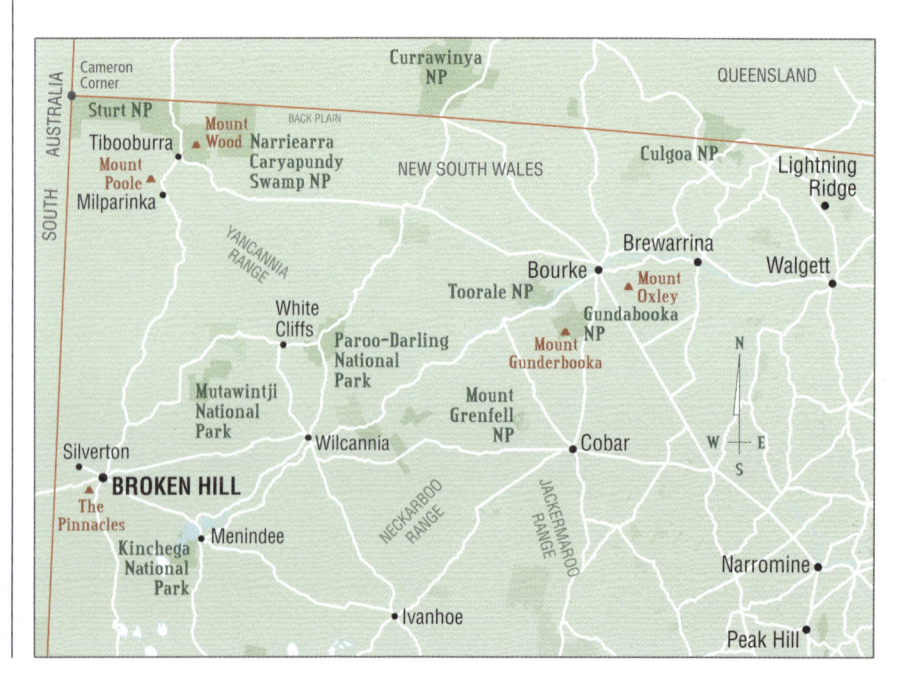

CHEAT SHEET

- Allow at least a week to 10 days for a proper exploration.
- Best time to visit: during the cooler winter months – avoid the hot summer months if you can, when the flies can be annoying.
- Main towns: Bourke (*see* p. 109), Broken Hill (*see* p. 109), Cobar (*see* p. 110).
- The Bandjigali, Barindji, Barkindji, Barranbinya, Danggali, Gunu, Kamilaroi, Karenggapa, Ngemba, Wailwan, Wandjiwalgu, Wiljali and Wongaibon are the Traditional Owners of the NSW outback region. Mount Grenfell and Gundabooka National Park are both home to some of the most significant rock-art sites in western NSW. The fish traps at Brewarrina are thought to be more than 40,000 years old.
- Don't miss: art galleries and outdoor sculptures at Broken Hill; a drink at the famous Silverton Pub; fossicking for opals in Lightning Ridge; and sleeping underground in White Cliffs.

Top: Broken Hill has many tourist attractions
Opposite: Mount Oxley near the town of Bourke

TOP ATTRACTIONS

BREWARRINA FISH TRAPS: The traditional story states that these traps were created by Baiame and his two sons, Booma-ooma-nowi and Ghinda-inda-mui. Gurrungga was created when Baiame threw his net over the river and his two sons built the shape of the net. The Ngemba People of Brewarrina know them as 'Baiame's Ngunnhu'. Anthropologists claim the traps are impressive evidence of early engineering, river hydrology and knowledge of fish biology. Around 500m long, these traps relied on the currents to sweep the fish inside, where they would be confined when the water level dropped. Thousands of years ago, the traps formed the centrepiece of a seasonal festival, regularly attended by up to 50,000 people from Aboriginal groups along the east coast. At night corroborees and shared stories were held around campfires in a language common to the region. The traps preserve the memory of these ancient times. Guided tours are available from the visitor centre.

CAMERON CORNER: Where Queensland, NSW and SA meet. The Dog Fence, the longest fence in the world, runs through here from Jimbour in Queensland to the Great Australian Bight in SA. It's 133km north-west of Tibooburra.

GUNDABOOKA NATIONAL PARK: This park 74km south-west of the town of Bourke (*see* p. 109) is a woodland haven for wildlife. There are more than 130 species of birds, including the endangered pink cockatoo, pied honeyeater and painted honeyeater. Kangaroos, wallaroos and endangered bats also make their homes here. Mount Gundabooka offers great walking tracks and a spectacular lookout. The Ngemba and Paakintji Peoples have a history of ceremonial gatherings in the area and rock art can be seen at the Mulgowan Heritage Site. The park also provides camping and barbecue facilities; contact Bourke NPWS (02) 6830 0200. Take a driving tour of nearby **Toorale National Park** and State Conservation Area, which has cultural significance to the Kurnu-Baakandji People. It also has a rich pastoral history.

KINCHEGA NATIONAL PARK: The Paakantji People are the Traditional Owners and used fish traps and speared fish from canoes. The park contains shell midden sites dating back over 35,000 years, and you can take a Discovery tour with local guides to find out more. When full, the lakes here support waterbirds such as egrets, cormorants, black swans and spoonbills, and other wildlife. There are giant river red gums growing along the banks of the Darling River, and campsites along the river to the north. Attractions include the wreck of the paddlesteamer *Providence*, the old homestead and woolshed at old Kinchega Station, and accommodation in the restored shearers' quarters. There is also a cemetery near the homestead. Activities include swimming, fishing and canoeing.

MILPARINKA: This small settlement is now almost a ghost town, although the Albert Hotel continues to do business here. Historic buildings include a restored courthouse, the remains of an old police station, a bank, a general store and a post office. Depot Glen Billabong is where Charles Sturt was marooned for six months in 1845 while searching for an inland sea (*see* p. 113).

MOUNT GRENFELL HISTORIC SITE: The 5km Ngiyambaa Walkabout leads visitors on a scenic tour with breathtaking views of the Cobar area. There are hundreds of Aboriginal stencils and paintings of great cultural significance in spectacular reds, yellows and ochres on rock overhangs along the trail. Picnic and barbecue facilities are available. Off Barrier Hwy. It's 67km north-west of Cobar (see p. 110).

MUTAWINTJI NATIONAL PARK: Bushwalks lead through rugged terrain of colourful gorges, rockpools and creek beds, and rock engravings and paintings tell stories of creation. Significant ceremonies have been held here and the land was returned to its Traditional Owners – the Malyankapa and Pandjikali People – in 1998, and a historic site in the centre containing a vast gallery of rock art is accessed by tour only. Tri State Safaris offers day tours of the national park from Broken Hill; (08) 8088 2389.

STURT NATIONAL PARK: Occupying 310,000ha of Corner Country – the point where three states meet – is this semi-desert park, which begins on the edge of town. It is the Traditional Land of the Wangkumara and Malyangapa Peoples, and there are middens and stone relics here. It is noted for its wildlife – wedge-tailed eagles, kangaroos and myriad reptiles. The landscape is diverse, ranging from ephemeral lakes to jump-ups, grassy plains and the rolling dunes of the Strzelecki Desert. The Dingo Fence (see Broken Hill) runs along the western and northern boundaries of the national park. Temperatures range from well over 40°C in summer to below 0°C at night in winter. Lake Pinaroo in the west is the site where Charles Sturt once built a fort to protect his party's supplies and sheep. There is an outdoor pastoralist museum and camping and homestead accommodation at Mount Wood, and short walking trails that lead from here and the park's three other campsites. You can do a self-guided tour or join a guided tour.

OTHER ATTRACTIONS

BACK O' BOURKE EXHIBITION CENTRE: This fascinating facility is set among river red gums on the Darling River, and uses interactive and audiovisual displays to immerse visitors in the story of the outback, from local bushrangers to stories of early exploration. Kidman Way, Bourke; (02) 6872 1321.

GREAT COBAR MUSEUM: This centre in Cobar (see p. 110) has displays on the local mining of copper, gold and silver-lead-zinc, an authentic re-creation of a local woolshed and displays on First Nations culture. Learn about the chronic water shortages in the early days of European settlement and the bush skills the settlers needed to survive in the harsh environment. The Centenary of Federation Walking Track begins here and is a 2hr scenic walk past mines and a slag dump. Barrier Hwy, Cobar; (02) 6836 2448.

HOT ARTESIAN BORE BATHS: The baths have an average temperature of 42°C and are free and open 24/7. The baths are 2km north-east of Lightning Ridge (see p. 110).

LINE OF LODE MINERS MEMORIAL AND VISITOR CENTRE: Perched on top of the mullock heap at the centre of Broken Hill; open 6am–9pm; Federation Way; (08) 8087 1318.

LIVING DESERT: Magnificent sandstone sculptures set on a hillside near Broken Hill. It is particularly striking at sunrise and sunset and there are walking trails through the mulga-dotted landscape; brochure available from Broken Hill visitor centre; Nine Mile Rd.

Back O'Bourke Exhibition Centre **Opposite top:** The Living Desert Reserve in Broken Hill **Opposite bottom:** The Historic Barwon Bridge in Brewarrina

VISITOR INFORMATION

Broken Hill Visitor Information Centre
Cnr Blende and Bromide sts
(08) 8080 3560
brokenhillaustralia.com.au

KEY TOWNS

BOURKE
Population 1535

Don't believe the common meaning of 'back o' Bourke' (middle of nowhere) – this town is the gateway to the real outback. When Bourke was first explored by Europeans, Charles Sturt commented that it was 'unlikely to become the haunt of civilised man'. He'd be very surprised to see the town today, which is the centre of the wool, cotton and citrus regions on the Darling River.

SEE & DO **Gundabooka National Park:** *see* Top Attractions; **Back O' Bourke Exhibition Centre:** see Other Attractions. **Fred Hollows' Grave and Memorial:** the eye surgeon and famous humanitarian is buried in the cemetery; Cobar Rd. **Historic wharf replica:** a reminder of the days when Bourke was a busy paddlesteamer port. There's also an old Crossley engine next to the wharf; Sturt St. **Paddleboat cruise:** go on a 1hr cruise of the Darling River on the *PV Jandra*; Kidman's Camp; (02) 6872 1321. **Fort Bourke Stockade replica:** memorial to Sir Thomas Mitchell, who built the original fort; 20km SW. **Mount Oxley:** home to wedge-tailed eagles and offering views of plains from the summit. A permit is needed for access to the mountain (collect from visitor centre, 02 6872 1321); 40km SE.

BREWARRINA
Population 931

This historic outback town on the banks of the Barwon River is affectionately known as 'Bre'. It was developed in the 1860s as a river port, but later thrived because of its position on a Cobb & Co. route. Brewarrina was once a meeting place for Aboriginal Peoples, with sacred sites including burial and ceremonial grounds, pointing to a culture that revolved around the river. By far the most impressive relics are the ancient stone fish traps of the Ngemba People, estimated to be 40,000 years old – and among the oldest constructions in the world.

SEE & DO **Brewarrina Fish Traps:** *see* Top Attractions. **Aboriginal Cultural Museum:** displays on aspects of Aboriginal life, from tales of the Dreamtime to the present; open Mon–Fri; Bathurst St. **Barwon Bridge:** one of two surviving examples of the first series of lift-span bridges in the state (1889); Bridge Rd. **Narran Lake Nature Reserve:** wetlands and a breeding ground for native and migratory birds; access permits from visitor centre; 50km NE. **Culgoa National Park:** wildlife unique to the western floodplains including falcons, stripe-faced dunnarts and pied bats; information from visitor centre; 100km N. **Fishing:** plentiful Murray cod in the Barwon River. **Start of Darling River Run:** self-drive tour; brochure from visitor centre.

★ BROKEN HILL
Population 17,456

Originally the intermittent home for the Wilyakali People, the area was described by explorer Charles Sturt as some of the most barren and desolate land he'd ever seen. But that might have been because he was disappointed not to discover his long-sought-after inland sea (*see* box, p. 113). In fact, the desert landscape is rich with beauty, as well as silver – the discovery of which led to the establishment of Broken Hill, NSW's 'Silver City'. A syndicate of seven men quickly bought much of the land and in 1885 they discovered the world's largest silver-lead-zinc-lodes; later that same year they decided to form a company and float shares. That company – Broken Hill Proprietary – is now BHP Group Limited, one of the world's largest mining companies. Broken Hill is also the centre of the West Darling pastoral industry, which has millions of merino sheep cordoned off by a 600km 'dog-proof' fence. As you would expect of a hot, arid mining town, Broken Hill has plenty of pubs. Note that Broken Hill operates on Central Standard Time, half an hour behind the rest of NSW.

SEE & DO **Line of Lode Miners Memorial; Living Desert:** *see* Other Attractions for both. **Art galleries:** around 20 in town including Pro Hart Gallery, Wyman St; Jack Absalom Gallery, Chapple St; and Broken Hill Regional Art Gallery, Argent St. **Silver City Mint and Art Centre:** the oldest regional gallery in the state and home of the largest acrylic canvas painting in the world (100m wide); Chloride St. **Sulphide Street Railway & Historical Museum:** displays on old mining and rail services. Also incorporates the Hospital Museum and Migrant Museum; open Sat–Sun 10am–3pm (Mar–Dec); Sat–Sun 9am–1pm (Jan–Feb); Blende St; (08) 8088 4660. **Albert Kersten Mining and Minerals Museum:** also known as the GeoCentre with displays of minerals, mining specimens and a silver tree; Tues–Fri 10am–4pm, Sat 10am–2pm; 2 Bromide St; (08) 8080 3501. **Joe Keenan Lookout:** view of town and mining dumps; Marks St. **Mosque:** one of the first mosques in Australia, built by the Afghan community in 1891; open by appt; 246 Buck St; (08) 8088 3187. **Twin Lakes:** popular picnic spot at lakes used as a water source for mines; off Wentworth Rd, South Broken Hill. **Heroes, Larrikins and Visionaries of Broken Hill Walk and Silver Trail self-guided historical town drive:** brochures from visitor centre. **Markets:** Beryl St; 2nd Sat of each month. **Royal Flying Doctor Service base and visitor centre:** headquarters, radio room and aircraft hangar open to visitors for guided tour, film and Mantle of Safety Museum; at airport; (08) 8080 3714; 10km S.

Outback Astronomy: guided stargazing shows; 0427 055 225; 10km NE. **Dingo Fence:** longest fence in the world at 5300km from Jimbour in Queensland to the Great Australian Bight in SA. Originally constructed in the 1880s to prevent rabbit invasion, now maintained to keep dingoes out of sheep-grazing areas; 150km NW.

COBAR
Population 3369

The story goes that in 1869, Charles Campbell and Thomas Hartman, with Aboriginal guides, Boney and Frank, were heading south from Bourke and stopped at Kuparr waterhole, near present-day Cobar, and noticed the water was an unusual colour. They took samples and showed them to the publicans at the Gilgunnia Pub, who identified copper ore inside the samples. From this discovery, the Cobar mining industry was born. The mines made Cobar so prosperous that at one point the town had a population of 10,000 and its own stock exchange. Mines still operate, including the CSA Copper Mine, which is the second deepest in Australia. Today Cobar is a surprisingly green and picturesque outback town.

SEE & DO **Great Cobar Museum:** *see* Other Attractions. **Fort Bourke Hill Lookout:** view over Cobar's first open-cut mine and the entrance to the still-operating underground mine; Kidman Way. **Golden Walk:** tour the operating Peak Gold Mine or view from observation deck; Kidman Way; (02) 6830 2265. **Self-guided heritage walks:** historic buildings including the courthouse and the Great Western Hotel (with the longest iron-lace verandah in NSW), and mining and agricultural sites around town; brochure from visitor centre. **Canbelego–Nymagee Tourist Drive:** this is mining country, and the round trip from Cobar takes you through historic mining towns. **The Old Reservoir and Devil's Rock:** Devil's Rock was a site for ceremonial rites for the Ngemba People. Good swimming and watersports at the reservoir; 3km N.

LIGHTNING RIDGE
Population 1396

Lightning Ridge still has the feel of a frontier town, even though opals – including the town's famous black opals – have been mined in this area since 1902. Like most frontier towns, Lightning Ridge has a lot of character, from the replica Egyptian tomb in the Chambers of the Black Hand to the quirky castle that you can rent as accommodation. You need to be creative and resilient to live here, as miners must provide their own electricity and water. This is a popular tourist town where you can take a tour of a mine or try your own hand at fossicking.

SEE & DO **Hot artesian bore baths:** *see* Other Attractions. **Bottle House Museum:** collection of bottles, minerals and mining relics; originally a miner's camp; Opal St; (02) 6829 0618. **The Big Opal:** large opal showroom and self-guided underground tours available Mon–Sun; Three Mile Rd; (02) 6829 0247. **John Murray Art Gallery:** exclusive outlet for original paintings, limited-edition prints, postcards and posters; Opal St; (02) 6829 1130. **Chambers of the Black Hand:** unique underground sculptures and carvings in sandstone walls of an old mine; tours 10.30am and 3pm (Apr–Nov), 10.30am (Dec–Mar); Three Mile Rd; (02) 6829 0221. **Displays of art and craft:** including beautiful displays of black opal in the

Top: Broken Hill and the mine beyond **Opposite:** Silverton Hotel is an iconic outback landmark

TOP EVENTS

- → MAR St Patrick's Race Day (Broken Hill)
- → EASTER Barwon River Rodeo (Brewarrina), Easter Festival (Lightning Ridge)
- → JUN Bre Big Fish (Brewrrrina)
- → JULY Opal and Gem Festival (Lightning Ridge)
- → SEPT Broken Heel Festival (Broken Hill)
- → OCT Festival of the Miners Ghost (Cobar), Gymkhana and Rodeo (Tibooburra)

TEMPERATURES

Jan: 23–37°C

July: 6–18°C

---

many opal showrooms; several locations; brochure from visitor centre. **Car Door Tours:** follow painted car doors to find attractions; brochure from visitor centre. **Opal Mine Adventure:** working mine with easy access and tours on demand. Also a cactus nursery nearby; off Bald Hill Rd; 2km N. **Opal fields:** Grawin (65km W) and Sheepyards (76km W); brochure from visitor centre. **Designated fossicking areas:** maps from visitor centre.

MENINDEE
Population 537

They don't always have water in them, but when they do the 20 or so lakes that surround the township of Menindee, 110km south-east of Broken Hill, are an oasis in the middle of the arid outback plains, all fed by the Darling River. There's also a local dam, which means that farmers can run vegetable farms and orchards, in stark contrast to the surrounding saltbush and red soil. The tiny settlement was also visited by a hat-trick of explorers: Major Thomas Mitchell, Charles Sturt, and Burke and Wills.

SEE & DO **Kinchega National Park:** *see* Top Attractions. **Maiden's Menindee Hotel:** Burke and Wills lodged here in 1860. Meals and accommodation are available; Yartla St. **Menindee Lakes:** in dry times, only the upper lakes have water, making them the most reliable for fishing, swimming, birdwatching and watersports, and the best place for camping; details from visitor centre. **Menindee Lake Lookout:** good views of the lake; 10km N. **Copi Hollow:** great spot for waterskiers, swimmers and powerboat enthusiasts, with campsites on the waterfront; 18km N.

SILVERTON
Population 48

The National Trust–classified town of Silverton was established when silver chloride was found 27km north-west of Broken Hill in 1883. It now has just a handful of inhabitants and is surrounded by stark, arid plains, making it popular with filmmakers wanting an outback setting. *Mad Max II* (1981), *Razorback* (1984), *Young Einstein* (1988), *The Adventures of Priscilla, Queen of the Desert* (1994) and *Dirty Deeds* (2002) were filmed here, and the Silverton Hotel displays photographs of the film sets on its walls.

SEE & DO **Silverton Heritage Walking Trail:** brochure from Broken Hill visitor centre and visit the **Silverton Gaol Museum**, 9.30am–4pm, Bourke St, (08) 8088 5317; **Silverton School Museum**, 9.30am–3.30pm (except Tues and Thurs), Loftus St, (08) 8088 7481; the **Mad Max Museum**, 10am–4pm; or one of the four art galleries in town. **Mundi Mundi Plain Lookout**, a further 10km N, affords views of the desolate yet awe-inspiring landscape. **Daydream Mine**, 13km NE, operated in the 1880s and is now open for 1hr surface and underground tours; 10am–2pm (Easter–Nov), 10–11.30am (Nov–Easter); (08) 8088 5682.

TIBOOBURRA
Population 95

Tibooburra is one of the hottest and most isolated towns in NSW. Its name is believed to mean 'heaps of rocks' in the language of the Wangkumara People, and the 450-million-year-old granite tors that surround the town are culturally significant. The Dreaming story is that three brothers were turned to stone after marrying women from another tribe, creating three large rocks (only one remains today). Gold was discovered in 1881 but a poor yield, outbreaks of typhoid and dysentery, and a lack of water meant the population explosion did not last.

SEE & DO **Sturt National Park:** *see* Top Attractions; **Pioneer Park:** features a replica of the whaleboat Charles Sturt carried with him on his 1844–46 expedition to find an inland sea (*see* box, p. 113); Briscoe St. **Courthouse Museum:** history of the region told with photographs, relics and documents in the restored 1887 courthouse; Briscoe St. **Tibooburra Local Aboriginal Land Council Keeping Place:** photographs and Aboriginal artefacts on display include a cockatoo-feather headdress; check opening times (08) 8091 3435; Briscoe St. **School of the Air:** most remote school in NSW servicing students of Tibooburra and the Cameron Corner region. Tours during school terms; Briscoe St. **Family Hotel:** pub walls have been painted by artists including Russell Drysdale, Clifton Pugh and Rick Amor; Briscoe St.

WALGETT
Population 1377

Walgett played a part in the famous Freedom Ride in 1965, when the local RSL was picketed for not allowing access to local Aboriginal ex-servicemen. The Freedom Ride bus was run off the road just out of town by a local farmer. The town is on the junction of the Barwon and Namoi rivers, and paddlesteamers used the town as a port in the 19th century. These days the river is more often used for fishing. A local archaeological dig established that there were human inhabitants in the area around 30,000 years ago.

SEE & DO **Norman 'Tracker' Walford Track:** signposted 1.5km scenic walk includes the first European settler's grave on the banks of the Namoi River; from levee bank at end of Warrena St. **Hot artesian springs:** relaxing and therapeutic baths at swimming pool; Montekeila St. **Come-By-Chance:** this town 'came by chance' to William Colless when all of the land in the area was thought to be allocated, but it was discovered that some had been missed. Colless came to own most of the buildings, including the police station, post office, hotel, blacksmith shop and cemetery. It is now an attractive and quiet town with riverside picnic spots, bushwalks and abundant wildlife. There are picnic races in Sept. 65km SE. **Grawin, Glengarry and Sheepyard opal fields:** go fossicking, but be warned that water is scarce so an adequate supply should be carried. Brochure from visitor centre; 70km NW.

SEARCHING FOR THE INLAND SEA

Despite having found the Darling River and mapped the course of the Murray River in 1828–30, explorer Charles Sturt is more famous for what he didn't find. Convinced that the centre of Australia was a vast inland sea, he set out to find it, with a boat, in 1844.

Travelling from Adelaide along the Murray and Darling rivers, past the site of modern-day Broken Hill, he became trapped at a place he called Depot Glen for six months in weather so hot that 'it made screws drop out of boxes, lead fell out of pencils and the men's nails became as brittle as glass'. He kept his men busy by building a cairn on a hilltop, and you can still see the grave of his second-in-command, James Poole, who died there. You'll find it near the modern ghost town of Milparinka.

Sturt eventually moved on and built a small stockade, which he called Fort Grey, to house his stock and supplies. It's in Sturt National Park, near Tibooburra, and you can camp there, although little remains of the stockade today. There's a replica of his boat, beached high and dry, in the park at Tibooburra (see p. 112) – the ultimate monument to wishful thinking!

Sturt's route took him through some of the most inhospitable land in the country, across the Strzelecki, Sturt Stony and Simpson deserts. These days parts of his route are navigable on the iconic Strzelecki and Birdsville 4WD tracks, the blood-red dunes still sweeping towards the horizon just as Sturt described in his journal: 'in parallel lines beyond the range of vision ... like the waves of the sea.'

WHITE CLIFFS
Population 156

White Cliffs is first and foremost an opal town. The first mining lease was granted in 1890, and a boom followed with an influx of 4500 people. The area is still known for its opals, particularly the unique opal 'pineapples' and the opalised remains of a plesiosaur, a 2m long, 100-million-year-old fossil found in 1976. The intense heat has forced many people to build their homes underground, often in the remains of old opal mines. The buildings left on the surface are surrounded by a pale and eerie moonscape with an estimated 50,000 abandoned opal digs.

SEE & DO **Solar Power Station:** the country's first solar power station was established by the Australian National University in 1981 at White Cliffs because it receives the most solar radiation in NSW. The row of 14 giant mirrored dishes is a striking sight between the blue sky and red earth. Next to council depot. **Outback Treasures:** opal jewellery and First Nations art; Smiths Hill; (08) 8091 6654. **Self-guided and guided historical walks and fossicking:** include the old police station (1897) and school (1900) and several fossicking sites; brochures and maps from visitor centre. **Underground accommodation:** various standards available in dugout premises. Underground temperatures come as a relief at 22°C; details from visitor centre. **Opal shops:** several in town sell local gems; details from visitor centre. **Paroo–Darling National Park:** the Traditional Land of the Paakantyi People, the section of this national park 20km east of town contains magnificent Peery Lake, part of the Paroo River overflow, where there are birdlife, and walking trails. Southern section of park has camping along the Darling River. **Wilcannia:** small town with many fine sandstone buildings, an opening bridge across the Darling River and an old paddlesteamer wharf. Also a self-guided historical walk available; brochure from council offices in Reid St; 93km S.

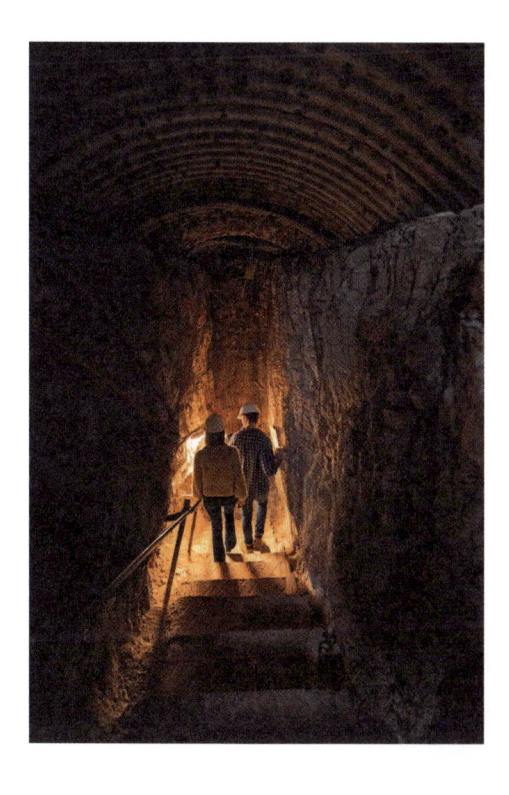

Bottom: Walk In Mine in Lightning Ridge **Opposite:** Sturt National Park is known for its wildlife

Victoria

HIGHLIGHTS

Tour the idyllic wine regions of central Victoria and sample some of Australia's finest shiraz in Heathcote. *See* p. 148.

Grab your mountain bike and whiz down bush tracks in the Yarra Valley and Dandenongs among towering mountain ash trees. *See* p. 122.

Cruise the Great Ocean Road: marvel at the iconic Twelve Apostles (those still standing), visit rainforests and waterfalls, and discover beautiful holiday towns along the magnificent stretch of coastline. *See* p. 164.

Drive, walk or cycle the majestic sandstone mountain ranges of Grampians National Park/Gariwerd for jaw-dropping views and amazing First Nations rock art. *See* p. 173.

Jump on your bicycle, freewheel the Murray to Mountains Rail Trail through Myrtleford and Bright and enjoy the region's fresh produce. *See* p. 190.

Get your adrenaline pumping at Alpine National Park, an adventure playground for 4WD-enthusiasts, hikers, mountain-bikers and cross-country skiers. *See* p. 191.

STATE FLOWER

Common Heath
Epacris impressa

The Black Spur is a dramatic drive through forest

Melbourne/Naarm at a glance

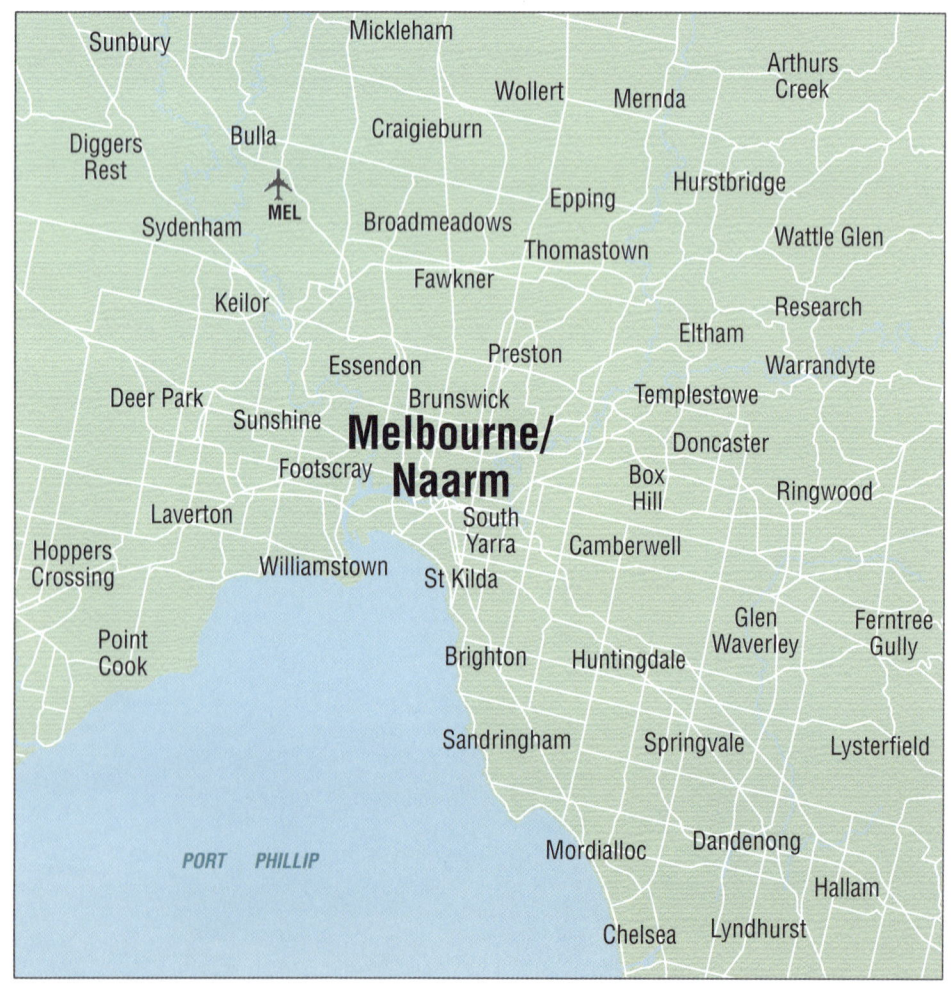

The Traditional Owners of the Melbourne/Naarm area are the Bunurong, Boon Wurrung and Wurrundjeri Peoples of the Kulin Nation.

Melbourne is Australia's **sporting and cultural capital** and a **UNESCO City of Literature**. It is famed for **city laneways, grandiose Victorian buildings, dazzling modern architecture** and a **renowned cafe scene**. The **bookshops, festivals, street art** and cosmopolitan culture make Melbourne the most **exciting metropolis** in the country.

Top: The Yarra River/Birrarung and city skyline **Middle:** The city's coffee scene is famous **Bottom:** The historic Block Arcade **Opposite:** Cafes and boutique shops fill Melbourne's many laneways

IF YOU LIKE …

GALLERIES
Alcaston Gallery
Australian Centre for Contemporary Art
Centre for Contemporary Photography
National Gallery of Victoria: NGV International
Outré Gallery
The Ian Potter Centre: NGV Australia

HISTORIC BUILDINGS
Flinders Street Station
Manchester Unity Building
Nicholas Building
Old Treasury and Parliament House, Spring Street
Royal Exhibition Building
St Patrick's Cathedral
St Paul's Cathedral

LANEWAYS AND ARCADES
Block Arcade for life's finer things
Degraves Street for coffee
Hardware Lane for bars and cafes
Hosier Lane for street art
Meyers Place for restaurants
Royal Arcade for a historic clock

MARKETS
Arts Centre Sunday Markets
Camberwell Sunday Market
Queen Victoria Market
St Kilda Esplanade Market
South Melbourne Market

MODERN ARCHITECTURE
Barak Building
Federation Square
Pixel Building
Storey Hall and Building 8, RMIT
The Webb Bridge in Docklands

MUSEUMS
Australian Centre for the Moving Image (ACMI)
Australian Sports Museum
Chinese Museum
Immigration Museum
Melbourne Museum and Bunjilaka Aboriginal Cultural Centre
Old Treasury Building
Scienceworks (for kids)

PARKS AND GARDENS
Albert Park
Birrarung Marr
Edinburgh Gardens
Fitzroy Gardens
Royal Botanic Gardens
Yarra Bend Park

VICTORIA

117

Daytrips from Melbourne/Naarm

BELLARINE PENINSULA
1.25hr from Melbourne CBD

The Bellarine Peninsula separates the waters of Port Phillip from the famously rugged coastline of Victoria's south-west. It's just over an hour from Melbourne's CBD to the gateway to the Bellarine, the regional city of Geelong. Start your day by checking out the city's historic buildings and charming waterfront, and get a coffee from one of the bustling local cafes.

Ready? It's time to head on to the quaint villages and excellent beaches! Drop into the charming seaside historic village of Queenscliff for fish and chips or a ride on a steam train; admire the immense horizon over Port Phillip at Portarlington; chill out on the peaceful river or stroll and shop boutiques at Barwon Heads; and make a splash in the surf beach at Ocean Grove. Oh, and don't forget to taste the offerings at the local wineries and craft breweries. *See* Geelong p. 161, Queenscliff p. 162.

THE DANDENONGS
1hr from Melbourne CBD

These scenic hills are a popular daytrip from Melbourne, with native rainforests of misty mountain ash and gullies of giant ferns, cool-climate gardens, galleries, craft shops and cafes among the many attractions.

Enjoy twinkling views of the cityscape or a ride on ever-popular steam train *Puffing Billy*. Take a walk in Dandenong Ranges National Park or visit the Dandenong Ranges Botanic Garden for the brilliant displays of rhododendrons, azaleas, camellias, cherry blossom and daffodils. If you're looking for a physical challenge, take on the 1000 Steps Walk (also known as the Kokoda Track Memorial Walk). *See* Olinda p. 126.

Top: Kangaroos with the infamous Hanging Rock beyond **Middle:** Passengers onboard Puffing Billy **Bottom left:** Hepburn Springs's Pavillion Café **Bottom right:** Sorrento Pier, Searoad ferry from Queenscliff to Sorrento

MORNINGTON PENINSULA
1hr from Melbourne CBD

This holiday region features fine-food producers, cool-climate vineyards, historic holiday villages, quiet coastal national parks, golf courses and plenty to keep the kids happy. About an hour from Melbourne, the area makes for a lovely daytrip dawdling down the eastern side of Port Phillip.

Go rummaging for treasure in vintage and antique junk shops at Tyabb or throw a line in at Sorrento or peruse the town's many independent and chain stores. You can also jump in the placid waters of a bay beach at Rosebud or hit the waves with your surfboard at an ocean beach. See Mornington p. 131, Sorrento p. 131.

MOUNT MACEDON AND HANGING ROCK
1hr from Melbourne CBD

Only an hour from Melbourne up the Calder Freeway, the European-style gardens of this area are a highlight, as are the wineries, cafes, nurseries and galleries. Hanging Rock is a place of legend and mystery and a good place for a picnic. Visit the towns of Woodend and Kyneton for cafes, antiques and boutique browsing.

For a more active trip, take a bike up by train from Melbourne and then tackle Mount Macedon. There's also the mysterious Hanging Rock, a Victorian pilgrimage famous from a literary thriller. See Mount Macedon p.156, Woodend p. 157.

PHILLIP ISLAND
1.5hr from Melbourne CBD

The nightly penguin parade on Phillip Island is one of Victoria's signature attractions – and it's only one-and-a-half hours from Melbourne. Drop into the Penguin Parade Visitor Centre for a greater understanding of these little icons. For the avid wildlife-watcher, seals and koalas are the other stars of the show. The island also boasts magnificent coastal scenery with blowholes, caves and spectacular rock formations. If you prefer to be part of the action, you'll find some great surf breaks, as well as sheltered bay beaches.

Phillip Island is a popular holiday destination, and perhaps the island's greatest attraction is its ability to absorb the summer crowds – you can always find your own patch of quiet island paradise. See Cowes p. 136.

SOVEREIGN HILL
1.25hr from Melbourne CBD

Located in the regional city of Ballarat, Sovereign Hill is an award-winning re-creation of a 19th-century goldmining village that conjures up the detail and drama of life during the gold rush. It's an outdoor museum and is great fun for families and kids.

Experience life during the gold rush in 1850s Ballarat: take an absorbing underground mine tour; watch rare 19th-century trades and crafts practised by skilled craftspeople; try your luck at gold panning; or take a coach ride. The kids will love the musket-firing demonstration. You can even stay the night at accommodation within the village, with full period costume thrown in! See Ballarat p. 151.

SPA COUNTRY AND BEYOND
1.5hr from Melbourne CBD

Soak away the blues in the mineral-rich waters of the historic Hepburn Springs spa complex, nestled among the hills and lakes of central Victoria about an hour and a half from Melbourne.

Nearby, Daylesford is a popular holiday town with gourmet food offerings, beautiful scenery and lovely gardens – perfect for a relaxing wander. See Daylesford p. 153.

WERRIBEE PARK AND THE OPEN RANGE ZOO
40min from Melbourne CBD

The key feature of Werribee Park is a beautifully preserved 1870s mansion with the interior painstakingly restored to its original opulence. The mansion is surrounded by 12ha of gardens, including a grotto and a farmyard area. Within the grounds is the Victoria State Rose Garden with more than 500 varieties of flowers.

Next to the park is the Werribee Open Range Zoo, developed around the Werribee River. The zoo covers 200ha and has a variety of animals native to the grasslands of Africa, Asia, North America and Australia, including giraffes, rhinos, meerkats, cheetahs, lions and gorillas. Guided safaris through the replicated African savannah are a must. Access from the Princes Hwy; contact Parks Victoria 13 1963 or the Open Range Zoo 1300 966 784.

YARRA VALLEY
1.25hr from Melbourne CBD

The wineries, fruit farms and forests of the Yarra Valley are right on Melbourne's doorstep. It's easy to mooch a day away around the valley.

Enjoying quality pinot noir at one of the valley's many wineries is guaranteed to get you into a more relaxed state of mind. Drop into Yarra Valley Dairy for superb local cheeses or have lunch in the foodie-friendly town of Healesville before walking it off while visiting Australian animals at Healesville Sanctuary. Cherry picking in this region is fun around Christmas. See Healesville p. 125, Yarra Glen p. 127.

Top: Surfing at Ocean Grove **Second from top:** The Penguin Parade, Phillip Island **Second from bottom:** Sovereign Hill, Ballarat **Bottom:** Werribee Open Range Zoo

Regions of Victoria

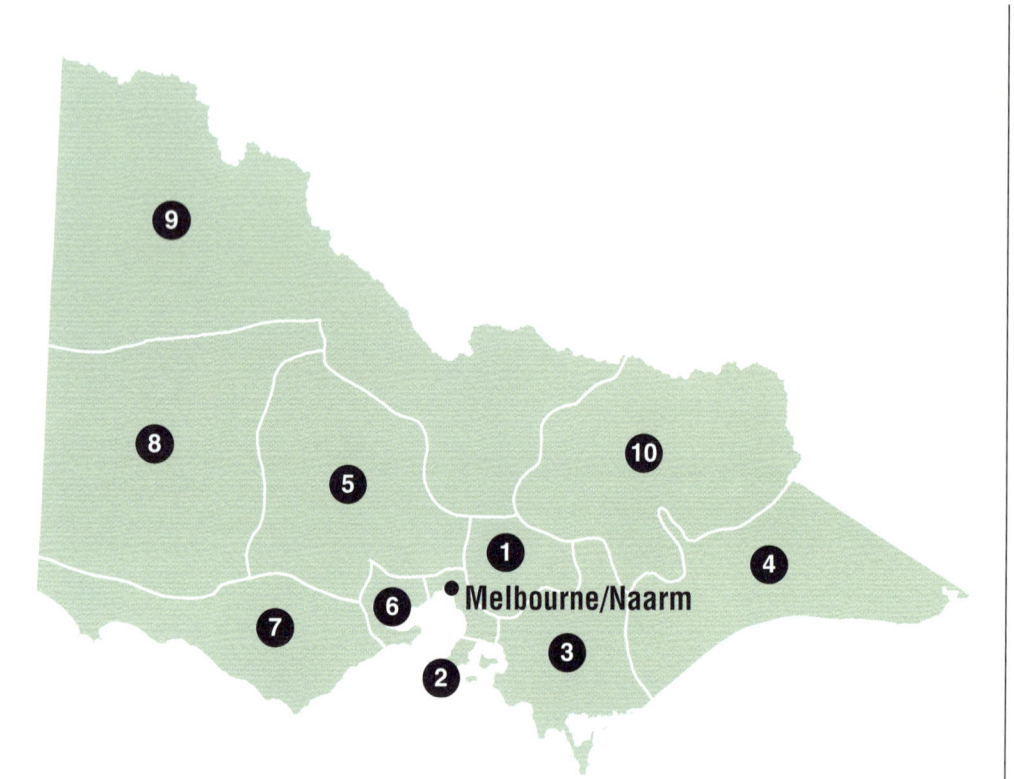

❶ YARRA VALLEY AND DANDENONGS P. 122

Emerald
Healesville ★
Marysville
Olinda ★
Warburton
Yarra Glen

❷ MORNINGTON PENINSULA P. 128

Flinders
Mornington
Sorrento ★

❸ PHILLIP ISLAND AND SOUTH GIPPSLAND P. 132

Cowes (Phillip Island) ★
Foster
Inverloch
Koo Wee Rup
Korumburra
Leongatha
Moe
Morwell
Port Albert
Traralgon
Walhalla
Warragul
Welshpool
Wonthaggi
Yarram

❹ EAST GIPPSLAND P. 140

Bairnsdale
Buchan
Cann River
Lakes Entrance ★
Maffra
Mallacoota ★
Orbost
Paynesville
Sale

❺ GOLDFIELDS AND SPA COUNTRY P. 146

Avoca
Bacchus Marsh
Ballarat ⭐
Bendigo ⭐
Castlemaine
Clunes
Creswick
Daylesford ⭐
Dunolly
Heathcote
Inglewood
Kilmore
Kyneton ⭐
Maldon
Maryborough
Mount Macedon
St Arnaud
Wedderburn
Woodend

❻ GEELONG AND THE BELLARINE PENINSULA P. 158

Barwon Heads ⭐
Drysdale
Geelong ⭐
Ocean Grove
Queenscliff ⭐
Winchelsea

❼ GREAT OCEAN ROAD AND SURF COAST P. 164

Aireys Inlet
Anglesea
Apollo Bay ⭐
Camperdown
Colac
Lorne ⭐
Port Campbell
Port Fairy ⭐
Portland
Torquay
Warrnambool

❽ GRAMPIANS/ GARIWERD AND CENTRAL WEST P. 172

Ararat
Casterton
Coleraine
Dimboola
Donald
Dunkeld
Edenhope
Halls Gap ⭐
Hamilton
Horsham
Jeparit
Nhill
Stawell
Terang
Warracknabeal
Wycheproof

❾ GOULBURN, MURRAY AND MALLEE P. 180

Cobram
Cohuna
Echuca ⭐
Euroa ⭐
Hopetoun
Kerang
Mildura ⭐
Murrayville
Nagambie
Ouyen
Pyramid Hill
Robinvale
Rochester
Rushworth
Seymour
Shepparton
Swan Hill
Yarrawonga
Yea

❿ HIGH COUNTRY P. 190

Alexandra
Beechworth ⭐
Benalla
Bright ⭐
Chiltern
Corryong
Eildon
Glenrowan
Mansfield
Milawa
Mount Beauty
Myrtleford
Omeo
Rutherglen
Tallangatta
Wangaratta
Wodonga
Yackandandah ⭐

Top: Beautiful Beechworth **Bottom:** Tawonga Gap lookout, High Country **Opposite:** Charming Port Fairy, at the end of the Great Ocean Road

Yarra Valley and Dandenongs

These ranges east of Melbourne are genuine crowd pleasers, with something for everyone. City dwellers come here to escape the urban crush; garden lovers for the **springtime flower displays**; nature lovers for the **towering forests of mountain ash** and fern-filled gullies; families love the **historic steam train rides** and interactive **wildlife sanctuary**; and foodies hit up the **food and wine trails** – the Yarra Valley produces some of the best cool-climate wine in the country.

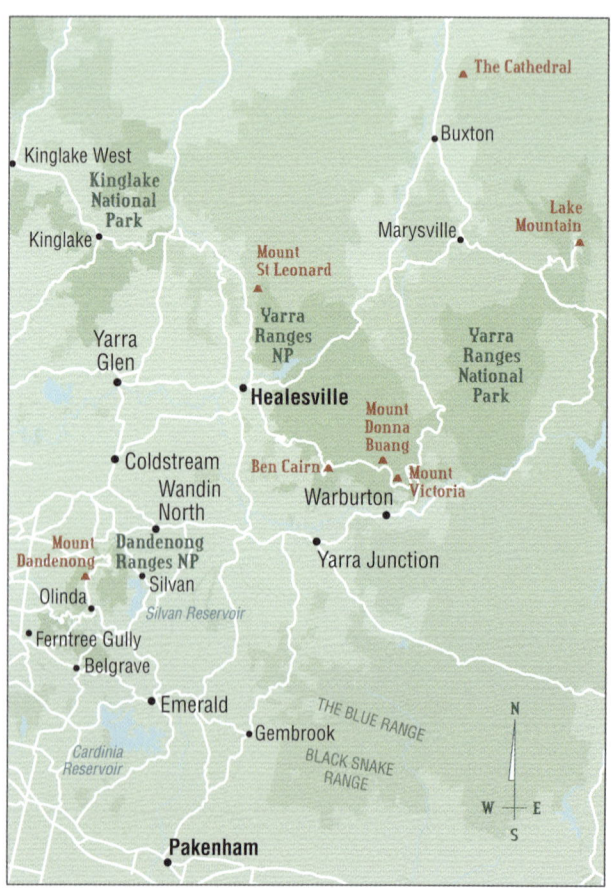

CHEAT SHEET

→ Allow at least two or three days for a proper exploration.

→ Best time to visit: year-round but the gardens are at their best in spring.

→ Main towns: Healesville (see p. 125), Emerald (see p. 125), Olinda (see p. 126), Marysville (see p. 125).

→ The Yarra Ranges are the Traditional Lands of the Wurundjeri People. This website features some great First Nations experiences in the Yarra Valley: visityarravalley.com.au/blog/10-ways-to-have-an-indigenous-experience-in-the-yarra-valley

→ Don't miss: a ride on Puffing Billy; winetasting in the Yarra Valley; TarraWarra Museum of Art; Healesville Sanctuary; Lady Talbot Forest Drive; Dandenong Ranges Botanic Garden.

Top: Jack Holman, Stone and Crow Cheese Company
Opposite: De Bortoli Yarra Valley Estate

TOP ATTRACTIONS

CATHEDRAL RANGE STATE PARK: The word 'imposing' does not do justice to the 7km rocky ridge that forms the backbone of this park near Marysville (see p. 125). Challenging hikes up the ridge to lookout points offer unparalleled views to the valley below but go prepared. Walks can include overnight stays at the Farmyard campground, so named because lyrebirds imitate the noises of the domestic animals in the farmyards below.

DANDENONG RANGES BOTANIC GARDEN: The gardens begin just east of Olinda township (see p. 126) and are something of a mecca for garden enthusiasts, with superb displays of rhododendrons and azaleas in season.

DANDENONG RANGES NATIONAL PARK: This park offers great walking tracks and picnic facilities. Visitors may be lucky enough to spot an elusive lyrebird, a species renowned for its ability to mimic sounds from other bird calls to human voices and even chainsaws. Most walking tracks leave from picnic grounds, such as the 1000 Steps Walk from Ferntree Gully Picnic Ground (south-west via the Mount Dandenong Tourist Rd) and the walk to Sherbrooke Falls from the Sherbrooke Picnic Ground (via Sherbrooke Rd from the Mount Dandenong Tourist Rd).

HEALESVILLE SANCTUARY: Australia's unique animals are on show at this 32ha reserve in Healesville (see p. 125). The sanctuary is one of the few places in the world to have successfully bred platypus in captivity and the devoted trainers put on a daily talk while interacting with these amazing aquatic animals. Allow at least half a day to visit and see the animal hospital or have a close-up encounter with your favourite Australian animal. Open 9am–5pm; Badger Creek Rd, Healesville; (03) 5957 2800 or 1300 966 784; pre-book at zoo.org.au/healesville; no tickets are available at the gate.

LAKE MOUNTAIN: Renowned for first-rate cross-country skiing, the area is also great for tobogganing, snow tubing and sled rides. When the snow melts and the wildflowers bloom, hikers can take the Summit Walk (4km return) over the mountain. Ski and walk brochure available from visitor centre.

PUFFING BILLY: Victoria's favourite steam train runs the 25km between Belgrave and Gembrook, stopping at Emerald Lake. If you time your trip for the last Sat of the month, you could catch the craft and produce market at Gembrook station. Also at Gembrook is the Motorist Museum. Recorded timetable and fare information on 1900 937 069, all other inquiries (03) 9757 0700.

TARRAWARRA MUSEUM OF ART: TarraWarra Estate has been operating as a vineyard since 1983, producing a selection of fine chardonnay and pinot noir. Here also is a striking building housing an extensive private collection of modern art. The collection focuses on the three key themes of Australian Modernism – landscape, figuration and abstraction – and works by artists such as Howard Arkley, Arthur Boyd and Brett Whiteley can be found within. Open Tues–Sun 11am–5pm; 311 Healesville–Yarra Glen Rd; (03) 5957 3100.

YARRA RANGES NATIONAL PARK: Here, tall mountain ash trees give way to pockets of cool temperate rainforest. **Mount Donna Buang** is a popular daytrip destination – especially during winter, when it is often snow-covered; it is 17km north-west of Warburton. At 1245m, the views from the lookout tower here are spectacular: you can see the Yarra Valley, Dandenong Ranges, Melbourne and beyond. There are picnic areas, and the **Rainforest Gallery** on the southern slopes of the mountain features a walkway and treetop viewing platform where you can see mountain ash and myrtle beech. Night-walk tours here reveal some of Victoria's unique nocturnal creatures. **Acheron Way** is a scenic 37km drive north through the national park to Marysville. Along the way are views of Mount Victoria and Ben Cairn.

YARRA VALLEY WINE REGION: With over 50 cellar doors and around 100 wineries, the Yarra Valley is home to some exceptional names. **De Bortoli** is Australia's oldest family-owned winery and is well recognised throughout the country. Owned by the legendary Moët & Chandon, **Domaine Chandon** makes sophisticated sparkling wines that can be enjoyed in the tasting room with full-length windows overlooking the vines. **Yering Station** produces excellent shiraz viognier as well as award-winning pinot noir. It is also the site of a produce store, a good restaurant, and the **Yarra Valley Farmers' Market** held in an old barn (3rd Sun of the month). To combine wine with art, head to **TarraWarra Estate** *See* Top Attractions TarraWarra Museum of Art. **Giant Steps/ Innocent Bystander** is a modern cellar door near Healesville.

OTHER ATTRACTIONS

BLUE LOTUS WATER GARDEN: Tropical themed water gardens with seasonal displays of magnificent lotus flowers and other exotic blooms, cafe, garden shop, fairy garden and picnic shelters. Open late Dec–mid-April; 2628 Warburton Hwy, Yarra Junction; (03) 5967 2061; tickets at bluelotusfarm.com.au.

GULF STATION: This National Trust–owned pastoral property near Yarra Glen, preserved as it was during early settler days and recently restored, features old-fashioned farming implements; open 1st Thurs each month or by appt; (03) 9656 9889.

KINGLAKE NATIONAL PARK: Beautiful messmate forests, fern gullies, panoramic lookouts and bushwalking tracks.

Black Spur **Opposite top:** Echidna at Healesville Sanctuary **Opposite bottom:** Hargreaves Hill Brewery in the Yarra Valley

VISITOR INFORMATION

Dandenong Ranges Information Centre
Upper Ferntree Gully Railway Station
visitdandenongranges.com.au

Yarra Valley
visityarravalley.com.au

KEY TOWNS

EMERALD
Population 5890

Emerald is a delightful little town set in the Dandenong Ranges. Over the weekend people come from the city into 'the hills' to take in the scenic forests and visit the cafes, galleries, and antique and craft stores.

SEE & DO **Puffing Billy:** see Top Attractions. **Emerald Lake:** the lake is a lovely, tranquil spot. Attractions include the largest model railway display in the Southern Hemisphere, paddleboats, cafe and tearooms, fishing and walking trails. Picnic shelters can be hired. **Galleries and craft shops:** a wide variety, specialising in locally made products; along Main St. **Cardinia Reservoir Park:** where picnic spots are shared with free-roaming kangaroos; and **Lake Aura Vale**, a popular spot for sailing; Belgrave-Gembrook Rd; 4km NW. **Australian Rainbow Trout Farm:** fish for rainbow trout or Atlantic salmon from one of the ponds. For more experienced anglers there is a 0.8ha lake; 26 Mulhalls Rd, Macclesfield; (03) 5968 4711; 8km N. **Sherbrooke Art Gallery:** an impressive collection of local artwork; open Fri-Mon 11am-3pm; Monbulk Rd, Belgrave; (03) 9754 4264; 11km NW. **Treetops Adventure:** tree-top challenge courses for all skill levels set in heritage gardens; Glen Harrow Park, Old Monbulk Rd, Belgrave; bookings essential (03) 9752 5354; treetopsadventure.com.au/location/belgrave; 12km NW.

★ HEALESVILLE
Population 8698

To the west of Yarra Ranges National Park and within easy reach of Melbourne, Healesville is a small mountain town surrounded by rolling hills, native bush and cultivated estates, especially vineyards and orchards. The bustling town has a great buzz and an assortment of quality restaurants and cafes, all focusing on local produce, especially the world-class Yarra Valley wines. On top of this, there is a host of art and craft boutiques and two major attractions – TarraWarra Museum of Art and the famous Healesville Sanctuary.

SEE & DO **Healesville Sanctuary; TarraWarra Museum of Art; Yarra Valley Wine Region:** see Top Attractions for all. **Silvermist Studio:** handmade jewellery gallery and goldsmith's workshop; open Wed-Mon 9am-5pm; 238 Maroondah Hwy; (03) 5962 5470. **Yarra Valley Railway:** train or open-air trolley rides from Healesville railway station to Tunnel Hill; open Sun 10am-4pm and public holidays; Healesville-Kinglake Rd; (03) 5962 2490. **Healesville Organic Farmers' Market:** Coronation Park, River St; Sat. **Community Market:** River St; 1st and 3rd Sun each month. **Coranderrk Aboriginal Station:** 3km S. **Maroondah Reservoir Park:** a magnificent park set in lush forests with walking tracks and a lookout nearby; 3km NE. **Donnelly's Weir Park:** starting point of the 5000km Bicentennial National Trail to Cooktown (Qld); the park also has short walking tracks and picnic facilities; 4km N. **Badger Creek Blueberry Winery:** makers of blueberry wines including a sparkling and a fortified variety; and apple and pear ciders; open Thurs-Mon 10am-5pm; 11 Garnook Grove, Badger Creek; (03) 5962 1601; 5km S. **Badger Weir Park:** picnic area in a natural setting; 7km SE. **Yarra Valley Chocolaterie and Ice Creamery:** over 250 different chocolate products; free chocolate tastings and plenty of room in the gardens to let the kids loose; 35 Old Healesville Rd; (03) 9730 2777; 12km W. **Mallesons Lookout:** views of Yarra Valley to Melbourne; 8km S. **Mount St Leonard:** good views from the summit; 14km N. **Coombe – The Melba Estate:** the former home of world-famous opera singer Dame Nellie Melba offers magnificent landscaped gardens, a quality dining restaurant: Coombe Yarra Valley, local wines, a gallery and a local produce shop; 675 Maroonday Hwy; (03) 9739 0173; 18km SW. **Lilydale-Warburton Rail Trail:** hire a bike and follow a disused railway line 38km through the valley, passing idyllic countryside with spectacular views and quiet country towns.

MARYSVILLE
Population 453

For 100 years, the beautiful subalpine village of Marysville was a much-frequented holiday destination for Melburnians with its cafes, galleries and popular guesthouses. Tragically, the town was almost totally destroyed by bushfire on 7 Feb 2009 in what came to be known as Black Saturday. With the help of the community, and state and federal governments, this idyllic township has been rebuilt and is once more welcoming visitors to the beauty of its natural surrounds. The magnificent 84m Steavenson Falls are nearby.

SEE & DO **Cathedral Range State Park:** see Top Attractions. **Lolly Shop:** old-fashioned candy store in a new purpose-built home; open Mon-Fri 10am-4pm, Sat-Sun 10am-5pm; 8 Murchison St; 0408 173 656. **Bruno's Art & Sculpture Garden:** gardens featuring sculptures by artist Bruno Torfs; open 10am-5pm; 51 Falls Rd; (03) 5963 3513. **Community Market:** Murchison St; 2nd and 4th Sun each month. **Lady Talbot Forest Drive:** this 46km route begins east of town. Stop en route to enjoy picnic spots, walking tracks and lookouts. **Buxton Trout & Salmon Farm:** drop a line in one of the well-stocked ponds, purchase smoked

VICTORIA

fish or enjoy a barbecue lunch; 2118 Maroondah Hwy, Buxton; (03) 5774 7370; 12km SE. **Steavenson Falls:** a short 700m walk from the waterfall carpark on Falls Rd, this 84m waterfall is spectacular and one of Victoria's highest. **Scenic walks:** many tracks in the area, including a 4km loop walk in Cumberland Memorial Scenic Reserve, 16km E; 4km Beeches Walk through ancient beech and mountain ash forests (accessed via Lady Talbot Forest Dr). **Big River State Forest:** camping, fishing and gold fossicking; 30km E.

⭐ OLINDA
Population 1773

Olinda is in the centre of the Dandenong Ranges, a landscape of towering mountain ash forests, lush fern gullies, waterfalls, English gardens and picnic spots. The ranges have been a retreat for Melburnians since the 1800s. Olinda and nearby Sassafras are known for their many galleries, cafes and tearooms serving Devonshire teas. The Rhododendron and Daffodil Festivals in late spring attract gardens lovers from all over.

SEE & DO **Dandenong Ranges National Park; Dandenong Ranges Botanic Garden:** see Top Attractions for both. **R.J. Hamer Arboretum:** good walking tracks through 100ha of rare and exotic trees; Olinda–Monbulk Rd, shortly after the turn-off to Dandenong Ranges Botanic Gardens. **Cloudehill Gardens:** twilight concerts are held here in summer; south of R.J. Hamer Arboretum. **Mount Dandenong Lookout:** spectacular views over Melbourne; picnic and barbecue facilities; 3km N. **Piggery Café:** rustic eatery in the grounds of the historic Burnham Beeches Estate with a trufferie and childrens playground: 1 Sherbrooke Rd, Shrebrooke; 6km N. **Alfred Nicholas Memorial Garden:** the original garden of the historic Burnham Beeches Estate with an ornamental lake with historic boathouse and flowering plants beneath mountain ash trees. The original Nicholas family home (built 1920s) is here; Sherbrooke; 4km SE. **Kawarra Australian Plant Garden:** an impressive collection of native plants; Kalorama; 4.5km N. **Markets:** art, craft, plants and homemade goods; nearby markets include Kallista Market (6km S) 1st Sat each month, and Upper Ferntree Gully Market (12km SE) every Sat and Sun. **Burrinja Cultural Centre:** contemporary art and performances; Upwey; 10km SW. **Silvan:** prominent flower-growing region with many tulip farms. The famous Tesselaar Tulip Farm hosts a popular festival each Sept–Oct with sales of flowers and bulbs, and traditional Dutch music and food; Monbulk Rd; 15km NE. **Silvan Dam:** an area to the north of this major Melbourne water supply has walking tracks, picnic and barbecue facilities; 1.4km E of Silvan. **Mont De Lancey:** a wonderfully preserved house, built in 1882 and set in landscaped gardens; includes a museum and a chapel; open 2nd Sat each month; Wandin North; 22km NE via Mount Evelyn.

WARBURTON
Population 1913

Established when gold was discovered in the 1880s, Warburton, hidden in the Yarra Ranges, still has the feeling of a town slightly off the grid. But don't be misled – this popular tourist town is an easy drive from Melbourne with access to Yarra Ranges National Park and a great biking trail.

Healesville Sanctuary
Opposite: Puffing Billy

TOP EVENTS

- APR PAVE Festival (Performing and Visual Arts in Emerald)
- MAY Puffing Billy Running Festival (Emerald)
- JUNE Film Festival (Warburton)
- JULY Christmas in July (Marysville)
- AUG–NOV Rhododendron and Daffodil Festivals (Olinda)
- OCT Shedfest local wine festival (Healesville)

TEMPERATURES

Jan: 15–26°C

July: 7–12°C

SEE & DO **Blue Lotus Water Garden:** see Other Attractions. **Waterwheel:** local history display and an old-style operating waterwheel 6m in diameter. An art gallery and wood-fire bakery is adjacent to the centre; Warburton Hwy. **River Walk:** 9km return walk, following a pretty stretch of the Yarra River; starts at Signs Bridge; Warburton Hwy. **Golf:** with great views across the river valley; Dammans Rd. **O'Shannassy Aqueduct Trail:** good walking and cycling track that follows the historic open-channelled aqueduct; details from visitor centre. **Valley Market:** 1st Sun each month. **Upper Yarra Museum:** local history displays; open Sun 11am–4pm; Warburton Hwy; 10km SW. **Upper Yarra Reservoir Park:** picnic and camping facilities; 23km NE. **Ada Tree:** a giant mountain ash over 300 years old; access from Powelltown. **Yellingbo Nature Conservation Reserve:** good for nature spotting. Home to the helmeted honeyeater, a state emblem; 25km SW. **Vineyards:** several in the region, many with tastings and sales, including Yarra Burn Winery, Five Oaks Vineyard and Brahams Creek Winery. **Rail trails:** former railway tracks now used for walking, bikeriding or horseriding; the main one being the Lilydale to Warburton trail; details from visitor centre.

YARRA GLEN
Population 2417

Yarra Glen is in the heart of the Yarra Valley wine region, nestled between the Yarra River and the Great Dividing Range. It is a gorgeous area featuring lush, vine-covered hills and fertile valleys, all within easy reach of Melbourne. Fine wines and top-quality local produce, fascinating antique, specialty gift and clothing shops, and restaurants are all in town to entice. For the more adventurous, there is hot-air ballooning, scenic helicopter flights and skydiving at nearby Coldstream airfield.

SEE & DO **Yarra Valley Wine Region:** see Top Attractions. **Gulf Station:** see Other Attractions. **Yarra Glen Grand Hotel:** imposing heritage-listed and National Trust–classified hotel, built in 1888 with a recently refurbished restaurant, stands like a sentinel in the main street; 19 Bell St; (03) 9730 1230. **Yarra Valley Antique Centre:** boasts large collections of genuine antique furniture, china and glass, vintage radios and other collectibles; Bell St. **Railway station:** old station on the 1888 Healesville–Lilydale railway line, rebuilt in 1915; King St. **Yarra Valley farmers' market:** historic barn at Yering Station; 3rd Sun each month. **Yarra Valley Dairy:** a working dairy with sales of specialty cheeses, clotted cream and local produce; 4km S. **Yarra Valley Trails Ponyland:** trail rides and riding lessons; 7km W. **Sugarloaf Reservoir Park:** sailing, fishing and walking, with barbecue and picnic facilities available; 10km W. **Yarra Valley Regional Food Trail:** a self-guided tour, taking in many gourmet food outlets; details from visitor centre.

Mornington Peninsula

This boot-shaped peninsula just south of Melbourne has **stylish resort towns, beaches** lined with colourful wooden bathing boxes, **historic bayside mansions, grand old hotels** and a **hinterland carpeted in grape vines**. With more than 260km of coastline it's a perpetually popular holiday spot for Melburnians to spend summertime, and the **food and wine scene** is superb.

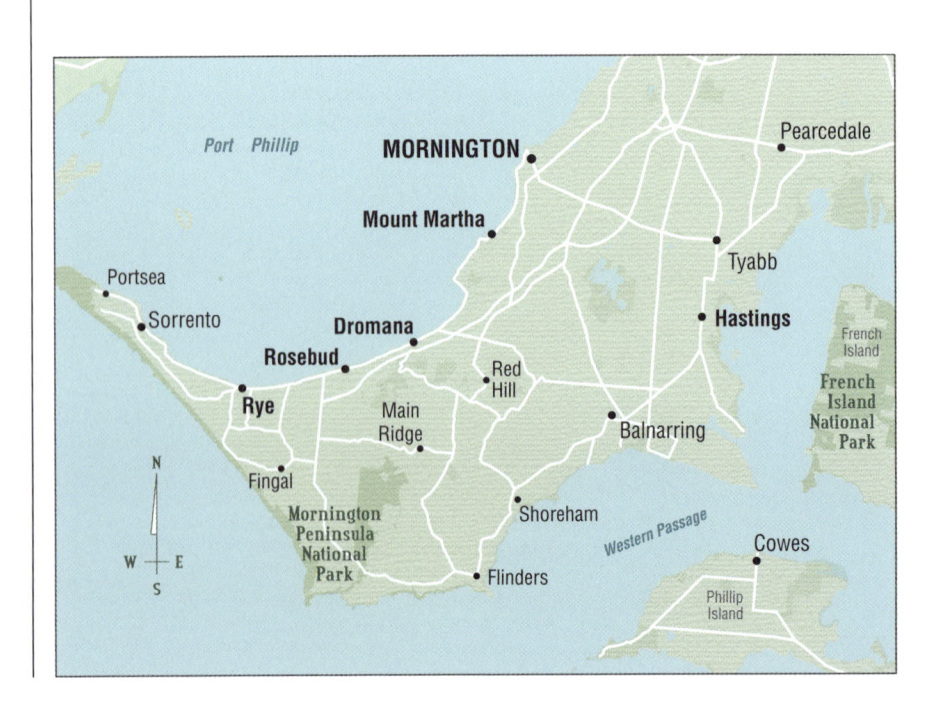

CHEAT SHEET

→ Allow at least two to three days for a proper exploration.

→ Best time to visit: Sept–April.

→ Main towns: Mornington (see p. 131), Flinders (see p. 131), Sorrento (see p. 131).

→ The Mornington Peninsula is the Traditional Land of the Boon Wurrung and Bunurong Peoples.

→ Don't miss: French Island; Peninsula Hot Springs; Cape Schanck; historic Point Nepean; beaches; and wineries.

TOP ATTRACTIONS

ARTHURS SEAT STATE PARK: At 314m, Arthurs Seat is the highest point on the Mornington Peninsula. The summit can be reached by foot or vehicle and offers panoramic views of the bay and surrounding bushland. Picnic facilities and a restaurant are on the summit. There are many short walks, plus the historic Seawinds Gardens with gardens and sculptures. The Enchanted Adventure is set in superb gardens, with a variety of mazes, treetop adventure courses and zip lines. Arthurs Seat Rd, near Dromana.

FRENCH ISLAND NATIONAL PARK: French Island served as a prison for most of the 20th century and was where inmates kept themselves entertained with their own 9-hole golf course. This unique reserve features a range of environments from mangrove saltmarsh to open woodlands. During spring more than 100 varieties of orchids come into bloom. The park is home to the most significant population of koalas in Victoria. Long-nosed potoroos and majestic sea-eagles can also be spotted. There is a variety of walking tracks on the island and bicycles can be hired from the general store. There are also guesthouses, and camping and picnic facilities. Contact Parks Victoria on 13 1963; access is via a 30-min ferry trip from Stony Point.

MOONAH LINKS GOLF COURSE: Two fantastic 18-hole golf courses, one designed specifically for the Australian Open; Peter Thomson Dr, Fingal.

MORNINGTON PENINSULA NATIONAL PARK: The park covers 2686ha and features a diverse range of vegetation, from the basalt cliff-faces of Cape Schanck to banksia woodlands, coastal dune scrubs and swampland and incorporates Sorrento, Rye and Portsea back beaches. Walks, picnics and swimming are the main attractions, but there is also the impressive rock formation of London Bridge, at Portsea. The rugged coastline offers good surfing. One of the park's many attractions is the **Cape Schanck Lighthouse**, built in 1859, which provides accommodation in one of the lighthouse keepers' houses. Historic **Point Nepean** was a quarantine processing station in the 1850s for newly arrived people to Australia, it was also a fort from the 1880s until the end of World War II in 1945 and retains its original fortifications and has information displays and soundscapes. Also available here is a 'hop-on-hop-off' tractor train with commentary, as well as bicycle hire. Point Nepean and historic Fort Nepean can be accessed by a daily transport service departing near the Point Nepean Information Centre. You can also choose to walk the paths or cycle to the tip of Point Nepean (bike hire is available). There are ocean beaches for swimming and surfing, while the Bushranger Bay Nature Walk, starting at Cape Schanck, and the Farnsworth Track at Portsea are just two of the many other walks on offer.

Top: Cape Schanck Lighthouse
Opposite: Sorrento Back Beach

MORNINGTON PENINSULA WINE REGION: Featuring many boutique wineries, the peninsula's signature styles are chardonnay and pinot noir, with shiraz, pinot gris and sauvignon blanc also grown here. **Paringa Estate** repeatedly receives gold medals for its pinot noir, while **Stonier** creates beautiful chardonnay. **Pt. Leo Estate** has an acclaimed outdoor sculpture park with more than 60 large-scale pieces and it continues to grow. Plenty of the wineries also have excellent restaurants, pairing food and wine with great views. **Red Hill Estate** is one of the biggest wineries on the peninsula and features a much-applauded restaurant, Max's. **Jackalope** offers both fine-dining at Doot Doot Doot and a more casual experience at Rare Hare, as well as picnics among the vines; its luxe hotel and spa are more reasons to linger longer. At **Montalto**, the acclaimed restaurant is set in a large, light-filled piazza with beautiful views and modern sculpture displays. At **Ten Minutes By Tractor**, both international and the winery's own wines are matched to the wonderfully flavoursome dishes. The **Wine Food Farmgate Trail** has an extensive program with seasonal information and a trail map. Contact visitor centres for details or download a map at visitmorningtonpeninsula.org.

PENINSULA HOT SPRINGS: Relaxing, outdoor, naturally heated pools open 24 hours. Private mineral pools, baths and massage therapies available as well as glamping accommodation; Springs La, Fingal; (03) 5950 8777.

OTHER ATTRACTIONS

ALBA Opened in late 2022, this thermal springs and spa has quickly become a sought-after wellness destination. Bathing experiences include a rain pool, geothermal pools and botanical pools and spa treatments are also available. Browns Rd, Fingal.

ASHCOMBE MAZE AND LAVENDER GARDENS: A large hedge maze surrounded by beautifully landscaped gardens, with a cafe and gift shop; closed Aug; Shoreham Rd, Shoreham; (03) 5989 8387; ashcombemaze.com.au. The maze is 8km north of Flinders (see p. 131).

HERONSWOOD HOUSE AND GARDEN: Historic house surrounded by formal show gardens and home of the Diggers Club, dedicated to preserving heirloom seeds and gardening traditions. There's also a cafe and garden shop; 105 Latrobe Pde, Dromana; (03) 5984 7318.

MOONLIT SANCTUARY WILDLIFE CONSERVATION PARK: Wildlife park featuring endangered native Australian animals; bookings are essential and you can even take an evening tour; Tyabb–Tooradin Rd, Pearcedale; moonlitsanctuary.com.au.

RED HILL: This is fine wine country, where vineyards are interspersed with noted art galleries, farm gates, cafes and restaurants. The **Red Hill Market** is legendary and is held on the 1st Sat of each month (Sept to May). It specialises in local crafts, clothing and fresh produce. The town also features a number of galleries and the **Ripe N Ready Cherry Farm**, where you can 'pick your own' cherries and berries in a pleasant setting (in season); Arkwells La.

VISITOR INFORMATION

Peninsula Visitor Information Centre
395B Point Nepean Rd, Dromana
(03) 5987 3078 or
1800 804 009
visitmorningtonpeninsula.org

TOP EVENTS

→ JAN Portsea Swim Classic (Portsea)

→ MAR Kite Festival (Rosebud); Peninsula Piers & Pinots (Flinders)

→ JUN Winter Wine Weekend (throughout wine region); Winter Music Festival (Mornington)

→ NOV Peninsula VineHop Festival (throughout wine region)

TEMPERATURES

Jan: 15–23°C

July: 6–14°C

Stand-up paddleboarding against the backdrop of Mount Martha's colourful beach boxes

KEY TOWNS

FLINDERS
Population 811

Flinders is set on the south coast of the Mornington Peninsula, a region famous for its wineries. During the 1880s, it became known as a health and recreation resort and a number of guesthouses and hotels emerged. Today Flinders remains a popular holiday spot, with its renowned cliff-top golf course and gastropub. Heritage buildings have wide verandahs, often shading antique and curio shops or excellent cafes, giving the town an enchanting and historical air. This, combined with the view across the bay to the Nobbies and Seal Rocks, makes it easy to understand the town's perennial appeal.

SEE & DO Ashcombe Maze and Lavender Gardens: see Other Attractions. **Foreshore Reserve:** popular for picnics and fishing from the jetty. **Cook Street Collective:** exhibits jewellery, photography, paintings and sculpture; open Fri–Mon 10am–4pm; 41 Cook St; (03) 5989 1022. **Historic buildings:** Bimbi, built in the 1870s, is the earliest remaining dwelling in Flinders; King St. Wilga is another fine Victorian-era home; King St. **Golf:** great views across Bass Strait; Bass St. **The Ranch:** western-themed adventure park with beach and bush horse trail rides; Cape Schanck; 11km W. **Sunny Ridge Strawberry Farm:** pick your own berries in season; 244 Shands Rd, Main Ridge 11km N. **Point Leo:** great surf beach; 12km NE via Shoreham. **Balnarring:** hosts a market specialising in handmade crafts; 3rd Sat each month Nov–May; 17km NE. Nearby is **Coolart Homestead**, an impressive Victorian mansion with historical displays, gardens, wetlands and a bird-observation area.

MORNINGTON
Population 25,759

Mornington was once the hub of the Mornington Peninsula, which is the reason this long arm of land was eventually given the same name. Today Melbourne's urban sprawl has just about reached the town, and it has virtually become a suburb. However, it retains a seaside village ambience, with a historic courthouse and post office museum that provide a glimpse of the past. The Rocks restaurant on the harbour offers a stunning view over the famous yachts. In the distance, colourful bathing boxes line Mills Beach.

SEE & DO Heronswood House and Garden; Moonlit Sanctuary Wildlife Conservation Park: see Other Attractions for both. **Historic Mornington Pier:** built in the 1850s, the pier remains popular today for walks and fishing. **Regional Gallery:** print and drawing collection, including works by Dobell, Drysdale and Nolan; open Tues–Sun 11am–4pm; Civic Reserve, Dunns Rd; (03) 5975 4395. Also in Civic Reserve is the **Mornington Botanical Rose Gardens** with over 4000 roses planted out in 86 beds. **Main Street Historical Walk:** self-guided tour of historical buildings, including the old post office, now a museum with local history displays; details and map from visitor centre. **Mornington Railway:** journey on a heritage steam train most Sun; 1 300 767 274. **Main Street Market:** each Wed. **Racecourse market:** home-grown and hand-made goods; 2nd Sun each month. **Mount Martha:** visit the Briars for its significant collection of Napoleonic artefacts and furniture. The town also features many gardens, plus wetlands great for birdwatching and bushland walks; 7km S. **Mulberry Hill:** former home of artist Sir Daryl Lindsay and author Joan Lindsay, who wrote *Picnic at Hanging Rock*; open 2nd Sun of the month; Golf Links Rd, Baxter; (03) 9656 9889; 14km NE. **Tyabb Packing House Antiques:** huge collection of antiques and collectibles; Mornington–Tyabb Rd, Tyabb; 16km E. **Hastings:** coastal town on Western Port with 2km walking trail through wetlands and mangrove habitat; 21km SE. **Beaches:** the stretch of coast between Mornington and Mount Martha features sheltered, sandy bays popular with holidaymakers.

★ SORRENTO
Population 2013

Sorrento is a holiday beach town with a luxe vibe. The peninsula nearby is famed for its idyllic natural landscapes, festivals, wines, beaches, gourmet offerings and affable communities. In 1803 Sorrento was the site of Victoria's first European settlement, a convict settlement that was abandoned soon after. The town, just inside Port Phillip Heads, is close to historic Point Nepean and major surf and bayside beaches. Its population swells significantly over summer as visitors flock to soak up the holiday-resort atmosphere. It has a variety of fashion and homewares stores, day spas, cafes, restaurants and accommodation. A ferry links Sorrento to Queenscliff (*see* p. 162) on the Bellarine Peninsula.

SEE & DO Manyung Gallery: showcasing the best of Australian paintings and sculpture, this is the Mornington Peninsula's oldest art space; open 10am–5pm, closed Wed; 113 Ocean Beach Rd; (03) 9787 2953. **Polperro Dolphin Swims:** swim with wild bottlenose dolphins in Port Phillip with eco-accredited operator; Sorrento Pier (late Sept–early May); (03) 5988 8437. **Collins Settlement Historic Site:** marks Victoria's first European settlement and includes early graves; on Sullivan Bay; contact Parks Victoria on 13 1963. **Historic buildings:** Hotel Sorrento on Hotham Rd and Continental Hotel on Ocean Beach Rd. Both are fine examples of early Victorian architecture, with the latter reputed to be the largest limestone building in the Southern Hemisphere. The visitor centre has details of self-guided historical walks. **Nepean Historical Society Museum and Heritage Gallery:** a collection of local artefacts and memorabilia in the National Trust–classified Mechanics Institute. Adjacent is **Watt's Cottage and the Pioneer Memorial Garden**; check ahead for opening hours; Melbourne Rd; (03) 5984 0255. **Day spas:** all types of relaxation therapies are available at health and wellness centres; details from visitor centre. **Blairgowrie:** a boutique bayside village with easy access to sailing; 3km NW. **Portsea:** an opulent holiday town with good swimming beaches. It hosts the Portsea Swim Classic each Jan; 4km NW. **Pope's Eye Marine Reserve:** an artificially created horseshoe-shaped island and reef, now popular for diving. Gannets nest here. Cruises available; ask at visitor centre; 5km offshore at Portsea. **Rye:** a beachside holiday spot with a large campground and a foreshore market (1st Sat each month); 8km E. **Rosebud:** a bayside resort town with gorgeous swimming beaches and local markets on weekends. Summer fishing trips depart from Rosebud pier. An international kite festival is held in Mar; 15km E. **McCrae Homestead:** National Trust drop-slab property built in 1844, making it one of Victoria's oldest homesteads; open Sun 11am–4pm Sun (except July and Aug); group bookings by appt; McCrae (03) 9656 9889; 17km E. **St Andrews Beach:** golf course; 209 Sandy Rd, Fingal; (03) 5988 6000; 18km SE.

Phillip Island and South Gippsland

The Bass Coast east of Melbourne is home to two of Victoria's best-loved attractions: the nightly **penguin parade** on Phillip Island and the coastal wilderness of **Wilsons Promontory National Park**. Explore a little further and you'll find more **beautiful beaches** and charming – sometimes downright quirky – towns and museums, **fabulous food and wine trails** and two of Victoria's best **rail trails**: Bass Coast Rail Trail and Great Southern Rail Trail.

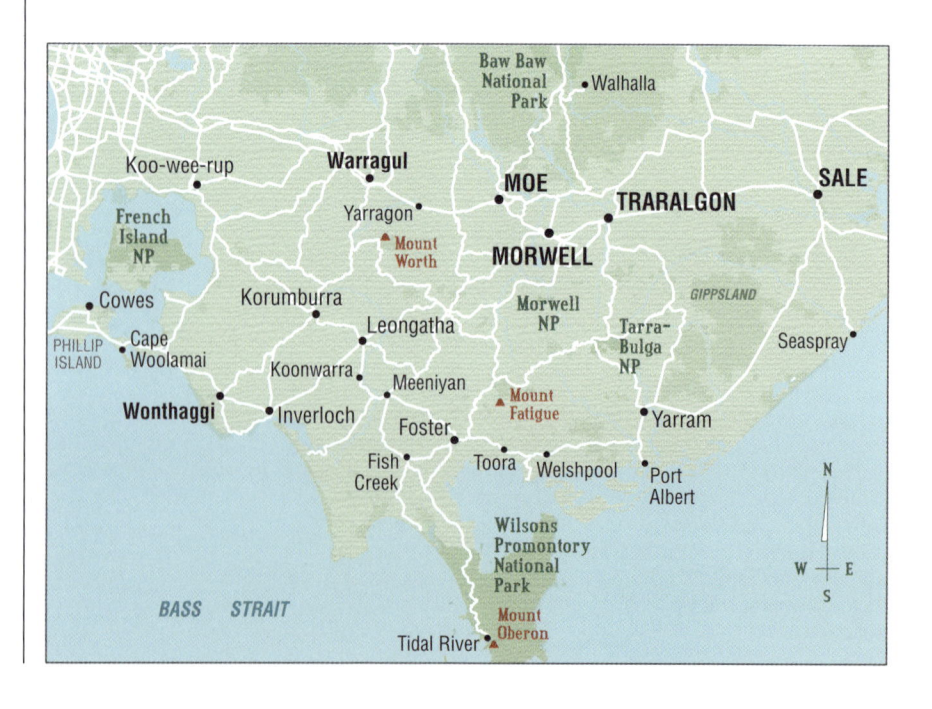

CHEAT SHEET

- → Allow at least four days for a proper exploration.
- → Best time to visit: year-round.
- → Main towns: Cowes (see p. 136), Foster (see p. 136), Wonthaggi (see p. 139).
- → Phillip Island and South Gippsland are the Traditional Lands of the Boon Wurrung, Bunurong and Gunaikurnai Peoples.
- → Don't miss: the penguin parade; a night camping at Wilsons Prom; coastal views on the Bunurong Coastal Drive; ride the rail trails; historic Walhalla.

Top: Corrigan Suspension Bridge in Tarra Bulga National Park **Opposite:** Squeaky Beach, Wilsons Prom

TOP ATTRACTIONS

BAW BAW NATIONAL PARK: The landscape ranges from densely forested river valleys to alpine plateaus and the activities on offer are equally varied – from canoeing river rapids and fishing for trout to skiing, horseriding and bushwalking. Wildflowers carpet the alpine areas in spring. Baw Baw Alpine Resort is 90km north of Moe, while the popular Aberfeldy picnic and camping area is accessed via a track north of Walhalla.

BUNURONG COASTAL DRIVE: Stretching for 14km between Inverloch and Cape Paterson is this coastal drive with magnificent views to Venus Bay and beyond. Carparks offer access to beaches and coastal walks along the drive. The waters offshore are protected within Bunurong Marine National Park, and offer opportunities to surf, snorkel, scuba dive or simply explore the numerous rockpools that are dotted along the coast.

COAL CREEK COMMUNITY PARK AND MUSEUM: This open-air museum offers all the fascination of life in a 19th-century coal-mining village, including history and memorabilia of the area. The village contains beautiful picnic areas, a bush tramway and cafe, and community events are held throughout the year. Open Fri–Mon 10am–4pm; South Gippsland Hwy; Korumburra; (03) 5655 1811.

GIPPSLAND GOURMET COUNTRY: The renowned 'Gippsland Gourmet Country' region takes in lush green pastures and state forests to reveal a diverse range of superb gourmet delights. Gippsland Gourmet encompasses some of the best food and wine producers in the region, including trout, venison, cheese, berries, potatoes, herbs and wine. It's sure to tempt your tastebuds, so grab a basket and get ready to fill it for an amazing picnic; details from local visitor centres.

GIPPSLAND WINE REGION: This dispersed wine region stretches from Phillip Island to Lakes Entrance, with the main cluster of wineries around Leongatha. **Bass Phillip** makes what is regarded as Australia's greatest pinot noir. **Phillip Island Winery** is responsible for another superb version, as well as an excellent botrytis riesling. Chardonnay is Gippsland's other specialty, evident from wineries such as **Narkoojee** and **Nicholson River**. The latter makes a particularly wonderful merlot and a blend called the Nicholson (merlot and shiraz).

KOALA CONSERVATION CENTRE: You can view these lovely creatures in their natural habitat from an elevated boardwalk; Phillip Island Rd, Rhyll; (03) 5951 2800.

PENGUIN PARADE: The nightly penguin parade is Phillip Island's most popular attraction. During this world-famous event, little penguins emerge from the sea after a tiring fishing expedition and cross Summerland Beach to their homes in the dunes. Tours run at sunset each night, and the penguins can be spotted from the boardwalks and viewing platforms. The site also has an interactive visitor centre with details about these adorable creatures. Note that no cameras are allowed beyond the visitor centre. Ventnor Rd, Summerlands; bookings on (03) 5951 2800.

PHILLIP ISLAND GRAND PRIX CIRCUIT: Home to the Australian Motorcycle Grand Prix and the Superbike World Championship as well as various Australian motor racing events, the circuit is steeped in both old and recent history, which is detailed thoroughly in the visitor centre. You can also try go-karting on a replica of the Grand Prix track; Back Beach Rd, Ventnor; (03) 5952 9400.

PORT WELSHPOOL: This popular coastal town has all the natural attractions that a seaside village could want. It is frequented by families who enjoy the safe beaches and fabulous coastal walks, and has fantastic views across to Wilsons Promontory. Fishing enthusiasts should drop a line from the historic jetty, or from a boat. The port's long link with the sea is detailed in the Port Welshpool and District Maritime Museum, which exhibits shipping relics and local history displays as well.

STATE COAL MINE: The demand for black coal created a thriving industry in Wonthaggi from 1909 until 1968, and the mine site has been retained to show visitors the lifestyle and working conditions of the miners. Daily underground tours offer close-up views of the coalface, a short walk into the East Area Mine and a cable-hauled skip ride to the surface. Above ground, visit the museum for an introduction to the history of the mine and of Wonthaggi itself, or take a walk around the historic buildings. Open 10am–4.30pm; Garden St, Wonthaggi; (03) 5672 3053 or Parks Victoria on 13 1963.

TARRA–BULGA NATIONAL PARK: Tarra-Bulga National Park is highly significant to the Gunaikurnai People creation storyline where Borun, carrying his canoe, travelled from the mountains in the north to the place called Tarra Warackel. It's a tranquil park with spectacular river and mountain views. Fern Gully Walk takes in the dense, temperate rainforests of mountain ash, myrtle and sassafras and leads across a suspension bridge high among the treetops. A walk to Cyathea or Tarra falls, surrounded by lush fern gullies, completes the rainforest experience. Look out for rosellas, lyrebirds and the occasional koala. The Tarra–Bulga Visitor Centre is on Grand Ridge Rd near Balook; from Yarram, access the park from Tarra Valley Rd.

THE NOBBIES CENTRE AND SEAL ROCKS: This interactive centre gives you an insight into local marine life, including Australia's largest colony of Australian fur seals, via cameras that you can control yourself. The Antarctic Journey exhibition highlights key iconic wildlife in one of the world's last great wilderness areas. Outside, the island features a cliff-side boardwalk with views of the fantastic natural landmark the Nobbies and out to Seal Rocks. Walk around to the Blowhole to hear the thunderous noise of huge waves crashing and look out for the nesting sites of vast colonies of seagulls and short-tailed shearwaters that migrate to the island annually. Informative displays explain each natural attraction. Ventnor Rd, Summerlands; (03) 5951 2800.

WEST GIPPSLAND ARTS CENTRE: Part of Warragul's fantastic, architect-designed civic centre complex, the centre is a mecca for art lovers from across the state. It houses a good permanent collection of contemporary visual arts and is known for the variety of theatre productions and events held here throughout the year. Cnr Smith and Albert sts, Warragul; (03) 5624 2456.

WILSONS PROMONTORY NATIONAL PARK: The Traditional Lands of the Gunaikurnai, Boon Wurrung and Bunurong Peoples, The Prom, as it's known by most Victorians, is well loved across the state for its wild and untouched scenery and great camping facilities. Its 130km coastline is framed by granite headlands, mountains, forests and fern gullies. Bordered on all sides by sea, it hangs from Victoria by a thin, sandy isthmus. Limited road access means opportunities for walking are plentiful. The park features dozens of walking tracks, ranging from easy strolls to more challenging overnight hikes that take visitors to one of 11 campsites only accessible by foot. Hikes range from beginner to intermediate, and permits are required. Families camp at Tidal River and the Wilsons Promontory Lightstation, built in 1859, has cottage accommodation. Detailed information is provided at the park's own visitor centre: the remnants of a commando training camp from World War II, or at parks.vic.gov.au.

YALLOCK-BULLUK MARINE AND COASTAL PARK: Honouring the Traditional Owners, the Yallock-Bulluk Clan of the Bunurong People, this is one of Victoria's most recently gazetted parks. This spectacular stretch of the Bass Coast includes many Aboriginal cultural heritage sites. 'Yallock' is the Bunurong word for creek or river. 'Bulluk' means swamp. Stretching 40km from San Remo to Inverloch it combines the Bunurong Coastal, Kilcunda-Harmers Haven Coastal, Punchbowl Coastal, Wonthaggi Heathlands Nature Conservation, and parts of the San Remo, Kilcunda and Cape Paterson foreshore reserves. In 2022, construction work began on the 45km Yallock-Bulluk Trail, which will eventually stretch the entire length of the park.

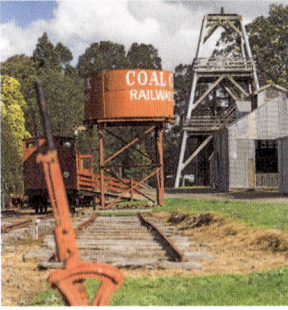

OTHER ATTRACTIONS

BASS COAST RAIL TRAIL:
16km trail that runs between Wonthaggi and Anderson. Suitable for walking and cycling, it is the only coastal rail trail in Victoria and has landscape that varies from flat farmland and bushland to rugged coastline, while crossing one of the most impressive trestle bridges in the state.

CAPE WOOLAMAI: The beach is renowned for its fierce and exciting surf (patrolled in season). From the beach there are a number of 2–4hr loop walks, many to the southern end of the cape and passing The Pinnacles rock formations on the way. South of Cape Woolamai township on Phillip Island.

FISH CREEK: A rural village, which attracts many visitors en route to the Prom. From the novelty of the giant mullet on top of the Promontory Gate Hotel to the fish-shaped seats around town, there is more to this unusually themed town than meets the eye, with galleries and vineyards nearby. Access the Great Southern Trail and walk, ride or cycle your way to Foster. Nearby Mount Nicol offers a lookout with spectacular views.

GIPPSLAND HERITAGE PARK:
Also known as Old Gippstown, this is a re-creation of a 19th-century community with over 30 restored buildings and a fine collection of fully restored horse-drawn carriages. Open Wed–Sun 10am–4pm; Lloyd St, Moe; (03) 5127 3082.

GREAT SOUTHERN RAIL TRAIL:
Following in the tracks of the now defunct South Gippsland Tourist Railway, this 72km cycling trail starts in Leongatha and goes through towns including Stony Creek and Foster before ending in Port Welshpool.

GREAT WALHALLA ALPINE TRAIL: Challenging two-day, 40km walk from Walhalla to Mount Baw Baw taking in the rivers, mountain ash and native wildflowers of Baw Baw National Park (see p. 133).

KOONWARRA: Situated between Leongatha and Meeniyan on the South Gippsland Hwy, Koonwarra became the first eco-wise town in Australia. The town prides itself on its commitment to sustainable lifestyles. On the 1st Sat of each month, Koonwarra holds a farmers' market. The town also boasts an organic cooking school, day spa, specialty shops, pottery and winery nearby.

LONG TUNNEL EXTENDED GOLD MINE: This goldmine in Walhalla (see p. 138) was one of the most prosperous in the state during the 19th century with over 13 tonnes of gold extracted. Guided tours take visitors through sites such as Cohen's reef and the original machinery chamber 150m below the ground. Tours run Mon–Sun at 1.30pm, Sat–Sun at 12pm and 3pm and on public holidays. Main St, Walhalla; 0412 285 913.

MORWELL NATIONAL PARK:
This park protects some of the last remnant vegetation of the Strzelecki Ranges, including pockets of rainforest and fern gullies. The area is the Traditional Land of the Woollum Woollum People, who hunted in the ranges. In the 1840s European settlers cleared much of the surrounding land. On the Fosters Gully Nature Walk, keep your eyes peeled for orchids (more than 40 species are found here) and native animals.

MOUNT WORTH STATE PARK:
A rich variety of native flora including the silver wattle and the Victorian Christmas bush are protected in this park. The Giant's Circuit walk takes in a massive old mountain ash 7m in circumference. Other walks include the Moonlight Creek and MacDonalds tracks, both of which are easily accessible. No camping is permitted; access via Grand Ridge Rd.

NOORAMUNGA MARINE AND COASTAL PARK: Surrounding Port Albert and comprising the waters and sand islands offshore, this marine park is a fishing enthusiast's delight. Snapper, flathead and Australian salmon can be caught from the surf beaches or from a boat. The shell middens that dot the shorelines prove that fishing and feasting on shellfish has been carried on here by the Gunai and Kurnai People for many thousands of years. This park is an important reserve for migratory wading birds. Camping is allowed but permits must be obtained.

PROM COUNTRY CHEESE:
Sheep cheese farm with tastings and lunch. Open Sat 11am–4pm Sept–Feb; 275 Andersons Inlet Rd, Moyarra/Bena; (03) 5657 3338.

TOORA: An internationally recognised wetland located on Corner Inlet, Toora is renowned for the huge variety of migratory birds that nest in the area. It is also home to Agnes Falls, a wind farm, a lavender farm and the Bird Hide, where you can watch migratory and native birdlife.

YARRAGON: Nestled in the foothills of the Strzelecki Ranges and with views of green rolling hills, Yarragon is a wonderful destination with an abundance of delightful shops, art and craft galleries and accommodation options.

Top: Mount Baw Baw **Middle:** Coal Creek Community Park & Village in Korumburra **Bottom:** Corrigan Suspension Bridge in Tarra-Bulga National Park

KEY TOWNS

★ COWES (PHILLIP ISLAND)
Population 6797

Situated on the north side of Phillip Island, Cowes is the island's major town and a popular base for holiday accommodation. The island is linked to the Mornington Peninsula by a passenger ferry service or to the Gippsland region via the San Remo bridge. The Cowes foreshore offers fantastic coastal walks and safe swimming beaches, with the focal point being the town's jetty. It is a popular fishing spot, as well as a departure point for several ferries. Wildlife-watching cruises to Seal Rocks operate from the jetty and are the best way to see the fur seals close-up.

SEE & DO **Penguin Parade; the Nobbies Centre and Seal Rocks; Koala Conservation Centre; Grand Prix Circuit:** see Top Attractions for all. **Seal-watching cruises:** depart from the jetty to Seal Rocks; bookings on 1300 763 739. **Farmers' market:** Churchill Island; 4th Sat each month. **Phillip Island Wildlife Park:** features native fauna, with opportunities to handfeed kangaroos and wallabies; Phillip Island Rd; (03) 5952 2038; 3km S. **A Maze'N Things:** family fun park featuring a large timber maze, a high rope course called a SkyTrail and Maxi Mini Golf; Phillip Island Rd; (03) 5952 2283; 6km SE. **Rhyll Inlet:** wetlands of international significance, with the marshes and mangroves providing an important breeding ground for wading birds. There are various loop walks, as well as an excellent view from the Conservation Hill Observation Tower; 7km E. **Wineries:** Phillip Island Winery offers tastings, sales and casual dining; Berrys Beach Rd; (03) 8595 2155; 7km SW. Purple Hen Wines also offers tastings and light meals; McFees Rd, Rhyll; (03) 5956 9244; 9km SE. **Churchill Island:** a road bridge provides access to this protected parkland, which features a historic homestead, a walking track and abundant birdlife; 16km SE. **Clip 'n Climb:** climbing and adventure centre with an augmented reality wall and virtual reality pods; 6–8 Industrial Way, Cowes; (03) 5952 6780. **National Vietnam Veterans Museum:** details the history of Australian involvement in the Vietnam War, displaying around 6000 artefacts; 25 Veterans Dr, Newhaven; (03) 5956 6400; 16km SE. **Panny's Amazing World of Chocolate:** has information on the chocolate-making process and a mosaic of Dame Edna made from 12,000 chocolate pieces; visitors can even make their own chocolate; Newhaven; (03) 5956 6600; 16km SE. **Pelicans:** see these unusual birds up close, with feeding time daily at 12pm; San Remo Pier (opposite the Fishing Co-op); 17km SE.

FOSTER
Population 1308

Most cars driving through Foster are stacked with tents and hiking gear – that's because this town is a popular stop-off (and base) for people visiting Wilsons Promontory. The town has a good pub, a few excellent cafes, and even a shop featuring the work of renowned children's author Alison Lester. Foster was originally a goldmining town settled in the 1870s.

SEE & DO **Historical Museum:** in old post office; Main St. **Stockyard Gallery:** Main St. **Hayes Walk:** view the site of Victory Mine, Foster's largest goldmine; starts in town behind the carpark. **Pearl Park:** picturesque picnic spot. **Foster North Lookout:** 6km NW. **Turtons Creek Reserve:** features mountain ash, blackwood and tree ferns, and a small waterfall. Bush camping is available; 18km N. **Coastal towns:** popular bases during summer months are Sandy Point, 22km S, Waratah Bay, 34km SW and Walkerville, 36km SW. **Cape Liptrap:** views over rugged coastline and Bass Strait; 46km SW.

VISITOR INFORMATION

Phillip Island Visitor Information Centre
895 Phillip Island Tourist Road, Newhaven
1300 366 422
visitphillipisland.com

Prom Country Visitor Information Centre
cnr Main and McDonald sts, Foster
(03) 5655 2233 or
1800 630 704
visitsouthgippsland.com.au

Latrobe Visitor Information Centre
The Old White Church,
41 Princes Hwy, Traralgon
1800 621 409
visitlatrobecity.com

Bass Coast
visitbasscoast.com

Central Gippsland
visitgippsland.com.au

Opposite: The foreshore at Cowes, Phillip Island

INVERLOCH
Population 6046

Inverloch is a small seaside town set on the protected waters of Anderson Inlet, east of Wonthaggi. It is characterised by long stretches of pristine beach that offer good surf and excellent fishing.

SEE & DO **Bunurong Environment Centre:** houses shell museum and natural history displays with special focus on dinosaur diggings; also sales of natural products; open Wed–Mon 10am–5pm; cnr Ramsay Blvd and The Espl; (03) 5674 3738. **Anderson Inlet:** the most southerly habitat for mangroves in Australia. This calm inlet is popular for windsurfing and watersports, and nearby Townsend Bluff and Mahers Landing offer good birdwatching; adjacent to town. **Fishing:** in nearby waterways such as the Tarwin River; 20km SE.

KOO WEE RUP
Population 3336

Koo Wee Rup and the surrounding agricultural area exist on reclaimed and drained swampland. It has given rise to Australia's largest asparagus-growing district. The town's name derives from the Bunurong word meaning 'blackfish swimming', a reference to the fish that were once plentiful in the swamp.

SEE & DO **Historical Society Museum:** local history; open Sun; Rossiter Rd. **Swamp Observation Tower:** views of remaining swampland and across to Western Port; South Gippsland Hwy; 2km SE. **Bayles Fauna & Flora Reserve:** native animals; 8km NE. **Tooradin:** offers good boating and fishing on Sawtells Inlet; 10km W. **Caldermeade Farm:** originally a premier beef cattle property but now a fully operational modern dairy farm focused on educating and entertaining visitors; 10km SE. **Tynong:** attractions include Gumbuya Park, a family fun park, Australian native food experiences at Peppermint Ridge Farm and Pakenham Racing Club; 20km NE. **Royal Botanic Gardens Cranbourne:** renowned, wonderfully maintained native gardens; 22km NW. **Moonlit Sanctuary:** walk around the 10ha of bushland for encounters with native wildlife; 24km E.

KORUMBURRA
Population 3869

Established in 1887, Korumburra stands firmly as the heritage centre of South Gippsland. The township was a primary producer of black coal for Victoria's rail industry until the last mine closed in 1958. Korumburra is set in the rolling green hills of South Gippsland, with scenic drives found in every direction.

SEE & DO **Coal Creek Community Park and Museum:** see Top Attractions. **Coal Creek farmers' market:** 2nd Sat each month. **Botanic Park:** features a variety of labelled trees and a popular creek-side walk; Bridge St. **Loch:** a thriving art and craft village with cosy eateries, antique stores and galleries; 18km NW. **Poowong:** beautiful country town nestled among the green hills of South Gippsland with Poowong Pioneer Chapel, built in 1878; 15km NW.

LEONGATHA
Population 5618

Leongatha is considered the commercial centre of South Gippsland. Idyllically positioned as a gateway to Gippsland destinations and attractions, any major road departing Leongatha provides access to popular attractions, all within an easy hour's drive.

SEE & DO **Leongatha Gallery:** featuring contemporary exhibits and local arts and craft; open Wed–Sun 10am–4pm; Michael Pl; (03) 5662 5370. **Great Southern Rail Trail:** commencement of 50km rail trail that winds between Leongatha and Foster. **Meeniyan:** a great place to visit for the art and craft enthusiast. Places of interest include Meeniyan Art Gallery and Lacy Jewellery Studio. Meeniyan hosts a garlic festival each Feb, with produce and novelty events; 16km SE. **Mossvale Park:** a tranquil setting for a picnic or barbecue. Music concerts and festivals are held here in Feb and Mar; 16km NE. **Mirboo North:** situated among the picturesque Strzelecki Ranges, the township is decorated with murals depicting the history of the area. Grand Ridge Brewery, Lyre Bird Forest Walk and the Grand Ridge Rail Trail are also located here; 26km NE.

MOE
Population 9375

Like many of the towns in this region, Moe is supported by the power industry, but it has managed to avoid becoming a grim industrial centre. Instead, there is a small-town feel and a number of pretty gardens and public parks.

SEE & DO **Gippsland Heritage Park:** see Other Attractions. **Edward Hunter Heritage Bush Reserve:** 3km S via Coalville St. **Trafalgar Lookout and Narracan Falls:** near Trafalgar; 10km W. **Old Brown Coal Mine Museum:** explore the history and memorabilia of the original township known as 'Brown Coal Mine' and the establishment of the power industry in the Latrobe Valley; cnr Third St and Latrobe River Rd, Yallourn North; 10km E. **Blue Rock Lake:** large dam on the Tanjil River with trout fishing and limited boating; 20km NW. **Thorpdale:** a town renowned for its potatoes. A bakery sells potato bread and a potato festival is held each Mar; 22km SW.

MORWELL
Population 14,068

Morwell is primarily an industrial town and Victoria's major producer of electricity. It nestles in the heart of the Latrobe Valley, which contains one of the world's largest deposits of brown coal. Among all the heavy machinery is the impressive

Centenary Rose Garden, featuring over 4000 rose bushes and regarded as one of the finest rose gardens in the Southern Hemisphere.

SEE & DO **Centenary Rose Garden:** off Commercial Rd. **Power Trail:** self-guided tour along Route 98; details and map from visitor centre. **Latrobe Regional Gallery:** hosts outstanding works of contemporary Australian art by local and national artists; open 10am–4pm; 138 Commercial Rd; (03) 5128 5700. **Gippsland Immigration Wall of Recognition:** acknowledges immigrants who contributed to the development of the Gippsland region; Gippsland Immigration Park, Princes Way; 1300 900 737. **Hazelwood Pondage:** warm water ideal for year-round watersports; 5km S. **Arc Yinnar:** artist-run gallery housed in an old butter factory; Main St, Yinnar; (03) 5163 1310; 12km SW. **Lake Narracan:** fishing and waterskiing; 15km NW. **Narracan Falls:** 27km W. **Scenic drives:** routes around the Strzelecki Ranges and Baw Baw ranges offer impressive views over the Latrobe Valley.

PORT ALBERT
Population 349

Port Albert is a tranquil port on the south-east coast. Looking at this peaceful village now, it is hard to believe that it was the first established port in Victoria, and that ships from Europe and America once docked at its jetty. Ships from China arrived here during the gold rush, bringing thousands of prospectors to the Gippsland goldfields. The sheltered waters of Port Albert, still a commercial fishing port, are popular with anglers and boat owners, which sees its population swell considerably during summer.

SEE & DO **Old Port Trail:** this 11km return trail between the township and the old port in Seabank, the former site of the town, winds through coastal vegetation little changed by white settlement. **Historic buildings:** include original government offices and stores, Customs House Inn and the Bank of Victoria, which now houses a maritime museum with photographs and relics from the town's past. Georgian and Victorian architectural styles are evident in over 40 buildings; Tarraville Rd. **Port Albert Art Gallery:** a gallery featuring works by Warren Curry; Tarraville Rd. **Maritime Art and Antiques:** marine relics on show and for purchase; Wharf St. **Christ Church:** built in 1856, this was the first church to be established in Gippsland; Tarraville; 5km NE. **Beaches:** Manns, for swimming, 10km NE; and Woodside, on Ninety Mile Beach, for good surfing, 34km NE. Note that both beaches are patrolled during summer. **St Margaret Island:** a protected area featuring a wildlife sanctuary; 12km E.

TRARALGON
Population 27,628

Traralgon is one of the Latrobe Valley's largest towns; a commerical hub located on the main Gippsland rail and road routes. Primarily a service centre for neighbouring agricultural communities (as well as timber and power generation), it retains a village atmosphere with historic buildings in its wide streets and attractive public gardens.

SEE & DO **Historic buildings:** include the old post office and courthouse; cnr Franklin and Kay sts. **Victory Park:** a great spot for picnics. There's also a band rotunda and miniature railway; Princes Hwy. **Miniature train rides:** Newman Park; 4th Sun each month. **Farmers' market:** 4th Sat each month. **Walhalla Mountain Rivers Trail:** this scenic drive (Tourist Route 91) winds through pretty hills to the north of town. **Loy Yang power station:** self-guided tours; details from visitor centre; 5km S. **Hazelwood Cooling Pond:** year-round warm water makes this a popular swimming spot; outskirts of Churchill; 20km SW.

WALHALLA
Population 35

You'll feel like you've entered Indiana Jones territory in Walhalla, a tiny town hidden in a steep, narrow valley in the Gippsland mountains. What would entice people to move here? Gold, of course. Be sure to take a tour of the old Long Tunnel Extended Gold Mine to hear more about the town's goldmining history. If you see a TV on in the pub when you visit, be impressed – the town was only connected to reticulated electricity in 1998.

SEE & DO **Long Tunnel Extended Gold Mine:** *see* Other Attractions. **Historic buildings and goldmining remains:** include the old post office, bakery and Windsor House, now a B&B. **Walks:** excellent walks in the town area, including one to a cricket ground on top of a 200m hill. Another walk leads to a historic cemetery with graves of early miners; details from visitor centre. **Museum:** local history displays plus goldmining artefacts; Main St. **Walhalla Goldfields Railway:** wonderfully restored old steam engine; departs from Thomson Station; details at walhallarail.com.au. **Gold panning:** try your luck along pretty Stringers Creek, which runs through town. **Ghost tours:** spook yourself with a night-time guided ghost tour of Walhalla using old-fashioned lanterns; (03) 5165 6250. **Thomson River:** excellent fishing and canoeing; 4km S. **Rawson:** a town built to accommodate those who helped construct the nearby Thomson Dam; 8km SW. **Erica:** visit this small timber town to see a timber-industry display at the Erica Hotel; 12km SW. **Moondarra State Park:** great for walks and picnics. Moondarra Reservoir is nearby; 30km S. **4WD tours:** to gold-era 'suburbs' such as Coopers Creek and Erica. Tours can be organised through Mountain Top Experience; (03) 5134 6876.

Top: Warragul Farmers Market
Bottom: Traralgon Post Office
Opposite: Walhalla

TOP EVENTS

- → FEB Garlic Festival (Meeniyan); South Gippsland Golf Classic (Leongatha); International Film Festival (Wonthaggi)
- → FEB–MAR World Superbike Championships (Phillip Island)
- → MAR Autumn Festival (Inverloch); Prom Coast Festival (Foster)
- → AUG Jazz Festival (Inverloch)
- → SEPT Leongatha Daffodil & Floral Show (Leongatha)
- → OCT Australian Motorcycle Grand Prix (Phillip Island); Supercars (Phillip Island); Literary Festival (Coal Creek)

TEMPERATURES

Jan: 16–24°C

July: 8–13°C

WARRAGUL
Population 19,134

Warragul is a thriving rural town with a growing commuter population, and is the dairying centre that supplies much of Melbourne's milk. An excellent base to explore the delightful countryside including the Baw Baw snowfields and Gippsland Gourmet Country, the town itself showcases 19th-century architecture, especially in the ornate facades and arched windows of Queen St.

SEE & DO West Gippsland Arts Centre; Gippsland Gourmet Country: see Top Attractions for both. Arts Market: Civic Park; 3rd Sat each month. Waterfalls: Glen Cromie, Drouin West (10km NW); Glen Nayook, south of Nayook (30km N); and Toorongo Falls, just north of Noojee (48km N). Neerim South: visit Tarago River Cheese Company for tastings and sales of top-quality cheeses, or enjoy a picnic or barbecue at the pleasant reserve near the Tarago Reservoir. Scenic drives through mountain country start from town; 17km N. Grand Ridge Road: 132km drive that starts at Seaview, 17km S, and traverses the Strzelecki Ranges to Tarra–Bulga National Park, see Top Attractions. Childers: Sunny Creek Fruit and Berry Farm; 31km SE. Noojee: a mountain town featuring a historic trestle bridge and the Alpine Trout Farm; 39km N.

WELSHPOOL
Population 361

Welshpool is a small dairying community in South Gippsland. On the coast nearby, Port Welshpool is a deep-sea port servicing the local fishing and oil industries. Barry Beach Marine Terminal, a short distance west of Port Welshpool, services the offshore oil rigs in Bass Strait.

SEE & DO Port Welshpool: see Top Attractions. Franklin River Reserve: great bushwalking with well-marked tracks; near Toora; 11km W. Agnes Falls: the highest single-span falls in the state at 59m, glorious after heavy rain; 19km NW. Scenic drive: head west to see magnificent views from Mount Fatigue; off South Gippsland Hwy. Fishing and boating: excellent along the coast.

WONTHAGGI
Population 8430

'Wonthaggi' means 'home' in the Boonwurrung language. Once the main supplier of coal to the Victorian Railways, Wonthaggi, near the beachside town of Cape Paterson, is South Gippsland's largest town. There are good tourist facilities in town and a number of pretty beaches nearby.

SEE & DO State Coal Mine: see Top Attractions. Bass Coast Rail Trail: see Other Attractions. Cape Paterson: waters offshore are protected by Bunurong Marine and Coastal Park and are good for surfing, swimming, snorkelling and scuba diving; 8km S. George Bass Coastal Walk: starts at Kilcunda; 11km NW. Ask at visitor centre for details of other walks. Gippsland Gourmet Country Road Cycling Loop: takes in central Gippsland's gourmet food and wine producers; details from visitor centre.

YARRAM
Population 1739

Yarram is deep in the dairy country of South Gippsland, and at the heart of some of its most beautiful locales, from the splendour of Ninety Mile Beach to the refreshingly cool atmosphere of Tarra–Bulga National Park. The term 'Yarram Yarram' is thought to be an Aboriginal phrase meaning 'plenty of water', however it is not known which language group the name is taken from.

SEE & DO Tarra–Bulga National Park: see Top Attractions. Won Wron Forest: great for walks, with wildflowers in spring; Hyland Hwy; 16km N. Beaches: there are many attractive beaches in the region, including Manns, for fishing, 16km SE; McLoughlins, 23km E; and Woodside Beach, which is patrolled in summer, 29km E. Tarra Valley: there are many great gardens; located just north-west of Yarram. Scenic drive: a 46km circuit goes from Yarram through Hiawatha taking in Minnie Ha Ha Falls on Albert River, where picnic and camping facilities are provided.

East Gippsland

The north-eastern coast of Victoria is a waterside holiday playground, where **rivers and lakes** converge in a maze of waterways separated from the ocean by a strip of coastal sand dunes known as **Ninety Mile Beach**. Much of the coastline is protected by **Croajingolong National Park**, and it's no surprise that this region attracts **sailors, anglers, bushwalkers** and **campers**, particularly in the summer months.

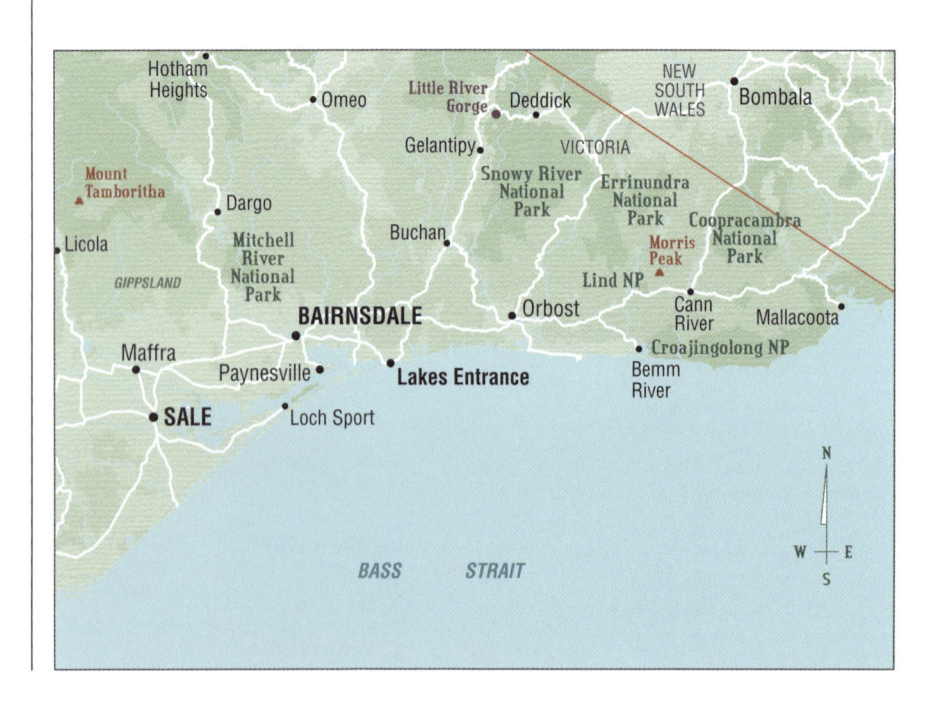

CHEAT SHEET

→ Allow at least four days for a proper exploration.

→ Best time to visit: Sept–April.

→ Main towns: Bairnsdale (*see* p. 143), Lakes Entrance (*see* p. 143), Mallacoota (*see* p. 144).

→ The Kurnai People are the Traditional Owners of this region. The Bataluk Cultural Trail follows the traditional routes used by the Gunai and Kurnai People for more than 30,000 years and includes 11 significant sites across the East Gippsland region. Download a map from batalukculturaltrail.com.au

→ Don't miss: the koala colony on Raymond Island at Paynesville; sightseeing cruise or sail on Gippsland Lakes; fresh seafood at Lakes Entrance; the beaches of Cape Conran; Mallacoota Inlet and the views from Point Hicks Lighthouse.

Top: East Gippsland Rail Trail **Opposite:** Mitchell River National Park

TOP ATTRACTIONS

BUCHAN CAVES RESERVE: The reserve features more than 350 limestone caves, of which the Royal and Fairy caves are the most accessible – the Fairy Cave alone is over 400m long, with impressive stalactites. Visitors can cool off in the spring-fed swimming pool after exploring the caves. Tours of the Royal and Fairy caves usually run daily but check ahead. Off Buchan Rd, north of town; (03) 5162 1900.

CAPE CONRAN COASTAL PARK: Rugged coastal scenery, excellent walks and good camping. The park was impacted by the 2020 bushfires but is now regenerating. Turn south after Cabbage Tree Creek or take the coastal route from Marlo.

CROAJINGOLONG NATIONAL PARK: This park takes up a vast portion of what has been dubbed the Wilderness Coast. It protects remote beaches, tall forests, heathland, rainforest, estuaries and granite peaks, as well as wildlife like wallabies, possums, goannas and lyrebirds. Offshore, you might be lucky enough to spot dolphins, seals or southern right and humpback whales. Tamboon and Mallacoota inlets are good spots for canoeing, while the area around the popular Point Hicks Lighthouse, built in 1890, was impacted by bushfires in 2019/20 and is expected to be closed to visitors into 2024. Access the park via a track west of town or various roads south of the Princes Hwy. Some parts of the park, including the 100km Wilderness Coast Walk, were impacted by heavy flooding in 2022, so check for alerts and closures at parks.vic.gov.au.

GIPPSLAND ART GALLERY: The gallery promotes the work of artists and craftspeople in central Gippsland as well as showing travelling exhibitions. Works range from traditional landscapes to visual statements on environmental and cultural issues, and may be in any medium from painting and photography to film and textiles, including the work of internationally recognised textile artist – and Sale resident –Annemieke Mein. Open Mon–Fri 9am–5.30pm, Sat–Sun 10am–4pm; Civic Centre, 68–70 Foster St, Sale; (03) 5142 3500.

GIPPSLAND LAKES: Five rivers end their journey to the sea here, forming a vast expanse of water tucked in behind Ninety Mile Beach. The lakes are a true playground for anyone with an interest in water activities, especially fishing and boating. Explore them on a sightseeing cruise, including one to Wyanga Park Winery, or on the ever-popular houseboats that can be hired over summer. Contact visitor centre for details. At the centre, the Lakes National Park offers birdwatching, walking, swimming and camping. Access is via boat from Paynesville or road and foot from the township of Loch Sport.

KROWATHUNKOOLONG KEEPING PLACE: This museum in Bairnsdale details the cultural history of the region's Kurnai People and provides an insight into the impact of European settlement; open Mon–Fri 10am–4pm; Dalmahoy St, Bairnsdale; (03) 5150 0737. To explore local First Nations history further, visit Howitt Park, Princes Hwy – a tree here has a 4m scar where bark has been removed to make a canoe. The **Bataluk Cultural Trail** from Sale to Cann River takes in these and other First

Nations sites of East Gippsland. Details of the trail from Krowathunkoolong or from visitor centre.

LAKE GUTHRIDGE PARKLANDS: This major recreational area in Sale comprises the Lake Guthridge and Lake Guyatt precincts, the Botanic Gardens and the Regional Aquatic Complex. The precinct showcases over 35ha of historically significant botanic gardens and walking trails, including an interpretative trail featuring contemporary artworks by Traditional Owners. It also provides sensory gardens, abundant seating, an adventure playground for children, tennis courts and a fauna park. Foster St, Sale.

RAYMOND ISLAND: This residential island, just east of Paynesville, is called Gragin by the Gunai and Kurnai People, who jointly manage the Raymond Island Gippsland Lakes Reserve at the north-eastern end of the island. The island is home to a large koala colony and sightings are almost guaranteed if you follow the self-guided koala walking trail; it starts near the ferry terminal. The island is small enough to explore on foot and can be accessed by a ferry (free for pedestrians) that departs from the foreshore in Paynesville.

SNOWY RIVER NATIONAL PARK: In the south of the park is Raymond Creek Falls. A 40min return walk leads to the falls, with a further 1hr walk leading to the Snowy River; 2WD access, check road conditions and seasonal road closures at parks.vic.gov.au. McKillops Bridge, via Deddick, is one of the most accessible parts of this park.

SNOWY RIVER SCENIC DRIVE: The drive takes in the Buchan and Snowy rivers junction and runs along the edge of Snowy River National Park to Gelantipy. Beyond Gelantipy is Little River Gorge, Victoria's deepest gorge. A short walking track leads to a cliff-top lookout. Near the gorge is McKillops Bridge, a safe swimming spot, a good site to launch canoes, and the starting point for two walking tracks. Care is required on the road beyond Gelantipy; 4WD is recommended. Details from Orbost visitor centre.

OTHER ATTRACTIONS

COOPRACAMBRA NATIONAL PARK: This park is in one of the most remote sections of Victoria. Ancient tetrapod footprints have been found in the red sandstone gorge of the Genoa River, and the surrounding granite peaks create a spectacular scene. The 35,000ha area protects unique ecosystems and rare flora and fauna. Only experienced and well-equipped hikers should undertake walks in the rugged and remote parts of this park. A 'trip intentions' form needs to be lodged at the Cann River or Mallacoota office of Parks Victoria prior to departure, and Parks staff must be notified upon return.

ERRINUNDRA NATIONAL PARK: The park is one of the largest remaining stands of cool temperate rainforest in Victoria and features giant eucalypt forests. There is a rainforest boardwalk and for keen hikers there are walking tracks, as well as camping and picnic facilities. Enjoy superb views from Ellery View, Ocean View Lookout and the peak of Mount Morris. In winter, snow and rain can make access difficult. Errinundra Rd, off Princes Hwy.

HOLEY PLAINS STATE PARK: The open eucalypt forests in this park near Sale are home to abundant wildlife, while swamps provide a habitat for many frog species. There is a good swimming lake, and bushwalking, picnicking and camping are all popular activities, particularly around Harriers Swamp. Access from Princes Hwy.

LIND NATIONAL PARK: The park includes the Euchre Valley Nature Drive through temperate rainforest gullies. It also supports open eucalypt forests with grey gum, messmate and silvertop ash. Watch for wildlife such as the pretty masked owl and the elusive long-footed potoroo. Picnic facilities available.

MCLEODS MORASS WILDLIFE RESERVE: A boardwalk extends over the freshwater marshland, allowing a close-up view of the many species of waterbirds found here (the morass can at times be harmful to animals and people, check conditions with Parks Victoria on 13 1963); southern outskirts of Bairnsdale, access via Macarthur St.

MITCHELL RIVER NATIONAL PARK: Set in the remnants of temperate rainforest, this park has giant kanooka trees, wildflowers and more than 150 species of birds. According to Gunai and Kurnai ancient stories, Nargun was a beast made all of stone except for his hands, arms and breast. The Den of Nargun can be found in the park, but please show respect and don't enter the cave. There is a circuit walk to Bluff Lookout and Mitchell River, and Billy Goat Bend is good for picnics.

VISITOR INFORMATION

Orbost Visitor Information Centre
Slab Hut, Nicholson St
(03) 5154 2424 or
1800 637 060

Bairnsdale Visitor Information Centre
240 Main St, Bairnsdale
(03) 5152 3444 or
1800 637 060
visiteastgippsland.com.au

Top: Art Gallery in Sale
Bottom: Bairnsdale
Opposite: Cape Conran

KEY TOWNS

BAIRNSDALE
Population 13,734

An attractive rural centre situated on the Mitchell River Flats and considered to be the western gateway to the lakes and wilderness region of East Gippsland. The area has a rich Koorie history brought to life through local landmarks, especially in Mitchell River National Park, where fascinating Gunai and Kurnai ancient stories are based around the Den of Nargun.

SEE & DO **Krowathunkoolong keeping place:** see Top Attractions. **Mitchell River National Park; McLeods Morass Wildlife Reserve:** see Other Attractions for both. **East Gippsland Art Gallery:** visual arts and resource centre; open Tues–Fri 10am–4pm, Sat 10am–2pm; 2 Nicholson St; (03) 5153 1988. **Historical Museum:** built in 1891, contains relics from Bairnsdale's past; open Wed, Sat and Sun 10am–3pm; 40 Macarthur St; (03) 5152 6363. **Self-guided heritage walks:** take in St Mary's Church, built in 1913, with wall and ceiling murals by Italian artist Francesco Floreani, and the courthouse, a magnificent, castle-like construction; details from visitor centre. **Farmers' market:** secondary college; 1st Sat each month. **Wineries:** include Nicholson River Winery and Tambo Winery, for tastings and sales; 10km E. **Nyerimilang Heritage Park:** homestead and semi-formal gardens overlooking the picturesque Gippsland Lakes; Nungurner Rd, Nungurner; 32km E. **Dargo:** historic township and major producer of walnuts. The road beyond Dargo offers a scenic drive through the High Country to Hotham Heights on unsealed road, so check conditions at parks.vic.gov.au; 93km NW.

BUCHAN
Population 201

Buchan offers some of the best caving in Victoria, with the Buchan Caves Reserve – where there is excellent camping – nearby. Apart from its caves, Buchan is primarily an agricultural town. Its only hotel burnt down in 2014, but was rebuilt thanks to a community crowdfunding campaign. Although the origin of the town's name is disputed, it is said to be derived from the Gunai and Kurnai term for either 'smoke-signal expert' or 'place of the grass bag'.

SEE & DO **Buchan Caves Reserve; Snowy River Scenic Drive:** see Top Attractions for both. **Suggan Buggan:** this historic townsite, surrounded by Alpine National Park, features an 1865 schoolhouse; 64km N.

CANN RIVER
Population 197

Most people driving the scenic route between Melbourne and Sydney along the Princes Hwy stop at Cann River. Although the town itself is small, its list of nearby attractions is big, with proximity to several national parks. This area was severely impacted by the 2020 bushfires, so please check ahead for road and bridge closures at parks.vic.gov.au.

SEE & DO **Croajingolong National Park:** see Top Attractions. **Coopracambra National Park:** see Other Attractions. **Point Hicks:** was the first land on the east coast of Australia to be sighted by Europeans (that we know of); 29km S.

★ LAKES ENTRANCE
Population 6527

Lakes Entrance is a lovely holiday town situated at the eastern end of the Gippsland Lakes, an inland network of waterways covering more than 400sqkm. The artificially created 'entrance' of the town's name allows the Tasman Sea and the lakes to meet, creating a safe harbour that is home to one of the largest fishing fleets in Australia. While many of the attractions in Lakes Entrance are based around the water, there is also opportunity for foodies to indulge with a variety of cafes and restaurants lining the Esplanade, plus sales of fresh fish and local wines.

SEE & DO **Griffiths Seashell Museum and Marine Display:** one of Australia's biggest marine life collections; 125 The Espl; (03) 5155 1538. **Lonsdale Eco Cruises:** discover the wildlife of the lakes, including seals, dolphins and birds such as pelicans; Cunninghame Quay; 0413 666 638. **Lakes-Explorer Sea Safari and Water Taxi:** explore the lakes and islands in a shallow-bottom boat with a knowledgeable guide; Post Office Jetty; 0458 511 438. **Surf Club Foreshore Market:** 1st Sun of the month. **Jemmys Point:** great views of the region; 1km W. **Lake Bunga:** nature trail along foreshore; 3km E. **Lake Tyers:** sheltered waters ideal for fishing, swimming and boating. Cruises depart from Fishermans Landing in town. Lake is 6–23km NE, depending on access point. **Lake Tyers Forest Park:** great for bushwalking, wildlife-spotting, picnicking and camping; 20km NE. **Metung:** a scenic town on Lake King with boat hire, cruises and a marina regatta each Jan. The town has a number of scenic walks and it's a good place to tap into Gippsland's creative streak with several artists' galleries and studios; 15km W.

MAFFRA
Population 4548

Maffra, settled in the 1840s, has the charm and old-style hospitality of another era. Surrounded by fertile dairy and farming lands watered by the Glenmaggie Irrigation Scheme established in 1919 Maffra, once famous for its sugar beet industry, continues to support its rich agricultural surrounds. It holds a great sense of history in its original shop verandahs and grand homesteads.

SEE & DO **Gippsland Vehicle Collection:** rotating display of vehicles, located in a historic vegetable-dehydrating factory; open Fri–Mon 10am–4pm; Maffra–Sale Rd; (03) 5147 3223. **Gippsland Plains Rail Trail:** recreational trail for cycling and walking that passes through town. The trail links Stratford in the east to Traralgon in the west by traversing dairy country. **Variety and Farmers' Market:** 1st Sun each month. **Stratford:** the scenic Avon River flows through town. Knobs Reserve is a site where the Gunai and Kurnai People once sharpened axe heads on sandstone grinding stones – it is part of the **Bataluk Cultural Trail**, which takes in significant First Nations sites throughout East Gippsland; 9km E. **Lake Glenmaggie:** popular watersports venue; 42km NW via Heyfield. **Alpine National Park:** sprawls from Licola, 75km NW, to the NSW border. Near Licola is Lake Tali Karng, which lies 850m above sea level and is a popular bushwalking destination during the warmer months. **Scenic drives:** the Traralgon to Stratford Tourist Route highlights attractions of the area. For stunning scenery, drive north along Forest Rd, through the Macalister River Valley to Licola and Mount Tamboritha in Alpine National Park; or to Jamieson (166km NW via Heyfield), with access to snowfields or Lake Eildon.

★ MALLACOOTA
Population 1118

The last coastal town before Victoria becomes NSW, Mallacoota is surrounded by Croajingolong National Park, East Gippsland's answer to Wilsons Promontory National Park (*see* p. 134), and is, unsurprisingly, a very popular holiday centre. Severely impacted by the 2020 bushfires when many buildings in and around town were lost, the surrounding forests and bushland have begun to regenerate and Mallacoota Inlet is still as beautiful as ever. Swimming, fishing, surfing, walking and boating are what Mallacoota excels at. Gabo Island is just offshore, with its remarkable pink granite lighthouse.

SEE & DO **Croajingolong National Park:** *see* Top Attractions. **Bunker Museum:** restored World War II bunker located at the airport; open Tues 9.30–11.30am. **The Narrows Walk:** picturesque shoreline walk along Mallacoota Inlet; details from visitor centre. **Artisans and Producers Market:** 1st Sat each month. **Surf beaches:** Bastion Point, 2km S; Bekta, 5km S. **Gabo Island Lightstation Reserve:** take a scenic daytrip or stay in the Lightkeeper's Residence; 11km E (offshore). **Gipsy Point:** a quiet holiday retreat overlooking the Genoa River; 16km NW.

ORBOST
Population 2024

Situated on the banks of the legendary Snowy River, Orbost is surrounded by spectacular coastal and mountain territory. For those who love arts and crafts, there are many shops in the area supplying and displaying local products.

SEE & DO **Errinundra National Park:** *see* Other Attractions. **Forest Park:** attractive reserve with restored and relocated 1872 Slab Hut; also houses the visitor centre with displays on rainforest ecology; Nicholson St; (03) 5154 2424. **Heritage walk:** weaves its way through town with storyboards, fingerboards and plaques explaining the historic buildings; begins at Slab Hut. **Historical Museum:** details local history with displays of artefacts; inside the Library on Ruskin St; (03) 5153 9500. **Exhibition Centre:** equipped with two galleries, one dedicated to the National Collection of Australian Wood Design, the other presenting monthly exhibitions; contact the centre for opening hours; Clarke St; 0449 734 598. **Marlo:** a popular fishing spot also known for its galleries and bush races in Jan; cruise the Snowy River on the PS *Curlip II*; 14km S. **Cabbage Tree Creek Flora Reserve:** 27km E. **Bemm River Scenic Reserve:** 1km signposted rainforest walk and

TOP EVENTS

- JAN; Snowy River Golf Classic (Orbost); Regatta (Metung)
- FEB Blues & Arts Festival (Bruthen); Music Festival (Paynesville)
- MAR Mardi Gras (Maffra); Music Festival (Sale)
- EASTER Australian Powerboat Racing Championships (Eagle Point)
- APR Wild Harvest Seafood Festival (Mallacoota); Gippsland Lakes Paddle Challenge (Lakes Entrance)
- MAY Shakespeare on the River Festival (Stratford)
- JUN–JUL Winter Festival (across the region)
- DEC Alpine Rally (Lakes Entrance)

TEMPERATURES

January: 14–26°C

July: 4–15°C

Top: Main Beach at Lakes Entrance **Opposite:** Lake Glenmaggie

picnic facilities; off Princes Hwy; 40km E. **Sydenham Inlet:** a good spot for bream fishing; 58km E. **Delegate River Tavern:** on the banks of the Delegate River near the NSW border; about 115km NE. **Baldwin Spencer Trail:** 262km scenic drive following the route of this explorer, taking in old mining sites and Errinundra National Park.

PAYNESVILLE
Population 3505

Paynesville is a popular tourist resort close to the rural city of Bairnsdale, on the McMillan Straits. The town is set on the Gippsland Lakes, and the beaches of the Tasman Sea, making it a favourite destination for fishing and waterskiing.

SEE & DO **Gippsland Lakes; Raymond Island:** see Top Attractions for both. **St Peter by the Lake Church:** built in 1961, this unique structure incorporates seafaring images in its design; The Espl. **Community Craft Centre:** displays and sells local arts and crafts; The Espl. **Farmers Market:** Foreshore Reserve; 4th Sat each month. **Eagle Point:** a small fishing community set by Lake King. The Mitchell River empties here, where it forms curious silt jetties that stretch out into the distance; 2km NW.

SALE
Population 14,100

Situated by the Thomson River near the Latrobe River junction, Sale grew on the back of the gold rush and became Gippsland's first city in 1950. Although largely considered an industrial town, with the nearby Bass Strait oilfields providing a large part of its economy, Sale has a lot more to offer. The Port of Sale is being redeveloped and there are many good cafes and restaurants, and a number of fine-art galleries and craft outlets. The lakes near Sale are home to the unique Australian black swan – the bird that has become a symbol for the town.

SEE & DO **Gippsland Art Gallery; Lake Guthridge Parklands:** see Top Attractions for both. **Historical Museum:** local history memorabilia; open Wed and Sun 1.30–4pm; Foster St; details from visitor centre. **Historical buildings:** include Our Lady of Sion Convent in York St; Magistrates Court and Supreme Court, Foster St; St Paul's Anglican Cathedral featuring fine stained-glass windows, Cunninghame St; St Mary's Cathedral, Foster St. The bicentennial clock tower in the mall utilises the original bluestone base, ironwork and clock mechanisms; Raymond St. **RAAF base:** home of the famous Roulettes aerobatic team; Aerodrome St. **Gippsland Armed Forces Museum:** military history and memorabilia on display at a former World War II RAAF bombing and air gunnery school; open Sat–Mon 10am–4pm; West Sale Airport; (03) 5144 5500. **River Heritage and Wetlands Trail:** protected wetland area; a trail with interpretive panels leads from the historic canal to the Common Wetlands; south-east edge of town. **Producers Market:** showgrounds; 3rd Sat each month. **Fishing:** good fishing for trout in the Avon River near Marlay Point and also in the Macalister, Thomson and Latrobe rivers, especially at Swing Bridge; 5km S. **Marlay Point:** on the shores of Lake Wellington with boat-launching facilities provided; 25km E. **Seaspray:** a popular holiday spot on Ninety Mile Beach; offers excellent surfing and fishing; 32km S. **Golden and Paradise beaches:** two more townships on Ninety Mile Beach with great surfing and fishing; 35km SE. **Cycling:** various recreational trails, including the Tarra Trail and Gippsland Plains Rail Trail; details from visitor centre. **Loch Sport:** set on Gippsland Lakes and popular for camping and fishing; 65km SE.

Goldfields and Spa Country

North to north-west of Melbourne lies the historic Goldfields region. The extraordinary wealth of the 1850s and '60s gold rush fuelled the area's development, and is still seen in the **grand streetscapes and heritage buildings**. Weekends away are popular in this area's beautiful towns, where **gourmet eateries, boutique wineries, art galleries and natural mineral springs** intersect with fascinating heritage.

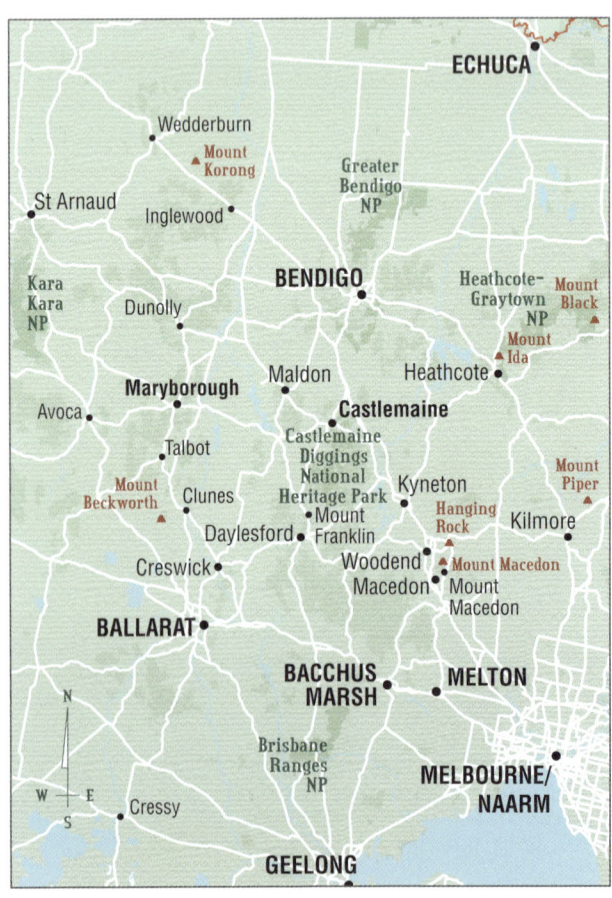

CHEAT SHEET

→ Allow at least four days for a proper exploration of the region.

→ Best time to visit: Sept–June.

→ Main towns: Ballarat (see p. 151), Bendigo (see p. 152), Daylesford (see p. 153).

→ The region is the Traditional Land of the Dja Dja Wurrung, Djabwurrung, Waddawurrung and Taungurung Peoples.

→ Did you know? The 1850s and 1860s were prosperous times for Victoria as gold was extracted from the ground in a frenzy. About $9 billion worth of gold was found in Bendigo alone, making it the seventh richest goldfield in the world.

→ Don't miss: an indulgent spa treatment at Hepburn Springs; treasure-hunting in Castlemaine; a glass of shiraz in Heathcote; delving into history in Bendigo.

Top: Art Gallery of Ballarat
Opposite: Bendigo's historic buildings and tram

TOP ATTRACTIONS

BENDIGO ART GALLERY: Well regarded for contemporary blockbuster exhibitions, often from the V&A in London, plus an extensive permanent collection with a focus on Australian artists, including Arthur Boyd, Tom Roberts and Arthur Streeton; open 10am–5pm; 42 View St, Bendigo; (03) 5434 6088; bendigoregion.com.au/bendigo-art-gallery

BENDIGO WINE REGION: Like neighbouring Heathcote (see p. 154), this area is responsible for some of the country's richest reds. Both its shiraz and cabernet sauvignon are wonderfully reliable varieties that could only be shaken by a very bad season. Wineries to visit are **Water Wheel** and the picturesque **Balgownie Estate**, with its lovely cafe and boutique cottages. Winemaker **Bress** also dabbles in traditional apple cider.

BUDA HISTORIC HOME AND GARDEN: Located in the town of Castlemaine (see p. 152), Buda is considered to have one of the most significant examples of 19th-century gardens in Victoria. The house itself is furnished with period pieces and art and craft created by the Leviny family, who lived here for 118 years. Ernest Leviny was a Hungarian silversmith and jeweller and named the house 'Buda' after Budapest. Five of his six daughters never married but remained at Buda and pursued woodwork, photography and embroidery. Open 12–4pm; 42 Hunter St, Castlemaine; (03) 5472 1032; budacastlemaine.org.

CENTRAL DEBORAH GOLD MINE: Perhaps the best way to get a feel for life in a goldmining town is to take a trip down this mine in Bendigo (see p. 152), where you can still see traces of gold in the quartz reef 20 storeys below the ground. The mine was the last commercial goldmine to operate in Bendigo. From 1939 to 1954, around a tonne of gold was excavated. 76 Violet St, Bendigo; (03) 5443 8322 for tour details.

CONVENT GALLERY: This magnificent building in Daylesford (see p. 153) was a former convent and girls school, now restored and surrounded by delightful cottage gardens with an art and sculpture park. The gallery features permanent and temporary exhibitions. Bad Habits cafe serves local produce and Devonshire tea. Open 10am–4pm; cnr Hill and Daly sts, Daylesford; (03) 5348 3211.

EUREKA CENTRE: The Museum of Australian Democracy in Ballarat (see p. 151) has displays about democracy and the social history of the gold rush. It's on the site of the Eureka Stockade of 3 December 1854; the original flag is also on display. To read more about the Eureka Stockade, see p. 157; cnr Eureka and Stawell sts, Ballarat; 1800 287 113.

GOLDEN DRAGON MUSEUM: This museum in Bendigo (see p. 152) commemorates the contribution of the Chinese community to life on the goldfields. On display are exhibitions depicting the daily life and hardships of Chinese immigrants and an impressive collection of Chinese memorabilia and processional regalia, including what is said to be the world's oldest imperial dragon, 'Loong' (which first appeared at the Bendigo Easter Fair in 1892), and the world's longest imperial dragon, 'Sun Loong'. Adjacent to the museum is the Yi Yuan Gardens (Garden of Joy) and Dai Gum San precinct. 1–11 Bridge St, Bendigo; (03) 5441 5044.

HANGING ROCK: A massive rock formation made famous by *Picnic at Hanging Rock*, the novel (1967) by Joan Lindsay that was later made into a film (1975). The story, about schoolgirls who mysteriously vanished while on a picnic in the reserve, became a famous legend. There is certainly something eerie about Hanging Rock with its strange rock formations, created by the erosion of solidified lava, and narrow tracks through dense bushland. Hanging Rock is renowned for the annual races held at its base, especially the New Year's Day and Australia Day races. The reserve also has a discovery centre and cafe. Access from South Rock Rd, off Calder Hwy. It's 8km north-east of Woodend (see p. 157).

HARD HILL TOURIST RESERVE: Hard Hill is a fascinating former mining district with original gold diggings and Government Battery. There is a good walking track through the site. Hard Hill is in a pleasant bushland setting, and picnic facilities are provided. Nearby is a fully operational eucalyptus distillery offering tours and selling eucalyptus products. It's on the northern outskirts of Wedderburn.

HEATHCOTE WINE REGION: Heathcote shiraz makes wine lovers go weak at the knees. Its depth is the result of the dark, red Cambrian soil and the continental climate. **Jasper Hill** is the most exclusive name in the area. Its elegant red wines can be hard to come by, so if you manage to find a bottle it is worth purchasing it on the spot. Other good wineries include **Heathcote Winery** with its cellar door located on the town of Heathcote's main street, **Wild Duck Creek Estate** and **Red Edge**. To find most of the region's wines – and a few local gins, beers and ciders – under one roof, head to **Heathcote Wine Hub**, which also stocks a full range of local gourmet produce.

HEPBURN SPRINGS SPAS: Dating back to 1894, the renovated Hepburn Bathhouse and Spa has state-of-the-art communal and private mineral bathing, spas and therapies using the renowned local mineral springs, plus a day spa for massage, facials and indulgent beauty treatments. Mineral Springs Reserve Rd, Hepburn Springs; (03) 5321 6000. There are other spas in the town, such as at **Peppers Mineral Springs Hotel**.

MACEDON RANGES WINE REGION: This is mainland Australia's coolest wine region and, like Tasmania, it's responsible for some very good sparkling wine. Most wineries are found east of the Calder Fwy around Romsey, Lancefield and Kyneton. **Hanging Rock Winery** achieves iconic status thanks to its position behind Hanging Rock (see Top Attractions), and its Non Vintage Macedon Cuvee sparkling wine is said to be one of the most complex sparkling wines in Australia. Also try the sauvignon blanc. **Curly Flat** is known for its excellent pinot noir and chardonnay, and **Granite Hills** for riesling and shiraz.

PYRENEES WINE REGION: Shiraz is the Pyrenees' premium drop and its big names are **Blue Pyrenees Estate** and **Taltarni**. **Dalwhinnie** has been highly praised for its Eagle Series Shiraz and is also doing well in a range of styles including chardonnay, cabernet sauvignon and pinot noir. **Redbank Winery** is known for its Sally's Paddock blend, comprising merlot, cabernet sauvignon, shiraz and cabernet franc; visitpyrenees.com.au.

SOVEREIGN HILL: This outdoor museum is a great family-friendly activity to get a taste for what life was like on the Victorian goldfields. Spread over 60ha, Sovereign Hill is a replica gold-mining town, complete with staff dressed in period costumes. Panning for gold is a popular activity, there's an old-fashioned lolly shop and stagecoach rides. In the evening the Aura immersive theatre show tells the story of gold's discovery using projections and 3D technology. Bradshaw St, Ballarat; (03) 5337 1199; sovereignhill.com.au.

SUNBURY WINE REGION: This small but historic wine region is found just beyond Melbourne airport. **Goona Warra Vineyard** was established in 1863, and its winery is set in an original bluestone building. **Craiglee**, just over the road, was established only a year later in 1864. Shiraz is the specialty of both labels, and Craiglee's shiraz has won several trophies.

TALBOT: This delightful historic town has many 1860–70s buildings, particularly in Camp St and Scandinavian Cres. Attractions include the Arts and Historical Museum in the former Methodist Church; second-hand bookstores and one of Victoria's largest farmers' markets selling local produce, 3rd Sun each month.

VICTORIAN GOLDFIELDS RAILWAY: This historic railway runs from Castlemaine to Maldon. The steam train journeys through box–ironbark forest in a region that saw some of the richest goldmining in the country. Castlemaine Railway Station, Kennedy St; (03) 5470 6658.

OTHER ATTRACTIONS

CASTLEMAINE ART MUSEUM: Founded in 1913, the gallery is housed in an elegant Art Deco building that was designed in 1931 by Peter Meldrum and is renowned for its collection of Australian art. Along with the permanent collection that includes pieces by Tom Roberts and Charles Blackman, it houses many exhibitions. Historical museum in the basement. Open Thurs–Sun 12–5pm; 14 Lyttleton St, Castlemaine; (03) 5472 2292.

CASTLEMAINE DIGGINGS NATIONAL HERITAGE PARK: The wealth on Castlemaine's streets springs from the huge hauls of gold found on the Mount Alexander Diggings, east and south of town. Towns such as Fryerstown, Vaughan and Glenluce – now almost ghost towns – supported breweries, schools, churches and hotels. Visitors can explore Chinese cemeteries, mineral springs, waterwheels and old towns. Details of self-guided walks and drives from Castlemaine visitor centre.

CRESWICK REGIONAL PARK: Forester La Gerche replanted the denuded hills around Creswick in the 1890s, and those hills and other natural history can be explored on the various walking trails, including the 30min Landcare Trail or the longer La Gerche Forest Walk. Visit St Georges Lake, once a mining dam and now popular for picnics and watersports, and Koala Park, an old breeding ground for koalas that was highly unsuccessful (they escaped over the fences). Slaty Creek is great for gold panning or picnics, with abundant birdlife.

ENFIELD STATE PARK: Great for bushwalking or horseriding, the park is home to many species of orchids and numerous animals including echidnas, koalas, bats and frogs. There is a pretty picnic ground at remote Long Gully, and numerous walking tracks. Also featured are the remnants of early goldmining settlements, including the Berringa Mines Historic Reserve. Access via Incolls and Misery Creek roads.

GREATER BENDIGO NATIONAL PARK: The park, which extends to the north and south of town, protects some high-quality box–ironbark forest and is popular for scenic driving, cycling, walking and camping. Relics of the region's goldmining and eucalyptus oil industries can be found within. Fauna includes over 170 species of birds including the grey shrike-thrush, a pretty songbird. In the early morning and late evening, look out for eastern grey kangaroos, black wallabies and echidnas. Detailed maps of the park are available at the Bendigo visitor centre. Access via Loddon Valley Hwy through Eaglehawk.

HEATHCOTE–GRAYTOWN NATIONAL PARK: One of Victoria's newest national parks, gazetted in 2002, Heathcote-Graytown was part of a statewide plan to preserve box-ironbark forest. It is understood that the box-ironbark forests date back many thousands of years. The national park is the Traditional Land of the Taungurung People. The forests provided food and material for tools and shelter. The close association with the forests continues today and significant First Nations sites can be found throughout the area. The park is an important nature reserve and is good for birdwatching, bushwalking or having a picnic. Mount Ida, Mount Black and Viewing Rock lookouts provide scenic views. Access from Northern Hwy and Heathcote–Nagambie Rd.

HEPBURN REGIONAL PARK: Surrounding Daylesford and Hepburn Springs (see p. 148), this park features goldmining relics, mineral springs and the impressive Mount Franklin, an extinct volcano, with panoramic views from the summit and picnic, barbecue and camping facilities around the base. There are good walking tracks.

KARA KARA NATIONAL PARK: The park protects an oasis of dense box–ironbark forest and woodland surrounded by agricultural land. More than 270 different species of native flora have been recorded here and provide a glimpse of what the area would have looked like before the land-clearing during and after the gold rush. Within the park are the Teddington Reservoirs, popular for brown trout and redfin fishing. The rugged terrain provides a great opportunity for bushwalkers or 4WD enthusiasts. Wedge-tailed eagles can be seen soaring above the steep, forested ranges. The park is 15km south of St Arnaud (see p. 156).

KOOYOORA STATE PARK: The park sits at the northern end of the Bealiba Range and features extensive box-ironbark forests. The Eastern Walking Circuit offers a great opportunity for bushwalkers, passing through strange rock formations and giant granite slabs. The Summit Track leads to Melville Caves Lookout. The caves were once the haunt of the notorious bushranger Captain Melville. Camping is allowed around the caves.

LAVANDULA SWISS ITALIAN FARM: A sprawling estate featuring fields of lavender, cottage gardens and sales of lavender-based products; free tours of the 1850s stone farmhouse. It's a lovely place to spend a few hours exploring the farm and gardens or in the La Trattoria eatery; open Fri–Tues 10.30am–5.30pm; only Sat–Sun and public/school holidays (June–Aug); 350 Hepburn-Newstead Rd,

Top: Hepburn Springs Bathhouse *Middle:* Tellurian Wines in Heathcote *Bottom:* Convent Gallery in Daylesford *Opposite:* Victorian Goldfields Railway

Shepherds Flat; (03) 5476 4393. The farm is 10km north of Daylesford (see p. 153).

LERDERDERG STATE PARK: Featuring the imposing Lerderderg Gorge, the 14,250ha park is a great venue for picnics, bushwalking and swimming, while the Lerderderg River is ideal for trout fishing. The area was mined during the gold rush, and remnants from the water races used for washing gold can still be found upstream from O'Brien's Crossing. Late winter and spring are good times to see wildflowers and blossoming shrubs. Look out for koalas nestled in giant manna gums and for the magnificent sulphur-crested cockatoo and the wedge-tailed eagle.

MARYBOROUGH RAILWAY STATION: So immense and impressive is this building that Mark Twain, on his visit to the town, remarked that Maryborough was 'a station with a town attached'. Rumour has it that the building was actually intended for Maryborough in Queensland. The beautifully preserved working station houses Railway Cafe and Tracks Bar in its Great Hall. Open Wed–Fri 10am–3pm, Sat–Sun 9am–3pm; Station St; (03) 5461 1362.

PADDYS RANGES STATE PARK: This park offers the chance to enjoy red ironbark and grey box vegetation on a scenic walk or drive. The majority of walks start from the picnic area. You can see old goldmines and relics or keep an eye out for the rare painted honeyeater and other birdlife. There is also fossicking within the park, but in designated areas only. Access to the park is just south of Maryborough.

PYRENEES RANGES STATE FOREST: Covering a large stretch of bushland, these ranges are great for bushwalking, picnics and camping. Visitors can see a variety of wildlife, including koalas, wallabies, kangaroos and goannas. Orchids and lilies can be found growing around the base of the ranges in season. An 18km walking track starts at the Waterfalls camping area and finishes at Warrenmang–Glenlofty Rd. Access via Sunraysia or Pyrenees Hwy.

TRENTHAM AND WOMBAT STATE FOREST: Trentham is a picturesque spa-country town also renowned for its gourmet pubs and restaurants, with a mixed history of gold, timber and farming. It has a charming streetscape and attractions include a historic foundry. Just north-east of town is Wombat State Forest and deep within is Victoria's largest single-drop waterfall, Trentham Falls.

WERRIBEE GORGE STATE PARK: Over time the Werribee River has carved through ancient seabed sediment and lava flows to form a spectacular gorge. The name 'Werribee' comes from the Waddawurrung word 'wearibi', meaning 'swimming place' or 'backbone', perhaps in reference to the snake-like path of the river. Rock climbing is permitted at Falcons Lookout, and a popular walk follows the Werribee River from the Meikles Point picnic area, providing views of the river and the gorge cliff-faces.

VISITOR INFORMATION

Ballarat Town Hall,
225 Sturt St
(03) 5337 4337 or
1800 446 633
visitballarat.com.au

Bendigo Visitor Information Centre
51–67 Pall Mall
(03) 5434 6060 or
1800 813 153
bendigoregion.com.au

Macedon Ranges
visitmacedonranges.com

Hepburn Shire
visithepburnshire.com.au

Opposite: Sovereign Hill in Ballarat

KEY TOWNS

AVOCA
Population 1129

The wide main street of Avoca features a few remaining heritage buildings, and the Avoca River flows to the west of town. Explorer Thomas Mitchell travelled through this area and found it much more to his liking than inland NSW, yet the town of Avoca wasn't established until the gold rush. Wine, agriculture and collectibles are the vogue now that the gold has run out.

SEE & DO **Pyrenees Wine Region:** *see* Top Attractions. **Pyrenees Ranges State Forest:** *see* Other Attractions. **Historic walk:** takes in the original courthouse, one of the oldest surviving courts in Victoria, as well as the police residence and Lalor's, one of the state's earliest pharmacies; map from visitor centre. **Cemetery:** Chinese burial ground from the goldmining period; on outskirts of town. **Avoca Chinese Garden:** this state-funded community garden honours the contribution of Chinese immigrants during the gold rush; 24–30 Dundas St.

BACCHUS MARSH
Population 21,692

Bacchus Marsh shares part of its name with the Roman god of wine, but is actually better known for the apples that grow so well in the fertile valley region between the Werribee and Lerderderg rivers. Considered a satellite town within commuting distance of Melbourne, Bacchus Marsh retains a certain charm with stunning heritage buildings and a rural atmosphere.

SEE & DO **Avenue of Honour:** visitors to the town are greeted by the sight of the renowned Avenue of Honour, an elm-lined stretch of road built in honour of the Australian soldiers who fought in World War I. Eastern approach to town. **Historic buildings:** include the Manor, the home of the town's founder, Captain Bacchus (now privately owned), and Border Inn, built in 1850, thought to be the first stop for Cobb & Co. coaches travelling to the goldfields; details from visitor centre. **Blacksmith's Cottage and Forge complex:** local history museum and book barn; 100–102 Main St. **Naturipe Fruits:** pick-your-own fruits and roadside sales; open 9am–5pm (Oct–Apr). **Long Forest Nature Conservation Reserve:** a great example of the distinctive mallee scrub that once covered the region; 2km NE. **St Anne's Vineyard:** with a bluestone cellar built from the remains of the old Ballarat Gaol; Western Fwy; 6km W. **Merrimu Reservoir:** attractive park area with picnic facilities; about 10km NE. **Organ Pipes National Park:** lava flows have created a 20m wall of basalt columns in this small park near Sunbury. The 'organ pipes' can be seen close-up via an easy walking trail. **Melton:** now virtually a satellite suburb of Melbourne, this town has a long and rich history of horse breeding and training. Visit the **Willows Homestead** to see exhibits detailing the life of early settlers (open Wed and Sun 1–4pm and by appt; (04) 0205 3175), picnic on the Werribee River at **Melton Reservoir**, or taste the fine wines in the nearby **Sunbury Wine Region** (*see* p. 148); 14km E. **Brisbane Ranges National Park:** good walking tracks, wildflowers during spring and the imposing, steep-sided Anakie Gorge; 16km SW. **Ballan:** try the refreshing mineral-spring water at Bostock Reservoir, or join in the festivities at the Vintage Machinery and Vehicle Rally in Feb, or the Autumn Festival (Mar); 20km NW. **Blackwood:** visit the Mineral Springs Reserve and Garden of St Erth. Blackwood is also the start of the 53km return scenic drive through the **Wombat State Forest**; 31km NW.

★ BALLARAT
Population 105,348

Ballarat is Victoria's largest inland city, featuring grand old buildings and wide streets that create an air of splendour. Built on the wealth of the region's goldfields, Ballarat offers one of the best opportunities in the region to get a taste of the past at Sovereign Hill. Fine dining in the many restaurants, a good cafe scene, music events, creative festivals, walking and ghost tours, and fun activities for the kids ensure it also has a contemporary edge. Lake Wendouree and the Botanic Gardens are charming places for a walk and lakeside cafes provide lovely places to enjoy the view. Ballarat is spelled as 'Ballaarat' in Wadawurrung language. Ballarat was the site of the infamous Eureka Stockade rebellion (*see* box p. 157).

SEE & DO **Sovereign Hill; Eureka Centre:** *see* Top Attractions for both. **Heritage And Arts Precinct:** view historic architecture, including Her Majesty's Theatre (built in 1875; Australia's oldest intact, purpose-built theatre, with classic old-world surroundings and a full performing arts program), and the Craig's Royal and George hotels; Lydiard St South. **Art Gallery of Ballarat:** holds a significant collection of Australian art, has regular exhibitions, including as part of the Ballarat International Foto Biennale, and is a good size so as not to be overwhelming; 40 Lydiard St North; (03) 5320 5858. **Botanic Gardens:** an impressive collection of mature trees, native and exotic plants, large greenhouses, and a lovely place for a wander; the Botanic Gardens host the **Ballarat Begonia Festival** on the March Labour Day weekend; Prime Minister Ave within the gardens features busts of all of Australia's prime ministers; Wendouree Pde. **Lake Wendouree:** features an adventure playground, picnic spots and the 6km Steve Moneghetti running and walking track. **Wildlife Park:** houses native Australian animals such as koalas, kangaroos, Tasmanian devils and crocodiles; cnr Fussel and York sts, Ballarat East; (03) 5333 5933. **Gold Museum:** details the rich goldmining history of the area; opposite Sovereign Hill, Bradshaw St; (03) 5337 1107; admission free with Sovereign Hill ticket. **Vintage Tramway:** via Wendouree Pde; rides Sat–Sun, public and school holidays. **Avenue of Honour and Arch of Victory:** honours those who fought in World War I; western edge of city. **Tours:** heritage tours and eating/drinking tours in the city's laneways; ask for details at visitor centre. **Fresh Produce Market:** Bridge Mall; 1st Sat every month. **Buninyong:** a little town south of Ballarat that features many fine art and craft galleries 11.5km S. **Ballarat Bird World:** home to many species of parrots, has raised walkways through the aviaries. 408 Eddy Ave, Mount Helen; 0409 002 527. The **Mount Buninyong Lookout** east of town offers great views. 13km SE. **Kirks and Gong Gong reserves:** ideal for picnics and bushwalking, these parks include many unique indigenous plants; on opposite sides of Daylesford Rd; 5km NE. **Kryal Castle:** replica of a medieval castle, with daily tours and family entertainment; Forbes Rd, Leigh Creek; (03) 5334 8500; 9km E. **Lal Lal Falls:** plunge 30m into the Moorabool River; 18km SE. **Lal Lal Blast Furnace:** fascinating 19th-century archaeological remains; 18km SE. **Lake Burrumbeet:** this 2100ha lake is a popular fishing spot, especially for redfin in spring and summer. Various boat ramps provide access; 22km NW. **Beaufort:** a small town on the shores of Lake Beaufort, an artificial lake surrounded by gardens, providing a picturesque location for picnics and leisurely walks; 54km W. South of town is **Lake Goldsmith**, home of a major rally of steam-driven machinery and vehicles each May and Oct. **Mooramong Homestead:** built in the 1870s and then altered during the 1930s by its ex-Hollywood owners. It is surrounded by beautiful gardens and a flora and fauna reserve; Glenelg Hwy, Skipton; (03) 9656 9889; 56km NW. **Great Grape Rd:** circuit visiting local wineries through Avoca, St Arnaud and Stawell.

★ BENDIGO
Population 100,649

The Bendigo area is on the Traditional Lands of the Dja Dja Wurrung and the Taungurung Peoples. The city was the location of one of the world's most exciting gold rushes, with more gold found here between 1850 and 1900 than anywhere else in the world. Elaborate buildings and monuments from this golden past line the main streets, offering an ever-present reminder of the riches from the goldfields. Today modern life weaves itself around this legacy with a vibrant pace. The town's new wealth can be seen in many areas including art, culture, festivals, dining, wine and shopping.

SEE & DO The Golden Dragon Museum; Central Deborah Gold Mine; Bendigo Art Gallery: *see* Top Attractions for all. **Self-guided heritage walk:** takes in landmarks including the Shamrock Hotel, built in 1897, cnr Pall Mall and Williamson St; Sacred Heart Cathedral, the state's largest cathedral outside Melbourne, cnr Wattle and High sts; Alexandra Fountain, built in 1881, one of the largest and most ornate fountains in regional Victoria, at Charing Cross; and the Renaissance-style post office and law courts at Pall Mall; details on heritage walks available from visitor centre. **Bendigo Pottery:** Australia's oldest working pottery centre, with potters at work, a cafe and sales; 146 Midland Hwy, Epsom; (03) 5448 4404; bendigopottery.com.au. **Dudley House:** National Trust–classified building; View St. **Pall Mall:** this tree-lined, French-style boulevard is probably country Australia's most impressive street. **Vintage Talking Trams:** run from Central Deborah Gold Mine on 8km city trip, including a stop at the Tram Depot Museum. Recorded commentary provided; bendigotramways.com. **Chinese Joss House:** National Trust–classified temple built by Chinese miners; included on the vintage tram trip; Finn St, North Bendigo; (03) 5442 1685. **Rosalind Park:** majestic parklands that sit beautifully in the centre of Bendigo offering stately gardens for leisure and relaxation, and include a lookout tower, the Cascades water feature and Conservatory Gardens; Pall Mall. **Discovery Science and Technology Centre:** features more than 100 hands-on displays; 7 Railway Pl; (03) 5444 4400; discovery.asn.au. **Bendigo Showgrounds Market:** Prince of Wales Showgrounds, Holmes St; every Sun. **Bendigo Farmers' Market:** fresh regional produce; Hargreaves St (Thurs); cnr Breen St and Belle Vue Rd (Sat); 2nd Sat and 4th Thurs each month. **Trove Makers' Market:** handcrafted arts, crafts and jewellery; Hargreaves St; usually 3rd Sun each month; trovebendigo.com.au. **One Tree Hill observation tower:** panoramic views; 4km S. **Eaglehawk:** site of the gold rush in 1852, it features remnants of goldmining days and fine examples of 19th-century architecture; details for self-guided heritage tour from visitor centre; 6.5km NW. **Mandurang:** features historic wineries and is the exact centre of Victoria; 8km S. **Great Stupa of Universal Compassion:** currently under construction but open for visitors; will be the largest stupa in the Western world when completed; 13km W.

CASTLEMAINE
Population 10,577

The drive into hilly Castlemaine, passing many old, yet perfectly maintained miners' cottages, heralds that this town did big mining business. In fact, it was the site of the greatest alluvial gold rush in the world, and you can read more about the story at Castlemaine Diggings National Heritage Park. The gold money that flowed through

TOP EVENTS

→ FEB Rock Ballarat Rockabilly Festival (Ballarat)

→ MAR Harvest Festival (Bacchus Marsh); Begonia Festival (Ballarat); Lost Trades Fair (Bendigo); State Festival (Castlemaine); ChillOut Queer Pride Festival (Daylesford); Detector Jamboree (Wedderburn)

→ EASTER Easter Festival (Bendigo); Easter Fair (Maldon)

→ MAY Booktown Festival (Clunes); Bendigo Writers Festival (Bendigo)

→ JUNE Jazz Festival (Castlemaine); Celtic Festival (Kilmore); Winter Arts Festival (Woodend)

→ JULY Australian Sheep & Wool Show (Bendigo)

→ AUG–OCT International Foto Biennale (odd numbered years, Ballarat)

→ SEPT Daffodil and Arts Festival (Kyneton); Vintage Machinery Rally (Wedderburn)

→ OCT Wine and Food Festival (Heathcote); Swiss Italian Festa (Hepburn Springs); Mount Tarrangower Historic Hillclimb and Folk Festival (both Maldon)

→ NOV Bendigo Swap Meet (Bendigo); Festival of Gardens (Castlemaine); Budburst Festival (throughout Macedon Ranges)

Opposite top: Peppers Mineral Springs Hotel, Hepburn Springs **Opposite bottom:** Maldon Market

---

Castlemaine in the 19th century can also be seen in its grand buildings. The town is a popular 'tree-change' destination, and has a vibrant artistic community, cafes and interesting shops.

SEE & DO **Buda Historic Home and Garden; Victorian Goldfields Railway:** see Top Attractions for both. **Castlemaine Art Museum; Castlemaine Diggings National Heritage Park:** see Other Attractions for both. **Theatre Royal Castlemaine:** hosts live music performances and films and also houses a brewery, pizza and wine bar; 30 Hargraves St; (03) 5472 1196. **Botanic Gardens:** one of Victoria's oldest and most impressive 19th-century gardens; cnr Walker and Downes rds. **Food and wine producers:** dotted throughout the area, including several at **The Mill** (Walker St) which also houses the Castlemaine Vintage Bazaar, a collection of art studios, a winery, brewery, cheese maker, chocolatier and other artisan food producers. **Old Castlemaine Gaol:** under new ownership, the gaol is set to reopen soon as an art gallery; information from visitor centre. **Mountain-biking:** maps and information from visitor centre. **Farmers' market:** Forest St; 1st Sun each month. **Wesley Hill Market:** 2.5km E; Sat. **Castlemaine Artists Market:** Western Reserve, Forest St, 1st Sun each month. **Chewton:** historic buildings line the streets of this former gold-rush town; 4km E. **Harcourt:** this town is known for its many wineries, including **Harcourt Valley Vineyard** and **BlackJack Vineyards**, with tastings and cellar-door sales; there are a number of cideries in the area, and the town hosts the Applefest in Mar; 9km NE. **Big Tree:** a giant red gum over 500 years old; Guildford; 14km SW. **Goldfields Track:** a 210km track for mountain biking or walking, stretching from Bendigo to Mount Buninyong; goldfieldstrack.com.au.

CLUNES
Population 886

The first registered gold strike in Victoria was made at Clunes on 7 July 1851 – and the rush was on! During the boom, Clunes was the fifth largest town in Victoria, and you can see most of that history on the main street today; Clunes is considered to be one of the best-preserved gold towns in the state. Historic buildings include the Clunes Railway Station, which was built in the 1870s. That's probably why the town was used as a setting for the movie *Ned Kelly* (2003), starring Heath Ledger. The town is now an International Booktown, and has a festival every May celebrating books and the town's many bookstores.

SEE & DO **Clunes Museum:** local history museum reveals the fascinating history of the town, particularly in the gold-rush era; open Wed–Mon; Fraser St. **Lee Medlyn Home of Bottles:** more than 6000 old and rare bottles on display in the former South Clunes State School; open Thurs–Sun 11am–4pm; Bailey St. **Esmond Park:** on the hills overlooking the town centre, featuring goldmining sites and relics, and a scenic lookout. **Market:** Fraser St; 2nd Sun each month. **Mount Beckworth:** popular picnic and horseriding reserve with panoramic views from the summit; 8km W.

CRESWICK
Population 2794

Creswick is an attractive and historic town, a symbol of the rich and heady life of the gold-rush days of the 1850s. Unfortunately, the goldmining also decimated the surrounding forests. Today the town is surrounded by pine plantations over 100 years old; they exist thanks to the initiative and foresight of local John La Gerche and – while they are no replacement for the Australian bush – they have given Creswick the title of 'the home of forestry'. Creswick was the birthplace of renowned Australian artist Norman Lindsay; you can see some of his paintings in the local historical museum.

SEE & DO **Creswick Regional Park:** See Other Attractions. **Historic walk:** self-guided tour, map from visitor centre. **Giant Mullock Heaps:** indicate how deep mines went; Ullina Rd. **Museum:** photos and memorabilia from the town's goldmining past as well as an exhibition of Lindsay paintings; open Sun, public holidays or by appt; Albert St. **Gold Battery:** est. 1897; Battery Cres. **Creswick Woollen Mills:** last coloured woollen mill of its type in Australia; offers product sales, regular demonstrations and exhibitions; Railway Pde. **Makers Market:** RSL Hall, Albert St; 1st Sat each month. **Crafters and Traders:** railway station; 3rd Sun each month. **Market:** community centre, Victoria St; 3rd Sat each month. **Smeaton:** a pretty little town famous for its potatoes; other attractions include the historic Smeaton House, the Tuki Trout Farm and Anderson's Mill; 16km NE.

★ DAYLESFORD
Population 3732

Daylesford is an idyllic destination for visitors and a popular weekend escape, located in the heart of Victoria's spa country. The town has beautiful gardens, picturesque mountain scenery, gourmet eating options and a laidback nonchalance. The roads are lined with trees that blaze with colour in autumn, and inside the gold rush–era buildings are restaurants, cafes, galleries and boutique shops. The area developed with the discovery of gold, which lured many Swiss–Italian settlers, but it was the discovery of natural mineral springs that proved a more lasting attraction. Of the 72 documented springs in the area, the most famous are the nearby Hepburn Springs. The water is rich with minerals that dissolve into it as it flows from the crest of the Great Dividing Range through underground rocks, and it is known for its rejuvenating and healing qualities.

SEE & DO **Convent Gallery; Hepburn Springs Spas:** see Top Attractions for both. **Lavandula Swiss Italian Farm; Hepburn Regional Park:** see Other Attractions for both. **Historical Museum:** features a collection of photographs from the region's past and artefacts from the Dja Dja Wurrung People; open Sat–Sun 1.30–4.30pm, public and school holidays (Tues, Wed and Thurs); Vincent St; (03) 5348 1453. **Lake Daylesford:** a lovely spot for picnics, with paddleboats and rowing boats for hire in the warmer months. The Tipperary walking track starts here and ends at the Mineral Springs Reserve. Access to the lake is from Bleakley St. **Wombat Hill Botanical Gardens:** established in 1861, these lovely gardens are situated on the hill overlooking town and Wombat Hill House cafe's pastries are hard to go past; Central Springs Rd. **Daylesford Spa Country Railway:** leaves railway station for Bullarto; runs Sun; Raglan St; 0476 527 999. **Daylesford farmers' market:** Vincent St; 1st Sat of the month. **Market:** for arts, crafts and local produce; Raglan St, near railway station; Sun morning. **Waterfalls:** several in area, including Sailors Falls, 5km S; Loddon Falls, 10km NE; Trentham Falls, 21km SE. **Breakneck Gorge:** early goldmining site; 5km N. **Lyonville Mineral Springs:** picnic and barbecue facilities; 15km SE. **Yandoit:** historic Swiss–Italian settlement; 18km NW.

DUNOLLY
Population 680

The towns of Dunolly, Wedderburn and Inglewood formed the rich goldfield region colloquially known in the 1850s as the 'Golden Triangle'. The district has produced more gold nuggets than any other goldfield in Australia, with 126 unearthed in Dunolly itself. The 'Welcome Stranger', considered to be the largest nugget ever discovered, was found in 1869 15km north-west of Dunolly, at Moliagul.

SEE & DO **Restored courthouse:** offers a display relating to gold discoveries in the area; open by appointment; 0448 017 436; Market St. **Original lock-up and stables:** viewable from street only; Market St. **Gold-themed tours of the region:** includes gold panning in local creeks; details from visitor centre. **Community Street Market:** Broadway; 2nd Sun each month. **Moliagul:** the Welcome Stranger Discovery Walk leads to a monument where the 'Welcome Stranger' nugget was found in 1869. Moliagul is also the birthplace of Rev. John Flynn, founder of the Royal Flying Doctor Service; 15km NW. **Laanecoorie Reservoir:** a great spot for swimming, boating and waterskiing, water levels permitting, with camping and picnic facilities; 16km E. **Tarnagulla:** a small mining town with splendid Victorian architecture and a flora reserve nearby; 16km NE.

HEATHCOTE
Population 1844

Heathcote, located near the outskirts of scenic Heathcote–Graytown National Park, see Other Attractions, with the McIvor Creek flowing by the town, is the place to come if you want to try some red wines. Originally established during the gold rush, Heathcote is now emerging as a major wine region with good red wines produced from a number of new vineyards.

SEE & DO **Heathcote Wine Region:** see Top Attractions. **Heathcote–Graytown National Park:** see Other Attractions. **Court House Crafts:** co-operative art and craft centre with displays relating to the gold rush; High St. **Pink Cliffs:** eroded soil from gold sluices gave the cliffs their remarkable pink colour; Pink Cliffs Rd, off Hospital Rd. **McIvor Range Reserve:** a range of walking tracks; off Barrack St; details of walks from visitor centre. **Lake Eppalock:** one of the state's largest lakes, great for fishing, watersports and picnics; 10km W.

INGLEWOOD
Population 779

Hidden in the scrub north of Bendigo is the town of Inglewood, one of the famous 'Golden Triangle' towns. Sizeable gold nuggets were found in this area during the gold rush – and gold is still being unearthed. You can pick up a fossicking map from the visitor centre if you want to try your luck. The town also has graceful and elaborate buildings from the lucrative gold-rush period. Inglewood is known as Blue Eucy town, due to the once vigorous blue mallee eucalyptus oil industry. The town was also the birthplace of famous Australian aviator Sir Reginald Ansett.

SEE & DO **Old eucalyptus oil distillery:** not in operation but can be viewed; Calder Hwy, northern end of town. **Old courthouse:** local historical memorabilia; open by appt; Southey St. **Streetscape:** historic buildings are evidence of the town's goldmining history. **Bridgewater on Loddon:** fishing and watersports and a bakery famous for its vanilla slice; 8km SE. **Loddon Valley wine region:** the warm climate and clay soils of this region are known for producing outstanding red varieties and award-winning chardonnays. Taste the wines at cellar doors like **Water Wheel Vineyards** at **Bridgewater on Loddon** (8km SE) and **Both Banks Vineyard** (19km SW).

KILMORE
Population 8786

Kilmore is Victoria's oldest inland town, known for its historic buildings and horseracing events. Like many towns in the central goldfields, Kilmore was the scene of a Kelly family saga. In this case, it was Ned Kelly's father who had a run-in with the law. In 1865 John 'Red' Kelly was arrested for killing a squatter's calf to feed his family, and was locked away in the Kilmore Gaol for six months. It was a crime

Top: Heathcote grape harvest
Bottom: Art Gallery of Ballarat
Opposite: Maldon's historic streetscape

TEMPERATURES

Jan: 14–29°C

July: 3–12°C

that Ned had actually committed. Soon after Red's release, he died of dropsy and was buried in the small town of Avenel, where the Kelly family lived for some time.

SEE & DO **Old Kilmore Gaol**: an impressive bluestone building, established in 1859, that is now a privately owned auction house. Sutherland St. **Hudson Park**: picnic/barbecue facilities; cnr Sydney and Foote sts. **Historic buildings**: Whitburgh Cottage, Piper St, and a number of 1850s shops and hotels along Sydney St; brochure from visitor centre. **Tramways Heritage Centre**: extensive display of cable cars and early electric trams at Bylands, with tram rides available; open Sun only; just south of town. **Broadford**: a small town featuring a historic precinct on High St; 17km ne. **Mount Piper Walking Track**: wildlife and wildflowers can be spotted along the way (1hr return); near Broadford. **Strath Creek**: walks to Strath Creek Falls and a drive through the Valley of a Thousand Hills; starts at outskirts of Broadford.

★ KYNETON
Population 5151

Part of Victoria's picturesque spa and garden country, Kyneton is a well-preserved town with many attractive bluestone buildings. It is known for its fantastic eateries and has developed into one of Victoria's top gastronomic destinations. It is a popular weekend getaway town and has boutiques and cafes. The annual daffodil festival is in Sept.

SEE & DO **Kyneton Museum**: in a former bank building, with a drop-log cottage in the grounds; open Fri–Sun 11am–4pm; 67 Piper St; (03) 5422 1228. **Stockroom**: dynamic arts hub with galleries showcasing local artists; also designer crafts, clothes, pottery and jewellery; 98 Piper St; (03) 5422 3415. **Botanic Gardens**: 8ha area scenically located above Pipers Creek. The gardens feature rare varieties of trees; Clowes St. **Historic buildings**: many in town, including Mechanics Institute on Mollison St and old police depot on Jenning St. **Campaspe River Walk**: scenic walk with picnic spots and a Sculpture Park with works from local artists; access from Piper St. **Black Hill Reserve**: beautiful bushwalks and possibly the largest granite monolith in Victoria; Ennis Rd. **The Golden Mile**: mile-long carpet of daffodils blooms beside the Calder Highway on the Bendigo side of town (late Aug to mid-Sept). **Farmers' market**: selling farmgate produce; Piper St; 2nd Sat each month. **Reservoirs**: several offering scenic locations for walks and picnics. Upper Coliban, Lauriston and Malmsbury reservoirs are all nearby. **Paramoor Winery**: a former Clydesdale horse farm, now a winery; Carlsruhe; 5km SE. **Malmsbury**: a town noted for its old bluestone buildings and very impressive railway viaduct bridge; it features historic Botanic Gardens; wineries are also in the area; 10km NW. **Turpins and Cascade falls**: with picnic area and walks; near Metcalfe; 22km N.

MALDON
Population 1381

Maldon is one of Victoria's best-known gold towns and a popular weekend getaway for Melburnians. The town has been wonderfully preserved, with the wide, tree-lined main street featuring old buildings and shopfronts. There is also a tourist steam train that runs to Castlemaine (*see* p. 152). Aside from the cafes and galleries, the town seems unchanged from the gold-rush days. Maldon was declared Australia's first 'notable town' by the National Trust in 1966.

SEE & DO **Historic town walk**: grab a brochure from the visitor centre and take to the wide, old footpaths to discover the historic delights of Maldon. See preserved 19th-century shopfronts and old stone cottages, many of which now house art galleries, antiques and boutiques. Highlights include the restored Dabb's General Store in Main St, and the Maldon Hospital in Adair St. **Museum**: displays on mining as well as domestic memorabilia from Maldon's past, in heritage building; open Wed and Sun 11.30am–2pm; High St. **Vintage Machinery and Museum**: machinery heaven for enthusiasts; call for opening times; Vincent Rd; (03) 5472 2202. **Beehive Mine Chimney**: southern end of Church St. **Anzac Hill**: the walk to the top is rewarded with magnificent views of the area; southern end of High St. **Market**: home grown and

VICTORIA

handmade goods at the Bill Woodfull Recreation Reserve on 2nd Sun of each month. **Mount Tarrangower Lookout Tower:** town and district views; 2km W. **Carman's Tunnel Mine:** guided mine tours feature relics from goldmining days; 2km SW. **Nuggetty Ranges and Mount Moorol:** 2km N. **Cairn Curran Reservoir:** great for watersports and fishing, water levels permitting; features picnic facilities and a sailing club near the spillway; 10km SW.

MARYBOROUGH
Population 7769

Maryborough is a small city set on the northern slopes of the Great Dividing Range. Its historic 19th-century buildings, particularly around the civic square, are a testament to the riches brought by the gold rush of the 1850s. Stroll through the streets to enjoy the cafes, craft shops and magnificent buildings, such as the National Trust–listed courthouse, post office and town hall.

SEE & DO **Maryborough Railway Station:** *see* Other Attractions. **Pioneer Memorial Tower:** Bristol Hill. **Worsley Cottage:** a historical museum featuring local relics; open Tues, Thurs 10am–12pm, Sun 2–4pm; (03) 5461 2518; Palmerston St. **Central Goldfields Art Gallery:** features an impressive collection of local artworks, housed in the old fire station; open Thurs–Sun 10am–4pm; Neill St; (03) 5461 6600. **Phillips Gardens:** Alma St. **Carisbrook:** historic town with oldest log gaol in the state; 7km E.

MOUNT MACEDON
Population 1450

Country mansions and superb 19th- and 20th-century European-style gardens sit comfortably in native bush at the surprisingly lush Mount Macedon. Many of the renowned and beautiful gardens are listed by the National Trust and open to the public in autumn and spring.

SEE & DO **Macedon Ranges Wine Region:** *see* Top Attractions **Macedon Regional Park:** bushwalking and scenic drives. The Camels Hump marks the start of a signposted walk to the summit of the mountain where a huge World War I memorial cross stands. Access via turn-off after Mount Macedon township. **Macedon:** a town at the foot of Mount Macedon. Home to the Church of the Resurrection, with stained-glass windows designed by Leonard French, and excellent plant nurseries; 6km SW.

ST ARNAUD
Population 2126

A former goldmining town surrounded by forests and scenic hill country, St Arnaud is a service centre for the district's farming community, and has a peaceful rural atmosphere. The main street is lined with well-preserved historic buildings, many of which feature impressive ornate lacework.

SEE & DO **Kara Kara National Park:** *see* Other Attractions. **Self-guided historic tour:** brochure available from visitor centre. **Queen Mary Gardens:** great spot for a picnic; Napier St. **Historical Society and Museum:** research room, displays and gift shop; 1–4pm Wed and Fri; Napier St; (03) 5495 1106. **Police lock-up:** built in 1862; Jennings St. **Great Grape Rd:** wine-themed circuit through Stawell and Ballarat; details from visitor centre.

WEDDERBURN
Population 650

Wedderburn, part of the 'Golden Triangle', was once one of Victoria's richest goldmining towns. Many large nuggets have been unearthed here in the past and – for some lucky people – continue to be discovered today. The town's annual Detector Jamboree, with music, historical re-enactments and family entertainment recognises the importance of gold in the development of so many towns.

SEE & DO **Hard Hill Tourist Reserve:** *see* Top Attractions. **Kooyoora State Park:** *see* Other Attractions. **Walking Tour of Town:** Tues–Wed 11am; bookings via visitor centre; (03) 5494 3489. **Coach House Gallery:** a 1910 building restored to its original appearance, with authentic, old-fashioned stock and coach-builders' quarters; open for group bookings; High St; (03) 5594 1257. **Nardoo Creek Walk:** takes in the key historic buildings around town; map from visitor centre. **Mount Korong:** bushwalking; 16km SE. **Wychitella Nature Conservation Reserve:** wildlife sanctuary set in mallee forest, home to mallee

Hanging Rock
Opposite: Woodend

THE EUREKA STOCKADE

The Eureka Stockade rebellion was a watershed moment in Australia's history and shed light on the dismal conditions of people working in the Victorian goldfields. The rebellion was fuelled by the discontent of goldfields workers and gathered momentum when the government introduced the miner's licence – a tax that required the payment of fees irrespective of the gold mined.

The workers on the goldfields were known as diggers, a term that reflected the strength of the Eureka movement, and the miners' prevailing 'mateship'. Australian soldiers have been called diggers since World War I, so the identity endures.

In 1854, about 25,000 diggers worked on the Ballarat goldfields. Starting in June that year, police conducted twice-weekly licence checks to enforce the taxation laws. Such actions were seen as harassment, so a large group of miners established the Ballarat Reform League in November 1854. They burnt their licences in protest later that month.

The government responded by ordering a licence hunt, and 500 miners gathered at the Eureka diggings, where they built the famous stockade and swore an oath on the Southern Cross Flag (now known as the Eureka Flag): 'We swear by the Southern Cross to stand truly by each other and fight to defend our rights and liberties'. On 3 December, police and military attacked the stockade. The short battle saw 22 of the outnumbered miners and five troopers killed, and many others badly wounded. Thirteen miners faced trial, but were acquitted.

Although they paid a terrible price, the miners did get changes after the rebellion. A royal commission recommended that the licensing laws be phased out and replaced with a new tax where miners only paid a tax on gold they actually found. Miners were also given the right to vote and elect representatives into the legislative council. Three years later, all white Victorian men were given the right to vote.

---

fowl; 16km N. **Fossickers Drive:** takes in goldmining sites, Dja Dja Wurrung rock wells and scar trees, local wineries and Melville Caves; details from visitor centre.

WOODEND
Population 4663

During the gold rushes of the 1850s, travellers sought refuge from mud, bogs and bushrangers at the 'wood's end' around Five Mile Creek, where a town eventually grew. In the late 19th century, Woodend became a resort town, and its lovely gardens and proximity to spectacular natural sights, such as Hanging Rock and Macedon Ranges Wine Region still make it a popular daytrip and weekend getaway.

SEE & DO **Hanging Rock; Macedon Ranges Wine Region:** see Top Attractions for both. **Bluestone Bridge:** built in 1862, the bridge crosses Five Mile Creek on the northern outskirts of town. **Clock Tower:** built as a World War I memorial; Calder Hwy. **Courthouse:** historic structure built in 1870; Forest St. **Farmers' market:** High St; 1st Sat each month. **Gisborne:** a variety of craft outlets. Gisborne Steam Park holds a steam-train rally each May; 16km SE. **Cope-Williams Winery:** weekend tastings and sales, surrounded by charming English-style gardens, tennis courts and a cricket green; 160 Glenfern Rd, Romsey; (03) 5429 5595; 19km E. **Lancefield:** historic buildings and wineries. The town also hosts a farmers' market, for local produce, on the 4th Sat each month; 25km NE. **Monegeetta:** in town is the Mintaro homestead, a smaller replica of Melbourne's Government House, but not open to the public; 27km E via Romsey.

Geelong and the Bellarine Peninsula

The Bellarine Peninsula is only 1.5hr from Melbourne and is a region full of **boutique wineries, bay and surf beaches, spectacular views, lighthouses, holiday towns** and **historic villages**. Geelong is a regional city and the gateway to the Bellarine, Surf Coast and Great Ocean Road. It is a **UNESCO City of Design** and has a picturesque waterfront area and botanic gardens.

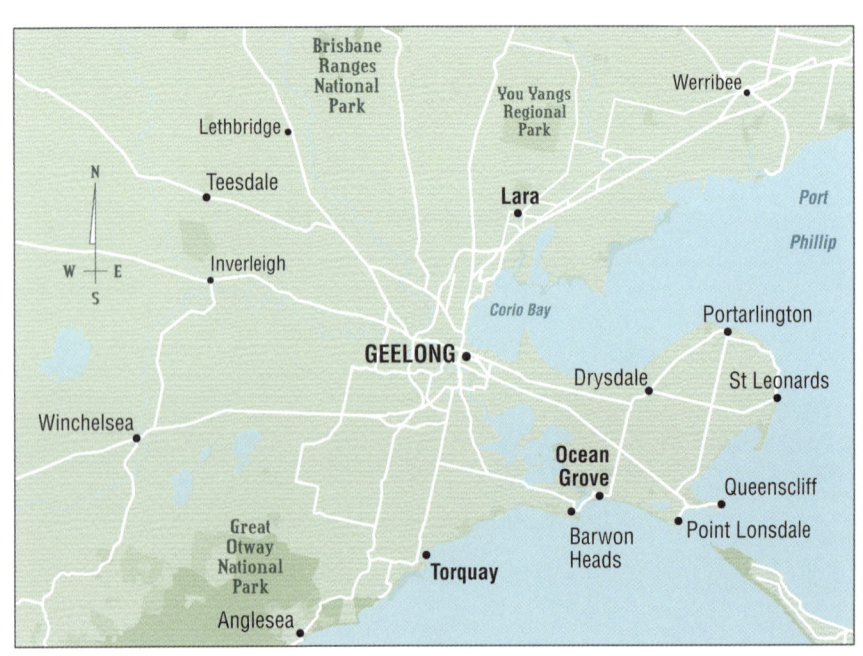

CHEAT SHEET

→ Allow three or four days for a proper exploration.

→ Best time to visit: Sept–April.

→ Main towns: Geelong (*see* p. 161), Barwon Heads (*see* p. 161), Ocean Grove (*see* p. 162), Portarlington (*see* p. 159), Queenscliff (*see* p. 162).

→ Geelong, the You Yangs and the Bellarine Peninsula are on the Traditional Lands of the Wadawurrung People. The Winchelsea area is the Traditional Lands of the Gulidjan People of the Eastern Marr Traditional Owner Group.

→ Don't miss: the Bellarine Peninsula's many wineries; the historic town of Queenscliff and its steam trains; Geelong's waterfront dining precinct; the popular holiday village of Barwon Heads.

Top: Geelong's Eastern Beach
Opposite: Queenscliff's Black Lighthouse and entrance to Port Phillip known as The Heads

TOP ATTRACTIONS

GEELONG AND THE BELLARINE WINE REGION: During the 1800s, the Geelong region had a large wine industry that competed with Rutherglen for prominence. But when the devastating phylloxera disease hit, all the vines were pulled out. Today the region has a plethora of quality boutique wineries once again, and two of its highly regarded labels are found at Bannockburn. **Bannockburn Vineyards** date from the 1970s, and **Wine by Farr** (no cellar door) produce shiraz, pinot noir and chardonnay of serious quality. Look out for the wines on local menus. **Scotchmans Hill** is a large winery and cellar-door complex on the Bellarine Peninsula with views over Port Phillip to Melbourne; nearby **Jack Rabbit's** vines also have views over the bay with a renowned restaurant; and across the road **Terindah Estate** lives up to its 'most beautiful' name translation. Other must-visit vineyards include **Lethbridge Wines**, **Clyde Park Vineyard**; and **Leura Park Estate**. Various cellar doors offer tastings and sales; map from visitor centres.

GEELONG WATERFRONT: This superbly restored promenade stretches along Eastern Beach and offers a variety of attractions. Visitors can relax in the historic 1930s-era sea baths, enjoy fine dining in seaside restaurants and cafes or stroll along the famous Bollards Trail featuring painted posts. The Waterfront district is on Eastern Beach Rd, with the beautiful old Cunningham Pier as a centrepiece.

MARINE DISCOVERY AND FRESHWATER CENTRE: Just outside the historic town of Queenscliff (*see* p. 162), this is a great family destination with aquariums and touch-tanks. The centre also runs various tours, including boat cruises on Port Phillip and 'rockpool rambles'. Open only for school holiday programs; Bellarine Hwy, Queenscliff; (03) 5258 3344.

NATIONAL WOOL MUSEUM: Housed in a historic bluestone woolstore in Geelong (*see* p. 161), the museum features audiovisual displays plus re-created shearers' quarters and a mill-worker's cottage. There are also interesting temporary exhibitions, including the annual Wildlife Photographer of the Year from the Natural History Museum in London, and a souvenir shop selling locally made wool products. 26 Moorabool St, Geelong; (03) 5272 4701.

PORTARLINGTON: A popular bayside holiday town with a restored flour mill featuring displays of agricultural history, a bay for swimming and fresh mussels for sale near the pier. It has a renowned bakery, Portarlington Bakehouse, and cafes that overlook the water. There is a market at Parks Hall on the last Sun of each month. A ferry service operates between Portarlington and Melbourne, see portphillipferries.com.au.

ST LEONARDS: A small beach holiday town, which includes Edwards Point Wildlife Reserve and a memorial commemorating the landing of Matthew Flinders in 1802 and of John Batman in 1835.

THE BLUES TRAIN: A unique dining and entertainment experience on board a steam train. It departs from and returns to Queenscliff Railway Station (*see* p. 162). Round trips provide four carriages, each with a different blues musician, and a carriage bar at each station platform; bookings at thebluestrain.com.au or at Ticketek on 132 849.

THE Q TRAIN: A boutique rail restaurant using heritage carriages and showcasing local food, beer, wine and cider. Runs from Drysdale Railway Station to Queenscliff Railway Station for lunch and dinner; Thurs–Sat; theqtrain.com.au.

YOU YANGS REGIONAL PARK: These granite outcrops, rising 352m above Werribee's lava plains, have an ancient link to the Wadawurrung People because they provided a much-needed water source – rock wells were created to catch water, and many of them can still be seen at Big Rock. The park is popular for mountain-biking, with over 50km of trails. There's also the 12km Great Circle Drive and the climb to Flinders Peak for fantastic views of Geelong, Corio Bay, Mount Macedon and Melbourne's skyline. The You Yangs are 22km north-east of Geelong (see p. 161).

OTHER ATTRACTIONS

BARWON PARK: Only the greatest estate would satisfy Elizabeth Austin, and so her husband, Thomas, acquiesced. Barwon Park, built in Winchelsea, west of Geelong, in 1869, was the biggest mansion in the Western District. Featuring 42 rooms furnished largely with original pieces, the bluestone building is an impressive example of 19th-century design. The name Austin might be familiar: Thomas Austin reputedly imported the first of Australia's devastating rabbit population and Elizabeth Austin contributed to major charities, and established the Austin Hospital in Melbourne. Open 11am–4pm Wed and Sun; 105 Inverleigh Rd, Winchelsea; (03) 5267 2209.

BELLARINE RAILWAY: Beautifully restored steam trains run between Queenscliff (see p. 162) and Drysdale (see p. 161), including themed Thomas the Tank Engine and Easter bunny train rides. Engines are on display around Queenscliff station. Check for running times and events; Symonds St, Queenscliff; (03) 5258 2069.

GEELONG ART GALLERY: This regional gallery is considered one of the finest in the state. The focus is on late 19th- and early 20th-century paintings by British artists and members of the Royal Academy, such as Tom Roberts and Arthur Streeton; Little Malop St, Geelong; (03) 5229 3645.

HMAS CANBERRA DIVE SITE: Opened to the public in Dec 2009, this purposely sunken warship was Victoria's first artificial site created specifically for diving. Divers can visit every area of the ship's 138m length, from the captain's cabin to the galley. Bookings must be made with a charter boat operator or dive shop to be taken to the dive site; hmascanberra.com.au. Contact Parks Victoria on 13 1963. The site is 4km south-east of Ocean Grove (see p. 162).

Top: Geelong Fountain in Eastern Beach **Bottom:** The Blues Train **Opposite top:** Geelong Art Gallery **Opposite bottom:** Narana Aboriginal Cultural Centre

VISITOR INFORMATION

Geelong and the Bellarine Visitor Information Centre
26 Moorabool St, Geelong
(03) 5222 2900 or
1800 755 611
visitgeelongbellarine.com.au

KEY TOWNS

⭐ BARWON HEADS
Population 4353

This village, situated on the banks of the Barwon River near Bass Strait, was the setting for ABC TV's classic show *SeaChange*, and is suitably picturesque. It's a popular holiday destination with boutique shops and cafes, and gets busy with traffic in summer. The town was properly established in the late 19th century when the post office opened. While the area is mainly about coastal activities, such as fishing and swimming in the river, cycling has increased in popularity because Barwon Heads is the hometown of 2011 Tour de France winner Cadel Evans.

SEE & DO **Golf courses:** golf courses include Thirteenth Beach and the Barwon Heads Golf Club. **Barwon Heads Bridge:** the recently restored wooden bridge is a heritage-listed structure. **Barwon Bluff Marine Sanctuary:** covering 17ha of ocean, the sanctuary is home to a vast array of marine life, as well as kelp forests and a couple of shipwrecks; contact Parks Victoria on 13 1963. **Jirrahlinga Koala and Wildlife Reserve:** home to an abundance of Australian wildlife, including koalas; open 10am–5pm; Taits Rd; (03) 5254 2484.

DRYSDALE
Population 4976

Drysdale, on the Bellarine Peninsula, is close to the beaches of Port Phillip and the area has a number of renowned wineries. Drysdale is now considered a satellite town of Geelong, yet retains a small town atmosphere.

SEE & DO **Geelong and Bellarine Wine Region:** see Top Attractions. **Bellarine Railway:** see Other Attractions. **Old Courthouse:** home of the Bellarine Historical Society; High St. **Tuckerberry Hill:** berry picking and produce tastings at Tuckerberry Hill Cafe; 35 Becks Rd; (03) 5251 3468. **Country Market:** at the reserve, near the football ground; 3rd Sun each month Oct–May. **Lake Lorne picnic area:** 1km SW.

⭐ GEELONG
Population 180,239

Situated on Corio Bay, Geelong is the largest regional city in Victoria. The town was first settled by Europeans in the 1830s, but Geelong and its surrounds are the Traditional Lands of the Waddawurrung People. It is the gateway to both the Great Ocean Road and Bellarine Peninsula, which means it gets a lot of passing tourist traffic. It is also a vibrant destination for visitors in its own right and was declared a UNESCO City of Design in 2017. A revitalisation of areas such as the fabulous waterfront has seen new bars and restaurants popping up and the city is also embracing an energetic arts scene. Geelong is a beautifully laid-out city, and a drive along the scenic Esplanade reveals magnificent old mansions built during its heyday.

SEE & DO **Geelong Waterfront; National Wool Museum:** see Top Attractions for both. **Geelong Art Gallery:** see Other Attractions. **Boom Gallery:** contemporary art and design gallery and workshop in historic woollen mill, with a cafe on site; open Mon–Sat 9am–4pm, Sun 9am–3pm; 11 Rutland St, Newtown; 0417 555 101. **Historic buildings:** there are over 100 National Trust classifications in Geelong, including Merchiston Hall, Osborne House and Corio Villa. The Heights Heritage House and Garden is a 14-room prefabricated timber mansion set in landscaped gardens; contact visitor centre for details of open days; Aphrasia St, Newtown. Christ Church, still in use, is the oldest Anglican Church in Victoria; Moorabool St. **Geelong Library and Heritage Centre (the Dome):** futuristic architectural design; drop in to see what's on, including activities for kids; open Mon–Fri 8am–8pm, Sat–Sun 10am–5pm; 51 Little Malop St; (03) 4201 0600. **Little Malop Street:** near the library and Geelong Art Gallery, a small street and nearby laneways of hip restaurants and bars. **Pakington Street:** a long stretch of cafes, restaurants and shops. **Botanic Gardens:** overlooking Corio Bay and featuring a good collection of native and exotic plants; part of Eastern Park; Garden St. **Johnstone Park:** picnic and barbecue facilities; cnr Mercer and Gheringhap sts. **Queens Park:** walks to Buckley Falls, rope playground; Queens Park Rd, Highton. **Barwon River:** extensive walking tracks and bike paths in parkland by the river. **Corio Bay beaches:** popular for fishing and sailing; boat ramps provided. **Walking tours:** volunteer-led walks give insight into the city's landmarks and heritage; inquire at visitor centre. **Waterfront Makers and Growers Market:** gourmet treats, local produce, music and arts and crafts; 1st Sun each month; Steampacket Gardens, Eastern Beach Rd. **Fyansford:** one of the oldest European settlements in the region, with historic buildings including the Balmoral Hotel and Fyansford Hotel. The Monash Bridge across the Moorabool River is thought to be the earliest reinforced-concrete bridge in Victoria; outskirts of Geelong; 7km W. **Narana Aboriginal Cultural Centre:** gallery, performance space and cultural display, along with a native garden; 'Narana' is understood to mean a deep listening and understanding. (03) 5241 5700; 9km S. **Adventure Park:** Victoria's first water park, with more than 20 attractions and rides; open Oct–Apr, confirm days with park; 1249 Bellarine Hwy, Wallington; (03) 5250 7200; 15km SE. **Avalon Airfield:** hosts the

VICTORIA

161

Australian International Air Show and Aerospace and Defence Exposition in odd-numbered years; off Princes Hwy; 22km NE. **Serendip Sanctuary:** a wildlife research station that includes nature trails, bird hides and a visitor centre; just south of the You Yangs; Windermere Rd, Lara; contact Parks Victoria 13 1963; 19km N. **Fairy Park:** miniature houses and scenes from fairytales; Ballan Rd, Anakie; (03) 5284 1262; 33km N. **Steiglitz:** once a gold town, now almost deserted. The restored courthouse is open on Sun; 37km NW.

OCEAN GROVE
Population 17,714

Ocean Grove is a popular summer holiday destination near the mouth of the Barwon River. The beaches around the town offer great surfing and swimming, with surf patrols operating during the summer months.

SEE & DO **HMAS Canberra Dive Site:** *see* Other Attractions. **Ocean Grove Nature Reserve:** This reserve contains the only significant example of woodland on the Bellarine Peninsula, preserved virtually as it was prior to European settlement. Several bird hides let visitors look out for any number of the 130 different species that have been recorded here; access is from Grubb Rd. **Bookgrove:** an indie bookstore that holds author events; 1/73 The Terrace; (03) 5255 5973. **Lake Connewarre State Game Reserve:** with mangrove swamps and great walks, the game reserve is home to a variety of wildlife, including 149 recorded species of birds; 7km N. **Wallington:** the town is home to Koombahla Park Equestrian Centre and **Adventure Park** water and theme park (*see* p. 161). A strawberry fair is held in Wallington in Mar; 8km N.

⭐ QUEENSCLIFF
Population 1516

Queenscliff is a charming historic seaside town on the Bellarine Peninsula. It began life as a resort for wealthy Victorians in the 1800s, as testified by lavish buildings on Gellibrand and Hesse streets, such as the Vue Grand Hotel. The town's wide main street is lined with cafes and restaurants, art galleries and bric-a-brac shops, and the nearby beaches become a playground for holidaymakers during summer. The town's spelling has some confusion, with Queenscliff used for the town and Queenscliffe for the Borough, which includes part of nearby Point Lonsdale. A ferry runs between Queenscliff and Sorrento (*see* p. 131), see searoad.com.au.

SEE & DO **Marine Discovery and Freshwater Centre; The Blues Train; The Q Train:** *see* Top Attractions for all. **Bellarine Railway:** *see* Other Attractions. **Maritime Museum:** the museum explores the town's long association with ships and the sea through a collection of maritime memorabilia. Open 11am–4pm; Wharf St; (03) 5258 3440. **Fort Queenscliff:** built in the aftermath of the Crimean War, it includes the unique 'Black Lighthouse'. Access is by tour only, see fortqueenscliff.com.au; entry via King St; (03) 5258 1488. **Historical Museum:** open Mon–Thurs 11am–3pm; Hesse St. **The Bookshop at Queenscliff:** a fabulous indie bookstore with a great range of fiction and non-fiction and kids books; 84 Hesse St; (03) 5258 4496. **Harbour:** a pretty marina with yachts and cafes overlooking the water, and an observation tower with 360-degree views of the bay. **Market:** with crafts and second-hand goods; Princess Park, Gellibrand St; last Sun each month (Sept–May). **Sea All Dolphin Swims:** swim with dolphins and other marine

Queenscliff's historic steam train rides **Opposite:** Barwon Heads Bluff boardwalk

TOP EVENTS

→ JAN Festival of Sails (Geelong); Mussel Festival (Portarlington); Great Australian Beer Festival (Geelong)

→ FEB Pako Festa (multicultural event, Geelong)

→ MAR Festival of the Sea (Barwon Heads)

→ MAY Queenscliffe Literary Festival (Queenscliff)

→ JUNE National Celtic Festival (Portarlington)

→ NOV Queenscliff Music Festival (Queenscliff)

TEMPERATURES

Jan: 20–40°C

July: 7–14°C

life in the beautiful waters of Bass Strait; dolphinswims.com.au. **Point Lonsdale:** This peaceful holiday village offers a front bay beach popular with families, and a rough ocean (back) beach for surfers. The main street has cafes, an IGA supermarket and a few shops, as well as a deck and playground overlooking the front beach. The Rip View carpark provides a great view of the treacherous entrance to Port Phillip known as 'the Rip'. There is a pier, popular for fishing, and the **Point Lonsdale Lighthouse**, built in 1902, opens for tours on Sun morning; bookings required; 0490 550 837. A market is held in the Point Lonsdale Primary School grounds; 2nd Sun of each month; 4km SW. **Lake Victoria:** an important waterbird habitat; 5km W via Point Lonsdale. **Harold Holt Marine Reserve:** incorporates Mud Island and coastal reserves.

WINCHELSEA
Population 2032

This charming little town on the Barwon River west of Geelong was first developed with cattle runs in the 1830s. Many of the historic buildings that grew from this development can still be seen around town, the most impressive being the nearby Barwon Park Homestead – a mansion built by famous settlers of the district, Thomas and Elizabeth Austin. Winchelsea soon became a key stopover for travellers taking the road from Colac to Geelong, and it still serves that purpose for travellers on the Princes Hwy.

SEE & DO

Barwon Park: *see* Other Attractions. **Barwon Bridge:** an impressive arched bridge, built from stone in 1867; Princes Hwy. **Antiques and collectibles:** many shops in town that outline its history; Main St and Princes Hwy. **Winchelsea Historical Trail:** map available from visitor information centre, or check township information boards. **Barwon Hotel:** known locally as the 'bottom pub' of the town, offers country-style fare; Main St. **Winchelsea Tavern:** renovated Art Deco 'top pub'; Princes Hwy. **Old Shire Hall:** beautifully restored bluestone building; Princes Hwy. **Marjorie Lawrence Trail:** details the life of one of the world's most adored dramatic sopranos from the 1900s; details from visitor centre. **Country Dahlias Gardens:** beautiful gardens, best viewed during spring, with sales of dahlia plants; open Mar–Apr; Mathison Rd; 5km S.

Great Ocean Road and Surf Coast

The Great Ocean Road is one of Australia's iconic attractions, and winds its way between the **wild beaches** of the south-west coast and the **forested, mountainous hinterland**. One of the hardest things about the drive is concentrating on the road, rather than the view! The route is dotted with charming **seaside villages**, as well as an almost ridiculous level of natural attractions. The Surf Coast boasts the **surf town of Torquay** and nearby **world-famous Bells Beach**.

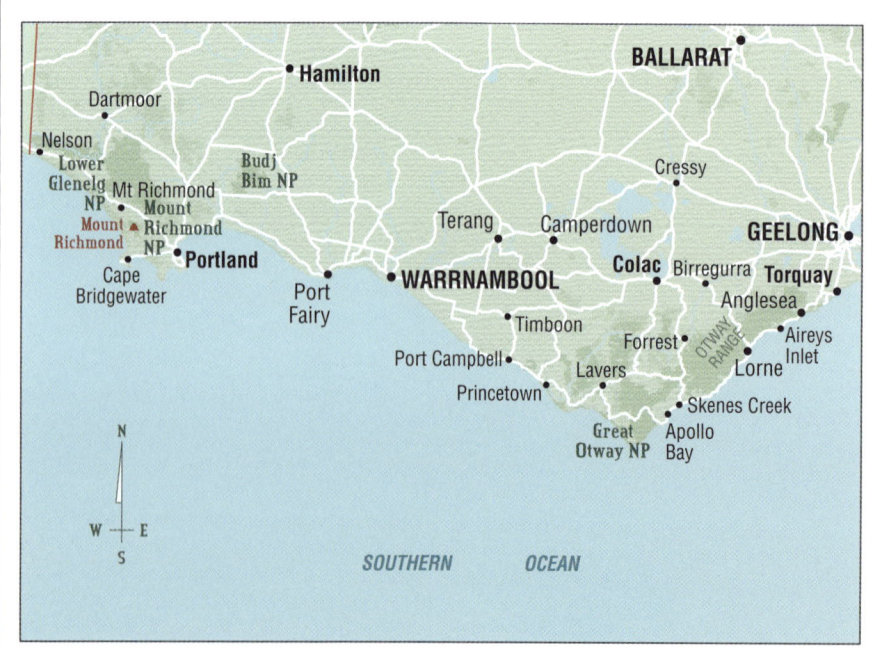

CHEAT SHEET

→ Allow a week for a proper exploration, although two or three days will work too.

→ Best time to visit: Sept–April.

→ Main towns: Torquay (see p. 171), Anglesea (see p. 168), Lorne (see p. 169), Apollo Bay (see p. 168) Warrnambool (see p. 171), Portland (see p. 170).

→ The southern coastal areas of Victoria are the Traditional Lands of the Wadawuurung, Eastern Maar and Gunditjmara Peoples, an area believed to be made up of several language groups, clans and nations.

→ Did you know? The Great Ocean Road, carved into rock along Victoria's southern coastline, is actually a memorial to those killed in the line of duty during World War I. It was built by thousands of returned soldiers. The backbreaking work was done entirely with picks, shovels and horse-drawn carts.

→ Don't miss: Bells Beach; the Otways; waterfalls around Lorne; the mountain-biking town of Forrest; historic Port Fairy; Cape Bridgewater. The famous Twelve Apostles are just east of Port Campbell in Port Campbell National Park.

Top: Cape Otway Lighthouse
Opposite: View from Teddy's lookout, Lorne

TOP ATTRACTIONS

AUSTRALIAN NATIONAL SURF MUSEUM: The world's biggest surfing museum. See how board technology has developed over the last century, find out exactly what makes a good wave, and learn about the history of surfing at Bells Beach. A theatre here screens classic 1960s and 1970s surf flicks and the latest surf videos. The museum adjoins the flagship surf shops of many of the leading brands. Beach Rd, Torquay.

BIRREGURRA: Renowned for its foodie culture, this township located at the foot of the Otway Ranges and the edge of volcanic plains holds local produce market with preserves, jams and ice-cream, Birregurra Park, 2nd Sun each month. Also home to acclaimed fine-dining restaurant **Brae**.

CAPE BRIDGEWATER: This cape is home to a 650-strong colony of Australian fur seals. A 2hr return walk leads to a viewing platform. Across the cape towards Discovery Bay are the Petrified Forest and the Blowholes – spectacular during high seas.

FLAGSTAFF HILL MARITIME MUSEUM: This reconstructed 19th-century maritime village in Warrnambool (see p. 171) is complete with a bank, hotel, schoolhouse and surgery. There are also two operational lighthouses and an authentic keeper's cottage, where relics retrieved from the *Loch Ard* – including the famous porcelain Loch Ard Peacock – are kept. On display is the Flagstaff Hill tapestry, an intricate work depicting themes of First Nations history, sealing, whaling, exploration, immigration and settlement. At night, visitors can watch the sound-and-light show *Tales of the Shipwreck Coast*, which details the story of the *Loch Ard*. Merri St, Warrnambool; (03) 5559 4600.

FORESTS AND WATERFALL DRIVE: 109km loop drive featuring impressive Otway Ranges scenery. Waterfalls include Beauchamp, Triplet and Hopetoun falls. Drive starts at Apollo Bay, travels west to Lavers Hill and around to Skenes Creek; map from visitor centres.

GREAT OCEAN WALK: Enjoy stunning views on this 100km walk between Apollo Bay and the Twelve Apostles. Walkers must register to use campgrounds en route. greatoceanwalk.com.au

GREAT OTWAY NATIONAL PARK: Formerly named Otway National Park, this 103,000ha park includes a range of environments, from the timbered ridges of the eastern Otways to fern gullies, waterfalls and some of the most rugged coastline in Victoria, particularly around Cape Otway and the stretch of coast towards Princetown. Many species of wildlife inhabit the park, including koalas and (seen especially around sunset) eastern grey kangaroos. It is an ideal location for a bushwalking adventure taking in sights through the park to the sea. Around Lorne there are more than 60 walking tracks of varying levels, and the rock platforms along the coast provide ideal spots for ocean fishing. Popular and peaceful Erskine Falls pour 30m over moss-covered rocks. As well as driving, you can walk to the falls from Lorne along the river. The Great Ocean Road, west of Apollo Bay, passes through the park. A popular walk in this hinterland section is the 800m **Maits Rest** circuit, which takes you along a boardwalk among fern gardens and giant rainforest trees up to 300 years old. Also nearby is the historic **Cape Otway Lighthouse**, built in 1848. Other highlights are **Melba Gully**, where, at dusk, visitors can witness a show of twinkling lights from glow worms, **Triplet Falls** and **Wreck Beach**, where there are the rusty anchors from two shipwrecks. Contact Parks Victoria on 13 1963.

LOGANS BEACH: Each year in June, southern right whales return to the waters along the south coast of Australia to give birth, raise their young and start the breeding cycle again. Each female seems to have a favourite spot to give birth, which means that many familiar fins keep reappearing at Logans Beach in Warrnambool (see p. 171). The beach features a purpose-built viewing platform above the sand dunes (binoculars or telescopes are recommended), and the local visitor centre releases information on whale sightings daily.

LOWER GLENELG NATIONAL PARK: The Glenelg River is a central feature of the park. It has cut an impressive 50m deep gorge through a slab of limestone. Watch for platypus, water rats, moorhens and herons around the water's edge. Bushwalking, camping, fishing and canoeing are all popular, and Jones Lookout and the Bulley Ranges offer great views. Also in the park are the Princess Margaret Rose Caves on the north side of the river – you can drive there via Nelson or Dartmoor. Contact Parks Victoria on 13 1963 to check on cave opening times.

OTWAY FLY: A steel-trussed walkway perched high among the temperate rainforest treetops of the Otway Ranges. The 'Fly' is 25m high and stretches for 600m. It is accessible to all ages and levels of mobility. Get a bird's-eye view of ancient myrtle beech, blackwood and mountain ash while looking out for a variety of wildlife, including pygmy possums and the raucous yellow-tailed black cockatoo. A springboard bridge takes you over Youngs Creek, where you might spot a shy platypus. Inquiries on 1800 300 477.

SURF COAST: It is no wonder the coast running from Torquay through to Eastern View (past Anglesea) is dubbed the Surf Coast. Submerged reefs cause huge waves that are a surfer's paradise. Most famous is Bells Beach, around 5km SW of Torquay. The clay cliffs provide a natural amphitheatre for one of the best surf beaches in the world and the longest running surf competition, the Rip Curl Pro, which started in 1973 and attracts top competitors. Other good surf beaches include Jan Juc, Anglesea and Fairhaven. To see the coast on foot, take the 30km **Surf Coast Walk**, starting at Torquay and travelling south to Moggs Creek. surfcoastwalk.com.au

Top: Redwoods near Beech Forest **Opposite top:** Brae at Birregurra **Opposite bottom:** Surfing at Kennett River

THE TWELVE APOSTLES AND PORT CAMPBELL NATIONAL PARK: Most known for the famous Twelve Apostles, Port Campbell National Park is a major attraction on the Great Ocean Road, with magnificent rock formations jutting out into the ocean. Particularly impressive when viewed at dusk (also when penguins can be seen) and dawn, the key coastal features are the **Arch**; **London Bridge**; **Loch Ard Gorge**; and the world-famous **Twelve Apostles**, which begin 12km SE of Port Campbell and stretch along the coast. These spectacular limestone stacks were part of the cliffs until wind and water left them stranded in wild surf off the shore. There are only eight of the stacks remaining; the ninth stack collapsed into the ocean in 2005. Other notable features are the **Grotto**, **Bay of Islands** and **Bay of Martyrs**. There are walking tracks throughout the park, and you can take a scenic boat ride or helicopter for a bird's-eye view of the rocks. Stop in at the visitor centre for details.

TIMBOON: A pretty town in the centre of a dairy district. **Timboon Cheesery** offers tastings and sales of gourmet cheeses, while **Timboon Railway Shed Distillery** offers a variety of spirits. A scenic drive goes from Port Campbell to the town. It is also on one end of the Camperdown–Timboon (Crater to Coast) Rail Trail. Pick your own berries in season at nearby **Berry World**; 16km north of Timboon.

TOWER HILL WILDLIFE RESERVE: This is a beautiful piece of preserved bushland featuring an extinct volcano and a crater lake with tiny islands. There are easy self-guided nature walks and Worn Gundidj Visitor Centre in the reserve has cultural displays and authentic First Nations products.

OTHER ATTRACTIONS

CALIFORNIAN REDWOODS: Set in the heart of the Otways, this a must-visit for the atmosphere of awe and reverence in which the forest envelops you. The redwood forest is 12km north-west of Apollo Bay (see p. 168).

CRATER LAKES: These spectacular crater lakes near Camperdown (see p. 168) provide an interesting history of volcanic activity over the past 20,000 years, as well as opportunities for watersports and fishing. Travelling west of town, join in the watersports and swimming at South Beach. The lakes are regularly stocked with Chinook salmon and redfin. For a scenic picnic spot, and some of the best fishing in the area, visit Lake Purrumbete. By far one of the most impressive lakes is Lake Corangamite, Australia's largest permanent salt lake. The best viewing spot is Red Rock Lookout.

FORREST: An old timber and logging town in the Otway Ranges, with an excellent brewery. The town has become renowned for its mountain biking and there are 16 fun and diverse mountain-bike trails for two-wheeled explorers. There's fishing, walking and picnics at the West Barwon Reservoir (2km S), or you can spot a platypus as you walk around Lake Elizabeth, formed by a landslide in 1952.

MARITIME DISCOVERY CENTRE: The centre in Portland (see p. 170) features a 13m sperm whale skeleton, and the lifeboat used to rescue 19 survivors from the *Admella* shipwreck in 1859. Another wreck, the *Regia*, is displayed in 2m of water. The information centre is also here. Lee Breakwater Rd, Portland.

WILDLIFE WONDERS: This conservationist project takes you on a guided walk through the bush, learning about the flora and fauna of the Otways. Includes a stop at the Research Base, with up-to-date information from the Conservation Ecology Centre; open 10am–5pm; 475 Great Ocean Road, Apollo Bay; 1300 099 467.

KEY TOWNS

AIREYS INLET
Population 979

Aireys Inlet is on the Traditional Land of the Waddawurrung People. It is one of the prettiest towns on the Great Ocean Road and is famed for being home to the Split Point Lighthouse. While there are many attractions in town to entice, its lure lies in its proximity to the stunning ochre cliffs and secluded beaches of the Great Ocean Road, and to some of the best national parks in Victoria.

SEE & DO **Split Point Lighthouse:** this famous lighthouse is still operating and is visible for kilometres on the Great Ocean Road. Tours run 11am–2pm year-round; (03) 5263 1133. **Eagles Nest Fine Art Gallery:** a small gallery featuring the work of local artists; open Fri–Mon 10am–5pm; 48 Great Ocean Road; (03) 5289 7366. **Great Escape Books:** a wonderful indie bookstore with a great range of interiors books, fiction, children's books and gifts; open 10am–5pm. **Farmers' market:** Aireys Inlet Community Hall; 2nd Sun each month. **Surf Coast Walk:** this ocean walk continues for 66km along the Great Ocean Road and takes you along pristine beaches and imposing cliffs; details from visitor centre. **Eagle Rock Marine Sanctuary:** found off the coast of Aireys Inlet, this marine sanctuary protects an abundance of marine life.

ANGLESEA
Population 3191

Angelsea is on the Traditional Land of the Waddawurrung People. Located on a pretty and sheltered part of the Surf Coast, Anglesea is a popular holiday town just before the start of the main Great Ocean Road. The main beaches are patrolled from Christmas through to Easter, making it a favourite destination for both swimmers and beginner surfers.

SEE & DO **Coogoorah Reserve:** set on the Anglesea River, the name of this park means 'swampy reed creek'. Coogoorah was established after the 1983 Ash Wednesday fires and now features a network of boardwalks weaving through the distinctive wetland vegetation. Keep an eye out for local birdlife, including the peregrine falcon. There is an excellent playground with a picnic area called Inverlochy. **Anglesea Golf Course:** golfers share the greens with kangaroos; Golf Links Rd; (03) 5263 1582. **Viewing platform:** overlooks open-cut brown coal mine and power station; behind town in Coalmine Rd. **Paddleboats:** for hire on the banks of the Anglesea River. **Markets:** local crafts and produce, by the Anglesea River; runs during summer, Easter and Melbourne Cup weekend. **J.E. Loveridge Lookout:** 1km W. **Point Roadknight Beach:** a shallow, protected beach, popular with families; 2km SW. **Ironbark Basin Reserve:** features ocean views, local birdlife and good bushwalking. The **Point Addis Koorie Cultural Walk** leads through the reserve, highlighting sites of significance; 7km NW, off Point Addis Rd. **Surf schools:** learn to surf with a lesson available at nearby beaches; details from visitor centre.

⭐ APOLLO BAY
Population 1491

Apollo Bay is on the Traditional Land of the Eastern Maar People. It was named after a local schooner and is a popular seaside town with fish and chip and ice-cream shops, cafes, gift stores and two supermarkets. It was the resting place of many shipwrecks and is situated near Great Otway National Park with a wonderful contrast between rugged coastline and tranquil green hills. The town is popular with fishing enthusiasts and it's also a great place to buy local lobster – the Fishermen's Co-op beside the working harbour is a local hotspot for fresh seafood, caught daily.

SEE & DO **Great Otway National Park; Otway Fly; Forests and Waterfall Drive:** see Top Attractions for all. **Wildlife Wonders:** see Other Attractions. **Apollo Bay Museum:** housed in a former cable station this museum features artefacts from Australia's telecommunications history and informative displays exploring the history of the region; open Sat–Sun 2–5pm, school and public holidays; 6250 Great Ocean Road; (03) 5237 7441. **Foreshore Market:** each Sat. **Farmers' Market:** Apollo Bay Youth Club Hall; 3rd Sun every month. **Marriners Lookout:** with views across Skenes Creek and Apollo Bay; 1.5km NW. **Barham Paradise Scenic Reserve:** in the Barham River Valley, it is home to a variety of distinctive moisture-loving trees and ferns; 7km NW. **Charter flights:** views of the Twelve Apostles, the Bay of Islands and the Shipwreck Coast; details from visitor centre.

CAMPERDOWN
Population 2884

Located at the foot of Mount Leura, a volcanic cone, Camperdown is more famous for its natural attractions than for the town itself, being situated on the world's third-largest volcanic plain. But that should not detract from Camperdown; National Trust–listed Finlay Ave features 2km of regal elm trees, while in the town centre the Gothic-style Manifold Clock Tower stands as a tribute to the region's European settlers.

SEE & DO **Crater Lakes:** see Other Attractions. **Manifold Clock Tower:** an imposing structure built in 1896; open 1st Sun each month or by appt; cnr Manifold and Pike sts. **Historical**

VISITOR INFORMATION

Great Ocean Road Visitor Information Centre
100 Great Ocean Road, Apollo Bay
1300 689 297
visitgreatoceanroad.org.au
visitotways.com

Torquay Visitor Information Centre
Surf City Plaza, Beach Rd, Torquay

Opposite top: Lorne Pier
Opposite bottom: Warrnambool Art Gallery

Society Museum: displays First Nations artefacts, local historical photographs, and household and farming implements; open Tues 10am–3pm and 1st Sun of the month; Manifold St. **Courthouse**: built in 1886–87, described as one of the most distinctive courthouses in Australia; Manifold St. **Rotary market**: Finlay Ave; 1st Sun each month. **Camperdown–Timboon Rail Trail**: walking or riding track through bush, following historic railway line. **Mount Leura**: extinct volcano close to the perfect cone of Mount Sugarloaf. At the base is an interpretive centre; a lookout offers excellent views over crater lakes and volcanoes, and north across the plains to Gariwerd (Grampians); 1km S. **Botanic Gardens**: feature rare examples of Himalayan oak and a lookout over Lakes Bullen Merri and Gnotuk; 3km W. **Cobden Miniature Railway**: operates 3rd Sun each month; Cobden; 13km S.

COLAC
Population 12,348

Colac is on the Traditional Land of the Gulidjan and Gadubanud People represented by the Eastern Maar. Colac was built by the shores of Lake Colac on the volcanic plain that covers much of Victoria's Western District. It's a large inland farming town and a gateway to the Otways if you don't want to drive the Great Ocean Road.

SEE & DO **Heritage walk**: self-guided tour of the history and architectural wonders of Colac; details from visitor centre. **Performing Arts and Cultural Centre**: incorporates the COPACC Gallery and the Historical Centre, open Thurs, Fri and Sun 2–4pm; cnr Gellibrand and Rae sts; (03) 5232 9400. **Botanic Gardens**: unusual in that visitors are allowed to drive through the gardens. Picnic, barbecue and playground facilities are provided; open 10am–4pm; Fyans St; (03) 5232 9400. **Barongarook Creek**: prolific birdlife, and a walking track leading from Princes Hwy to Lake Colac; on the northern outskirts of town. **Red Rock Lookout**: features spectacular views across 30 volcanic lakes, including **Lake Corangamite**. At the base of the lookout is the **Red Rock Winery**. Near Alvie; 22km N. **The Volcano Discovery Trail**: goes from Colac to Millicent in SA, and follows the history of volcanic activity in the region; details from visitor centre. **Old Beechy Rail Trail**: 45km trail that follows one of the state's former narrow-gauge railway lines from Colac to Beech Forest, suitable for walkers and cyclists. The trail starts at Colac railway station; details from visitor centre. **Art and craft galleries**: at Barongarook (12km SE); details from visitor centre. **Otway Estate**: with its well-known Prickly Moses ale range, views of the Otways, and Oktoberfest event; 10–30 Hoveys Rd, Barongarook; (03) 4245 1124; 13km S. **Tarndwarncoort Homestead**: wool displays and sales; off Warncoort Cemetery Rd; 15km E.

★ LORNE
Population 1248

Lorne is on the Traditional Land of the Wadawurrung, Eastern Maar and Gunditjmara Peoples. Lorne is one of Victoria's most attractive and lively coastal resorts. The approach into town along the Great Ocean Road is truly spectacular, with the superb mountain scenery of the Otways on one side and the rugged Bass Strait coast on the other. The village of Lorne was established in 1871 and quickly became popular with pastoralists from inland areas, leading to its development around picturesque Louttit Bay. When the Great Ocean Road opened in 1932, Lorne became much more accessible, yet the area has remained relatively unspoiled. Today the village has boutique shops, surf shops, cafes, restaurants, a cinema and a large foreshore area with activities for kids. There are good beaches, surfing, fishing, and bushwalking and waterfalls in the hills – activities made all the more enjoyable by the area's pleasant, mild climate.

SEE & DO **Great Otway National Park**: *see* Top Attractions. **Teddys Lookout**: excellent bay views; behind the town, at the end of George St. **Shipwreck Trail**: walk along the beach passing the numerous shipwreck sites along this stretch of coast; details from visitor centre. **Foreshore Reserve**: great spot for a picnic, with barbecues, a skate park and a playground. Lorne Sea Baths has mini-golf and a pool; Lorne Foreshore, 81 Mountjoy Pde; (03) 5289 2077. **Qdos**: contemporary art gallery; a focal point for Lorne's vibrant arts scene; open Fri–Sun (winter), Thurs–Sun (spring, autumn, summer); 35 Allenvale Rd; (03) 5289 1989. **Lorne Books**: a well-established indie bookstore that has been in Lorne for over 20 years, with an excellent selection of fiction, non-fiction and kids books; 108a Mountjoy Pde; (03) 5289 2489. **Cumberland River Valley**: walking tracks and camping; 4km SW. **Mount Defiance Lookout**: 10km SW. **Wye River**: a small coastal village with a great beachside cafe, good for rock and surf fishing, surfing and camping. 17km SW. **Kennett River**: a small coastal hamlet with walking trails, a campground and the likelihood of seeing koalas. 23km SW.

PORT CAMPBELL
Population 231

This peaceful seaside resort – the base of a small crayfishing industry – is in the centre of Port Campbell National Park on the Great Ocean Road. The Twelve Apostles, one of Victoria's most famous attractions, is nearby.

SEE & DO **The Twelve Apostles**: *see* Top Attractions. **Historical Museum**: open Wed, Thurs and Sat; weekends only in winter Lord St. **Fishing**: good from rocks and pier; boat charters available. **Mutton Bird Island**: attracts short-tailed shearwaters, best viewed at dawn and dusk Sept–Apr; just off coast. **Great Ocean Road Wildlife Park:** 19km SE. **12 Apostles Gourmet Trail:** map from visitor centre.

⭑ PORT FAIRY
Population 3424

This atmospheric coastal hamlet has a charming old-world feel, with bluestone buildings and a small fleet of fishing boats lining the old wharf. These remain from the day when Port Fairy was a whaling industry centre with one of the largest ports in Australia. While Port Fairy comes alive in March during its renowned Port Fairy Folk Festival, it has a lively community, great beaches and a lighthouse. Like many coastal towns, it has seen an influx of people moving there during the coronavirus pandemic.

SEE & DO **Art galleries and studios:** diverse collection of places showcasing local artists; includes painting, photography and crafts; details from visitor centre, including an Art Walk map. **History Centre:** displays relating to local history housed in the old courthouse; check ahead for opening hours; Gipps St; (03) 5568 2263. **Battery Hill:** old fort and signal station at the river mouth; end of Griffith St. **Port Fairy Wharf:** sales of fish and crayfish when in season; or drop a line in and catch your own; picturesque backdrop of Norfolk pines and heritage buildings. **Historic buildings:** many are National Trust–classified, including the splendid timber home of Captain Mills, Gipps St; Mott's Cottage, Sackville St; Caledonian Inn, Bank St; Seacombe House, Cox St; St John's Church of England, Regent St; and the Gazette Office, Sackville St. **Farmers' market:** Railway Pl, Bank St; 3rd Sat each month (Feb–Dec). **Community Market:** Railway Pl, Bank St; 2nd and 4th Sat each month, weekly (Jan). **Griffiths Island:** connected to town by a causeway, this island is home to a large colony of short-tailed shearwaters. Each year they travel across the Pacific Ocean from North America to nest in the same burrows (Sept–Apr). Also on the island is a much-photographed charming lighthouse, built in 1859. **The Crags:** rugged coastal rock formations; 12km W. **Yambuk:** a small township centred around an old inn with Yambuk Lake, a popular recreation area with a giant slide, nearby; 17km W. **Lady Julia Percy Island:** off-shore volcano home to a fur seal colony; charters and eco-tours can be arranged from Port Fairy Wharf; 22km off coast. **Codrington Wind Farm:** Victoria's first wind-power station; 27km W. **Mahogany walking track:** a demanding 6hr walk (one-way from Port Fairy to Warrnambool, can return by bus) via the beach taking in a magnificent stretch of coastline; details from visitor centre. **Walks:** historic buildings, shipwrecks and more; details from visitor info centre. **Port Fairy–Warrnambool Rail Trail:** a scenic walking/cycling trail taking in 37km of beautiful south-west scenery.

PORTLAND
Population 10,450

Portland is the Traditional Land of the Gunditjmara People. It is the most westerly of Victoria's major coastal towns and the only deep-water port between Melbourne and Adelaide. It was also the first permanent European settlement in Victoria, founded in 1834 by the famous pastoralist Henty family. The township, which features many National Trust–classified buildings, overlooks Portland Bay. The Kerrup–Tjmara People, who once numbered in the thousands, were the original inhabitants of the district and referred to it as Pulumbete, meaning 'Little Lake' – a reference to the scenic lake now known as Fawthorp Lagoon.

SEE & DO **Maritime Discovery Centre:** *see* Other Attractions. **Botanical Gardens:** established in 1857, with both native and exotic plant life. A restored 1850s bluestone worker's cottage is within the grounds and open to the public; Cliff St. **Historic buildings:** more than 200 around town, many National Trust–classified. The best way to explore buildings such as the courthouse, Steam Packet Inn and Mac's Hotel is to take a self-guided walk; details and map from visitor centre. The restored Portland Cable Tram also runs along the town's historic foreshore; ask at the visitor centre for departure times. **History House:** a historical museum and family research centre in the old town hall; open 10am–12pm and 1–4pm; Cliff St; (03) 5522 2266. **Fawthorp Lagoon:** prolific birdlife; Glenelg St. **World War II Memorial Lookout Tower:** displays of memorabilia on the way up the 133 steps to magnificent 360-degree views across Portland and the ocean, where whales and dolphins can sometimes be spotted; open 9am–4pm Bentinck St; (03) 5523 3938. **Whale-watching:** other good spots for whale-watching include the cliff-top overlooking the bay for blue whales in summer and Ploughed Field park overlooking Nuns Beach for southern right whales in winter; brochure and details from visitor centre. **Cape Nelson Lighthouse:** an 1884 lighthouse perches on the top of tall cliffs, lightstation tours 11am and 2pm; 11km SW. **Discovery Bay Coastal Park:** Cape Bridgewater, *see* p. 165, is included in this park, though the majority of it is remote and relatively untouched. The Great South West Walk (see below) offers the best chance to take in the park's scenery. Behind Cape Bridgewater are the Bridgewater Lakes (19km W) – popular for waterskiing and fishing. A walking track leads from here to the beach. **Mount Richmond National Park:** a 'mountain' formed by an extinct volcano. The area has abundant spring wildflowers and native fauna, including the elusive potoroo; 25km NW. **Heywood:** home to the Pioneer Wagon Shed & Museum, and the Wood, Wine and Roses Festival (Feb). The World Heritage-listed **Budj Bim Cultural Landscape** (*see* p. 173), the Traditional Lands of the Gunditjmara People is also

TOP EVENTS

- JAN Pier to Pub swim race (Lorne); Hooked on Portland (music and fishing in Portland); NightJar Festival (Torquay); Beachfest and Wunta Fiesta (both Warrnambool)
- FEB Seafood Festival (Apollo Bay)
- MAR Open Mic Music Festival (Aireys Inlet); Folk Festival (Port Fairy); Kana Festival (Colac)
- APR Great Ocean & Otway Classic Ride (Torquay); Rip Curl Pro (Bells Beach)
- MAY Great Ocean Road Running Festival (across the region)
- JULY Robert Burns Scottish Festival (Camperdown)
- NOV Sculpture Biennale (even numbered years, Lorne)
- DEC Rodeo (Warrnambool); Falls Festival (NYE, Lorne)

TEMPERATURES

Jan: 14–23°C

July: 7–14°C

Opposite top: Port Fairy surfing
Opposite bottom: Apollo Bay

located here; 28km N. **Nelson:** a charming hamlet near the mouth of the Glenelg River. There is good waterskiing in the area; 70km NW. **Great South West Walk:** this epic 250km walking trail takes in the full range of local scenery – the Glenelg River, Discovery and Bridgewater bays and Cape Nelson are some of the highlights. It is possible to do just small sections of the walk; maps and details from visitor centre.

TORQUAY
Population 18,534

Torquay is on the Traditional Land of the Wadawurrung and Eastern Marr People. Torquay was one of the first holiday towns on Victoria's coast, and remains one of the most popular. It has a couple of shopping areas, surf-brand flagship stores and a lot of choice for cafes and restaurants. It was named in honour of the famous English resort, but its heritage is very different. Not only do Torquay and its coast have some of the best surf beaches in the world, but Torquay was also the birthplace of world leaders in surfboards, wetsuits and other apparel, including Rip Curl and Quiksilver, founded here in the 1960s and 1970s.

SEE & DO **Australian National Surf Museum:** see Top Attractions. **Surf City Plaza:** this modern plaza houses some of the biggest names in surfing retail alongside smaller outlets. **Beaches:** include the popular front beach and the surf back beach. **Fishermans Beach:** a good spot for fishing, with a sheltered swimming beach and a large sundial on the foreshore. **Tiger Moth World:** theme park based around the 1930s Tiger Moth biplane. Joy-flights available; Blackgate Rd; (04) 4761 5100. **Saltair Spa:** spa treatments and therapies; Ashmore Rd; (03) 5261 9977. **Surf schools:** programs available to suit all abilities, with many courses run during summer school holidays; details from visitor centre.

WARRNAMBOOL
Population 32,894

Warrnambool is the Traditional Land of the Gunditjmara People. It is a large regional centre near the end of the wonderfully scenic Great Ocean Road. It has stunning natural and cultural attractions, headed up by the whale-watching season and the town's famed maritime museum, which holds impressive relics from nearby wrecks. It's. There are opportunities to really get out and enjoy the great outdoors here, including a walking/cycling trail to Port Fairy, coastal strolls, horseriding and kayaking. Warrnambool is on a notorious section of coastline that has seen more than 80 shipwrecks. The best known wreck was that of the *Loch Ard* in 1878, which claimed the lives of all but two of those on board. Warrnambool offers a range of accommodation and dining as well as a fantastic swimming beach. Southern right whales can be spotted from Logans Beach (June to Sept).

SEE & DO **Flagstaff Hill Maritime Museum; Tower Hill Wildlife Reserve; Logans Beach:** see Top Attractions for all. **Main beach:** a safe swimming beach with a walkway along the foreshore from the breakwater to near the mouth of the Hopkins River. **Lake Pertobe Adventure Playground:** a great spot for family picnics; also minigolf and flying foxes; opposite main beach, Pertobe Rd. **Art Gallery:** local artwork, plus European and avant-garde collections; open Mon–Fri 10am–5pm, Sat–Sun 10am–3pm and public holidays; 26 Liebig St; (03) 5559 4949. **Botanic Gardens:** pretty regional gardens designed by Guilfoyle (a curator of Melbourne's Royal Botanic Gardens) in 1879; Botanic Rd. **Aboriginal Soldiers Memorial:** dedicated to all Aboriginal men and women from south-west Victoria who served their country proudly along with fellow Australians since World War I; Merri St, Cannon Hill. **Fletcher Jones Gardens/Markets:** award-winning landscaped gardens and market in front of former Fletcher Jones factory; cnr Flaxman St and Raglan Pde; (03) 5562 9936. **Portuguese Padrao:** monument to early Portuguese explorers; Cannon Hill, southern end of Liebig St. **Heritage walk:** 3km self-guided walk taking in the many historic buildings around town; details from visitor centre. **Deep Blue Hot Springs Sanctuary:** open-air thermal rock pools opposite the harbour; Warm Bay Rd; (03) 5559 2000; thedeepblue.com.au. **Hopkins River:** great for fishing and boating, with Blue Hole, at the river's mouth, a popular spot for family swimming and rockpool exploration. Cruises are available; east of town. **Proudfoots Boathouse:** National Trust–classified boathouse on the Hopkins housing a restaurant and bar; Simpson St. **Wollaston Bridge:** an unusual bridge, built over 100 years ago; northern outskirts of town. **Tours and charters:** fishing, whale-watching and diving tours (including shipwreck sites); contact visitor centre for details. **Rundell's Mahogany Trail Rides:** 1–2 hours of horseriding along the beach, also also twilight rides and horse care days; Millers La; 0408 589 546. **Port Fairy to Warrnambool Rail Trail** and **Mahogany walking track:** see Port Fairy. **Fresh Market:** Pertobe Rd; 1st and 3rd Sun morning. **Hopkins Falls:** a scenic picnic spot, particularly impressive in winter after heavy rain. In spring hundreds of elvers (baby eels) migrate up the falls, creating a most unusual sight; 16km NE. **Koroit:** National Trust–classified buildings, good local arts and crafts shops, botanic gardens, and an Irish festival in Apr; 19km NW.

Grampians/Gariwerd and Central West

The **towering sandstone and heavily forested mountains** of the Grampians/Gariwerd rise out of the otherwise flat terrain and stand sentinel over the western plains, as they have done for millions of years. The Djab Wurrung and Jardwadjali People have a deep cultural connection to these mountains and there are numerous **significant rock-art sites**. But this region also offers **charming country towns, renowned regional galleries, UNESCO World Heritage–listed Budj Bim National Park** and **Little Desert National Park**.

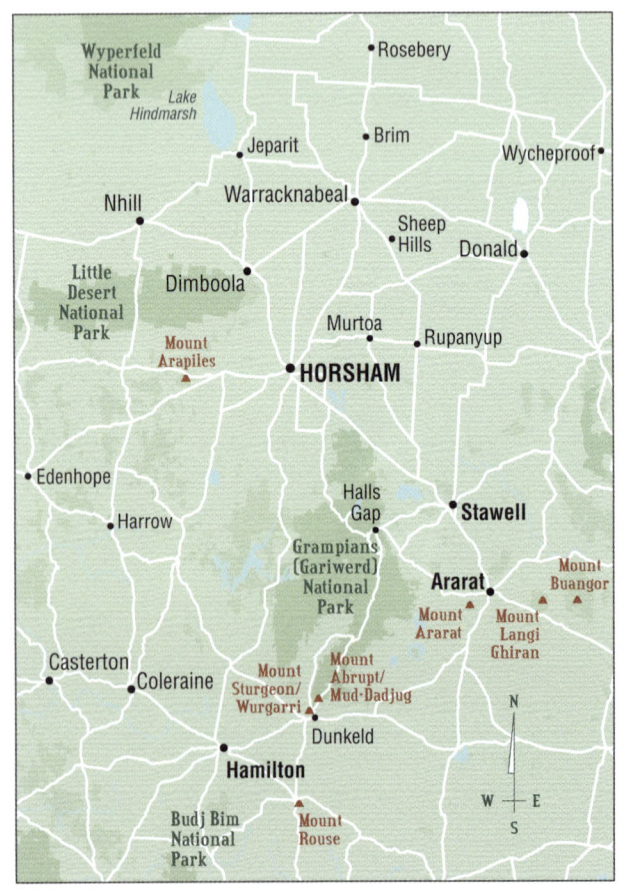

CHEAT SHEET

→ Allow at least four days for a proper exploration.

→ Best time to visit: Sept–April.

→ Main towns: Ararat (see p. 176), Dunkeld (see p. 177), Halls Gap (see p. 178).

→ Gariwerd – including its land, skies and waters – are culturally significant to Traditional Owners, represented by Barengi Gadjin Land Council Aboriginal Corporation, Eastern Maar Aboriginal Corporation and Gunditj Mirring Traditional Owners Aboriginal Corporation. To learn about local culture and organise to visit rock-art sites, drop into Brambuk – the National Park and Cultural Centre or the the Budja Budja Aboriginal Co-operative, both in Halls Gap.

→ Don't miss: Hamilton Gallery; Gum San Chinese Heritage Centre in Aarat; painted silos on the Silo Trail; lookouts over the Grampians/Gariwerd and the scenic drive through the mountains between Dunkeld and Halls Gap.

Top: Gateway to Little Desert National Park **Opposite:** Hiking in Grampians National Park

TOP ATTRACTIONS

ARARAT GALLERY TAMA (TEXTILE ART MUSEUM AUSTRALIA): Regional art gallery with Australia's most significant collection of textile art along with travelling exhibitions; open 10am–4pm; cnr Vincent St and Western Hwy, Ararat; (03) 5355 0220.

AUSTRALIAN KELPIE CENTRE: Museum dedicated to the history of the much-loved working dog; 139 Henty St, Casterton; (03) 5554 2440.

BRAMBUK – THE NATIONAL PARK AND CULTURAL CENTRE: Brambuk features interactive displays and written information about the Grampians/Gariwerd's attractions, bringing to life the culture of the local Jardwadjali and Djab Wurrung Peoples. 277 Grampians Rd, Halls Gap; (03) 5361 4000.

BUDJ BIM NATIONAL PARK: The wider **Budj Bim Cultural Landscape** is the Traditional Land of the Gunditjmara People, whose connection stretches back thousands of years, as evidenced by remnants of large, settled communities and eel farms, one of the oldest and most extensive aquaculture systems in the world. In 2019 the national park was inscribed by UNESCO as Australia's only World Heritage Site listed purely for First Nations cultural value, although its significance for the Gunditjmara People has been ongoing for millennia. The dormant volcano Budj Bim is responsible for much of the surrounding landscape, and a key feature of this national park is a large volcanic crater lake. A range of walks lets visitors explore the scoria cones and caves formed 20,000 years ago from erupting volcanoes. The resulting lava flows created channels in the land, which the Gunditjmara People developed into weirs, dams and traps for fish and eels. The three main craters hold a 700m long lake, Lake Surprise, fed by underground springs. Excellent walking trails and camping are available. The Tae Rak Aquaculture Centre opened in 2022 and is a hub for cultural tours and information and houses a gift shop and cafe.

BUNJIL'S SHELTER: This is the richest site for Aboriginal rock art in Victoria. It depicts the creator figure, Bunjil, sitting inside a small alcove with his two dingoes. Bunjil created the geographical features of the land, and then created people, before disappearing into the sky to look down on the Earth as a star. The site is thought to have been used for ceremonies by the local Djab Wurrung and Jardwadjali Peoples. Off Pomonal Rd. It's 11km south of Stawell (see p. 179).

GRAMPIANS NATIONAL PARK: Occupation of the area known as the Grampians dates back over 5000 years (some evidence suggests up to 30,000 years). To local Koorie communities, this magnificent mountain range is known as Gariwerd. Within the 168,000ha park is a startling array of vegetation and wildlife, including 200 bird species and a third of Victoria's native flora species. The heathlands abound in colourful shows of wildflowers including Grampians boronia, blue pincushion lily and Grampians parrot-pea. More than 20 of the park's roughly 1000 plant species are not found anywhere else in the world. Natural highlights of Grampians/Gariwerd include MacKenzie Falls, the largest of the park's many waterfalls; Zumsteins picnic ground, a beautiful spot with tame and friendly kangaroos; and the Balconies, a rock ledge once known as the Jaws of Death, offering views over Victoria Valley. The most popular section of the park is the Wonderland Range, true to its name with features including Elephants Hide, Grand Canyon, Venus Baths and Silent Street. The southern section of the park, near Dunkeld, includes Victoria Valley Rd, a scenic drive that stops at Freshwater Lake Reserve, popular for picnics. Also near Dunkeld are various hiking destinations and the Chimney Pots, a formation popular for rock climbing. However, there has recently been a greater understanding of the cultural significance of the Grampians/Gariwerd and a recognition not to climb in some areas, with climbing currently banned across around one-third of the park; check with Parks Victoria to find open areas. There are more than 90 bushwalks available in the park, all varying in length and degree of difficulty. In 2021, the Grampians Peaks Trail was launched. The 13-stage, 160km hiking trail extends the length of the Grampians/Gariwerd, with custom-built shelters and campsites sprinkled along it. Visitors are advised to consult a ranger before embarking on one of the longer treks. For further information, contact Brambuk – The National Park and Cultural Centre on (03) 5361 4000.

GRAMPIANS WINE REGION: This region is famous for sparkling whites and traditional old shiraz. Between Stawell and Ararat, the small town of Great Western encompasses some winemaking treasures. Dating from the 1860s, **Seppelt** is famous for the historic underground tunnels that form its cellars. Its name goes hand in hand with sparkling white wine, although most of the grapes for this variety are actually grown elsewhere. If you're after local sparkling, try Seppelt's sparkling shiraz. **Best's** most prized wine is its Thomson Family Shiraz. The winery has its own set of historic buildings and a small plot of vines possibly found nowhere else in the world. East of Ararat, **Mount Langi Ghiran Vineyards** produces what might be the region's best shiraz, as well as a great cabernet sauvignon. Many more of the region's wineries can be accessed on the **Great Grape Rd**, a circuit through Ballarat and St Arnaud.

GUM SAN CHINESE HERITAGE CENTRE: Gum San means 'hill of gold', a fitting name for this impressive centre built in traditional Southern Chinese style and incorporating the principles of Feng Shui. The centre celebrates the contribution of the Chinese community both to Ararat, which is said to be the only goldfields town founded by Chinese prospectors, and to the surrounding goldfields region. The experience is brought to life with interactive displays and an original Canton lead-mining tunnel, uncovered during the building of the centre. Open Mon–Sun 11am–4pm; 31–33 Lambert St (Western Hwy), Ararat; (03) 5352 1078.

HAMILTON GALLERY: This gallery is one of regional Australia's finest, featuring a diverse collection of fine arts and museum pieces dating back to the earliest European settlements in Australia. Many trinkets and treasures of the region's first stately homes are on display, as well as English and European glass, ceramic and silver work. There is also a good collection of colonial-era art from the Western District. Guided heritage tours of the gallery and district are available. Open Mon–Fri 10am–5pm, Sat 10am–12pm and 2–5pm, Sun 2–5pm; 107 Brown St, Hamilton; (03) 5573 0460.

LAKE HINDMARSH: Victoria's largest freshwater lake is fed by the Wimmera River, although it's periodically dry. Boating, waterskiing and fishing are all popular pastimes (Schulzes Beach and Four Mile Beach have boat ramps and camping facilities), with pelicans and other waterbirds existing at the lake in breeding colonies. Picnic and camping spots are available on the lake's shores. Contact the visitor centre on (03) 5391 3086 for an update on water levels.

LITTLE DESERT NATIONAL PARK: During spring, more than 600 varieties of wildflowers and more than 40 types of ground orchids flourish in this 132,647ha park. With nearly 600km of tracks, it is ideal for four-wheel driving, but perhaps the best way to appreciate the colourful spring display is on foot: for keen hikers, there is the 84km Desert Discovery Walk. The Little Desert Lodge is in the central section of the park, south of the town of Nhill, and is a departure point for day tours and a popular place to stay. There are walking trails in the central and western sections. The eastern block (the section nearest to Dimboola) has picnic and camping facilities and good walking tracks. The park is home to the distinctive mallee fowl, and the large ground-nests built by the male birds can be seen during breeding season. Kangaroos, possums and bearded dragons are just some of the other wildlife that inhabit the park.

MOUNT ARAPILES–TOOAN STATE PARK: This park is divided into two blocks, the larger Tooan block and the smaller Mount Arapiles block. The first recorded ascent of Mount Arapiles, a 369m sandstone monolith, was by Major Thomas Mitchell in 1836. Today it is a popular rock-climbing destination with over 2000 marked routes. Should you choose not to scale one of the various rock faces, great views are still available from the walking tracks, or you can drive to the summit. Nature study is another possibility – a huge 14 per cent of the state's flora is represented in the Mount Arapiles section alone; access is from the Wimmera Hwy.

MURTOA: This town lies on the edge of Lake Marma, which has dried out in recent times. The Water Tower Museum (open Sun and by appointment) displays the history of the area as well as James Hill's 1885–1930 taxidermy collection of some 500 birds and animals. On the eastern side of town, among the grain silos, is an unusual relic called the Stick Shed. The roof of this now empty storage shed is held up with 640 unmilled tree trunks, and the interior is an evocative sight; open 10am–2pm; 1465 Wimmera Hwy, Murtoa; 0434 227 921.

STAWELL GIFT HALL OF FAME MUSEUM: In 1878 the Stawell Athletic Club was formed by local farmers and businessmen who were keen to have a sports day each Easter. The club put up the prize pool of £110, and the race was on. The annual Stawell Gift has run almost continually since (at Easter), and is now one of the most prestigious races in the world. The race has been run at Central Park since 1898. Visit the museum to discover the glory and heartbreak of the race since its inception. Open Tues–Sat 10am–4pm; Main St, Stawell; (03) 5358 1326.

WIMMERA–MALLEE PIONEER MUSEUM: This unique museum details what life was like for early settlers in the Wimmera through a collection of colonial-era buildings furnished in the style of the period. The buildings are spread over a 4ha complex and include log cabins, a church and a blacksmith's shop. The museum also features displays of restored farm machinery. Charles St, Jeparit; open Mon, Wed and Fri 10am–3pm, Sat–Sun 1–4pm; (03) 5397 2101.

OTHER ATTRACTIONS

DERGHOLM STATE PARK: The park features a great diversity of vegetation, including woodlands, open forests, heaths and swamps. An abundance of wildlife thrives, including echidnas, koalas, kangaroos, reptiles and the endangered red-tailed black cockatoo. A key attraction is Baileys Rocks, unique giant green-coloured granite boulders.

DERRINALLUM AND MOUNT ELEPHANT: Mount Elephant rises to almost 200m behind the small township of Derrinallum – it doesn't sound like a lot, but across the plains of the Western District you can see it from up to 60km away. A gash in the elephant's western side is the result of decades of quarrying. The mountain is actually the scoria cone of an extinct volcano, and inside is a 90m deep crater. Now owned by the community, there is a walking trail to the top. Lake Tooliorook on the other side of town offers good fishing for trout and redfin, and watersports.

HAMILTON BOTANIC GARDENS: First planted in 1870 and classified by the National Trust in 1990, these gardens have long been regarded as among the most impressive in rural Victoria. Designed by the curator of the Melbourne Botanic Gardens, William Guilfoyle, the gardens feature his 'signature' design elements of sweeping lawns interrupted by lakes, islands, and contrasting plant and flower beds. Keep an eye out for the free-flight aviary, enormous English oaks and historic band rotunda. Cnr French and Thompson sts, Hamilton.

HARROW: One of Victoria's oldest inland towns, Harrow has many historic buildings in Main St, including the **Hermitage Hotel**, the police station and an early log gaol. The **Johnny Mullagh Cricket Centre** is in recognition of Johnny Mullagh, known as one of the most impressive players of the 1868 Aboriginal team that became the first sporting team from Australia to tour internationally and the **National Bush Billycart Championship** is held here in Mar.

HORSHAM REGIONAL ART GALLERY: This is one of Victoria's key regional galleries, with an extensive collection housed in a refurbished and extended 1930s Art Deco building. Most of the artwork is centred on the Mack Jost collection of Australian art, with contemporary Australian photography another specialty. Open 10am–4pm; 78 Wilson St, Horsham; (03) 5382 9575.

J WARD MUSEUM: Ararat's original gaol, 'J Ward' served as an asylum for the criminally insane for many years and offers an eerie glimpse into the history of criminal confinement. Guided tours reveal in chilling detail what life was like for the inmates. Open for guided tours; Girdlestone St, Ararat; (03) 5352 3357.

LAKE BULOKE: The lake is filled by the floodwaters of the Richardson River, so its size varies greatly with the seasons. This extensive wetland area is home to a variety of birdlife and is a popular venue for fishing, picnicking and bushwalking. The end of the park closest to Donald is a protected bird sanctuary. The lake is 10km north of Donald.

MOUNT BUANGOR STATE PARK: The park features the Fern Tree Waterfalls and the three impressive peaks of Mount Buangor, Mount Sugarloaf and Cave Hill. The diverse terrain with many varieties of eucalypts offers great sightseeing, bushwalking and picnicking. There are more than 130 species of birds, as well as eastern grey kangaroos, wallabies and echidnas. Access to the southern section is via Ferntree Rd off the Western Hwy. Mount Buangor and Cave Hill can be accessed from the main Mount Cole Rd in the Mount Cole State Forest.

MOUNT NAPIER STATE PARK: Features Byaduk Caves (lava caves) near the park's western entrance, part of a giant, 24km lava flow stretching to Budj Bim, see p. 173. The caves are a wonderland of ropey lava, columns, stalactites and stalagmites. Only one cave is accessible to the public.

SIR REGINALD ANSETT TRANSPORT MUSEUM: Birthplace of Ansett Airlines, the museum tells the story of Ansett and Australia's aviation history in one of the airline's original hangars; open 10am–4pm; 21 Ballarat Rd, Hamilton; (03) 5571 2767.

Opposite top: Boroka Lookout over Halls Gap *Opposite bottom:* Cockatoo at Brambuk: The National Park and Cultural Centre

KEY TOWNS

ARARAT
Population 7015

In 1857 a group of 700 Chinese miners walking from Robe in SA to the Victorian goldfields stopped at what is now Ararat to drink from the spring – and they found alluvial gold! Although there were squatters in the area before then, it was gold that really established the town. The Traditional Owners are the Djab Wurrung People.

SEE & DO **Gum San Chinese Heritage Centre; Ararat Gallery TAMA (Textile Art Museum Australia); Grampians Wine Region:** see Top Attractions for all. **J Ward Museum:** see Other Attractions. **Alexandra Park and Botanical Gardens:** an attractive formal garden featuring ornamental lakes, fountains and an orchid glasshouse; Vincent St. **Historical self-guided tours (walking or driving):** of particular note are the bluestone buildings in Barkly St, including the post office, town hall, civic square and war memorial; details from visitor centre. **Langi Morgala Museum:** an eclectic museum that also houses the largest collection of First Nations artefacts in Victoria; open Tues–Thurs 10am–3pm, Sat 1–4pm; Queen St; (03) 5352 3117. **Green Hill Lake:** great for fishing and water activities; 4km E. **One Tree Hill Lookout:** 360-degree views across the region; 5km NW. **Langi Ghiran State Park:** Mount Langi Ghiran and Mount Gorrin form the key features of this park. A popular walk starts at the picnic area along Easter Creek, then goes to the Old Langi Ghiran Reservoir and along the stone water-race to a scenic lookout; access via Western Hwy, Kartuk Rd; 14km E. **Mount Cole State Forest:** adjoins Mount Buangor State Park, with bushwalking, horseriding, four-wheel drive tracks and trail-bike riding. The Ben Nevis Fire Tower offers spectacular views; 35km E.

CASTERTON
Population 1336

Casterton is a Roman name meaning 'walled city', given to the town because of the natural wall of hills surrounding the valley in which it lies. These hills, and the Glenelg River that flows through town, create an idyllic rural atmosphere. The region is colloquially known as 'Kelpie Country' because it is the birthplace of this world-famous breed of working dog. In the mid-1800s a prized Scottish collie female pup from nearby Warrock Homestead was sold to a stockman named Jack Gleeson, who named her 'Kelpie' – she was bred out with various 'black and tan' dogs, and so began the long line of the working man's best friend.

SEE & DO **Australian Kelpie Centre:** see Top Attractions. **Historical Museum:** housed in the old railway station, the museum displays local artefacts; open by appt; McKinlay St. **Art galleries:** visit the numerous art galleries around town. **Ess Lagoon:** regularly stocked with trout, there's good fishing; McPherson St on the northern edge of town. **Mickle Lookout:** a great view across the town; Moodie St, off Robertson St on the eastern edge of town. **Long Lead Swamp:** waterbirds, kangaroos, emus and a trail-bike track; Penola Rd; 11km W. **Geological formations:** in particular, The Hummocks 12km NE, and The Bluff, viewable from Dartmoor Rd, 20km SW. Both rock formations are around 150 million years old. **Warrock Homestead:** a unique collection of 33 buildings erected by its founder, George Robertson. The homestead was built in 1843 and is National Trust–classified; open by appointment; 0417 938 533; 26km N. **Bilston's Tree:** 50m high and arguably the world's largest red gum; Glenmia Rd; 30km N.

COLERAINE
Population 867

Coleraine is a small, picturesque town supported by the wool and beef industries. For a small town it has plenty of attractions, including a chocolate factory, a garden with more than 2000 species of native flowers and a vintage car display.

VISITOR INFORMATION

Halls Gap & Grampians Visitor Information Centre
117 Grampians Rd, Halls Gap
(03) 5361 4444 or
1800 065 599
visitgrampians.com.au

TOP EVENTS

→ FEB Grampians Music Festival (Halls Gap); Henley on Lake Wallace Festival (Edenhope)

→ MAR Jailhouse Rock Festival (Ararat); Country Music Festival (Horsham); National Bush Billycart Championship (Harrow).

→ EASTER Stawell Gift (foot race, Stawell); Y-Fest (Warracknabeal)

→ MAY Grampians Grape Escape (Hall Gap)

→ JUNE–JULY Australian Kelpie Muster (Casterton)

→ OCT Golden Gateway Festival (Ararat); 3 Peaks Festival (Dunkeld); Spring Garden & Sustainability Lifestyle Festival (Horsham)

TEMPERATURES

Jan: 16–27°C

July: 6–10°C

Opposite: Ararat vineyards, with Mount Langi Ghiran in the background

SEE & DO **Peter Francis Points Arboretum:** two thousand species of native flora are found here, including 500 species of eucalyptus. 'The Points' sprawls up the hillside behind the town, with great views from the top, on Portland–Coleraine Rd. **Eucalyptus Discovery Centre** in town is designed to complement the arboretum and give an insight into the natural history and commercial applications of eucalypts. Whyte St. **Glenelg Fine Confectionery:** immerse yourself in the rich aroma of German-style continental chocolates; tastings available; Whyte St. **Historic Railway Station:** also site of the visitor centre, it displays and sells local arts and crafts; Pilleau St. **Coleraine Classic Cars:** open by appt; Whyte St. **Bochara Wines:** wine-tasting available Fri–Sun; Glenelg Hwy. **Balmoral:** historic township west of the Grampians; 49km N. Nearby features include the Glendinning Homestead, just east of town, with gardens and a wildlife sanctuary. The town is also the gateway to Rocklands Reservoir, for watersports and fishing, and Black Range State Park, for bushwalking.

DIMBOOLA
Population 1315

Dimboola, on the Wimmera River, is a key access point to Little Desert National Park. The Traditional Owners are the Wotjobaluk People. The district was known as 'Nine Creeks' because of the many little streams that appear when the river recedes after floods. Many of the early settlers were German.

SEE & DO **Little Desert National Park:** see Top Attractions. **Historic buildings:** include the Mechanics Institute in Lloyd St and the Victoria Hotel, a grand two-storey structure with grapevines hanging from the verandahs (cnr Wimmera and Victoria sts). **Walking track:** follows a scenic stretch of the Wimmera River and the Nine Creeks Reserve. The track can be followed all the way to the Horseshoe Bend camping ground in the Little Desert National Park, see Top Attractions, 7km away; details about walks from visitor centre. **Pink Lake:** a salt lake that appears a deep pinkish colour, particularly impressive at sunset, but has dried up in recent years; 9km NW. **Ebenezer Mission Station:** founded in 1859 in an attempt to bring Christianity to the local Aboriginal people. The site contains fascinating ruins of the original buildings, a cemetery and a restored limestone church; off the Dimboola–Jeparit Rd; Barengi Gadjin Land Council (03) 5381 0977; 15km N. **Kiata Lowan Sanctuary:** the first part of Little Desert National Park to be reserved, in 1955. Home to the mallee fowl; Kiata; 26km W.

DONALD
Population 1375

Donald is on the scenic Richardson River and referred to by locals as 'Home of the Duck', owing to the many waterbirds that live in the region. The town also features Bullocks Head, a tree on the riverbank with a growth that looks like its namesake. The 'bull' is also used as a flood gauge – according to how high the waters are, the 'bull' is either dipping his feet, having a drink or, when the water is really high, going for a swim.

SEE & DO **Lake Buloke:** see Other Attractions. **Bullocks Head Lookout:** beside Richardson River; Byrne St. **Steam Train Park:** a restored steam locomotive, an adventure playground and barbecue facilities; cnr Hammill and Walker sts. **Historic Police Station:** dates back to 1865; Wood St. **Shepherds hut:** built by early settlers; Wood St. **Agricultural Museum:** an impressive collection of agricultural machinery; Hammill St. **Scilleys Island:** reserve on the Richardson River featuring wildlife, walking tracks and picnic facilities; access by footbridge from Sunraysia Hwy. **Kooka's Country Cookies:** tours and sales; Sunraysia Hwy. **Fishing:** There is good fishing for redfin and trout in the many waterways close to town. Good spots include Lake Cope Cope, 10km S; Lake Batyo Catyo and Richardson River Weir, both 20km S; Watchem Lake, 35km N; and the Avoca River, which runs through Charlton, 43km NE. **Mount Jeffcott Wildflower Reserve:** flora, kangaroos and views over Lake Buloke; 20km NE.

DUNKELD
Population 511

Dunkeld is considered the southern gateway to the Grampians/Gariwerd, and its natural beauty has been recognised since the explorer Major Thomas Mitchell camped here in 1836. It was originally named Mount Sturgeon after the mountain that towers over the town. Both Mount Sturgeon and Mount Abrupt (to the north of town) have been renamed to recognise the ancient First Nations heritage of the landscape; they are now known as Mount Wuragarri and Mount Murdadjoog, respectively.

SEE & DO **Arboretum:** exotic species from all over the world have been planted here, with a sandstone labyrinth a new addition to the grounds. Ideal for walking, cycling, fishing and picnics. Old Ararat Rd. **Historical Museum:** housed in an old church, the museum features displays on the history of the local First Nations people, the wool industry and the journeys of explorer Major Mitchell. Check ahead for opening hours; cnr Wills and Templeton sts; 1800 807 056. **Dunkeld Old Bakery:** operational as a bakery since 1887, now with cafe; Martin St; (03) 5577 2663. **Roz Greenwood Old and Rare Books:** open Sat–Sun 10am–4pm; Parker St; 0417 360 362. **Waiting Room Art Gallery:** open Sat 11am–5pm, Sun 10am–4pm or by appt; Parker St; (03) 5577 2281. **Bushwalking:** walking trails include Mount Wuragarri, Mount Murdadjoog and the Piccaninny Walk.

EDENHOPE
Population 713

Just 30km from the SA border, Edenhope is set on the shores of Lake Wallace, a haven for waterbirds. The town is renowned as the site where, in 1868, Australia's first all-Indigenous cricket team trained – their coach was T.W. Wills, who went on to establish Australian Rules football. A cairn in Lake St honours the achievements of this early cricket team.

SEE & DO **Edenhope Antiques:** offers an extensive variety of antique wares; Elizabeth St. **Lake Wallace:** walking tracks and birdwatching hides; Wimmera Hwy. **Dergholm State Park:** Wander among boulders, wildflowers and one of Australia's largest river red gums; 26km S. **Fishing:** redfin, trout and yabbies in many lakes and swamps nearby. Availability depends on water levels; contact visitor centre for locations.

★ HALLS GAP
Population 363

The little town of Halls Gap is set in the heart of the Grampians/Gariwerd and is the northern gateway to Grampians National Park. It's a beautiful, leafy place to base yourself for an exploration of the surrounding mountains and lush bushland. The town itself has its own charm – shops, galleries and cafes lend a casual atmosphere that befits the location, while in the evening long-billed corellas arrive to roost opposite the shops in the main street. It was named after Charles Browning Hall, who was the first European to discover the gap and valley in 1841. The valley was later developed by cattle-station owners, but the town really took off in the early 1900s when tourists, nature-lovers and botanists caught on to the beauty and diversity of the mountain ranges that would later become Grampians National Park.

SEE & DO **Brambuk – The National Park and Cultural Centre; Grampians National Park:** see Top Attractions for both. **Steve Morvell Wildlife Art Studio and Gallery:** home of world-renowned wildlife artist; wonderful local wildlife captured on canvas; 159 Grampians Rd; (03) 5356 4820. **Grampians Adventure Golf and MOCO Gallery:** 18-hole minigolf course set on 0.8ha; also has a gallery showcasing works by local artists; 481 Grampians Rd; 0400 595 683; 4km S. **Halls Gap Zoo:** explore the park's nature track and view the animals, many of which roam free; 4061 Ararat–Halls Gap Road; (03) 5356 4668; 7km SE. **Scenic drive:** from Halls Gap drive to Boroka Lookout, Reed Lookout and MacKenzie Falls, and break for lunch at the Zumsteins picnic area.

HAMILTON
Population 9577

Hamilton is a prominent rural centre in the heart of a sheepgrazing district. This industry is such an important part of the town's economy that it has been dubbed the 'Wool Capital of the World'. It is both the geographical and business hub of the Western District. A thriving country city, Hamilton is filled with cultural experiences, whether gazing at botanical, artistic or architectural beauty, browsing through great shops or putting in a bid as part of a 50,000-head sheep sale.

SEE & DO **Hamilton Art Gallery:** see Top Attractions. **Hamilton Botanic Gardens; Sir Reginald Ansett Transport Museum:** see Other Attractions for both. **Lake Hamilton:** attractive landscaped artificial lake used for swimming, sailing, yachting and rowing, and featuring an excellent walking/bike track; Rippon Rd, off Mill Rd. **Pastoral Museum:** features farm equipment, tractors, engines, household items and small-town memorabilia; check website for open day dates; Ballarat Rd; (03) 5571 1595; hamiltonpastoralmuseum.com.au. **Hamilton History Centre:** features the history of early Western District families and town settlement; open Sun–Fri 2–5pm; Gray St (03) 5572 4933. **Farmers' and Craft Market:** last Sat each month. **Tarrington:** established by German settlers and originally named Hochkirch, this area is fast becoming a well-known pinot noir grape-producing area; 12km SE. **Waterfalls:** Nigretta Falls has a viewing platform; 15km NW; also Wannon Falls; 19km W. **Cavendish:** a small town en route to Gariwerd (Grampians), notable for the three beautiful private gardens open during spring; 25km N. **Penshurst:** a lovely historic town at the foot of Mount Rouse. Excellent views from the top of the mountain, where there is a crater lake; 31km SE.

HORSHAM
Population 16,289

Known as one of the prettiest towns in Victoria, Horsham is the major centre for the Wimmera district, north-west of the Grampians/Gariwerd. It's on the way to Little Desert National Park, and is also near rock-climbing mecca Mount Arapiles. The Wotjobaluk, Jaadwa, Jadawadjali, Wergaia and Jupagik Nations are the Traditional Owners of the Horsham area. Although the Wimmera is a renowned wheat-growing region, Horsham is also a centre for fine wool production.

SEE & DO **Little Desert National Park:** see Top Attractions. **Horsham Regional Art Gallery:** see Other Attractions. **Botanic Gardens:** picturesquely set on the banks of the Wimmera River; cnr Baker and Firebrace sts. **Wimmera River:** key attraction for the town, with scenic picnic spots along the river's edges. Visit the river at dusk for spectacular sunsets. **Haven Market:** Haven Recreation Reserve; 1st Sat each month. **Jung:** market on last Sat each month; 10km NE. **Fishing:** redfin and trout in local lakes, depending on water levels. Reasonable levels at Taylors Lake; 18km SE.

JEPARIT
Population 326

This little town in the Wimmera lies 5km south-east of Lake Hindmarsh, which is the largest natural freshwater lake in Victoria (although it can dry up for years in times of drought). Former prime minister Sir Robert Menzies was born here in 1894.

SEE & DO **Wimmera–Mallee Pioneer Museum and Lake Hindmarsh:** see Top Attractions. **Menzies Square:** site of the dwelling where Menzies was born, with displays on Menzies, plus a children's play area; cnr Charles and Roy sts. **Wimmera River Walk:** 6km return; starts at museum. **Rainbow:** a charming little Wimmera township, with Pasco's Cash Store, an original country general store, and Yurunga Homestead, a beautiful Edwardian home with a large collection of antiques and original fittings (northern edge of town, open 2-4pm Sun); 35km N. **Pella:** former German settlement with Lutheran church and old schoolhouse; 40km NW via Rainbow. **Lake Albacutya:** fills only when Lake Hindmarsh overflows; 44km N.

NHILL
Population 1949

Nhill is exactly halfway between Melbourne and Adelaide, and claims to have the largest single-bin silo in the Southern Hemisphere. It is known for its successful resettlement of Karen refugees from Myanmar. The town is a good starting point for tours of Little Desert National Park.

SEE & DO **Little Desert National Park:** see Top Attractions. **Aviation Heritage Centre:** commemorating the town's history of aviation and its days as a World War II RAAAF base with five rebuilt aircraft on display; open Sat–Sun 10am–4pm; Aerodome Rd; (04) 9065 7770. **Historical Society Museum:** open Thurs, Fri or by appt; McPherson St. **Cottage of John Shaw Neilson (lyric poet):** open by appt; Jaypex Park, Victoria St. **Boardwalk:** scenic walk from Jaypex Park to Nhill Lake. **Self-guided historical walk:** details from visitor centre. **Mallee Dam:** lately dry, once offered fantastic birdwatching with bird hides provided; 20km SW.

STAWELL
Population 5627

Pastoral runs were established in the Stawell (rhymes with ball) region in the 1840s, but it was the discovery of gold in 1853 by a shepherd at nearby Pleasant Creek that was the catalyst for creating a town. Stawell remains a goldmining centre with Victoria's largest mine. However, it is actually better known as the home of the Stawell Gift, Australia's richest footrace, and is the gateway to the Grampians/Gariwerd.

SEE & DO **Grampians National Park; Stawell Gift Hall of Fame Museum; Bunjil's Shelter:** see Top Attractions for all. **Big Hill Lookout and Stawell Gold Mine viewing area:** the Pioneers Lookout at the summit of this local landmark presents magnificent 360-degree views of the surrounding area. Continue down Reefs Rd to Stawell Gold Mine viewing area to hear about the daily operations of Victoria's largest gold-producing mine. **Fraser Park:** displays of mining equipment; Main St. **Pleasant Creek Court House Museum:** local history memorabilia; Western Hwy. **Stawell Ironbark Forest:** spring wildflowers, including rare orchids; northern outskirts of town, off Newington Rd. **The Sisters Rocks:** huge granite tors; beside Western Hwy; 3km SE. **Tottington Woolshed:** rare example of a 19th-century woolshed; road to St Arnaud; 55km NE. **Great Grape Rd:** circuit through Ballarat and St Arnaud, stopping at wineries, including Best's and Garden Gully; details from visitor centre.

TERANG
Population 2020

Terang is in a fertile dairy-farming district. It is a well laid-out town with grand avenues of deciduous trees, and is known throughout the state for its horseracing carnivals.

SEE & DO **Lions Walking Track:** 4.8km, beside dry lake beds and majestic old trees; begins behind Civic Centre on High St. **Historic buildings:** many examples of early 20th-century commercial architecture. A Gothic-style Presbyterian church is in High St. **Lake Keilambete:** two and a half times saltier than the sea and reputed to have therapeutic properties; must obtain permission to visit because it is surrounded by private land; 4km NW. **Noorat:** birthplace of Alan Marshall, author of *I Can Jump Puddles*. The Alan Marshall Walking Track here involves a gentle climb to the summit of Mount Noorat, an extinct volcano, with excellent views of the crater, the surrounding district and the Grampians/Gariwerd; 6km N.

WARRACKNABEAL
Population 2227

The town's name means 'the place of the big red gums shading the watercourse', a name that is both beautifully descriptive and accurate, especially for the part of town around Yarriambiack Creek. Warracknabeal is a major service town at the centre of a wheat-growing district.

SEE & DO **Historical Centre:** includes a pharmaceutical collection, clocks, and antique furnishings of child's nursery; open afternoons; Scott St. **Black Arrow Tour:** a self-guided driving tour of historic buildings. **Walks:** including the Yarriambiack Creek Walk; details from visitor centre. **National Trust–classified buildings:** include the post office, the Warracknabeal Hotel and the original log-built town lockup. **Lions Park:** by the pleasant Yarriambiack Creek with picnic spots and a flora and fauna park; Craig Ave. **Wheatlands Agricultural Machinery Museum:** displays of farm machinery from the last 100 years; Henty Hwy; 3km S.

WYCHEPROOF
Population 562

Wycheproof is renowned for the long wheat trains that travel down the middle of the main street, towing up to 60 carriages behind them. There are many historic buildings in town, as well as rare, old peppercorn trees.

SEE & DO **Mount Wycheproof:** at a mere 43m, Mount Wycheproof has been named the smallest mountain in the world. A walking track leads up and around the mountain. Emus and kangaroos can be seen up close in a fauna park at the mountain's base. **Willandra Museum:** farm machinery, old buildings and historical memorabilia; open by appt; Calder Hwy. **Centenary Park:** aviaries, two log cabins and barbecue facilities; Calder Hwy. **Tchum Lakes:** artificially created lakes, great for fishing and watersports, depending on water levels; 23km W. **Birchip:** visitors to town are greeted by the town's beloved 'Big Red' mallee bull in the main street. Also in town is the Soldiers Memorial Park with large, shady Moreton Bay fig trees, a great spot for a picnic; 31km W.

SILO ART TRAIL

Taking art appreciation to new heights, the Silo Art Trail is Australia's largest outdoor gallery. A team of renowned artists – including Rone, Kaff-eine and Adnate – met with the locals and created a series of murals painted onto grain silos, aiming to reflect the spirit of these regional communities. Over 200km long, this drive takes in awe-inspiring art on silos in eight small towns from Rupanyup near Horsham to Patchewollock in the north-west and includes the towns of Nullawil, Sea Lake, Brim, Sheep Hills, Lascelles, and Rosebery. See siloarttrail.com for map.

Opposite top: Cattle graze in Casterton
Opposite bottom: Victorian wind farm near Hamilton

Goulburn, Murray and Mallee

Forming the border between Victoria and New South Wales, a journey along the mighty **Murray River** – on land or on water, by car or by paddlesteamer – is an epic adventure that harks back to a time when the river was a floating highway. The many towns along its length overflow with history. From the **irrigated farmlands** and vast **orchards** and **vineyards** of the Sunraysia, the landscape gets drier as you head south-west into the Mallee, where **salt lakes** and **dunes** are a taste of the outback.

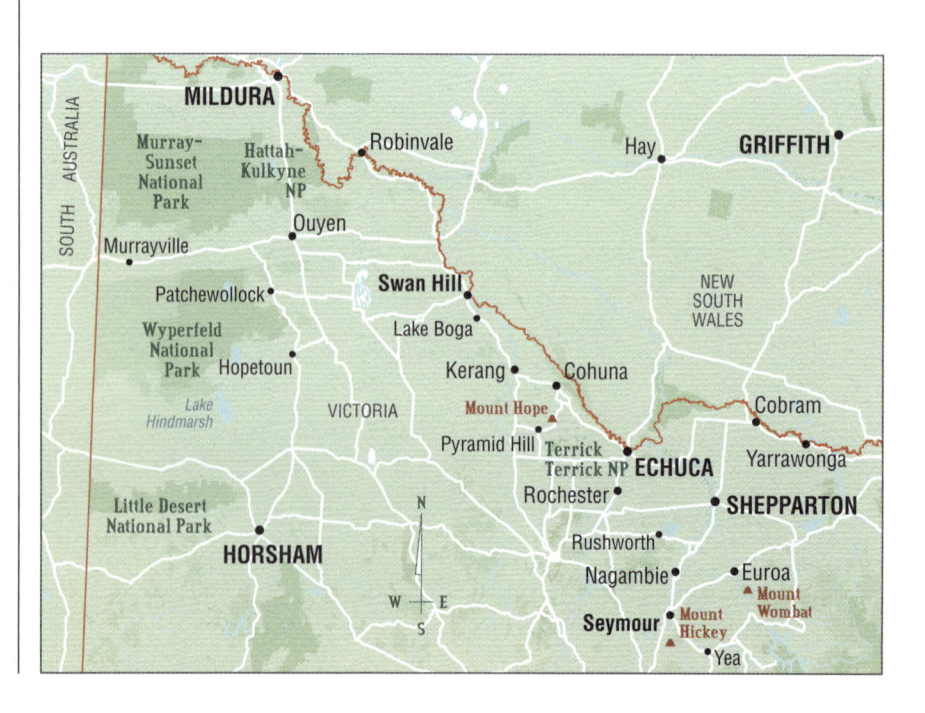

CHEAT SHEET

→ Allow at least a week to 10 days for a proper exploration.

→ Best time to visit: year-round, although winter can be cold for water-based activities.

→ Main towns: Mildura (*see* p. 186), Echuca (*see* p. 184), Swan Hill (*see* p. 189), Shepparton (*see* p. 188).

→ The land in this region is the homeland of the Baraba Baraba, Barkindji, Kureinji, Latji Latji, Ngurraiilam, Wadi Wadi, Wemba Wemba, Wergaia and Yorta Yorta Peoples , and Taungurung Clans. The Murray River is called Millewa or Tongala.

→ Need to know: In late 2022, many Murray River towns and communities were impacted by severe flooding. Check ahead of time before travelling to see which activities and attractions are open.

→ Did you know? The Murray River is Australia's longest, and the third longest navigable river in the world, second only to the Amazon and the Nile. It rises in the NSW Snowy Mountains and spills into the sea near Goolwa in South Australia, some 2520km to the west. There are 37 golf courses along its length.

→ Don't miss: river beaches, houseboating, paddlesteamer rides, river red gum forests and river cruises in Barmah National Park; silo art; the pink lakes; golf; wineries of the Goulburn Valley and Mildura.

Top: The Murray River at Yarrawonga **Opposite left:** River red gums grow in Barmah State Park **Opposite right:** Tahbilk Winery

TOP ATTRACTIONS

BARMAH NATIONAL PARK: Barmah National Park is in north-central Victoria, on the Country of the Yorta Yorta People. This Ramsar-listed park combines with NSW's Millewa forest to form the largest river red gum forest in the country. Nearby are Barmah Lakes, a good location for fishing and swimming. Canoes, barbecue boats and pontoons are available for hire. Walking trails take on various Yorta Yorta lands. Ulupna Island, in the eastern section of the park (near Strathmerton), has river beaches, camping and a large population of koalas. Barmah Muster, a festival celebrating Barmah's drovers, is held in the park in Apr.

LAKE BOGA: The town has an interesting history as an RAAF flying-boat repair depot during World War II. The depot serviced over 400 flying boats, one of which can be seen at the Flying Boat Museum. The underground museum is in the original communications bunker in Willakool Dr; open 9am–4pm; (03) 5037 2850. At Lake Boga, the water mass is popular for watersports, fishing and camping, and is home to a variety of bird species that can be seen on the various walks.

MILDURA ARTS CENTRE AND RIO VISTA: Houses an impressive permanent collection, including Australia's largest display of Orpen paintings, works by Degas and Brangwyn, frequent temporary exhibitions and performing arts. Outside, a delightful sculpture trail winds through landscaped gardens. Open 10am–5pm; 199 Cureton Ave, Mildura; (03) 5018 8330.

MURRAY DARLING WINE REGION: The Mediterranean-style climate combined with irrigated lands has contributed to making this wine region Victoria's largest. The area is well regarded for its varieties of chardonnay, cabernet sauvignon and shiraz. Among the large-scale wineries such as **Lindemans Karadoc**, smaller boutique wineries offer specialty wines for tastings and sales. Brochures available from Mildura visitor centre.

MURRAY–SUNSET NATIONAL PARK: Millions of years ago this area – the Traditional Country of the Latji Latji, Ngintait and Nyeri Nyeri Peoples – was submerged beneath a sea. When the sea retreated, large sand ridges and dunes were left. Now there is a variety of vegetation including grasslands, saltbush and mallee eucalypts. In spring, wildflowers abound; look out for Victoria's largest flower, the Murray lily. Access roads to the park are off Mallee Hwy. The Pink Lakes – saltwater lakes with a distinctive, pinkish hue – are a key attraction and are especially remarkable at sunset. There are many good walking tracks near the lakes, as well as excellent camping facilities.

NAGAMBIE WINE REGION: **Tahbilk Winery** has a small pocket of its original 1860 shiraz vines, which continue to produce wine that's worth its weight in gold. The winery also makes stunning marsanne (from its vines planted in 1927, the oldest in Australia) and cabernet sauvignon. It is worth spending some time at Tahbilk to explore the winery's wetland, wildlife reserve and three-tiered chateau and buildings, which are classified by the National Trust. You can then hop on a cruise along the Goulburn River to the other big name in the area, **Mitchelton**. This winery has reintroduced Preece Wines to its portfolio. Within the grounds are the cellar door, Muse Restaurant, Mitchelton Gallery of Aboriginal Art and the iconic Ashton Tower with views of the Goulburn River. The addition of the boutique Mitchelton Hotel/Day Spa has added to the winery's charms. Mitchelton regularly hosts Day on the Green events.

PADDLESTEAMER CRUISES: Paddleboats depart for river cruises at Mildura, Swan Hill and Echuca. Mildura's include the steam-driven PS *Melbourne*; PV *Rothbury* for daytrips to Gol Gol Hotel and Trentham Winery; and PV *Mundoo* for lunch and dinner cruises; bookings (03) 5023 2200.

PORT OF ECHUCA DISCOVERY CENTRE: The massive red-gum wharf has been restored to the grandeur of its heyday, with huge paddlesteamers anchored here. The wharf is accessed from the Discovery Centre, which has a visitor centre, interactive displays on the port's history and its famous paddlesteamers. Guided tours of the port area, including a nighttime ghost tour, and cruises on original paddlesteamers are available. Open 9am–5pm; Murray Espl, Echuca; (03) 5481 0500.

RUSHWORTH STATE FOREST: The largest natural ironbark forest in the world, Rushworth State Forest is also renowned for its orchids and wildflowers. Picnics and bushwalks are popular activities in this reserve, where over 100 species of birds, along with echidnas and kangaroos, can be seen. Access via Whroo Rd; 3km S of Rushworth.

SWAN HILL PIONEER SETTLEMENT: This museum re-creates life in the Murray and Mallee regions from the 1830s to the 1930s. There are barber shops and chemists, and rides available on the PS *Pyap* or horse-drawn carts. There is also the Heartbeat of the Murray sound and light show; bookings required. Cultural sites, such as canoe trees, can be found in the park (end of Gray St on Little Murray River). Open 9.30am–4pm; Monash Dr, Swan Hill; (03) 5036 2410.

SWAN HILL WINE REGION: The region takes advantage of the Murray River and the Mediterranean-style climate. The first vines were planted here in 1930, but the proliferation of vineyards really began when Sicilian immigrants arrived on the Murray after World War II. Today cellar doors offer tastings and sales of shiraz, pinot gris and most other varietals.

OTHER ATTRACTIONS

GOULBURN WEIR: The construction of this weir resulted in the creation of Lake Nagambie. It is the diversion weir on the Goulburn River for the Goulburn–Murray Irrigation District and feeds water by channel and pipeline to Bendigo, among other places. A walkway runs across the weir offering views of the structure and lake. Picnic and barbecue facilities are available.

GUNBOWER ISLAND: This island, surrounded by Gunbower Creek and the Murray River near Cohuna, is a Ramsar wetland of international importance, with a great variety of waterbirds and stands of river red gum forest. A 5km canoe trail flows through Safes Lagoon. Bushwalking is another highlight. The island is popular with campers.

HATTAH–KULKYNE NATIONAL PARK: This park protects an area of 48,000ha that includes typical mallee country with both low scrub and open native pine woodlands. The freshwater Hattah Lakes are seasonally filled by creeks connected to the Murray River, which brings the area to life with plants and waterbirds. Activities within the park include bushwalking, canoeing, fishing and scenic drives. There are picnic and camping facilities at Mournpall and Lake Hattah.

KINGS BILLABONG WILDLIFE RESERVE: Situated on the Murray River floodplain, home to river red gums and abundant birdlife. Attractions include Psyche Pump Station, Bruces Bend Marina and Kings Billabong Lookout.

KYABRAM FAUNA PARK: This park, owned by the Kyabram community, is home to over 140 animal species – from wombats to waterfowl. It has been built from the ground up on a piece of degraded farmland, and is now heavily involved in breeding programs for endangered species such as the eastern barred bandicoot. There is a walk-through aviary and a reptile house. (03) 5852 2883.

ROCHESTER SPORTS MUSEUM: Memorabilia and sporting stories including the history of Sir Hubert Opperman, affectionately known as Oppy, a champion cyclist who competed in the Tour de France. A statue of Oppy is opposite the museum. Open Thurs–Sun 10am–4pm. Moore St, Rochester.

TERRICK TERRICK NATIONAL PARK: The park is a large Murray pine forest reserve with granite outcrops, including Mitiamo Rock. There is a variety of good walking tracks, and the park is a key nesting area for the brolga.

WYPERFELD NATIONAL PARK: Outlet Creek connects the network of lake beds that are the main highlight for visitors to this park. They fill only when Lake Albacutya overflows; it in turn fills only when Lake Hindmarsh overflows. The Traditional Owners are the Wotjobaluk People. Once a corroboree ground, the main lake bed, Wirrengren Plain, has flooded only once in the last 100 years. Eastern grey kangaroos can be seen grazing on Wirrengren and the other lake beds, and the Eastern Lookout Nature Drive is a great way to see the range of vegetation in the park – river red gums, black box, mallee and cypress pine, and wildflowers in spring. The park is home to the endangered mallee fowl, a turkey-size bird that makes nesting mounds up to 5m across. A variety of walking trails leaves from the two campgrounds – Wonga Campground in the south and Casuarina Campground in the north, near the lakes.

YEA WETLANDS DISCOVERY CENTRE: Explore the Yea River floodplain and habitats supporting platypus, koalas and insect life, including the rare damselfly. The discovery centre has interpretive displays on the local ecology and the importance of water. 2 Hood St, Yea; (03) 5797 2106.

Top: Vineyards at Swan Hill winery **Opposite:** Pioneer Settlement, Swan Hill

KEY TOWNS

COBRAM
Population 5389

At Cobram and nearby Barooga (across the NSW border) the Murray River is bordered by sandy beaches, making it a great spot for fishing, watersports and picnics. The stretch of land between the township and the river features river red gum forests and lush wetlands, with walking tracks leading to the various beaches. The town is supported by peach, nectarine, pear and orange orchards and dairies, earning it the nickname 'peaches and cream country'.

SEE & DO **Historic log cabin:** built in Yarrawonga in 1875, then moved piece by piece to its current location in Federation Park. **Thompsons Beach:** Australia's largest inland beach, located off Mookarii St. **Log Cabin market:** Federation Park; last Sat each month. **Farm Gate Trail:** explore the region from Yarrawonga to Barmah and sample some local produce; brochure from visitor centre. **Quinn Island Flora and Fauna Reserve:** home to abundant birdlife and First Nations artefacts, including scar trees, flint tools and middens, the island can be explored on a self-guided walk; on the Murray River, accessed via a pedestrian bridge off River Rd. **Golf course:** across the river in NSW is this renowned 36-hole course; Golf Course Rd, Barooga; (03) 5873 4304; 5km NE. **The Big Strawberry:** strawberry-picking during warmer months; Goulburn Valley Hwy, Koonoomoo; (03) 5871 1300; 11km NW. **Cactus Country:** Australia's largest cacti gardens; 4986 Murray Valley Hwy, Strathmerton; (03) 5874 5271; 16km W. **Ulupna Island:** part of Barmah National Park, *see* Top Attractions, turn-off after Strathmerton.

COHUNA
Population 1870

Cohuna's claim to fame is that its casein factory developed produce that became part of the diet of the astronauts flying the Apollo space missions. Apart from its space history, Cohuna is a peaceful town located on the Murray River and near Gunbower Island, a popular camping and hiking destination with abundant wildlife, including kangaroos and emus.

SEE & DO **Gunbower Island:** *see* Other Attractions. **Cohuna Historical Museum:** housed in the former Scots Church, the museum features memorabilia relating to explorer Major Mitchell; Sampson St. **Wetlander Cruises:** explore Gunbower Creek in this charming boat. You can pick a cruise with meals included for a more luxe experience; Southern Rd; 17km NW. **Kow Swamp:** bird sanctuary with picnic spots and fishing at Box Bridge; 23km S. **Section of Major Mitchell Trail:** 1700km trail that retraces this explorer's footsteps from Mildura to Wodonga via Portland. From Cohuna, follow the signposted trail along Gunbower Creek down to Mount Hope; 28km S. **Torrumbarry Weir:** during winter the entire weir structure is removed, while in summer waterskiing is popular; 40km SE.

⭐ ECHUCA
Population 15,056

A delightful town on the banks of the Murray River, Echuca is all about days gone by, with a historic waterfront area and working paddlesteamers. Visitors are transported back in time by the sight of the beautiful old boats plying the waters and can enjoy this scenic stretch of the river from a houseboat, or while waterskiing or swimming. The town has a good selection of cafes, shops and accommodation. The town is at the junction of the Murray, Campaspe and Goulburn rivers and was once Australia's largest inland port. There are also nearby river red gum forests to explore. In October 2022, the Murray River peaked at almost 95m, flooding large parts of Echuca; call ahead to check on any lingering damage or closures.

SEE & DO **Port of Echuca Discovery Centre:** *see* Top Attractions. **Historic buildings:** many along Murray Espl including the Star Hotel, with an underground bar and escape tunnel, and the Bridge Hotel, built by Henry Hopwood, the founder of Echuca, who ran the original punt service. **Sharp's Magic Movie House and Penny Arcade:** penny-arcade machines and movie house showing classics; Murray Espl. **TwistED Science:** a wonderfully interactive science discovery centre for families and kids with hands-on activities; open Wed–Sun (school terms) and Mon–Sun (school holidays), book ahead for a session; 2 Radcliffe St; 1300 984 823; twistedscience.com.au. **Echuca Historical Society Museum:** housed in former police station; open 10am–2pm; Dickson St. **National Holden Motor Museum:** dedicated to Australia's iconic cars with some beautifully restored older models; Warren St; (03) 5480 2033. **Great Aussie Beer Shed and Heritage Farm Museum:** a shrine for everything related to Australian beer with astonishing collection of paraphernalia and extensive collection of 19th-century farming equipment; Mary Ann Road; (03) 5480 6904. **Echuca Farmers' Market:** Alton Reserve, Hare St; 1st, 3rd and 5th Sat each month. **Moama:** attractions include the Horseshoe Lagoon nature reserve; 2km N. **Billabong Ranch Adventure Park:** family fun with plenty of activities, including horseriding, minigolf and pedal boats; also has carriages for tours starting in Murray Espl, Echuca; (03) 5483 5122; 11km E. **Mathoura:** set among the mighty red gums, Mathoura is a charming

VISITOR INFORMATION

Echuca Visitor Centre
2 Heygarth St
(03) 5480 7555 or
1800 804 446
echucamoama.com

Mildura Visitor Information Centre
180–190 Deakin Ave
(03) 5018 8380 or
1800 039 043
visitmildura.com.au
visitthemurray.com.au

Wimmera and Mallee
visitwimmeramallee.com.au

Murray town over the NSW border. Fishing is popular, with sites including Gulpa Creek and the Edward and Murray rivers. To see the Millewa Forest in its splendour, take the Moira Forest Walkway or, for that authentic Murray River experience, visit nearby Picnic Point, popular for camping, picnics, waterskiing and fishing; 40km N. **Nathalia:** a town on Broken Creek with historic buildings. Walking tracks along the creek take in fishing spots, old homesteads and a lookout; 57km E.

★ EUROA
Population 3116

Euroa was the scene of one of Ned Kelly's most infamous acts. In 1878 the notorious bushranger staged a daring robbery, rounding up some 50 hostages and making off with money and gold worth nearly £2000. The Strathbogie Ranges, once one of the Kelly Gang's hideouts, provide a scenic backdrop to the town, and the region really comes to life in spring when stunning wildflowers bloom. During this time and in autumn, a number of private gardens are open to the public. The town itself is charming with a small selection of excellent cafes, shops and picnic areas.

SEE & DO **Farmers Arms Hotel Museum:** the museum features displays explaining the history of Ned Kelly and Eliza Forlonge; Eliza and her sister are said to have imported the first merino sheep into Victoria. Open Wed and Sun 1–4pm; 25 Kirkland Ave. **Walking trail:** self-guided trail to see the rich history and architecture of the town, including the National Bank building and the post office, both in Binney St; brochure available from visitor centre. **Seven Creeks Park:** good freshwater fishing, particularly for trout; Kirkland Ave. **Miniature steam-train rides:** Turnbull St; last Sun each month. **Faithfull Creek Waterfall:** 9km NE. **Longwood:** includes the delightful White Hart Hotel and horse-drawn carriage rides; 14km SW. **Gooram Falls:** a scenic drive takes in the falls and parts of the Strathbogie Ranges; 20km SE. **Locksley:** popular for gliding and parachuting; 20km SW. **Polly McQuinns Weir:** historic river crossing and reservoir; Strathbogie Rd; 20km SE. **Mount Wombat Lookout:** spectacular views of surrounding country and the Australian Alps; 25km SE. **Avenel Maze:** Ned Kelly–themed maze; open weekends, school and public holidays 10am–5pm; 37km SW.

HOPETOUN
Population 509

This small Mallee town, south-east of Wyperfeld National Park, was named after the first governor-general of Australia, the Earl of Hopetoun. The earl was a friend of Edward Lascelles, who played a major role in developing the Mallee Country by working to eradicate vermin, mainly rabbits, developing water strategies to cope with the dry conditions, and enticing settlers to the region. Today Hopetoun is surrounded by productive broad acre farmland, and is the gateway to the three major national parks of the Mallee: Wyperfeld, Hattah–Kulkyne, and Murray–Sunset.

SEE & DO **Murray–Sunset National Park:** *see* Top Attractions. **Wyperfeld National Park; Hattah–Kulkyne National Park:** *see* Other Attractions for both. **Hopetoun House:** the residence of Lascelles, the man who worked to transform the Mallee into farming land, the building is now a National Trust–classified private home; Evelyn St. **Mallee Mural:** depicts history of the region; wall of Dr Pete's Memorial Park, cnr Lascelles and Austin sts. **Lake Lascelles:** good for boating, swimming and fishing. Camping facilities available; access from end of Austin St. **Corrong Homestead:** the house of the first European settler in town, Peter McGinnis; tours by appt through Gateway Beet; Evelyn St. **Patchewollock:** the northern gateway to Wyperfeld National Park, and also home of the Patchewollock Hotel; 50km NW.

Camping riverside at Swan Hill **Opposite top:** Birdlife on the Murray **Opposite bottom:** Farmers Markets, Mildura

KERANG
Population 3696

Kerang, situated on the Loddon River just south of the NSW border, lies at the southern end of the Kerang wetlands and lakes. They extend from Kerang 42km north-west to Lake Boga and offer a wonderland for watersport's enthusiasts and birdwatchers; the lakes contain what are reputedly the world's largest ibis breeding grounds. The town itself is a centre for its agricultural surrounds.

SEE & DO **Lester Lookout Tower:** town views; cnr Murray Valley Hwy and Shadforth St. **Walking tracks:** follow the river on the Loddon River Walking Track or take a self-guided historical walking tour. **Historical Museum:** focuses on cars and antique farm machinery; open Sun afternoon; 17 Museum Dr. **Reedy Lakes:** a series of three lakes. Apex Park, a recreation reserve for swimming, picnicking and boating, is set by the first lake, and the second features a large ibis rookery. Picnic facilities are available at the third lake; 8km NW. **Koondrook:** this historic town used to be a hub for paddlesteamers in the early 1900s. The town has a new redgum wharf with sculptures and murals that showcase local and First Nations history; Arbuthnot Sawmills, a working mill that offers tours; 24km NE. **Leaghur State Park:** on the Loddon River floodplain, this peaceful park is the perfect spot for a leisurely walk through the black-box woodlands and wetlands; 25km SW. **Murrabit:** a historic timber town on the Murray surrounded by picturesque forests, with a country market, 1st Sat each month; 27km N. **Fishing:** Meran, Kangaroo and Charm lakes all offer freshwater fishing; details from visitor centre.

⭐ MILDURA
Population 34,565

Mildura provides visitors with a diverse range of alluring attractions and a dynamic culinary scene, and can be used as a base for access to some of the state's best protected areas. The Murray River flowing by the town and sunny, mild weather throughout the year make conditions ideal for a calendar packed with exciting events and festivals. Its development has been aided by the expansion of irrigation, which has allowed the area around the city to become a premier fruit-growing region.

SEE & DO **Paddlesteamer Cruises; Arts Centre and Rio Vista:** see Top Attractions for both. **Kings Billabong Wildlife Reserve:** see Other Attractions. **Art Galleries: Riverfront Gallery** on Hugh King Dr and the new **NAP Contemporary**, opened in 2022, with a fine collection of modern art and a permanent collection of First Nations art; 90 Deakin Ave. **Mildura Brewery:** produces natural and specialty beers inside the former Art Deco Astor Theatre; view the brewing process or eat at the Brewery Pub; open 12pm–late; 20 Langtree Ave; (03) 5021 5399. **Sunraysia farmers' market:** Jaycee Park; 1st and 3rd Sat each month. **Mildura City Market:** Langtree Mall; 2nd and 4th Sun each month. **Orange World:** tours of citrus-growing region; Silver City Hwy, Buronga; (03) 5023 5197; 6km N. **Australian Inland Botanic Gardens:** unique semi-arid botanic gardens; River Rd, Buronga; (03) 5023 3612; aibg.org.au; 8km NE. **Red Cliffs:** a centre for the local citrus and dried fruit industries. The town features the 'Big Lizzie' steam traction engine; 15km S.

MURRAYVILLE
Population 214

While Victoria might not be as famous for its outback as other states in Australia, this

TOP EVENTS

- → FEB Riverboats Music Festival (Echuca)
- → MAR Bridge to Bridge Swim (Cohuna); Head of the River and On Water Festival (Nagambie); Shepparton Festival (Shepparton)
- → EASTER River Beaches Festival (Cobram); Australian Tractor Pull Championship (Quambatook); Yachting regatta (Lake Boga).
- → APR Barmah Muster (Barmah National Park)
- → JUNE Steam Rally (Echuca)
- → JULY Winter Blues Festival (Echuca); Writers Festival (Mildura)
- → AUG Almond Blossom Festival (Robinvale)
- → SEPT Country Music Festival (Mildura)
- → OCT Tastes of the Goulburn (Seymour)
- → NOV Big Cohuna Festival (Cohuna); Springnats car festival (Shepparton); Music Festival (Euroa)
- → DEC Lake Mulwala Cod Classic (Yarrawonga)

TEMPERATURES

Jan: 15–32°C

July: 3–13°C

Opposite: *PS Pevensey* paddlesteamer, Echuca

small town, on the Mallee Hwy near the SA border, is near the two best examples of outback landscape in Victoria – Big Desert Wilderness Park to the south and Murray–Sunset National Park to the north. Settled in 1910, Murrayville is known for the wonderful wildflowers and wildlife nearby.

SEE & DO **Murray–Sunset National Park:** *see* Top Attractions. **Historic buildings:** include the restored railway station and the old courthouse. **Walking tracks:** several, including the Pine Hill Walking Trail in the town. **Cowangie:** a small, historic town with several 19th-century buildings, including Kow Plains Homestead; 19km E. **Big Desert Wilderness Park:** the Traditional Country of the Wotjobaluk People, this is a remote park with no access other than by foot. True to its name, this park has remained relatively untouched and includes many reptile species and plants that have adapted to arid conditions; the track south of town takes you close to the park boundary.

NAGAMBIE
Population 2036

Nagambie sits within the Traditional Lands of the Taungurung People. The name was said to be a local Aboriginal word meaning 'lagoon' or 'still waters'. Nagambie is between Seymour and Shepparton on the Goulburn Valley Hwy. The town is on the shores of Lake Nagambie, which was created by the construction of Goulburn Weir, in 1891. Activities such as waterskiing, speedboating and especially rowing are popular on the lake.

SEE & DO **Nagambie Wine Region:** *see* Top Attractions. **Goulburn Weir:** *see* Other Attractions. **Black Caviar Trail:** the racehorse who won every race she ever ran was born in Nagambie and there's a bronze statue of the famous horse beside the lake on High St. In and around the town are 15 of the trail's 25 sites ; trail maps available from the visitors centre. **The Jetty:** fine dining, lakeside apartments and spa; High St; (03) 5794 2189. **Nagambie Brewery and Distillery:** atmospheric waterfront dining; Wed–Sun, High St; (03) 7019 8170. **Community Market:** 1st Sat each month. **Farmers' market:** at Tahbilk Winery, last Sun each month except Dec.

OUYEN
Population 1022

Ouyen was once little more than a station on the Melbourne–Mildura train route, but it has since grown to become an important service town. It is at the centre of the Mallee region, which was developed in the early 1900s – relatively late when compared with other regions of rural Victoria. This was mainly due to the difficulties in clearing the land as well as the harsh climate. Other towns may have big bananas, prawns or pineapples, but here you'll find the world's largest mallee root stump (according to Guinness World Record officials) proudly displayed beside the highway at the southern entrance to the town, an enduring symbol of what the early famers had to overcome. The current success of agriculture in the region, in particular wheat-growing, is a testament to their perseverance. The town is a gateway to Hattah–Kulkyne National Park.

SEE & DO **Hattah–Kulkyne National Park:** *see* Other Attractions. **Roxy Theatre:** functioning tropical-style theatre, only one of its type in southern Australia; Oke St.

PYRAMID HILL
Population 475

Pyramid Hill's namesake is an unusually shaped, 187m high hill. The town, which is located in a wheat-growing district about 30km from the NSW border and features several lovely Art Deco buildings, was a source of inspiration to notable Australian author Katherine Susannah Pritchard, who based a character in her book *Child of the Hurricane* on a woman she met while staying in Pyramid Hill during World War I.

SEE & DO **Terrick Terrick National Park:** *see* Other Attractions. **Pyramid Hill:** a climb to the top of this eerily symmetrical hill reveals views of the surrounding irrigation and wheat district. There are abundant wildflowers in spring. **Historical Museum:** features local story displays; open Tues 10am–3pm; McKay St. **Mount Hope:** named by explorer Major Mitchell, who 'hoped' he would be able to spot the sea from the mountain's peak. Now known for its wildflowers; 16km NE. **Boort:** nearby lakes provide a habitat for swans, ibis, pelicans and other waterbirds, and a place for watersports, fishing and picnics; 40km W.

ROBINVALE
Population 2441

Robinvale is set on the NSW border beside a pretty stretch of the Murray River, surrounded by irrigated fruit farms and vineyards. The Robinswood Homestead, built in 1926, was home to the town's founder, Herbert Cuttle. Herbert's son, Robin, was killed during World War I, so Herbert named both the homestead and the town in Robin's honour.

SEE & DO **Rural Life Museum:** housed in the information centre, with locally grown almonds for sale; open Sat and by appt; Bromley Rd. **Murray River:** the beaches around Robinvale are popular for picnics and fishing, while in the river waterskiing and swimming are favourite summer pastimes. **Euston Weir and Lock on Murray:** created as an irrigation water store, it features a 'fish ladder' that enables fish to jump over the weir. Picnic and barbecue facilities are provided; Pethard Rd, south-west edge of town. **Robinvale Wines:** tastings and sales of distinctive, preservative-free wines. Also a children's playground; Sea Lake Rd; 5km S. **Olive oil:** this region is renowned for its award-winning olive oil; producers include Robinvale Estate; Tol Tol Rd; 8km SE.

ROCHESTER
Population 2802

On the way to Echuca from Bendigo, Rochester is a small agricultural town on the Campaspe River, known for tomato-growing and rich dairying. It has a lovely main street, some impressive silo art and there are lakes and waterways near town where you can take a rod and try your hand at freshwater fishing. Rochester suffered major flooding in October 2022, with up to 1000 homes and businesses inundated, so call ahead to check on any continuing closures.

SEE & DO Rochester Sports Museum; Kyabram Fauna Park: see Other Attractions for both. **Silo Art:** gigantic murals of a squirrel glider and azure kingfisher by artist Jimmy D'vate adorn the GrainCorp silos on Ramsay St. **Heritage walk:** take in the town's attractive old buildings. **Campaspe River Walk:** a pleasant, signposted walk by the river. **Campaspe Siphon:** an impressive engineering feat, where the Waranga–Western main irrigation channel was redirected under the Campaspe River; 5km N. **Fishing:** nearby channels, rivers and lakes are popular with anglers for redfin and carp. Lakes include Greens Lake and Lake Cooper (14km SE), also good for picnicking and watersports. **Elmore:** here is the Campaspe Run Rural Discovery Centre, which celebrates the history of the famous Sunshine Harvester which was developed in the area by Hugh Victor McKay and revolutionised grain farming; 17km S.

RUSHWORTH
Population 972

Situated off the Goulburn Valley Hwy, this delightful little town was once a goldmining settlement. The original site of the township was known as Nuggetty owing to the numerous gold nuggets found during the 19th century. Rushworth has retained much of its original character, with well-preserved early buildings lining the main street.

SEE & DO Rushworth State Forest: see Top Attractions. **Historic buildings:** many along High St are National Trust–classified, including St Paul's Anglican Church, the Band Rotunda, the former Imperial Hotel, the Glasgow Buildings and the Whistle Stop. Read the 'Walk Through Time' plaques on the buildings for more information. **Museum:** housed in the old Mechanics Institute with displays relating to the town's goldmining heritage; open 10am–12pm Sat; cnr High and Parker sts; (03) 5856 1583. **Growlers Hill Lookout Tower:** views of the town, Rushworth State Forest and the surrounding Goulburn Valley; Reed St. **Jones's Eucalyptus Distillery:** eucalyptus oil is extracted from blue mallee gum; Parramatta Gully Rd, just south of town. **Waranga Basin:** an artificial diversion of the Goulburn Weir constructed in 1916, now a haven for boating, fishing, swimming and watersports; 6km NE. **Whroo Historic Reserve:** Balaclava Hill, an open-cut goldmine, along with camping and picnic facilities, the Whroo cemetery and an Aboriginal waterhole; 7km S. **Murchison:** a small town set on the picturesque Goulburn River. Town attractions include the Italian war memorial and chapel; Meteorite Park, the site of a meteorite fall in 1969; Longleat Winery; and Campbells Bend Picnic Reserve; 19km E. **Days Mill:** a flour mill with historic buildings dating from 1865; 24km NE via Murchison. **Town ruins:** not all towns survived the end of the region's gold rush. Ruins of Angustown, Bailieston and Graytown are all to the south of Rushworth.

SEYMOUR
Population 6016

Seymour is on the Traditional Land of the Taungurung People. The town is a commercial, industrial and agricultural centre on the Goulburn River. The area was recommended for a military base by Lord Kitchener during his visit in 1910. Nearby Puckapunyal became an important training place for troops during World War II, and remains a major army base today. Seymour was flooded in October 2022 when the Goulburn River hit its highest levels since 1974 floods.

SEE & DO Royal Hotel: featured in Russell Drysdale's famous 1941 painting *Moody's Pub*; Emily St. **Old Courthouse:** built in 1864, it now houses local art; Emily St. **Restaurant and Art Gallery:** in the old post office; Emily St. **Goulburn River:** a walking track goes by the river and the Old Goulburn Bridge remains as a historic relic. **Goulburn Park:** for picnics and swimming; cnr Progress and Guild sts. **Railway Heritage Centre:** restored steam engines and carriages; open by appt; Railway Pl. **Australian Light Horse Memorial Park:** Goulburn Valley Hwy. **Wine by Sam:** Winery in a former dyeworks factory; Anzac Ave. **Farmers' Market:** 1st Sun each month; Mechanics Institute, Main Rd, Tallarook. **Tallarook State Forest:** popular for bushwalking, camping, rock climbing and horseriding, the key features are Mount Hickey, the highest point in the park and the location of a fire-lookout tower, and Falls Creek Reservoir, a scenic picnic spot. 10km S. **Wineries:** several in the area, including Somerset Crossing (2km S), Fowles (21km NE), **RAAC Memorial and Army Tank Museum:** Puckapunyal army base; 25km W.

SHEPPARTON
Population 49,862

Shepparton is the Traditional Land of the Yorta Yorta Nations. It is is a thriving regional city and is considered the 'capital' of the Goulburn Valley. It is a popular destination for conferences and sporting events, and so has plenty of modern accommodation and good restaurants in town. It is also home to many orchards irrigated by the Goulburn Irrigation Scheme and in recent years has become renowned for its street art and murals. Shepparton suffered major flooding in

Top: Seymour Railway Heritage Centre **Bottom:** Nagambie Brewery

October 2022, so check ahead in case of any continuing closures in the town.

SEE & DO **Art Museum (SAM):** features Australian paintings and ceramics; open 10am–4pm; 530 Wyndham St; (03) 4804 5000. **Bangerang Cultural Centre:** artefacts and artworks from Aboriginal communities across Australia, with a focus on local communities of the Murray and Goulburn Valleys; open Mon–Fri 9am–4pm; 45 Parkside Dr; (03) 5831 1020. **Heritage Centre Museum:** four galleries built around the town's oldest surviving building, the 1873 Public Hall; open Tues–Sat afternoons; High St. **Victoria Park Lake:** scenic picnic spot; Wyndham St. **Reedy Swamp Walk:** prolific birdlife; at the end of Wanganui Rd. **Moooving Art:** mobile interactive public art of life-size cow sculptures; various locations in Shepparton and surrounds including Monash Park and the visitor centre. **MOVE, the Museum of Vehicle Evolution:** Australian historic and classic vehicles; open 10am–4pm; Goulburn Valley Hwy; (03) 5823 5833. **SPC Factory Sales:** open Mon–Sat; 197–205 Corio St. **KidsTown Adventure Playground:** a fun attraction with a maze, flying fox, enormous playground, miniature railway and camel rides; Midland Hwy; (03) 5831 4213; 3km W. **Mooroopna:** a small town in the fruit-growing district. It hosts a street parade and festival on New Year's Eve; 5km W. **Kialla:** Australian Botanic Gardens: native plants in extensive themed gardens: Botanic Gardens Ave, 5km SW. **Tatura Irrigation and Wartime Camps Museum:** a museum with displays on local World War II internment camps. **Tatura Hot Bread** is known for its award-winning baked goods; 17km SW.

SWAN HILL
Population 10,869

The Wemba Wemba, Latji Latji, Tatti Tatti, Waddi Waddi and Barapa Barapa Peoples are the original Custodians of Country of the land known as Swan Hill. In 1836, explorer Thomas Mitchell named this spot Swan Hill because of the black swans that kept him awake all night. The town's swans remain but there are many other attractions in this pleasant city on the Murray Valley Highway.

SEE & DO **Pioneer Settlement:** *see* Top Attractions. **Regional Art Gallery:** an impressive permanent collection plus touring exhibitions; open Tues–Fri 10am–5pm, Sat–Sun 10am–4pm; Horseshoe Bend; (03) 5036 2430. **Now and Then history walk:** various sites in town including the Burke and Wills Tree; Curlewis St; details from visitor centre. **Farmers' Market:** Riverside Park; 1st Sun each month. **Rotary Country Market:** railway carpark, Curlewis St; 3rd Sun each month. **Nyah:** good market with local produce; 2nd Sat each month; 27km NW. **Tooleybuc:** situated in NSW, has riverside walks and an adventure playground; 46km N.

YARRAWONGA
Population 8661

Yarrawonga and its sister town Mulwala, across the NSW border, are separated by a pleasant stretch of the Murray River and the attractive Lake Mulwala. The 6000ha lake was created in 1939 during the building of the Yarrawonga Weir, which is central to irrigation in the Murray Valley. Yarrawonga's proximity to such great water features has made it a popular holiday resort. The sandy beaches and calm waters are ideal for watersports, and are also home to abundant wildlife. The Lake Mulwala Cod Classic, the biggest fishing competition in Australia, is held here on the first full weekend in Dec.

SEE & DO **Yarrawonga and Mulwala foreshores:** great locations for walks and picnics, with shady willows, water slides, barbecue facilities and boat ramps. **Cruises:** cruises along the Murray on the paddleboat *Paradise Queen*; details from visitor centre. **Rotary Market:** local crafts and second-hand goods; showgrounds; 3rd Sun each month. **Farmers' Market:** foreshore; 4th Sun each month. **Fishing:** Murray River for Murray cod and yellow-belly. **Farm Gate Trail:** visit regional food producers; details from visitor centre.

YEA
Population 1279

This town sits by the Yea River, a tributary of the Goulburn River. Hume and Hovell, the first European explorers through the region, discovered this wonderfully fertile area – a discovery that led in part to the settlement of the rest of Victoria. Near Yea–Tallarook Rd there are beautiful gorges and fern gullies, a reminder of what Yea looked like thousands of years ago.

SEE & DO **Yea Wetlands Discovery Centre:** *see* Other Attractions. **Historic buildings:** Beaufort Manor, now a function centre, High St; General Store, now a restaurant, High St. **Market:** local craft and produce; Station St; 1st Sat each month Nov–Apr. **Cheviot Tunnel:** historic rail tunnel built from handmade bricks. Now part of the Great Victorian Rail Trail, it's the longest tunnel on any rail trail in Victoria; 7km W. **Murrindindi Scenic Reserve:** see the impressive Murrindindi Cascades and a variety of wildlife including wombats, platypus and lyrebirds; 31km SE. **Grotto:** a beautiful old church set in the hillside; Caveat; 35km N. **Wilhelmina Falls:** spectacular falls and a great spot for walks and picnics; access via Melba Hwy; 32km SE. **Philip Lobley Wines:** vineyard and bakery; 39km S. **Scenic drives:** many in the region; maps from visitor centre.

High Country

The Victorian Alps, north-east of Melbourne, are a source of delight for adventure-seekers. Activities include **hiking, horseriding, canoeing**, and of course – when snow dusts the slopes in winter months – **skiing and snowboarding. The Great Alpine Road** is the state's highest altitude road and a wonderful touring route. A sprinkling of towns and their hinterlands provide **gourmet eateries, fresh local produce, outstanding wineries,** and **walking and cycling trails** to discover it all.

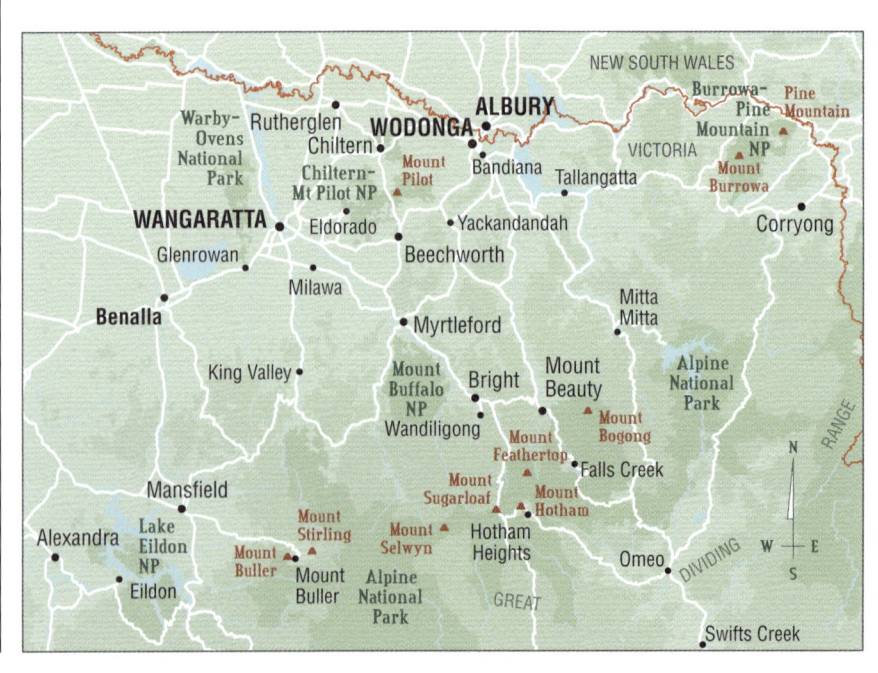

CHEAT SHEET

→ Allow at least a week for a proper exploration.

→ Best time to visit: year-round depending on your adventure activity of choice.

→ Main towns: Benalla (see p. 194), Bright (see p. 195), Mansfield (see p. 197).

→ It is understood that the High Country is the Traditional Land of the Dhudhuroa, Gunai Kurnai, Taungurung, Waywurru and Jaithmathang Peoples; sites such as Cloggs Cave in north-eastern Victoria have yielded evidence of 8500-year-old stone tools.

→ Did you know? The High Country is home to some famous characters and events, including the last stand of infamous bushranger Ned Kelly and his gang, and the exploits of poet A.B. 'Banjo' Paterson's 'The Man From Snowy River'.

→ Don't miss: Alpine National Park; Beechworth; the Prosecco Road in the King Valley; craft brews and cycling the Murray to Mountains Rail Trail.

Top: Mount Buller is a popular ski resort **Opposite:** Hiking in Mount Buffalo National Park

TOP ATTRACTIONS

ALPINE NATIONAL PARK: Covering 646,000ha in four sections, this is Victoria's largest national park, containing the highest mountain in the state, Mount Bogong (1986m). Most of Australia's south-east rivers have their source here. The area is known for its outstanding snowfields during winter, and bushwalking and wildflowers in summer. Other activities include horseriding, canoeing, rafting and mountain-bike riding.

BEECHWORTH GAOL: Built in 1859, the original wooden gates of this gaol were replaced with iron ones when it was feared prisoners would break out in sympathy with Ned Kelly during his trial. The gaol is now privately owned but open to the public for guided tours. Tours daily at 11am and 1pm; cnr Ford and William sts, Beechworth.

BEECHWORTH HISTORIC AND CULTURAL PRECINCT: This fantastic precinct provides a snapshot of 19th-century Beechworth during the goldrush. Featuring fine, honey-coloured granite buildings, the area incorporates the telegraph station, gold office, Chinese prospectors' office, town hall and powder magazine. Of particular interest is the courthouse, site of many famous trials including Ned Kelly's, and where former Governor-General Sir Isaac Isaacs began his legal career. Also in the precinct is the **Robert O'Hara Burke Memorial Museum**, with the interesting 'Street of Shops' exhibition where 19th-century Beechworth shops are brought to life.

BEECHWORTH WINE REGION: According to many wine writers, this boutique region is one to watch. With only small quantities being produced and much of it quickly whisked away by a discerning clientele, Beechworth's wines can be hot property. **Castagna Vineyard** grows its grapes biodynamically and is known for its superb Genesis Syrah Viognier. **Giaconda** produces outstanding chardonnay, while Demeter-certified **Sorrenberg** is a leader in gamay and does a wonderful blend of cabernet sauvignon, cabernet franc and merlot.

BONEGILLA MIGRANT EXPERIENCE: A rare example of postwar immigrant accommodation camps, the first Australian home for some 300,000 postwar immigrants from over 50 countries; Mon, Wed, Thurs, Sat–Sun 10am–4pm; 132 Bonegilla Rd, Bonegilla (10km E of Wodonga); (02) 6020 6912.

CRAIG'S HUT: The High Country is synonymous with courageous and hardy cattlemen, transformed into Australian legends by Banjo Paterson's iconic ballad *The Man from Snowy River*. The men built huts on the high plains for shelter during summer cattle drives. Craig's Hut on Mount Stirling is a replica of one such shelter, used as a set on the 1982 film *The Man from Snowy River*. It burnt down in the 2006 bushfires, but was rebuilt and reopened in Jan 2008. The last 2km of the track to the hut is 4WD or there's a fairly steep walking track from the Circuit Rd picnic area on Mount Stirling.

GLENROWAN WINE REGION: Known for its full-bodied reds and fortified wines, there's lots of cellar doors to choose from. If you drop into **Taminick Cellars** you'll find a fourth-generation family winery, and you can also enjoy a craft beer at the Black Dog brewery on site.

GREAT ALPINE ROAD: The 307km Great Alpine Rd begins in Wangaratta, crosses Mount Hotham and finishes in Bairnsdale. Prosecco Rd leads south through the beautiful King Valley offering many delicious stops at local wineries and gourmet food producers, with natural beauty detours including Paradise Falls and Powers Lookout. A network of minor roads allows you to fully explore the area, including a number of tiny, unspoiled townships such as Whitfield, Cheshunt and Carboor.

KING VALLEY WINE REGION: Given that this region is known for its cheese, make sure to enjoy its wines with a decadent cheese platter. Italian heritage is evident in many of the vineyards. Varieties such as sangiovese, nebbiolo and barbera rub shoulders with cabernet sauvignon, chardonnay and merlot. **Brown Brothers** is the biggest name with the most established cellar door – a barn-like building featuring some enormous oak barrels of ageing wine. It also incorporates the Epicurean Centre restaurant, which is perfect for long, lazy lunches. To the west, **Sam Miranda** is known for its chardonnay. Heading south are **Pizzini**, whose sangiovese is one of Australia's best, and **Dal Zotto**.

MOUNT BUFFALO NATIONAL PARK: This 31,000ha national park is the state's oldest, declared in 1898. A plateau of boulders and tors includes the Horn, the park's highest point and a great place for views at sunrise. Walking tracks are set among streams, waterfalls, stunning wildflowers, and snow gum and mountain ash forest. There is summer camping, swimming and canoeing at Lake Catani, and rock climbing and hang-gliding are also popular. In winter, Dingo Dell and Cresta Valley are popular with families to enjoy snow play and tobogganing.

MURRAY TO MOUNTAINS RAIL TRAIL: 100km-plus track between Wangaratta and Bright, with offshoots to Beechworth, Rutherglen and Milawa, follows historical railway lines with 94km of bitumen sealed track. Suitable for cycling and walking, the trail ventures into pine forests, natural bushland and open valleys and links several townships. A gentle gradient makes the track appropriate for all ages and levels of fitness; details from visitor centre.

RUTHERGLEN WINE REGION: Winemaking in Rutherglen has been more or less continuous since 1839, and many of the wineries go back well beyond 100 years. **Campbells**, **Jones**, **St Leonards** and **Warrabilla** produce the bold reds – shiraz and durif – for which the region is renowned. But Rutherglen is even better known for its world-class fortified wines, mostly muscat and tokay. In this category, **Chambers Rosewood** and **Morris** lead the way. Look out for **All Saints** (see below), and **Pfeiffer**, **Chambers** and **Scion**. The countryside of grassy paddocks and big old gum trees is dotted with many beautiful historic buildings, and some of the wineries are located on the banks of the Murray River.

THE MAN FROM SNOWY RIVER MUSEUM: Banjo Paterson's famous 'The Man from Snowy River' poem evoked the lives of the High Country's settlers. This charming museum proudly does the same, with local exhibits, tools used by Traditional Owners, memorabilia and photos depicting the hardships of local life, as well as a unique collection of historic skis. The museum also contains the magnificent knitted rug of Australia that Jim Simpson created when he was a POW in Germany in World War II. 103 Hanson St, Corryong.

OTHER ATTRACTIONS

ALL SAINTS ESTATE: Situated in the respected Rutherglen district and 5km south-west of Corowa, All Saints is a winery like no other. Behind the hedge fence and imposing set of gates lies an enormous medieval castle built by the original owner, George Smith, based on the Castle of Mey in Scotland. All Saints offers a large cellar-door operation, a pair of excellent restaurants, KIN and Bonnie, and beautiful gardens. (02) 6035 2222.

BENALLA ART GALLERY: Set beside Lake Benalla, the gallery has an impressive collection including contemporary Australian art, works by Sidney Nolan, Arthur Streeton, Tom Roberts and Arthur Boyd, and a substantial collection of Aboriginal art including works by Emily Kame Kngwarreye, Rover Thomas and Albert Namatjira. Built in 1975, the gallery is a striking work of modern architecture. Bridge St, Benalla; (03) 5760 2619.

BURROWA–PINE MOUNTAIN NATIONAL PARK: Pine Mountain is one of Australia's largest monoliths. Mount Burrowa is home to wet-forest plants and unique wildlife, including wombats and gliders. Both mountains provide excellent and diverse opportunities for bushwalkers, campers, climbers and birdwatchers. The Cudgewa Bluff Falls offer fabulous scenery and bushwalking; main access is from the Cudgewa Valley Rd, which runs off Murray Valley Hwy.

Top: Historic sign at Beechworth
Bottom: Beechworth streetscape
Opposite: Wandiligong's autumn splendour

CHILTERN–MOUNT PILOT NATIONAL PARK: This park stretches from around Chiltern south to Beechworth and protects remnant box-ironbark forest, which once covered much of this part of Victoria. Also featured are significant goldmining relics, including the impressive Magenta Goldmine; around 2km E. An introduction to the forest scenery and goldmining history is on the 25km scenic drive signposted from Chiltern. Other activities include canoeing and rafting, fishing, and cycling and walking trips along the many marked trails; access via Hume Hwy and the road south to Beechworth.

ELDORADO: A fascinating old goldmining township named after the mythical city of gold. The main relic of the gold era is a huge dredge, the largest in the Southern Hemisphere, which was built in 1936. There is a walking track with information boards around the lake where the dredge now sits. The Eldorado Museum provides details of the town's mining past, alongside World War II relics and a gemstone collection; open most Sunday afternoons. The town is 20km north-east of Wangaratta (see p. 199).

LAKE EILDON NATIONAL PARK: Comprising the lake and surrounding woodlands, hills and wilderness areas, this national park provides a venue for many water- and land-based activities. When full, Lake Eildon has six times the capacity of Sydney Harbour. Hire a boat or houseboat from the outlets in Eildon to explore the waters, or enjoy the thrills of waterskiing with the picturesque foothills of the Australian Alps providing a backdrop. There are various nature walks, scenic drives and panoramic lookout points.

MOUNT GRANYA STATE PARK: This landscape contrasts steep, rocky slopes and open eucalypt forests. Bushwalking is a popular pastime and the display of wildflowers in spring is magnificent. There is a pleasant picnic spot at Cottontree Creek, and a short walk leads to the Mount Granya summit, which offers spectacular views of the Alps.

ORIENTAL CLAIMS: The Claims was a major goldmining area near Omeo, and remains the highest alluvial goldfield in Australia. French–Canadians, Americans and Europeans all worked alongside Australians and Chinese during the gold boom. The word 'Oriental' in the mine's name may conjure an image of Chinese prospectors, but 'Oriental Claims' was actually the name of a European company. There are a variety of walks around the site and visitors should look out for the flora, including wild orchids. High cliffs, left by the hydraulic sluicing process, offer impressive views across town, and signs throughout the Parks Victoria–managed site explain the history of the Claims. It's 1.5km west of Omeo on Great Alpine Rd.

REEF HILLS STATE PARK: The park offers scenic drives, bushwalks, picnics and horseriding. There are more than 100 species of birds, including gang-gang cockatoos and crimson rosellas, plus animals such as eastern grey kangaroos, sugar gliders and bats. It's on the western side of the Midland Hwy 4km south-west of Benalla.

WANDILIGONG: A National Trust–classified hamlet near Bright, the area contains well-preserved historic buildings from the town's goldmining days. The tiny village is set in a rich green valley, with the Diggings Walk a dominant feature, which loops through some of the area's former goldfields; Centenary Ave. The Wandiligong Nut Festival in April is Australia's only celebration of the nut.

WARBY–OVENS NATIONAL PARK: The 'Warbys', as they are known locally, extend for 25km north of Glenrowan (see p. 196). The steep ranges provide excellent viewing points, especially from Ryans Lookout. Other lookouts include the Pangarang Lookout near the Pine Gully Picnic Area and the Mount Glenrowan Lookout, the highest point of the Warbys at 513m. There are well-marked tracks for bushwalkers and a variety of pleasant picnic spots amid open forests and woodlands, with wildflowers blossoming during the warmer months.

WINTON WETLANDS: Formed from Lake Mokoan, the wetlands can be reached by a 14km cycling track from Benalla (see p. 194) and offer glamping, birdwatching, a hub and cafe, art and First Nations cultural heritage sites.

KEY TOWNS

ALEXANDRA
Population 2480

Alexandra was apparently named after Alexandra, Princess of Wales – although, coincidentally, three men named Alexander discovered gold here in 1866. Situated in the foothills of the Great Dividing Range, Alexandra is supported primarily by agriculture. Nearby, the Goulburn River is an important trout fishery.

SEE & DO **Alexandra Timber Tramways:** museum housed in the original railway station that offers an insight into the timber industry around Alexandra; open 2nd Sun each month; Station St. **Art and craft galleries:** many around town displaying and selling local art, pottery and glassware. **Alexandra on Perkins Market:** Perkins St; 4th Sat each month. **McKenzie Nature Reserve:** in virgin bushland, with orchids and wildflowers during winter and spring. **Self-guided tourist drives:** the Skyline Rd from Alexandra to Eildon features lookouts along the way; information from visitor centre. **Trout fishing:** in the Goulburn, Acheron and Rubicon rivers. **Bonnie Doon:** Made famous in the cult classic movie, *The Castle*, this small town is a good base for exploring the lake region. Activities include trail-riding, bushwalking, watersports and scenic drives; 37km NE, near Lake Eildon.

★ BEECHWORTH
Population 3291

One of northern Victoria's most picturesque towns, Beechworth has faded grandeur in its historic buildings, combined with a lovely natural setting – especially in autumn. Local breweries, wineries, cafes, shops and farm produce are the icing on the cake. Set in the picturesque surrounds of the Australian Alps, Beechworth is one of the state's best preserved 19th-century gold towns, with over 30 buildings listed by the National Trust. Beechworth's grand buildings are evidence that in the 14 years from 1852 when it was first discovered, over four million ounces of gold were mined here. There is a delightful tale about Beechworth's heyday: the story goes that Daniel Cameron, a political candidate vying for support from the Ovens Valley community, rode at the head of a procession through the town on a horse shod with golden shoes. Sceptics claim they were merely gilded, but the tale offers a glimpse into the wealth of Beechworth during the gold rush.

SEE & DO **Beechworth Historic and Cultural Precinct; Beechworth Gaol; Beechworth Wine Region:** see Top Attractions for all. **Walking tours:** Ned Kelly–themed and other historic walking tours operate daily, and ghost tours are available at the former Mayday Hills Asylum; bookings at visitor centre. **Craft breweries:** Popular **Bridge Road Brewers** sits along the town's main street, while **Billson's** has returned the art of beer to a historic brewery building. **Beechworth Honey:** interpretive display on the history of honey; includes a glass-fronted live bee display and honey tour. A wide range of premium Australian honey is on offer in the concept shop; open 9am–5.30pm; cnr Ford and Church sts; (02) 6033 2322. **Harry Power's Cell:** under the shire offices, where the 'gentleman bushranger' was once briefly held; Albert Rd. **Beechworth Farmers' Market:** 1st Sat of the month; Christ Church, Church St. **Quercus Flea Market:** 1st Sat each month (Oct–May); Quercus Hall. **Beechworth Hidden Wineries:** 2nd weekend each month (excluding winter); select wineries open their cellars to visitors; brochure available from the visitor centre on Ford St; 1300 366 321. **Golden Horseshoes Festival:** a celebration of the town's past, with street parades and a variety of market stalls; Easter. **Beechworth Cemetery:** a fascinating piece of goldfields history. More than 2000 Chinese goldminers are buried here. Twin ceremonial Chinese burning towers stand as a monument to those who died seeking their fortune far from home. Northern outskirts of town. **Beechworth Historic Park:** surrounds the town and includes Woolshed Falls Historical Walk through former alluvial goldmining sites. **Gorge Scenic Drive or Walk (5km):** starts north of town. **Beechworth Forest Drive:** takes in Fletcher's Dam; 3km SE towards Stanley. **Kellys Lookout:** at Woolshed Creek; about 4km N. **Mount Pilot Lookout:** views of Murray Valley 5km N. **Stanley:** a historic goldmining settlement with fantastic views of the Alps from the summit of Mount Stanley; 10km SE.

BENALLA
Population 9742

Benalla is determined to be land belonging to the Yorta Yorta Nations. If you're driving from Melbourne, you'll notice the Rose Gardens beside the highway a short distance before Lake Benalla – gardens for which Benalla has become known as the 'Rose City'. The town was the home of Sir Edward 'Weary' Dunlop and has a museum display and a statue in his honour at the Botanic Gardens. Benalla is also gaining fame for its annual street art festival, Wall to Wall, during which visiting artists create street art to add to the 50-plus murals around the town, and workshops, tours and interactive activities attract people of all ages.

SEE & DO **Benalla Art Gallery:** see Top Attractions. **Reef Hills State Park; Winton Wetlands:** see Other Attractions for both. **Ceramic Art Mural:** a Gaudi-inspired community construction, this fascinating 3D mural is opposite the art gallery on Lake

Top: Eurobin Station along the Murray to Mountains Rail Trail
Bottom: Streets of Bright

VISITOR INFORMATION

Alpine Visitor Centre
119 Gavan St, Bright
(03) 5755 0584 or
1800 111 885
visitbright.com.au
victoriashighcountry.com.au

Rutherglen Visitor Information Centre
57 Main St, Rutherglen
(02) 6033 6300 or
1800 622 871
explorerutherglen.com.au

Wangaratta Visitor Information Centre
100–104 Murphy St, Wangaratta
(03) 5721 5711 or
1800 801 065
visitwangaratta.com.au

TEMPERATURES

Jan: 11–29°C

July: 2–12°C

Benalla. **Costume and Kelly Museum:** has period costumes, a Ned Kelly exhibit and a feature display of Benalla's 'famous sons'; open Tues–Sat 10am–3.30pm; Mair St. **Lake Benalla:** created in Broken River, it has good recreation and picnic facilities and is a haven for waterbirds. **Botanic Gardens:** features a splendid collection of roses and a memorial statue of Sir Edward 'Weary' Dunlop; Bridge St. **Aeropark:** centre for the Gliding Club of Victoria, offering hot-air ballooning and glider flights; northern outskirts of town; bookings (03) 5762 1058. **Lakeside Craft and Farmers' Market:** near the Civic Centre; 4th Sat each month. **1950s-style cinema:** showing classic films at Swanpool; 23km S.

★ BRIGHT
Population 2481

It's easy to spend time outdoors discovering this beautiful town with its idyllic valley and riverside setting and rail trail begging for two-wheel exploration. Bright is situated in the Ovens Valley in the foothills of the Victorian Alps. A particularly striking element of the town is its avenues of deciduous trees, at their peak during the autumn months. The Autumn Festival is held annually in celebration of the spectacular seasonal changes. The Ovens River flows through the town, providing a delightful location for picnics or camping. The town has lots of shops and cafes, ski hire shops and also offers off-the-mountain accommodation for nearby Mount Hotham, Mount Buffalo and Falls Creek (*see* box below).

SEE & DO

Mount Buffalo National Park; Murray to Mountains Rail Trail: *see* Top Attractions for both. **Centenary Park:** a riverside park with a deep weir, children's playground and picnic facilities; Gavan St. **Art Gallery and Cultural Centre:** community-owned gallery, displays with fine art and handicrafts sales; 28 Mountbatten Ave; (03) 5750 1660. **Bright Brewery:** enjoy award-winning beers; 121 Great Alpine Rd; (03) 5755 1301. **Historical Museum:** in the old railway station building, with artefacts and photographs from the town's past; check opening hours with visitor centre; Railway Ave. **Walking tracks:** well-marked tracks around the area include Canyon Walk along the Ovens River, where remains of gold-workings can be seen; details from visitor centre. **Bright Electric Bikes:** cruise around town or on the Murray to the Mountains Rail Trail on these state-of-the-art electric bikes; vintage-style pedal bikes also available; Delany Ave; (03) 5755 1309. **Make It. Bake It. Grow It.:** regional produce and products made by local designers; Howitt Park, 3rd Sat of the month. **Wandiligong:** *See* Other Attractions; 6km S. **Huggins Lookout:** access from Zivan Ct or McFadyens La; 2km SW. **Ringer Reef Winery:** open for sales and tastings; 6835 Great Alpine Rd; 8km NW. **Harrietville:** a former goldmining village located just outside the Alpine National Park. Attractions include Pioneer Park, an open-air museum and picnic area; Tavare Park, with a swing bridge and picnic and barbecue facilities; a trout farm; and a lavender farm; 20km SE.

SNOWY HOT SPOTS

The Victorian ski season runs between early June and early Oct.

DINNER PLAIN
Home to Australia's longest toboggan run, this relaxed village – one of the few snow resorts that are dog friendly – is surrounded by Alpine National Park. Other activities on offer include beginner skiing, walking, dog-sledding, horse riding and Australia's first indoor–outdoor alpine spa.

FALLS CREEK
Surrounded by Alpine National Park, Falls Creek is a winter playground for downhill and cross-country skiers and snowboarders. There's a variety of runs and terrain, including some to suit beginners and a ski school. Novelty tours are also available, such as the Snowmobile Tours. Each Aug, Falls Creek hosts the Kangaroo Hoppet cross-country ski race. In spring and summer, take a walk on the Bogong High Plains or fly-fish in one of the lakes and rivers nearby.

MOUNT BULLER
Victoria's largest and best alpine snowsports resort is Mount Buller, whose summit stands 1805m above sea level. The 22 lifts, including the six-seater ABOM Express (first of its kind in Australia), give access to 180ha of ski trails, from gentle 'family runs' to heart-stopping double black diamond chutes. If you are a beginner, take on the friendly Bourke Street (Green Run) to find your 'ski legs', or join one of the ski school programs. There are also three terrain parks at Boggy Creek and Terrain Park, or cross-country skiing at nearby Mount Stirling. Mount Buller Village offers resort accommodation. In summer, the mountain has some of Australia's best mountain biking.

MOUNT HOTHAM
This popular downhill ski resort is suited to both budding and experienced skiers. Skiing areas range from the beginners' Big D Playground through to the more advanced slopes around Mary's Slide and the black diamond chutes of Heavenly Valley.

Paragliding/hang-gliding: the region around Bright is renowned for these sports; details at visitor centre. **Adventure activities**: plenty of activities are available in the area, such as climbing, caving, abseiling, mountain-biking and kayaking; information at visitor centre.

CHILTERN
Population 1208

Walking down the main street of Chiltern, you could almost imagine that you're back in the gold-rush boom, with historical buildings including Dow's Pharmacy. Chiltern boomed after the discovery of gold in the 1850s, and some miners abandoned nearby towns like Beechworth to rush over. After the rush, the town settled back into farming, and it is still surrounded by rich pastoral farmland.

SEE & DO **Chiltern–Mount Pilot National Park:** *see* Other Attractions. **Athenaeum Museum:** historic building with heritage display; call to check opening times; Conness St; (03) 5726 1280. **Dow's Pharmacy:** old chemist shop with original features; open Fri 10am–3pm and by appt; Conness St; (03) 9656 9889. **Star Theatre:** formerly the Grape Vine Hotel, boasts the largest grapevine in Australia, planted in 1867 and recorded in the Guinness World Records; Main St. **Federal Standard Printing Works:** one of the last surviving newspaper printeries from the gold rush era – you can watch the news being printed on a still functioning printing press dating from the 1870s. The equipment is maintained and demonstrated by volunteers (all retired printers), so opening hours can vary but generally open 11am–3pm 2nd weekend of the month and by appt for groups; Main St; (03) 5726 1611. **Lakeview House:** former home of author Henry Handel Richardson; open 11am–2pm Wed, Sat and 3rd Sun of the month; Victoria St; (03) 9656 9889. **Lake Anderson:** picnic and barbecue facilities; access via Main St.

CORRYONG
Population 1186

Welcome to authentic *Man from Snowy River* country. This area offers superb mountain scenery and excellent trout fishing in the Murray River and its tributaries, with the town being known as the home and final resting place of Jack Riley, the original 'Man from Snowy River'. A life-size statue depicting 'that terrible descent' made famous by Banjo Paterson's poem sits in the town. An annual festival honours Riley's memory with a feature event called the 'Challenge' to find his modern-day equivalent. Corryong is also the Victorian gateway to Kosciuszko National Park across the NSW border.

SEE & DO **The Man From Snowy River Museum:** *see* Top Attractions. **Burrowa–Pine Mountain National Park:** *see* Other Attractions. **Jack Riley's grave:** Corryong cemetery. **Man from Snowy River Statue:** Hanson St. **Galleon Park:** features a large wooden galleon for kids to play on; Murray Valley Hwy. **Playle's Hill Lookout:** for a great view of the township; Donaldson St. **World War II memorials:** statue of 'Horrie the Wog Dog', who was adopted in Egypt during World War II and smuggled back into Australia after the war; Chainsaw Statue commemorating farmers who went to war. **Nariel:** Nariel Creek is a good spot for trout fishing. The town hosts the Nariel Creek Folk Music Festival each Dec; 8km SW. **Towong:** historic Towong Racecourse is where scenes from *Phar Lap* were filmed. Gangster Squizzy Taylor once stole the takings from the races in the 1930s; 12km E. **Lookouts:** lookout with views over Kosciuszko National Park at Farren's Lookout Towong, 12km NE; Embery's Lookout over Mount Mittamatite, 16km N. **Walwa:** hire canoes and mountain bikes from Upper Murray Cottages; 47km NW. **Touring routes:** Murray River Rd, Lakeside Loop, Murray Valley Highway onto Alpine Way, Mitta Valley Loop; details from visitor centre.

EILDON
Population 725

Once you hit Eildon, you know that the delights of Lake Eildon are only a short distance away. The Goulburn River was dammed to create Lake Eildon in the 1950s and Eildon was originally established as a service town for dam workers, although the focus is now on holidaymaking. Lake Eildon is the state's largest constructed lake, irrigating a vast stretch of northern Victoria and providing hydro-electric power. In recent years, low water levels have revealed homesteads that were submerged when the dam was constructed. The lake and the surrounding national park are popular summer holiday destinations, especially for watersports, fishing and boating.

SEE & DO **Lake Eildon National Park:** *see* Top Attractions. **Lake Eildon Wall Lookout:** 1km N. **Eildon Pondage and Goulburn River:** for excellent fishing – there is no closed season for trout in Lake Eildon or the Eildon Pondage. **Mount Pinniger:** for views of Mount Buller, the Alps and the lake; 9km E. **Waterfalls:** include Snobs Creek Falls and Rubicon Falls; 28km SW via Thornton.

GLENROWAN
Population 355

Glenrowan has had fun with the Ned Kelly legend (*see* box text), building a giant statue of Ned that towers over shops in Gladstone St, as well as Ned Kelly's Last Stand, a unique take on telling Ned's story through animatronics (although visitors are divided over whether the entry price is worth it). Almost as legendary as Ned Kelly is the Glenrowan Wine Region, and fruit orchards in the area.

SEE & DO **Glenrowan Wine Region:** *see* Top Attractions. **Warby–Ovens National Park:** *see* Other Attractions. **Kate's Cottage:** gifts and souvenirs in the front, and out back is the Ned Kelly Museum with an extensive collection of

Top: Gateway Village Farmers Market in Wodonga **Bottom:** Hero mountain bike trail in Bright

TOP EVENTS

→ JAN Alpine Classic cycling (Bright); Corryong Cup Hang-gliding Competition

→ FEB Adventure Travel Film Festival (Bright)

→ MAR The High Country Hop (Beechworth); Wall to Wall Festival (Benalla); Myrtleford Festival; Tastes of Rutherglen; Dragon Boat Regatta (Wodonga); Yackandandah Folk Festival; Spring Ditch (Stanley)

→ EASTER Golden Horseshoes Festival (Beechworth); Rodeo (Omeo)

→ APR Nut Festival (Wandiligong); Man From Snowy River Bush Festival (Corryong); Music Festival (Mount Beauty); Autumn Festival (Bright); Man from Snowy River Rodeo (Corryong)

→ MAY Harvest Celebration (Beechworth); La Fiera Italian Festival (Myrtleford)

→ JUNE Trails, Tastings and Tales (Glenrowan); Winery Walkabout (Rutherglen)

→ AUG Kangaroo Hoppet ski race (Falls Creek)

→ SEPT Goulburn Fishing Festival (Eildon)

→ OCT North East Wine and Food Festival (Wodonga)

→ OCT–NOV Open Gardens (Alexandra); Spring Festival (Bright); Wangaratta Festival of Jazz and Blues

→ NOV Celtic Festival (Beechworth); Benalla Festival; Campdraft (Corryong); High Country Festival (Mansfield); La Dolce Vita Festival (King Valley)

THE MOST FAMOUS BUSHRANGER OF THEM ALL

Victoria's High Country is Ned Kelly country, and the exploits of the Kelly Gang are immortalised in folklore. Learn more about the life and times of Australia's most well-known bushranger in towns like Wangaratta, Beechworth and Glenrowan. The latter is particularly famous for Ned Kelly's last stand in 1880, where the Kelly Gang dressed in homemade suits of metal armour and had their final bloody confrontation with police.

Before his execution by hanging in Old Melbourne Gaol in 1880, Ned Kelly had already become an Australian legend. Then, as now, he divided opinion: some saw him as a Robin Hood character, a larrikin who was known for speaking out about discrimination against poor Irish settlers, and for protesting against police harassment; others viewed him as a villain, a murderous criminal (he killed three policemen in 1878). His final reported words before the hangman are etched into history: 'Such is life'.

Ned Kelly's life has featured in paintings (most famously by Sidney Nolan), film, songs and poems. In fact, the members of the Kelly gang are among the most referenced historical figures in Australian history. While touring Victoria's High Country, you can make up your own mind: Australia's Robin Hood fighting for the oppressed or a criminal who deserved the hangman's noose?

Kelly memorabilia and an interpretive display, also a replica of the Kelly Homestead; Gladstone St. **Ned Kelly's Last Stand:** two computer-animated shows of Kelly's capture starting every half-hour; Gladstone St. **Kelly Gang Siege Site Walk:** discover the sites and history that led to the famous siege on this self-guided walk (brochure available).

MANSFIELD
Population 3999

Mansfield is located at the junction of the Midland and Maroondah hwys. It is within easy reach of Lake Eildon's network of rivers, Alpine National Park, Mansfield State Forest and Mount Buller (see box p. 195). Activities ranging from hiking to horseriding and skiing make it an ideal destination for anyone with a love of outdoor adventure, no matter what the season.

SEE & DO **Alpine National Park:** see Top Attractions. **Troopers' Monument:** monument to police officers shot by Ned Kelly at Stringybark Creek; cnr High St and Midland Hwy. **Mansfield Mullum Wetlands Walk:** along reclaimed railway line; starts from behind the visitor centre. **Self-guided town walk:** take in buildings of historical significance. **Great Victorian Rail Trail:** the longest rail trail in Victoria, this route meanders for 134km from Mansfield to Tallarook. **Farmers' market:** 4th Sat each month. **Delatite Winery:** Stoneys Rd; 7km SE. **Mount Samaria State Park:** scenic drives, camping and bushwalking; 14km N. **Lake Nillahcootie:** popular for boating, fishing and watersports; 20km NW. **Howqua Hills Historic Area:** popular free camping on the Howqua River, particularly with large groups and horseriders. This area has an early settler cottage; 30km SE.

Jamieson: an old goldmining town on the Jamieson River with historic buildings; 37km S. **Scenic drive:** take the road over the mountains to Whitfield (62km NE), in the King River Valley, passing through remarkable scenery, including Powers Lookout (48km NE) for views over the valley. **Lake William Hovell:** for boating and fishing; 85km NE. **Mount Skene:** great for bushwalking, with wildflowers in summer; 85km SE via Jamieson. **Fishing:** good spots include the Delatite, Howqua, Jamieson and Goulburn rivers. **Horse trail-riding:** a different way to explore the region, from short trails to 10-day treks; details from visitor centre. **Mountain-biking:** summer months reveal an expanding network of downhill and cross-country trails at nearby Mount Buller and Mount Stirling.

MILAWA
Population 270

Milawa is the perfect destination for lovers of fine food and wine. The Milawa Gourmet Region boasts more than 13 wineries, including the renowned Brown Brothers vineyard (see King Valley Wine Region, p. 192). Other fresh local produce outlets sell olives, honey, cheese, chocolates and berries.

SEE & DO **Milawa Mustards:** a wide range of locally produced mustards; set in attractive cottage gardens; Milawa-Bobinawarrah Rd; (03) 5727 3202. **Milawa Cheese Company:** sales and tastings of specialist, gourmet cheeses; Factory Rd; (03) 5727 3589. **Brown Brothers:** cellar-door tastings and sales; Bobinawarrah Rd; (03) 5720 5547. **Oxley:** home to many wineries as well as the Blue Ox Berries and King River Cafe; 4km W.

MOUNT BEAUTY
Population 910

At the foot of Mount Bogong, Victoria's highest mountain at 1986m, Mount Beauty calls to all of those who enjoy adventure activities, with mountain-biking, hang-gliding and bushwalking being just a few of the many activities on offer. If you prefer a lower level of adrenalin, there are more leisurely pursuits like golf, swimming and fishing in the surrounding area, but don't leave without heading to a lookout for a view over the alpine region.

SEE & DO **Mount Beauty Pondage:** for watersports and fishing; just north of Main St. **Wineries:** cool-climate vineyards. **Scenic walks:** several scenic walking tracks; details from visitor centre. **Markets:** Hollonds St; 1st Sat each month. **Tawonga Gap:** features a lookout over valleys; 13km NW. **Bogong:** scenic walks around Lake Guy and nearby Clover Arboretum for picnics; 15km SE. **Scenic drives:** to Falls Creek and the Bogong High Plains (not accessible in winter beyond Falls Creek); details from visitor centre.

MYRTLEFORD
Population 2846

You'll find Myrtleford in the pretty Ovens Valley, part of Victoria's alpine High Country and one of the gateway towns to the summer and winter playground of Mount Hotham (*see* box p. 195). The town has cafes, shops and ski hire. The town is the centre of the thriving agricultural district, and all sorts of things are grown near town, including tobacco back in the day – you can still see the old tobacco kilns in the surrounding countryside.

SEE & DO **Mount Buffalo National Park; Murray to Mountains Rail Trail:** *see* Top Attractions for both. **Museum:** housed in the former state school with local history displays and farming equipment. Check ahead for opening hours; Elgin St; (03) 5727 1417. **The Phoenix Tree:** a sculpture created by Hans Knorr from the trunk of a red gum; Lions Park. **The Big Tree:** a huge old red gum; Smith St. **Swing Bridge over Myrtle Creek:** Standish St. **Reform Hill Lookout:** a scenic walking track from Elgin St leads to the lookout, which has great views across town; end of Halls Rd. **Parks:** Rotary Park in Myrtle St and Apex Park in Standish St are both delightful picnic spots. **Michelini Wines:** Great Alpine Rd. **Farmers Market:** local produce; Great Alpine Rd; 4th Sat of the month. **Gapsted Wines:** The area's largest vineyard, with cellar door and restaurant; 8km NW. **Eurobin:** a number of farms near the town with sales of local produce, including Bright Berry Farm, offering homemade jams and berries (Dec–Mar); 16km SE. **Fishing:** in the Ovens and Buffalo rivers and Lake Buffalo (25km S).

OMEO
Population 242

Omeo, a picturesque town in the Victorian Alps, is a peaceful farming community but it wasn't always so. During the 1800s gold rush, Omeo was an unruly frontier town, which early Australian novelist Rolf Boldrewood described as the roughest goldfield in Australia. Despite being damaged in the 1939 Black Friday bushfires, several historic buildings still remain.

SEE & DO **Oriental Claims:** *see* Other Attractions. **Historic Park:** the park preserves a piece of Omeo's rich history in a peaceful, bushland setting. Many distinctive structures from the 19th century can be seen – buildings on display include the old courthouse, which now houses a museum, a log gaol, police cookhouse and stables. Open 10am–2pm; (03) 5159 1515; Day Ave (Great Alpine Rd). **Livingstone Park and Creek:** walking tracks and swimming area adjacent to the Oriental Claims. **Lake Omeo:** scenic natural landscape, dry for most of the year; Benambra; 21km NE. **Benambra:** gateway to Alpine National Park; 24km N. **Anglers Rest:** historic **Blue Duck Inn**, a remote destination pub and a good base for horseriding, whitewater rafting and fly fishing; 29km NW. **Swifts Creek:** this town, situated at the junction of Swifts Creek and Tambo River, has the Great Alpine Art Gallery; 40km S. **Taylors Crossing suspension bridge:** part of the scenic Alpine Walking Track and also a great base for camping and fishing the Mitta Mitta River; off Tablelands Rd; 44km NE. **Dinner Plain:** 46km W; *see* box p. 195. **Ensay:** small but picturesque town that is home to the well-known Ensay Winery; 70km S. **Mitta Mitta and Cobungra rivers:** great trout fishing, waterskiing and whitewater rafting (only available in spring); details from visitor centre. **High Country tours:** explore the high plains around Omeo – on horseback, by 4WD or, for keen hikers, on challenging bushwalks; details from visitor centre.

RUTHERGLEN
Population 2324

Visitors to Rutherglen often leave with a fortified wine or two in their bags, as the surrounding wine-growing district does a particularly good fortified drop. There are numerous notable wineries nearby, so take a day or two to explore. Aside from its produce, the town itself has a main street with charmingly preserved 19th-century buildings.

SEE & DO **Rutherglen Wine Region:** see Top Attractions. **Rutherglen Wine Experience:** interpretive displays of Rutherglen's wine history; visitor centre, Main St. **Common School Museum:** local history displays and a re-creation of a Victorian-era schoolroom; behind Main St. **Historic tours:** take a self-guided walk, bike ride or drive, following maps provided at the visitor centre. **Lake King:** originally constructed in 1874 as Rutherglen's water storage, it is now a wildlife sanctuary and offers a scenic walk and a number of sculptures, along with good fishing (but no swimming). **Great Northern:** marked by mullock heaps associated with the first alluvial goldmine in the district. Historical details are provided on site; Great Northern Rd, 5km E. **Lake Moodemere:** found near the winery of the same name, the lake is popular for watersports and features scarred red gum trees where you can still see where the Whroo People removed bark to make canoes and shields; 8km W. **Old customs house:** a relic from the time when a tax was payable on goods from NSW; 10km NW.

TALLANGATTA
Population 1016

When the old town of Tallangatta was going to be submerged in 1956 after the level of the Hume Weir was raised, the residents simply moved the entire township 8km west. Tallangatta now has an attractive lakeside location and sits directly north of the alpine region.

SEE & DO **The Hub:** local art and craft, and Lord's Hut, the only remaining slab hut in the district; Womaatong St. **Lake Hume:** Tallangatta is on the shores of this enormous and attractive lake, formed by the construction of Hume Weir. It is now a picturesque spot for swimming, waterskiing, windsurfing, camping and fishing. The foreshore reserves are perfect for barbecues. **Eskdale:** craft shops and trout fishing in the Mitta Mitta River; 33km S. **Lake Dartmouth:** great for trout fishing and boating; hosts the Dartmouth Cup Fishing Competition over the June long weekend. Also here is the Witches Garden featuring unique medicinal plants; 58km SE. **Mitta Mitta:** remnants of a large open-cut goldmine, a gallery, Butcher's Hook Craft Shop and renovated Mitta Mitta Pub. Hosts the Mighty Mitta Muster on Sun of the long weekend in Mar; 60km S. **Australian Alps Walking Track:** passes over Mount Wills; 108km S via Mitta Mitta. **Scenic drives:** to Cravensville, or to Mitta Mitta along Omeo Hwy or to Tawonga and Mount Beauty.

WANGARATTA
Population 19,712

Wangaratta lies in a rich agricultural district in north-eastern Victoria that produces a diverse range of crops including kiwifruit, wine grapes, walnuts and wheat. An entry for both the Murray to the Mountains Rail Trail and the Great Alpine Rd, it offers the services of a rural city while retaining country-town warmth. A short drive in any direction will lead to world-class wineries, gourmet food and some spectacular views.

SEE & DO **Eldorado:** see Other Attractions. **Self-guided heritage walk:** historic sites and buildings, such as the majestic Holy Trinity cathedral, Vine Hotel Cellar Museum and the Wangaratta Historical Museum; details from visitor centre. **Cemetery:** headless body of infamous bushranger Daniel 'Mad Dog' Morgan is buried here; Tone Rd. **Art Gallery:** changing exhibitions by national and regional artists; open Tues–Sun 10am–4pm; 56 Ovens St; (03) 5722 0865. **Bullawah Cultural Trail:** explore ancient stories, knowledge and culture of the Pangerang People along the 2.4km track; start Apex Park. **Reids Creek:** popular with anglers, gem fossickers and gold panners; near Beechworth; 28km E.

WODONGA
Population 20,259

Wodonga and its twin town, Albury (in NSW, see p. 100), sit astride the Murray River. These twin cities blend city style and country pace, history and contemporary attractions, art and adventure. The Murray and nearby Lake Hume have plenty of attractions to appeal to water lovers.

SEE & DO **The Bonegilla Migrant Experience:** see Top Attractions. **Junction Place:** this urban renewal project doubled the size of Wodonga's CBD by breathing new life into the historic railway station and rail yards transforming it into a cafe and fine-dining precinct with restaurants, boutiques, a brewery, markets and events. **Gateway Village:** includes woodwork shops and cafes. Also houses a visitor centre; Lincoln Causeway. **Huon Hill Lookout:** maps from visitor centre. **Sumsion Gardens at Belvoir Park:** a pretty lakeside park with walking track, picnic and barbecue facilities; Church St. **Farmers' market:** Gateway Village; Sat. **Army Museum:** Anderson Rd, South Bandiana; 4km SE. **Hume Weir:** good spot for walks and picnics; 15km E. **Tours:** winery and fishing tours, as well as scenic drives through the Upper Murray region, the mountain valleys of north-east Victoria and the Riverina; details from visitor centre.

★ YACKANDANDAH
Population 1113

Yackandandah, with its avenues of English trees and traditional buildings, is so rich with history that the entire town is National Trust classified. It is situated in the heart of the north-east Goldfields region. Many of the town's creeks still yield alluvial gold.

SEE & DO **Historic buildings:** the post office, several banks and general stores, with the Bank of Victoria now preserved as a museum; open Sat–Sun 10.30am–3.30pm; High St; (02) 6027 0627. Explore these and other buildings on a self-guided walk; details from visitor centre. **The Old Stone Bridge:** a beautiful old structure, built in 1857; High St. **Arts and crafts:** many outlets in town, including Sluga Gallery; open Fri–Sun 10.30am–4 pm; High St; (02) 6027 1797. **Antiques:** High St has an array of antiques and bric-a-brac for sale on weekends. **Kirbys Flat Pottery and Gallery:** studio of renowned potter, John Dermer; open Sat–Sun 10.30am–5 pm; Kirbys Flat Rd; (02) 6027 1416; 4km S. **Indigo Valley:** a picturesque area with a scenic drive leading along the valley floor to Barnawatha; 6km NW. **Allans Flat:** a great destination for a picnic at the Dredge waterhole or visit Schmidt's Strawberry Winery, with tastings and sales; Osbornes Flat Rd; (02) 6027 1454; 10km NE.

Opposite: The Big Ned Kelly in Glenrowan

South Australia

HIGHLIGHTS

Catch a game of cricket or AFL football at the Adelaide Oval.

Spend a few days camping, bushwalking and wildlife spotting in the semi-arid Ikara–Flinders Ranges National Park. See p. 247.

Get to know the wildlife on Kangaroo Island: koalas, seals, sea lions, cockatoos, dolphins and (of course) kangaroos. See p. 211.

Travel from cellar door to cellar door on a winery tour of the famous Barossa Valley. See p. 214.

Hire a houseboat and spend a few days chugging up and down the Murray River. See p. 232.

Fill up on oysters and superb seafood in Coffin Bay, on the far-flung Eyre Peninsula. See p. 259.

STATE FLOWER

Sturt's desert pea
Swainsona formosa

SOUTH AUSTRALIA

The Fleurieu Peninsula

201

The Traditional Owners of the Adelaide/Tarndanya area are the Kaurna People.

Adelaide/Tarndanya at a glance

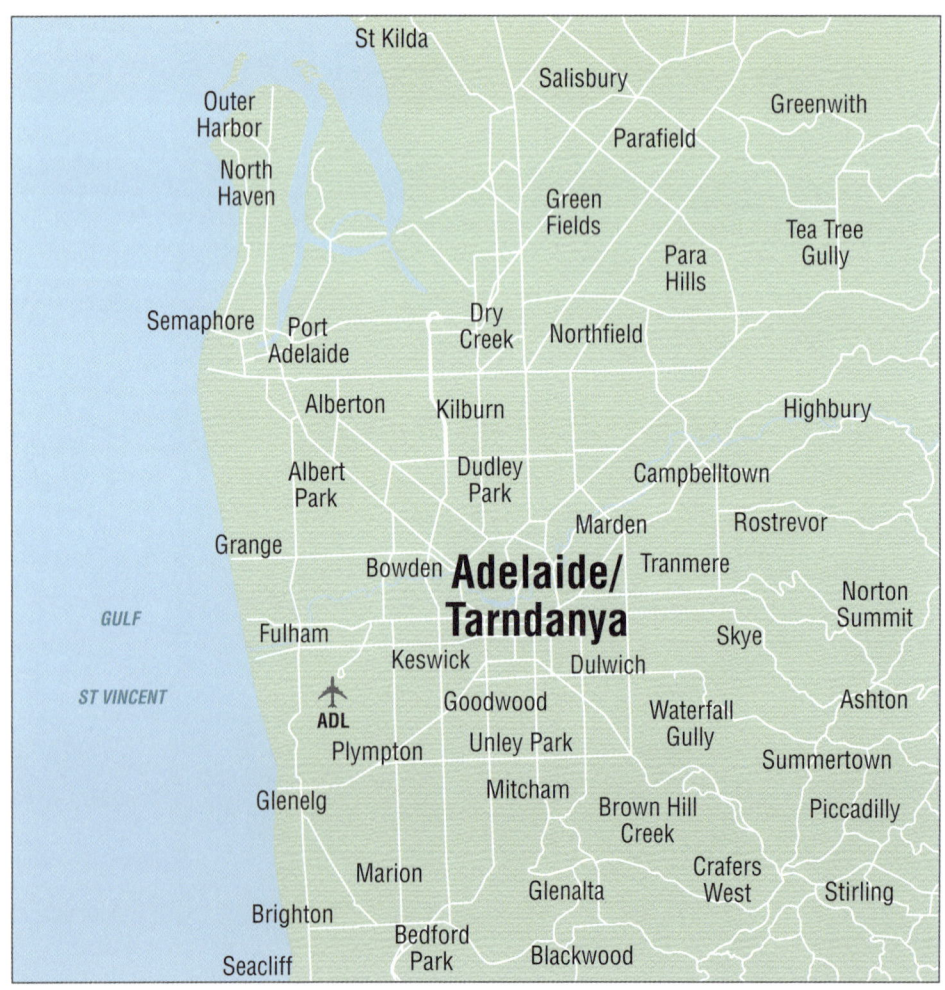

Adelaide is Australia's fifth biggest city – with just over 1.3 million locals – but you'd never know it. **Encircled by parks, flanked by hills and fringed by beaches**, the atmosphere here is cultured, low-key and nature loving. Despite its small size, it's a city that punches above its weight with **food, wine and festivals**.

Top: Adelaide Oval **Middle:** Art Gallery of South Australia **Bottom:** Haigh's Chocolates **Opposite:** Glenelg Beach pier

IF YOU LIKE ...

BEACHES
Brighton Beach
Glenelg Beach
Grange Beach
Henley Beach
Semaphore Beach

EAT STREETS
Goodwood Road
Gouger Street
Hutt Street
Leigh Street
O'Connell Street
Peel Street
Rundle Street

FESTIVALS AND EVENTS
Tour Down Under, Jan
Adelaide Festival, Feb–March
Adelaide Fringe, Feb–March
WOMADelaide, March
Adelaide Cabaret Festival, June
Feast Festival, Nov

HISTORIC PUBS
The Archer
The Austral
Exeter Hotel
Gilbert Street Hotel
Grace Emily Hotel

MARKETS
Adelaide Central Market
Adelaide Farmers' Market
Gilles at the Grounds
Plant 4 Bowden
Stirling Market

MUSEUMS
Art Gallery of South Australia
Bradman Collection at Adelaide Oval
Migration Museum
National Railway Museum
South Australian Maritime Museum
South Australian Museum

SHOPPING
King William Road
Melbourne Street, North Adelaide
Queen Street, Croydon
Rundle Mall
The Parade, Norwood

SOUTH AUSTRALIA

Daytrips from Adelaide/Tarndanya

ADELAIDE HILLS WINERIES
20min from Adelaide CBD

From Adelaide, drive 20min up the South Eastern Freeway into the Adelaide Hills, the crescent-shaped ridgeline embracing Adelaide's plains. These hills are technically the Mount Lofty Ranges – a smidge over 700m high, but lofty enough for perfect cool-climate grape-growing conditions.

Weave through the leafy roads and historic towns to discover some of South Australia's best wineries. The Lane Vineyard near Hahndorf has show-stopping views and fabulous food to accompany its top-flight chardonnay and sparkling white. Deviation Road winery bottles some serious shiraz and sauvignon blanc. Other big names like Shaw + Smith, Longview and Nepenthe will round out your wine-hued daytrip. See Hahndorf p. 218.

BIRDWOOD AND WOODSIDE
30min from Adelaide CBD

Visiting the Adelaide Hills is all about indulging in good food and wine. At Woodside, a 37km drive from Adelaide, you can get a good dose of each. The main lures are in the backblocks: Woodside Cheese Wrights and Melba's Chocolates are artisan producers where you can try before you buy. Also at Woodside are the Bird in Hand, Petaluma and Barristers Block winery cellar doors.

Nearby, historic Birdwood is famous for its cars. Every September, the Bay to Birdwood sees dozens of classic cars (and costumed crew) winding through the Adelaide Hills to the National Motor Museum – home to hundreds more rare cars and motorbikes. See Birdwood p. 217.

Top: Mount Lofty Estate
Middle: Spirit of Coorong
Bottom left: Bird in Hand cellar door **Bottom right:** Shopping in the German village of Hahndorf

GOOLWA AND COORONG NATIONAL PARK
1.5hr from Adelaide CBD

The Coorong is a salty system of lakes and lagoons where the mighty Murray River empties into the sea. Explore the national park wilds via camping and 4WD trips, or take a daytrip to Goolwa and access the Coorong on a scenic cruise.

In the 1870s Goolwa was a bustling river port, with dozens of paddleboats trading up and down the Murray all the way into New South Wales. These days this historic town, 82km south of Adelaide on the Fleurieu Peninsula, offers cafes, atmospheric old pubs, a riverside craft brewery and excellent boat trips on the river. *See* Goolwa p. 211.

ENCOUNTER COAST
1.5hr from Adelaide CBD

Around 83km south of Adelaide, the Fleurieu Peninsula's southern shores are known as the Encounter Coast – named after explorer Matthew Flinders's 1802 encounter here with Nicolas Baudin, a rival explorer from France. These days it is beaches, bikeways and wildlife that attract the visitors.

At Victor Harbor, check out the South Australian Whale Centre and the famous horse-drawn tram to Granite Island; at Port Elliot swim at gorgeous Horseshoe Bay. The easygoing Encounter Bikeway and heritage SteamRanger train (aka the Cockle Train) connect Victor Harbor to Goolwa, via Port Elliot. *See* Port Elliot p. 212, Victor Harbor p. 213.

MURRAY RIVER TOWNS
1.5hr from Adelaide CBD

At 2508km, the Murray River is certainly Australia's longest river. For much of this distance it bends and loops through South Australia, and supplies Adelaide with its drinking water. To see the 'Old Man River' up close, take a daytrip 76km east of Adelaide to the historic river towns of Mannum and Murray Bridge.

Murray Bridge is a large regional centre spread across the hillsides above the river. Down on the riverbanks you'll find grassy parklands (picnic lunch, anyone?) and riverboat cruises. Some 32km upstream is Mannum, a photogenic town with an endearing old pub or two, houseboats, river cruises, the Mannum Dock Museum of River History and the wide brown Murray slowly snaking past. *See* Mannum p. 237, Murray Bridge p. 238.

HAHNDORF
30min from Adelaide CBD

The Adelaide Hills town of Hahndorf, 25km south-east of Adelaide, is an alluring little hamlet soaked in history. Founded by pious Lutheran settlers from Prussia in 1839, the town proudly shows its Germanic roots along the main street where old stone pubs serve frothy steins of Löwenbräu beer.

But Hahndorf is not all beery good times – it's also a super place for lunch, with some brilliant cafes and internationally flavoured eateries. Daytrippers from Adelaide settle in for a long lazy lunch, followed by a slow-paced promenade, ice-cream in hand, ducking into galleries and craft shops along the way. There are some lovely winery cellar doors nearby too. *See* Hahndorf p. 218.

SOUTHERN BEACHES
45min from Adelaide CBD

Feel like a beach break? Tracking south of the city along the eastern shore of the gleaming Gulf St Vincent, Adelaide's southern beaches make for a stress-free daytrip. You can swim, fish, beachcomb or just sit on the sand with a good book, a cold drink and a picnic.

Adelaide's city beaches are great for a swim but there's not much surf here (Kangaroo Island to the south cuts off the ocean swell). Aldinga Beach is good for fishing; Maslin Beach is 'clothing optional'; and Port Willunga Beach is the prettiest of the lot, with impressive cliffs, safe swimming, a cliff-top cafe and a handsome swathe of yellow sand.

PORT ADELAIDE
30min from Adelaide CBD

Just 14km north-west of the CBD, Port Adelaide is technically a suburb of Adelaide. But this endearing enclave of historic buildings, museums and raffish pubs makes an interesting daytrip from the big smoke – especially if the adored local AFL football team, Port Power, has had a win on the weekend!

The Port Adelaide Visitor Centre has information on dolphin-spotting cruises, walking tours and kayaking trips around the Port River's mangroves and shipwrecks. The South Australian Maritime Museum offers lots of salty history, and the excellent National Railway Museum is just up the road.

Top: Port Willunga **Second from top:** Coorong National Park **Second from bottom:** Granite Island **Bottom:** Port Elliot Beach

Regions of South Australia

❶ FLEURIEU PENINSULA AND KANGAROO ISLAND P. 208

Aldinga Beach
Goolwa
Kingscote
   (Kangaroo Island) ★
McLaren Vale
Port Elliot
Strathalbyn
Victor Harbor ★
Willunga
Yankalilla

❷ ADELAIDE HILLS AND BAROSSA VALLEY P. 214

Angaston
Birdwood
Gawler
Hahndorf ★
Lyndoch
Nuriootpa
Tanunda

❸ CLARE VALLEY AND MID-NORTH P. 220

Balaklava
Burra
Clare ★
Jamestown
Kapunda
Mintaro
Peterborough

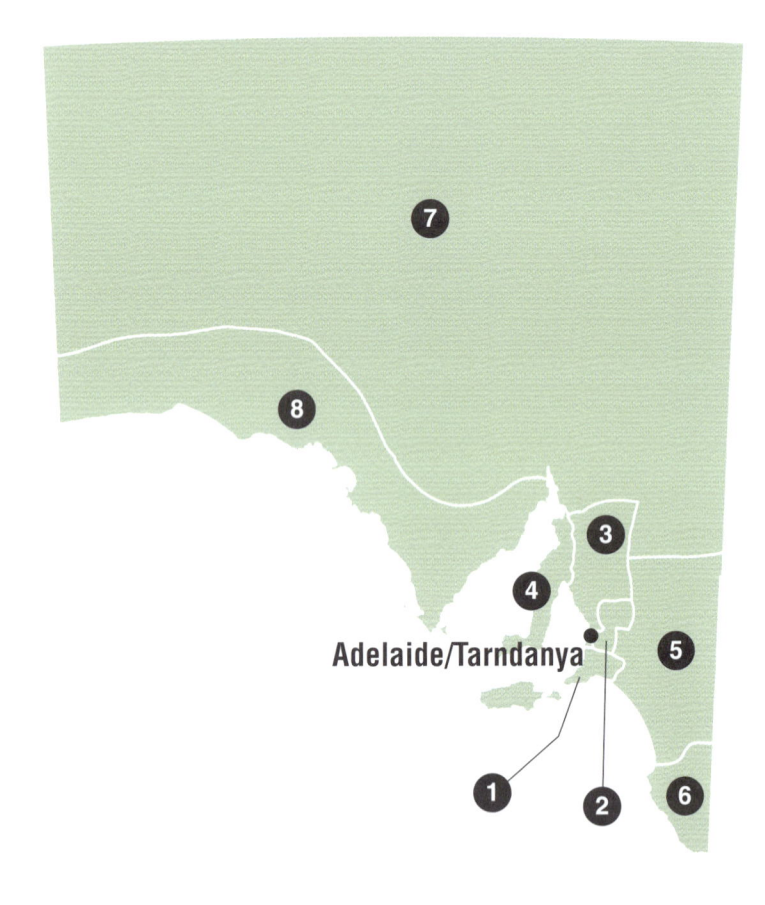

Adelaide/Tarndanya

❹ YORKE PENINSULA P. 226

Ardrossan
Crystal Brook
Edithburgh
Kadina
Maitland
Minlaton
Moonta
Port Broughton
Port Pirie
Port Victoria
Stansbury
Wallaroo
Yorketown

❺ THE MURRAY P. 232

Barmera
Berri
Bordertown
Keith
Loxton
Mannum
Meningie
Morgan
Murray Bridge
Pinnaroo
Renmark ★
Swan Reach
Waikerie

❻ LIMESTONE COAST P. 240

Beachport
Kingston S.E.
Millicent
Mount Gambier ★
Naracoorte
Penola
Port MacDonnell
Robe ★

❼ FLINDERS RANGES AND OUTBACK P. 246

Andamooka
Arkaroola ★
Blinman
Coober Pedy ★
Hawker
Innamincka
Marree
Melrose
Oodnadatta
Port Augusta
Quorn
Roxby Downs
Wilmington
Wilpena ★
Woomera

❽ EYRE PENINSULA AND NULLARBOR P. 256

Ceduna
Coffin Bay
Cowell
Elliston
Kimba
Port Lincoln ★
Streaky Bay
Tumby Bay
Whyalla
Wudinna

Top: Driving into Wilpena Pound Resort, Flinders Ranges **Bottom:** Sellicks Beach, Fleurieu Peninsula **Opposite:** Yalumba, Barossa Valley

SOUTH AUSTRALIA

207

Fleurieu Peninsula and Kangaroo Island

Jutting into the sea south of Adelaide, the Fleurieu Peninsula is prime holiday territory for Adelaide locals, with **beaches, a burgeoning foodie culture and the seductive McLaren Vale wine region**. A 20km ferry ride offshore, vast **Kangaroo Island (aka 'KI') offers wilderness, wildlife and beachy isolation** (and more wineries if you're still in the mood).

Top: Feeding pelicans at Kingscote in Kangaroo Island
Opposite: Granite Island, near Victor Harbor

CHEAT SHEET

→ Give yourself two or three days to explore the Fleurieu Peninsula, with another three (minimum) on Kangaroo Island.

→ Best time to visit: the Fleurieu Peninsula is a summery beach destination, but the McLaren Vale wine region is at its most atmospheric during the autumn harvest, when the vine leaves change colour. Visit Kangaroo Island during summer when the attractions keep longer hours, or winter to have the place all to yourself.

→ Main towns: Kingscote (see p. 211), McLaren Vale (see p. 212), Willunga (see p. 213).

→ The Fleurieu Peninsula is the Traditional Lands of the Kaurna, Ngarridjeri and Peramanguk Peoples.

→ Did you know? Kaurna Miyurna, Ngarrindjeri, Ramindjeri and Barngalla People were the first to live on Kangaroo Island about 65,000 years ago, when it was still attached to the mainland. The island's traditional name, Karta Pintingga, or 'Island of the Dead', comes from a Ngarrindjeri Creation story.

→ Don't miss: McLaren Vale wine region; Willunga Farmers' Market; Seal Bay; Remarkable Rocks; Admirals Arch.

TOP ATTRACTIONS

COCKLE TRAIN: The oldest steel-railed railway in Australia (since 1887) travels around Encounter Bay from Goolwa Wharf (see p. 211) to Victor Harbor (see p. 213), stopping at Port Elliot (see p. 212). It forms part of the longer SteamRanger tourist railway from Mount Barker (see Hahndorf, p. 218); operates Sun, Wed and public/school holidays; bookings (08) 8263 5621 or 1300 655 991.

D'ARENBERG CUBE: A $15 million five-storey architectural showpiece inspired by a Rubik's Cube with tasting rooms, art installations, a wine inhalation room – also known as the 'wine fog room' – wine museum, and two virtual fermenters as well as degustation-dining restaurant, in addition to the popular **d'Arry's Verandah Restaurant** in the neighbouring 19th-century homestead; 58 Osborn Rd, McLaren Vale; (08) 8329 4888.

DEEP CREEK NATIONAL PARK: Deep Creek was previously a conservation park, but declared a national park in 2021. Take one of the many walks along rugged coastal cliffs, tranquil creeks, majestic forests and scenic waterfalls. Walks range from easy and short to more challenging long-distance hikes. Keep an eye out for the western grey kangaroos at dusk on the Aaron Creek Hiking Trail or drop a line at Blowhole Creek and Boat Harbour beaches. The park can be accessed 26km south-west of Yankalilla (see p. 213).

ENCOUNTER BIKEWAY: Scenic coastal route between Goolwa (see p. 211) and and The Bluff (Rosetta Head).

FLEURIEU WINE REGION: With vineyards covering just about every other part of the Fleurieu Peninsula, including McLaren Vale and Langhorne Creek, it is not surprising that they eventually crept south. This is a region to watch, with a climate conducive to vines and some high-quality wines already being produced.

FLINDERS CHASE NATIONAL PARK: Occupying Kangaroo Island's western end, this vast park protects hundreds of square kilometres of forest and isolated coastline – gradually recovering from the 2020 bushfires which razed much of the park's beautiful bushland. Unaffected by the fires, one of the park's most popular features is the precariously balanced pile of granite boulders called the **Remarkable Rocks**, which are gradually being eroded by wind and sea to form amazing globular shapes. Nearby is the **Cape du Couedic Lighthouse** (1909), and a colony of New Zealand fur seals that you can eyeball from the boardwalk above **Admirals Arch**, a sea cave with the waves surging in.

GRANITE ISLAND RECREATION PARK: Victor Harbor's Granite Island has a long and varied history. The island, known as Kaiki, is part of the local Ramindjeri Nation's landscape. The male Creator Ngurunderi created the island by throwing a spear into the sea, so it has always been of great importance to this community. In 1837 a whaling station was established on the island and today it is a recreation park. This history is detailed on the Kaiki Trail, a 1.5km walk around the island. You may also be lucky enough to see one of the resident little penguins, although sadly their population numbers have declined sharply in the past few years. Another highlight is the **Oceanic Victor** underwater aquarium, which also offers swim-with-tuna encounters and tours daily; (08) 8552-7137. The island is linked to the mainland by a 630m causeway – check ahead that it's open as it was being renovated at the time of research (Oceanic Victor is also closed while this renovation continues). Walk or take the horse-drawn tram, the last one remaining in the Southern Hemisphere; tram departs from entrance to the causeway at 10.30am daily. Tickets available at visitor centre or on the tram.

KANGAROO ISLAND WINES: Make sure to take home a bottle or two of local wine. Around eight vineyards are scattered across the eastern side of the island, although only a few have cellar doors. The pick of the bunch is **Dudley Wines**, with its architecturally sassy cellar door perched over a steeply sloping section of coastline on the Dudley Peninsula (12km E of Penneshaw). It's a super spot for lunch and a bottle of chilled chardonnay. Open 10.30am–4.30pm Mon–Sun; 1153 Cape Willoughby Rd, Cuttlefish Bay.

LANGHORNE CREEK WINE REGION: This productive area lies to the east of McLaren Vale on the floodplains of the Bremer and Angas rivers. Langhorne Creek boasts the oldest recorded cabernet sauvignon vines in the world and families that have been making wine for over five generations. The wines produced have an endearing softness as well as depth of flavour and are highly awarded. **Bleasdale Vineyards** dates back to 1850 and its wines are the classic Langhorne Creek label sold at reasonable prices. **Zonte's Footstep** also has good, value-for-money wines. Other wineries to visit in the area include **Lake Breeze Wines** and **Temple Bruer**, which is certified organic.

MCLAREN VALE WINE REGION: In this world-class wine region, shiraz is the drop of choice, although the grenache, chardonnay and sauvignon blanc are also very respectable. **Coriole** bottles wonderful shiraz as well as olive oil, while the wines at hilltop d'Arenberg are as good as the views from the top of the **d'Arenberg Cube** (see above). Other top McLaren Vale wineries include **S.C. Pannell**, **Paxton**, **Wirra Wirra** and **Hardys Tintara**. Pick up a cellar-door map from the McLaren Vale visitor centre (see p. 212), nominate someone else to drive and get tasting. For gin lovers, **Never Never Distilling Co.** is one of the area's best distilleries.

SEAL BAY CONSERVATION PARK: This park on Kangaroo Island protects a colony of Australian sea lions, a species that faced extinction on the SA coast during the 1800s. Guided beach tours provide close-up encounters with the snoozing beasts. There are also views down to the beach from the 400m boardwalk that runs through dunes to an observation deck. Additional tours run on summer evenings. Open 9am–4pm; Seal Bay Rd, Kanagaroo Island; (08) 8553 4463.

SOUTH AUSTRALIAN WHALE CENTRE: This unique centre in Victor Harbor (see p. 213) focuses on the 25 species of whale and dolphin and other marine life found in southern Australian waters, with the aim of educating and conservation. Past atrocities, from when Granite Island had a whaling station, are displayed alongside interactive displays and presentations that reveal the wonders of the amazing creatures. Between May and Oct, southern right whales mate and breed in Encounter Bay. The centre offers **whale cruises** and sighting information, as well as a hotline for the latest sightings (in season). At the time of writing, the centre was closed for major renovations. Railway Tce, Victor Harbor; (08) 8551 0750.

OTHER ATTRACTIONS

HINDMARSH ISLAND: Captain Sturt located the mouth of the Murray River from here in 1830 – visit the Captain Sturt Lookout and monument. The island is popular for both freshwater and saltwater fishing. The island is 5km east of Goolwa (see p. 211).

MILANG: This old riverboat town on the shores of Lake Alexandrina, South Australia's largest freshwater lake, is now a popular holiday destination. The lake offers fishing, sailing and windsurfing. In town, visit the Port Milang Railway for its local history display and pick up a Heritage Trail brochure for a self-guided walk. Each Australia Day weekend the Milang–Goolwa Freshwater Classic fills the town with visitors who come to watch hundreds of yachts begin the race.

ONKAPARINGA RIVER NATIONAL PARK: SA's second-longest river (after the mighty Murray) winds through valleys and steep rocky gorges to Gulf St Vincent. Walks in Onkaparinga Gorge are impressive but very steep; there are more easy-going trails on the northern side of the gorge. The estuary section of the park is an altogether different environment – wide and open-skied – best explored in a kayak or along the 5km interpretive trail. Keep an eye out for native birds and the 27 species of native orchids found here. Access via Main South Rd, Old Noarlunga; (08) 8278 5477.

STAR OF GREECE: In 1888 the *Star of Greece* plunged to the ocean floor in a wild storm. The ship was only a short distance from land, but at 3am, and in gigantic swells, 17 of the 28 people on board drowned. Today a portion of the vessel can be seen from shore at low tide. A plaque lies on the seabed for the benefit of divers, but for those wanting to stay dry, pictures of the wreck line the walls of the Star of Greece fine-dining restaurant. Port Willunga.

Top: Little Sahara, Kangaroo Island **Middle:** Wilunga Markets **Bottom:** Town of Kingscote

VISITOR INFORMATION

Kangaroo Island Gateway Visitor Information Centre
3 Howard Dr, Penneshaw
(08) 8553 1185 or
1800 811 080
tourkangarooisland.com.au

McLaren Vale and Fleurieu Visitor Centre
796 Main Rd, McLaren Vale
(08) 8323 9944 or
1800 628 410
mclarenvale.info

TOP EVENTS

- JAN Regatta Week (Goowla)
- FEB Fleurieu Film Festival (McLaren Vale)
- APR Festival Fleurieu (odd-numbered years, across the region); Wooden Boat Festival (odd-numbered years, Goolwa); Glenbarr Highland Gathering (Strathalbyn)
- JULY Almond Blossom Festival (Willunga)
- AUG Collectors, Hobbies and Antique Fair (Strathalbyn)
- SEPT Rock 'n' Roll Festival (Victor Harbor)
- OCT Fleurieu Folk Festival (Wilunga)

TEMPERATURES

Jan: 15–23°C

July: 8–15°C

KEY TOWNS

ALDINGA BEACH
Population 10,667

The rolling hills of the southern Mount Lofty Ranges form the backdrop to Aldinga Beach, a long curve of white sand facing Gulf St Vincent. About 1.5km off the coast is one of the state's best diving spots – the Aldinga Drop Off, an underwater cliff where divers say the marine life has to be seen to be believed. The township – to the west of the original Aldinga, which grew as a small farming centre in the mid-1800s – is a popular holiday spot.

SEE & DO **Star of Greece:** *see* Other Attractions. **Aldinga Beach:** the main attraction here is the beach itself: a wide, sandy swimming beach where you can launch a boat; The Espl. **Aldinga Scrub Conservation Park:** walk through remnant coastal vegetation; the park is ablaze with colourful wildflowers in spring; end of Dover St, off Aldinga Beach Rd; 1km S. **Aldinga:** Uniting Church cemetery has the graves of those who died in the *Star of Greece* shipwreck; 4km NE. **Beaches:** many north and south of Aldinga Beach including Port Willunga Beach, with the remains of an old jetty and caves built in the cliff by anglers (3km N); Sellicks Beach, with boat access and good fishing (8km S); and Maslin Beach, Australia's first official nudist beach (10km N). **Lookouts:** one south of Sellicks Beach (11km S) and another over the Myponga Reservoir (23km S).

GOOLWA
Population 8756

Goolwa is a rapidly growing holiday town on the last big bend of the Murray River before it reaches open waters. In 2007 Goolwa became the first town in Australia to be declared a Cittaslow, or 'slow town' – joining a network of towns in Europe and throughout the world which aim to improve the quality of life in towns. Goolwa was originally surveyed as the capital of SA, but Adelaide was later thought to be a better option. Goolwa did, however, boom as a river port from the 1850s to the 1880s, in the golden days of the riverboats. The area is excellent for fishing – freshwater in the Murray and saltwater in the Southern Ocean and the Coorong – as well as boating, surfing, watersports, birdwatching and photography.

SEE & DO **Cockle Train; Encounter Bikeway:** *see* Top Attractions for both. **National Trust Museum:** documents the history of Goolwa and early navigation of the Murray River; open Tues–Thurs and Sat–Sun 2–4pm; 11 Porter St; (08) 8555 2221. **South Coast Regional Arts Centre:** explore the restored old court and police station and see exhibitions by local artists; open Mon–Fri 9am–5pm; 1 Goolwa Tce; (08) 8555 7289. **Goolwa Beach and Boardwalk:** popular surfing and swimming beach with large cockles (kuti in Ngarrindjeri language) to be dug up (in season); end of Beach Rd. **Steam Exchange Brewery:** taste some locally brewed beers down on the riverfront; open Wed–Sun 11.30am–4.30pm; Goolwa Wharf; (08) 8555 3406. **Goolwa Barrages:** desalination barrier preventing salt water from reaching the Murray River and lower lakes; Barrage Rd. **Armfield Slipway:** a working exhibition of wooden boatbuilding and restoration; open Tues and Fri 9am–4pm; Barrage Rd. **River Dolls of Goolwa:** largest private collection of dolls on display in South Australia, plus a lolly shop; open Wed–Mon 11am–5pm, Tues 1–5pm; 33 Cadell St; 0447 988 084. **Cruises:** day tours to the mouth of the Murray, the Coorong, the Barrages and lower lakes; details and bookings at visitor centre. **Goolwa Heritage Walk:** brochure available from visitor centre. **Goolwa Wharf Markets:** Jaralde Park; 1st and 3rd Sun of each month. **Kuti Shack:** among the sandhills of Goolwa Beach, serves dishes that use local ingredients and heroes the pipi (kuti). **Currency Creek Game Reserve:** feeding grounds, breeding rookeries and hides for many waterbirds; access by boat only; 3km E. **Currency Creek:** Lions Park is a popular picnic spot with a walking track along the creek. Near town is a First Nations canoe tree (a eucalypt carved to make a canoe) and also the **One Paddock Currency Creek Winery** with a restaurant and a 3km wetlands walking trail; winery open Thurs–Sun 11am–4pm; 291 Winery Rd, Currency Creek; (08) 8555 4069; 7km N.

★ KINGSCOTE (KANGAROO ISLAND)
Population 1915

In the early days of Australia's European settlement, Kangaroo Island was a haven for some of the country's most unsavoury characters – escaped convicts and deserters from English and American whaleboats. These men formed gangs, and hunted more than their fair share of whales, seals, kangaroos, wallabies and possums. They also went on raids to the mainland (and as far afield as Tasmania) to kidnap Aboriginal women and children. It was a lawless place. Two centuries on, the main ruggedness here is along the island's south coast, where the surf surges in from the Southern Ocean and the seals are now left in peace. The north shore is a rippling line of bays and coves, with grassy hills arcing down into Investigator Strait. On the shores of Nepean Bay is Kingscote, the island's biggest town and the state's first official settlement (1836). If not for a lack of fresh water, Kingscote, not Adelaide, might have become the SA capital! The breezy town has all you'll need to set up base for a few days: pubs, restaurants, banks, a supermarket and a petrol station.

SEE & DO **Seal Bay Conservation Park; Flinders Chase National Park:** see Top Attractions for both. **Island Beehive:** tour the honey factory or just enjoy some honeycomb ice-cream and buy a pot of honey to take home; 59 Playford Hwy; (08) 8553 0080. **Hope Cottage Museum:** National Trust museum in an 1859 cottage, exploring the town's long colonial and maritime history with rooms crammed with memorabilia; open 1–4pm; Centenary Ave; (08) 8553 2656. **Kangaroo Island Gallery:** central gallery selling beautiful local artworks from ceramics and glassworks to paintings and jewellery; open 10am–5pm; 1 Murray St; (08) 8553 2868. **Fine Art Kangaroo Island:** traditional and contemporary artworks get an airing in two renovated heritage buildings in the main retail precinct; open Wed–Sat 10am–5pm; 91 Dauncey St; 0417 832 037. **St Alban's Church:** check out the impressive stained-glass windows and early settler memorials at this modest little church; open 9am–4pm; cnr Drew and Osmond sts; (08) 8553 2065. **Pioneer Historical Cemetery:** SA's oldest cemetery contains the remains of early settlers dating back to 1836; Reeves Point, off Seaview Rd; (08) 8553 4500. **Fishing:** Kingscote jetty is a hot spot for anglers; off Anzac Dr. **Farmers' Market:** 1st Sun of the month in Penneshaw. **Kangaroo Island Spirits:** 'KIS' is a local gin maker (as well as liqueurs and vodka), creatively using interesting local ingredients; open Wed–Mon 11am–5.30pm; 856 Playford Hwy, Cygnet River; (08) 8553 9211. **Emu Bay:** the closest swimming beach to Kingscote, with fishing from the jetty; North Coast Rd; 17km NW. **Emu Ridge Eucalyptus Oil Distillery:** production and sales of super-scented eucalyptus-oil products; open 9am–4pm; Wilsons Rd, off South Coast Rd; (08) 8553 8228; 20km S. **Clifford's Honey Farm:** sales and free tastings of Kangaroo Island's unique honey, produced by a pure strain of local Ligurian bees; 1157 Elsegood Rd, Haines; (08) 8553 8295; 30km S. **Prospect Hill Lookout:** grab some stunning sea and island views from the spot where Matthew Flinders surveyed Kangaroo Island; Hog Bay Rd, between American River and Penneshaw; 35km SE. **American River:** a low-key fishing village overlooking the sheltered spans of Eastern Cove and Pelican Lagoon, both havens for birdlife. It was named after a crew of American shipbuilders who built a boat here in the early 1800s; 40km SE. **Stokes Bay:** a natural rock tunnel leads to a rockpool, perfect for swimming (especially with kids). There's a beachy cafe here too; North Coast Rd; 50km W. **Little Sahara:** hulking sand dunes surrounded by bush; you can hire sandboards here and hurtle down the sandy slopes; South Coast Rd; 55km SW. **Penneshaw:** a buzzy little town on the Dudley Peninsula where the ferry arrives from Cape Jervis on the mainland. Town highlights include a National Trust maritime museum, monthly farmers' market, and a beaut pub with water views; 60km E. **Vivonne Bay:** popular beach for surfing and fishing (beware the undertow – swim safely near the jetty, boat ramp and in Harriet River); South Coast Rd; 63km SW. **Antechamber Bay:** photogenic beach area, excellent for bushwalking, camping, swimming and beach and river fishing (whiting and bream); 72km SE. **Hanson Bay Wildlife Sanctuary:** this privately-owned wildlife sanctuary, famous for its koala spotting opportunities, was all but destroyed in the 2020 fires, but tours resumed in September 2022 and it remains one of the best places to see koalas on the island. 7797 South Coast Rd, Karatta; (08) 8559 7344; 94km SW. **Scott Cove:** from here you can view the highest coastal cliffs in the state, rising a rather amazing 263m from the sea; off Playford Hwy, near Cape Borda; 100km W. **Cape Borda Lightstation:** although the surrounding bushland was razed in the fires, the historic lighthouse, built in 1858, was spared and is open for pre-booked self-guided tours; book online at parks.sa.gov.au/parks/cape-borda-lightstation; Playford Hwy, Flinders Chase National Park; (08) 8553 4465; 105km W.

MCLAREN VALE
Population 3277

Where the vines meet the sea, McLaren Vale is a world-class wine region and its vines are interlaced with orchards and gourmet-produce farms. If you need non-liquid sustenance, there are some quality eateries along the town's main street. Visit in autumn when the vines turn russet red, or late winter when the almond blossoms are blushing pink.

SEE & DO **D'arenberg Cube; Mclaren Vale Wine Region:** see Top Attractions for both. **Onkaparinga River National Park:** see Other Attractions. **McLaren Vale and Fleurieu Visitor Information Centre:** the complete package: landscaped grounds, vine rows, art exhibitions, local craft and produce and a cafe; open Mon–Fri 9am–5pm, Sat–Sun 10am–4pm; 796 Main Rd; (08) 8323 9944. **Shiraz Trail:** 8km walking and cycling track from McLaren Vale visitor centre through the vines to nearby Willunga; map from visitor centre. Part of the longer (37km) Coast to Vines Rail Trail from Marino Rocks to Willunga. **Lloyd Brothers Wine and Olive Company:** grows over 26 varieties of olives, packaging them up into all manner and description, plus arts, crafts and gourmet produce; open 11am–5pm; 69 Warners Rd; (08) 8323 8792. **The Menz FruChocs Shop:** SA-produced fruity chocolates; open 10am–5pm; 203 Main Rd; (08) 8323 9105. **Goodieson Brewery:** low-key, family-run brewery among the grape vines; open 11am–5pm; 194 Sand Rd; 0409 676 542. **Willunga Farmers' Market:** Willunga Town Square; Sat. **Gulf St Vincent beaches:** safe swimming beaches include Port Willunga, O'Sullivan, Christies, Maslin (clothing optional) and Moana; 7km W. **Old Noarlunga:** self-guided tour of historic colonial buildings; brochure available from visitor centre. Walks into Onkaparinga National Park kick off from here; 7km NW. **Port Noarlunga Reef Underwater Trail:** marked underwater trail along the reef for curious divers and snorkellers; Port Noarlunga jetty, The Espl; 11km NW.

PORT ELLIOT
Population 2251

Port Elliot is a charming historic town set on scenic Horseshoe Bay. Its popularity as a holiday destination lies in the fabulous beaches and the relaxed coastal atmosphere. The town was established in 1854, the year Australia's first public (horse-drawn) railway began operating between Goolwa and the town. Port Elliot's intended purpose as an ocean port for the Murray River was, however, unsuccessful. The bay proved less protected than was first thought and the port was moved to Victor Harbor.

SEE & DO **Cockle Train:** see Top Attractions. **National Trust Historical Display:** interpretive centre in the old railway station detailing local history; The Strand. **The Strand:** historic street of art and craft shops, cafes and restaurants, with local institution Port Elliot Bakery around the corner on North Terrace. **Freeman Nob:** ocean views and coastal walks; end of the Strand. **Horseshoe Bay:** safe family beach with fishing from jetty. **Boomer Beach:** popular surfing beach; western edge of town. **Maritime Heritage Trail:** the town's story illustrated in foreshore displays. **Heritage walk:** brochure from railway station. **Market:** Lakala Reserve; 1st and 3rd Sat each month. **Basham Beach Regional Park:** scenic coastal trails with interpretive signage and southern right whale sightings during their migration season, June–Sept; just north-east of Port Elliot. **Middleton:** coastal town with old flour mill and fabulous beaches; 3km NE. **Crows Nest Lookout:** excellent views of the coast; 6km N.

STRATHALBYN
Population 6429

This heritage town has some of the most picturesque and historic streetscapes in country SA and is renowned for its beautiful gardens, historic buildings and antique shops. It has a predominantly Scottish heritage, first settled by Dr John Rankine, who emigrated with other Scotsmen in the late 1830s. The town is set on the Angas River, with the Soldiers Memorial Gardens following the watercourse through the town.

SEE & DO **National Trust Museum:** history display in the courtroom, Victorian-era relics in the courthouse, and a historical room and photographic displays in the Old Police Station; open Tues–Thurs and Sat–Sun 1.30–4pm; Rankine St. **Old Railway Station:** includes the visitor centre, the Stationmaster's Art Gallery and the station for the tourist railway from Mount Barker, the *SteamRanger* (see Hahndorf, p. 218); South Tce. **St Andrew's Church:** impressive church with castle-like tower; Alfred Pl. **Original Lolly Shop:** old-fashioned lollies and fudge; High St. **Antiques, art and craft shops:** outlets in High St. **Heritage walk:** self-guided trail featuring over 30 heritage buildings and the architectural delights of Albyn Tce; brochure available from visitor centre. **Lookout:** views over town and district; 7km SW. **Ashbourne:** buy local produce at roadside stalls; 14km W.

★ VICTOR HARBOR
Population 16,709

Today Victor Harbor is a popular holiday town and Granite Island a recreation park, but in the 1830s the crystal waters of Encounter Bay – and the Southern Ocean beyond – throbbed with whalers and sealers and Granite Island housed a whaling station. The naming of Encounter Bay comes from the unexpected meeting in the bay between early explorers Matthew Flinders and Nicolas Baudin.

SEE & DO **Cockle Train; Granite Island Recreation Park; South Australian Whale Centre:** see Top Attractions for all. **Victor Harbor National Trust Museum:** National Trust museum that covers First Nations, whaling, settler and recent local history. A museum walk finishes at the Old Customs House, which has period furnishings; open 11am–3pm; Flinders Pde. **Hindmarsh River Estuary:** peaceful picnic and fishing spot with boardwalk through coastal scrub; 1km NE. **Urimbirra Wildlife Park:** popular fauna park with a wetland bird sanctuary, crocodile-feeding and children's farmyard; Adelaide Rd; 5km N. **Big Duck Boat Tours:** spectacular 45min and 90min tours taking in Encounter Bay and coastal parts of Victor Harbor. Leaves from Granite Island causeway; (08) 8555 2203. **Nangawooka Flora Reserve:** tranquil walks through native bushland with over 1250 native plant varieties on show; opposite Urimbirra Wildlife Park. **The Bluff (Rosetta Head):** 500-million-year-old mass of granite, well worth the 100m climb for the views; 5km SW. **Newland Head Conservation Park:** known for its wild surf and coastal vegetation, this park protects the headland and Waitpinga and Parsons beaches, which offer surf-fishing opportunities and beach walks; turn-off 15km SW. **Hindmarsh Falls:** pleasant walks and spectacular waterfall (during winter); 15km NW. **Mount Billy Conservation Park:** mallee and forest park renowned for its rare orchid species; 18km NW. **Inman Valley:** features Glacier Rock, said to be the first recorded discovery of glaciation in Australia; 19km NW.

WILLUNGA
Population 2300

This historic town sits at the southern edge of the McLaren Vale wine region and is surrounded by farmlands and olive groves. The town grew rapidly around the slate quarries, which drove the town's economy until the late 1800s. Fortunately, by that time Willunga already had a thriving new industry – almonds. Its name is derived from a First Nations word 'willa-unga', meaning 'the place of green trees'. The weekly Saturday farmers' market is one of the state's best.

SEE & DO **Fleurieu Wine Region:** see Top Attractions. **Courthouse Museum:** National Trust museum with local history displays in the original 1855 courtroom, cells and stables; guided 'Willunga Walks and Talks' tours; open 2nd Sun of the month 1pm–4pm; High St; (08) 8556 2195. **Quarry:** operated for 60 years (1842–1902), now a National Trust site; Delabole Rd. **Historical walk:** self-guided walk featuring historic pug cottages, colonial architecture and an Anglican church with an Elizabethan bronze bell; brochure from museum. **Farmers' market:** Hill St; Sat mornings. **Quarry Market:** country market with local produce and crafts; Aldinga Rd; 2nd Sat each month. **Mount Magnificent Conservation Park:** explore virtually untouched rocky landscapes and vegetation popular for picnics and scenic walks. The highlight is the walk to the Mount Magnificent summit for coastal views; 12km SE. **Mount Compass:** a small farming town featuring the Wetlands Boardwalk. Many farms open for viewing and sales, offering both primary products and gourmet food; 14km S. **Kyeema Conservation Park:** completely burnt out in the 1983 Ash Wednesday fires and then again in the fires of 1994 and 2001, this park is evidence of nature's ability to constantly regenerate. It is home to over 70 species of birdlife and offers good hiking and camping. Part of the Heysen Trail passes through it; 14km NE.

YANKALILLA
Population 795

Since the first land grant in 1842, Yankalilla has been the centre of a thriving farming industry. It is a growing settlement just inland from the west coast of the Fleurieu Peninsula, but it still retains its old country flavour. It has even adopted the slogan 'Yankalilla Bay – you'll love what we haven't done to the place'.

SEE & DO **Deep Creek National Park:** see Top Attractions. **Historical Museum:** local history and interpretive trail; open Mon–Fri 9am–4pm, Sat–Sun and public holidays 10am–4pm; Main South Rd. **Anglican Church:** historic and known for an apparition of the Blessed Virgin Mary at Our Lady of Yankalilla Shrine, first sighted here in 1996; Main St. **Normanville:** a seaside town with beach and heritage-listed sand dunes. Shipwrecks are popular with divers; 3km W. **Myponga Conservation Park:** popular bushwalking and birdwatching park; 9km NE. **Myponga:** a historic town with fantastic views from the Myponga Reservoir; 14km NE. **Second Valley:** a peaceful picnic spot with a jetty for fishing; 17km SW. **Rapid Bay:** this seaside town offers excellent fishing and diving opportunities. Sightings of the endangered leafy sea dragon in the bay make diving a must for any enthusiast; 27km SW. **Talisker Conservation Park:** an interpretive trail explains the old silver-mine workings in the park; 30km SW. **Cape Jervis:** breathtaking sea and coastal views on entering town. Vehicular ferries to Kangaroo Island depart from here, and it is also the starting point of the 1200km Heysen Trail (bushwalking trail) to the Flinders Ranges. Morgan's and Fishery beaches nearby have good fishing; 35km S.

Adelaide Hills and Barossa Valley

South Australia is flush with wine regions including the cool-climate wineries of the Adelaide Hills – but the most celebrated of them all is the Barossa Valley, **one of the oldest and most productive grape-growing areas** in Australia. Alongside **myriad cellar doors**, you'll find **picturesque towns**, **superb eateries**, **accessible wilderness** and **German heritage**. These regions hold great cultural heritage and significance for Peramangk, Ngadjuri and Kaurna Nations, each with distinct cultural expressions which connect community and people to place, flora and fauna.

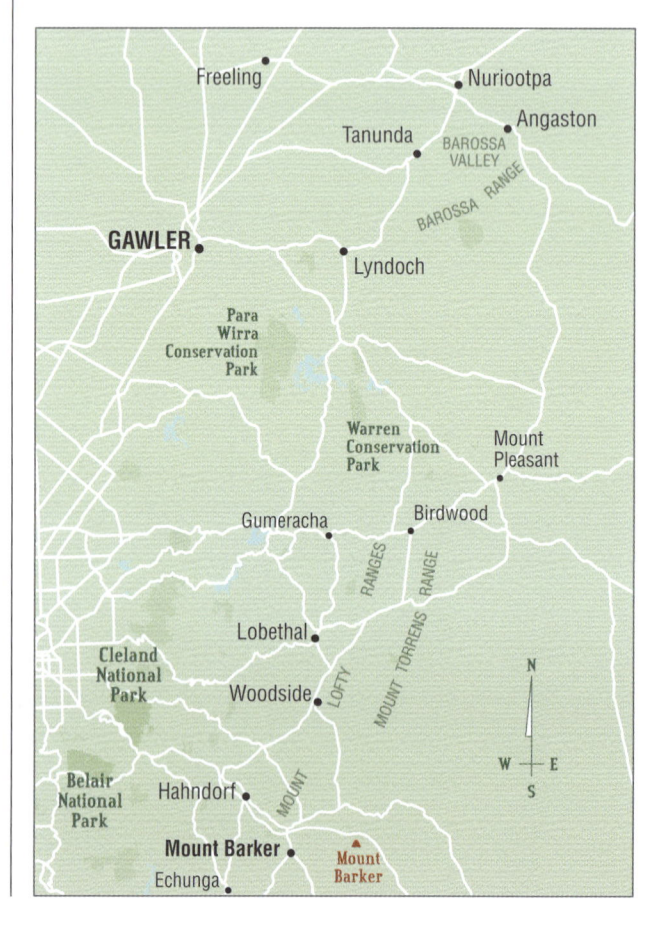

CHEAT SHEET

→ Give yourself three or four days to explore.

→ Best time to visit: time your trip to coincide with one of the Barossa's big-ticket events – the biennial Barossa Vintage Weekend in April is a favourite. Or arrive in autumn when the vine leaves change from green to vermilion.

→ Main towns: Angaston (*see* p. 217), Hahndorf (*see* p. 218), Nuriootpa (*see* p. 219), Tanunda (*see* p. 219).

→ The Peramangk and Ngadjuri Peoples are the Traditional Owners of this region.

→ Did you know? Cool-climate wines such as chardonnay, pinot noir and sparkling are the specialty of the Adelaide Hills, while the Barossa is all about big, beefy red wines. If you're more of a white wine fan, detour an hour north to the compact Clare Valley, where riesling reigns supreme.

→ Don't miss: Barossa Valley wineries; Barossa Farmers' Market; wining and dining in Angaston and Tanunda; German beer, wursts and pretzels in Hahndorf; Hans Heysen's home and studio, also in Hahndorf; the National Motor Museum in Birdwood.

Top: Biking in the Barossa
Opposite: Yalumba, Barossa Valley

TOP ATTRACTIONS

BEERENBERG STRAWBERRY FARM: This family-run farm in Hahndorf (*see* p. 218) has been here for generations, with rutted rows of strawberries lining the surrounding hillsides. Inside you can buy all sorts of jams and condiments, or head into the fields and pick your own punnet. Open 9am–5pm (picking Nov–May); 1 Mount Barker Rd, Hahndorf; (08) 8388 7272.

BELAIR NATIONAL PARK: The Traditional Owners are the Kaurna People who know the park's area as 'Piradli', meaning 'baldness', which refers to the area's appearance when looking south from the Adelaide Plains – 'bald like the moon'. Aboriginal peoples continue to play an active role in caring for their Country, including in parks across South Australia. This is the first national park in SA (1891) and is right in Adelaide's south-eastern suburbs, protecting a compact, forested valley. Things to see and do include well-defined bushwalking trails for all levels of fitness, cycling and horseriding tracks, tennis courts and picnic areas. You'll find the estimable **Old Government House** here, built in 1859 to serve as the governor's summer residence; open 1st and 3rd Sun each month and on some public holidays 1–4pm; Upper Sturt Rd, Belair; (08) 8278 5477. The park can be accessed 19km west of Hahndorf (*see* p. 218).

CLELAND NATIONAL PARK: Cleland was previously a conservation park, but declared a national park in 2021. This leafy park on the steep slopes of Mount Lofty protects stringybark forest highlands, grassy lowlands, waterfalls and walking trails – the uppermost of which rewards the hiker with panoramic city views from Mount Lofty Summit. **Cleland Wildlife Park** is here too, with native animals aplenty: kids will love the daily animal-feeding shows and there's guided night tours and a cafe. Open 9.30am–5pm; 365 Mount Lofty Summit Rd, Crafers; (08) 8339 2444. The park is 14km north-west of Hahndorf (*see* p. 218).

EDEN VALLEY WINE REGION: Another history-rich region abutting the Barossa Valley to the east, but with a cooler climate that creates different wines. **Henschke** has a shiraz plot that dates back to the winery's inception in 1868, and the **Hill of Grace** label vies with the Barossa's **Penfolds Grange** as Australia's classic red. **Pewsey Vale** and **Heggies Vineyard** make fine examples of riesling; you can buy them at the **Yalumba Wine Room**; 40 Eden Valley Rd.

MOUNT LOFTY BOTANIC GARDENS: SA's largest botanic gardens are on the eastern face of Mount Lofty, with lovely lakes and walking trails past cool-climate garden species; open Mon–Fri 8.30am–4pm, Sat–Sun 10am–5pm; 16 Lampert Rd, Crafers; (08) 8370 8370. The garden is 14km north-west of Hahndorf (*see* p. 218).

NATIONAL MOTOR MUSEUM The largest collection of vehicles in the Southern Hemisphere, this impressive museum contains more than 300 vintage cars, motorcycles and commercial vehicles housed in the 1852 flour mill in Birdswood (*see* p. 217). The vehicles are lovingly restored, often from simply a shell. Visit the workshop complex to see the process of restoration as coach builders and mechanics work tirelessly on these old machines. The building's original history as a flour mill can be seen in the Mill Building. Shannon St, Birdwood; (08) 8568 4000.

THE CEDARS: Historic paintings, gardens and home of famous landscape artist Hans Heysen (1877–1968) in the town of Hahndorf (*see* p. 218); open Tues–Sun 10am–4.30pm; Heysen Rd, Hahndorf; (08) 8388 7277.

OTHER ATTRACTIONS

A.H. DODDRIDGE BLACKSMITH SHOP: This is the town of Angaston's (*see* p. 217) original blacksmith, started by Cornish immigrant William Doddridge. The shop closed in 1966 and 15 years later it was purchased by local townspeople. On Sat and Sun it operates as a working smithy, complete with the original bellows that Doddridge brought from England. Murray St, Angaston.

BAROSSA MUSEUM: Situated in Tanunda's (*see* p. 219) former post and telegraph office (1866), its collections specialise in German heritage; open Fri–Tues 10am–5pm; 47 Murray St, Tanunda.

CHURCH HILL STATE AREA: The 2.4km historical walking trail in Gawler (*see* p. 218) guides visitors past stately buildings, several churches, the old school, the courthouse, modest workers' cottages and grand homes, many with original cast-iron lacework – a fascinating snapshot of town planning in the 1830s. Excellent trail brochures are available at the Gawler visitor centre.

MAGGIE BEER'S FARM SHOP: Just 5km from Nuriootpa (*see* p. 219), you can have tastings and sales of gourmet farm produce from renowned cook, food writer and TV presenter Maggie Beer. Tuck into a gourmet lunch (book ahead) and catch a cooking demonstration; open 10am–4.30pm; 50 Pheasant Farm Rd Nuriootpa; (08) 8562 4477.

PARA WIRRA RECREATION PARK: The three First Nations connected to Para Wirra are the Peramangk, Ngadjuri and Kaurna Nations. The name Para Wirra comes from the Kaurna language – 'pari' means river, creek or gully; 'wirra' means forest, so it is the forest where a waterway flows. Today, Para Wirra Recreation Park is an important area for all three Nations, and National Parks are working with them to develop and promote cultural interpretation of the park. The park has a large recreational area with extensive facilities including tennis courts, picnic and barbecue areas, and walking trails ranging from short 800m walks to more extensive 7.5km trails. The park consists of mostly eucalypts and is home to a large variety of native birds – including inquisitive emus that meander around the picnic areas. The historic Barossa Goldfield Trails (1.2km or 5km loop walks) cover the history of the old goldmines. The park is 12km south-west of Lyndoch (*see* p. 219).

THE TOY FACTORY: A family business manufacturing wooden toys from a shop adjacent to an 18m giant rocking horse; Gumeracha. It's 7km west of Birdwood (*see* p. 217).

BAROSSA WINE REGION

The Barossa is Australia's eminent wine region, a landscape of historic villages spreading out to vine-covered hills and grand buildings on old wine estates. Shiraz is the premier drop, with semillon the star of the whites. Some of the old shiraz vines date back to the 1840s, and several winemaking families, many with German backgrounds, are into their sixth generation.

At the **Chateau Dorrien Winery** on the Barossa Valley Way there is an interesting mural depicting Barossa heritage. For some history on Barossa winemaking, the **Jacob's Creek Visitor Centre** has a display gallery next to its wine-tasting area; open 10am–5pm; 2129 Barossa Valley Way, Rowland Flat; (08) 8521 3000.

There are upwards of 150 wineries in the valley: senior names include **Yalumba** (1849), which is officially part of the Eden Valley, **Penfolds** (1844) and **Seppelt** (1851). You can sample the iconic Penfolds Grange at **Penfolds Barossa Valley** and even visit the **Winemakers' Laboratory** to blend your own wine to take home in a personalised bottle. **Seppeltsfield** is a must-visit winery with its elegant bluestone buildings and gardens. Its range of fortified wines includes Spanish styles and classic tawnys – the jewel is Para Liqueur, a tawny released when it is 100 years old. Seppeltsfield Dr, the road to the winery, is interesting in itself – an unexpected palm-lined avenue slicing through the vines.

Other big names to visit include **Peter Lehmann Wines** and **Wolf Blass**. Smaller gems include **Charles Melton Wines**, known for its Rose of Virginia rosé and **Nine Popes** blend of shiraz, grenache and mourvedre; nearby **Rockford Wines** has beefy reds seldom seen in other Australian states; **Torbreck** bottles excellent shiraz and shiraz viognier; and low-key **Langmeil Winery,** home to what is believed to be the world's oldest shiraz vineyard, is worth a stop too. Close to Tanunda is the cellar door at **Chateau Tanunda** with a range of winery tours and tasting experiences.

VISITOR INFORMATION

Adelaide Hills Visitor Information Centre
68 Main St
(08) 8393 7600
adelaidehills.org.au

Barossa Visitor Information Centre
66–68 Murray St, Tanunda
(08) 8563 0600 or
1300 852 982
barossa.com

KEY TOWNS

ANGASTON
Population 2184

Angaston takes its name from George Fife Angas, who purchased the original plot of land on which the town now stands. He was a prominent figure in the South Australian Company and many of the town's public buildings were funded by him. In a sense, the town's strong German heritage was also funded by him because he sponsored many Lutherans to make the journey to SA. Angaston still has strong ties with its history. In town are a German butcher shop that has been making wursts (sausages) for more than 60 years, a blacksmith shop over a century old, and a cafe and specialty food shop named the South Australian Company Store. Jacarandas and Moreton Bay figs line the main street.

SEE & DO **A.H. Doddridge Blacksmith Shop:** *see* Other Attractions. **Gully Gardens:** locally grown, hand-picked and dried fruits straight from the fruit orchards; Gawler Park Rd. **Barossa Valley Cheese Company:** cheese made on the premises; open Thurs–Sun; Murray St. **Angaston Heritage Walk:** brochure from visitor centre. **Barossa Cycle Track:** 7km rail trail, starts on Washington St; bike hire available at Angaston Hardware. **Farmers' market:** behind Vintners Bar & Grill, Nuriootpa Rd; Sat mornings. **Mengler Hill Lookout:** views over the Barossa Valley; 8km SW. **Kaiserstuhl Conservation Park:** a small pocket of native flora and fauna, with walking trails; 10km S. **Butcher, Baker, Winemaker Trail:** between Lyndoch and Angaston; visit wineries and gourmet-food producers along the way. Voucher booklet available for purchase, which allows you VIP experiences and rewards points; details and brochure from visitor centre.

BIRDWOOD
Population 932

The small, picturesque town of Birdwood is set in the Torrens Valley in the northern part of the popular Adelaide Hills district. The region's beauty would have been a welcome sight for German settlers escaping religious persecution in the 1840s. Like many of the German-settled towns in the area, Birdwood was originally named after a Prussian town, Blumberg. However, anti-German sentiment during World War I created a feeling of unrest and the town's name was changed to Birdwood after the commander of the ANZAC forces at Gallipoli, Sir William Birdwood. The Bay to Birdwood Run is a vintage motoring event attracting more than 1600 vehicles. It's held in Sept in even-numbered years.

SEE & DO **National Motor Museum:** *see* Top Attractions. **The Toy Factory:** *see* Other Attractions. **Blumberg Hotel:** imposing 1865 inn harking back to German-settler days; Main St. **Lobethal:** The quaint town of Lobethal features historic German-style cottages and an 1842 Lutheran seminary. The town lights up each Christmas in the 'Lights of Lobethal' festival. 13km SW. **Chain of Ponds Wines:** boutique winery with tastings, sales, viewing platform, restaurant and B&B (1880s cottage); 9km W. **Herbig Tree:** an extraordinary insight into Friedrich Herbig and the hollow red gum tree where he raised a family in the 1850s. School museum and early settler cemetery also onsite; Springton; group bookings only (08) 8568 2287; 15km NE. **Malcolm Creek Vineyard:** boutique winery with cellar door and friendly deer; open Sat–Sun and public holidays; Bonython Rd, Kersbrook; 20km NW. **Roachdale Reserve:** self-guided nature trail with brochure; 23km NW via

Z Wine, Barossa Valley

Kersbrook. **Torrens Gorge:** spectacular cliffs and streams make this a popular spot for picnics; 25km W. **Warren Conservation Park:** difficult trails, including part of the long-distance Heysen Trail, lead to views over countryside and Warren Gorge; adjacent to Samphire Wines and Pottery. **Mount Crawford Forest:** walkers, horseriders and cyclists will enjoy the forest tracks of this park, which is scattered in various locations north, west and south-west of Birdwood; visit the information centre on Warren Rd (signposted turn-off between Kersbrook and Williamstown) for a map.

GAWLER
Population 28,562

Set in the fork of the North and South Parra rivers and surrounded by rolling hills, it is no wonder that in 1839 Gawler was picked as the site of SA's first country town. The grand architecture of that era can be seen in its stately homes and buildings, especially in the Church Hill State Heritage Area. Just 40km north of central Adelaide, Gawler is a major service centre to a thriving agricultural district and has a substantial Adelaide commuter population.

SEE & DO **Church Hill State Heritage Area:** see Other Attractions. **Old Telegraph Station Museum:** this National Trust museum displays the history of Gawler's early settler past; open Tues–Fri 1–4pm; 59 Murray St; (08) 8523 1082. **Lions Market:** produce and bric-a-brac; Sun 8am–12pm; Gawler Railway Station, 23rd St. **The Food Forest:** award-winning permaculture farm on the Gawler River, producing 160 varieties of organically certified food; tours by appt only; 80 Clifford Rd, Hillier; (08) 8522 6450. **Dead Man's Pass Reserve:** so named because an early settler was found dead in the hollow of a tree. It has picnic facilities and a walking trail; southern end of Murray St, Gawler East. **Community Art Gallery:** local artwork on display in the town's old Station Master's house; open weekends; Gawler Railway Station, 23rd St; 0481 356 515. **Adelaide Soaring Club:** glider flights over Gawler and region; Gawler Aerodrome, Ward Belt Rd, Buchfelde; (08) 8522 1877. **Roseworthy Agricultural Museum:** farming museum featuring vintage equipment, located at the Roseworthy campus of the University of Adelaide; open 10am–4pm Wed and 3rd Sun each month; Mudla Wirra Rd, Roseworthy; (08) 8303 7739; 15km N. **Freeling:** rural town with a self-guided historical walking trail; 17km NE. **Two Wells:** named for two First Nations wells found by settlers, forgotten, then recovered in 1967. A few shops sell local crafts; Old Port Wakefield Rd; 2km W. **Stockport Observatory:** run by the Astronomical Society of SA, this impressive observatory has public viewing nights – call for information; Observatory Rd, Stockport; (08) 8338 1231; 30km N.

★ HAHNDORF
Population 2313

A short hop from the city in the heart of the Adelaide Hills lies Hahndorf, Australia's oldest surviving German settlement. Prussian Lutheran refugees fleeing religious persecution in their homelands settled the area in the late 1830s, bringing with them their beer, their wursts (sausages) and their sauerkraut – three things you'll have a hard time avoiding in Hahndorf today! In fact, many of the town's businesses and attractions are still run by descendants of the original German settlers. Around the town you'll find gentle hills, historic stone villages, wineries, gourmet-produce farms and native bushland, all of which makes Hahndorf one of SA's busiest tourist destinations – expect plenty of company as you wander up and down the main street.

SEE & DO **Beerenberg Strawberry Farm; Belair National Park; Cleland National Park; Mount Lofty Botanic Gardens; The Cedars:** see Top Attractions for all. **Main St:** a long, straight parade of historic buildings, German-style bakeries, pubs, restaurants, cafes, buskers and art and craft shops. **Hahndorf Academy:** a local history museum with a gallery displaying works of local artists, including Hans Heysen; open 10am–5pm; 68 Main St; (08) 8388 7250. **Hahndorf Farm Barn:** interactive farm animal shows, with petting and feeding – great for the kids; open 10am–4pm; 2282 Mount Barker Rd; (08) 8388 7289. **Hahndorf Hill Winery:** boutique cool-climate winery with tastings and sales; open 10am–5pm; 38 Pains Rd; (08) 8388 7512. **Hahndorf Walking Tours:** guided walks around Hahndorf's historic highlights; operates daily, tour times vary; (08) 8388 1185. **Historic Hahndorf:** a self-guided walking-tour brochure listing historic properties, available from visitor centre. **The Lane Vineyard:** wine tastings and restaurant meals, with sublime Adelaide Hills views; 5 Ravenswood La, Hahndorf. **SteamRanger Highlander:** tourist train operating from Mount Barker, with regular trips to Strathalbyn and beyond to a coastal track between Goolwa and Victor Harbor (this section is known as the Cockle Train, *see* Goolwa, p. 211); open Mon–Fri 8.30am–5.30pm, Sat 9am–5pm, train times vary; off Dutton Rd, Mount Barker; 1300 655 991; 6km SE. **Bridgewater Mill:** historic mill with upmarket restaurant; 6km W. **Aldgate:** historic village featuring the old Aldgate Pump – literally an old pump once used for watering horses, across the road from a pub of the same name – and the National Trust–listed Stangate House, with its photogenic camellia garden; 8km W. **Stirling:** the Adelaide Hills's most urbane town, with myriad cafes and eateries, an excellent pub, a village green–like oval, monthly street market (4th Sun) and European gardens; 10km W. **Jupiter Creek Goldfields:** walking trails with interpretive signs, where the yellow stuff was discovered in 1852; off

Top: Grünthal Brew microbrewery, Adelaide Hills **Bottom:** Mount Lofty Estate, Adelaide Hills **Opposite:** Seppeltsfield, Barossa Valley

TOP EVENTS

→ JAN Santos Tour Down Under (across the region); Adelaide Hills Crush Festival (across the Adelaide Hills)

→ EASTER Racing Carnival (Oakbank)

→ APR Barossa Vintage Festival (odd-numbered years across the Barossa region)

→ JULY Winter Reds Festival (Hahndorf)

→ AUG Barossa Gourmet Weekend (across the Barossa region)

→ SEPT Bay to Birdwood Run (even-numbered years; Birdwood)

→ DEC Lights of Lobethal festival (Lobethal)

TEMPERATURES

Jan: 15–30°C

July: 5–14°C

Shepherd Rd, Echunga; 12km SW. **Melba's Chocolate Factory:** artisan chocolate factory with tastings and sales; open 9am–4.30pm Mon–Sun; 22 Henry St, Woodside; (08) 8389 7868; 13km NE.

LYNDOCH
Population 1883

Lyndoch is one of the oldest towns in SA. The first European explorers, led by Colonel Light in 1837, described the area around Lyndoch as 'a beautiful valley'. The undulating landscape and picturesque setting attracted Lutheran immigrants and English gentry, who began growing grapes here. By 1850 Johann Gramp had produced his first wine from the grapes at Jacob's Creek and today the picturesque town sits amongst vineyards.

SEE & DO **Para Wirra Recreation Park:** see Other Attractions. **Spinifex Arts & Crafts:** retail shop selling exclusive quality handcrafted goods including pottery, quilts, folk art and paintings of local scenes. All goods are locally made in the Barossa region; Barossa Valley Way. **Helicopter and balloon flights:** scenic flights over the Barossa region; contact visitor centre for details. **Historic Lyndoch Walk:** self-guided walk featuring buildings from the mid-1800s, including many built from locally quarried hard ironstone; brochure from visitor centre. **Sandy Creek Conservation Park:** on undulating sand dunes, with walking trails and birdlife. See western grey kangaroos and echidnas at dusk; 5.5km W. **Lyndoch Lavender Farm and Cafe:** wander through rows of over 60 lavender varieties. The nursery and farm shop offer lavender-product sales; open Mon–Sun Sept–Feb, Mon–Fri Mar–Apr; cnr Hoffnungsthal and Tweedies Gully rds; 6km SE. **Barossa Reservoir and Whispering Wall:** acoustic phenomenon allowing whispered messages at one end to be audible at the other end, 140m away; 8km SW.

NURIOOTPA
Population 6204

Check the pulse of the Barossa in Nuriootpa, the valley's main service hub. The long history of winemaking in the Barossa wouldn't have been so long if it weren't for practical, down-to-earth Nuriootpa. But it wasn't wine that built 'Nuri', it was beer – the town actually began life as a pub. As a trade route was being established northwards to the Kapunda copper mines, the canny William Coulthard foresaw the demand for rest and refreshment. He built the Old Red Gum Slab Hotel in 1854 and the town grew around it. The North Para River runs through Nuriootpa, its course marked by parks and picnic spots.

SEE & DO **Maggie Beer's Farm Shop:** see Other Attractions. **Coulthard Reserve:** popular park close to the main street, great for a picnic or spotting ducks on the North Para River. Nuriootpa swimming pool is here too; off Penrice Rd. **Barossa Bike Hire:** cruise around the Barossa vineyards under your own steam; open 9am–5pm; 5 South Tce; 0400 537 770. **Barossa Farmers' Market:** in the historic Vintners Sheds between Nuriootpa and Angaston; Sat morning. **Light Pass:** a small, historic township with age-old Lutheran churches and Luhrs Pioneer German Cottage, displaying German artefacts; Light Pass Rd; 3km E.

TANUNDA
Population 4394

Tanunda is at the heart of the Barossa and surrounded by vineyards. The modern-day township grew out of the village of Langmeil, which was the focal point for early German settlement. The German Lutherans planted vines and many of the Barossa's shiraz vines date back to those early days. Tanunda has good eateries and fine examples of Lutheran churches.

SEE & DO **Barossa Museum:** see Other Attractions. **Gourmet produce:** specialty stores include Tanunda Bakery for German breads (Murray St) and Apex Bakery for traditional pastries (Elizabeth St). **Heritage walk:** includes many historic Lutheran churches; more details available from visitor centre in Murray St. **Bethany:** this pretty village was the first German settlement in the Barossa, and it has a great winery sitting on a hilltop. The creekside picnic area, early settler cemetery, attractive streetscapes and walking trail along Rifle Range Rd make it well worth a visit; 5km SE.

Clare Valley and Mid-North

Neighbouring Barossa Valley might steal all the limelight, but Clare Valley is an epicurean delight, especially for those that prefer their wines white. Renowned for its **exceptional rieslings**, Clare is one of South Australia's oldest wine regions. History buffs will love exploring the mid-north, with its **wealth of well-preserved old mining towns** and **heritage railways**.

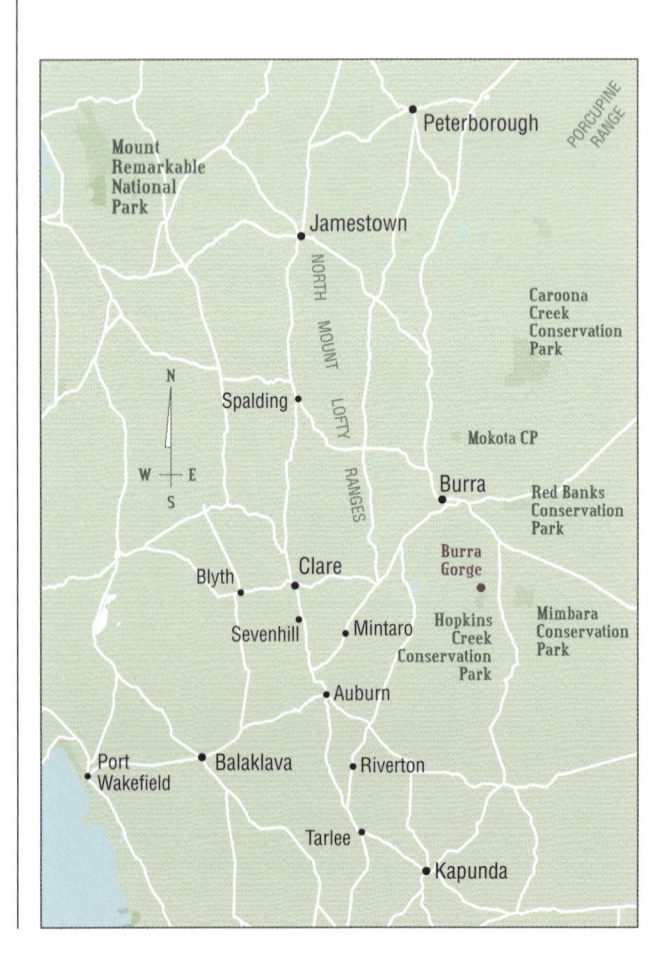

CHEAT SHEET

→ Allow at least two or three days.

→ Best time to visit: year-round.

→ Main towns: Clare (see p. 223), Peterborough (see p. 225).

→ The Ngadjuri People are the Traditional Owners of the land in this region.

→ Don't miss: cycling (or walking) the Riesling Trail; winetasting in the Clare Valley; historic Burra; Martindale Hall and Spring Gully Conservation Park.

Top: Kilikanoon Wines
Opposite: Jim Barry Wines

TOP ATTRACTIONS

BURRA HERITAGE PASSPORT: This 'passport' allows visitors to discover the major heritage sites of Burra – armed with an unlimited-access 'key' and a brief history of each site outlined in the information booklet included. The passport takes you to the **Burra Historic Mine Site** (off Market St), with an ore dressing tower and powder magazine offering views of the open-cut mine and town. At the site is **Morphetts Enginehouse Museum**, featuring engine displays and magnificent views across the mine site. Another site covered in the passport is the **Burra Creek Miners' Dugouts** (alongside Blyth St) – these dugouts, cut into the creek beds, housed 1800 people during the boom. Visit the **Unicorn Brewery Cellars** (Bridge Tce) that date back to 1873, the police lock-up and stables (Tregony St) – these were the first built outside Adelaide – and **Redruth Gaol** (off Tregony St), which served as a gaol, then a girls' reformatory from 1856 to 1922 and the **Market Square Museum**, an old-style general store, post office and restored family home. You can also visit the ruins of a private English township called **Hampton**, on the northern outskirts of town. Passports are available from the Burra (see p. 223) visitor centre in Market Sq and include access to the town's museums.

CLARE VALLEY WINE REGION: This is Australia's best region for riesling, and a very good region for shiraz and cabernet sauvignon. Vineyards are sprawled over the gently undulating country between Auburn and Clare, with historic stone buildings dotting the landscape. Jesuit priests established **Sevenhill Cellars** in 1851 to ensure a steady supply of altar wine. The winemaking is still overseen by Jesuits, with riesling and shiraz the standout varieties. Visit the stone cellars and St Aloysius Church. The well-known brand **Annie's Lane** was also established in 1851 (though under a different name), and produces excellent riesling, semillon, shiraz and grenache mourvedre. Other impressive wineries include **Grosset** and **Skillogalee**.

MARTINDALE HALL: This 1879 mansion in Mintaro (see p. 225) was built for Edmund Bowman who, the story goes, commissioned it for the woman he wanted to marry, who was from English high society. The lady declined his offer of marriage, and Bowman lived there on his own until 1891. Today visitors can explore the National Trust, Georgian-style home with its Italian Renaissance interior. The mansion featured extensively in the 1975 film *Picnic at Hanging Rock*. Open Wed–Mon 10am–4pm; Manoora Rd, Mintaro; 0417 838 897.

STEAMTOWN HERITAGE RAIL CENTRE: With a 100-year-old rail history this dynamic museum in Peterborough (see p. 225), located around the old locomotive workshops, is a collection of historic rolling stock, including a converted Morris car that rides the tracks. Also on display is Australia's only three-gauge roundhouse and turntable. Main St, Peterborough; (08) 8651 3355.

OTHER ATTRACTIONS

BALAKLAVA COURTHOUSE GALLERY: The arts are alive and well in Balaklava (*see* p. 223), as shown by this community-run art gallery that has a changing program of local and visiting exhibitions, plus a popular art prize in July. Open Thurs and Sun 2–4pm, Fri 10am–4pm; Edith Tce, Balaklava.

BUNDALEER FOREST RESERVE: This plantation forest, established in 1876, was Australia's first purpose-planted forest. Walking tracks start from the Jamestown (*see* p. 224) Arboretum, Georgetown Rd and the picnic area, and range from botanic walks to historic trails past building ruins and extensive dry-stone walls. The longer Mawson (cycling) and Heysen (walking) trails also travel through the reserve, as does a scenic drive from Jamestown, which then continues towards New Campbell Hill, Mount Remarkable and the Bluff. Each Easter Sunday the Bilby Easter Egg Hunt is held in the reserve. Spalding Rd. The reserve is 9km south of Jamestown.

KAPUNDA MUSEUM: Excellent folk museum with a short film about Kapunda's (*see* p. 224) history and displays of old agricultural machinery, an original fire engine and other vehicles in the pavilion. Detailed mining history is in Bagot's Fortune interpretive centre; open Thurs–Tues 1–4pm; Hill St, Kapunda; 0402 026 835.

PORT WAKEFIELD: Behind the National Hwy's long line of takeaways and petrol stations is a quiet town that began life as a cargo port to carry the copper mined in Burra's Monster Mine back to Port Adelaide. It is set on the mangrove-lined Wakefield River at the top of Gulf St Vincent. The wharf, which has a floor of mud at low tide, is now used by the local fishing industry. This is a popular spot for fishing, crabbing and swimming. The town is 25km west of Balaklava (*see* p. 223).

Morphett's Enginehouse Museum **Opposite:** Clare Valley Wine Tours

VISITOR INFORMATION

Clare Valley Wine Food and Tourism Centre
8 Spring Gully Rd
(08) 8842 2131 or
1800 242 131
clarevalley.com.au

KEY TOWNS

BALAKLAVA
Population 1956

Balaklava is set on the Wakefield River in an area dominated by traditional wheat and sheep farms. It sprang up as a stopping point between the Burra copper fields and Port Wakefield, but a grain merchant from Adelaide, Charles Fisher, soon turned the focus to agriculture. He built grain stores here before there was any sign of grain. This proved a canny move, as it lured farmers to the area. The town features old sandstone buildings and a 'silent cop' – a curious 'keep left' sign in the middle of a roundabout.

SEE & DO **Courthouse Gallery; Port Wakefield:** see Other Attractions for both. **Museum:** old household items and local memorabilia; open 1st Sun each month or by appt 2–4pm; Old Centenary Hall, May Tce; 0409 286 177. **Urlwin Park Agricultural Museum:** old agricultural machinery, two old relocated banks and a working telephone exchange; open 2nd and 4th Sun each month or by appt 2.30–4.30pm; Short Tce; (08) 8862 1854. **Walking trail:** scenic 3km track along the riverbank. **Devils Garden:** a picnic spot among river box gums, once a 'devil of a place' for bullock wagons to get through as the black soil quickly turned to mud; 7km NE. **Rocks Reserve:** walking trails and unique rock formations by the river; 10km E. **Balaklava Gliding Club:** offers weekend 'air experience flights' with an instructor; Whitwarta Airfield; (08) 8864 5062; 10km NW.

BURRA
Population 922

The Burra region became a hive of activity when two shepherds found copper in 1845. Settlements were established based on the miners' countries of origin: Aberdeen for the Scottish, Hampton for the English, Redruth for the Cornish and Llwchwr for the Welsh. The combined settlement grew to be the second largest in SA, but the miners were fickle – with riches promised on the Victorian goldfields, they did not stay for long. In 1877 the Monster Mine closed. Luckily, Burra did not turn into a ghost town, but became a farming centre. The rich heritage of its past has been carefully preserved by the community, resulting in the town being declared a State Heritage Area in 1993. The Burra Heritage Passport gives you access to mine sites, the ruins of a private township, a gaol and museum. Burra is in the Bald Hill Ranges, named for the 'naked' hills around the town.

SEE & DO **Burra Heritage Passport:** see Top Attractions. **Bon Accord Mine Complex:** National Trust interpretive centre with working forge and model of Burra Mine. Guided tours available Mon–Fri 10am–1pm, Sat–Sun 11am–2pm; Railway Tce. **Malowen Lowarth Cottage:** restored 1850s Cornish miners' cottage, open Sat 2–4pm, Sun 9.30–11.30am; Kingston St. **Art Gallery:** local and touring exhibitions; Market St. **Antique shops:** in Commercial and Market sts. **Burra Creek:** canoeing and picnicking. **Burra Trail Rides:** horseriding adventures in Bald Hills Range. **Burra Gorge:** picnics, camping and walking tracks around gorge and permanent springs; 23km SE. **Dares Hill Drive:** scenic 90km drive with lookout; begins 30km N near Hallett; map available from visitor centre. **Conservation parks:** bushwalking, birdwatching and camping opportunities in the conservation parks surrounding Burra; details from National Parks and Wildlife Service South Australia, parks.sa.gov.au

★ CLARE
Population 3379

Clare is known as the 'Garden of the North'. In the mid-1800s, Edward John Eyre reported favourably on the area and pastoral settlement followed; the town came to be known as Clare after the county in Ireland. The land has proved as favourable as Eyre claimed and Clare continues to boast a rich agricultural industry, including the famous Clare Valley wine region. The first vines were planted by Jesuit priests at Sevenhill in 1851. The Sevenhill Cellars are still operated by Jesuit

SOUTH AUSTRALIA

Brothers and the monastery buildings, including the historic St Aloysius Church, are of special interest.

SEE & DO **Clare Valley wine region:** *see* Top Attractions; **Old Police Station Museum:** previously a prison, a casualty hospital and housing for government employees, it is now a National Trust museum with historic artefacts and photographs; open Fri and Sun 1–3pm, other times by appt; Neagles Rock Rd; (08) 8842 2376. **Lookouts:** Billy Goat Hill from Wright St and Neagles Rock Lookout on Neagles Rock Rd. **Town walk:** self-guided trail; brochure from visitor centre. **Watervale:** a historic town with a self-guided walk; brochure available from the visitor centre; 12km S. **Blyth:** a little country town overlooking the western plains. Take a short walk on the interpretive botanical trail or picnic at Brooks Lookout. Medika Gallery, originally a Lutheran church, offers an art gallery and Australian craft sales; 13km W. **Auburn:** the birthplace in 1876 of poet C.J. Dennis; take a self-guided walk through National Trust historic precinct in St Vincent St; 26km S. **Scenic drive:** travel south to Spring Gully Conservation Park with its walking tracks and rare red stringybarks.

JAMESTOWN
Population 1389

Jamestown survived the demise of wheat crops in the late 1800s to become an important service town to the thriving agricultural farmlands of the Clare Valley. John Bristow Hughes took up the first pastoral lease in 1841 and from then the town grew rapidly on the strength of stud sheep and cattle farms, cereals, dairy produce and timber. A look at the names of towns in SA will reveal that the governors, politicians and surveyors of the day were bent on commemorating themselves or people they liked. Jamestown followed this trend, named after Sir James Fergusson, then state governor.

SEE & DO **Bundaleer Forest Reserve:** *see* Other Attractions. **Railway Station Museum:** a National Trust museum detailing local rail and Bundaleer Forest history and featuring the Both-designed iron lung (invented at Caltowie); open 10.30am–3.30pm Mon–Fri; Mannanarie Rd; (08) 8664 2036. **Heritage murals:** on town buildings. **Belalie Creek:** picnic in one of the parks along the banks; floodlit at night. **R.M. Williams Centre:** open-air, interpretive centre on the life of one of Australia's most iconic businessmen. **Town and cemetery walks:** self-guided tours; brochure available from caravan park. **Sheep Markets:** livestock market at saleyards on Murchland Dr, Thurs. **Appila Springs:** scenic picnic and camping spot; 31km NW via Appila. **Spalding:** a town in the Broughton River valley. Picnic areas and excellent trout fishing; 34km S.

KAPUNDA
Population 2633

The town name 'Kapunda' is thought to be from an Ngadjuri word, meaning 'water jump out', possibly in relation to nearby springs. Copper was discovered in Kapunda by Francis Dutton, a sheep farmer, in 1842. It was to be

Town of Kapunda

TOP EVENTS

- → FEB–MAR Adelaide Plains Cup Festival (Balaklava)
- → APR Autumn Garden Festival (Clare); Farm 4x4 Outdoor Expo (Kapunda)
- → MAY Gourmet Week (Clare)
- → SEPT–OCT Celtic Festival (Kapunda)

TEMPERATURES

Jan: 13–30°C

July: 3–14°C

the highest-grade copper ore found in the world. Settlement followed, and Kapunda came into existence as Australia's first copper mining town. When the mines closed in 1878, Australia's 'cattle king' Sir Sidney Kidman moved in, eventually controlling 26 million hectares of land across Australia. Kapunda is between two wine districts – the Barossa Valley and the Clare Valley – but you'll find a better range of accommodation in Clare or the Barossa itself.

SEE & DO

Kapunda Museum: see Other Attractions. **Community Gallery:** significant regional gallery with local and touring art exhibitions; cnr Main and Hill sts. **'Map Kernow':** 8m bronze statue commemorating early miners, many of whom emigrated from Cornwall in England; end of Main St at southern entrance of town. **High school's main building:** former residence of Sir Sidney Kidman; West Tce. **Gundry's Hill Lookout:** views over township and surrounding countryside; West Tce. **Heritage trail:** 10km self-guided tour through town and historic Kapunda Copper Mine; *Discovering Historic Kapunda* brochure available at visitor centre. **Pines Reserve:** nature and wildlife reserve; 6km NW on road to Tarlee. **Anlaby Station:** historic Dutton Homestead and gardens, once a setting for large prestigious parties. Also a coach collection and historic station buildings; open for groups and on open garden days; Anlaby Rd; (08) 8566 2465; 16km NE. **Tarlee:** historic local-stone buildings; 16km NW. **Riverton:** a historic town in the Gilbert Valley, once a stopover point for copper-hauling bullock teams. Many historic buildings remain, including the heritage-listed railway station and Scholz Park Museum, which incorporates a cottage, blacksmith and wheelwright shop; open 12–3pm last Sun of the month; 30km NW. **Scenic drive:** 28km drive north-east through sheep, wheat and dairy country to Eudunda.

MINTARO
Population 218

Although it is in the Clare Valley region, Mintaro's prosperity is not linked with the valley's booming wine industry. Instead, its buildings date back to the 1840s and '50s, when bullock drays carried copper from the Monster Mine at Burra to Port Wakefield in the south. Many of the buildings use local slate. In 1984 Mintaro became the first town in SA to be classified a State Heritage Area. It has the National Trust–listed Georgian-style mansion Martindale Hall, gardens, a hedge maze and heritage-listed colonial-era buildings.

SEE & DO

Martindale Hall: see Top Attractions. **Timandra Garden:** one of the town's fine garden displays; enter via Timandra Nursery, Kingston St. **Mintaro Maze:** kids will love getting lost in the hedge maze, comprising over 800 conifers; open Thurs–Mon 10am–4pm; Jacka St. **Reillys Wines:** wine-tastings, cellar-door sales and a restaurant; Burra Rd. **Mintaro Wines:** wine-tastings and sales; Leasingham Rd. **Heritage walk:** self-guided trail includes 18 heritage-listed colonial-era buildings and two historic cemeteries; brochure available. **Polish Hill River Valley:** a sub-region of the Clare Valley wine region, with cellar doors offering tastings and sales; between Mintaro and Sevenhill. **Waterloo:** features the historic Wellington Hotel, once a Cobb & Co. staging post; 23km SE.

PETERBOROUGH
Population 1428

Peterborough is a town obsessed with the railway. Its very existence and growth can be claimed by that industry. In 1881 the line to Jamestown was opened and over the next few years the town became a key intersection between all the major SA towns. Locals boast about how, in a mammoth one-day effort, 105 trains travelled the Broken Hill to Port Pirie line. The rail passion continued even after many of the lines closed, and today each entrance to the town has a welcoming model steam train.

SEE & DO

Steamtown Heritage Rail Centre: see Top Attractions. **Town hall:** a beautiful, ornate 1927 building with its original theatre and a Federation wall-hanging in the foyer; Main St. **Town Carriage Museum:** local history on display inside an old train carriage; Main St; (08) 8651 3355. **Social History Museum** and **Meldonfield Miniatures:** local history and a world of miniature horse-drawn carriages modelled on the style used in the 1800s; YMCA Building Main St; contact visitor centre for opening times. **Printing Works:** original print shop with historic presses and printed material, left exactly as it was when the business closed; open Wed–Fri 10am–1pm or by appt; 9 Jervis St; 0408 220 248. **Victoria Park:** features a lake and islands with deer and kangaroo enclosure, and a playground; Queen St. **Town walk and drive:** self-guided tour; brochure from visitor centre. **Terowie:** an old railway town with well-preserved 19th-century main street. Self-guided drive or walk tour; brochure *A Tour of Terowie* available from tearooms; 24km SE. **Magnetic Hill:** stop the car, turn off the engine, put it in neutral and watch it roll uphill; 32km NW via Black Rock.

Yorke Peninsula

The Yorke Peninsula is a **laid-back beach shack sort of place** that's popular with holidaymakers from Adelaide. Chill out on the **beaches**, explore the **coastal national parks** with their **shipwrecks** and **lighthouses** and follow the **seaside scenic drives**. Or take a deep dive into the peninsula's **rich Cornish heritage** – thanks to the copper mining boom – it's home to the **best Cornish pasties** in the country.

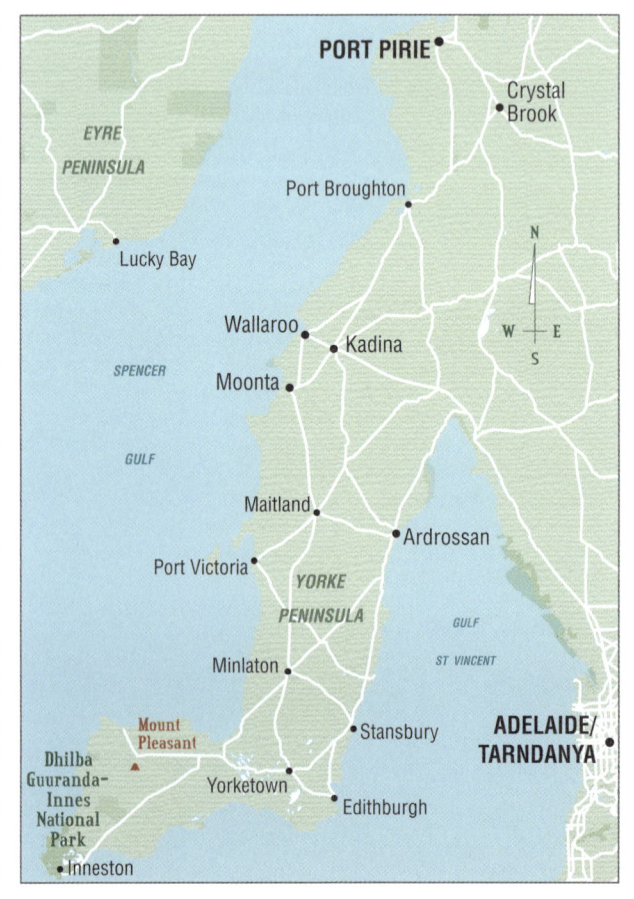

CHEAT SHEET

→ Allow at least three or four days for a proper exploration, longer if you just want to relax by the seaside for a few days.

→ Best time to visit: summer is very popular.

→ Main towns: Minlaton (see p. 230), Port Pirie (see p. 230), Yorketown (see p. 231).

→ The Yorke Peninsula is the Traditional Land of the Narungga/Nharangga People.

→ Don't miss: jetty fishing; coastal walks; the Red Devil plane; the scenic drive to Troubridge Point; sunset at West Cape Lighthouse; Innes National Park; the ghost town of Inneston; and a pastie from the Cornish Kitchen in Moonta.

Top: Cape Spencer Lighthouse
Opposite: Dhilba Guuranda-Innes National Park

TOP ATTRACTIONS

DHILBA GUURANDA-INNES NATIONAL PARK: This national park was previously called Innes National Park but in 2020 renamed as Dhilba Guuranda-Innes National Park, in recognition of its Narungga Traditional Owners. In summer, soak up the sun at beaches or bays with excellent (but challenging) surf breaks at Chinamans Reef, Pondalowie Bay and West Cape, where you'll find the glimmering **West Cape Lighthouse** made of stainless steel. In winter, keep an eye out at Stenhouse Bay and Cape Spencer for migrating southern right whales. A new lookout at Chinaman's Hill was being constructed at the time of research and visitor facility upgrades were scheduled for Stenhouse Bay and Shell Beach. Diving is popular, especially near the Gap, an eroded gap in a 60m high cliff. Other activities include beach and jetty fishing, and walking on coastal and inland tracks. Accommodation is something special in this park – enjoy fabulous coastal camping in the mallee scrub or stay at the heritage lodge in the old mining township of Inneston, now a ghost town with self-contained overnight accommodation in the abandoned (but very comfortable) buildings.

MOONTA MINES STATE HERITAGE AREA: Take a historical walk or drive from Moonta (see p. 230) to this significant heritage area. Interpretive walking trails guide the visitor to the major sites, including the Hughes Pump House, shafts, tailing heaps and ruins of mine offices. A 50min historical railway tour runs from the museum (tour times vary). Also on the site is a historic 1880 pipe organ in the Moonta Mines Heritage Uniting Church; Cornish lifestyle history and memorabilia at the Moonta Mines Museum; and the furnished National Trust Miners Cottage and Heritage Garden; opening times vary. Enjoy old-style sweets at the Moonta Mines Sweet Shop; via Verran Tce, Moonta.

REGIONAL TOURISM AND ARTS CENTRE: This award-winning centre in Port Pirie (see p. 230) comprises an eclectic mix of exhibitions, art and information. A lifelike fibreglass model of the largest white pointer shark taken from SA waters is on display (a 5.5m specimen known as 'Shakka') or try the virtual-reality shark cage-dive, if you're game. Local and regional history are presented through a series of artworks, and you can take a ride on the miniature railway **Pirie Rail Express**, which replicates the journey from Port Pirie to Broken Hill (1st and 3rd Sun each month 11.30am–2.30pm). There are local and touring art exhibitions in the art gallery. Open Mon–Fri 9am–5pm, Sat–Sun 10am–2pm; 3 Mary Elie St, Port Pirie; (08) 8633 8700.

STUMP-JUMP PLOUGH: A lonely stump-jump plough stands in the cliff-top park opposite East Tce in Androssan (see p. 229). Mallee scrub once covered much of this area and caused endless grief to early farmers because it was so difficult to clear. The invention of the stump-jump plough made it possible to jump over stumps left in the ground and plough on ahead. The plough's design was perfected in Ardrossan. The original factory, on Fifth St, now houses a historical museum. Open 10am–4pm; (08) 8837 4195.

THE FARM SHED MUSEUM AND TOURIST CENTRE: This multi-faceted centre in Kadina (see p. 229) is home to the Dry Land Farming Interpretive Centre; Matta House, which is the former home of the mining manager's family; a 1950s-style schoolroom; Kadina story, a display of the town's history; and the visitor information centre; Moonta Rd, Kadina; (08) 8821 2333.

OTHER ATTRACTIONS

BUTLER MEMORIAL: In a hangar-like building in the main street of Minlaton (see p. 230) stands the *Red Devil*, a fighter plane – thought to be the only one of its type left in the world – that fought in France and, less romantically, flew mail between Adelaide and Minlaton. The pilot, Aviator Captain Harry Butler, was born in Minlaton and the National Trust museum in the historic general store nearby features a local history display and memorabilia from Captain Butler; open Tues–Fri 9.30am–1pm, Sat 9.30am–12pm; Main St Minlaton.

CYP MUSEUM: Housed in the former school in Maitland (see p. 230), this National Trust museum documents local First Nations and settlement history; open Sun, public and school holidays 2–4pm, other times by appt; cnr Gardiner and Kilkerran tces, Maitland; (08) 8832 2220.

HISTORIC AND FOLK MUSEUM: Located in historic Port Pirie (see p. 230) town buildings, including the old customs house (1882) and the Victorian pavilion-style railway station (1902), the town's National Trust museum houses a history display and rooms furnished in early 1900s style; open Mon–Sat 10am–4pm, Sun 1–4pm; 73–77 Ellen St, Port Pirie; (08) 8632 3435.

WALLAROO HERITAGE AND NAUTICAL MUSEUM: This National Trust museum in Wallaroo's (see p. 231) original 1865 post office features shipwreck displays, maps, charts, model ships and records, as well as local cultural and religious history. Meet George, the unlucky giant squid eaten and then recovered from a whale's belly 30 years ago. Open 10am–4pm and public holidays; Jetty Rd, Wallaroo; (08) 8823 3015.

DIVE THE SHIPWRECK TRAIL

Discover the south coast of Yorke Peninsula with *The Investigator Strait Maritime Heritage Trail* brochure that includes the history and maps of 26 dive sites. By far the worst recorded shipwreck was that of the *Clan Ranald*, a huge steel steamer that, through incompetence and greed, was wrecked in 1909 just west of Troubridge Hill. The disaster claimed 40 lives – 36 bodies were later buried in the Edithburgh Cemetery. **Wardang Island Maritime Heritage Trail** is a scuba-diving and overland trail that includes eight shipwreck sites with underwater plaques around Wardang Island and six interpretive signs at Port Victoria; a waterproof self-guided brochure available from visitor centre in Port Victoria. SA's most complete shipwreck is the *Zanoni* 15km south-east of Ardrossan off Rogues Point. The wreck was lost for over 100 years, but was eventually rediscovered by some local fishermen. It lies virtually in one piece on the seabed. Some artefacts from the ship can be found at the Ardrossan Historical Museum, but divers wanting to see the wreck in situ need a permit from Heritage South Australia. environment.sa.gov.au; (08) 8204 1910.

Top: Edithburgh Tidal Pool

VISITOR INFORMATION

Maitland Information Centre
3 Robert Street, Maitland
(08) 8832 2174
visityorkepeninsula.com.au

Port Pirie Regional Tourism and Arts Centre
3 Mary Elie St, Port Pirie
(08) 8633 8700 or
1800 000 424

TOP EVENTS

→ APR Saltwater Classic - wooden and classic boat regatta (even-numbered years, Stansbury and Port Vincent); Folk Fair (Laura)

→ MAY Kernewek Lowender Cornish Festival (odd-numbered years, Kadina, Wallaroo, Moonta)

→ JUNE Winter Fun Fishing Competition (Port Broughton)

→ SEPT Yorke Peninsula Field Days (odd-numbered years, Paskeville); Blessing of the Fleet (Port Pirie)

→ OCT Moonta Open Gardens (Moonta); Rubber Duck Race (Port Broughton); Country Music Festival (Port Pirie); Yorkes Classic (Innes National Park)

TEMPERATURES

Jan: 16–30°C

July: 7–15°C

KEY TOWNS

ARDROSSAN
Population 1188

A cluster of bright white grain silos sits atop the red clay cliffs at Ardrossan, an industrial town. The town has two jetties – one for the export of grain, salt and dolomite, and the other for the benefit of local anglers. Ardrossan is well known for its blue swimmer crabs that are found under the jetty or in the shallows at low tide. The best season for crabbing is between Sept and Apr.

SEE & DO **Stump-Jump Plough:** *see* Top Attractions. **Walking trail:** 3km track along cliff-tops to Tiddy Widdy Beach; begins at the boat ramp in town. **BHP Lookout:** view of Gulf St Vincent and dolomite mines; 2km S. **Clinton Conservation Park:** mangrove swamps and tidal flats with an array of birdlife; begins after Port Clinton (25km N), and stretches around the head of Gulf St Vincent.

CRYSTAL BROOK
Population 1322

Crystal Brook serves the sheep and wheat country at the southern point of the Flinders Ranges. It once formed part of a vast sheep station, Crystal Brook Run, which extended from the current town to Port Pirie in the north-west. The country feel of the town begins on entering the tree-lined main street.

SEE & DO **Heritage Centre:** local history collection in the town's first two-storey building; open Sun and public holidays 2–4pm, or by appt; Brandis St; (08) 8636 2142. **Crystal Crafts:** local craft; Bowman St. **Creekside parks:** popular spots for picnics. **The Big Goanna:** we love our things big in Australia, be it fruit, rocking horses, or, in this case, reptiles. **Bowman Park:** enjoyable walks, including part of the Heysen Trail, around ruins of the Bowman family property, Crystal Brook Run (1847); 8km E. **Koolunga:** a small community and home to the mythical bunyip – in 1883, two attempts to capture the beast were unsuccessful. Also craft outlets and the Bunyip River Walk on the banks of Broughton River; 10km E. **Gladstone:** set in rich rural country in the Rocky River Valley. Heriatge-listed Gladstone Gaol was closed to the public at the time of research, so check ahead to see if tours have recommenced. Discover the town's history on foot by picking up a map from the caravan park; 21km NE. **Redhill:** riverside walk, museum, craft shop and antique shop; 25km S. **Laura:** boyhood home of C.J. Dennis, author of *The Songs of a Sentimental Bloke*, and known for its cottage crafts, art galleries and historic buildings; 32km N. West of town is the Beetaloo Valley and Reservoir, a pleasant picnic spot in the cooler months.

Snowtown: surrounded by large salt lakes that change colour according to weather conditions. Lake View Drive is a scenic 6km drive around the lakes. Lochiel–Ninnes Rd Lookout provides panoramic country and lake views; 50km S.

EDITHBURGH
Population 497

Edithburgh is located on the foreshore at the south-eastern tip of Yorke Peninsula and is a popular coastal holiday destination overlooking Gulf St Vincent and Troubridge Island. This is an area synonymous with shipwrecks and, although reflecting tragic maritime days of old, it is a source of excitement for the diving enthusiast. Despite the construction of a lighthouse in 1856, over 26 vessels were wrecked on the coast between West Cape in Innes National Park and Troubridge Point just south of Edithburgh.

SEE & DO **Museum:** a community museum with local history of the town and region featuring a historical maritime collection; open Sun and public holidays 2–4pm, or by appt; Edith St; (08) 8852 6273. **Native Flora Park:** walk through eucalypts and casuarinas and see a variety of birdlife; Ansty Tce. **Bakehouse Arts and Crafts:** local handicrafts and produce in a historic 1890 building; Blanche St. **Town jetty:** built in 1873 to service large shipments of salt found inland, it offers views to Troubridge Island and is popular with anglers; end of Edith St. **Natural tidal pool:** excellent for swimming; foreshore. **Nature walks:** south to Sultana Point or north to Coobowie. **Sultana Point:** fishing and swimming; 2km S. **Coobowie:** a coastal town popular for swimming; 5km N. **Troubridge Island Conservation Park:** home to penguins, black-faced shags and crested terns; contact Troubridge Island Escape to stay the night in the lighthouse keeper's cottage. **Scenic drive:** west along the coast to Innes National Park.

KADINA
Population 4666

Kadina is the commercial centre and largest town on the Yorke Peninsula. It exists solely as a result of the digging habits of wombats. In 1860 upturned ground from wombat diggings revealed copper. This was the starting point of copper mining on the Yorke Peninsula. The wombats were commemorated by the naming of Kadina's 1862 hotel: Wombat Hotel. Kadina, along with Wallaroo and Moonta, formed part of a copper triangle colloquially named Little Cornwall because of the number of Cornish immigrants recruited to work in the mines.

SEE & DO **The Farm Shed Museum and Tourist Centre:** *see* Top Attractions. **Victoria Square Park:** historic band rotunda and Wallaroo Mine Monument; Main St.

Heritage walk: self-guided walk includes historic hotels such as the Wombat and the Royal Exchange with iron-lace balconies and shady verandahs; brochure from visitor centre.

MAITLAND
Population 1079

Maitland appears as a miniature version of Adelaide, with the town layout in the same pattern of radiating squares. It is in the heart of the Yorke Peninsula and is central to a rich agricultural region.

SEE & DO **CYP Museum:** *see* Other Attractions. **St John's Anglican Church:** stained-glass windows depict biblical stories in an Australian setting; cnr Alice and Caroline sts. **Cultural tours:** a range of tours through Adjahdura Land (Yorke Peninsula), with an Adjahdura guide; bookings and inquiries 0429 367 121. **Heritage town walk:** interpretive walk; brochure from council in Elizabeth St. **Barley Stacks Wines:** Yorke Peninsula's original commercial vineyard. Cellar-door tastings and sales 10am–5pm; Lizard Rd; (08) 8834 1258; 13km S. **Balgowan:** this town has safe, sandy beaches and is popular with anglers; 15km W.

MINLATON
Population 759

This small rural centre was originally called Gum Flat, because of the giant eucalypts in the area, but its name was later changed to Minlaton – believed to be from a Narrungga word 'minlacowie' which means fresh waterhole, combined with the Anglo Saxon word 'ton'.

SEE & DO **Museum** and **Butler Memorial:** *see* Other Attractions. **Gum Flat Gallery:** art workshop and gallery; open 10am–2pm Wed; Main St. **HJ & Brian Cook Native Animal Reserve:** popular spot for picnics, with kangaroos, emus and up to 43 species of birds; Maitland Rd.

Minlaton Walking Trail: a trail to the only naturally occurring stand of river red gums in the Yorke Peninsula. See a number of historic landmarks including an old horse dip and ancient First Nations wells, catch a glimpse of the local birdlife at the bird hide, and learn about the area through interpretive signs. **Ramsay Park:** native flora and fauna park; east between Minlaton and Port Vincent. **Port Rickaby:** quiet swimming and fishing spot; 16km NW.

MOONTA
Population 4627

The towns of Moonta, Kadina and Wallaroo form the 'Copper Coast' or 'Little Cornwall', so called because of abundant copper finds and the significant Cornish population. Like so many other copper discoveries in SA, Moonta's was made by a local shepherd – in this case, Paddy Ryan in 1861. It was to prove a fortunate find: Moonta Mining Company paid over £1 million in dividends. Thousands of miners, including experienced labourers from Cornwall, flocked to the area but the mines were abandoned in the 1920s because of the slump in copper prices and rising labour costs. Moonta has survived as an agricultural service town with an increasing tourist trade, thanks to the nearby beaches and historic sites.

SEE & DO **Moonta Mines State Heritage Area:** *see* Top Attractions. **The Cornish Kitchen:** home to possibly the best Cornish pastries outside of Cornwall, Ellen St. **All Saints Church of England:** features a locally constructed copper bell; cnr Blanche and Milne tces. **Queen Square:** park for picnics, with the imposing town hall opposite; George St. **Heritage walks and drives:** self-guided trails to see heritage stone buildings and historic mine sites; brochure from visitor centre. **Moonta Bay:** a popular seaside town for fishing and swimming. See native animals at the Moonta Wildlife Park; 5km W.

PORT BROUGHTON
Population 1116

This holiday town has a quiet coastal feel in winter and bustles with sun-seeking holidaymakers in summer. Set on a quiet inlet on Spencer Gulf, it has a long fishing history. In the 1900s the fishing fleets operated from the jetty. Today the town is still a major port for fishing boats and each week truckloads of blue swimmer crabs depart for city restaurants.

SEE & DO **Heritage Centre:** local history museum in the old school; Edmund St. **Sailboat hire and fishing charters:** from foreshore. **Town jetty:** popular fishing spot. **Historical walking trail:** grab the booklet, *Walk Around Port Broughton* from the visitor centre and navigate the historic sights of the town, including the heritage plaques on the foreshore. **Fisherman Bay:** fishing, boating and holiday spot with over 400 holiday shacks; 5km N along the coast.

PORT PIRIE
Population 13,708

Industry in its splendour greets visitors at this major industrial and commercial centre. The oil tanks, grain silos and 250m high Nyrstar smokestack all tower over the city, while on the waterfront huge local and overseas vessels are loaded and discharged. Broken Hill Proprietary Company (BHP) began mining lead in 1889 and various SA ports at that time vied for BHP's smelting business. Port Pirie eventually won, and created what is today the largest lead smelter in the world. Wheat and barley from the mid-north are also exported from here. Port Pirie shows great character in its old buildings and attractive main street, and Spencer Gulf and the Port Pirie River offer swimming, waterskiing, fishing and yachting.

SEE & DO **Regional Tourism and Arts Centre:** *see* Top Attractions. **Historic and Folk Museum:** *see* Other Attractions. **Memorial Park:** features the *John Pirie* anchor (from the first ship to navigate the Port Pirie River), memorials, and the Northern Festival Centre; Memorial Dr. **Fishing:** reliable local spots include the main wharf and John Pirie Bridge. **Heritage walk:** self-guided town walk past 31 historic sites; brochure from visitor centre. **Solomontown Beach:** enjoy a picnic, a stroll along the boardwalk or a swim in the Port Pirie River at the town's popular artificial beach; Beach Rd. **Weeroona Island:** low-lying island (also known as Port Flinders) with good fishing and a 3km birdwatching trail; accessible by car via a causeway; 13km N. **Port Germein:** a quiet beachside town with a tidal beach safe for swimming.

At 1.5km, the town's jetty is one of the longest in Australia, and is a hotspot for fishing for blue swimmer crabs; 23km N. **Telowie Gorge:** Home to the southernmost colony of yellow-footed rock wallabies in the Flinders Ranges region, this deep gorge is part of Wapma Thura–Southern Flinders Ranges National Park. 'Wapma Thura' means 'Snake People' in the language of the Traditional Owners, the Nukunu People; 24km NE.

PORT VICTORIA
Population 321

A tiny township on the west coast of Yorke Peninsula, Port Victoria was tipped to be a thriving port town after land surveyor James Hughes travelled up the coast in 1840. Hughes studied the coastline from his schooner, *Victoria*, and reported favourably on the region. It became an important port for grain exports, with windjammers transporting wheat from here to Europe. The town still proudly proclaims that it is the 'last of the windjammer ports'.

SEE & DO **Maritime Museum:** includes displays, relics and artefacts of the great era of the windjammer; open Sat–Sun and public holidays 2–4pm; Main St. **Jetty:** original 1888 jetty with good swimming and fishing; end of Main St. **Geology trail:** 4km interpretive track along the foreshore explains the coast's ancient volcanic history; brochure from visitor centre. **Goose Island Conservation Park:** important breeding area for several bird species and the Australian sea lion; 13km offshore; access by private boat. **Wardang Island:** this large island is a reserve, and permission for access is required from Goreta (Point Pearce) Aboriginal Community Council; (08) 8871 7059; near Goose Island.

STANSBURY
Population 480

Situated on the lower east coast of Yorke Peninsula and with views of Gulf St Vincent, Stansbury was originally known as Oyster Bay because of its claim to the best oyster beds in the state. The town has always serviced the farms inland, but its mainstay today is tourism. The bay is excellent for fishing and watersports, including diving and waterskiing.

SEE & DO **Schoolhouse Museum:** this local history museum in Stansbury's first school features cultural and environmental displays as well as the headmaster's rooms furnished in early 1900s style; open Wed and Sun 2–4pm, Mon–Sun in Jan; North Tce. **Oyster farms:** see daily operations of local oyster farms and eat some fresh oysters. **Fishing:** popular spots include the jetty, rocks and beach. **Mills Gully Lookout:** popular picnic spot with panoramic views of bay, town and Gulf St Vincent; northern outskirts of town. **Coastal trails:** walking and cycling trails past reserves, lookouts and a historic cemetery; start at foreshore caravan park; brochure from visitor centre. **Klein Point Quarry:** SA's largest limestone quarry; 5km S. **Lake Sundown:** one of the many salt lakes in the area and a photographer's delight at sunset; 15km NW. **Port Vincent:** popular holiday destination with good swimming, yachting and waterskiing; 17km N.

WALLAROO
Population 4241

Vast grain silos greet visitors to Wallaroo, a coastal town and shipping port on the west coast of Yorke Peninsula. The town is an interesting mix of tourism and industry. The safe beaches and excellent fishing prove popular with holidaymakers, while the commercial port controls exports of barley and wheat. Wallaroo exists thanks to a lucky shepherd's discovery of copper in 1859. Vast deposits were uncovered and soon thousands of Cornish miners arrived. The area boomed until the 1920s, when copper prices dropped and the industry slowly died out. Wallaroo's buildings and old Cornish-style cottages are a reminder of its colourful past. Wallaroo and nearby towns Moonta and Kadina are part of the 'Copper Coast' or 'Little Cornwall'.

SEE & DO **Wallaroo Heritage and Nautical Museum:** see Other Attractions. **Boat hire and charters:** for the ultimate gulf-fishing experience. **Self-guided historical walk:** highlight is the 1865 Hughes chimney stack, which contains over 300,000 bricks and measures more than 7sqm at its base; brochure available from museum or town hall. **Ferry:** to avoid the extra driving distance to the Eyre Peninsula, *Spencer Gulf Searoad* runs a ferry service between Wallaroo and Lucky Bay; bookings (08) 8823 0777. **Bird Island:** crabbing; 10km S.

YORKETOWN
Population 667

Yorketown is a small rural community at the south end of Yorke Peninsula. The surrounding landscape is dotted with many inland salt lakes, some of which are still mined. In the late 1840s farmers were eager to take up land here because it was prime crop-producing land. The town was settled in 1872 and has remained an important service centre since.

SEE & DO **Innes National Park:** see Top Attractions. **Courthouse Photographic Display:** historic photographs of the area; open Fri mornings or by appt; (08) 8852 1385. **Bublacowie Military Museum:** personal stories, memorabilia and documents, and also a craft centre; open Mon, Tues and Sun; 25km N. **Corny Point:** coastal town featuring a lighthouse and lookout, and fishing and camping; 69km NW. **Daly Head:** great surfing spot with nearby blowhole; 75km W. **Marion Bay:** popular with surfers and visitors to nearby Innes National Park; 79km SW.

Top: Beach path to Inneston
Opposite: Wallaroo ferry port

The Murray

It's a fabulous adventure to follow the twists and turns of Australia's greatest river – the mighty Murray – to where it seeps into the sea. You can do it by road or on the water in a **houseboat, paddlewheeler, kayak** or **canoe**. Beyond the waterway you'll find charming riverside towns full of beautiful **Art Deco architecture, quirky museums** and plenty of places to sample the delicious **local wines and produce**.

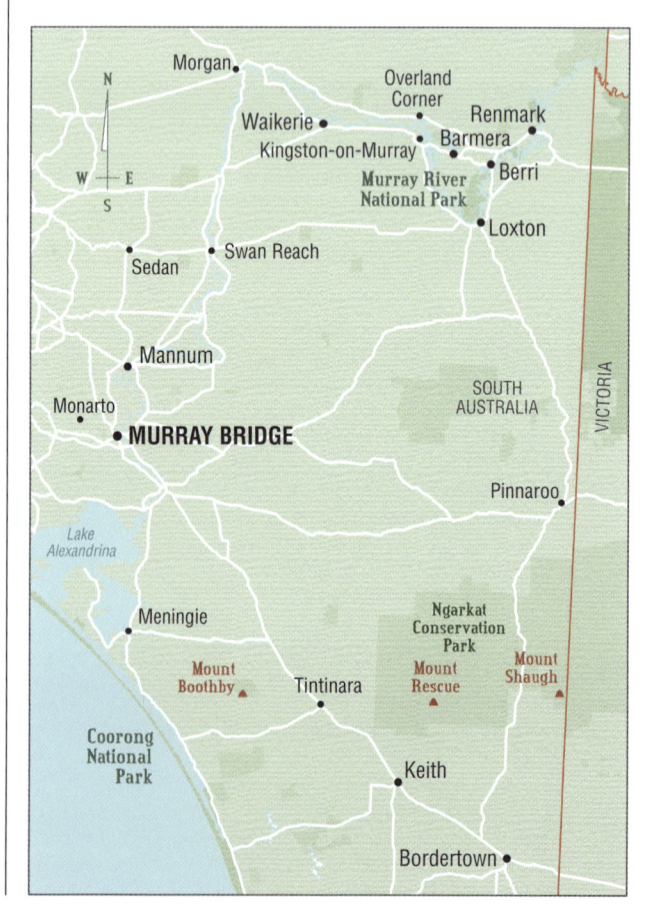

CHEAT SHEET

→ Allow at least three or four days to explore the region.

→ Best time to visit: year-round.

→ Main towns: Berri (see p. 236), Murray Bridge (see p. 238), Renmark (see p. 238).

→ The riverlands of the Murray are the Traditional Lands of the Latje Latje, Meru, Ngaiawang and Ngarrindjeri Peoples.

→ Don't miss: Banrock wetlands (and wine); a river cruise on an historic paddlesteamer; a stroll through riverland gardens; birdwatching in The Coorong.

→ Need to know: The floods of late 2022 and early 2023 swept along The Murray and into towns and communities, so check ahead before visiting to ensure attractions and activities are open.

→ Did you know? The Kurangk (Coorong), is the Traditional Land of the Ngarrindjeri Nation, and has sustained the people since Creation. Ancient shell middens which can be found on the Younghusband Peninsula are testament to this ongoing connection.

Top: Murray River houseboat
Opposite: *Murray Princess*, Mannum

TOP ATTRACTIONS

BANROCK STATION WINE & WETLAND CENTRE: Fruity wines mix with a cacophony of birds and frogs at Banrock Station. In these new times of sensitive agriculture, Banrock is working with environmental organisations to breathe life back into a pocket of wetland that was ruined by irrigation (almost 70 per cent of all Murray wetlands have been affected). The natural cycles of flooding and drying have seen the return of black swans, native fish and ibis, and a boardwalk gives visitors a close-up look. Kingston-on-Murray; (08) 8583 0299. It's 10km west of Barmera (see p. 236).

BIG BEND: The Murray River's tallest cliffs are home to diverse fauna and flora.; spectacular night tours are available; inquiries (08) 8570 1097; 20km downstream of Swan Reach (see p. 239).

COORONG NATIONAL PARK: Listed as a 'wetland of international importance', this park's waterways, islands and vast saltpans demonstrate a diverse ecological environment invaluable for the refuge and habitat of migratory and drought-stricken birds. Throughout the park are reminders of the long history and ongoing connection of the Traditional Owners, the Ngarrindjeri People. In the 1980s, archaeologists documented the location, size and content of various middens in The Coorong, showing that the middens form the largest, most extensive evidence of Aboriginal inhabitation in the region. There are a number of ways to see the park: take a boat, canoe or cruise on the waterways; walk one of the varied tracks offered; drive your 4WD onto the Southern Ocean beach; or simply sit and soak up the park's atmosphere. Walking is the best way to access great coastal views, birdwatching spots and historic ruins. The most comprehensive walk in the park is the Nukan Kungun Hike. This 25km hike starts at Salt Creek and includes smaller, side trails, including the informative walk to Chinaman's Well, the ruins of a temporary settlement that sprang up en route to the goldfields. The hike ends at the 42 Mile Crossing Sand Dune Walk, which leads to the wild Southern Ocean; (08) 8575 1200.

LOXTON HISTORICAL VILLAGE: The Riverland's early settler history comes to life in the 30 historic buildings in Loxton (see p. 237), all fully furnished in the styles of the late 1880s to mid-1900s. A highlight is the pine-and-pug building, Settler's Hut, built to represent the original hut occupied by the town's namesake, boundary rider William Loxton. Visit on one of the Village Alive days held twice yearly in the village, when locals dress up in period costume and the whole village steps back 100 years. Allan Hosking Dr, Loxton; (08) 8584 7194.

MANNUM DOCK MUSEUM: This excellent museum in Mannum (see p. 237) documents the changing history of the Mannum region through First Nations habitation, European settlement and river history to the present day. Outside is the renowned Randell's Dry Dock, where the grand lady of the Murray, *PS Marion*, is moored. Passenger cruises on the restored paddlesteamer still operate. Randell St, Mannum; (08) 8569 1303.

MURRAY RIVER NATIONAL PARK, KATARAPKO SECTION: Two distinct Australian vegetation regions merge in this park: the famous Murray River floodplains and the equally renowned Mallee region. The Murray Pine Drive gives visitors a taste of these two distinctive terrains. There are also walking trails from which you can spot the park's inhabitants, including echidnas, goannas and kangaroos. Off Katarapko Cres, just south of Berri; (08) 8595 2111.

PADTHAWAY WINE REGION: Though Padthaway's soil is not quite as rich as that of the Coonawarra region (see p. 241), it is a wonder that this region is not more prominent. With vines growing in terra rossa (red earth), wineries include **Padthaway Estate**, where visitors can also taste the wines of **Browns of Padthaway** in the 1850s old stables that has been converted to a cellar door and is situated near the red gums and stringybarks of Padthaway Conservation Park. The wine region is away from river country but worth a side trip. For more cellar doors, see: padthawaywineregion.com

PORT OF MORGAN MUSEUM: This comprehensive museum is dedicated to the rail- and river-trade history of Morgan (see p. 237). In the old railway buildings are museum exhibits focusing on the paddlesteamers and trains that were the lifeblood of the town. The Landseer Building has vintage vehicles and a 12m mural depicting the old Murray River lifestyle. Other highlights are the restored wharf and permanently moored PS *Mayflower*. Open Mon–Fri 10am–4pm; Morgan Riverfront; (08) 8540 0073.

RIVERLAND BIOSPHERE RESERVE: This 9000sqkm reserve incorporates the mallee country and arid outback landscapes of Chowilla Regional Reserve and Danggali Conservation Park. Chowilla comprises floodplains interspersed with native woodland and scrubland; fishing, canoeing and birdwatching are why you're here. The history of the floodplains is explained on the Old Coach Road Vehicle Trail. Danggali is a vast wilderness area with interesting trails to explore, including Nanya's Pad Interpretive Drive (100km circuit, 2WD accessible) and Tipperary Drive (100km circuit, 4WD only); both are excellent introductions to the mallee scrub. The 10km Target Mark Walking Trail is a bushwalking option. Maps from visitor centres; (08) 8595 2111.

RIVERLAND WINE REGION: Chances are you've tasted some of the Riverland region's grapes as more than 30 per cent of all Australian grapes are grown here. The region is currently working on enhancing the visitor experience by opening more cellar doors and focusing on quality, as well as quantity. For details, see: riverlandwine.com.au

Top: Canoeing at Coorong National Park **Opposite:** Dark Sky Tour with Jugglehouse

OTHER ATTRACTIONS

MALLEE TOURIST AND HERITAGE CENTRE: Established in 1999, this centre in Pinnaroo (*see* p. 238) dwarfs its former home in the old railway station, which is now a Pioneer Women's Museum. The new building comprises the D.A. Wurfel Grain Collection, featuring the largest cereal collection in Australia (1300 varieties); working letter presses in the Printing Museum; dioramas, interpretive displays and photos depicting local history in the Heritage Museum; and a collection of restored farm machinery in the Gum Family Collection. Open 10am–1pm or by appt; Railway Tce Sth, Pinnaroo; (08) 8577 8644.

MONARTO SAFARI PARK: This open-range 1000ha zoo features Australian, African and Asian animals. It also runs a breeding program for rare and endangered species. Jump on a safari bus tour to see the animals up close. On the way you might encounter the huge giraffe herd or some cheetahs, zebras or rhinoceroses. Tours depart hourly 10.30am–3.30pm. There are also walking tracks through native bushland and mallee country; last entry 3pm; 3401 Old Princes Hwy, Monarto; (08) 8534 4100. It is 10km west of Murray Bridge (*see* p. 238).

NGARKAT GROUP OF CONSERVATION PARKS: Protecting 262,700ha of sand dunes, mallee and heath are four adjacent conservation parks – Ngarkat, Scorpion Springs, Mount Rescue and Mount Shaugh. The walking trails are an excellent introduction to the region's vegetation. Birdwatching is particularly good at Rabbit Island (Mount Rescue) and Comet Bore (Ngarkat). For panoramic views, hike to the summit of Mount Rescue, Goose Hill or Mount Shaugh. Visitors can drive through the parks on the Pinaroo–Bordertown Rd. 34km south of Pinnaroo via Princes Hwy or via Snozwells Rd near Tintinara.

OLIVEWOOD: National Trust–listed historic building in Renmark (*see* p. 238), formerly the Chaffey homestead (the Canadian brothers who brought irrigation to Renmark), decked out in period furnishings with famous olive trees in the orchard; cnr Renmark Ave and 21st St, Renmark; (08) 8586 6175.

OVERLAND CORNER: This was the first settlement in the area, a convenient stop en route for drovers and people travelling to the goldfields. By 1855 a police post had been established to deal with the odd bushranger and quell the problems flaring between drovers and Traditional Owners. In 1859 the Overland Corner Hotel opened its doors. Its thick limestone walls and red gum floors have seen many floods. An 8km walking track into the adjacent Herons Bend Reserve leaves from the hotel. 19km NW of Barmera.

RIVER MURRAY INTERNATIONAL DARK SKY RESERVE: In 2019, this 3200sqkm stretch was accredited by the International Dark-Sky Association for its unpolluted skies. The 'core' area is the **Swan Reach Conservation Park** in the Mallee, and it's a great place to see the Milky Way. Astronomy tours are available.

ROCKY'S HALL OF FAME AND PIONEERS MUSEUM: Dean 'Rocky' Page established Barmera's (*see* p. 236) famous country music festival and was a well-known musician in his own right. Within the centre is an array of country music memorabilia and a display of replica guitars with the handprints of the legends who used them. The pièce de résistance is Slim Dusty's hat. Open Mon and Wed–Fri; Barwell Ave, Barmera; (08) 8588 1463.

RUSTONS DISTILLERY: Distilllery and rose garden 7km south-west of Renmark (*see* p. 238), grab a glass of gin to try among the 50,000 rose bushes from 4000 varieties; Moorna St, off Sturt Hwy; (08) 8586 6191.

YOOKAMURRA SANCTUARY: This sanctuary represents an initiative to restore 1100ha of land to its original state. The mallee vegetation that was found here before European habitation has been replanted. The Australian Wildlife Conservancy-owned property has infrequent open days for the public. Keep an eye out for the rare and endangered numbat or the bilby and woylie; Pipeline Rd, Sedan. The sanctuary is 21km west of Swan Reach (*see* p. 239).

KEY TOWNS

BARMERA
Population 1895

Barmera lies in the middle of a swooping hairpin bend of the Murray River, but it is hard to tell where the river stops and where the floodplains and tributaries begin in the area to the west of town. The wetlands eventually flow into Lake Bonney, a large body of water to the north of Barmera. Swimming, waterskiing, sailing and fishing are popular activities on the lake. The town was established in 1921 as a settlement for returned World War I soldiers, who were all promised a patch of well-irrigated farmland.

SEE & DO **Banrock Station Wine & Wetland Centre:** see Top Attractions. **Rocky's Hall of Fame and Pioneers Museum:** see Other Attractions. **Donald Campbell Obelisk:** commemorates an attempt in 1964 to break the world water-speed record, but 347.5km/h was not quite enough to make the books; Queen Elizabeth Dr. **Barmera Main Street Market:** 1st Sun each month, Oct–June. **Cobdogla Irrigation and Steam Museum:** has the world's only working Humphrey Pump, used in the early days of irrigation. Also local memorabilia and steam-train rides; open Tues and Sun; 5km W. **Napper's Old Accommodation House:** ruins of a hotel built in 1850 on the shores of the lake; turn east over Napper Bridge; 10km NW. **Loch Luna Game Reserve:** linking Lake Bonney and the Murray, these wetlands form an important refuge for waterbirds and are one of the few inland nesting sites for sea eagles. Chambers Creek, which loops around the reserve, is popular for canoeing; turn west over Napper Bridge; 16km NW. **Moorook Game Reserve:** these wetlands surround Wachtels Lagoon; 16km SW. **Loveday Internment Camps:** you can go on a guided tour or self-guided drive to the camps where Japanese, Italian and German POWs were held during World War II; details from visitor centre.

BERRI
Population 4143

Orange products and wine are big business in this Riverland town, which is surrounded by orchards and vineyards and is one of the major growing and manufacturing centres of the country's biggest orange-juice company. The name 'Berri' has nothing to do with fruit, though. It comes from 'bery bery', thought to mean 'bend in the river' in the language of the Meri People. The town was established in 1911, the year after irrigation of the Murray began.

SEE & DO **Community Mural:** enormous community-painted mural commemorating the past and present fruit industry; Old Sturt Hwy. **Berri Lookout Tower:** panoramic views of river, town and surrounds from a converted water tower; cnr Fiedler St and Vaughan Tce. **Lions Club Walking Trail:** 4km riverfront walk from Berri Marina to Martin Bend Reserve, a popular spot for picnics and waterskiing, via a First Nations mural and totems under the bridge. **Canoe Adventures:** guided canoe/kayak tours along the Murray River; 0421 167 645. **Monash:** a small irrigation town best known for the free family attractions at the Monash Adventure Park on Morgan Rd. Enjoy delicate handmade chocolates at the Chocolates and More store opposite the park; 12km NW.

BORDERTOWN
Population 2840

In spite of its name, Bordertown is actually 18km from the SA–Victoria border in the fertile country of the Tatiara district. Thought to be a Bodaruwitj word meaning 'good country', Tatiara's name is justified by the region's productive wool and grain industries. Look out for Bordertown's famous white kangaroos, Australia's only known colony. Another claim to fame is that former Australian prime minister Bob Hawke was born here.

SEE & DO **Padthaway Wine Region:** see Top Attractions. **Bordertown Wildlife Park:** native birds and animals, including pure-white kangaroos; Dukes Hwy. **Walkway Gallery:** in foyer of civic centre; Woolshed St. **Bordertown Recreation Lake:** popular spot for fishing, canoeing and walking, with artwork on display; northern outskirts of town. **Clayton Farm Heritage Museum:** features vintage farm machinery and a National Trust–classified thatched-roof building and woolshed; 3km S. **Mundulla:** a historic township featuring the heritage-listed Mundulla Hotel; 10km SW. **Bangham Conservation Park:** a significant habitat for the red-tailed black cockatoo; 30km SE.

KEITH
Population 1140

Keith is a farming town in the area formerly known as the Ninety Mile Desert. Settlers found the original land unpromising, but the area has since been transformed from infertile pasture to productive farmland with the addition to the soil of missing trace elements and water piped from the Murray.

SEE & DO **Congregational Church:** National Trust church with 11 locally made leadlight windows depicting the town's life and early settler history; Heritage St. **Early Settler's Cottage:** limestone historic cottage; open by appt; Heritage St; (08) 8755 1118. **Keith Water Feature:** water sculpture; Heritage St. **Monster Conservation Park:** scenic views and picnic spots; 10km S. **Mount Boothby Conservation Park:** mallee

VISITOR INFORMATION

Barmera Visitor Information Centre
Cnr Barwell Ave and Fowles St
(08) 8588 2289 or
1300 768 468

Renmark Paringa Visitor Information Centre
84 Murray Ave
(08) 8586 6704 or
1300 661 704
destinationriverland.org.au

Top: Fresh produce by the Sturt Highway Bottom: Restored farm tractors in Loxton

scrub, granite outcrops and wildflowers in spring; 58km NW via Tintinara.

LOXTON
Population 3947

The area around Loxton was originally largely settled by German immigrants, but the town's boom began when servicemen returned from World War II, enticed by irrigated allotments. The success of current-day industries, such as the production of citrus fruits, wine, dried fruit, wool and wheat, is due to their skill on the land. Loxton's delightful setting on the Murray River has made the town the 'Garden City of the Riverland'.

SEE & DO **Loxton Historical Village:** see Top Attractions. **The Pines Historical Home:** resplendent gardens and filled with antique furniture and fine china. Tours of the house 2pm every Sun, followed by afternoon tea on request; Henry St; 0427 820 815. **Pepper tree:** grown from a seed planted by William Loxton over 110 years ago; near the historical village. **Nature trail:** along riverfront; canoes for hire. **Heritage walk:** brochure from visitor centre. **Salena Estate:** wine-tasting and sales; Bookpurnong Rd; (08) 8584 1333; 12km N. **Lock 4:** picnic and barbecue area on Murray River; 14km N. **MV *Loch Luna* Eco Cruise:** relaxing 3hr cruise around the Nockburra and Chambers creeks; departs daily (except Sat) from Kingston-on-Murray at 9.30am; 0449 122 271; 35km NW.

MANNUM
Population 2537

Mannum is one of the oldest towns on the Murray River. It was the romantic heart of the old paddlesteamer days. In 1853 the 'Father of Mannum', William Randell, built the first Murray River paddlesteamer, *Mary Ann* (named after his mother), in order to transport his flour to the Victoria goldfields. The paddlesteamer set out from Mannum in 1853 and started a boom in the river transport industry. Another first for Mannum was Australia's first steam car, built in 1894 by David Shearer. In January 2023, floods hit the town of Mannum; check ahead before visiting to see what's open.

SEE & DO **Mannum Dock Museum:** see Top Attractions. **River Murray International Dark Sky Reserve:** see Other Attractions. **Mary Ann Reserve:** popular recreation reserve on the riverbank with a replica of PS *Mary Ann*'s boiling engine. PS *River Murray Princess* is moored here between cruises. **Ferry service:** twin ferries operate to the eastern side of the river. **River cruises and houseboat hire:** afternoon, day and overnight cruises are available from the town wharf. Alternatively, hire a houseboat to discover the Murray River your own way. Contact visitor centre for details. **Town lookout:** off Purnong Rd to the east. **Scenic and historical walks:** brochures from visitor centre. **Mannum Falls:** picnics and scenic walks, best visited in winter (after rains) when the waterfall is flowing; 6km SE. **Kia Marina:** the largest river marina in SA; boats and houseboats for hire; 8km NE. **Lowan Conservation Park:** mallee vegetation park with varied wildlife, including fat-tailed dunnarts, mallee fowl and western grey kangaroos; turn-off 28km E at Bowhill. **Purnong:** scenic drive north-east, runs parallel to excellent Halidon Bird Sanctuary; 33km NE.

MENINGIE
Population 860

Today Meningie is an attractive lakeside town, but it was once a wilderness area, home to the Ngarrindjeri People, who had a self-sufficient lifestyle on the water. They made canoes to fish on the waterways and shelters to protect themselves from the weather. However, European invasion – after Captain Charles Sturt's journey down the Murray from 1829 to 1830 – soon wiped out much of the population, largely through violence and the introduction of smallpox. Stretching south from the mouth of the Murray and located just south of Meningie, the justifiably famous Coorong, with its lakes, birdlife, fishing and deserted ocean beaches, attracts visitors year-round.

SEE & DO **Coorong National Park:** see Top Attractions. **The Cheese Factory Museum:** community museum with special interest in the changing population of Meningie and the Coorong; open Tues–Sun; Fiebig Rd. **Coorong Cottage Industries:** local craft and produce; The Chambers, Princes Hwy. **Pelican Path:** also known as Yunti Ngopun Ngami, meaning 'together we walk' in Ngarrindjeri language, this 400m interpretive trail follows the foreshore and highlights the Aboriginal and European environmental history of the region. **Scenic drive:** follows Lake Albert to the west, adjacent to Lake Alexandrina, which is the largest permanent freshwater lake in the country (50,000ha). Ferry crossing at Narrung.

MORGAN
Population 326

This town was once a thriving river port and a stop on the rail trade route to Adelaide. Settlers saw the potential of the region, and Morgan boomed as soon as it was declared a town in 1878. Now it is a quiet holiday destination, but evidence of its boom days can still be seen in the streetscapes and the historic wharf and rail precinct.

SEE & DO **Port of Morgan Museum:** see Top Attractions. **Houseboats:** for hire; contact visitor centre for details. **Heritage walk:** self-guided trail covers 41 historic sites, including the impressive wharves (1877) standing 12m high, the customs house and courthouse, the sunken barge and steamer, and the rail precinct; details and brochure from visitor centre. **Morgan Conservation Park:** a diverse landscape of river flats, sand dunes and mallee scrub with abundant birdlife; across the Murray River from Morgan. **White Dam Conservation Park:** well known for red and western grey kangaroo populations; 9km NW. **Cadell:** scenic 12km drive east from Morgan via a ferry crossing (operates 24hrs) to Cadell, a major citrus-growing region.

MURRAY BRIDGE
Population 17,457

Murray Bridge, just as its name suggests, is all about bridges. The town was established in 1879 when a road bridge was built over the Murray River. The plan to make the river a major trade route from east to west and back had become a reality. In 1886 the construction of a railway line between Adelaide and Melbourne cemented the town's importance. Today watersports, cruises and an unhurried river atmosphere make Murray Bridge SA's fourth-largest urban hub and a pleasant spot to visit.

SEE & DO **Monarto Safari Park:** *see* Other Attractions. **Captain's Cottage Museum:** local history museum in an old stone house; open Sat–Sun and public holidays 10am–4pm; 12 Thomas St; (08) 8539 1142. **Murray Bridge Regional Gallery:** regular art exhibitions from local artists, plus touring exhibitions; open Tues–Sat 10am–4pm, Sun 11am–4pm; 27 Sixth St; (08) 8539 1420. **Sturt Reserve:** offers fishing, swimming, picnic and playground facilities, a skate ramp as well as a caged local bunyip (coin-operated); Sturt Reserve Rd. **Thiele Reserve:** a popular waterskiing spot on the eastern bank of the river; Thiele Rd. **Avoca Dell:** riverside picnic spot with boating facilities, waterskiing, minigolf and a caravan park; Avoca Dell Dr. **Swanport Wetlands Reserve:** recreational reserve with raised walkways and bird hides; adjacent to Swanport Bridge; off Princes Hwy. **River cruises:** on the Murray River; contact visitor centre for details. **Town and riverside walks:** brochures from visitor centre. **Sunnyside Reserve Lookout:** sweeping views across the wetlands and Murray River; Karoonda Rd, off Princes Hwy; 10km E. **Willow Point Wines:** cellar-door tastings and sales of ports, sherries and muscats; open 10am–5pm; 1041 Jervois Rd, White Sands; (08) 8532 2632; 10km S. **Ferries–McDonald and Monarto conservation parks:** walking trails through important mallee conservation areas, prolific birdlife, and blossoms in spring; Ferries McDonald Rd; 16km W. **Tailem Bend:** historic railway town with broad views across the Murray River. Over 90 historic buildings are displayed at the Old Tailem Town re-created early settler village; open 9am–5pm; Princes Hwy; (08) 8572 3838; 25km SE. **Wellington:** situated where Lake Alexandrina meets the Murray River, with a free 24hr vehicle ferry across the water; 32km S. **Karoonda:** the heart of the Mallee, Karoonda is known for the meteorite that fell nearby in 1930 (on display at the council office, see also the monument at RSL Park). Other natural attractions include the limestone caves of Bakara Plains and walking trails in Pioneer Historical Park; 66km E.

PINNAROO
Population 575

In the 19th century the harshness of the land prevented settlers from properly establishing a wheat farming community here. Instead, they chose the more fertile conditions further south-west. The arrival of the rail in 1906 and the influx of farming families allowed the community to grow and the agricultural industry to develop into what it is today. You can find out more about the history at the Mallee Tourist and Heritage Centre in town and also explore the Ngarkat group of conservation parks from Pinnaroo.

SEE & DO **Mallee Tourist and Heritage Centre; Ngarkat group of conservation parks:** *see* Other Attractions for both. **Animal Park and Aviary:** South Tce. **Karte Conservation Park:** includes a walking trail through low scrub and 40m high sand dunes; 30km NW. **Billiatt Conservation Park:** the 1km walk through mallee scrub and dune country ends with panoramic views from Trig Point; 37km NW. **Lameroo:** Mallee town with historic 1898 Byrne pug-and-pine homestead (Yappara Rd) and railway station (Railway Tce); 40km W. **Peebinga Conservation Park:** important reserve for the rare western whipbird; Loxton Rd; 42km N.

⭑ RENMARK
Population 4703

Renmark lives and thrives on the Murray River – a laidback river town awash with vines and fruit trees. It's a regional hub, a functional sort of place with a grassy riverfront and houseboats chugging past. It is hard to believe that the lush landscape around Renmark, flush with verdant orchards and vineyards, was once a dry, sandy wasteland. In 1887 the Canadian-born Chaffey brothers were granted 30,000 acres (12,000ha) by the SA government to test their irrigation scheme, piping water from the mighty Murray River. Theirs was the first of its type to succeed in Australia, and today the farmlands here are still irrigated with river water.

SEE & DO **Olivewood; Rustons Distillery:** *see* Other Attractions. **PS Industry:** this 1911 grand lady of the river still paddles up and down the river on 90min cruises, 1st Sun of the month; bookings at visitor centre; 84 Murray Ave; (08) 8586 6704. **Renmark Hotel:** historic Art Deco community-owned pub, with accommodation, restaurants and bars; open 9am–late Mon–Sun; cnr Murray Ave and Para St; (08) 8586 6755. **Canoe the Riverland:** guided paddles on the river, exploring hidden nooks and crannies; tours depart visitor centre; 0475 754 222. **Paringa:** small riverside community (population 950) featuring a historic suspension bridge (1927), Bert Dix Memorial Park and nearby Headings Cliffs

Opposite: Enjoying the views

TOP EVENTS

→ FEB Mardi Gras and Nippy's Loxton Gift (both Loxton); Riverland Dinghy Derby (Renmark)

→ EASTER Horse Show (Waikerie)

→ APR Riverland Harvest Festival & Great Grape Stomp (Loxton);

→ APR-MAY Riverland Rock 'n' Roll Festival (Waikerie)

→ SEPT Riverland Field Days (Barmera); Australian International Pedal Prix (Murray Bridge)

→ OCT Barmera Sheepdog Trials; Riverland Wine and Food Festival (Berri); Spring Show (Loxton); Rose & Garden Festival (Renmark)

TEMPERATURES

Jan: 16–34°C

July: 4–17°C

Lookout; 4km E. **Angove:** leading Riverland wine producers, with cellar-door tastings and sales (sip some St Agnes Brandy); open Mon–Fri 10am–5pm, Sat 11am–4pm, Sun 10am–3pm; Bookmark Ave; (08) 8580 3148; 5km SW. **Murray River National Park, Bulyong Island section:** just upstream from Renmark, offering terrific canoeing, boating, fishing and birdwatching; access via Murtho Rd, Paringa; (08) 8595 2111; 8km N. **Woolshed Brewery:** the Riverland's own craft beer brewery; open Mon–Sun 11am–5pm; 65 Wilkinson Rd, Paringa; (08) 8595 8188; 21km NE.

SWAN REACH
Population 274

Swan Reach's picturesque Murray River scenery and excellent fishing make the town a popular holiday destination. This quiet little township was once one of five large sheep stations; the original homestead is now the Swan Reach Hotel. Swan Reach was established as one of the first river ports for Murray River trade, but the introduction of rail and Morgan's rise as one of the state's busiest ports saw the era of paddlesteamers in Swan Reach decline.

SEE & DO **Big Bend:** see Top Attractions. **River Murray International Dark Sky Reserve** and **Yookamurra Sanctuary:** see Other Attractions for both. **Museum:** local history displays with special focus on Swan Reach's flood history, the waters having devastated the town in the early 1900s; open Wed 10am–1pm, Sat 10am–12pm; Nildottie Rd. **Ridley and Swan Reach conservation parks:** both parks represent typical western Murray vegetation and protect the habitat of the hairy-nosed wombat; 7.5km S and 10km W, respectively. **Ngaut Ngaut Boardwalk:** guided tours of archaeological site, established when an ancient skeleton was discovered; Nildottie; 14km S. **Bakara Conservation Park:** mallee-covered plains and sand dunes, important habitat for the mallee fowl; 32km E. **Brookfield Conservation Park:** bushwalking in limestone country to see hairy-nosed wombats, red kangaroos and a variety of bird species; 40km NW.

WAIKERIE
Population 1670

Waikerie, the citrus centre of Australia, is surrounded by an oasis of irrigated orchards and vineyards in the midst of the mallee-scrub country of the Riverland. Owing to its position on cliff-tops, the area around Waikerie was not a promising settlement. But, in an experiment by the SA government in 1894 that attempted to alleviate unemployment and decentralise capital, 281 people were relocated from Adelaide – and an instant town was born. Waikerie has beautiful views of the river gums and sandstone cliffs along the Murray River and is a popular spot for fishing, boating and waterskiing. The skies above are a glider's paradise due to the fantastic thermals and flat landscape.

SEE & DO **Rain Moth Gallery:** local art exhibitions; Peake Tce; call 0435 648 282 for opening hours. **Harts Lagoon:** wetland area with bird hide; Ramco Rd. **Houseboat hire:** scenic trips along the Murray; contact visitor centre for details. **Bush Safari:** camel or 4WD tours to the river and outback country north-east of Waikerie; bookings (08) 8543 2280. **Scenic walk:** along cliff-top to lookout; northern outskirts of town. **Waikerie Gliding Club:** offers recreational flights, beginner courses and cross-country training; Waikerie Aerodrome, off Sturt Hwy, east side of town; inquiries (08) 8541 2644. **Maize Island Conservation Park:** this waterbird reserve has fantastic cliffs and lagoons. Beware of strong currents when swimming; 2km N. **Pooginook Conservation Park:** both dense and open mallee country, home to kangaroos, hairy-nosed wombats and the ever-busy mallee fowl; 12km NE. **Stockyard Plain Disposal Basin Reserve:** varied plant and birdlife – over 130 bird species identified; key available from visitor centre; 12km SW. **Broken Cliffs:** popular fishing spot; Taylorville Rd; 15km NE. **Birds Australia Gluepot Reserve:** important mallee area that forms part of the Bookmark Biosphere Reserve. Also significant bird refuge, with over 17 threatened Australian species to be seen on the 14 walking trails; 64km N.

Limestone Coast

Stretching from the Victorian border almost all the way to The Coorong east of Adelaide, the Limestone Coast contains many wonders, from mysterious **cyan-coloured lakes** to **fossil hordes, sinkhole gardens, underground waterfalls, UNESCO-listed caves** and a fabled strip of special soil that produces some of the **world's best cabernets**. Home to Australia's first saint, it's a place with plenty of **fascinating history** to unearth.

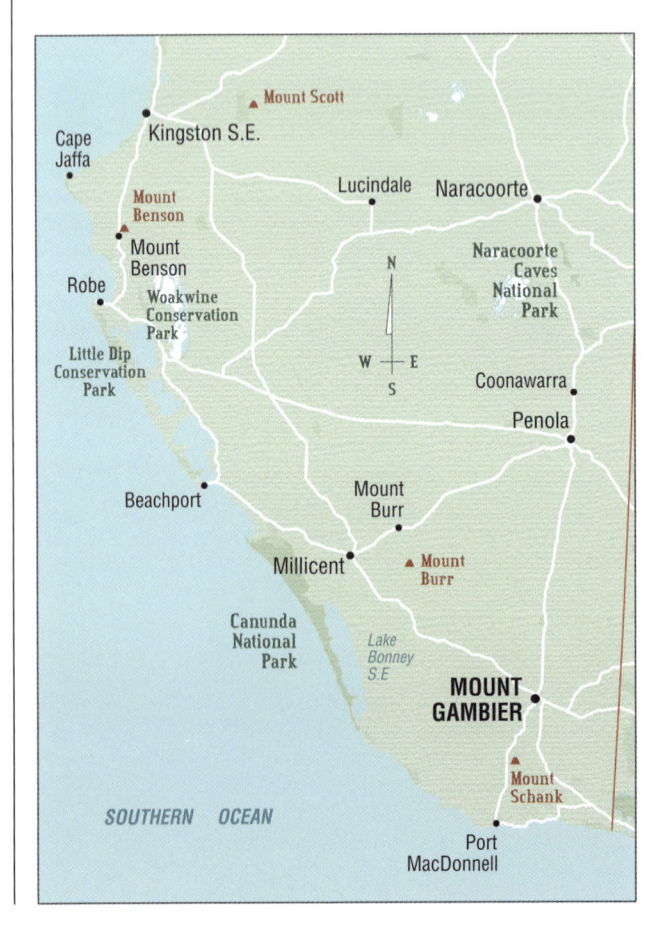

CHEAT SHEET

→ Allow at least three or four days for a proper exploration.

→ Best time to visit: year-round.

→ Main towns: Mount Gambier (*see* p. 244), Penola (*see* p. 244), Robe (*see* p. 245).

→ The Limestone Coast is the Traditional Land of the Buandig and Ngarrindjeri Peoples.

→ Don't miss: winetasting in the Coonawarra; the sunken gardens and Blue Lake of Mount Gambier; World Heritage-listed Naracoorte Caves; feasting on lobster; Beachport jetty; the Bowman Scenic Drive.

Top: Umpherston Sinkhole garden, Mount Gambier
Opposite: Robe's obelisk

TOP ATTRACTIONS

BEACHPORT CONSERVATION PARK: This park is a succession of white beaches, sand dunes and rugged limestone cliffs, with the southern shore of Lake George lying inland. The coast is dotted with ancient shell middens and is accessed primarily by 4WD or on foot. Five Mile Drift, a beach on Lake George, is a good base for swimming, sailing and windsurfing. Access to the coast side is via Bowman Scenic Dr, which begins at the lighthouse; access to the Lake George side is via Railway Tce North, Beachport.

BLUE LAKE: Drive up the slopes of the extinct volcanic cone of Mount Gambier itself to check out this amazing lake, so-called because its water changes from dull, blue-grey during winter to an unbelievable, iridescent blue between Nov and Mar. You can take a walk around the rim of the crater on a 3.6km walking track, or Aquifer Tours runs elevator trips down an old well shaft to the water's edge; check ahead for tour times. Tours run Mon–Sun year-round, times vary, check ahead; cnr Bay Rd and John Watson Dr, Mount Gambier; (08) 8723 1199.

CANUNDA NATIONAL PARK: The massive sand-dune system of the southern part of the park rises to cliffs and scrublands in the north. These two sections provide quite different experiences. In the north (accessed via Southend and Millicent) the walking trails pass along cliff-tops and through the scrubland. In the south (accessed via Carpenter Rocks and Millicent) the beaches and wetlands provide picturesque coastal walks. You can surf, 4WD, birdwatch, bushwalk and fish (excellent from the beaches and rocks). (08) 8735 1177. The park is accessed 18km north-west of Millicent (*see* p. 243).

CAVE GARDENS: This 50m deep sinkhole cave in the middle of downtown Mount Gambier (*see* p. 244) was used as a water supply by early settlers. It's now a sunken garden with a suspended viewing platform; cnr Watson Tce and Bay Rd, Mount Gambier.

COONAWARRA WINE REGION: Unlike many other Australian wine regions, Coonawarra was a planned horticulture scheme – and a very successful one. John Riddoch, a Scottish immigrant, acquired extensive lands in SA's south-east in the late 1800s. He subdivided 800ha of his landholding specifically for orchards and vineyards. Prominent wine professionals such as Wolf Blass damned this region as a place that could never produce decent wine, and the original John Riddoch wine estate was nearly sold to the Department of Forestry and Lands (thankfully, David Wynn purchased the property and it is now Wynns Coonawarra). In the 1950s, large wine companies such as Penfolds and Yalumba finally began recognising the depth of the region's reds, and opinions began to change. Coonawarra's famed terra rossa (red earth) combined with the region's particular climate is now known to create some of the best cabernet sauvignon in the country, as well as excellent shiraz, merlot, riesling and chardonnay. **Wynns Coonawarra** produces world-class shiraz and cabernet sauvignon, some for purchase at reasonable prices. Other excellent wineries to visit are **Balnaves of Coonawarra**, **Brands of Coonawarra**, **Majella** and **Zema Estate**. The town of Penola (*see* p. 244) is a good access point for the wine region.

EWENS PONDS AND PICCANINNIE PONDS CONSERVATION PARKS: For a unique snorkelling or diving experience, visit the crystal-clear waters of these parks, both located near the town of Port MacDonnell (*see* p. 244). At Ewens Ponds there are three ponds, connected via channels. Snorkel on the surface to see the amazing plant life underwater, or go diving for the ultimate experience. The deep caverns in Piccaninnie Ponds offer visitors an insight into the underwater world. Snorkellers can gaze into the depths of the Chasm, while divers can explore the limestone-filtered waters of the Cathedral, so named because of its regal white walls. While no experience is necessary for snorkelling, divers require qualifications. Inquiries and bookings through SA Parks and Wildlife (08) 8735 1177.

MARY MACKILLOP PENOLA CENTRE: Details the lives of Mary MacKillop and Father Julian Tenison (who shared Mary's dream) through photos, memorabilia and displays in this 1860s-style schoolhouse in Penola (see p. 244); Portland St, Penola.

MOUNT BENSON WINE REGION: The first vines were planted less than two decades ago, and this region near Robe (see p. 245) is still revealing its true colours. The large venture of **Norfolk Rise**, established by an international company, indicates the area's promise. Make sure to try its shiraz. Other wineries to visit are **Cape Jaffa Wines** and **Ralph Fowler Wines**.

NARACOORTE CAVES NATIONAL PARK: For thousands of years the 28 Naracoorte Caves – today protected by national park and UNESCO World Heritage listing – have acted as a natural trap for animals, providing an environment that was just right for fossilisation. Twenty fossil deposits have been found throughout the 600ha park – an incredible record of Australia's evolution over the last 500,000 years. Guided walking tours of four caves take in the chambers, extensive stalagmite and stalactite deposits and fossil collections. The Victoria Fossil Cave Tour is an introduction to the ancient animal history of Australia, while the natural delights of the caves, including helictites and fabulous domed ceilings, are accessed on the 30min Alexandra Cave Tour. The world of bats is celebrated on the Bat Tour, the highlight being unhindered views of the bats' activity from infra-red cameras. Adventure caving allows visitors to see the caves in their raw state, while also providing an opportunity for exciting squeezes and crawls through some very tight spaces. For caving beginners, try the Stick-Tomato tour. For more experienced cavers, enjoy the crawls and sights on the Starburst Chamber Tour. The Fox Cave Tour is the ultimate caving experience, with access to the cave system by a small entrance, leading to great fossil collections, vast speleothem development and incredible scenery. You can get details about these tours from Wonambi Fossil Centre, located within the park; (08) 8760 1210.

PORT MACDONNELL MARITIME MUSEUM: The long maritime history of the stretch of coast near Port MacDonnell (see p. 244) is littered with stories of shipwrecks and bravery. Here photos and salvaged artefacts bring the old days to life. A particularly tragic story is the wreck of the *Admella* on an off-coast reef in 1859. Only 24 of the 113 people aboard survived. There is also a focus on community history and on the rock lobster industry. Cnr Charles and Milstead sts, Port MacDonnell; (08) 8738 3000.

UMPHERSTON SINKHOLE: A sunken garden on the floor of a collapsed cave in Mount Gambier (see p. 244) and it's floodlit at night. The water level was once much higher (people used to row boats here!); Jubilee Hwy E, Mount Gambier.

OTHER ATTRACTIONS

ENGELBRECHT CAVE: Guided tours of the limestone cave system that extends beneath Mount Gambier's (see p. 244) city streets; cafe onsite; open 9.30am–3pm; 26 Chute St, Mount Gambier; (08) 8723 5552.

LITTLE DIP CONSERVATION PARK: Features a complex, moving sand-dune system, salt lakes, freshwater lakes and abundant wildlife. Drive or walk through native bush to beaches for surfing and beach-fishing; some areas are 4WD only. The park is 11km south of Robe (see p. 245).

MILLICENT MUSEUM: In the town of Millicent (see p. 243), the visitor centre houses the Living History Museum, including a shipwreck room, farm machinery shed, a First Nations room, a natural history room, a T-Class locomotive and the largest collection of restored horse-drawn vehicles in SA; open Mon–Fri 9am–5pm, Sat–Sun 10am–4pm; 1 Mt Gambier Rd, Millicent; (08) 8733 2417.

MOUNT GAMBIER VISITOR CENTRE: Features a full-scale replica of *HMS Lady Nelson* (the ship that first spied the peak of Mount Gambier in 1800) and interactive displays on the region's history and geography; open Mon–Fri 9am–5pm, Sat–Sun 10am–4pm; 35 Jubilee Hwy E, Mount Gambier; (08) 8724 9750.

OLD WOOL AND GRAIN STORE MUSEUM: The old store in the town of Beachport (see p. 243) contains a whaling and fishing display including harpoons and whaling pots, as well as relics from shipwrecks off the coastline. Upstairs rooms are furnished in the style of the day. Natural history display features local and migratory seabirds. Open 10am–4pm; 5 Railway Tce, Beachport; (08) 8735 8013.

VISITOR INFORMATION

Mount Gambier Visitor Centre
35 Jubilee Hwy E
(08) 8724 9750 or
1800 087 187
discovermountgambier.com.au

Penola Coonawarra Visitor Information Centre,
27 Arthur St, Penola
(08) 8737 2855 or
1300 045 373
coonawarra.org

Top: Naracoorte Caves National Park **Bottom:** Umpherston Sinkhole

KEY TOWNS

BEACHPORT
Population 530

Beachport started out as a whaling port but today people flock here for summer holidays to relax on the beautiful sandy beaches and swim in the bay. The crayfish industry is thriving and the town has SA's second-longest jetty, favoured by anglers young and old, with regular catches including whiting, flathead and garfish. The Bowman Scenic Drive provides stunning views over the Southern Ocean with access to sheltered coves and rocky headlands for the adventurous to explore. It is also a great place for whale-watching.

SEE & DO **Beachport Conservation Park:** see Top Attractions. **Old Wool and Grain Store Museum:** see Other Attractions. **Lanky's Walk:** a short walk through bushland to Lanky's Well, where Lanky Kana, a member of the local Bunganditj People, camped while working as a police tracker; begins on Railway Tce North; details on this and other walks from visitor centre. **Pool of Siloam:** this small lake, seven times saltier than the sea, is said to be a cure for all manner of ailments. Also a popular swimming spot; end of McCourt St. **Lighthouse:** the original lighthouse was located on Penguin Island, a breeding ground for seals and penguins offshore from Cape Martin, where the current Cape Martin Lighthouse (1960) now stands. It offers good views of the island from the cape; south of town. **Woakwine Cutting:** an incredible gorge, cut through Woakwine Range by one man to drain swampland and allow farming; with viewing platform, information boards and machinery exhibit; 10km N.

KINGSTON S.E.
Population 1637

Known as the 'Gateway to the South East', Kingston S.E. is at the southern end of Coorong National Park on Lacepede Bay. The area is the Traditional Land of the Ngarrindjeri, river people of the Coorong and the Murray River. This famous lobster town was established in 1858 and its shallow lakes and lagoons are a haven for birdlife and a delight for photographers.

SEE & DO **National Trust Museum:** historic museum; open 10am–12pm during school holidays, or by appt; Cooke St; (08) 8767 2033. **Cape Jaffa Lighthouse:** built in the 1860s on the Margaret Brock Reef, it was dismantled and re-erected on its current site in the 1970s; open 10am–3pm during school holidays, or by appt; Marine Pde; 0427 854 175. **Analematic Sundial:** an unusual sundial, one of only eight in the world; on an island in the creek adjacent to Apex Park in East Tce. **Power House engine:** historic engine that produced the town's energy until 1974; Lions Park, Holland St. **The Big Lobster:** 17m high 'Larry Lobster'; Princes Hwy. **Butchers Gap Conservation Park:** this important coastal park provides a winter refuge for bird species. Follow the walking trail from the carpark; 6km SW. **The Granites:** rocky outcrops, a striking sight from the beach; 18km N. **Cape Jaffa:** scenic drive south-west from Kingston S.E. leads to this small fishing village popular with anglers and divers. The Cape Jaffa Seafood and Wine Festival is usually held here each Jan; 18km SW. **Mount Scott Conservation Park:** part of a former coastal dune system, with walks through stringybark forest; 20km E. **Jip Jip Conservation Park:** features a prominent outcrop of unusually shaped granite boulders; 50km NE.

MILLICENT
Population 4760

Millicent is a prosperous country community located in the heart of the Limestone Coast region. It is named after Millicent Glen, wife of one of the early settlers and daughter of the first Anglican Bishop of Adelaide. In 1876 the ship *Geltwood* was wrecked off Canunda Beach, with debris, bodies and cargo littering the sands. Relics from the *Geltwood* can be found in the town's award-winning Millicent Museum. The town's subtle woody aroma is from the surrounding pine forests, which support a pulp mill, a paper mill and sawmill.

SEE & DO **Canunda National Park:** see Top Attractions. **Millicent Museum:** see Other Attractions. **Lake McIntyre:** boardwalks and bird hides to view the lake's prolific birdlife, native fish and yabbies; off Saleyards Rd. **Mayura Station Tasting Room:** wagyu dinners on Thu, Fri and Sat nights; bookings essential; Canunda Frontage Rd; (08) 8733 4333. **Woakwine Range Wind Farm:** dozens of giant turbines dominate the Woakwine Range skyline, comprising the largest wind-farm development in the Southern Hemisphere. Take a drive along the Wind Farm Tourist Drive – maps available from the visitor centre; Frontage Rd, Tantanoola; 2km S. **Mount Muirhead Lookout:** a large viewing platform provides views of Millicent, pine plantations and Mount Burr Range. It is also the start of the Volcanoes Discovery Trail (brochure from visitor centre); Mt Burr Rd; 6km NE. **Mount Burr:** a historic timber town, the first to plant pines for commercial use on the Limestone Coast; 10km NE. **Tantanoola Caves Conservation Park:** daily tours of an imposing dolomite cavern in an ancient limestone cliff. Also walks and picnic areas; open 10am–3pm; Princes Hwy; (08) 8734 4153; 21km SE. **Glencoe Woolshed:** National Trust limestone woolshed once occupied by 38 shearers; open Mon–Sat 9am–5pm, Sun 11am–5pm; Glencoe Rd; 0432 881 842; 29km SE.

⭐ MOUNT GAMBIER
Population 26,734

SA's second-biggest town, Mount Gambier boasts an incredible collection of volcanic caves and lakes and sits at the base of an extinct volcano. The area has an amazing array of craters and lakes above ground and limestone caves beneath. Lieutenant James Grant named Mount Gambier in 1800 – he sighted it from *HMS Lady Nelson*. The original settlement was known as Gambier Town. Today Mount Gambier sits at the centre of a vast pine plantation region and is surrounded by farming and dairy country … but everyone's here to see the amazing Blue Lake and the caves around town.

SEE & DO **Blue Lake; Cave Gardens; Umpherston Sinkhole:** *see* Top Attractions for all. **Mount Gambier Visitor Centre; Engelbrecht Cave:** *see* Other Attractions for both. **Old Courthouse:** a National Trust–listed dolomite building with a local history museum inside; open Thurs–Sun 10am–4pm, reduced winter hours; 42A Bay Rd; (08) 8725 7011. **Riddoch Arts and Cultural Centre:** changing exhibitions of local and touring art and sculpture; open Mon–Fri 10am–5pm, Sat–Sun 10am–2pm; 1 Bay Rd; (08) 8723 2563. **Centenary Tower:** picturesque views of the city and surrounding countryside from 190m above sea level; open when flag is flying; Elliott Dr; (08) 8724 9750. **City Heritage Walk:** self-guided wander around the town's old edifices, many constructed of white Mount Gambier stone; brochure from visitor centre; (08) 8724 9750. **Mount Schank:** outstanding views of the surrounding district from the 158m peak of an extinct volcano, via 2 very steep summit tracks; off Post Office Rd, Mount Schank; 17km S.

NARACOORTE
Population 5223

Naracoorte dates from the 1840s but its growth has been slow. In the 1850s it was a stopover for Victorian gold escorts and miners. Since then it has developed a rich agricultural industry. Today it is renowned for its natural attractions, including parks and gardens but more significantly the Naracoorte Caves, which are in a national park protected as a UNESCO World Heritage–listed Site.

SEE & DO **Naracoorte Caves National Park:** *see* Top Attractions. **The Sheep's Back:** a comprehensive museum in the former flour mill (1870) details the history and community of the wool industry, with a craft and souvenir shop and information centre; MacDonnell St; (08) 8762 1399. **Art Gallery:** local and touring exhibitions; open Wed–Sun; Ormerod St; (08) 8762 3390. **Pioneer Park:** restored 1876 V-class steam locomotive on display; MacDonnell St. **Walking trail:** starts at the town centre and winds 5km along the Naracoorte Creek. **Wrattonbully wine region:** a recently established wine region focusing mainly on red varieties; 15km SE. **Bool Lagoon Game Reserve:** wetland area of international significance, a haven for ibis and more than 100 waterbird species. It includes boardwalks and a bird hide; 30km S. **Lucindale:** a small country town featuring a Historical Society Museum and Jubilee Park with a lake, island and bird haven; 41km E.

PENOLA
Population 1376

Penola is one of the oldest towns in south-east SA, and has some excellent wineries nearby. The town is noted for its association with Mary MacKillop, a Josephite nun who, in 1866, established Australia's first school to cater for children, regardless of their family's income or social class. In 2010 she was canonised by the Vatican, making her the first Australian to be declared a saint. Penola is also noted for its literary roots – several Australian poets have been inspired by its landscape and lifestyle.

SEE & DO **Coonawarra Wine Region; Mary MacKillop Penola Centre:** *see* Top Attractions for both. **Petticoat Lane:** heritage area of original cottages, including Sharam Cottage, the first built in town; many are now retail outlets. **John Shaw Neilson Acquisitive Art Gallery:** incorporates the Local History Exhibition and John Shaw Nielson art collection inside the visitor centre; Arthur St. **Toffee and Treats:** sells old-fashioned sweets; Church St. **Heritage walk:** details from visitor centre. **Yallum Park:** a magnificent two-storey Victorian home with original decorations; by appt 0418 854 505; 8km W. **Penola Conservation Park:** signposted woodland and wetland walk; 10km W. **Nangwarry Forestry Museum:** features a fascinating array of mill machinery, firefighting equipment, photographs and other artefacts from a bygone era; 18km S.

PORT MACDONNELL
Population 660

Port MacDonnell is a quiet fishing town that was once a thriving port. The rich maritime history, fascinating natural pools and coastal scenery attract visitors year-round. The establishment of the breakwater in 1975 has ensured the southern rock lobster trade many more years of fruitful operation and the fleet is now the largest in Australia.

SEE & DO **Port MacDonnell Maritime Museum; Ewens Ponds and Piccaninnie Ponds Conservation Parks:** *see* Top Attractions for both. **Clarke's Park:** popular picnic spot with natural spring; northern outskirts. **Fishing:** anglers will enjoy fishing from the jetty and landing. Boat charters are available for deep-sea catches of tuna; details from visitor centre. **Heritage walk:** includes historic cemetery with hidden headstones; contact visitor centre. **Cape Northumberland Heritage and Nature Park:** a coastal park famous for its sunrises and sunsets. Other highlights include a historic lighthouse,

Top: Water views near the town of Robe **Bottom:** Marina in Robe **Opposite:** Piccaninnie Ponds Conservation Park

TOP EVENTS

→ JAN Surf Fishing Contest (Kingston SE); Seafood and Wine Festival (Cape Jaffa)

→ FEB Taste the Limestone Coast (Naracoorte); Petanque Festival (Penola); Boating Show (Robe)

→ MAR South East Country Music Festival (Mount Gambier)

→ MAR-APR Geltwood Festival (Millicent)

→ EASTER Surfing Classic (Robe)

→ MAY Penola Coonawarra Arts Festival; Generations in Jazz Festival (Mount Gambier); Arts Festival (Penola)

→ JUL Coonawarra Cellar Dwellers

→ SEPT Blessing of the Fleet (Robe)

→ OCT Cabernet Celebrations (Penola)

→ NOV Lions National Brass Band Festival (Mount Gambier)

TEMPERATURES

Jan: 10–26°C

July: 5–14°C

a penguin colony and unusual rock formations; just west of town. **Dingley Dell Conservation Park:** the historic 1862 restored cottage that is located here was once the home of Australian poet Adam Lindsay Gordon and features displays on his life and work; cottage open by appt; (08) 8735 1177; 2km W. **Germein Reserve:** 8km boardwalk (loop track) through wetlands; opposite Dingley Dell. **Southern Ocean Shipwreck Trail:** over 89 vessels came to grief on the section of coast from the Victorian border to the Murray River mouth. The drive trail includes 10 interpretive sites; brochure from visitor centre.

★ ROBE
Population 1156

Robe is one of the state's most significant historic towns, a fishing port famous for its crayfish, and a popular holiday destination renowned for its secluded beaches. During the Victorian gold rush in the mid-1800s, around 16,500 Chinese people disembarked here and travelled overland to the goldfields to avoid the Poll Tax enforced at Victorian ports. Robe had a thriving export trade before rail was introduced, which has left a legacy of historic buildings, from quaint stone cottages to the Caledonian Inn.

SEE & DO Mount Benson Wine Region: see Top Attractions. **Little Dip Conservation Park:** see Other Attractions. **The Robe Institute:** incorporates the visitor centre, library and Historic Interpretation Centre with photographic and audiovisual displays on Robe's history; Mundy Tce. **Robe Customs House:** historic 1863 building, once the hub of Robe's export trade, now a museum featuring Chinese artefacts and displays; check opening times at visitor centre; Royal Circus. **Caledonian Inn:** built in 1858-9, this stone pub features internal doors salvaged from shipwrecks; 1 Victoria St; (08) 8768 2029. **Art and craft galleries:** throughout town, especially in Smillie and Victoria sts. **Deep Sea Fishing Charters:** sightseeing cruise also on offer; bookings (08) 8768 1807. **Crayfish fleet:** begins with the Blessing of the Fleet and anchors in Lake Butler (Robe's harbour). Sells fresh crayfish and fish; Oct–Apr. **Walk and scenic drive tours:** self-guided tours available. Take the town walk past 81 historic buildings and sites; brochures from visitor centre. **Lake Fellmongery:** popular spot for waterskiing; 1km SE. **Long Beach:** 17km of pristine beach for surfing and swimming. Cars are allowed on the sand; 2km N. **Beacon Hill:** panoramic views of Robe, lakes and coast from lookout tower; Beacon Hill Rd; 2km SE. **The Obelisk:** navigational marker at Cape Dombey; scenic access via cliff walk from the Old Gaol at Robe; 2km W.

Flinders Ranges and Outback

South Australia's **endless arid outback** remains sparsely populated and hauntingly beautiful, dotted with **quirky towns** and **crisscrossed with 4WD tracks**. Just a day's drive from Adelaide/Tarndanya, the Flinders Ranges offer all of this and more. **Coober Pedy's famous underground buildings** and **Kati Thanda–Lake Eyre** are must-sees in this region too.

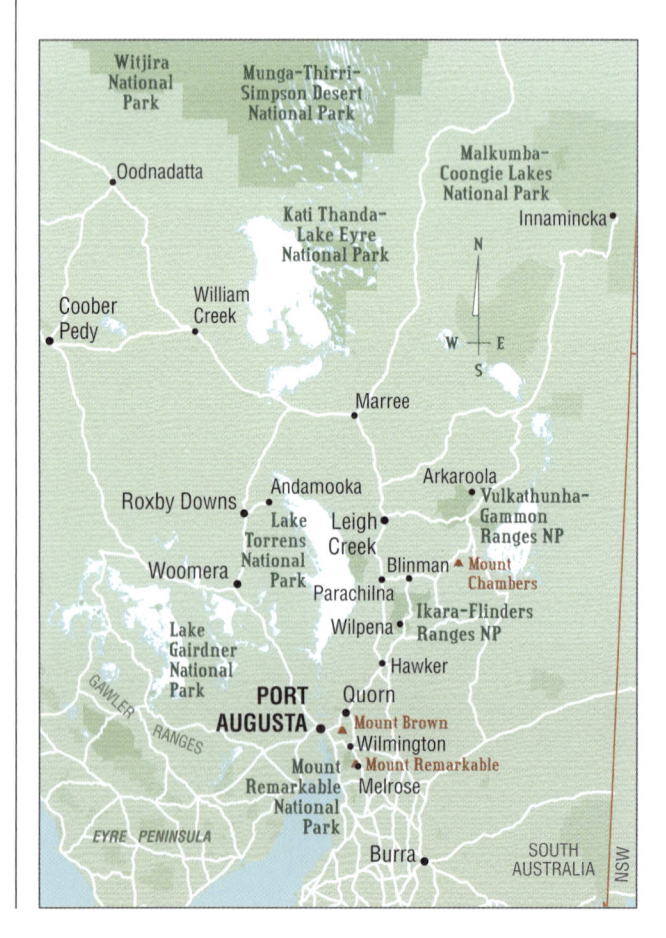

CHEAT SHEET

→ You'll need a good two weeks to get the most out of the huge South Australian outback and impressive Ikara–Flinders Ranges National Park.

→ Best time to visit: don't leave your outback trip too late in the year; after September, things get seriously hot here! Time your visit for spring when the wildflowers are blooming, or winter when the weather is at its most moderate.

→ Main towns: Coober Pedy (*see* p. 250), Port Augusta (*see* p. 253), Quorn (*see* p. 253).

→ The Flinders Ranges are the Traditional Lands of the Adnyamathanha People, who have many sacred sites throughout the region. Northern South Australia is the Traditional Lands of many cultural groups, including the Arabana, Banggarla, Dhirari, Dieri, Kokatha, Kurani, Malyangaba, Pirlatapa, Yandruwandha and Yawarawarka Peoples.

→ Did you know? The legendary Oodnadatta Track between Marree and Marla follows the route of the old Great Northern Railway, long since re-routed 100km to the west.

→ Don't miss: Mount Remarkable National Park; Ikara (Wilpena Pound); Prairie Hotel; Oodnadatta Track; noodling (fossicking) for opals in Coober Pedy; Australian Arid Lands Botanic Garden.

Top: Relaxing at Wilpena Pound Resort **Opposite:** Rawnsley Park Station, Flinders Ranges

TOP ATTRACTIONS

ARKAROOLA RIDGETOP TOUR: This, the signature attraction of the Vulkathunha-Gammon Ranges National Park, is a 4WD tour along an insanely steep track at **Arkaroola Wilderness Sanctuary**. The original track, built for mining exploration, wound through the creek beds, but run-off from the ridges washed the road away in just a few years. The idea was formed to create a track along the ridges themselves. A few bulldozers later, the track was complete. This is a guided tour, but Arkaroola Wilderness Sanctuary also has 100km of self-guided 4WD tracks, including the popular Echo Camp Backtrack; (08) 8648 4848.

COOBER PEDY'S UNDERGROUND CHURCHES: The underground opal town of Coober Pedy is unique and Little St Peter and St Paul's Catholic Church was the first underground church in the world; open 10am–4pm; cnr Hutchison St and Halliday Pl. Other interesting churches include the Catacomb Church with televised sermons beamed in from afar, open 10am–4pm, 746 Catacomb Rd; and the Serbian Orthodox Church with its lofty carved rock interiors; Saint Elijah Dr, Coober Pedy.

IKARA–FLINDERS RANGES NATIONAL PARK: The Adnyamathanha People (meaning hills or rock people) are the Traditional Custodians of the Ikara-Flinders Ranges National Park. Their connection with the land stretches back many thousands of years. There are many significant cultural sites to be found in the park, including ancient rock paintings and engravings at Arkaroo Rock, Sacred Canyon and Perawurtina Cultural Heritage Site, however it is important to be respectful and responsible while travelling in the park. In the 1850s stock runs were established at Arkaba, Wilpena and Aroona: foreign plant and animal species were introduced and the natural balance of the ranges was altered. Within 50 years many endemic animals had been pushed to extinction. Today, the Ikara-Flinders Ranges National Park is co-managed by a board consisting of Adnyamathanha and Department of Environment, Water and Natural Resources representatives, and conservationists are trying to restore natural balances, aiding the recovery of the yellow-footed rock wallaby. The central ranges offer fabulous hiking, with more than a dozen established trails providing historical, geological or scenic perspectives. For a look into early European settlement take the 5.4km return Hills Homestead Walk into the extraordinary natural rock formation of Ikara (Wilpena Pound). The Bunyeroo Gorge Hike is a 7.5km return trail revealing abundant wildlife and rock formations. The Brachina Gorge Geological Trail is a 20km drive, time-travelling through the long geological history of the ranges – look for yellow-footed rock wallabies on the rocky slopes. Other than the road to Blinman, roads north of Wilpena are unsealed but are generally 2WD accessible. In 2021 a nomination was made for the Flinders Ranges to be included on the UNESCO World Heritage List; at the time of writing, it had a Tentative Listing. Full World Heritage status isn't expected until 2025. Wilpena Pound Visitor Information Centre is the place to pay park fees, pick up a park guide or book scenic flights and 4WD tours. Wilpena Rd, via Hawker; (08) 8648 0048.

INNAMINCKA REGIONAL RESERVE: This spectacular, isolated reserve lures plenty of 4WD off-roaders and nature lovers. It covers 13,800sqkm and comprises important desert wetland areas including Coongie Lakes, an internationally significant wetland area that's waterbird heaven. Closer to Innamincka (see p. 251) is Cullyamurra Waterhole, on Cooper Creek, a super spot for some bush camping and fishing, with First Nations rock carvings accessible by foot at the eastern end of the waterhole. A 4WD is essential in most of the park; after heavy rains roads become impassable. A Desert Parks Pass is required; (08) 8648 5328.

KANKU–BREAKAWAYS CONSERVATION PARK: The Breakaways – 40sqkm of arid, flat-topped outcrops and stony gibber desert – is really something to marvel at, as is the wildlife that has adapted to these harsh conditions. Entry permits to the park are available from the Coober Pedy visitor centre. Nearby you'll bump into the Dog Fence, a 5300km long mesh barrier built to protect sheep properties in the south from roaming wild dogs of the north. Off Stuart Hwy; (08) 8672 4617. The park is 30km north of Coober Pedy (see p. 250).

KATI THANDA–LAKE EYRE NATIONAL PARK: Of international significance, Kati Thanda–Lake Eyre is dry most of the time – it has filled to capacity on only three occasions in the last 150 years. When water does fill parts of the lake (usually due to heavy rains in Queensland funnelled south via creeks and rivers), birds flock to it. Avoid visiting in the hotter months (Nov–Mar). Kati Thanda–Lake Eyre North is accessed via the Oodnadatta Track (see box p. 255), 195km west of Marree. Kati Thanda–Lake Eyre South is accessed via the 94km track north of Marree (along this track is Muloorina Station, which offers camping alongside the Frome River). Both access routes are 4WD only. Kati Thanda–Lake Eyre South also meets the Oodnadatta Track about 90km west of Marree, where there are good views of the lake. A Desert Parks Pass is required for the park and is available from Marree Post Office or call the Desert Parks Hotline on (08) 8648 5328. Scenic flights are a rewarding option, from both Marree and William Creek.

MOON PLAIN: The eerie lunar landscape of Moon Plain, littered with rocks on red sand, has been the backdrop for many movies, especially those with a sci-fi bent. Coober Pedy–Oodnadatta Rd. Moon Plain is 15km north-east of Coober Pedy (see p. 250).

MOUNT REMARKABLE NATIONAL PARK: This national park is part of the southern Flinders Ranges and popular with bushwalkers. Marked trails through the park's gorges and ranges vary in scope from short scenic walks to long three-day hikes. Highlights include pretty Alligator Gorge and the tough but worthwhile 5hr return walk from Melrose to the summit of Mount Remarkable (960m), with breathtaking views from the top. Access to the park by vehicle is via Mambray Creek or Wilmington. Foot access is from carparks and Melrose (see p. 252). (08) 8634 7068.

MUNGA-THIRRI–SIMPSON DESERT NATIONAL PARK: Australia's largest national park was formed in Nov 2021. It includes what was previously the Simpson Desert Conservation Park and Regional Reserve. Includes 4WD tracks across enormous dune desert east of Witjira. It is closed from 1 Dec to 15 March. Travellers must be totally self-sufficient; check for condition updates regularly. Details and bookings from Port Augusta National Parks Wildlife Service South Australia office. (08) 8648 5300.

OLD TIMERS MINE: This fascinating underground museum in Coober Pedy (see p. 250) is in an original 1916 mine, boarded up for years before being rediscovered and turned into a tourist attraction. Inside are three large opal seams and an interpretive centre with a self-guided walk. Mining equipment demonstrations happen above ground daily. Open 8.30am–5.30pm; 1 Crowders Gully Rd, Coober Pedy; (08) 8672 5555.

PICHI RICHI RAILWAY: Historical tourist train travels through dramatic countryside return from Quorn (see p. 253) to Port Augusta (see p. 253); bookings online, call 1800 777 245, or through Quorn Visitor Centre.

PRAIRIE HOTEL: A historic hotel at Parachilna offering cuisine with a bush-tucker twist as well as first-rate accommodation. Hotel staff can arrange 4WD tours, scenic flights and visits to nearby Nilpena Station on the edge of Lake Torrens to sample the outback life; High St, Parachilna; (08) 8648 4844.

UMOONA OPAL MINE AND MUSEUM: This engaging underground hub gives Coober Pedy (see p. 250) a good once-over, from detailed town history to a First Nations interpretive centre and an excellent documentary on Coober Pedy screened in an underground cinema. Experience 'dugout' life in an underground home or get an insight into opal mining on a mine tour. Open 8am–6pm; 14 Hutchison St, Coober Pedy; (08) 8672 5228.

VULKATHUNHA–GAMMON RANGES NATIONAL PARK: This park is directly south of Arkaroola (see p. 250). The Adnyamathanha People believe that the Dreamtime serpent, Arakaroo, drank adjacent Lake Frome dry and carved out Arkaroola Gorge as he slithered back to his resting spot inside Mainwater Pound. His restlessness is the cause of the earthquakes. Features include the surprisingly lush Weetootla Gorge, fed by a permanent spring, and Italowie Gorge, the unlikely spot where

Opposite: Stargazing at Arkaroola Wilderness Sanctuary observatory

an impoverished R.M. Williams began making boots. Park Headquarters at Balcanoona; (08) 8648 0049.

WADLATA OUTBACK CENTRE: This award-winning complex in Port Augusta (*see* p. 253) covers the natural history of the outback and Flinders Ranges, as well as the people who have called it home throughout the ages. Discover the landscape of 15 million years ago in the Tunnel of Time, and hear Adnyamathanha Creation stories (Yura Muda) to explain how landforms and resources were created and why each are equally important. Open Mon–Fri 9am–4pm, Sat–Sun 10am–3pm; 41 Flinders Tce, Port Augusta; (08) 8641 9193.

WILLIAM CREEK: The smallest town in SA (population five or six!) is about halfway along the Ooodnadatta Track (*see* box p. 255). Don't miss a cold beer at the 1887 pub and a scenic flight over Kati Thanda–Lake Eyre; Oodnadatta Track.

WITJIRA NATIONAL PARK: This arid park is famous for the Dalhousie Springs. These thermal springs emerge from the Great Artesian Basin deep below the surface and are said to be therapeutic (visitors can swim in the main spring). They are also a habitat for many fish species that can adapt to the changing water conditions. A Desert Parks Pass is required; they are available from Mount Dare Homestead (which has fuel and supplies), the Pink Roadhouse or National Parks and Wildlife Service South Australia; see: parks.sa.gov.au.

OTHER ATTRACTIONS

AUSTRALIAN ARID LANDS BOTANIC GARDEN: This unique botanic garden has 200ha of arid-zone vegetation on Port Augusta's (*see* p. 253) northern outskirts with great walking trails. Guided tours Mon–Fri 10am; birdwatching brochures available. Cafe onsite; Stuart Hwy, Port Augusta; (08) 8641 9116.

COOBER PEDY OPAL FIELDS GOLF CLUB: Tee-off on this unique 18-hole grass-less course – the only golf club in the world with reciprocal playing rights with the 'home of golf', St Andrews in Scotland. Night golf by appt (minimum four people); open 9am–5pm; 1509 Rowe Dr, Coober Pedy.

MAIL RUN TOUR: This overland adventure is a typically offbeat way of exploring Coober Pedy (*see* p. 250) and beyond. Travelling with the local mailman, the tour passes waterholes and traverses scenic desert landscapes on its delivery run to Oodnadatta, William Creek and the remote cattle stations in between. Covering 600km over outback roads and the legendary Oodnadatta Track, you'll hear stories and history of the landscape and people. Tours Mon and Thurs 9am; (08) 8672 5226.

MAWSON TRAIL: This 900km bike trail from Adelaide ends in Blinman. It is named after famous Australian explorer Sir Douglas Mawson and traverses Mount Lofty and Ikara–Flinders Ranges National Park; for details contact Bicycle SA; (08) 8411 0233.

MELROSE NATIONAL TRUST MUSEUM: This museum in the tiny outback town of Melrose (*see* p. 252) documents local history, with a particular focus on early law enforcement. Original stone buildings include the courthouse and lock-up; open Fri–Wed 10am–4pm, Thurs 10am–1pm; Stuart St, Melrose; (08) 8666 2141.

PAINTED DESERT: Rich ochre colours dapple the Arckaringa Hills, also noted for desert flora and fauna; Oodnadatta Rd. It's 150km north of Coober Pedy.

YARTA PURTLI – PORT AUGUSTA CULTURAL CENTRE: Volunteer-run arts hub in Port Augusta (*see* p. 253), featuring local and touring art and cultural exhibitions, plus workshops and regular talks; open Mon–Fri 10am–4pm, Sat 10am–1pm; 6 Beauchamp La, Port Augusta; (08) 8641 9176.

KEY TOWNS

ANDAMOOKA
Population 260

Queen Elizabeth was gifted an Andamooka Opal in 1954 on her first visit to Australia. The opal weighed 203 carats and glistened in blues, reds and greens. It was the result of an extensive search for the most beautiful opal in the state, yet Andamooka itself is a misshapen collection of tin sheds, dugouts and fibros in the middle of the desert. With constant water shortages, no local council and an all-consuming drive to find opals, residents have become experts in making do. The town offers old-fashioned outback hospitality to an increasing number of tourists.

SEE & DO **Opal showrooms:** showrooms in town include Andamooka Opal Showroom Underground Opal and Mineral Museum, attached to Dukes Bottlehouse Motel. **Historic miners huts:** a handful of old semi-dugouts line the creek bed in the centre of town, complete with old tools and furnishings. Access is by tour, which includes a visit to an underground mine; details from post office. **Cemetery:** with miners' nicknames on the headstones. **Fossicking:** noodling is the term for fossicking and you can try your hand at it in unclaimed mullock dumps surrounding town; details from post office. **Lake Torrens:** one of the state's largest salt lakes stretches away to the south-east; 4WD recommended for access.

⭐ ARKAROOLA
Population 32

Arkaroola is set in an incredible landscape of ranges laced with precious minerals, waterholes nestled inside tall gorges and places with tongue-twister names like Nooldoonooldoona and Bararranna. What's more, the Flinders Ranges are still alive, rumbling with up to 200 small earthquakes a year. It was a place that geologist Reg Sprigg found fascinating, and worth conserving. He purchased the Arkaroola property in 1968 and created a wildlife sanctuary for endangered species. Today a weather station, seismograph station and observatory (tours available) add to its significance, and the spectacular 4WD tracks entice many visitors. The village has excellent facilities for such a remote outpost.

SEE & DO **Arkaroola Ridgetop Tour; Vulkathunha–gammon Ranges National Park:** *see* Top Attractions for both. **Waterholes:** many picturesque waterholes along Arkaroola Creek and tributaries west and north-east of the village. **Bolla Bollana Smelter ruins:** where the ore from surrounding mines was once treated. It includes a Cornish beehive-shaped kiln; 7km NW. **Paralana Hot Springs:** the only active geyser in Australia, where water heated by radioactive minerals bubbles through the rocks. Swimming or extended exposure is not recommended; 27km NE. **Big Moro Gorge:** rockpools surrounded by limestone outcrops. The gorge is on Nantawarrina Aboriginal Land; obtain permit from Nepabunna Community Council, (08) 8648 3764; nepabunnatourism.com.au; 59km S. **Astronomy Tours:** some of the best star-watching conditions in the Southern Hemisphere at three magnificent observatories; (08) 8648 4848. **Scenic flights:** over the ranges or further afield; details from village reception.

BLINMAN
Population 43

During the 19th century numerous mining townships dotted the northern lands of what is now Ikara–Flinders Ranges National Park. Blinman is the sole surviving town surveyed at the time. The discovery of copper here in 1859 was accidental; the story goes that a shepherd, Robert Blinman, used to watch his sheep from a boulder and one day he absentmindedly broke off a chunk and discovered it was copper. Historic buildings in the main street are reminders of those rich (and temporary) days.

SEE & DO **Blinman Heritage Mine:** a 1km self-guided walk explains the history and geology of the site; for a guided tour call (08) 8648 4782; just north-east of Blinman. **Wadna:** cultural tours of Adnyamathanha region of the ancient Flinders Ranges; see: wadna.com.au. **Great Wall of China:** impressive limestone ridge; Wilpena Rd; 10km S. **Angorichina Tourist Village:** starting point for 4km walk along creek bed to Blinman Pools, permanent spring-fed pools in scenic surrounds. Accommodation ranges from tents to cabins; (08) 8648 4842; 14km W. **Glass and Parachilna gorges:** 10km NW and 15km W of town are these two beautiful gorges. Parachilna Gorge is the end point of the 1200km Heysen Trail (bushwalking trail), which begins at Cape Jervis; for information contact National Parks and Wildlife Service South Australia; see: parks.sa.gov.au. **Scenic drive:** travel east through Eregunda Valley (around 20km E), then north-east to Mount Chambers Gorge (around 75km NE), with its rockpools and First Nations carvings; further north is Vulkathunha–Gammon Ranges National Park.

⭐ COOBER PEDY
Population 1437

Go underground in Coober Pedy, the opal capital of the world! On 1 February 1915, a group of gold prospectors discovered opal in the area surrounding Coober Pedy. One hundred years later the town is the biggest opal field on the planet, providing around

VISITOR INFORMATION

Wadlata Outback Centre
41 Flinders Tce,
Port Augusta
(08) 8641 9194 or
1800 633 060
flindersandoutback.com.au

Ikara Flinders Ranges National Park
parks.sa.gov.au/parks/
ikara-flinders-ranges-
national-park

Opposite top: Arkaroola Wilderness Sanctuary **Opposite bottom:** Coober Pedy Desert Cave Hotel

80 per cent of the world's gem-quality opals. The name Coober Pedy is thought to come from from the First Nations phrase 'kupa piti', loosely translating to 'white man's hole in the ground'. However in 1975 the local Aboriginal people of the town adopted the name 'Umoona', which means 'long life' and is also their name for the mulga tree. The town's unique underground style of living was instigated by soldiers returning from World War I who were used to trench life. Today much of the population calls these dugouts home – ideal places to escape severe summer temperatures and cold winter nights. The landscape is desolate and otherworldly, dotted with thousands of mines and 'blowers' – truck-mounted devices used to sort the stones from the dirt. The town is also home to a unique grass-less golf course, and a public swimming pool that gets some serious use in summer. It's important to note that Coober Pedy's opal fields are pocked with diggings and you need to beware of unprotected mine shafts; don't wander around after dark – joining a tour is a much safer option. Trespassers on claims can be fined a minimum of $1000. In Jan 2022, Coober Pedy experienced severe flooding and supplies had to be airlifted in. Coober Pedy is the last stop for petrol between Cadney Homestead (151km north) and Glendambo (252km south).

SEE & DO Underground Churches; Umoona Opal Mine and Museum; Old Timers Mine; Moon Plain; Kanku–Breakaways Conservation Park: see Top Attractions for all. **Coober Pedy Opal Fields Golf Club; Mail Run Tour:** see Other Attractions for both. **Faye's Underground Home:** Faye's is a real retro time-warp, an underground home excavated in the 1960s (seemingly very little has changed since); open Mon–Sat 8.30am–5pm, Sun 2–5pm; Old Water Tank Rd; (08) 8672 5029. **Big Winch:** monument and lookout over the dusty town rooftops; also home to the **360° Cinema Experience** with 40min shows every hour on the half hour from 12.30pm–6.30pm. There's also a cafe. Open Thurs–Mon 12–8pm; Italian Club Rd, 0417 902 224. **Tom's Working Opal Mine:** on the outskirts of town, Tom's is the place to try your hand at noodling (fossicking) for opals; tours 10am and 2pm; 1993 Stuart Hwy; 1800 196 500. **Wrightsair:** scenic outback flights over Kati Thanda–Lake Eyre, the Oodnadatta Track and the Painted Desert; Airport Rd; (08) 8670 7962.

HAWKER
Population 226

This small outback town was once a thriving railway centre, and historic buildings are still well preserved in its streets. Hawker was also once an agricultural region producing bumper crops of wheat but serious drought sent the crops into decline and the industry died. Hawker is the place to begin exploring the fantastic natural attractions of the southern Flinders Ranges.

SEE & DO Fred Teague's Museum: local history displays; Hawker Motors, cnr Wilpena and Cradock rds. **Jeff Morgan Gallery:** including a 30m painting of the view from Wilpena Pound; Cradock Rd. **Heritage walk:** self-guided walk on numbered path; brochure from visitor centre. **Scenic flights and 4WD tours:** contact visitor centre for details. **Jarvis Hill Lookout:** walking trail with views over the countryside; 7km SW. **Yourambulla Caves:** First Nations rock paintings in hillside caves; 12km SW. **Willow Waters:** popular picnic spot with a short walk to Ochre Wall; 20km E, off Cradock Rd. **Moralana Scenic Drive:** 22km drive with superb views of Wilpena Pound and the Elder Range; leaves Hawker–Wilpena Rd; 23km N. **Cradock:** a tiny town with National Heritage-listed St Gabriel's Church (1882); 26km SE. **Kanyaka Homestead Historic Site:** ruins of the homestead, stables and woolshed once part of a large sheep run, with informative displays explaining the history of each ruin; 28km SW. **Long-distance trails:** close to Hawker you can pick up sections of the Heysen (walking) and Mawson (cycling) trails; information from visitor centre.

INNAMINCKA
Population 21

About as far-flung as you can get in SA, Innamincka is a quirky desert outpost. On Cooper Creek at the northern end of the Strzelecki Track, this tiny desert settlement revolves around a pub and trading post. The first European explorer to visit the area was Charles Sturt, who discovered the Cooper in 1846 while vainly searching for an inland sea. It was also the final destination of the ill-fated Burke and Wills expedition. In 1860 all but one of Burke and Wills's party perished near the creek. John King survived with the help of the Yandruwandha People who he lived with for more than two months before being found by a search party. Innamincka was once a customs depot and service centre for surrounding pastoral properties, but now mainly services travellers, many of whom arrive from the south via the Strzelecki Track (4WD vehicles only). It's important to note that motorists intending to explore the Strzelecki Track should ring the Transport SA Road Condition Hotline on 1300 361 033 to check conditions before departure. There are no supplies or petrol between Lyndhurst and Innamincka. For more about the Strzelecki Track, see box p. 255.

SEE & DO Innamincka Regional Reserve: see Top Attractions. **Australian Inland Mission:** built in 1928 to service the medical needs of remote pastoral properties, this mission was attended by a rotating staff of two nurses on horseback. Injured workers, flood victims and even fallen jockeys from the races called on their expertise. The mission was abandoned in the early 1950s when the Royal Flying Doctor Service began providing services; opening hours vary; Strzelecki Track;

(08) 8675 9909. **Boat hire and tours:** fishing and cruising trips on Cooper Creek; Innamincka Hotel, 2 South Tce; (08) 8675 9901. **Memorial plaques:** commemorating explorers Charles Sturt and Burke and Wills; Cordillo Rd; 2km N. **Burke and Wills Dig Tree:** visit the famous Dig Tree where supplies were buried for their ill-fated expedition; Bullah Bullah Waterhole, Adventure Way (across border in Queensland); 71km E. **Strzelecki Regional Reserve:** barren but beautiful sand-dune desert country with birdwatching and camping at Montecollina Bore; Strzelecki Track; (08) 8648 5300; 167km SW.

MARREE
Population 65

Marree is the perfect image of a tiny outback town. It is frequented by 4WD enthusiasts taking on the legendary Birdsville and Oodnadatta tracks (*see* box p. 255). The settlement was established in 1872 as a camp for the Overland Telegraph Line as it was being constructed, and also became a railhead for the Great Northern Railway (which was later known as the *Ghan*). The town soon serviced all travellers and workers heading north, including the famous Afghan traders who drove their camel trains into the desert and played a significant role in opening up the outback. It's important to note that care must be taken when attempting the Birdsville and Oodnadatta tracks. These tracks are unsealed, with sandy patches. Heavy rain in the area can cut access for several days. Motorists are advised to ring the Northern Roads Condition Hotline on 1300 361 033 before departure.

SEE & DO **Marree Heritage Park:** includes Tom Kruse's truck that once carried out the famous outback mail run on the Birdsville Track in the 1950s. **Camel sculpture:** made out of railway sleepers. **Scenic flights:** including over Kati Thanda–Lake Eyre and the Marree Man, a 4km long carving in a plateau of a First Nations hunter. The carving, visible only from the air, appeared mysteriously in 1998, and is slowly fading; contact visitor centre for details.

MELROSE
Population 342

Melrose, a quiet settlement at the foot of Mount Remarkable, is the oldest town in the Flinders Ranges. Mount Remarkable is a culturally significant place for the Nukunu and Adnymathanha Nations. These First Nations continue to have shared responsibilities for their Country, and play an important role in protecting significant and sacred sites, land management and restoration of cultural expressions. Pastoral properties were established on the mountainous slopes of the ranges, but Melrose's population boomed when copper deposits were found nearby in 1846. Bushwalking through Mount Remarkable National Park is a highlight of any visit to this area. The arid north country meets the wet conditions of southern regions to provide a diverse landscape to explore.

SEE & DO **Mount Remarkable National Park:** *see* Top Attractions. **Melrose National Trust Museum:** *see* Other Attractions. **4WD tours:** to local landmarks; contact visitor centre for operators. **Heritage walk:** self-guided walk includes ruins of Jacka's Brewery and Melrose Mine; brochure from visitor centre. **Cathedral Rock:** an impressive rock formation on Mount Remarkable Creek; just west of Melrose. **Murray Town:** a farming town with nearby scenic lookouts at Box Hill, Magnus Hill and Baroota Nob. Remarkable View Wines offers tasting and sales on weekends. Starting point for a scenic drive west through Port Germein Gorge; 14km S. **Booleroo Centre:** this service town

TOP EVENTS

- MAY Races & Gymkhana (Oodnadatta)
- JUNE Opal Festival (Coober Pedy); Pichi Richi Marathon (Quorn)
- JULY Camel Cup (Marree); Bronco Branding (Oodnadatta)
- AUG Picnic Races & Gymkhana (Innamincka)

TEMPERATURES

Jan: 21–36°C

July: 6–19°C

Opposite: The Pink Road House in Oodnadatta

to a rich farming community features the Booleroo Steam Traction Preservation Society's Museum; annual Rally Day is held in Mar/Apr; open by appt; (08) 8667 2185; 15km SE. **Wirrabara:** silo art and antiques and a producers market on the 3rd Sun of the month; 25km S.

OODNADATTA
Population 102

Oodnadatta is a gutsy outback town on the legendary Oodnadatta Track. It was once a major railway town, but the line's closure in 1981 left it largely deserted. For tens of thousands of years, this place was also a stop on an old trade route for First Nation peoples. Today many travellers use it to refuel and gather supplies before heading out to the major desert parks to the north. The name Oodnadatta is derived from the Arrernte word 'utnadata', which means 'mulga blossom'.

SEE & DO **Munga-Thirri-Simpson Desert National Park:** see Top Attractions. **Painted Desert:** see Other Attractions. **Pink Roadhouse:** a town icon, and also the place to go for information on local road conditions and outback travel advice; Ikaturka Tce. **Railway Station Museum:** well-preserved sandstone station (1890), now a local museum; key available from roadhouse. **Oodnadatta Track** (see box p. 255: runs from Marree (404km SE) through Oodnadatta and joins the Stuart Hwy at Marla (212km NW). **Neales River:** swim in permanent waterholes.

PORT AUGUSTA
Population 12,788

At the head of Spencer Gulf, Port Augusta is the most northerly port in SA. The difficulty of land transportation in the 1800s prompted the town's establishment in 1854. There was a major wool and wheat shipping depot here until its closure in 1973 – but by that stage Port Augusta's power stations were already the city's chief income generators. Port Augusta is also a supply centre for outback areas, an important link on the *Indian–Pacific* railway and a stopover for the Adelaide-to-Darwin *Ghan* train.

SEE & DO **Wadlata Outback Centre:** see Top Attractions. **Yarta Purtli – Port Augusta Cultural Centre; Australian Arid Lands Botanic Garden:** see Other Attractions for both. **Gladstone Square:** landscaped square surrounded by historic sites, including the courthouse, barracks and Presbyterian church; cnr Jervois and Marryatt sts. **McLellan Lookout:** site of Matthew Flinders' landing in 1802, with views of the power stations; end of Edinburgh Tce. **Water Tower Lookout:** spectacular town and gulf views from the balcony of this 1882 tower; Mitchell Tce. **Matthew Flinders Lookout:** excellent view of Spencer Gulf and the Flinders Ranges; open 7.30am–dusk; end of McSporran Cres. **Boat cruises and Flinders Ranges 4WD tours:** contact visitor centre. **Heritage walk:** self-guided town walk includes courthouse and the magnificent stained glass in St Augustine's Church; brochure from visitor centre. **Curdnatta Art Gallery:** high-quality painting, pottery and fabric art; open Thurs–Fri 10am–2pm, Wed and Sat 10am–12pm, 105 Commercial Rd; (08) 8641 0195.

QUORN
Population 1150

Nestled in a valley in the Flinders Ranges, Quorn was established as a town on the Great Northern Railway line in 1878. The line was built by Chinese and British workers and operated for over 45 years (it closed in 1957). Part of the line through Pichi Richi Pass has been restored as a tourist railway, taking passengers on a scenic 33km round trip via Port Augusta. The town's old charm has not been lost on movie producers – the historic streetscapes and surrounding landscapes have been used in many films.

SEE & DO **Pichi Richi Railway:** see Top Attractions. **Silo Light Show:** free 30min Son et lumière featuring local stories and history projected onto the silos in the Railway Precinct; nightly at sunset, check with visitor centre for times. **Railway Workshop Tours:** guided tours of the workshop where locomotives travelling on the Pichi Richi line are maintained and restored. Tours by appt; book at visitor centre. **Junction Art Gallery:** local art exhibition; Railway Tce. **Outback Colours Art Gallery:** Seventh St. **Town walks:** the Walking Tour of Quorn and the Quorn Historic Buildings walk; brochures from visitor centre. **Quorn Native Flora Reserve:** stone reserve, which was once the town's quarry, with informative brochure available that details the reserve's flora; Quarry Rd; 2km NW. **The Dutchman's Stern Conservation Park:** colourful rocky outcrops observed on two trails through the park. The Ridge Top Trail (8.2km return) offers spectacular views of the Flinders Ranges and Spencer Gulf; 8km W. **Devil's Peak Walking Trail:** panoramic views up steep climb to the summit (closed Nov–Apr, fire season); 10km S. **Mount Brown Conservation Park:** mixed landscape of ridges and woodland. The loop trail, starting at Waukarie Falls, offers a side climb to the Mount Brown summit; Richman Valley Rd; 15km S. **Warren Gorge:** imposing red cliffs popular with climbers. Also the habitat of the rare yellow-footed rock wallaby; 23km N. **Buckaringa Gorge Scenic Drive:** drive past Buckaringa Sanctuary and Proby's Grave (he was the first settler at Kanyaka Station) to a lookout accessed via a short walk; begins 35km N.

ROXBY DOWNS
Population 3671

In 1975 Roxby Downs station was a hard-working property on the red sand dunes of central SA. That was until a body of copper and uranium, the largest in the world, was discovered near a dam. The resultant town of Roxby Downs was built in 1988 to accommodate the employees of the Olympic Dam mining project and has many modern facilities.

SEE & DO **Cultural and Leisure Precinct:** incorporates the visitor centre, cinema, cafe, swimming pool, art gallery with local and touring exhibitions, and interpretive display on town and dam history; 1 Richardson Pl; (08) 8671 5941. **Arid Recovery:** 123sqkm of native landscape with sunset tours (non-summer months only) to see reintroduced native animals, including bilbies and burrowing bettongs; contact visitor centre for tour details and bookings. **Emu Walking Trail:** self-guided, 3km nature walk through town; brochures from the visitor centre. **Olympic Dam Mine:** an extensive underground system of roadways and trains services the mine that produces refined copper, uranium oxide, gold and silver. A 20-minute video at the visitor centre provides an overview of the mine, including a virtual underground tour. 16km N.

WILMINGTON
Population 472

In 1861, Robert Blinman had the foresight to build an inn, called the Roundwood Hotel, at the base of Horrocks Pass, and soon the Cobb & Co. coaches were stopping there on their passenger routes. The town was built around that first hotel, and before long the farming community was thriving. Named Beautiful Valley by European explorers, the name was changed to Wilmington in 1876, although Beautiful Valley still persists in many local establishments. Today the town retains much of its old-time feel and is renowned for its stone buildings.

SEE & DO **Wilmington Hotel:** built around 1876, the hotel is one of the town's oldest buildings and was first called the Globe Hotel. Original Cobb & Co. coach stables are at the rear of the building; Main North Rd. **Sansouci Puppet Museum and Gallery**: more than 1,000 puppets, marionettes and ventriloquist dolls on display in Australia's only puppet museum; call for opening times, Main Rd; (08) 8667 5356. **Mount Maria Walking Trail:** 2km walking trail starting from town leads to vantage point over Wilmington; brochure available from general store. **Spring Creek Mine Drive:** 24km scenic loop beginning south of town, passing mountain and farm scenery and an old copper mine (now the town's water supply). **Horrocks Pass and Hancocks Lookout:** this historic pass was named after explorer John Horrocks who traversed the pass in 1846. Hancocks Lookout, at the highest point of the pass, offers magnificent views to Spencer Gulf; 8km W off road to Port Augusta. **Winninowie Conservation Park:** coastal park of creeks and samphire flats, home to abundant birdlife; 26km SW. **Hammond:** historic ghost town; 26km NE. **Bruce:** historic railway town featuring 1880s architecture; 35km N. **Carrieton:** historic buildings and Yanyarrie Whim Well in town. A rodeo is held here each Dec; 56km NE. See First Nations carvings a further 9km along Belton Rd.

★ WILPENA

Shady Wilpena is a resort as well as a camping, tours and information hub within Ikara–Flinders Ranges National Park. An oasis on the desert fringe, Wilpena sits on the edge of Ikara (Wilpena Pound). In 1902 the Hill family, wheat farmers, built a homestead inside the pound, but they abandoned it after a flood washed away the access road in 1914. The pound is a vast natural amphitheatre surrounded by peaks that change colour with the light, and is a fantastic destination for bushwalking. Don't miss a cold beer at the resort bar.

SEE & DO **Ikara–Flinders Ranges National Park:** *see* Top Attractions. **Wilpena Pound Resort:** partly powered by the largest solar-power system in the Southern Hemisphere, this place is a real desert-edge oasis, with accommodation, camping, a swimming pool, restaurant and bar, plus petrol and national park visitor centre with info on bushwalks, 4WD tours and scenic flights; visitor centre open 8am–5pm; Wilpena Rd, via Hawker; (08) 8648 0004. **Sacred Canyon Cultural Heritage Site:** First Nations rock carvings and paintings; 19km E. **Rawnsley Park Station:** camping and holiday-unit accommodation, scenic flights, horseriding, 4WD tours and the terrific Woolshed Restaurant; restaurant open Mon–Sun 5–8pm and Wed–Sun 12–2pm; Old Wilpena Rd, Hawker; (08) 8648 0700; 25km S. **Moralana Scenic Drive:** 22km route between Elder Range and south-west wall of Wilpena Pound, with plenty of lookouts and picnic spots en route; Moralana Gorge Rd; 30km S.

WOOMERA
Population 132

Woomera and its testing range were established in 1947 as a site for launching British experimental rockets during the Cold War era. The town was a restricted area until 1982. The Woomera Prohibited Area remains in force today and is still one of the largest land-based rocket ranges in the world. Until 2003, Woomera was the site of a controversial detention centre for refugees.

SEE & DO **Heritage and Visitor Information Centre:** provides a detailed history of the area through videos, exhibitions, rocket relics and photographic displays. It also includes a bowling alley. Tours of the Rocket Range can be booked and depart here; Dewrang Ave. **Missile Park:** open-air defence display of rockets, aircraft and weapons; cnr Banool and Dewrang aves. **Baker Observatory:** viewing the night sky through a computer-controlled telescope; contact visitor centre for details.

EPIC OUTBACK TRACKS

Like most folks on mainland Australia, South Australians tend to cling to the coast where there's a bit more rain, a bit of a sea breeze and a sporting chance of growing a few veggies in the backyard. Although we know now that the South Australian desert isn't the most hospitable of places to live, intrepid explorers – the likes of John McDouall Stuart, Edward John Eyre, Charles Sturt and Harry Redford – forged tracks through the outback to see what they could see. Three of these tracks – the Oodnadatta, Birdsville and Strzelecki – have become so ingrained in Australian outback folklore that their very mention will invoke an excited intake of breath and the jangling of 4WD keys.

The 620km **Oodnadatta Track** crosses the dusty red desert between Marree in the north Flinders Ranges and Marla on the Stuart Highway (which runs north–south between Darwin in the Northern Territory and Port Augusta in South Australia). The track follows the route taken by John McDouall Stuart on his 1859 expedition. Stuart's path later became the route of the Central Australian Railway (built in the 1870s, but long since re-routed further west) and the original Overland Telegraph Line, which opened in 1872, linking Port Augusta and Darwin.

These days the Oodnadatta Track is a popular 4WD route, passing the southern verges of Kati Thanda–Lake Eyre and the far-flung outposts of William Creek and Oodnadatta itself (*see* p. 253). A cold beer at the William Creek Hotel is a quintessentially Australian experience! Highlights along the track include the Dog Fence (around 40km W of Marree) and the railway-siding ruins at Curdimurka Siding and Bore (90km W of Marree) from the original Great Northern Railway line to Alice Springs. A short distance beyond Curdimurka is Wabma Kadarbu Mound Springs Conservation Park, with a series of springs – fed by water from the Great Artesian Basin – supporting a small ecosystem of plants and animals. The real attraction, however, is the landscape itself: vast open skies and beautifully desolate red-sand wilderness Between Marree and Marla, fuel is available only at William Creek (202km NW of Marree) and Oodnadatta (405km NW of Marree). It's important to note that care must be taken when attempting the Birdsville and Oodnadatta tracks. These tracks are unsealed, with sandy patches. Heavy rain in the area can cut access for several days. Motorists are advised to ring the Northern Roads Condition Hotline on 1300 361 033 before departure.

The **Birdsville Track** is an old stock route between Marree in South Australia and Birdsville in Queensland, 517km to the north across the Tirari and Sturt Stony deserts. The route was opened up by drovers in the 1860s who were looking to get their cattle from Queensland to waiting rail carriages in Port Augusta, and later Marree – a much quicker route than crossing most of Queensland to get to Brisbane. The track is more remote than the Oodnadatta, but the old pubs at Marree and Birdsville are enough of an enticement to keep you rolling – especially when the legendary Birdsville Cup horseraces are happening in September. Highlights on the track include the failed date palm plantation at Lake Harry Homestead (30km N) and the meeting of the Tirari and Strzelecki deserts at Natterannie Sandhills (140km N, after Cooper Creek crossing). Cooper Creek may have to be bypassed if flooded (with a 48km detour to a ferry). Between Marree and Birdsville, fuel is available only at Mungerannie Roadhouse (204km N of Marree).

The rugged **Strzelecki Track** meanders across 459km of isolated outback landscape between Lyndhurst and Innamincka (*see* p. 251) in north-eastern South Australia. As on the Birdsville Track, there's not much in between the two towns – just the wide-open wilds of the Strzelecki Desert. The route was opened up by Harry Redford in 1871, but it wasn't until the discovery of natural gas at Moomba in the 1960s that the track became passable to anything more comfortable than a camel. Innamincka on Cooper Creek (discovered by Charles Sturt in 1846) is where explorers Burke and Wills died in 1860. These days there's a pub and a trading post here, and some brilliant campsites and swimming holes along Cooper Creek, within Innamincka Regional Park. It's important to note that motorists intending to explore the Strzelecki Track should ring the Transport SA Road Condition Hotline on 1300 361 033 to check conditions before departure. There are no supplies or petrol between Lyndhurst and Innamincka.

Opposite top: Emu in the Flinders Ranges **Opposite bottom:** Arkaroola Wilderness Sanctuary

Eyre Peninsula and Nullarbor

The Eyre Peninsula – the triangle of land between Adelaide and the Great Australian Bight – is where the **outback meets the sea**. Here you'll find not just one of the most **dramatic coastlines** in the country, but also the legendary Coffin Bay oysters. Drop a fishing line from one of the jetties, enjoy **waterfront camping** and head out on **scenic drives**. In fact, the one thing you won't find out here are crowds.

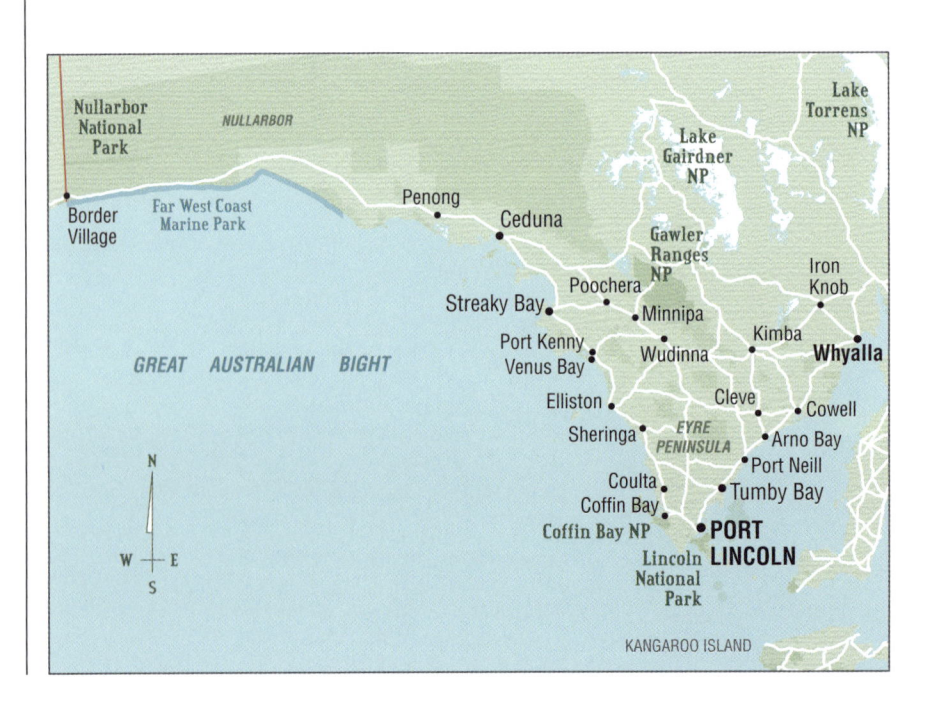

CHEAT SHEET

→ Allow at least a week for a proper exploration.

→ Best time to visit: year-round depending, although the water is too cold for swimming in winter.

→ Main towns: Ceduna (see p. 259), Port Lincoln (see p. 261), Whyalla (see p. 263).

→ The Eyre Peninsula is the Traditional Lands of the Banggarla, Nawu and Wirangu Peoples, whose land also stretches into the Nullarbor along with the homelands of the Kokatha, Mirning and Ngalea Western Desert Peoples.

→ Don't miss: oysters and fresh seafood; Point Labbat sea lion colony; whale watching at Head of Bight; Penong's windmills; coastal tracks and trails in Coffin Bay and Lincoln national parks; Elliston's Great Ocean Drive.

Top: Watching for sea lions in Coffin Bay **Opposite:** Sand dunes at Lincoln National Park

TOP ATTRACTIONS

COFFIN BAY NATIONAL PARK: A picturesque mix of rugged coastal landscapes, calm bays and waterways, extending south and west of Coffin Bay township. Conventional vehicles can access the eastern section of the park where there are walks through she-oak stands and samphire swamps, all a-twitter with native birds. 4WD vehicles and bushwalkers can access the western part of the park, which includes Gunyah Beach, Point Sir Isaac, Coffin Bay Peninsula and remote beaches and campsites.

ELLISTON'S GREAT OCEAN DRIVE: Scenic cliff-top drive north of the town of Elliston (see p. 260) to adjacent Anxious Bay, with fabulous coastal views and a number of sculptures dotted along the clifftops. Along the way is Blackfellows, reputedly one of the best surf breaks in Australia.

FAR WEST COAST MARINE PARK: This reserve protects the fragile ecosystem of the Great Australian Bight. It has spectacular wildlife sights, including breeding and calving southern right whales (June–Oct). Spend a day observing these giant creatures from the viewing platform at Head of Bight. There are also views of the Bunda Cliffs, which begin at the head and trail all the way to the WA border. Whale-watching permits are purchased from the visitor and interpretive centre on site. Visitor centre open 8am–5pm (June–Oct), 8.30am–4pm (Nov–May); (08) 8625 6201.

GAWLER RANGES NATIONAL PARK: This rugged national park offers fantastic gorge and rocky-outcrop scenery, spectacular when the spring wildflowers are in bloom. There are no marked trails, but highlights of drive tours include the Organ Pipes, a large and unique formation of volcanic rhyolite, the Kolay Mirica Falls and Yandinga Gorge. Some areas are accessible by 2WD, but 4WD is generally recommended; roads may be impassable after rain.

KOPPIO SMITHY MUSEUM: The early 1900s come to life in this extensive National Trust museum in the Koppio Hills near Tumby Bay (see p. 262). Consisting of the restored Blacksmith's Shop (1903), historic log cottage 'Glenleigh' (1893) and schoolrooms, the museum houses an eclectic collection of First Nations artefacts, early settler furniture, firearms and early machinery. Open Tues–Sun. It's 30km south-west of Tumby Bay.

LINCOLN NATIONAL PARK: This magnificent coastal park has a network of walking trails through rugged wilderness areas to fantastic coastal scenery. The park is an important sanctuary for migrating birds. To see the park from above, take the 1.1km return hike up Stamford Hill. At the top are Flinders Monument and panoramic views of the coast. For a true uninterrupted wilderness experience, grab a key and permit from the visitor centre and head on to Memory Cove (4WD recommended), a calm bay with a fantastic beach. There is also a replica of the plaque placed by Matthew Flinders in 1802 in memory of eight crew members lost in seas nearby. 4WD enthusiasts will enjoy the challenges of the Sleaford Bay coast. The park is reached from Port Lincoln (see p. 261).

NULLARBOR NATIONAL PARK: Part of the largest karst landscape in the world, the caves, dolines, blowholes and rock holes of this region form a significant First Nations cultural landscape, connected by ancient tracks. Some of these tracks were used to trade the flint mined on Mirning Country with other groups as far away as Kati Thanda. Koonalda Cave has particular historical and cultural significance for the Mirning People – the cave contains markings made by Aboriginal people some 22,000 years ago. Murrawijinie Caves are the only ones open to public – other caves are closed due to unsafe conditions. Vast and mainly flat, the park's most beautiful scenery is along the coast where the cliffs stretch for 200km overlooking the Southern Ocean. Visitors should take care along the unstable cliff edges. Rare and endangered species such as the Major Mitchell cockatoo and the peregrine falcon are often sighted. Watch out for the southern hairy-nosed wombat.

POINT LABATT CONSERVATION PARK: From the cliff-top viewing platform, see the rare and endangered Australian sea lions sleeping on the beach. This colony is the only permanent one on the Australian mainland. The park can be accessed 50km south-east of Streaky Bay (see p. 262).

TALIA CAVES: Spectacular sea caves with waves crashing on the edge. Another good spot for beach fishing. It's 45km north of Elliston (see p. 260).

WHYALLA MARITIME MUSEUM: The central attraction is HMAS Whyalla, a 650-tonne corvette, the largest permanently landlocked ship in Australia. It was the first ship built in the BHP shipyards. Guided tours of the ship are included in the entry price and run at 11.30am and 1.30pm daily. The lives of the four wartime corvettes built by BHP are documented, as are histories of the shipbuilding industry and maritime heritage of Spencer Gulf. Open 10am–4pm; Lincoln Hwy, Whyalla; (08) 8645 7900.

OTHER ATTRACTIONS

FRANKLIN HARBOUR HISTORICAL MUSEUM: In Cowell (see p. 259), the old post office and its attached residence (1888) is now operated by the National Trust and features local history displays; open 10am–2pm; Main St, Cowell; (08) 8629 2686.

HALFWAY ACROSS AUSTRALIA GEM SHOP AND THE BIG GALAH: Standing 8m high, the Big Galah is in front of the gem shop, which sells local gemstones, carved emu eggs, opal and locally mined jade, including rare black jade; Eyre Hwy, Kimba.

MOUNT DUTTON BAY WOOLSHED: Restored heritage-listed jetty and woolshed (1875), the latter now a shearing and farming museum. There's a cafe here too; open Mon–Fri 10am–4pm; Woolshed Dr, Mount Dutton Bay; (08) 8685 4031. It's 40km north of Coffin Bay (see p. 259).

MOUNT LAURA HOMESTEAD MUSEUM: This National Trust museum in Whyalla (see p. 263) features the original homestead with progressive city-history displays, period furnishings in the 1914 Gay St Cottage, and the Telecommunications Museum; open Mon–Fri 10am–3pm, Sun 1–4pm, or by appt; Ekblom St, Whyalla; (08) 8645 4213.

MOUNT WUDINNA RECREATION RESERVE: The mountain is thought to be the second-largest granite outcrop in the Southern Hemisphere. At its base is a picnic area, a 30min return interpretive walking trail, and original stone walls used as water catchments. Enjoy scenic views at the mountain's summit. On the road to the reserve look out for Turtle Rock. It's 10km north-east of Wuddina (see p. 263).

PENONG WINDMILL MUSEUM: Open-air collection of historic windmills – including 'Bruce', the biggest windmill in Australia – all lovingly restored by a band of locals knowns as the Windmill Warriors; Eyre Hwy, Penong; 0428 141 352.

PORT BONYTHON AND POINT LOWLY: This coast east of Whyalla (see p. 263) offers beautiful views of Spencer Gulf, fishing from rocks, and dolphin sightings. Lowly Beach is a popular swimming beach and the Freycinet Trail is a scenic drive from just before Port Bonython along Fitzgerald Bay to Point Douglas (parts of the road are gravel). It's 34km east Whyalla.

VENUS BAY: A fishing village renowned for catches of King George whiting, trevally, garfish and many more. Its waters are safe for swimming and watersports, and nearby beaches are good for surfing. Needle Eye Lookout close by provides fantastic views, with southern right whale sightings June–Oct.

YANGIE TRAIL: Get your boots on and tackle this 10km trail, starting at Coffin Bay (see p. 259) and tracking south-west through Coffin Bay National Park to Yangie Bay Lookout, from where there are awesome views to Point Avoid and Yangie Bay; off Long Beach Rd; (08) 8688 3111.

VISITOR INFORMATION

Port Lincoln Visitor Information Centre
3 Adelaide Pl, Port Lincoln
(08) 8683 3544 or
1300 788 378
eyrepeninsula.com

Opposite: Almonta Beach in Coffin Bay National Park

KEY TOWNS

CEDUNA
Population 2290

The name Ceduna is derived from a First Nations word 'chedoona', meaning 'resting place', which is apt for those who have just traversed the Nullarbor. Ceduna is also the last major town for those about to embark on the journey west – the place to check your car and stock up on food and water, but it's also a beautiful seaside town worth spending some time relaxing in. Ceduna was established in 1896, and is situated on the shores of Murat Bay with sandy coves, sheltered bays and offshore islands. In the 1850s there was also a whaling station on St Peter Island (visible from Thevenard).

SEE & DO **School House Museum:** historic artefacts, including those from British atomic testing at Maralinga; open Mon–Tues and Fri–Sat 10am–12pm, Wed 2–4pm, Thurs 10am–4pm; 2 Park Tce; (08) 8625 3343. **Arts Ceduna:** Original paintings, local pottery and ceramics from First Nations artists from around Eyre Peninsula; 2 Eyre Hwy; (08) 8625 2487. **Oyster tours:** to Denial Bay and Smoky Bay; book at visitor centre. **Ceduna Oyster Bar:** fresh oysters year-round; open Mon–Fri 9.30am–5pm, Sat 10am–4pm; Eyre Hwy; (08) 8626 9086. **Local beaches:** swimming, boating, waterskiing and fishing. The foreshore is an ideal spot for walks and picnics (sharks have been known to frequent these waters – seek local advice). **Encounter Coastal Trail:** 4km interpretive trail from the foreshore to Pinky Point at Thevenard. **Denial Bay:** visit the McKenzie ruins to see an early settler home and the heritage-listed landing where cargo was brought to shore. Denial Bay jetty is good for fishing and crabbing, or you can take an oyster farm tour; 14km W. **Davenport Creek:** see pure-white sandhills and swim in the sheltered creek. Beyond the sandhills are excellent surfing and waterskiing; 40km W. **South-east towns and beaches:** Decres Bay for swimming, snorkelling and rock-fishing (10km SE); Laura Bay with cove-swimming near the conservation park (18km SE); Smoky Bay for safe swimming, fishing and boating (40km SE); Point Brown for surf beaches, salmon fishing and coastal walks (56km SE). **Cactus Beach:** renowned for its perfect left- and right-hand surf breaks for serious surfers; 94km W. **Fowlers Bay:** surrounded by a conservation park, Fowlers Bay offers long, sandy beaches and excellent fishing; 139km SW. **North-east conservation parks and reserves:** comprising Yellabinna, Yumbarra, Pureba, Nunnyah and Koolgera, an extensive wilderness area of dunes and mallee country. Rare species of wildlife live here, including dunnarts and mallee fowl. It's important to note that a 4WD is essential, and visitors must be experienced in outback travel; north of Ceduna. **Googs Track:** 4WD trek from Ceduna to the Trans-Australia railway track (154km N) through Yumbarra Conservation Park and Yellabinna Regional Reserve, continuing east to Glendambo on the Stuart Hwy; contact visitor centre for details.

COFFIN BAY
Population 667

A photogenic summer-holiday town and fishing village on the shores of a beautiful estuary, Coffin Bay is overrun with visitors in summer, when the population quadruples. The town was originally named Oyster Town after the abundant natural oysters in the bay. The Barngarla and Nauo People used the rich food resources of the coast long before the arrival of Matthew Flinders, but sadly the oysters were dredged to extinction last century. Today the town cultivates oysters in equal abundance, and the industry keeps the town afloat when the tourists go home. The bay – despite some of the spooky stories some locals will tell you – was named by Matthew Flinders in 1802 in honour of his friend Sir Isaac Coffin. Out on the water there is excellent sailing, waterskiing, swimming and fishing.

SEE & DO **Coffin Bay National Park:** *see* Top Attractions. **Yangie Trail; Mount Dutton Bay Woolshed:** *see* Other Attractions. **Oyster Walk:** 12km foreshore walkway through bushland from a lookout (stellar views of Coffin Bay itself) to Long Beach, passing the waterways where cutters used to dredge for native oysters in the late 1800s. **Experience Coffin Bay:** cruises on Coffin Bay; check out oyster leases and passing dolphin pods; book tours at experiencecoffinbay.com.au; 0428 261 805 or 0428 261 806. **Fishing:** dangle a line in the bay or head for the game-fishing areas further out to sea; boat hire and charters available; Coffin Bay jetty, The Espl. **Kellidie Bay Conservation Park:** a limestone landscape popular for walking and canoeing; off Coffin Bay Rd; (08) 8688 3111; 1km E. **Farm Beach:** super white-sand swimming spot; Farm Beach Rd, Farm Beach; 50km N. **Gallipoli Beach:** one of the film locations used in the 1981 Peter Weir film *Gallipoli*, with safe swimming; off Flinders Hwy, Coulta; 55km N.

COWELL
Population 1004

This pleasant Eyre Peninsula township is on the almost landlocked Franklin Harbour – its entrance is merely 100m wide. Matthew Flinders sailed past here in 1802 and, understandably, mistook the harbour for a large lagoon. The sandy beach is good for swimming and the fishing is excellent. Oyster farming is a relatively new local industry, and fresh oysters can be purchased year-round. The world's oldest and perhaps largest jade deposit is in the

SOUTH AUSTRALIA

259

district. Discovered in the Minbrie Range in 1965, the deposit is believed to have been formed around 1700 million years ago by the shifting of the Earth's surface.

SEE & DO **Franklin Harbour Historical Museum:** see Other Attractions. **Ruston Proctor Steam Tractor Museum:** open-air agricultural museum; Lincoln Hwy. **Cowell Jade Motel:** showroom and sales of local jade jewellery; Lincoln Hwy. **Foreshore and Mangrove Boardwalk:** ideal for a picnic, with barbecue area and adventure playground for the kids; The Espl. **Scenic drive:** 20km drive south to Port Gibbon along a coast renowned for its history of wrecked and sunken ketches; interpretive signs detail the history at each site. **Franklin Harbour Conservation Park:** coastal peninsula park of sand dunes and mangrove habitat, popular for bush camping and fishing; 5km S. **May Gibbs Memorial:** marks the location of children's author May Gibbs's first home; Cleve Rd; 10km S. **The Knob:** good fishing from sheltered beach and rocks; 13km S. **Lucky Bay:** safe swimming and the start of a 4WD track to Victoria Point with great views of the harbour. Spencer Gulf Searoad operates a ferry from here to Wallaroo on the Yorke Peninsula; bookings (08) 8823 0777; 16km E. **Port Gibbon:** old shipping port with remains of original jetty. Sea lions are visible from the short walk to the point; 25km S. **Yeldulknie Weir and Reservoir:** picnics and walking; 37km W. **Cleve:** a service town with murals depicting its early days and an observation point at Tickleberry Hill; 42km W. **Arno Bay:** a holiday town with sandy beaches and a jetty for fishing. Regular yacht races are held on Sun in summer; 44km SW.

ELLISTON
Population 333

Nestled in a range of hills on the shores of picturesque Waterloo Bay is the small community of Elliston. The rugged and scenic coastline is spectacular and – with its excellent fishing and swimming beaches – Elliston is becoming a popular holiday destination. The waters of the bay used to have rich abalone beds, but fierce exploitation in the 1960s decimated them. Thanks to a hatchery and rehabilitation, the abalone population is once again flourishing. The 12km stretch of coast north of Elliston, known as Elliston's Great Ocean Drive, is said to rival the landscape of Victoria's Great Ocean Road (see p. 164), but on a smaller scale.

SEE & DO **Elliston's Great Ocean Drive:** see Top Attractions. **Town Hall Mural:** represents the history of the town and district; Main St. **Jetty:** the heritage-listed 1889 jetty has been restored and is lit at night. **Waterloo Bay Massacre Monument:** commemorates the murder of more than 200 Wirangu People in 1880, acknowledging a historical injustice to allow community to reflect. **Elliston Coastal Trail:** a 13.6km walking and driving track that stretches along the coast either side of the town centre and can be broken up into shorter sections or a beach loop. **Anxious Bay:** good fishing from beach and ledges for King George whiting. The boat ramp here provides access to Waldegrave Island (4km offshore) and Flinders Island (35km offshore), both good for fishing and seal-spotting (seek local advice about conditions before departing). **Locks Well:**

TOP EVENTS

- JAN Tunarama (Port Lincoln)
- EASTER uneARTh Festival (Whyalla)
- APR SALT arts and culture festival (Port Lincoln)
- JUNE–AUG Australian Salmon Fishing Competition (Elliston), Cuttlefish spawning (Whyalla)
- OCT Oysterfest (Ceduna)

TEMPERATURES

Jan: 16–26°C
July: 8–17°C

Top: Swimming with sea lions at Seal Cove **Opposite:** Ben Yuan National Park

a long stairwell down to a famous salmon-fishing and surf beach with coastal lookout; 12km SE. **Walkers Rock:** good beaches for swimming and rock fishing; 15km N. **Lake Newland Conservation Park:** significant dunes separate the park's salt lakes and wetlands from the sea. Walk along bush tracks or try a spot of fishing; 26km N. **Scenic drive:** to Sheringa; 40km SE. From Sheringa Beach, a popular fishing spot, see whales, dolphins and seals offshore.

KIMBA
Population 608

A small town on the Eyre Peninsula, Kimba is 'halfway across Australia' according to the huge sign on the Eyre Highway. The peninsula is named after explorer Edward John Eyre, who traversed the harsh landscape in 1839 before heading off to tackle the Nullarbor. Early settlers thought the country too arid for settlement and it wasn't until demand for wheat production grew, and rail services were extended to the area in 1913, that the Kimba region developed. It is now major sheep- and wheat-farming country.

SEE & DO Halfway Across Australia Gem Shop and the Big Galah: *see* Other Attractions. **Kimba and Gawler Ranges Historical Museum:** a 'living' museum featuring local history and a Pioneer House (1908), a blacksmith's shop and 'Clancy' the fire truck; open Sun 1.30–4pm, Tues–Thurs 9–11am and 2–4pm (closed Jan) or by appt; Eyre Hwy; (08) 8627 2436. **Silo Art:** spectacular mural across Viterra silos, part of the Australian Silo Art Trail; Eyre Hwy. **Roora Walking Trail:** meanders through 3km of bushland to White Knob Lookout; starts at north-eastern outskirts of town. **Lake Gilles Conservation Park:** habitat for mallee fowl; 20km NE. **Caralue Bluff:** popular for rock climbing; 20km SW. **Carappee Hill Conservation Park:** bush camping and walking; 25km SW. **Darke Peak:** excellent views from the summit and a memorial at the base to John Charles Darke, an explorer who was speared to death in 1844; 40km SW. **Pinkawillinie Conservation Park:** the largest mallee vegetation area on the peninsula and a habitat for small desert birds, emus and western grey kangaroos; turn-off 50km W.

★ PORT LINCOLN
Population 14,404

Sheltered waters, a Mediterranean climate and scenic coastal roads make this town a popular holiday spot. Port Lincoln is set on attractive Boston Bay, which is three times the size of Sydney Harbour. Each January, this township celebrates the life of the tuna – one of the few festivals in Australia devoted to a fish, and a fair indication of the importance tuna has to this town. Lincoln Cove, the marina, is the base for Australia's largest, and most expensive, tuna fleet and tuna-farming industry. The townsite was reached by Matthew Flinders in his expedition of 1802, and he named it in honour of his home, Lincolnshire, in England.

SEE & DO Lincoln National Park: *see* Top Attractions. **Mill Cottage:** National Trust museum with early settler artefacts and paintings; open Wed and Sun 2–4pm or by appt; Flinders Hwy. **Railway Museum:** relics of the railway past are displayed in a historic 1926 stone building; open Wed 1–4pm; Railway Pl. **Axel Stenross Maritime Museum:** features original boatbuilding tools and working slipway; open Tues, Thurs and Sun 9.30am–4.30pm, Sat and public holidays 1–4.30pm, tours by appt; Lincoln Hwy; (08) 8682 3624. **Settler's Cottage:** stone cottage with historic photos and documents; open Sun 2–4pm or by appt (closed July and Aug); in Flinders Park, Flinders Hwy. **Nautilus Art Centre:** local art and travelling exhibitions; open Mon–Fri 10am–3pm, Sat 10am–1pm; 66 Tasman Tce; (08) 8621 2351. **Lincoln Cove:** includes marina, leisure centre with water slide, holiday charter boats and the base for the commercial fishing fleet (tastings of local catches available). Guided walking tours of the marina are available from the visitor centre; off Ravendale Rd. **Boston Bay:** swimming, waterskiing, yachting and excellent fishing. **Yacht and boat charters:** for diving, game fishing, day fishing and for viewing sea lions, dolphins and birdlife around Sir Joseph Banks Group Conservation Park and Dangerous Reef; contact visitor centre for details. **Aquaculture Cruise:** offers you a chance to view the working tuna farms (when in season) and to taste some mouth-watering local sashimi; a sea lion colony can also be visited; contact visitor centre for details. **Boston Island boat tours:** cruises around bay and island; contact visitor centre for details. **Adventure tours and safaris:** offshore and land adventures offered, including close-up tuna tours, shark expeditions and 4WD safaris;

contact visitor centre for details. **Old Mill Lookout:** panoramic views of town and bay; Dorset Pl. **Parnkalla Walking Trail:** 14km trail with coastal views and abundant wildlife. It forms part of the longer Investigator Walking Trail from North Shields to Lincoln National Park; brochure from visitor centre. **Winters Hill Lookout:** views to Boston Bay, Boston Island and Port Lincoln; Flinders Hwy; 5km NW. **Boston Bay Winery:** tastings and sales; open 12pm–4pm; Lincoln Hwy; (08) 8684 3600; 6km N. **Glen-Forest Tourist Park:** native animals, bird-feeding, minigolf course, Segway rides and vineyard with cellar door tastings and sales; Greenpatch; 15km NW. **Poonindie Church:** quaint old church built in 1850 with the unique feature of 2 chimneys; 20km N. **Constantia Designer Craftsmen:** guided tours of world-class furniture factory and showroom by appt; open Mon–Fri; on road to Whalers Way; (08) 8682 3977. **Whalers Way:** cliff-top drive through privately owned sanctuary inhabited by seals, ospreys, kangaroos and emus; permit from visitor centre; 32km S.

STREAKY BAY
Population 967

This pretty holiday town is also a fishing port and agricultural centre for the cereal-growing hinterland. The town's surrounding bays and coves, sandy beaches and towering cliffs bring the visitors. The bay was first sighted in 1627 by Dutch explorer Peter Nuyts, but it wasn't fully explored until 1802 by Matthew Flinders. Flinders named the bay after the 'streaky' colour of the water, caused by seaweed oils.

SEE & DO **Point Labatt Conservation Park:** see Top Attractions. **National Trust Museum:** early settler history displays in the old school, as well as a restored settler cottage and a restored doctor's surgery; open 9am–4pm Tues and Fri, or by appt; Montgomerie Tce; (08) 8626 1443. **Powerhouse Museum:** display of old working engines; open Tues and Fri 2–5pm; Alfred Tce. **Shell Roadhouse:** great white shark replica (original caught with rod and reel); Alfred Tce. **Fishing:** for King George whiting, southern rock lobster, salmon, mullaway, garfish, abalone and shark (check with PIRSA & Fisheries centre). **Scenic drives:** include Westall Way Scenic Drive, which starts 9km S, taking in rock formations, high cliffs, quiet pools and the Yanerbie Sand Dunes. Also the drive west of town to Cape Bauer and the Blowhole (20km NW), for views across the Bight. **Calpatanna Waterhole Conservation Park:** bushwalking in coastal park to an important First Nations waterhole; excellent birdwatching; 28km SE. **Murphy's Haystacks:** a much-photographed cluster of pink granite boulders, with interpretive signage and paths; 40km SE. **Baird Bay:** a small coastal town with an attractive beach for swimming, boating and fishing; Baird Bay Ocean Eco Experience offer swims with sea lions and dolphins; (08) 8626 5017;

45km SE. **Acraman Creek Conservation Park:** this mangrove and mallee park is an important refuge for coastal birds. Popular activities include canoeing and fishing; 2WD access to beach, 4WD to Point Lindsay; turn-off 53km N. **Port Kenny:** this small township on Venus Bay offers excellent fishing, boating and swimming, with sea lion and dolphin tours available; 62km SE. **Poochera Museum:** displays about rare dinosaur ants discovered in Poochera in 1977; open Wed 9.30am–3pm; 62km E.

TUMBY BAY
Population 1511

Tumby Bay is a pretty coastal town on the east coast of the Eyre Peninsula. Matthew Flinders discovered the bay in 1802, settlers arrived in the 1840s and the jetty was built in 1874 to ship the grain produce, but it took until the early 1900s for any official settlement to be established. Now the famous long crescent beach, white sand and blue water attract holidaymakers.

SEE & DO **Koppio Smithy Museum:** see Top Attractions. **National Trust Museum:** depicts early settler history in an old timber schoolroom; open Tues–Thurs, Fri, Sun 10am–5pm, Mon 2–4pm, Sat 10am–12pm or by appt; West Tce; (08) 8688 4210. **Silo Art:** iconic mural on Viterra silos of two boys jumping off the Tumby Bay jetty. Part of the Australian Silo Art Trail; cnr Lincoln Hwy and Bratten Rd. There are also several wall art murals in various locations around town. **Excell Blacksmith and Engineering Workshop Museum:** original workshop and equipment dating from the early 1900s; open 4th Sun each month, plus 2nd Sun Sept–Apr 2–4pm or by appt; Barraud St; (08) 8688 2037.

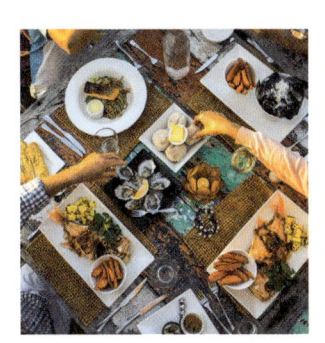

Mangrove boardwalk: 70m walkway with interpretive signs explaining ecology of mangroves; Berryman St. **Fishing:** from the recreational jetty, beach, rocks or boats (hire and charters available). **Trinity Haven Scenic Drive:** travels south from town along the coast and offers scenic coastal views and secluded beaches and bays. **Island Lookout Tower and Reserve:** views of town, coast and islands. Enjoy a picnic in the reserve; Harvey Dr; 3km S. **Lipson Cove:** popular spot for anglers. Walk to the coastal sanctuary on Lipson Island at low tide; 10km NE. **Ponta and Cowleys beaches:** fishing catches include snapper and bream; 15km NE. **Moody Tanks:** State Heritage-listed water-storage tanks once used to service passing steam trains; 30km W. **Port Neill:** an old port town with a safe beach for fishing and watersports. Also Ramsay Bicentennial Gardens, and vintage vehicles at Vic and Jill Fauser's Living Museum. Port Neill Lookout, nearby, provides fantastic views of the coast; 42km NE. **Sir Joseph Banks Group Conservation Park:** comprising around 20 islands and reefs, this park is a breeding area for migrating coastal birds and the Australian sea lion colony at Dangerous Reef; boat access is from Tumby Bay, Port Lincoln and 250m north of Lipson Cove.

WHYALLA
Population 20,880

Whyalla, northern gateway to the Eyre Peninsula, has grown from the small settlement of Hummock Hill to the second-largest provincial city in SA. The small city is modern and offers good beaches, excellent fishing and boating. It became known for its heavy industry since iron ore was found in the 1890s around Iron Knob and the steelworks opened in 1964. Each year, from May to Aug, an incredible number of cuttlefish spawn on the rocky coast just north – a must-see for diving and snorkelling enthusiasts.

SEE & DO **Maritime Museum:** *see* Top Attractions. **Mount Laura Homestead Museum:** *see* Other Attractions. **Tanderra Craft Village:** art and craft shops, market and tearooms in the original BHP workers quarters; open 10am–4pm last weekend each month; next to Maritime Museum; (08) 8644 0105. **Whyalla Wetlands:** park and wetlands area with walking trails and a picnic and barbecue area; Lincoln Hwy. **Foreshore and marina:** safe beach, fishing, unique circular jetty (the only one of its kind in the Southern Hemisphere), picnic and barbecue area, access to Ada Ryan Gardens, and a marina with boat-launching facilities. **Ada Ryan Gardens:** bird aviaries with picnic facilities under shady trees; Cudmore Tce. **Steelworks Tour:** 2hr guided tour explains steelmaking process; departs 9.30am Mon, Wed and Fri; book at visitor centre. **Hummock Hill Lookout:** views of city, gulf, steelworks and coast from World War II observation post; Queen Elizabeth Dr. **Flinders and Freycinet Lookout:** Farrel St; Whyalla; visitor guide from visitor centre. **Whyalla Conservation Park:** 30min walking trail through typical semi-arid flora and over Wild Dog Hill; 10km north off Lincoln Hwy. **Iron Knob:** a mining town with museum and mine lookout tours (depart from the museum: call for times); (08) 8646 2129; 53km NW.

WUDINNA
Population 516

The enormous silos in Wudinna are indicative of the town's major grain industry, predominantly wheat and barley, grown here since the first pastoral lease was granted in 1861. Wudinna was proclaimed a town in 1916 and has since grown as a service centre to the Eyre Peninsula. The surrounding countryside reveals unusually shaped granite outcrops – the area is known as granite country.

SEE & DO **Gawler Ranges National Park:** *see* Top Attractions. **Mount Wudinna Recreation Reserve:** *see* Other Attractions. **Wudinna Granite Trail:** signposted 25km tourist drive to all major rock formations in the area. **Mount Polda Rock Recreation Reserve:** walking trail for excellent birdwatching with views from the top of Polda Rock; 7km NE. **Ucontitchie Hill:** isolated and unique granite formations, similar to Kangaroo Island's Remarkable Rocks; 32km S. **Minnipa:** home to the Agricultural Centre, which provides invaluable research into sustainable dryland farming. Nearby are granite formations of geological significance, including Yarwondutta Rock (2km N), Tcharkuldu Rock (4km E) and the wave-like formation of Pildappa Rock (15km N); 37km NW. **Koongawa:** memorial to explorer John Charles Darke; 50km E.

Top: Delicious dishes at Mocean Café in Streaky Bay **Bottom:** Local sights at Tumby Bay **Opposite:** Four-wheel driving in Coffin Bay National Park

Western Australia

WESTERN AUSTRALIA

HIGHLIGHTS

Follow your nose to Margaret River. Cherished for its towering karri forests, pristine beaches and gourmet fare, this is a premium wine destination like no other. See p. 285.

Enjoy a 4WD adventure, ancient rock art and fabulous waterfalls along the legendary Gibb River Road in the Kimberley. See p. 322.

If you fear heights, don't look down as you explore the forest canopy along the stunning Valley of the Giants Tree Top Walk. See p. 275.

Snorkel the UNESCO World Heritage–protected Ningaloo Reef and swim with whale sharks, the biggest fish on the planet. See p. 310.

Explore the gorges of Karijini National Park and take a dip in one of its many rockpools. See p. 319.

Tour the fascinating Dampier Peninsula with a First Nations guide, and try the ancient art of mudcrabbing. See p. 324.

STATE FLOWER

Red and green kangaroo paw
Anigozanthos manglesii

Margaret River region

Perth/Boorloo at a glance

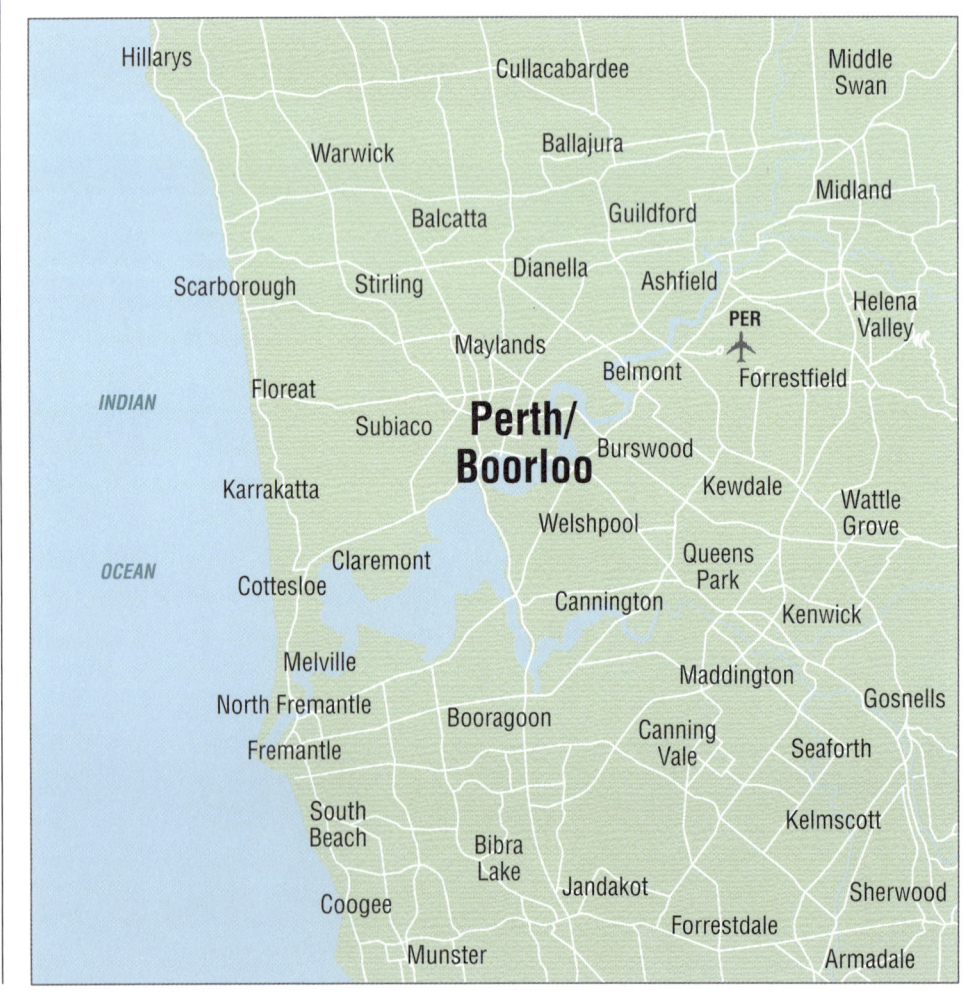

The Traditional Owners of the Perth/Boorloo area are the Whadjuk Noongar People.

Australia's most isolated city has a population fiercely proud of their beachside bliss – and who can blame them? Draped about the inner-city bushland of Kings Park and the Swan River's undulating expanse – with its **sublime coves, inlets and hidden beaches** – is a **modern, dynamic city** that is confident of its place in the world.

Top: View of Perth from Kings Park **Middle:** Fremantle Markets **Bottom:** Shopping in Perth **Opposite:** Bike riding around Perth

IF YOU LIKE …

BEACHES
City Beach
Cottesloe Beach
Leighton Beach
Scarborough Beach
Trigg Beach

FESTIVALS AND EVENTS
Fringe World, Jan–Feb
Perth Festival, Feb–Mar
Perth Comedy Festival, Apr–May
Kings Park Festival, Sept
Perth International Jazz Festival, Nov

GALLERIES
Aboriginal Art Gallery – Kings Park
Art Gallery of Western Australia
Fremantle Arts Centre
Lawrence Wilson Art Gallery
Perth Institute of Contemporary Arts

MARKETS
Farmers' Market on Manning
Fremantle Markets
Perth City Farm Market
Perth Upmarket
Wanneroo Markets

MUSEUMS
Museum of Performing Arts
Western Australian Cricket Association Museum
Western Australian Maritime Museum
WA Museum Boola Bardip
Western Australian Shipwrecks Museum

NOTABLE BUILDINGS
Bell Tower
His Majesty's Theatre
Old Court House
Optus Stadium
Perth Town Hall

PARKS
Araluen Botanic Park
Hyde Park
Kings Park
Sir James Mitchell Park
Whiteman Park

WESTERN AUSTRALIA

Daytrips from Perth/Boorloo

AVON VALLEY
1hr from Perth CBD

This region's enchanting historical towns and countryside attract people to the area; the townships of Toodyay, York and Northam evoke images of yesteryear, while the Avon River provides a lovely natural setting for a picnic or stroll along its grassy banks.

While exploring, try some adventure activities such as hot-air ballooning, skydiving, paragliding or shoot down the white-water rapids of the Avon River. For a more relaxed pace, take a scenic row visiting the valley's picturesque villages and enjoy strolling among the magnificent wildflowers in spring. *See* Northam p. 296, Toodyay p. 298, York p. 299.

DARLING RANGES
45min from Perth CBD

The Darling Ranges are Perth's bush oasis and a favourite with locals looking for a healthy dose of nature, with spectacular scenery, stunning vistas and charming villages all waiting to be discovered. Follow the Great Eastern Highway for a tour of the ranges and their more than 23,000ha of protected escarpment and jarrah forest.

Be wowed by the immense forest-fringed Mundaring Weir; canoe or swim at Lake Leschenaultia; have a picnic lunch in one of the area's magnificent forests; hike the Railway Reserves Heritage Trail or Bibbulmun Track; or hit the Munda Biddi Cycle Trail. For a break from nature, simply meander around the many arts and craft studios and tearooms. *See* Mundaring p. 295.

Top: Little Armstrong Bay, Rottnest Island/Wadjemup **Middle:** Yanchep National Park **Bottom left:** Sandalford, Swan Valley **Bottom right:** A quokka at Rottnest Island/Wadjemup

MANDURAH
1hr from Perth CBD

This traditional beachside holiday haunt has had new life breathed into it in recent years. It's now a sophisticated marine playground where visitors can sample some very fine seafood.

Apart from crabbing, prawning, fishing and dolphin-spotting, lazing in the sublime sun and taking a lazy dip are favourite pastimes of those who visit this charmed coastal area. Be sure to drop into the Mandurah Ocean Marina and investigate its waterfront market stalls, shops and Performing Arts Centre. To fully explore this waterside wonderland, consider hiring a boat. *See Mandurah p. 284.*

NEW NORCIA
1hr, 45min from Perth CBD

A Benedictine monastery dominates the quiet town of New Norcia, 130km north-east of Perth. This is Australia's only monastic settlement and it's overflowing with character.

Don't miss the New Norcia Museum and Art Gallery, which reveals the fascinating story of the town's foundation and also houses some remarkable artworks. A guided tour of the town is recommended, as is a cold drink on the sprawling verandah of the New Norcia Hotel afterwards. *See New Norcia p. 295.*

ROTTNEST ISLAND/WADJEMUP
2.5hr from Perth CBD

Powder-white beaches, turquoise waters, friendly quokkas and eye-catching natural scenery – and that's just what you experience as the ferry pulls into Thomson Bay! Just 20km offshore, and accessible by ferry from Fremantle, Hillarys Boat Harbour or the Barrack Street jetty in Perth, the island is a favourite escape for city folk wanting to indulge in some serious R&R. It's locally known as 'Rotto' and originally named Wadjemup by the Whadjuk People of the Noongar Nation.

In keeping with the island's serenity, no private cars are allowed – and shoes are optional! You get around by foot, bus or – most visitors' preferred method – bicycle. Divide your time between the many beach coves, where you can swim and snorkel around coral reefs to your heart's content, and the scenic and historic attractions of the island. *See Thomson Bay p. 296.*

SWAN VALLEY
30min from Perth CBD

The Swan Valley is fabled for its Mediterranean-inspired wines. Exploring the region's many family-owned cellar doors – and the sophisticated craft-brewing scene – is an enchanting way to spend an afternoon, as is taking in one of its many quality eateries.

Other attractions in the Swan Valley include the historic town of Guildford – best discovered on one of its excellent heritage walks; the Maze, a huge water-slide playground; Caversham Wildlife Park; and Walyunga National Park. *See Mundaring p. 295.*

YANCHEP NATIONAL PARK
50min from Perth CBD

Nestled on the coast north of Perth, Yanchep has long been one of the city's favourite recreation destinations. While Perth's northern suburban sprawl continues to creep, this pristine coastal region feels a world away and maintains its rustic and relaxed beach-meets-bush vibe.

There is plenty to explore in the adjacent national park, best done on foot – choose from walking trails with varied distances and levels of difficulty. Have your photo taken with a resident koala; see didgeridoo and dance performances; or take a guided tour of Crystal Cave where stalactites hang above the inky waters of an underground pool. There are also collapsed cave systems, gorges and haunted historic remains all awaiting exploration. *See Yanchep p. 299.*

Top: Beach in Mandurah
Second from top: Mundaring Weir
Second from bottom: The chapel in St Ildephonsus College, New Norcia
Bottom: Rottnest Island/Wadjemup

WESTERN AUSTRALIA

Regions of Western Australia

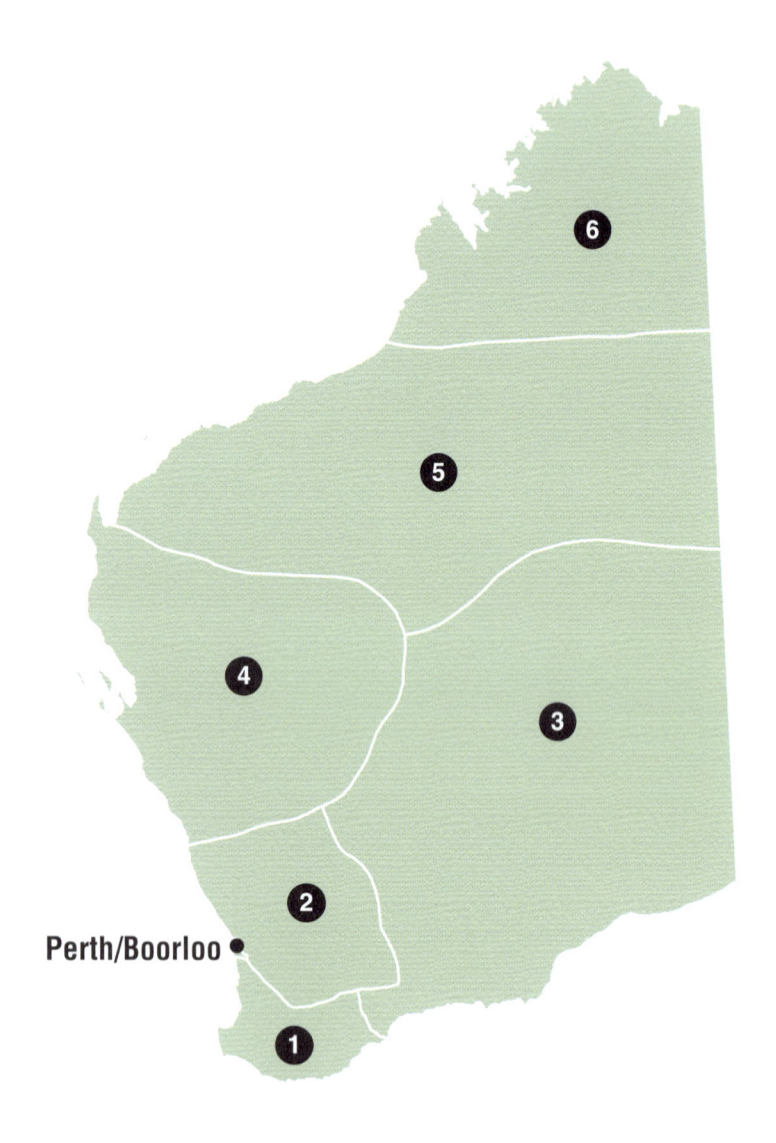

❶ THE SOUTH-WEST AND GREAT SOUTHERN P. 272

Albany ★
Augusta
Australind
Balingup
Boyup Brook
Bremer Bay
Bridgetown
Bunbury ★
Busselton
Collie
Cranbrook
Denmark
Donnybrook
Dunsborough
Dwellingup
Harvey
Katanning
Kojonup
Mandurah
Manjimup
Margaret River ★
Mount Barker
Nannup
Northcliffe
Pemberton
Pinjarra
Rockingham
Walpole
Yallingup

Perth/Boorloo

❷ THE HEARTLANDS
P. 288

Beverley
Carnamah
Cervantes
Corrigin
Gingin
Hyden
Jurien Bay
Kellerberrin
Kulin
Lake Grace
Lake King
Merredin
Moora
Mundaring
Narrogin
New Norcia
Northam
Pingelly
Rottnest Island/
    Wadjemup ★
Southern Cross
Toodyay
Wagin
Wickepin
Yanchep
York

❸ NULLARBOR AND THE GOLDFIELDS
P. 300

Balladonia
Caiguna
Cocklebiddy
Coolgardie
Esperance ★
Eucla
Kalgoorlie–Boulder ★
Laverton
Leonora
Madura
Norseman
Ravensthorpe

❹ CORAL COAST AND MID-WEST
P. 308

Carnarvon
Coral Bay ★
Cue
Denham
Dongara–Port Denison
Exmouth ★
Gascoyne Junction
Geraldton
Greenough
Kalbarri ★
Meekatharra
Morawa
Mount Magnet
Mullewa
Northampton
Yalgoo

❺ PILBARA P. 318

Karratha
Marble Bar
Newman
Onslow
Port Hedland
Roebourne
Tom Price

❻ THE KIMBERLEY
P. 322

Broome ★
Derby
Fitzroy Crossing
Halls Creek
Kununurra ★
Wyndham

WESTERN AUSTRALIA

Top: Kayaking near Esperance **Middle:** Kalgoorlie-Boulder mine tour **Bottom:** Whale watching near Albany **Opposite:** Wildflowers at Karijini National Park

The South-West and Great Southern

This verdant region begins at the gateway city of Bunbury, 190km south of Perth, and cuts a triangular swathe across the south-west corner of the state. The area features **gourmet eateries, boutique wineries, powder-sand beaches, world-class surf and towering karri forests.**

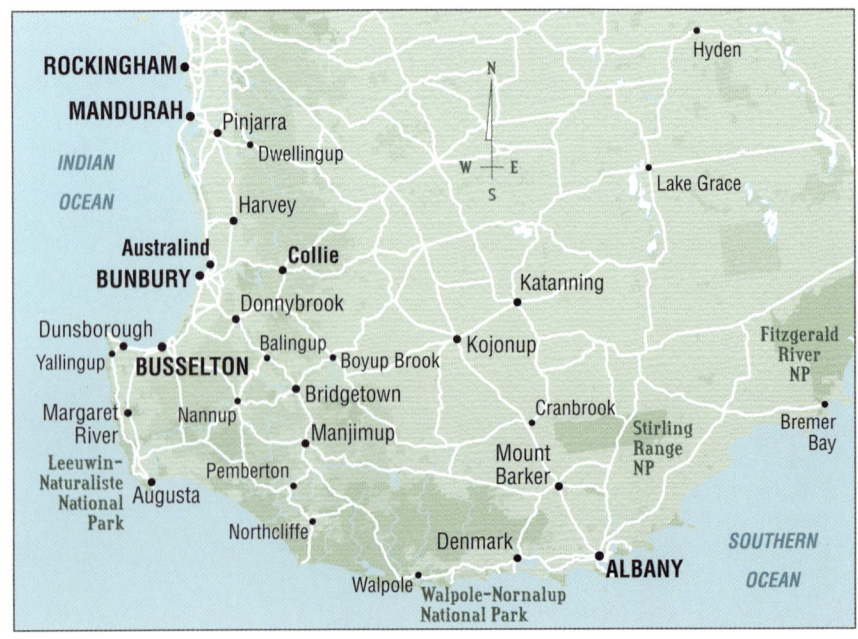

CHEAT SHEET

→ Allow at least two to three weeks for a proper exploration.

→ Best time to visit: Oct–May, although wildflowers are spectacular Aug–Nov and the cold winter months are best for whale watching.

→ Main towns: Albany (see p. 278), Bunbury (see p. 280), Busselton (see p. 281).

→ The South-west is the Traditional land of the Noongar Nation, including the Bibbulman, Goreng, Kaniyang, Minang, Pinjarup, Wardandi and Wiilman Peoples. Visit Kodja Place in Kojonup to learn more about the area's First People and take in the monument to the Pinjarra Massacre for reflection. Joining a Koomal Dreaming tour is an ideal way to discover Noongar culture.

→ Did you know? The first Europeans permanently settled in Western Australia in 1827 in what is now Albany, and soon after began whaling. The South-West is one of the world's 34 biodiversity hot spots, and its jarrah, karri and tingle forests are some of the region's greatest natural attractions.

→ Don't miss: Busselton's jetty; the legendary bakery at Dunsborough; a glass of pinot noir in Denmark; gastronomic grandeur in Margaret River; sensational surf in Yallingup; the awe-inspiring Valley of the Giants Tree Top Walk.

Top: Busselton Jetty Underwater Observatory
Opposite: Pemberton region

TOP ATTRACTIONS

BUSSELTON JETTY: The longest timber jetty in the Southern Hemisphere was built over a 95-year period, beginning in 1865, principally for the export of timber. Over 5000 ships from all over the world docked here through the ages of sail, steam and diesel, before the port closed in 1972. The jetty stretches a graceful 1.8km into Geographe Bay and has always been a popular spot for fishing, snorkelling and scuba diving because of the variety of marine life. Today you can take a small tourist train from one end to the other. At the seaward end is an underwater observatory featuring an observation chamber with viewing windows 8m beneath the surface revealing vividly coloured corals, sponges and fish. Tours are available, bookings essential. At the entry to the jetty is a new skate park and huge playground – complete with pirate ship – that kids will love; end of Queen St, Busselton.

DOLPHIN DISCOVERY CENTRE: Wild bottlenose dolphins regularly visit Koombana Bay in Bunbury (see p. 280). The centre has interpretive displays on dolphins and other marine life and offers visitors the chance to swim with dolphins under ranger guidance. A 360-degree digital Dolphinarium, opened in 2011, is the first of its kind in Australia. Dolphin visits usually occur in the mornings but times and days of visits are unpredictable. If you prefer not to get wet, take a dolphin-spotting cruise on the bay. Open 8am–4pm Nov–Apr, 9am–2pm May–Oct; Lot 830 Koombana Dr, Bunbury; (08) 9791 3088.

FITZGERALD RIVER NATIONAL PARK: This huge 242,739ha park, lying between Bremer Bay (see p. 279) and Hopetoun (see p. 307) to the east, is renowned for its scenery and flora. A staggering 1800 species of flowering plants have been recorded. Royal hakea, endemic to this region, is one of the most striking. Quaalup Homestead (1858), restored as a museum, offers meals and accommodation in the park. Point Ann has a viewing platform for whale-watching (southern rights, June–Oct). Campgrounds, barbecues and picnic areas available.

GLOUCESTER NATIONAL PARK: In this park is Pemberton's most popular tourist attraction, the **Gloucester Tree**. With its fire lookout teetering 61m above the ground and a spine-tingling 153 rungs spiralling upwards, this is not a climb for the faint-hearted. The Gloucester Tree is one of eight tree towers constructed from the late 1930s as fire lookouts. As the extremely tall trees in the southern forests offered few vantage points for fire-lookout towers, it was decided to simply build a cabin high enough in one of the taller trees to serve the purpose. Also within the park are the Cascades, a scenic spot for picnicking, bushwalking and fishing.

GREAT SOUTHERN WINE REGION: There are several impressive strings to the Great Southern's bow: riesling, chardonnay, pinot noir, cabernet sauvignon and shiraz. In Frankland River, **Alkoomi** is one of the region's oldest wineries, and **Ferngrove Vineyards** has won several awards. In Mount Barker (see p. 285), **Plantagenet** is a large, long-standing operation excelling in a range of styles, while **Gilberts** makes stunning riesling with the region's hallmark hints of lime and apple. A summer wine festival is held each Feb in Porongurup. The local **Castle Rock Estate** has superb riesling and pinot noir, and sweeping views of the Porongurup Range. In Denmark you'll find the big names of **Howard Park**, which has the MadFish brand, and **West Cape Howe Wines** – plus a burgeoning natural wine scene spearheaded by newcomer **Brave New Wine**.

HISTORIC WHALING STATION:
This is the only whaling museum in the world created from what was once a working whaling station. Even before the Cheynes Beach Whaling Company closed in 1978, Albany's (*see* p. 278) oldest industry was a major tourist attraction. At its peak, the company's chasers took up to 850 whales a season. View the restored whale-chaser *Cheynes IV*, whale skeletons, the old processing factory, an aircraft display and the world's largest collection of marine mammal paintings. A 3D theatrette occupies one of the old whale-oil storage tanks. It's within the Discovery Bay Tourism Experience, which includes the Australian Wildlife and Botanic Garden. (08) 9844 4021; it's 25km south-east of Albany.

LEEUWIN–NATURALISTE NATIONAL PARK:
This park extends 120km from Cape Naturaliste in the north to Cape Leeuwin in the south. Near Augusta (*see* p. 278) is the Old Water Wheel, built in 1895 from timber that has since calcified, giving it the appearance of stone. At Hamelin Bay (18km north-west of Augusta), a windswept beach and the skeleton of an old jetty give little indication of the massive amounts of jarrah and karri that were once transported from here. In the heyday of the local timber industry, the port's exposure to the treacherous north-west winds resulted in 11 shipwrecks. These now form the state's most unusual Heritage Trail: the **Hamelin Bay Wreck Trail**, which is for experienced divers. Close to Dunsborough at the northern end of the park is Cape Naturaliste, with its lighthouse, museum and whale-watching platform (humpback whales linger offshore Sept–Nov). Walking tracks offer glorious views of the coastline. **Sugarloaf Rock** is a dramatic formation just south of the lighthouse – it is also a habitat of the endangered red-tailed tropic bird. Lying beneath the Leeuwin–Naturaliste Ridge that separates the hinterland from the coast is one of the world's most extensive and beautiful limestone cave systems. **Mammoth Cave** is home to the fossil remains of prehistoric animals and you can take an audio self-guided tour. A few kilometres away is **Lake Cave**, with its famous reflective lake and delicate formations. Book your guided tour at the visitor centre in Margaret River (*see* p. 285). Further south, also in the national park, are Jewel and Moondyne caves. **Jewel Cave** is renowned for its limestone formations, including the longest straw stalactite found in any tourist cave.

MANJIMUP AND PEMBERTON WINE REGIONS:
Well before wineries were established here, Dr John Gladstones studied the climate of the wider region and claimed that Manjimup had similar conditions to Bordeaux. As in Bordeaux, merlot grows well here. Visit **Chestnut Grove** to taste some of the region's best merlot, as well as its verdelho. The much denser wine region of Pemberton has vineyards squeezed in between the marri and karri forests. Wineries include **Peo's Estate**, **Smithbrook** and **Truffle Hill Wines** (also WA's first truffiére).

MARGARET RIVER WINE REGION:
Although the first grapevines were only planted in the area in 1967, Margaret River is now considered to be one of the top wine-producing regions in Australia with cabernet sauvignon and chardonnay at the core of its reputation. While the region accounts for only three per cent of Australia's total wine grape harvest it commands over 20 per cent of the country's premium wine market. The *terroir* is perfect for grape-growing: cool frost-free winters, good moisture-retaining soils and low summer rainfall provide a long, slow ripening period. Acclaimed by Australian wine critic James Halliday as the 'golden triangle' are three outstanding wineries. **Leeuwin Estate** is renowned for making Australia's most exquisite chardonnay, and sells its exclusive wines as part of the winery's Art Series, with labels designed by leading contemporary Australian artists. The actual artworks can be viewed at the cellar door's art gallery, which includes works by the likes of Sir Sidney Nolan. The grounds also host the popular annual Leeuwin Concert Series. The second outstanding winery, **Voyager Estate**, with its distinctive Dutch architecture and elegant rose garden, is a lovely place for tasting top-shelf wines. The third in the trio, **Cape Mentelle**, offers fantastic chardonnay and semillon sauvignon blanc. Other outstanding wineries include **Vasse Felix**, **Moss Wood**, **Ashbrook Estate** and **Cullen**. Premium craft brewing, cider making and distilling has also taken root in the region, with the best examples being **Colonial**, **Black Brewing**, **The Beer Farm**, **Eagle Bay Brewing**, **Bootleg**, **Margaret River Distilling Company** and **Cheeky Monkey**.

Top: Valley of the Giants, Walpole **Opposite:** Valley of the Giants Tree Top Walk

PORONGURUP NATIONAL PARK: This is a park of dramatic contrasts, from stark granite outcrops and peaks to lush forests of magnificent karri trees. Many unusual rock formations, such as Castle Rock and Balancing Rock, make the range a fascinating place for bush rambles. The Tree in the Rock, a mature karri, extends its roots down through a crevice in a granite boulder. The Castle Rock Granite Skywalk offers a stunning vantage point. The park is 24km east of Mount Barker (see p. 285).

STIRLING RANGE NATIONAL PARK: Surrounded by a flat, sandy plain, the Stirling Range rises abruptly to over 1000m, its jagged peaks veiled in swirling mists. The cool, humid environment created by these low clouds supports 1500 flowering plant species, many unique to the area, earning the park recognition as one of the top 10 biodiversity hotspots in the world. This National Heritage-listed park is one of WA's premier destinations for bushwalking and Bluff Knoll, at 1073m, is one of the state's most challenging hikes. Best time to visit is Oct–Dec. The park is 10km from Cranbrook (see p. 281).

TORNDIRRUP NATIONAL PARK: Torndirrup, near Albany (see p. 278), is one of the most-visited parks in the state, featuring abundant wildflowers, wildlife and bushwalking trails. Granite outcrops and cliffs alternate with dunes, and sandy heath supports peppermint, banksia and karri. The park is renowned for its rugged coastal scenery, including such features as the Gap, a chasm with a 24m drop to the sea; and the Natural Bridge, a span of granite eroded by huge seas to form a giant arch. Exercise extreme caution on this dangerous coastline: king waves can rush in unexpectedly.

VALLEY OF THE GIANTS: Here you can wander over a walkway suspended 38m above the forest floor, the highest and longest tree-top walkway of its kind in the world. The Ancient Empire interpretive boardwalk weaves its way through the veteran tingle trees. Twilight walks are available during holiday season; (08) 9840 8263. It's 16km east of Walpole (see p. 287).

WALPOLE–NORNALUP NATIONAL PARK: The many forest attractions include Valley of the Giants (see previous entry), Hilltop Drive and Lookout Circular Pool and the Knoll. The park is probably best known for its huge, buttressed red tingle trees (some more than 400 years old), which are unique to the Walpole area.

WHALE-WATCHING: Charter boats and coastal vantage points offer sightings of migrating humpback whales (June–Aug) and southern right whales (June–Oct), plus pods of dolphins and fur seals; contact Augusta visitor centre (see p. 278) for details.

WILLIAM BAY NATIONAL PARK: This relatively small 1867ha park protects stunning coastline and forest between Walpole (see p. 287) and Denmark (see p. 282). It is renowned for its primeval windswept granite tors. Green's Pool, a natural rockpool in the park, remains calm and safe for swimming and snorkelling all year round. The area is very popular in peak season, and parking is limited, so plan ahead. Nearby are the Elephant Rocks, massive boulders resembling elephants; Madfish Bay, a good fishing spot; and Waterfall Beach for swimming.

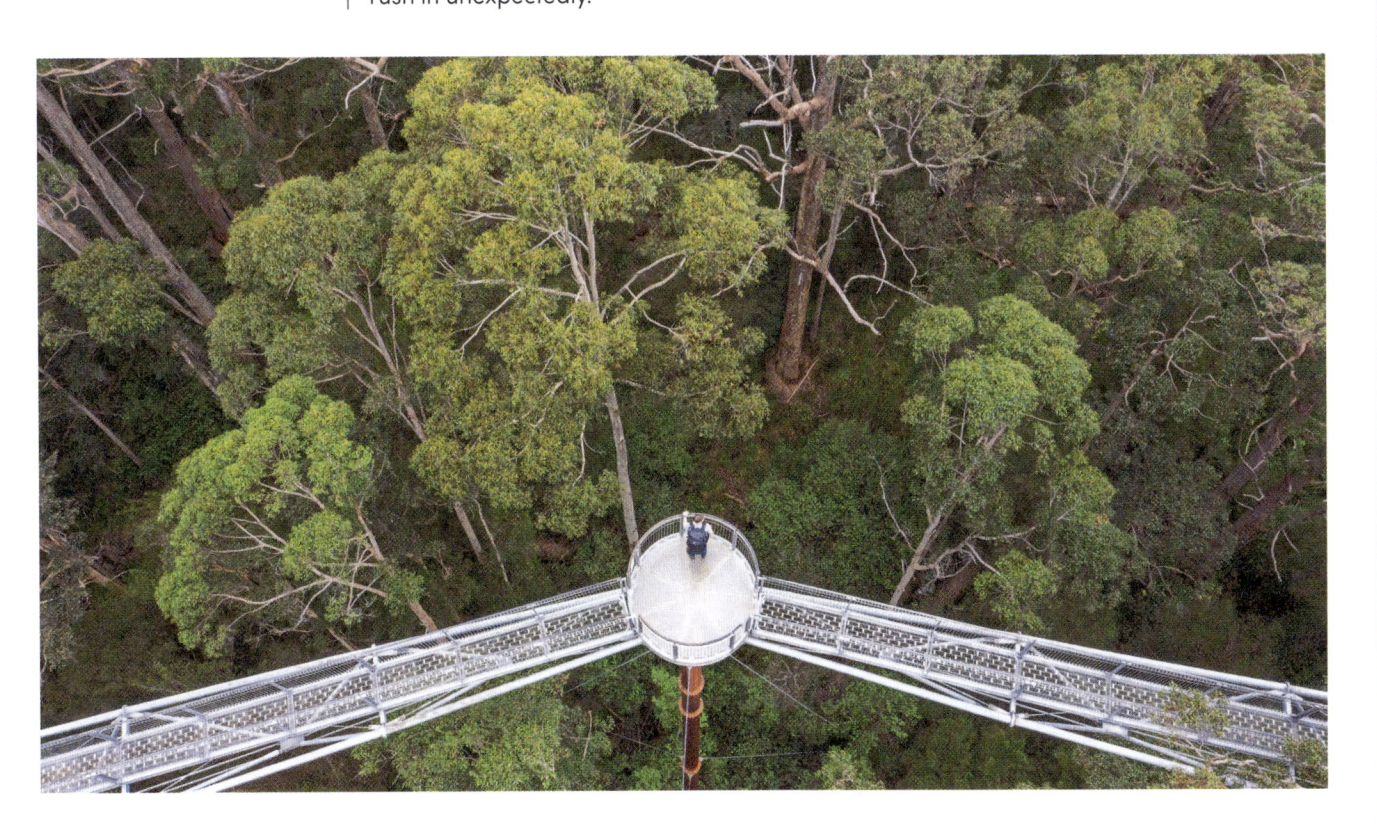

OTHER ATTRACTIONS

BLACKWOOD VALLEY WINE REGION: This low-key region between Margaret River and Great Southern began producing wine in 1976. The climate is perfect for the full ripening of cabernet sauvignon grapes, while chardonnay and shiraz are also good performers, with more than 50 wineries in the area.

BRIERLEY JIGSAW GALLERY: The only public jigsaw gallery in the Southern Hemisphere, Brierley in Bridgetown (see p. 280) has more than 170 jigsaws ranging from the world's smallest wooden puzzle to a huge 9000-piece jigsaw. A highlight is an 8000-piece jigsaw of the Sistine Chapel. It's at the back of the visitor centre, Hampton St, Bridgetown; (08) 9761 1740.

CAPE LEEUWIN LIGHTHOUSE: This limestone lighthouse, built in 1895, marks the most south-westerly point of Australia and is the tallest lighthouse on the Australian mainland. Climb 176 steps to the top. It's 8km south of Augusta (see p. 278).

CARNABY BEETLE AND BUTTERFLY COLLECTION: Keith Carnaby was such a leading light in the field of entomology that beetles have been named after him. His collection of jewel beetles, part of which is on display at the Boyup Brook Tourist Information Centre (see p. 279), is regarded as the best outside the Natural History Museum in London. Cnr Bridge and Abel sts, Boyup Brook.

EDENVALE: Built in 1888 with locally fired clay bricks, Edenvale in Pinjarra (see p. 286) was the home of Edward McLarty, member of the state's Legislative Council for 22 years. Nearby is Liveringa (1874), the original residence of the McLarty family, now an art gallery. There is a Heritage Rose Garden featuring 364 varieties of roses, a quilters' display in the Old School House and a machinery museum. Cnr George and Henry sts, Pinjarra.

FOREST DISCOVERY CENTRE: This centre in Dwellingup (see p. 282) records WA's jarrah forest heritage and promotes fine wood design. The building is formed from rammed earth and features an interpretive centre, fine-art gallery and shop. Acacia Rd, Dwellingup; (08) 9538 1395.

GREATER BEEDELUP NATIONAL PARK: Here you'll find the Walk Through Tree, a 75m, 400-year-old karri with a hole cut in it big enough for people to walk through. The Beedelup Falls, a total drop of 106m, are rocky cascades best seen after heavy rain. Nearby are trails and a suspension bridge. The park is 18km west of Pemberton (see p. 286).

HARVEY DICKSON'S COUNTRY MUSIC CENTRE: This entertainment shed in Boyup Brook (see p. 279) is decorated wall-to-wall and floor-to-rafter with music memorabilia spanning 100 years. The 'record room' containing hundreds of records also has Elvis memorabilia. There is a rodeo in Oct, with basic bush camping facilities. Open by appt; Arthur River Rd, Boyup Brook; (08) 9765 1125.

HOTHAM VALLEY TOURIST RAILWAY: Travel from Pinjarra (see p. 286) to Dwellingup (see p. 282) by train, taking in lush green dairy country before climbing the steep and spectacular Darling Range and finishing in the heart of the jarrah forest. The train is steam-hauled May–Oct and diesel-hauled Nov–Apr; check times online or with the Pinjarra visitor centre, or contact (08) 6278 1111.

LANE POOLE RESERVE: There's opportunities here for picnicking, swimming, canoeing, rafting, fishing, camping and walking. **Trees Adventure Park** is here too and has ziplines and high-rope courses suitable for all ages; Tues–Sun; (08) 9463 4063. Walking trails include sections of the Bibbulmun Track (see box p. 277), the 18km King Jarrah Track from Nanga Mill, the 17km Nanga Circuit and a 1.5km loop from Island Pool. The reserve is 10km south of Dwellingup (see p. 282).

LESCHENAULT INLET: Offers recreational attractions ranging from the simple pleasure of fishing from the Leschenault Inlet Fishing Groyne to picnicking, camping and bushwalking in the Peninsula Conservation Park. The park is a haven for native wildlife with over 60 species of birds recorded. Only walking or cycling is permitted in the park, except for 4WD beach access from Buffalo Rd (1km S). The Leschenault Waterways Discovery Centre has an interpretive gazebo. Old Coast Rd, Australind.

PEEL AND GEOGRAPHE WINE REGIONS: On the way to Margaret River from Perth, you might consider visiting the Peel wine region around the town of Mandurah (see p. 284), or Geographe further to the south. **Peel Estate** produces one of Australia's best shiraz wines. In Geographe, **Capel Vale** is also known for shiraz that packs a punch and riesling made from grapes grown elsewhere. **Hackersley** and **Willow Bridge Estate** are other wineries to visit.

Top: Vineyards, Pemberton
Middle: Gourmet fare at Voyager Estate, Margaret River **Bottom:** Albany's Historic Whaling Station

PENGUIN ISLAND: Take a trip to this offshore island, which is home to a colony of little penguins. The Discovery Centre allows you to see the penguins up close in an environment similar to their natural habitat and to learn about them through daily feedings, commentaries and displays. The island also provides picnic areas, lookouts and a network of boardwalks, and you can swim, snorkel or scuba dive at any of the pristine beaches. The island is open to the public in daylight hours Sept–June. Ferries to the island leave regularly from Mersey Pt, south of Rockingham. The ferry also provides bay cruises and snorkelling tours. See: penguinisland.com.au

PIONEER MUSEUM: The town of Northcliffe (see p. 285) came into existence as a result of the Group Settlement Scheme, a WA government plan to resettle returned World War I soldiers and immigrants by offering them rural land to farm. The scheme was enthusiastically backed by English newspaper magnate Lord Northcliffe (hence the town's name). Unfortunately, by the 1920s, when the scheme began, all the good land in the state had already been settled. The Group settlers were left to contend with inhospitable country and, with only crosscut saws and axes, they were faced with the daunting task of clearing some of the world's biggest trees from their land. It is not surprising that by the mid-1930s all of the Group Settlement projects in the south-west timber country had failed. A visit to the Pioneer Museum with its excellent displays is the best way to understand the hardships the Group settlers experienced. Open 10am–3pm; Wheatley Coast Rd, Northcliffe; (08) 9776 7777.

TIMBER AND HERITAGE PARK: A must-see for any visitor to Manjimup (see p. 284), this 10ha park includes the state's only timber museum, an exhibition of old steam engines, an 18m climbable fire-lookout tower, and a historic village with an early settler's cottage, blacksmith's shop, old police station and lock-up, one-teacher school and early mill house. The bushland surrounds provide delightful spots for picnics or barbecues. Cnr Rose and Edwards sts, Manjimup.

TOURIST COALMINE: Step back in time in Collie (see p. 281) and gain an insight into the mining industry and the working conditions in underground mines. This replica mine was constructed in 1983 to commemorate the 100-year anniversary of the discovery of coal here. Tours by appointment only; contact visitor centre; Throssell St, Collie.

TUART FOREST NATIONAL PARK: The majestic tuart tree grows only on coastal limestone 200km either side of Perth. Known locally as the Ludlow Tuart Forest, this 2049ha park protects the largest natural tuart forest in the world. It also has the tallest and largest specimens of tuart trees on the Swan Coastal Plain, up to 33m high and 10m wide. Enjoy scenic drives, forest walks, ziplining and picnics in this magnificent setting. The forest is 12km south-east of Busselton (see p. 281).

WARREN NATIONAL PARK: This park near Pemberton (see p. 286) boasts some of the most easily accessible virgin karri forest. The Dave Evans Bicentennial Tree has another fire lookout with picnic facilities and walking tracks nearby.

BIBBULMUN TRACK

At 963km, this is WA's longest walking trail and one of the longest continuously marked trails in Australia. It stretches from Kalamunda, a suburb on the outskirts of Perth, to Albany. On the way it passes through some of the state's most picturesque southern towns, including Dwellingup, Collie, Balingup, Pemberton, Northcliffe, Walpole and Denmark. Named after a local Noongar language group, the Bibbulmun Peoples, the track is marked by a stylised image of the Waugal (rainbow serpent), a spirit-being from the Dreaming. Whether you are taking a short walk or a five-week hike, easy-access points enable walkers of all ages and fitness levels to experience the Bibbulmun Track. Walk the track in springtime and see the bush at its best with WA's amazing array of wildflowers. Near Walpole you'll encounter the massive red tingle trees of the Valley of the Giants (see p. 275). Other well-known natural attractions on the track include Mount Cook (the highest point in the Darling Range), Beedelup Falls and the Gloucester Tree lookout. For maps and more information, head to bibbulmuntrack.org.au.

KEY TOWNS

⊛ ALBANY
Population 31,128

Picturesque Albany is a city on the south coast and a popular tourist destination with a crumbling colonial-era quarter, a redeveloped waterfront, dramatic coastline, and a reputation with foodies for its outstanding local produce (including the region's world-class wines). On Boxing Day 1826, Major Edmund Lockyer, with a party of soldiers and convicts from NSW, came ashore to establish a military and penal outpost, the site of the state's first European settlement. Ninety years later, Albany was the embarkation point for Australian troops during World War I, and it maintains a reputation as the birthplace of the ANZAC legend. A whaling industry began in the 1940s and defined the town until the closure of Cheynes Beach Whaling Company in 1978. Nowadays, whale-watching has taken its place.

SEE & DO **Historic Whaling Station; Torndirrup National Park:** see Top Attractions for both. **Historic buildings:** as WA's oldest town, Albany boasts more than 50 buildings of historical significance dating back to settlement. Two of the oldest were built in the 1830s: **Patrick Taylor Cottage** on Duke St and the **Old Farm at Strawberry Hill** on Middleton Rd, site of the first government farm in WA. Other heritage buildings include the restored **Old Gaol** (1851) with its collection of social history artefacts. **Albany Heritage Park:** 260ha parkland reserve which stretches from the Port of Albany to the shores of Middleton Beach. It offers a unique blend of natural, cultural and historical attractions from the wonder of wildflowers to pre-Federation military installations at Princess Royal Fortress, as well as the **National Anzac Centre,** Australia's foremost museum honouring the ANZAC legend. Off Marine Dr. **St John's Church:** discover the origin of the Dawn Service at Padre White's church, the first consecrated in WA; York St. **Albany Entertainment Centre:** architecturally stunning performing arts centre on the foreshore with breathtaking harbour views; Toll Pl. **Discovery Bay Tourism Experience:** incorporates the Historic Whaling Station, Australian Wildlife and Botanic Garden, and 12km of boardwalks through protected wetlands; Frenchman Bay. **Museum of the Great Southern:** exhibitions and programs as well as information on the region's natural and social history. Star exhibit is the **Brig Amity,** a full-scale replica of the brig that brought Albany's first settlers from Sydney in 1826; Residency Rd; (08) 9841 4844. **Fish traps:** discover the ancient stone fish traps built 7500 years ago by Minang People; Oyster Harbour. **Princess Royal Fortress:** Albany's first federal fortress, commissioned in 1893 and fully operational until the 1950s, now houses historic barracks and gun emplacements; off Forts Rd. **Lookouts:** lookouts at the peaks of Mount Clarence and Mount Melville have 360-degree views. Near the top of Mount Clarence is the Desert Mounted Corps Memorial statue, a recast of the original statue erected at Suez in 1932; Apex Dr. **John Barnesby Memorial Lookout:** the lookout at the top of Mount Melville is 23m high, with observation decks; Melville Dr. **Mount Clarence Downhill:** downhill mountain-bike trail adjacent to the peak; Apex Dr. **Whale-watching:** cruises daily from the town jetty; June–Oct. **Farmers' market:** Collie St; Sat. **Boatshed Markets:** Princess Royal Dr; Sun. **The Sandalwood Shop:** skincare products, perfumes, therapeutics and distillery; (08) 9845 6817; 12km N. **Point Possession Heritage Trail:** views and interpretive plaques; Vancouver Peninsula; 20km SE. **Fishing:** Emu Point (8km NE), Oyster Harbour (15km NE), Jimmy Newhill's Harbour (20km S), Frenchman Bay (25km SE). **Diving:** former HMAS *Perth* was scuttled in 2001 as an artificial dive reef; Frenchman Bay; 25km SE. **West Cape Howe National Park:** walking, fishing, swimming and hang-gliding; 30km W. **Two Peoples Bay Nature Reserve:** sanctuary for the noisy scrub bird (thought to be extinct but rediscovered in 1961), and the critically endangered Gilbert's potoroo; 40km E.

AUGUSTA
Population 1211

The town of Augusta is the state's third-oldest settlement and sits high on the slopes of Hardy Inlet, overlooking the mouth of the Blackwood River and the waters of Flinders Bay. Just beyond it lies Cape Leeuwin with its unforgettable signpost dividing the oceans: the Southern Ocean to the south and the Indian Ocean to the west.

SEE & DO **Leeuwin-Naturaliste National Park; Whale Watching:** see Top Attractions for both. **Cape Leeuwin Lighthouse:** see Other Attractions. **Augusta Historical Museum:** Augusta's difficult beginning in 1830 is documented in this collection of artefacts and photographs. Blackwood Ave; (08) 9758 0465. **The Landing Place:** where the first European settlers landed in 1830; 3km S. **Whale Rescue Memorial:** commemorates the 1986 rescue of beached pilot whales; 4km S. **Matthew Flinders Memorial:** Flinders began mapping the Australian coastline from Cape Leeuwin in Dec 1801; 5km S. **Alexandra Bridge:** picnic and camping spot with towering jarrah trees and beautiful wildflowers in season; 10km N. **Boranup Forest Maze and Lookout:** the maze offers a short walking track under trellis, while the lookout provides a picnic area with panoramic views towards the coast;

VISITOR INFORMATION

Albany Visitor Centre
221 York St,
Albany
(08) 6820 3700
theamazingsouthcoast.com

Margaret River Visitor Centre
100 Bussell Hwy
Margaret River
(08) 9780 5911
margaretriver.com
australiassouthwest.com

Top: Cherry Orchard, Manjimup *Bottom:* Dining at Voyager Estate, Margaret River

18km N. **Augusta–Busselton Heritage Trail:** 100km trail traces the history of the area through the early settler Bussell and Molloy families, who settled in Augusta only to move further up the coast looking for suitable agricultural land; contact visitor centre for map. **Blackwood River:** meanders 500km through wheat-belt plains and forested valleys to its broad estuary at Augusta. Secluded spots between Nannup and Alexandra Bridge offer tranquil camping, fishing, swimming and canoeing. **Cruises:** Blackwood River and Hardy Inlet. **Marron in season:** fishing licence required and available at the post office; Blackwood Ave.

AUSTRALIND
Population 15,988

Australind is one of Western Australia's most popular sea-change destinations and is one of the fastest-growing towns in regional WA. Located on the Leschenault Estuary and bordered by the Collie River, it offers fishing, crabbing, prawning, swimming, boating, sailing and windsurfing.

SEE & DO **Leschenault Inlet:** *see* Other Attractions. **St Nicholas Church:** built in 1840 and reputedly the smallest church in Australia at only 3.6m wide and 8.2m long; Paris Rd. **Henton Cottage:** originally a hotel, the 1841 heritage building now houses the visitor centre and an antiques and collectibles shop; cnr Old Coast and Paris rds. **Featured Wood Gallery & Museum:** fine furniture and craft made from the local timbers of jarrah, she-oak, marri, banksia and blackbutt. Also includes a museum of Australian and American West history; Piggott Dr; (08) 9797 2411. **Pioneer Memorial:** site of the first settlers' landing in 1840; Old Coast Rd. **Cathedral Ave:** scenic 2km drive through arching paperbark trees, offering sightings of kangaroos and black swans, especially at sunset; off Old Coast Rd. **Pioneer Cemetery:** graves dating back to 1842 and beautiful wildflowers in season; Old Coast Rd; 2km N. **Binningup and Myalup:** pleasant beach towns north of Leschenault. **Australind–Bunbury Tourist Drive:** coastal scenery, excellent crabbing and picnic spots; contact visitor centre for brochure.

BALINGUP
Population 280

This small town in the Blackwood River Valley is surrounded by rolling hills, forests and orchards. Balingup is renowned for its glowing summer sunsets, amazing autumn colours and misty winter mornings.

SEE & DO **Balingup Fruit Winery:** unique award-winning fruit wines, chutneys, jams and fruits; Brockman St; (08) 9764 1172. **Tinderbox:** herbal and natural products; South Western Hwy. **Old Cheese Factory Craft Centre:** antiques, art and craft centre; Balingup–Nannup Rd; (08) 9764 1018. **Golden Valley Tree Park** This 60ha arboretum boasts a superb collection of exotic and native trees. Other attractions include a tree information gazebo, walking trails, a lookout and the historic Golden Valley Homestead. Old Padbury Rd; 2km S. **Jalbrook Alpacas and Knitwear Gallery:** feed alpacas and buy alpaca knitwear; accommodation also available; (08) 9764 1616; 2km E. **Balingup Heights Scenic Lookout:** stunning views of town and orchards; off Balingup–Nannup Rd; 2.5km W. **Greenbushes:** boasts WA's first metal-producing mine (1888), still in production and now the world's largest tantalum producer. The Discovery Centre has interactive displays and walking trails, and there is an excellent lookout at the mine; 10km W. **Bibbulmun Track:** sections of this trail pass through Balingup (*see* box p. 277).

BOYUP BROOK
Population 540

Boyup Brook is on the tranquil Blackwood River in the heart of WA's grass-tree country. The town's name is thought to derive from a local Noongar word 'booyup', meaning 'place of big stones', which was given to nearby Boyup Pool. Wildflowers are abundant in Sept and Oct.

SEE & DO **Blackwood Valley wine region; Carnaby Beetle and Butterfly Collection; Harvey Dickson's Country Music Centre:** *see* Other Attractions for all. **Pioneers' Museum:** displays of historic agricultural, commercial and domestic equipment; open Mon, Wed, Fri 10am–3pm or by appt; Jayes Rd. **Sandakan War Memorial:** honours 1500 World War II Australian POWs sent to Sandakan on a death march by the Japanese; Sandakan Park. **The Flax Mill:** built during World War II for processing flax needed for war materials. At its peak it operated 24hrs a day and employed over 400 people. A scale model of the mill can be viewed onsite, which is now the caravan park; off Barron St. **Heritage walk:** follows 23 plaques around town centre; self-guided pamphlet available from visitor centre. **Bicentennial Walking Trail:** pleasant walk around town and beside the Blackwood River. **Gregory Tree:** remaining stump of a tree blazed by explorer Augustus Gregory in 1845; Gibbs Rd; 15km NE. **Haddleton Flora Reserve:** displays of boronia in season. Not suitable for campers or caravans; 50km NE.

BREMER BAY
Population 211

Bremer Bay on the south coast is a wide expanse of crystal-clear blue water and striking white sand. Offshore Bremer Canyon is one of the best places in the southern hemisphere to see orcas. The main beach, only a 10min walk from the town, has a sheltered cove for swimming and fishing. Just north of Bremer Bay is magnificent Fitzgerald River National Park, with its four rivers, dramatic gorges, wide sand plains, rugged cliffs, pebbly beaches and displays of wildflowers between Aug and Oct.

WESTERN AUSTRALIA

SEE & DO **Fitzgerald River National Park:** see Top Attractions. **Watersports:** fishing, boating, swimming, surfing, waterskiing, scuba diving, stand-up paddle boarding, bay cruises and seasonal orca-watching tours are the town's main attractions. **Rammed-earth buildings:** the Bremer Bay Hotel–Motel on Frantom Way and Catholic Church on Mary St are excellent examples of rammed-earth construction. **Orca watching:** with the largest congregation of orca in the southern hemisphere, Bremer Bay is the place to see these elusive whales. Orca-watching trips depart Jan–Mar. **Wellstead Homestead Museum:** the first residence in the area, now incorporating historic accommodation, a gallery, museum with family heirlooms, historic farm equipment, vintage cars and onsite cafe, serving up homegrown and locally sourced produce; Peppermint Grove, Wellstead Rd; (08) 9837 4313; 9km SW. **Surfing:** nearby beaches include Native Dog Beach, Dillon Bay, Fosters Beach and Trigelow Beach; ask at visitor centre for directions.

BRIDGETOWN
Population 2300

Bridgetown is a picturesque timber town nestled among rolling hills on the banks of the Blackwood River. Spanning the river is the longest wooden bridge in the state, made of the area's famous jarrah.

SEE & DO **Brierley Jigsaw Gallery:** see Other Attractions. **Bridgedale:** historic house constructed in 1862 of local timber and bricks made from riverbank clay; South Western Hwy. **Blackwood River Park Markets:** Sun mornings each fortnight. **The Cidery:** discover the history of Bridgetown's apple industry and sample fresh juice, cider and award-winning beers. Open Sun–Mon; cnr Forrest St and Gifford Rd; (08) 9761 2204; 2km N **Geegelup Heritage Trail:** this 52km walk retraces the history of agriculture, mining and timber in the region. It starts at Blackwood River Park. **Scenic drives:** choose from 8 scenic drives in the district through green hills, orchards and valleys into karri and jarrah timber country; self-guided maps available at visitor centre. **Sutton's Lookout:** excellent views off Phillips St and Hester Hill, 5km N. **Bridgetown Jarrah Park:** ideal place for a picnic or bushwalk. **The Tree Fallers and Shield Tree trails:** commemorate the early timber history of the town; Brockman Hwy; 20km W. **Karri Gully:** bushwalking and picnicking; 20km W.

★ BUNBURY
Population 75,196

Known as the 'city of three waters', Bunbury is surrounded by the Indian Ocean, Koombana Bay and the Leschenault Inlet. This is a water-lover's paradise with fishing, crabbing, diving, kayaking, sailing and white sandy beaches. Bunbury is also known for its wild dolphins that come close to the beach at Koombana Bay. Bunbury was settled by Europeans in 1838 and the Koombana Bay whalers were a source of initial prosperity. Today the port is the main outlet for the timber and mining industries. Sadly, the town's namesake was involved in massacres of Noongar People in the 1800s.

SEE & DO **Dolphin Discovery Centre:** see Top Attractions. **Historic buildings:** many date back to the early decades of the settlement, including the 1865 Rose Hotel, cnr Victoria and Stephen sts; contact visitor centre for details. **King Cottage:** built in 1880 and one of the oldest buildings in Bunbury, this cottage was built by Henry King using homemade bricks. It now displays items of domestic life from the early 20th century; 77 Forrest Ave; (08) 9721 7546. **Sir John Forrest Monument:** born in Picton on the outskirts of Bunbury in 1847, Sir John Forrest was elected the first premier of WA in 1890 and entered federal parliament in 1901; cnr Victoria and Stephen sts. **Bunbury Regional Art Gallery:** built in 1887, formerly a convent for the Sisters of Mercy and now the largest art gallery in the South-West; open 10am–4pm; 64 Wittenoom St; (08) 9792 7323. **Miniature Railway Track:** take a ride on this 800m track through the trees at Forrest Park; 9.30am on the 3rd Sun of each month; Blair St. **Lookouts:** Boulter's Heights, Haig Cres and Marlston Hill; Apex Dr. **Lighthouse:** painted in black-and-white check, this striking landmark has a lookout at the base; end of Ocean Dr. **Basaltic rock:** formed by volcanic lava flow 150 million years ago; foreshore at end of Clifton St, off Ocean Dr. **Mangrove boardwalk:** 200m elevated boardwalk lets you view the southernmost mangrove colony in WA, estimated to be 20,000 years old; Koombana Dr. **Wildlife Park:** handfeed kangaroos, see quokkas, wombats, swamp wallabies and more, and enjoy the South-West's largest walk-through aviary, with 60 species of native birds; open Thurs– Mon 10am–5pm; Prince Phillip Dr; (08) 9792 7274. **Heritage trail:** 12km walk from the Old Railway Station; contact visitor centre for brochure. **St Mark's Anglican Church:** built in 1842, this is the second-oldest church in WA. The churchyard contains the graves of many early Bunbury settlers; 5km SE at Picton. **Featured Wood Gallery & Museum:** craft and furniture made by local artisans; 12 Piggott Dr, Australind; (08) 9797 2411; 10km N. ***Lena* Dive Wreck:** apprehended by the navy in 2002 for illegal fishing, the *Lena* was sunk three nautical miles from Bunbury as a dive wreck; suitable for snorkelling and diving for all levels of experience; dive tours include Octopus Garden Marine Charters and the Dive Shed; contact visitor centre for details. **Wineries:** at the heart of the Geographe wine region, many offer cellar-door tastings, including Willow Bridge Estate (20km E) in the Ferguson Valley, and Capel Vale Wines (27km S); contact visitor centre for details. **Abseiling tours:** on the quarry face of Wellington Dam; contact visitor centre.

Top: Valley of the Giants Treetop Walk, Walpole **Middle:** Albany's Historic Whaling Station **Bottom:** Dolphins swimming at Penguin Island

TOP EVENTS

- JAN Festival of Busselton
- FEB Country Music Festival and Ute Muster (Boyup Brook); Geographe Bay Race Week (Busselton); Porongurup Festival (Mount Barker)
- MAR Augusta River Festival; Harvest Festival (Harvey); Crab Fest (Mandurah); Music Festival (Nannup)
- MAR–APR Taste Great Southern (Albany, Denmark)
- APR Small Farm Field Day (Balingup); Pumpkin Festival (Dwellingup); Margaret River Surf Pro
- MAY Forest Rally (Busselton, Nannup); Festival of Triathlon (Busselton); Groovin the Moo (Bunbury); Readers & Writers Festival (Margaret River)
- JUNE Truffle Kerfuffle (Manjimup); Festival of Voice (Denmark); Pinjarra Festival
- AUG Medieval Carnivale (Balingup); State Downriver Kayaking Championships (Bridgetown); Flower & Garden Festival (Nannup)
- SEPT Festiv Arty (Collie)
- SEPT–OCT Great Southern Treasures Bloom Festival (across the Great Southern regions)
- OCT Rodeo (Boyup Brook)
- OCT–NOV Festival of Country Gardens (Balingup, Bridgetown, Manjimup); Brave New Works (arts festival, Denmark)
- NOV Margaret River Gourmet Escape; Blues Festival (Bridgetown)
- DEC Cherry Harmony Festival (Manjimup)

BUSSELTON
Population 27,233

Busselton was officially recognised as a town in 1834 – it is situated on the shores of Geographe Bay and the picturesque Vasse River. Sheltered from most prevailing winds, the tranquil waters of the bay are an aquatic playground edged with 30km of white-sand beaches that draw droves of holidaymakers to these pretty shores each summer. Over the past three decades, the traditional industries of timber, dairying, cattle and sheep have been joined by grape-growing and winemaking. Fishing is also important, particularly for crayfish and salmon in season.

SEE & DO **Busselton Jetty:** see Top Attractions. **Tuart Forest National Park:** see Other Attractions. **Ballarat Engine:** first steam locomotive in WA; Pries Ave. **St Mary's Anglican Church:** built in 1844 of limestone and jarrah, with a she-oak shingle roof. The churchyard has many early settler graves, including John Garrett Bussell's, after whom Busselton was named; Peel Tce. **ArtGeo Cultural Complex:** local art, heritage and culture, including many historic buildings such as the restored gaol cells in the Old Courthouse; gallery open Thurs–Tues; Queen St; (08) 9751 4651. **Historical Museum:** originally a creamery, now houses historic domestic equipment; open Wed–Mon; Peel Tce. **Vasse River Parkland:** barbecue facilities; Peel Tce. **Wonnerup House:** built in 1859, now a National Trust museum and fine example of colonial architecture, furnished in period style; 10km N. **Cape Naturaliste Lighthouse:** offers panoramic views of the Indian Ocean and surrounding area; 37km W. **Ngilgi Cave:** limestone cave with family area; 32km W. **Augusta–Busselton Heritage Trail:** contact visitor centre for map.

COLLIE
Population 7599

Collie is WA's only coalmining town. The surrounding area was first explored in 1829 when Captain James Stirling led a reconnaissance party to the land south of Perth. The region was originally considered ideal for timber production and as pasturelands, but the discovery of coal along the Collie River in 1883 changed the region's fortunes. Set in dense jarrah forest, near the winding Collie River, the town has many parks and gardens. The drive into Collie on the Coalfields Hwy along the top of the Darling Scarp offers spectacular views.

SEE & DO **Tourist Coalmine:** see Other Attractions. **Coalfields Museum:** historic photographs, coalmining equipment, rocks and minerals, woodwork by local miner Fred Kohler, a doll house and art, all displayed in the historic Roads Board building; 161 Throssell St; (08) 9734 2051. **Collie Art Gallery:** opened in 2015, it is the first fit-for-purpose A-class gallery to be built since the Art Gallery of WA; open Thurs to Mon 10am–4pm; Throssell St; (08) 9734 2921. **Railway Station:** the rebuilt station houses railway memorabilia, a scale model of the Collie township with model trains, tearooms and a giftshop; Throssell St. **Soldiers' Park:** bordering the Collie River, features include a war memorial, rose garden, gazebo and children's playground; Steere St. **All Saints Anglican Church:** impressive Norman-style church distinctive for its unusual stained-glass windows, extensive use of jarrah timbers and elaborate mural, which in 1922 took renowned stage artist Philip Goatcher eight months to complete. Tours by appt; contact visitor centre; Venn St. **Central Precinct Historic Walk:** self-guided walking tour of historic buildings; contact visitor centre for map. **River Walk:** pleasant walk along riverbank; contact visitor centre for map. **Mural Trail:** more than 40 murals adorn the buildings around town, leading to the largest dam mural in the world – a very impressive 8000 square metres – called Reflections, at nearby Wellington Dam, completed in 2021. Maps are available at the visitor centre, or see colliemuraltrail.com. **Agricultural Markets:** Wallsend Showgrounds, Bridge St; 1st Sat each month. **Wellington National Park:** Covering 4000ha, this park is characterised by jarrah forest. Picnic, swim, canoe or camp at Honeymoon Pool or Potters Gorge, or go rafting in winter on the rapids below the Wellington Dam wall. 18km W. **Minninup Pool:** located where the Collie River is at its widest, it's ideal for swimming, canoeing or picnicking; off Mungalup Rd; 3km S. **Stockton Lake:** camping and waterskiing; 8km E. **Harris Dam:** beautiful picnic area; 14km N. **Motorplex:** the home of regional motor sports in WA for car, bike and kart racing, hosts regular events; Powerhouse Rd; (08) 9734 7477; 17km E. **Munda Biddi Trail:** starting in the hills near Perth, this bike trail winds through scenic river valleys and forests south to Collie and beyond; details from visitor centre. **Bibbulmun Track:** this long-distance hiking trail passes through Collie (see box p. 277). **Wellington Dam Mural:** biggest dam mural in the world; 20km W.

CRANBROOK
Population 505

The small town of Cranbrook greets travellers with a large sign announcing that it is the 'Gateway to the Stirlings'. A mere 10km away is Stirling Range National Park, a mecca for bushwalkers and climbers. The nearby Frankland area has gained a national reputation for its premium-quality wines. The Stirling Ranges and Porongorups are culturally important to the Noongar People of the area.

SEE & DO **Stirling Range National Park:** see Top Attractions. **Station House Museum:** restored and furnished 1930s-style; open by appt; Gathorne St. **Wildflower walk:** 300m walk to Stirling Gateway, featuring orchids in spring; Salt River Rd. **Sukey Hill Lookout:** expansive views of farmland, salt lakes and Stirling Range; off Salt River Rd; 5km E. **Lake Poorrarecup:** swimming and waterskiing; 40km SW. **Wineries:** the nearby Frankland River region boasts several wineries, including **Alkoomi**, **Frankland Estate** and **Ferngrove**; 50km W. **Wildflower drive and heritage trail:** contact visitor centre for brochure. **Gnowangerup Aboriginal Museum & Keeping Place:** a fascinating museum of Noongar history; (08) 9827 1007; 65KM NW.

DENMARK
Population 2944

Denmark lies at the foot of Mount Shadforth, overlooking the tranquil Denmark River and Wilson Inlet. It is surrounded by forests of towering karri trees that sweep down to meet the Southern Ocean. The Noongar name for the Denmark River is 'kwoorabup', meaning 'place of the brush tailed wallabies'. Once a timber town, Denmark is home to an impressive array of artisan producers and farmgate shops specialising in everything from chocolates and cider to boutique cheese.

SEE & DO **Valley of the Giants; William Bay National Park:** see Top Attractions for both. **Historical Museum:** in old police station; open Tues 2–4pm, Thurs and Sun 10am–12pm; Mitchell St. **Arts and crafts:** galleries abound, including studios in the Old Butter Factory in North St; contact visitor centre for details. **Mount Shadforth Lookout:** magnificent views; Mohr Dr. **Berridge and Thornton parks:** shaded picnic areas; along riverbank in Holling Rd. **Ocean Beach:** one of the finest surfing beaches in WA; 8km S. **Monkey Rock:** lookout with panoramic views; 10km SW. **Bartholomews Meadery:** honey, honey wines, gourmet honey ice-cream and other bee products, as well as a live beehive display; 20km W. **Pentland Alpaca Stud and Tourist Farm:** diverse collection of animals, including alpacas, koalas, emus, kangaroos, highland cattle, birds, llamas and many more; cnr McLeod and Scotsdale rds; (08) 9840 9262; 20km W. **Whale-watching:** viewing platform above Lowlands Beach (southern right whales June–Oct); 28km E. **Fishing:** at Wilson Inlet, Ocean Beach (8km S) and Parry Beach (25km W). **West Cape Howe National Park:** Torbay Head, WA's most southerly point, and Cosy Corner, a protected beach for swimming; 30km SW. **Wineries:** many wineries open for cellar-door tastings, including **Howard Park Wines**, **West Cape Howe** and **Forest Hill**, the state's oldest cool-climate vineyard; contact visitor centre for map. **Scenic drives:** the 25km Mount Shadforth Scenic Drive and the 34km Scotsdale Tourist Drive both feature lush forests, ocean views, wineries and galleries; contact visitor centre for maps. **Heritage trails:** 3km Mokare trail, 5km Karri Walk or 9km Wilson Inlet trail; contact visitor centre for maps. **Bibbulmun Track:** a section of this world-class 963km long-distance trail passes through Denmark (see box p. 277).

DONNYBROOK
Population 2786

Donnybrook is the centre of the oldest and largest apple-growing area in WA. This is a home of the Granny Smith apple and where Lady William apples were developed. Gold was found here in 1897 but mined for only four years. Donnybrook is famous for its sandstone, which has been used in construction statewide since the early 1900s. In Perth, the GPO, St Mary's Cathedral and University of Western Australia buildings have all been faced with Donnybrook stone. The quarry can be seen from the Upper Capel Road out of town.

SEE & DO **Memorial Hall:** built of Donnybrook stone; Bentley St. **Anchor and Hope Inn:** (1862) the oldest homestead in the district, now a private property; view outside from South Western Hwy. **Boyanup:** features South West Rail and Heritage Centre; 12km NW. **Ironstone Gully Falls:** barbecue area en route to Capel; 19km W. **Gnomesville:** surprising roadside collection of garden gnomes; by the side of the Wellington Mills roundabout on the road between Dardanup and Lowden; 25km SE.

DUNSBOROUGH
Population 7182

Dunsborough is a picturesque coastal town on the south-western tip of Geographe Bay. Just west of the town is Leeuwin–Naturaliste National Park, with its dramatic coastline and wildflower displays. Many of the wineries of the South-West region are only a short drive away.

SEE & DO **Leeuwin–Naturaliste National Park:** see Top Attractions. **Blackwood Valley Wine Region:** see Other Attractions. **Country Life Farm:** animals galore, plus merry-go-round, giant slide and bouncing castles; Caves Rd; (08) 9755 3707; 1km W. **Wreck of HMAS Swan:** the largest accessible dive-wreck site in the Southern Hemisphere; tour bookings and permits at visitor centre; off Point Picquet, just south of Eagle Bay; 8km NW. **Beaches:** to the north-west, popular for fishing, swimming and snorkelling, include Meelup (5km), Eagle Bay (8km) and Bunker Bay (12km). **Tours and activities:** whale-watching charters (Sept–Nov); deep-sea fishing charters; scuba diving, snorkelling and canoeing; wildflower displays.

DWELLINGUP
Population 332

Set among pristine jarrah forest, this is a thriving timber town that was virtually destroyed in 1961 when lightning started a bushfire that lasted for five days, burnt 140,000ha of forest and destroyed several nearby towns. Dwellingup was the only town to be rebuilt, and is now a forest-management centre. The Hotham Valley Tourist Railway operates here and

TEMPERATURES

Jan: 16–23°C

July: 9–17°C

Opposite top: Concrete fermenters at Voyager Estate
Opposite bottom: National ANZAC Centre, Albany
Overleaf: Windows Estate, Yallingup

the town is an established centre for adventure activities and popular with mountain-bike riders.

SEE & DO **Forest Discovery Centre; Hotham Valley Tourist Railway; Lane Poole Reserve:** see Other Attractions for all. **Historical and Visitor Information Centre:** includes a photographic display depicting early 1900s life in the mill towns of the region, as well as a 1939 Mack Fire Truck, the only one in WA; Marrinup St. **Community Hotel:** the last community-owned hotel in WA; Marrinup St. **Wine Tree Cidery:** small batch wines and ciders made from local fruits; open weekends; Holyoak Rd; (08) 9538 1076. **Marrinup Forest Tour:** unique 16km vehicle-and-walking tour that takes in many features of the Darling Scarp including the Marrinup POW camp and remnants of old mills and towns of days gone by; contact visitor centre for map. **Etmilyn Forest Tramway:** takes visitors 8km through farms and old-growth jarrah forest to the historic settlement of Etmilyn. **Bibbulmun Track:** long-distance walking trail runs through the middle of the town (see box p. 277).

HARVEY
Population 2797

On the Harvey River, 18km from the coast, the thriving town of Harvey is surrounded by fertile, irrigated plains. Bordered by the Darling Range, Harvey offers a wealth of attractions, from the scenic drives through the escarpment to the pristine white beaches with excellent sunsets and fishing on the coast.

SEE & DO **Tourist and Interpretive Centre:** tourist information and display of local industries and May Gibbs characters; James Stirling Pl. **Big Orange:** lookout, one of Australia's big icons; Third St. **Harvey Museum:** memorabilia housed in renovated railway station; open 2–4pm 1st, 3rd and 5th Sun each month or by appt; (08) 9729 1685; Harper St. **Stirling Cottage:** replica of the home of Governor Stirling, which later became the home of May Gibbs, author of Snugglepot and Cuddlepie, it's now a cafe; James Stirling Pl tourist precinct. **Heritage Gardens:** picturesque country gardens on the banks of the Harvey River; James Stirling Pl tourist precinct. **Internment Camp Memorial Shrine:** the only roadside shrine of its type in the world, built by World War II POWs in the 1940s; collect key from visitor centre; South Western Hwy. **Heritage trail:** 6.2km self-guided walk includes historic buildings and sights of town; map available at visitor centre. **Mosaics and murals:** unique collection throughout the region; Uduc Rd, South Western Hwy, and entrances to Myalup and Binningup. **Harvey Dam:** landscaped park with viewing platform, amphitheatre, barbecues and playground. Fishing is allowed in season with permit; 3km E. **Harvey Cheese:** gourmet cheese tasting and sales; (08) 9729 3949; 3km S. **Beaches:** Myalup Beach provides good swimming, surfing and beach fishing; 21km W. Binningup Beach is protected by a reef that runs parallel to shore and is ideal for sheltered swimming, snorkelling, beach fishing and boating; 25km SW. **Wineries:** more than 10 wineries open to the public, only a short distance from town; contact visitor centre for details.

KATANNING
Population 3641

Katanning lies in the middle of a prosperous grain-growing and pastoral area. A significant development in the town's history was the 1889 completion of the Great Southern Railway, which linked Perth and Albany. Construction was undertaken at both ends, and a cairn north of town marks the spot where the lines were joined.

SEE & DO **All Ages Playground and Miniature Steam Railway:** scenic grounds with playground equipment for all ages. Covered shoes required to ride the train, which runs on the 2nd and 4th Sun of each month; cnr Great Southern Hwy and Clive St. **Kobeelya:** a majestic residence (1902) with seven bedrooms, ballroom, billiard room, tennis courts and croquet lawn, now a conference centre; Brownie St. **Old Winery Ruins:** inspect the ruins of the original turreted distillery and brick vats, with old ploughs and machinery on display; Andrews Rd. **Historical Museum:** the original school building has been converted into a museum of local memorabilia; Taylor St. **Sale yards:** one of the biggest yards in Australia, sheep sales every Wed at 8am; viewing platform for visitors; Daping St. **Heritage Rose Garden:** with roses dating from 1830; Austral Tce. **Piesse Memorial Statue:** unveiled in 1916, this statue of Frederick H. Piesse, the founder of Katanning, was sculpted by P.C. Porcelli, a well-known artist in the early days of WA; Austral Tce. **Art Gallery:** a changing display and local collection; Austral Tce. **Farmers' markets:** Pemble St; 3rd Sat each month. **Police Pools (Twonkwillingup):** site of the original camp for the district's first police officers. Enjoy swimming, picnicking, birdwatching and bushwalking; 3km S. **Lake Ewlyamartup:** picturesque freshwater lake ideal for picnicking, swimming, boating and waterskiing, particularly in early summer when the water level is high; 22km E. **Katanning-Piesse Heritage Trail:** 20km self-drive and walking trail; map at visitor centre.

KOJONUP
Population 878

Kojonup is famous for being the first shire in Australia to have more than a million sheep. In spring its hills are painted with gold from the flowering of the annual canola crop. A military outpost was established here in 1837, and you can still visit the military barracks today.

SEE & DO **The Kodja Place:** fascinating and fun displays about the land and its people, with stories of Noongar

Traditional Owners and European settlement. It also includes the **Australian Rose Maze**, the only rose garden in the world growing exclusively Australian roses; 143 Albany Hwy. **A.W. Potts Kokoda Track Memorial:** a life-size statue of the brigadier facing towards his beloved farm, Barrule; Albany Hwy. **Centenary of Federation Wool Wagon:** commemorates the significance of the sheep industry to the Kojonup community; Albany Hwy. **Kojonup Spring:** grassy picnic area; Spring St. **Military barracks:** built in 1845, this is one of the oldest surviving military buildings in WA and features historical information about the building; open by appt; Spring St. **Elverd Cottage:** display of early settler tools and farm machinery; open by appt; Soldier Rd. **The Kodja Place Bush Tucker Walk:** follows the old railway line east where 3000 trees and shrubs indigenous to the area have been planted; map from visitor centre. **Historic trail:** self-guided walk to 52 historic sights; map from visitor centre. **Myrtle Benn Memorial Flora and Fauna Sanctuary:** walk one of the numerous trails among local flora and fauna, including many protected species; Tunney Rd; 1km W. **Farrar Reserve:** scenic bushland and wildflower display in season; Blackwood Rd; 8km W. **Australian Bush Heritage Block:** natural woodland featuring wandoo and species unique to the South-West; 16km N. **Lake Towerinning:** boating, waterskiing, horseriding, camping; 40km NW.

MANDURAH
Population 8804

Mandurah, which has long been a popular holiday destination for Perth residents, is today the southernmost point of Perth's ever-expanding commuter belt. The Murray, Serpentine and Harvey rivers meet at the town to form the vast inland waterway of Peel Inlet and the Harvey Estuary. This river junction was once a meeting site for First Nations groups who travelled here to barter. The town's name is derived from the Bindjareb word 'mandjar', meaning 'trading place'. The river and the Indian Ocean offer a variety of watersports and excellent fishing and prawning. But the aquatic activity for which Mandurah is perhaps best known is crabbing. It brings thousands of people during summer weekends, wading the shallows with scoop nets and stout shoes.

SEE & DO **Peel and Geographe Wine Regions:** *see* Other Attractions. **Christ's Church:** built in 1870, this Anglican church has hand-worked pews believed to be the work of early settler Joseph Cooper. Many of the district's settlers are buried in the churchyard, including Thomas Peel, the founder of Mandurah. In 1994 the church was extended and a belltower added to house eight bells from England. Cnr Pinjarra Rd and Sholl St. **Hall's Cottage:** (1832) restored home of one of the original settlers, Henry Hall; open Sun 10–3pm; Leighton Pl, Halls Head. **Mandurah Community Museum:** (1898) originally a school then a police station, now houses displays on Mandurah's social, fishing and canning histories; 3 Pinjarra Rd; (08) 9550 3680. **King Carnival:** fun-fair attractions including ferris wheel and minigolf; open Fri–Sun and school holidays; Leighton Pl; (08) 9581 3735. **Mandjar Markets:** off Mandurah Tce on Eastern Foreshore; 2nd and 4th Sun Oct–May. **Coopers Mill:** the first flour mill in the Murray region, located on Cooleenup Island near the mouth of the Serpentine River. Joseph Cooper built it by collecting limestone rocks and sailing them across to the island every morning. Accessible only by water; contact visitor centre for information. **Yalgorup National Park:** swamps, woodlands and coastal lakes abounding with birdlife. Lake Clifton is one of only three places in Australia where the living fossils called thrombolites survive. A boardwalk allows close-up viewing; 45km S.

MANJIMUP
Population 4138

Manjimup is the gateway to the South-west region's tall-timber country. Magnificent karri forests and rich farmlands surround the town. While timber is the main economic activity here, Manjimup is also the centre of a thriving fruit-and-vegetable industry and is the birthplace of the delicious Pink Lady apple. More recently the town has gained renown as a gourmet hub, thanks in part to the popular Manjimup truffle.

SEE & DO **Manjimup and Pemberton Wine regions:** *see* Top Attractions. **Timber and Heritage Park:** *see* Other Attractions. **One Tree Bridge:** In 1904 a single enormous karri tree was felled so that it dropped across the 25m wide Donnelly River, forming the basis of a bridge. Winter floods in 1966 swept most of the bridge away; the 17m piece salvaged is displayed near the original site beside information boards. Nearby is Glenoran Pool, a scenic spot for catching rainbow trout and marron in season, with walking trails and picnic areas. Graphite Rd; 21km W. **King Jarrah:** estimated to be 600 years old, this massive tree is the centrepiece for several forest walks; Perup Rd; 3km E. **Fonty's Pool:** dammed in 1925 by Archie Fontanini for the irrigation of vegetables, it is now a popular swimming pool and picnic area in landscaped grounds; Seven Day Rd; 7km S. **Dingup Church:** built in 1896 by the early settler Giblett family, this church is one of the few remaining local soapstone buildings; Balbarrup Rd; 8km E. **Pioneer Cemetery:** poignant descriptions on headstones testify to the hardships faced by the first settlers; Perup Rd; 8km E. **Diamond Tree:** one of eight tree towers constructed from the late 1930s as fire lookouts, in use 1941–47 but now closed to climbers; 9km S. **Fontanini's Nut Farm:** seasonal chestnuts, walnuts, hazelnuts and fruit; closed at the time of writing, so check ahead for reopening details; Seven Day Rd; 10km S. **Nyamup:** old mill town redeveloped as a tourist village; 20km SE. **Four Aces:** four giant karri trees, 220–250 years old and 67–79m high, standing in a straight line; Graphite Rd; 23km W. **Great Forest Trees Drive:** self-guided drive through Shannon National Park; contact visitor centre for map; 45km S. **Lake Muir Lookout/Bird Observatory:** boardwalk over salt lake to bird hide; 55km E.

★ MARGARET RIVER
Population 7430

Margaret River is synonymous with world-class wines, magnificent coastal scenery, excellent surf breaks and spectacular cave formations. In addition, the region boasts a thriving arts scene, boutique breweries, gourmet food outlets and restaurants with views of sweeping vineyards and the sparkling ocean. The bustling township lies on the Margaret River near the coast, 280km south-west of Perth.

SEE & DO **Leeuwin–Naturaliste National Park; Margaret River Wine Region:** *see* Top Attractions for both. **Rotary Park:** picnic area on the riverbank with a display steam engine; Bussell Hwy. **St Thomas More Catholic Church:** one of the first modern buildings built of rammed earth; Wallcliffe Rd. **Fudge Factory:** fudge and chocolate made before your eyes; open 10am–5pm; 152 Bussell Hwy; (08) 9758 8881. **Arts and crafts:** many in town. **Margaret River Brewhouse:** try local brews in the backyard of an iconic shack on the edge of town, surrounded by forest; Bussell Hwy; (08) 9757 2614. **Margaret River Farmers' Market:** The best one-stop shop for local produce, every Sat morning year-round. **Town Square Markets:** every Sun in summer, 2nd Sun each month rest of year. **Amaze'n Margaret River:** family-friendly venue with giant hedge maze, ground puzzles, outdoor games and picnic area; open Thurs–Mon 9am–5pm; cnr Bussell Hwy and Gnarawary Rd; (08) 9758 7439; 4km S. **Eagles Heritage:** the largest collection of birds of prey in Australia, with free-flight displays on Tues–Thurs and Sat–Sun, 11am and 1.30pm; Boodjidup Rd; (08) 9757 2960; 5km SW. **Surfers Point:** the centre of surfing in Margaret River and home to the Margaret River Pro; 8km W, just north of Prevelly. **Candy Cow:** free tastings of fudge, nougat and honeycomb; cnr Bussell Hwy and Bottrill St, Cowaramup; (08) 9755 9155; 13km N. **Gnarabup Beach:** good swimming beach; 13km W. **The Berry Farm:** jams, pickles, naturally fermented vinegars, fruit and berry wines; 43 Bessell Rd, Rosa Glen; (08) 9757 5054; 15km SE. **Ellenbrook Homestead:** this wattle-and-daub homestead (1857) was once the home of Alfred and Ellen Bussell, the district's first European settlers; open Thurs–Sat 10am–4pm; (08) 9755 5173. Nearby is the beautiful **Meekadarabee Waterfall**, a place known to Traditional Owners as 'the bathing place of the moon'; 15km NW. **Margaret River Dairy Company:** free tastings of cheese and yoghurt; Bussell Hwy, Metricup; (08) 9750 6600; 17km N. **Olio Bello:** boutique, handmade olive oil, with tastings available; Armstrong Rd, Cowaramup; (08) 9755 9771; 17km NW. **Arts and crafts:** many in area, including Boranup Gallery selling furniture made with local wood such as jarrah, paintings, sculptures and more; Caves Rd; (08) 9757 7585; 20km S. **Margaret River Chocolate Company:** free chocolate tastings, interactive displays and viewing windows to watch the chocolate products being made; cnr Harmans Mill and Harmans South rds, Metricup; (08) 9755 6555; 30km NW. **Bushtucker River and Winery Tours:** experience the region through its wine, wilderness and food; (08) 9757 9084.

MOUNT BARKER
Population 1898

Mount Barker lies in the Great Southern region of WA, with the Stirling Range to the north and the Porongurups to the east. The area was settled by Europeans in the 1830s. Vineyards were first established here in the late 1960s and today it is renowned as a major wine-producing area with excellent local produce.

SEE & DO **Great Southern Wine Region; Porongurup National Park:** *see* Top Attractions for both. **Old Police Station Museum:** a gaol built by convicts in 1867–68, it now houses memorabilia; open Sat–Sun 10am–3pm or by appt; Albany Hwy, north of town; 0448 512 651. **Lookout and TV tower:** easily pinpointed on the summit of Mount Barker by the 168m high television tower, it offers panoramic views of the area from the Stirling Ranges to Albany; 5km SW. **St Werburgh's Chapel:** small mud-walled chapel (1872) overlooking Hay River Valley; 12km SW. **Kendenup:** historic town, location of WA's first gold find; 16km E. **Porongurup:** hosts a wine festival each Mar and boasts many small wineries; 24km E. **Mount Barker Heritage Trail:** 30km drive tracing the development of the Mount Barker farming district; contact visitor centre for map.

NANNUP
Population 538

Nannup is a historic and perfectly preserved timber town in the Blackwood Valley south of Perth. Known as 'The Garden Village', it has beautiful private and public gardens, tulip farms, daffodils and wildflowers. The countryside is a series of lush, rolling pastures alongside jarrah forests and pine plantations.

SEE & DO **Heritage trail:** 2.5km of historic and cultural sites of significance; contact visitor centre for map; 16 Warren Rd. (The visitor centre also sells a selection of local wares and products.) **Old Flood Tree:** at the Old Railway Bridge, it records the levels of floods through the town. **Marinko Tomas Memorial:** memorial to the local boy who was the first serviceman from WA killed in the Vietnam War; Warren Rd. **Munda Biddi Trail:** passing through Nannup, a world-class mountain-bike trail. **Arts, crafts and antiques:** many outlets in town. **Market:** Warren Rd; Sat morning fortnightly. **Kondil Park:** bushwalks and wildflowers in season; 3km W. **Barrabup Pool:** largest of several pools, ideal for swimming, fishing and camping. Also has barbecue facilities; 10km W. **Cambray Cheese:** award-winning sheep and cow cheeses, visitors can watch the milking and cheesemaking; samples available; 12km N. **Donnelly River Wines:** open for cellar-door tastings Thurs–Sun 10am–5pm; 0418 253 622; 45km S. **Blackwood River:** camping, swimming, canoeing and trout fishing. **Self-guided walks:** wildflower (in spring), waterfall (in winter) and forest walks; contact visitor centre for maps. **Scenic drives:** through jarrah forest and pine plantations, including 40km Blackwood Scenic Drive; contact visitor centre for maps.

NORTHCLIFFE
Population 288

Magnificent virgin karri forests surround the township of Northcliffe. Just a kilometre from the town centre is the spectacular Northcliffe Forest Park. Not far away is the coastal settlement of Windy Harbour, a popular swimming beach.

SEE & DO **Pioneer Museum:** *see* Other Attractions. **Canoe and bike hire:** contact visitor centre for details. **Northcliffe Forest Park:** follow the Hollow Butt Karri and Twin Karri walking trails or enjoy a picnic, look out for purple-crowned lorikeets, scarlet robins and, in spring, a profusion of wildflowers; Wheatley Coast Rd. **Warren River:** trout fishing and sandy beaches; 8km N. **Mount Chudalup:** spectacular views of the surrounding D'Entrecasteaux National Park and coastline from the summit of this giant granite outcrop; 10km S. **Moon's Crossing:** delightful picnic spot; 13km NW. **Lane Poole Falls and Boorara Tree:** 3km walking trail leads to the falls, passing the Boorara Tree with 50m high fire-lookout cabin; 18km SE. **Point D'Entrecasteaux:** limestone cliffs, popular with rock climbers, rise 150m above the sea where 4 viewing platforms provide superb views; 27km S. **Windy Harbour:** swimming, snorkelling, fishing, camping and whale-watching (from platform, best times Sept–Nov); 27km S. **Cathedral Rocks:** watch seals and dolphins; 27km S. **Salmon Beach:** surf beach offers salmon fishing Apr–June; 27km S. **The Great Forest Trees Drive:** 50km self-guided scenic drive takes in the karri giants at Snake Gully Lookout, the Boardwalk and Big Tree Grove; contact visitor centre for map. **Bibbulmun Track:** section of this long-distance walking trail links the three national parks around Northcliffe: D'Entrecasteaux (5km S), Warren (20km NW) and Shannon (30km E); see box p. 277. **Munda Biddi Trail:** this long-distance mountain-bike route passes right through town; Pemberton is a day's ride away for a good taster.

PEMBERTON
Population 617

Pemberton sits in a quiet valley surrounded by some of the tallest trees in the world and, in spring, brilliant wildflowers. This is the heart of karri country, with 4000ha of protected virgin karri forest in the nearby Warren and Greater Beedelup national parks. Pemberton is a centre for high-quality woodcraft and is renowned for its excellent rainbow trout and marron fishing.

SEE & DO **Gloucester National Park:** see Top Attractions. **Greater Beedelup National Park; Warren National Park:** see Other Attractions for both. **Karri Forest Discovery Centre and Pioneer Museum:** interpretive centre includes museum with collection of historic photographs and forestry equipment; at visitor centre. **Craft galleries:** many in town, including the Fine Woodcraft Gallery in Dickinson St and the Peter Kovacsy Studio specialising in large scale glass sculptures in Jamieson St. **CWA Markets:** Brockman St; 4th Sat each month. **Lavender and Berry Farm:** enjoy berry scones, lavender biscuits and other unusual produce; Browns Rd; 4km N. **Big Brook Dam:** the dam has its own beach, picnic and barbecue facilities, trout and marron fishing in season, and walking trails; 7km N. **Big Brook Arboretum:** established in 1928 to study the growth of imported trees from around the world; 7km N. **Founder's Forest:** part of the 100 Year Old Forest, with karri regrowth trees over 120 years old; 10km N. **Wineries:** more than 28 wineries in the area, many offering tours, tastings and sales; contact visitor centre for details. **Pemberton Tramway:** tramcars based on 1907 Fremantle trams operate daily through tall-forest country to the Warren River Bridge; (08) 9776 1322. **Fishing:** in rivers, an inland fishing licence is required for trout and marron; contact post office for details and permits. **Tours:** river tours, scenic bus tours, 4WD adventure tours, self-guided forest drives, walking trails and eco-tours; contact visitor centre for details. **Drive trails:** include the Heartbreak Trail, a one-way drive through the karri forest of Warren National Park; contact visitor centre for maps. **Walk trails:** include the 1hr return Rainbow Trail; contact visitor centre for maps. **Bibbulmun Track:** walking trail passes through Pemberton (see box p. 277).

PINJARRA
Population 3883

Pinjarra is prettily set on the Murray River. Predominantly a dairying, cattle-farming and timber-producing area, Pinjarra was also once known as the horse capital of WA, when horses were bred for the British Army in India. Today horseracing, pacing and equestrian events are a major part of Pinjarra culture. The Alcoa Refinery north-east of town is the largest alumina refinery in Australia.

SEE & DO **Hotham Valley Tourist Railway:** see Other Attractions. **Edenvale Heritage Precinct:** built in 1888 with locally fired clay bricks, Edenvale was the home of Edward McLarty, member of the state's Legislative Council for 22 years. Nearby is Liveringa (1874), the original residence of the McLarty family, now an art gallery. There is a **Heritage Rose Garden** featuring 364 varieties of roses, a quilters' display in the Old School House and a machinery museum. Cnr George and Henry sts. **Suspension bridge:** across the Murray River, with picnic areas at both ends; George St. **Heritage trail:** 30min river walk follows series of tiles explaining the heritage of the area; contact visitor centre for map. **Railway Markets:** Lions Park; 2nd Sun morning each month. **Ranger Red's Zoo & Conservation Park:** set in lush native flora, includes opportunities to feed and interact with the animals and has picnic area and barbecues; (08) 9531 4322; 2km N. **Old Blythewood:** beautiful National Trust property built in 1859 by John McLarty, who arrived in Australia in 1839; 4km S. **Alcoa Mine and Refinery Tours:** includes the mining process, and the world's biggest bulldozer. Choose from three different tours (weekly tour from Pinjarra (Wed), monthly tour from Waroona, or tailor-made trips); bookings essential, contact Alcoa Discovery Centre on (08) 9530 2400; 6km NE. **Alcoa Scarp Lookout:** good views of coastal plain, surrounding farming area and Alcoa Refinery; 14km E. **North Dandalup Dam:** recreation lake, picnic area and coastal views from lookout; 22km NE. **South Dandalup Dam:** barbecues and picnic areas; 30km E. **Lake Navarino:** formerly known as Waroona Dam, it is good for watersports, fishing, walking and horseriding; 33km S. **Coopers Mill:** first flour mill in the Murray region, located on Cooleenup Island near the mouth of the Serpentine River. It is accessible only by water; contact visitor centre for details.

ROCKINGHAM
Population 15,312

Lying on the edge of Cockburn Sound just 47 km south of Perth, the coastal city of Rockingham offers sheltered waters ideal for swimming, snorkelling, sailing, windsurfing, fishing and crabbing. It is on the Traditional Lands of the Noongar Nation. The port town was established in 1872 to ship timber from Jarrahdale to England, and was named for the unfortunate boat that ran aground here in 1830. Rockingham became the busiest port in WA until the end of the 19th century, after which all port activities were shifted north to Fremantle. It was only due to the development of the industrial area nearby at Kwinana in the 1950s and the establishment of HMAS *Stirling* Naval Base on Garden Island in the 1970s that the town was revitalised. Today its magnificent beaches and relaxed demeanour are its main attractions – alongside its pristine environmental surrounds.

SEE & DO **Penguin Island:** see Other Attractions. **Museum:** folk museum featuring local history exhibits including displays on the Group Settlement farms, the timber industry, domestic items and antique photographic equipment; open Tues–Thurs and Sat–Sun 1–4pm; cnr Flinders La and Kent St; 0451 851 413. **Rockingham Art Centre:** art classes and exhibitions; 11 Kent St; (08) 9528 0333. **Mersey Point Jetty:** departure point for cruises and island tours; Shoalwater. **Kwinana Beach:** hull of wrecked SS *Kwinana*. **Cape Peron:** the lookout was once the main observation post for a World War II coastal battery; Point Peron Rd. **Bell and Churchill Park:** barbecues in shaded grounds; Rockingham Rd. **Sloan's Cottage:** restored early settler cottage; Leda; 2km W. **Lake Richmond:** walks, flora and fauna, and thrombolites (domed rock-like structures like the famous stromatolites of Hamelin Pool near Denham, built by ancient micro-organisms); 4km SW. **Wineries:** in the area include **Peel Estate** (17km SE); contact visitor centre for details. **Secret Harbour:** surfing, snorkelling and windsurfing; 20km S. **Serpentine Dam:** major water storage with brilliant wildflowers in spring, bushland and the nearby Serpentine Falls; 48km SE. **Garden Island:** home to HMAS *Stirling* naval base, two-thirds of the island is open to the public but is accessible only by private boat during daylight hours. **Shoalwater Bay Islands Marine Park:** extends from just south of

Garden Island to Becher Pt. Cruises of the park are available; contact visitor centre for details. **Dolphin Watch Cruises:** swim with dolphins between Pt Peron and Garden Island; Sept–May; contact visitor centre for details. **Scenic drives:** including Old Rockingham Heritage Trail, a 30km drive that takes in 23 points of interest in the Rockingham–Kwinana area, and Rockingham–Jarrahdale Timber Heritage Trail, a 36km drive retracing the route of the 1872 timber railway.

WALPOLE
Population 336

Walpole is entirely surrounded by national park, protecting some of the most impressive forest in Australia. The area is renowned for its striking ocean and forest scenery, and is an idyllic setting for outdoor activities. The town of Walpole was established in 1930 through the Nornalup Land Settlement Scheme for city families hit by the Great Depression.

SEE & DO **Walpole–Nornalup National Park; Valley of the Giants:** *see* Top Attractions for both. **Pioneer Cottage:** re-creation of a historic cottage to commemorate the district's early settlers; South Coast Hwy. **Markets:** Pioneer Park, South Coast Hwy, Sept–Apr, contact visitor centre for exact dates. **Giant Red Tingle:** a 25m circumference defines this tree as one of the 10 largest living things on the planet; 2km E. **Hilltop Lookout:** views over Frankland River out to Southern Ocean; 2km W. **John Rate Lookout:** panoramic views over the mouth of the Deep River and of the nearby coastline and forests; 4km W. **Mandalay Beach:** site of the 1911 shipwreck of the Norwegian *Mandalay*. A boardwalk has descriptive notes about the wreck. Also popular for fishing; 20km W. **Dinosaur World:** a collection of native birds and reptiles, and exotic birds; 25km E. **Mount Frankland National Park:** noted for its exceptional variety of birdlife, it also offers breathtaking views from the top of Mount Frankland, known as 'Caldyanup' to the Noongar People; 29km N. **Peaceful Bay:** small fishing village with an excellent beach for swimming; 35km E. **Fernhook Falls:** ideal picnic spot with boardwalk, at its best in winter when it is popular for canoeing and kayaking; 36km NW. **Walking trails:** many trails in the area, including self-guided Horseyard Hill Walk Trail through the karri forest and the signposted Coalmine Beach Heritage Trail from the coastal heathland to the inlets; contact visitor centre for maps. **Tours:** take a guided cruise through the inlets and rivers, hire a boat or canoe, or go on a forest tour or wilderness eco-cruise; contact visitor centre for details.

YALLINGUP
Population 1195

Yallingup, from the Wardandi language, is known for its limestone caves and world-class surf breaks, and is also an ideal location for swimming, fishing and beachcombing. Nearby Leeuwin–Naturaliste National Park, offers eye-widening scenery, interesting bushwalks and beautiful wildflowers in season. Art and craft galleries abound and many of the wineries of the South-West region are only a short drive from the town – although leave your car behind to really appreciate them.

SEE & DO **Leeuwin–Naturaliste National Park:** *see* Top Attractions. **Maze:** fun for all the family, with a timber maze, indoor puzzles and games, cafe and playground. Open Tues–Sun; 3059 Caves Rd; (08) 9756 6500. **Yallingup Beach:** surfing, scuba diving, whale-watching and salmon fishing in season. **Ngilgi Cave:** (pronounced 'Nillgee') an interpretive area details the history of this cave, known for its stunning display of stalactite, stalagmite and shawl rock formations; daily adventure tours available; contact visitor centre; 2km E. **Canal Rocks and Smiths Beach:** interesting rock formation plus fishing, surfing, swimming, snorkelling and diving; 5km SW. **Gunyulgup Galleries:** more than 80 artists and craftspeople are represented, with paintings, prints, ceramics and sculpture on display and for sale; cnr Gunyulgup Valley and Koorabin drs; (08) 9755 2177; 9km SW. **Yallingup Galleries:** fine art and design with a focus on custom-built furniture; cnr Gunyulgup Valley Dr and Caves Rd; (08) 9755 2372; 9km SW. **Quinninup Falls:** falls that are particularly attractive in winter and can be reached only by 4WD or on foot – the long-distance Cape to Cape Track passes right by them; 10km S. **Wineries and breweries:** many award-winning wineries and boutique breweries in the area offer tastings and sales; contact visitor centre for details.

Forest drive, Margaret River region

The Heartlands

The heartland of southern Western Australia is also known as the Wheatbelt. A huge expanse of farmland south-west of Perth, it's dotted with **small character-laden towns**. Closer to the capital, the Swan Valley and Perth Hills are all about fruit production, including some **very good wines**. The heartlands also includes a place close to the heart of all Perthites: **Rottnest Island/ Wadjemup**, or Rotto as it is fondly known. If you've ever wondered how the west has fun, catch the ferry to this beautiful place to find out.

CHEAT SHEET

→ Allow at least a week.

→ Best time to visit: year-round, although summer – a lovely time to visit the coastal towns and Rottnest Island (Wadjemup) – can be very hot in inland areas.

→ Main towns: Northham (*see* p. 296), Mundaring (*see* p. 295), York (*see* p. 299).

→ Most of this region is the Traditional Lands of the Noongar Nation, including the Balardung, Nyaki-Nyaki, Pinjarup, Wajuk and Yuat Peoples. For a sobering perspective of the colonial impact upon the lives of Whajuk Noongar, visit Wadjemup (Rottnest Island), where more than 4000 First Nations men and boys were incarcerated. In 2020, the Wadjemup Project began, and Noongar Elders will determine the commemoration of the men and boys buried on Wadjemup and the use of the former prison.

→ Don't miss: surfing Wave Rock; the Tin Horse Highway; winetasting in the Swan Valley and Perth Hills; the amazing Pinnacles near Cervantes; meeting the friendly quokkas on Rottnest Island (Wadjemup); the historic buildings of York.

Top: Rottnest Island/Wadjemup
Opposite: The Pinnacles, Nambung National Park

TOP ATTRACTIONS

AVON VALLEY NATIONAL PARK: In the 1860s, bushranger Moondyne Joe hid in the forests, caves and wildflower fields of the lush Avon Valley. The park preserves and protects this landscape, offering spectacular scenery with abundant wildflowers in season. Being at the northern limit of the jarrah forests, the jarrah and marri trees mingle with wandoo woodland. This mix of trees creates diverse habitats for fauna, including a wide variety of birdlife. The Avon River, which in summer and autumn is a series of pools, swells to become impressive rapids during winter and spring. These rapids provide the backdrop for the Avon Descent, a well-known annual whitewater race held every Aug, which begins in Northam and passes through the park. The park is ideal for camping, bushwalking, canoeing and picnicking, although all roads are unsealed. Whitewater rafting available.

DRYANDRA WOODLAND NATIONAL PARK: One of the few remaining areas of virgin forest in the wheat belt, Dryandra is a paradise for birdwatchers and bushwalkers. The open, graceful eucalypt woodlands of white-barked wandoo, powderbark and thickets of rock she-oak support many species of flora and fauna, including numbats (the state's animal emblem), woylies, tammar wallabies, brush-tailed possums and many others. Over 100 species of birds have been identified, including the mound-building mallee fowl. Tune your radio to 100 FM for 'Sounds of Dryandra', a 25km radio drive trail with six stops featuring tales of the local Noongar People, early forestry days, bush railways and Dryandra's unique wildlife. There are day-visitor facilities and accommodation and walk trails. **Barna Mia Animal Sanctuary**, within the Dryandra Woodland, has guided spotlight walks at night that reveal threatened marsupials, including the bilby and boodie. Bookings essential; Dept of Parks & Wildlife on (08) 9881 9200 Mon–Fri or Narrogin visitor centre on Sat, which also has maps. The woodland is 22km north-west of Narrogin (*see* p. 295).

JOHN FORREST NATIONAL PARK: Declared a national park in 1947, this is one of the oldest and best-loved picnic spots in the Perth Hills. A drive through the park offers vantage points with superb views across Perth and the coastal plain. A popular walk is the Heritage Trail on the western edge. It passes waterfalls and an old rail tunnel, and there is a lovely picnic spot beside Rocky Pool. The park is 6km west of Mundaring (*see* p. 295).

NAMBUNG NATIONAL PARK: In the Pinnacles Desert, hundreds of limestone pillars rise out of a stark landscape of yellow sand, reaching over 3m in places. They are the eroded remnants of a bed of limestone, created from sea-shells breaking down into lime-rich sands. See formations like the Indian Chief, Garden Wall and Milk Bottles. The sandy loop drive is one-way and not suitable for caravans. The park allows day visits. The park is 17km south of Cervantes (*see* p. 291).

SWAN VALLEY AND PERTH HILLS WINE REGIONS: The Swan Valley begins where the suburbs of Perth end, giving wine lovers the chance to leave their car behind and catch a ferry up the river. Dating back to 1830, this winemaking region is flat and hot. Fortified wines were once a staple, but are now made by only a few companies such as **Talijancich** and **John Kosovich Wines**. **Houghton** is responsible for one of the biggest white wine brands in the country, Houghton White Burgundy. The other major winery of the valley is **Sandalford**. Contact visitor centre in the Guildford Courthouse for map (Cnr Meadow and Swan sts; (08) 9207 8899). Recognised as an official appellation in 1999, Perth Hills may not have the winemaking history of the Swan Valley, but that isn't stopping local vignerons from making some exciting wine. Some of the region's best producers include **Millbrook**, **Myattsfield**, **Aldersyde Estate** and **Fairbrossen**, although new names and cellar doors seem to pop up with pleasing regularity.

WAVE ROCK: Resembling a breaking wave, this 100m long and 15m high granite cliff near Hyden owes its shape to wind action over the past 2.7 billion years. Vertical bands of colour are caused by streaks of algae and chemical staining from run-off waters. At Wave Rock Visitor Centre see the largest lace collection in the Southern Hemisphere with fine examples of antique lace, including lace worn by Queen Victoria. There are local wildflower species on display, an Australiana collection at the **Pioneer Town Museum**, fauna in a natural bush environment and a walking trail. Many gnamma holes, where the Noongar People collected water for centuries, are nearby. As is the town of Hyden (*see* p. 292).

OTHER ATTRACTIONS

AVONDALE DISCOVERY FARM: Avondale is an agricultural research station in Beverley (*see* p. 291) with displays of historic farming machinery and tools. The 1850s homestead is furnished in period style and set in traditional gardens. It also has an animal nursery, Clydesdale horses and a picnic area with barbecues and a children's playground. A land-care education centre houses interactive displays. Waterhatch Rd, Beverley.

CORRIGIN PIONEER MUSEUM: In the town of Corrigin (*see* p. 291), this museum houses a superb collection of old agricultural equipment including an original Sunshine harvester and some early steam-driven farm machinery. A small working steam train carries passengers on a short circuit around the museum and local rest area. Open Wed and Sun 1–4pm; Kunjin St, Corrigin.

GNAROJIN PARK: This park in Narrogin (*see* p. 295) is a national award winner for its original designs and artworks portraying local history and culture, which include the Centenary Pathway, marked with 100 commemorative tiles, Newton House Barbecue and Noongar Cultural Sites. Gordon St, Narrogin.

GRAVITY DISCOVERY CENTRE: This modern centre offers hands-on and static scientific displays on gravity, magnetism and electricity. It includes the biggest public astronomy centre in the Southern Hemisphere and the largest telescope in WA. Military Rd, Yeal; (08) 9575 7577. The centre is 15km south-west of Gingin (*see* p. 291).

NEW NORCIA MUSEUM AND ART GALLERY: The museum tells the story of New Norcia's history as an Aboriginal mission. The art gallery houses priceless religious art from Australia and Europe as well as Spanish artefacts, many of which were gifts from Queen Isabella of Spain. The museum gift shop features New Norcia's own produce, including bread, nutcake, pan chocolatti, biscotti, wine, honey and olive oil; Great Northern Hwy; (08) 9654 8056.

YANCHEP NATIONAL PARK: On a belt of coastal limestone, this 2842ha park has forests of massive tuart trees, underground caves and spring wildflowers. Within the park, attractions include the historic Tudor-style Yanchep Inn; the Crystal Cave featuring magnificent limestone formations (daily tours available); a koala boardwalk; rowing-boat hire on freshwater Loch McNess; self-guided walks; and Noongar cultural tours (available on weekends and public holidays). Boomerang Gorge follows an ancient collapsed cave system and has an interpretive nature trail with access for people with disabilities. Grassy areas with barbecues and picnic tables make a perfect setting for a family outing.

WAGIN HISTORICAL VILLAGE: Explore 24 relocated or re-created historic buildings and machinery providing a glimpse of early settler rural life in Wagin (*see* p. 298). The buildings are furnished with original pieces, and audio commentaries are available. Open 10am–4pm; Kitchener St, Wagin; (08) 9861 1232.

Top: Sandalford Estate, Swan Valley **Bottom:** The Pinnacles, Nambung National Park

VISITOR INFORMATION

Dryandra Country Visitor Centre
cnr Park and Fairway sts, Narrogin
(08) 9881 2064
dryandratourism.org.au

Perth Hills Mundaring Visitor Centre
7225 Great Eastern Highway, Mundaring,
(08) 9290 6645
perthhillsmundaring.com.au

Rottnest Island Visitor Centre
at the end of the main jetty, Thomson Bay
(08) 9372 9730
rottnestisland.com

Nambung National Park
visitpinnaclescountry.com.au

Turquoise Coast
visitturquoisecoast.com.au

KEY TOWNS

BEVERLEY
Population 869

Beverley is a small town set on the banks of the Avon River and 130km east of Perth. Its main street boasts some beautifully preserved buildings, representing Federation to Art Deco architectural styles. This farming community, while having long been associated with wheat and wool, also produces grapes, olives, emus, deer and yabbies.

SEE & DO **Avondale Discovery Farm:** see Other Attractions. **Beverley Station Arts:** art exhibitions and sales in the Tudor-style (1889) railway station; Vincent St. **Dead Finish Museum:** the oldest building in town (1872) houses memorabilia; open Sun 11am–3pm Mar–Nov or by appt through visitor centre; Hunt Rd. **Brookton:** attractions of this nearby town include the Old Police Station Museum and the Brookton Pioneer Heritage Trail; 32km S.

CARNAMAH
Population 314

Carnamah is a typical wheat-belt town servicing the surrounding wheat and sheep properties. From late July through to Dec the shire of Carnamah and the rest of the wheat belt blossoms into a wildflower wonderland.

SEE & DO **Historical Society Museum:** displays historic domestic equipment and old farm machinery; Fri 1.30pm–5pm; Macpherson St. **Tathra National Park:** this park, with its diverse range of spring wildflowers, is named after the Nyungar word for 'beautiful place'. 25km SW. **Macpherson's Homestead:** an excellent example of early settler architecture (1869), once the home of Duncan Macpherson, the first settler in the area; open by appt; Bunjil Rd; (08) 9951 1690; 1km E. **Yarra Yarra Lake:** this salt lake changes from pink in summer to deep blue in winter. View it from Lakes Lookout; 16km S. **Eneabba:** spectacular wildflowers surround this mining town; 74km W. **Lake Indoon:** a freshwater lake popular for sailing, boating, camping, picnics and barbecues (swimming is forbidden due to poor water quality); 85km W.

CERVANTES
Population 480

This small but thriving fishing town was established in 1962 and named after the American whaling ship *Cervantes*, which sank off the coast in 1844. The town's fishing fleet nearly doubles in the rock-lobster season, and in spring the town is surrounded by spectacular displays of wildflowers with vistas of wattles stretching from horizon to horizon. Not far from Cervantes is one of Australia's best-known landscapes, the Pinnacles, in Nambung National Park.

SEE & DO **Nambung National Park:** see Top Attractions. **Thirsty Point:** lookout has superb views of the bay and Cervantes islands. A trail connects the lookouts between Thirsty Point and Hansen Bay; off Seville St. **Lake Thetis Stromatolites:** one of WA's six known locations of stromatolites, the oldest living organisms on Earth; 5km S. **Kangaroo Point:** good picnic spot; 9km S. **Hangover Bay:** a stunning white sandy beach ideal for swimming, snorkelling, windsurfing and surfing; 13km S.

CORRIGIN
Population 625

Corrigin was established in the early 1900s and was one of the last wheat-belt towns to be settled. Today the town has a healthy obsession with dogs, as demonstrated by its Dog Cemetery and its national record for lining up 1527 utes with dogs in the back.

SEE & DO **Corrigin Pioneer Museum:** see Other Attractions. **RSL Monument:** a Turkish mountain gun from Gallipoli; McAndrew Ave. **Dog Cemetery:** loving dog owners have gone to the considerable expense of having elaborate headstones placed over the remains of their faithful four-footed friends. There are more than 80 dogs buried in the cemetery. There is even one statue almost 2m high. Brookton Hwy; 7km W. **Wildflower scenic drive:** signposted with lookout; 3km W. **Gorge Rock:** large granite outcrop with picnic area; 20km SE.

GINGIN
Population 902

Gingin is one of the oldest towns in WA, having been settled in 1832, only two years after the establishment of the Swan River colony. It has the charm of historic stone buildings within a lovely natural setting. Situated 84km north of Perth, it is an ideal destination for a daytrip.

SEE & DO **Gravity Discovery Centre:** see Other Attractions. **Historic Buildings:** enjoy a pleasant self-guided stroll around the town on the Gingin Walkabout Trail, which features many fine examples of early architecture including Philbey's Cottage and St Luke's Anglican Church, both made from local stone. Contact visitor centre for map. **Granville Park:** in the heart of the town with free barbecue facilities, playground and picnic area. **Self-guided walks:** stroll along the Gingin Brook on the Jim Gordon VC Trail; contact the visitor centre (7 Brockman St) for maps. **Moore River National Park:** conservation area featuring banksia woodlands and wildflower displays in spring; 20km NW.

HYDEN
Population 384

The small wheat-belt town of Hyden is synonymous with its famous nearby attraction, Wave Rock, originally known as Hyde's Rock in honour of a sandalwood cutter who lived in the area. A typing error by the Lands Department made it Hyden Rock, and the emerging town soon became known as Hyden. The area around the town boasts beautiful wildflowers in spring, including a wide variety of native orchids.

SEE & DO **Wave Rock:** see Top Attractions. **Hippos Yawn:** rock formation; 5km E via Wave Rock. **Lake Magic:** good sunset spot; 8km N. **Salt Baths:** experience weightlessness in this free swimming pool near Lake Magic on Wave Rock Rd. **The Humps and Mulkas Cave:** First Nations wall paintings; 22km N via Wave Rock. **Rabbit-proof fence:** see the fence where it meets the road; 56km E.

JURIEN BAY
Population 1600

Jurien Bay is located within a sheltered bay protected by reefs and islands. Its wide beaches and sparkling waters make it ideal for swimming, waterskiing, windsurfing, snorkelling, diving and surfing. The Jurien Bay boat harbour services the lobster fishing fleet and has facilities for holiday boating and fishing. The town was settled in the mid-1850s and the jetty was constructed in 1885 to enable a more efficient route to markets for locally produced wool and hides.

SEE & DO **Jurien Bay Charters:** boat and fishing charters, scuba diving, sea lion tours; bookings at dive shop; Carmella St. **Old jetty site:** plaque commemorates site of original jetty. Remains of the jetty's timber piles have been discovered 65m inland from high-water mark, which indicates the gradual build-up of coastline over time; Hastings St. **Market:** Bashford St; usually last Sat each month. **Jurien Bay Marine Park:** this marine park extends from Wedge Island to Green Head and encompasses major sea lion and seabird breeding areas. The reefs are populated by a range of plants and animals including the rare Australian sea lion, and the seagrass meadows are a breeding ground for western rock lobsters. **Lions Lookout:** views of town and surrounds; 5km E. **Drovers Cave National Park:** rough limestone country with numerous caves, all of which have secured entrances limiting public access; 4WD access only; 7km E. **Grigsons Lookout:** panoramic views of ocean and hinterland; wildflowers July–Nov; 15km N. **Lesueur National Park:** with over 900 species of flora, representing 10 per cent of the state's known flora, Lesueur is an important area for plants conservation and as a world biodiversity hotspot. Not to be missed in wildflower season. Enjoy coastal views from a lookout; 23km E. **Stockyard Gully Reserve:** walk through 300m Stockyard Gully Tunnel along winding underground creek; 4WD access only; 50km N. **Turquoise Way:** cycling and walking track that follows the coast 14km south from town to Hill River, with plentiful swim stops along the way.

KELLERBERRIN
Population 798

Centrally located in the wheat belt, Kellerberrin is 200km east of Perth. In springtime, magnificent displays of wildflowers adorn the roadsides, hills and plains around the town.

SEE & DO **Pioneer Park and Folk Museum:** located in the old Agricultural Hall, displays include local artefacts, farming machinery and photographic records. Pick up the key from tourist information or Dryandra building next door; cnr Leake and Bedford sts. **Centenary Park:** children's playground, in-line skate and BMX track, maze, heritage walkway and barbecue facilities all in the centre of town; Leake St. **Golden Pipeline Lookout:** interpretive information at viewing platform with views of the countryside and pipeline; via Moore St. **Durokoppin Reserve:** take a self-guided scenic drive through this woodland area, which is beautiful in the wildflower season; contact visitor centre for map; 27km N. **Kokerbin Rock:** the 3rd largest monolith in WA. These granite outcrops (which are found throughout the wheat belt) hold great significance to local First Nations people because of the natural water catchments they form and the game they attract. The Devils Marbles and a historic well are also at the site. Restricted vehicle access to the summit, but the walk rewards with panoramic views; 30km S. **Cunderdin:** museum housed in the No. 3 pumping station has displays on the pipeline, wheat-belt farming and the Meckering earthquake; 45km W. **Golden Pipeline Heritage Trail:** one of the main stops along

TOP EVENTS

→ JAN Lancelin Ocean Classic

→ FEB Rottnest Channel Swim (Rottnest Island/Wadjemup)

→ MAR Port to Pub (open water swimming, Rottnest Island); Woolorama (Wagin)

→ MAY Moondyne Festival (Toodyay)

→ JUNE Running Festival (Rottnest Island/Wadjemup)

→ AUG Avon Descent (Northam, York); King of the Cross (motorcycle races, Southern Cross)

→ SEPT Wave Rock Weekender music festival (Hyden); Gateway Merredin Festival (Merredin); Machinery Field Days (Newdegate)

→ OCT Kulin Bush Races; Spring Festival (Narrogin), York Festival (York)

→ OCT–NOV Perth Hills Spring Festival (Mundaring)

→ NOV Darlington Arts Festival (Mundaring)

TEMPERATURES

Jan: 16–32°C

July: 8–16°C

Opposite: Wave Rock near Hyden

the trail, which follows the water pipeline of C.Y. O'Connor from Mundaring Weir to the goldfields; guidebook available at visitor centre (see box p. 302).

KULIN
Population 294

The sheep- and grain-farming districts surrounding Kulin provide spectacular wildflower displays in season. The flowering gum, *Eucalyptus macrocarpa*, is the town's floral emblem. A stand of jarrah trees, not known to occur elsewhere in the wheat belt, grows near the town. The Kulin Bush Races on the first weekend in October has expanded from horseracing to a major attraction including live music, an art and craft show, foot races and Clydesdale horserides. In the months prior to the Kulin Races, tin horses appear in the paddocks lining the road on the way to the racetrack.

SEE & DO **Tin Horse Hwy:** starting in town and heading to the Jilakin racetrack, the highway is lined with horses made from a wide variety of materials. **Kulin Herbarium:** specialising in local flora; open by appt; Johnston St. In spring, guided wildflower trail walks are available Wed, Thurs and Fri at 10.30am. **Butler's Garage:** built in the 1930s, this restored garage houses a museum of cars and machinery; open Wed and Sat 10am–2pm; cnr Johnston and Stewart sts. **Memorial Slide and Swimming Pool:** the longest waterslide in regional WA; pool open summer months only Tues–Fri 12–6pm, Sat–Sun and public holidays 11am–6pm; check for opening hours of water slide; Holt Rock Rd; (08) 9880 1222. **Macrocarpa Walk Trail:** 1km self-guided signposted walking trail through natural bush; brochure available at visitor centre; 1km W. **Jilakin Rock and Lake:** granite monolith overlooking a 1214ha lake; 16km E. **Hopkins Nature Reserve:** important flora conservation area; 20km E. **Buckleys Breakaways:** unusual pink-and-white rock formations; 70km E. **Dragon Rocks Nature Reserve:** wildflower reserve with orchids and wildlife; 75km E.

LAKE GRACE
Population 477

The area around Lake Grace is a major grain-growing region, producing wheat, canola, oats, barley, lupins and legumes. Sandy plains nearby are transformed into a sea of colour at the height of the wildflower season in Sept and Oct.

SEE & DO **Inland Mission Hospital Museum:** the only remaining inland mission hospital in WA, this fully restored building (est. 1926) is now a fascinating medical museum. Approach via Apex Park along the interpretive walkway; open Mon–Fri; Stubbs St. **Mural:** artwork of early settler women was begun in 1912; Stubbs St. **Memorial Swimming Pool:** includes water playground for children; open Tues–Fri 5.30–7am, Mon–Sun 12–6pm Dec–Apr; Bishop St. **Wildflower walk:** easy walk through natural bushland, with informative signage; details at visitor centre; 19 Stubbs St; 3km E. **Lake Grace:** combination of two shallow salt lakes that gives the town its name; 9km W. **Lake Grace Lookout:** ideal spot to view the north and south lakes system; 12km W. **Holland Track:** in 1893 John Holland and his partners cut a track from Broomehill through bushland to Coolgardie in the goldfields. Hundreds of prospectors and their families trudged along this track in search of fortune, and cartwheel ruts are still evident today. A plaque marks the place where the track crosses the road; Newdegate Rd; 23km E. **Dingo Rock:** now on private property, this reservoir for water run-off was built by labourers from Fremantle Gaol. Wildflowers are beautiful in season; details at visitor centre; 25km NE. **Newdegate:** small town with an early settler museum in the heritage-listed Hainsworth building. One of WA's major agricultural events, the Machinery Field Days, is held here in Sept each year; 52km E.

LAKE KING
Population 84

This small rural town lies on the fringe of sheep- and grain-farming country. With a tavern and several stores, Lake King is a stopping place for visitors travelling across the arid country around Frank Hann National Park to Norseman (adequate preparations must be made because there are no stops en route). Outstanding wildflowers in late spring include rare and endangered species.

SEE & DO **Self-guided walks:** signposted walking trails. **Lake King and causeway:** 9km road across the salt lake studded with native scrub and wildflowers. Lookout at eastern end; 5km W. **Pallarup Reserve:** early settler well and lake with abundant wildflowers in season; 15km S. **Mount Madden:** cairn and lookout with picnic area that forms part of the Roe Heritage Trail; 25km SE. **Frank Hann National Park:** good example of inland sand-plain-heath flora with seasonal wildflowers. The rabbit-proof fence forms a boundary to the park; access is subject to weather conditions; 32km E. **Roe Heritage Drive Trail:** offers panoramic views from the Roe Hill Lookout and retraces part of J.S. Roe's explorations in 1848; map available at Lake Grace visitor centre.

MERREDIN
Population 2384

Merredin started as a shanty town where miners stopped on their way to the goldfields. In 1893 the railway reached the town and a water catchment was established on Merredin Peak, guaranteeing the town's importance to the surrounding region.

SEE & DO **Cummins Theatre:** Heritage-listed theatre that was totally recycled from Coolgardie in 1928. Used regularly for local productions, events and visiting artists; open Mon–Fri 10am–4pm;

WESTERN AUSTRALIA

SPOT ENDANGERED NATIVE WILDLIFE IN WA

The fauna of Western Australia is rich and diverse and, with a little luck and a keen eye, you may spot these endangered creatures in their natural habitat.

QUOKKA
At the time of European settlement, quokkas were common in the south-west of Western Australia. Today, although some do exist on the mainland, quokkas are most plentiful on Rottnest Island (Wadjemup), 18 km offshore from Perth. Willem de Vlamingh, a Dutch explorer, referred to Rottnest Island as 'Rottenest' (rats' nest) after he mistook the quokkas for large rats.

NUMBAT
This small marsupial has a squirrel-like tail, a narrow head and a small body with coarse fur – it is also known as the banded anteater. The main populations occur east of Manjimup at Perup Nature Reserve in the south-west, although this endangered critter has been reintroduced in various spots throughout the state.

GILBERT'S POTOROO
A small, rat-kangaroo-like creature with dense fur and a slender snout, this critically endangered potoroo (Australia's rarest mammal, and the world's rarest marsupial) was listed as extinct until 1994 when five were captured in Two Peoples Bay Nature Reserve, near Albany.

BILBY
Looking a bit like a bandicoot with giant ears and a thick tail, the nocturnal bilby is perhaps cutest of all the Western Australian natives you might hope to meet. Of the two original bilby species, only the greater bilby survives. A major reintroduction program to help save this vulnerable species was introduced in Francois Peron National Park and Shark Bay.

Bates St. **Military Museum:** significant collection of restored military vehicles and equipment; open 10am–3pm; Great Eastern Hwy. **Railway Museum:** prize exhibits are the 1897 locomotive that once hauled the Kalgoorlie Express and the old signal box with 95 switching and signal levers; open 10am–1pm Mon–Sun, 11am–2pm; Great Eastern Hwy. **Pioneer Park:** picnic area adjacent to the highway including a historic water tower that once supplied the steam trains; Great Eastern Hwy. **Merredin Peak Heritage Walk:** self-guided walk that retraces the early history of Merredin and its links with the goldfields and the railway; contact visitor centre for map; 85 Barrack St; (08) 9041 1666. **Merredin Peak Heritage Trail:** leads to great views of the countryside, and a rock catchment channel and dam from the 1890s. Adjacent to the peak is the interpretation site of a World War II field hospital that had over 600 patients in 1942; off Benson Rd. **Tamma Parkland Trail:** a 1.2km walk around this 23ha of bushland will give an insight into the flora and fauna of the area; South Ave. **Pumping Station No 4:** built in 1902 but closed in 1960 to make way for electrically driven stations, this fine example of early industrial architecture was designed by C.Y. O'Connor; 3km W. **Totadgin Conservation Park:** interpretive walk, Hunt's Well and mini rock formation similar to Wave Rock. Picnic tables and wildflowers in spring; 16km SW. **Rabbit-proof fence:** roadside display gives an insight into the history of this feature; 25km E. **Mangowine Homestead:** now a restored National Trust property, in the 1880s this was a wayside stop en route to the Yilgarn goldfields. Nearby is the Billyacatting Conservation Park with interpretive signage; open Mon–Fri 1–4pm, Sat–Sun and public holidays 10am–4pm; Nungarin; (08) 9046 5149; 40km NW. **Shackleton:** site of Australia's smallest bank; 85km SW. **Kokerbin Rock:** superb views from summit; 90km SW. **Koorda:** small town with a museum and several wildlife reserves in the area; 140km NW.

MOORA
Population 1591

On the banks of the Moore River, Moora is the largest town between Perth and Geraldton. The area in its virgin state was a large salmon-gum forest. Many of these attractive trees can still be seen.

SEE & DO **Moora town walk:** leads visitors past outdoor art and historical buildings; contact visitor centre for more information; 65 Padbury St; (08) 9653 1053. **Painted Roads Initiative:** murals by community artists on and in town buildings. **Westways Wildflower Farm:** one of the largest exporters of dried wildflowers in WA, with dried flowers, seeds and souvenirs for sale and an interpretive education centre; 4WD tours through the wildflowers are also available; open Easter–Christmas; Midlands Rd, Coomberdale; (08) 9651 8010; 19km N. **Watheroo National Park:** site of Jingamia Cave; 50km N. **Moora Wildflower Drive:** from Moora to Watheroo National Park, identifying flowers on the way; contact visitor centre for map.

Top: Fishing, Rottnest Island/Wadjemup
Bottom: New Norcia

MUNDARING
Population 3190

Mundaring is the gateway to the Swan Valley and Perth Hills wine regions and virtually an outer suburb of Perth – being only 34km east. Nearby, the picturesque Mundaring Weir is the water source for the goldfields – 500km further east. It's also the starting point for the Munda Biddi Trail, a 1060km mountain-bike route to Albany (munda biddi means 'path through the forest' in Noongar).

SEE & DO Swan Valley and Perth Hills Wine Regions; John Forrest National Park: *see* Top Attractions for both. **Arts Centre:** contemporary WA fine art and design with comprehensive exhibition program; Great Eastern Hwy; (08) 9295 3991. **District Museum:** displays on the diverse history of the shire; Great Eastern Hwy. **Sculpture Park:** collection of sculptures by WA artists, set in natural bush park with grassed areas for picnics and children's playground; Jacoby St. **Market:** Nichol St, 2nd Sun each month. **Mundaring Weir:** the Mundaring Weir is the starting point of the 560km Golden Pipeline Heritage Trail to Kalgoorlie, which follows the route of C.Y. O'Connor's water pipeline, taking in towns and heritage sites. The hilly bush setting also makes the weir a popular picnic spot. Nearby, the **Perth Hills Discovery Centre** is run by Nearer to Nature, which provides hands-on activities including bush craft, animal encounters, bushwalks and information about First Nations culture; (08) 9295 2244. The **Mundaring Weir Gallery**, built in 1908 as a Mechanics Institute Hall, showcases the work of local craftspeople; open 11.30am–5pm Fri–Sun and public holidays; cnr Hall and Weir Village rds; (08) 9295 0200. **Karakamia Sanctuary:** Australian Wildlife Conservancy (AWC) native wildlife sanctuary with guided dusk walks; bookings essential; (08) 9572 3169; Lilydale Rd, Chidlow; 8km NE. **Calamunnda Camel Farm:** camel rides; open Thurs–Sun; 361 Paulls Valley Rd; (08) 9293 1156; 10km S. **Lake Leschenaultia:** swimming, canoeing, bushwalks and camping with a cafe and picnic and barbecue facilities; 12km NW. **Kalamunda National Park:** walking trails through jarrah forest, including the first section of the 963km Bibbulmun Track; 23km S. **Kalamunda History Village:** collection of historic buildings; open Mon–Wed and Fri 10am–3pm, Sat–Sun 10am–4pm; 23km S. **Lesmurdie Falls National Park:** good views of Perth and Rottnest Island (Wadjemup) near spectacular falls over the Darling Escarpment; 29km S. **Walyunga National Park:** beautiful bushland and wildflowers, and venue for the Avon Descent, a major whitewater canoeing event held each Aug; 30km NW. **Araluen Botanic Park:** jarrah, eucalypt and marri trees frame the rockpools, cascades and European-style terraces of these beautiful 59ha gardens. Offering walking trails, picnic and barbecue areas and, in spring, magnificent tulip displays; 55km S.

NARROGIN
Population 3745

Narrogin, 192km south-east of Perth on the Great Southern Hwy, is the commercial hub of a prosperous agricultural area. The town's name is derived from a Noongar word 'gnarojin', meaning 'waterhole'. The area attracts birdwatchers and walkers to the nearby Dryandra Woodland.

SEE & DO Dryandra Woodland: *see* Top Attractions. **Gnarojin Park:** *see* Other Attractions. **History Hall:** local history collection; Egerton St. **Old Courthouse Museum:** built in 1894 as a school, it later became the district courthouse; open 10am–4pm Mon–Fri, 10am–12pm Sat; Egerton St; (08) 9881 6758. **Arts Space:** exhibitions; open Tues–Thurs 10am–4pm; Federal St; (08) 9881 6987. **Lions Lookout:** excellent views; Kipling St. **Heritage trail:** self-guided walk around the town's historic buildings; contact visitor centre for map. **Foxes Lair Nature Reserve:** 60ha of bushland with good walking trails, wildflowers in spring and 40 species of birds; maps and brochures from visitor centre; Williams Rd; 1km SW. **Yilliminning and Birdwhistle Rocks:** unusual rock formations; 11km E.

NEW NORCIA
Population 57

This is Australia's only monastic town and it still operates as a monastery. In 1846 Spanish Benedictine monks established a mission here 132km north of Perth in the secluded Moore Valley, and named it after the Italian town of Norcia, the birthplace of the order's founder, St Benedict. The imposing Spanish-inspired buildings of New Norcia, surrounded by the gum trees and dry grasses of the wheat belt, provide a most unexpected vista. Visitors may join the monks at daily prayers.

SEE & DO New Norcia Museum & Art Gallery: *see* Other Attractions. **Abbey Church:** this fine example of bush architecture was built using a combination of stones, mud plaster, rough-hewn trees and wooden shingles. Built in 1846, it is the oldest Catholic church still in use in WA and contains the tomb of Dom Rosendo Salvado, the founder of New Norcia and its first abbot. Hanging on a wall is the painting of Our Lady of Good Counsel, given to Salvado before he left for Australia in 1845. One of New Norcia's most famous stories relates how, in 1847, Salvado placed this revered painting in the path of a bushfire threatening the mission's crops. The wind suddenly changed direction and the danger was averted. Next to the church, the 'Rock of Remembrance' is an interactive memorial that serves as acknowledgement and an apology for the abuse and neglect inflicted here. **Monastery:** daily tours of the interior. A guesthouse allows visitors to experience monastic life for a few days. **New Norcia Hostel:** this magnificent building, featuring a massive divided central staircase and high, moulded pressed-metal ceilings, was opened in 1927 to accommodate parents of the children who were boarding at the town's colleges. Groups of 10 or more can still stay here. **Old Flour Mill:** the oldest surviving building in New Norcia dates from the 1850s. **Heritage trail:** 2km self-guided walk highlights New Norcia's historic and cultural significance and the role of the Benedictine monks in colonial history; contact visitor centre for map. **Guided tour:** 2hr tour of the town with an experienced guide takes you inside buildings not otherwise open to the public; tours depart from museum (not on Christmas Day and Boxing Day). **Mogumber:** town with one of the state's highest timber-and-concrete bridges; 24km SW. **Piawaning:** magnificent stand of eucalypts north of town; 31km NE. **Bolgart:** site of historic hotel; 49km SE.

NORTHAM
Population 6679

Northam lies in the heart of the fertile Avon Valley. The Avon River winds its way through the town and on its waters you'll find white swans – a most unusual sight in a state where the emblem is a black swan. White swans were first brought to Northam from England in the 1900s and have since flourished. Northam is also synonymous with hot-air ballooning, being one of the few places in WA ideally suited to it, and is home to the famous Avon Descent, a 133km whitewater race down the Avon and Swan rivers to Perth held in August.

SEE & DO **Historic buildings:** of the many historic buildings in Northam, two are particularly noteworthy: Morby Cottage (1836), on Avon Dr, the home of Northam's first settler, John Morrell, and now a museum open Sun 11am–3pm or by appt; and the National Trust–classified Sir James Mitchell House (1905), cnr Duke and Hawes sts, with its elaborate Italianate architecture. Take the 90min self-guided walk for a full tour of the town; contact visitor centre for map. **Bilya Koort Boodja Centre for Nyoongar Culture and Environmental Knowledge:** interactive educational experience highlights the rich Aboriginal and environmental presence in the region; open 9am–4pm; Minson Ave. **Old Railway Station Museum:** displays include a steam engine and renovated carriages, plus numerous artefacts from the early 1900s; open Sun–Mon and Fri–Sat 11am–3pm; Fitzgerald St West; (08) 9621 1739. **Visitor centre:** encompasses displays showcasing the area's significant postwar immigrant history, a wheat-belt exhibition and the Avon Valley Arts Society; Grey St; (08) 9622 2100. **Suspension bridge:** the longest pedestrian suspension bridge in Australia crosses the Avon River; Minson Ave. **Mount Ommanney Lookout:** excellent views of the township and agricultural areas beyond; 1.5km W. **Hot-air ballooning:** take off from Northam Airfield, Mar–Nov; bookings essential; **Windward Balloon Adventures**, 104 Withers St; (08) 9621 2000; 2km NE. **Meckering:** a small town made famous by a 1968 earthquake, which created a huge fault line here; 35km E. **Cunderdin Museum:** housed in the No. 3 pumping station, has displays on the pipeline, farming and the Meckering earthquake; (08) 9635 1291; 50km E.

PINGELLY
Population 722

Located 158km south-east of Perth on the Great Southern Hwy, Pingelly is part of the central-southern farming district. Sandalwood was once a local industry, but today sheep and wheat are the major industries.

SEE & DO **Courthouse Museum:** built in 1907, now houses historic memorabilia and photographs; Parade St. **Apex Lookout:** fine views of town and countryside; Stone St. **Moorumbine Heritage Trail:** walk or drive through this old townsite featuring early settlers' cottages and St Patrick's Church, built in 1873; contact council office for map; 8km E. **Tutanning Nature Reserve:** botanist Guy Shorteridge collected over 400 species of plants from here for the British Museum between 1903 and 1906; 22km E. **Boyagin Nature Reserve:** widely recognised as one of the few areas of original flora and fauna left in the wheat belt, this picnic reserve has important stands of powderbark, jarrah and marri trees and is home to numbats and tammar wallabies. It is also a place of huge importance to the Noongar People, as they used the rocks as a signalling place to warn other groups that the mounted police were coming and they should hide. 26km NW.

⭐ ROTTNEST ISLAND/ WADJEMUP
Population 166

Rottnest Island/Wadjemup's Traditional Owners are the Whadjuk Noongar People. Although only 11km long and 5km wide, the island boasts crystal-clear waters for swimming, coral reefs for snorkelling and diving, a range of beautiful sandy beaches and secluded coves and of course its much-adored native marsupial, the quokka – the estimated population of these friendly critters is around 10,000. Thomson Bay, a protected north-easterly bay that faces the mainland, is the island's largest and oldest settlement. As the site of the island's main jetty, it is the arrival and departure point for all ferries travelling to and from Perth, Fremantle and Hillarys. The visitor centre and accommodation office are at the end of the jetty. There are no private vehicles on the island so it's best to hire a bike or bring one onboard the ferry (although you can get a shuttle bus around if cycling isn't your thing!).

SEE & DO **Historic buildings:** originally established in 1838 as a prison for Aboriginal men and boys from the mainland, the Rottnest settlement has a number of convict-built buildings, including the Wadjemup Museum, built in 1857 as a haystore and granary, which now features displays and photographs on the history

Opposite: Rottnest Island/ Wadjemup

of the island. The Salt Store, built in 1968 to hold the bagged salt collected from the island's salt lakes, is now an art gallery, exhibition space and information centre. The octagonal 'Quod' (1864), which once served as a prison and later became part of the Rottnest Lodge – its prison cells transformed into hotel rooms – has now been shuttered and plans are now afoot to create a place of respect and reflection that documents the island's dark history as a prison, from where many never returned. The adjacent burial ground of unmarked graves remains a testament to this brutal chapter in Rottnest's lesser-known history. The Wadjemup Project, initiated in 2020, means Noongar Elders will oversee the commemoration of the burial ground and the building. **Vincent Way:** overlooking Thomson Bay, is one of the oldest streetscapes in Australia. The original building of the Hotel Rottnest, built in 1864 as the summer residence for the governors of WA, has now been revamped and joined by an alfresco beachside courtyard, bars and accommodation. Tours covering different aspects of Rottnest's history are run daily by the Rottnest Voluntary Guides; brochures on self-guided walking trails also available; contact visitors centre for details. **Bike hire:** as the use of vehicles, except by the authorities, is prohibited on Rottnest, cycling is the usual mode of transport for visitors and helmets are mandatory. Bring your own on the ferry or rent one from the ferry operators or Pedal & Flipper, just behind the Hotel Rottnest; hours vary seasonally; (08) 9292 5105. **Bus services:** A shuttle runs between the main accommodation areas on the island. The **Island Explorer** and **Bayseeker** are all-day jump-on-jump-off services that do a regular circuit of the island – best to buy a ticket ahead from the visitors centre in the peak summer holiday season. **Shopping precinct:** just a short walk from the main jetty is the settlement's small pedestrian mall of shops, including a general store, surfwear shop, pharmacy, historic bakery and other food outlets. **Rottnest Movies and Mini Golf:** when you need a break from Rottnest's natural wonders, this nostalgic fun park from yesteryear offers minigolf, arcade games and movie screenings in the island's original picture hall, complete with canvas deck chairs. **Water-based activities:** Thomson Bay offers plenty of water-based activities, from swimming at the sheltered beach to snorkelling and fishing; snorkelling equipment available for hire at Pedal & Flipper bike hire. **Wadjemup Lighthouse:** the original lighthouse, built in 1849 by Noongar prisoners, was WA's first lighthouse. This was replaced in 1881 by a lighthouse with a rotating beam, which is still standing. **Oliver Hill:** take a scenic train ride up to Oliver Hill, where the evidence of Rottnest Island's military past, including a tunnel system, can be found. The gun battery was built in the 1930s to defend the WA coastline and Fremantle harbour. Find out more on one of the daily 'Guns and Tunnels' tours; contact visitor centre for details. **Beaches:** the island has over 60 beaches, the most popular of which is the Basin, only a short walk or bike ride from Thomson Bay, and so named because the coral reef forms a basin-like swimming pool. **Vlamingh's Lookout:** this lookout boasts panoramic views of the island; on the way, stop at the old cemetery, where the gravestones testify to the hardships of the early settlers. **Snorkelling and diving:** with some 360 species of fish, over 20 species of coral and 13 historic shipwrecks in its coastal waters, Rottnest is a perfect location for snorkelling and diving; a snorkel trail at Parker Point features underwater interpretative plaques. **Surfing and bodyboarding:** Strickland Bay, Salmon Bay and Stark Bay are the island's best spots for waves. **Birdwatching:** its A-Class Reserve status and varied habitat – coastal, woodlands, heath, salt lakes and swamps – means the island is home to a wide range of bird species; the osprey nest at Salmon Point is estimated to be 70 years old. **Wadjemup Bidi walking trail:** explore the natural beauty of the island on foot. 'Bidi' means 'trail' or 'track' in the Noongar language and the trail is broken into five sections, ranging from the 5.9km Karlinyah Bidi along the northern beaches to the 10km Wardan Nara Bidi along Salmon Bay. Bring plenty of drinking water; allow 1.5–2hrs by bike to get to the island's west end, or take the bus on the Discovery Tour (contact visitor centre for details); 11km W. **Rottnest Island Marine Reserve:** lying in the path of the warm Leeuwin ocean current, the waters around Rottnest support an unusually rich diversity of marine life, including coral reefs, tropical fish, sharks and migrating humpback whales, dolphins and sea lions. Day-long boat tours are available or, if short on time, take the 90min Adventure Tour (Sept–Apr); Rottnest Express; 1300 467 688.

SOUTHERN CROSS
Population 572

A small, flourishing town on the Great Eastern Hwy, Southern Cross is the centre of a prosperous agricultural and pastoral region. Its claim to fame is as the site of the first major gold discovery in the huge eastern goldfields and, although it never matched the fever pitch of Kalgoorlie, Southern Cross remains the centre for a significant gold-producing area.

SEE & DO **Yilgarn History Museum:** originally the town courthouse and mining registrar's office, it now houses displays on mining, agriculture, water supply and military involvement; open Mon, Wed–Fri and Sun; Antares St. **Historic buildings:** including the post office in Antares St, the Railway Tavern in Spica St and the restored Palace Hotel in Orion St. **Hunts Soak:** once an important water source, now a picnic area; 7km N. **Frog Rock:** large rock with wave-like formations; popular picnic spot; 34km S. **Baladjie Rock:** granite outcrop with spectacular views; 50km NW. **Karalee Rock and Dam:** this dam was built to provide water for steam trains and is now popular for swimming and picnics; 52km E.

TOODYAY
Population 953

This National Trust–classified town is nestled in the Avon Valley and surrounded by picturesque farming country and bushland. The name originates from 'duidgee', which means the 'place of plenty'. Founded in 1836, Toodyay was one of the first inland towns to be established in the colony. It was a favourite haunt of WA's most famous bushranger, Joseph Bolitho Johns, who was known as 'Moondyne Joe'.

SEE & DO **Avon Valley National Park:** see Top Attractions. **Historic buildings:** some original buildings from the early settlement of Toodyay still stand, including Stirling House (1908), Connor's Mill (1870s) with displays of working flour-milling equipment, the Old Newcastle Gaol (1865) built by convict labour and where Moondyne Joe was imprisoned, and the police stables (1870) built by convict labour from random rubblestone. Self-guided walk available; pamphlet at visitor centre; 7 Piesse St; (08) 9574 9380. **Duidgee Park:** popular picnic spot on the banks of the river, has a miniature railway and a walking track; check at visitor centre for running times; Harper Rd. **Newcastle Park:** contains a unique stone monument of Charlotte Davies, the first white female to set foot on the soil of the Swan River Colony. Also has a children's playground; Stirling Tce. **Pelham Reserve and Lookout:** nature walks, a lookout with views over the town and a memorial to James Drummond, the town's first resident botanist; Duke St. **Coorinja Winery:** dating from the 1870s; open for tastings and sales Fri, Sat, Mon 10am–5pm; 4km SW. **Ringa Railway Bridge:** constructed in 1888, this timber bridge has 18 spans, but is not readily accessible; details from visitor centre; 6km SW. **Windmill Hill Cutting:** the deepest railway cutting (34m) in Australia; 6km SE. **Emu Farm:** one of the oldest in Australia. Birds range free in natural bushland. Also crafts and emu products for sale; 15km SW.

Cartref Park Country Garden: 2ha park of English-style landscaped gardens and native plants, with prolific birdlife; 16km NW. **Toodyay Pioneer Heritage Trail:** honouring the early settler spirit in the Avon Valley, this 20km self-drive trail retraces the route of the first settlers; contact visitor centre for map. **Avon Valley Tourist Drive:** 95km scenic drive includes Toodyay, Northam, York and Beverley; contact visitor centre for map. **Hotham Valley Steam Railway:** the famous steam-train service runs special trips including a restaurant train each Saturday with a five-course meal.

WAGIN
Population 1311

Wagin, 177km east of Bunbury, is the sheep capital of WA. The importance of the wool industry is celebrated in the annual Woolorama, one of the largest rural shows in the state, and its Giant Ram, known locally as Bart.

SEE & DO **Wagin Historical Village:** see Other Attractions. **Giant Ram and Ram Park:** 9m high statue – take this photo opportunity by the horns; Arthur River Rd. **Heritage trail:** self-guided walk around the town; contact visitor centre in the Historical Village. **Puntapin Rock:** spectacular views over the town and surrounding farmlands from the top of the rock. Enjoy the picnic and barbecue facilities nearby; Bullock Hill Rd; 4km SE. **Mount Latham:** interesting rock formation with walking trails, a lookout and abundant wildflowers in season; Arthur River Rd; 8km W. **Lake Norring:** swimming, sailing and waterskiing; picnic and barbecue facilities; water levels vary considerably; check conditions at visitor centre; 17km SW. **Lake Dumbleyung:** where Donald Campbell established a world water-speed record in 1964. Swimming, boating and birdwatching are subject to water levels that vary considerably; check conditions at visitor centre; 18km E. **Wait-**

jen Trail: self-guided 10.5km signposted walk that follows ancient Noongar Dreaming. The word 'wait-jen' means 'emu footprint' in the Noongar language; contact visitor centre for map. **Wheat Belt Wildflower Drive:** self-guided drive that includes the Tarin Rock Nature Reserve; contact visitor centre.

WICKEPIN
Population 266

The first European settlers arrived in the Wickepin area in the 1890s. This small town has some literary fame and excellent Edwardian architecture. Albert Facey's internationally acclaimed autobiography, *A Fortunate Life*, details early settler times. The poet and playwright Dorothy Hewett was born in Wickepin in 1923.

SEE & DO **Historic buildings in Wogolin Road:** excellent examples of Edwardian architecture. **Facey Homestead:** the home of author Albert Facey has been relocated and restored with its original furniture; opening times vary, key available from newsagent. **Tarling Well:** the circular stone well marks the original intended site for the town; 8km W. **Malyalling Rock:** unusual rock formation; 15km NE. **Toolibin Lake Reserve:** see a wide variety of waterfowl while you enjoy a barbecue; 20km S. **Yealering and Yealering Lake:** historic photographs on display in town, and swimming, boating, windsurfing and birdwatching at lake; 30km NE. **Harrismith Walk Path:** self-guided trail through wildflowers in season, including orchids and some species unique to the area; contact visitor centre for brochure. **Albert Facey Heritage Trail:** 86km drive brings to life the story of Albert Facey and the harshness of life in the early settler days; contact visitor centre for map.

YANCHEP
Population 11,009

Only 58km north of Perth, Yanchep is a rapidly developing recreational area and popular tourist destination. It provides safe, sandy beaches and good fishing areas, as well as natural attractions such as the series of caves found within Yanchep National Park. The town derives its name from the Noongar word 'yanjet', which means 'bullrushes', a feature of the area.

SEE & DO **Yanchep National Park:** *see* Other Attractions. **Yanchep Lagoon:** good swimming and fishing beach; off Lagoon Dr. **Marina:** charter fishing boat hire at Two Rocks; 6km NW. **Guilderton:** peaceful town at the mouth of the Moore River. Estuary provides safe swimming, and upper reaches of the river can be explored by boat or canoe (hire on river foreshore). Also good fishing; 37km N. **Ledge Point:** great destination for diving, with dive trail to 14 shipwrecks. Also the starting point for Lancelin Ocean Classic, a major windsurfing race each Jan; 62km N. **Lancelin:** great base for fishing and boating because of a natural breakwater offshore. White sandy beaches provide safe swimming, and sand dunes at the edge of town have designated areas for off-road vehicles and sand-boarding; 71km N.

YORK
Population 2399

On the banks of the Avon River in the fertile Avon Valley, York is one of the best-preserved and restored 19th-century towns in Australia. It is now classified by the National Trust as 'York Historic Town'. There are a significant number of carefully preserved historic buildings here, many made from local stone and some built of mudbrick. Settled in 1831, only two years after the establishment of the Swan River Colony, York was the first inland European settlement in WA.

SEE & DO **Historic buildings:** the town's three remaining hotels are fine examples of early coaching inns, while the Romanesque-style Town Hall (1911) with its ornate facade reflects the wealth brought into the town by the gold rush. Contact the York Visitor Centre, located in the town hall, for details; 81 Avon Tce. **Avon Park:** picturesque park on the banks of the river with playground, barbecue facilities and toilets – adjacent free RV camping area; Lowe St. **Motor Museum:** vehicles on display represent the development of motor transport; Avon Tce. **Old York Mill:** built in 1892, the mill includes shops featuring local artisanal wares and products, a cafe and playground; 10 Henrietta St. **York Residency Museum:** historic and personal artefacts, ceramics and silverware reflect aspects of civic and religious life in early York; Brook St. **Old Courthouse Complex:** buildings date from the 1840s and includes courtrooms, police station, troopers' cottage, gaol cells and stable yard; Avon Tce. **Suspension bridge and walk trail:** built in 1906, the bridge crosses the Avon River at Avon Park. A 1.5km nature and heritage walk starts at the bridge; Lowe St. **Mount Brown Lookout:** provides 360-degree views over town and surrounds; 3km SE. **Gwambygine Park:** picturesque picnic area overlooking the river; 10km S. **Wildflower wanders:** self-drive tours and walking trails, contact visitor centre for maps and itineraries. **Toapin Weir and Mount Stirling:** panoramic views; 64km E. **Self-drive trails:** eight different routes including the Avon Ascent through Perth's scenic hinterland to a series of special places in the Avon Valley; contact visitor centre for maps.

Top: Mundaring Weir
Bottom: Lobster Shack, Cervantes **Opposite:** Connor's Mill, Toodyay

Nullarbor and the Goldfields

Don't be misled by all the dots on the map when planning a road trip across the Nullarbor, as most of them are little more than a roadhouse. Driving across **the longest, straightest, loneliest road in the country is an adventure** you won't soon forget, and there is much more to see and do along the way than you might think, including lots of short side tracks that lead to lookouts over **a coastline that will take your breath away**. There are also many more trees than the name implies – Nullarbor is Latin for 'no trees'. Often forgotten in the rush to get to the coast, the **abandoned villages and historic towns of the goldfields** are fascinating places to explore.

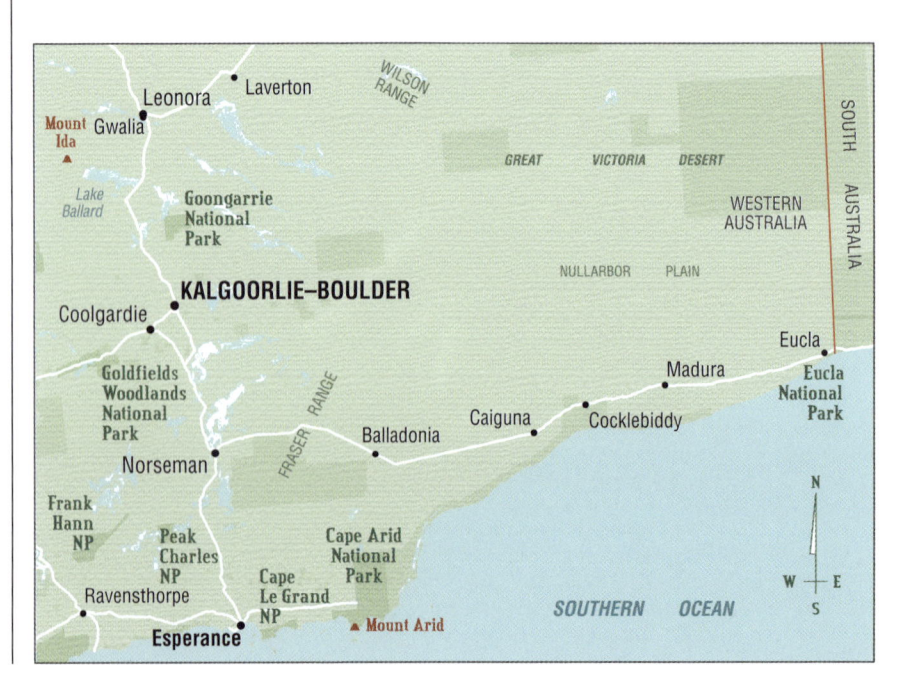

CHEAT SHEET

→ Allow a week for a proper exploration: you'll need three days at a minimum to drive across the Nullarbor.

→ Best time to visit: May–Sept.

→ Main towns: Esperance (see p. 304), Kalgoorlie (see p. 305).

→ The lands of the Nullarbor and Goldfields are the Traditional Lands of the Kalaamaya, Malpa, Mirning, Ngalea, Ngatjumay, Nyanganyatjara, Wangkathaa and Wudjari Peoples.

→ Need to know: Distances can be vast; 4WD often needed; fuel, water and food stops are limited in parts of the region. Research before travelling, including for any required permits.

→ Don't miss: Great Ocean Drive in Esperance; seeing where Skylab crashed landed in Balladonia; goldfields heritage in Kalgoorlie and the ghost town of Gwalia; the arresting statues in the middle of Lake Ballard; the half-buried ruins of Eucla.

Top: Kalgoorlie–Boulder
Opposite: Cape Le Grand National Park

TOP ATTRACTIONS

CAPE LE GRAND NATIONAL PARK: This dreamy coastline is filled with pristine beaches, including Hellfire Bay and Thistle Cove. At Lucky Bay, kangaroos can often be spotted lying on the beach. Visit Whistling Rock, which 'whistles' under certain wind conditions, and climb Frenchmans Peak for breathtaking views. There are magnificent displays of wildflowers in spring, and many bushwalks. You can camp at Cape Le Grand and Lucky Bay. The park is 56km east of Esperance (see p. 304).

ESPERANCE MUSEUM: This is one of WA's outstanding regional museums. See exhibits about shipwrecks, including the famous *Sanko Harvest*, and learn of Australia's only recorded pirate, the bloodthirsty Black Jack Anderson, who roamed the Recherche Archipelago. There is also a comprehensive display about *Skylab*, which crashed and spread debris through the area in 1979. Open Thurs–Sun 1.30–4.30pm; James St, Esperance; (08) 9083 1580.

EUCLA TELEGRAPH STATION RUINS: Opened in 1877 (just 33 years after Samuel Morse invented the telegraph), the Eucla Telegraph Station helped link WA with the rest of Australia and the world, often sending over 20,000 messages a year. The first message, sent to Perth in Dec 1877, stated simply, 'Eucla line opened. Hurrah.' The ruins are being slowly buried by shifting sand dunes. It's about 4km south of Eucla (see p. 304).

GREAT OCEAN DRIVE: One of Australia's most spectacular scenic drives, this 38km loop road on the outskirts of Esperance (see p. 304) passes wind farms, which supply 30 per cent of the town's electricity, and some of the region's best known natural attractions, including sheltered swimming at Twilight Cove, and Pink Lake, rendered the colour of lipstick by algae. There are coastal lookouts, and sightings of southern right whales from June to Oct.

GWALIA: A mining ghost town that has been restored to show visitors what life was like in the gold-rush days, featuring miners' cottages and camps. The original mine manager's office includes the largest steam winding engine in the world and a headframe designed in 1898 by Herbert Hoover – the first mine manager of the Sons of Gwalia mine and later the 31st President of the United States. Gwalia is about 12km from Leonora (see p. 306).

LAKE BALLARD: A collection of 51 black steel sculptures created by world-renowned artist Antony Gormley are scattered across the vast 10sqkm white salt plain of Lake Ballard. Made using scans of locals from the nearby town of Menzies, these taut, stick-like body-forms are best seen at sunrise and sunset. Lake Ballard is about a 1hr, 40min drive from Leonora (see p. 306) or a 2hr, 20min drive from Kalgoorlie–Boulder (see p. 305).

MUSEUM OF THE GOLDFIELDS: Panoramic views of Kalgoorlie–Boulder (see p. 305) from the massive mining headframe at the entrance. Displays include a million-dollar gold collection, nuggets and jewellery. See the narrowest pub in the Southern Hemisphere, a re-created 1930s miner's cottage and heritage buildings; guided tours; open 10am–3pm; 17 Hannan St, Kalgoorlie; (08) 9021 8533.

SUPERPIT LOOKOUT: Peer into the depths of this enormous open-mining operation in Kalgoorlie–Boulder (see p. 305) from the lookout at the end of Outram St, Boulder (visit during blasting; check times at visitor centre); daily tours (free on market day); scenic flights are also available; (08) 9022 1100.

OTHER ATTRACTIONS

90 MILE STRAIGHT: Snap a selfie beside the signpost marking the western end of the longest straight stretch of road in Australia, which runs for 90 miles (146.6km) between Balladonia (see p. 303) and Caiguna (see p. 303).

EUCLA NATIONAL PARK: This small park extends between Eucla (see p. 304) and Border Village. On the coast near the SA border is Wilsons Bluff Lookout, with views to the east following the Bunda Cliffs into the distance. Closer to Eucla are the enormous sculptural shapes of the Delisser Sandhills.

EYRE BIRD OBSERVATORY: Housed in the fully restored 1897 Eyre Telegraph Station, Australia's first bird observatory offers birdwatching, bushwalking and beachcombing in Nuytsland Nature Reserve, 50km south-east of Cocklebiddy (see p. 303). Over 240 species of birds have been recorded at Eyre, including Major Mitchell cockatoos, brush bronzewings, honeyeaters and mallee fowl. It is near the site where Edward John Eyre found water and rested during his Nullarbor journey in February 1841. Courses, tours and whale-watching (June–Oct) as well as accommodation can be arranged on (08) 9039 3450; 4WD access only.

GOLDEN QUEST DISCOVERY TRAIL: 965km drive that traces the gold rushes of the 1890s through Coolgardie, Kalgoorlie–Boulder, Menzies, Kookynie, Gwalia, Leonora and Laverton; pick up the map and book at the Kalgoorlie Visitor Centre (see p. 305).

GOLDFIELDS EXHIBITION MUSEUM: Local photographs and exhibits inside Coolgardie's old Warden's Court include a display on the famous Varischetti mine rescue. In 1907, Modesto Varischetti was trapped underground in a flooded mine for nine days; he survived in an air pocket until divers eventually found him. The dramatic rescue captured world attention. Bayley St, Coolgardie.

HANNANS NORTH TOURIST MINE: Gold-rush days and modern-day mining come together at Hannans North Tourist Mine just outside of Kalgoorlie–Boulder (see p. 305). Here you can pan for gold, clamber onto a giant haulage truck, and try your hand at the legendary game of two-up; free barbecue and picnic facilities. Open Sun–Fri 9am–4pm; off Goldfields Hwy; (08) 9022 1664. The mine is 7km north of Kalgoorlie–Boulder.

RECHERCHE ARCHIPELAGO: The Esperance region is known as the Bay of Isles because of this collection of 110 islands dotted 250km along the coast, which provide a haven for seals and sea lions. Half- and full-day cruises (subject to minimum numbers and weather) take guests through the archipelago and land on Woody Island. If you are lucky, you might see fur seals, sea lions, dolphins and, in season, southern right whales. For an extraordinary camping experience, try a safari hut on Woody Island. These canvas huts set high on timber decking overlook an idyllic turquoise bay framed by eucalyptus trees. Woody Island also has an interpretive centre to provide information to visitors; 0484 327 580, woodyisland.com.au

GOLDEN PIPELINE HERITAGE TRAIL

Follow the course of the pipeline from Mundaring Weir to Mount Charlotte. Finding a reliable water supply to support the eastern goldfields' booming population became imperative after the 1890s gold rush. C.Y. O'Connor's solution was radically brilliant: the construction of a reservoir at Mundaring in the hills outside Perth and a 556km water pipeline to Kalgoorlie–Boulder. His project was criticised relentlessly by the press and public, which affected O'Connor deeply. On 19 Mar 1902 he went for his usual morning ride along the beach in Fremantle. As he neared Robb Jetty, he rode his horse into the sea and shot himself. The pipeline was a success, delivering the promised 22 million litres of water a day to Kalgoorlie, and continues to operate today. On the coast just south of Fremantle, a half-submerged statue of a man on a horse is a poignant tribute to this man of genius; guidebook at Kalgoorlie Visitor Centre.

VISITOR INFORMATION

Esperance Visitor Centre
Museum Village,
48 Dempster St, Esperance
(08) 9083 1555 or
1300 664 455
visitesperance.com

Kalgoorlie–Boulder Visitor Centre
316 Hannan St, Kalgoorlie
1800 004 653 or
(08) 9021 1966
kalgoorlietourism.com
australiasgoldenoutback.com

Top: Superpit goldmine in Kalgoorlie **Bottom:** Ruins of the telegraph station, Eucla **Opposite:** Marking the 90 Mile Straight

KEY TOWNS

BALLADONIA
Population 5

Balladonia lies on the Eyre Hwy on the western edge of the Nullarbor Plain. Its closest towns are Norseman (174km to the west) and Caiguna (176km to the east). This arid desert shrubland is one of the world's oldest landscapes, containing seashells millions of years old from when the area was ocean floor. Balladonia made world headlines in 1979 when space debris from NASA's *Skylab* landed 40km east on Woorlba Station.

SEE & DO **Museum:** learn about the crash-landing of *Skylab*, local First Nations culture, early European explorers, Afghan cameleers and other chapters in the area's history. Balladonia Roadhouse, Eyre Hwy; (08) 9039 3453. **Newman Rocks:** superb views from rocky outcrop, with picnic and camping areas onsite; 50km W. **Cape Arid National Park and Israelite Bay:** great birdwatching and fishing; access via 4WD track, south of town; check track conditions at roadhouse.

CAIGUNA
Population 8

The tiny community of Caiguna, on the Nullarbor Plain, consists of a 24hr roadhouse, caravan park, motel, restaurant and service station. The nearest towns are Balladonia, 176km west, and Cocklebiddy, 64km east. To the south is the coastal wilderness of Nuytsland Nature Reserve. From immediately east of Caiguna until Border Village, locals operate on Central Western Time, 45min ahead of the rest of WA.

SEE & DO **Caiguna Blowhole:** a hole in the flat limestone landscape where the Earth seemingly breathes in and out; 5km W.

COCKLEBIDDY
Population 15

This tiny settlement on the Nullarbor Plain comprises a roadhouse with motel units, caravan sites and camping facilities. It features one of the oldest telegraph stations in WA. Nuytsland Nature Reserve extends southwards: a 400,000ha strip running along the Great Australian Bight. Locals operate on Central Western Time, 45min ahead of the rest of the state.

SEE & DO **Eyre Bird Observatory:** *see* Other Attractions. **Cocklebiddy Caves:** largest of the Nullarbor caves but closed to public; 5km W. **Twilight Cove:** fishing and whale-watching spot with views of 70m-high limestone cliffs overlooking the Great Australian Bight; 4WD access only; 32km S.

COOLGARDIE
Population 773

This town was the first settlement in the eastern goldfields. After alluvial gold was found in 1892, Coolgardie grew in 10 years to a town of 15,000 people, 23 hotels, six banks and two stock exchanges. The main street, Bayley St, lined with some magnificent buildings, was made wide enough for camel trains to turn around in. There are 23 buildings in the town centre that have been listed on the National Estate register, many of them on Bayley St. As in many outback towns, the heat and the isolation led to innovation, in this case that of the Coolgardie safe, which used water and a breeze to keep food cool before the days of electricity.

SEE & DO **Goldfields Exhibition Museum:** *see* Other Attractions. **Historic Buildings:** more than 100 markers are positioned at buildings and historic sites across the town, using stories and photographs to recapture the gold-rush days. The index to markers is in Bayley St, next to the visitor centre. **Ben Prior's Open-Air Museum:** unusual collection of machinery and memorabilia; cnr Bayley and Hunt sts. **Warden Finnerty's House:** striking 1895 example of early Australian architecture and furnishings; open Sat–Wed 11am–4pm but confirm it's open at the visitor centre before visiting; McKenzie St. **Gaol tree:** used in early gold-rush days, before a gaol was built; Hunt St. **Lindsay's Pit Lookout:** this lookout is over an open-cut goldmine; Ford St. **Cemetery:** the town's historic cemetery gives you an inkling of the harshness of the early gold-rush years. The register of burials records that of the first 32 burials, the names of 15 were unknown, and many entries for 'male child' and 'female child' note 'fever' as the cause of death. 1km W. **Camel Farm:** offers rides on the 'ships of the desert'; (08) 9026 6159; 4km W. **Gnarlbine Rock:** originally a First Nations well, then one of the few water sources for the early prospectors; 30km SW. **Kunanalling Hotel:** once a town of more than 800 people, the ruins of the hotel are all that remain; 32km N. **Victoria Rock:** camping, and spectacular views from the summit; 55km SW. **Burra Rock:** popular camping and picnic area; 55km S. **Rowles Lagoon Conservation Park:** picnicking and camping spots available, although recently there has been no water; 65km N.

★ ESPERANCE
Population 10,218

Esperance was a sleepy backwater until farming took off in the area in the 1950s. The town is now a laidback place with a great arty vibe, a beach lifestyle and a truly magnificent setting on the Bay of Isles. The majestic scenery, the pristine beaches and the proximity of many national parks draw visitors to this town. It is also the last major settlement before travellers cross the Nullarbor heading east. Take the Great Ocean Dr, 38km of postcard-perfect scenery, and you'll understand why Esperance is one of the fastest growing towns in WA.

SEE & DO **Esperance Museum; Great Ocean Drive; Cape Le Grand National Park:** see Top Attractions for all. **Museum Village:** collection of historic buildings housing craft shops, pottery shops, art galleries, cafes and visitor centre; Dempster St. **Cannery Arts Centre:** a premier exhibition space for the arts in Esperance; Norseman Rd; (08) 9071 3599. **Mermaid Leather:** unique range of leather products made from fish and shark skins; Wood St; (08) 9071 5248. **Esperance art trail:** trail map from visitors centre. **Museum Village Markets:** Dempster St; most Sun mornings, call visitor centre for dates. **Rotary Lookout:** views of bay, town and archipelago; Wireless Hill; 2km W. **Esperance Bird and Animal Park:** interact with animals or photograph them from a distance; (08) 9076 1067; 13km N. **Esperance Stonehenge:** full-scale replica of the original UK Stonehenge; 18km E. **Kepwari Trails:** trailwalking, birdwatching, wildflowers and a self-guided canoe trail; 4km N. **Monjingup Lake Nature Reserve:** walking trails, birdwatching and wildflowers in spring; 20km W. **Stokes National Park:** beautiful coastal and inlet scenery; 80km W. **Cape Arid National Park:** birdwatching, fishing, camping and 4WD routes; 120km E. **Whale-watching:** southern right whales visit bays and protected waters to calve (June–Oct); along the Great Ocean Dr and at Cape Arid.

EUCLA
Population 37

Eucla is the largest settlement on the Nullarbor Plain, located just near the SA border. The ruins of a telegraph station exist at the original townsite and beyond the ruins are the remains of a jetty, a reminder of early settler days when supplies were transported by boat. Eucla is today located on the Hampton Tableland and operates on Central Western Time, 45min ahead of the rest of WA.

SEE & DO **Eucla Telegraph Station Ruins:** see Top Attractions. **Eucla National Park:** see Other Attractions. **Eucla Museum:** local history, including exhibits of the telegraph station, told through newspaper clippings and old photographs; Eucla Motel. **Travellers' Cross:** dedicated to travellers and illuminated at night; on the escarpment, west of town. **1-hole golf course:** part of the Nullarbor Links – the longest golf course in the world, stretching 1365km from Ceduna to Kalgoorlie; north of town. **Border Village:** quarantine checkpoint for people entering WA (travellers should ensure they are not carrying fruit, vegetables, honey, used fruit and produce containers, plants or seeds); 13km E.

★ KALGOORLIE–BOULDER
Population 29,068

Kalgoorlie is the centre of WA's goldmining industry and with its historical buildings and frontier feel, it's the ultimate Wild West town. There are some outstanding museums here and opportunities to see

Stairs to beach, Esperance

TOP EVENTS

→ MAR Norseman Cup

→ MAY–JUNE Golden Gift and Festival (Leonora)

→ JUNE Goldfields Cyclassic (Kalgoorlie)

→ SEPT Wildflower festivals (Esperance and Ravensthorpe)

→ OCT Back to Boulderfest (Kalgoorlie)

TEMPERATURES

Jan: 19–34°C

July: 5–17°C

the region's journey from old gold-rush town to modern mining behemoth. It was once known as Hannan's Find in honour of Paddy Hannan, the first prospector to report of the epic discovery. In June 1893 Hannan was among a party who set out from Coolgardie to join the goldrush at Mount Yule. After a stop at Mount Charlotte, the main party of 150 continued on, leaving Hannan and two others behind to search out water. Some idle 'specking' (looking on the ground for nuggets) led them to stumble on the richest goldfield the world had known – it soon grew to encompass the 'Golden Mile' (discovered in August 1893 by Sam Pearce and William Brookman), which is reputedly the world's richest square mile of gold-bearing ore. Rapid development of Kalgoorlie and nearby Boulder followed, with thousands of people travelling to the field from all over the world, reaching a maximum population of about 30,000 in 1903. In their heyday Kalgoorlie and Boulder boasted eight breweries and 93 hotels.

SEE & DO **Museum of the Goldfields; Superpit Lookout:** see Top Attractions for both. **Hannan's North Tourist Mine; Golden Quest Discovery Trail:** see Other Attractions for both. **Historic Buildings:** although only a few kilometres apart, Kalgoorlie and Boulder developed independently for many years. The amalgamated towns now form a city with two main streets, each lined with impressive hotels and civic buildings. Built at the turn of the 20th century, when people were flocking to the area, many of these buildings display ornamentation and fittings that reflect the confidence and wealth of the mining interests and are fine examples of early Australian architecture. **Kalgoorlie Town Hall** (1908), cnr Hannan and Wilson sts, has hosted many a famous performer on its stage, including Dame Nellie Melba and Percy Grainger. It now displays a collection of memorabilia; tours Tues and Thurs 10.30am. The **Kalgoorlie Miner Building** on Hannan St was the first three-storey building in town. **Burt St in Boulder:** regarded as one of the most significant streetscapes in WA. Buildings to see include the **Grand Hotel** (1897), the **Old Chemist** (1900) and the **post office** (1899), which was once so busy it employed 49 staff. The well-preserved **Boulder Town Hall**, built in 1908, is home to one of the world's last remaining Goatcher stage curtains. Phillip Goatcher was one of the greatest scenic painters of Victorian times and his hand-painted drop curtains graced theatres in London, Paris and New York. The self-guided walking trail will take you on a tour of 40 historic buildings; contact the visitor centre for a brochure. **Paddy Hannan's Statue:** a monument to the first man to discover gold in Kalgoorlie; Hannan St. **Questa Casa Bordello:** the only original brothel left in Kalgoorlie is also one of the world's oldest; unique tours available, contact visitor centre. **St Mary's Church:** built in 1902 of Coolgardie pressed bricks, many of which are believed to contain gold; cnr Brookman and Porter sts, Kalgoorlie. **WA School of Mines Mineral Museum:** displays include over 3000 mineral and ore specimens and many gold nuggets; open Mon–Fri 9am–4pm, closed on school holidays; Egan St, Kalgoorlie. **Goldfields Arts Centre:** art gallery and theatre; Cassidy St, Kalgoorlie. **Goldfields Aboriginal Art Gallery:** local art and artefacts for sale; open Mon–Fri 9.30am–4.30pm; Dugan St, Kalgoorlie. **Paddy Hannan's Tree:** a plaque marks the spot where Paddy Hannan first discovered gold; Outridge Tce, Kalgoorlie. **Mount Charlotte:** the reservoir holds water pumped from the Mundaring Weir in Perth via the pipeline of C.Y. O'Connor. A lookout provides good views of the city; off Goldfields Hwy, Kalgoorlie. **Hammond Park:** miniature Bavarian castle made from thousands of local gemstones. There is also a sanctuary for kangaroos and emus, plus aviaries for a variety of birdlife; Memorial Dr, Kalgoorlie. **Arboretum:** a living museum of species of the semi-arid zone and adjacent desert areas, this 26.5ha parkland has interpretive walking trails and recreation facilities; Hawkins St, adjacent Hammond Park. **Miners' Monument:** tribute to mine workers; Burt St, Boulder. **WMC Nickel Pots:** massive nickel pots and interpretive panels describe the story of the development of the nickel industry in the region; Goldfields Hwy. **Royal Flying Doctor Visitor Centre:** climb on board an authentic RFDS plane and learn about the RFDS with interpretive displays in the recently upgraded visitor centre; closed at the time of writing, so check ahead with the visitor centre; Airport, Hart Kerspien Dr; (08) 9093 7595. **Karlkurla Bushland:** pronounced 'gullgirla', this natural regrowth area of bushland offers a 4km signposted walking trail, picnic areas and lookout over the city and nearby mining areas; Riverina Way. **Boulder Market Day:** Burt St; 3rd Sun each month. **Bush Two-Up:** visit the original corrugated-iron shack and bush ring where Australia's only legal bush two-up school used to operate; games Sun 1.30pm; off Goldfields Hwy; 8km E. **Kanowna Belle Gold Mine lookouts:** wander the ghost town remains of Kanowna and see day-to-day mining activities from 2 lookouts over a previously mined open pit and processing plant; 20km E. **Broad Arrow:** see the pub where scenes from the Googie Withers movie *Nickel Queen* were shot in the 1970s. Every wall is autographed by visitors; 38km N. **Kambalda:** nickel-mining town on Lake Lefroy (salt). Head to Red Hill Lookout for views across the expanse; 55km S. **Prospecting:** visitors to the area may obtain a miner's right from the Dept of Mineral and Petroleum Resources in Bayley St, Coolgardie; (08) 9026 7930; dmp.wa.gov.au; strict conditions apply.

LAVERTON
Population 407

Surrounded by old mine workings and modern mines, Laverton is on the edge of the Great Victoria Desert. In 1900 Laverton was a booming district of gold strikes and mines, yet gold-price fluctuations in the late 1950s made it almost a ghost town. In 1969 nickel was discovered at Mount Windarra, which sparked a nickel boom. Early in 1995 a cyclone blew through Laverton, leaving it flooded and isolated for three months. Mines closed down and supplies were brought in by air. Today the town has two major goldmines and one of the world's largest nickel-mining operations. The wildflowers are brilliant in season too. It's important to note that permits are required to travel through Aboriginal reserves and communities – they can be obtained from the Department of Indigenous Affairs in Perth, and the Central Lands Council in Alice Springs. Water is scarce so ensure you carry plenty. Fuel, supplies and accommodation are available at the Tjukayirla, Warburton and Warakurna roadhouses along Great Central Rd. Check road conditions before departure at the Laverton Police Station or Laverton Shire Offices; roads can be closed due to heavy rain.

SEE & DO **Historic Buildings:** restored buildings include the courthouse, the Old Police Station and Gaol, and the Mount Crawford Homestead. The original Police Sergeant's House is now the local museum with displays of local memorabilia. Contact visitor centre for details. **Great Beyond Explorers Hall of Fame:** uses cutting-edge technology to bring to life the characters and stories of the early European explorers of the region. It also houses the visitor centre; Augusta St. **Cross-Cultural Centre:** houses the Laverton Outback Gallery, a collection of art and artefacts made and sold by the local Wongatha People; Augusta St. **Giles Breakaway:** scenic area with interesting rock formation; 25km E. **Lake Carey:** swimming and picnic spot exhibiting starkly contrasting scenery; 26km W. **Windarra Heritage Trail:** walk includes rehabilitated mine site and interpretive plaques; Windarra Minesite Rd; 28km NW. **Empress Springs:** named after Queen Victoria by a European explorer in 1896, the springs are an important water source for Wongatha People. The spring is in limestone at the end of a tunnel that runs from the base of a 7m deep cave. A chain ladder allows access to the cave. Enclosed shoes and torch required; 305km NE. **Warburton:** the Tjulyuru Arts and Culture Regional Gallery showcases the art and culture of the Ngaanyatjarraku people; 565km NE. **Outback Way and Anne Beadell Hwy:** travel the 1200km to Uluru from Laverton via the Great Central Rd; or drive 1350km to Cooper Pedy in SA on the Anne Beadell Hwy. All roads are unsealed, but the Great Central Rd is regularly maintained. Sections of the Anne Beadell Hwy require a high-clearance 4WD.

LEONORA
Population 567

Leonora, in the north-eastern goldfields, is the service centre for the mining, exploration and surrounding pastoral region. Gold was found in the area and the first claims were pegged in 1896. By 1908 Leonora boasted seven hotels and was the largest town on the north-eastern goldfields. Many of the original buildings were constructed of corrugated iron and hessian, because these were versatile materials and light to transport. You can get a glimpse of these structures at nearby Gwalia, a town once linked to Leonora by tram.

SEE & DO **Gwalia; Lake Ballard:** see Top Attractions for both. **Historic buildings:** The Leonora Heritage Trail showcases buildings from the turn of the century, including the police station, courthouse, fire station, Masonic Lodge and historic miners' cottages; details at visitor centre. **Tank Hill:** excellent view over town; Queen Victoria St. **Mount Leonora:** sweeping views of the surrounding plains and mining operations; 4km S. **Malcolm Dam:** picnic spot at the dam, which was built in 1902 to provide water for the railway; 15km E. **Kookynie:** tiny township with restored shopfronts, and historic memorabilia on display at the Grand Hotel. The nearby Niagara Dam was built in 1897 with cement carried by camel from Coolgardie; 92km SE. **Menzies:** small goldmining town with an interesting historic cemetery; 110km S.

MADURA
Population 18

Madura, comprising a roadhouse, motel and caravan park on the Eyre Hwy, lies midway between Adelaide and Perth on the Nullarbor Plain. It is

Top: Antony Gormley's 'Inside Australia' outdoor gallery at Lake Ballard

remarkable, given the isolation of the area, that Madura Station was settled in 1876 to breed horses, which were then shipped across to India for use by the British Army. Now Madura is surrounded by private sheep stations. Locals operate on Central Western Time, 45min ahead of the rest of WA.

SEE & DO **Blowholes:** smaller versions of the one found at Caiguna. Look for the red marker beside the track; 1km N. **Madura Pass Lookout:** spectacular views of the Roe Plains and Southern Ocean; 1km W on highway.

NORSEMAN
Population 555

Norseman is the last large town on the Eyre Hwy for travellers heading east towards SA. Gold put Norseman on the map in the 1890s with one of the richest quartz reefs in Australia. The town is steeped in goldmining history, reflected in its colossal tailings dump. If visitors could stand atop this dump they'd have up to $50 million in gold underfoot (although the rock has been processed, much residual gold remains). The story behind the town's name has become folklore. The settlement sprang up in 1894 when a horse named Norseman, owned by prospector Laurie Sinclair, pawed the ground and unearthed a nugget of gold; the site proved to be a substantial reef.

SEE & DO **Historical Museum:** mining tools and household items; located in the School of Miners building. **Phoenix Park:** open-plan park with displays, stream and picnic facilities; Prinsep St. **Statue of Norseman:** bronze statue by Robert Hitchcock commemorates Norseman, the horse; cnr Roberts and Ramsay sts. **Camel Train:** corrugated-iron sculptures represent the camel trains of the early settler days; Prinsep St. **Gem fossicking:** gemstone permits from the visitor centre. **Cobb & Co. Heritage Trail:** 50km loop from Norseman along the Cobb & Co. coach route, includes the township of Dundas and the Lady Mary mine, contact visitor centre for more information. **Beacon Hill Lookout:** spectacular at sunrise and sunset, this lookout offers an outstanding 360-degree panorama of the salt lakes, Mount Jimberlana, the township, tailings dump and surrounding hills and valleys; Mines Rd; 2km E. **Mount Jimberlana:** reputed to be one of the oldest geological areas in the world. Take the walking trail to the summit for great views; 5km E. **Dundas Rocks:** barbecue and picnic area amid granite outcrops near old Dundas townsite, where the lonely grave of a 7-month-old child is one of the only signs that the area was once inhabited by miners and their families. Travel here via Goldfields Hwy (22km S) or along the 33km heritage trail that follows an original Cobb & Co. route (map available from visitor centre). **Buldania Rocks:** picnic area with beautiful spring wildflowers; 28km E. **Bromus Dam:** freshwater dam with picnic area; 32km S. **Peak Charles National Park:** good-weather track for experienced walkers and climbers to Peak Eleanora, with a magnificent view of saltpans, sand plains and dry woodland from the top; 50km S, then 40km W off Goldfields Hwy. **Cave Hill Nature Reserve:** a granite outcrop with a cave set in its side and a dam nearby. Popular spot for camping, picnicking and rock climbing; access via Widgiemooltha; 90km N. **Granite and Woodlands Discovery Trail:** a 300km self-drive tour from Norseman to Hyden along the gravel Hyden–Norseman Rd; the trail is divided into 16 sections with natural and historical points of interest along the way. Short walks and picnic facilities en route. Stunning wildflowers in spring. Check road conditions; trail brochure available from the Shire of Dundas; (08) 9039 1205.

RAVENSTHORPE
Population 350

Ravensthorpe is encircled by the Ravensthorpe Range. This unspoiled bushland is home to many plants unique to the area such as the Qualup bell, warted yate and Ravensthorpe bottlebrush. Gold was discovered here in 1898 and by 1909 the population had increased to around 3000. Coppermining reached a peak in the late 1960s; the last coppermine closed in 1972. Many old mine shafts can be seen around the district and fossicking is a favourite pastime.

SEE & DO **Historical Society Museum:** local history memorabilia; in Dance Cottage near visitor centre, Morgans St. **Historic buildings:** many in town including the impressive Palace Hotel (1907) and the restored Commercial Hotel (now a community centre); both in Morgans St. **Rangeview Park:** local plant species, picnic and barbecue facilities; Morgans St. **WA Time Meridian:** a plaque on a boulder marks the WA time meridian; at first rest bay west of town. **Old Copper Smelter:** in operation 1906–18, now site of tailings dumps and old equipment; 2km SE. **Archer Drive Lookout:** extensive views over farms and hills; 3km N in Ravensthorpe Range. **Mount Desmond Lookout:** magnificent views in all directions; Ethel Daw Dr; 17km SE in Ravensthorpe Range. **Hopetoun:** seaside village with pristine beaches ideal for swimming, surfing, windsurfing, fishing and boating. Summer Festival each June. Walk on the Hopetoun Trail Head Loop (part of the Hopetoun–Ravensthorpe Heritage Walk) or visit Fitzgerald River National Park to the west; *see* Bremer Bay; 49km S. **Scenic drives:** include the 170km circular Hamersley Drive Heritage Trail; contact visitor centre for maps. **Rock-collecting:** check locally to avoid trespass.

Coral Coast and Mid-West

Big skies, big distances, big attractions. If you love a roadtrip, you will love this Western Australian odyssey. The destinations in this region will sear themselves in your mind with their **timeless landscapes and natural beauty.** Marvel at **dramatic gorges** carved by rivers over millennia, **turquoise seas, coral reefs, white sand beaches,** surreal rock formations, ancient rock art and living fossils.

CHEAT SHEET

→ Given the vast distances involved, allow at least two weeks for a proper exploration.

→ Best time to visit: June–Sept; May if you're keen to swim with whale sharks, spring for wildflowers.

→ Main towns: Carnarvon (see p. 312), Exmouth (see p. 314), Geraldton (see p. 314), Meekatharra (see p. 316).

→ Just some of the many Traditional Owners of the land in this vast region include the Amangu, Badimaya, Malkana, Maya, Nhanta, Payungu, Purduna, Thalanyji, Tharrgari, Tjupany, Warriyangga, Watjarri and Yinggarda Peoples. Visit the Yamaji Art Centre in Geraldton for information on the 195km Yamaji Drive Trail which takes you to 14 sites of significance to the local First Nations People.

→ Don't miss: the coral reef and fish life of Ningaloo Marine Park; gorges and jagged cliffs in Kalbarri; Shell Beach; meeting the wild dolphins of Monkey Mia; spring wildflowers that carpet the whole region.

Top: Cape Range National Park **Opposite:** The spectacular Coral Coast

TOP ATTRACTIONS

CAPE RANGE NATIONAL PARK: This rugged landscape of arid rocky gorges is edged by the stunning coastline of Ningaloo Marine Park. Wildlife is abundant, with emus, euros (wallaroos), rock wallabies and red kangaroos often sighted. In late winter there is a beautiful array of wildflowers including the Sturt's desert pea and the superb bird flower. Attractions within the park include Shothole Canyon, an impressive gorge; Mangrove Bay, a sanctuary zone with a bird hide overlooking a lagoon; and Mandu Mandu Gorge, where you can walk along an ancient river bed. Yardie Creek is the only gorge with permanent water. Turquoise Bay is a popular beach for swimming and snorkelling (watch for currents). The Milyering Discovery Centre, made of rammed earth and run by solar power, is 52km from Exmouth on the western side of the park and offers information on both Cape Range and Ningaloo. Contact (08) 9949 2808.

CARNARVON SPACE AND TECHNOLOGY MUSEUM: Celebrating Carnarvon's (see p. 312) role in the manned space program, this museum was opened by astronaut Buzz Aldrin. A huge 29m wide reflector dish, part of the old NASA station, is part of the museum, which contains an interactive command module; Mahony Ave, Brown Range (8km e of Carnarvon); (08) 9941 9901.

DIRK HARTOG ISLAND: WA's largest and historically significant island is named after Dutchman Dirk Hartog who landed here in 1616 – 154 years before James Cook reached Australia (although more than 40,000 years after the First Nations Peoples). Hartog left behind an inscribed pewter plate, which was removed in 1697 by his countryman Willem de Vlamingh and replaced with another plate. The original was returned to Holland; Vlamingh's plate is now housed in the WA Maritime Museum in Fremantle. Flights and cruise bookings at Shark Bay World Heritage Discovery & Visitor Centre in Denham (see p. 313).

DUGONGS: The Shark Bay World Heritage Area has the largest seagrass meadows in the world, covering about 4000sqkm. These meadows are home to around 10,000 dugongs, 10 per cent of the world's remaining population. An endangered species, the dugong is nature's only vegetarian sea mammal. Also known as a sea cow, it can live for up to 70 years and grow up to 3m long. Tours are available to see dugongs in the wild. Contact Shark Bay World Heritage Discovery and Visitor Centre in Denham (see p. 313) for details.

HAMELIN POOL STROMATOLITES: The shores of Hamelin Pool are dotted with stromatolites, the world's largest and oldest living fossils. These colonies of micro-organisms resemble the oldest and simplest forms of life on earth, dated at around 3.5 billion years old. The Hamelin Pool stromatolites are relatively new colonies – about 3000 years old. They thrive here because of the extreme salinity of the water, the occurrence of calcium bicarbonate and the limited water circulation. The visitor boardwalk above the stromatolites was destroyed by Cyclone Seroja in 2021, but these extraordinary life forms can still be viewed from the beach. Close by is the Flint Cliff Telegraph Station and the Post Office Museum (1884). Hamelin Pool is 88km south-east of Denham (see p. 313).

HMAS SYDNEY II MEMORIAL: Built on Mount Scott overlooking Geraldton (see p. 314) to commemorate the loss of 645 men from HMAS *Sydney II* on 19 Nov 1941. The ship sank after an encounter with the German raider HSK *Kormoran*. The wrecks of both ships were found in Mar 2008. Seven pillars representing the seven seas hold aloft a 9m high domed roof formed of 645 interlocking figures of seagulls. At night an eternal flame lights the cupola. Near the memorial is the bronze sculpture of a woman looking out to sea, representing the women left behind waiting for those who would not return. The fifth and final element of the memorial is a remembrance pool, its black granite walls engraved with 644 seagulls and the remaining 2m seagull sculpture in the centre of the pool indicating the coordinates of the sunken vessel. Tours daily at 10.30am; Gummer Ave, Geraldton.

KALBARRI NATIONAL PARK: Gazetted in 1963, this park has dramatic coastal cliffs along its western boundary, towering river gorges and seasonal wildflowers, many of which are unique to the park. The Murchison River has carved a gorge through sedimentary rock known as Tumblagooda sandstone, creating a striking contrast of brownish red and purple against white bands of stone. Embedded in these layers are some of the earliest signs of animal life on Earth. There are many lookouts including Nature's Window at the Loop, which overlooks the Murchison Gorge, and the breathtaking scenery at Z Bend Lookout, although the most dramatic of all are the new twin cantilevered skywalks that project out over the rim of the Inyaka Wookai Watju (the West Loop) 100m above the river below. The Loop is closed after 7am in the summer months (Nov–Mar) due to extreme temperatures. Along the 20km coastal section of the park, lookouts such as Mushroom Rock, Pot Alley and Eagle Gorge offer panoramic views and whale-watching sites; there is a walking and cycling trail along these sea cliffs. Dolphins, whale sharks and whales frequent the coastal waters, and the fishing is excellent. Bushwalking, rock climbing, abseiling, canoeing tours, rafting, river cruises, camping safaris and coach tours are all available.

MONKEY MIA: The daily shore visits by the wild bottlenose dolphins at Monkey Mia are a world-famous phenomenon. The dolphins swim into the shallows, providing a unique opportunity for humans to make contact with them. It began in the 1960s when a local woman started feeding the dolphins that followed her husband's fishing boat to the shoreline. Feeding still occurs, although now it is carefully monitored by rangers to ensure that the dolphins maintain their hunting and survival skills. Visiting times, and the number of dolphins, vary. For a total marine encounter, dugong-watching cruises can also be arranged from here. Monkey Mia is 26km north-east of Denham (see p. 313).

MOUNT AUGUSTUS NATIONAL PARK: Mount Augustus is the world's largest monolith, twice the size of Uluru. It is also known as Burringurrah, named after a boy who, in Wajarri legend, broke tribal law by running away from his initiation. On capture, he was speared in the upper right leg. The spear broke as the boy fell to the ground, leaving a section protruding from his leg. It is said that, as you look at Mount Augustus, you can see the shape of the boy's body with the stump of the spear being the small peak at the eastern end called Edneys Lookout. The monolith is over 1750 million years old, cloaked in thick scrub, and offers many interesting rock formations, caves and rock-art sites. Rock-art sites are culturally sensitive areas and visitors should seek advice at the Mount Augustus Outback Tourist Resort before entering them. Camping and powered sites are available at Mount Augustus Outback Tourist Resort; (08) 9943 0527.

MUSEUM OF GERALDTON: Exhibits focus on the cultural and natural heritage of the Geraldton region. Maritime displays include finds from Australia's oldest shipwrecks, notably the original stone portico destined to adorn the castle gateway in the city of Batavia and lost to the sea when the *Batavia* sank in 1629; Museum Pl, Batavia Coast Marina; (08) 9431 8393. In the Geraldton Marina is a replica of the *Batavia* longboat; you can book harbour sailings on the last Sun of each month; check with visitor centre for details. For the story of the *Batavia*, see Houtman Abrolhos Islands entry, p. 311.

NINGALOO MARINE PARK: This park protects the 260km long Ningaloo Reef, the longest fringing coral reef in Australia. It is the only large reef in the world found so close to a continental land mass: about 100m offshore at its nearest point and less than 7km at its furthest. This means that even novice snorkellers can access the coral gardens. The reef is home to over 500 species of fish, 250 species of coral, manta rays, turtles and other marine creatures, with seasonal visits from humpback whales, dolphins and whale sharks. Ningaloo Reef is famous for its whale sharks, and from Apr to July visitors can swim with these gentle giants. Ningaloo Visitor Centre in Exmouth (see p. 314) provides tour information and the reef is easy to access from the tiny town of Coral Bay (see p. 312).

SHELL BEACH: 120km of unique coastline comprising countless tiny coquina shells. It's 45km south-east of Denham (see p. 313).

WILDFLOWERS: The Upper Gascoyne is one of the most resplendent locales for wildflowers in the world, with a dazzling array of native blooms, including Sturt's desert pea, grevilleas, sandalwood, banksia, hibiscus and bush tomato. Visit July–Sept. See Community Resource Centre for maps and itineraries; 4 Scott St; Gascoyne Junction; (08) 9943 0988.

Top: Dirk Hartog Island
Bottom: Mangrove shoots at Yardie Creek, Cape Range National Park

OTHER ATTRACTIONS

CARNARVON HERITAGE PRECINCT: On Babbage Island, and connected to the township of Carnarvon (see p. 312) by a causeway. The historic **One Mile Jetty**, built in 1897, was the longest jetty in WA's north, stretching for 1493m into the Indian Ocean, before it was destroyed by a cylcone in early 2021. Other attractions include the **Lighthouse Keeper's Cottage Museum**, **Railway Station Museum**, and **Pelican Point**.

CENTRAL GREENOUGH HISTORIC SETTLEMENT: Precinct of 11 restored stone buildings in the town of Greenough (see p. 315), dating from the 1860s, including a school, police station, courthouse, gaol and churches. Fully re-created interior and furnishings. Self-guided maps are available, or tours by appt; cnr Brand Hwy and McCartney Rd, Grenough; (08) 9926 1084.

CHURCH OF THE HOLY CROSS: From 1915 to 1939, the famous WA priest-architect Monsignor John C. Hawes designed a large number of churches and church buildings in WA's mid-west region. Morawa (see p. 316) boasts two of them: the Church of the Holy Cross and an unusually small stone hermitage known as the Old Presbytery. The latter, which Hawes used when visiting the town, is reputed to be the smallest presbytery in the world with only enough room for a bed, table and chair. Both buildings are part of the Monsignor Hawes Heritage Trail. Church is usually open; if not, contact council offices; Davis St, Morawa.

HOUTMAN ABROLHOS ISLANDS: These 122 reef islands span 100km of ocean and are the main source of rock lobster for the local lobster fishing industry – they also have a fascinating history. There are 16 known shipwrecks in the Abrolhos Islands, the most infamous of which is that of the Dutch ship *Batavia* from 1629. Captain Pelsaert and 47 of the survivors sailed north to Batavia (modern-day Jakarta) for help. When they returned nearly 15 weeks later, they discovered that a mutiny had taken place and 125 of the remaining survivors had been massacred. All of the mutineers were hanged, except for two who were marooned on the mainland, becoming Australia's first known European inhabitants. There is no record of their subsequent fate. The wreck was discovered in 1963 and some skeletons of victims of the mutiny have been found on Beacon Island. The islands now offer diving, snorkelling, surfing, windsurfing, fishing and birdwatching. Access is via boat or plane; tours and charters are available; contact Geraldton Visitor Centre for bookings: (08) 9956 6670. You can view a replica of the *Batavia* in the Geraldton Marina (see p. 314).

IRWIN DISTRICT MUSEUM: Housed in Dongara's (see p. 313) Old Police Station, Courthouse and Gaol (1870), the museum features exhibits on the history of the buildings, the introduction of rabbits to WA and the Irwin Coast shipwrecks. Open Mon–Sat 10am–12pm; Waldeck St, Dongara; (08) 9927 1323.

KENNEDY RANGE NATIONAL PARK: Along with great scenery, the park is home to fossils of the earliest known species of banksia in Australia, and marine fossils that reflect the history of the region as an ocean bed. Ideal for sightseeing, hiking and bush camping, trails start from the camping area and pass through gorges where you can see honeycomb-like rock formations. Visit late autumn and early spring.

OUR LADY OF MOUNT CARMEL CHURCH: This small church in Mullewa (see p. 317) is widely considered to be the crowning achievement of noted priest-architect Monsignor John C. Hawes. Built of local stone, this gem of Romanesque design took seven years to build with Hawes as architect, stonemason, carpenter, modeller and moulder. The adjoining Priest House is now a museum in honour of Hawes, housing his personal belongings, books, furniture and drawings (cnr Doney and Bowes sts, Mullewa). Both of these buildings are part of the Monsignor Hawes Heritage Trail, which also features the Pioneer Cemetery (Mullewa–Carnarvon Rd) and a site at the old showground just outside town, where a rock carved by Monsignor Hawes was once a simple altar where he held mass for the local First Nations people (Mount Magnet Rd). Details and a map of the trail are available from the visitor centre on the cnr Maitland Rd and Jose St, Mullewa; (08) 9961 1500.

WALGA ROCK: This monolith is 1.5km long and 5km around the base. It has several Wajarri rock paintings. One of the most extraordinary paintings, considering that the rock is over 300km from the sea, is of a white, square-rigged sailing ship. It is believed to depict one of the Dutch ships that visited WA's mid-west shores in the 17th century. This area is of profound cultural importance to the Wajarri People and the art is to be admired and respected. Walga Rock is 50km west of the town of Cue (see p. 313).

KEY TOWNS

CARNARVON
Population 4162

Carnarvon is a large coastal town at the mouth of the Gascoyne River. The town has great services for passing travellers, and a tropical feel. The waterfront area makes for a very pleasant evening stroll. The river and the fertile red earth surrounding the town are crucial to its thriving agricultural industry. In 1876, the region's founding fathers, Aubrey Brown, John Monger and C.S. Brockman, overlanded 4000 sheep from York. Carnarvon was gazetted in 1883 and developed into the centre of an efficient wool-producing area. Camel teams, driven by Afghan camel drivers, brought the wool to Carnarvon from the outlying sheep stations. This is the reason for the extraordinary width of the town's main street (Robinson St), which, at 40m, gave the camel teams enough room to turn around.

SEE & DO **Carnarvon Space and Technology Museum:** see Top Attractions. **Carnarvon Heritage Precinct:** see Other Attractions. **Fascine Town Beach:** a good spot for a picnic; Olivia Tce. **Murals:** up to 15 buildings in the town, including the Civic Centre, are adorned with murals painted by local artists. **Carnarvon Food Trail:** follow this self-drive tour of the plantations, orchards and fresh produce outlets in Carnarvon; contact visitor centre for brochure. **Bumbak's Plantation:** seek out delicious homemade preserves, jams, fruit ice-creams and other treats; 449 North River Rd. **Gascoyne Growers' Markets and Courtyard Markets:** Civic Centre; Sat mornings May–Oct. **Blowholes:** jets of water shoot up to 20m in the air after being forced through holes in the coastal rock. When you arrive at the Blowholes, you are greeted by a huge sign declaring 'KING WAVES KILL' – a cautionary reminder that this picturesque coastline has claimed the lives of over 30 people in freak waves; 73km N. Nearby, a sheltered lagoon provides good swimming and snorkelling (1km S). A further 7km north of the Blowholes is a cairn commemorating the loss of *HMAS Sydney* in 1941. **Bibbawarra Artesian Bore:** hot water surfaces at 65°C; picnic area nearby; 16km N. **Bibbawarra Trough:** 180m long, believed to be the longest in the Southern Hemisphere; adjacent to bore; 16km N. **Miaboolya Beach:** good fishing, crabbing and swimming; 22km N. **Rocky Pool:** picnic area and deep billabong ideal for swimming (after rains) and wildlife-watching; Gascoyne Rd; 55km E.

★ CORAL BAY
Population 245

Coral Bay is famous for one thing: its proximity to Ningaloo Marine Park. Ningaloo Reef boasts an incredible diversity of marine life and beautiful coral formations. At Coral Bay, the coral gardens lie close to the shore, which makes access to the reef as easy as a gentle swim. Lying at the southern end of Ningaloo Marine Park, Coral Bay has pristine beaches and a near-perfect climate: it is warm and dry regardless of the season, and the water temperature only varies from 18°C to 28°C. Swimming, snorkelling, scuba diving, and beach, reef and deep-sea fishing (outside sanctuary areas) are available year-round.

Clear, blue waters of Coral Bay

VISITOR INFORMATION

Shark Bay World Heritage Discovery & Visitor Centre
53 Knight Tce, Denham
(08) 9948 1590 or
1300 367 072
sharkbayvisit.com.au

Ningaloo Visitor Information Centre,
2 Truscott Cres, Exmouth
(08) 9949 3070
visitningaloo.com.au
australiascoralcoast.com

SEE & DO **Ningaloo Marine Park:** see Top Attractions. **Point Cloates:** the wrecks of the *Zvir*, *Fin*, *Perth* and *Rapid* lie on the reef just off the point; 4WD access only; 8km N. **Tours:** glass-bottomed boat cruises, snorkel and dive tours, kayak tours, fishing charters, scenic flights and marine wildlife-watching tours to see whale sharks (Apr–July), humpback whales (June–Nov) and manta rays (all year); contact visitor centre for details.

CUE
Population 135

This town was once known as the 'Queen of the Murchison'. In 1891 Mick Fitzgerald and Ned Heffernan found large nuggets of gold not far from what was to become the main street. It was their prospecting mate, Tom Cue, who registered the claim on their behalf, and when the town was officially proclaimed in 1894, it bore his name. Within 10 years the population of this boom town had exploded to about 10,000 people. While Cue's population has dwindled since, the legacy of those heady gold-rush days is evident in its remarkably grandiose buildings.

SEE & DO **Walga Rock:** see Other Attractions. **Heritage Buildings:** many early buildings still stand and are classified by the National Trust. A stroll up the main street takes in the elegant band rotunda, the former Gentleman's Club (now the shire offices, housing a photographic display of the region's history), the Old Gaol, the courthouse, the post office and the police station. One block west in Dowley St is the former Masonic Lodge, built in 1899 and reputed to be the largest corrugated-iron structure in the Southern Hemisphere. **Day Dawn:** once Cue's twin town, thanks to the fabulous wealth of the Great Fingall Mine. The mine office, a magnificent century-old stone building now perched precariously on the edge of a new open-cut mine, is all that remains of the town; 5km W. **Milly Soak:** popular picnic spot for early Cue residents. A tent hospital was set up nearby during the typhoid epidemic; three lone graves are the only reminder of the thousands who died; 16km N. **Heritage trail:** includes the abandoned towns of Big Bell and Day Dawn; contact visitor centre for brochure. **Fossicking:** areas surrounding the town; contact visitor centre for details.

DENHAM
Population 723

On the middle peninsula of Shark Bay, Denham is the most westerly town in mainland Australia. Dirk Hartog, the Dutch navigator, landed on an island at the bay's entrance in 1616, the first known European to land on the continent. Centuries later, in 1858, Captain H.M. Denham surveyed the area and a town bearing his name was established. The Shark Bay region was once known for its pearling and fishing, and the streets of Denham were literally paved with pearl shells. In the 1960s, however, the local roads board poured bitumen over the pearl shells, and so destroyed this unique, but bumpy, road surface. Fortunately, several buildings made from coquina shell block still stand in the town. Today Shark Bay is renowned for the wild dolphins that come right up to the beach at Monkey Mia (pronounced 'my-a'). As a World Heritage area, it also protects dugongs, humpback whales, green and loggerhead turtles, important seagrass feeding grounds and a colony of stromatolites, the world's oldest living fossils.

SEE & DO **Monkey Mia; Dirk Hartog Island; Shell beach, Dugongs; Hamelin Pool Stromatolites:** see Top Attractions for all. **Shell-block buildings:** St Andrews Anglican Church (cnr Hughes and Brockman sts) and the Old Pearlers Restaurant (cnr Knight Tce and Durlacher St) were both built from coquina shell block. **Town Bluff:** popular walk for beachcombers; from town along beach to bluff. **Pioneer Park:** contains the stone on which Captain Denham carved his name in 1858; Hughes St. **Little Lagoon:** ideal fishing and picnic spot; 3km N. **Francois Peron National Park:** Peron Homestead has a 'hot tub' of artesian water; 4WD access only; 7km N. **Ocean Park:** marine park with aquarium and touch pool; 9km S. **Eagle Bluff:** habitat of sea eagles and a good viewing spot for sharks and stingrays; 20km S. **Blue Lagoon Pearl Farm:** working platform where black pearls are harvested; Monkey Mia; 26km NE. **Steep Point:** westernmost point on mainland, with spectacular scenery; 4WD access only; 260km W. **Zuytdorp Cliffs:** extend from beneath Shark Bay region south to Kalbarri; 4WD access only.

DONGARA–PORT DENISON
Population 2841

The twin towns of Dongara–Port Denison proclaim to be the 'Lobster Capital' of the state, with offshore reefs supporting a profitable industry. The main street of Dongara is lined with Moreton Bay fig trees, while Port Denison provides local anglers with a large marina and harbour.

SEE & DO **Irwin District Museum:** see Other Attractions. **Russ Cottage:** a beautifully restored farm-worker's cottage (1870). The hard-packed material of the kitchen floor was made from scores of anthills, and the flood-level marker near the front door indicates how high the nearby Irwin River rose during the record flood of 1971; open Sun 10am–12pm or by appt; St Dominics Rd, Dongara. **Church of St John the Baptist:** built in 1884, its pews were made from the driftwood of shipwrecks and its church bell is said to have come from Fremantle Gaol; cnr Waldeck and Church sts, Dongara. **Dongara Activity Park:** archery, minigolf, croquet, karts, barbecue and playground facilities; cnr Matsen Rd and Brand Hwy; (08) 9927 2864. **Cemetery:** headstones dating from 1874 and a wall of remembrance to Dominican sisters; brochure from visitor centre; Dodd St, Dongara. **Town heritage trail:** 1.6km walk that features 28 historic Dongara sites; contact visitor centre for map. **Fisherman's Lookout:** one of two obelisks built in 1869, with panoramic views; Point Leander Dr, Port Denison. **Monthly Market:** Priory Gardens; 1st Sat each month.

★ EXMOUTH
Population 2806

Exmouth has a great array of eating and accommodation options for weary travellers. There's an upbeat feel about the place which, although remote, can get very busy with tourists given its location – close to some of the state's best tourist attractions. One of the newest towns in Australia, Exmouth was founded in 1967 as a support town for the Harold E. Holt US Naval Communications Station, the main source of local employment. Excellent year-round fishing and its proximity to Cape Range National Park and Ningaloo Reef, now grease the wheels of its tourist trade.

SEE & DO **Ningaloo Marine Park; Cape Range National Park:** see Top Attractions for both. **Bundegi Beach:** sheltered waters here provide great swimming, snorkelling and kayaking; 14km N. **Navy Pier:** the best shore dive in the country; by tour only, contact Dive Ningaloo 0456 702 437; 7km N. **Jurabi Turtle Centre:** see nesting turtles and hatchlings (Nov–Mar); Yardie Creek Rd; 13km N. **Harold E. Holt Naval Communication Station:** the centre tower in its antenna field, at 388m, is one of the tallest structures in the Southern Hemisphere; not open to public; 5km N. **Vlamingh Head Lighthouse and Lookout:** built in 1912, Australia's only kerosene-burning lighthouse served as a beacon to mariners until 1967. The lookout offers panoramic 360-degree views; 19km N. **Learmonth Jetty:** popular fishing spot, rebuilt after cyclone Vance; 33km S. **Wildlife-watching:** coral-spawning (Mar–Apr); boat cruises and air flights to see whale sharks (Apr–Jul) and humpback whales (Aug–Nov). From lighthouse (17km N), or with whale-watching boat tours. Coral-viewing boat cruises also available; contact visitor centre for details.

GASCOYNE JUNCTION
Population 65

Lying at the junction of the Lyons and Gascoyne rivers, Gascoyne Junction is a small administration centre for the pastoral industry. Sheep stations in the area, ranging in size from around 36,000 to 400,000ha, produce a wool clip exceeding 1.5 million kg annually. Floods destroyed much of the town in 2010, but it has since been rebuilt.

SEE & DO **Mount Augustus National Park; wildflowers:** see Top Attractions for both. **Kennedy Range National Park:** see Other Attractions.

GERALDTON
Population 32,717

Situated on the extremely picturesque Batavia Coast, Geraldton is the largest town in the mid-west region. As a port city, it is the major centre for the wheat belt and is renowned for its rock-lobster industry. Geraldton is also regarded as one of the best windsurfing locations in the world and has superb swimming and surfing beaches. The nearby Houtman Abrolhos Islands are the site of 16 known shipwrecks. The most infamous is that of the Dutch ship *Batavia* (see Houtman Abrolhos Islands entry, p. 311), which foundered on a reef in 1629.

SEE & DO **HMAS Sydney II Memorial; Museum of Geraldton:** see Top Attractions for both. **Houtman Abrolhos Islands:** see Other Attractions. **Historic buildings:** explore the town's historic architecture dating back to the mid-1800s, with works by noted architect-priest Monsignor John Cyril Hawes a highlight. Many of the buildings have been restored and are open to the public, including the **Old Geraldton Gaol** (1858), which is now a craft centre, and the **Bill Sewell Complex** (1884), which was built as a hospital and subsequently became a prison. In Cathedral Ave, **St Francis Xavier Cathedral** offers tours (Mon and Fri 10am, Wed 4pm), and the **Cathedral of the Holy Cross** has one of the largest areas of stained glass in Australia. **Yamaji Art Centre** sells local art and has information on the 195km Yamaji Drive Trail which takes you to cultural and historic sites significant to the Yamaji People: open Mon–Fri 9am–4pm; 189 Marine Tce; (08) 9965 3440. Brochures for **Historic Walk Trails** available from visitor centre. **Geraldton Regional Art Gallery:** the original Geraldton Town Hall (1907) converted to house art exhibitions and workshops; open Tues–Fri 9am–4pm, Sat–Sun 9.30am–1.30pm; 24 Chapman Rd; (08) 9964 7170. **Point Moore Lighthouse:** assembled in 1878 from steel sections prefabricated in England, and standing 34m tall, this is the only lighthouse of its kind in Australia; information on nearby pillar; Marine Tce. **Markets:** Maitland Park, Sat; Old Railway Station, Sun. **Fishing:** good fishing spots at Sunset Beach (6km N) and Drummond Cove (10km N). **Mill's Park Lookout:** excellent views over Moresby Range and coastal plain; 10km NE. **Chapman Valley:** picturesque farmlands and fields of springtime wildflowers on display July–Oct; 20km NE. **Scenic flights:** tours over nearby Abrolhos Islands, Murchison Gorges or the coastal cliffs of Kalbarri; contact visitor centre. **Scenic drive:** Indian Ocean Dr, with its coastal views, is a beautiful alternate route for travelling between Geraldton and Perth via Dongarra, bypassing much of the Brand Hwy.

Top: Vineyards in Carnarvon
Bottom: Geraldton Museum
Opposite: Hiking, Ningaloo

TOP EVENTS

- → FEB Kalbarri Fishing Classic
- → MAR Gamex game fishing competition (Exmouth)
- → EASTER Gascoyne Dash (Carnavon and Gascoyne Junction)
- → MAY Carnar-fin fishing competition (Carnarvon); Gascoyne River Music Festival (Gascoyne Junction)
- → AUG–SEPT Gascoyne Food Festival (Carnarvon); Wildflower Show (Mullewa)
- → SEPT–OCT Landor Races (Gascoyne Junction)
- → OCT Sunshine Festival (Geraldton); Iwarra Wilungga (Aboriginal cultural festival; Geraldton)
- → NOV Blessing of the Fleet (Dongara-Denison); Festival of Lights (Geraldton)

TEMPERATURES

Jan: 18–32° C

July: 9–20° C

GREENOUGH
Population 344

Lying 24km south of Geraldton, the Greenough Flats form a floodplain close to the mouth of the Greenough River. At its peak in the 1860s and 1870s, Greenough (pronounced 'Grennuff') was a highly successful wheat-growing area. However, the combined effects of drought, crop disease and floods led to the area's decline and from 1900 the population dropped dramatically. The historic hamlet has now been extensively restored and is classified by the National Trust.

SEE & DO **Central Greenough Historic Settlement:** see Other Attractions. **Greenough Museum & Gardens:** folk display located in an original limestone cottage; tours available; Brand Hwy; (08) 9926 1890. **Leaning trees:** a unique sight, these trees have grown sideways under the influence of the harsh, salt-laden winds; view from Brand Hwy on Greenough Flats. **Wildlife and Bird Park:** privately owned rescue and rehabilitation reserve; Company Rd; (08) 9926 1171. **Walkaway Railway Station:** built in the style of a traditional British railway station, it now houses a railway and heritage museum; open Tues–Sun; Evans Rd; (08) 9926 1976; 10km E. **Flat Rocks:** surfing, swimming and rock fishing. A round of the state surfing championships is held here in June every year; 10km S. **Ellendale Pool:** this deep, freshwater swimming hole beneath sandstone cliffs is an ideal picnic area; 23km E. **Greenough River Nature Trail:** self-guided walk; contact visitor centre. **Walkaway Heritage Trail:** 57km self-drive tour of the area; contact visitor centre.

★ KALBARRI
Population 1270

Kalbarri was established in 1951 and is now a popular holiday town. It is draped around the mouth of the Murchison River, and surrounded by epic countryside, including giant sea cliffs flanked by Kalbarri National Park. The park is famous for its magnificent gorges, up to 130m deep along the river. Just south of the township, a cairn marks the spot where in 1629 Captain Pelsaert of the Dutch East India Company marooned two crew members implicated in the Batavia shipwreck and massacre. These were the first, albeit unwilling, white inhabitants of Australia, see Houtman Abrolhos Islands entry, p. 311, for the story. Although Kalabrri was almost destroyed by cyclone in early 2021, the town is in the process of rebuilding and is welcoming visitors again.

SEE & DO **Kalbarri National Park:** see Top Attractions. **Pelican feeding:** daily feeding Apr–Feb by volunteers on the river foreshore; starts 8.45am; off Grey St. **Kalbarri Entertainment Centre:** also known as the 'Pirate Park' with trampolines, minigolf, amusement arcade; Magee Cres. **Kalbarri Skywalk:** Wander out onto a pair of dizzying skywalks, overhanging the Murchison River Gorge in Kalbarri National Park. **Wildflower tours:** tour Kalbarri National Park's vivid display of wildflowers to view over 1100 species of WA wildflowers. Stop in at the visitor centre for the latest wildflower viewing information and wildflower tour times, itineraries and special features; July–Oct; Ajana–Kalbarri Rd; 3km E. **Murchison House Station:** a selection of tours available at of one of the oldest and largest stations in WA, which includes historic buildings, military vehicles, cemetery and wildflowers; Apr–Oct; Ajana–Kalbarri Rd; murchisonhousestation.com.au; 4km E. **Big River Ranch:** enjoy horseriding through the countryside; Ajana–Kalbarri Rd; 3km E. **Wittecarra Creek:** cairn marking the site where two of the mutineers from the Dutch ship Batavia were left as punishment for their participation in the murders of 125 survivors of the wreck; 4km S.

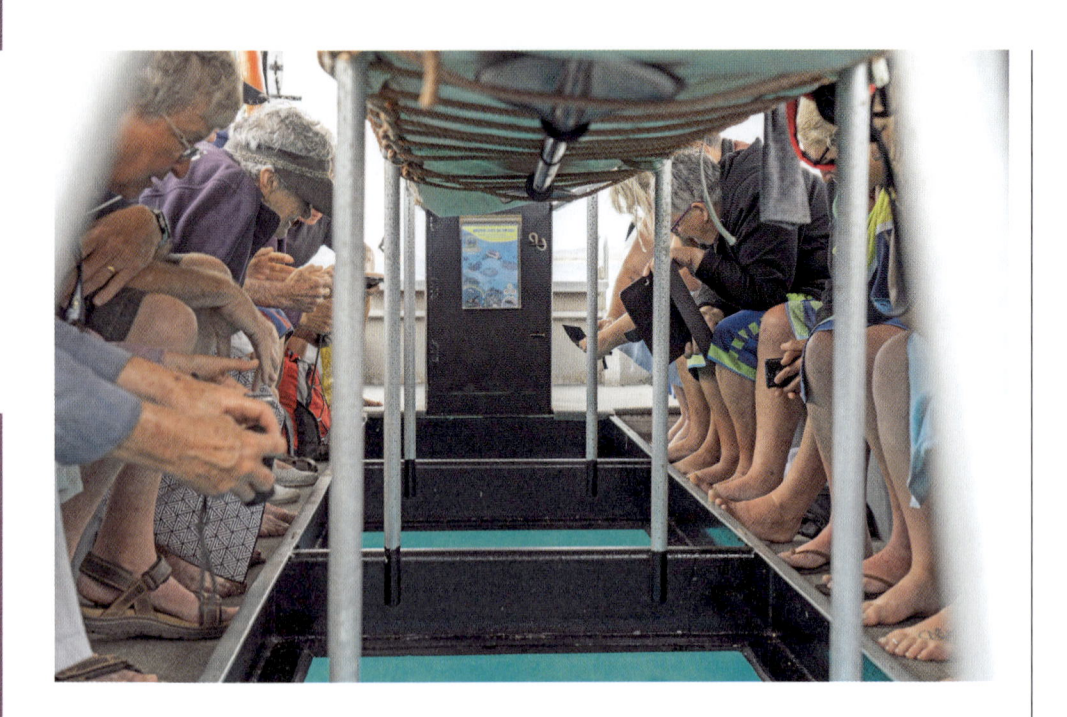

MEEKATHARRA
Population 675

The name Meekatharra is believed to be a Yamatji word meaning 'place of little water' – an apt description for a town sitting on the edge of a desert. Meekatharra is now the centre of a vast mining and pastoral area. It came into existence in the 1880s when gold was discovered in the area. However, the gold rush was short-lived and it was only the arrival of the railway in 1910 that ensured the town's survival. The town became the railhead at the end of the Canning Stock Route, a series of 54 wells stretching from the East Kimberley to the Murchison. The stock route was built at the expense of local First Nations People, however, who were deprived of water in order that they would reveal to explorers where the water was located. The railway was closed in 1978, but the town continues to provide necessary links to remote outback areas through its Royal Flying Doctor Service.

SEE & DO **Royal Flying Doctor Service:** operates an important base in Meekatharra; open to visitors 9am–2pm; Main St. **Old Courthouse:** National Trust building; Darlot St. **Museum:** photographic display and items of memorabilia from Meekatharra's past; open Mon–Fri 8am–4.30pm; Shire offices, Main St. **State Battery:** relocated to the town centre in recognition of the early prospectors and miners; Main St. **Meeka Rangelands Discovery Trail:** walk or drive this trail for insight into the town's Traditional Owners and its mining past and landscapes; maps at visitor centre. **Peace Gorge:** this area of granite formations is an ideal picnic spot; 5km N. **Bilyuin Pool:** swimming (but check water level in summer); 88km NW. **Old Police Station:** remains of the first police station in the Murchison; Mount Gould; 156km NW.

MORAWA
Population 443

Morawa, a small wheat-belt town, has the distinction of being home to the first commercial iron ore to be exported from Australia. In springtime the area around Morawa is ablaze with wildflowers.

SEE & DO **Church Of The Holy Cross and Old Presbytery:** see Other Attractions. **Historical Museum:** housed in the old police station and gaol with displays of farm machinery, household items and a collection of windmills; open 9.30am–4pm Mon–Sat; cnr Prater and Gill sts; (08) 9971 1777. **Koolanooka Mine Site and Lookout:** scenic views and a delightful wildflower walk in season; 9km E. **Perenjori:** nearby town has historic St Joseph's Church, designed by Monsignor Hawes, and the Perenjori–Rothsay Heritage Trail, a 180km self-drive tour taking in Rothsay, a goldmining ghost town; 18km SE. **Bilya Rock Reserve:** with a large cairn, reportedly placed there by John Forrest in the 1870s as a trigonometrical survey point; 20km N. **Koolanooka Springs Reserve:** ideal for picnics; 26km E.

MOUNT MAGNET
Population 576

In 1854 the hill that rises above this Murchison goldmining town was named West Mount Magnet by surveyor Robert Austin after he noticed that its magnetic ironstone was playing havoc with his compass. Now known by its traditional name, Warramboo Hill affords a remarkable view over the town and mines. Mount Magnet offers visitors a rich mining history, rugged granite breakaway countryside and breathtaking wildflowers in season. Take care as there are dangerous old mine shafts in the area.

Top: Glass boat viewing at Exmouth

SEE & DO **Mining and Pastoral Museum:** a collection of mining and early settler artefacts and includes a Crossley engine from the original State Battery; Hepburn St. **Heritage trail:** see the surviving historic buildings and sites of the gold-rush era on this 1.4km walk; contact visitor centre for map. **The Granites:** rocky outcrop with picnic area and rock paintings created by the Badimia People; 7km N. **Heritage drive:** 37km drive to local historic and natural sights, including views of old open-cut goldmine. Also takes in the Granites and various ghost towns; contact visitor centre for map.

MULLEWA
Population 312

Mullewa, 92km north-east of Geraldton, is in the heart of wildflower country. In spring, the countryside surrounding the town bursts forth with one of the finest displays of wildflowers in WA. The wreath flower is the star attraction of the annual Mullewa Wildflower Show. Mullewa is also the hometown of Yamatji man Ernie Dingo, who has entertained Australian television viewers for decades.

SEE & DO **Wildflowers:** *see* Top Attractions. **Our Lady Of Mount Carmel Church:** *see* Other Attractions. **Tenindewa Pioneer Well:** an example of the art of stone pitching that was common at the time of construction, reputedly built by Chinese labourers en route to the Murchison goldfields. Also walking trails; 18km W. **Bindoo Hill:** glacial moraine where ice-smoothed rocks dropped as the face of a glacier melted around 225 million years ago; 40km NW. **Coalseam Conservation Park:** remnants of the state's first coal shafts, now a picnic ground; 45km SW. **Tallering Peak and Gorges:** ideal picnic spot; Mullewa–Carnarvon Rd; check accessibility at visitor centre; 59km N. **Wooleen Homestead:** stay on a working sheep and cattle station in the central Murchison district. Visit Boodra Rock and First Nations sites, and experience station life; (08) 9963 7973; 194km N.

NORTHAMPTON
Population 821

Northampton, nestled in the valley of Nokarena Brook 47km north of Geraldton, was awarded Historic Town status by the National Trust in 1993. It was declared a townsite in 1864. A former lead-mining centre, its prosperity is now based on sheep and wheat-farming. The town has also produced it's fair share of AFL stars, including Brownlow Medallist Patrick Cripps.

SEE & DO **Chiverton House Museum:** unusual memorabilia housed in what was originally the home of Captain Samuel Mitchell, mine manager and geologist. Surrounding gardens include a herbarium and restored farm machinery; open Mon, Wed, Fri–Sun 10am–12pm and 2–4pm; Hampton Rd. **Mary St Railway Precinct:** railway memorabilia at the site of the town's 2nd railway station, built 1913; eastern end. **Church of Our Lady in Ara Coeli:** designed in 1936 by Monsignor John Hawes, WA's famous priest-architect; Hampton Rd (*see also* Our Lady Of Mount Carmel Church, Other Attractions). **Gwalla Church and Cemetery:** ruins of town's first church (1864); Gwalla St. **Hampton Rd Heritage Walk:** 2km walk past 37 buildings of historical interest, including the Miners Arms Hotel (1868) and the Old Railway Station (1879); contact visitor centre for map. **AFL metal figurines:** celebrates nine hometown AFL legends along Hampton Road, outside the Miners Arms Hotel. **Alma School House:** built in 1916 as a one-teacher school; 12km N. **Willigully Cave paintings:** stencilled artwork created by the Nhanda decorate the walls of these caves at the mouth of the Bowes River; 17km W. **Oakabella Homestead:** one of the first farms in WA to plant canola, or rapeseed as it was then known. Take a guided tour of the historic homestead and outbuildings; open Mar–Jan; 18km S. **Horrocks Beach:** beautiful bays, sandy beaches, good swimming, fishing and surfing; 20km W. **Lynton Station:** ruins of labour-hiring depot for convicts, used in 1853–56; 35km NW. **Hutt Lagoon:** appears pink in midday sun; 45km NW. **Port Gregory:** beach settlement, ideal for swimming, fishing and windsurfing; 47km NW. **Warribano Chimney:** Australia's first lead smelter; 60km N.

YALGOO
Population 313

Alluvial gold was discovered in the 1890s in Yalgoo and today gold is still found in the district. Visitors are encouraged to try their luck fossicking.

SEE & DO **Courthouse Museum:** exhibits of local artefacts; Gibbons St. **Gaol:** built in 1896 and recently relocated to the museum precinct, it has photographs illustrating the town's history; Gibbons St. **Chapel of St Hyacinth:** designed by Monsignor John Cyril Hawes and built in 1919 for the Dominican Sisters who lived in a wooden convent school near the chapel; Henty St. **Heritage walk:** self-guided town walk; pamphlet available at visitor centre in the Council offices, 37 Gibbons St, (08) 9962 8042. **Cemetery:** the history of Yalgoo as told through headstones; 5km W. **Joker's Tunnel:** a tunnel carved through solid rock by early prospectors and named after the Joker's mining syndicate, it has panoramic views near the entrance; 10km SE. **Meteorite crater:** discovered in 1961, a portion of the meteorite is held at the WA Museum in Perth; 100km N. **Gascoyne Murchison Outback Pathways:** three drives exploring outback history: the Wool Wagon Pathway, the Kingsford Smith Mail Run and the Miners Pathway; see outbackpathways.com for maps.

Pilbara

Often overshadowed and overlooked by travellers keen to get to the Kimberley just to the north, the Pilbara is one of Australia's unsung treasures. **Spectacular gorges, breathtaking waterfalls** and **sparkling rockpools** make up an incredible natural attraction in an otherwise harsh landscape. Many of the gorges have walking tracks, so you can fully appreciate the rugged beauty of their yawning chasms.

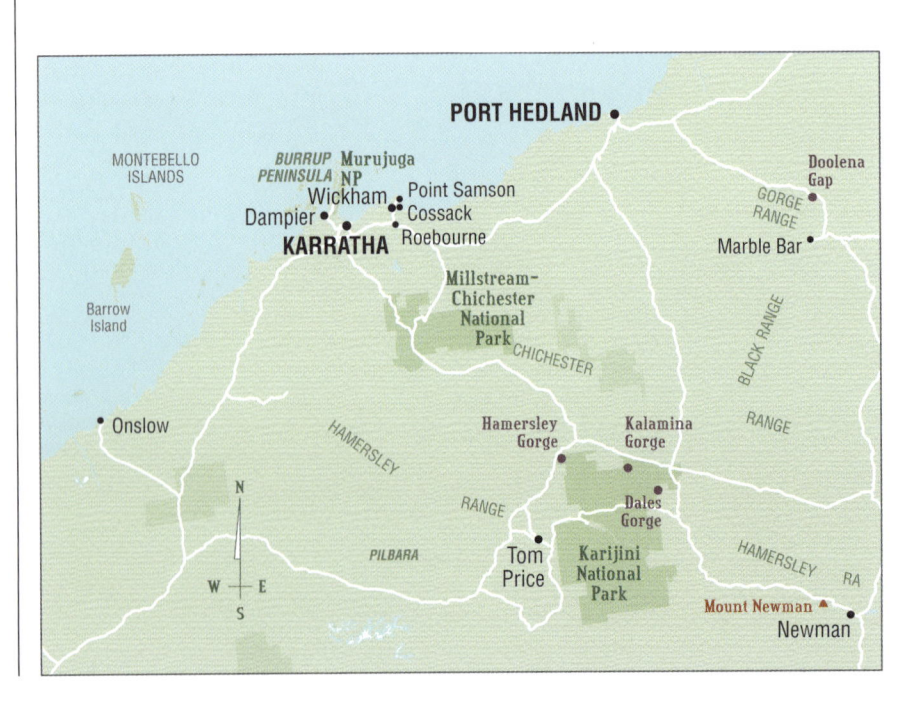

Top: Karijini National Park
Opposite: Taking a dip at Python Pool, Millstream-Chichester National Park

CHEAT SHEET

→ Allow at least a week to 10 days because like most parts of WA this area is big.

→ Best time to visit: June–Oct. The coastline between Exmouth and Broome is one of the most cyclone-prone regions in Australia. Cyclone season runs between Nov and April, so keep an eye on local news services if travelling in the north during this time.

→ Main towns: Karratha (see p. 320), Newman (see p. 320), Port Headland (see p. 321).

→ There are more than 31 cultural groups that belong to the area, which is the Traditional Lands of the Banjima, Jaburrara, Jurruru, Kariyarra, Kurrama, Martu, Ngarla, Ngarluma, Nhuwala, Nyamal, Nyangumarda, Palyku, Pinikura, Yindjibarndi, Yinhawangka and other peoples of the Western Deserts. Explore fascinating rock-art sites, especially the sacred Burrup Peninsula.

→ Need to know: Distances are vast; 4WD often needed; fuel, water and food stops are limited. Research before travelling, including for any required permits.

→ Did you know? The Pilbara region is home to the biggest mining operations in Australia, digging up and shipping out large quantities of salt, iron-ore, copper, fertilisers and natural gas.

→ Don't miss: hiking into the gorges of Karrijini; the outback oasis of Millstream Chicester National Park; a mine tour of Mount Whaleback in Newman.

TOP ATTRACTIONS

KARIJINI NATIONAL PARK: Karijini was the name given to this area by the Traditional Owners, the Banyjima, Kurrama and Innawonga Peoples. The second-largest national park in WA, this park features ochre-coloured rock faces with bright-white snappy gums, bundles of spinifex dotting the red earth and chasms up to 100m deep. The waterfalls and rockpools of Karijini offer some of the best swimming in the state. The park protects the many different wildlife habitats, plants and animals of the Pilbara. The landscape is dotted with huge termite mounds and the rock piles of the rare pebble mouse; other species in the park include red kangaroos and rock wallabies, and reptiles from legless lizards to pythons. **Dales Gorge**, which contains Jubura (Fern Pool), a cooling swimhole and deeply sacred spot for the Traditional Owners, is one of the most popular and accessible gorges, while at **Hamersley Gorge**, a wave-like rock formation acts as a backdrop to a swimming hole and natural spa. **Oxer Lookout** reveals where the Joffre, Hancock, Weano and Red gorges meet. Mount Bruce, the second-tallest peak in the state, offers spectacular views, both natural and of the enormous Marandoo iron-ore mine. The Karijini Visitor Centre is located off the road to Dales Gorge and has information on camping.

MILLSTREAM–CHICHESTER NATIONAL PARK: Rolling hills, spectacular escarpments and tree-lined watercourses with hidden rockpools characterise this park. The remarkable oasis of **Millstream** is an area of tropical, palm-fringed, freshwater springs, well known to the Afghan cameleers of the Pilbara's past. The spring-fed **Chinderwarriner Pool** has an almost mirage-like quality. Other notably scenic spots are Python, Deepreach and Circular pools, and Cliff Lookout. The Millstream Homestead Visitor Centre, housed in the Gordon family homestead (1919), has displays dedicated to the local Yinjibarndi People, early settlers and the natural environment.

MURUJUGA NATIONAL PARK (BURRUP PENINSULA): There are more than 10,000 ancient engravings on the Burrup Peninsula alone, including some of the earliest examples of art in Australia. The Traditional Owners of the rock art are the Ngarluma-Yindjibarndi, the Yaburara-Mardudhunera and the Woon-goo-tt-oo Peoples. The area is a very culturally sensitive site and should be treated with great care and respect. A debate is raging over the damage being done to this magnificent outdoor gallery by the adjacent gas project; check with visitor centre in Karratha (see p. 320) for locations.

OTHER ATTRACTIONS

COSSACK: Although now a ghost town, Cossack's beautiful stone buildings have been restored and nine are classified by the National Trust. It was once named Tien Tsin after the boat that brought the first settlers there in 1863 and it was the first port in the north-west region, as well as a pearling centre in the late 1800s. The town comes alive in late July and early Aug when it hosts the annual Cossack Art Awards, which attracts thousands of people. The town is 14km north of Roebourne (see p. 321).

MOUNT WHALEBACK MINE TOURS: The mine in Newman (see p. 320) produces over 100 million tonnes of iron ore every year. Tours (minimum four people) run daily at 9.15am May–Sept, Mon–Fri Oct–April; book through visitor centre in Newman; (08) 9175 2888.

NORTH-WEST SHELF GAS PROJECT VISITOR CENTRE: Displays on the history and technology of Australia's largest natural-resource development, with panoramic views over the massive onshore gas plant; opening times vary seasonally; Burrup Rd, Dampier; (08) 9158 8292.

STAIRCASE TO THE MOON: Like the Broome version (see p. 324), this beautiful illusion is created when a full moon rises over the shore at low tide. The reflection of the moon is broken into bars by the ridges on the wet mudflats, creating the image of a 'stairway' leading up to the moon. It lasts for about 15min and can be seen in several places around the Pilbara region. Check with Port Hedland and Karratha visitor centres for locations, dates and times.

KEY TOWNS

KARRATHA
Population 17,013

Karratha is a local word for 'good country'. Founded in 1968 as a result of expansion of the iron-ore industry, Karratha is now WA's leading oil and gas hub. For visitors, Karratha is an ideal centre from which to explore the fascinating Pilbara region.

SEE & DO **Millstream–Chichester National Park; Murujuga National Park:** see Top Attractions for both. **North-West Shelf Gas Project Visitor Centre:** see Other Attractions. **Yaburara Heritage Trail:** 3hr walk features rock carvings by the Ngarluma People; pamphlet available at visitor centre. **Dampier:** port facility servicing the iron-ore operations at Tom Price and Paraburdoo, home of the famous Red Dog; 22km N. **Hamersley Iron Port Facilities:** 3hr tour and audiovisual presentation daily; bookings essential, through visitor centre; 22km N. **Cleaverville Beach:** scenic spot ideal for camping, boating, fishing and swimming; 26km NE. **Dampier Archipelago:** 42 islands and islets, ideal for swimming, snorkelling, boating, fishing and whale-watching; take a boat tour from Dampier; 34km NW. **Montebello Islands:** site of Australia's first shipwreck, the *Tryal*, which ran aground and sank in 1622. In 1952, Britain also conducted Atomic bomb tests near Trimouille and Alpha islands. It is now a good spot for snorkelling, beachcombing, fishing and diving; beyond Dampier Archipelago; 141km W.

MARBLE BAR
Population 153

Marble Bar has gained a dubious reputation as the hottest town in Australia. For 161 consecutive days in 1923–24 the temperature here did not drop below 37.8°C (100°F). This mining town was named after a bar of mineral deposit that crosses the nearby Coongan River and was originally mistaken for marble. It proved to be jasper, a coloured variety of quartz.

SEE & DO **Government buildings:** built of local stone in 1895, now National Trust listed; General St. **Comet Gold Mine:** this mine operated from 1936 to 1955. The Comet is now a museum and tourist centre with displays of gemstones, rocks, minerals and local history. 10km S. **Marble Bar Pool:** site of the famous jasper bar (splash water on it to reveal its colours) and a popular swimming spot; 4km W. **Corunna Downs RAAF Base:** ruins of a secret base built in 1943 for long-range attacks on the Japanese-occupied islands of the Indonesian archipelago; 40km SE. **Doolena Gorge:** watch the cliff-face glow bright red as the sun sets; 45km NW.

NEWMAN
Population 4239

Located in the heart of the Pilbara, this mining town was established in the 1960s by the Mount Newman Mining Company to house the workforce for nearby Mount Whaleback, the largest open-cut iron-ore mine in the world. At the same time, a 426km railway was constructed between Newman and Port Hedland to transport the ore for export to Japan.

SEE & DO **Mount Whaleback Mine Tours:** see Other Attractions. **Mining and Pastoral Museum:** interesting display of relics from the town's short history, including the first Haulpak (giant iron-ore truck) used at Mount Whaleback; located at visitor centre. **Martumili Artists:** Aboriginal art from artists who live in western desert and Pilbara communities; cnr Kalgan and Newman Dr; (08) 9175 1020. **Ophthalmia Dam:** swimming, sailing, barbecues and picnics (no camping); 20km E. **Mount Newman:** excellent views; 25km NW. **Wanna Munna:** site of ancient rock carvings made by the Nyiyaparli People; 74km W. **Eagle Rock Falls:** permanent pools and picnic spots nearby; 4WD access only; 80km NW. **Rockpools and waterholes:** Kalgans Pool (65km NE), Three Pools (75km N) and Weeli Wolli (99km W). **Newman Waterholes and Art Sites Tour:** maps available at visitor centre.

ONSLOW
Population 813

Onslow, on the north-west coast between Exmouth and Karratha, is today the supply base for offshore gas and oil fields but also an attractive tree-shaded town that has had many incarnations in its time. This part of the coast is among the north's most cyclone-prone and Onslow has often suffered severe damage. The town was originally located at the Ashburton River mouth and a bustling pearling centre and in the 1890s gold was discovered nearby. In 1925 the townsite was moved to Beadon Bay after cyclones caused the river to silt up. During World War II, submarines refuelled here and the town was bombed twice. In the 1950s it was the mainland base for Britain's nuclear experiments at Montebello Islands. In 1963 Onslow was almost completely destroyed by a cyclone.

SEE & DO **Goods Shed Museum:** memorabilia from the town's long history and collections of old bottles, shells and rocks; in visitor centre; Second Ave. **Beadon Creek and Groyne:** popular fishing spot. **Ian Blair Memorial Walkway:** 1km scenic walk; starts at Beadon Point and finishes at Sunset Beach. **Heritage trail:** contact visitor centre for map. **Termite mounds:** with interpretive display; 10km S. **Mackerel Islands:** excellent fishing destination. Charter boats are available

VISITOR INFORMATION

Karratha Tourism and Visitor Centre
Lot 4548 De Witt Rd
(08) 9186 8055

Port Hedland Visitor Centre
13 Wedge St, Port Hedland
(08) 9173 1711
australiasnorthwest.com

TOP EVENTS

→ APR Karijini Experience (Karijini National Park)

→ JUL FeNaClNG Festival (Karratha); Races (Marble Bar)

→ JUL–AUG Cossack Art Awards

→ AUG Dampier Classic (game fishing, Karratha); Fortescue Festival (Newman)

→ AUG–SEPT North West Festival (Port Hedland)

TEMPERATURES

Jan: 26–36°C

July: 13–27°C

Opposite top: Port Hedland
Opposite bottom: Snorkelling off the Montebello Islands

for daytrips or extended fishing safaris; contact visitor centre for details; 22km off the coast. **Ashburton River:** swimming, camping and picnicking; 45km SW. **Old townsite heritage trail:** self-guided walk around original townsite; contact visitor centre for map; 45km SW.

PORT HEDLAND
Population 15,298

Port Hedland is a mining hub with a rich history and growing cultural identity. The iron-ore boom that began in the early 1960s saw the town grow at a rapid rate and it currently handles the largest iron-ore export tonnage of any Australian port. It was named after Captain Peter Hedland, who reached this deep-water harbour in 1863. There are two main centres: Port Hedland, on the coast, and South Hedland, 13km inland. It's important to wear strong shoes when walking on rocky reef areas as poisonous stonefish frequent this stretch of coast, especially Nov–Mar; make local inquiries before swimming.

SEE & DO **Don Rhodes Mining Museum:** open-air museum with displays of historic railway and mining machinery; Wilson St; (08) 9173 1711. **Town, harbour and mine tours:** various tours that include a boat cruise on the working harbour, Fortescue mine visit, the world's largest bulk loading port, salt operations and exploring the township with a local; book through visitor centre. **Heritage trail:** 1.8km self-guided walk around town; contact visitor centre. **Courthouse Gallery+Studio:** works by national and local artists, including makers studios; Edgar St; (08) 9141 0041. **Dalgety House:** museum and interpretive centre documenting the area's history; open 10am–2pm May–Oct; Wedge St; (08) 9173 4300. **Pretty Pool:** picnic, fish and swim at this scenic tidal pool; Taylor St, Port Hedland; 8km NE. **Dampier Salt:** see giant cone-shaped mounds of salt awaiting export; Wilson St, Port Hedland; (08) 9173 0200; 8km S. **Turtle-watching:** flatback turtles nest in the area Oct–Mar at Pretty Pool, Cooke Point and Cemetery Beach. **Street art:** explore the town's laneways and discover contemporary street art from Australian and international artists.

ROEBOURNE
Population 700

Named after John Septimus Roe, WA's first surveyor-general, Roebourne was established in 1866 and is the oldest town on the north-west coast. As the centre for early mining and pastoral industries in the Pilbara, it was connected by tramway to the pearling port of Cossack and later to Point Samson. Now Cossack is a ghost town and Point Samson is known for its watersports, fishing and whale-watching. Roebourne is also known for the high-profile case of 16-year-old Yindjibarndi boy John Pat, who died in police custody after being brutally beaten by five off-duty police in 1983. Pat's death led to the Royal Commission into Aboriginal Deaths in Custody. The bulk of the 339 recommendations in the 1991 report are still to be implemented.

SEE & DO **Cossack:** *see* Other Attractions. **Ganalili Centre:** Aboriginal art and culture; the centre also houses the visitor information centre and library. **Historic buildings:** some original stone buildings remain, many of which have been classified by the National Trust. The Old Gaol was designed by the well-known colonial architect George Temple Poole; Queen St. **Mount Welcome:** offers views of the coastal plains and rugged hills surrounding the town. Spot the railroad from Cape Lambert to Pannawonica, and the pipeline carrying water from Millstream to Wickham and Cape Lambert; Fisher Dr. **Wickham:** the company town for Robe River Iron Ore offers a spectacular view from Tank Hill Lookout; 12km N. **Point Samson:** good fishing, swimming, snorkelling and diving. Boat hire, whale-watching and fishing charters are available; 19km N. **Cleaverville:** camping and fishing; 25km N. **Harding Dam:** ideal picnic spot; 27km S. **Millstream–Chichester National Park:** *see* Karratha, 150km S. **Emma Withnell Heritage Trail:** 52km historic self-drive trail, named after the first European woman in the north-west, takes in Roebourne, Cossack, Wickham and Point Samson; map available at visitor centre.

TOM PRICE
Population 2874

The huge iron-ore deposit now known as Mount Tom Price was discovered in 1962 in the heart of the Pilbara, after which the Hamersley Iron Project was established. A mine, two towns (Dampier and Tom Price) and a railway line between them, all followed. Today the town is an oasis in a dry countryside. On the edge of the Hamersley Range and at an altitude of 747m, this is the state's highest town.

SEE & DO **Karijini National Park:** *see* Top Attractions. **Kings Lake:** constructed lake with nearby park offering picnic and barbecue facilities (no swimming); 2km W. **Mount Nameless (Jarndunmunha) Lookout:** stunning views of the district around Tom Price; 6km W via walking trail or 4WD track. **Mine tours:** marvel at the sheer vastness of Rio Tinto's open-cut iron-ore mine; bookings essential, arrange through visitor centre. **Rio Tinto/Railway Access Road:** this private road is the most direct route between Tom Price and Karratha via Karijini and Millstream national parks. It requires a permit to travel along it; available from visitor centre. **Travellers note:** *To the north-east is Wittenoom, an old asbestos-mining town. Although the mine was closed in 1966, there is still a health risk from microscopic asbestos fibres present in the abandoned mine tailings in and around Wittenoom. If disturbed and inhaled, blue asbestos dust may cause cancer. The Ashburton Shire Council advocates avoidance of the Wittenoom area.*

The Kimberley

This remote region is Western Australia's undisputed adventure-travel highlight. The dramatic splendour of the tropical landscape – **surging rivers, thunderous waterfalls, deep chasms, bulging boab trees** – is governed by the wet and dry seasons. The area is rich in First Nations culture, displayed in the amazing art, petroglyphs and sacred sites found here, spanning back at least 40,000 years. There are two main routes in the area: the tarmac-sealed Great Northern Highway, which connects Broome to Kununurra, skirting the Kimberley region to the south; and the rough, dirt 4WD-only Gibb River Road, which crawls through **isolated and at times spectacular territory**, joining Derby to Kununurra.

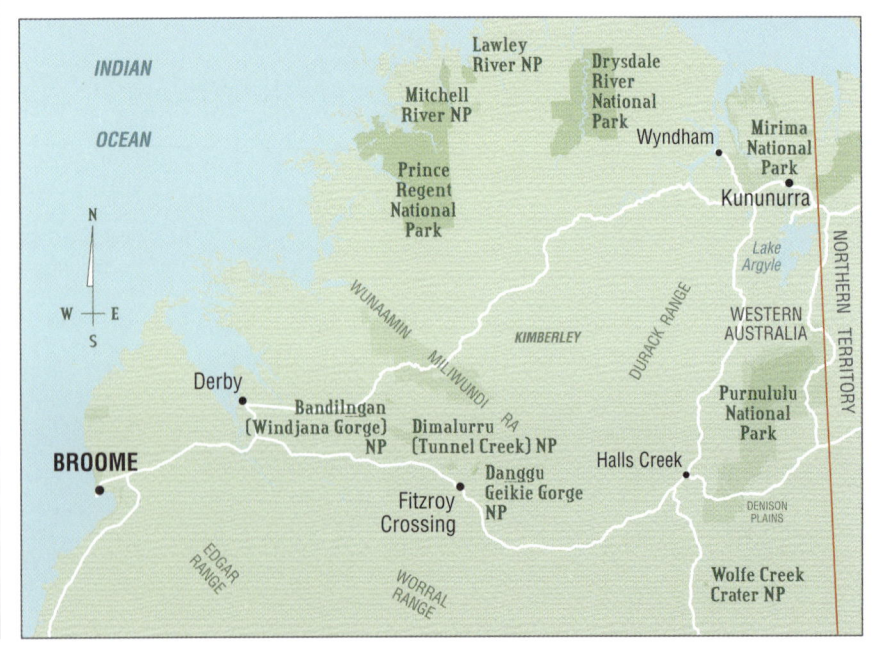

Top: Kimberley waterfalls
Opposite: Cockburn Ranges

CHEAT SHEET

→ Allow at least two weeks because this area is vast: Broome to Kununurra is 1040km.

→ Best time to visit: June–Aug.

→ Main towns: Broome (see p. 325), Kununurra (see p. 326).

→ There are more than 100 Aboriginal communities across the Kimberley. Broome is on the homelands of the Jukun People; Cape Leveque is on Bardi land, Kunnurra is the Traditional Lands of the Mriwoong. The Gibb River Road and Great Northern Highway pass through the lands of the Doolboong, Gooniyandi, Jaru, Kija, Ngarinyin, Nyikina, Punuba and Unggumi Peoples. The region is home to some of the finest rock-art sites in Australia – best seen by organised tour.

→ Need to know: The Kimberley has some spectacular natural swimming pools, but it is also crocodile country. Distances in this remote region are vast; 4WD often needed; fuel, water and food stops are limited. Research before travelling, including for any required permits. In January 2023, the Kimberley flooded and many communities were affected, and the Fitzroy River Bridge collapsed. Check conditions with local authorities before travelling, and to see whether national parks and attractions are open.

→ Did you know? Bunuba man Jandamarra lived during the 1870s–90s and is remembered as a First Nations warrior for defending his people against the police.

→ Don't miss: Aboriginal art galleries; Broome; a flight over Purnululu (Bungle Bungle Range); the adventure of the Gibb River Road.

TOP ATTRACTIONS

BANDILNGAN (WINDJANA GORGE) NATIONAL PARK: A 350-million-year-old Devonian reef rises majestically above the plains. An easy walking trail winds through the gorge, taking in primeval life forms fossilised within the gorge walls. The gorge is 145km east of Derby (see p. 325).

BUCCANEER ARCHIPELAGO: In Broome (see p. 325) and Derby (see p. 325), you can arrange scenic flights over this magnificent landscape that stretches north-east of the Dampier Peninsula. Also known as the Thousand Islands, this is a dramatic coastal area of rugged red cliffs, epic waterfalls and secluded white sandy beaches. Here you'll find whirlpools created by massive 11m tides and the horizontal two-way waterfall of Talbot Bay.

CABLE BEACH: With its 22km of pristine white sands fringing the turquoise waters of the Indian Ocean, Cable Beach in Broome (see p. 325) is one of the most stunning beaches in the world. Every day the beach is washed clean by high tides ranging from 4m to 10m. It takes its name from the telegraph cable laid between Broome and Java in 1889. The luxurious **Cable Beach Resort**, which fronts onto the beach, is a popular tourist destination. The quintessential Broome activity is to ride a camel along this famous beach.

COCKBURN RANGES: Explore this 600m towering escarpment from the Gibb River Rd, visiting **El Questro** and **Home Valley** stations with gorge hikes, swimming holes, lookouts, 4WD tracks, fishing and evening entertainment. Accommodation and camping are available at both sites.

DANGGU GEIKIE GORGE NATIONAL PARK: Danggu Geikie Gorge has cliffs and sculptured rock formations carved by water through an ancient limestone reef. The Fitzroy River is home to sharks, sawfish and stingrays that have, over centuries, adapted to the fresh water. Freshwater crocodiles up to 3m long and barramundi are plentiful, and best seen on a guided boat tour. Heritage and cultural tours are run by Bunuba guides; bookings essential. Park rangers run tours on the geology, wildlife and history of the area. The park closed following the January 2023 floods when it experienced significant damage, so check ahead before visiting. Entry to the park is restricted during wet season (Dec–Mar). The park is 18km north-east of Fitzroy Crossing (see p. 326)

DIMALURRU (TUNNEL CREEK) NATIONAL PARK: The Traditional Owners of this park are the Bunuba People. Wear solid shoes, carry a torch and be prepared to get wet wading through pools as you explore the 750m long cave that runs through Napier Range. The roof has collapsed near the centre of the tunnel and there are five species of bats here. Nearby Pigeon's Cave was the hideout of an 1890s Bunuba resistance leader, Jandamarra. It's 184km east of Derby (see p. 325).

GIBB RIVER ROAD: 4WD road between Derby and Wyndham traverses some of the most incredible gorge country of the Kimberley; contact visitor centres in Broome, Derby or Kununurra for guidebook and current road conditions, especially following the January 2023 floods.

LAKE ARGYLE: The view of the hills that pop out of the main body of water is said to resemble a crocodile basking in the sun and is known locally as Crocodile Ridge. Birdwatching, camping, bushwalking, mountain biking, fishing, sailing, canoeing and lake cruises are all available. The lake is 72km south of Kununurra (see p. 326).

MITCHELL RIVER NATIONAL PARK: The Traditional Owners and joint managers of this park are the Wunambal Gaambera People. It's one of the Kimberley's newest national parks and protects this scenic and biologically important area.

Mitchell Falls (Punamii-Uunpuu) and **Surveyors Pool** are the two main attractions for visitors. The area is remote with no phone or internet and you need a scenic flight or a 4WD to access the park; it's about a 16hr drive from Kununurra (see p. 326); you need an Uunguu Visitor Pass (UVP) before you visit; see wunambalgaambera.org.au.

PURNULULU NATIONAL PARK: This World Heritage Area in the outback of the East Kimberley is home to the **Bungle Bungle Range**, a remarkable landscape of tiger-striped, beehive-shaped rock domes intersected by narrow, palm-lined gorges where pools reflect sunlight off sheer walls. A scenic flight is the best way to gain a perspective of the Bungle Bungles's massive size and spectacular scenery (details from Kununurra visitor centre, see p. 326). The most visited site in Purnululu is Cathedral Gorge, which is a fairly easy walk. A couple of days and a backpack allow you to explore nearby Piccaninny Creek and Gorge, camping overnight. On the northern side of the park is Echidna Chasm, a narrow gorge totally different from those on the southern side. Purnululu is also rich in Gija and Jaru art, and there are many traditional burial sites within its boundaries. Before entering this area please ensure that all cultural protocols are respected by getting advice from the visitors centre. The impact of European domination has left many cultural scars and the remaining sacred sites must be respected. Purnululu is open to visitors (Apr–Dec) and is accessible by 4WD, airplane or helicopter. The park has its own dedicated visitors centre open from May-Oct. There are two campsites and some limited accommodation; visitors must carry in all food and water.

STAIRCASE TO THE MOON: This beautiful optical illusion is caused by a full moon reflecting on the exposed mudflats of Roebuck Bay in Broome (see p. 325) at extremely low tides. Three nights approx. monthly Mar–Oct; Town Beach, Broome; check dates and times at visitor centre.

OTHER ATTRACTIONS

ARGYLE HOMESTEAD MUSEUM: Built in 1884 by the Durack family (of *Kings in Grass Castles* fame) and relocated when the lake was formed, the building is a fine example of an early station homestead; open 8am–4pm Mon–Sun Apr–Dec; Parker Rd; (08) 9168 1177. The museum is 70km south of Kununurra (see p. 326).

DAMPIER PENINSULA: This remote area north of Broome (see p. 325) boasts unspoiled coastline (4WD access only). Record-breaking game fish have been caught in the surrounding waters. Charters and tours leave from Dampier. The Sacred Heart Church at Beagle Bay was built by Pallottine monks in 1917 and boasts a magnificent pearl-shell altar. Lombadina is a former mission now home to an Bardi community that offers four-wheel driving, whale-watching, fishing and mud-crabbing tours; contact (08) 9192 4936. On the eastern side of the peninsula is Cygnet Bay Pearl Farm, the oldest Australian and family-owned pearl farm, with 1hr and day tours and onsite accommodation; contact (08) 9192 4283. **Cape Leveque**, at the north end of the peninsula, is well known for its pristine beaches and rugged pindan cliffs.

FIVE RIVERS LOOKOUT: Views of the Kimberley landscape from the highest point of the Bastion Range, particularly good for viewing the striking sunsets. Also a good picnic area with barbecue facilities. It's 5km north of Wyndham (see p. 327).

GANTHEAUME POINT: Dinosaur footprints believed to be 130 million years old can be seen at very low tide. A plaster cast of the tracks has been embedded at the top of the cliff. Nearby, view the almost perfectly round Anastasia's Pool, built by a lighthouse keeper for his wife. It's 5km north-east of Broome (see p. 325).

MIRIMA NATIONAL PARK: The park on the edge of Kununurra township (see p. 326) is fondly known to locals as the 'mini Bungle Bungles' due to its similarly striking rock formations. One of its famed features is the boab trees that grow on the rock faces, the seeds having been carried there by rock wallabies and left in their dung. There are walking trails within the park, and between May and Aug guided walks are available. Details at visitor centre.

PARRY LAGOONS NATURE RESERVE: Enjoy birdwatching from a shaded bird hide at Marlgu Billabong or scan the wide vistas of the flood plain and distant hills afforded from the lookout at Telegraph Hill. It's 20km south-east of Wyndham (see p. 327).

PEARL LUGGERS: Experience Broome's (see p. 325) pearling heritage by visiting two restored pearling luggers in Chinatown. Tours Mon–Sun; Dampier Tce, Broome; (08) 9192 0022.

WILLIE CREEK PEARL FARM: This pearl farm is a highly awarded attraction, with bus, boat and helicopter transfers available; daily tours; (08) 9192 0000. It's 35km north of Broome (see p. 325).

WOLFE CREEK CRATER NATIONAL PARK: Wolfe Creek Crater is the second-largest meteorite crater in the world. Named after Robert Wolfe, a Halls Creek prospector, it is 870–950m across and was probably formed by a meteorite weighing at least several thousand tonnes crashing to Earth a million years ago. Scenic flights afford magnificent views. It's 150km south of Halls Creek (see p. 326).

Top: Paddle boarding at Cable Beach, Broome
Bottom: Purnululu National Park **Opposite:** Cathedral Gorge, Purnululu National Park

VISITOR INFORMATION

Broome Visitor Centre
1 Hamersley St
(08) 9195 2200
visitbroome.com.au

Kununurra Visitor Centre
75 Coolibah Dr
(08) 9168 1177
visitkununurra.com
australiasnorthwest.com

KEY TOWNS

★ BROOME
Population 14,660

Broome is distinguished by its pearling history, cosmopolitan character and startling natural assets, including white sandy beaches, turquoise water and red soils. The discovery of pearling grounds off the coast in the 1880s led to the foundation of the Broome township in 1883. A melting pot of nationalities flocked to its shores in the hope of making a fortune. Japanese, Malays and Koepangers joined the Yawuru pearl divers, while Chinese people became the shopkeepers in town. By 1910 Broome was the world's leading pearling centre. In those early, heady days, more than 400 pearling luggers operated out of Broome. The industry suffered when world markets collapsed in 1914, but stabilised in the 1970s as cultured-pearl farming developed. Today remnants of Broome's fascinating past are everywhere, with the town's multicultural population ensuring a dynamic array of cultural influences. Broome's beaches are ideal for swimming Apr–Oct, and there is good fishing year-round.

SEE & DO Buccaneer Archipelago; Cable Beach; Staircase to the Moon: see Top Attractions for all. **Pearl Luggers; Gantheaume Point; Willie Creek Pearl Farm; Dampier Peninsula:** see Other Attractions for all. **Chinatown:** an extraordinary mix of colonial-era and Asian influences, Chinatown was once the bustling hub of Broome where pearl sheds, billiard saloons and Chinese eateries flourished; now it is home to some of the world's finest pearl showrooms. **Buildings on Hamersley St:** distinctive Broome-style architecture including the courthouse, made of teak inside and corrugated iron outside; Captain Gregory's House, a classic old pearling master's house, built in 1917, now an art gallery; and Matso's brewery, once the Union Bank Building. **Short St Gallery:** heritage building holding regular exhibitions of First Nations artwork; Short St; (08) 9192 2658. **Broome Historical Society & Museum:** pearling display and collection of historical photographs on Broome's past; Robinson St. **Japanese Cemetery:** the largest Japanese cemetery in Australia contains the graves of more than 900 Japanese pearl divers, dating back to 1896. This is a sobering reminder of the perils of the early pearling days when the bends, cyclones and sharks claimed many lives; cnr Port Dr and Savannah Way. **Sun Pictures:** believed to be the world's oldest operating outdoor cinema, opened in 1916; Carnarvon St. **Sisters of St John of God Convent:** built in 1926 by Japanese shipbuilder Hori Gorokitchi in the 1920s using traditional methods that emphasise the external framing of the building; cnr Barker and Weld sts. **Deep Water Port and Jetty:** good for fishing and ship watching; Port Dr. **Jetty to Jetty Heritage Trail:** 3.4km walk taking in many key sites and features a guided phone app; contact visitor centre for maps and details. **Courthouse Markets:** Hamersley St; Sat morning year round, plus Sun morning Apr–Oct. **Town Beach Night Markets:** Robinson St; every Thurs evening Jun–Sept and the first two nights of the Staircase to the Moon; check with visitor centre for dates and times. **Malcolm Douglas Crocodile Park:** home to some of Australia's biggest crocodiles and plenty of other wildlife; Broome Hwy; 16km NE. **Reddell Beach:** enjoy the dramatic sight of Broome's distinctive red soils, known as 'pindan', meeting white sands and brilliant blue water; 7km SW. **Buccaneer Rock:** at the entrance to Dampier Creek, this landmark commemorates Captain William Dampier and HMS *Roebuck*; 15km E. **Broome Bird Observatory:** see some of the 300-plus species of migratory wader birds that arrive each year from Siberia; Crab Creek Rd; 17km E.

DERBY
Population 3009

It is said that Derby, known as the 'Gateway to the Gorges', is where the real Kimberley region begins. The first town settled in the Kimberley, it features some spectacular natural attractions nearby: the Devonian Reef Gorges of Bandilngan (Windjana) and Dimalurru (Tunnel Creek) are only a few hours' drive along the Gibb River Rd, and the magnificent islands of the Buccaneer Archipelago are just a short cruise away.

Although King Sound was first explored in 1688, it wasn't until the early 1880s that the Port of Derby was established as a landing point for wool shipments and Derby was proclaimed a townsite. The first jetty was built in 1885, the same year that gold was discovered at Halls Creek. Miners and prospectors poured into the port on their way to the goldfields, but by the 1890s, as the gold fever died down, the port was used almost exclusively for the export of live cattle and sheep. In 1951 iron-ore mining began at Cockatoo Island, which revitalised the town. Derby is now a service centre for the region's rich pastoral and mining industries. In January 2023, floods hit the region after ex-tropical cyclone Ellie, and Derby was evacuated. Check conditions with local authorities before travelling.

SEE & DO **Buccaneer Archipelago; Gibb River Road; Bandilngan (Windjana Gorge) National Park; Dimalurru (Tunnel Creek) National Park:** see Top Attractions for all. **Old Gaol:** built in 1906, this is the oldest building in town; Loch St. **Wharfinger House Museum:** built in the 1920s for the local harbourmaster, to a design that is typical of the tropics, the building now houses an extensive collection of historical memorabilia and First Nations artefacts. Key from visitor centre; Loch St. **Jetty:** some of the highest tides in Australia, up to 12m, can be seen from the jetty. Now used to export ore from various local mines; Jetty Rd. **Market:** Clarendon St; each Sat May–Sept. **Prison tree:** 1000-year-old boab tree formerly used as a prison; 7km S. **Myall's Bore:** beside the bore stands a 120m long cattle trough reputed to be the longest in the Southern Hemisphere; 7km S. **Gorges:** Lennard Gorge (190km E), Bell Gorge (214km E), Manning Gorge (306km E), Barnett River Gorge (340km NE) and Sir John Gorge (350km E); 4WD access only.

FITZROY CROSSING
Population 1022

Fitzroy Crossing is in the heart of the Kimberley region. As its name suggests, the original townsite was chosen as the best place to ford the mighty Fitzroy River. In the wet season, the river can rise over 20m and spread out up to 15km from its banks. In January 2023, floods inundated the town after ex-tropical cyclone Ellie hit the region. The bridge at Fitzroy Crossing collapsed. Road trains and barges delivered essential goods to the cut-off local communities. Check with local authorities ahead of time before visiting this area.

SEE & DO **Danggu Geikie Gorge National Park:** see Top Attractions. **Crossing Inn:** first established in the 1890s as a shanty inn and trade store for passing stockmen, prospectors and drovers, it has operated on the same site ever since, and is one of the very few hotels in the state to keep its true outback atmosphere. Stop off for a meal and a drink at Crossing Inn Homestead. Skuthorp Rd; (08) 9191 5080.

Fitzroy Crossing Visitor Centre: locally made arts, crafts and cafe. **Mangkaja Arts Centre:** studio and gallery of local artists' paintings; 8 Bell Road; (08) 9191 5833. **Causeway Crossing:** concrete crossing that was the only way across the river until the new bridge was built in the 1970s; Geikie Gorge Rd; 4km NE. **4WD tours:** to Tunnel Creek and Windjana Gorge; bookings essential, contact visitor centre for details. **Mimbi Caves:** take a tour of the Devonian Reef system; (08) 9191 5355; Great Northern Hwy; 90km E.

HALLS CREEK
Population 1572

In the heart of the Kimberley region and on the edge of the Great Sandy Desert, Halls Creek was the site of the first payable gold discovery in WA. In 1885 Jack Slattery and Charlie Hall (after whom the town is named) discovered gold, thereby sparking a gold rush that brought over 15,000 people to the area. In 1917 a seriously injured stockman named James 'Jimmy' Darcy was taken into Halls Creek. With neither doctor nor hospital in the town, the local postmaster carried out an emergency operation using a penknife as instructions were telegraphed by morse code from Perth. The Perth doctor then set out on the 10-day journey to Halls Creek via cattle boat, model-T Ford, horse-drawn sulky and, finally, on foot, only to discover that the patient had died the day before his arrival. The event inspired Reverend John Flynn to establish the Royal Flying Doctor Service in 1928, a development that helped to encourage settlement throughout the outback.

SEE & DO **Russian Jack Memorial:** tribute to a prospector who pushed his sick friend in a wheelbarrow to Wyndham for medical help; Thomas St. **Trackers' Hut:** restored original hut of First Nations trackers; Robert St, behind police station. **China Wall:** white quartz formation said to resemble the Great Wall of China; 6km E. **Caroline's Pool:** deep pool ideal for swimming (in wet season) and picnicking; 15km E. **Old Halls Creek:** remnants of original town including graveyard where James Darcy is buried; prospecting available; 16km E. **Palm Springs:** fishing, swimming and picnicking; 45km E. **Warlayirti Artists Art Centre:** contemporary Aboriginal art centre and gallery; check centre is open before visiting; 0407 123 478; Balgo via Tanami Rd; 259km S.

★ KUNUNURRA
Population 4515

Set in a farmland oasis and with great services and transport links, Kununurra is located in the East Kimberley region, not far from the NT border. Kununurra is a welcome sight for weary travellers. There is plenty to keep visitors busy for a few days, including access to the art and culture of the Miriuwung and Gajerrong People. The town was established in the 1960s alongside Lake Kununurra on

Top: Dining in Broome **Bottom:** Parry Creek Farm, Wyndham **Opposite:** Birdwatching in the Kimberley

TOP EVENTS

→ MAY Ord Valley Muster (Kununurra)

→ JULY Boab Festival and Mowanjum Festival (both Derby); Rodeo (Fitzroy Crossing and Halls Creek)

→ AUG–SEPT Shinju Matsuri (pearl festival, Broome)

→ NOV Mango Festival (Broome)

TEMPERATURES

Jan: 26–33°C

July: 14–29°C

---

the Ord River, at the centre of the massive Ord River Irrigation Scheme, which has transformed a dusty, million-acre cattle station into a habitat for waterbirds, fish and crocodiles; the hills and ridges of the former station have become islands. Lake Argyle to the south, in the Carr Boyd Range, was created by the damming of the Ord River and is the largest body of fresh water in Australia.

SEE & DO **Lake Argyle; Purnululu National Park:** see Top Attractions for both. **Argyle Downs Homestead Museum; Mirima National Park:** see Other Attractions for both. **Historical Society Museum:** artefacts and photos provide a historical overview of the town; check with visitor centre for opening times; 72 Coolibah Dr; (08) 9169 3331. **Waringarri Aboriginal Arts:** large and varied display of art and artefacts for sale; open Mon–Fri 8.30am–4.30pm, Sat 10am–2pm May–Oct; 16 Speargrass Rd; (08) 9168 2212. **Birdland Functional Art:** outstanding pottery, ceramics and other functional art for sale; 22 Poincettia Way; (08) 9168 1616. **Kellys Knob Lookout:** panoramic view of town and Ord Valley; off Speargrass Rd. **Celebrity Tree Park:** arboretum on the shore of Lake Kununurra. Lily Creek Lagoon at the edge of the park is a good spot for birdwatching. The boat ramp was once part of the road to Darwin; off Victoria Hwy. **Kununurra Markets:** fresh produce and the usual market bric-a-brac; also artistic delights such as jewellery and zebra rock; Whitegum Park; Sat. **Lake Kununurra:** formed after the completion of the Diversion Dam as part of the Ord River Scheme, the lake is home to a large variety of flora and fauna and is ideal for sailing, rowing, waterskiing and boat tours; details at visitor centre; 2km S. **City of Ruins:** unusual sandstone formation of pinnacles and outcrops that resemble the ruins of an ancient city; off Weaber Plains Rd; 6km N. **Ord River and Diversion Dam:** abundance of wildlife, spectacular scenery and a variety of watersports and cruises available; details at visitor centre; 7km W. **Ivanhoe Crossing:** permanently flooded causeway is an ideal fishing spot; Ivanhoe Rd; 12km N. **Hoochery Distillery:** visit a traditional old 'Country and Western' saloon bar or take a tour of the renowned distillery; see visitors centre for tour times; 300 Weaber Plains Rd; (08) 9168 2467; 15km N. **Middle Springs:** picturesque spot with diverse birdlife; 4WD access only; 30km N. **Black Rock Falls:** spectacular waterfall during the wet season that spills over rocks stained by the minerals in the water; 4WD access only; entry subject to weather and road conditions; 32km N. **The Grotto:** ideal swimming hole (in the wet season) at the base of 140 stone steps; 70km NW. **Scenic flights:** flights from town take visitors over the remarkable Bungle Bungles, Mitchell Plateau or Kalumburu; details and bookings at visitor centre.

WYNDHAM
Population 941

Wyndham is the most northerly town and safe port in WA. The entrance to the town is guarded by the 'Big Croc', a 20m long concrete crocodile.

SEE & DO **Five Rivers Lookout; Parry Lagoons Nature Reserve:** see Other Attractions for both. **Historical Society Museum:** in the old courthouse building, its displays include a photographic record of the town's history, artefacts and machinery; O'Donnell St. **Warriu Dreamtime Park:** bronze statues representing the Traditional Owners of the area; Koolama St. **Pioneer Cemetery:** gravestones of some of the area's early settlers; Great Northern Hwy. **Three Mile Valley:** here you will find the big picture scenery that makes the Kimberley region so spectacular, with rough red gorges and pools of clear, cold water during the wet season. Walking trails lead the visitor through the brilliant displays of wildflowers in season; 3km N. **Afghan Cemetery:** containing the graves of Afghan camel drivers who carried supplies throughout the Kimberley region. All the gravestones face towards Mecca; 1km E. *Koolama* **wreck site:** the *Koolama* was hit by Japanese bombs near Darwin during World War II in 1942. After limping along the coast to Wyndham, it sank just 40m from the jetty. The spot is marked by unusual swirling in the water; 5km NW. **Moochalabra Dam:** completed in 1971, the dam was constructed to provide an assured water supply to the Wyndham area. The construction is unique in Australia, designed to allow overflow to pass through the rock on the crest of the hill. 4WD access only; King River Rd; 18km SW. **Wandjina rock paintings:** 4WD access only; well signposted off the King River Rd; 18km SW. **Prison Tree:** 2000–4000-year-old boab tree once used by local police as a lock-up; King River Rd; 22km SW. **The Grotto:** this waterhole, estimated to be 100m deep, is a cool oasis offering year-round swimming; 36km E.

Northern Territory

HIGHLIGHTS

Marvel at some of the world's oldest rock-art sites in Kakadu National Park. See p. 337.

Soak up the tropical lifestyle of Darwin. Check out World War II museums and tunnels; galleries showcasing artworks by Traditional Owners; beachside markets; and top cafes. See p. 330.

Ride a bike or do a base walk around mesmerising Uluru – this mammoth rock will imprint itself in your memory. See p. 350.

Start early to walk the circuit along the rim of Kings Canyon in Watarrka National Park, and enjoy the magnificent views of the canyon's gaping chasms. See p. 350.

Explore the mighty gorges of Tjoritja/West MacDonnell Ranges and cool off in one of the beautiful swimming holes. See p. 350.

From Darwin explore the white sandy beaches of the Cobourg Peninsula and Arnhem Land on a 4WD tour.

Near Alice Springs/Mparntwe visit the wild Finke Gorge National Park. See pp. 352, 349.

STATE FLOWER

Sturt's desert rose
Gossypium sturtianum

Kakadu National Park

The Traditional Owners of the Darwin/Garramilla area are the Larrakia People.

Darwin/Garramilla at a glance

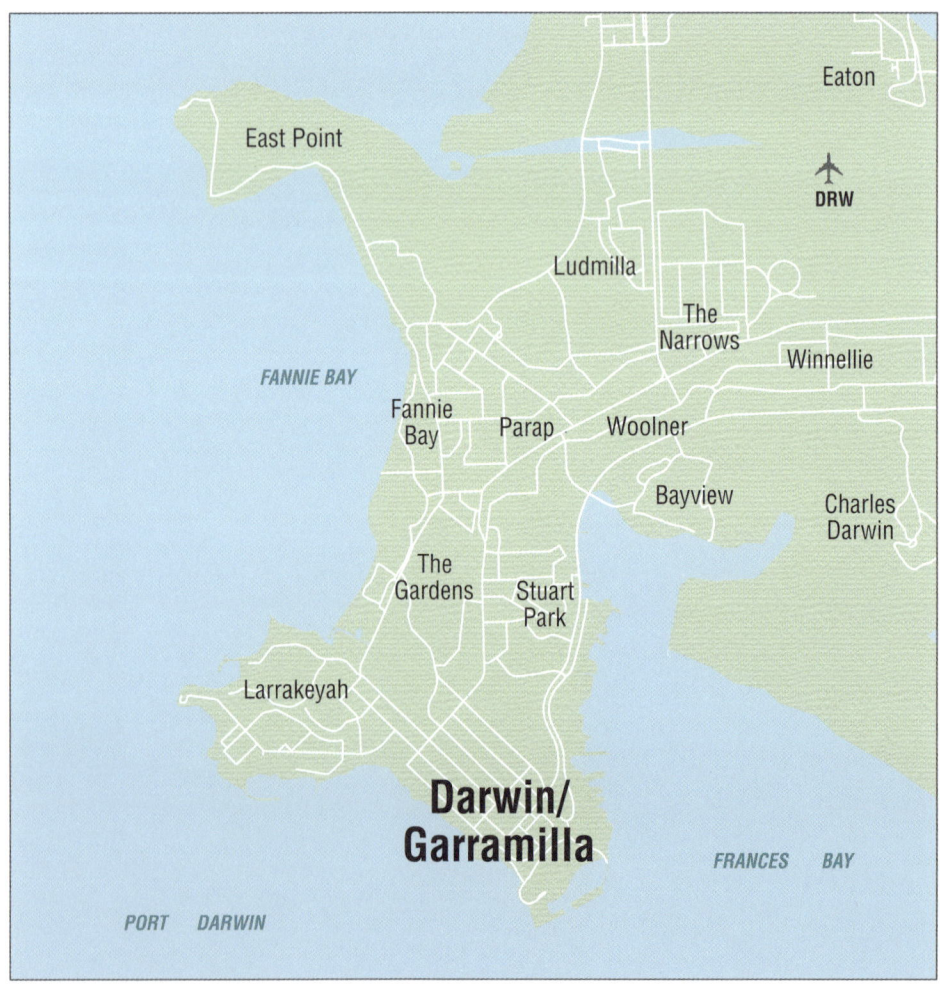

Darwin, Australia's northern outpost, is wrapped around a natural ocean inlet with **spectacular beaches** and a real **tropical vibe**. It's a true **cultural melting pot**, with First Nations, Asian and European culture making for a fascinating mix of attractions, historic sites, events and food. The city's **remoteness** and its **turbulent history** – including being bombed in World War II – have made the people of Darwin proud, resilient and independent.

Top: Sunset at Mindil Beach **Middle:** The city's waterfront gardens **Bottom:** Darwin cityscape **Opposite:** Mindil Markets

IF YOU LIKE …

FESTIVALS AND EVENTS
Bombing of Darwin Day, Feb
Tiwi Islands Grand Final and Art Sale, March
Arafura Games, April (biennial)
Bass in the Grass, May
Beer Can Regatta, July
Darwin Aboriginal Art Fair, Aug
Darwin Festival, Aug
Darwin International Laksa Festival, Nov

GALLERIES
Darwin SArt Trail
Mbantua Gallery
Mason Gallery

MARKETS
Malak Marketplace
Mindil Beach Sunset Market
Nightcliff Markets
Parap Village Market
Rapid Creek Markets

MUSEUMS
Aviation Museum
Crocosaurus Cove
Defence of Darwin Experience
Museum and Art Gallery of the Northern Territory
Royal Flying Doctor Service Darwin Tourist Facility
World War II Oil Storage Tunnels

SHOPPING
Darwin Waterfront
Harriet Park/Smith Street
Parap Shopping Village
The Mall and Knuckey Street
Casuarina Shopping Centre

SUNSET VIEWS
Cullen Bay Beach
East Point Reserve
Mindil Beach
Nightcliff Foreshore
Stokes Hill Wharf
Trailer Boat Club

WALKS AND TOURS
Darwin Hop-on Hop-off bus
Sunset Cruises
Tiwi Island Tours
Walk Darwin
World War II Bombing of Darwin Tours

NORTHERN TERRITORY

Daytrips from Darwin/Garramilla

ADELAIDE RIVER AND FOGG DAM CONSERVATION RESERVE
45min to 1.25hr from Darwin CBD

Have you ever fancied being on a boat as a croc leaps out of the water next to you to get its jaws around a piece of meat dangling over the river? If so, the Adelaide River is the place for you! Several operators put on tours to see this astonishing, and frankly quite terrifying, spectacle. For more tranquil options, check out Adelaide River Tours for an extensive wildlife cruise.

The wetlands of Fogg Dam Conservation Reserve are protected, with an astounding population of waterbirds and birdwatching opportunities. Window on the Wetlands has great views and information on the area's history. The Limilngan-Wulna People are the Traditional Owners of the area. *See* p. 338.

LITCHFIELD NATIONAL PARK
1.5hr from Darwin CBD

Cool waterholes and plunging waterfalls make Litchfield a popular destination for locals and visitors. The 1500sqkm national park attracts campers and hikers, and is a popular daytrip from Darwin.

Swimming or floating under the escarpments is top of the attractions, especially in the dry season when the spectacular waterholes are usually safe from crocs – although always check with rangers and read the warning signs. The best places for a dip are Buley Rockhole, Florence Falls and Wangi Falls. In the wet season, waterfalls rage down the escarpment and are a must for photographers. *See* p. 338.

Top: Florence Falls, Litchfield National Park **Middle:** Mary River wetlands **Bottom left:** Fishing, Tiwi Islands **Bottom right:** Tiwi Island Retreat

TIWI ISLANDS
1.5hr (including flight) from Darwin CBD

Bathurst and Melville islands comprise the Tiwi Islands. They are known for the Traditional lifestyle of the Tiwi People. Although the Tiwi Islands are just 80km north of Darwin, there's no public transport, so you'll need to take a tour with the option of travelling either by a 20min flight or a 4hr ferry ride.

Visit the Patakijiyali Museum and Tiwi Design art centre, and tour the local mission precinct. The traditional and unique fabric designs make a special gift. If you're here in March, don't miss the Tiwi Football (Australian Rules) Grand Final.

MARY RIVER
1.5hr from Darwin CBD

Drive along the Arnhem Highway to reach Mary River, one of eight rivers slicing its way through the Top End. It's an unforgettable region with floodplains, woodlands, billabongs and monsoon forests.

Best visited from May to Sept, Mary River and Corroboree Billabong offer excellent opportunities for wildlife-watching, fishing, four-wheel driving and bushwalking. Couzen's Lookout has stunning sunset views and Shady Camp is one of the best fishing and camping spots around. *See* p. 341.

TERRITORY WILDLIFE PARK AND BERRY SPRINGS NATURE PARK
45min from Darwin CBD

These two destinations are popular with locals and visitors alike. Australian wildlife and ecosystems are showcased at the vast, natural Territory Wildlife Park. Top attractions include an aquarium, monsoon vine forest, goose lagoon and the birds of prey free-flight display.

Next door the delightful Berry Springs Nature Park is the closest waterhole to Darwin (heed warning signs about crocs). It's a series of lovely, spring-fed swimming holes perfect for lazing about in. There are picnic areas shaded by palms and paperbark trees, grassy lawns and walking tracks with plenty of birdlife. *See* p. 338.

KATHERINE AND NITMILUK NATIONAL PARK
3.5hr from Darwin CBD

From Darwin, head down the highway to Katherine, the stopping-off point to visit Nitmiluk National Park. This must-see natural attraction of 13 linked gorges can be experienced by cruise, canoeing, walking or picnicking. Or try a helicopter tour – the overhead view is a majestic sight, especially at the height of the wet season.

Further afield, explore the thermal springs at Mataranka, the plunge pools at Leliyn (Edith Falls) or the art galleries featuring work by Traditional Owners in and around Katherine. *See* p. 346.

Top: Territory Wildlife Park **Second from top:** Swimming at Florence Falls **Second from bottom:** Giant termite mound in Litchfield National Park **Bottom:** Tiwi weaving

Regions of Northern Territory

❶ TOP END
P. 336

Adelaide River
Batchelor
Jabiru ⭐
Nhulunbuy
Noonamah
Pine Creek

❷ GULF COUNTRY
P. 342

Borroloola
Daly Waters
Elliott
Katherine ⭐
Mataranka
Timber Creek

❸ RED CENTRE
P. 348

Aileron Hotel Roadhouse
Alice Springs/Mparntwe ⭐
Arltunga Historical Reserve
　Visitor Centre
Barrow Creek
Hermannsburg
Tennant Creek
Ti Tree
Wauchope
Yulara ⭐

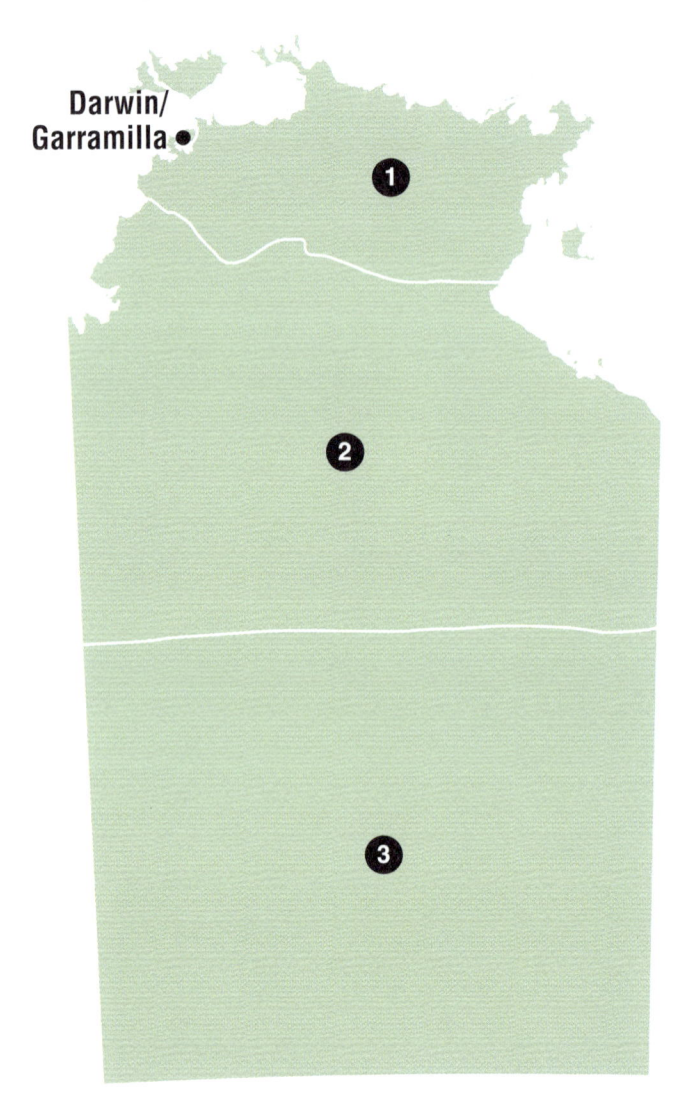

Opposite: Kununurra

NORTHERN TERRITORY

Top End

Welcome to the legendary Top End, where every day is an adventure. UNESCO World Heritage–listed **Kakadu National Park** is an absolute highlight, but **Litchfield National Park**, closer to Darwin, is every bit as spectacular. These parks have **plunging waterfalls, wetlands with birdlife galore, escarpments and lookouts**. Camping is a very special experience that capitalises on the Top End's **rugged natural beauty**. For those with a sense of adventure and time to spare, **Arnhem Land rewards with its rich and vibrant Yolngu culture and breathtaking beaches**.

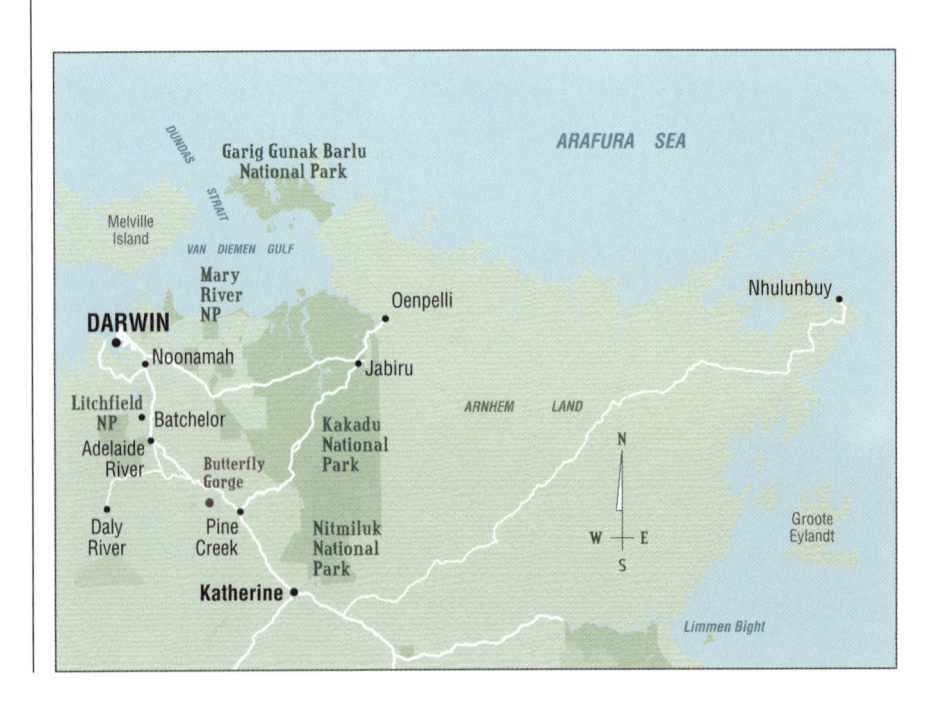

Top: Cruising on Yellow Water/Ngurrungurrudjba, Kakadu National Park
Opposite: The adventure of the Savannah Way

CHEAT SHEET

→ Litchfield is an easy daytrip from Darwin, but allow four days for a proper exploration of Kakadu. Add a week or longer to do a tour into Arnhem Land.

→ Best time to visit: June–Sept is the dry season, but Kakadu is accessible year-round and is even more spectacular in the Wet – a helicopter flight over the escarpment with the rugged sheer rocks and waterfalls is a real treat! Sept–Oct is the best time for barramundi fishing.

→ Main towns: Jabiru (see p. 340), Nhulunbuy (see p. 341).

→ The Traditional Owners of Kakadu National Park are the Bininj in the north and Mungguy in the south, and the park is jointly managed with Parks Australia: many people still practise culture in Traditional ways in Kakadu, and the park has one of the greatest concentrations of rock-art sites in the world. Arnhem Land (roughly the same size as Iceland) is Yolngu land, and largely governed by Traditional law. Yirrkala (near Nhulunbuy) is the birthplace of Native Land Rights in Australia.

→ Need to know: a national parks pass is required to visit Kakadu. Check online (parksaustralia.gov.au/kakadu/plan/passes) or at one of the visitor centres. If you're travelling to Gunbalanya or Arnhem Land, you'll also need permits (see p. 337).

→ Don't miss: rock-art galleries; a cruise on Yellow Water Billabong in Kakadu; floating in a plunge pool beneath a waterfall in Litchfield; fishing for barramundi; a crocodile spotting cruise on Adelaide River; and watching artists at work in art centres.

TOP ATTRACTIONS

ADELAIDE RIVER JUMPING CROCODILE CRUISES: Get up close and personal with wildlife as you watch crocodiles leap out of the water to catch food; several tours daily. Contact the visitor centre, 1300 138 886; Arnhem Hwy. It's 111km south-east of Darwin.

BUKU-LARRNGGAY MULKA: This renowned community-based art centre near Nhulunbuy (see p. 341) in north-eastern Arnhem Land is one of Australia's premier galleries. It was established in 1975 and supports the Yolngu People of Yirrkala and surrounding communities. The gallery is well known for bark paintings, memorial poles and woodcarvings including didgeridoos. A permit is not required to visit. Open Mon–Fri 8am–4.30pm, Sat 9am–12pm; (08) 8987 1701. En route to the gallery visit Rainbow Cliffs and Shady Beach, both covered by your permit from Dhimurru Aboriginal Corporation (see Nhulunbuy, p. 341).

DALY RIVER: Copper was discovered here in 1883 and mining began in 1884, which led to a bloody conflict between miners and the Traditional Owners. Today the town, located on the banks of the river, is a small community with some good camping facilities and is a very popular destination for fishing. Renowned for its large barramundi, there are two major fishing competitions every year, the Barra Nationals and the Barra Classic, plus Million Dollar Fish, running from Oct–Mar.

KAKADU NATIONAL PARK: A UNESCO World Heritage site listed for both its natural value and cultural significance, Kakadu is a place of rare beauty and grand landscapes, abundant flora and fauna, astonishing rock art and Dreaming. The Traditional Owners are the Bininj in the north and Mungguy in the south. Kakadu is a special place. It's important to respect the land and its people, and refrain from entering restricted areas, such as sacred sites, ceremonial sites and burial grounds. Kakadu encompasses the floodplain of the South Alligator River system and is bordered to the east by the massive escarpment of the Arnhem Land Plateau. The wide-ranging habitats, from arid sandstone hills, savannah woodlands and monsoon forests to freshwater floodplains and tidal mudflats, support an immense variety of wildlife – some rare, endangered or endemic. There are over 50 species of mammal, including kangaroos, wallabies, quolls, bandicoots, bats and dugongs, as well as a plethora of reptiles and birdlife. With around 5000 rock-art sites, the park has the world's largest and possibly oldest collection of rock art, which reveals the complex culture of the Traditional Owners since the Creation Time, when their ancestors are believed to have created all landforms and living things. Burrungkuy (Nourlangie Rock) is one of Kakadu's main rock-art areas. The **Nourlangie Art Site** walk takes visitors through a variety of rock-art styles, including prime examples of Kakadu X-ray art (see p. 339), which shows the anatomy of humans and animals in rich detail. The **Yellow Water/Ngurrungurrudjba** area is a spectacular wetland with prolific birdlife, especially in the dry season. Boat tours give visitors a close-up view of the birdlife and NT's crocodiles. Other highlights of the park include **Barrkmalam/Jim Jim Falls** and **Gungkurdul/Twin Falls**, reached via a 4WD track off the Kakadu Hwy. An incredible volume of water cascades over **Barrkmalam/Jim Jim Falls** in the wet season, when the falls can only be seen from the air. Not to be missed is sunset at **Ubirr** rock, with free ranger tours daily June–Sept. Traditional Owners once camped in the rock shelters there, leaving the legacy of a remarkable rock-art site. A 1km circuit covers the main natural galleries, which feature portrayals of extinct animals, including a thylacine (Tasmanian tiger) and animated figures in motion. Another highlight is a shorter sidetrack that climbs steeply to Nardab Lookout, a rocky vantage point with sensational views. Also in Kakadu, stop in at the **Warradjan Aboriginal Cultural Centre** in Cooinda, which features interactive and educational displays and exhibitions, as well as a gift shop. You need a Parks Pass to enter Kakadu National Park (book.parksaustralia.gov.au/passes/kakadu). **Gunbalanya/Oenpelli** in Arnhem Land is accessed across the East Alligator River (Cahill's Crossing) via a causeway at low tide (dry season only) and is about 60km north-east of Jabiru. **Injalak Arts** provides a fascinating insight into the local art and runs rock-art tours; a permit from the Northern Land Council is required to enter Gunbalanya; apply online (nlc.org.au/apply-for-permit).

LITCHFIELD NATIONAL PARK:
A world of waterfalls, gorges, pockets of rainforest, giant termite mounds and rock formations that resemble lost civilisations feature in this park that's easily accessible from Darwin. There are fantastic swimming spots, many beneath the waterfalls – most offer crocodile-free swimming but read the signs before you take the plunge into places like the rainforest-fringed pool at **Wangi Falls**, where you'll also find the Wangi Falls Cafe; usually open Mon–Sun. You can also swim beneath cascading **Florence Falls** or relax in the waters of **Buley Rockhole**. On the way to the waterfalls check out the magnetic termite mounds, so-called because they all align north–south. Do not miss the Lost City; these impressive sandstone pillar formations eerily resemble the ruins of a long-forgotten civilisation; access to this section of the park is by 4WD only.

TERRITORY WILDLIFE PARK:
This 400ha bushland park features native animals in their natural habitat. They can be seen from walking trails or an open train. Wander through the perspex tunnel in the aquarium and visit the nocturnal house or goose lagoon. Check out the daily program of events and don't miss the free-flying bird of prey display. Open 9am–4pm; Cox Peninsula Rd, Berry Springs; (08) 8988 7200.

OTHER ATTRACTIONS

ADELAIDE RIVER WAR CEMETERY: Australia's only war cemetery on native soil contains the graves of 434 military personnel. The adjacent civil section contains the graves of nine post-office staff killed on 19 February 1942, during the bombing of Darwin.

BUTTERFLY GORGE NATURE PARK: This park is a wilderness of sheer cliff-faces, dense vegetation and scenic, shady river walks. Butterfly Gorge was named for the butterflies that settle in its rock crevices and is a beautiful and safe swimming and picnic spot. Open only during the dry season (May–Sept); access is by 4WD only. The park is 113km north-west of Pine Creek (see p. 341).

FOGG DAM: Built in the 1950s to provide irrigation to the Humpty Doo Rice Project, the dam is a refuge for an amazing range of wildlife, especially waterbirds. Walks include the Monsoon Forest Walk, a 2.7km trail exploring a wide range of habitats, and there are also ranger-guided walks; off the Arnhem Hwy; (08) 8988 8009.

MOUNT BUNDY STATION: Alongside the Adelaide River this cattle station offers 4WD tours, fishing, walking, swimming and a wide range of accommodation including camping; (08) 8976 7009. It's 3km north-east of Adelaide River township (see p. 339).

ROBIN FALLS: A pleasant 30min walk to falls that flow most of the year. It's 15km south of Adelaide River township (see p. 339).

TJUWALIYN (DOUGLAS) HOT SPRINGS PARK: Laze in the natural thermal hot springs or the cool pools downstream. There are sacred sites to the Wagiman women, and men are asked to not visit them; off Stuart Hwy. At the time of writing, the park was closed due to water supply issues so it's best to check ahead; go to nt.gov.au or call the Ranger Station on (08) 8999 3947.

UMBRAWARRA GORGE NATURE PARK: Good swimming, rock climbing and walking trails and camping.

Top: Florence Falls, Litchfield National Park **Bottom:** General store at Daly River

VISITOR INFORMATION

Tourism Top End
6 Bennett St, Darwin
(08) 8980 6000 or
1300 138 886
tourismtopend.com.au;
northernterritory.com

KEY TOWNS

ADELAIDE RIVER
Population 243

Adelaide River is a small town with a sprawling pub and several important attractions. It is located midway between Darwin and Pine Creek and makes an ideal stopover if you've been on the road for a while. During the dry season a small market operates in the middle of the town. A settlement was established here as a base for workers on the Overland Telegraph Line in the early 1870s. The building of the Northern Australia Railway, which operated from 1888 to 1976, further increased its significance on the north–south track. During World War II, the town was a major military base for 30,000 Australian and US soldiers. Follow the river down to the Adelaide River War Cemetery, a peaceful and moving place.

SEE & DO **Adelaide River Jumping Crocodile Cruises:** see Top Attractions. **Adelaide River War Cemetery; Mount Bundy Station:** see Other Attractions for both. **Adelaide River Inn and Resort:** this hotel was a favourite watering hole for soldiers during World War II and still has war photographs and memorabilia adorning the walls. Hard to ignore is its main attraction, Charlie the Buffalo, taxidermied, from the film *Crocodile Dundee*. Meals and accommodation are available. Stuart Hwy; (08) 8976 7047. **Adelaide River Railway Station:** National Trust–classified station (1888), now a museum featuring relics of local history, including the railway construction and World War II; open 9am–5pm (Apr–Sept); Stuart Hwy; (08) 8976 7101. **Old Stuart Hwy Scenic Route:** runs for 61km from Adelaide River, past Robin Falls (15km S) and the turn-off to Daly River to rejoin the Stuart Hwy just north of Hayes Creek.

BATCHELOR
Population 371

Batchelor was initially established as an experimental farming region to assess the economic viability of the NT. During World War II a large air-force base was set up, strategically placed to defend the northern part of Australia. After the war, Batchelor became prominent with the discovery of uranium at nearby Rum Jungle in 1949. Today the town thrives on tourism, particularly because of its proximity to Litchfield National Park.

SEE & DO **Litchfield National Park:** see Top Attractions. **Rum Jungle:** Czech immigrant Bernie Havlik worked at Rum Jungle and was a gardener there until his retirement in 1977. As a gardener he had been frustrated by a rocky outcrop that was too large to move and too difficult to keep tidy, so he decided to build over it. Havlik spent five years constructing a mini replica of the original Karlstein Castle that still stands in Bohemia. He added finishing touches, despite serious illness, and died just after its completion;

FIRST PEOPLE'S ROCK ART IN THE NORTHERN TERRITORY

First Nations People have inhabited the Australian continent for at least 65,000 years. Their extraordinary history and connection to the land is recorded in artwork at special and sacred rock sites.

Rock art portrays representations of life, with paintings of animals, rituals and tales connected to the Dreaming; they are important links to Creation stories and the spirituality of ancestors. Rock-art sites are often found in gorges and on rocky outliers, and are incredibly precious. Carbon dating in Arnhem Land has shown that rock art there is some of the most ancient in the world.

The opportunity to see rock art is a highlight of any visit to the Northern Territory. The quality of the art, its age and the often spectacular natural setting make for an absorbing and moving experience.

As an example, in Kakadu National Park the rich repository of rock art is one of the major reasons it attained UNESCO World Heritage status. Paintings here are up to 20,000 years old, making it one of the oldest records of human existence in the world. You'll find traditional X-ray art, depicting the insides of animals, and there are even images of early European contact; and art in the Yam Figure style – yams incorporated into human forms – which are about 8000 years old.

Rock art is incredibly fragile. Always treat the sites with respect and be careful not to do anything to degrade or damage the paintings. Don't touch the rocks, and never try to scramble over them for a better view. And of course, never remove any objects without permission from the Traditional Owners.

TOP END CROCODILES

Estuarine or saltwater crocodiles, or 'salties', are the world's largest reptile. They have a fearsome reputation in the Northern Territory ... and it's well deserved. Nothing has knocked the saltwater crocodile off the top of the food chain in Australia's north in the last 100 million years. Due to their numbers, which have increased in recent years (saltwater crocodiles are a protected species), you have a good chance of crossing paths with one on a visit to the Northern Territory. The biggest you will likely see is four or five metres long (big enough!), but males can grow to a staggering seven metres – a full-grown male croc is an awesome and seriously scary sight. The highest concentration of salties in the Top End is around Darwin and, in particular, the Mary River.

Remember that salties are found in salt and fresh water, often far inland. They live along tidal rivers, in floodplains and freshwater wetlands. Salties are aggressive, and are quite happy to munch on a foolish or unlucky human.

The smaller freshwater crocodiles have a narrower snout, and are found in freshwater rivers or billabongs. They – unlike their saltie cousins – are not dangerous to humans unless provoked.

Check with local authorities about croc danger, and keep in mind these safety tips:

1. Obey all crocodile warning signs – they are there for a reason, even if you don't see any crocodiles.
2. Do not assume that a body of water is safe if no sign is present – this includes shallow pools, drainage canals and ditches.
3. Keep a close eye on kids around water sources.
4. When camping, pitch your tent or park your camper well away from the water, and preferably on high ground. If setting up camp on a beach, be aware that estuarine crocodiles sometimes wander around on the shore at night.
5. If you are fishing, stand well back from the water's edge. Never wade into the water.
6. If you're in a boat or kayak, do not dangle your arms or legs over the side; that's just asking for trouble.

The local newspaper, the *NT News*, invariably has regular stories of gruesome croc attacks (including decapitation). Such holiday horrors are avoidable with a bit of common sense.

If you're keen to see a croc in action, the 'jumping crocs' in the Adelaide River (*see* p. 339) will get your adrenaline pumping, and Crocosaurus Cove (*see* p. 331) brings the crocs to city folk, with massive salties in purpose-built aquariums right in the middle of Darwin's CBD.

Rum Jungle Rd. **Lake Bennett Resort:** this resort has a plethora of birdlife and native fauna that can be enjoyed in the many serene picnic areas. A range of activities are available, including canoe hire, golf, swimming and barramundi fishing. Dining and accommodation are onsite; Chinner Rd; 0437 513 198; 18km NE. **Rum Jungle Lake:** canoeing, kayaking, diving and swimming; 10km W.

★ JABIRU
Population 755

Located at the easterly end of Kakadu National Park, Jabiru was first established because of the nearby uranium mine. But the mine closed in early 2021 and Jabiru is now a tourist destination supporting the thousands who come to explore Kakadu each year. Facilities include accommodation, camping, a supermarket, bank and a large town swimming pool. In 2021, Jabiru was returned to the Mirarr Traditional Owners.

SEE & DO **Kakadu National Park:** *see* Top Attractions. **Mercure Kakadu Crocodile Hotel:** this NT icon is a 250m crocodile-shaped building that really only resembles a crocodile from the air. The entrance (the mouth of the crocodile) leads to a cool marble reception area, designed to represent a billabong, and accommodation is in the belly of the beast. There's a full range of accommodation options, a restaurant and bar. Flinders St; (08) 8979 9000. **Bowali Visitor Centre:** interpretive displays on Kakadu and its ecology; plus tour bookings, permits, a gallery and cafe. Access is via a 1.5km walking track from Jabiru. **Scenic flights:** over Kakadu parklands to see inaccessible sandstone formations standing 300m above vast floodplains, seasonal waterfalls, wetland wilderness, remote beaches and ancient rock-art sites; 6km E. **Indigenous cultural tours:** day tours and cruises, including the Guluyambi Cultural Cruise on the East Alligator River; contact Bowali Visitor Centre.

Top: You can get off-the-beaten track in Kakadu
Bottom: Termite mound, Kakadu

TOP EVENTS

- APR NT Barra Classic (Daly River)
- MAY Taste of Kakadu
- MAY Barra Nationals (Daly River)
- JUNE Gold Rush Festival and Gold Panning Championships (Pine Creek)
- JUNE Merrepen Arts Festival (Daly River)
- JULY–AUG Garma Festival (Nhulunbuy)
- OCT Kakadu Bird Week
- OCT–MAR Million Dollar Fish (across the Top End)

TEMPERATURES

Jan: 25–32°C

July: 19–31°C

NHULUNBUY
Population 3267

The eastern Arnhem Land region is the land of the Yolngu People. It is known for its rugged, sublime landscapes and picture-postcard beaches. Getting here is an adventure but it is well worthwhile for visitors with some adventure and extra time up their sleeve. Located on the north-eastern tip of Arnhem Land on the Gove Peninsula, Nhulunbuy and its surrounds are held freehold by the Yolngu People. The town was originally established to service the bauxite-mining industry. Access is by a year-round daily air service from Darwin or Cairns, or, with a permit, by 4WD only, through Arnhem Land via the Central Arnhem Road. It is over 1000km from Darwin. The annual Garma Festival (July–Aug) is the largest meeting of First Nations Elders, federal politicians and policy makers in the country, as well as a celebration of culture. Visitors intending to drive to Nhulunbuy must obtain permits from the Northern Land Council beforehand (nlc.org.au or phone 08 8920 5100) and from Dhimurru Aboriginal Corporation (dhimurru.com.au). Allow two weeks for processing for permits. It's 4WD only; conventional caravans are not allowed; conditions also apply. Suggested itineraries for the area are available at easternhemland.com.au.

SEE & DO **Buku-Larrnggay Mulka:** see Top Attractions. **Gayngaru Wetlands Interpretive Walk:** the path surrounds an attractive lagoon that is home to around 200 bird species. There are two viewing platforms and a bird hide, as well as signs near local flora explaining their uses in Traditional food and bush medicine. **Ray Marika Lookout:** at the summit of Nhulunbuy, the hill that gave the town its name. **Scenic flights:** several airlines offer scenic flights and transfers to nearby islands; refer to easternhemland.com.au. **Dhamitjinya (East Woody Island) and Galaru (East Woody Beach):** Gove Peninsula has long sandy beaches, tropical clear-blue water and amazing sunset views; 3km N.

NOONAMAH
Population 328

Located 45km south of Darwin, Noonamah is close to Litchfield National Park and within easy reach of the Arnhem Hwy and Kakadu National Park. It makes a good base from which to experience wildlife, native bushland and safe swimming spots (something of a rarity, considering the NT's crocodile population). The Melbourne Cup Frog Races are usually held on the first Tues in Nov.

SEE & DO **Kakadu National Park; Litchfield National Park:** see Top Attractions for both. **Didgeridoo Hut and Art Gallery:** this Aboriginal-owned art gallery has a diverse range of artworks and sometimes there are artists in residence; open Mon–Sun 9am–7pm; Arnhem Hwy, Humpty Doo; (08) 8988 4457; 8km N. **Berry Springs Nature Park:** safe swimming in spring-fed pools in a monsoon forest, with pleasant walking trails and picnic areas; 13km SW. **Jenny's Orchid Garden:** a huge and colourful collection of tropical orchids – many on sale – and a tea house; Niel Crt, Howard Springs; (08) 8983 1641; 22km NW. **Howard Springs Nature Park:** take a walk, have a swim or relax with a picnic in the shade by the children's pool; 23km NW. **Manton Dam:** safe swimming, fishing, watersports and shady picnic spots; 25km S. **Fishing:** excellent barramundi fishing at Mary River Crossing (45km E of Fogg Dam turn-off); several 4WD tracks lead north from there to prime fishing spots in Mary River National Park, including Corroboree Billabong.

PINE CREEK
Population 318

This town was named Pine Creek by Overland Telegraph workers because of the prolific pine trees growing along the banks of the tiny creek. During the 1800s it was the centre of Chinese settlement on the Top End goldfields. Today the town benefits from an active mining industry and is a regular stop for travellers going up and down the Stuart Hwy.

SEE & DO **Butterfly Gorge Nature Park:** see Other Attractions. **Railway Precinct:** this area and station (1888) is at the terminus of the uncompleted 19th-century transcontinental railway system and now houses photographs and memorabilia; open intermittently May–Sept. The nearby historic **Beyer Peacock steam train** was built at Manchester in England in 1877 and the adjacent **Miners Park** points to an important visible link between the railway and the mines. There are interpretive signs and displays of old mining machinery that reflect life on the goldfields. Nearby is the historic **Walk through Time**, a footpath of tiles painted by local artists; Main Tce. **Water Gardens:** ponds with walking trails, birdlife and picnic spots; Main Tce. **Pine Creek National Trust Museum:** once a doctor's residence, military hospital, then post office, and considered the oldest prefabricated structure in the Territory, the building now houses a historical collection, including a display on the Overland Telegraph; Railway Tce. **The Pine Creek Lookout:** panoramic views of the open-cut goldmine that was once Enterprise Hill but is now a water-filled pit. **Town walk:** takes in historic buildings and mining sites; get a brochure from Lazy Lizard Tavern. **Lake Copperfield:** safe swimming in deep-water lake and picnicking on foreshore; 6km SW. **The Moline Rockhole:** attractive, secluded waterhole; 4WD access only (via Kakadu Hwy); 65km NE. **Gold fossicking:** several locations; licence required (available along with maps from visitor centre).

Gulf Country

A journey along the edge of the Gulf of Carpentaria at the Top End of Australia on the **Savannah Way** – an epic trans-continental driving route from Cairns to Broome – is a true adventure. Be blown away by the dramatic scenery **of Nitmiluk Gorge,** luxuriate in **thermal pools**, marvel at **sandstone spires** and take a deep dive into Australia's past. If you have a 4WD, get off the beaten path and tackle the tracks of **Judbarra/ Gregory National Park** for some spectacular **riverside camping spots.**

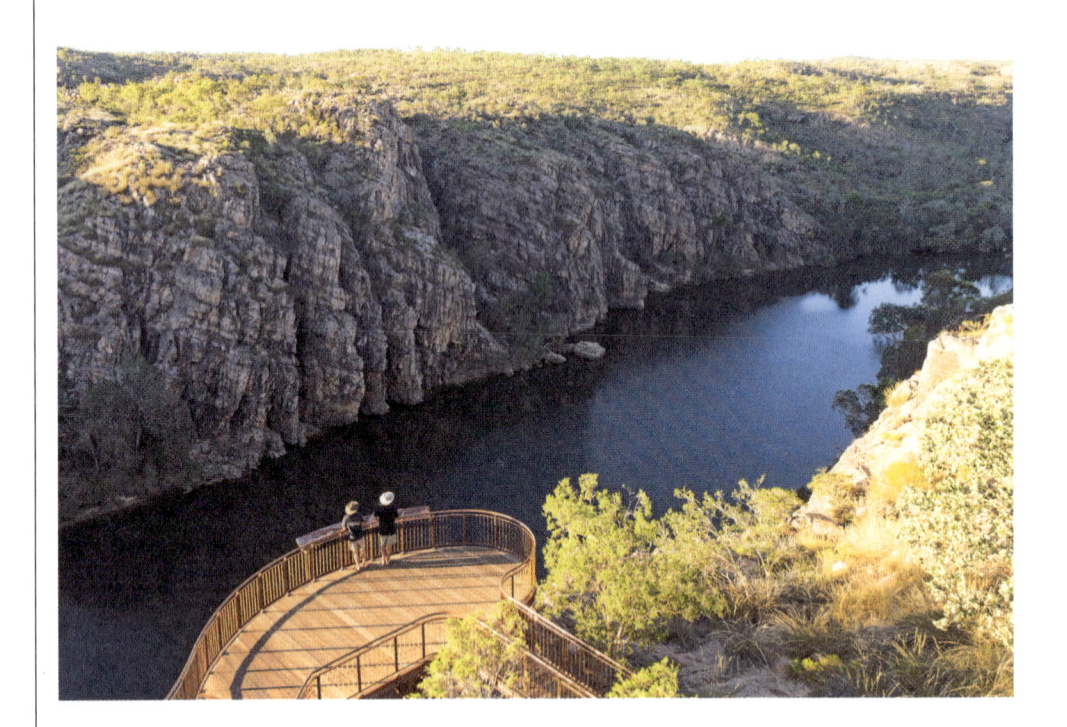

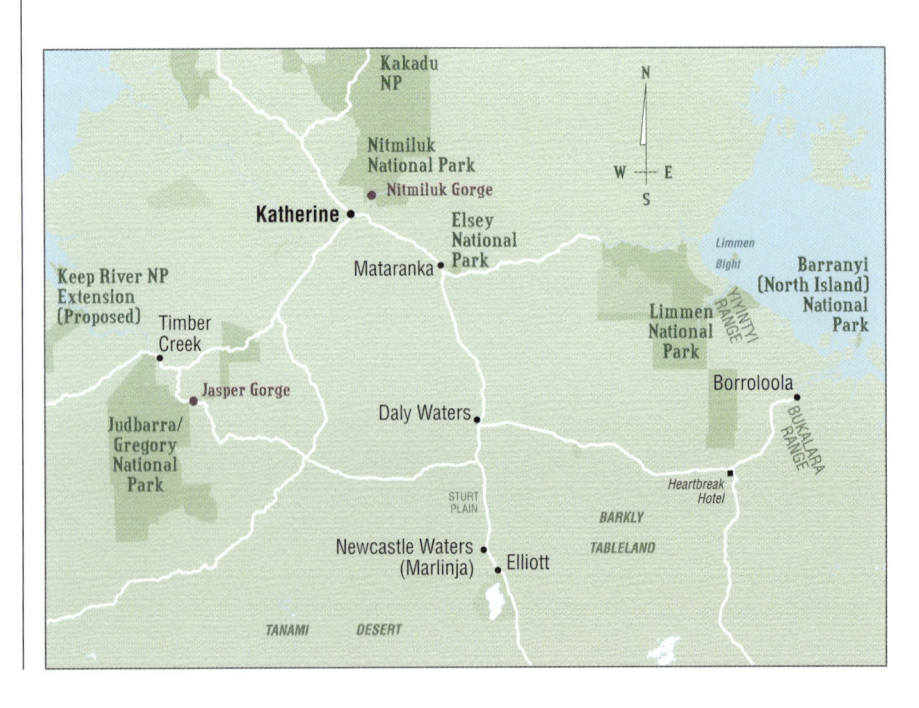

CHEAT SHEET

→ Allow at least a week for proper exploration.

→ Best time to visit: May–Sept.

→ Main town: Katherine (see p. 346).

→ Like most of the Northern Territory, First Nations cultures enrich almost every corner of the Gulf Country. There are many nations that call this part of the continent home, including the Jawoyn People, who are the Traditional Owners of the land around Katherine and Nitmiluk National Park.

→ Need to know: you don't need a 4WD to explore Gulf Country, although if you do it will mean you can get into some of the more remote areas. Be adequately prepared with appropriate shoes, clothing, sunscreen, supplies and water and stay on marked trails. This is saltwater crocodile country: for safety information see box p. 340.

→ Don't miss: a cruise, canoe trip or guided tour in Nitmiluk Gorge; soaking in the hot springs of Mataranka; Cape Crawford's surreal Lost City; and exploring the wilderness of Judbarra/Gregory National Park.

Top: Swimming at the springs at Mataranka
Opposite: Viewing deck, Nitmiluk National Park

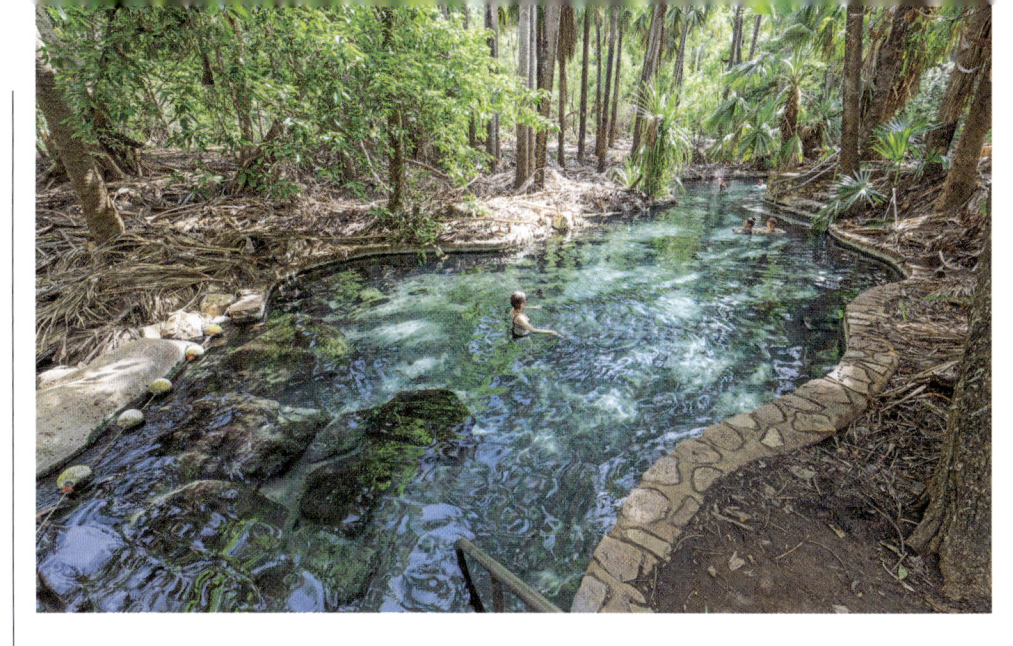

TOP ATTRACTIONS

CAPE CRAWFORD: This tiny outpost is an excellent base for exploring Bukalara Rocks (60km E) and the Lost City (20km SE), both part of the Caranbirini Conservation Reserve. Bukalara Rocks are a mass of chasms winding through ancient sandstone structures (the area is very remote and a local guide is recommended; ask at the Heartbreak Hotel). The Lost City is a collection of sandstone turrets, domes and arches formed by water seeping through cracks and eroding the sandstone. It is an important Gadanji ceremonial site and accessible only by air or 4WD (flights can be arranged from Cape Crawford). Cape Crawford is the site of the iconic Heartbreak Hotel, one of the outback's most remote stopovers; (08) 8975 9928. It's 110km south-west of Borroloola (see p. 345).

DALY WATERS PUB: Known as one of the great authentic Australian pubs with characters to match, the corrugated-iron pub was built in 1934 and wandering around the grounds is almost like visiting a museum. It is famous for its Beef and Barra barbecue nights during the dry season. Accommodation is available at the hotel, the campground or cabins across the road. Stuart St; (08) 8975 9927.

ELSEY NATIONAL PARK: The park encircles the Roper River, with rainforest, paperbark woodlands and tufa limestone formations at the small but beautiful **Mataranka Falls**; the walk from Twelve Mile Yards leads to the falls. The Roper River offers excellent barramundi fishing but fishing regulations apply. There are scenic walking tracks through pockets of rainforest with wildlife observation points and camping areas. **Bitter Springs** thermal pools are an ideal place to relax and unwind.

JUDBARRA/GREGORY NATIONAL PARK: This is the NT's second largest national park with two sections covering 13,000sqkm of ranges, gorges, sandstone escarpments, remnant rainforest, eucalypts and boab trees. The land is still used by the Traditional Owners, and one of Australia's largest rock-art sites can be seen here. There are opportunities for boating, canoeing, bushwalking, scenic flights and cruises, as well as European heritage sites to see. A boab tree known as **Gregory's Tree** (just off the Victoria Hwy) stands at the site of explorer Augustus Charles Gregory's campsite and bears inscriptions from 1885. The tree also has significance for the Ngariman People and is a registered sacred site. The park has a huge network of 4WD tracks with access only in the dry season. The old Bullita Homestead still stands and includes traditional timber stockyards, interpretive displays and shady camping spots. There are saltwater crocodiles throughout the national park so do not swim. Check ahead for current park access details and safety tips (nt.gov.au/parks/find-a-park/judbarra-gregory-national-park).

NITMILUK NATIONAL PARK: Near Katherine, this 292,800ha wilderness featuring Nitmiluk Gorge is owned by the Jawoyn People and managed jointly with Parks and Wildlife Commission NT. High above the floodline, on the overhangs of the ancient rock walls, is rock art that is thousands of years old. The best way to explore the gorge is on daily cruises or by hiring a canoe (bookings at visitor centre). You can also swim or explore the 100km network of bushwalking tracks. Other highlights include a ferry or hike to Southern Rockhole or a detour to Leliyn (Edith Falls). Fauna in Nitmiluk includes kangaroos and wallabies in higher reaches and rare birds such as the hooded parrot and Gouldian finch. Magnificent scenery can be enjoyed from helicopter tours, scenic flights and boat cruises, especially during the Wet. For more information and bookings contact the Nitmiluk Visitor Centre at the park; 1300 146 743.

OTHER ATTRACTIONS

BARRANYI (NORTH ISLAND) NATIONAL PARK: Sun-drenched wilderness with long sandy beaches and excellent angling; no permit is required but visitors are requested to register with Borroloola Ranger Station.

CUTTA CUTTA CAVES NATURE PARK: The only accessible tropical limestone caves in the NT, with fascinating stalactite and stalagmite formations 15m underground; regular tours daily; 1300 146 743.

FLORA RIVER/GIWINING NATURE PARK: Great campsites, interesting mineral formations and cascades along the river; saltwater crocodiles so do not swim; 4WD recommended.

JASPER GORGE: Scenic gorge with permanent waterhole and rock art; 48km SE of Timber Creek; 4WD recommended.

KATHERINE HOT SPRINGS: On the banks of the Katherine River, with picnic facilities and walking trails; nearby is the **Low Level Nature Reserve**, featuring a weir built by US soldiers during World War II, now a popular waterhole for picnicking; both are 3km south of Katherine.

KATHERINE MUSEUM: Built as an air terminal in 1944–45, the museum houses artefacts, maps, photographs and farming displays. There is also memorabilia relating to Dr Clyde Fenton, who, as a pioneer medical aviator and Katherine's Medical Officer between 1934 and 1937, travelled an area of 8,000,000sqkm in a second-hand Gypsy Moth. The plane is on display; open Mon–Fri 9am–4pm; Sat 9am–2pm (April–Nov); Gorge Rd; (08) 8972 3945.

KEEP RIVER NATIONAL PARK: On the WA border, the park includes the traditional land of the Miriwoong and Kadjerong Peoples. There are a number of walks that lead to important rock-art sites, including Jinumum and Ginger Hill. Other attractions include rugged sandstone formations similar to the Bungle Bungles (Purnululu National Park). There are designated camping areas and good walking tracks. Check ahead for access details (nt.gov.au/parks/find-a-park/keep-river-national-park).

KING ASH BAY: On the McArthur River and popular for fishing and camping year-round; (08) 8975 9800.

LIMMEN RIVER FISHING CAMP: Ideal conditions for barramundi and mud crabs. Accommodation is available but check road access in the wet season.

LIMMEN NATIONAL PARK: Fascinating sandstone pinnacles and towers; camping, birdwatching and fishing. The park is isolated and accessible only in the dry season. Check with Parks and Wildlife Commission NT for access details (nt.gov.au/parks/find-a-park/limmen-national-park).

MATARANKA HOMESTEAD: Enjoy a swim in the beautiful thermal pool here surrounded by palm trees. There are self-contained cabins, motel rooms and powered campsites. The 1982 movie *We of the Never Never* was filmed here, and the replica of the original homestead is still part of the attractions; (08) 8975 4544.

RENNER SPRINGS: Roadside stop on the Stuart Hwy, said to mark where the tropical Top End gives way to the dry Red Centre. It was named after Frederick Renner, doctor to workers on the Overland Telegraph Line in the 19th century. Renner discovered the springs when he noticed flocks of birds gathering in the area. Fuel, supplies and meals are available, and there are pleasant picnic and barbecue facilities; (08) 8964 4505.

SEVEN EMU STATION: Owned and operated by the Shadforth family – Garawa People – for four generations this working cattle station is believed to be the first pastoral lease in the country to be purchased by an Aboriginal family. Enjoy camping and fishing and tour the wildlife sanctuary, but you'll need a 4WD to get there; (08) 8975 9904.

VICTORIA RIVER ROADHOUSE: Accommodation and camping where the Victoria Hwy crosses the Victoria River. Cruises and fishing trips are available. There are also several scenic walks in the area including the Nawulbinbin Walk, a 1.7km loop walk (10km W).

VISITOR INFORMATION

Katherine Visitor Information Centre
Cnr Katherine Tce (Stuart Hwy) and Lindsay St
(08) 8972 2650 or 1800 653 142
visitkatherine.com.au; northernterritory.com/katherine-and-surrounds

TOP EVENTS

→ EASTER Barra Classic (Borroloola)
→ MAY Never Never Festival (Mataranka)
→ JUNE–JULY Barunga Festival (near Katherine)

TEMPERATURES

Jan: 24–35°C

July: 13–30°C

Keep River National Park
Opposite: Katherine Hot Springs

KEY TOWNS

BORROLOOLA
Population 755

Located beside the McArthur River, Borroloola is a small settlement known for its fishing and incredible surrounding scenery, and is a particular favourite with 4WD enthusiasts. It lies at the heart of the Gulf Country, at the junction of the Savannah Way and the sealed all-weather Carpentaria Hwy. The town is on land belonging to the Yanyuwa Traditional Owners, but no permit is required to enter. Borroloola also offers access to the waters around North Island/Barranyi National Park.

SEE & DO **Cape Crawford:** *see* Top Attractions. **Old Police Station Museum:** built in 1886, the museum is the oldest surviving outpost in the NT and displays memorabilia and photographs that illustrate the town's history. It is managed by the NT National Trust; Johns St; 0438 331465. **Fishing charters:** river and offshore fishing trips; bookings at visitor centre. **Scenic flights:** over town and the islands of the Sir Edward Pellew Group; brochures at visitor centre.

DALY WATERS
Population 55

This tiny town has a significant amount of history plus there's a fun and famous pub and plenty of accommodation options. It makes a great stopover between Alice Springs/Mparntwe and Darwin/Garramilla. Scottish Explorer John McDouall Stuart stopped here during his north–south journey in 1862 across Australia and carved an S on a nearby tree; 10 years later, the Overland Telegraph Line came through. Believe it or not the town also boasts Australia's first international airport.

SEE & DO **Daly Waters Pub:** once a supply point for drovers and now a major tourist attraction. It is also part of the historic Stuart Trail which links the town's seven historical sites, including the original buildings surrounding Stuart's Tree. **Daly Waters Aviation Complex:** check out the display on local aviation in the oldest hangar in the NT (1930); the key is available from the pub. **Historic marker:** commemorates the joining of the north and south sections of the Overland Telegraph Line; 79km S. **Larrimah:** remains of historic World War II building at Gorrie Airfield, and museum with relics of the war and the local transport industry.

ELLIOTT
Population 287

Elliott is right in the middle of the NT, on the Stuart Hwy. A popular stopping point for travellers, it is also rich in military history. It was named after Lieutenant Snow Elliott, the officer in charge of an army camp here during World War II. Nearby is the once-thriving old droving town of Newcastle Waters, which features historic buildings and a bronze statue, The Drover. It is a haven for birds – and photographers.

★ KATHERINE
Population 5980

The best reason to come to Katherine is to visit the gorges at nearby Nitmiluk National Park. For opportunities to speak with the Traditional Owners, the Jawoyn People, contact the visitor centre. Take a self-guided walk or hire a bike – there is plenty to explore in and around Katherine. On the south side of the Katherine River, the town has always been a busy and important area for the Traditional Owners, who used the river and gorge as meeting places. Explorer John McDouall Stuart 'named' the river on his way through in 1862 after the second daughter of James Chambers, one of his expedition sponsors. The town grew up around an Overland Telegraph station. Note that opening hours for attractions and national parks are subject to the weather during the wet season.

SEE & DO **Nitmiluk National Park:** *see* Top Attractions. **Katherine Museum; Katherine Hot Springs:** *see* Other Attractions for both. **Godinymayin Yijard Rivers Arts and Culture Centre:** performing arts centre that also showcases local artworks; Tues–Sat; Stuart Hwy; (08) 8972 3751. **Top Didj Cultural Experience:** learn about Traditional culture through painting, fire lighting and spear throwing; also a wide range of local art on display; open Apr–Oct; 0414 888 786. **O'Keefe House:** one of the oldest houses in town, was built during World War II and used as the officers' mess. It became home to Sister Olive O'Keefe, whose work with the Flying Doctor and Katherine Hospital from the 1930s to the 1950s made her a NT identity; Riverbank Dr. **Katherine Outback Experience:** a live performance bringing to life an outback cattle station. Includes horse-breaking and working dog demonstrations; 115 Collins Rd; 1300 818 612. **Mimi Aboriginal Art & Craft:** Aboriginal community-owned and -operated gallery with workshops and art from all around the Territory. Sometimes artists are available to share stories; 34 Katherine Tce; Mon–Fri 8.30am–4.30pm or by appointment; (08) 8971 0036. **Knotts Crossing:** site of this region's first Overland Telegraph station (1870s), around which the township of Katherine developed; Giles St; 2km E. **Katherine Community Market:** farmers' market in Lindsay St; Sat 8am–12pm (April–Nov).

MATARANKA
Population 327

Visitors are lured to Mataranka for a dip in its refreshing thermal springs – check out Bitter Springs in Elsey National Park or the pools at Mataranka Homestead – and a sense of literary history: Jeannie Gunn, author of *We of the Never Never*, lived at nearby Elsey Station in the early 20th century. The town has adopted the term 'Never Never', using it to name a museum and a festival.

SEE & DO **Elsey National Park:** *see* Top Attractions. **Mataranka Homestead Resort:** *see* Other Attractions. **The Never Never Museum:** outdoor displays of early settler life, railway and military history, and the Overland Telegraph; Mon–Fri 9am–4pm; next to the Roper Gulf Shire Offices, Stuart Hwy; (08) 8975 4576. **Giant termite mound:** sculpture with recorded information; Stuart Hwy. **Elsey Cemetery:** graves of outback settlers immortalised by Jeannie Gunn, who lived on Elsey Station from 1902 to 1903; 20km SE. **Old Elsey Homestead:** a cairn marks the site of the original homestead near the cemetery; 20km SE.

TIMBER CREEK
Population 278

The Ngaliwurra People are the Traditional Owners of the Timber Creek area. In 1855, explorer A.C. Gregory followed the Victoria River south from the Timor Sea and his boat was wrecked at what is now Timber Creek. Cattle and sheep graziers came to the area many years later, following the Overland Telegraph Line from SA. Victoria River Downs became one of the largest properties in Australia. In the town's heyday the river access played a major role in the history of the NT. Timber Creek is now an important stop on the journey from the Kimberley in WA to the major centres of the NT, and is a gateway to Judbarra-Gregory National Park.

SEE & DO **Judbarra/Gregory National Park:** *see* Top Attractions. **Timber Creek Police Station Museum:** displays of historic artefacts in restored police station (1908); Mon–Fri 10am–12pm; off Victoria Hwy. **Katherine Visitor Information Centre:** for information on **boat and fishing tours, river cruises** (with many opportunities to see crocodiles) and **scenic flights**; (08) 8972 2650.

Top: A water buffalo near the turn-off to Judbarra/Gregory National Park
Opposite: Kayaking at Nitmiluk

BUYING A YIDAKI (DIDGERIDOO) IN THE NORTHERN TERRITORY

A yidaki, often called a didgeridoo, is a popular souvenir to take home from a trip to the Northern Territory. It is an artwork as well as a musical instrument and, for First Nations People, it possesses deep cultural significance. According to the AIATSIS website, the term 'didgeridoo' was coined by anthropologist Herbert Basedow, 'who likened the word to the sound of it being played'. Yidaki is the name for this instrument in Yolngu matha, the language of the Yolngu People, and other communities have their own names for it. It's also worth noting that cultural protocols dictate that the yidaki is only played by men.

The NT is a great place to buy the genuine article, and a certificate of authenticity should be available if it was made and decorated by a First Nations artist. To test its authenticity, run your finger around the inside of the instrument – it should be rough; if it's even and smooth then it was probably bored out by a drill. Mass-produced didgeridoos or 'fakes' are usually made in a factory instead of individually by an artist, and are generally way overpriced.

A genuine yidaki is made from eucalypt wood, naturally hollowed out by termites. Each instrument is unique depending on the tree it came from, how it was cut and then decorated. Before you buy it, listen to the drone the yidaki makes – this can vary from low and deep to high-pitched. What you choose is simply based on your preference. The yidaki's mouthpiece is often moulded with beeswax (unless the end is naturally smooth). Beeswax mouthpieces create a better seal when playing, and are soft, making it more comfortable to play your yidaki.

Katherine is the major centre for artists making didgeridoos, so the instruments tend to be cheaper here, and most vendors are happy to provide a buyer with a quick lesson. The main two galleries are Mimi Aboriginal Art & Craft (see p. 346) and Top Didj Cultural Experience (see p. 346). But there are many other outlets, especially in Alice Springs/Mparntwe and Darwin/Garramilla, where an authentic didgeridoo can also be purchased. Buku-Larrnggay Mulka in Yirrkala is another excellent option, and many businesses now have online shops.

Red Centre

Travelling through Australia's red heart is a mesmerising experience of landscapes and **First Nations culture. Wide open spaces of red rock, horizons of vast blue skies, canyons, gorges and one very big 'rock'!** From Alice Springs/Mparntwe you can **drive the Red Centre Way** and head south on the Stuart Highway to **Uluṟu–Kata Tjuṯa National Park**. Then take the route to **Kings Canyon to walk the rim of the gorge** before checking out the **escarpments, gorges and waterholes** of **Tjoritja/West MacDonnell Ranges** on the way back to Alice Springs/Mparntwe.

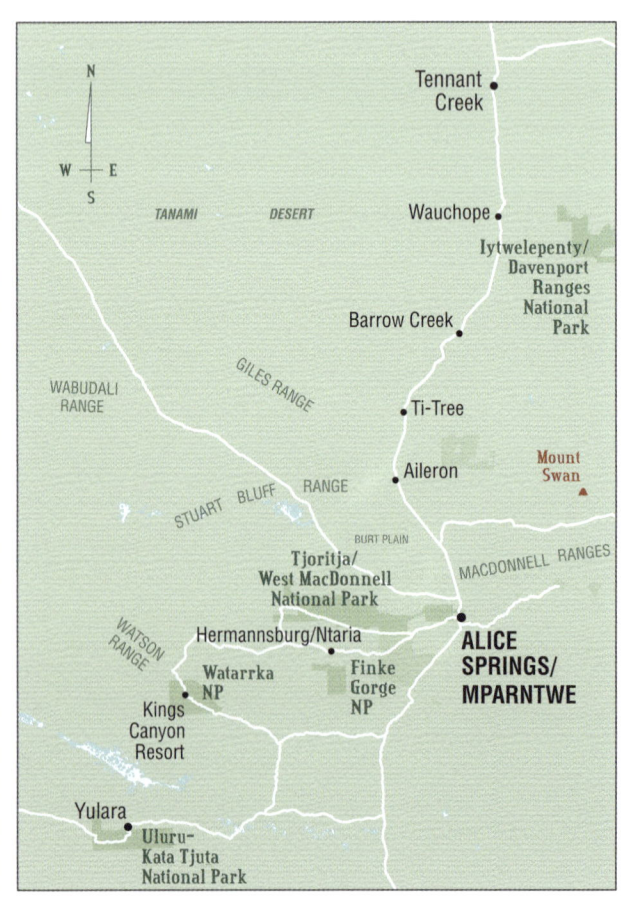

CHEAT SHEET

→ Allow at least a week for a proper exploration. It's a little over 1000km to drive the Red Centre Way loop, so plan to spend at least five days and immerse yourself in the experience of the Centre.

→ Best time to visit: May–Sept

→ Main towns: Alice Springs/Mparntwe (see p. 352), Tennant Creek (see p. 354).

→ First Nations cultures enrich almost every corner of the Red Centre. Uluru is on Anangu land and is the most famous sacred space. Climbing Uluru is no longer allowed out of respect to the Anangu People's Dreaming, Tjukurpa – and because of safety concerns. Alice Springs/Mparntwe is Central Arrernte Country. The East MacDonnell Ranges are home to some extraordinary rock art.

→ Did you know? It is believed two-thirds of Uluru lies beneath the ground.

→ Need to know: be adequately prepared with appropriate shoes, clothing, sunscreen, supplies and water for walking, stay on marked trails, and check road conditions and 4WD requirements ahead of travel.

→ Don't miss: sunrise and sunset at Uluru and the Sounds of Silence dinner; the Kings Canyon Rim Walk and splashing about in a waterhole in Tjoritja/West MacDonnell Ranges.

Opposite: Finke Gorge National Park

TOP ATTRACTIONS

ALICE SPRINGS DESERT PARK: David Attenborough was so impressed by this desert park that he proclaimed, 'There is no museum or wildlife park in the world that could match it'. The park invites visitors to explore the arid lands and the relationship between plants, animals and people. A walking trail leads through three habitats: desert rivers, sand country and woodland. There are films, interactive displays, free audio-guides, guided day tours, nocturnal tours (to experience the Central Australian desert at night), and talks about flora and fauna. You can also learn about the ingenuity of the First Peoples to survive in such harsh conditions. Open 7.30am–6pm; Larapinta Dr; (08) 8951 8788.

ARALUEN CULTURAL PRECINCT: This hub of museums and art galleries includes some of the best cultural attractions in Alice Springs/Mparntwe (see p. 352). At the Araluen Arts Centre, four galleries feature work from the Central Desert and a magnificent stained-glass window by local artist Wenten Rubuntja. The Museum of Central Australia offers an insight into the geological and natural history of the Red Centre, with interpretive displays and impressive fossils. Also in the precinct are the Strehlow Research Centre, Central Craft, the Central Australian Aviation Museum and the Yeperenye Sculpture, depicting a Dreamtime caterpillar. One ticket covers entry to all attractions. Cnr Larapinta Dr and Memorial Ave, Alice Springs/Mparntwe; (08) 8951 1121.

CHAMBERS PILLAR HISTORICAL RESERVE/ITIRKAWARA: Chambers Pillar, named by John McDouall Stuart in 1860, but known as Itirkawara to the Pertame (Southern Arrernte) and Luritja Peoples, is a 40m high solitary rock pillar left standing on a Simpson Desert plain after 340 million years of erosion. It served as a landmark for early settlers and explorers and is best viewed at dawn or dusk; (08) 8952 1013. It's 160km south of Alice Springs/Mparntwe (see p. 352).

FINKE GORGE NATIONAL PARK: For millions of years the Finke River has carved its way through the weathered ranges, creating red-hued gorges and wide valleys. There are astonishing rock formations and dry creek beds that wind through sandstone ravines where rare flora flourishes. It is easy to see here what inspired artist Albert Namatjira. The park's most famous feature, Palm Valley, is home to about 12,000 red cabbage palms (*Livistona mariae*), which are unique to Australia. The 46,000ha area is great for bushwalking: a 1.5km climb leads to Kalarranga Lookout; the 5km Mpaara Walk, with informative signs, explains the Dreaming of Western Arrernte culture; and the 2km Arankaia and 5km Mpulungkinya walks explore the lush oasis of Palm Valley. Park access is by 4WD only but check road conditions first; (nt.gov.au/parks/find-a-park/finke-gorge-national-park). It's 138km west of Alice Springs/Mparntwe (see p. 352) and 20km south of Hermannsburg (see p. 353).

GLEN HELEN GORGE: This gorge is a breathtaking sandstone formation created by the erosive action of the Finke River over thousands of years. There is a beautiful walk along the Finke River with towering cliffs providing a habitat for black-footed wallabies. The gorge is 133km west of Alice Springs/Mparntwe (see p. 352).

KARLU KARLU–DEVILS MARBLES CONSERVATION RESERVE: An iconic outback destination near Wauchope (see p. 355), where massive red-and-orange boulders sit precariously on top of each other, like a sculpture park in the desert. There's camping and a walking track around the rock formations.

MEREENIE LOOP: This unsealed road links Tjoritja/West MacDonnell Ranges, Hermannsburg, Glen Helen and Palm Valley with Watarrka National Park. One of the many highlights includes the **Tnorala (Gosse Bluff) Conservation Reserve** where a huge crater, 25km in diameter, was formed when a comet struck Earth over 130 million years ago – there are excellent views from Tylers Pass. A 4WD is necessary and a map and permit for travelling through Aboriginal land can be obtained from Tourism Central Australia in Alice Springs/Mparntwe, Hermannsburg or Glen Helen.

N'DHALA GORGE NATURE PARK: The shady gorge features tracks that provide access to a large number of rock-art sites with carvings and paintings, including more than 6000 petroglyphs. The carvings are of two distinct types – finely pecked and heavily pounded – and are thought to represent two different periods. There are also rare plants in the park, such as the peach-leafed poison bush and the undoolya wattle. The park is 53km south-west of Arltunga Historical Reserve (see p. 353) and 90km east of Alice Springs/Mparntwe (see p. 352) and then there is 11km of 4WD-only track into the park. Check ahead for road conditions (nt.gov.au/parks/find-a-park/ndhala-gorge-nature-park).

RUBY GAP NATURE PARK: This is the site of Central Australia's first mining rush, in 1886, when rubies were thought to have been found. After the stones proved to be relatively valueless garnets, the boom went bust and people left. The stunning gorges are now popular sites for bushwalking and camping. Access is by 4WD only. Track closures are possible Nov–Apr due to wet conditions, so check ahead (nt.gov.au/parks/find-a-park/ruby-gap-nature-park). The park is 150km east of Alice Springs/Mparntwe (see p. 352).

TJORITJA/WEST MACDONNELL NATIONAL PARK: The majestic MacDonnell Ranges, once higher than the Himalayas, were formed over 800 million years ago. Over time the ancient peaks have been dramatically eroded. What remains is a spectacular environment of rugged gorges, hidden waterholes, remnant rainforest and an unexpectedly large number of animal species and flora. The jewel of the ranges is **Ormiston Gorge/Kwartatuma**, a hidden and glorious waterhole, while the **Ochre Pits** are a natural quarry once mined by Arrernte People who used the ochre in their rock art, painting and ceremonial decoration. **Standley Chasm/Angkerle Atwatye**, a spectacular, narrow, sheer-sided gorge, is particularly striking at midday when the sun lights up the rocks, and **Simpsons Gap** is one of the most prominent gaps in the ranges. The **Larapinta Trail** is a huge 223km walk, divided into 12 sections, covering the major sites along the ranges; each section can be walked separately and keys for the food drops are available from the visitor centre; deposit and $10 fee. Contact the Parks and Wildlife Commission NT at Ormiston Gorge/Kwartatuma (08) 8956 7799; or Simpsons Gap (08) 8951 8250; (nt.gov.au/parks/find-a-park/tjoritja-west-macdonnell-national-park).

TREPHINA GORGE NATURE PARK: Known for its sheer quartzite cliffs, river red gums and sandy creek bed. Several waterholes attract native wildlife and provide a beautiful setting for bushwalking, swimming, camping and picnicking; (08) 8956 9765. It's 85km east of Alice Springs/Mparntwe (see p. 352) and ensure you check road conditions ahead of visiting (nt.gov.au/parks/find-a-park/trephina-gorge-nature-park).

ULURU: Australia's most recognisable natural landmark, Uluru features stunning rock-art sites created by the Traditional Owners, the Anangu People, over the past 30,000 years. Uluru can be viewed by walking, cycling (bike hire onsite) or taking a tour (including on Segways) around the base. The rock-art sites highlight the rock's significance for the Anangu People. Uluru is Tjukurpa (often interpreted as Dreaming – creation and connection between land/people/ancestors) to the Anangu People. In October 2019, climbing on Uluru was officially banned, following more than 30 years of work by the Traditional Owners, who sought respectful recognition of Uluru's cultural significance as a sacred place, as well as protecting the safety of visitors. It is well worth reading online the Statement by Sammy Wilson, Chair of the Board of Management of Uluru-Kata Tjuta National Park, to more fully understand the significance. Ensure you stay on marked trails, and only walk during the cooler hours of the day. The changing colours of Uluru at sunrise and sunset are not to be missed. Nearby **Kata Tjuta** is just as impressive as Uluru. Highlights include remarkable rock formations, the Valley of the Winds walk, fantastic views and flora and fauna. There is a three-day pass to enter Uluru-Kata Tjuta National Park that can be bought online (parksaustralia.gov.au/uluru).

WATARRKA NATIONAL PARK: This park's many rock holes and gorges provide refuge from the harsh conditions for many species of plants and animals. The great attraction is **Kings Canyon**, an enormous amphitheatre with sheer sandstone walls rising to 270m. The 870m Carmichael Crag is known for its majestic colours, which are particularly vibrant at sunset. There are also well-signed trails. The 6km (3–4hr) Kings Canyon Rim Walk is recommended for experienced walkers. Wander through prehistoric cycads in the lush Garden of Eden and unusual rock formations such as the Lost City. The Kings Creek Walk is a 1hr return walk along the creek to a lookout. You can pre-book tours of the park run by Traditional Owners and scenic flights (nt.gov.au/parks/find-a-park/watarrka-national-park).

YEPERENYE (EMILY AND JESSIE GAPS) NATURE PARK: Located in the East MacDonnells, Emily Gap and Jessie Gap contain Aboriginal rock art and are important spiritual sites to the Eastern Arrernte People. The rock art forms a 'Dreamtime Trail' and should not be touched, out of respect. The caterpillar beings of Alice Springs/Mparntwe originated where Emily Gap lies today; they formed Emily Gap and other topographical features around Alice Springs/Mparntwe. Both gaps are popular barbecue and picnic places.

OTHER ATTRACTIONS

ALICE SPRINGS TELEGRAPH STATION HISTORICAL RESERVE: An area protecting original stone buildings and equipment, with historical display, mountain-bike trails, bushwalking and wildlife. There is also a kiosk here.

CORROBOREE ROCK CONSERVATION RESERVE: Significant Eastern Arrernte site for sacred men's business with a short walk and information signs; (08) 8956 9765. It's 43km east of Alice Springs/Mparntwe (see p. 352).

EWANINGA ROCK CARVINGS CONSERVATION RESERVE: These soft sandstone outcrops form natural galleries of sacred ancient petroglyphs created by Arrernte men as men's space. The walking track is about 680m long and forms a natural gallery. Stay on the path, and custodians request that visitors do not climb on rocks or interfere with the paintings; (08) 8952 1013. The reserve is 35km south-east of Alice Springs/Mparntwe (see p. 352).

GEMTREE CARAVAN PARK: Prospecting for zircons, guided fossicking tours and gem-cutting at a caravan park. There's a camp oven dinner and show Wed and Sat nights Easter–Oct; (08) 8956 9855; it's 135km north-east of Alice Springs/Mparntwe (see p. 352).

HENBURY METEORITES CONSERVATION RESERVE: Contains 12 craters created when meteorites (comprising 90 per cent iron) crashed to earth 4700 years ago. The largest of the meteorites was over 100kg, and a small chunk is at the Museum of Central Australia in Alice Springs/Mparntwe; (08) 8951 1121. It's 147km south-west of Alice Springs/Mparntwe (see p. 352).

IYTWELEPENTY–DAVENPORT RANGES NATIONAL PARK: Isolated area with important heritage for the Alyawarr, Wakaya, Kaytete and Warumungu People. There are ecology sites here; high-clearance vehicles and experienced 4WD access only; advise someone of your travel plans.

KINGS CANYON RESORT: Kings Canyon Resort, in Watarrka National Park, is an excellent base from which to explore the region. It has various accommodation, a petrol station, supermarket, laundry, tennis courts and swimming pools. There are also many dining options. Luritja Rd; (08) 8956 7442 or 1300 731 551; kingscanyonresort.com.au

KINGS CREEK STATION: A working cattle and camel station with campsites and accommodation near Watarrka National Park/Kings Canyon. There are quad-bike, helicopter and camel tours; (08) 8956 7474; kingscreekstation.com.au.

MAC AND ROSE CHALMERS CONSERVATION RESERVE: This 4.7sqkm reserve is the first parcel of land to be placed under a perpetual conservation covenant as part of the Voluntary Conservation Covenants on Private Land program. This reserve is owned by Chris Chalmers, and is named after his parents. It supports a wide variety of flora and fauna including the kultarr – a small carnivorous marsupial; all enquiries to Mount Swan (08) 8956 9097 or (08) 8956 9045.

NYINKKA NYUNYU ART AND CULTURE CENTRE: This centre in Tennant Creek (see p. 354) was built near a Warumungu sacred site and its name means 'home of the spiky-tailed goanna'. Dioramas illustrate the history of the area, an Aboriginal art gallery showcases the Tennant Creek art movement, and bush tucker talks, dance performances and displays explain the Warumungu People's relationship with the land. The centre is set in landscaped gardens, featuring plants used for bush tucker and medicine. Open Tues–Fri 9am–3.30pm, Sat 10am–2pm; Paterson St, Tennant Creek; (08) 8962 6020.

OLIVE PINK BOTANIC GARDENS: Named after an anthropologist who worked with Central Desert communities, this is one of Australia's only arid-zone botanic gardens. Covering 16ha on the edge of Alice Springs/Mparntwe (see p. 352), it contains more than 600 Central Australian plant species. The Bean Tree Cafe is a great spot to take a break; 8am–6pm; cnr Barrett Dr and Tuncks Rd, Alice Springs/Mparntwe; (08) 8952 0190.

RAINBOW VALLEY CONSERVATION RESERVE: Stunning freestanding sandstone cliffs that change colour at sunrise and sunset; access by 4WD only; (08) 8952 1013. It's 97km south-west of Alice Springs/Mparntwe (see p. 352).

WYCLIFFE WELL: This roadhouse was the first in the NT to be allowed to sell water (at a penny a gallon). Once a market garden supplying troops during World War II, it now features pleasant grassed camping areas as well as motel and cabin accommodation. The area is said to be at a cross-section of energy lines and has had many alleged UFO sightings (ranked 5th in the world for the number of sightings). Wycliffe Well also claims to have Australia's largest range of beers, but any connection between that and the UFO sightings is hearsay. (08) 8964 1966. It's 17km south of Wauchope (see p. 355).

Top: Karlu Karlu/Devil's Marbles *Bottom:* Expert 4WD guided tour through Finke Gorge National Park *Opposite:* Glen Helen Gorge

KEY TOWNS

AILERON HOTEL ROADHOUSE

Aileron Hotel Roadhouse is strategically situated along the Stuart Hwy 135km north of Alice Springs/Mparntwe and is a welcome oasis with a swimming pool, local First Nations art for sale, a playground, picnic and barbecue facilities. A 17m tall sculpture of Charlie Portpot, a local rainmaker, stands beside the roadhouse. Aileron Hotel Roadhouse offers meals, accommodation and camping. It's a great stopover for a break or an overnight stay; (08) 8956 9703; aileronroadhouse.com.au

SEE & DO **Native Gap Conservation Reservation:** a sacred Aboriginal site with picnic area surrounded by cypress pines and offering magnificent views of the Hahn Range; 12km SE. **Ryan Well Historical Reserve:** named after Ned Ryan, a 19th-century stonemason and bushman who was an expert at sinking wells. Ryan Well was hand-dug in 1889 as part of an attempt to encourage settlement in the NT and to support the movement of stock along the Overland Telegraph Line. Today there is a plaque beside the well explaining the process of raising water. Across the road are the ruins of Glen Maggie Homestead, built in 1914 and once used as a telegraph office. 7km SE.

★ ALICE SPRINGS/MPARNTWE
Population 24,855

'The Alice' is located in a harsh but ruggedly beautiful landscape, essentially in the middle of a vast desert. Situated on the Todd River in the MacDonnell Ranges, Alice Springs/Mparntwe is almost 1500km from the nearest capital city. It makes an ideal base for exploring Australia's Red Centre. The town offers many facilities for travellers, including a wide range of accommodation, cafes and attractions. There are also fascinating opportunities to learn about First Peoples' vibrant culture and ties to the land. The Arrernte People are the Traditional Owners of the area. First Nations art is a highlight of any visit here and don't forget to do a circuit of the shops if you're looking for local art or souvenirs. In 1871, Overland Telegraph Line surveyor William Whitfield Mills discovered a permanent waterhole just north of today's city. Mills named the water source after Alice Todd, wife of SA Superintendent of Telegraphs, Sir Charles Todd. A repeater station was built on the site. In 1888 the SA government gazetted a town 3km to the south. It was called Stuart until 1933, when the name Alice Springs was adopted. Supplies came to the slow-growing settlement by camel train from Port Augusta in SA. The railway line from Adelaide, known as the *Ghan* after the original Afghan camel drivers, was completed in 1929 and stops in Alice Springs/Mparntwe.

SEE & DO **Alice Springs Desert Park; Araluen Cultural Precinct; Glen Helen Gorge; N'dhala Gorge Nature Park; Ruby Gap Nature Park; Trephina Gorge Nature Park:** see Top Attractions for all. **Alice Springs Telegraph Station Historical Reserve; Corroboree Rock Conservation Reserve; Ewaninga Rock Carvings Conservation Reserve; Gemtree Caravan Park; Olive Pink Botanic Gardens; Rainbow Valley Conservation Reserve:** see Other Attractions for all. **Adelaide House:** originally a hospital designed by Rev. Flynn, now a museum displaying the pedal-radio equipment he used and other artefacts and photographs; open Mon–Fri 10am–4pm, Sat 10am–12pm; Todd Mall; (08) 8952 1856. **Alice Springs Reptile Centre:** houses the largest reptile display in Central Australia, including goannas, lizards, pythons and some of the world's most venomous snakes; open 9.30am–5pm; Stuart Tce; (08) 8952 8900. **Royal Flying Doctor Service Tourist Facility:** operational base since 1939, with daily tours and presentations and an interactive museum. It also includes an innovative holographic show that explains the founding and evolution of the RFDS; open Mon–Sat 9.30am–4.30pm; Stuart Tce; (08) 8958 8411. **Women's Museum of Australia:** national project dedicated to highlighting women's roles in Australia's history; open Mon–Fri 11am–3pm; includes the Old Alice Springs Gaol (get key from

VISITOR INFORMATION

Tourism Central Australia
41 Todd Mall, Alice Springs/
Mparntwe
(08) 8952 5800 or
1800 645 199
discovercentralaustralia.com

Top: National Road Transport Hall of Fame *Bottom:* Glen Helen Gorge *Opposite:* Kings Canyon

the Residency or Old Hartley St School; alternatively, enquire at visitor centre; Todd Mall), 2 Stuart Tce; (08) 8952 9006. **Anzac Hill:** the most visited landmark in Alice Springs/Mparntwe, this war memorial features panoramic views of the town and Tjoritja/MacDonnell Ranges; Anzac Hill Rd. **Alice Springs School of the Air:** the first of its kind in Australia, with a classroom size of 1.3 million sqkm. See interpretive displays and hear lessons being broadcast; Head St; (08) 8951 6800. **Megafauna Central:** megafauna displays and 8-million-year-old fossils found at the Alcoota Scientific Reserve 150km north-east of Alice Springs/Mparntwe; open Mon, Wed–Fri 10am–4pm, Sat–Sun 10am–2pm; 21 Todd Mall; (08) 8951 1121. **Old Hartley Street School:** originally constructed in 1930 and closed in 1965, the school was added to several times as the population surged, reflecting the changing styles and requirements of school design; open Mon–Fri 10.30am–2.30pm (subject to the availability of volunteers, so call ahead to confirm); Hartley St; (08) 8952 4516. **The Residency:** a grand home completed in 1928 and housing Central Australia's regional administrator until 1973. It has welcomed many VIPs, including Queen Elizabeth II, and now showcases local history; open Mon–Fri 10am–3pm (March–Nov) and every Sun when Todd Mall Markets are on; cnr Parsons and Hartley sts; (08) 8953 6073. **Old Timers Traeger Museum:** a unique museum set in a retirement home and run by volunteer residents. It displays photographs and memorabilia from the early days of settlement in Central Australia; open 2–4pm late (Mar–Oct); 446 South Stuart Hwy; 0413 876 870. **National Road Transport Hall of Fame:** an impressive collection of old trucks, cars and motorbikes; also includes the Old Ghan Heritage Railway, a re-creation of a 1930s railway station featuring a museum, restored locomotives and carriages; Norris Bell Ave; (08) 8952 7161. **Pyndan Camel Tracks:** ride a camel through the picturesque Ilparpa Valley alongside Tjoritja/West MacDonnell Ranges; 0416 170 164; 15km SW. **Tropic of Capricorn marker:** bicentennial project marking the Tropic of Capricorn; 30km N. **Tours:** experience scenic attractions and First Nations culture by foot, bus or coach, train, 4WD safari, camel, horse, plane, helicopter or hot-air balloon; brochures at visitor centre; Todd Mall. **Todd Mall Markets:** local produce, arts, crafts and food; Todd Mall; every 2nd Sun from mid-Feb to early Dec.

ARLTUNGA HISTORICAL RESERVE

The ruins of this town have been well preserved by the dry climate. It was named Arltunga because it sounded like 'Annurra ntinga', which is Eastern Arrernte for 'the smelly water in the nearby rockholes'. The Eastern Arrernte People had lived in the area for at least 22,000 years before Europeans arrived. When gold was discovered in 1887, prospectors travelled 600km from the Oodnadatta railhead, often on foot, to get there. When the prospectors arrived, the local Aboriginal People were mostly sent to the Santa Teresa mission. When the gold ran out, people left, and the only remaining signs of life today are at the visitor centre.

SEE & DO **N'dhala Gorge Nature Park:** *see* Top Attractions. **Police station and gaol:** have been restored. **Mines:** some are accessible. **Visitor centre:** displays on the history of the town; open 8am–5pm; (08) 8956 9770.

BARROW CREEK
Population 11

Although its appearance today is that of a small wayside stop on the highway, Barrow Creek was originally an important telegraph station. It was also the site of an 1874 punitive expedition against the Kaytetye People by police after a telegraph station master and linesman were killed during an assault by a group of Kaytetye men. This attack (thought to have been in retribution to the abuse of a Kaytetye woman) is the only known planned attack on staff of the Overland Telegraph. The restored stone building of the Old Telegraph Station (1872) is set against the breathtaking backdrop of the Forster Ranges. It is one of 15 telegraph stations that formed the original network from Port Augusta (in SA) to Port Darwin. Stuart Hwy.

SEE & DO **Barrow Creek Hotel:** outback pub (1932), with original bar, cellar and tin ceilings and memorabilia of the area on display; Stuart Hwy; (08) 8956 9753. **Cemetery:** graves of early settlers and local characters; information available at the hotel.

HERMANNSBURG
Population 551

This Aboriginal community occupies the site of a former mission station established by German Lutherans in 1877. During the first 14 years, the Lutherans recorded the Arrernte language and culture, compiled an Arrernte dictionary and translated the New Testament into the local language. From 1894 to 1922 the mission was run by Pastor Carl Strehlow, who restored and constructed most of the existing buildings. His son, T.G.H. Strehlow, assembled a vast collection of items relating to the Arrernte way of life. Renowned artist and Arrernte man Albert Namatjira, the first Aboriginal person to paint landscapes in a European style, was born at the mission in 1902, and produced art under the acclaimed Hermannsburg School. In 1982 the mission and its land was returned to the Arrernte People. The National Heritage–listed mission site comprises about 13 main buildings, mostly stone. Visitors have access to the shop, petrol station and historic precinct and there is a caravan park.

SEE & DO **Finke Gorge National Park:** *see* Top Attractions. **Historic Precinct:** The National Heritage buildings include the Kata Anga Tea Rooms (in

Strehlow's historic house), which has a reputation for delicious apple strudel; the old manse (1888), currently a watercolour gallery housing work by First Nations artists of the Hermannsburg School (guided tours available); the old schoolhouse (1896); the tannery (1941); and the Old Colonists House (1885), now a museum displaying historic items from the missionary era; (08) 8956 7402. **Monument to Albert Namatjira:** 6m red sandstone memorial to the legendary artist; Larapinta Dr; 2km E. **Wallace Rockhole Aboriginal community:** cultural tours and camping; 46km SE.

TENNANT CREEK
Population 2949

Tennant Creek is midway between Alice Springs/Mparntwe and Katherine and, according to legend, emerged when a beer truck broke down here. Gold was found in the area in the early 1930s and the town grew rapidly in the wake of Australia's last great gold rush. Gold exploration still continues in the Barkly Tableland, an area larger than Victoria.

SEE & DO **Nyinkka Nyunyu Art and Culture Centre:** *see* Other Attractions. **Tuxworth Fullwood Museum:** housed in a World War II army hospital (1942) and listed by the National Trust, this museum has a photographic collection, displays of early mine buildings and equipment, a 1930s police cell and a steam tractor engine; open May–Sept, check times with the visitor centre; Schmidt St. **Purkiss Reserve:** a pleasant picnic area with a swimming pool nearby; Ambrose St. **Self-guided tours:** scenic drives and heritage walks including an old Australian Inland Mission, built in 1934 of prefabricated corrugated-iron, and the Catholic Church, built in 1911 and relocated from Pine Creek in 1936; brochures and maps from the visitor centre. **Battery Hill:** features an underground mine, a 10-head stamp battery and two museums. There are daily tours of the underground mine, where working machinery demonstrates gold extraction. **Bill Allen Lookout:** just past the battery, offers panoramic views, with plaques identifying significant sites. Off Peko Rd; 3.5km E. **Tennant Creek Cemetery:** settler graves; 2km S. **Tingkkarli/Lake Mary Ann:** reservoir ideal for swimming, canoeing, windsurfing and picnics; 7am–6.30pm (Apr–Sept), 6.30am–7pm (Oct–Mar); 6km NE. **Telegraph Station:** restored stone buildings (1872), once the domain of telegraph workers, whose isolated lives are revealed by interpretive signs; the key is available from Tennant Creek Visitor Centre; 11km N. **Kunjarra/The Pebbles:** spectacular in their quantity, these are smaller relatives of Karlu Karlu/Devils Marbles (huge balancing boulders found north of Wauchope). The site is a sacred Munga Munga Dreaming place and a women's place, and people are welcome to visit but not to climb the rocks; 16km NW (6km of unsealed road). **Arlpwe Art and Culture Centre:** meet the artists at this off-the-beaten-track gallery; midway between Tennant Creek and Ti Tree and 22km E off the Hwy; call to confirm opening times (08) 8964 1640.

TOP EVENTS

- APR Parrtjima A Festival in Light (Alice Springs/Mparntwe)
- APR–MAY Alice Springs Cup Carnival
- JUN Finke Desert Race
- JUNE–JULY Beanie Festival (Alice Springs/Mparntwe)
- JULY–AUG Desert Harmony Festival (Tennant Creek)
- AUG Henly-on-Todd Regatta (Alice Springs/Mparntwe)

TEMPERATURES

Jan: 22–36°C

July: 4–20°C

Top: Thorny devil, Uluru Kata-Tjuta National Park
Opposite: Field of Light Uluru

TI TREE

This rest stop on the Stuart Hwy took its name from nearby Ti Tree Wells, the source of plentiful sweet water in the 1800s. Today this desert region supports remarkably successful fruit and vegetable industries.

SEE & DO **Ti Tree Park:** a picnic area and playground; Stuart Hwy. **Central Mount Stuart Historical Reserve:** the sandstone peak was noted by John McDouall Stuart as the geographical centre of Australia; no facilities but a monument at the base; 18km N.

WAUCHOPE
Population 10

Wauchope (pronounced 'walk-up', unlike the town of the same name on the NSW mid-north coast which is pronounced 'war-hope') was established to cater for the wolfram-mining and cattle-farming communities nearby. Today it is a tourist stopover, thanks to its proximity to the popular Karlu Karlu–Devils Marbles Conservation Reserve. The hotel is really the only place to go in town.

SEE & DO **Wycliffe Well:** see Top Attractions. **Devils Marbles Hotel:** formerly known as the Wauchope Hotel, it catered for workers at the old wolfram mines back in the 1930s. Today this desert oasis offers fuel and various standards of accommodation including an adjacent campground. It also has a swimming pool, a beer garden and a good, licensed restaurant (or takeaway). **Karlu Karlu–Devils Marbles Conservation Reserve** is only 8km up the highway; make sure to visit at sunrise or sunset. Stuart Hwy; (08) 8964 1963; devilsmarbleshotel.com.au

★ YULARA
Population 853

Yulara is a tourist resort village that was built specifically to cater for visitors coming to see Uluru and Kata Tjuta. It offers excellent visitor facilities and a myriad of tour options, from guided walks to segway tours, camel safaris, bus trips, 4WD excursions, bike rides and scenic flights, as well as food and accommodation for all budgets. Advance bookings for accommodation are essential.

SEE & DO **Uluru:** see Top Attractions. **Visitor Information Centre:** displays of geology, history, flora and fauna with a spectacular photographic collection; audio tour available; you can also book helicopter, coach and safari tours; 8am–7pm; (08) 8957 7324. **Mingkiri Arts:** Aboriginal art gallery with resident artists at work; Town Square. **Gallery of Central Australia (GOCA):** Aboriginal art and design featuring artists exclusively from the Central Desert region; adjacent Desert Gardens Hotel off Yulara Dr. **Uluru–Kata Tjuta Cultural Centre:** designed in the shape of two snakes, the centre has displays of First Nations culture and sales of artwork; on approach road to Uluru; (08) 8956 1128; 17km S. **Sounds of Silence dinner:** an unforgettable buffet dinner experience at sunset and under the outback night sky overlooking Uluru-Kata Tjuta National Park. Book at ayersrockresort.com.au. **Field of Light:** art installation by artist Bruce Munro lights up the desert at the base of Uluru with more than 50,000 spindles of light. Tickets, available from ayersrockresort.com.au, include return transport from Yulara.

Queensland

HIGHLIGHTS

Explore Brisbane by CityCat on one of the best value river cruises around. See p. 358.

Snap a selfie at Cape York, the northernmost tip of mainland Australia. See p. 408.

Snorkel or dive to discover the Great Barrier Reef. See p. 408.

Share a beer with some larger-than-life Aussie characters in an outback pub. See p. 380.

Drive the Beach Highway on the Sunshine Coast. See p. 360.

Get up close and personal with humpback whales in Hervey Bay. See p. 397.

STATE FLOWER

Cooktown orchid
Dendrobium phalaenopsis

Whitsunday Islands National Park

Brisbane/Meanjin at a glance

The Traditional Owners of the Brisbane/Meanjin area are the Turrbal and Yuggera Peoples.

Subtropical Brisbane basks in **sunshine year-round**, although the summertime thunderstorms that roll through the city can offer a spectacular sound-and-light show. With weather this good, it's no surprise that some of the **city's best things to see and do are in the great outdoors**. But if you do venture indoors, you'll find the city also has **flourishing art and foodie scenes**.

Top: Fish Lane **Middle:** Dining at QAGOMA **Bottom:** Museum of Brisbane **Opposite:** Cruising along the Brisbane River

IF YOU LIKE …

FESTIVALS AND EVENTS
Brisbane Comedy Festival, Feb–March
World Science Festival Brisbane, March
Ekka (Royal Queensland Show), Aug
Brisbane Festival, Sept
Woodford Folk Festival, Dec–Jan

GALLERIES
Gallery of Modern Art (GoMA)
Queensland Art Gallery and Gallery of Modern Art (QAGOMA)
QUT Art Museum
State Library of Queensland
Tony Gould Gallery, Queensland Performing Arts Centre (QPAC)

MUSEUMS
Commissariat Store
Museum of Brisbane
Queensland Maritime Museum
Queensland Museum
Queensland Police Museum

PARKS AND GARDENS
Brisbane Botanic Gardens Mount Coot-tha
City Botanic Gardens
New Farm Park
Roma Street Parkland
South Bank Parklands

SHOPPING
Given and La Trobe terraces, Paddington
Grey Street, South Bank
James Street, Fortitude Valley
Queen Street Mall
Valley Markets, Fortitude Valley

VIEWS OF THE RIVER
Abseil or walk the Kangaroo Point cliffs
Dine at the Howard Smith Wharves
Ride a ferry or CityCat
Take on the Story Bridge Adventure Climb
Walk or cycle along the Promenade in South Bank
Walk the mangrove boardwalk in the City Botanic Gardens

WILDLIFE ENCOUNTERS
Daisy Hill Koala Centre
Lamington National Park
Lone Pine Koala Sanctuary
Walkabout Creek Discovery Centre, D'Aguilar National Park
Wild dolphins at Moreton Island

QUEENSLAND

Daytrips from Brisbane/Meanjin

BEACH HIGHWAY
2hr from Brisbane CBD

The quickest way to get to the northern end of the Sunshine Coast, if you've only got one day, is via Beach Highway between Rainbow Beach and Noosa, a glorious 70km drive along the beach – yes, you read that right, the beach is actually a designated road. The catch is you'll need a 4WD and to time your trip for low tide, but there are plenty of tours available if you don't fancy getting behind the wheel yourself. As far as great ocean roads go, it's hard to beat. See Noosa Heads p. 388.

BRIBIE ISLAND
1.5hr from Brisbane CBD

Linked to the mainland by a bridge, Bribie Island is a fantastic offshore escape without the need to get on a ferry and it's only 65km north of Brisbane. Enjoy beautiful coastal scenery, hire a boat and explore the Pumicestone Passage (if you're lucky you may see dolphins, dugongs or turtles), or go fishing, birdwatching or crabbing.

There are several easy, marked bushwalking trails that crisscross the island, or you can explore it by 4WD. It's a delightful destination year-round, although wildflowers are at their most impressive in spring. See Caboolture p. 367.

BRISBANE HINTERLAND
1hr from Brisbane CBD

You don't have to go very far out of Brisbane's CBD to get into the bush – the mountainous hinterland north-west of the city is a largely untouched swathe of bushland and rainforest.

Take a lovely long drive to explore this beautiful area and revel in expansive views from mountain-top lookouts, explore pockets of glorious rainforest and discover quiet country towns like Kilcoy and Woodford. Cool off in one of many swimming holes, trek to waterfalls and soak in the views from hilltop cafes or lakeside picnic areas. See Brisbane Hinterland p. 364.

Top: Horseriding along Rainbow Beach **Middle:** Snorkelling at Tangalooma Wrecks, Moreton Island/Mulgumpin **Bottom left:** Tamborine Mountain Coffee Plantation **Bottom right:** HOTA, Home of the Arts, Surfers Paradise

GOLD COAST
1hr from Brisbane CBD

A combination of golden beaches and the most varied theme-park attractions in Australia make the Gold Coast one of the country's most popular holiday playgrounds. The region's 42km coastline stretches from Southport to Coolangatta – with most of the nonstop action found in the built-up areas around Surfers Paradise, Broadbeach, Main Beach and Southport.

There's something for everyone on the 'Goldy', with top-notch eateries, high-end shopping, glitzy live shows and fun-filled family adventures. *See* Surfers Paradise p. 375.

GOLD COAST HINTERLAND
1hr from Brisbane CBD

Explore the Gold Coast's wilder side in the mountainous hinterland beyond the beach. The drive there is steep, winding and narrow, but the cool air and the views from the plateau make it all worth it.

Explore the villages of Mount Tamborine, Tamborine Village, North Tamborine and Eagle Heights – shoppers should head for Gallery Walk on Long Road – or lace up the walking boots and hit one of the many trails through the World Heritage–listed rainforests in Lamington, Springbrook or Tamborine national parks. *See* North Tamborine p. 374.

MORETON ISLAND/MULGUMPIN
3hr from Brisbane CBD

One of the largest sand islands in the world, Moreton Island/Mulgumpin is almost entirely national park, with an astonishingly diverse range of wildlife, freshwater lakes, wetlands, forests and achingly beautiful coastline. The island is famous for the pod of wild dolphins that nightly swims up to the sheltered waters to be hand-fed in front of the island's only resort.

You can snorkel or dive the 15 sunken wrecks just off the beach, go sand boarding or quad biking over the towering dunes, or explore the 420km or so of 4WD tracks. *See* Moreton Island/Mulgumpin p. 365.

SUNSHINE COAST HINTERLAND
1hr from Brisbane CBD

Driving the back roads of the Sunshine Coast hinterland and winding through the very pretty Mary Valley is a great one-day road trip from Brisbane. It's the verdant scenery that will steal the show, but other highlights include the late Steve Irwin's Australia Zoo at Beerwah where you can also visit a wildlife hospital.

At the nearby Glass House Mountains you'll get a superb view of the rocky volcanic peaks from Mary Cairncross Scenic Reserve, a patch of rainforest near the mountain-top village of Maleny. Maleny itself is crammed with art galleries, boutiques, second-hand bookshops, restaurants and cafes. *See* Kenilworth p. 386, Landsborough p. 387, Maleny p. 387.

SCENIC RIM
1hr from Brisbane CBD

Head beyond the popular tourist trail to explore the Scenic Rim, the lush ring of rainforest-clad mountains, hills and pretty valleys that arcs around the Gold Coast hinterland. Small towns such as Boonah, Killarney and Kalbar are full of classic Queensland architecture, while the larger town of Warwick has grand stone buildings, including a very impressive town hall.

Must-see sights include Queen Mary Falls, the views at Spicers Gap and picnic-perfect Lake Moogerah. *See* Boonah p. 373, Killarney p. 380, Warwick p. 381.

Top: Boonah farmland **Second from top:** Parasailing on the Gold Coast **Second from bottom:** Maleny Botanic Gardens & Bird World **Bottom:** Scenic Rim Eat Local Month festival

Regions of Queensland

❶ BRISBANE HINTERLAND
P. 364

Caboolture
Esk
Gatton
Ipswich
Kingaroy
Laidley
Murgon
Nanango
Strathpine

❷ GOLD COAST AND HINTERLAND
P. 370

Beaudesert
Boonah
Burleigh Heads
Nerang
North Tamborine
Surfers Paradise ★

❸ DARLING DOWNS
P. 376

Allora
Chinchilla
Clifton
Crows Nest
Dalby
Goondiwindi
Killarney
Miles
Oakey
Roma
St George
Stanthorpe
Texas
Toowoomba ★
Warwick

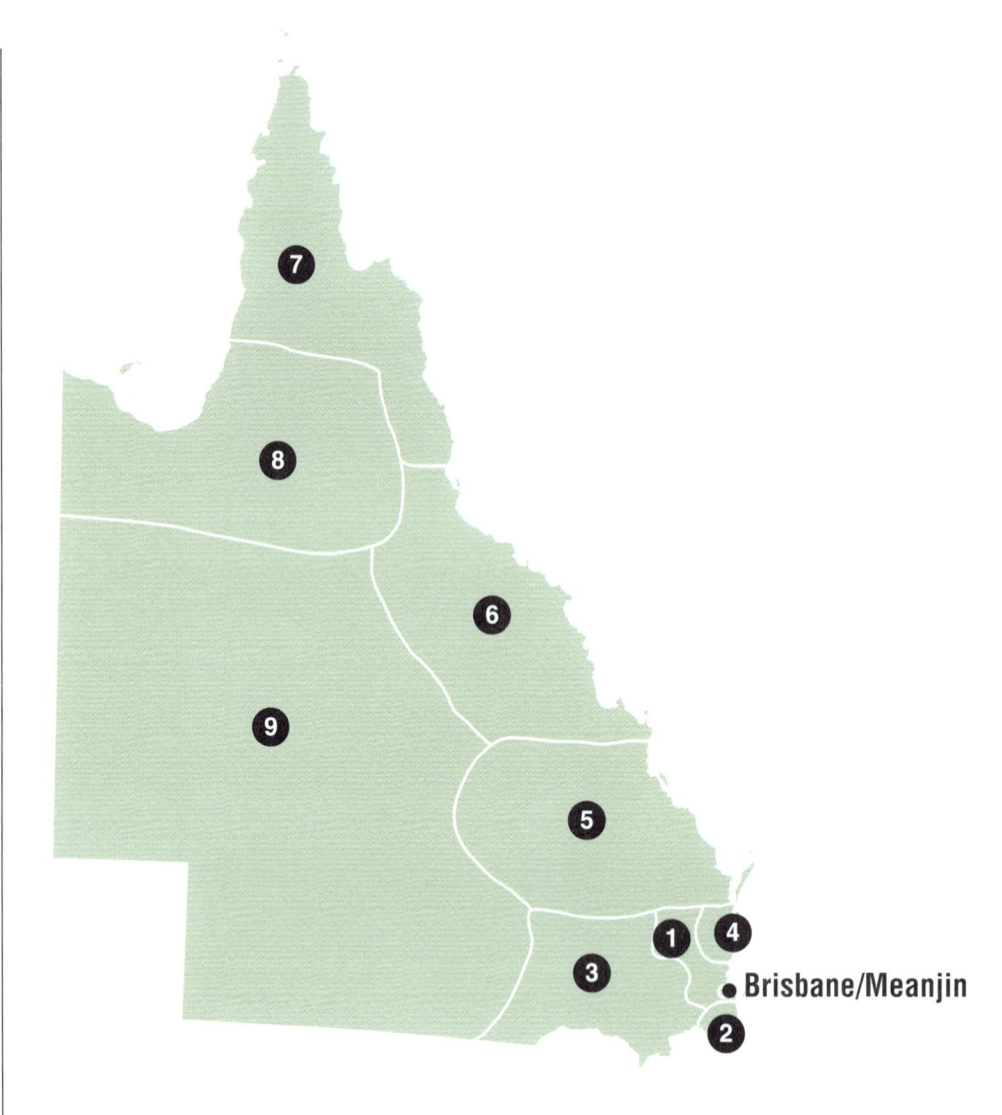

④ SUNSHINE COAST P. 382

Buderim
Caloundra
Gympie
Kenilworth
Landsborough
Maleny
Maroochydore
Mooloolaba
Nambour
Noosa Heads ★
Pomona
Tin Can Bay
Yandina

⑤ CAPRICORN AND K'GARI (FRASER ISLAND) COAST P. 390

Biggenden
Biloela
Blackwater
Bundaberg ★
Childers
Emerald
Gayndah
Gin Gin
Gladstone
Hervey Bay (including K'gari/Fraser Island) ★
Maryborough
Miriam Vale
Monto
Mount Morgan
Mundubbera
Rockhampton
Springsure
Taroom
Theodore
Yeppoon

⑥ WHITSUNDAY COAST P. 400

Airlie Beach ★
Ayr
Bowen
Cardwell
Charters Towers
Clermont
Ingham
Mackay
Moranbah
Proserpine
Ravenswood
Sarina
Townsville ★

⑦ CAIRNS AND THE TROPICAL NORTH P. 408

Atherton
Babinda
Cairns ★
Cooktown
Daintree
Gordonvale
Herberton
Innisfail
Kuranda
Laura
Mareeba
Millaa Millaa
Mission Beach ★
Mossman
Mourilyan
Palm Cove
Port Douglas ★
Ravenshoe
Thursday Island
Tully
Weipa
Yungaburra

⑧ GULF SAVANNAH P. 420

Burketown
Chillagoe
Croydon
Karumba
Mount Surprise
Normanton

⑨ OUTBACK P. 424

Aramac
Barcaldine
Birdsville
Blackall
Boulia
Camooweal
Charleville
Cloncurry
Cunnamulla
Eulo
Hughenden
Isisford
Julia Creek
Jundah
Kynuna
Longreach ★
Mitchell
Mount Isa
Muttaburra
Quilpie
Richmond
Tambo
Winton ★

Top: Whitehaven Beach, Whitsundays **Bottom:** Snorkelling off Lady Musgrave Island **Opposite:** Outback road, Julia Creek

QUEENSLAND

363

Brisbane Hinterland

Escape the hustle and bustle of Brisbane in the ring of **lushly forested hills and ridges** that flank the city, where everything is green and cool. Or **bask in the golden sands of the islands of Moreton Bay**. North Stradbroke/Minjerribah is a favourite, but Moreton/Mulgumpin and Bribie islands are just as special. They may only be a short ferry ride from the city centre but once you're there you'll feel like you're a million miles away.

CHEAT SHEET

→ The region is perfect for daytrips or long weekends.

→ Best time to visit: year-round. May to Oct is a great time to see whales.

→ Main towns: Caboolture (*see* p. 367), Ipswich (*see* p. 367), Kingaroy (*see* p. 368).

→ The Turrbal and Yuggera Peoples are the Traditional Owners of the location of Meanjin, known as Brisbane. Much of the hinterland is on Barunggam, Wakka Wakka, and Yuggera land; North Stradbroke/Minjerribah and Moreton Island/Mulgumpin are Quandamooka land. Visit Salt Water Murris on North Stradbroke/Minjerribah to see local art and take a tour with Straddie Adventures for a cultural paddling experience.

→ Don't miss: the beaches of Straddie; feeding wild dolphins on Moreton Island/Mulgumpin; forest walks; art galleries; country pubs and quirky shopping.

Top: St Helena Island
Opposite: Moreton Island/Mulgumpin

TOP ATTRACTIONS

BRIBIE ISLAND: This island is separated from the mainland by Pumicestone Passage, where mangroves flourish and dugongs, dolphins, turtles and more than 350 species of birds live. National park covers about a third of the island and offers secluded pristine white beaches. Follow the Bicentennial Bushwalks to discover the park on foot, boat along Pumicestone Passage or 4WD along the ocean beach (permit required). Fishing and surfing are popular at Woorim Beach, just north of which are World War II bunkers. Woorim itself is an old-fashioned resort. See migratory birds in summer at **Buckleys Hole Conservation Park** on the south-west tip of the island, where there are also picnic spots and walking tracks to the beach. Bridge access to island east of Caboolture (*see* p. 367).

BUNYA MOUNTAINS NATIONAL PARK: The Bunya Mountains sit on an isolated spur of the Great Dividing Range, a cool, moist region of waterfalls, with green-and-scarlet king parrots. This important park and Queensland's second-oldest (declared in 1908) contains the world's largest natural bunya-pine forest, much depleted by early timber-getters. It is a significant site for the First Nations Peoples of the area as feasts were held here with the bunya nuts as the main fare. There are many walking trails for both beginners and the experienced, including the 8.4km return Cherry Plain Track, and the easy 4km Scenic Circuit from the Dandabah camping area, which winds through rainforest to Pine Gorge Lookout. Have a bush picnic and see the many butterflies, or go spotlighting to glimpse owls and mountain possums.

D'AGUILAR NATIONAL PARK: This natural bushland forest park has a scenic drive from the south-east corner to lookouts, mountain towns and attractive landscapes, ending at Lake Wivenhoe. It has pristine rainforest, towering trees, cascading waterfalls, deep pools, mountain streams and incredible wildlife. In the southern section of the park (formerly called Brisbane Forest Park), the small settlement of Mount Glorious is a base for forest walking tracks. Wivenhoe Lookout, 10km further on, has superb views west to Lake Wivenhoe. There are many picnic spots – Jollys Lookout is a highlight, with views over Brisbane, the valley and north to the Glass House Mountains. A guide to the park's walks is available from the park headquarters at 60 Mt Nebo Rd, The Gap.

IPSWICH ART GALLERY: This large regional art gallery is housed in Ipswich's (*see* p. 367) restored Old Town Hall, and incorporates Australia's first dedicated gallery for children. See the local and visiting exhibitions and heritage displays; take part in special events and family activities. Look out for local artist Davida Allen's Archibald Prize–winning portrait of her father-in-law. D'Arcy Doyle Pl, Ipswich; (07) 3810 7222.

MORETON ISLAND/MULGUMPIN: 'Mulgumpin' means 'place of sandhills' in the Jandai language of Quandamooka Country. Almost all of this large island is within the Gheebulum Kunungai National Park. The island is mainly sand, with 280m Mount Tempest possibly the world's highest stable sandhill. On the east coast is an unbroken 36km surf beach, with calmer beaches on the west coast. Get to the island by passenger or vehicular ferry from Scarborough or the Brisbane River. A 4WD and a permit are required for self-drive touring.

NORTH STRADBROKE/ MINJERRIBAH: 'Straddie' is a coastal and bushland island paradise, with contained pockets of development – the sort of place that people go for quiet weekends away immersed in nature. Blue Lake National Park is an ecologically significant wetland; access is by 4WD or a 45min walk. Other island walking trails include the popular North Gorge Headland Walk. Explore the island with a Quandamooka guide from Straddie Adventures – kayaking, sandboarding, 4WD trips and guided walks – while learning about local culture and lore. Travel to the island by vehicular ferry from Cleveland to Dunwich, the site of a 19th-century quarantine and penal centre.

WORKSHOPS RAIL MUSEUM: Located in the North Ipswich (see p. 367) railyards, this museum offers historical displays, interactive exhibitions and an impressive variety of machinery. See workers restoring old steam trains, or marvel at the model railway depicting Queensland. Hear stories about the history of rail – and look into the future. North St, Ipswich; (07) 3432 5100.

OTHER ATTRACTIONS

BOAT MOUNTAIN CONSERVATION PARK: The flat-topped crest in this park looks like an upturned boat, hence the name. The views from the top are panoramic and take in the surrounding agricultural valley. There are two lookout walks and an excellent 1.8km circuit track. Watch for the bandicoot digs along the way. The park is 20km north-east of Murgon via Boat Mountain Rd.

CABOOLTURE REGIONAL ART GALLERY: Travelling exhibitions as well as showcasing the work of emerging regional artists; Tues–Sat 10am–4pm; Hasking St; Caboolture; (07) 5433 2800.

DAS NEUMANN HAUS: Restored and refurbished in 1930s style, this 1893 historic home is the oldest in the Laidley (see p. 368) shire. It was built by a German immigrant, whose carpentry skills can be seen in the excellent detailing of the building's facade and interior. It houses a local-history museum and exhibits local art and craft. Open 10am–3pm; William St, Laidley.

JACK SMITH SCRUB REGIONAL PARK: This park comprises valuable remnant dry rainforest that used to cover the region before clearing for agriculture began. Have a picnic overlooking the South Burnett Valley before taking the 20min return track through scrub to see the abundant birdlife of the park. It's 13km north of Murgon (see p. 369).

ST HELENA ISLAND: This low, sandy island, 8km from the mouth of the Brisbane River, was used as a prison from 1867 to 1932. It was dubbed 'the hell-hole of the South Pacific'. Historic ruins remain and are protected in the island's national park. Tours of the island depart from the Brisbane suburbs of Manly and Breakfast Creek.

SOUTH BURNETT WINE REGION: This is a young winemaking region; the first vines were only planted in 1993. However, South Burnett now has more than a dozen wineries. The Semillon at **Clovelly Estate** has won a swag of gold medals, and the winery also does good cold-pressed olive oils. Enjoy million dollar views as you sip and swirl at **Crane Wines** high on the Booie Ranges, or if you prefer old-world varieties like Viognier, Nebbiolo and Sangiovese, head to **Nuova Sculoa** in Moffatdale. For details of these and other cellar doors in the region visit discoversouthburnett.com.au

THE PALMS NATIONAL PARK: Located at the Brisbane River headwaters is this vine forest and subtropical rainforest park. Have a bush picnic and then take the 20min Palm Circuit track through natural vegetation and along boardwalks.

VISITOR INFORMATION

Ipswich Visitor Information Centre
Queens Park
(07) 3281 0555
discoveripswich.com.au

Moreton Bay region
visitmoretonbayregion.com.au

Top: Barambah Ridge Winery and Vineyard, Murgon
Bottom: Ipswich welcome sign
Opposite: Bunya Mountains National Park

KEY TOWNS

CABOOLTURE
Population 29,534

At the northern edge of Greater Brisbane and the southern opening to the Sunshine Coast, Caboolture is surrounded by subtropical fruit farms. The town was settled in 1842 after the restricted land around Moreton Bay penal colony was opened up. The historical village north of town exhibits much of this history. Bribie Island to the east has spectacular aquatic and wildlife attractions, which bring many visitors to the region.

SEE & DO **Bribie Island:** see Top Attractions. **Regional Art Gallery:** see Other Attractions. **Trail of Reflections:** self-guided trail of 18 open-air artworks and sculptures around town that illustrate the history of the area; starts in King St; details from visitor centre. **Market:** Showgrounds, Beerburrum Rd; Sun mornings. **Ferryman cruises:** cruise the waters of Pumicestone Passage; 0408 214 980. **Historical Village:** more than 50 restored buildings of historical importance house museums with themes including maritime and transport; open Mon–Sun 9.30am–3.30pm; Beerburrum Rd; 2km N. **Warplane Museum:** displays of World War II memorabilia and restored fighter planes. Tiger Moth and Mustang flights and gliding are available; Airfield, McNaught Rd; 2km E. **Sheep Station Creek Conservation Park:** walks through open forest; see remains of the old bridge on original road leading from Brisbane to Gympie; 6km SW. **Abbey Museum:** traces growth of Western civilisation with displays of art and antiques; open Mon–Sat 10am–4pm; just off road to Bribie Island; 9km E. **Woodford:** the town has one of the largest narrow-gauge steam locomotive collections in Australia; Margaret St; 22km NW. **Mount Mee State Forest:** boardwalks through subtropical rainforest and lookouts over Neurum Valley, Moreton Bay and surrounds; 23km W. **Donnybrook, Toorbul and Beachmere:** coastal fishing towns to the east.

ESK
Population 1230

Esk is a heritage town in the Upper Brisbane Valley renowned for its beautiful lakes and dams where watersports are popular. Deer roam in the grazing country north of town, progeny of a small herd presented to the state by Queen Victoria in 1873.

SEE & DO **Antiques and local crafts:** numerous shops in town. **Market:** Pipeliner Park, Highland St; Sat. Known as the Valley of the Lakes, this region is popular for swimming, fishing and boating. **Lake Wivenhoe** is the source of Brisbane's main water supply. Walk to the Fig Tree Lookout for a panoramic view or ride a horse around the lake; 25km E. **Lake Somerset** is on the Stanley River and a popular waterskiing spot; 25km NE. **Atkinson Dam** also attracts watersports enthusiasts; 30km S. **Somerset Canoe Trails:** canoe and kayak on the Brisbane River and Somerset region dams; canoe trail map available from the visitor centre. **Coominya:** small historic town; 22km SE. **Skydiving:** take a tandem dive over the valley; contact visitor centre for details. **Brisbane Valley Rail Trail:** Australia's longest rail trail (161km) is a picturesque rural bike ride that runs right through town. **Kilcoy:** small and unassuming farming town that claims to be the home of the Yowie, Australia's equivalent of the Bigfoot or Yeti. There is a large wooden statue of the supposed creature in town; 60km N.

GATTON
Population 6852

Located in the Lockyer Valley west of Brisbane, Gatton is situated in the heart of the south-east's 'Salad Bowl' region and is blessed with fertile black soils, with many fruit and vegetable farms found in and around town. In Gatton's town centre, the Great Dividing Range provides a scenic backdrop to historic buildings – it was founded in 1855 – sports and recreation facilities and quaint ale houses.

SEE & DO **Queensland Transport Museum:** large private collection of vehicles on display, including tanks and vintage trucks; 34 Lake Apex Dr; (07) 5466 3426. **Historical Society Museum:** complex of 11 buildings depicting the social history of the region; open by appt; Freemans Rd; 0409 873 495. **Lake Apex:** this park and complex include a historic village with preserved heritage buildings, memorabilia and First Nations carvings. Follow the walking tracks to see the diverse birdlife; Old Warrego Hwy. **Plaque:** a plaque commemorating the 1974 floods can be found next to Davies Bridge, which also went under in 2011. **Markets:** Lake Apex, 1st Sun each month. **Helidon:** town noted for its sandstone – used in many Brisbane buildings – and spa water; 16km W. **Glen Rock Regional Park:** at the head of East Haldon Valley, this park boasts rainforest gorges, creeks and excellent valley views; 40km S. **Tourist drive:** 82km circuit through surrounding countryside that includes farm visits; contact visitor centre for details.

IPSWICH
Population 229,208

Ipswich is Queensland's oldest provincial city and was first settled as a town in 1827. The city centre has diverse heritage buildings, art galleries and museums, trendy cafes, and vintage and antique shops. The impressive Workshops Rail Museum honours Ipswich as the birthplace

QUEENSLAND

367

of Queensland Railways, while Australia's largest RAAF base is in the suburb of Amberley.

SEE & DO **Workshops Rail Museum; Ipswich Art Gallery:** see Top Attractions. **Ipswich Nature Centre:** native flora, animals and a bird aviary; Queens Park, Goleby Ave. **Pillar of Courage:** memorial to 2011 floods; Queen St, Goodna. **Heritage trail:** a self-guided walk to see the renowned heritage buildings, churches and excellent domestic architecture of Ipswich, including Claremont (1856) and the Old Town Hall (1860); brochures available from visitor centre. **Showplace Markets:** Showgrounds, Warwick Rd; Sun. **Handmade Expo:** arts and crafts; 2nd Sat of each month Mar–Nov. **Queensland Raceway:** home to the Queensland 500 and host of the V8 Supercar Series. Winternationals Drag-racing Championship runs every June; 15km W. **Wolston Farmhouse:** historic home at Wacol; open Sat 12pm–2.30pm, Sun 10am–2.30pm; 16km E. **Rosewood:** heritage town featuring St Brigid's Church, one of the largest wooden churches in Queensland; 20km W. **Recreational reserves:** popular picnic and leisure spots to the north-east of Ipswich include College's Crossing (7km), Mount Crosby (12km) and Lake Manchester (22km).

KINGAROY
Population 10,147

Kingaroy is a large and prosperous town in the South Burnett region. The town's name derives from the Wakka Wakka word 'kingaroori', meaning 'red ant'. Found in the area, this unique ant has gradually adapted its colour to resemble the red soil plains of Kingaroy. The town is the centre for Queensland's peanut and navy-bean industries, and its giant peanut silos are landmarks. The region's wine industry is also thriving and Bunya Mountains National Park is just 58km away. Kingaroy is also the former home of the late Sir Joh Bjelke-Petersen, the state's longest-serving premier.

SEE & DO **Bunya Mountains National Park:** see Top Attractions. **South Burnett Wine Region:** see Other Attractions. **Heritage Museum:** formerly the Kingaroy Power House, the museum depicts the history of Kingaroy under the themes of people, power and peanuts. Historical displays include machinery, photos and videos on the peanut and navy-bean industries; Haly St. **Art Gallery:** local and regional artists; open Mon–Fri 10am–4pm, Sat 9am–1pm; Haly St. **The Peanut Van:** sales of local peanuts in a variety of flavours; Kingaroy St. **Apex Lookout:** panoramic views of town; Apex Park, Fisher St. **Market:** Kingaroy Showgrounds, 3rd Sat of the month 6.30am–12pm. **Observatory:** nightly astronomical shows when conditions are favourable; by appt; Geoff Raph Dr Kingaroy airport; (07) 4164 6194; 5km S. **Mount Wooroolin Lookout:** excellent views over Kingaroy's farmlands; 3km W. **Wooroolin:** quaint town with many heritage buildings including the Grand Hotel (1916). The Gordonbrook Dam is an excellent spot for picnics and birdwatching from the hides; 18km N. **Scenic glider flights:** (07) 4162 2191.

LAIDLEY
Population 3976

Located west of Brisbane in the Lockyer Valley, the township of Laidley boasts classic Queensland architecture. A landscape dominated by agricultural farmland has earned the region the nickname of 'Queensland's Country Garden'. It produces an abundance of seasonal fruit and vegetables, and farmers showcase their fresh produce at the weekly Country Market. Memorials, museums and statues commemorate Laidley's rich history as a wagon-stop route, later replaced by a rail line between Ipswich and Toowoomba.

SEE & DO **Das Neumann Haus:** see Other Attractions. **Street market:** Patrick St; Fri. **Country Market:** Ferrari Park; 4th Sat each month. **Historical walk:** self-guided walk to heritage sites; contact visitor centre for details. **Pioneer Village:** original buildings from old township including blacksmith shop and slab hut; 1km S. **Narda Lagoon:** flora and fauna sanctuary with picturesque suspension footbridge over lagoon; adjacent to pioneer village. **Lake Dyer:** beautiful spot for fishing, picnics and camping; 1km W. **Lake Clarendon:** birdwatching area; 17km NW. **Laidley Valley Scenic Drive:** attractive drive to the south of Laidley through Thornton.

TOP EVENTS

- MAR South Burnett Wine and Food in the Park Festival (Kingaroy)
- APR–MAY Clydesdale and Heavy Horse Field Days (Gatton)
- MAY Multicultural Festival (Gatton); Pumpkin Festival (Goomeri)
- JUN Winternationals Drag-racing Championship (Ipswich)
- JULY Abbey Medieval Festival (Caboolture); V8 Supercars (Ipswich); SPARK Ipswich (arts festival, Ipswich)
- AUG; StoryArts Festival (Ipswich)
- SEPT Spring Festival (Laidley); Heritage Country Muster (Nanango)
- OCT Jacaranda Festival (Goodna/Ipswich)
- NOV Murgon Music Muster
- DEC Woodford Folk Festival

TEMPERATURES

Jan: 20–32°C

July: 8–22°C

Top: Bunya Mountains National Park Opposite: Workshops Rail Museum at Ipswich

MURGON
Population 1966

Murgon, known as 'the beef capital of the Burnett', is one of the most attractive towns in southern Queensland. European settlement dates from 1843, but the town did not really develop until after 1904, when the railway arrived and the large stations of the area were divided up. The town's name comes from a lily pond, found on Barambah Station, which was the site of the first pastoral property in the area.

SEE & DO **Boat Mountain Conservation Park; Jack Smith Scrub Regional Park; South Burnett Wine Region:** see Other Attractions for all. **Queensland Dairy & Heritage Museum:** static and interactive displays illustrating the history of the dairy industry, with special focus on the development of butter; Gayndah Rd. **Cherbourg:** small First Nations community featuring the Ration Shed Precinct displaying a pictorial history of the area; check before visiting as permits were required to enter the community during Covid-19; 5km SE. **Wondai:** attractions include the Regional Art Gallery, Heritage Museum and South Burnett Timber Industry Museum. Town hosts Garden Expo in Sept; 13km S. **Bjelke-Petersen Dam:** popular spot for watersports and fishing (boat hire available). The dam is home to the Annual Fishing Competition in Oct; 15km SE. **Goomeri:** known as 'clock town' for its unique memorial clock in the town centre. It has numerous antique stores and holds the Pumpkin Festival in May; 19km NE. **Kilkivan:** Queensland's first discovery of gold was here in 1852. Try fossicking for gold or visit the lavender farm and historical museum. 44km NE. **Lake Boondooma:** watersports, fishing and the Fishing Competition in Feb; 74km NW via Proston. **Kilkivan to Kingaroy Rail Trail:** Murgon makes a good night's stop midway along this half-sealed, half-unsealed 88km rail trail. **Fossicking:** semi-precious stones in Cloyna and Windera region; details from visitor centre.

NANANGO
Population 3438

Nanango is one of the oldest towns in Queensland. Gold was mined here from 1850 to 1900 and fossickers still try their luck today. The industrial Tarong Power Station and Meandu Coal Mine are nearby, yet Nanango still retains a welcoming country atmosphere.

SEE & DO **The Palms National Park:** see Other Attractions. **Tarong Power Station Display:** adjacent to visitor centre. **Market:** showgrounds; 1st Sat each month. **Tipperary Flat:** tribute park to early settlers with old goldmining camp, displays and walking track; 2km E. **Seven-Mile Diggings:** gold and gem fossicking; currently not open to any motorised transport – visitors are asked to park where signed and walk to the diggings; permit from visitor centre; 11km SE. **Yarraman:** historic timber town with heritage centre and regional mud maps; 21km S. **Blackbutt:** picturesque timber town with country markets 3rd Sun each month; 41km SE.

STRATHPINE
Population 10,647

Strathpine is north of Brisbane in the Pine Rivers region, a district that includes the forested areas and national parks closest to the capital. Taking advantage of this rural setting so close to the city are a number of art and craft industries.

SEE & DO **D'aguilar National Park, South D'aguilar Section:** see Top Attractions. **St Helena Island:** see Other Attractions. **Lake Samsonvale:** fishing, watersports and bushwalking; 8km NW. **Old Petrie Town:** heritage park that holds markets each Sun and the popular Twilight Markets last Fri each month (Jan–Oct) then every Fri (Nov–Dec); 9km N. **Osprey House:** environmental centre with resident raptors, koalas and great birdwatchng; Dohles Rocks Rd, Griffin; 18km N.

Gold Coast and Hinterland

The Gold Coast, with its glittering glass towers, **theme parks, shopping** and **nightlife** needs no introduction; it's been a **favourite holiday destination** since the first meter maids shashayed down the street in their gold lamé bikinis back in 1965, although it's the **golden beaches and endless surf** that really draw the crowds. The **World Heritage–listed national parks** west of the high-rise coastal strip are laced with walking tracks and waterfalls, lush valleys, **boutique wineries, quirky shops, art studios and laid-back country towns,** and feel a world away from the coastal razzle dazzle.

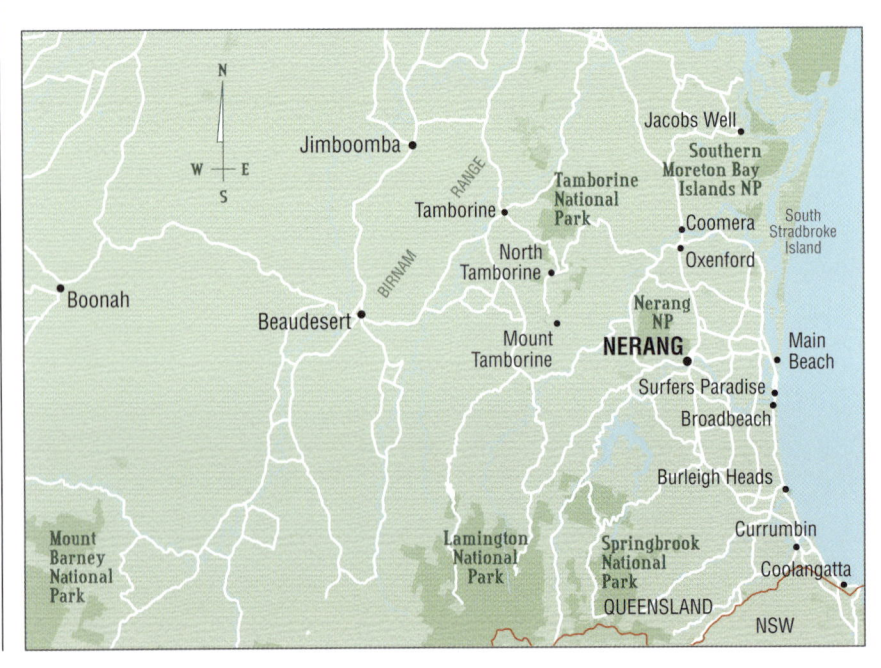

CHEAT SHEET

- Allow at least two days.
- The Gold Coast is very popular during school holidays. Warm enough for swimming for most of the year, it really is a year-round destination. Escape the summer humidity in the cooler highlands.
- Main towns: Surfers Paradise (see p. 375).
- The Gold Coast is Yugambeh Country.
- Did you know? The Gold Coast is home to Australia's tallest building, Q1, built in 2005. The views from the Observation Deck on the 77th and 78th floors are truly spectacular.
- Don't miss: getting wet at Surfers Paradise; walking through the rainforest in Lamington or Tamborine national parks; Natural Arch in Springbrook National Park; fine dining in Main Beach or Burleigh Heads.

Top: Warrie Circuit, Springbrook National Park
Opposite: SkyPoint Climb, SkyPoint Observation Deck

TOP ATTRACTIONS

BROADBEACH: The cosmopolitan heart of the Gold Coast has sophisticated wine bars, chic cafes, sun-drenched beaches and a vibrant nightlife. Visit Pacific Fair, Queensland's largest shopping centre, hit the Star casino, or stroll down to Kurrawa Beach, home of Australia's major surf-lifesaving competition.

CURRUMBIN WILDLIFE SANCTUARY: A 20ha reserve owned by the National Trust. There are free-ranging animals in open areas, the Crocodile Wetlands with raised walkways over pools of freshwater and saltwater crocodiles, a walk-through rainforest aviary and a miniature railway. Highlights are the twice-daily feeding of wild rainbow lorikeets, the free-flight bird show and animal hospital; 28 Tomewin St, Currumbin; (07) 5534 1266.

LAMINGTON NATIONAL PARK: Part of a World Heritage area, this popular park preserves a wonderland of rainforest and volcanic ridges, crisscrossed by 160km of walking tracks. The main picnic, camping and walking areas are at Binna Burra and Green Mountains, sites of the award-winning Binna Burra Mountain Lodge and O'Reilly's Rainforest Retreat. Don't miss the Tree Top Walk for an up-close look at the canopy. Access to the Green Mountains section is via Canungra; Binna Burra is accessed via Beechmont. Some sections of the park were burned in bushfires in 2019-20, but the park has fully re-opened.

MAIN RANGE NATIONAL PARK: A World Heritage–listed park of rugged mountains and landscapes with superb lookouts. There are walks starting at the Cunninghams Gap and Spicers Gap campsites. See the varied birdlife, including the satin bowerbird, on the 8.4km return Box Forest track. There are also short walks around Dalrymple Creek and spectacular views from Mount Castle and Sylvesters lookouts. In the south of the park near Killarney (see p. 380) is Queen Mary Falls, close to the NSW border. Most of the vegetation is open eucalypt, but in the gorge below the falls is subtropical rainforest. Follow the 2km Queen Mary Falls circuit to the lookout for a stunning view of the 40m falls and continue down to the rockpools at the base. If you are lucky, the rare Albert's lyrebird might be seen on the walk or the endangered brush-tailed rock wallaby on the cliffs. Access park from Cunningham Hwy; it's 40km west of Boonah (see p. 373).

SKYPOINT OBSERVATION DECK: At 230m above sea level in one of the tallest residential buildings in the world, the Q1 SkyPoint Observation Deck offers breathtaking panoramic views from Brisbane to Byron Bay. The SkyPoint Climb will take you up to the crow's nest on the outside of the building, 270m in the air; Hamilton Ave, Surfers Paradise.

SOUTH STRADBROKE ISLAND: This resort island, separated from North Stradbroke/Minjerribah (see p. 366) by the popular fishing channel Jumpinpin, is a peaceful alternative to the Gold Coast. It boasts quiet coves to the west and lively ocean beaches to the east, separated by wetland and remnant rainforest. See the abundant bird and butterfly species and discover the pleasures of windsurfing and sailing on either a daytrip or longer stay. Cars are not permitted; once on the island, visitors must walk or cycle. Access by ferry or private boat from Runaway Bay Marina.

SPRINGBROOK NATIONAL PARK: This rainforest park forms part of the Scenic Rim of mountains. The Springbrook section has an information centre, from which a short walk leads to a spectacular lookout over the Gold Coast. Access is via Springbrook; 39km SW of Nerang. The Natural Bridge section features an unusual rock arch over Cave Creek. Take the 1km rainforest walk to see the Natural Bridge where Cave Creek plunges through an eroded hole to a cavern below. There are tours to see the glow worms or a 3km night trail through rainforest; bookings on (07) 5533 5239.

QUEENSLAND

371

The Mount Cougal section of the park near Burleigh Heads contains a subtropical rainforest remnant and is part of the Gondwana Rainforests of Australia World Heritage Area. Mount Cougal's twin peaks and the Currumbin Valley are an interesting and diverse landscape. There is a scenic drive through the valley and a walking track through rainforest, past cascades, to the remains of an old bush sawmill. End of Currumbin Creek Rd; it's 27km south-west of Burleigh Heads (see p. 373).

TAMBORINE NATIONAL PARK: This picturesque mountain park protects remnant subtropical rainforest. Waterfalls, such as **Curtis Falls**, cliffs and beautiful walks make it a popular spot for visitors. The scenic drive visits the major waterfalls and lookouts and there are 22km of walks on offer. Walk highlights are the 5.4km Jenyns Falls circuit track and the 3km Witches Falls circuit track. Park access points are on Tamborine–Oxenford Rd; parks.des.qld.gov.au/parks/tamborine.

THEME PARKS: The Gold Coast is the theme park capital of Australia, with four major theme parks in the Surfers Paradise area (see p.375). **Warner Bros. Movie World** is 'Hollywood on the Gold Coast' with thrilling rides, stunts and shows that will interest all ages. Just down the road is **Wet'n'Wild Water Park**. Enjoy the thrill-seeking rides or relax on artificial Calypso Beach. **Dreamworld** has a diverse range of attractions including the 'Biggest Tallest Fastest' thrill rides, ABC Kids World, Tiger Island, sheep-shearing and crocodile feeding shows. There is also a corroboree. Next to Dreamworld is **Whitewater World**, which boasts the latest technology in water slides. Also popular is **Sea World** in Main Beach, which has marine exhibits as well as thrill rides and live shows.

OTHER ATTRACTIONS

BRISBANE TO GOLD COAST WINE REGION: Wineries are scattered from the Sunshine Coast hinterland down to the Gold Coast, with the tourist trade understandably the focus. Between Brisbane and the Gold Coast, the state-of-the-art **Sirromet Wines** grows the majority of its grapes in the Granite Belt and makes them into various wines here. It is also home to the popular **Lurleen's** restaurant. Further south is **Albert River Wines**, which is particularly skilled in shiraz varieties, and has some lovingly restored historic buildings.

DAVID FLEAY WILDLIFE PARK: Presents Queensland's native animals in a natural setting with the only display of Lumholtz's tree kangaroos and mahogany gliders in the world. The park also has crocodile feeding in summer. There are also First Nations-heritage programs; West Burleigh Rd, Burleigh Heads; (07) 5576 2411.

HOTA (HOME OF THE ARTS): Cultural hub including the new HOTA Gallery (contemporary and historical Australian art), theatres, cinema, a sculpture walk, and Evandale Park and lake; Bundall Rd, Surfers Paradise.

MAIN BEACH: This wealthy area just north of Surfers Paradise is awash with trendy boutiques and chic eateries. The Southport Spit (or just 'the Spit') is home to Sea World and the lavish Palazzo Versace hotel, as well as many specialty shops, restaurants, outdoor cafes and weekend entertainment at Marina Mirage and Mariners Cove. It is also a hotspot for fishing, while diving can be done at the nearby wreck of the *Scottish Prince*.

MOUNT BARNEY NATIONAL PARK: A remote park where the rugged peaks of Barney, Maroon, May and Lindesay mountains stand as remnants of the ancient Focal Peak Shield Volcano. The walks are not for the inexperienced, and picnicking at Yellow Pinch at the base of Mount Barney is an alternative. The challenging 10hr ascent to Mount Barney's summit on the Logan's Ridge track rewards walkers with spectacular views. 13 7468.

MOUNT TAMBORINE WINE REGION: Flying under the radar of many wine lovers, the Mount Tamborine wine region has a charming collection of boutique wineries to visit. **Tamborine Mountain Distillery:** award-winning distillery with a range of liqueurs, schnapps, vodkas and spirits; Beacon Rd. **Mount Tamborine Winery:** tastings and sales; Long Rd (Gallery Walk). **Cedar Creek Estate:** tastings and sales; Hartley Rd.

NERANG NATIONAL PARK AND NERANG STATE FOREST: On the north-west fringe of Nerang is this hilly rainforest and open eucalypt reserve. An excellent way of exploring the landscape is on the 2.8km return Casuarina Grove Track through rainforest and along the creek. Look out for the black cockatoos. These parks are popular with horseriders and cyclists. There are 12km of cycling tracks.

VISITOR INFORMATION

Gold Coast Visitor Information Centre
2 Cavill Ave,
Surfers Paradise
1300 309 440
destinationgoldcoast.com

Gold Coast Hinterland
visitscenicrim.com.au

Curtis Falls, Tamborine National Park **Opposite top:** SkyPoint Climb **Opposite middle:** Hiking through Lamington National Park **Opposite bottom:** SkyPoint Bar & Bistro with panoramic ocean views

KEY TOWNS

BEAUDESERT
Population 8127

Beaudesert lies in the valley of the Logan River, in the Gold Coast hinterland. The town was built on the Traditional Land of the Yugambeh People. It was built up around the homestead of Edward Hawkins – his property was immense, comprising land from the coast to the Logan River. The land around here is rich, and the area is known for its excellent beef cattle and fruit and vegetable produce – it's worth visiting for the country markets alone.

SEE & DO **The Centre:** arts and cultural centre, a hub for musicians, artists, comedians and film buffs. State-of-the-art auditorium for large performances as well as intimate spaces; Brisbane St. **Museum:** displays of old machinery and tools; Brisbane St. **Community Arts Centre:** art gallery, teahouse and craft shop; Enterprise Dr. **Market:** Westerman Park; 1st Sat each month. **Darlington Park:** recreation area with picnic and barbecue facilities; 12km S. **Tamrookum:** has a fine example of a timber church; tours by appt; 24km SW. **Bigriggen Park:** recreation area with picnic and barbecue facilities; 30km SW. **Rathdowney:** great views from Captain Logan's Lookout in John St; 32km S.

BOONAH
Population 2721

Boonah is set in the picturesque Fassifern Valley, surrounded by hills and once noted as a 'beautiful vale' by 19th-century explorers. A little expedition in the surrounding region will reveal the beauty and ruggedness of the area. West of town is Main Range National Park, part of the Scenic Rim.

SEE & DO **Main Range National Park:** *see* Top Attractions. **Cultural Centre:** incorporates regional art gallery; open Mon–Fri, gallery open Wed–Sun 10am–4pm; High St. **Gliding tours:** flights over the Scenic Rim; contact Boonah Gliding Club 0407 770 213. **Country market:** Springleigh Park; 2nd and 4th Sat each month 7am–12pm. **Templin:** has a historical village museum chronicling the history of the area (open Sun only); 5km NW. **Kalbar:** historic German town with magnificent buildings including St John's Lutheran Church; 10km NW. **Moogerah Peaks National Park:** excellent for birdwatching, with lookouts over the Fassifern Valley. Frog Buttress at Mount French is one of the best rock-climbing sites in Queensland; contact QPWS on 13 7468 for more information; 12km W. **Lakes Maroon and Moogerah:** ideal for camping and watersports; 20km S and SW.

BURLEIGH HEADS
Population 10,572

Burleigh Heads is a Gold Coast suburb situated between Coolangatta and the tourist hub of Surfers Paradise. It is known for its breathtaking scenery, highlighted by stunning Burleigh Head National Park. The famed south-easterly swells and surrounding parklands make the beaches at Burleigh Heads some of the best in the world, attracting international surfing tournaments. The relaxed charm of Burleigh Heads can be enjoyed from under the beachside pines and pandanus palms or in a restaurant overlooking the Pacific.

QUEENSLAND

373

SEE & DO **Springbrook National Park; Currumbin Wildlife Sanctuary:** see Top Attractions for both. **David Fleay Wildlife Park:** see Other Attractions. **Burleigh Head National Park:** take the 2.8km Ocean View circuit to experience the coastal vegetation, rainforest and mangroves or go to Tumgun Lookout to watch for dolphins and humpback whales (seasonal); access from Goodwin Tce; 13 7468. **Jellurgal Aboriginal Cultural Centre:** rainforest walk, shell middens, guided tours, daily shows at 11am; 1711 Gold Coast Hwy; (07) 5525 5955. **Car Boot Sale:** Stocklands Shopping Centre carpark; 2nd Sun each month. **Coolangatta Markets:** beachfront; 2nd Sun each month. **Art and Craft Market:** beachfront; last Sun each month. **Palm Beach:** popular golden-sands beach that has won Queensland's Cleanest Beach Award three times; 4km SE. **Honeyworld:** live displays, Walks with Bees tour, honey making and sales; opposite Currumbin Sanctuary; (07) 5598 4548; 8km SE. **Greenmount and Coolangatta beaches:** sheltered white-sand beaches with beautiful views of the coast; 13km SE. **Rainbow Bay:** sheltered beach excellent for swimming. Walk along the coast to Snapper Rocks; 15km SE. **Snapper Rocks:** top surf area with the 'Superbank', one of the world's longest point breaks; 15km SE. **Point Danger:** named by James Cook as he sailed by. It offers excellent panoramic views over the ocean and coast. Catch a glimpse of dolphins from the Captain Cook Memorial Lighthouse; 15km SE. **Tom Beatson Outlook (Razorback Lookout):** excellent views; behind Tweed Heads; 16km SE.

NERANG
Population 17,048

Nerang is in the Gold Coast hinterland. Today the town is more similar in character to the dense urban coast below than to the small rural centre it started out as in the 1860s. The gorgeous Nerang River flows through town, providing a popular spot for picnics, boating, fishing and watersports.

SEE & DO **Springbrook National Park; Lamington national park:** see Top Attractions for both. **Nerang National Park and Nerang State Forest:** see Other Attractions. **Farmers' market:** Lavelle St; Sun morning. **Carrara:** nearby town offers scenic balloon flights over the Gold Coast and holds weekend markets; (07) 5578 2244; 5km SE. **Lakelands Golf Club:** Lakelands Dr, Merrimac; (07) 5579 8700; 10km SE. **Hinze Dam (also called Advancetown Lake):** sailing and bass fishing; 10km SW. **Historic River Mill:** 1910 arrowroot mill, now a cafe, nursery and museum; Beaudesert–Nerang Rd; 10km W. **Mudgeeraba:** holds the Somerset Storyfest writers festival; in Mar. Nearby is the Gold Coast War Museum with military memorabilia and skirmish paintball; 12km S. **The Links Hope Island:** golf course; Hope Island Rd, Hope Island; (07) 5530 9000. **Sanctuary Cove Golf and Country Club:** Gleneagles Dr, Hope Island; (07) 5699 9000; 21km N.

NORTH TAMBORINE
Population 8001

North Tamborine is one of the towns on the Tamborine Mountain ridge in the Gold Coast hinterland. Numerous galleries, arts

Birds of Prey Show, O'Reilly's Rainforest Retreat
Opposite: Surfers at Surfers Paradise Beach

TOP EVENTS

- JAN Magic Millions Racing Carnival (Surfers Paradise)
- FEB–MAR Beyond the Sand festival (sand sculpture Surfers Paradise)
- MAR Campdraft (Beaudesert); Mountain Show (North Tamborine)
- APR Gold Coast Cup Outrigger Canoe Marathon (Burleigh Heads); Gold Coast Film Festival (Surfers Paradise)
- MAY Gold Coast Open surfing competition (Burleigh Heads); Country Show (Boonah); Blues on Broadbeach Music Festival (Surfers Paradise)
- JUNE–JULY Cooly Rocks On 50s & 60s nostalgia festival (Coolangatta); Scenic Rim Eat Local Month, including the Winter Harvest Festival (across the region)
- AUG Rodeo (Boonah); BLEACH* Festival (across the region)
- SEPT Arts Festival (Boonah)
- OCT Scarecrow Festival (North Tamborine); Gold Coast 500 (Surfers Paradise)
- NOV Coolangatta Gold ironman and ironwoman race (Coolangatta)

TEMPERATURES

Jan: 21–29°C

July: 9–21°C

and crafts shops and boutique wineries make it a popular getaway, along with the nearby towns of Tamborine Village, Eagle Heights and Mount Tamborine. Tamborine National Park covers most of the mountain – the Witches Falls section was Queensland's first national park, listed in 1908.

SEE & DO **Tamborine National Park:** see Top Attractions. **Mount Tamborine Wine Region:** see Other Attractions. **Tamborine Rainforest Skywalk:** canopy walk and 30m-high cantilevered lookout as well as a café and eco-gallery; Geissmann Dr; (07) 5545 2222. **Hang-gliding:** off Tamborine Mountain; Main Western Rd; contact visitor centre. **Produce market:** Showgrounds (green shed); Sun mornings. **Tamborine Mountain Country Markets:** Showgrounds, Main Western Rd; 2nd Sun morning each month. **Eagle Heights:** pretty village to the north-east with the Gallery Walk on Long Rd featuring many local crafts; Botanical Gardens in Forsythia Dr are set on 9ha of rainforest with a variety of plants; historic buildings are on show at the Heritage Centre, Wongawallen Rd; open Sun 11am–3pm.. **Thunderbird Park:** wildlife sanctuary, horseriding, laser skirmish, ropes course and fossicking for 'thunder eggs'; Tamborine Mountain Rd.

★ SURFERS PARADISE
Population 26,412

Surfers Paradise is the Gold Coast's signature beach. It's come a long way since the first big hotel was built here in the 1930s alongside a clutch of beach shacks, and today is an international holiday destination where high-rise hotels and apartments compete for attention – among them, one of the world's tallest residential towers, Q1 Resort and Spa. It's a popular place for families to holiday, with beaches, shopping and Australia's main theme parks, clustered here.

SEE & DO **Theme Parks; Skypoint Observation Deck; Broadbeach:** see Top Attractions for all. **Main Beach; HOTA:** see Other Attractions for both. **Orchid Avenue:** famous strip with the best live music in town. **Ripley's Believe It or Not:** the 12 galleries of extraordinary feats, facts and figures will surprise and amaze. There are interactive displays and movies that bring events to life; Cavill Mall. **Adventure activities and tours:** try surfing lessons or scenic flights to see Surfers Paradise in a new light, or take a tour to the Gold Coast hinterland; contact visitor centre for details. **Quack'R Duck:** take an adventure on both land and water in this amphibious vehicle; departs Elkhorn Ave. **Markets:** The Espl, between Hanlan St and Elkhorn Ave; Wed, Fri and Sat evening. **Farmers' market:** Marina Mirage Shopping Centre; Sat morning. **Broadbeach Market:** Kurrawa Park; 1st and 3rd Sun each month. **Cararra Markets:** Gooding Dr; every Sat and Sun. **Miami and Nobby beaches:** both beaches are separated by a headland known as Magic Mountain. Miami is home to many diehard surfers; 6km S. **The Broadwater:** sheltered waterways excellent for boating (hire available), watersports and shore walks; access from Labrador and Southport; 5km N. **Surfers Riverwalk:** scenic 9km walk from Sundale Bridge at Southport to Pacific Fair at Broadbeach. **Sanctuary Cove:** famous area for championship golf courses, the exclusive Pines and the immaculate Palms. Hire a houseboat or take a cruise; 23km NW. **Surf World Gold Coast:** museum dedicated to all things surfing, including Australia's largest collection of surfboards, surfing memorabilia, photographs and films about the history of surfing and beach culture; 1st floor, 35 Tomewin St, Tugun; 18km S.

Darling Downs

The Darling Downs and Granite Belt is where Queenslanders go when they need to chill out. Up here, in the highlands of the south-east, in the time of year the locals call Brass Monkey Season, it gets cold enough to **warm up beside a roaring fireplace**. The cool climate produces an amazing array of **wonderful produce** and **Queensland's best wines**. In spring, the region is ablaze with **colourful flowers** and the many **parks and gardens** are reason enough to visit. There's nowhere else in the Sunshine State quite like it.

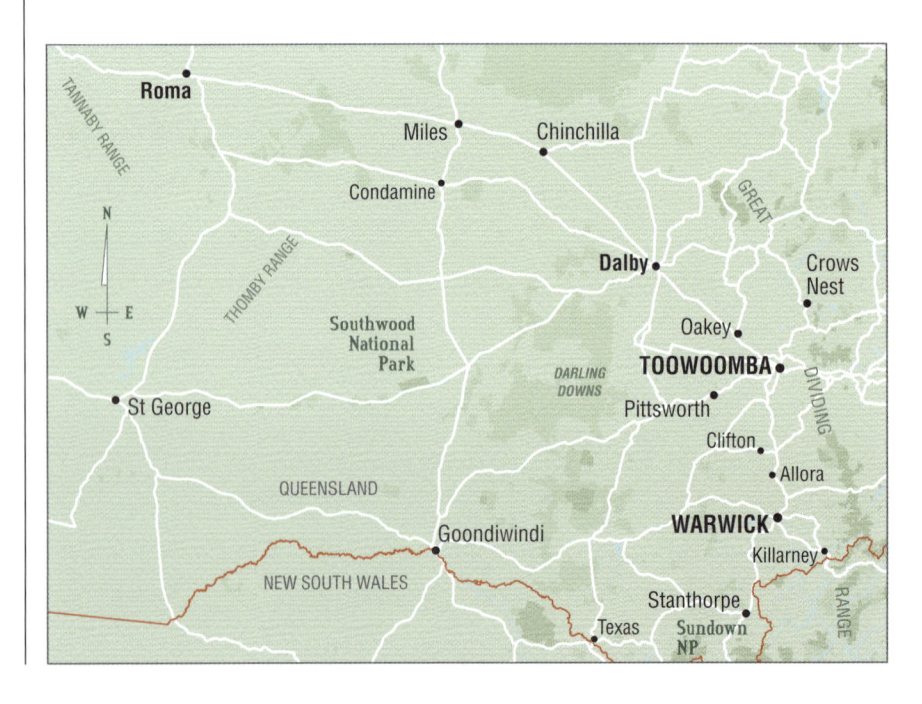

CHEAT SHEET

→ Allow three or four days to explore the region.

→ Escape the heat or embrace the cold: this really is a year-round destination, that is particularly popular in spring, when flower festivals are major drawcards.

→ Main towns: Stanthorpe (*see* p. 381), Toowoomba (*see* p. 381), Warwick (*see* p. 381).

→ The countryside of the Darling Downs and Granite Belt regions are the Traditional Lands of the Barunggam, Bigambul, Giabal, Yuggera, Jarowair, Kooma and Mandandanjii Peoples.

→ Don't miss: Queen Mary Falls near Killarney; wine tasting on the Granite Belt Wine Trail; four-wheel driving in Condamine Gorge; a beer at the Nindigully Pub; a riverwalk at Goondiwindi; and stopping to smell the flowers at Toowoomba.

Top: Toowoomba's Cobb & Co. Museum **Opposite:** Carnival of Flowers in Toowoomba

TOP ATTRACTIONS

COBB & CO. MUSEUM: This museum in Toowoomba (*see* p. 381), traces the history of horse-drawn vehicles in the Darling Downs region. The complex includes the National Carriage Collection, featuring an open-plan training centre that hosts workshops that teach heritage skills including blacksmithing, saddlery, silversmithing and glass art, with a viewing area for visitors. There is also an interactive discovery centre for children. Guided tours run at 10.30am and 2.30pm daily. Open 10am–4pm; 27 Lindsay St, Toowoomba; (07) 4659 4900.

GRANITE BELT WINE REGION: This is Queensland's version of the Hunter Valley, also making successful semillon and shiraz. The region is called the Granite Belt because of the granite bed that lies beneath the northern extension of the New England Tableland. Vineyards are found at an altitude of around 800m and, although grapes were first planted in the 1960s, it is the recent vintages that have caused a stir. **Ballandean Estate** is known for an interesting German variety, sylvaner. **Boireann** is a relative newcomer growing Italian and French grapes, with a rapidly growing reputation for wines like shiraz viognier.

JONDARYAN WOOLSHED: Built in 1859 and still shearing under steam power, this woolshed is a memorial to pioneers of the wool industry. The complex includes the huge woolshed, historic buildings, and machinery and equipment collections. Visitors can see the shearing and sheepdog demonstrations or sit down to some billy tea and damper. Events are held throughout the year, including the Working Draught-horse Expo in June and the Australian Heritage Festival in Aug. It's 22km north-west of Oakey (*see* p. 380).

THE BIG RIG: This unique complex is set on an old oil derrick and features historic oil rigs and machinery displays. Photographs, memorabilia and multimedia displays provide a comprehensive history of oil and gas discovery and usage in Australia from 1900 to the present day. A highlight is the evening sound-and-light show (Tues, Thurs, Sun). Adjacent to the complex is a historic slab hut, recreational area and 1915 miniature train that travels on a 1.4km circuit; 2 Riggers Rd, Roma.

TOOWOOMBA'S PARKS AND GARDENS: No trip to the 'Garden City' would be complete without a visit to some of the superb parks and gardens. **Lake Annand** is a popular recreation spot with boardwalks, bridges and ducks. There are imposing European trees in **Queens Park**, which includes the **Botanic Gardens**. **Laurel Bank Park** features the unique Scented Garden, designed for the visually impaired. Birdwatchers should visit Waterbird Habitat where native birds can be watched from observation platforms and floating islands. The impressive **Japanese Garden** at the University of Southern Queensland is the largest in Australia; a thousand visitors a week stroll the 3km of paths at Ju Raku En, which showcases the harmony and beauty of ancient Japanese garden design with its lake, willowy beeches, islands, bridges, stream and pavilion.

OTHER ATTRACTIONS

AUSTRALIAN ARMY FLYING MUSEUM: Every aircraft flown by the Australian army since World War II is represented at the museum through originals and replicas. Other aircraft can also be viewed, from the early wood Box Kite to the hi-tech Blackhawk helicopter; at Army base on Corfe Rd, Oakey.

AUSTRALIAN RODEO HERITAGE CENTRE: Follow the history and relive the glory of the Australian Professional Rodeo Association's greatest champions; open Mon–Fri 10am–3pm, or by appt; Alice St, Warwick.

CHINCHILLA HISTORICAL MUSEUM: A varied collection of memorabilia including steam engines, a replica 1910 sawmill and a slab cottage. Also an excellent display of local petrified wood known as 'Chinchilla Red'; open Thurs–Mon 9am–4pm; Villiers St, Chinchilla.

CROWS NEST NATIONAL PARK: This popular park near Crows Nest features a variety of landscapes, including granite outcrops and eucalypt forest. The wildlife is spectacular: see the platypus in the creek and the brush-tailed rock wallabies on the rocky cliffs. A steep track from the creek leads to an excellent lookout over Crows Nest Falls; follow this further to Koonin Lookout for views over the gorge, known locally as the Valley of Diamonds.

DARLING DOWNS ZOO: Queensland's newest zoo is situated in serene countryside where you can view native and exotic animals from Africa, South America and Asia. The zoo has a shady picnic area as well as barbecue facilities and a small kiosk. Gatton–Clifton Rd; it's 10km east of Clifton (see p. 379).

GLENGALLAN HOMESTEAD AND HERITAGE CENTRE: Restored 1867 sandstone mansion. Documents and photos chronicle its history as a pastoral station; open Wed–Sun; New England Hwy. It's 11km south of Allora (see p. 379).

LAKE BROADWATER CONSERVATION PARK: The 350ha lake is an important breeding ground for waterfowl. There are more than 240 species of bird that can be seen from the short walks around the lake. Waterskiing and boating are popular on the main body of the lake when it is full (permit required).

PITTSWORTH PIONEER HISTORICAL VILLAGE: Featuring a single-teacher school, early farming machinery and a display commemorating Arthur Postle, or the 'Crimson Flash', once the fastest runner in the world; village open Thurs–Fri 10am–1pm, Sun 10am–2pm or by appt; Pioneer Way, Pittsworth; 0436 399 168. It's 46km south-west of Toowoomba (see p. 381).

RAVENSBOURNE NATIONAL PARK: A small park comprising remnant rainforest and wet eucalypt forest with over 80 species of birds, including the black-breasted button-quail that can be seen feeding on the rainforest floor on the Cedar Block track. Many bushwalks start at Blackbean picnic area; Esk–Hampton Rd. It's 25km south-east of Crows Nest (see p. 379).

SOUTHWOOD NATIONAL PARK: This brigalow–belah forest park was once known as 'Wild Horse Paradise'. Have a bush picnic and look for the black cockatoos in the belah trees, or visit at night and go spotlighting for feathertail gliders. 4WD is recommended. Access from Moonie Hwy.

SUNDOWN NATIONAL PARK: Rugged national park of gorges and high peaks. Go birdwatching to see herons and azure kingfishers along the river or take the short Red Rock Gorge Lookout Track for spectacular views.

VISITOR INFORMATION

Toowoomba Visitor Information Centre
86 James St, Toowoomba
1800 331 155

Warwick Visitor Centre
Town Hall, 72 Palmerin St, Warwick
(07) 4661 3122 or
1800 060 877

Southern Queensland
southernqueensland country.com.au

Granite Belt
granitebeltwinecountry.com.au

TEMPERATURES

Jan: 24–35°C

July: 13–30°C

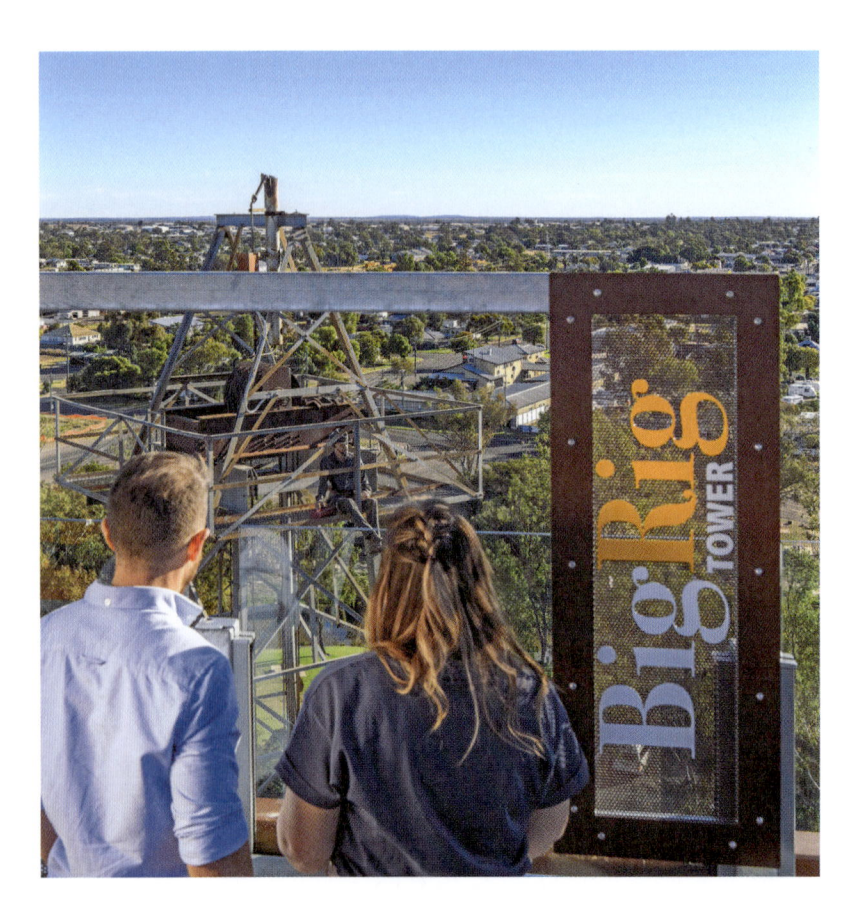

The Big Rig Museum at Roma

TOP EVENTS

- FEB Melon Festival and Rodeo (odd-numbered years, Chinchilla)
- MAR Apple and Grape Harvest Festival (even-numbered years, Stanthorpe); Torture on the Border triathlon (Texas); CelticFest (Warwick); Royal Show (Toowoomba); Festival of Hell triathlon (Goondiwindi)
- EASTER Easter on the MacIntyre Festival (Goondiwindi)
- JULY Jumpers and Jazz Festival (Warwick)
- AUG Delicious and Delightful multicultural festival (Dalby); Historic Leyburn Sprints (Leyburn)
- SEPT Carnival of Flowers (Toowoomba); Polocrosse Carnival (Chinchilla); Spring Sensations (Dalby); Gourmet in Gundy (Goondiwindi); Back to the Bush (inc Wildflower Festival, Miles); Beef, Bells and Bottle Tree Festival (even-numbered years, Miles); Country Music Roundup (Texas)
- OCT Grandfather Clock Campdraft (Chinchilla); Country Week (inc Rose and Iris Show, Clifton), Australian Small Winemakers Show (Stanthorpe); Rose and Rodeo Festival (Warwick); Australian Camp Oven Festival (Millmerran); Condamine Bell Campdraft (Condamine)
- NOV Pig Races (Nindigully)

KEY TOWNS

ALLORA
Population 843

Charming Allora is the centre for its rich agricultural surrounds, explored and settled with stud farms in the 1840s. Allora's main street is noted for its well-preserved historic buildings and old-time country feel.

SEE & DO **Glengallan Homestead:** see Other Attractions. **Museum:** noted for its replica of the Talgai Skull, dating back 15,000 years; open by appt; 0408 753 085; old courthouse, Drayton St. **St David's Anglican Church:** built in 1888 and said to be one of the finest timber churches in country Queensland; Church St. **Glengallan farmers' markets:** 1st Sun each season.

CHINCHILLA
Population 6292

Chinchilla is a prosperous town in the western Darling Downs. Explorer Ludwig Leichhardt named the area in 1844 as a corrupted version of the word his Aboriginal guides used for the native cypress pines, 'jinchilla' and there are still many of the trees in town. Today Chinchilla is known as the 'melon capital' of Australia because it produces around 25 per cent of the country's melons. The biennial Melon Festival and Rodeo is held in February in odd-numbered years.

SEE & DO **Chinchilla Historical Museum:** see Other Attractions. **Lapunyah Art Gallery:** touring exhibitions and work by local artists; open Mon–Fri 10am–4pm, Sat 9am–12pm; Heeney St. **Pioneer Cemetery:** historic headstones include a monument to Ludwig Leichhardt; Warrego Hwy. **Cactoblastis Memorial Hall:** dedicated to the insect introduced from South America to eradicate the prickly pear cactus; Boonarga, 8km E. **Fossicking:** for petrified wood at nearby properties; licences and details from visitor centre. **Fishing:** good spots include Charleys Creek and the Condamine River; details from visitor centre. **Chinchilla Weir:** popular spot for boating and waterskiing, plus freshwater fishing for golden perch and jewfish; 10km S.

CLIFTON
Population 1299

Clifton is south of Toowoomba in the fertile agricultural lands of the Darling Downs. The charming street facades are an appealing backdrop when the town becomes a vision of colour during the renowned annual Rose and Iris Show in October.

SEE & DO **Darling Downs Zoo:** see Other Attractions. **Historical Museum:** in the old butter factory, with displays of early implements and farm life; open Fri–Mon 10am–2pm; King St. **Alister Clark Rose Garden:** largest Queensland collection of these roses; Edward St. **Nobby:** this small town provided inspiration to writer Arthur Hoey Davis (Steele Rudd), author of *On Our Selection* and creator of the famous Dad and Dave characters. Rudd's Pub (1893) has a museum of early settler memorabilia. Nearby is the burial site of Sister Kenny along with a memorial and museum dedicated to her – she was renowned for her unorthodox method of treating poliomyelitis. 8km N.

CROWS NEST
Population 1808

On the western slopes of the Great Dividing Range north of Toowoomba is the small town of Crows Nest. It was named after a Kabi-Kabi man the European settlers referred to as 'Jimmy Crow', who made his home in a hollow tree near the present police station. He was an invaluable source of directions for passing bullock teams staying overnight in the area. A memorial to him can be found in Centenary Park.

SEE & DO **Crows Nest National Park; Ravensbourne National Park:** see Other Attractions for both. **Carbethon Folk Museum and Pioneer Village:** interesting old buildings and over 20,000 items of memorabilia documenting the history of the shire; open 10am–3pm; Thallon St. **Bullocky's Rest and Applegum Walk:** a 1.5km track follows the creeks to Hartmann Park and a lookout over Pump Hole; visit in late winter to see the beautiful wildflowers; entry from New England Hwy. **Holland Wines:** a vast collection of exquisite wines available; 5km N. **Lake Cressbrook:** this excellent spot for windsurfing and boating is set among picturesque hills. Fish the lake for silver perch; 17km E. **Beutel's Lookout:** picnic area with scenic views across the Brisbane Valley; adjacent to Ravensbourne National Park; 25km SE. **Goombungee:** historic town with museum; once famous for running rural ironman and ironwoman competitions on 26 Jan; 32km W.

DALBY
Population 12,082

Sitting at the crossroads of the Warrego, Moonie, Condamine and Bunya highways, Dalby was a small rural town until the soldier resettlement program after World War II; the population influx allowed the surrounding agricultural industry to thrive. It is now a relaxed country town with uncluttered landscapes, interesting local pubs and home-grown produce. Dalby was inundated by several floods in the first half of 2022, though town life has returned to normality.

SEE & DO **Lake Broadwater Conservation Park:** see Other Attractions. **Thomas Jack Park:** beautifully landscaped park with playground equipment and tranquil lagoon; cnr Drayton and

Condamine sts. **Art Centre:** in the Cultural Centre complex, Drayton St. **Pioneer Park Museum:** comprises historic buildings, household and agricultural items and a craft shop; Black St. **The Crossing:** an obelisk marks the spot where explorer Henry Dennis camped in 1841; Edward St. **Historic cairn:** pays homage to the Cactoblastis, the Argentinean caterpillar that controlled prickly pear in the 1920s; Myall Creek picnic area, Marble St. **Myall Creek Walk:** walk along the banks of Myall Creek to see varied birdlife. **Heritage walk:** self-guided walk provides insight into the town's history; brochure from visitor centre. **Jimbour:** attractive French homestead and formal gardens with regular gourmet picnic events; see jimbour.com; 29km N. **Bell:** small town at the base of Bunya Mountains with traditional arts and crafts stores; 41km NW. **Cecil Plains:** cotton town with a historic pub and Cecil Plains Homestead. Also a popular spot for canoeing down Condamine River; 42km S.

GOONDIWINDI
Population 5439

Goondiwindi is situated beside the picturesque MacIntyre River in the western Darling Downs. Explored by Allan Cunningham in 1827 and settled by pastoralists in the 1830s, the town derives its name from a Bigambul word 'gonnawinna', meaning 'resting place of the birds'. Goondiwindi is one of the largest cotton-growing areas in Australia.

SEE & DO **Customs House Museum:** explore local history in the restored 1850 customs house; open Mon–Tues, Fri–Sat 9am–1pm; McLean St. **Victoria Hotel:** renowned historic pub with tower; Marshall St. **Town Tours:** bus tours include visits to a cotton farm and a grain depot; contact visitor centre. **River Walk:** abundant birdlife and wildlife on 2km walk along MacIntyre River; starts at Riddles Oval, Lagoon St. **'Goondiwindi Grey' Statue:** tribute to famous racehorse Gunsynd; Apex Park, MacIntyre St. **Fishing:** some of Queensland's best fishing in and around the town, particularly for Murray cod and yellow-belly. **Botanic Gardens of Western Woodlands:** 25ha of native plants in the Darling Basin. Also here is a lake popular for swimming and canoeing; access from Brennans Rd; 1km W. **Toobeah:** small town famous for its horse events; 48km W.

KILLARNEY
Population 685

The attractive small town of Killarney is on the banks of the Condamine River close to the NSW border. It is appealingly situated at the foothills of the Great Dividing Range and is surrounded by beautiful mountain scenery.

SEE & DO **Main Range National Park, Queen Mary Falls section** (*see* p. 371) 11km E. **Brown's and Dagg's waterfalls:** stand behind Brown's Falls and see the 38m Dagg's Falls; 4km S. **Cherrabah Resort:** offers horseriding and fabulous bushwalking; 7km S. **Condamine Gorge** (also known as Cambanoora Gorge): 20km-long scenic drive popular with 4WDs with 14 river crossings and several good picnic spots; 14km NE.

MILES
Population 1349

Miles is in the Western Downs. Ludwig Leichhardt passed through this district on three expeditions and named the place Dogwood Crossing. The town was later renamed Miles in honour of a local member of parliament. After spring rains, this pocket of the Darling Downs is ablaze with wildflowers.

SEE & DO **Dogwood Crossing, Miles:** this modern cultural centre combines history and art in an innovative space and has changing exhibitions from local and regional artists. There is an IT centre and library onsite. Murilla St. **Historic Village:** all types of early buildings, a war museum, shell display and lapidary exhibition; Murilla St. **Wildflower excursions:** some of the most beautiful wildflowers in Australia; details from visitor centre. **Condamine:** small town known for inventing the Condamine Bell, a bullfrog bell that, hung around bullocks, can be heard up to 4km away. A replica and history display are in Bell Park. There is excellent fishing on the Condamine River, and the town holds a famous campdraft in Oct; 33km S. **The Gums:** tiny settlement with historic church and nature reserve; 79km S. **Glenmorgan:** the Myall Park Botanic Gardens; 134km SW.

OAKEY
Population 4319

Oakey is an agricultural town surrounded by beautiful rolling hills and black-soil plains. It is also the base for the aviation division of the Australian Army.

SEE & DO **Jondaryan Woolshed:** *see* Top Attractions. **Australian Army Flying Museum:** *see* Other Attractions. **Bernborough:** bronze statue of famous racehorse; Campbell St. **Oakey Historical Museum:** local memorabilia; Warrego Hwy.

ROMA
Population 6522

Roma is in the Western Downs region and was named after the wife of Queensland's first governor. Roma boasts a few historic 'firsts' for Queensland and Australia. In 1863 Samuel Symons Bassett brought vine cuttings to Roma, and Queensland's first winemaking enterprise began (Romavilla Winery continued running until 2016), at the same time that cattle rustler and bushranger Captain Starlight faced trial in Roma. Australia's first natural gas strike was at Hospital Hill in 1900. The excellent Big Rig documents the oil and gas industry since this discovery.

SEE & DO **The Big Rig:** *see* Top Attractions. **Roma Cultural Centre:** features a large 3D clay mural by a local artist depicting Roma's history; cnr Bungil and Quintin sts; 1300 007 662. **Heroes Avenue:** heritage-listed street of 140 bottle trees commemorating local soldiers who died in World War I; Wyndham and Bungil sts. **Roma Saleyards:** largest inland cattle market in Australia with sales and free tours from 8.30am on Tues (year-round); Warrego Hwy; (07) 4622 8676; 4km E. **Surat:** small town featuring the Cobb & Co. Changing Station complex with museum, art gallery and aquarium. Try fishing for Murray cod on Balonne River; 78km SE.

ST GEORGE
Population 2508

St George is on the banks of the Balonne River in the Western Downs and was 'discovered' by explorer Sir Thomas Mitchell on St George's Day, 1846, giving the town its name. It is often called the inland fishing capital of Queensland with lakes and rivers nearby, which also support the area's rich cotton, grape and grain industries.

SEE & DO **Heritage Centre:** historic buildings and a local history museum; Victoria St; (07) 4625 5168. **The Unique Egg:** carved, illuminated emu eggs; open Mon–Fri 9am–4pm, Sat 9am–12pm; Balonne Sports Store, Victoria St; (07) 4625 3490. **Town murals:** around town, depicting scenes of the town's history. **Riversands Wines:** boutique winery on the banks of the Balonne River; Whytes Rd; (07) 4625 3643. **Riverbank Walkway:** 2km walkway starts below the Jack Taylor Weir, marked by the Sir Thomas Mitchell cairn commemorating the explorer's landmark crossing in 1846; western outskirts. **Beardmore Dam:** popular spot for watersports and picnics in surrounding parklands, with excellent fishing for yellow-belly and Murray cod; 21km N. **Ancient rock**

well: hand-hewn by First Nations People, possibly thousands of years ago; 37km E. **Nindigully:** town where the movie *Paperback Hero* was filmed. It features Nindigully Pub, which has the oldest continuous licence in Queensland, since 1864; George Rd; (07) 4625 9637; 44km SE. **Thallon:** small town with excellent swimming and fishing at Barney's Beach on the Moonie River. Known for its landmark grain silos, painted with colourful murals; 76km SE. **Bollon:** large koala population in river red gums along Wallan Creek and a heritage centre in George St; 112km W. **Thrushton National Park:** undeveloped park of mulga scrub, sand plains and woodlands; access in dry weather only and 4WD recommended; 13 7468; 132km NW. **Culgoa Floodplain National Park:** in the Murray–Darling basin, with over 150 species of birds and is excellent for birdwatchers. There are no formal walking tracks and visitors must be self-sufficient. 4WD recommended; access via Brenda Rd, Goodooga; 13 7468; 200km SW.

STANTHORPE
Population 4873

Stanthorpe is the main town in the Granite Belt and mountain ranges along the NSW border. The town came into being after the discovery of tin at Quartpot Creek in 1872, but the mineral boom did not last. The climate is cool, said to be the coldest in Queensland, but the numerous wineries in the vicinity offer a warm welcome. Embrace the cold during winter, coined here as Brass Monkey Season. Visit in spring to see fruit trees, wattles and wildflowers.

SEE & DO **Granite Belt Wine Region:** see Top Attractions. **Heritage Museum:** displays the region's past in historic buildings, such as a schoolroom, gaol and shepherd's hut; open Wed–Sun; High St. **Regional Art Gallery:** touring and local exhibitions; open Mon–Fri, Sat–Sun afternoons; Weeroona Park, Marsh St. **Market in the Mountains:** Showgrounds; 2nd Sun each month. **Mount Marlay:** excellent views; 1km E. **Storm King Dam:** popular spot for picnics, canoeing, waterskiing, and fishing for Murray cod and silver perch; 26km SE. **Heritage trail:** historical drive of surrounding towns; brochure from visitor centre.

TEXAS
Population 707

Texas lies alongside the Dumaresq River (pronounced Dumeric) and the Queensland–NSW border. Its name comes from an 1850s land dispute in the area, viewed as similar to a quarrel between the then Republic of Texas and Mexico. The town was originally on the river flat, 2km from its current position but severe floods forced the move. Remains of the original town can be seen on the river off Schwenke St.

SEE & DO **Heritage Centre and Tobacco Museum:** in the old police building (1893), with memorabilia that shows 100 years of the tobacco industry, horse-drawn vehicles, mini shearing shed and the gaol; open Sat or by appt; Flemming St; (07) 4653 1392. **Art Gallery:** local and touring art exhibitions; open Tues–Sat; High St. **Texas Rabbit Works:** holds photos and memorabilia of the rabbit skins factory, antiques and collectibles; open by appt for tours; Mingoola Rd; (07) 4653 1106 or 0448 762 016. **Beacon Lookout:** regional views; 3km SE on Stanthorpe Rd. **Cunningham Weir:** site where Allan Cunningham crossed the Dumaresq River in 1827; 31km W off Texas–Yelarbon Rd. **Glenlyon Dam:** excellent fishing spot; 45km SE. **Inglewood:** Texas's twin town, at the centre of Australia's olive industry, sits on the banks of the lovely Macintyre Brook. Visit Inglewood Heritage Centre for local memorabilia (open Mon, Wed, Fri 10am–2pm or by appt; 0407 581 098). Tour the local olive groves and follow the scenic drives in the area; brochure available; 55km N. **Coolmunda Reservoir:** picnics, boating and fishing; 75km NE via Inglewood. **Dumaresq River:** winding river popular for canoeing and fishing, and hiking through wilderness areas along its banks.

★ TOOWOOMBA
Population 108,398

Toowoomba shines with a distinctive charm, courtesy of its tree-lined streets, colonial-era architecture and more than 150 parks and gardens – at their most vibrant in autumn and spring. The city is perched 700m above sea level on the rim of the Great Dividing Range and, unlike most of Queensland, enjoys four distinct seasons. Its proximity to Brisbane and its local gourmet produce make it a popular weekend destination.

SEE & DO **Parks and Gardens; Cobb & Co. Museum:** see Top Attractions for both. **Pittsworth Pioneer Historical Village:** see Other Attractions. **Regional Art Gallery:** changing exhibitions at Queensland's oldest gallery; open Tues–Sat 10.30am–3.30pm, Sun 1–4pm; 531 Ruthven St; (07) 4688 6652. **Royal Bull's Head Inn:** National Trust–listed building (1859) with small museum; open first Sun of each month 10am–4pm; Brisbane St, Drayton; (07) 4637 2278. **Empire Theatre:** live theatre in restored Art Deco building, opened in 1911. The adjacent Empire Church Theatre is another live theatre venue; 56 Neil St; 1300 655 299. **Picnic Point:** views of Lockyer Valley, mountains and waterfall. Enjoy the recreational facilities and walks through bushland; Tourist Dr, eastern outskirts. **Farmers' markets:** Campbell and Lindsay sts; Sat. **Highfields:** growing town featuring Orchid Park, quaint shopping and historical village with vintage machinery and buildings; 12km N. **Cabarlah:** small community that has the Black Forest Hill Cuckoo Clock Centre and holds excellent country markets on the last Sun each month; 19km N. **Lake Cooby:** fishing, walking and picnic facilities; 35km N. **Yandilla:** here you'll find the quaint All Saints Anglican Church (1877), the oldest building in the shire; 77km SW. **Millmerran:** colourful murals illustrate the history of this industrial town. The town's historical museum is open by appt; see millmerranmuseum.com.au; 87km SW. **Scenic drives:** take in places such as Spring Bluff, with an old railway station and superb gardens (16km N); drives also to Murphys Creek and Heifer Creek.

WARWICK
Population 14,110

Warwick is an attractive city, known for its beautiful sandstone buildings set alongside the willow-shaded Condamine River. It is known as the 'Rose and Rodeo City', as the Warwick Rodeo dates back to the 1850s, and the parks and gardens have an abundance of roses. There is even the City of Warwick Rose (or Arofuto Rose). Though the lands were already the home to the Githabul People, the area was re-explored by Allan Cunningham in 1827. In 1840 the Leslie brothers established a sheep station at Canning Downs. Warwick was eventually established in 1849 on the site that Patrick Leslie selected. The surrounding pastures support horse and cattle studs.

SEE & DO **Australian Rodeo Heritage Centre:** see Other Attractions. **Pringle Cottage Museum Complex:** five historic buildings, including a sandstone cottage (1870) housing a large historic photo collection, vehicles and machinery; open Tues and Thurs 9am–12pm, Fri 10am–3pm, Sat–Sun 12–3pm; Dragon St. **Art Gallery:** local and touring exhibitions; open Tues–Sun; Albion St. **Leslie Park:** see the roses that Warwick is famous for; cnr Palmerin and Fitzroy sts. **Lookout:** viewing platform for regional views; Glen Rd. **Historic walk or drive:** self-guided tour of sandstone buildings; brochure from visitor centre. **Leslie Dam:** watersports, fishing and swimming; 15km W. **Heritage drive:** 80km cultural drive in region; brochure from visitor centre.

Sunshine Coast

A natural alternative to the skyscraper razzle-dazzle of the Gold Coast, the Sunshine Coast lives up to its name: **basking in sunshine year-round**, particularly in winter, when days are mild more often than not, and the water is warm enough for swimming. It encompasses a **beautiful hinterland**, including the Glass House Mountains, Blackall Range, the Mary Valley, and **more than 100km of beaches**, as well as **charming villages** and the holiday resort town of Noosa. It's the type of place you go for a weekend but end up staying a week.

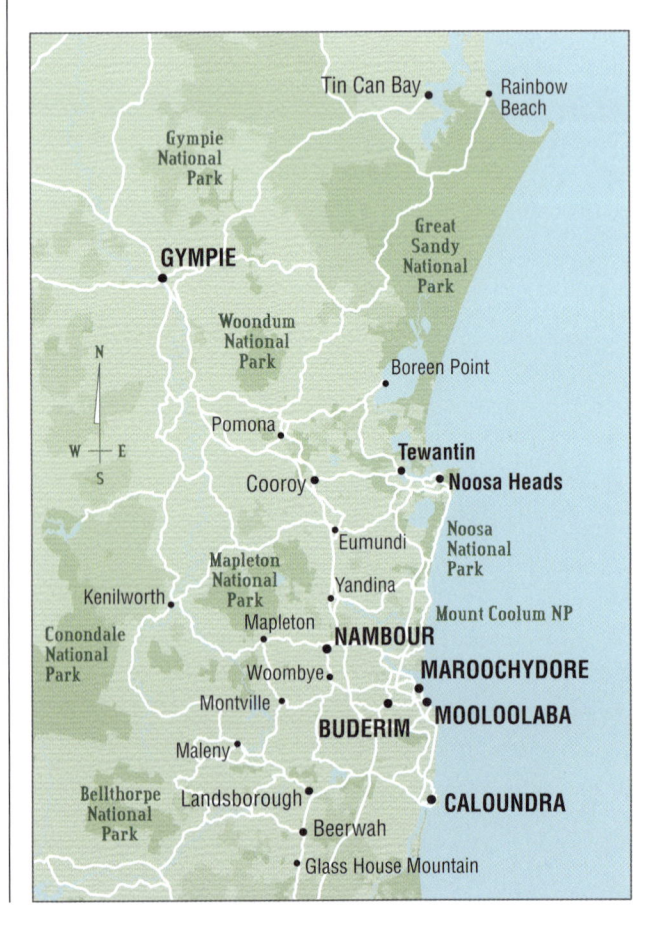

CHEAT SHEET

→ Allow two or three days to explore the region.

→ The area is popular during summer school holidays, so book ahead.

→ The Beach Highway is 4WD only. Avoid driving on the beach two hours either side of high tide. And you'll need a permit; they are available from qpws.usedirect.com/qpws or call 13 7468. It's very popular on weekends and summer holidays – go mid-week to beat the crowds.

→ Main towns: Caloundra (see p. 386), Maleny (see p. 387), Maroochydore (see p. 387), Mooloolaba (see p. 388), Noosa Heads (see p. 388).

→ Kabi Kabi (Gubbi Gubbi) and Jinibara Peoples are the Traditional Owners of the region now known as the Sunshine Coast.

→ Don't miss: Australia Zoo; Mary Cairncross Scenic Reserve; Kenilworth Cheese Factory; Eumundi Markets; the Coloured Sands; Noosa National Park; Noosa ferry; Rainbow Beach; Sea Life Sunshine Coast; and Carlo Sandblow, one of the largest piles of wind-blown sand on the Queensland coast.

Top: Mount Ngungun, Glass House Mountains National Park **Opposite:** Noosa Main Beach

TOP ATTRACTIONS

AUSTRALIA ZOO: Made famous by the late 'Crocodile Hunter', Steve Irwin, and still run by his family, this zoo now covers 28ha and is home to a wide range of native and exotic animals, from koalas and wombats to tigers and rhinos. See otters catching fish, birds of prey tackling the skies, the ever-popular crocodile demonstrations, or feed kangaroos by hand. The complex also has important breeding programs for threatened and endangered species, and an animal hospital; Steve Irwin Way, Beerwah; (07) 5436 2000; australiazoo.com.au.

EUMUNDI: This historic town has a variety of excellent galleries to visit, including some with First Nations art. The impressive artisan markets are famous for their size with over 600 stalls. The quality of the fresh produce, locally made art and craft, along with the wonderful atmosphere, make it a major Sunshine Coast attraction; Wed and Sat.

GLASS HOUSE MOUNTAINS NATIONAL PARK: This park protects eight rugged volcanic mountain peaks. These 20-million-year-old crags, the giant cores of extinct volcanoes, mark the southern entrance to the Sunshine Coast. Glass House Mountains Rd leads to sealed and unsealed routes through the mountains, with some spectacular lookouts along the way. The open eucalypt and mountain-heath landscape is a haven for many threatened and endangered animals. Three tracks lead to mountain lookouts that provide panoramic views of the Sunshine Coast hinterland. There are picnic grounds, and challenges aplenty for rockclimbers, but only experienced walkers should attempt climbing to any of the summits. However, the Traditional Owners, the Jinibara People and the Kabi Kabi (Gubbi Gubbi) People, ask people not to climb Beerwah and Tibrogargan, which are sacred mountains. The national park is 13km south-west of Landsborough (see p. 387).

GREAT SANDY NATIONAL PARK: This park has stunning coloured sands, beaches, lakes, forests and sand dunes, all of which are protected. Many rare and threatened species call it home. There are walks for all ranges of fitness and stamina, from short circuit walks to overnight hikes. For the serious walker, there is the 3- to 5-day Cooloola Wilderness Trail with bush camping. For less strenuous activity, picnic in the rainforest at Bymien or see the Teewah Coloured Sands, which rise in 40,000-year-old cliffs. It is thought that oxidisation or decaying vegetation has caused the colouring; Kabi Kabi (Gubbi Gubbi) Peoples legend attributes it to the slaying of a rainbow serpent. The park is separated from Noosa by the Noosa River and is accessed via vehicle ferry from Tewantin. Access from the north is via Rainbow Beach; 4WD recommended; 13 7468.

KENILWORTH STATE FOREST: This diverse park is in the rugged Conondale Ranges. The rainforest, tall open forest and exotic pines are home to birds and wildlife, including the threatened yellow-bellied glider. There are signposted walks, but a highlight is the steep 4km return hike from Booloumba Creek to the summit of Mount Allan, where the forest and gorge views are breathtaking. Visit Booloumba Falls from the Gorge picnic area (3km return) or picnic in the riverine rainforest at Peters Creek. Turn-off to the park is 6km south-west of Kenilworth (see p. 386).

MARY CAIRNCROSS PARK: This beautiful park on the outskirts of Maleny (see p. 387) was donated to the community in 1941 as protected rainforest after the fierce logging days of the early 1900s. Walk through the rainforest to see superb panoramic views.

MARY VALLEY HERITAGE RAILWAY: Known locally as the 'Valley Rattler', this restored 1923 steam train takes visitors on a 40km journey through the picturesque Mary Valley. A variety of train trips is on offer and the Historic Gympie Station refreshment rooms cafe serves delicious food and wine. Visitors can also inspect the heritage carriages; inquiries (07) 5482 2750.

NOOSA NATIONAL PARK: This largely untouched rocky coastal park offers walks of varying length through rainforest and heathland. Escape the summer crowds at Noosa by taking the Tanglewood Track across the headland to Hells Gate, a popular lookout and whale-viewing spot. Return via the coastal track for scenic ocean views. Access the park via Park Rd in Noosa Heads, the coastal boardwalk from Hastings St, or Sunshine Beach; info and maps from the visitor centre in Noosa.

RAINBOW BEACH: This relaxing coastal town to the east of Tin Can Bay across the inlet offers a pristine sandy beach popular with surfers. The week-long Family Fishing Classic is held here each July/Aug. Tours include dolphin ferry cruises, safaris and 4WD tours. The road south (4WD) leads to the coloured sands and beaches of the Cooloola section of Great Sandy National Park. Take time to learn about the Kabi Kabi (Gubbi Gubbi) Dreaming stories that tell the story of Rainbow Beach.

SEA LIFE SUNSHINE COAST: This award-winning aquarium in Mooloolaba (see p. 388) has a fantastic 80m walkway through seawater 'ocean', with displays of the Great Barrier Reef and underwater creatures. There are daily shows, including the seal show and crocodile feeding. Spend 15min swimming with a seal or dive in with sharks (bookings essential). The Touch Tank is a less daunting alternative. Wharf Complex, Parkyn Pde, Mooloolaba; visitsealife.com/sunshine-coast.

THE BIG PINEAPPLE: The 16m fibreglass pineapple makes this retro landmark tourist attraction hard to miss. The grounds are home to **Wildlife HQ Zoo**, a zipline course and an amphitheatre for music events. 76 Nambour Connection Rd, Woombye; (07) 5442 3102.

THE GINGER FACTORY: This award-winning complex in Yandina (see p. 389) is devoted to everything ginger. Visitors can see Gingertown, watch ginger-cooking demonstrations, see ginger being processed and ride on the historic Queensland Cane Train through subtropical gardens with acres of tropical plants, water features and a plant nursery – a highlight is the stunning flowering gingers. Pioneer Rd, Yandina; 1800 067 686.

OTHER ATTRACTIONS

ALEXANDRA HEADLAND: Popular coastal town with views to the Maroochy River and Mudjimba Island. Extensive beaches and parklands on the foreshore. Surf lessons and board hire are available from Mooloolaba Wharf; just north of Mooloolaba (see p. 388).

AMAMOOR STATE FOREST: More than 120 native animal species shelter in this protected forest, a remnant of the woodlands and vegetation that used to cover the Cooloola region. See the platypus in Amamoor Creek at dusk or take the Wonga walk or Cascade circuit track starting across the road from Amama. The renowned outdoor music festival, the Gympie Music Muster, is held in the forest on the last weekend in Aug. The forest is 30km south of Gympie (see p. 386).

BOREEN POINT: This sleepy town is on the shores of Lake Cootharba. The town features a 2.4km walk from Teewah Land to Noosa's north shore beaches, boardwalks into the surrounding wetlands and boat hire is available on Lake Cootharba. Try the many watersports on offer, including canoeing and kayaking. Windsurfing and yachting competitions are held here throughout the year.

BOTANIC GARDENS AND BIRD WORLD: 7ha of privately-owned gardens with waterfalls and four walk-though bird aviaries as well as cafe and picnic grounds. Guided tours are available; Maleny-Stanley River Rd; (07) 5344 0010.

BUDERIM FOREST PARK: Subtropical rainforest reserve and a great place for a picnic or barbecue. In the south, via Quorn Cl, is the Edna Walling Memorial Garden and Serenity Falls; in the north, via Lindsay Rd, is Harry's on Buderim restaurant and a boardwalk along Martins Creek.

CURRIMUNDI LAKE CONSERVATION PARK: This unspoiled coastal park offers quiet walks beside the lake and through to the beach. Canoe and swim in the lake or see the finches and friarbirds in the remnant wallum heath. In spring the wildflowers are glorious. Access from Coongara Espl, Caloundra.

KONDALILLA NATIONAL PARK: This park has scenic walks, subtropical rainforest and the spectacular Kondalilla Falls. The 4.6km return Falls Circuit track passes rockpools on the way to the falls, which drop 90m. The park is 21km north of Maleny (see p. 387), via Montville.

MALENY–BLACKALL RANGE TOURIST DRIVE: This 28km scenic drive is one of the best in south-east Queensland. Drive north-east from Maleny (see p. 387) through to Mapleton, stopping off at museums, antique shops, fruit stalls and tearooms along the way, as well as taking in spectacular views. The drive can be extended to Nambour.

MAPLETON FALLS NATIONAL PARK: Volcanic columns jut out of Pencil Creek just before the creek's water falls 120m to the valley floor. Walk to the falls lookout or see panoramic views of the Obi Obi Valley from Peregrine Lookout. Birdwatchers will delight at the early morning and dusk flights of the park's numerous bird species. The park is 3km south-west of Mapleton.

MOUNT COOLUM NATIONAL PARK: Located above the surrounding sugarcane fields, the mountain offers cascading waterfalls after rain. The park is generally undeveloped, but take the rough 800m trail to the summit to be rewarded with panoramic views of the coast. It's 19km north of Maroochydore (see p. 387).

NOOSA RIVER AND THE EVERGLADES: The river extends over 40km north into Great Sandy National Park. Take a cruise into the mirrored Everglades and to Harry's Hut, a relic of timber-cutting days. Kayak and canoe hire on offer, as well as camping facilities; contact Noosa visitor centre for details; (07) 5430 5000.

PIONEER COTTAGE: This restored 1876 National Trust timber cottage is one of Buderim's earliest houses and retains many of its original furnishings. Now home to the local historical society, it has exhibits on the history of the town and its surrounds. Open 11am–3pm; Ballinger Cres, Buderim; (07) 5450 1966.

QUEENSLAND AIR MUSEUM: Founded by members of the Aviation Historical Society of Australia in 1973, this museum in Caloundra (see p. 386) collects important relics of Queensland's aviation heritage. Memorabilia on display includes old fighter planes and bombers; open 10am–4pm. Airport, 7 Pathfinder Dr, Caloundra; (07) 5492 5930.

Opposite: Driving along Rainbow Beach

KEY TOWNS

BUDERIM
Population 31,430

Buderim is just inland from the Sunshine Coast, high on the fertile red soil of Buderim Mountain, a plateau overlooking the surrounding bushland and ocean. With its wide streets and abundance of small art and craft galleries, it escapes the crush of nearby towns like Maroochydore and Mooloolaba.

SEE & DO **Pioneer Cottage; Buderim Forest Park:** see Other Attractions for both. **Foote Sanctuary:** rainforest walks and more than 80 bird species; car entry via Foote St. **Arts and crafts galleries:** various shops selling locally made items; Main St.

CALOUNDRA
Population 56,213

This popular holiday spot at the southern tip of the Sunshine Coast boasts a diverse population of retirees and young Brisbane commuters keen on the seaside lifestyle. The nearby beaches offer a variety of watersports – the calm waters of Golden Beach are especially popular with windsurfers. The fishing between Bribie Island and the mainland in Pumicestone Passage is excellent.

SEE & DO **Queensland Air Museum; Currimundi Lake Conservation Park:** see Other Attractions for both. **Regional Art Gallery:** local and touring art exhibitions; open Tues–Fri 10am–4pm, Sat–Sun 10am–2pm; Omrah Ave. **Ben Bennett Bushland Park:** easy walks through natural bushland; Queen St. **Caloundra Cruise:** morning, lunchtime and sunset cruises. Pumicestone Passage cruises have scenic views of Bribie Island and Moreton Bay; bookings on (07) 5492 8280. **Kayak tours:** paddle in the tranquil Moreton Bay Marine Park; details from visitor centre. **Street Fair:** Bulcock St; Sun. **Pelican Waters Golf Club:** a Greg Norman–designed course; 38 Mahogany Dr, Pelican Waters; (07) 5437 5000; 8km S. **Opals Down Under:** opal-cutting demonstrations and 'scratch patch' where visitors fossick for their own gemstones; Glenview; 14km NW. **Aussie World:** family fun park in native garden setting, with about 25 rides and games, Side Show Alley and an Aussie-themed pub; Palmview; 18km NW. **Surrounding beaches:** includes patrolled beaches of Bulcock, Kings and Dicky; excellent fishing at Moffat and Shelly beaches. **Scenic drives:** taking in the beaches to the north, the Blackall Range with art galleries and views of the Sunshine Coast, and the Glass House Mountains with magnificent walks and scenery; details from visitor centre.

GYMPIE
Population 19,435

On the Mary River, north of the Sunshine Coast, is the heritage town of Gympie. Gympie's streets are lined with attractive jacarandas, silky oaks, cassias, poincianas and flame trees. The area is the Traditional Land of the Kabi Kabi (Gubbi Gubbi) People, who carry on their connection to Country and the many sacred sites across the area today. The area was re-settled when James Nash discovered gold in the area in 1867 and started Queensland's first gold rush. The field proved extremely rich – four million ounces had been found by the 1920s. The gold slowed to a trickle, but the dairy and agricultural industries were already well established. The 2022 floods damaged much of the city, with flood waters reaching the highest level in over a century.

SEE & DO **Mary Valley Heritage Railway:** see Top Attractions. **Amamoor State Forest:** see Other Attractions. **Woodworks Museum:** exhibits memorabilia from old logging days including a steam-driven sawmill; open Mon–Sat; Fraser Rd. **Deep Creek:** gold-fossicking area, Counter St; permits from visitor centre. **Public gallery:** local and visiting art exhibitions in heritage building; Nash St. **Heritage walk:** self-guided walk includes the Stock Exchange and Town Hall; details from visitor centre. **Trail rides:** horseriding through Kiah Park and Mary Valley; details from visitor centre. **Farmers Market:** Showgrounds; 2nd and 4th Sun each month. **Gold Mining and Historical Museum:** delve into the area's goldmining history. It includes Andrew Fisher House (Fisher was the first Queenslander to become prime minister); 5km S. **Mothar Mountain:** rockpools and forested area for bushwalking and excellent views; 20km SE. **Imbil:** picturesque town with excellent valley views. There is a market every Sun, and the nearby Lake Borumba offers great conditions for watersports and fishing – especially for golden perch and saratoga. Take the 14km Imbil Forest Drive through scenic pine plantations just south of town; 36km S. **Mary Valley Scenic Way:** enjoy this scenic route through towns of the valley, pineapple plantations and grazing farms; it runs south between Gympie and Maleny, via Kenilworth.

KENILWORTH
Population 272

West of the Blackall Range in the Sunshine Coast hinterland is Kenilworth. This charming town is known for its handcrafted cheeses and excellent bushwalking. The spectacular gorges, waterfalls, creeks and scenic lookouts make Kenilworth State Forest a popular spot for bushwalking, camping and picnics.

VISITOR INFORMATION

Glass House Mountains Visitor and Interpretive Centre
Bruce Pde & Steve Irwin Way, Glass House Mountains
(07) 5458 8848 or 1300 847 481
visitsunshinecoast.com

Gympie Region Visitor Information Centre, Lake Alford
24 Bruce Hwy, Gympie
(07) 5478 5183 or 1800 444 222
visitgympieregion.com.au

Noosa
visitnoosa.com.au

SEE & DO
Kenilworth State Forest: see Top Attractions. **Kenilworth Dairies:** tastings and sales of local cheeses; Charles St. **Historical Museum:** machinery, dairy display and audiovisual show; open 10am–2pm Sun Feb–Nov; Alexandra St; (07) 5446 0581. **Wineries:** tastings and sales at boutique wineries; 4km N. **Kenilworth Bluff:** steep walking track to lookout point; 6km N. **Conondale National Park:** this small forest reserve west of the Mary River is suitable only for experienced walkers. Take the 37km scenic drive, starting in the adjacent Kenilworth Forest, to enjoy the rugged delights of the park; 13 7468. **Lake Borumba:** picnics and watersports, and home to a fishing competition each Mar; 32km NW.

LANDSBOROUGH
Population 4635

Landsborough is just north of the magnificent Glass House Mountains, in the hinterland. It was named after the explorer William Landsborough and was originally a logging town for the rich woodlands of the Blackall Ranges. It is a 5min drive from the famous Australia Zoo.

SEE & DO
Australia Zoo; Glass House Mountains National Park: see Top Attractions for both. **Historical Museum:** this excellent local museum documents the history of the shire through memorabilia, photographs and artefacts; open Wed–Fri and Sun 9am–3pm; Maleny St. **Market:** School of Arts Memorial Hall; Sat 8am–1pm. **Dularcha National Park:** scenic park with excellent walks; contact QPWS on 13 7468; 1km NE. **Big Kart Track:** largest outdoor go-kart track in Australia, open for day and night racing and includes a kids' track with double-seater karts; 5km N. **Beerburrum State Forest:** short walks and drives to lookouts; access from Beerburrum; 11km S.

MALENY
Population 2976

A steep road climbs from the coast to Maleny, at the southern end of the Blackall Range. The surrounding area is lush dairy country, although farmland is increasingly being sold for residential development. The town's peaceful community lifestyle and picturesque position, with views to the coast and Glass House Mountains, make it popular with artists.

SEE & DO
Mary Cairncross Park: see Top Attractions. **Botanic Gardens and Bird World, Maleny–Blackall Range Tourist Drive** and **Kondalilla National Park:** see Other Attractions for all. **Arts and crafts galleries:** excellent quality galleries throughout town. **Markets:** RSL Hall, Bunya St; Sun. **Baroon Pocket Dam:** popular spot for fishing and boating. Follow the boardwalks through rainforest; North Maleny Rd; 8km N. **Montville:** main street lined with cafes, giftshops, potteries and art and craft galleries. The town also has a growing wine industry; 16km NE. **Flaxton:** charming tiny village surrounded by avocado orchards. Visit the local craft stores and public gardens; 19km NE. **The Barn on Flaxton:** antiques store with local food and wine; 21km N via Flaxton.

MAROOCHYDORE
Population 20,629

A popular beach resort, Maroochydore is also the business centre of the Sunshine Coast. The parklands and birdlife on the Maroochy River and the excellent, patrolled surf beaches began to attract a growing tourist interest in the 1960s – and the town has never looked back.

SEE & DO
Mount Coolum National Park: see Other Attractions. **Maroochy River:** enjoy diverse birdlife and parklands on the southern bank with safe swimming.

QUEENSLAND

Mary Cairncross Scenic Reserve near Maleny
Opposite top: Ginger plant at Buderim **Opposite bottom:** Maleny Botanic Gardens and Bird World

387

The Esplanade: atmospheric strip of cafes and shops. **Sunshine Plaza:** the region's biggest shopping mall; Horton Pde. **Sunshine Coast Craft Beer Tours:** local company that takes you brewery-hopping around the best craft beer spots. Tours run from Maroochydore; see sunshinecoastcraftbeertours.com.au for details. **Cotton Tree Markets:** King St; Sun mornings. **Market:** cnr Fishermans Rd and David Low Way; Sun mornings. **Scenic flights:** take a helicopter, seaplane or balloon flight for a bird's-eye view of the Sunshine Coast and hinterland, and over Moreton Bay; details from the visitor centre. **Twin Waters Golf Club:** 151 Ocean Dr; (07) 5457 2444; 8km N. **Bli Bli:** Watersports Complex, which includes a catch-and-release barramundi fishing park. Take a cruise through Maroochy River wetlands; 9km NW. **Marcoola:** coastal town with quiet beach; 11km N. **Coolum Beach:** coastal resort town with long sandy beach; 17km N. **Cruise Maroochy:** eco-cruises through wetlands, rainforest and creek ecosystems; details from visitor centre.

MOOLOOLABA
Population 8202

Mooloolaba is a popular holiday destination. Its fabulous beaches, restaurants, nightlife and resort-style shopping contribute to the constant influx of families and young people eager for the sun. Mooloolaba Harbour is the base for a major prawning and fishing fleet and the local seafood, particularly the famous Mooloolaba prawns, are renowned for their freshness and flavour.

SEE & DO **Sea Life Sunshine Coast:** see Top Attractions. **Mooloolaba Harbour:** popular spot for parasailing, scuba diving and cruises; contact visitor centre for tour operators. **Alexandra Headland:** popular coastal town with views to the Maroochy River and Mudjimba Island. Extensive beaches and parklands on the foreshore. Surf lessons and board hire are available from Mooloolaba Wharf; just north of Mooloolaba. **Mooloolah River National Park:** take a canoe down Mooloolah River, ride along the bike trail or walk on the fire trails in this remnant wallum heath park; straddles Sunshine Motorway; (07) 5494 3983; 6km SW. **Yachting and fishing:** trips to offshore reefs; details from visitor centre.

NAMBOUR
Population 20,918

Nambour is a large, unpretentious service town in the Sunshine Coast hinterland, on Kabi Kabi (Gubbi Gubbi) Country. Post-settlement development began in the 1860s and sugar has been the main crop since the 1890s. Sugarcane farming has been in decline since the early 2000s and the mill is now closed, but part of the old cane tramway can still be seen embedded in the main street. The town's name is derived from the Kabi Kabi word for the local flowering tea tree.

SEE & DO **The Big Pineapple:** see Top Attractions. **Mapleton Falls National Park:** see Other Attractions. **Mapleton:** attractive arts and crafts town in the Blackall Range; 15km W. **Mapleton National Park:** with an excellent drive through bunya pines and blackbutt forests starting just north of Mapleton. You can walk to the top of the waterfall from Poole's Dam and take the short Piccabeen Palm Groves Walk. The drive ends with spectacular views from Point Glorious.

★ NOOSA HEADS
Population 5120

Noosa Heads, commonly known as Noosa, is a coastal resort town on Laguna Bay. The relaxed lifestyle, weather and year-round swimming make this a popular holiday destination. Cosmopolitan Hastings St offers a relaxed cafe lifestyle and boutique shopping, and within walking distance are the natural attractions of superb coastal scenery and the protected coves, surfing beaches and seascapes of Noosa National Park.

SEE & DO **Noosa National Park; Eumundi; Great Sandy National Park:** see Top Attractions for all. **Noosa River and the Everglades:** see Other Attractions. **Noosa Main Beach:** one of Australia's few north-facing beaches; safe family swimming; beginners' surfing lessons available. **Boutique shopping:** browse clothing stores, gift shops and art galleries on stylish Hastings St. **Adventure sports:** on spectacular coastal waters of the Coral Sea and inland waterways. Activities include kitesurfing, high-speed boating and kayaking; book at the visitor centre. **Horseriding:** beach and bushland rides on Noosa's North Shore; book at visitor centre. **Farmers' market:** AFL ground, Weyba Rd, Noosaville; Sun. **Laguna Lookout:** views of Noosa River, lakes and hinterland; on Noosa Hill, access via Viewland Dr. **Sunshine Beach:** golden beach popular for

Top: Sunshine Beach **Opposite:** Majestic Theatre, Pomona

388

TOP EVENTS

→ JAN Ginger Flower & Food Festival (Yandina)

→ MAR Festival of Surfing (Noosa)

→ JUNE Eat and Drink Festival (Noosa); Downunder Beachfest (retro cars, Caloundra)

→ JULY City Bowls Carnival (Caloundra); Winter Jazz Festival (Nambour); Noosa Alive! arts festival (Noosa); King of the Mountain (running event, Pomona); Art Festival (Mary Valley)

→ AUG Music Muster (Gympie); Fishing Classic (Rainbow Beach)

→ SEPT Music Festival (Maleny); Jazz Party (Noosa); Kenilworth Celebrates (arts festival)

→ SEPT–OCT Music Festival (Caloundra)

→ OCT Sunshine Coast Marathon (Maroochydore); Garden Festival (Buderim)

→ OCT–NOV Scarecrow Festival (Mary Valley)

TEMPERATURES

Jan: 22–29°C

July: 11–21°C

---

surfing; 3km SE. **Noosaville:** family-friendly area with Noosa River as focal point; departure point for river cruises; 5km SW. **Peregian Beach:** beachside village with alfresco cafes, restaurants and boutique shops; 13km S. **Lake Cooroibah:** ideal for boating, sailing and windsurfing; access by car or boat from Noosaville, 14km NW. **Tewantin:** Noosa Marina in Parkyn Crt has restaurants, boat hire and cruises; 7km W. **Tewantin State Forest:** hilly rainforest and eucalypt forest reserve with 10min walk to Mount Tinbeerwah Lookout offering a panoramic view over Noosa River, lakes and hinterland; 10km W via Tewantin.

POMONA
Population 1735

This small and relaxed farming centre is in the northern hinterland of the Sunshine Coast. Mount Cooroora rises 439m above the town. Each July mountain runners from around the world attempt the base–summit and back again race, the winner being crowned King of the Mountain. The town is named for the Roman goddess of fruit and orchards.

SEE & DO **Majestic Theatre:** authentic silent-movie theatre with cinema museum and regular old silent movie screenings; Factory St. **Noosa Shire Museum:** tribute to the shire's past in old council chambers; Factory St. **Railway Station Gallery:** converted station featuring local art; open Mon–Fri 10am–4pm, Sat 10am–2pm; Station St. **Country market:** Stan Topper Park; Sat. **Cooroy:** large residential area with excellent art gallery and cultural centre in the Old Butter Factory. The Noosa Botanic Gardens and Lake Macdonald are nearby; 10km SE.

TIN CAN BAY
Population 2274

Tin Can Bay is a well-known fishing and prawning region north-east of Gympie. Though the exact origins of the name are unknown, it is believed to be derived from a Kabi Kabi (Gubbi Gubbi) word. The town is a relaxing hamlet offering watersports and houseboating on the quiet waters of Tin Can Bay inlet.

SEE & DO **Rainbow Beach:** see Top Attractions. **Environmental walkway:** a 9.5km trail for birdwatching on the Tin Can Bay foreshore. **Boat and yacht hire:** cruise the inlet and Sandy Strait; Tin Can Bay Marina. **Norman Point boat ramp:** see wild dolphins up close, usually between 7.30am and 8am; access point to waterways. **Carlo Point:** great for fishing and swimming. There is also boat access to the inlet, with houseboats and yachts available for hire; 43km E via Rainbow Beach. **Inskip Point:** camp along the point or take the car ferry to Fraser Island; 53km NE via Rainbow Beach.

YANDINA
Population 2595

Yandina is in the Sunshine Coast hinterland and is a historic town, dating back to 1868, with heritage buildings. It is home to the Ginger Factory, the largest of its kind anywhere, giving rise to Yandina's title of 'Ginger Capital of the World'.

SEE & DO **The Ginger Factory; Eumundi:** see Top Attractions. **Yandina Historic House:** local-history display, arts and crafts, art gallery and visitor centre; Pioneer Rd. **Nutworks:** see processing of macadamia nuts and taste-test the results, also includes a chocolate factory; opposite the Ginger Factory. **Fairhill Native Plants and Botanic Gardens:** fabulous nursery and gardens – a must for any native-plant buff; also includes a cafe in garden setting; Fairhill Rd. **Heritage trail:** self-guided trail around town; brochure from visitor centre. **Country Market:** town centre; Sat. **Wappa Dam:** popular picnic area; west of Yandina.

Capricorn and K'gari (Fraser Island) Coast

From UNESCO World Heritage–listed **K'gari (Fraser Island)** – the largest sand island in the world – to the **whale-watching playground** of Hervey Bay and north to Rockhampton on the Tropic of Capricorn, this stretch of the Queensland coastline is packed with fascinating diversions. Don't be tempted to rush through this region to get further north, because there are **beautiful beaches, rare wildlife encounters, grand historic towns** and **Australian icons**, like Bundy Rum, to discover and explore.

CHEAT SHEET

- → Allow at least two weeks because there is plenty to see and do.
- → Best time to visit: May to Oct is the best time to see whales but the warmer months are best for swimming; Nov to March is also the best nesting turtles at Mon Repos.
- → Main towns: Bundaberg (see p. 394), Gladstone (see p. 396), Hervey Bay (see p. 397), Maryborough (see p. 397), Rockhampton (see p. 398), Yeppoon (see p. 399).
- → The Butchulla People are the Traditional Owners of K'gari (Fraser Island); join a Djinang Walking Tour with Hervey Bay Eco Marine Tours to discover significant sites and history. Other custodians of the lands we call the Capricorn and Fraser Coast include the Bayali, Darumbal, Gangulu, Kabi Kabi (Gubbi Gubbi), Gureng Gureng and Wadjigu Peoples.
- → Don't miss: driving across K'gari (Fraser Island); whale watching in Hervey Bay; snorkelling coral cays in and around Heron Island; seeing how Bundy Rum is made in Bundaberg; and watching turtles nest in Mon Repos Conservation Park.

Top: Carnarvon Gorge
Opposite: Lake McKenzie, K'gari (Fraser Island)

TOP ATTRACTIONS

BLACKDOWN TABLELAND NATIONAL PARK: Covering mountains and lowlands, including some beautiful waterfalls. It is the traditional home of the Ghungalu People, whose stencil art can be seen on the 2.8km Mimosa Culture Track. Walk through to Rainbow Falls Gorge and swim in rockpools. It's accessible from Blackwater (see p. 394) and Emerald (see p. 395).

BUNDABERG BOTANIC GARDENS: Many buildings from Bundaberg's (see p. 394) past stand within this picturesque setting. Bundaberg proudly claims the aviator Bert Hinkler as one of its own. In 1928 Hinkler was the first to successfully fly from England to Australia on a flight that took just over 15 days. **Hinkler Hall of Aviation** and the **Hinkler House Memorial Museum** – Bert Hinkler's relocated Southampton home – are a tribute to him and to aviation history, and feature replica aircraft, memorabilia and a flight simulator. **Fairymead House Sugar Museum**, a restored sugar plantation home, recalls the town's early years of sugar production, and the nearby **Historical Museum** chronicles the general history of the area. To see more of the grounds, take the restored **Sugarcane Railway** around the lakes; runs most Sun; Mt Perry Rd, Bundaberg.

BYFIELD NATIONAL PARK: This coastal park offers views of the ocean from its long beaches. Explore the open woodlands and forest or take in coastal views from the headlands at Five Rock and Stockyard Point. Fishing and boating are popular at Sandy Point at the south of the park. 4WD only; experience in sand driving is essential. The park is 32km north of Yeppoon (see p. 399).

CAPRICORNIA CAYS NATIONAL PARK AND HERON ISLAND: This park, 60–100km offshore from Gladstone (see p. 396), protects the nine coral islands and cays that form the southern end of the Great Barrier Reef. The islands are important nesting sites for seabirds and loggerhead turtles. **North West Island** has walking tracks through forests dominated by palms and she-oaks. The most popular activities are diving and snorkelling in the spectacular reefs, or visiting the renowned dive sites on **Heron Island**, where there is also a 109-room resort. Camping is allowed seasonally on three other cays. Access is by private boat or charter from Gladstone; air access to Heron Island; there is seasonal closure to protect nesting wildlife.

CARNARVON NATIONAL PARK: This large national park features a variety of landscapes, but by far the most popular is the gorge section roughly halfway between Roma (see p. 380) and Springsure (see p. 399). Here the Carnarvon Creek winds through the steep-sided Carnarvon Gorge, flanked by white sandstone cliffs. It's a 19km return walk through the gorge, with short side trails to fern-filled side gorges, caves and the rock engravings, stencils and paintings at Cathedral Cave and the Art Gallery. The 87km Carnarvon Great Walk takes up to six days. The remote Ka Ka Mundi section of the park, 130km west of Springsure is in Queensland's brigalow belt and features undulating plains and sandstone cliffs. See king parrots and fig birds around the springs and creeks, or learn about the area's pastoral history at the old cattleyards near the springs. The Mount Moffatt Section of the park 256km north of Mitchell (see p. 433) is mainly for driving, with short walks to scenic spots. See the sandstone sculptures of Cathedral Rock, Marlong Arch and Lot's Wife, or visit the Tombs for the ancient stencil art of the Nuri and Bidjara Peoples. The high-country woodlands and forest are home to a variety of wildlife, and birdwatching for raptors and lorikeets is exceptional. 4WD recommended. The remote Salvator Rosa Section, 130km east of Tambo (see p. 434) is a perfect spot to escape the crowds. The attractive Nogoa River and Louisa Creek flow through the valley. See the spectacular rock formations, Belinda

Springs and other natural attractions on the self-guided trail, which starts at the Nogoa River camping area. The turn-off to the gorge section of the park is 199km north of Roma (see p. 380) on the Carnarvon Developmental Rd.

GAYNDAH MUSEUM: An award-winning museum with several historic buildings, displays, photographs and memorabilia that illustrate the town's history from small settlement to thriving agricultural centre – a highlight is a restored 1864 cottage. Simon St; Gayndah; (07) 4161 2226.

GREAT KEPPEL ISLAND: A popular island-holiday destination with 17 beaches to explore, swim and relax on. There is snorkelling and diving offshore and walks exploring the island's centre, including an interesting cultural trail. Great Keppel is the Traditional Land of the Woppaburra People who won a Native Title Claim on their lands in Dec 2021. Access is by ferry from Keppel Bay Marina at Rosslyn Bay Harbour, which is 7km south of Yeppoon (see p. 399).

GREAT SANDY STRAIT: The Mary and Susan rivers to the south of Hervey Bay run into this strait where you can see spectacular migratory birds, including the comb-crested jacana. Look out for dugongs, the world's only plant-eating marine mammals. You can fish at the mouth of the Mary River, around River Heads. Hire a houseboat to travel down the strait; contact visitor centre in Hervey Bay for details; 1800 811 728.

K'GARI (FRASER ISLAND): UNESCO World Heritage–listed K'gari (Fraser Island) is the largest sand island in the world. The Traditional Owners, the Butchulla People, were granted Native Title rights in 2014, and in September 2021 the World Heritage area was officially renamed K'gari, meaning 'paradise'. It's important for visitors to respect the wishes of the Butchulla People and leave the lands and seas of K'gari as they are found. The island is an ecological wonder with lakes and forests existing purely on sand. The island has an oasis of beaches, beautifully coloured sand cliffs, more than 40 freshwater lakes and spectacular rainforests. Although it was impacted by bushfires in late 2020, the forests are regenerating and the island's iconic attractions were not affected. Idyllic **Lake McKenzie** is definitely one of the most beautiful of its freshwater lakes – its shallow water is dazzling aquamarine and ringed by white sandy beaches backed by paperbark trees. The island is also home to a variety of wildlife, including migratory birds and rare animals such as the ground parrot and Illidge's ant-blue butterfly. Offshore, see the turtles, dugongs and dolphins soak up the warm waters and, between Aug and Nov, look out for migrating humpback whales. There is a variety of walks around the island, as well as swimming spots and scenic drives. The surf coast, on the island's east, takes in the beautiful **Seventy Five Mile Beach**; the Cathedrals, 15m sheer cliffs composed of different-coloured sands; the wreck of the *Maheno*, a trans-Tasman luxury liner; and Eli Creek, a freshwater creek filtering through the dunes, where visitors can float beneath the pandanus trees. Care should be taken around the island's dingo population: stay with children, walk in groups, never feed or coax the dingoes and keep all food and rubbish in vehicles or campground lockers. They are thought to be the purest strain of dingoes in eastern Australia. By the time these native dogs arrived on the mainland – they came with Asian seafarers around 5000 years ago – K'gari was already disconnected from the continent, and the dingoes swam across Great Sandy Strait. Unlike most mainland dingoes, they have not been hybridised by contact with domestic dogs. Vehicle and camping permits from parks.des.qld.gov.au/parks/kgari-fraser.

LADY ELLIOT ISLAND: A small coral cay with 19 major dive sites, bird rookeries, a turtle-nesting site and whale-watching opportunities. Low-key resort (maximum 140 people), ranging from budget to island suites. Air access to Lady Elliot from Hinkler Airport at Bundaberg (see p. 394); contact visitor centre for details; (07) 4153 8888.

MON REPOS CONSERVATION PARK: This park 15km north-east of Bundaberg (see p. 394) contains the largest and most accessible mainland loggerhead turtle rookery in eastern Australia. Between Nov and Mar these giant sea turtles come ashore to lay their eggs. Hatchlings leave their nests for the sea from mid-Jan to late Mar. Access to the park is restricted during these times – guided night tours depart from the park information centre for viewing turtles up close. When turtles are not hatching, snorkelling and exploring rockpools are popular activities. Book online via bundabergregion.org/turtles

ROCKHAMPTON BOTANIC GARDENS: These heritage-listed gardens are more than 130 years old. There are tropical displays, an orchid and fern house, a Japanese-style garden and the bird haven of Murray Lagoon. The city zoo (within the gardens) has free entry and koala, chimpanzee, otter and lorikeet feedings and an aviary show every afternoon. Access via Spencer and Ann sts, Rockhampton.

SAPPHIRE GEMFIELDS: To the west of Emerald (see p. 395) is the largest sapphire area in the Southern Hemisphere, incorporating Rubyvale, Sapphire, Anakie and Willows gemfields. The towns feature walk-in mines, fossicking parks, gem-faceting demonstrations, jewellers and museums. Obtain a licence and map of the mining areas from local stores or the Department of Natural Resources in Emerald to start fossicking. Rubyvale offers a tag-along fossicking tour of the gemfields; details from Emerald's visitor centre.

OTHER ATTRACTIONS

AUBURN RIVER NATIONAL PARK: In this small park the Auburn River flows through a sheer-sided gorge and over granite boulders in the riverbed. Dry rainforest grows on the upper part of the tough track that leads down the side of the gorge to the river. An easier walk is the 150m trail to the lookout above the Auburn River. Opposite the campsite catch a glimpse of the nesting peregrine falcons. 4WD is recommended in wet weather; 13 7468. The park is 40km south-west of Mundubbera (see p. 398).

BLACKWATER INTERNATIONAL COAL CENTRE: Interactive and interpretive touch-screen displays, a cafe, mine tours and an ornate Japanese garden to recognise Blackwater's sister town, Fujisawa in Japan. Capricorn Hwy, Blackwater; (07) 4982 7755.

BUNDABERG RUM DISTILLERY: Learn about the distillation process on daily tours; Avenue St, Bundaberg; (07) 4348 3443.

BURRUM COAST NATIONAL PARK: Split into two sections, this national park 57km south of Bundaberg (see p. 394) offers a variety of landscapes and activities. The northern Kinkuna section is relatively undeveloped. The vegetation along the beach is rugged, and birdwatching in the wallum heath is a highlight. Access is via Palm Beach Rd; 14km south-west of Bundaberg; 4WD and sand-driving experience are necessary. The southern Woodgate section has boardwalks and established tracks from where you can see abundant wildlife. Access is via Woodgate, a small town with an ocean beach.

CANIA GORGE NATIONAL PARK: Part of Queensland's sandstone belt, this park has cliffs, gorges and caves of spectacular colours. The rock art is a reminder of the area's ancient heritage. See the park's goldmining history on the 1.2km return Shamrock Mine track or experience breathtaking park views from the Giant's Chair Lookout, reached on the longer Fern Tree Pool and Giant's Chair circuit. The park is 25km north-west of Monto (see p. 398).

DEEPWATER NATIONAL PARK: Diverse vegetation covers this coastal park, including paperbark forests, swamp mahogany, Moreton Bay ash and subtropical rainforest. Walk along the beaches or enjoy the birdlife of Deepwater Creek. Bush camp at Wreck Rock, and explore the rockpools. 4WD access only. The park is 63km north-east of Miriam Vale (see p. 398), via Agnes Water.

EXPEDITION NATIONAL PARK: This remote park features the 14km Robinson Gorge. Only experienced walkers should attempt the rough track down into the gorge. A 4km return track leads to an excellent lookout. The Cattle Dip Lookout overlooks a waterhole reached via the 8km return Shepherds Peak Trail or from the carpark at the lookout. 4WD recommended; most of the road is gravel.

FLYING HIGH BIRD PARK: The native vegetation is home to 600 bird species. Follow the boardwalk tracks to see many Australian parrots and finches. Cnr Bruce Hwy and Old Creek Rd, Apple Creek; it's 5km north of Childers (see p. 395).

GOOD NIGHT SCRUB NATIONAL PARK: A dense remnant hoop pine rainforest in the Burnett Valley, this park is home to over 60 species of butterfly. Have a bush picnic at historic Kalliwa Hut, used during the logging days of the park. Drive up to One Tree Hill (4WD only) for a panoramic view over the area. The park is 10km south of Gin Gin (see p. 395).

ISLA GORGE NATIONAL PARK: This highland park has gorges and spectacular rock formations. The camping area overlooks the gorge and sunset is the time to see the colours of the sandstone cliffs. A 2km return walk leads to the Isla Gorge Lookout. You turn off to the park 35km south of Theodore (see p. 399).

MOUNT ARCHER NATIONAL PARK: On the north-east outskirts of Rockhampton (see p. 398) in the Berserker Ranges, this park is a backdrop to the city. Take a scenic drive up the mountain to Frazer Park for panoramic views. Explore the open forest and subtropical vegetation of the mountain on the 11km walk from top to bottom. Be advised that the return trip is quite strenuous. Other shorter walks lead to scenic lookouts. Access to the summit is via Frenchville Rd; access to the base via German St, Rockhampton (see p. 398).

MOUNT WALSH NATIONAL PARK: Featuring the impressive Bluff Range, this wilderness park commands the skyline. Walks take in rugged granite outcrops and gullies and are for experienced bushwalkers only but there are views from the picnic area. Maryborough Rd. The park is 8km south of Biggenden (see p. 394).

MUSEUM OF ART: One of regional Australia's best art collections, featuring the likes of Nolan, Drysdale, Boyd and Blackman; opened in new premises – six times the size of its previous space – in 2022; Quay St, Rockhampton (see p. 389).

QUEENSLAND HERITAGE PARK: Originally at the Expo '88 in Brisbane, the 28m tall silo now finds its home in Biloela (see p. 394). Inside are exhibitions on the history of the Callide and Dawson valleys. Dawson Hwy, Biloela; (07) 4992 2400.

Opposite top: Carnarvon National Park **Opposite bottom:** Heron Island

KEY TOWNS

BIGGENDEN
Population 657

This agricultural town is known as the 'Rose of the Burnett' and is proud of its impressive range of roses in the main street. Situated in a valley, the majestic ranges of Mount Walsh National Park tower over the town.

SEE & DO **Mount Walsh National Park:** see Other Attractions. **Historical Museum:** exhibits history of the shire and life of early settlers; open Thurs and 2nd Sat each month, or by appt; Brisbane St; (07) 4127 5137. **Mount Woowoonga:** bushwalking in a forestry reserve; picnic and barbecue facilities; 10km NW. **Coalstoun Lakes National Park:** protects two volcanic crater lakes. Walk up the northern crater for a view over the rim; 20km SW. **Coongara Rock:** a volcanic core surrounded by rainforest; 4WD access only; 20km S. **Chowey Bridge:** 1905 concrete arch railway bridge, one of two surviving in the country; 20km NW. **Brooweena:** small town with Early Settlers Museum; Biggenden Rd; 30km SE. **Paradise Dam:** this 30,000-megalitre dam took four years to build and has a tourist centre. Walking track and fishing areas nearby; barbecue facilities; 35km NW.

BILOELA
Population 5667

This thriving town in the fertile Callide Valley is part of the Banana Shire but don't expect to find any bananas grown here. The area was actually named after a bullock called 'Banana', whose job was to lure wild cattle into enclosures, a difficult feat that was much applauded by local stockmen.

SEE & DO **Queensland Heritage Park:** see Other Attractions. **Spirit of the Land Mural:** amazing mural depicting the history of women in the shire; State Farm Rd. **Greycliffe Homestead:** original slab hut converted to a museum showcases the area's settler heritage; open by appt; Gladstone Rd; (07) 4992 1862. **Mount Scoria Conservation Park:** known locally as the 'Musical Mountain' because of the basalt columns at the top that ring when hit with another rock. Walks and trails around the mountain. 17km S. **Thangool:** renowned for its race days; (07) 4995 8190; 10km SE. **Callide Dam:** excellent for boating, fishing and swimming; 12km NE. **Callide Power Station:** near Callide Dam. **Callide Mine Lookout:** view over Biloela, the mine and the dam; 18km NE. **Kroombit Tops National Park:** sandstone escarpments and gorges; 1300 656 191; 33km E; **Baralaba:** historic village; 95km SE.

BLACKWATER
Population 4567

Blackwater is known as the coal capital of Queensland. The coal is transported directly from coalmines south of town to Gladstone by train. The name 'Blackwater' is not a reference to the effects of mining operations, but comes from the discolouration of local waterholes caused by tea trees.

SEE & DO **Blackdown Tableland National Park:** see Top Attractions. **Blackwater International Coal Centre:** see Other Attractions. **Lions Park:** displays the flags of 37 nations to commemorate the nationality of every worker on the coalmines. In terms of size and variety, the display is second only to that of the United Nations building in New York; Capricorn Hwy to the west of town. **Helicopter flights over Blackwater Coal Mine:** see the mine in action; details from visitor centre. **Bedford Weir:** excellent for fishing; 20km N. **Comet:** discover the Leichhardt Dig Tree, where the explorer buried letters and marked the tree 'dig'; 30km W.

★ BUNDABERG
Population 52,370

Bundaberg, the southernmost access point to the Great Barrier Reef, is proud of its parks and gardens, heritage buildings, vineyards, breweries and scenic walks. Its world-famous amber spirit, Bundaberg Rum attracts visitors to taste and tour its distillery. Between Nov and March turtles nest at Mon Repos Beach and the nightly tour to Mon Repos Conservation Park is hugely popular. Fields of towering sugarcane border the town and nearby Burnett River.

SEE & DO **Bundaberg Botanic Gardens; Mon Repos Conservation Park; Lady Elliot Island:** see Top Attractions for all. **Bundaberg Rum Distillery; Burrum Coast National Park:** see Other Attractions for both. **Bundy Kegs & Schmeider's Cooperage:** demonstrations of barrel making; Alexandra St. **Regional Art Gallery:** three galleries devoted to local and visiting art exhibitions; cnr Barolin and Quay sts. **Baldwin Swamp Conservation Park:** stroll along boardwalks and pathways through waterlily lagoons, abundant birdlife and native fauna; Steindl St. **Alexandra Park and Zoo:** historic band rotunda, spacious picnic lawns, cactus garden, zoo (free admission); riverbank, Quay St. **Whaling Wall:** a six-storey-high whale mural by Robert Wyland; Bourbong St. **Heritage city walk:** self-guided walking tour of 12 significant sites and buildings; starts at School of Arts Building, Bourbong St. **Bundaberg Barrel:** giant barrel building houses Bundaberg Brewed Drinks. With interactive tours, a holographic

VISITOR INFORMATION

Bundaberg Visitor Information Centre
36 Avenue St,
Bundaberg East
(07) 4153 8888 or
1300 722 099
bundabergregion.org

Hervey Bay Visitor Information Centre
227 Maryborough–Hervey Bay Rd
1800 811 728
visitfrasercoast.com

Capricorn Spire Visitor Information Centre
176 Gladstone Rd,
Rockhampton
(07) 4936 8000
explorerockhampton.com.au

Sandstone Wonders
sandstonewonders.com

Opposite top: Biloela Opposite bottom: Rockhampton

3D adventure and free sampling; Bargara Rd. **Shalom College markets:** local crafts; Fitzgerald St; every Sun. **Hummock Lookout:** panoramic view of Bundaberg, cane fields and coast; 7km NE. **Meadowvale Nature Park:** rainforest and walkway to Splitters Creek; 10km W. **Sharon Nature Park:** rainforest, native fauna and walkway to Burnett River; 12km SW. **Bargara:** coastal town with a popular surf beach and year-round fishing on artificial reef. Turtles often nest at nearby Neilson Park, Kelly's and Rifle Range beaches; 13km NE. **Fishing spots:** area renowned for its wide variety of fishing. Excellent spots at Burnett Heads (15km NE), Elliott Heads (18km SE) and Moore Park (21km NW). **Mystery craters:** 35 small craters in sandstone slab. Their origin causes much debate; they're more than 25 million years old; 25km SW. **Littabella National Park:** lagoons and billabongs surrounded by tea tree forest. Many sand tracks for the 4WD enthusiast can be found at nearby Norval Park Beach; 13 7468; 38km NW. **Lady Musgrave Island:** excellent spot for snorkelling, fishing and camping. Sea access from Bundaberg Port; 107km N.

CHILDERS
Population 1361

Childers is a picturesque National Trust town and part of the state's sugarcane belt. With leafy streets and a lovely outlook over the surrounding valleys, the town has some heritage buildings and interesting museums.

SEE & DO **Burrum Coast National Park; Flying High Bird Park; Good Night Scrub National Park:** *see* Other Attractions for all. **Pharmaceutical Museum:** collection of memorabilia, including leather-bound prescription books; open Mon–Fri 9am–3pm, Sat 9am–1pm; Churchill St. **Historical complex:** area of historic buildings including school, cottage and locomotive, as well as First Nations artefacts; Taylor St. **Baker's Military and Memorabilia Museum:** 16,000 items on display covering all the major wars, including uniforms and communications equipment; open Mon–Sat (open Sun by appt); Ashby La. **Childers Art Space (CHARTS):** Churchill St. **Snakes Downunder:** informative exhibits on native snakes; open Mon–Tues and Thurs–Sun 9.30am–3pm; Lucketts Rd. **Historic Childers:** self-guided town walk past historic buildings; highlight is the Old Butcher's Shop (1896) in Churchill St. **Memorial:** a fire engulfed a backpackers' hostel in 2000, tragically killing 15 people; Churchill St. **Buxton and Walkers Point:** unspoiled fishing villages to the east. **Woodgate:** coastal town to the north-east with 16km beach.

EMERALD
Population 14,089

An attractive town with many classic Queenslander-style buildings at the heart of the Central Highlands, Emerald serves as a gateway to Blackdown Tableland and Carnarvon national parks and outback Queensland. Also nearby are the largest sapphire fields in the Southern Hemisphere where you can try fossicking. The area was home to the Western Kangoulu People who now hold Native Title over parts of the land. It was re-settled as a service town while the railway from Rockhampton to the west was being constructed. Several fires ravaged the town in the mid-1900s, destroying much of this early history.

SEE & DO **Blackdown Tableland National Park; Carnarvon National Park; Sapphire Gemfields:** *see* Top Attractions for all. **Pioneer Cottage Complex:** historic cottage and lock-up gaol with padded cells. There is also a church plus a communications museum; Morton Park, Clermont St. **Botanic Gardens:** walk around a native display, herb garden and melaleuca maze. Also visit a traditional bush chapel, all-abilities playground and 6km of walking tracks along the Nogoa River. **Railway station:** restored 1900 National Trust–classified, with attractive lacework and pillared portico; 100 Capricorn Hwy; (07) 4982 4142. **Fossilised tree:** 250 million years old; in front of town hall. **Mosaic pathway:** 21 pictures depict 100 years of Emerald history; next to the visitor centre. **Van Gogh Sunflower Painting:** one in a series of four large reproductions in the world; Morton Park, Clermont St. **Lake Maraboon/Fairbairn Dam:** popular spot for watersports and fishing, especially for the redclaw crayfish; 18km S. **Capella:** first town settled in the area. See its history at the Capella Pioneer Village; 51km NW.

GAYNDAH
Population 1695

Gayndah is one of Queensland's oldest towns. The Traditional Owners of Gayndah are the Wakka Wakka People. A European settlement was founded on their lands in 1849, competing with Brisbane and Ipswich to be the state's capital. Main Street's heritage buildings and landscaped gardens illustrate the long history of the town, which is now central to a rich citrus-growing industry.

SEE & DO **Gayndah Historical Museum:** *see* Top Attractions. **Market:** Jaycees Park; 1st Sun each month. **Lookouts:** several in area offering views over Burnett Valley; closest to town is Archers Lookout, atop the twin hills 'Duke and Duchess' overlooking town. **Claude Warton Weir:** an excellent spot for fishing and picnics; 3km W. **Ban Ban Springs:** natural springs and picnic area; 26km S.

GIN GIN
Population 914

Some of Queensland's oldest cattle properties surround this pastoral town. The district is known as 'Wild Scotsman Country' after James McPherson, a bushranger who was captured here in 1866.

SEE & DO
Good Night Scrub National Park: see Other Attractions. **Historical Society Museum:** displays memorabilia of settler past in 'The Residence' – a former police sergeant's house. The old sugarcane locomotive *The Bunyip* forms part of the historic railway display; open Mon–Fri 8.30am–3.30pm, Sat 8.30am–12pm, other times by appt; Mulgrave St. **Courthouse Gallery:** fine-arts gallery in refurbished old courthouse; Mulgrave St. **Market:** Historical Museum; Sat. **Lake Monduran:** an excellent spot for watersports and fishing (permit from kiosk). Catch a barramundi or Australian bass, or walk the 6km of tracks in the bush surrounds; 24km NW. **Boolboonda Tunnel:** longest non-supported tunnel (192m) in the Southern Hemisphere. It forms part of a scenic tourist drive; brochure available from visitor centre; 27km W. **Mount Perry:** small mining town, home to mountain-bike racing in June; 55km SW.

GLADSTONE
Population 34,703

Set among hills with natural lookouts over the harbour and southern end of the Great Barrier Reef, Gladstone is a modern city and popular for swimming, surfing and fishing – especially for mud crabs and prawns. The area is the lands of the Bailai, Gurang, Gooreng Gooreng and Taribelang Bunda Peoples. Matthew Flinders landed at Port Curtis, Gladstone's deep-water harbour, in 1802, but the town did not truly develop until the 1960s. Today it is an outlet for central Queensland's mineral and agricultural wealth – a prosperous seaboard city with one of Australia's busiest harbours. It is the gateway to national parks, Heron Island and the coral islands and cays protected in Capricornia Cays National Park.

SEE & DO
Capricornia Cays National Park and Heron Island: see Top Attractions. **Tondoon Botanic Gardens:** displays of all native species of the Port Curtis region with free weekday guided tours by appointment. Also offers a recreational lake and Mount Biondello bushwalk; Glenlyon Rd. **Regional Art Gallery and Museum:** local and regional art with history exhibitions; open Mon–Sat; cnr Goondoon and Bramston sts. **Maritime Museum:** artefacts and memorabilia document 200 years of port history; open Fri–Sun and public holidays; Francis Ward Dr. **Potters Place:** fine-art gallery and craft shop; Dawson Rd. **Gecko Valley Winery:** cellar door, cafe and gallery; open Fri–Sun; Glenlyon Rd. **Barney Point Beach:** historic beach including Friend Park; Barney St. **Waterfall:** floodlit at night; Flinders Pde. **Boyne Island:** beautiful foreshore parks and beaches; home to the Boyne Tannum HookUp fishing competition in May. The Boyne Island aluminium smelter is Australia's largest. The island and its twin town of Tannum Sands are linked by bridge; 25km SE. **Tannum Sands:** small community offering sandy beaches with year-round swimming, picturesque Millennium Espl along the beach and 15km of scenic walkways known as the Turtle Way. Wild Cattle Island, an uninhabited national park at the southern end of the beach, can be reached on foot at low tide; 25km SE. **Calliope:** small rural community with excellent fishing in nearby Calliope River with abundant mud crabs, salmon and flathead. The Calliope River Historical Village documents its history in restored buildings and holds regular markets; 26km SW. **Lake Awoonga:** a popular spot for swimming, skiing (permit required) and fishing. It has walking tracks and recreational facilities; 30km S. **Mount Larcom:** views from the summit; 33km W. **Castle Tower National Park:** a rugged park of granite cliffs and the outcrops of Castle Tower and Stanley mountains. Only experienced walkers should attempt the climb to Mount Castle Tower summit, where there are superb views over the

TEMPERATURES
Jan: 23–32°C

July: 10–23°C

Military and Colonial Museum in Maryborough

TOP EVENTS

- MAR Rockfest (Biloela); Agnes Water Longboard Classic (Agnes Water)

- EASTER Central Highlands Easter Sunflower Festival (Emerald); Harbour Festival (Gladstone); Amateur Fishing Classic (Burrum Heads)

- MAY Golden Mount Festival (Mount Morgan); Beef Australia (Rockhampton); Boyne Tannum HookUp (Boyne Island)

- JUNE Taste Bundaberg Festival; Orange Festival (odd-numbered years, Gayndah); Relish food and wine Festival (Maryborough)

- JULY Childers Festival (Childers); Rodeo (Springsure); Seafood Festival (Gladstone)

- JUL–AUG Whale Festival (Hervey Bay)

- AUG Gemfest (Emerald); Calliope River Village Music Festival; Coal and Country Festival (Moura); Village Arts Festival (Yeppoon)

- SEPT Mary Poppins Festival (Maryborough); Crafts Fair and Vintage Machinery Rally (Capella); Capricorn Food and Wine Festival (Rockhampton)

- OCT Arts Festival (Brigalow); Rodeo (Blackwater); Lake Monduran Fishing Classic; Tropical Pinefest (Yeppoon); Arts Festival (Bundaberg)

- NOV Lake Cania Fishing Classic (Lake Cania); Milbi Festival (Bundaberg)

Boyne Valley and Gladstone; access by foot or boat from Lake Awoonga; access by car from Bruce Hwy; 40km S. **Kroombit Tops National Park:** this mountain park is on a plateau with sandstone cliffs and gorges, waterfalls and creeks. Drive the 90min return loop road to explore the landscapes and walk to the site of a WWII bomber crash; 4WD recommended; 75km SW via Calliope. **Curtis Island National Park and Conservation Park:** at the north-east end of the island is this small park with a variety of vegetation and excellent spots for birdwatching. There are no walking tracks, but the three-day hike along the east coast is worthwhile; access by boat from Gladstone or the Narrows. **Great Barrier Reef tours:** cruises depart from the Gladstone Marina; Bryan Jordan Dr.

★ HERVEY BAY
Population 57,722

Hervey (pronounced 'Harvey') Bay is a natural bay known for its calm and safe waters, ideal for families. The urban centre that spreads out along the bay's southern shore is the thriving city of Hervey Bay. The region's climate is ideal, with hot days cooled by trade winds during the summer. An influx of people visit during winter for a chance to see migrating humpback whales frolic in the bay's warm waters between July and Nov. Fishing is a popular recreational activity, especially off the town's kilometre-long pier. Hervey Bay is a 15min drive from River Heads, the ferry departure point for World Heritage–listed K'gari (Fraser Island).

SEE & DO K'gari (Fraser Island); **Great Sandy Strait:** see Top Attractions for both. **Burrum Coast National Park:** see Other Attractions. **Whale-watching tours:** half- and full-day tours to see the migratory whales off the coast, departing from Boat Harbour; contact visitor centre for details. **Botanic Gardens:** peaceful vistas and orchid conservatory; Elizabeth St. **Historical Village and Museum:** recalls early settler days inside 20 historic buildings, including Acutt Cottage, the old church and sugar machinery; open Fri–Sat 1–4.30pm, Sun 10.30am–4.30pm; Zephyr St. **Reefworld:** natural aquarium with Great Barrier Reef's coral and sea life, featuring shark and turtle feeding; Pulgul St. **M & K Model Railways:** award-winning miniature village and model trains; ride the replica diesel train; open by appt Tues–Sat; Old Maryborough Rd; (07) 4124 1979. **Dayman Park:** memorial commemorates the landing of Matthew Flinders in 1799 and also the Z-Force commandos who trained there on the Krait in World War II. **Scenic walkway:** cycle or walk 15km along the waterfront. **Pier Park Community Markets:** Pier St; Wed & Sat 7am–1pm. **Toogoom:** quiet seaside resort town. Feed the pelicans on the boardwalk; 15km W. **Burrum Heads:** pleasant holiday resort at the mouth of the Burrum River with excellent beaches and fishing. Visit at Easter for the Amateur Fishing Classic; 20km NW. **Hervey Bay Eco Marine Tours:** cultural tours of Hervey Bay and K'gari (Fraser Island) with a Butchulla guide; (07) 4125 6888. **Scenic flights:** over Hervey Bay and K'gari (Fraser Island) in a small plane; contact visitor centre for details.

MARYBOROUGH
Population 22,237

Maryborough is an attractive city on the banks of the Mary River. Its fine heritage buildings and famous timber Queenslander architecture date back to the early years of settlement, when Maryborough was a village, port and important immigrant destination in the mid-1800s. Today the Mary River is a popular spot for boating and fishing. In early 2022, Maryborough was devastated by two floods in a six-week period. Check ahead to see what is open.

SEE & DO Portside Precinct: this area is home to around 13 heritage-listed buildings that now house museums, restaurants and galleries. The Portside Centre includes the **Customs House Museum**, which depicts the area's industries and early immigration and Kanaka (Pacific Islander forced labourers) history, and **Bond Store Museum**, which documents the history of the region from a river port to the present day; open Mon–Fri 9am–4pm, Sat–Sun 10am–1pm. Here you will also find the Mary River Parklands and Gatakas Artspace; Wharf St. **Military and Colonial Museum:** fascinating look at local military and colonial-era history; open Mon–Fri 9.30am–3.30pm, Sat–Sun 9.30–2pm; Wharf St. **Mary Poppins statue:** statue of the famed and magical nanny in honour of author Pamela Lyndon Travers (P.L. Travers), who was born in the town in 1899; cnr Kent and Richmond sts. **The Story Bank:** the birthplace of P.L. Travers, now a colourful and whimsical museum, opened in 2019; Richmond St. **Mary Ann Steam Engine:** replica of Queensland's first steam engine with rides in Queens Park every Thurs and last Sun each month; Lennox St. **Queens Park:** unusual domed fernery and waterfall; cnr Lennox and Bazaar sts. **Elizabeth Park:** extensive rose gardens; Kent St. **ANZAC Park:** includes Ululah Lagoon, a scenic waterbird sanctuary where black swans, wild geese, ducks and waterhens may be handfed; cnr Cheapside and Alice sts. **Heritage walk:** self-guided walk past 22 historic buildings, including the impressive City Hall, St Paul's bell tower (with pealing bells) and National Trust–listed Brennan and Geraghty's Store. The walk starts at City Hall, Kent St; brochure available from visitor centre. **Heritage drive:** a highlight is the original site of Maryborough (until 1885), where a series of plaques document its history. Drive starts at City Hall; brochure available from visitor centre. **Ghost tours:** discover the town's ghostly past; details from the visitor centre. **Heritage Markets:** cnr Adelaide and Ellena sts; Thurs. **Teddington Weir:** popular for watersports; 15km S. **Tiaro:** excellent fishing for Mary River cod in surrounding waterways. See the historic Dickabram Bridge over the river, and visit nearby Mount Bauple National Park; 24km SW. **Tuan Forest:** bushwalking; 24km SE.

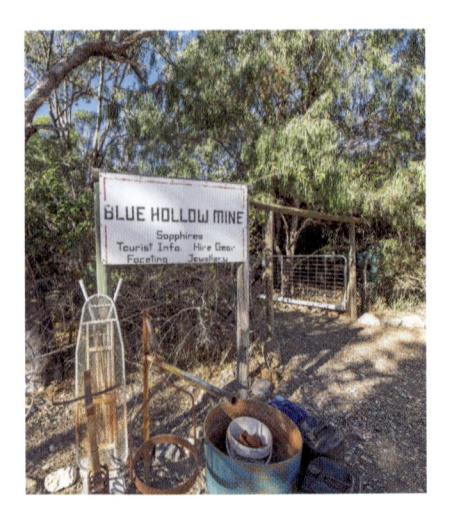

MIRIAM VALE
Population 385

Miriam Vale lies in the hinterland of the Discovery Coast. The town is renowned for its charming hospitality, its historic fig trees in the main street and its mud-crab sandwiches. The hinterland and coastal national parks are ideal places for bushwalking, four-wheel driving and horseriding.

SEE & DO **Deepwater National Park:** *see* Other Attractions. **Eurimbula National Park:** rugged coastal park with walks along the beach, canoeing on Eurimbula Creek, fishing, and scenic views from Ganoonga Noonga Lookout. 4WD recommended; 13 7468; access between Miriam Vale and Agnes Water; 50km NE. **Agnes Water:** this coastal town has the most northerly surfing beach in Queensland and the town holds the surfing competition Agnes Waters Longboard Classic each Mar. A local history museum includes documents of Cook's voyage in 1770; 57km NE. **1770:** James Cook, while on his discovery voyage, made his second landing on Australian soil at this town site. Today the seaside village has the Joseph Banks Environmental Park and is the departure point for daytrips and fishing charters to the Great Barrier Reef and Lady Musgrave Island; 63km NE.

MONTO
Population 1021

Monto, one of the youngest towns in the Capricorn region, was settled in 1924. It is the centre of a rich dairy and beef cattle district and is set on a plateau surrounded by rolling hills.

SEE & DO **Cania Gorge National Park:** *see* Other Attractions. **Historical and Cultural Complex:** variety of historic artefacts and a mineral display; Flinders St. **Lake Cania:** excellent spot for watersports, fishing (permit required) and walking to lookout. Annual Lake Cania Fishing Classic is held here every Nov; 11km N via Cania Gorge Picnic Area. **Kalpower State Forest:** hoop pine and rainforest vegetation. 4WD or walk rugged tracks to lookouts; 40km NE. **Wuruma Dam:** swimming, sailing and waterskiing; 50km S.

MOUNT MORGAN
Population 2487

The quaint historic gold-mining town of Mount Morgan is said to be the largest single mountain of gold in the world – now a big crater and the largest excavation in the Southern Hemisphere. Mount Morgan's gold supply was discovered and mined from the late 1800s. In the mine's heyday, around 1910, the town was home to about 14,000 people.

SEE & DO **Railway station:** historic station with tearooms, rail museum and a restored 1904 Hunslett Steam Engine that operates regularly; Railway Pde; (07) 4938 2312. **Historical Museum:** varied collection of memorabilia traces history of this mining town; Morgan St. **Historic suspension bridge:** built in the 1890s and spans the Dee River. **Historic cemetery:** features the Chinese Heung Lew (prayer oven) and the Linda Memorial to men killed in underground mines (1894–1909); off Coronation Dr. **The Big Stack:** 76m high 1905 brick chimney used to disperse mining fumes; at the mine site. **The Big Dam:** good boating and fishing; 2.7km N via William St. **Wowan:** former dairy service centre with a museum in a 1919 butter factory; 40km SW.

MUNDUBBERA
Population 1066

Mundubbera is on the banks of the Burnett River and is a major citrus-growing area. Fruit pickers flock to the town in the cooler months.

SEE & DO **Auburn River National Park:** *see* Other Attractions. **Historical Museum:** local history; Leichhardt St. **Heritage Centre:** several displays of early settlement history; Durong Rd. **Regional Art Gallery:** changing program of local and interstate artists; Lyons St; **Jones Weir:** popular spot for fishing; Bauer St. **'Meeting Place of the Waters':** 360-degree town mural; cnr Strathdee and Stuart–Russell sts. **Pioneer Place:** gorgeous park with picnic facilities in the middle of town. **Morning Market:** Uniting Church; 3rd Sat each month. **Enormous Ellendale:** the big mandarin, another addition to the 'big' monuments of Queensland; outskirts of town at the Big Mandarin Caravan Park. **Golden Mile Orchard:** impressive orchard with tours; 5km S. **Eidsvold:** town at the centre of beef cattle country featuring the Historical Museum Complex, Tolderodden Environmental Park and the R.M. Williams Australian Bush Learning Centre; 37km NW.

ROCKHAMPTON
Population 63,151

Rockhampton is a prosperous city that straddles the Tropic of Capricorn. It is known as the beef capital of Australia, with about 2.5 million cattle in the region. Quay St is Australia's longest National Trust–classified streetscape, with more than 20 heritage buildings set off by flowering bauhinia and brilliant bougainvilleas.

SEE & DO **Rockhampton Botanic Gardens:** *see* Top Attractions. **Mount Archer National Park** and **Museum of Art:** *see* Other Attractions for both. **Heritage walk:** self-guided 2km trail of 15 spots around city centre, including the impressive copper-domed Customs House, built in 1901; brochure available from visitor centre or online. **Archer Park Rail Museum:** interactive displays document the history of rail transport in Rockhampton. A restored Purrey Steam Tram operates every Sun 10am–1pm, Feb–Nov; open Mon–Thurs 10am–3pm, Sun 9am–1pm; cnr Denison and Cambridge sts. **Kershaw Gardens:** this popular recreation area was significantly damaged during cyclone Marcia in February 2015; the Northern Precinct and kid-friendly Central Precinct have been redeveloped but he Southern Precinct remains closed indefinitely; Bruce Hwy. **Great Western Hotel:** operates rodeos at an indoor arena, with live bull-rides on Wed and Fri nights; Stanley St. **Fitzroy River:** a barrage in Savage St that separates tidal saltwater from upstream freshwater provides opportunities for barramundi fishing. **Capricorn Spire:** marks the line of the Tropic of Capricorn; Curtis Park, Gladstone Rd. **Markets:** Heritage Village; held six times a year, Sun mornings. **Dreamtime Cultural Centre:** displays of Aboriginal and Torres Strait Islander culture set on an ancient tribal site; guided tours available; open Mon–Fri 9am–3.30pm; 7km N on Bruce Hwy. **Heritage Village:** heritage buildings with unusual clock collection, vintage vehicles and farm animals; open 10am–4pm (except public holidays); Parkhurst; 9km N. **St Christopher's Chapel:** open-air wood and stone chapel built by American servicemen in World War II; Emu Park Rd; 20km E. **Capricorn Caves:** guided tours and wild caving adventures through limestone cave system; visit in Dec/Jan when a beam of sunlight light enters the cave with spectacular effect known as the Summer Solstice Light Spectacle; 23km N. **Mount Hay Gemstone Tourist Park:** thunder-egg fossicking and sales; 38km W. **Capricorn Coast Scenic Loop tourist drive:** through coast and hinterland.

SPRINGSURE
Population 731

Mount Zamia towers over Springsure, a small valley town in the Central Highlands. The land was taken over by European settlers in 1860s, which set in motion a series of massacres of the local Aboriginal People and of retaliatory attacks on the settlers, although only the deaths of the settlers are recorded. The town features a number of historic sites and natural attractions for visitors to explore.

SEE & DO **Carnarvon National Park:** *see* Top Attractions. **Yumba-Burin (resting place):** in Cemetery Reserve, containing three bark burials (around 600 years old). **William St Parklands:** incorporates Rich Park Historical Complex and the Bauhinia Bicentennial Art Gallery. **Historic Hospital:** heritage-listed building (1868) includes museum. **Minerva Hills National Park:** the park includes the Boorambool and Zamia mountains and has unusual wildlife, such as the fawn-footed melomys. There's also a 2.2km walking track to a great lookout; have a bush picnic at Freds Gorge. Part of road unsealed; 13 7468; 4km W. **Old Rainworth Fort:** National Trust buildings built in 1862; open Fri–Wed 10am–3pm; 10km S.

TAROOM
Population 578

Taroom is on the banks of the Dawson River in the Capricorn region. Since settlers took up land in 1845, cattle farming has been the main local industry.

SEE & DO **Expedition National Park:** *see* Top Attractions. **Museum:** old telephone-exchange equipment, farm machinery and items of local history; open by appt; Kelman St; 0409 663 701. **Leichhardt Park:** site of Leichhardt's memorial; Yaldwyn St. **Coolibah tree:** in Taroom's main street was marked 'L.L.' by explorer Ludwig Leichhardt on his 1844 trip from Jimbour House near Dalby to Port Essington, north of Darwin (the tree is still there; the initials are not). **Palm Tree Creek:** rare Livistona palms; 15km N. **Lake Murphy Conservation Park:** pristine lake with birdlife, and picnic and camping spots. It was the site of Leichhardt's camp in 1844; 30km N. **Glebe Weir:** waterskiing and fishing; 40km NE. **Wandoan:** the local heritage trail in the town visits 23 sights, including the Waterloo Plain Environmental Park; brochure from visitor centre in Zupp Rd; 59km S.

THEODORE
Population 451

Theodore, once called Castle Creek, was named after Edward (Red Ted) Theodore, union leader and then Queensland premier from 1919 to 1925. With its rich black soils, the town is surrounded by pastoral and grazing properties with sheep, cattle, sorghum, wheat and cotton. It was the site of Queensland's first irrigation project. Located on the Dawson River, irrigation has resulted in palm-lined streets and a tropical air.

SEE & DO **Isla Gorge National Park:** *see* Other Attractions. **Theodore Hotel:** only cooperative hotel in Queensland; The Blvd. **Dawson Folk Museum:** provides local history; open by appt; Second Ave; 0429 931 264. **Theodore Weir:** popular spot for fishing; southern outskirts of town. **Moura:** major cattle town that holds the annual Coal and Country Festival in Aug; 48km NW. **Cracow:** where gold was mined from the famous Golden Plateau mine 1932–76; 49km SE.

YEPPOON
Population 18,789

The popular coastal resort of Yeppoon lies on the shores of Keppel Bay. Yeppoon and the beaches to its south – Cooee Bay, Rosslyn Bay, Causeway Lake, Emu Park and Keppel Sands – are known as the Capricorn Coast. Great Keppel Island lies 13km offshore and is a popular holiday and daytrip destination offering great swimming, snorkelling and diving.

SEE & DO **Great Keppel Island; Byfield National Park:** *see* Top Attractions for both. **The Esplanade:** shops, galleries and cafes overlooking parkland and crystal-clear water. **Shell World:** collection of more than 20,000 shells; Scenic Hwy. **Market:** showgrounds; Sat mornings. **Fig Tree Markets:** Merv Anderson Park; 1st Sun each month. **Boating:** bareboat and fishing charters, sea access to Great Keppel Island and nearby underwater observatory, and water taxis to Keppel Bay islands; all from Keppel Bay Marina; 7km S. **Cooberrie Park Wildlife Sanctuary:** flora and fauna reserve where you can cuddle a koala; 15km N. **Emu Park:** small village community with historical museum and interesting 'singing ship' memorial to Captain Cook – the sea breezes cause hidden organ pipes to make sounds; 19km S. **Byfield State Forest:** the extremely rare Byfield fern is harvested here. Walks include the 4.3km Stony Creek circuit track through rainforest and the boardwalk along Waterpark Creek; adjacent to Byfield National Park, *see* Top Attractions. **Keppel Sands:** this popular spot for fishing and crabbing is home to the Joskeleigh South Sea Island Museum; 38km SW. **Keppel Bay Islands National Park:** this scenic group of islands is popular for walks, snorkelling, reef-walking and swimming; private boat or water taxi from Keppel Bay Marina; 13 7468. **Koorana Crocodile Farm:** commercial crocodile farm, home to 3000 crocodiles, with 90min guided tours every morning and afternoon; (07) 4934 4749. **Scenic flights:** over islands and surrounds from Hedlow Airport (between Yeppoon and Rockhampton); details from visitor centre.

Great Keppel Island
Opposite: Mine in Emerald

Whitsunday Coast

The Whitsunday region – Queensland's mid tropics – stretches north from Mackay to Townsville and includes the southern Great Barrier Reef and the idyllic **74 islands of the Whitsundays**, named by Cook on Whit Sunday 1770. Pastimes here are all about enjoying the warm **sun, sand and sea, sailing, snorkelling, diving, beachcombing,** luxuriating at **island resorts,** and **exploring the rainforest.**

CHEAT SHEET

→ Distances between some towns are huge. Allow at least a week to explore the region, but don't try to see it all.

→ Best time to visit: summer is hot, humid and stormy, and stinger season in the water so time your visit for the winter months, when it's still warm enough to get wet but stinger free.

→ Main towns: Airlie Beach (see p. 404), Charters Towers (see p. 405), Mackay (see p. 406), Townsville (see p. 407).

→ This section of the Queensland Coast and hinterland is the Traditional Land of the Gia, Ngaro, Biri, Yuru and Yuwibara Peoples.

→ Did you know? Whitehaven Beach, on Whitsunday Island, the largest of the 74 Whitsunday Islands, claims to have the whitest sand in the world, an assertion disputed by Hyams Beach in southern NSW and Lucky Bay near Esperance in south-west WA. The devil's in the fine print, and they are all blindingly beautiful. Best way to sort fact from fiction is to see them all for yourself!

→ Don't miss: sailing in the Whitsundays; snorkelling the Great Barrier Reef; Reef HQ: the world's largest living coral reef aquarium; seeing platypus in the wild in Eungella National Park; Buffy the giant cane toad in Sarina; a trip to Magnetic Island/ Yunbenun; and a walk along the Strand in Townsville.

Top: Finch Hatton Gorge, Eungella National Park
Opposite: Magnetic Island/ Yunbenun

TOP ATTRACTIONS

EUNGELLA NATIONAL PARK: This ecologically diverse park is home to some unusual plants and animals, including the Mackay tulip oak and the Eungella gastric brooding frog. A highlight of the visit is seeing the platypus in Broken River from a viewing deck. Visit the Finch Hatton Gorge section of the park with its waterfalls, swimming holes and walking tracks. The more adventurous could try sailing through the rainforest canopy on the Forest Flying eco-tour. Finch Hatton Gorge turn-off is just before Eungella. Broken River is 6km south of Eungella.

GIRRINGUN NATIONAL PARK: Travel through UNESCO World Heritage rainforest on road (access during dry weather only) to the three-tier, 91m Blencoe Falls. The Wallaman Falls section is in the Herbert River Valley and features waterfalls, gorges and tropical rainforest. See the crimson rosellas on the 4km return walk from the Falls Lookout to the base of Wallaman Falls – look out for platypus and water dragons. Take a scenic drive around the Mount Fox section of the park or walk the 4km return ascent to the dormant volcano crater. There are no formal tracks and the ascent is for experienced walkers only. 4WD is recommended in both sections during the wet season.

HINCHINBROOK ISLAND NATIONAL PARK: An amazing variety of vegetation covers this island national park, including rainforest, wetlands, forests and woodlands. The 32km Thorsborne Trail on the east coast is renowned for its spectacular scenery as it winds past waterfalls and along pristine beaches. Many people allow four days for the walk, camping on a different beach each night. Hikers must be self-sufficient and bookings are essential (limited number of walkers allowed). Shorter walks leave from the camping areas at Macushla and The Haven. Access the island via ferry from Cardwell (see p. 405) or Lucinda (see p. 406).

MAGNETIC ISLAND/ YUNBENUN: More than half of this beautiful island is covered by Magnetic Island/Yunbenun National Park. The sandy beaches, granite headlands and hoop pine rainforest make this an attractive daytrip or stay overnight in the private accommodation on offer, which ranges from budget to deluxe. See the natural attractions by taking some of the many walks around the island or hire a bike for a different view. Snorkel and swim at Alma Bay and see spectacular views from the World War II forts. Access from Townsville (see p. 407) by passenger and car ferry.

MOUA (MUSEUM OF UNDERWATER ART): In what's thought to be the first underwater art museum in the Southern Hemisphere, MOUA in Townsville (see p. 407) is a series of installations by underwater sculptor Jason deCaires Taylor. The Ocean Siren sculpture, which changes colour after dark according to the ocean temperature, can be seen rising from the sea from The Strand in Townsville, others are scattered across four locations in the Great Barrier Reef Marine Park off the coast of Townsville. New artworks were being readied for installation at the time of research. Ask at the Townsville visitor centre for local dive operators who run trips to art sites.

ORPHEUS ISLAND NATIONAL PARK: This rainforest and woodland park is a continental resort island in the Palm Islands surrounded by a marine park and fringing reefs. Snorkel and dive off the beaches or take in the wildlife on the short track from Little Pioneer Bay to Old Shepherds Hut; access is by private or charter boat from Lucinda (*see* p. 406) or Taylors Beach (*see* p. 406). There's a five-star resort (maximum 74 people) and three national park campgrounds; camping permits from Ingham parks office.

REEF HQ GREAT BARRIER REEF AQUARIUM: Home to the headquarters for the Great Barrier Reef Marine Park Authority, this underwater observatory in Townsville (*see* p. 407) is informative and visually breathtaking. Its living reef is the largest 'captive' reef in the world. Get up close at the touch pools or see marine feeding and dive shows. At the time of research it was closed for refurbishment but was expected to re-open in 2023; check reefhq.com.au for updates. Flinders St East, Townsville; (07) 4750 0800.

WHITSUNDAY ISLANDS

The Whitsundays offer the sort of tropical idyll that we're used to seeing on Instagram or on postcards. There are white sandy beaches, turquoise waters and low-key or luxe islands aplenty to choose from. Become your own version of Robinson Crusoe as you take your pick from these dreamy islands:

DAYDREAM ISLAND
A small island of volcanic rock, coral and dense tropical foliage. Daydream has one resort that reopened in 2019 after a $100 milliion redevelopment following cyclone damage in 2016. Facilities include a Kids Club, tennis, outdoor cinema, watersports centre, snorkelling, diving, and reef and island trips. Luxury resort (maximum 900 people).

HAMILTON ISLAND
A large island with a wide range of facilities and activities, shops, marina and fauna park. There's windsurfing, sailing, fishing, scuba diving, parasailing, helicopter rides, tennis, squash, and reef and inter-island trips. Resort (maximum 1500 people).

HAYMAN ISLAND
Close to the outer reef, with fishing, sightseeing trips, scenic flights, diving, watersports, Kids Club and whale-watching excursions. Big-game enthusiasts strive to catch black marlin off the island, Sept–Nov. Luxury resort (maximum 450 people).

HOOK ISLAND
Part of Whitsunday National Park, this mostly uninhabited island has impressive waterfalls and beautiful butterflies at Butterfly Bay. See also Airlie Beach p. 404.

LONG ISLAND
The closest island to the mainland, mostly national park, with 13km of walking tracks, sheltered bays, wildlife and wonderful views. Two boutique resorts, one at Palm Bay (maximum 60 people) and one at Paradise Bay on the southern point of the island (maximum 20 people), which is accessible only by helicopter.

WHITSUNDAY ISLAND
Uninhabited national park, with a beautiful 7km white silica beach and complex mangrove system. Camping only (maximum 40 people); details from Airlie Beach parks office.

OTHER ATTRACTIONS

BOWLING GREEN BAY NATIONAL PARK: This coastal park offers much for the self-sufficient visitor. Granite mountains blend with a variety of landscapes including saltpans and mangrove country. Walk along Alligator Creek to see cascades and waterfalls. Stay overnight at the Alligator Creek campsite and go spotlighting to glimpse brush-tail possums and sugar gliders. Turn-off Bruce Hwy 28km south-east of Townsville (see p. 407); the park is 6km further.

CAPE PALMERSTON NATIONAL PARK: This remote park features rugged coastal landscapes of headlands, swamps and sand dunes. Watch for the soaring sea eagles overhead or the birdlife around the swamp. There are spots for bush camping. The park has no official walking tracks, but the outlook from the cape is spectacular. 4WD recommended; the park is 46km south-east of Sarina (see p. 407), via Ilbilbie.

CARDWELL BUSH TELEGRAPH: This complex in Cardwell (see p. 405) comprises the old post office and telegraph station (in operation 1870–1982) and the original magistrates court and gaol cells. An informative history of communications and the region is provided through interpretive displays. Open Mon–Fri 9am–4.30pm, Sat–Sun 9am–1pm; Bruce Hwy, Cardwell; (07) 4066 2412.

CONWAY NATIONAL PARK: Covering 35km of coastline, this park is renowned for its natural beauty and as the habitat of the endangered Proserpine rock wallaby. Walks start in Airlie Beach and Shute Harbour. Mount Rooper Lookout is a highlight, featuring a panoramic view over Hamilton, Dent, Long and Henning islands. The park is 30km east of Proserpine (see p. 406).

DALRYMPLE NATIONAL PARK: This small national park on the Burdekin River comprises mainly woodland and is an important area for native animals including rock wallabies and sugar gliders. A highlight is the four-million-year-old solidified lava wall, the Great Basalt Wall, parts of which are accessible from this park. The site of the old Dalrymple township is also of interest. Walking here is suitable only for experienced, well-equipped bushwalkers; remember to tell someone your plans. The park is 46km north of Charters Towers (see p. 405).

GHOSTS OF GOLD HERITAGE TRAIL: This informative tour reveals the rich history of Charters Towers in the district known as 'One Square Mile'. More than 60 heritage-listed buildings are in the precinct. Of particular interest are the re-created workings of the Stock Exchange in Mosman St; the once heavily mined Towers Hill (1.5km W) with interpretive walking trails; and the Venus Gold Battery in Millchester Rd, an old gold-processing plant where the 'ghosts' come alive. Starts in the orientation centre behind the visitor centre at 74 Mosman St; (07) 4761 5533.

HIBISCUS COAST: Comprises the quaint coastal towns of Seaforth, Ball Bay and Cape Hillsborough. Steep, rainforest-clad hills plunge to rocky headlands and white sandy beaches in this lovely and surprisingly peaceful district north of Mackay. Cape Hillsborough National Park offers the most pristine scenery, as well as tidal rockpools and walking trails. Kangaroos are often seen hopping along the deserted beaches, especially early in the morning.

MUSEUM OF TROPICAL QUEENSLAND: This museum in Townsville (see p. 407), features artefacts from *HMS Pandora*, a British vessel wrecked on the reef in 1791; 70–102 Flinders St, Townsville; (07) 4726 0600.

PALUMA RANGE NATIONAL PARK: The Jourama Falls section of the park (24km S) is at the foothills of the Seaview Range. Walk the 1.5km track through rainforest and dry forest to the Jourama Falls Lookout (take care crossing the creek) to see the vibrant birdlife, including azure kingfishers and kookaburras. The Mount Spec section of the park (40km S) features casuarina-fringed creeks in the lowlands and rainforest in the cooler mountain areas. Drive to McClelland's Lookout for a spectacular view and take the two short walks from there to see the varied park landscapes. The park is 49km south of Ingham (see p. 406).

SARINA SUGAR SHED: Australia's only fully operational miniature sugar mill and distillery. Take a tour and watch the complex process of turning sugarcanes into granules. There are also multimedia presentations and a novelty shop onsite; Railway Sq, Sarina; (07) 4943 2801.

SS YONGALA WRECK: This world-famous wreck, which sank near Cape Bowling Green during a cyclone in 1911, lay undiscovered for half a century. Despite being under water for more than 100 years, details such as the engine room, toilets, portholes and most of the ship's name are still evident. The marine life is excellent, with beautiful corals, giant groupers and trevally, barracuda, stingrays, turtles and hundreds of other sea creatures. For experienced divers only; various tour operators.

Top: Museum of Underwater Art (MOUA), Townsville
Bottom: Eungella National Park
Opposite: Hamilton Island jetty

KEY TOWNS

★ AIRLIE BEACH
Population 1312

Airlie Beach sits at the centre of the thriving Whitsunday coast. This tropical holiday town offers a cosmopolitan blend of bars, restaurants and shops just metres from the beach. From Coral Sea Marina, daytrips to the outer Great Barrier Reef and Whitsunday islands are on offer. Watersports available include sailing, snorkelling, diving and fishing. Nearby Shute Harbour, along with the Port of Airlie ferry terminal, services the majority of the Whitsunday Islands (see box p. 402).

SEE & DO **Conway National Park:** see Other Attractions. **Airlie Beach Lagoon:** safe, year-round swimming in landscaped environment; foreshore. **Whale-watching:** tours depart Coral Sea Marina, July–Sept; details from visitor centre. **Sailing:** choose from traditional sailing, adventure or luxury crewed; details from visitor centre. **Skydiving:** tandem skydive and take in the stunning views from very high above; (07) 4838 4040. **Community market:** Airlie Beach Espl; Sat mornings. **Crocodile safaris and fishing trips:** to nearby coastal wetlands; details from visitor centre. **Scenic flights:** various tours over the 74 Whitsunday islands; details from visitor centre.

AYR
Population 8200

This busy town south-east of Townsville is surrounded by sugarcane fields – the most productive in Australia. It is also the largest mango-growing area in the country. On the north side of the Burdekin River, it is linked to Home Hill to the south by the 1103m Silver Link Bridge, which ensures the towns are not cut off when the river floods.

SEE & DO **SS Yongala Wreck:** see Other Attractions. **Burdekin Cultural Complex:** 500-seat theatre, library and music loft. The forecourt has distinctive artworks and the Living Lagoon water feature; Queen St. **Gubulla Munda:** this 60m carpet snake sculpture is the totem for the Juru People, the Traditional Owners of the area. Nearby Juru Walk passes through remnant dry tropical rainforest; Bruce Hwy, southern entrance to Ayr. **Market:** Plantation Park, Bruce Hwy; 1st and 3rd Sun of the month. **Home Hill:** this small town is just south of Ayr over the Silver Link. The towering melaleuca trees along the main street bear plaques commemorating the town's early settler families. The Silver Link Interpretive Centre in Eighth Ave gives a photographic history of the Burdekin River Bridge. Ashworth's Tourist Centre houses Ashworth's Jewellers, the Rock Shop and the Treasures of the Earth Display. 12km S. **Hutchings Lagoon:** watersports; 5km NW. **Brandon Heritage Precinct:** includes district's oldest church, St Patrick's (1897), now a local history museum. Ye Olde Machinery Place has an antique farm machinery display; 6km N. **Alva Beach:** beach walks, birdwatching, swimming and fishing; 18km N. **Mount Kelly:** great views of surrounding farmlands; 15km SW. **Charlie's Hill:** World War II historic site; 24km S. **Groper Creek:** great fishing spot with camping available; 24km SE. **Horseshoe Lagoon:** birdwatching; 35km N. **Mount Inkerman:** good views at the top, plus picnic and barbecue facilities; 30km S. **Burdekin Dam:** biggest dam in Queensland, holding the equivalent of four Sydney Harbours. Fishing, picnic facilities and camping available; 180km NW.

BOWEN
Population 9612

At the northern end of the Whitsundays, Bowen is surrounded by eight pristine beaches and bays, all within a 5km radius. Snorkelling is available and swimming and fishing are expected – you're in the tropics, after all. In addition, the foreshore area has been redeveloped to include information on the making of Baz Luhrmann's 2008 film *Australia*, part of which was made in Bowen. The town and the surrounding area are also well known for mangoes.

SEE & DO **Historical Murals:** around the buildings of Bowen's town centre are 25 murals by local and national artists, each illustrating an aspect of the region's history. **Bays and Beaches:** Rose and Horseshoe bays are connected by walking tracks with panoramic views over the ocean. Impressive corals and fish are found at Grays, Horseshoe, Murray and Rose bays. Fishing is available at the jetty or the mouth of the Don River. Diving is also available. The recently redeveloped foreshore incorporates fun family activities including a water park. **Historical Museum:** open Mon–Fri 9.30am–3.30pm, Sun 10am–12pm Sept–Apr (closed Feb–Mar); Gordon St. **Summergarden Theatre:** styled on the classic movie houses of southern California. Currently used to screen films and stage performances; Murroona Rd. **Muller's Lagoon:** a must for birdwatching. **Flagstaff Hill:** lookout offers 360-degree views. **Big Mango:** tribute to the local Kensington Pride mango, grown since the 1880s. A shop sells all things mango, the sorbet is the highlight; Bruce Hwy, Mount Gordon; 7km S. **Gloucester Island National Park:** secluded islands 23km offshore, part of the Great Barrier Reef, boasting beaches and rainforest. Campers must be self-sufficient and obtain a permit. Access via private boat from Dingo Beach, Hideaway Bay, Bowen or Airlie Beach; 13 7468; 20km E. **Cape Upstart National Park:** remote granite headland flanked with sandy beaches; self-sufficient visitors only; access by boat, ramps at Molongle

VISITOR INFORMATION

Charters Towers Visitor Information Centre
74 Mosman St,
Charters Towers
(07) 4761 5533
visitcharterstowers.com.au

Townsville Visitor Information Centre
Townsville Bulletin Square,
Flinders St, Townsville
(07) 4721 3660
townsvillenorthqueensland.com.au

The Whitsundays Visitor Information Centre
12505 Bruce Hwy,
Proserpine
(07) 4945 3967
tourismwhitsundays.com.au

Top: Museum of Tropical Queensland **Bottom:** Airlie Beach

TOP EVENTS

- **JAN** Goldfield Ashes cricket carnival (Charters Towers)
- **APR** Burdekin Auto Festival (Ayr); Ten Days in the Towers (Charters Towers)
- **MAY** Coral Sea Battle Memorial Commemoration (Cardwell); Country Music Festival (Charters Towers); Mud Trials (buggy racing, Sarina)
- **JUNE** Gold Cup Campdraft (Clermont); Australian Italian Festival (Ingham)
- **JULY** Festival of the Arts (Mackay); Australian Festival of Chamber Music (Townsville); Rodeo (Charters Towers)
- **AUG** Race Week Festival of Sailing and Great Barrier Reef Festival (both Airlie Beach); Gold and Coal Festival (Clermont); Triathlon and Multisport Festival (Townsville); Arts Festival (Ingham)
- **AUG–SEPT** Yunbenun (Magnetic Island) Race Week; Burdekin Water Festival (Ayr)
- **SEPT** Sarina Beach Coconut Festival
- **OCT** Maraka Festival (Ingham); Global Grooves multicultural festival (Mackay); Seafest (Cardwell); Harvest Festival (Home Hill)
- **NOV** Festival of Music (Airlie Beach)

TEMPERATURES

Jan: 22–32°C

July: 12–23°C

Bay and Elliot River; 13 7468; 50km NW. **Collinsville:** The Coalface Experience celebrates Australia's coalmining heritage; (07) 4785 5452; 82km SW. **Lake Proserpine:** great barramundi fishing year-round; permit required; 41km SE.

CARDWELL
Population 1245

Cardwell is a coastal town overlooking Rockingham Bay and the nearby islands. Ferries transport visitors to nearby Hinchinbrook Island, the largest island national park in Australia. Between the island and the mainland is Hinchinbrook Channel (Cardwell is at the northern edge), a popular spot for fishing and a sheltered area for houseboats.

SEE & DO **Hinchinbrook Island; Girringun National Park:** see Top Attractions for both. **Cardwell Bush Telegraph:** see Other Attractions. **Rainforest and Reef Information Centre:** interpretive centre that acquaints visitors with landscape, flora and fauna of northern Queensland; Bruce Hwy, near jetty. **Coral Sea Battle Memorial Park:** large war memorial that commemorates the World War II battle off the coast between Australian–US forces and the Japanese; beachfront. **Boat hire and cruises:** explore the tropical waters and islands to the east at the helm of a yacht, houseboat or cruiser, or travel with an organised cruise; details from visitor centre. **Snorkelling and scuba-diving tours:** details from visitor centre. **Jetty Market:** 1st Sat each month. **Scenic drive in Cardwell State Forest:** this 26km circuit from Cardwell takes in a lookout, waterfalls, swimming holes and picnic spots; begins on Braesnose St. **Girramay National Park:** boardwalk through extensive mangrove forests and a variety of other vegetation to the beach, with spectacular view of islands. This park is a habitat of the endangered mahogany glider; 13 7468; 4km N. **Five Mile Swimming Hole:** attractive picnic and swimming spot safe from crocodiles, sharks and stingers; 7km S. **Dalrymple Gap:** original service path and stone bridge through range; 15km S. **Brook Islands:** nesting area for Torresian imperial pigeons (Sept–Feb). Excellent snorkelling on reef of three northern islands; sea access only; 30km NE. **Murray Falls:** climb the steep 1km path to viewing platform over falls and surrounds; 42km NW.

CHARTERS TOWERS
Population 8040

Charters Towers is in the Burdekin Basin south-west of Townsville. The town's gold rush began on 25 December 1871 when an Indigenous servant Jupiter discovered gold while looking for lost horses. He brought gold-laden quartz to his employer, Hugh Mosman, who rode to Ravenswood to register the claim, and the gold rush was on. Between 1872 and 1916 Charters Towers produced ore worth £25 million. At the height of the gold rush it was Queensland's second-largest city and was commonly referred to as 'The World' because of its cosmopolitan population. This rich history can be seen in the preserved streetscapes of 19th- and 20th-century architecture, with many beautiful buildings including the Bank of Commerce, now restored as the New World Theatre Complex. To the north-west of Charters Towers is the 120km Great Basalt Wall, a lava wall created from the Toomba basalt flow.

SEE & DO **Ghosts Of Gold Heritage Trail; Dalrymple National Park:** see Other Attractions for both. **Folk Museum:** local historical memorabilia; Mosman St. **Civic Club:** once a gentlemen's club, this remarkable building (1900) still contains the original billiard tables; Ryan St. **Rotary Lookout:** panoramic views over region; Fraser St. **National Trust markets:** Stock Exchange Arcade; 1st and 3rd Sun each month. **Greenvale:** near the Gregory Development Rd, with a roadhouse, caravan park, golf course and the well-known Three Rivers Hotel, made famous by Slim Dusty's song of the same name; 290km NW. **Burdekin Falls Dam:** recreation area with barramundi fishing; 165km SE via Ravenswood. **Blackwood National Park:** a woodland park of undulating hills and stony ridges. See the Belyando blackwood trees that give the park its name, and walk on fire trails to discover the park's interesting birdlife, including squatter pigeons and speckled warblers; 13 7468; 180km S.

CLERMONT
Population 2079

Clermont is in the central highlands south-west of Mackay. The town was established over 130 years ago, after the discovery of gold at Nelson's Gully. At first the settlement was at Hoods Lagoon, but was moved to higher ground after a major flood in 1916 in which 63 people died. To the east of Clermont are the prominent cone-shaped mountains of Peak Range National Park. The Wolfgang Peak between Clermont and Mackay is particularly spectacular.

SEE & DO **Hoods Lagoon and Centenary Park:** walk the boardwalks in this picturesque setting to see the colourful birdlife. The park has interesting memorials and monuments that include the Sister Mary MacKillop grotto and a war memorial. The tree marker at the flood memorial plaque demonstrates how high the water rose. Access via Lime St. **Railway Wagon Murals:** paintings on four original wagons depict industries within the Belyando Shire; Hershel St. **The Stump:** memorial to the 1916 flood; cnr Drummond and Capricorn sts. **Cemetery:** headstones dating back to 1860s and mass grave of 1916 flood victims; 2.5km NE. **Clermont Historical Centre:** museum exhibits historic artefacts and machinery, including the steam engine used to shift the town after the flood, and historic buildings such as the old Masonic lodge, with displays of local family histories; open Wed–Sat 9am–3pm; 1300 472 227; 4km NW. **Remnants of**

Copperfield: old coppermining town with museum in original Copperfield store, a chimney stack and a cemetery containing 19th-century graves of copperminers; 5km S. **Theresa Creek Dam:** popular spot for waterskiing, sailboarding and fishing (permit required). Bushwalks nearby; off Peakvale Rd; 17km SW. **Fossicking for gold:** obtain licence and fossicking kit to start your search in nearby area; details from visitor centre; Cnr Herschel and Karmoo sts; (07) 4983 3311.

INGHAM
Population 4334

Ingham is a major sugar town near the Hinchinbrook Channel. Originally, Kanaka labourers (from the Pacific Islands) were employed in the surrounding sugarcane fields, but after their repatriation at the beginning of the 20th century, Italian immigrants took their place (the first Italians arrived in the 1890s). This strong Italian heritage is celebrated in the Australian Italian Festival each June. Ingham is at the centre of a splendid range of national parks. Wallaman Falls in Girringun National Park is a highlight as the largest single-drop falls in Australia.

SEE & DO **Orpheus Island; Girringun National Park:** *see* Top Attractions for both. **Paluma Range National Park:** *see* Other Attractions. **Hinchinbrook Heritage Walk and Drive:** displays at each historic site in Ingham and the nearby township of Halifax illustrate the dynamic history of the shire. It starts at the Shire Hall in Ingham; brochure available from visitor centre. **Memorial Gardens:** picturesque waterlily lakes and native tropical vegetation; they include Bicentennial Bush House with displays of orchids and tropical plants; open Mon–Fri; Palm Tce. **Conroy Hall Markets:** McIlwraith St; 2nd Sat each month. **Raintree Market:** Rotary Park; 1st and 3rd Sun each month. **Tyto Wetlands:** 90ha of wetlands with birdlife and wallabies. See the rare grass owl from the viewing platform; outskirts of town. **Cemetery:** interesting Italian tile mausoleums; 5km E. **Forrest Beach:** sandy 16km beach overlooking Palm Islands; stinger-net swimming enclosures are installed in summer; 20km SE. **Taylors Beach:** popular family seaside spot for sailing with excellent fishing and crabbing in nearby Victoria Creek; 24km E. **Lucinda:** coastal village on the banks of the Herbert River at the southern end of the Hinchinbrook Channel. Take a safari or fishing tour through the channel; stinger-net swimming enclosures are installed in summer; 27km NE. **Broadwater State Forest:** swimming holes, walking tracks and birdwatching; 45km W.

MACKAY
Population 80,455

The city of Mackay is an intriguing blend of 1900s and Art Deco heritage buildings mixed with modern-day architecture. The area is on the Traditional Land of the Yuwibara People. It was re-settled in the 1860s by explorer Captain John Mackay, the city's namesake. Sugar was first grown here in 1865. Mackay is now known as Queensland's 'sugar city': it produces around one-third of Australia's sugar crop and has the world's largest bulk sugar-loading terminal. Tourism is a growth industry in Mackay with the natural delights of the Great Barrier Reef just off the coast and spectacular inland national parks nearby.

SEE & DO **Eungella National Park:** *see* Top Attractions. **Hibiscus coast:** *see* Other Attractions. **Artspace Mackay:** this modern art gallery forms part of the Queensland Heritage Trails Network and has changing exhibitions of both local and international artwork. Tues–Sun; Gordon St. **Bluewater Lagoon:** waterfront dining area, with lots of public art to admire, as well as the heritage-listed Leichhardt Tree, which played a significant part in the city's maritime history as an 'anchor' for ships and free swimming area with children's water-play park. **Old Town Hall:** houses the Heritage Interpretive Centre with displays on Mackay's history and visitor information; Sydney St. **Regional Botanic Gardens:** follow the picturesque boardwalk over a lagoon and explore specialised gardens of central-coast flora; Lagoon St. **Queens Park:** includes the Orchid House with more than 3000 orchids; Goldsmith St. **Heritage walk:** self-guided walk to 22 heritage buildings; brochure available from visitor centre. **City cemetery:** 1.5km heritage walk; Greenmount Rd. **Museum:** local artefacts with a research area, and souvenirs for sale; open Tues, Thurs and Sat 10am–2pm (closed Dec and Jan); Casey Ave. **Great Barrier Reef tours:** snorkelling, diving, reef fishing and sailing tours; details at visitor centre. **Paxton Night Markets:** River St; 2nd Fri Feb–Dec. **Greater Whitsunday Farmers Markets:** Bluewater Quay; Wed mornings. **Northern beaches:** visit fabulous beaches including Harbour (patrolled, fishing), Town, Blacks (area's longest beach), Bucasia, Illawong, Eimeo, Lamberts (excellent lookout) and Shoal Point. **That Sapphire Place:** sapphire display and gem-cutting demonstrations; 10am–4pm Wed-Sat; 20km W. **Greenmount Homestead:** restored historic home with museum; open Mon–Wed and last Sun of the month 9am–1pm; Walkerston; 20km W. **Homebush:** small town offers art and craft gallery, orchid farms and self-drive tour through historic area; 25km S. **Melba House:** the home where Dame Nellie Melba spent the first year of her married life; now home to Pioneer Valley Visitor Centre; Marian; 28km W. **Mirani:** small town in the Pioneer Valley with museum and historic pub; 38km W. **Kinchant Dam:** popular spot for watersports and fishing; 40km W. **Smith Islands National Park:** the largest island of this group is Goldsmith, with long sandy beaches and snorkelling in surrounding reefs; access is by private boat or water taxi; 70km NE via Seaforth. **South Cumberland Islands National Park:** this group of nine islands off Mackay's coast is popular for boating and also an important rookery for flatback and green turtles; access is by private boat or water taxi. **Nebo:** historic town of Mackay region, with local artefacts and early settler history at the museum; 93km SW.

MORANBAH
Population 8899

Moranbah is a modern mining town south-west of Mackay. The area is the Traditional Lands of the Barada Barna and Widi Peoples. The town was developed in 1969 to support the huge open-cut coalmines of the expanding Bowen Coal Basin. Coking coal is railed to the Hay Point export terminal just south of Mackay.

SEE & DO **Federation Walk:** 1km scenic walk starts at Grosvenor Park; Peak Downs Hwy. **Heritage walk:** self-guided trail past interesting sites and heritage buildings of town; brochure from visitor centre. **Tours to Peak Downs Mine:** leaves from town square the last Wed each month; bookings at visitor centre. **Isaacs River:** recreational area with historic monuments and a hiking trail in dry weather; 13km S. **Lake Elphinstone:** camping, recreation activities, waterskiing, boating and fishing; 70km N.

PROSERPINE
Population 3440

Proserpine is the inland sugar town and service centre of the Whitsunday Shire. It was named after the Roman goddess of fertility, Persephone, for the rich and fertile surrounding lands.

SEE & DO **Conway National Park:** *see* Other Attractions. **Historical Museum:** local history dating back to Federation; open Mon–Fri 9am–4pm, by appt Sat-Sun; Bruce Hwy. **Entertainment Centre:** hosts shows by visiting and local artists and has regular cinema screenings;

16 Main St. **Pioneer Park and Mill Street Park:** beautiful shady picnic areas. **Lake Proserpine at Peter Faust Dam:** boat hire, waterskiing, fishing and swimming. Cedar Creek Falls are nearby; 20km NW, on Crystalbrook Rd. **Midge Point:** coastal community and an ideal spot for bushwalking, fishing, crabbing and swimming; 41km SE. **Crocodile safaris:** take a nature tour on a tractor-drawn open-air 'wagon train' and cruise through a mangrove river system on Proserpine River; bookings (07) 4948 3310.

RAVENSWOOD
Population 297

Ravenswood is on the Traditional Land of the Gudjal People. Once a boom town in the 1860s, today Ravenswood is home to a modest population and a range of historic buildings and ruins that recall the region's goldmining past. Queensland's first major inland European settlement, the area reached its peak at the start of the 20th century when mine manager Archibald Lawrence Wilson, 'the uncrowned king of Ravenswood', attracted investors and workers to the region to extract more than 12,000kg of gold. Ravenswood is a National Trust–certified town, and a stroll down Main St will take you past the stately Imperial Hotel to the ruins of the Mabel Mill.

SEE & DO **Historic Buildings:** many have been restored or are still in use. The town was once home to more than 30 pubs; the **Imperial Hotel** (c. 1902) is a beautiful Edwardian building and one of two bars that remain in use. Clad in multicolour brickwork, the entry to the pub's lavish interior is via swinging saloon doors. The ruins of the **Mabel Mill** are an impressive monument to the mining past of this town, as are chimney stacks, which can be seen south of the town centre. The **Railway Hotel** has recently been restored and the historical school building, built in the 1870s, is still in use. Regular tours of the area are run by the local Heritage Cottage. **Courthouse Museum:** displays on the town's history, people and mining industry; Wed–Mon 10am–3pm; (07) 4770 2047. **White Blow Environmental Park:** this park is well known locally for its milky quartz outcrop, which gives White Blow its name. There is also an attractive open-woodland forest; 5km NE.

SARINA
Population 3487

Sarina is in the hinterland of what has been dubbed the Serenity Coast, at the base of the Connor Range. It is central to the Queensland sugar belt. To the east and south are fine beaches, many of which are renowned fishing spots.

SEE & DO **Sarina Sugar Shed; Cape Palmerston National Park:** see Other Attractions for both. **Art and Craft Centre:** excellent variety of local art and craft, as well as visitor centre; Bruce Hwy. **'Field of Dreams' Historical Centre:** local industry history and memorabilia; open Tues, Wed and Fri 9am–2pm (open Tues and Wed only in Feb–Mar); Railway Sq. **Market:** Showgrounds; last Sun each month. **Beaches:** including Grasstree and Half Tide beaches to the north-east (Grasstree hosts an annual motorcycle race; date depends on tidal conditions); also Sarina Beach (east), popular for boating, fishing and swimming, with a lookout over the coast, and Armstrong Beach (south), great for swimming, prawning and fishing. **Hay Point Lookout:** viewing gallery at Hay Point and Dalrymple Bay coal terminal complex – informative video and excellent views; 12km N. **Salonika Beach:** attractive beach with amazing wildlife, including loggerhead turtles and whales in season; adjacent to Hay Point Lookout. **Lake Barfield:** picnic area and bird sanctuary; 12km N. **Carmila:** small town with beach just to the east; 65km S. **Clairview:** popular spot for beach fishing and crabbing; 73km S. **St Lawrence:** once a major port, this town is now a tribute to days past with many historic buildings, including the Anglican church (1898) and the remains of the convict-built wharf and abattoir. The local cemetery has graves dating back to the mid-1800s. The town also has wetlands nearby with a walking track and interpretive signs along with abundant birdlife; 110km S.

★ TOWNSVILLE
Population 173,724

This bustling coastal city boasts diverse landscapes, activities for all ages and a certain charm. The lands now known as Townsville are home to a number of Aboriginal clans, the Wulgurukaba of Gurambilbarra and Yunbenun, Bindal, Gugu Badhun and Nywaigi Peoples. The township was established in 1864 to service a new cattle industry. The many historic buildings found around the city are a reminder of this heritage. Today the city is known for its cosmopolitan feel and fast growth. Its landscaped foreshore, the Strand, has excellent cafes and restaurants, as well as tropical parks, a water-park playground for kids, free barbecues and views to Magnetic Island/Yunbenun. It connects to the Jezzine Barracks parkland, where there are stunning public artworks and war memorials, via a coastal walkway.

Wallaman Falls

SEE & DO **Reef HQ Great Barrier Reef Aquarium; Magnetic Island/Yunbenun; MOUA:** see Top Attractions for all. **Museum of Tropical Queensland; Bowling Green Bay National Park:** see Other Attractions for both. **Maritime Museum:** maritime items of historical significance; open 10am–3pm; 42–68 Palmer St; South Townsville; (07) 4721 5251. **The Strand Rockpool:** year-round swimming (closed Wed); The Strand. **Perc Tucker Regional Gallery:** local and touring exhibitions; open Mon–Fri 10am–5pm, Sat–Sun 10am–2pm; Flinders Mall; (07) 4727 9011. **Botanic Gardens:** Anderson Park, Kings Rd. **Town Common Conservation Park:** a coastline park with prolific birdlife, Aboriginal Plant Trail and forest walks; Cape Pallarenda Rd. **Castle Hill Lookout:** off Stanley St. **Ferry Terminal:** for Magnetic Island/Yunbenun, see Top Attractions, and daytrips and dive cruises to the Great Barrier Reef; Sir Leslie Thiess Dr. **Adventure activities:** numerous tour operators offer scuba diving, jetskiing, waterskiing, abseiling, whitewater rafting and more; contact visitor centre for details. **Strand Night Markets:** 1st Fri of each month. **Cotters Markets:** Flinders St, Sun; **Horseshoe Bay Market:** Beachside Park, Yunbenun (Magnetic Island); second and last Sun each month (Apr–Jan). **Billabong Sanctuary:** covering 10ha of rainforest, eucalypt forest and wetlands. See koala feeding and crocodile shows; Bruce Hwy; (07) 4778 8344; 17km SE. **Giru:** small community with waterfalls, bushwalks and swimming nearby; 50km SE.

Cairns and the Tropical North

Tropical North Queensland is the only place in the world where **two World Heritage–listed areas** converge: **the Wet Tropics**, a vast area of tropical rainforest that stretches some 450km along the coast from Townsville to Cooktown, and **the Great Barrier Reef**, the world's largest collection of coral reefs. Combine these two bucket-list attractions with **a lush hinterland boasting a fascinating history, a string of practically perfect beaches and tropical islands**, and it's easy to see why this region is one of Australia's most popular holiday destinations.

Top: Myall Beach, Cape Tribulation **Opposite:** Green Island

CHEAT SHEET

- Allow around five days to explore the region, and a couple of extra weeks if you want to head up to the tip of Cape York (see box p. 414).

- Best time to visit: winter, known as the dry season. 'Stinger' season is from Oct to May. Swimming is not recommended during this time because box jellyfish and Irukandji jellyfish are prevalent in the waters.

- Main towns: Cairns (see p. 413), Port Douglas (see p. 417).

- More than half of Cape York's population identify as Aboriginal or Torres Strait Islander and several communities at the Tip and around Laura and Cooktown welcome travellers to camp on their land. The Quinkan rock art galleries near Laura are superb. The area around Cairns is the Traditional Lands of the Djabuganjdi, Djirbalngan, Kuku-yalanji, Mbaabaram, Wargamaygan and Yidinjdji Peoples. Join a tour with a Traditional Owner at Mossman Gorge to see the world's oldest rainforest.

- Did you know? Although the Great Barrier Reef spans more than 2000km of Queensland's coastline, Cairns and Port Douglas are the closest northern gateways to the coral beds of the outer reef.

- Don't miss: Museum of Tropical Queensland; Innisfail's Art Deco trail; Atherton's Hou Wang Temple; Cairns Regional Gallery; Cairns Aquarium; Mareeba Wetlands; Skyrail Rainforest Cableway; Kuranda Scenic Railway; Hartley's Crocodile Adventures; Mossman Gorge Centre, Cape Tribulation.

TOP ATTRACTIONS

ATHERTON TABLELAND: This 900m high tableland is a productive farming district, thanks to the high rainfall and rich volcanic soil. Near Yungaburra is the remarkable Curtain Fig Tree, a strangler fig that has subsumed its host, sending down a curtain of roots. Volcanic lakes and waterfalls, including Millaa Millaa Falls and Zillie Falls, are among the other scenic attractions.

BARRON GORGE NATIONAL PARK: This national park is managed by its Traditional Owners, the Djabugay People. Most people experience this park via the Scenic Railway or Skyrail, but those who want to get away from the crowds could set out on one of the park's bushwalking tracks leading into pockets of World Heritage wilderness. Perhaps you'll spot a Ulysses butterfly, cassowary or tree kangaroo. If you haven't already seen Barron Falls from the train or Skyrail, make your way to Barron Falls lookout, 3km from Kuranda. Access to the national park is via Cairns or Kuranda.

CAIRNS AQUARIUM: Showcases Wet Tropics habitats and around 15,000 creatures in a three-level building; behind-the-scenes tours available; 5 Florence St, Cairns; (07) 4044 7300.

CAIRNS BOTANIC GARDENS: Established in 1886 as a recreational reserve, these are now the only wet tropical botanic gardens in Australia. The gardens display tropical plants from around the world, including a number of endangered species and more than 200 species of palm. Follow the boardwalks through remnant lowland swamp to adjacent Centenary Lakes to see turtles and mangrove birds. Access gardens via Collins Ave; Edge Hill, Cairns.

COOKTOWN MUSEUM: Housed in the old convent school (1888), this museum documents First Nations life prior to European settlement, also Cook's voyages and the 1870s gold-rush past. Relics include the anchor from the *Endeavour*. Helen St, Cooktown; (07) 4069 5386.

DAINTREE NATIONAL PARK: Arguably Australia's most beautiful and famous rainforest. The lush tangle of green protected within it is an incredible remnant from the days of Gondwana, forming part of the Wet Tropics World Heritage Area. This park, which is split into two distinct sections – **Mossman Gorge** and **Cape Tribulation** – will dazzle visitors with its diverse landscapes, which, apart from beautiful rainforest, include canopies of sprawling fan palms, deserted mangrove-lined beaches and boulder-strewn gorges. The Mossman Gorge section takes visitors into the rainforest's green and shady heart via an easy 2.7km walk to the Mossman River. The Cape Tribulation section is a rich mix of coastal rainforest, mangroves, swamp and heath.

FITZROY ISLAND: A low-key destination with a national park, white coral beaches and magnificent flora and fauna for bushwalking, diving and snorkelling. To the east are impressive snorkelling sites at Welcome and Sharkfin bays. A 99-room resort and a camping ground with 20 tent sites provide accommodation.

GAB TITUI CULTURAL CENTRE: This museum and gallery on Thursday Island (see p. 418) preserves the cultural heritage of the Torres Strait Islands and documents the art, culture, geography and history in an excellent exhibition; Victoria Pde, Thursday Island; (07) 4069 0888.

GREAT BARRIER REEF: Take a tour, charter a boat or fly to see some of the spectacular sights just offshore. Michaelmas and Upolo cays to the north-east are important sites for ground-nesting seabirds. The surrounding waters are excellent for reef swimming. You can also take a trip to the outer Barrier Reef, which is known for its spectacular underwater scenes and huge variety of marine life. For tours contact the visitor centre in Cairns (see p. 413) or Port Douglas (see p. 417).

GREEN ISLAND: A true coral cay covered with thick, tropical vegetation. The surrounding reef is home to magnificent tropical fish; they can be seen from a glass-bottom boat, in the underwater observatory or by snorkelling or helmet diving. This popular daytrip destination from Cairns (see p. 413) has a small resort (maximum 90 people).

LIZARD ISLAND NATIONAL PARK: The Dingaal People are the Traditional Owners of Dyiigurra, known as Lizard Island. The national park actually comprises six islands to the north-east of Cooktown (see p. 414) and is surrounded by the blue waters and coral reefs of the northern Great Barrier Reef. Four of the islands are important seabird nesting sites. Lizard Island itself is a resort island popular for sailing and fishing. You can also snorkel in the giant clam gardens of Watsons Bay or walk to Cooks Look for a spectacular view. There are 11 species of lizard here, and green and loggerhead turtles nest in late spring. Regular flights depart from Cairns; charter flights depart from Cairns and Cooktown; charter or private boat hire is available at Cooktown; 13 7468.

MOSSMAN GORGE CENTRE: Entrance to Mossman Gorge, with gallery, cafe and information centre. Ngadiku Dreamtime walks conducted by Traditional Owners are available. Access to the gorge is by shuttle bus every 15min 8am–6pm. Mossman Gorge Rd; (07) 4099 7000.

PARONELLA PARK: This 5ha park was the vision of immigrant sugarcane worker José Paronella. After making his fortune, he started building a mansion on the site (1930–46). Floods and other natural disasters have ruined the grand buildings, despite rebuilding efforts. Now visitors can walk through the ruins, admire the rainforest and birdlife, swim near the falls and have Devonshire tea at the cafe. The park is 17km south-west of Innsifail (see p. 415).

RINYIRRU (LAKEFIELD) NATIONAL PARK CAPE YORK PENINSULA ABORIGINAL LAND (CYPAL): The Lama Lama and Kuku Thaypan Peoples, the Bagaarrmugu, Mbarimakarranma, Muunydyiwarra, Magarrmagarrwarra, Balnggarrwarra and Gunduurwarra clans and related families are the Traditional Owners – and joint managers – of this vast area, Queensland's second largest national park. An important place of cultural significance to the Traditional Owners, there are many occupation, ceremonial and story places in the park. A visit to Rinyirru is a highlight of any visit to Cape York. The large rivers and waterholes are excellent for fishing and boating in the dry season, but become inaccessible wetlands in the wet season. In the south is the Old Laura Homestead, once en route to the Palmer River Goldfields, and in the north are plains dotted with notable anthills. See the threatened gold-shouldered parrot and spectacled hare-wallaby in the rainforest fringes of the Normanby and Kennedy rivers. 4WD is recommended; access only in the dry season (Apr–Nov); 13 7468.

SCENIC RAILWAY AND SKYRAIL: The Scenic Railway is an engineering feat more than 100 years old with tunnels, bridges and incredible views of Barron Falls. It begins at Caravonica Lakes (11km N of Cairns) and ends 34km later in the lush garden setting of Kuranda Station (see p. 416). Travel by rail on the way up and take the Skyrail, a journey via gondola across the treetops, on the way back (or vice versa). (07) 4036 9333.

SPLIT ROCK AND GUGU YALANJI ROCK-ART SITES: These rock-art sites have continued significance for the Quinkan People. Hidden behind a tangle of trees in the chasms and crevices of the sandstone escarpment, a diorama of lore and culture unfolds. The Quinkan spirits – the reptile-like Imjim and stick-like Timara – can be found hiding in dark places. There are also dingos, flying foxes, kangaroos, men, women and many hundreds of other things, both obvious and mysterious. More sites exist nearby, though only these two are accessible to the public. Bookings through the Quinkan Cultural Centre in Laura; (07) 4060 3457.

TULLY GORGE NATIONAL PARK: This park incorporates the Tully Gorge and the raging waters of the Tully River. It is the Traditional Land of the Jirrbal and Gulngay Peoples. Visit the Tully Gorge Lookout for gorge views, take the Rainforest Butterfly Walk and visit the Cardstone Weir boardwalk to watch rafters negotiate the rapids. Head to the top reaches of the river for superb scenery and swimming. Tully Falls are part of the Tully Falls National Park. Visit during the dry season only (May–Dec).

WATERFALL CIRCUIT: This 17km circuit road includes the Zillie, Ellinjaa and Mungalli falls, as well as the popular Millaa Millaa Falls, a great spot for swimming, with walks leading to other waterfalls. The circuit road is mostly sealed and the route leaves and rejoins Palmerston Hwy east of Millaa Millaa township.

WOOROONOORAN NATIONAL PARK: Part of the Wet Tropics World Heritage Area, more than 500 types of rainforest trees mean the landscape in this park is both diverse and breathtaking. The state's two highest mountains are here, Mount Bartle Frere (1622m) and Mount Bellenden Ker (1592m). Swim in the watering hole at Josephine Falls, located at the base of Mount Bartle Frere, or see the Babinda Boulders, a large group of rocks worn smooth by tropical rains. Walks include a 5km return track leading to spectacular gorge views at Crawford's Lookout and a short 800m track to glimpse the Tchupala Falls. Also visit the Mamu Canopy Rainforest Walk, which has views of the North Johnstone Gorge.

OTHER ATTRACTIONS

ATHERTON CHINATOWN AND HOU WANG TEMPLE: Atherton (see p. 413) once had a large population of Chinese people working for local timber cutters. This museum tells their stories through photographic exhibits, artefacts, interactive displays and oral histories. Tours of the restored Hou Wang Temple, built in 1903, are run throughout the day. Open Tues–Sat 10am–2pm; 86 Herberton Rd, Atherton.

AUSTRALIAN SUGAR HERITAGE CENTRE: This large museum was opened in 1977. Its permanent displays feature a collection of photographs, books, documents and an incredible display of machinery that includes a steam engine, reputedly one of the largest ever built. See the audiovisual display on the history of Australia's sugar industry and tour the art gallery. Cnr Bruce Hwy and Peregrine St, Mourilyan; (07) 4063 2477.

BEDARRA ISLAND: This island of untouched tropical beauty is off-limits to day visitors and children under 16. The exclusive resort (maximum 20 people) offers bushwalking, snorkelling, fishing, swimming, paddleboarding, kayaking and tennis. It's 16km south-east of Mission Beach (see p. 417).

COOKTOWN BOTANIC GARDENS: The oldest botanic gardens in Queensland, with native, European and exotic plants. The 'Cooktown Interpretive Centre: Nature's Powerhouse' has botanical and wildlife illustrations, and there are also walking trails to Cherry Tree and Finch bays; Walker St, Cooktown; (07) 4069 5763.

CRATER LAKES NATIONAL PARK: The two volcanic lakes, Lake Eacham and Lake Barrine, are surrounded by rainforest and offer watersports, bushwalking and birdwatching. Look for the eastern water dragons along the 3km track around Lake Barrine or take a wildlife cruise on the lake. There is a children's pool at Lake Eacham, a self-guided trail through the rainforest and a 3km circuit shore track. Both lakes are popular recreation areas. 13 7468.

EUBENANGEE SWAMP NATIONAL PARK: This important park protects the last of the remnant coastal lowland rainforest around Alice River, which is part of the Wet Tropics Region. See the rainforest birds on the walk from Alice River to the swamp where jabirus and spoonbills feed. 13 7468. It's 13km north-west of Innisfail (see p. 415).

FAMILY ISLANDS: The Family Islands National Park protects this chain of islands, which are the The Traditional Land of the Bandjin and Djiru Aboriginal People. The most northerly of the group, Dunk Island, has spectacular forest, rainforest, 14km of walking tracks and is home to bright blue Ulysses butterflies. The former resort has been derelict since it closed after damage during cyclone Yasi in early 2011, but daytrips operate and camping is available. The less-developed islands of Wheeler and Coombe are perfect for bush camping (visitors must be self-sufficient). Permits are necessary; 13 7468. The islands are accessible by water taxi from Mission Beach.

GOLDSBOROUGH VALLEY: The lowland rainforest along the Goldsborough Valley is protected as part of Wooroonooran National Park. Walk to the falls along the 1.6km Kearneys Falls track and learn about the culture and customs of the Traditional Owners,

Babinda Boulders

the Yidinj People, from the informative displays. The 18km historic Goldfields Trail travels through nearby Wooroonooran National Park to the Boulders near Babinda.

HARTLEY'S CROCODILE ADVENTURES: Crocodile park in a natural bush setting, with a lagoon that is home to around 25 saltwater crocs. Captain Cook Hwy, Wangetti Beach; (07) 4055 3576; 40km N of Cairns.

HERBERTON MINING MUSEUM: Explore local mining history in this richly informative museum, with displays of antique machinery, an array of minerals and rocks, and multimedia shows. A short walking track takes you past the mining relics that made up the Great Northern Claim, now a heritage-listed site; 1 Jacks Rd, Herberton; (07) 4096 3474.

HERBERTON RANGE NATIONAL PARK: The temperate climate attracts a variety of wildlife in this rainforest park, including the attractive golden bowerbird. Walk to the summit of Mount Baldy for panoramic views over the tableland (the steep ascent should be attempted only by experienced walkers); Rifle Range Rd, between Atherton and Herberton.

INNOT HOT SPRINGS: These natural thermal springs reputedly have healing powers. The spring water was originally bottled and sent to Europe as a healing remedy until the 1900s. The springs are 32km south-west of Ravenshoe.

JARDINE RIVER NATIONAL PARK: This remote park is on the north-east tip of Cape York Peninsula. It was known to early explorers as the 'wet desert' because of its abundant waterways but lack of food. These waters attract varied birdlife including the rare palm cockatoo. See Fruit Bat Falls from the boardwalk, or fish in restricted areas. 4WD access only; visit May–Oct. Off Peninsula Development Rd, south of Bamaga; 13 7468.

LAKE TINAROO: With 200km of shoreline, Lake Tinaroo is ideal for fishing, waterskiing and sailing. Walking tracks circle the lake, and dinghies and houseboats are available for hire. The Danbulla Forest Drive is a scenic 28km drive.

MALANDA: A small town in the middle of rich dairy-farming country, Malanda claims the longest milk run in the world (to Alice Springs) and boasts the still-operating 19th-century Majestic Theatre. On the southern outskirts of town are the Malanda Falls Conservation Park, with signposted rainforest walks, and the Malanda Falls Environmental Centre, which has displays on local history, vulcanology, flora and fauna. The Malanda Falls flow into the local swimming pool.

MOUNT HYPIPAMEE NATIONAL PARK: Set on the Evelyn Tableland, this park boasts high-altitude rainforests and a climate that attracts birdlife and possums, including the green and lemuroid ringtail possums. The park is known locally as 'The Crater' because of its sheer-sided, 70m wide volcanic explosion crater. Walk to the viewing deck for the best vantage point, or see the Dinner Falls cascade down the narrow gorge.

WESTERN CAPE CULTURAL CENTRE — ACHIMBUN: Established to introduce visitors to the culture of western Cape York, the centre has cultural displays, artworks and information about the ecosystems of the cape. A large grassy area overlooking the Embley River is a nice place to enjoy a coffee. The centre is also planning a major redevelopment, which will add a food outlet and retail store, an Aboriginal Arts Centre and Cultural Park and a new stage for cultural events. Bush food and medicines will be planted throughout the precinct. A highlight of the centre is the ceramic mural depicting sacred images of the local First Nations People. There is also information about the ecosystems of the Cape. Open Mon–Fri 10am–2pm, Mar–Nov; Evans Landing, Weipa; (07) 4069 7945.

WILDLIFE HABITAT: This sanctuary covers an area of 2ha and is home to more than 1600 animals. Walk along the boardwalks through the four habitats of north Queensland – rainforest, wetlands, woodlands and grasslands. The regular guided tours are a great way to see the sanctuary, and you'll make your visit memorable with the special daily events including Breakfast with the Birds and koala encounters (with the chance to touch and photograph one). Cnr Captain Cook Hwy and Port Douglas Rd, Port Douglas; (07) 4099 3235.

VISITOR INFORMATION

Cairns & Tropical North Visitor Information Centre,
51 The Espl, Cairns
(07) 4051 3588
tropicalnorthqueensland.org.au

Innisfail Visitor Information Centre
Anzac Memorial Park,
Bruce Hwy, Innisfail
0428 228 962

Tropical Coast
tropicalcoasttourism.com.au

Atherton Tablelands
athertontablelands.com.au

Opposite: Zillie Falls, Atherton Tableland

KEY TOWNS

ATHERTON
Population 7348

Originally called Prior's Pocket and renamed in 1885, this town is the commercial hub of the Atherton Tableland. It is an area renowned for its volcanic crater lakes, waterfalls and fertile farmlands. Surrounding the town is dense rainforest that abounds in birdlife, and the nearby parks and forests offer a variety of watersports, bushwalking and other outdoor activities.

SEE & DO **Atherton Tableland:** *see* Top Attractions. **Atherton Chinatown and Hou Wang Temple; Lake Tinaroo:** *see* Other Attractions for both. **Hallorans Hill Conservation Park:** walk to the rim of this extinct volcanic cone on the Atherton Tableland, where there is a great lookout plus informative displays; off Kennedy Hwy. **The Crystal Caves:** explore underground tunnels and chambers lined with crystals, fossils and fluorescent minerals. The above-ground shop sells a range of jewellery and gemstones; 69 Main St. **Tolga Bat Hospital:** get up close and learn about Australia's four species of flying foxes. Open 3–6pm (bookings essential); 134 Carrington Rd; (07) 4091 2683. **Hasties Swamp National Park:** local and migratory birds visit this swamp, including whistling ducks and magpie geese; 3km S. **Tolga:** this town has a railway museum and craft outlets; 5km N. **Wongabel State Forest:** important wildlife refuge in the Wet Tropics World Heritage Area. An informative heritage trail gives an insight into First Nations culture and history; Kennedy Hwy; 8km S.

BABINDA
Population 1113

A small sugar town south of Cairns, Babinda boasts abundant wildlife, secluded swimming holes and untouched rainforest in its surrounds. It is the gateway to Wooroonooran National Park.

SEE & DO **Wooroonooran National Park:** *see* Top Attractions. **Arts and crafts:** several galleries in town. **Deeral:** departure point for cruises through rainforest and saltwater crocodile haunts of the Mulgrave and Russell rivers; 14km N. **Bramston Beach:** small community behind long palm-lined beach; Bruce Hwy S to Miriwinni, then 12km E. **Russell River National Park:** small park on the coast with good birdwatching and canoeing; no facilities, 4WD access; 13 7468; 6km N of Bramston Beach.

★ CAIRNS
Population 153,181

This modern, colourful city is the capital of the tropical north and the gateway to the Great Barrier Reef. The city centre is an unusual mix of modern architecture and original Queenslander homes, with the city's focal point a large artificial lagoon on the Esplanade, studded with sculptures and picnic areas. Walking and cycling paths trace the bay foreshore and blend city life with the natural attractions of the Coral Sea. With Cairns's superb location – the Great Barrier Reef and islands to the east, the mountain rainforests of the Wet Tropics and plains of the Atherton Tableland to the west, and palm-fringed beaches to the north and south – it's a good base from which to explore the wonders and adventures of this region.

SEE & DO **Cairns Botanic Gardens; Cairns Aquarium; Great Barrier Reef; Scenic Railway and Skyrail; Fitzroy Island; Green Island:** *see* Top Attractions for all. **Hartley's Crocodile Adventures:** *see* Other Attractions. **Foreshore Promenade:** landscaped area with safe swimming lagoon; pool closed Wed mornings; foreshore. **Cairns Art Gallery:** local artists exhibit in this National Trust–classified building; open Mon–Fri 9am–5pm, Sat 10am–5pm, Sun 10am–2pm; cnr Shields and Abbott sts; (07) 4046 4800. **Mount Whitfield Conservation Park:** two major walking tracks through a forested mountain range to the summit for views of Cairns and the Coral Sea; behind botanic gardens; access via Collins Ave, Edge Hill. **McLeod Street Pioneer Cemetery:** honours local settlers. **Tanks Art Centre:** multipurpose centre in revamped World War II oil-storage tanks, including gallery with local art; call for event listings; 46 Collins Ave, Edge Hill; (07) 4032 6600. **Australian Armour and Artillery Museum:** largest collection of armoured vehicles and artillery in the Southern Hemisphere, including items from World War I; 2 Skyrail Dr; (07) 4048 1665. **Game fishing:** contact visitor centre for details. **Dive schools:** contact visitor centre for details. **Rusty's Markets:** Grafton and Sheridan sts; Fri–Sun. **Beaches:** incredible 26km of beaches extending from Machans Beach on north bank of Barron River (10km N), to Ellis Beach (26km N). **Bungee jumping:** choose from a variety of jumps and other thrills in the rainforest; 10am–5pm; 5 McGregor Rd, Smithfield; (07) 4057 7188; 13km N. **Crystal Cascades:** walk by cascades and a secluded freshwater swimming hole; end of Redlynch Valley; 18km SW. **Lake Morris and Copperlode Dam:** walking tracks; 19km SW. **Barron and Freshwater valleys:** bushwalking, hiking, whitewater rafting and camping; contact visitor centre for details; W and NW of Cairns. **Safaris:** 4WD to Cape York and the Gulf Country; contact visitor centre for details.

QUEENSLAND

COOKTOWN
Population 1797

Cooktown is the last main town before the wilderness that is Cape York. It is the Traditional Lands of the Eastern Kuku Yalanji People. In 1770 James Cook beached the *Endeavour* here for repairs after running aground on the Great Barrier Reef. In 1874 gold was discovered on the Palmer River, and Cooktown became a gold-rush port with 37 hotels and a transient population of some 18,000 people, including 6000 Chinese fossickers who established a thriving community. Nearby are some of the most rugged and remote national parks in Australia. They form part of the Wet Tropics World Heritage Area and are a special experience for today's intrepid explorers. Before driving to remote areas check road conditions and restrictions with Queensland Parks and Wildlife Service, 1 Ferrari St, Cooktown, 13 7468 or (07) 4069 5777.

SEE & DO **Cooktown Museum; Lizard Island National Park:** *see* Top Attractions for both. **Cooktown Botanic Gardens:** *see* Other Attractions. **History Centre:** chronicles the history of the town from goldrush to the present; Mon–Sat 9am–3pm; 121 Charlotte St. **Historic cemetery:** documents the varied cultural heritage of Cooktown and includes the grave of tutor, early immigrant and heroine Mary Watson; Boundary Rd. **Chinese shrine:** to many who died on the goldfields; near cemetery. **Cooktown Wharf:** dates back to 1880s and is an excellent spot for fishing. **The Milbi Wall:** collage of Traditional art by local First Nations People; near wharf. **Fishing:** Spanish mackerel and barramundi at the wharf. **Walking trails:** plenty around town and outlying areas, including the Scenic Rim and Wharf and Foreshore Walk; details from visitor centre. **Market:** Lions Park; Sat. **Discovery Festival:** re-enactment of Cook's landing with First Nations performances and various markets; during Queen's Birthday long weekend, June. **Endeavour River National Park:** just north of town is this park of diverse landscapes, including coastal dunes, mangrove forests and catchment areas of the Endeavour River. Most of the park is accessible only by boat (ramps at Cooktown); southern vehicle access is via Starcke St, Marton. **Black Mountain (Kalkajaka) National Park:** impressive mountain range of granite boulders and a refuge for varied and threatened wildlife; Cooktown Developmental Rd; 25km S. **Helenvale:** small town with historic Lions Den Hotel (est. 1875) and rodeo in June; 30km S. **Rossville:** town with markets every 2nd Sat; 38km S. **Ngalba Bulal National Park:** this remote coastal park is

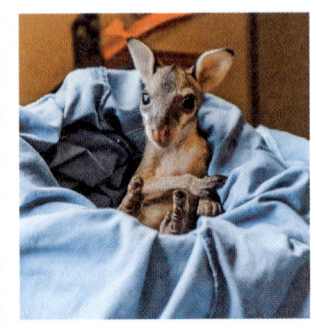

CAPE YORK

There's nothing quite like the Cape. An adventure playground for those who like getting off the beaten track and camping, it offers challenging (some may say extreme) four-wheel driving, superb fishing and spectacular scenery, from pristine white-sand beaches (sadly off limits for swimming thanks to the resident sharks and saltwater crocodiles, who also inhabit the wild rivers that cover the Cape like a veil of lace), rainforests and lily-covered wetlands brimming with birdlife to vast savannah lands studded with towering termite mounds.

But before you go, here's some things you need to know:

The Cape is roughly 1000km from Cairns to the Tip, and it's not the type of place you want to rush, so allow plenty of time, two to three weeks at the very least.

Roads are closed during the wet season, which can start in late Oct (but more often than not, it doesn't rain until Dec) and last until June (although most roads and parks reopen in May).

Almost all roads on the Cape are 4WD only. The Old Telegraph Track is notorious for its deep and tricky river crossings.

The PDR (Peninsula Development Road) is an easier option – it is progressively being sealed to Weipa but beyond that the road to the tip is still very dusty and deeply corrugated.

The region is popular during winter school holidays in July. Campgrounds are often full and you may have to queue to cross rivers. All campsites in national parks need to be prebooked online at qpws.usedirect.com/qpws (if you have difficulty, call 13 7468). There's little mobile phone coverage on the Cape but there are internet kiosks at most ranger stations.

Roadhouses along the way offer good camping, hot showers and basic meals (think hamburgers and steaks).

Almost all rivers are home to saltwater crocodiles: obey all warning signs.

Main towns: Cooktown (*see* p. 414), Laura (*see* p. 416), Weipa (*see* p. 419).

Don't miss: James Cook Museum, Quinkan rock-art galleries at Laura, Umagico, The Tip, Lockhart River Arts, Chilli Beach in Kutini-Payamu (Iron Range) National Park, Laura Dance Festival.

Top: Wildlife rescue at Wildlife Habitat Port Douglas
Bottom: Mission Beach

TOP EVENTS

- MAR Feast of the Senses (Innisfail)
- MAY Great Wheelbarrow Race (Mareeba to Chillagoe)
- JUNE Adventure Festival (Cairns); Discovery Festival (Cooktown), Annual Races (Laura); Fishing Classic (Weipa)
- JULY Quinkan Dance Festival (odd-numbered years, Laura); Rodeo (Mareeba)
- AUG Indigenous Art Fair (Cairns); Maize Festival (Atherton); Tropical Writers Festival (odd-numbered years, Cairns); Bullride (Weipa); Tour of the Tropics Cycling Festival (Cairns); RRR Mountain Bike Challenge (Port Douglas)
- AUG–SEPT Cairns Festival
- SEPT Winds of Zenadth Cultural Festival (Thursday Island); Game Fishing Tournament (Innisfail); Spring Festival (Kuranda)
- OCT Savannah in the Round Music Festival (Mareeba); Reef Feast (Palm Cove); Torimba Festival (Ravenshoe); Tablelands Folk Festival (Yungaburra); Harvest Festival (Babinda)

TEMPERATURES

Jan: 24–31°C

July: 17–26°C

an attractive mix of rainforest, beaches and fringing reefs, with a variety of wildlife including the rare Bennett's tree kangaroo. Walk on the old donkey track, once used by tin miners (remains of tin workings can be seen); access by boat or the walking track, which starts at Home Rule Rainforest Lodge, Rossville, 38km S. **Elim Beach and the Coloured Sands:** beach with white silica sandhills and surrounding heathlands. The Coloured Sands are found 400m along the beach. This is Traditional land, permit required from Hope Vale Community Centre; 65km N. **Cape Melville National Park Cape York Peninsula Aboriginal Land (CYPAL):** this rugged park on the Cape York Peninsula has glorious coastal scenery. Much of the plant life is rare, including the foxtail palm. Visitors must be self-sufficient; 4WD access only in dry weather; southern access via Starcke homestead, western access via Kalpower Crossing in Rinyirru (Lakefield) National Park (CYPAL); 140km NW. **Flinders Group National Park:** comprising seven continental islands in Princess Charlotte Bay. There are two self-guided trails taking in bushfoods and rock-art sites on Stanley Island. Access by charter or private boat or sea plane; 195km NW. **Sport fishing safaris:** to nearby waterways; details from visitor centre. **Bicentennial National Trail:** 5330km trail that runs from Cooktown to Healesville in Vic., for walkers, bike riders and horseriders; it is possible to do just a section of the trail; details from visitor centre.

DAINTREE
Population 93

The unspoiled township of Daintree lies in the tropical rainforest of Far North Queensland, at the heart of the Daintree River catchment basin, surrounded by the McDowall Ranges. Daintree began as a logging town in the 1870s. Now tourism is the major industry with the Daintree River and World Heritage rainforest nearby. Saltwater crocodiles are found in the mangrove-lined creeks and tributaries of the Daintree River.

SEE & DO **Daintree National Park:** see Top Attractions. **Daintree Discovery Centre:** informative displays for visitors; a boardwalk and aerial walkway passes through the rainforest canopy; 11km SE. **Cape Tribulation:** beaches and reefs; reef tours and horseriding on beach can be arranged via most accommodation tour desks or Mason's Tours in Cape Tribulation; (07) 4098 0070; access via Daintree River cable ferry (car ferry runs 6am–12am); 48km N. **River cruises:** to see saltwater crocodiles and plentiful birdlife.

GORDONVALE
Population 6035

Gordonvale is a sugar-milling town just south of Cairns with well-preserved streetscapes, historic buildings and the 922m high Walsh's Pyramid that forms the backdrop to the town. People flock to the mountain in Aug for a race to the top. The town's less glorious claim to fame is that cane toads were released here in 1935 in an attempt to eradicate sugarcane pests.

SEE & DO **Goldsborough Valley:** see Other Attractions. **Mulgrave Settlers Museum:** with displays and dioramas depicting early settler life in the shire. Includes blacksmith's shop, old store and a Chinese display; open Mon–Sat 10am–2pm Mar–Nov; Gordon St. **Mulgrave River:** runs next to Gordonvale and is popular for swimming, canoeing, kayaking and bushwalking.

HERBERTON
Population 984

Known as the 'Village in the Hills', Herberton sits about 1000m above sea level on the south-west ranges of the Atherton Tableland. The first settlement on the tableland, it was established in 1880 when two prospectors discovered tin in the area. It was a thriving and lively tin-mining town, the most important in the Herbert River field, until the mine's closure in 1978.

SEE & DO **Mining Museum; Mount Hypipamee; Herberton Range national parks:** see Other Attractions for all. **Spy and Camera Museum:** houses some of the world's rarest, oldest and smallest cameras; see Russian spy cameras and cameras from Hitler's Germany; Grace St. **Ghost walks:** several times a year the ghosts of former miners and Herberton residents 'materialise' to retell their stories; dates vary, details from visitor centre.

INNISFAIL
Population 7173

Innisfail has seen destruction by cyclone more than once but the town is resilient. The parks and walks on the riverside, as well as the classic Art Deco buildings in the town centre, add to the charm of this town. The area is renowned for its sugar industry and the excellent fishing in nearby rivers, beaches and estuaries.

SEE & DO **Eubenangee Swamp National Park:** see Other Attractions. **Historical Society Museum:** documents local history; Edith St. **Lit Sing Gung Chinese Temple:** reminder of Chinese presence during gold-rush days; Owen St. **Warrina Lakes and Botanical Gardens:** recreational facilities and walks; Charles St. **Historical town walk:** see classic Art Deco architecture and historic shire hall on self-guided or guided town walk; details from visitor centre. **Market:** ANZAC Memorial Park; 3rd Sat morning each month. **Flying Fish Point:** popular spot for swimming, camping and fishing; 5km NE. **Mamu Rainforest Canopy Walkway:** 350m elevated cantilevered walkway with a 37m viewing tower; 30km NW. **Ella Bay National Park:** small coastal park with beach and picnic spot; 13 7468; 8km N. **North Johnstone River Gorge:** walking tracks to several picturesque waterfalls; 18km W via Palmerston Hwy. **Crawford Lookout:** for spectacular views of North Johnstone River; 38km W off Palmerston Hwy.

KURANDA
Population 2456

This small village is set in tropical rainforest on the banks of the Barron River north-west of Cairns. Its beautiful setting attracted a strong hippie culture in the 1960s and 1970s and, while it still has a bohemian feel, tourism is now its focus. There are many nature parks and eco-tourism experiences on offer, along with plenty of art and craft workshops, cafes and a daily market. Even transport to and from the town has been developed into an attraction – the Scenic Railway and Skyrail, both with jaw-dropping views over World Heritage–listed rainforest.

SEE & DO **Scenic Railway and Skyrail; Barron Gorge National Park:** *see* Top Attractions for both. **Butterfly Sanctuary:** large enclosure, home to more than 1500 tropical butterflies, including the blue Ulysses and the Australian birdwing (the country's largest butterfly); Rob Veivers Dr. **Birdworld:** more than 50 species of birds, including the flightless cassowary and some endangered species; in the heritage markets. **Koala Gardens:** Australian animals in a natural setting; close to the heritage markets. **Kuranda Arts Cooperative:** arts and craft centre where you can meet the artists and watch them work; Mon–Sun; Coondoo St (next to the Butterfly Sanctuary). **Doongal Aboriginal Arts & Artefacts:** supports many First Nations' artists, features rainforest art and didgeridoos; Coondoo St. **Emu Ridge Gallery:** fossil and gemstone museum featuring a 9m replica of an Allosaurus dinosaur skeleton; Therwine St. **Honey House:** free tastings and live bee displays; open 9am–3.30pm; Therwine St. **Riverboat tours:** depart daily from the riverside landing below the railway station. **Jumrum Creek Walk:** 750m rainforest walk in Jumrum Creek Conservation Park, in the middle of the township; links to the village circuit walk; Barang St. **Heritage Markets:** Rob Veivers Dr; Mon–Sun. **Original Rainforest Markets:** behind the Kuranda Market Arcade; Mon–Sun. **Rainforestation Nature Park:** rainforest tours, tropical fruit orchard, Pamagirri Aboriginal Dance troupe, Dreamtime walk, and a koala and wildlife park; 35km E.

LAURA
Population 101

Laura is a tiny town in Far North Queensland that boasts only a few buildings, including the quaint old pub nestled in the shade of mango trees. The area to the south-east of town is known as Quinkan Country after the spirits depicted at the incredible Split Rock and Gugu Yalangi rock-art sites. Every two years Laura hosts one of the biggest First Nations events on Australia's calendar – the three-day Laura Quinkan Dance Festival in July – when around 25 Cape York and Gulf First Nations communities gather at a traditional meeting ground by the Laura River and celebrate with traditional dance, music, and art and craft; check anggnarra.org.au for updates.

SEE & DO **Split Rock and Gugu Yalangi Rock-art Sites; Rinyirru (Lakefield) National Park (CYPAL):** *see* Top Attractions for both. **Quinkan and Regional Cultural Centre:** featuring an interpretive display on the history of Quinkan Country. Guided tours, which include rock-art sites, can also be booked from the centre; Peninsula Development Rd; (07) 4060 3457. **Lakeland Downs:** bananas and coffee are the main fare cultivated from the area's rich volcanic soil, which is also ideal for a variety of fruit and vegetables; 62km S.

MAREEBA
Population 8585

Mareeba was the first town settled on the Atherton Tableland by pastoralist John Atherton in 1877. Tobacco production began in the 1950s, but was deregulated in the early 2000s. Today the area produces mangoes, coffee and sugarcane. The morning balloon flights over the tableland and Mareeba Valley are spectacular.

SEE & DO **Heritage Museum:** local history exhibits and information centre; Centenary Park, Byrnes St. **Barron River Walk:** walk along the banks to swimming hole. **Bicentennial Lakes:** park with plantings to encourage wildlife. Explore the park on the walking tracks and bridges; Rankine St. **Coffee Works:** see the production of coffee and taste-test the results; 136 Mason St. **The Australian Coffee Centre & Skybury Plantation:** this complex offers a coffee laboratory and restaurant. Open 9am–5pm; 136 Ivicevic Rd. **Market:** Centenary Park; 2nd and 5th Sat each month. **Makotrac International Racetrack:** fast go-karts and an 18-hole minigolf course; open Tues–Sun; Springs Rd, 2km W. **de Brueys Boutique Wines:** taste tropical fruit wines, liqueurs and ports; Fichera Rd, 4km E. **Golden Drop Winery:** try the white wine made from Kensington Red mangoes; Bilwon Rd, Biboohra; 7km N. **Granite Gorge:** impressive boulder and rock formation; 12km SW off Chewko Rd. **Emerald Creek Falls:** walk 1.9km and see the water as it tumbles down the mountain between massive boulders; Cobra Rd; 12km SE. **Davies Creek National Park:** walk the 1.1km Davies Creek Falls circuit to see the falls crashing over boulders; 13 7468; 22km E.

MILLAA MILLAA
Population 314

Millaa Millaa is at the southern edge of the Atherton Tableland, and is central to a thriving dairy industry. The 17km Waterfall Circuit and rainforest-clad Wooroonooran National Park, are just two of the natural attractions that bring visitors to town.

SEE & DO **Waterfall Circuit; Wooroonooran National Park:** *see* Top Attractions for both. **Eacham Historical Society Museum:** documents history of local area, with special interest in dairy and timber industries; Main St; (07) 4097 2725. **Millaa Millaa Lookout:** panoramic views of tablelands and national parks; 6km W. **Misty Mountains walking trails:** short- and long-distance tracks through World Heritage–listed Wet Tropics, many of which follow traditional paths of the Jirrbal and Mamu Peoples; details from visitor centre.

⭐ MISSION BEACH
Population 872

Mission Beach and its surrounding areas are the lands of the Dijru People who now hold Native Title of parts of this area. The beach that features in the town's name is a 14km long strip of golden sand fringed by coconut palms and World Heritage–listed wet tropical rainforest. Artists, potters, sculptors and jewellers have settled in the area, which is now reliant on the strong tourism industry of the coast and nearby islands.

SEE & DO **Family Islands; Bedarra Island:** see Other Attractions for both. **Porter Promenade:** woodcarving sculptures and rainforest arboretum; next to visitor centre. **Ulysses Link Walking Trail:** this 1.5km pathway along the foreshore features local history, sculptures and mosaics. **Great Barrier Reef tours:** cruises and day tours to islands and reefs depart from Clump Point Jetty daily. **Boat, catamaran and jetski hire:** details from visitor centre. **Beach Market:** Ulysses Day Park, Porter Prom; 1st and 3rd Sun morning each month. **Monster Markets:** Ulysses Day Park, Porter Prom; last Sun morning each month (Easter–Nov). **Clump Mountain National Park:** this scenic park boasts remnant lowland rainforest, an important habitat for the southern cassowary. A highlight is the 4km Bicton Hill Track to the summit lookout over Mission Beach and coast; just north of Mission Beach on Bingil Bay Rd; 13 7468. **Historic Tales and Trails:** links places of interest in and around Mission Beach, including the memorial to the ill-fated 1848 Cape York expedition of Edmund Kennedy and an adjacent display of First Nations culture, and Yasi Circle, built after the cyclone in 2011; Rotary Park, Wongaling Beach. **Wet Tropics walking trails:** the area around Mission Beach offers spectacular rainforest walks, including the Lacy Creek Forest circuit (1.2km) in the major cassowary habitat of Djiru National Park, the Kennedy Trail (7km) past lookouts and along beaches, and the trails in Licuala State Forest; brochure available from visitor centre. **Adventure activities:** includes tandem parachuting, kayak trips and whitewater rafting; details from visitor centre.

MOSSMAN
Population 1744

The town of Mossman, in Far North Queensland, is set among green mountains and fields of sugarcane. Originally named after the explorer Hugh Mosman, the town changed the spelling of its name from Mosman to Mossman to avoid being confused with the Sydney suburb.

SEE & DO **Daintree National Park; Mossman Gorge Centre:** see Top Attractions. **Kuku Yalanji Cultural Habitat Tours:** Kubirri Warra brothers Linc and Brandon Walker lead small-group walking tours on Cooya Beach, teaching traditional hunting and fishing; bookings essential on (07) 4098 3437. **Market:** Foxton Ave; Sat. **SUP tours:** Walk (well, stand-up paddle board) on the crystal-clear waters of the Mossman River; 0427 498 042. **Wonga:** small town with an excellent beach and orchid gardens; 18km N.

MOURILYAN
Population 391

Mourilyan is the bulk-sugar outlet for the Innisfail area. The history of this thriving industry can be seen at the Australian Sugar Heritage Centre.

SEE & DO **Paronella Park:** see Top Attractions. **Australian Sugar Heritage Centre:** see Other Attractions. **Etty Bay:** quiet tropical beach with caravan and camping facilities; 9km E.

PALM COVE
Population 2450

Serene Palm Cove, north-west of Cairns, has white sandy beaches and streets lined with palm trees. It is essentially a resort village, with waterfront cafes and restaurants and locals and tourists alike soaking up the relaxed Far North Queensland atmosphere. The lifestyle is based around the water – fishing off the jetty, horseriding along the beach and swimming in the Coral Sea's crystal-clear blue water.

SEE & DO **Hartley's Crocodile Adventures:** see Other Attractions. **Reef tours:** to Green Island and the Great Barrier Reef; depart Palm Cove jetty Mon–Sun. **Day tours:** to Atherton Tableland and surrounds; details from visitor centre. **Clifton Beach:** resort village with park-lined beach; 3km S. **Rex Lookout:** stunning coastal views; 17km N.

⭐ PORT DOUGLAS
Population 3650

Port Douglas lies on the serene waters of a natural harbour in tropical north Queensland. Surrounded by lush vegetation and pristine rainforests, here you'll enjoy a relaxed village lifestyle with shops, galleries and restaurants. Its tropical mountain setting, the pristine Four Mile Beach and its proximity to the Great Barrier Reef make Port Douglas an ideal holiday destination. Drive from Cairns to Port Douglas to experience one of the most scenic coastal drives in Australia.

SEE & DO **Great Barrier Reef:** see Top Attractions. **Wildlife Habitat:** see Other Attractions. **Flagstaff Hill:** commands excellent views of Four Mile Beach and Low Isles; end of Island Point Rd. **Dive schools:**

Opposite top: Fresh fruit at Rusty's Markets, Cairns
Opposite middle: Millaa Millaa Falls **Opposite bottom:** Kuranda Scenic Railway

details from visitor centre. **Great Barrier Reef tours:** more than 100 operators offer reef tours to the outer Great Barrier Reef and Low Isles; details from visitor centre. **Cane-toad racing:** most nights at Chillys Pizza and Trattoria, 2 Mowbray St. **Market:** Anzac Park; Sun. **Tours:** horseriding, sea-kayaking, rainforest tours, Lady Douglas paddlewheel cruises, 4WD safaris and coach tours to surrounding areas; details from visitor centre.

RAVENSHOE
Population 786

At 930m, Ravenshoe is the highest town in Queensland. Situated on the Atherton Tableland, it is surrounded by World Heritage rainforest, with 350 species of birds, 14 species of kangaroos and 12 species of possums. Once a town with a thriving logging industry, an alternative-lifestyle population has now moved in. It's also home to Queensland's highest pub, but that's not the township's only claim to fame: Millstream Falls, 3km from the town centre, is the widest waterfall in Australia.

SEE & DO **Innot Hot Springs:** see Other Attractions. **Nganyaji Interpretive Centre:** showcases the lifestyle of the local Jirrbal People, including hunting techniques and community life; Moore St. **Scenic train ride:** heritage steam-train ride to nearby Tumoulin; see visitor centre. **Millstream Falls National Park:** enjoy the 1km return walk past falls and rockpools to Millstream Falls, the widest single-drop waterfall in Australia; 13 7468; 3km SW. **Tully Falls:** walk 300m to Tully Falls (flowing in wet season) and the gorge; 25km S. **Lake Koombooloomba:** popular spot for swimming, watersports, camping and fishing for barramundi; 34km S. **Mount Garnet:** old tin-mining town with prospecting sites nearby; 47km W.

THURSDAY ISLAND/WAIBEN AND THE TORRES STRAIT
Population 6929

This group of around 100 islands off the northern tip of Cape York make up the lands and seas of the Torres Strait Islander People. The Torres Strait Islander People are of Melanesian descent, including the late Eddie Mabo, famous for his successful 1992 land claim in Australia's High Court. The islands stretch from the tip of Cape York Peninsula to Papua New Guinea and include 17 that are inhabited. The first Europeans passed through the islands in the 1600s, and by the late 1800s a pearling industry was established, which continues today along with crayfishing, prawning and trochus snail industries. Thursday Island is the administrative centre.

SEE & DO **Gab Titui Cultural Centre:** see Top Attractions. **Green Hill Fort** was built in the late 19th century, decommissioned in 1927, and used as a signal station in World War II. You can do a tour here and the views are sweeping. Other surrounding islands worth a visit are **Friday Island**, where you can see pearls being cultivated at **Kazu**; **Horn Island/ Narupai**, which was an important posting for Australian troops in World War II;

SALTWATER CROCODILES

Saltwater (or estuarine) crocodiles are found in the mangrove-lined creeks and rivers, as well as in estuaries and the sea. Never cross tidal creeks or swim in creeks. Never prepare food at water's edge or camp close to waterholes. Obey all warning signs and ask at local visitor centres for current advice. *See* box p. 340 for more safety tips. Beware of marine stingers between Oct and Mar.

Opposite: Green Hill Fort, Thursday Island/Waiben

and **Badu Island**, where you can enjoy traditional dances, arts and crafts and food. Getting to the islands involves either a flight from Cairns, a trip on a cargo vessel from Cairns (through Sea Swift (07) 4035 1234) or a ferry ride from Seisia at the tip of Cape York (through Peddells (07) 4069 1551).

TULLY
Population 2252

At the foot of Mount Tyson, Tully receives one of the highest annual rainfalls in Australia – around 4200mm. This abundance of rain supports swift rapids on the Tully River – an attraction for any whitewater-rafting enthusiast. The river, which descends from the Atherton Tableland through rainforest gorges, is Queensland's premier rafting river, with more than 45 individual rapids up to grade 5. The area was settled in the 1870s by a family keen on growing sugarcane, and the town grew when the government decided to build a sugar mill in 1925. Sugarcane remains a major industry.

SEE & DO **Tully Gorge National Park:** *see* Top Attractions. **Tully Sugar Mill:** informative tours during the crushing season (approximately June–Nov); tickets from the visitor centre. **Golden Gumboot:** 7.9m high gumboot erected to celebrate Tully's status as Australia's wettest town. **Alligator's Nest:** beautiful rainforest with swimming in stream; 10km S. **Tully Heads:** estuary and beachside fishing; separated from Hull Heads by Googorra Beach; 22km SE. **Echo Creek Walking Trail:** take this guided trail through rainforest, walking a Jirrba trading route with Jirrba guides; turn-off after Euramo; 30km SW. **Murray Upper State Forest:** rainforest walks to cascades, rockpools and Murray Falls; turn-off 38km S. **Misty Mountains walking trails:** day walks or longer (up to 44km) in Wet Tropics World Heritage Area; details from visitor centre. **Whitewater rafting:** operators run from Tully to the renowned rapids of the Tully River; details from visitor centre.

WEIPA
Population 4097

This coastal part of Cape York is the Traditional Land of the Alngith People. The area was reputedly the first in Australia to be explored by Europeans, in 1605. The town of Weipa was built in 1961 on the site of a mission station and Aboriginal reserve, and is now home to the world's largest bauxite mine. Although the town is remote, it offers a full range of services for travellers. Roads to the Cape may become impassable during the wet season (Nov–Apr). Motorists are advised to check the RACQ Road Conditions Report on 13 1940 (or online at racq.com.au) before departing. Permits for travel over Traditional Land can be sought in Weipa; details from visitor centre. Beware of crocodiles in rivers, estuaries and coastal areas.

SEE & DO **Jardine River National Park:** *see* Top Attractions. **Western Cape Cultural Centre:** *see* Other Attractions. **Tours of bauxite mine:** guided tours provide insight into the mining process at Weipa; details from town office. **Fishing tours:** Weipa's fishing spots can be explored on tours; details from town office. **Boat and houseboat hire:** details from town office. **Markets:** Sat. **Oyala Thumotang National Park (CYPAL):** wilderness park of open forests, swamps and dense rainforest. There is excellent birdlife around lagoons and bushwalking along Archer River. 4WD access only; visit May–Nov; 13 7468; turn-off 29km N of Coen. **Mapoon:** camping and scenery; permit required; 85km N. **Kutini–Payamu National Park:** this important lowland tropical rainforest park is a haven for wildlife. There is good fishing at Chilli Beach, and bush camping for self-sufficient visitors only. 4WD recommended; visit only Apr–Sept; 216km E. For more information, contact QPWS on 13 7468.

YUNGABURRA
Population 1052

Yungaburra is a historic town on the edge of the Atherton Tableland. Once a resting spot for miners, it was slow to develop. The tourism boom did not hit until the coastal road opened from Cairns in 1926. Today the town offers craft shops, galleries, cafes and restaurants.

SEE & DO **Crater Lakes National Park:** *see* Other Attractions. **Historical precinct walk:** take this self-guided walk past heritage buildings, including the popular Lake Eacham Hotel in Cedar St; brochure available from visitor centre. **Platypus-viewing platform:** see the elusive animal at sunrise and sunset; Peterson Creek, Gillies Hwy. **Galleries, craft and gem shops:** various outlets in town. **Market:** renowned produce and craft market; Gillies Hwy; 4th Sat each month. **Curtain Fig Tree:** spectacular example of strangler fig with aerial roots in curtain-like formation; 2.5km SW. **Tinaburra:** a great spot for swimming and watersports on Lake Tinaroo; boat ramp provides access; nearby Seven Sisters are seven volcanic cinder cones; 3km N. **Heales Outlook:** spectacular views over Gillies Range; 16km NE. **Tinaroo Falls Dam outlet:** views over lake; 23km N.

Gulf Savannah

An adventure of epic proportions awaits as you drive across the vast grasslands of the Gulf of Carpentaria on the **Savannah Way** – the 3700km-long transcontinental road from Cairns to Broome across the top of Australia. Expect big skies, vast distances, great fishing and, if you're there in spring, the mysterious Morning Glory cloud that rolls across the sky. Some of the region's most fascinating attractions are hidden below ground, in the **limestone caves** of Chillagoe and **lava tubes** at Undara.

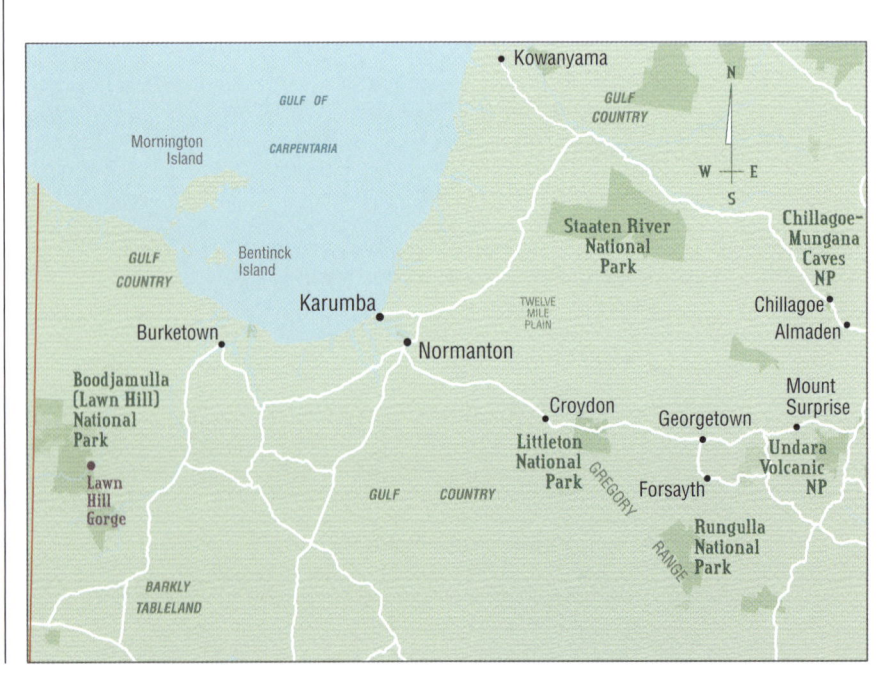

CHEAT SHEET

→ Distances between some towns are huge. Allow at least a week to explore the region.

→ Best time to visit: summer is extremely hot and wet and subject to flooding; plan your trip for the winter months. Sept and Oct is the best time to see the Morning Glory cloud. Barra fishing is best from April to June.

→ Main towns: Burketown (see p. 422), Karumba (see p. 423).

→ The Gulf of Carpentaria is home to many nations of First Nations People, including the Gangalidda, Gawara, Gkuthaarn and Kukatj. See the region through a cultural lens with the help of Yagurli Tours, based in Burketown (yagurlitours.com.au). Yagurli means fish, but aside from fishing charters they also have sunset river cruises, stargazing and four-wheel-drive tagalong tours.

→ Don't miss: guided tours of Undara lava tubes; Chillagoe Caves; fishing for barramundi or at least a barra pie at Burketown if you don't catch your own; a campdraft or rodeo if there's one on; a soak at Talaroo Hot Springs; watching the sunset at Karumba; and a ride on the *Savannahlander* train.

Top: Boodjamulla (Lawn Hill) National Park **Opposite:** Undara Experience, Undara Volcanic National Park

TOP ATTRACTIONS

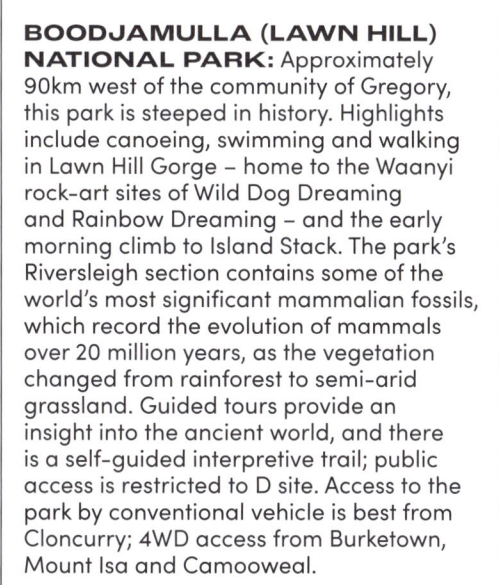

BOODJAMULLA (LAWN HILL) NATIONAL PARK: Approximately 90km west of the community of Gregory, this park is steeped in history. Highlights include canoeing, swimming and walking in Lawn Hill Gorge – home to the Waanyi rock-art sites of Wild Dog Dreaming and Rainbow Dreaming – and the early morning climb to Island Stack. The park's Riversleigh section contains some of the world's most significant mammalian fossils, which record the evolution of mammals over 20 million years, as the vegetation changed from rainforest to semi-arid grassland. Guided tours provide an insight into the ancient world, and there is a self-guided interpretive trail; public access is restricted to D site. Access to the park by conventional vehicle is best from Cloncurry; 4WD access from Burketown, Mount Isa and Camooweal.

CHILLAGOE–MUNGANA CAVES NATIONAL PARK: The impressive rugged limestone outcrops and magnificent caves of this park are studied by scientists world-wide. The cave system was originally an ancient coral reef and is home to a wide variety of bats. Fossilised bones, including those of a giant kangaroo, have been discovered in the caves. Guided tours only; tickets from The Hub in Chillagoe (caves subject to closure during heavy rain). Above ground are the magnificent Wullumba rock paintings at Balancing Rock.

UNDARA VOLCANIC NATIONAL PARK: Undara, an Ewamian word for 'long', accurately describes the tubes in Undara Volcanic National Park east of Mount Surprise. The cooling molten lava of an erupted volcano formed the 90km of hollow underground lava tubes. At 160km, one of the lava flows here is the longest on Earth. Tours are necessary to visit the tubes; bookings on 1800 990 992 with Undara Experience. See the egg-cup-shaped crater on the 2.5km Kalkani Crater circuit or go birdwatching to see some of the park's 120 bird species.

OTHER ATTRACTIONS

COBBOLD GORGE: Guided boat tours, helicopter flights and stand-up paddleboard trips through a sandstone gorge with Australia's first fully glass bridge. Visits only by tour and bookings essential (07) 4062 5470; cobboldgorge.com.au.

GULFLANDER: This historic 152km railway journey from Normanton (see p. 423) to Croydon (see p. 422) reveals the remote beauty of the Gulf Savannah; train departs Normanton at 8.30am Wed and returns from Croydon on Thurs afternoons. *Gulflander* also runs regular sunset tours with billy tea and damper, and other short trips; 1800 577 245; gulflander.com.au.

SAVANNAHLANDER: This unique train journey shows the rugged delights and beautiful landscapes between Mount Surprise (see p. 423) and Cairns (see p. 413). Departing from Mount Surprise Station each Sat, the train stops at various towns in the Gulf Savannah region. There are also trips between Mount Surprise and Forsayth. Bookings on (07) 4053 6848; savannahlander.com.au.

TALAROO HOT SPRINGS: Owned and operated by the Ewamian Traditional Owners, these oasis-like hot springs west of Mount Surprise bubble to earth at around 60°C and are funnelled into private soak pools and a public pool. Walking tours of the mound spring are run by Ewamian guides. There is a campground on site; talaroo.com.au.

THE HUB: This major interpretive centre is constructed from local materials including marble and copper. Informative displays cover the geographical history of the Chillagoe cave system and local landscape (dating back two billion years), the town's mining and settlement past and the region's First Nations heritage. Queen St, Chillagoe; (07) 4094 7111.

KEY TOWNS

BURKETOWN
Population 167

Burketown is on the edge of the Gulf of Carpentaria, the dividing line between the wetlands to the north and the Gulf Savannah plains to the south. It is the Traditional Land of the Gangalidda Garawa People. The town was named after the ill-fated explorer Robert Burke, who was the first European (with exploring partner William John Wills) to arrive in the area. Regularly in spring, the natural cloud phenomenon known as Morning Glory takes over the horizon at dawn between Burketown and Sweers Island. The clouds appear as rolling tube-like formations and can extend for more than 1000km.

SEE & DO **Yagurli Tours:** explore local First Nations' culture, including a sunset tour, a 4WD tour to Australia's largest salt pans and a stargazing tour with state-of-the art telescopes; yagurlitours.com.au. **Museum and Information Centre:** in the original post office, with displays on the history of the area plus local arts and crafts; open Apr–Oct; Musgrave St; (07) 4745 5111. **Artesian bore:** operating for over 100 years and quite a sight to see due to the build-up of minerals; The Great Top Rd. **Original Gulf Meatworks:** remains of 1860s meat processing plant. **Colonial Flat:** site of the Landsborough Tree. Blazed by William Landsborough on his search for Burke and Wills, it became the depot camp for search parties and the resting place of Landsborough's ship *Firefly* – the first ship to enter the Albert River; 5km E. **Nicholson River wetlands:** breeding ground for crocodiles, fish and birds; 17km W. **Bluebush Swamp:** large wetland area, ideal for birdwatchers; 30km SW. **Sweers Island:** excellent spot for lure and fly fishing, plus golden beaches and over 100 species of birds; access by aircraft or boat, details from visitor centre; 30km N. **Leichhardt Falls:** picturesque flowing falls in rainy months; 71km SE. **Gregory Township:** the old Gregory Downs Hotel was originally built to service the coach run from Burketown. Meals and accommodation; 113km S.

CHILLAGOE
Population 150

Chillagoe is a small outback town west of Cairns and the Atherton Tableland. Once a thriving mining town after silver and copper deposits were found in 1887, the town was practically deserted after the smelter closed in 1940. Chillagoe's history and the well-preserved First Nations rock art and limestone caves in the area make it a popular spot with visitors. The road to Chillagoe has been upgraded over the past decade, but it is still subject to flooding and can be impassable after heavy rain.

SEE & DO **Chillagoe–Mungana Caves National Park:** see Top Attractions. **The Hub:** see Other Attractions. **Heritage Museum:** displays on local history and relics of old mining days; Hill St. **Historic cemetery:** headstones from early settlement; Railway Line Rd. **Historical walks:** self-guided or guided walks taking in the old State Smelter and disused marble quarry just south of town; details from visitor centre. **Mungana:** Wakaman rock paintings at the Archways. Also a historic cemetery; 16km W. **Almaden:** small town where cattle wander the main street; 30km SE. **4WD self-guided adventure trek:** mud maps and clues provided; details from visitor centre.

CROYDON
Population 215

Croydon is a small town on the grassland plains of the Gulf Savannah. It marks the eastern terminus for the *Gulflander* train service. The train line was established in the late 1800s to service Croydon's booming gold industry. Many original buildings dating from 1887 to 1897, and classified by the National Trust and Australian Heritage Commission, have been restored to the splendour of the town's goldmining days.

SEE & DO *Gulflander:* see Other Attractions. **Historical precinct:** many restored buildings bring the rich history of Croydon to life; highlights include the old courthouse with original furniture, and the old hospital featuring original hospital documents. **Outdoor Museum:** displays mining machinery from the age of steam; Samwell St. **Old Police**

VISITOR INFORMATION

Burketown Visitor Centre
Cnr Musgrave and Burke
sts (Apr–Oct)
(07) 4745 5111
burketown.com.au

The Hub
Queen St, Chillagoe
(07) 4094 7111
athertontablelands.com.au

Gulf Savannah
tropicalnorthqueensland.
org.au/where-to-go/gulf-
savannah-outback

TOP EVENTS

- EASTER Barra Classic (Normanton)
- APR Outback by the Sea Festival and Anglers Classic fishing competition (both Karumba)
- MAY Great Wheelbarrow Race and Rodeo (Chillagoe)
- JUNE Poddy Dodgers Festival (Croydon); Normanton Show & Rodeo
- JULY Chillagoe Festival (Chillagoe)
- AUG Campdraft (Mount Surprise)
- SEPT Campdraft and Morning Glory (Burketown)

TEMPERATURES

Jan: 25–34°C

July: 14–28°C

Opposite: Salt pans, Burketown, Yagurli Tours

Precinct and Gaol: historic documents and access to gaol cells; Samwell St. **Mining Museum:** interesting display of early mining machinery including battery stamper; 1km N. **Historic cemetery:** includes Chinese gravestones; 2km S. **Chinese temple site:** heritage-listed archaeological site preserving 50 years of Chinese settlement that followed the gold discoveries of the 1880s. Take the heritage trail to see how the Chinese lived; on road to Lake Belmore. **Lake Belmore:** one of many sites for birdwatching, along with beautiful picnic areas and barbecue facilities. Also swimming, waterskiing and fishing (limits apply); 5km N.

KARUMBA
Population 487

Karumba is at the mouth of the Norman River in the Gulf Savannah. It is the easiest access point for the Gulf of Carpentaria, the key reason the town is the centre for the Gulf's booming prawn and barramundi industries. During the 1930s the town was an important refuelling depot for the airships of the Empire Flying Boats, which travelled from Sydney to England. Fishing enthusiasts will enjoy the untouched waters of the Gulf and nearby rivers.

SEE & DO **Les Wilson Barramundi Discovery Centre:** barramundi display and information; Riverside Dr; (07) 4745 9359. **Ferryman River Cruises:** tours include birdwatching, gulf sunset and night crocodile spotting; depart Karumba boat ramp; (07) 4745 9155. **Charters and dinghy hire:** discover the renowned fishing spots in the Gulf or on the Norman River on a charter, or hire a dinghy; Karumba Port. **Heritage walk:** self-guided walk; brochure from Karumba library. **Market:** Sunset Tavern; Sun 8am–12pm, Apr–Sept. **Wetland region:** extending 30km inland from Karumba are the wetlands, habitat of the saltwater crocodile and several species of birds, including brolgas and cranes. **Cemetery:** early settlement cemetery from when Karumba was known as Norman Mouth telegraph station; on road to Karumba Point, 2km N. **Karumba Point:** boat hire available; note presence of saltwater crocodiles; 3km N.

MOUNT SURPRISE
Population 138

Mount Surprise is a historic rail town in the Gulf Savannah. The region has excellent gemfields for fossicking, especially for topaz, quartz and aquamarine. The town is on the edge of the Undara lava field and the lava caves can be explored in Undara Volcanic National Park. The *Savannahlander* train departs from here and travels to Cairns.

SEE & DO **Undara Volcanic National Park:** *see* Top Attractions. *Savannahlander;* **Talaroo Hot Springs:** *see* Other Attractions for both. **Old Post Office Museum:** documents the bush history of the region in a historic 1870 building; opposite railway station. **O'Brien's Creek:** renowned for quality topaz; obtain a licence before fossicking; 37km NW. **Forty Mile Scrub National Park:** vine-thicket park on the McBride Plateau with informative short circuit track; (07) 4046 6600; 56km E. **Georgetown:** small town once one of many small goldmining settlements on the Etheridge Goldfields; noted for its gemstones, especially agate, and gold nuggets; 82km W. **Forsayth:** old mining town; 132km SW. **Agate Creek:** fossick for gemstones; 187km SW via Forsayth.

NORMANTON
Population 1326

Normanton thrived as a port town in the late 1800s when the gold rush was on in Croydon. The Normanton-to-Croydon railway line, established at that time, today runs the award-winning *Gulflander* tourist train. More recently, Australia's largest saltwater crocodile, known as Krys or Savannah King, was shot at nearby Archers Creek in 1957. A life-size replica of his body, over 8m long, can be seen in the council park.

SEE & DO *Gulflander: see* Other Attractions. **Railway station:** National Trust–listed Victorian building; Matilda St. **Indigenous Stock Workers and Rodeo Riders Display:** opened in 2019, this display tells the story of the Kurtijar, Kukatj and Gkuthaarn Peoples who were instrumental in the cattle industry of the region; at the Information Centre. **Original well:** settlers used it for drawing water; Landsborough St. **Giant Barramundi:** big monument to the fish; Landsborough St. **Scenic walk and drive:** self-guided tours to historic buildings including the Old Gaol in Haig St and the restored Bank of NSW building in Little Brown St; brochure available from information centre in the Burns Philip Building. **Norman River fishing tours:** fishing trips and boat hire for barramundi; details from visitor centre; Cnr Landsborough and Caroline sts; (07) 4747 8444. **Lakes:** attract jabirus, brolgas, herons and other birds; on the outskirts of Normanton. **Shady Lagoon:** bush camping, birdwatching and wildlife; 18km SE. **Fishing:** catching barramundi is very popular in the area – try the spots at Norman River in Glenore (25km SE), Walkers Creek (32km NW) or off the bridges or banks in Normanton. **Burke and Wills cairn:** last and most northerly camp of Burke and Wills (Camp 119) before their fatal return journey; off the Savannah Hwy; 30km SW. **Bang Bang Jump Up rock formation:** a solitary hill on the surrounding flat plains with excellent views; Matilda Hwy; 106km SW. **Kowanyama Aboriginal community:** excellent barramundi fishing, guesthouse and camping; permit to visit required from Kowanyama Community Council; 359km NE.

Outback

Almost anywhere you choose to go in the vast Queensland outback is an adventure. It stretches west of the Great Dividing Range through to the Gulf of Carpentaria in the north, across the Channel Country in the south and out to the endless red sand hills of the Simpson Desert in the west. Home to some of **Australia's richest fossil fields**, it's **a place where dinosaurs once roamed**. Learn about the region's fascinating characters from the **many museums**, or meet them on **outback stations** and in **classic outback pubs**.

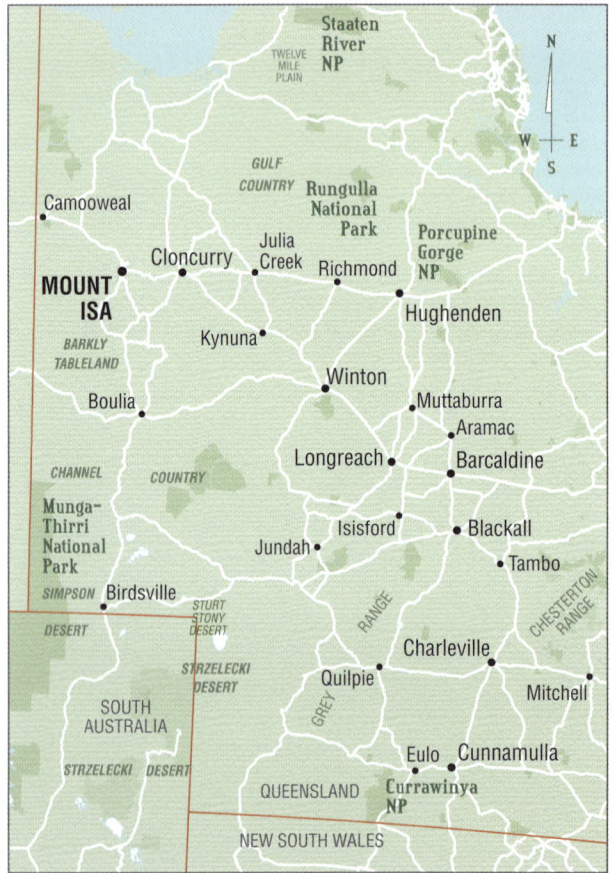

Top: Eromanga Natural History Museum **Opposite:** Cosmos Centre, Charleville

CHEAT SHEET

- → Distances between some towns are huge. Allow at least a week to explore the region, but don't try to see it all.

- → Best time to visit: summer is extremely hot; plan your trip for the winter months when days are warm but nights are very cold.

- → Main towns: Cunnamulla (see p. 430), Longreach (see p. 432), Mount Isa (see p. 433), Winton (see p. 435).

- → Outback Queensland covers more than a million square kilometres that belong to many First Nations clans. The South West Queensland Indigenous Cultural Trail (SWQICT) visits seven heritage sites that hold significance to First Nations People, from Dirranbandi to St George, Surat, Roma, Mitchell, Charleville and Cunnamulla. swqict.com

- → Did you know? The world's largest underground river – the Great Artesian Basin – is the lifeblood of outback Queensland. The first artesian wells in Queensland were struck at Thurlugoona near Cunnamulla in 1887.

- → Need to know: some areas in this region are very remote and require a 4WD, so check road conditions ahead with Queensland Parks and Wildlife Service (parks. des.qld.gov.au).

- → Don't miss: Lark Quarry Conservation Park; Australian Age of Dinosaurs; Australian Stockman's Hall of Fame; Qantas Founders Museum; Kronosaurus Korner; Mount Isa Mines Rodeo.

TOP ATTRACTIONS

AUSTRALIAN AGE OF DINOSAURS: Amazing natural history museum where you can see palaeontologists working on dinosaur bones – and help them – and walk through Dinosaur Canyon to imagine how life once was here. Guided tours daily and annual digs are held in May. Open Mon–Sat (Nov–Mar) and Mon–Sun (Apr–Oct). The museum is 25km east of Winton (see p. 435).

AUSTRALIAN STOCKMAN'S HALL OF FAME AND OUTBACK HERITAGE CENTRE: Opened in 1988 by Queen Elizabeth II, this impressive centre in Longreach (see p. 432) is a tribute to the early settler men and women who came to outback Australia and worked hard to build the agricultural industry. Its many educational and interactive displays include everything from Australia's First Nations heritage to the challenges of outback education and the life of the modern-day stockman. Highlights include live stockman shows, a photo gallery, an old blacksmith's shop, a 1920s kitchen and a fully equipped cutaway flying doctor's plane. Landsborough Hwy, Longreach; (07) 4658 2166.

AUSTRALIAN WORKERS HERITAGE CENTRE: This centre in Barcaldine (see p. 428) is a tribute to the working men and women of Australia – the shearers, teachers, police officers and other workers who helped build the nation. The interpretive displays also cover the events leading to the formation of the Labor Party. Open 8.30am–4pm; Ash St, Barcaldine; (07) 4651 1579.

BILBY TOURS: One of Australia's most rare and endangered animals, bilbies are captively bred in Charleville (see p. 430). Get up close and personal with these marsupials on the night tour; details from Charleville visitor centre; (07) 4656 8359.

COMBO WATERHOLE CONSERVATION PARK: On the Diamantina River, the park is an important dry-weather wildlife refuge. The events described in 'Waltzing Matilda' allegedly occurred in this park, which has waterholes lined with coolibahs. It is said that Samuel Hoffmeister, at the time of the Shearers' Strike, drank his last drink at the Blue Heeler Hotel and then killed himself at Combo waterhole (south of town). This story stirred Paterson to write the now-famous ballad. See the Chinese-labour-constructed historic stone causeways from the 1880s or take the 40min return waterhole walk. The turn-off to the park is 16km east of Kynuna (see p. 432).

COSMOS CENTRE: This centre in Charleville (see p. 430) explores the Australian night sky and its significance to First Nations culture. There are multimedia displays, nightly shows and interactive areas where the wonders of the sky are observed through powerful Meade Telescopes. The outback night sky has never looked so beautiful! Qantas Dr, Charleville; (07) 4654 7771.

CURRAWINYA NATIONAL PARK: The lakes and waterholes of the Paroo River form an important refuge for the abundant birdlife of this park. The 85km circuit track for vehicles starts at the ranger station and is the best way to view the park. See the black swans and grebes at Lake Wyara or go canoeing at Lake

Numulla. For an excellent outlook over the park, climb the Granites. 4WD necessary to reach the lakes. The park is 60km south-west of Eulo (see p. 431).

EROMANGA NATURAL HISTORY MUSEUM: In 2006 the fossilised bones of a giant plant-eating sauropod taller than a B-double truck and twice the size of a T-Rex was found on a cattle station near Cooper Creek; in 2021 it was confirmed as a new species, called *Australotitan cooperensis*, aka the Southern Titan, but is nicknamed Cooper. It's just one of the 98-million-year-old fossils on display at the new purpose-built museum on the property where Cooper was found. Guided tours are available and you can also learn how to prepare fossils for display. 1 Dinosaur Drive, Eromanga; (07) 4656 3084.

FLINDERS DISCOVERY CENTRE: Learn about the Flinders Shire history in this complex in Hughenden (see p. 431). The fossil exhibition's centrepiece is the 7m replica skeleton of *Muttaburrasaurus langdoni*, a dinosaur found in Muttaburra – it was the first entire fossil skeleton found in Australia. The Historical Society also documents the shire history in their display. Gray St, Hughenden; (07) 4741 2970.

JOHN FLYNN PLACE MUSEUM AND ART GALLERY: This museum in Cloncurry (see p. 430) celebrates the visionary John Flynn and the creation of the Royal Flying Doctor Service. The museum pays homage to this crucial part of outback life and the early settlers who had a vision for the service. There is also the **Fred McKay Art Gallery**, with changing exhibits of local art and the Alfred Traegar Radio Gallery. Open Mon–Fri 8am–4.30pm, Sat–Sun 9am–3pm, May–Sept; cnr Daintree and King sts, Cloncurry; (07) 4742 4100.

KRONOSAURUS KORNER: This marine-fossil museum in Richmond (see p. 434) has a renowned collection of vertebrate fossils, all found in the Richmond Shire. The museum and exhibition space holds more than 200 exhibits, including the 100-million-year-old armoured dinosaur Minmi, Australia's best-preserved dinosaur. There is also an activity centre, children's discovery area and fossil preparation area where visitors can watch the paleontologists at work. Guided museum tours, as well as tours to nearby fossicking sites with a paleontologist, are available (groups of 10 or more, bookings essential). Goldring St; Richmond; (07) 4741 3429.

LARK QUARRY CONSERVATION PARK: This park features the preserved tracks of a dinosaur stampede from 93 million years ago – the only track of this type known in the world. The 'trackways' are sheltered and can be visited on a tour (details from visitor centre). The park also offers a short walk past ancient rock formations, the Winton Formation, to a lookout over the region. The park is 110km south-west of Winton (see p. 435).

MUNGA-THIRRI NATIONAL PARK: West of Birdsville, this arid national park, formally known as Simpson Desert National Park, is the largest in Queensland. The parallel wind-blown sand dunes are enormous – up to 90m high, about 1km apart, and can extend up to 200km. Poeppel's Corner, 136km west of Birdsville, marks the boundary between Queensland, the NT and SA. The park is 65km west of Birdsville and a 4WD is essential. *See important note in Birdsville entry*, p. 428.

OUTBACK AT ISA: This modern complex in Mount Isa (see p. 433) incorporates a fascinating multimedia experience showing highlights of Queensland's outback and incorporating the Riversleigh Fossil Centre where ancient animals and landscapes come alive. There are major exhibits revealing more about the mining industry's development; take a guided tour of the 1.2km of underground tunnels in the Hard Times Mine. The history of Mount Isa is explored in the Sir James Foots building, and the Outback Park offers a scenic lagoon and informative walking trail. Open 8.30am–5pm (9am–4pm Jan–Feb); Marian St, Mount Isa; 1300 659 660.

PORCUPINE GORGE NATIONAL PARK: The coloured sandstone cliffs of this park are a delight and contrast with the greenery surrounding Porcupine Creek. The gorge, known locally as the 'mini Grand Canyon', has been formed over millions of years. See it from the lookout just off Kennedy Development Rd. Walk down into the gorge on the 1.2km track, but be warned: the steep walk back up is strenuous. The park is 61km north of Hughenden (see p. 431).

QANTAS FOUNDERS MUSEUM: This modern museum in Longreach (see p. 432) details the commercial-flight history of the second-oldest airline in the world. Explore the restored 1922 hangar, which features displays on early flights and a replica Avro 504K. Visit the exhibition hall to see how flying has evolved over the last century, take a behind-the-scenes tour of a 747 and walk out onto the wing or take off in a flight simulator. In 2020, the museum opened Luminescent Longreach, an animation, sound and light show projected on to retired Qantas planes and telling the history of aviation. Longreach Airport, Landsborough Hwy, Longreach; (07) 4658 3737.

WALTZING MATILDA CENTRE: Created as a tribute to the life of the swagman and the famous song, this museum also tells the story of the township of Winton (see p.435) and its involvement in World War II. Elderslie St, Winton; (07) 4657 1466.

Top: Cosmos Centre
Bottom: Kronosaurus Korner

OTHER ATTRACTIONS

BLADENSBURG NATIONAL PARK: The vast plains and ridges of this park provide an important sanctuary for a variety of wildlife, including kangaroos, dunnarts and emus. The Traditional Owners of the area are the Koa People. Skull Hole (40km S) has paintings and bora ceremonial grounds and is believed to be the site of a late 1880s Indigenous massacre. Walking should only be attempted by experienced bushwalkers. 'Route of the River Gums', a self-drive tour, showcases the region's landscapes. The drive starts 8km south of Winton (see p. 435).

DIAMANTINA NATIONAL PARK: This remote park 147km south-east of Boulia (see p. 429) is rich in colours and landscapes. Follow the 157km Warracoota self-guided circuit drive to view the sand dunes, claypans and ranges and many rare and threatened species in their native habitat, including the greater bilby, kowari and peregrine falcon. Canoe or fish in the winding creeks and rivers. 4WD access only; roads may become impassable after rain; check road conditions before travelling.

GREAT ARTESIAN SPA: There's nothing better than a good soak after a long day on the road, and the naturally heated mineral waters of the Great Artesian Basin are also therapeutic. With relaxing pools in a garden setting, this is Queensland's largest open-air spa; Cambridge St, Mitchell; (07) 4624 6923.

IDALIA NATIONAL PARK: Renowned habitat of the yellow-footed rock wallaby, which can be spotted at Emmet Pocket Lookout (which also has amazing panoramic views) or along the Bullock Gorge walking track. A self-guided drive begins at the information centre, 12km beyond the park entrance. The park is 113km south-west of Blackall via Yaraka Rd, at Benlidi siding turn south.

KENNIFF COURTHOUSE: This courthouse in Mitchell (see p. 433) was in use from 1882 to 1965. It held the murder trials for the Kenniff Brothers, infamous bushrangers who killed a policeman and station manager in 1902. The courthouse is now a museum with a bushranger exhibition, and art and craft sales. The landscaped grounds incorporate a community mosaic, an artesian windmill and a billabong. Cambridge St, Mitchell.

LOCHERN NATIONAL PARK: Waterholes created by the Thomson River are a sanctuary for a variety of birds, including brolgas and pelicans. Drive the 16km Bluebush Lagoon circuit to see kangaroos and emus. You must be self-sufficient. Check road conditions at parks.des.qld.gov.au/parks/lochern before departing – floods are usual here and roads may be impassable in wet weather.

MARIALA NATIONAL PARK: The park was formerly used to breed Cobb & Co. horses in the early 1900s. It is remote with spectacular contrasts – the rich red earth mixed with green vegetation of mulga trees and shrubs. The threatened yellow-footed rock wallaby and pink cockatoo find refuge here. There are no formal walking trails. You can bush camp, but you must be self-sufficient. 4WD is recommended; roads may become impassable in the wet season. The park is 130km north-east of Quilpie.

MUTTABURRASAURUS INTERPRETATION CENTRE: See a life-sized replica of the muttaburrasaurus and learn all about this plant-eating, land-living dinosaur that roamed the district around 100 million years ago; Bruford St, Muttaburra.

UNEARTHED VISITOR INFORMATION CENTRE AND MUSEUM: This Cloncurry (see p. 430) museum features Robert O'Hara Burke's water bottle and there's also memorabilia from the abandoned uranium mining town of Mary Kathleen, a gem collection, the breastplate of George, King of Friezland, and First Nations artefacts. Outdoors is historical machinery. Open Mon–Fri 8.30am–4.30pm, Sat–Sun 9am–4pm; Mary Kathleen Memorial Park, 48 McIlwraith St, Cloncurry.

WELFORD NATIONAL PARK: This park protects mulga lands, Channel Country and Mitchell grass downs. See the rare earthern homestead (1882) listed by the National Trust (not open to the public) and see pelicans and whistling kites at the many waterholes of the Barcoo River. There are two self-guided drives that start at the campground: one through the mulga vegetation to scenic Sawyers Creek; the other a desert drive past impressive red sand dunes. 4WD recommended; roads are impassable in wet weather. The park is 20km south of Jundah (see p. 432).

WILIYAN-NGURRU NATIONAL PARK: On the Barkly Tableland, this national park, formerly known as Camooweal Caves National Park, is still evolving as water continues to filter through the soluble dolomite to the extensive cave system. The caves are linked by vertical shafts and public entry to the caves is not allowed, although there is a viewing area at Great Nowranie cave. The Traditional Owners, the Indjalandji-Dhidhanu People, call the caves 'Wiliyan-ngurru'. The park is home to Mitchell grassland and spinifex, open eucalypt woodland and waterbirds. 4WD is recommended. The park is 24km south of Camooweal (see p. 429).

KEY TOWNS

ARAMAC
Population 226

Aramac is a small service town west of the Great Dividing Range. The town was once known as Marathon, but renamed by explorer William Landsborough who found the initials of an earlier explorer Robert Ramsay Mackenzie (RR Mac) carved on a tree. The town's only water supply is from two bores that tap into the Great Artesian Basin.

SEE & DO **Harry Redford Interpretive Centre:** photographic exhibition of cattle drives, also local arts and crafts; Gordon St. **White Bull replica:** commemorating Captain Starlight's arrest for cattle-stealing; Gordon St. **Tramway Museum:** with old rail motor and historical exhibits; McWhannell St. **Lake Dunn:** this freshwater lake and its surrounds have great appeal to birdwatchers. It is also popular for swimming and fishing. Follow signs to 'The Lake'. 68km NE. **Forest Den National Park:** this remote park is an important wildlife sanctuary due to its semi-permanent waterholes. Have a picnic next to Torrens Creek and go birdwatching at dusk. 4WD recommended; Torrens Creek Rd; 110km N. **Gray Rock:** large sandstone rock engraved with the names of hundreds of Cobb & Co. travellers. This was once the site of a hotel – a nearby cave was used as the hotel's cellar; 35km E. **Lake Galilee:** 15,000ha saltwater lake with large waterfowl population; parts of access road unsealed; 100km NE.

BARCALDINE
Population 1243

This pastoral and rail town is located some 100km east of Longreach. Known as the 'Garden City of the West', it was the first Australian town to tap the waters of the Great Artesian Basin, an event commemorated by the town's giant windmill. After the 1891 Shearers' Strike, the Australian Labor Party was born here, beneath the Tree of Knowledge. The town has some National Trust–classified buildings, murals and the Australian Workers Heritage Centre.

SEE & DO **Australian Workers Heritage Centre:** *see* Top Attractions. **Tree of Knowledge:** was a large ghost gum, which stood outside the railway station. It was fatally poisoned in 2006, but is now preserved inside a striking timber memorial, beautifully lit at night; Oak St. **Folk Museum:** display of historical memorabilia from the area; cnr Gidyea and Beech sts. **Roses 'n' Things:** sit among over 800 roses of various varieties while enjoying Devonshire tea; Coolibah St. **National Trust–classified buildings:** Masonic lodge, Beech St; Anglican church, Elm St; shire hall, Ash St. **Murals and musical instruments:** Barcaldine is home to several murals, including one painted by the late D'Arcy Doyle. There are also two musical instruments in the parks, which visitors are free to play; Oak St. **Between the Bougainvilleas Heritage Trail:** this award-winning heritage trail showcases Barcaldine's varied and colourful history; details from visitor centre. **Bike hire:** a gold-coin donation will allow you to cycle around the town at your leisure and take in all the sites. **Mini steam-train rides:** depart Folk Museum; last Sun each month (Mar–Oct). **Bicentennial Park:** has botanical walk through bushland; Blackall Rd; 9km S. **Lloyd Jones Weir:** great fishing and birdwatching venue; 15km SW.

BIRDSVILLE
Population 110

Birdsville is a tiny town at the northern end of the Birdsville Track, a major cattle route that was developed in the 1880s. The Wangkangurru-Yarluyandi People maintain a deep connection with the desert landscape that surrounds Birdsville. Birdsville is an essential supply centre for local pastoralists and travellers to outback Queensland, including 4WD enthusiasts keen to take on the Birdsville Track and the Simpson Desert. In 1900 the town boasted three hotels, several stores, a customs office and a cordial factory but with the abolition of interstate tolls after Federation, the town's prosperity slowly declined. Birdsville is in the Channel

VISITOR INFORMATION

Longreach Visitor Information Centre
Qantas Park, Eagle St, Longreach
(07) 4658 4141
experiencelongreach.com.au

Outback at Isa
19 Marian St, Mount Isa
(07) 4749 1555
discovermountisa.com.au

Winton Visitor Information Centre
50 Elderslie St, Winton
(07) 4657 1466 or 1300 665 115
experiencewinton.com.au

Opposite: Australian Workers Heritage Centre, Barcaldine

Country, named after the prolific river systems of the Diamantina and Georgina rivers, and the Cooper and Eyre creeks, that come together as one massive wetland after the rains. It's important to understand that travel in this area can be hazardous. Visit only between Apr and Oct. Motorists are advised to check the RACQ Road Conditions Report (13 1940; racq.com.au) for information before departing for the Birdsville Track and to advise police if heading west to Munga-Thirri National Park. There is no hotel or fuel at Betoota, 164km east, but fuel is available at Windorah, 375km east.

SEE & DO **Munga-Thirri National Park:** see Top Attractions. **Birdsville Bakery:** enjoy homemade pies (including curried camel) and a full menu for breakfast and lunch; Tues–Sun; Billabong Blvd; (07) 4656 4697. **Adelaide St:** ruins of Royal Hotel (1883), a reminder of Birdsville's boom days. **Birdsville Hotel:** (1884) still an important overnight stop for travellers; (07) 4656 3244. **Waddi trees:** 14km N. **Big Red:** huge sand dune; 35km W. **Birdsville Cup Racing Carnival:** the first meeting of the annual horseracing event was held in 1882 and the tradition continues on the claypan track south-east of town; it's held 1st Fri and Sat in Sept, when the population swells to over 6000. **Big Red Bash:** this annual music festival on the edge of the Simpson Desert in July, is even bigger than the races, drawing crowds of more than 10,000. **Bedourie:** Eyre Creek runs through the town providing waterholes that are home to the endangered bilby and peregrine falcon; 191km N.

BLACKALL
Population 1064

Blackall is west of the Great Dividing Range in sheep and cattle country. There is an outdoor public gallery of sculpture and artworks.

SEE & DO **Blackall Sculpture Trail:** nine artworks along the trail; the artwork called *Roly Poly* is a popular location for sunset pics. **Fossilised tree stump:** preserved tree stump estimated to be possibly 225 million years old; Shamrock St. **Major Mitchell Memorial Clock:** commemorates the founding of the town of Blackall in 1846; Shamrock St. **The Black Stump:** the reference point used when the area was surveyed in 1886. Beautiful mural painting of the stump at the site; Thistle St. **Jackie Howe Memorial:** Blackall was once home to the legendary sheep-shearer Jackie Howe who, in 1892 set the record of shearing 321 sheep in 7hrs 40min at Alice Downs Station. This statue recognises him; Shamrock St. **Ram Park:** incorporates the living history of the Blackall district, with shearing occurring all year round; Shamrock St. **Pioneer Bore:** first artesian bore sunk in Queensland, with display of replica drilling plant; Aqua St. **Blackall Wool Scour:** restored steam-driven wool-processing plant with demonstrations of machinery (steam operating May–Sept only); Evora Rd; 4km N.

BOULIA
Population 218

Boulia is the capital of the Channel Country and is on the Burke River, named after the ill-fated explorer Robert O'Hara Burke. The town is famous for random appearances of the mysterious Min Min light, a ball of light that sometimes reveals itself to travellers at night. The isolated Diamantina National Park nearby is a haven for threatened species.

SEE & DO **Diamantina National Park:** see Top Attractions. **Stonehouse Museum:** built in 1888, this National Trust–listed site was one of the first houses built in western Queensland. It is now a museum housing the history of the Jones family, as well as First Nations artefacts and photographs; Pituri St. **Min Min Encounter:** high-tech re-creation of the Min Min light, with outback characters as your guide; Herbert St. **Red Stump:** warns travellers of the dangers of the Simpson Desert; Herbert St. **Corroboree Tree:** last known such tree of the Pitta Pitta community; near Boulia State School. **Ruins of police barracks:** 19km NE. **Cawnpore Hills:** good views from summit; 108km E. **Burke and Wills Tree:** on the west bank of the Burke River; 110km NE. **Ruins of Min Min Hotel:** burned down in 1918, where the Min Min light was first sighted; 130km E.

CAMOOWEAL
Population 152

North-west of Mount Isa, Camooweal is the last Queensland town before the NT border. This area is of great spiritual significance to the Indjalandji-Dhidhanu People. It was once the centre for enormous cattle drives travelling south. Some say it is a suburb of Mount Isa, which would make the 188km of Barkly Hwy between Mount Isa and Camooweal one of the longest main streets in the world!

SEE & DO **Wiliyan-ngurru National Park:** see Other Attractions. **Historic buildings:** the Drovers store; Barkly Hwy. **The Drovers Camp:** historical displays, toilets and picnic area. Guided tours 10am–5pm May–Sept; Barkly Hwy. **Shire hall:** built in 1922, this historic building has wide verandahs, timber louvres and pressed tin ceiling. **Cemetery:** headstones tell local history; 1km E. **Boodjamulla (Lawn Hill) National Park:** around 300km N via Gregory.

CHARLEVILLE
Population 2551

Charleville is in the heart of mulga lands on the banks of the Warrego River and at the centre of a rich sheep and cattle district. By the late 1890s the town had its own brewery, 10 hotels and 500 registered bullock teams. Cobb & Co. recognised the value of Charleville's location on a major stock route and opened a coach-building factory in 1893. Charleville also has strong links with aviation: the first London–Sydney flight landed here in 1919, Qantas's first fare-paying service took off in 1922 and record-setting aviator Amy Johnson landed nearby in 1930. Charleville marks the terminus of the *Westlander* rail service from Brisbane.

SEE & DO **Cosmos Centre; Bilby Tours:** see Top Attractions for both. **Royal Flying Doctor Service Visitor Centre:** museum displaying memorabilia from the past and present. View the documentary entitled *A Day in the Life of the Flying Doctor*; John Flynn Way. **Historic House Museum:** a wonderful example of early Queensland architecture. Machinery displays including steam engine and a rail ambulance in restored Queensland National Bank building; Alfred St. **Vortex Gun:** in 1902 this 5m-long gun was used in an unsuccessful rain-making experiment; Bicentennial Park, Matilda Hwy. **Heritage trail:** self-guided walk past heritage buildings; audio or brochure from visitor centre. **Tregole National Park:** this semi-arid national park has a vulnerable and fragile ecosystem. It is largely made up of ooline forest – dry rainforest species dating back to the Ice Age. Follow the 2.1km circuit track to see the diverse vegetation and birds of the park. 99km E via Morven. **Monument:** marks the spot where Ross and Keith Smith landed with engine trouble on the first London–Sydney flight; 19km NW.

CLONCURRY
Population 2524

Cloncurry is an important mining town in the Gulf Savannah region. In 1861 John McKinlay, leading a search for Burke and Wills, reported traces of copper in the area. Six years later, pastoralist Ernest Henry discovered the first copper lodes. During World War I, Cloncurry was the centre of a copper boom and the largest source of the mineral in Australia. Copper prices slumped postwar and a pastoral industry was developed. Today main industries include grazing and mining for copper and gold. The town's interesting history extends to aviation. Qantas was conceived here – the original hangar can still be seen at the airport – and the town became the first base for the famous Royal Flying Doctor Service in 1928.

SEE & DO **John Flynn Place Museum and Art Gallery:** see Top Attractions. **Unearthed Visitor Information Centre and Museum:** see Other Attractions. **Shire hall:** built 1939; Scarr St. **Cemeteries:** cultural background of Cloncurry can be seen in the Old Cemetery with the grave of Dame Mary Gilmore (Sir Hudson Fyshe Dr), Afghan Cemetery (part of Old Cemetery), and the Chinese Cemetery (Flinders Hwy). **Original Qantas hangar:** airport; Sir Hudson Fyshe Dr. **Historic buildings:** the courthouse and post office are heritage listed. Also see Brodie Hardware Store, Central Hotel and the Post Office Hotel; details from visitor centre. **Rotary Lookout:** over Cloncurry and the river; Mount Isa Hwy; 2km W. **Chinamen Creek Dam:** peaceful area with abundant birdlife; 3km W. **Burke and Wills cairn:** near Corella River; 43km W. **Kuridala:** this one-time mining town is now a ghost town. Explore the ruins including the old cemetery; 88km S. **Fossicking:** for amethysts and other gemstones; details from visitor centre.

CUNNAMULLA
Population 1124

Cunnamulla is on the Warrego River, north of the NSW border. It is the biggest wool-loading station on the Queensland railway network, with two million sheep in the area. Explorers Sir Thomas Mitchell and Edmund Kennedy were the first European visitors, arriving in 1846 and 1847 respectively, and by 1879 the town was thriving with regular Cobb & Co. services to the west. The wetland birdlife in the area, particularly the black swans, brolgas and pelicans, is spectacular.

SEE & DO **Cunnamulla Fella Centre Art Gallery and Museum:** gallery showcases different artist exhibitions throughout the year, while the museum displays the rich history and heritage of the town and wider Paroo shire; Jane St. **Robber's Tree:** in 1880 Joseph Wells held up the local bank but could not find his escape horse. Locals bailed him up in a tree that is now known as the Robber's Tree; Stockyard St. **Yupunyah Tree:** planted by Princess Anne; cnr Louise and Stockyard sts. **Outback Botanic Gardens and Herbarium:** Matilda Hwy. **Heritage trail:** discover the days of the late 1880s on this self-guided trail; details from visitor centre. **Wyandra:** small town featuring Powerhouse Museum and heritage trail; 100km N. **Noorama:** remote sheep station that holds picnic races each Apr; 110km SE.

Cunnamulla is a wool station
Opposite: Flinders Discovery Centre, Hughenden

TOP EVENTS

- APR Way Out West Fest (music festival, Winton); Picnic Races (Noorama); Dirt 'n' Dust Festival (Julia Creek)
- MAY Tree of Knowledge Festival (Barcaldine); Sheep and Wool Show (Isisford)
- JUNE Outback Writers Festival (Winton)
- JUNE–JULY Vision Splendid outback film festival (Winton); Outback Queensland Masters (golf series across the region)
- JULY Big Red Bash (Birdsville); Camel Races (Boulia); Rockhana Gem & Mineral Festival (Cloncurry); Fishing Competition, Festival, Horse and Motorbike and Gymkhana (all Isisford); Opal Festival (Winton); Country Music Festival (Hughenden); Cunnamulla Fella Roundup (Cunnamulla)
- AUG Isa Rodeo (Mount Isa); Drovers Camp Festival (Camooweal); Better in Blackall Festival
- SEPT Birdsville Cup; Ballyneety Rodeo (Aramac); Bilby Festival (Charleville); International Yabby Race (Windorah); Outback Food, Wine and Music Festival (Longreach); Quilpie & District Show & Rodeo (Quilpie); Outback Festival (odd-numbered years, Winton)
- OCT Lake Moondarra Fishing Classic (Mount Isa)
- NOV Charleville Cup

EULO
Population 94

Eulo is on the banks of the Paroo River in south-west Queensland and was once a centre for opal mining. The town was originally much closer to the river but, after severe flooding, moved to where it currently stands. Eulo's population is variable as beekeepers travel from the south every winter so their bees can feed on the precious eucalypts in the area.

SEE & DO **Currawinya National Park:** see Top Attractions. **Eulo Queen Hotel:** owes its name to Isobel Robinson who ran the hotel and reigned over the opal fields in the early 1900s; Leo St. **World War II air-raid shelter:** part of Paroo Pioneer Pathways; self-guided brochure available from visitor centre. **Destructo Cockroach Monument:** commemorates the death of a champion racing cockroach; near Paroo Track, where annual lizard races are held. **Eulo Queen Opal Centre:** opals, First Nations art and jewellery on display and for purchase; Leo St. **Lizard Lounge:** beautiful picnic area inspired by the frill-necked lizard; Cunnamulla Rd. **Fishing:** on the Paroo River; details from visitor centre. **Yowah:** small opal-mining town where visitors can fossick for opals or take a tour of the minefields. The 'Bluff' and 'Castles' provide excellent views over the minefields. Yowah holds Opal Festival in July, which includes an international opal-jewellery competition; 87km NW. **Lake Bindegolly National Park:** walk to the lakes to see pelicans and swans. The 9.2km lake circuit track may flood after rain. No vehicles are allowed in the park; 100km W. **Thargomindah:** pick up a mud map at the visitor centre for Burke and Wills Dig Tree site; (07) 4655 3173; 130km W. **Noccundra Waterhole:** good fishing spot on Wilson River; 260km W.

HUGHENDEN
Population 1004

Hughenden is on the banks of the Flinders River, Queensland's longest river. The first recorded Europeans to pass through here were members of Frederick Walker's 1861 expedition, who were searching for the explorers Burke and Wills. Two years later Ernest Henry selected a cattle station and Hughenden came into existence. The black volcanic soil in the region is rich with fossilised bones, particularly those of dinosaurs.

SEE & DO **Flinders Discovery Centre; Porcupine Gorge National Park:** see Top Attractions for both. **Historic Coolibah Tree:** blazed by Walker in 1861 and again by William Landsborough in 1862 when he was also searching for Burke and Wills and their two companions; east bank of Station Creek, Stansfield St East. **Basalt Byways:** discover the Flinders Shire landscapes on these 4WD tracks. Cross the Flinders River and see the Flinders poppy in the valleys. The longest track is 156km; access on Hann Hwy; 7.3km N. **Prairie:** small town with mini-museum and historic relics at Cobb & Co. yards; 44km E. **Mount Emu Goldfields:** fossicking and bushwalking; 85km N. **Torrens Creek:** the town, a major explosives dump during World War II, was nearly wiped out by 12 explosions when firebreaks accidentally hit the dump; 88km E. **Kooroorinya Falls:** the small falls cascade into a natural waterhole, excellent for swimming; walk and go birdwatching in surrounding bushland; 109km SE via Prairie. **White Mountains National Park:** rugged park with white sandstone outcrops and varied vegetation. Burra Range Lookout on Flinders Hwy has excellent views over the park. There are no walking tracks; 13 7468; 111km E. **Chudleigh Park Gemfields:** gem-quality peridot found in fossicking area (licence required); 155km N. **Moorrinya National Park:** important conservation park protecting 18 different land types of the Lake Eyre Basin. The park is home to iconic Australian animals, such as koalas, kangaroos and dingos, and includes remains of the old sheep-grazing property Shirley Station. Walking is for experienced bushwalkers only; 13 7468; 178km SE via Torrens Creek.

ISISFORD
Population 218

Isisford is a small outback community south of Longreach. In the mid-1800s large stations were established in the area. This brought hawkers, keen on trading their goods to the landowners. Two such hawkers were brothers William and James Whitman who, after their axle broke trying to cross the Alice River, decided to stay and established Isisford in 1877. Once called Wittown, after the brothers, it was renamed in 1880 to recall the nearby Barcoo River ford and Isis Downs Station. The town provided inspiration to iconic Australian poet Banjo Paterson, in particular his poems 'Bush Christening' and 'Clancy of the Overflow'.

SEE & DO **Outer Barcoo Interpretation Centre:** features the world-class fossil exhibit of *Isisfordia duncani*, reputedly the ancestor of all modern crocodilians. Also local arts and crafts, town relics and theatrette; St Mary St. **Big Yellowbelly:** 12m-long fish sculpture made with corrugated-iron and windmill parts by the community to celebrate the annual yellowbelly fishing contest held on the last weekend of July. **Whitman's Museum:** photographic exhibition documents Isisford's history; St Mary St. **Barcoo Weir:** fishing and bush camping. **Oma Waterhole:** popular for fishing and watersports, and home to a fishing competition and festival mid-year (subject to rains); 15km SW.

JULIA CREEK
Population 377

Julia Creek became known as 'The Gateway to the Gulf', after the road to Normanton was sealed in 1964. Settler Donald MacIntyre established Dalgonally Station in 1862; Julia Creek is named after his niece. The district's main industries are cattle, sheep and mining. It is also home to a rare and endangered marsupial, the Julia Creek dunnart, a tiny nocturnal hunter found only within a 100km radius of town.

SEE & DO **At the Creek:** an award-winning visitor centre, focusing on water, country and people exhibits. **Spirit of the ANZAC Sculpture:** at the RSL. **Duncan McIntyre Museum:** local early settler and cattle history; Duncan was an explorer who led a search for Leichhardt; Burke St. **Monument:** a monument to brothers Donald and Duncan McIntyre can be seen by the grave site; Dalgonally Station boundary. **Opera House:** photographic display of McKinlay Shire; open Mon–Fri; Julia St. **Historical walk:** stroll the 38 signposted historical sites around the town; map from visitor centre. **World War II bunkers:** remains of concrete bunkers used to assist navigation of Allied aircraft; western outskirts near airport. **Punchbowl waterhole:** popular area for swimming and fishing on the Flinders River; 45km NE. **Sedan Dip:** popular swimming, fishing and picnicking spot, and location for Aug races; 100km N.

JUNDAH
Population 131

Jundah is at the centre of the Channel Country and its name comes from a Kuungkari word for 'women'. Gazetted as a town in 1880, the area was important for opal mining for 20 years, but lack of water caused the mines to close. The waterholes and channels of the Thomson River are filled with yabbies and fish. The spectacular rock holes, red sand dunes and beauty of Welford National Park, are the natural attractions of this outback town.

SEE & DO **Welford National Park:** *see* Other Attractions. **Museum:** documents the area's early settler heritage; Perkins St. **Post office:** beautiful shopfront mural; Dickson St. **Stonehenge:** named not for the ancient English rock formation, but for the old stone hut built for visiting bullock teams. Nearby on the Thomson River are brolgas and wild budgerigars; 68km NE. **Windorah:** holds the International Yabby Race in Sept; 95km S.

KYNUNA
Population 52

Kynuna is a tiny outback town famous for inspiring Banjo Paterson to write his iconic poem, 'Waltzing Matilda', about events in nearby Combo Waterhole Conservation Park.

SEE & DO **Combo Waterhole Conservation Park:** *see* Top Attractions. **Blue Heeler Hotel:** famous hotel with illuminated blue heeler statue on the roof. **Roadhouse:** obtain a mud map from the roadhouse to find the original Swagman's Billabong. **McKinlay:** although the town is tiny, its famous Walkabout Creek Hotel was originally known as McKinlay Hotel and is the local watering hole in the film *Crocodile Dundee*, which starred famed Australian larrikin Paul Hogan. 74km NW.

★ LONGREACH
Population 2738

Longreach is the largest town in central-west Queensland. Lying on the Tropic of Capricorn, this 'boom and bust' country is affected by flooding rains and devastating drought. It epitomises the outback and features the renowned Australian Stockman's Hall of Fame, devoted to the outback hero. In 1922 Longreach became the operational base for Qantas and remained so until 1934 and the Qantas Founders Museum is here. Longreach is bisected by the Thomson River, the vast length of which is this town's namesake.

SEE & DO **Australian Stockman's Hall of Fame and Outback Heritage Centre; Qantas Founders Museum:** *see* Top Attractions for both. **Lochern National Park:** *see* Other Attractions. **Powerhouse Museum:** displays of old agricultural machinery, power station and local history; open Mon–Fri 10.30am–12.30pm and 1.30–3.30pm; Swan St. **Botanic Gardens:** walking and cycling trails; Landsborough Hwy. **Qantas Park:** replica of original Qantas booking office, which now houses the information centre; Eagle St. **Heritage buildings:** highlights include the courthouse (1892) in Galah St and the railway station (1916) in Sir Hudson Fysh Dr. **Outback Pioneers:** offers horse-drawn adventure tours; Eagle St; (07) 4658 1776. **CWA Markets:** Qantas Park, Eagle St; 2nd Sat morning of month, May–Oct. **Thomson River:** fishing, bushwalking and swimming; 4.6km NW. **Thomson River cruises:** contact visitor centre for details. **Ilfracombe:** once a transport nucleus for the large Wellshot Station to the south, an interesting outdoor machinery museum now runs the length of this town on the highway. Another feature

Opposite: Outback at Isa

TEMPERATURES

Jan: 24–36°C

July: 9–25°C

is the historic Wellshot Hotel, with a woolpress bar and local memorabilia; 27km E. **Starlight's Lookout:** said to be a resting spot of bushranger Captain Starlight. Enjoy the scenic view; 56km NW. **Sheep and cattle station tours:** visit local stations to try mustering and shearing; contact visitor centre for details. **Camden Park Station:** a working cattle and sheep station where you can tour the historic shearing shed and cattle yards and meet Outback Dan, a fifth-generation farmer. The station hosted Queen Elizabeth II and Prince Phillip in 1970; see camdenparkstation.com.au.

MITCHELL
Population 835

Mitchell, a gateway to the outback, is on the banks of the Maranoa River at the western edge of the Darling Downs. It is located on the Great Artesian Basin so does not suffer the dry heat or exhibit the arid landscape typical of the region. This area is the Traditional Land of the Gunggari People who have also held Native Title over the area since June 2012. The town was named after Sir Thomas Mitchell, explorer and Surveyor-General of NSW, who visited the region in 1846. Its long pastoral history is shown in the fine examples of heritage buildings on the main street. The Mount Moffatt section of Carnarvon National Park (*see* p. 391) is good for four-wheel driving and 256km north of here.

SEE & DO Kenniff Courthouse; Great Artesian Spa Complex: *see* Other Attractions for both. **Graffiti murals:** depict the past, present and future of the Booringa Shire; around town. **Mitchell on Maranoa Art Gallery:** Cambridge St. **Horse-drawn wagon tours:** in season; details from visitor centre. **Neil Turner Weir:** birdwatching and picnics; 3.5km NW. **Fisherman's Rest:** good fishing spot; 6km W. **Maranoa River Nature Walk:** informative 1.8km circuit walk starting at Fisherman's Rest. **Kenniff statues:** depict the story of the brothers at their last stand; 7km S.

MOUNT ISA
Population 17,936

Mount Isa is found on the Traditional Lands of the Kalkadoon (Kalkatungu) People who are descendants of an Indigenous Australian tribe living in this region of Queensland for thousands of years. This tribe has been called 'the Elite of the Aboriginal warriors of Queensland', but in 1884 they were massacred at Battle Mountain by settlers and police. Today, Mount Isa is the most important industrial, commercial and administrative centre in north-west Queensland. John Campbell Miles discovered a rich silver-lead deposit in 1923, and now Mount Isa Mines operates one of the world's largest silver-lead mines. The city is also one of the world leaders in rodeos, holding the third-largest on the second weekend in August, attracting rough-riders from all over the state and almost doubling the town's population.

SEE & DO **Outback at Isa:** see Top Attractions. **School of the Air:** discover how distance education works in the outback; Abel Smith Pde; (07) 4744 8333. **City Lookout:** overview of city and mine area; Hilary St. **Underground Hospital and Tent House:** tours of World War II hospital and examples of a miner's lifestyle in 1930s and 1940s; Deighton St. **Rodeo Walk of Fame:** walk the road paved with the names of Mount Isa rodeo legends; Rodeo Dr. **Mine:** the mine's lead smelter stack is Australia's tallest free-standing structure (265m); details from visitor centre. **Donaldson Memorial Lookout:** lookout and walking track; off Pamela St. **Market:** library carpark, Sat. **Lake Moondarra:** artificial lake for picnics and barbecues, swimming, watersports and birdwatching. Home of the Fishing Classic in Sept; 20km N. **Mount Frosty:** old limestone mine and swimming hole (not recommended for children); 53km E. **Lake Julius:** canoe at the lake or see cave paintings and an old goldmine on the nature trails; 110km NE. **Station visits:** feel the outback spirit at one of the stations in the area; details from visitor centre. **Safari tours:** to Boodjamulla (Lawn Hill) National Park and Riversleigh Fossil Fields; details from visitor centre. **Air-charter flights:** to barramundi fishing spots on Mornington and Sweers islands in the Gulf of Carpentaria; details from visitor centre.

MUTTABURRA
Population 158

Muttaburra is a tiny outback community. The name Muttaburra is from the local Mootaburra language, meaning 'the meeting of waters'. A skeleton of an unknown dinosaur was found in 1963 in a creek close to the Thomson River. It was named muttaburrasaurus, and the bones are now in the Queensland Museum but there is a life-sized replica in the Muttaburrasaurus Interpretation Centre.

SEE & DO **Muttaburrasaurus Interpretation Centre:** see Other Attractions. **Dr Arratta Memorial Museum:** this museum has medical and hospital displays with original operating theatres and wards; tours by appt; (07) 4658 7287. **Cassimatis General Store and Cottage:** restored store depicts the original family business in early 1900s. The adjacent cottage was home to the Cassimatis family; tours by appt; (07) 4658 7287. **Agate fossicking:** 5km W. **Pump Hole:** swimming and fishing for golden perch and black bream; 5km E. **Broadwater:** part of Landsborough River for fishing, birdwatching, bushwalking and camping; 6km S.

QUILPIE
Population 451

Quilpie is on the banks of the Bullo River in the outback's famous Channel Country. The town was once a rail centre for the area's large sheep and cattle properties. Today it is better known as an opal town and, in particular, for the 'Boulder Opal'. The world's largest concentration of this opal is found in the area surrounding Quilpie. The town takes its name from the Margany word 'quilpeta', meaning 'stone curlew'. In 2006 the fossilised bones of a new dinosaur species, called *Australotitan cooperensis*, was found and you can see it at Eromanga Natural History Museum.

SEE & DO **Eromanga Natural History Museum:** see Top Attractions. **Museum and gallery:** historical and modern exhibitions; closed Sat–Sun from Oct–Mar; visitor centre, Brolga St. **St Finbarr's Catholic Church:** unique altar, font and lectern made from opal-bearing rock; Buln Buln St. **Opal sales:** various town outlets. **Lyn Barnes Gallery:** outback-inspired paintings; Brolga St. **Lake Houdraman:** popular watersports and recreation area; river road to Adavale; 6km NE. **Baldy Top:** large geological formation with spectacular views; 6km S. **Opal fields:** guided tours (no general access); details from visitor centre; 75km W. **Toompine:** historic hotel, cemetery and designated opal-fossicking areas nearby; 76km S.

RICHMOND
Population 459

This small town on the Flinders River in the Gulf Country serves the surrounding sheep and cattle properties. The town's main street is lined with beautiful bougainvilleas. In recent years Richmond has become the centre of attention as an area rich in marine fossils dating back around 100 million years, when outback Queensland was submerged under an inland sea.

SEE & DO **Kronosaurus Korner:** see Top Attractions. **Cobb & Co. coach:** restored coach with informative display; Lions Park, Goldring St. **Lake Fred Tritton:** recreational lake for waterskiing, picnics and walks. Enjoy the Richmond Community Bush Tucker Garden, which showcases beautiful native plants and was a finalist for the Banksia Environmental Awards; eastern outskirts. **Cambridge Store:** replica of the old Cambridge Downs Homestead from the late 1800s; contains memorablia and machinery from early settler days; Goldring St. **Heritage walk:** follow the self-guided trail with informative history at each stop. It includes the historic flagstone and adobe building, Richmond Hotel, St John the Baptist Church and the Pioneer Cemetery; brochure available from visitor centre. **Fossicking sites:** self-guided tours to nearby areas; details from Kronosaurus Korner.

TAMBO
Population 283

Tambo is the oldest town in central-western Queensland. The town was established in the mid-1860s to service the surrounding pastoral properties, which it continues to do today. This long history can be seen in the heritage buildings on

Top: Mount Isa **Middle:** Tree of Knowledge ghost gum tree, Barcaldine **Bottom:** Australian Stockman's Hall of Fame and Outback Heritage Centre

HUNTING DINOSAURS

Once upon a time (somewhere between 65 and 120 million years ago), outback Queensland was a lush and fertile place, where large herds of dinosaurs and other super-sized animals roamed. The waters and rainforests have long since disappeared, but the sediments of the ancient muddy seabed provided the perfect resting place for many creatures and these plains are now some of the richest dinosaur and fossil fields in the world.

LARK QUARRY CONSERVATION PARK
Around 110km south-west of Winton is the world's only known site of a dinosaur stampede, now marked by the Dinosaur Stampede National Monument. *See* Top Attractions.

AUSTRALIAN AGE OF DINOSAURS
This purpose-built museum on the outskirts of Winton has three parts – a fossil preparation lab, collection room, and Dinosaur Canyon, where life-sized sculptures recreate a vanished world. *See* Top Attractions.

KRONOSAURUS KORNER
In 1932 the bones of a carnivorous kronosaurus – 12m long, with teeth as long as a school ruler and a head twice the size of *T. rex*'s – were unearthed in Richmond, 230km north of Winton. Learn all about it at Kronosaurus Korner. *See* Top Attractions.

FLINDERS DISCOVERY CENTRE
You can't drive through the tiny town of Hughenden, 115km east of Richmond, without saying hello to Mutt, a life-size model of a 7m high muttaburrasaurus. *See* Top Attractions.

RIVERSLEIGH
A World Heritage site, these fossil fields, 285km north-west of Mount Isa, in Boodjamulla (Lawn Hill) National Park are some of the richest in the world. The Riversleigh Fossil Centre is at Outback at Isa. *See* Top Attractions.

EROMANGA NATURAL HISTORY MUSEUM
Eromanga is 106km west of Quilpie and the Eromanga dinosaurs are Australia's largest. *See* Top Attractions.

Arthur St. The Salvator Rosa section of Carnarvon National Park (*see* p. 391) is 130km east of here.

SEE & DO **Old Post Office Museum:** display of historic photographs; Arthur St. **Tambo Teddies Workshop:** produces popular all-wool teddies; Arthur St. **Grassland Art Gallery:** regional artists and touring exhibitions; Arthur St. **Coolibah Walk:** nature walk along banks of the Barcoo River. **Wilderness Way:** a 420km self-guided drive visiting rock art, historic settlement sites and the Salvator Rosa section of the Carnarvon National Park (*see* p. 391). Check road conditions before departing; brochure from council office.

★ WINTON
Population 856

The area surrounding Winton is known as Matilda Country – Australia's most famous song, 'Waltzing Matilda', was written by Banjo Paterson at nearby Dagworth Station in 1895. Combo Waterhole (*see* p. 432) was the setting for the ballad and the tune had its first airing in Winton. A less auspicious event in Winton's history was the declaration of martial law in the 1890s following the Shearers' Strike. In 1920 the first office of Qantas was registered here. Interestingly, the town's water comes from deep artesian bores at a temperature of 83°C. But a bigger wow factor is that this area forms part of Australia's Dinosaur Trail.

SEE & DO **Waltzing Matilda Centre; Australian Age of Dinosaurs; Lark Quarry Conservation Park:** *see* Top Attractions for all. **Bladensburg National Park:** *see* Other Attractions. **North Gregory Hotel:** built in 1878, this historical structure, where legend has it that 'Waltzing Matilda' was first performed, has been ravaged by fire three times, but its current refurbishment has returned it to all its retro glory with lots of 1950s glamour; 67 Elderslie St. **Royal Theatre:** historic open-air movie theatre and museum, one of the oldest still operating in Australia; Elderslie St. **Corfield and Fitzmaurice Store:** charming National Trust–listed store with diorama of Lark Quarry dinosaur stampede; Elderslie St. **Arno's Wall:** ongoing concrete-wall creation proudly containing 'every item imaginable'; Vindex St. **Opalton:** see the remains of the historic town or try fossicking for opals in one of the oldest fields in Queensland; licence available from visitor centre; 115km S.

Tasmania

HIGHLIGHTS

Scale a peak in Tasmania's alpine heartland at Cradle Mountain–Lake St Clair National Park. *See* p. 461.

Travel in the Posh Pit of the MONA Roma ferry upriver from Hobart's waterfront to the avant-garde Museum of Old and New Art (MONA). *See* p. 451.

Visit the sombre Port Arthur Historic Site on the isolated Tasman Peninsula/ Turrakana. *See* p. 441.

Spend Saturday morning browsing and grazing at Hobart's famous Salamanca Market's 300 stalls. *See* p. 439.

Hike to the lofty lookout to take a selfie above the impossibly scenic Wineglass Bay in Freycinet National Park. *See* p. 445.

Wander through the easily accessible city wilds of Launceston's Cataract Gorge. *See* p. 467.

STATE FLOWER

Tasmanian blue gum
Eucalyptus globulus

Maria Island's isthmus and Riedle Bay beach

Hobart/nipaluna at a glance

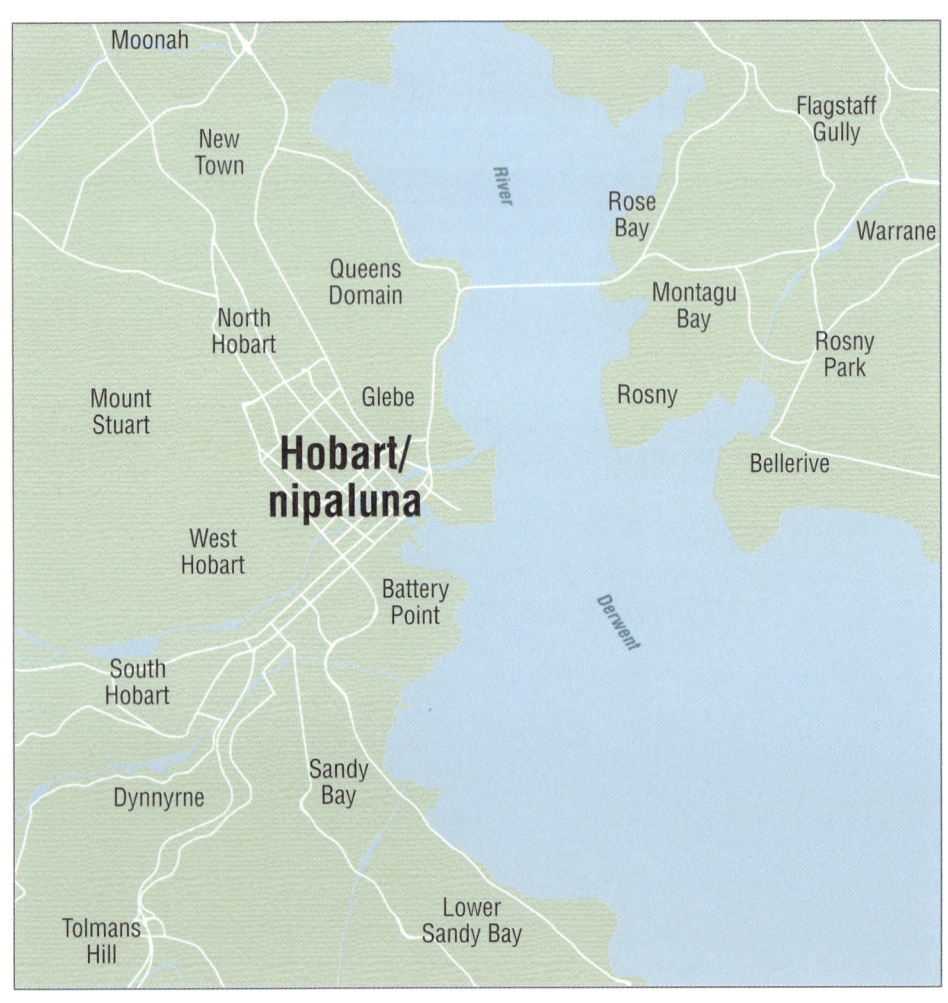

The Traditional Custodians of the Hobart/nipaluna area are the muwinina People, one of the palawa network of clans.

Backed by towering kunanyi/Mount Wellington and fronting the scenic Derwent Estuary, Hobart is a **compact and endearing city**, with **buzzing food and arts scenes and tangible history**. Wherever you stroll – among the **docks and boats** or the charming streets of **historic Battery Point** – there is a photogenic moment at every turn.

Top: Salamanca Market **Middle:** Tasmanian Museum and Art Gallery **Bottom:** View from kunanyi/Mount Wellington **Opposite:** Hobart with kunanyi/Mount Wellington as its backdrop

IF YOU LIKE ...

EAT STREETS
Elizabeth St, from the City to NoHo (North Hobart)
Hampden Rd, Battery Point
Salamanca Place
Sandy Bay Rd, Sandy Bay
Waterfront from MACq 01 to Elizabeth Street Pier

FESTIVALS AND EVENTS
Taste of Summer, Dec–Jan
Mona Foma, Jan
Australian Wooden Boat Festival, Feb (biennial; odd-numbered years)
Tasmanian Wine Festival, March
Ten Days on the Island, March (biennial; odd-numbered years)
Dark Mofo, June
Festival of Voices, June–July
Sydney–Hobart Yacht Race, Dec

HISTORIC PUBS
Customs House Hotel
Hope & Anchor Tavern
New Sydney Hotel
Shipwrights Arms Hotel
The Duke

HISTORY HOTSPOTS
Battery Point cottages and laneways
Cascades Female Factory Historic Site
Penitentiary Chapel Historic Site
Salamanca Place
Theatre Royal

MUSEUMS
GASP! Glenorchy Arts and Sculpture Park
Maritime Museum of Tasmania
Mawson's Huts Replica Museum
MONA (Museum of Old and New Art)
Tasmanian Cricket Museum
Tasmanian Museum and Art Gallery (TMAG)

PARKS AND GARDENS
Franklin Square
Royal Tasmanian Botanical Gardens
St David's Park
University Rose Gardens
Waterworks Reserve

VIEWS
Hobart Historic Cruises
kunanyi/Mount Wellington summit
Mount Nelson Signal Station
Rosny Point Lookout
Tasman Bridge walkway

Daytrips from Hobart/nipaluna

BRUNY ISLAND/LUNAWANNA-ALLONAH
2hr from Hobart CBD

Roll out of bed early and drive to the small Channel Highway town of Kettering, 32km south of Hobart. From here two car ferries chug over to Bruny Island/lunawanna-allonah – a 20min trip across the D'Entrecasteaux Channel. On this underpopulated isle you'll find beautiful unspoiled coastal scenery and plenty of chances to stock up on a variety of land- and sea-based gourmet produce. Catch a wild jet-boat ride around Bruny's towering coastal cliffs from the little beachside village of Adventure Bay/kaparati or take the road south to the Cape Bruny Lighthouse where you can take a guided tour up the spiral staircase inside for wild ocean views. Between North and South Bruny the sandy isthmus known as the Neck has a must-climb lookout with unforgettable coastal views. See Adventure Bay/kaparati p. 453.

CHANNEL HIGHWAY TOWNS
20min from Hobart CBD

There's a network of newer, straighter roads tracking south from Hobart, but the original south-bound road – the very wiggly and scenic Channel Highway – is a much more attractive route with plenty of beaches, history and lunch spots along the way. Your first stop is in leafy Taroona, once home to Crown Princess Mary of Denmark, and where the 1870 Shot Tower offers knockout views from its 48m stone turret. Drive a little further and the pretty beachside suburbs of Kingston and Blackmans Bay have safe swimming and seaside cafes.

Further south, pull in at the quirky Margate Train for shopping and a pancake; sample handmade nougat and chocolates at Kettering; and taste hand-smoked ocean trout and sheep cheese at Woodbridge. See Kettering and Kingston p. 454.

Top: Port Arthur Historic Site **Middle:** Bruny Island Cheese Co. **Bottom left:** Wooden Boat Centre, Franklin **Bottom right:** Tasmanian devils at Bonorong Wildlife Sanctuary

HUON VALLEY
45min from Hobart CBD

They don't call lutruwita/Tasmania the 'Apple Isle' for nothing. The Huon Valley – a 38km drive south-west of Hobart – is where most of the apples come from. Close to the main hub of Huonville is the rustic Apple Shed, housing an apple-industry museum and home to Willie Smith's natural organic apple ciders. On the Huon River, there's a quick-fire jet-boat tour to thrill you; the more sedate Wooden Boat Centre at Franklin has displays on traditional boat building.

This is also wine country, so a visit to classy Home Hill Winery at Ranelagh is recommended for tastings; for lunch, alternative Cygnet has quality cafe fare. *See* Cygnet p. 453, Huonville p. 454.

DERWENT VALLEY
1hr from Hobart CBD

Just 35km north-west of Hobart the Derwent narrows considerably as you roll into the 1808 township of New Norfolk. It's a picker's delight with antique shops and foodie attractions, including paddock-to-plate fine dining at the Agrarian Kitchen Eatery at Willow Court.

Further afield in the valley there are paddock-to-pint brews at Two Metre Tall brewery's Farm Bar, a treasure trove of small fruits at Westerway's raspberry farm and more historic stone buildings than you can point a camera at in National Trust–listed Hamilton. *See* Hamilton p. 473, New Norfolk p. 455.

MOUNT FIELD NATIONAL PARK
1hr from Hobart CBD

Some parts of Tasmania are mountainous enough to catch a good coating of winter snow. At Mount Field National Park, 80km north-west of Hobart, you can ski in winter, bushwalk in summer and get a good breath of fresh air any time of the year. It's a short walk from the visitor centre to Russell Falls, a much-photographed cascade tumbling 48m over two rocky tiers. Other short walks extend to Horseshoe Falls and Lady Barron Falls, with longer hikes taking you up into the park's wild alpine moorlands.

Getting to Mount Field is a super-scenic experience, tracking through the little towns and hop fields of the Derwent Valley. *See* Mount Field National Park p. 451.

THE MIDLANDS
1.5hr from Hobart CBD

The Midlands Highway follows the original carriage route between Hobart in the south and Launceston, Tasmanian's northern hub. En route is a string of heritage towns where you can really dig into the colonial-era history of this region.

The town of Oatlands (1821) is home to Australia's best-preserved collection of Georgian buildings. Don't miss Callington Mill (1837), now home to a namesake distillery. Snug little Ross is undeniably pretty, with the Ross Bridge (1836), Ross Female Factory (women's convict prison) and Tasmanian Wool Centre all worthy stops. Campbell Town has another convict-built bridge (1838), the engaging Campbell Town Museum and some handy lunch spots. *See* Campbell Town p. 471, Oatlands and Ross p. 475.

PORT ARTHUR
1.5hr from Hobart CBD

The Port Arthur Historic Site, 95km south-east of Hobart on the Tasman Peninsula/Turrakana, is famous for all the wrong reasons. Between 1830 and 1877, 12,500 convicts did hard time here; and in 1996 a gunman killed 35 people at the site. Visiting this place can be a profoundly moving experience.

Port Arthur's isolation – on a peninsula at the bottom of Tasmania's east coast – made it the perfect convict prison. Admission to the site includes a guided walking tour of the convict ruins and a boat cruise around the sheltered harbour. Surrounding attractions include Remarkable Cave and the Tasmanian Devil Unzoo at Taranna. *See* Port Arthur p. 446.

RICHMOND
30min from Hobart CBD

A short 26km hop north-east of Hobart is historic Richmond, founded in 1824 as a military post and stagecoach stopover between Hobart and Port Arthur. With an immaculately preserved cache of colonial-era buildings, the town is a true step-back-in-time daytrip. Among its must-see attractions and photo opportunities are Australia's oldest road bridge (1823), and Australia's oldest gaol (1825).

The surrounding Coal River Valley is a significant wine-producing area with plenty of cellar doors, and close by Bonorong Wildlife Sanctuary and Zoodoo Zoo are excellent wildlife parks that kids will love. *See* Richmond p. 455.

Top: Callington Mill in Oatlands **Second from top:** Get Shucked Oysters on Bruny Island/lunawanna-allonah **Second from bottom:** Port Arthur Historic Site **Bottom:** New Norfolk at sunrise

Regions of Tasmania

**❶ EAST COAST
P. 444**

Bicheno
Coles Bay ★
Dunalley
Fingal
Port Arthur ★
St Helens
St Marys
Sorell
Swansea
Teralina/Eaglehawk Neck
Triabunna

**❷ SOUTH-EAST
P. 450**

Adventure Bay/kaparati
  (Bruny Island/
  lunawanna–allonah)
Bothwell
Cygnet
Dover
Geeveston
Hastings Caves
Huonville
Kettering
Kingston
New Norfolk
Pontville
Richmond

**❸ WESTERN
WILDERNESS P. 456**

Corinna/Kurina
Queenstown
Rosebery
Strahan ★
Zeehan

**❹ NORTH-WEST
P. 460**

Burnie
Currie (King Island)
Devonport
Latrobe
Penguin
Port Sorell
Sheffield
Smithton
Stanley ★
Ulverstone
Waratah
Wynyard

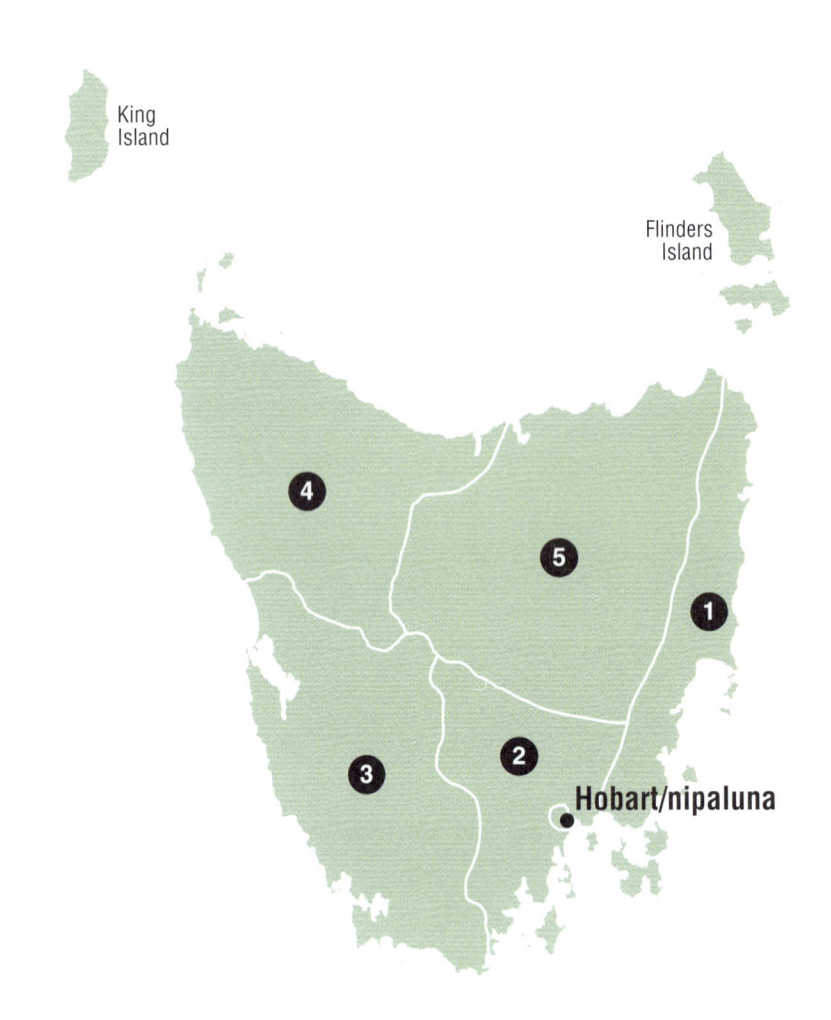

**❺ MIDLANDS AND
NORTH-EAST P. 466**

Beaconsfield
Beauty Point
Bridport
Campbell Town
Deloraine
Derby
Evandale
Exeter
George Town
Gladstone
Hadspen
Hamilton
Launceston ★
Lilydale
Longford
Miena
Mole Creek
Oatlands
Ross
Scottsdale
Westbury
Whitemark (Flinders Island)

Opposite: Roads in Tassie's wilderness areas can be remote and rugged

TASMANIA

East Coast

Tasmania's sunny, beachy east coast has long been where Hobartians come to escape for a weekend at the beach shack – family holiday cabins that are often intergenerational. But you'll find as many tourists as locals here, exploring historic sites like the **convict ruins at World Heritage-listed Port Arthur and Maria Island/ wukaluwikiwayna, wineries** and **superb national parks**, or just enjoying fish-and-chips on the beach.

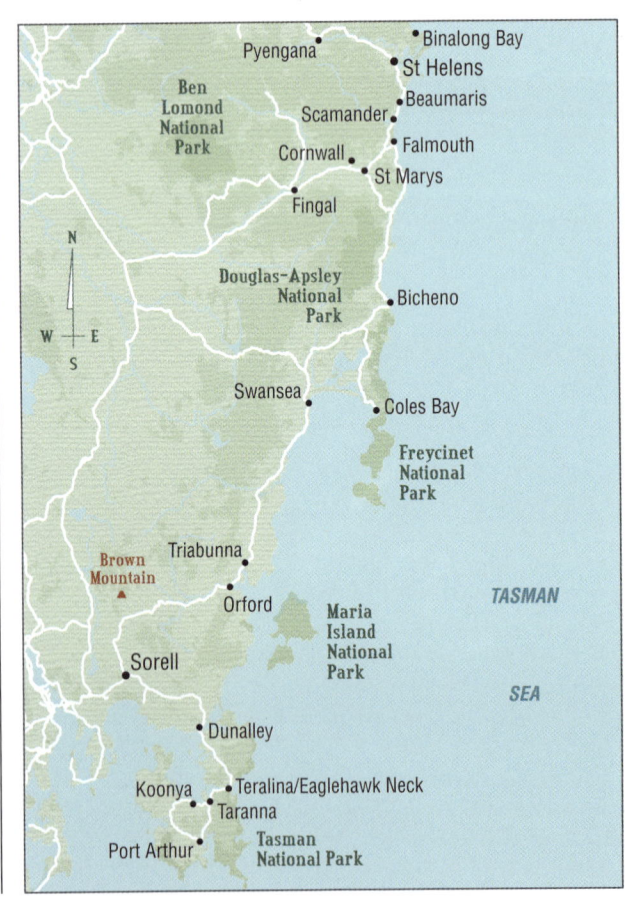

CHEAT SHEET

- → Block out a week or two to explore the east coast from bottom to top or top to bottom.

- → Best time to visit: summer is the right time to head for the east coast, but you'll find cheaper accommodation and less crowded walking tracks in the shoulder-season months of Mar/Apr and Oct/Nov.

- → Main towns: Coles Bay (see p. 447), St Helens (see p. 448), Swansea (see p. 449).

- → Tasmania's east coast is the Traditional Lands of the palawa.

- → Did you know? Maria Island National Park, a 15km ferry trip from Triabunna, has been designated a safe breeding ground for Tasmanian devils, the iconic native species under threat from Devil Facial Tumour Disease (DFTD).

- → Don't miss: Port Arthur Historic Site; Wineglass Bay; historic Darlington on Maria Island/ wukaluwikiwayna; Spiky Bridge; East Coast Heritage Museum; and the dramatic rock formations in Tasman National Park.

Top: Maria Island's Darlington penal settlement **Opposite:** The area's famed lichen-covered rocks

TOP ATTRACTIONS

BAY OF FIRES CONSERVATION AREA: The picture-perfect Bay of Fires name came from Captain Tobias Furneaux who saw First Nations campfires burning along the shore as he sailed past in 1773. From Eddystone Point to the northern part of the Bay of Fires has always been called larapuna by its Traditional Owners. This area features glorious coastal scenery, middens, good beach fishing and camping. The upmarket four-day guided **Bay of Fires Lodge Walk** takes in the scenery to the north; taswalkingco.com.au/bay-of-fires-lodge-walk. Award-winning Aboriginal-owned and operated **wukalina Walk** of four days/three nights covers the Bay of Fires; wukalinawalk.com.au.

BICHENO PENGUIN TOURS: Join a tour at dusk in the town of Bicheno (see p. 447) to watch impossibly cute little penguins return home from the sea. On most nights they waddle right past you as they make their way through the coastal vegetation to their sandy burrows. At the peak of the season, close to 600 birds inhabit the rookery. It's a magical and environmentally sensitive wildlife experience. Open Mon–Fri 9am–5.30pm, Sat–Sun 10am–5pm; 70 Burgess St, Bicheno; (03) 6375 1333.

COAL MINES HISTORIC SITE: Tasmania's first operational mine, run by convicts, is now a World Heritage site with self-guided tours around a series of interpretive panels; Coal Mine Rd, Saltwater River; 1800 659 101. The site is 30km north-west of Port Arthur (see p. 446).

FREYCINET NATIONAL PARK: This is a world-renowned park for its stunning coastal scenery, challenging rock climbs, abundant wildlife and range of walking tracks. The park is covered in wildflowers, including 60 varieties of ground orchid. Visitors can take the 1hr walk to the lookout over stunning and iconic Wineglass Bay, or the 2.5hr return walk to the beach. There are many swimming beaches and guided trips along the park's coastline by boat or kayak. Freycinet Visitor Centre (at park entrance); (03) 6256 7000.

GREAT EASTERN DRIVE: This 176km road trip takes in the east coast's many holiday towns, picturesque bays, beaches and national parks, as well as wineries and seafood stops. You can swim, walk or simply enjoy the views. It covers ground from Orford in the south to Binalong Bay in the north, and you can do it in a weekend or take a week; greateasterndrive.com.au

MARIA ISLAND NATIONAL PARK: Maria Island is a national park, uninhabited now and with a fascinating First Nations and convict history. Known as wukaluwikiwayna by the puthikwilayti tribe, who made regular canoe crossings to the island for thousands of years, it became a penal settlement in 1825 and was then used as a convict probation station from 1842 until 1850. After the convicts were moved to Port Arthur, the island was leased to Italian merchant Diego Bernacchi, who envisaged first a Mediterranean idyll and then a cement works. Both projects were short-lived. Today bushwalks are popular. The swirling sandstone patterns of the Painted Cliffs are magnificent and the historic penal settlement of Darlington is interesting. Wild wombats abound on the island and taking the Maria Island Pledge means you promise to protect the wombats and landscape (see: eastcoasttasmania.com/maria-island-pledge). There's a daily ferry to the island from Triabunna.

Contact PWS on 1300 135 513. Four-day guided walks of the island, staying in luxury accommodation, are available through Maria Island Walk. Bookings (03) 6234 2999.

PORT ARTHUR HISTORIC SITE: This astonishing collection of heritage buildings and ruins illuminates the lives of the Port Arthur convicts and their guards. From the 1830s to the 1870s, over 12,000 convicts from Britain, some of whom did nothing more than steal food to survive, were shipped to Port Arthur, dubbed 'Hell on Earth'. They lived under threat of the lash and experimental punitive measures that often drove them to madness. This grim past is offset by the stark beauty of the site's sandstone ruins and the glassy, often misty, waters of the bay. Entry tickets (valid for two consecutive days) include a guided walking tour, access to the visitor centre, interpretation gallery and museum, and a harbour cruise. Lantern-lit ghost tours depart at dusk, while additional tours of the colony's cemetery on the Isle of the Dead unravel further sad yet fascinating stories. The whole complex has a strangely serene atmosphere, despite the suffering and horrors endured here, both back in the convict days and in 1996 when a gunman killed 35 people here. Open 10am–5pm; 6973 Arthur Hwy; (03) 6251 2310.

ST COLUMBA FALLS: Dropping nearly 90m, these awesome falls flow down a granite cliff-face to the South George River. Walks lead to a viewing platform; St Columba Falls Rd, Pyengana. The falls are 31km west of St Helens (see p. 448).

TASMAN NATIONAL PARK: The major part of Tasman National Park is on the Tasman Peninsula/Turrakana and has some of the most striking scenery in the state. Tasman Blowhole, Tasmans Arch and Devils Kitchen are the key attractions, occurring in rocks that are Permian in age (about 250 million years old). There are numerous walks throughout the park, including the full track reaching from Doo Town to Fortescue Bay, and there are fantastic shorter walks to Bivouac Bay, Waterfall Bay and Cape Hauy. One spot not to miss is the remarkable Remarkable Cave, an eroded tunnel through the cliffs with waves surging in and out. From the top of the steep stairs down into the cavern you'll enjoy spectacular views along the coastline to Cape Raoul. The cave is also the starting point for a 5hr return walk to Crescent Bay and Mount Brown. Contact PWS on 1300 135 513.

TASMANIAN DEVIL UNZOO: The world's first 'unzoo' – unfenced, with most animals free to come and go – features Tasmanian devils, quolls, eagles, wallabies, owls and wombats. The Tasmanian devil feeding time is worth waiting for (10am, 11am, 12.30pm, 1.30pm and 3pm and 5pm; 4.30pm in winter). Arthur Hwy, Taranna; (03) 6250 3230.

OTHER ATTRACTIONS

DOUGLAS–APSLEY NATIONAL PARK: Rocky, steep and untamed, Douglas–Apsley is a compact national park comprising Tasmania's last undisturbed area of dry eucalypt forest. The Denison, Douglas and Apsley rivers all run through here, traversing some gorgeous gorges, waterfalls and safe swimming holes. Terrific bushwalking trails, too. Off Tasman Hwy; (03) 6359 2217. The park is 14km north-west of Bicheno (see p. 447).

EAST COAST NATUREWORLD: This busy park in Bicheno (see p. 447) offers close encounters with the region's diverse fauna. Devils in the Dark tours to see the nocturnal antics of Tasmanian devils are also available. Open 9.30am–4pm; 18356 Tasman Hwy, Bicheno; (03) 6375 1311.

EVERCREECH FOREST RESERVE: This reserve is home to the impressive White Knights, the tallest white gums in the world, including a specimen 89m high. A 20min circuit walk passes through a man-fern grove and blackwoods, then up a hill for a superb view. There is also a 45min return walk to Evercreech Falls, and many picnic and barbecue spots. On the road to Mathinna. It's 30km north of Fingal (see p. 448).

KATE'S BERRY FARM: Cool-climate berries, chocolate and delicious indulgences in a farmgate cafe on a hill overlooking Swansea (see p. 449); open Fri–Tues 9.30am–4.30pm; 12 Addison St, Swansea; (03) 6257 8428.

SORRELL FRUIT FARM: Offers pick-your-own and ready-picked. In season it has many types of berries, apricots, cherries, pears, nectarines and peaches. There is also a large gift shop and a cafe serving Devonshire teas and light lunches. Open Oct–May; 174 Pawleena Rd, Sorell; (03) 6265 3100.

SPIKY BRIDGE: Built by convicts in 1843, the bridge was pieced together without mortar or cement. The spikes – vertical fieldstones – prevented cattle from falling over the sides. The beach nearby has good rock-fishing but check conditions with locals. The bridge is 7.5km south of Swansea (see p. 449).

SWANSEA BARK MILL: The only restored black wattle–bark mill in Australia has machinery that still processes the bark for tanning leather. It has a cafe and tavern too. Tasman Hwy, Swansea; (03) 6257 8094.

TESSELLATED PAVEMENT: These rocks appear to have been tiled, but their formation is entirely natural – earth movements have fractured the pavement over the years. It's 1km north of Teralina/Eaglehawk Neck (see p. 449).

VISITOR INFORMATION

Port Arthur Historic Site
6973 Arthur Hwy,
Port Arthur
(03) 6251 2300 or
1800 659 101
portarthur.org.au

Freycinet Peninsula
parks.tas.gov.au/explore-our-parks/freycinet-national-park
wineglassbay.com

St Helens Visitor Information Centre,
61 Cecilia St, St Helens
(03) 6376 1744

East Coast
eastcoasttasmania.com

Opposite top: Wombat on Maria Island **Opposite bottom:** Cape Pillar in Tasman National Park

KEY TOWNS

BICHENO
Population 797

The quintessential east coast holiday town, Bicheno (pronounced 'bish-eno') is a seaside charmer today but it has a chequered history. It was established as a whaling and sealing port in 1803, pre-dating the official settlement of Van Diemen's Land by a few months. After a short stint as a coal port in the early 1850s, during which time the population boomed, Bicheno relaxed back into what it does best – fishing. It's a popular holiday destination, with the mildest climate in Tasmania, sandy beaches, dive spots and decent surf. Native rock orchids, unique to the east coast, bloom here during Oct and Nov.

SEE & DO **Bicheno Penguin Tours:** *see* Top Attractions. **East Coast Natureworld; Douglas–Apsley National Park:** *see* Other Attractions for both. **Scuba diving:** Bicheno is one of the best temperate dive locations in the world, with whales and dolphins passing by. **Foreshore Footway:** 3km track with great views, from Redhill Beach to the blowhole via The Gulch natural harbour; off Gordon St. **Wauba's memorial:** the abuse of local First Nations women was widespread in the whaling days. One of these women, Wauba Debar, became a heroine after saving two white men from drowning during a storm. Landmarks around town bear her name, and her grave can be seen in Lions Park. **Whalers Lookout:** climb atop this bulbous granite outcrop for some super sea views; off Foster St. **Glass Bottom Boat:** stay warm and dry while you drift above Bicheno's watery depths in Tasmania's only glass-bottom boat; open 9am–4pm Oct–May; The Espl, The Gulch; (03) 6375 1294. **East coast wineries:** the sunny east coast is a great place to grow chardonnay. To the south-west of Bicheno heading towards Swansea you'll find a string of cellar doors, including those at **Spring Vale Wines**, **Devil's Corner** and **Freycinet Vineyard**; Tasman Hwy; 18km SW. **Scenic flights:** Freycinet Air wings over Bicheno and beyond; flights daily; 109 Friendly Beaches Rd, Friendly Beaches; (03) 6375 1694.

★ COLES BAY
Population 515

Coles Bay is a little village of holiday homes and weekender shacks with a growing selection of upmarket accommodation, including the ultra-luxurious Saffire Freycinet. It is a popular summertime family camping destination and a peaceful base from which to explore the area. The spectacular scenery of the Hazards and Freycinet Peninsula is on its doorstep and there are walking trails to secluded beaches, lookouts and remote capes close by. The exquisite Wineglass Bay is regarded by many as one of the world's best beaches.

SEE & DO **Freycinet National Park:** *see* Top Attractions. **Freycinet Marine Farm:** working oyster farm with guided tours and sampling; open 9am–4pm; tour bookings online at oysterbaytours.com; 9km NW. **Moulting Lagoon Game Reserve:** wetlands of international importance with many bird species; 12km NW. **Fishing:** Great Oyster Bay is a renowned fishing spot – species include flathead and Australian salmon. Coles Bay is also a base for big-game fishing, particularly southern bluefin tuna in autumn; contact visitor centre for tour details.

DUNALLEY
Population 304

A quaint fishing village, Dunalley is on the canal separating the Forestier and Tasman peninsulas from mainland Tasmania.

SEE & DO **Tasman Monument:** erected in 1942, this monument commemorates the landing of Abel Tasman and his crew. The actual landing occurred to the north-east on the Forestier Peninsula, near the fairly inaccessible Cape Paul Lamanon. Imlay St. **Dunalley Fish Market:** offering a huge range of seafood delicacies, the market has sales, samples and a barbecue area; 11 Fulham Rd. **Denison Canal:** Australia's only purpose-built, hand-dug sea canal. The swing bridge that spans the canal has become quite a spectacle for visitors. **Bangor Vineyard Shed:** cellar door and restaurant with award-winning wines, events and views; 20 Blackman Bay Rd. **Marion Bay:** popular swimming beach, **Cape Bernier Vineyard** for tastings and sales and **Bream Creek Vineyard**; 14km NE.

FINGAL
Population 350

Poet James McAuley wrote of Fingal's 'blonding summer grasses', 'mauve thistledown' and the river that 'winds in silence through wide blue hours, days'. Indeed, the crags of Ben Lomond National Park and the lush valley make Fingal a quiet inspiration for many writers. The town was established in 1827 as a convict station and distinguished itself by becoming the headquarters of the state's coal industry – and home of the World Coal Shovelling Championships and Roof Bolting Championships. Just north of Fingal, at Mangana, Tasmania's first payable gold was discovered in 1852.

SEE & DO **Everchreech Forest Reserve:** *see* Other Attractions. **Historic Buildings:** there are many heritage buildings throughout the township, particularly in Talbot St. They include Holder Brothers General Store (1859), St Peter's Church (1867) and the Fingal Hotel (c.1840).

Self-guided walking tour map is available from the Avoca Museum and Information Centre, Avoca. **Avoca:** small township with many historical buildings; 27km SW. **Mathinna Falls:** magnificent 4-tier waterfall over a drop of 80m, with an easy 30min return walk to falls base; 36km N.

★ PORT ARTHUR
Population 247

Tasmania's most famous convict heritage site is a hauntingly beautiful place. The UNESCO World Heritage–listed Port Arthur Historic Site, on the super-scenic Tasman Peninsula/tukana, was Australia's most infamous penal settlement. Beyond the convict ruins, there is also Tasman National Park, with its many walks or you can explore Tasman Island on a cruise.

SEE & DO Coal Mines Historic Site; Port Arthur Historic Site; Tasman National Park: see Top Attractions for all. **Tasman Island Cruises:** excellent 3hr cruises exploring the beautiful coastal scenery of Tasman National Park, departing either Hobart or Port Arthur; booking office open 9am–5pm; 6961 Arthur Hwy; (03) 6250 2200. **Remarkable Cave:** part of Tasman National Park; 446 Safety Cove Rd; (03) 6214 8100; 6km S. **Fortescue Bay:** marvellous beach and camping spot within Tasman National Park; Fortescue Rd; (03) 6214 8100; 18km E.

ST HELENS
Population 1573

Pack your fishing rods and steer your boat (or car) to St Helens. At the head of Georges Bay, St Helens is the largest town on Tasmania's east coast. Like most places on the coast it's a holiday hub, but it's big enough to sustain a sizeable permanent population too, many of whom are fisherfolk (the East Australian Current runs past offshore – tuna, marlin and shark aplenty!). For land-based and inshore anglers, the long, narrow estuary of Georges Bay is full of fish, or you can order some for dinner at one of the town's good seafood eateries. These days, the town is known just as much for its mountain biking. The aquamarine waters, lichen-covered granite outcrops and footprint-free white-sand beaches of larapuna/Bay of Fires are also close by.

SEE & DO Bay of Fires Conservation Area; St Columba Falls: see Top Attractions for both. **St Helens History Room:** see memorabilia and models of local history, from a mine waterwheel and a horse-drawn hearse to a vintage church organ and life-sized Tasmanian tiger; St Helens Visitor Information Centre, 61 Cecilia St; (03) 6376 1744. **Fishing trips:** St Helens is famous for its fishing; there's flathead in Georges Bay, bream and trout in the Scamander River and blue-water game fishing offshore. Charter boats, tours and dinghy hire available; check with the visitor centre for details. **St Helens Saturday Market:** Portland Hall; Sat morning. **St Helens Mountain Bike Trail:** A stacked loop of fun trails, plus the epic 42km Bay of Fires trail, ending on a white-sand beach; 6km S. **Binalong Bay:** this compact, photogenic holiday town with its gorgeous white-sand beach sits at the southern end of larapuna/Bay of Fires. Expect excellent surf and rock fishing. 11km NE. **St Helens Point:** walks with eye-popping coastal scenery along Maurouard Beach; pick up a brochure from St Helens visitor centre; off St Helens Point Rd, Stieglitz; 9km S. **Beaumaris:** wide, empty surf beach and glassy lagoons; Tasman Hwy, Beaumaris; 12km S. **Blue Tier Forest Reserve:** mountain-bike trails, walks with wheelchair access and interpretive sites; grab a map from St Helens visitor centre; off Tasman Hwy, Weldborough; 27km NW. **Pyengana Dairy Company:** superb cheddar cheeses to taste and buy, and a cheesy cafe; open 9am–4pm; St Columba Falls Rd, Pyengana; (03) 6373 6157; 27km W.

ST MARYS
Population 494

The main centre of the Break O'Day Plains, St Marys is a small town overshadowed by the magnificent St Patricks Head in the eastern highlands. The roads to and from St Marys wind through forests or down through the valley.

SEE & DO **Rivulet Park:** platypus, Tasmania native hens and picnic and barbecue facilities; Main St. **St Marys Cranks and Tinkerers Museum;** quirky collection of train and mining stuff in the old St Marys Railway Station. Open Mon–Fri 9am–4pm; Esk Main Rd. **St Marys Hotel:** iconic building; Main St. **St Patricks Head:** challenging 1hr 40min return walk to top of rocky outcrop for great 360-degree views of coast and valley; 1.5km E. **South Sister:** an easier lookout alternative to St Patricks Head, a 10–15min walk leads through stringybarks and silver wattles to spectacular views of Fingal Valley; 3km NW. **Cornwall:** miners' wall and Cornwall Collectables shop; 6.5km W. **Falmouth:** small coastal township with convict-built structures, beaches and fishing; 14km NE. **Scamander:** holiday town with sea and river fishing, good swimming, and walks and drives through forest plantations; 17km N.

SORELL
Population 3180

The south-eastern town of Sorell was founded in 1821 and was important in early colonial times for providing most of the state's grain. It was named after Governor Sorell, who attempted to curb bushranging in Tasmania, but ironically the town was later targeted by bushranger Matthew Brady, who released the prisoners from gaol and left the soldiers imprisoned in their place. Today Sorell is a fast-growing town and tourist gateway to the Tasman Peninsula/Turrakana and en route to Tasmania's east coast.

Top: Port Arthur Historic Site
Bottom: Tessellated Pavement

TOP EVENTS

- → JAN Regatta (St Helens)
- → FEB Garlic Festival (Koonya)
- → APR East Coast Harvest Odyssey (ECHO Festival) (Swansea)
- → JUNE Bay of Fires Winter Arts Festival (St Helens)
- → OCT Freycinet Challenge (Coles Bay)
- → NOV Food and Wine Festival (Bicheno)

TEMPERATURES

Jan: 13–22°C

July: 6–14°C

SEE & DO **Sorrell Fruit Farm:** see Other Attractions. **Historic Buildings:** there are three churches listed in the National Estate, most notably St George's Anglican Church (1826). Other heritage buildings include the Old Rectory (c. 1826), Old Post Office (c. 1850), Bluebell Inn (c. 1864) and Sorell Barracks (1827). **Orielton Lagoon:** important migratory wading bird habitat. **Pioneer Park:** popular picnic spot; Parsonage Pl. **Market:** Memorial Hall and Oval, Gordon St; Sun (weekly in summer, fortnightly in winter). **Southern Tasmanian wine region:** many vineyards east of town; brochure from visitor centre. **Beaches:** around Dodges Ferry and Carlton; 18km S.

SWANSEA
Population 711

On the shores of Great Oyster Bay, Swansea has magnificent views to Freycinet Peninsula. It is part of the Glamorgan/Spring Bay shire, the oldest rural municipality in the country, and there are many fine heritage buildings.

SEE & DO **Swansea Bark Mill; Spiky Bridge; Kate's Berry Farm:** see Other Attractions for all. **Historic walk:** self-guided tour takes in charming heritage buildings including Morris's General Store (1838), run by the Morris family for over 100 years, and the Community Centre (c. 1860), featuring the unusually large slate billiard table made for the 1880 World Exhibition; brochure from visitor centre. **Waterloo Point:** 1km walking track leads to viewing area to see short-tailed shearwaters at dusk and middens; Esplanade Rd. **Melshell Oyster Shack:** slurp down a dozen freshly harvested oysters; 10am–4pm; 7 Yellow Sandbanks Rd, Dolphin Sands; (03) 6257 0269; 12km NE. **Coswell Beach:** good spot for viewing little penguins at dusk; 1km S along coast from Waterloo Point. **Duncombes Lookout:** splendid views; 3km S. **Mayfield Beach:** safe swimming beach with walking track from camping area to Three Arch Bridge. There is also great rock and beach fishing; 14km S. **Vineyards: Milton, Spring Vale, Freycinet** and **Craigie Knowe** vineyards all have cellar-door sales; 15km N. **Lost and Meetus Falls:** bushwalks past beautiful waterfalls in dry eucalypt forest. Sheltered picnic area is nearby; 50km NW.

TERALINA/EAGLEHAWK NECK
Population 391

Teralina/Eaglehawk Neck is a pleasant fishing destination with small holiday retreats and striking scenery. Situated on the narrow isthmus between the Forestier and Tasman peninsulas, Teralina/Eaglehawk Neck was the perfect natural prison gate for the convict settlement at Port Arthur. Few prisoners escaped by sea, so Teralina/Eaglehawk Neck was essentially the only viable way out. The isthmus was guarded by soldiers and a line of ferocious, tethered dogs. Most convicts knew not to bother, but William Hunt (convict and former strolling actor) tackled the isthmus in a kangaroo skin. As two guards took aim with their muskets, their efforts were cut short by a plaintive shout coming from the kangaroo, 'Don't shoot! It's only me – Billy Hunt!'

SEE & DO **Port Arthur Historic Site; Tasman National Park; Tasmanian Devil Unzoo:** see Top Attractions for all. **Tessellated Pavement:** see Other Attractions. **Bronze dog sculpture:** marks the infamous dogline; access by short walking track off Arthur Hwy. **Scuba diving:** the area has a huge range of dive sites including the spectacular formations of Sisters Rocks, the seal colony at Hippolyte Rock, the SS *Nord* wreck and amazing sea-cave systems; Eaglehawk Dive Centre; bookings on (03) 6250 3566. **Surfing:** good surf beaches at Teralina/Eaglehawk Neck and Pirates Bay. **Pirates Bay Lookout:** views across the bay, past the eastern side of Teralina/Eaglehawk Neck to the massive coastal cliffs of the Tasman Peninsula/Turrakana; 1.5km N. **Doo Town:** holiday town in which most of the houses bear names with variations of 'doo'; 3km S.

TRIABUNNA
Population 722

Triabunna is one of the only places in Tasmania that has retained its Traditional name in some form; the area was called trayapana. When Maria (pronounced 'mar-eye-ah') Island/wukaluwikiwayna was a penal settlement, Triabunna (pronounced 'try-a-bunnah') was a garrison town and whaling base. After an initial boom, this small coastal town settled into relative obscurity, as a centre for the scallop and abalone industries. It is now a small holiday town and where the ferry for Maria Island departs from.

SEE & DO **Maria Island National Park:** see Top Attractions. **Tasmanian Seafarers' Memorial:** commemorates those who lost their lives at sea; The Espl. **Spring Bay Maritime and Discovery Centre:** maritime displays and art; 17 The Espl. **Orford:** another holiday town situated on the Prosser River and with good beaches; it's a pleasant walk along along the Old Convict Road on the banks of the Prosser Rive; 7km SW. **Thumbs Lookout:** stunning views of Maria Island/wukaluwikiwayna; 9km SW. **Church of St John the Baptist:** heritage church (1846) with a stained-glass window (rumoured to have been taken from England's Battle Abbey) depicting John the Baptist's life; Buckland; 25km SW.

South-East

Reaching the end of road takes on a whole new meaning when you drive to Cockle Bay south of Hobart, because it's **as far south as you can go** on four wheels in Australia. The south-east region is famous for its **apple orchards**, but it also has **beautiful rainforests** and fascinating history, including pretty **Georgian towns**. A highlight is to catch the ferry across to Bruny Island/lunawanna-allonah for **fabulous local produce and seascapes**.

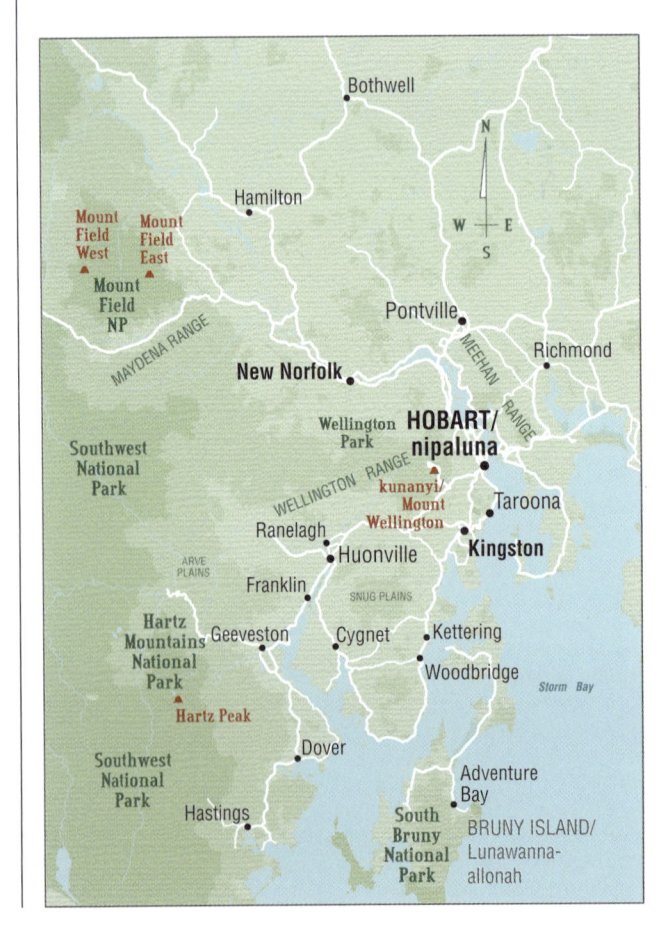

CHEAT SHEET

→ Allow two to three days to tour the region, and a couple of extra days if you want to explore Bruny Island/lunawanna-allonah.

→ Best time to visit: during summer, when the weather is mildest, although always be prepared for a cool change. It's very pretty in spring when the apple orchards are covered in blossoms.

→ Main towns: Cygnet (see p. 453), Huonville (see p. 455), New Norfolk (see p. 455).

→ Tasmania's south-east is the Traditional Lands of the palawa, including the Nuenonne People. One of the most well-known – for all the wrong reasons – is Trukanini (pronounced tru kah nee nee; often called Truganini), one of the last Tasmanian Aboriginal women to survive the onslaught of European settlement. Her story is both horrific and unbearably sad, including witnessing the kidnapping and murder of several of her family members at a young age. There is a monument to her tragic life and death on Bruny Island/lunawanna-allonah.

→ Don't miss: shopping for antiques in New Norfolk; Russell Falls in Mount Field National Park; Tahune Airwalk; driving as far south as you can drive in Australia to Cockle Bay; cider tastings; and Bruny Island/lunawanna-allonah.

Top: Richmond bridge
Opposite: The town of Franklin, Huon Valley

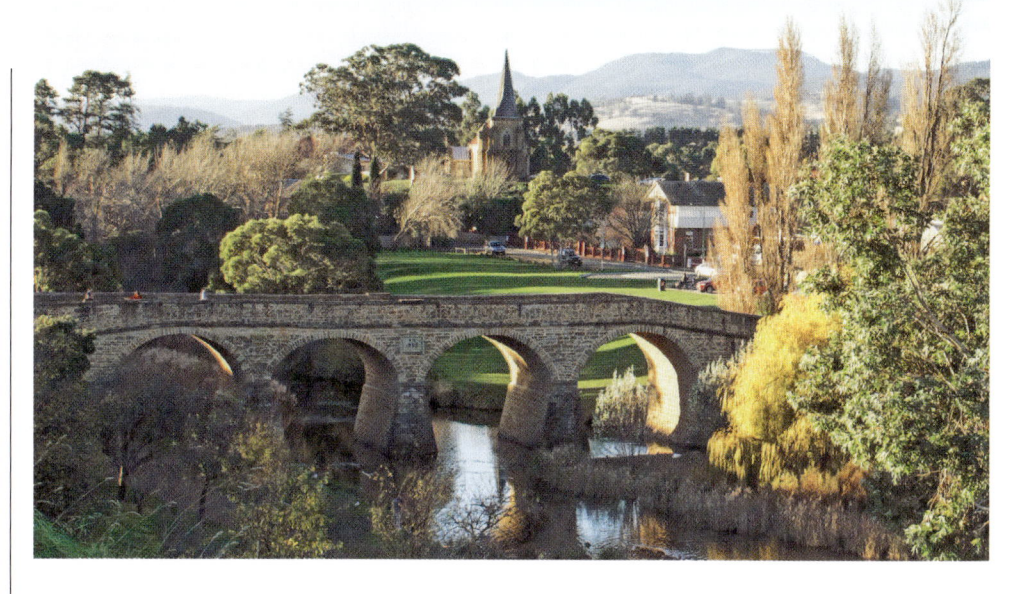

TOP ATTRACTIONS

BRUNY ISLAND CRUISES: Vying for the title of Tasmania's top eco experience, this 3hr cruise takes in the seal colonies, dolphins, humpback whales and birdlife beneath South Bruny's monumental sea cliffs. The ecology and history of the coastline are served up in equal portions. Departs Adventure Bay/kaparati daily; departures also available from Hobart and Kettering. Open 9am–5pm; 1005 Adventure Bay Rd, Bruny Island/lunawanna-allonah; (03) 6293 1465.

GEEVESTON VISITOR CENTRE: Formerly known as the Forest and Heritage Centre, this is much more than just a visitor centre. Comprising four different sections, including the Forest Room and Hartz Gallery, the centre offers a comprehensive look at forest practices with computer games, timber species exhibits and a woodturning viewing area. Church St, Geeveston; (03) 6297 1836.

HASTINGS CAVES AND THERMAL SPRINGS: This is the only cave system in Tasmania occurring in dolomite rather than limestone. Newdegate Cave, which began forming more than 40 million years ago, has stalactites, stalagmites, columns, shawls, flowstone and the more unusual helictites (distorted stalactites), making it – and especially Titania's Palace within it – one of Australia's most beautiful caves. There are 245 steps leading to its vast chambers of formations. Tours run throughout the day but bookings are essential: (03) 6298 3209. Near Newdegate Cave is a thermal pool surrounded by native bushland. It remains at 28°C year-round and is an extremely popular swimming and picnic spot. The Sensory Trail, an easy walk through magnificent forest, starts near the pool.

MONA: Just 11km north of Hobart is the justifiably renowned gallery, the Museum of Old and New Art (MONA). Founded by David Walsh in 2011, the gallery burst on to the world's art scene with its curation of cutting-edge contemporary and ancient artworks. It's mostly underground and a sensory visitor experience as you descend into it. There are permanent and temporary exhibitions, including – at time of research – installations by James Turrell. The acclaimed restaurant Pharos is part of the MONA complex. You can catch the museum's high-speed cataraman, the MONA Roma, from Brooke Street Pier in Hobart and be at MONA in 25min – the ferry has a Posh Pit if you want to travel in real style. The museum makes a great stop if you're driving from Hobart to New Norfolk (see p. 455); 655 Main Rd, Berriedale.

MOUNT FIELD NATIONAL PARK: Tasmania's first national park, Mount Field's best-known attractions are the feathery cascades of Russell and Lady Barron falls. Walking trails pass through lush ferns and rainforests, while the Pandani Grove walk traverses the glaciated landscapes of the alpine country around Lake Dobson. An onsite visitor centre has interpretive displays and a cafe. Mount Field National Park Visitor Information Centre; open 9am–5pm, reduced winter hours; 66 Lake Dobson Rd, National Park; (03) 6288 1149.

RICHMOND GAOL HISTORIC SITE: In the historic and charming town of Richmond (see p. 455), this is one of Australia's best-preserved convict prisons, built (by convicts) in 1825 and once the abode of prisoner Ikey Solomon, said to be the inspiration for Dickens's character Fagin, from *Oliver Twist*. Open 9am–5pm; 37 Bathurst St, Richmond; (03) 6260 2127.

SHOT TOWER: One of the state's most historic industrial buildings (with a National Trust 'A' classification), was completed in 1870 and is in the Hobart suburb of Taroona. There are wonderful views of the Derwent Estuary from the top of the 66m structure and a museum and a tearoom at the base. Open 9am–5pm; 318 Channel Hwy, Taroona; (03) 6227 8885.

SOUTH BRUNY NATIONAL PARK: Much of South Bruny is occupied by this woody national park, crisscrossed with bushwalking trails from easy to challenging. Just east of Adventure Bay/ kaparati is an easy walk to Grass Point from where a more arduous circuit of Fluted Cape kicks off. The Labillardiere Peninsula in the park's south is a walker's delight with tracks through eucalypt woodlands and coastal heath full of wildflowers. Check with the visitor centre; off Adventure Bay Rd, Bruny Island; (03) 6293 1419.

TAHUNE AIRWALK: Opened in 2001, this is one of the longest and highest forest canopy walks in the world. It stretches 597m through the treetops of the Tahune Forest Reserve and, at its highest point, is 48m above the forest floor. Cable hang gliding and river rafting adventures are also available; Arve Rd 28km west of Geeveston; (03) 6251 3903.

WILLIE SMITH'S APPLE SHED: Museum, cidery, distillery and restaurant, with history about the Huon Valley's early settlers and a seasonal display of more than 300 varieties of apples. 2064 Huon Hwy, Huonville; (03) 6266 4345.

OTHER ATTRACTIONS

ARVE FOREST DRIVE: Scenic drive following the Arve River Valley that takes in the Look-In Lookout (an information booth and lookout perch), the Big Tree Lookout (remarkable, large swamp gum), picnic areas and the Keoghs Creek Walk (a great short streamside walk). The drive starts in Geeveston (see p. 453).

AUSTRALASIAN GOLF MUSEUM: Displays of golfing memorabilia and history in Bothwell, the town that's home to Ratho Farm, Australia's oldest golf course (c.1830s); Market Pl, Bothwell; (03) 6259 4033.

BLIGH MUSEUM OF PACIFIC EXPLORATION: This compact curio on Bruny Island/lunawanna-allonah (see p. 453) is constructed from handmade convict bricks; you'll find displays on island history, focusing on the explorers Bligh, Furneaux, Cook and d'Entrecasteaux; 876 Adventure Bay Rd, Bruny Island; (03) 6293 1117.

BONORONG WILDLIFE SANCTUARY: This environmentally attuned wildlife park is a safe haven for injured and threatened Tasmania native animals, including Tasmanian devils, frogs, birds, quolls, pademelons and bettongs. Open 9am–5pm; 593 Briggs Rd, Brighton; (03) 6268 1184.

COCKLE CREEK: The southernmost point of Australia that can be reached by car, Cockle Creek is surrounded by beautiful beaches and mountainous terrain and is at the end of the multi-day South Coast Walking Track. It's 42km south of Dover (see p. 453).

HARTZ MOUNTAINS NATIONAL PARK: The Huon Valley used to be wholly glaciated and this national park displays some remarkable glacial features and morainal deposits. Hartz Lake is the largest of the glacial lakes that surround the 1255m high Hartz Mountain. There are walking tracks through forests of Tasmanian waratah, snow gums, yellow gum and alpine heath, and Waratah Lookout affords fantastic views. Self-guided brochure and park pass are available from the visitor centre. Off Arve Rd. The park is 23km south-west of Geeveston (see p. 453).

OLD HOBART TOWN MODEL VILLAGE: Taking three years to build, this intricate model of Hobart in the 1820s is a real labour of love. Open 9am–5pm; 21A Bridge St, Richmond; (03) 6260 2502.

PEPPERMINT BAY HOTEL: This is one of Tasmania's most popular gastronomic experiences, with a first-class restaurant and a store full of local products. There are fine views across the waterfront. The **Peppermint Bay Cruise** departs from Hobart and tours D'Entrecasteaux Channel along the way. 3435 Channel Hwy, Woodbridge; (03) 6267 4088; cruise bookings on 1800 751 229.

RATHO FARM: Home to the first game of golf in Australia, Ratho was the elegant 'gentleman's residence' of Alexander Reid in the early 1800s, situated in the historic town of Bothwell (see p. 453). It is a stone house with wooden Ionic columns. The famous golf course is still intact and in use. Lake Hwy, Bothwell.

SALMON PONDS: The first rainbow- and brown-trout hatchery in Australia, in operation since 1864. There's a pancake restaurant and barbecue huts in heritage gardens. Open 9am–3pm; 70 Salmon Ponds Rd, Plenty; (03) 6261 5663. It's 10km north-west of New Norfolk (see p. 455).

SOUTHWEST NATIONAL PARK: Tasmania's largest national park offers walking tracks of varying difficulty, beautiful scenic drives and plentiful fishing. Contact Parks & Wildlife Service in Huonville for up-to-date information on track and weather conditions; (03) 6264 8460.

ZOODOO ZOO: This Wildlife Park is on a 330ha farm, and is home to native fauna including Tasmanian devils, pademelons and wallabies, plus imported wonders such as lions, zebras and pythons. The kids will love it! Open 9am–5pm; 620 Middle Tea Tree Rd; (03) 6260 2444. It's 7km west of Richmond (see p. 455).

Top: Starry sky at Cape Bruny Lighthouse **Bottom:** Echidna at Bonorong Wildlife Sanctuary

VISITOR INFORMATION

Hobart Travel Centre
20 Davey St, Hobart
(03) 6238 4222
hobarttravelcentre.com.au
hobartandbeyond.com.au

Bruny D'Entrecasteaux Visitor Centre
Ferry Terminal, Kettering
(03) 6263 4494
brunyisland.org.au

Huon Valley
discovertasmania.com.au/places/hobart-and-south/huon-valley

KEY TOWNS

ADVENTURE BAY/KAPARATI (BRUNY ISLAND/LUNAWANNA-ALLONAH)
Population 218

Beach yourself in laidback Adventure Bay, known in palawa kani as kaparati, for your Bruny Island/lunawanna-allonah stay, a 20min car-ferry ride from Kettering (see p. 454), south of Hobart. Adventure Bay is the main town on largely undeveloped Bruny Island, a highlight of any Tassie trip. The island comprises two main land masses – North Bruny and South Bruny – joined by a narrow isthmus known as the Neck. One side of the isthmus is scoured by the waves of the Tasman Sea; the other faces onto the D'Entrecasteaux Channel. In the 1770s, James Cook and Tobias Furneaux interacted amicably with Adventure Bay's Nuenonne People, but the sealers and whalers who subsequently came to Bruny decimated the population. Amid the island's spectacular scenery, various memorials stand as stark reminders of the grim past. Adventure Bay itself remains a low-key holiday town, with a shop, a caravan park and a loose collection of holiday shacks.

SEE & DO Bruny Island Cruises; South Bruny National Park: see Top Attractions. **Bligh Museum of Pacific Exploration:** see Other Attractions. **Truganini Memorial:** 100 years after the death of Bruny Island/lunawanna-allonah born Trukanini (Truganini), her ashes were scattered in the sea off Bruny, as she had wished (see p. 451 for more of her story). At the Neck (the isthmus between North and South Bruny) there's a boardwalk and stairway up a steep dune to a memorial and lookout with 360-degree views; 11km N. **Birdlife:** little penguins and short-tailed shearwaters (aka muttonbirds) inhabit Bruny's ocean beaches; look for them at dusk at the Neck in summer; Bruny Island Main Rd; 11km N. **Cape Bruny Lighthouse:** the second oldest lighthouse in Australia (1836), designed by noted architect John Lee Archer; guided tours are available and the views are spectacular; Lighthouse Rd, South Bruny National Park via Lunawanna; 29km SW. **Nebraska Beach:** on North Bruny, with safe swimming and picnic facilities; Nebraska Rd, Dennes Point; 40km N. **Cloudy Bay:** a magnificent, isolated surf beach; Cloudy Bay Rd; 18km S.

BOTHWELL
Population 379

Bothwell is a charming historic town and boasts more than 50 National Trust–classified buildings. Australia's first golf course was created in Bothwell in 1837, making golf a point of pride.

SEE & DO Australasian Golf Museum; Ratho Farm: see Other Attractions. **Heritage Walk:** Bothwell has 53 colonial-era cottages, churches, houses and official buildings around Queens Park. Notable are the Georgian brick **Slate Cottage** and **St Luke's Church.** The best way to appreciate the historic buildings is by a self-guided walking tour; pamphlet from visitor centre at the Australasian Golf Museum, see Other Attractions. **Trout fishing:** some of Australia's best freshwater fishing in the region. A favourite among trout anglers is the Ouse River, which joins the Derwent north of Hamilton. Other spots include the Clyde, Jordan and Coal rivers east of the Derwent, and the Tyenna, Styx and Plenty rivers west of the Derwent; contact visitor centre for details.

CYGNET
Population 1057

Cygnet is a picturesque town in the Huon Valley and a fruit-growing and artistic community. In spring, the surrounding area blooms with magnificent wattle, apple and pear blossoms.

SEE & DO **Living History Museum:** memorabilia, historic photos; open Fri–Sun; Mary St. **Town square:** Presbytery, Catholic church (with stained-glass windows dedicated to lost miners) and convent; popular photo spot. **Near and Far:** handcrafts and gifts; Mary St. **Birdwatching:** black swans and other species inhabit Port Cygnet; viewing areas off Channel Hwy. **Wineries:** many including Hartzview Vineyard, known for pinot noir, ports and liqueurs. There are cellar-door tastings and sales; Gardners Bay; 10km SE. **Beaches:** good boat-launching facilities and beaches at Randalls Bay (14km S), Eggs and Bacon Bay (15km S) and Verona Sands (18km S). **Ninepin Point Marine Nature Reserve:** reef; near Verona Sands; 18km S. **Fishing:** sea-run trout and brown trout from the Huon River; west and south of town. **Berry orchards:** orchards with pick-your-own sales.

DOVER
Population 521

Dover lies beside the waters of Esperance Bay and the D'Entrecasteaux Channel, with the imposing figure of Adamsons Peak in the background. The three islands directly offshore are called Faith, Hope and Charity. The town is a popular destination for yachting enthusiasts.

SEE & DO **Commandant's Office:** well-preserved remnant of Dover's penal history; Beach Rd. **Faith Island:** several historic graves; access by boat. **Walking trails:** epic Tasmanian Trail to Devonport, as well as Dover Coast and Duckhole Lake tracks; details from visitor centre. **Beaches:** safe swimming beaches surround town.

TASMANIA

453

GEEVESTON
Population 658

Geeveston, on the cusp of enormous Southwest National Park, is driven by thriving timber and forestry industries, and slow-moving timber trucks frequent the roads. The other principal industry, apple farming, is responsible for the magnificent apple blossom in late Sept. Geeveston is the gateway to Hartz Mountains National Park.

SEE & DO **Geeveston Visitor Centre; Tahune Airwalk:** *see* Top Attractions for both. **Arve Forest Drive; Hartz Mountains National Park:** *see* Other Attractions for both. **Swamp Gum:** the trunk of a logged eucalypt 15.8m in length and weighing 57 tonnes, stands on the highway as the town's mascot.

HASTINGS
Population 54

Hastings lies in Tasmania's far south and is known for the eponymous stunning dolomite caves to its west. The caves were discovered in 1917 by a group of timber workers who, among others, flocked to the small town in more prosperous days.

SEE & DO **Hastings Caves and Thermal Springs:** *see* Top Attractions. **Cockle Creek:** *see* Other Attractions. **Southport:** seaside town and one of the oldest settlements in the area; good fishing, swimming, surfing and bushwalking; 6km SE. **Hastings Forest Tour:** this self-drive tour begins off Hastings Rd west of town, leads north to the Esperance River, then heads to Dover. Short walks and picnic spots en route; map available from visitor centre.

HUONVILLE
Population 2071

Huonville produces more than half of Tasmania's apples and is surrounded by blossoming fields of apples, cherries, plums, pears and berries. Willie Smith's Apple Shed tells the history of the orchards and growers. Although Huonville is relatively small, it is a prosperous community and the largest town in the Huon Valley.

SEE & DO **Willie Smith's Apple Shed:** *see* Top Attractions. **Huon River Jet Boats:** exciting 35min jet-boat rides along Huon River rapids; bookings on (03) 6264 1838; The Espl. **Market:** Town Hall, Main Rd; 1st and 3rd Sun each month. **Ranelagh:** has the atmosphere of a charming English village, complete with an old oast house to process the hops; 5km NW. **Wooden Boat Centre Tasmania:** workshop and interpretive centre; Main St, Franklin; 8km SW. **Pelverata Falls:** stunning waterfall with medium-to-difficult walk over scree slope; 14km SE. **Fishing:** good trout fishing in Huon River and tributaries.

KETTERING
Population 408

The area around Kettering was explored in 1792 by Bruni D'Entrecasteaux, after whom the adjoining channel is named. The town was settled in the 1800s by timber cutters, sealers and whalers, and the community was a transient one. Kettering is now principally the launching point to Bruny Island/lunawanna-allonah, but is charming in its own right with a sheltered harbour full of yachts and fishing vessels.

SEE & DO **Peppermint Bay:** *see* Other Attractions. **Oyster Cove Marina:** well-known marina with boats for hire, skippered cruises and fishing charters; Ferry Rd. **Nutpatch Chocolates:** Handmade fine chocolates; open 10am–4pm; 2956 Channel Hwy; 0428 870 891. **Woodbridge Hill Handweaving Studio:** weaving tuition and sales of products woven from silk, cotton, linen, wool, alpaca, mohair and collie-dog hair; open Mon–Thurs 9am–5pm, Fri and Sun 9am–1pm (call ahead in winter; 0408 187 479); 269 Woodbridge Hill Rd; 4km S. **Channel Historical and Folk Museum:** displays of historical memorabilia of the D'Entrecasteaux Channel region; open Sun–Fri; 1755 Channel Hwy, Margate; 12km N. **Coningham:** good swimming and boating beaches; 6km N. **Snug Falls:** pleasant 1hr return walk to falls; 8km N. **Grandvewe Sheep Cheesery and Hartshorn Distillery:** range of sheep's cheese as well as gin and vodka distilled from sheep cheese whey; Birchs Bay; 9km S. **Bruny Island ferry:** trips throughout the day from Ferry Rd Terminal; for information on the island, *see* Adventure Bay/kaparati (p. 453).

KINGSTON
Population 12,288

This pleasant seaside suburb sits just beyond Hobart's city limits. It has a laidback and relaxed feel and beaches.

SEE & DO **Shot Tower:** *see* Top Attractions. **Brookfield Markets:** bric-a-brac and crafts at Brookfield, Margate; Wed to Sat. **Kingston Beach:** popular, family-friendly beach with plenty of shade and nice cafes nearby; 3km SE. **Kingston Beach Golf Course:** well-regarded 18-hole course with specific holes picked by international

Top: Chocolates and cheese at Coal River Farm

TOP EVENTS

- JAN Folk Festival (Cygnet)
- FEB Mona Foma music and arts festival (Hobart and Launceston)
- FEB–MAR International Highland SpinIn and Fibre Festival (odd-numbered years, Bothwell)
- MAR A Taste of the Huon (Huonville)
- APR Derwent Valley Autumn Festival (New Norfolk)
- JUNE Dark Mofo
- JUL Huon Valley Mid Winter Festival (Huonville)
- NOV Agricultural Show (Huonville)

TEMPERATURES

Jan: 9–22°C

July: 1–12°C

---

players as their favourites; 1 Channel Hwy; (03) 6229 8300. **Boronia Hill Flora Trail:** 2km track follows ridge line between Kingston and Blackmans Bay through remnant bush; begins at end of Jindabyne Rd and finishes at Peter Murrell Reserve, renowned for its many native orchids; Kingston. **Blackmans Bay blowhole:** small blowhole at the northern end of the beach; Blowhole Rd; 7km S. **Alum Cliffs walk:** excellent scenic 45min return walk from rom Kingston Beach along the coastal cliffs to Taroona. **Margate Train:** 1950s passenger train (non-operational) with tearooms in the buffet car, and collectibles, lollies and book shops in other carriages. Sun market; 1567 Channel Hwy, Margate; 9km S. **Scenic drives:** south through Blackmans Bay, Tinderbox and Howden, with magnificent views of Droughty Point, South Arm Peninsula, Storm Bay and Bruny Island/lunawanna-allonah from Piersons Point. **Fishing:** good bream fishing at Browns River, for sport but not for the pan.

NEW NORFOLK
Population 6153

New Norfolk is 'olde worlde' – an antiques and history hub in the beautiful Derwent Valley. This National Trust–classified town has colonial-era buildings, heritage gardens and hop fields in nearby Bushy Park. The town was named after European settlers from the abandoned Norfolk Island penal settlement who were granted land here. New Norfolk is near Mount Field National Park and an easy daytrip from MONA or Hobart.

SEE & DO Mount Field National Park; MONA: see Top Attractions for both. **Salmon Ponds:** see Other Attractions. **Church of St Matthew:** reputedly the oldest church in Tasmania (1823). One of the stained-glass windows behind the nativity scene features the likeness of 9-year-old Nancy Hope Shoobridge, a local girl who died in 1890; 6 Bathurst St; (03) 6261 2223. **Bush Inn Hotel:** claimed as the longest continuously licensed pub in Tasmania (built 1815, licensed 1825), with resident ghost; 49–51 Montagu St; (03) 6261 2256. **Pulpit Rock Lookout:** sweeping valley and town views; Pulpit Rock Rd. **Antique and collectibles outlets:** a dozen of Tasmania's best antiques and collectibles shops, most within easy walking distance; map from visitor centre. **Two Metre Tall Brewery:** excellent craft beers and ciders at the Farm Bar; open Thurs–Sun 12am–4pm; 2862 Lyell Hwy, Hayes; (03) 6261 1930; 13km NW. **Possum Shed:** locally made crafts and collectibles, and riverside cafe with delicious coffee; open Wed–Sun 10am–4pm; 1654 Gordon River Rd, Westerway; 31km NW. **Styx Big Tree Reserve:** small reserve with the tallest flowering plants in the world, the giant swamp gums (*Eucalyptus regnans*), the biggest of which is 92m tall; off Gordon River Rd, Styx Valley via Maydena; 73km W.

PONTVILLE
Population 675

On the banks of the Jordon River, this former garrison town, established in 1821, sits on land that was once a palawa travelling route between Tasmania's north and south. One of the soldiers based here in the early days of settlement, Private Hugh Germain, is allegedly responsible for the unusual names found in the region, such as Bagdad, Jericho, Lake Tiberius and Jordan River. Legend has it that Germain carried with him copies of *Arabian Nights* and the Bible and found his inspiration within. There is a wealth of history in and around the town.

SEE & DO Bonorong Wildlife Sanctuary: see Other Attractions. **Historic Buildings:** buildings from Pontville's early days include the Romanesque **St Mark's Church** (1841), the **Sheiling** (1819) and the **Row** (thought to have been built in 1824 as soldiers' quarters). **Lark Distillery:** an extensive 1819 estate now making whisky with tasting room and cellar door, tasting room; guided tours are available, book online at larkdistillery.com; 76 Shene Rd; 4km N. **Historic towns:** Brighton (3km S), Tea Tree (7km E), Bagdad (8km N), Broadmarsh (10km W) and Kempton (19km N).

RICHMOND
Population 934

Just 27km north of Hobart, Richmond is an improbably picturesque colonial-era village and a popular daytrip destination. It is one of the most important historic towns in Tasmania. Richmond Bridge is the oldest surviving bridge in Australia, built by convicts under appalling conditions in 1823. It's also reputed to be haunted. But Richmond isn't all grim: there are some lovely places to sleep and eat here, boutiques and gift shops, an old-fashioned lolly shop, a maze and the wineries of the Coal River Valley are nearby.

SEE & DO Richmond Gaol Historic Site: see Top Attractions. **Old Hobart Town Model Village** and **Zoodoo Zoo:** see Other Attractions. **Amaze Richmond:** two-stage maze with surprise ending, plus puzzle corner, gardens and big Devonshire teas; 13 Bridge St; (03) 6260 2451. **History walk:** self-guided tour around the many heritage buildings throughout town, including **Ivy Cottage**, **St Luke's Church of England**, **St John's Church**, the old **Village Store** and the boozy **Richmond Arms** pub; pick up a map from Old Hobart Town Model Village. **Richmond farmers' and makers market:** every Sat. **Coal River wine region:** cellar-door tastings and sales at the cool-climate wineries between Richmond and Hobart, including **Frogmore Creek** (9km S), **Pooley Wines** (1km W) and **Puddleduck Vineyard** (6km S); you can also visit **Coal River Farm** in Cambridge for artisan chocolates and cheese and an onsite restaurant. **Scenic drive:** go exploring from Campania to Colebrook.

Western Wilderness

On a crowded planet where real wilderness is increasingly rare, it's reassuring to know that places like **Tasmania's World Heritage–listed South-west Wilderness** still exist. The region's **old mining towns** may be slowly scrubbing themselves up, but **the forests, rivers and mountains** here remain unchanged, as they have been for millennia.

CHEAT SHEET

→ Allow at least one week to explore Tassie's wild west, and longer if you're heading off on a bushwalk – highly likely in this wilderness of walking trails.

→ Best time to visit: Tasmania's western wilderness zone is wet and windy, battered by the Roaring Forties winds and receiving up to 3m of rain annually. Visit in summer!

→ Main towns: Queenstown (see p. 459) and Strahan (see p. 459).

→ Tasmania's south-west is the traditional homelands of the palawa and pakana, including the peerapper and toogee Peoples.

→ Did you know? The hillsides around Queenstown – once the richest mining town in the world – have long been denuded of vegetation, the result of pollution from copper mines and smelters. These days pollution levels from all the region's mines are strictly controlled, and you might even see a few patches of green re-emerging.

→ Don't miss: West Coast Wilderness Railway; Gordon River cruises; Ocean Beach; West Coast Heritage Centre.

Top: West Coast Heritage Centre, Zeehan **Opposite:** takayna/Tarkine wilderness near Corinna/kurina

TOP ATTRACTIONS

GALLEY MUSEUM: This extensive museum is housed in 21 rooms of the Imperial (1898), Queenstown's (see p. 459) first brick hotel, and displays over 800 photographs and historic west coast memorabilia. The maternity ward is especially interesting. Cnr Sticht and Driffield sts, Queenstown; (03) 6471 1483.

GORDON RIVER CRUISES: Day-long cruises and evening dinner cruises depart from Strahan (see p. 459) and journey across the harbour and up the river to Heritage Landing, where there's a short walk to see a 2000-year-old Huon pine. Cruises include tours of Sarah Island. Book at the visitor centre in Strahan: (03) 6472 6800.

MONTEZUMA FALLS: This waterfall is the highest in Tasmania at 104m. It is accessed from the former township of Williamsford on a 3hr return walk through rainforest. There is a viewing platform and swing bridge at the falls. It's 11km south-west of Rosebery (see p. 459).

PIEMAN RIVER CRUISE: This 4hr return lunch cruise aboard *Arcadia II* travels down the Pieman River/ruyinrim through untouched riverside rainforest to rugged Pieman Head, or there's a shorter cruise aboard *Sweetwater* to Savage River and Lovers Falls. You can return on foot through the forest from Savage River if you choose. Leaves from Corinna/kurina (see p. 459); daily; (03) 6446 1170.

SARAH ISLAND HISTORIC SITE: The ruins of this fascinating World Heritage-listed convict station are still out in Macquarie Harbour. A particularly cruel environment, Sarah Island was shut down in 1833, but not before convict Alexander Pearce had managed to escape. Pearce and seven others set off for Hobart but found the terrain too tough an adversary to overcome. Pearce, alone when discovered, was suspected of cannibalism. The following year he escaped again, once more killing and consuming his cohort. Pearce finally made it to Hobart, where he was recaptured and executed. Gordon River cruises stop for a tour of the island; check with the visitor centre in Strahan (see p. 459).

WEST COAST HERITAGE CENTRE: This fascinating heritage complex in Zeehan (see p. 459) includes the original **Zeehan School of Mines and Metallurgy** building (1894), which houses extensive photography galleries depicting the region's early mining community. There are world-class collections of minerals including Tasmania's unique fire-red crocoite, as well as displays of railway history, locomotives and mining machinery. Also at the West Coast Heritage Centre, visitors can walk through a **Masonic Lodge Hall** and explore the gorgeous old **Gaiety Theatre** (1898), once Australia's largest theatre, where Edwardian films are shown daily and there is a fine collection of theatre posters. 114 Main St, Zeehan; (03) 6471 6225.

WEST COAST VISITOR INFORMATION CENTRE: This jauntily designed centre in Strahan (see p. 459) has an impressive historical display on Tasmania's south-west, including First Nations history, European settlement, and more recent events such as the fight to save the Franklin River from being dammed in the early 1980s. But the amphitheatre offers the real highlight: an audiovisual slideshow and a nightly performance of *The Ship That Never Was*, about a convict escape. Open 10am–6.30pm; The Espl, Strahan; (03) 6472 6800 or 1800 352 200.

WEST COAST WILDERNESS RAILWAY: This restored 1896 rack-and-pinion railway winds through pristine forested valleys between Queenstown and Strahan, crossing 40 bridges. Bookings on (03) 6471 0100.

OTHER ATTRACTIONS

FRANKLIN–GORDON WILD RIVERS NATIONAL PARK: This 4463sqkm park has UNESCO World Heritage listing as part of the Tasmanian Wilderness World Heritage Area, after the state government tried to dam the Franklin River in the 1980s. Protests against the damming were so heated and widespread that the federal government and High Court stepped in and vetoed the proposal, saving the dense temperate rainforest and wild rivers that make up the park. Visitors can go kayaking and whitewater rafting, and there are many bush trails for experienced hikers. A four-day walk to Frenchmans Cap takes in magnificent alpine scenery as it scales one of Tasmnia's most prominent peaks. The 40min return walk to Donaghys Hill (much easier) overlooks the Franklin and Collingwood rivers. Gordon River cruises depart from Strahan. Off Lyell Hwy; Parks & Wildlife Service Strahan (03) 6472 6020.

OCEAN BEACH: Tasmania's longest beach (36km) offers long beach walks and beach fishing. The Roaring Forties wind is strong here and the ocean swells can be huge. See short-tailed shearwaters in their burrows (Oct–Mar) and no-one else within miles; Ocean Beach Rd. It's 6km west of Strahan.

STRATHGORDON: The place to see Tasmania's massive hydro-electricity industry in action. Drive along Gordon River Rd past Lake Pedder and Lake Gordon to the Gordon Dam (abseiling down the dam wall will get your heart pumping) to peer down onto the underground Gordon Power Station; Gordon River Rd; 332km SE (by road) of Strahan.

VISITOR INFORMATION

West Coast Visitor Information Centre
12 The Espl, Strahan
(03) 6472 6800 or
1800 352 200
westcoasttas.com.au

TOP EVENTS

→ JAN Mount Lyell Strahan Picnic (Strahan)
→ FEB Rosebery Festival
→ OCT Unconformity (biennial arts festival, Queenstown)

TEMPERATURES

Jan: 11–21°C

July: 5–12°C

The fascinating old mining town of Queenstown

KEY TOWNS

CORINNA/KURINA

Tiny Corinna/kurina has fascinating late 19th-century goldmining heritage and is at the southern end of the rainforest wilderness of takayna/Tarkine. It has become an eco travel destination. If you are coming from the south, you'll cross the Pieman River/ruyinrim on a barge called the Fatman.

SEE & DO **Pieman River Cruise:** see Top Attractions. **Corinna Wilderness Experience:** self-guided kayak tours; bookings (03) 6446 1170. **Walks:** various walks from the accessible Huon Pine Walk to the Whyte River Walk with boardwalks and more challenging ones. **Tarkine Hotel:** a tavern serving Tasmanian produce, wines and beers. Food is served only in summer.

QUEENSTOWN
Population 1772

The discovery of gold and other mineral resources in the Mount Lyell field in the 1880s led to the rapid building of the town of Queenstown. Continuous mining here from 1893 to 1994 produced over 670,000 tonnes of copper, 510,000kg of silver and 20,000kg of gold. Operations began again in 1995 before ceasing in 2014. The town has modern facilities, but its wide streets and historic buildings give it an old-mining-town flavour. In certain lights the hillsides, denuded through a combination of felling, wildfire, erosion and poisonous fumes from the smelter, reflect the sun's rays and turn amazing shades of pink and gold. The landscape is often compared to a moonscape. The road into Queenstown from the south is a steep switchback route through bare and often misty hills, adding to the town's unusual beauty.

SEE & DO **Galley Museum; West Coast Wilderness Railway:** see Top Attractions for both. **Spion Kop Lookout:** views of Queenstown and surrounding mountains; off Bowes St. **Paragon Theatre:** cinema; McNamara St. **RoamWild Tours:** guided tours of Queenstown and its fascinating mining history from underground and surface tours of the current workings to lost mines deep in the forest. Also tours of the unique Lake Margaret hydro-electricity facility; bookings 0407 049 612. **Iron Blow Lookout:** walkway overlooking the original open-cut mine where gold was discovered in 1883; Gormanston; 6km E. **Linda:** ghost town; 7km E. **Mount Jukes Lookout:** superb panoramic views; 7km S. **Lake Burbury:** excellent brown and rainbow trout fishing; picnic areas; 8km E. **Nelson Falls:** short walk through temperate rainforest leads to falls; 23km E. **Valley views:** spectacular views from Lyell Hwy as it climbs steeply out of town.

ROSEBERY
Population 749

Like the nearby towns of Queenstown, Strahan and Zeehan, Rosebery found its economic niche in mining. The region is also known for its ancient rainforests, home to the Tasmania's endemic Huon pine, which grows so slowly there are specimens that are among the oldest living things on Earth.

SEE & DO **Montezuma Falls:** see Top Attractions for both. **Mine:** gold was discovered at Rosebery in 1893 and zinc ore soon after. MMG operates an underground mine extracting zinc, lead, copper, silver and gold. A yearly open day is held at the mine and advertised locally; (03) 6473 1801. **Stitt Falls:** 10min rainforest walk from Stitt Park. **Wee Georgie Wood Steam Train:** a 2km ride along a scenic track on a fully restored heritage steam train; 1st Sun and last Sat–Sun each month 10am–3pm Oct–May; Tullah; weegeorgiewood.com.au; 12km NE. **Mount Murchison:** difficult but worthwhile 4hr return walk rising to a 1275m peak through ancient alpine forests; 14km SE. **Fishing:** good trout fishing in nearby Lakes Rosebery, Mackintosh and Murchison; north and east of town.

★ STRAHAN
Population 634

Super-scenic Strahan is the wild west coast's most urbane town: a little bit of polish in an otherwise rugged realm. A pretty little port on Macquarie Harbour, Strahan is the last stop before the long stretch of ocean to Patagonia. It might be one of the loneliest places on the planet, but Strahan was once dubbed 'The Best Little Town in the World' by the *Chicago Tribune* and attracts a steady stream of visitors. Strahan (pronounced 'strawn') came into being as a penal colony working in tandem with the isolated Sarah Island prison. These days Strahan is known for fine seafood and you can explore the Gordon River on a river cruise from here.

SEE & DO **West Coast Visitor Information Centre; West Coast Wilderness Railway; Gordon River Cruises; Sarah Island:** see Top Attractions for all. **Ocean Beach:** see Other Attractions. **Morrison's Huon Pine Sawmill:** one of the last remaining Huon pine sawmills in Tasmania; open by arrangement, tours; The Espl; (03) 6471 7235. **Ormiston House:** built in 1899 and a classic example of Federation architecture, surrounded by magnolia trees and expansive gardens. It's essentially an accommodation outfit these days; 1 The Espl; (03) 6471 7077. **Water Tower Hill Lookout:** views over the town rooftops and out across the harbour; Esk St. **Peoples Park:** a lush picnic spot in a botanic garden setting with a 45min return rainforest walk to Hogarth Falls; Hibiscus Crt, off The Espl. **Henty Sand Dunes:** vast sand dune system with sandboards and toboggans for hire; off Zeehan–Strahan Rd; 12km N. **Cape Sorell Lighthouse:** elegant 45m high lighthouse built in 1899 – purportedly the third-tallest in Australia; access via Macquarie Harbour south head; 23km SW.

ZEEHAN
Population 702

After silver-lead deposits were discovered here in 1882, Zeehan boomed and between 1893 and 1908, the mine yielded ore worth $8 million which led to its nickname, the 'Silver City of the West'. However, from 1910 the mine started to slow and Zeehan declined, threatening to become a ghost town. Fortunately, the nearby Renison Bell tin mine has drawn workers back to the area and the whole town is National Trust–classified.

SEE & DO **West Coast Heritage Centre:** see Top Attractions. **Historic buildings:** It's worth visiting the **West Coast Heritage Centre** to explore Zeehan's history, including historic buildings. Other buildings of historic interest include the post office, bank and St Luke's Church. **Scenic drives:** self-guided drives in town and nearby; brochure from visitor centre. **Fishing:** Trial Harbour (20km W) and Granville Harbour (35km NW) are popular fishing spots. **Lake Pieman:** boating and good trout fishing; 42km NW.

North-West

Tasmania's north-west corner is crammed full of natural wonders, from the iconic saw-toothed peaks of **Cradle Mountain** to the flat-topped circular headland known as **The Nut** in the charming town of Stanley. Drive the Bass Highway from Ulverstone to Stanley – it's the Apple Isle's version of the Great Ocean Road. Snap a selfie beside the **Big Penguin** – keep an eye out on the beaches after dark and you might be lucky enough to watch real ones waddle past. If you venture to remote King Island, you can taste some of the country's best beef and soft cheeses.

CHEAT SHEET

→ Allow around two-three days to explore the region, and a couple of extra days if you want to explore King Island.

→ Best time to visit: during summer, when the weather is mildest, although always be prepared for a cool change. The annual tulip festival is held at Table Cape near Wynyard in late September through to October.

→ Main towns: Burnie (see p. 463), Devonport (see p. 463), Stanley (see p. 465).

→ Tasmania's north-west is the Traditional Land of the palawa, including the peerapper, tommeginne, tyerrernotepanner and takayna Peoples.

→ Don't miss: King Island Dairy; the view from the top of The Nut at Stanley and the Edge of the World Lookout; Cradle Mountain and the murals of Sheffield.

Top: The House of Anvers chocolate, Latrobe
Opposite: Mount Gnomon Farm near Penguin

TOP ATTRACTIONS

AUSTRALIAN AXEMAN'S HALL OF FAME: This attraction honours the region's renowned axemen and the role of the town of Latrobe (see p. 464) in the creation of woodchop competitions. There's a cafe and gift shop. Bells Pde, Latrobe; (03) 6426 2099.

BASS HIGHWAY: The spectacular scenery on the Ulverstone to Stanley section of this highway recalls Victoria's Great Ocean Road. The route's highlights include the little penguins at Lillico Beach, Burnie and Stanley (see p. 465), the colourful fields of Table Cape Tulip Farm near Wynyard, and the picturesque town of Boat Harbour (see p. 462).

BASS STRAIT MARITIME CENTRE: See detailed models and displays from the days of sail through the age of steam, to the present sea-going passenger ferries. Open 10am–3pm; 6 Gloucester Ave, Devonport; (03) 6424 2790.

CRADLE MOUNTAIN–LAKE ST CLAIR NATIONAL PARK: Covering 124,942ha, this national park has over 25 major peaks, including the state's highest, Mount Ossa, and possibly its most spectacular, Cradle Mountain. The terrain is marked by pristine waterfalls, U-shaped valleys, dolerite formations, forests of deciduous beech, Tasmanian myrtle, pandani and King Billy pine, and swathes of wildflowers. There are many tracks for all levels of experience; visitors should always check for up-to-date information on conditions. The most famous walk is the six-day Overland Track, a 65km trail through alpine wilderness to Lake St Clair at the southern end of the park; it is one of Australia's best-known walks for experienced, well-equipped walkers; bookings are essential in summer and luxury guided walks are also available. Shorter trails include the Dove Lake Loop Track, a 2hr walk circling pretty Dove Lake in the shadow of Cradle Mountain; the 10min Rainforest Walk, through a patch of cool temperate rainforest behind the visitor centre; the easy 20min Weindorfers Forest Walk, through a glade of pines and myrtles; the 30min Enchanted Walk, beside pools and waterfalls; and the more arduous 8hr Summit Walk to the top of Cradle Mountain. For bookings, contact Parks & Wildlife Service, Mon–Fri (03) 6165 4254; for information, contact Cradle Mountain National Park Visitor Centre, 4057 Cradle Mountain Rd; (03) 6492 1110.

DON RIVER RAILWAY: Check out the largest collection of historic locomotives and carriages in Tasmania and hop on an hourly train ride along Don River to Coles Beach. Open Wed–Thurs and Sat–Sun 9am–4.30pm, trains run Wed–Sun; Forth Main Rd, Don; (03) 6424 6335.

EMU VALLEY RHODODENDRON GARDENS: Considered the city's floral emblem, the rhododendron has pride of place in the city of Burnie (see p. 463). These gardens have 22,000 wild and hybrid rhododendrons on display. The best time to visit is Sept–Nov and there's a floral festival here in Oct; off Cascade Rd, Burnie; (03) 6433 1805.

GUNNS PLAINS CAVES: Underground streams, limestone shawls and glow worms in well-lit, visitor-friendly caves. Tours daily on the hour from 10am, on the half-hour from 1.30pm. Caves Rd, Gunns Plains; (03) 6429 1388.

HIGHFIELD HISTORIC SITE: Dating back to 1832, the gracious old homestead of Highfield in Stanley (see p. 465) is the former headquarters of the Van Diemen's Land (VDL) Company. It has 12 rooms, a chapel, convict barracks, a schoolhouse, stables, a barn, workers' cottages and large gardens. Open 9.30am–4.30pm, reduced winter hours; Green Hills Rd, Stanley; (03) 6458 1100.

KING ISLAND DAIRY: Internationally recognised King Island Dairy has a tasting room stocked with its award-winning cheeses; North Rd, Currie; (03) 6462 0947.

PINMATIK/ROCKY CAPE NATIONAL PARK: With some of the best preserved palawa rock shelters and middens in Tasmania, the park at pinmatik/Rocky Cape incorporates Sisters Beach. Contact Parks & Wildlife Service on (03) 6458 1480 or 1300 827 727. The park is 29km north-west of Wynyard (see p. 465).

TABLE CAPE LOOKOUT: Brilliant views of the coast from 190m above sea level. En route to the lookout is **Table Cape Tulip Farm**, with tulips, daffodils and Dutch irises blooming Sept–Oct. From a lookout a short walk leads to the 1888 **Table Cape Lighthouse**. It's 5km north of Wynyard (see p. 465).

TASMANIAN ARBORETUM: A 58ha collection of Tasmanian plants, Southern Hemisphere conifers and Northern Hemisphere forest species. There are picnic areas, walking tracks and a lake where you can spy waterbirds and platypus. Open 9am–sunset; 46 Old Tramway Rd, Eugenana; (03) 6427 2690. Its 10km south of Devonport (see p. 463).

THE NUT: The Nut looms large above the charming seaside town of Stanley (see p. 465) and the surrounding sea and provides panoramic coastal views. To get to the top you can either walk up a very steep, challenging track, or take the chairlift. There's a 40min circuit walk around the cliffs at the top. Off Browns Rd, Stanley.

OTHER ATTRACTIONS

BOAT HARBOUR: A picturesque seaside village and popular holiday spot. Boat Harbour Beach (4km north-west of town) has good swimming, marine life in pools at low tide, fishing and waterskiing.

DEVILS@CRADLE: Located near the entrance to Cradle Mountain-Lake St Clair National Park, see Tasmanian devils up close; daytime keeper tours and after-dark feeding tours are available; 3950 Cradle Mountain Rd, Cradle Mountain; (03) 6492 1491.

DEVONPORT REGIONAL GALLERY: Displays the work of contemporary Tasmanian artists, part of the Devonport Arts Centre; open Mon–Fri 9am–5pm, Sat–Sun 9am–2pm; 145 Rooke Street, Devonport; (03) 6420 2900.

HOME HILL: A National Trust property, once home to prime minister Joseph Lyons and Dame Enid Lyons, who was the first woman elected to the House of Representatives in federal parliament in Australia, along with their 12 children (12!). Houses a rich collection of personal material, giving insight into the momentous events of mid-20th-century Australia. The property comprises a beautiful house, built in 1916, set in well-maintained gardens of wisteria and stately trees. Tours Wed–Thurs and Sat, other times by appt; 77 Middle Rd, Devonport; (03) 6424 8055.

LEVEN CANYON: From Cruikshank's Lookout down to the cantilevered Edge Lookout there are 697 steps, but they're worth the effort because the views of this 275m deep ravine are breathtaking. Picnic or barbecue in a bushland setting. Loongana Rd, Loongana.

LEVEN RIVER CRUISES: Choose a fun 2 or 4hr guided cruise or walking tour of the upper Leven River in Ulverstone (see p. 465). Tours leave daily, on foot or in a cute little passenger vessel; Public Pontoon; 0400 130 258.

TARKINE DRIVE: 60km loop through towering forest and steep valleys via the Sumac and Rapid River roads with many forest walks and lookouts including Sumac Lookout, Julius River forest walk, Lake Chisholm flooded sinkhole, the Milkshake Hills exquisite picnic areas and trails through rainforest, and lovely picnic areas at the Kanunnah and Tayetea bridges; Trowutta.

TASMAZIA: One of the world's largest hedge mazes with 'rooms' and 'doors' leading to the Three Bears Cottage. Along with seven other mazes, a cubby town, cafeteria and Lower Crackpot model village there's plenty of crazy fun to keep the kids going all day. Open 10am–4pm; 500 Staverton Rd, Promised Land; (03) 6491 1934. It's 14km south-west of Sheffield (see p. 464).

THE HOUSE OF ANVERS: The total chocolate experience – manufacturing viewing room, chocolate museum and tasting centre. Open 7am–6pm; 9025 Bass Hwy, Latrobe; (03) 6426 2958.

WARRAWEE FOREST RESERVE: An excellent place for platypus viewing, swimming, bushwalking and barbecues. A 5km walking track winds through the forest and a boardwalk has been installed around the lake to allow disabled access to trout fishing. Platypus watching tours are run by LandCare; ask at visitors centre in Latrobe (21 George St, (03) 6426 2240) for details.

WING'S WILDLIFE PARK: Get up close to Tasmanian devils at dinner time, let the kids explore the animal nursery and check out animals from far and wide. Tours available; open 10am–4pm and by appt; 137 Winduss Rd, Gunns Plains; (03) 6429 1151.

VISITOR INFORMATION

Devonport Visitor Information Centre
145 Rooke St
Market Square, Devonport
(03) 6420 2900
northwesttasmania.com.au

King Island
kingisland.org.au

Top: Family fishing boat at Rocky Cape National Park
Bottom: The Emu Valley Rhododendron Garden in Burnie

TOP EVENTS

→ JAN Henley-on-Mersey Festival (Latrobe); Regatta and Surf Lifesaving Championships (Port Sorell)

→ FEB FOKI (Festival of King Island); Flowerfest (Sheffield); Devil Country Muster (Smithton)

→ MAR Imperial 20 and Queenscliff to Grassy Yacht Race (both King Island); Devonport Regatta; Steamfest (Sheffield); Forth Valley Blues Festival (Ulverstone)

→ APR Mural Fest (Sheffield)

→ JULY Jazz Festival (Devonport);

→ AUG Chocolate Winterfest (Latrobe)

→ OCT Tulip Festival (Wynyard); Medieval Festival (Sheffield); Cradle Country Music Festival (Ulverstone); Mount Roland Folk Festival; Spring Festival (Burnie)

→ NOV King Island Golf Open (Currie); Melbourne to Stanley Yacht Race

→ DEC Running, Woodchopping and Cycling Carnivals (Devonport); Latrobe Gift footrace and Wheel Race

TEMPERATURES

Jan: 12–21°C

July: 4–12°C

KEY TOWNS

BURNIE
Population 20,267

The early European settlers believed the Burnie area to be agriculturally rich, but high rainfall and dense forests made farming virtually impossible. For 75 years, Burnie's main employer was a pulp and paper mill. The mill closed in 2010, but artisan paper is still made here as part of a thriving arts and crafts scene. Burnie is situated on a port, is Tasmania's fourth-largest city and has beautiful parks, charming Art Deco buildings and an ocean-front boardwalk.

SEE & DO **Emu Valley Rhododendron Gardens:** *see* Top Attractions. **Burnie Park:** this park has a modern playground and barbecues set among shaded lawns and seasonal garden beds. Burnie Inn, the city's oldest building, is in the park and has been restored as a teahouse; cnr Bass Hwy and West Park Gr. **West Beach:** popular swimming beach, a block from the CBD, with a boardwalk, restaurants and surf club; North Tce. **Penguin Observation Centre:** free guided viewing Oct–Mar; Parsonage Point; 0437 436 803. **Hellyers Road Distillery:** makers of single-malt whisky, vodka and liqueurs; tours, tastings, sales and licensed eatery; 153 Old Surrey Rd; (03) 6433 0439. **Farmers' market:** Wivenhoe showgrounds; 1st and 3rd Sat morning each month. **Fernglade:** tranquil riverside reserve with platypus, native orchids and diverse birdlife; walking tracks and picnic areas; off Old Surrey Rd; 5km W. **Lake Kara:** reservoir with good trout fishing; signposted from Hampshire; 30km S. **Guide Falls Farm:** exotic animal park, farm tours and gift shop; 309 West Ridgley Rd; 0474 821 588; 14km SW. **Guide Falls:** pretty falls with picnic areas and walking tracks; near Ridgley; 17km S.

CURRIE (KING ISLAND)
Population 659

Currie is the main town on King Island in Bass Strait. The island is well known for its gourmet produce, including superb soft cheeses and grass-fed beef. The Roaring Forties winds are responsible for many of the 57 shipwrecks scattered around the island. The island now has five lighthouses (to avoid any further disaster). There are no passenger ferries to King Island, so you'll need to fly from Hobart, Burnie (Wynyard), Launceston, or Melbourne, Victoria.

SEE & DO **King Island Dairy:** *see* Top Attractions. **King Island Cultural Centre:** local arts, community projects, resident artists and personal stories of King Island residents; Currie Harbour. **King Island Historical Society Museum:** memorabilia of the island; open Thurs–Mon 2–4pm in summer, closed in winter; Lighthouse St. **The Boathouse Gallery:** displays and sales of pottery, sculptures and paintings, plus barbecue facilities; Edward St. **King Island Maritime Trail:** interpretive self-guided tour of shipwreck sites; brochure from visitor centre. **Fishing:** excellent salmon, flathead and whiting fishing from east-coast beaches; morwong, warehou, yellowtail kingfish and squid fishing at British Admiral Reef; 3km S of Currie. **Penguins:** see them return to shore at dusk at Grassy; 25km SE. **Kelp Craft:** displays and sales of bull kelp handcrafts; open Tues 9.30am–2.30pm, Sun 10am–4pm; 2249 North Road, Reekara; 0458 569 591; 22km NE. **Naracoopa:** seaside town with pier and blowhole; 25km E. **Seal Rocks State Reserve:** covers 800ha, with calcified forest and stunning cliffs at Seal Rocks; 30km S. **Lavinia Nature Reserve:** 6400ha of ocean beaches, heath, dunes, wetland bird habitats, lagoons and a rare suspended lake formation. Lavinia Point has a popular surfing beach; 40km NE. **Cape Wickham:** at 48m high, this is the tallest lighthouse in the Southern Hemisphere. It's set on rugged cliffs; north of Egg Lagoon; 45km NE. **Surfing:** King Island has plenty of breaks, depending on the weather. **Golf:** The windblown, links-style Cape Wickham and Ocean Dunes have been listed among Australia's top 20 golf courses. Cape Wickham is 47km N of Currie, and Ocean Dunes is 4km N of Currie.

DEVONPORT
Population 24,591

Book a berth on the ferry to Devonport, the port town that links Tasmania with the Australian mainland. On the banks of the Mersey River, Devonport is the home base for the *Spirit of Tasmania* ferries that chug across Bass Strait to Geelong (and vice versa) carrying passengers and vehicles. Devonport is a functional port town framed by the dramatic headland of Mersey Bluff and some beautiful coastal reserves and parklands, with the whitecapped waters of the Strait offshore. The local economy is propelled along by farming, manufacturing and tourism.

SEE & DO **Don River Railway; Bass Strait Maritime Centre; Tasmanian Arboretum:** *see* Top Attractions for all. **Devonport Regional Gallery; Home Hill; House of Anvers Chocolate Factory:** *see* Other Attractions for all. **Mersey Bluff Lighthouse:** striking red-and-white striped icon completed in 1899 and part of the National Estate; Mersey Bluff. **Simon Martin Whips and Leathercraft:** leathercraft studio and expert traditional whip-maker supplying plaited kangaroo hide stockwhips to the world. Whip-cracking demonstrations on request; open Mon–Fri 8.30am–5pm; 306 Mersey Main Rd, Spreyton; (03) 6427 3946;

9km SE. **Braddons Lookout:** panoramic view of coastline; Braddons Lookout Rd, near Forth; 16km W. **Kelcey Tier Nature Walk:** 160ha of native bushland and 3.6km circuit walk with superb views of Devonport and the Mersey River; off Durkins Rd, Spreyton; 7km S.

KING ISLAND
See Currie p. 463

LATROBE
Population 4456

Latrobe was once Tasmania's third-largest settlement with inns, hotels, a hospital and no less than three newspapers in circulation. As it was the best place to cross the Mersey River, it became the highest profile town on the north coast. Since the early 19th century, however, Latrobe has ceded its importance as a port town and relaxed into a gentler pace. Latrobe was inundated by floods in October 2022, so check ahead for any closures.

SEE & DO **Australian Axeman's Hall of Fame:** see Top Attractions. **Warrawee Forest Reserve:** see Other Attractions. **Platypus tours:** with a LandCare guide; check at visitor centre for departure times and cost; bookings on (03) 6426 1774. **Court House Museum:** located in a heritage building under the National Trust register with over 600 prints and photographs; open Tues–Fri 1–4pm, other times by appt; Gilbert St; (03) 6426 1289. **Sheean Memorial Walk:** 3km return walk commemorating local soldiers; Gilbert St. **Bells Parade Reserve:** beautiful riverside picnic ground; River Rd. **Historic walk:** starts at western end of Gilbert St and turns into Hamilton St. **Relinquaire:** 20 rooms of antiques and collectibles; 139 Gilbert St; (03) 6426 2599. **Village Market:** Gilbert St; Sun. **Makers Market:** Axeman's Hall of Fame, Bells Pde; Sun. **Henry Somerset Orchid Reserve:** over 40 native orchids and other rare flora. Peak flowering time is Oct–Dec; Railton Rd; 7km S.

PENGUIN
Population 3330

This northern seaside holiday town was named after the little penguins that shuffle up nearby beaches. Images of the iconic bird are peppered around town. The largest example is the much-photographed Big Penguin, which stands 3m tall on the beachfront and is one of the town's premier attractions – alongside the renowned Sunday market.

SEE & DO **Dutch Windmill:** the windmill was presented to the town during Australia's bicentenary to commemorate the Dutch explorers and settlers. There is also a tulip display in spring and play equipment. Hiscutt Park, off Crescent St. **Johnsons Beach Reef:** popular walking spot at low tide when reef is exposed. **Perry-Ling Gardens:** originally a labour of love for two town residents, now a flourishing garden beside the road; Old Coast Rd to Ulverstone. **Market:** over 100 stalls undercover; Arnold St; Sun. **Dial Range Walks:** excellent tracks include the walk up Mount Montgomery (5km S) with magnificent views from the summit, and Ferndene Gorge (6km S). The Ferndene Bush Walk takes in an old silver-mine shaft, Thorsby's Tunnel. Brochures on walks from visitor centre highlight more trails; 78 Main Rd; (03) 6437 1421. **Mount Gnomon Farm:** Seasonal platter lunches (Sun), picnics and cider (Wed– Frid) and a beautiful garden (9km SW). **Pioneer Park:** beautiful gardens with picnic facilities and walks; Riana; 10km SW. **Scenic drive:** along the coast to Ulverstone.

PORT SORELL
Population 3869

This holiday town on the Rubicon River enjoys a mild and sunny climate nearly year-round. It was established in the early 1820s, but, sadly, many of its oldest buildings were destroyed by bushfires. The port is now a coastal retreat for retirees and beach lovers, and is the eastern gateway to Narawntapu National Park (see p. 468) and its abundant wildlife.

SEE & DO **Ghost Rock Vineyard:** wine tastings, sales and a modern cafe with views to the sea; open Mon–Sun in summer, Wed–Sun in spring and autumn, Fri–Sun in winter; 1055 Port Sorell Rd; (03) 6428 4005. **Jetty:** the estuary has good fishing for Australian salmon, whiting, flathead and bream. There are views to Bakers Beach and Narawntapu National Park; Darling St. **Port Sorell Conservation Area:** 70ha of coastal reserve with diverse flora and fauna. Guided tours available; bookings on (03) 6428 6072; Park Espl. **Market:** Memorial Hall; 1st and 3rd Sat each month Sept–May. **Shearwater:** holiday town with shopping centre and good beach access; 1.5km N. **Hawley Beach:** safe swimming, good fishing and historic Hawley House (1878) offering meals; 4km N. **Walk:** 6km return track from Port Sorell to Hawley Beach, offering excellent views of Narawntapu National Park; starts at beach end of Rice St.

SHEFFIELD
Population 1195

Inspired by the Canadian town of Chemainus, Sheffield has revitalised itself by commissioning artists to cover the town in murals depicting local history and scenery. As a result, the town has been transformed into Tasmania's largest outdoor gallery and a centre for artisans creating beautiful work in wood, glass, precious metals, stone and even chocolate.

SEE & DO **Tasmazia:** see Other Attractions. **Story of the Sheffield Murals:** audio tour that explains how the town went from rural decline to thriving outdoor art gallery; available from visitor centre. **Kentish Museum:** exhibits on local history and hydro-electricity; open Mon–Fri 10am–3pm; Main St. **Steam train:** Red Water Creek Steam and Heritage Society runs a train 1st weekend each month; cnr Spring and Main sts. **Badgers Range Kimberley's Lookout:** 90min return, with short, steep sections. Views along the walk; access from High St, Sheffield North. **Town Hall Market:** High St; every 3rd Sat. **Stoodley Forest Reserve:** experimental tree-farm forest, with a 40min loop walk through European beech, Douglas fir, radiata pine and Tasmanian blue gum and picnic areas; 7km NE. **Lake Barrington Estate Vineyard:** tastings and sales; open Wed–Sun Nov–Apr; West Kentish; 10km W. **Railton:** known as the 'Town of Topiary', Railton has over 100 living sculptures; 11km NE. **Mount Roland:** well-marked bushwalks to the summit, which rises to 1233m, with access from Claude Rd or Gowrie Park; 11km SW. **Lake Barrington:** internationally recognised rowing course created by Devils Gate Dam. Picnic and barbecue facilities along the shore; 14km SW. **Wilmot:** this 'Valley of Views' has magnificent views of the mountains of Cradle country and Bass Strait, novelty letterbox trail, and the original Coles store and family homestead; 38km W.

SMITHTON
Population 3282

This substantial town is renowned for its unique blackwood swamp forests. Smithton services the most productive dairying area in the state. With several large sawmills, it is also the centre of significant forestry reserves and the gateway to the takayna/Tarkine.

SEE & DO **Circular Head Heritage Centre:** artefacts and memorabilia detailing the area's early settler history; 8 King St; (03) 6452 3296. **Lookout tower:** excellent views from Tier Hill; Massey St. **Western Esplanade Community Park:** picnic spot overlooking the mouth of the Duck River; Western Espl. **Woolnorth tours:** tours visit spectacular Cape Grim cliffs, wind farm, Australia's largest dairy farm, which was created by royal decree in the 1820s; bookings on (03) 6452 1493. **River and Duck Bay:** good fishing and boating; 2km N. **Balfour Track:** 3hr return walk to an abandoned mining town along a packhorse trail cut by early prospectors; 48km. Blackwater Rd; 25km SW. **Surfing:** excellent, but turbulent, surf beaches near Marrawah where Rip Curl West Coast Classic is held in Mar; 51km SW. **Arthur River cruises:** trips into pristine wilderness of Arthur Pieman Protected Area; runs Sept–June; 70km SW. **Gardiner Point:** 'Edge of the World' plaque; 70km SW.

★ STANLEY
Population 504

Stanley is a picture-book fishing village with buckets of charm, historic buildings and amazing views. It was used as a location for the 2014 film *The Light Between Oceans*. The town sits in the base of an ancient volcanic outcrop called the Nut, with steep cliffs rising 152m on three sides. Matthew Flinders, upon eyeballing the Nut in 1798, commented that it looked like a 'cliffy round lump resembling a Christmas cake'. Today you can venture to the top on foot or by chairlift for magnificent views.

SEE & DO The Nut; Highfield Historic Site: *see* Top Attractions for both. **Historic buildings:** explore the old buildings around the wharf, including the bluestone former Van Diemen's Land (VDL) Company Store (1844) on Wharf Rd, and Ford's Store (1859), also on Wharf Rd; find details online, or pick up a map from the visitor centre. **Lyons Cottage:** birthplace of former prime minister Joseph Lyons (PM 1929–31), packed with interesting memorabilia; open 10am–4pm, Sept–end of May; 14 Alexander Tce; (03) 6458 1480. **Stanley Discovery Museum:** displays on local history; open 10am–3pm; Church St. **Penguins:** Follow the purpose-built boardwalk at the southern end of Godfreys Beach to watch little penguins come ashore at dusk. **Stanley Cemetery:** pay your respects at the graves of colonial architect John Lee Archer and explorer Henry Hellyer; Browns Rd. **Seal cruises:** boat trips to see offshore seal colonies; open Mon–Sun; Fishermans Dock; (03) 6458 1294 or 0419 550 134. **Dip Falls:** amazing double waterfall in dense rainforest and eucalypts, with a nearby picnic area; via Mawbanna off Bass Hwy; 40km SE.

ULVERSTONE
Population 12,723

At the mouth of the Leven River on the north-central coast, Ulverstone is renowned for its fine sweeping beaches and waterfront parklands. The rugged hinterland offers forest walks, caves to explore and breathtaking views into the Leven Canyon's deep ravine.

SEE & DO Bass Highway; Gunns Plains Caves: *see* Top Attractions for both. **Leven River Cruises; Leven Canyon; Wing's Wildlife Park:** *see* Other Attractions. **Hive Tasmania:** this new cultural centre incorporates the town visitor centre, history museum, gallery, Tasmania's largest planetarium and the state's only Science Centre; 50 Main St; (03) 6425 2839. **Ulverstone History Museum:** recreations of a general store, schoolhouse, railway station and blacksmith's foundry; open Mon–Sat 1.30–4.30pm; 50 Main St; (03) 6425 3835. **Pedal Buggies Tasmania:** pedal yourself and the kids around the town's picturesque waterfront and parks; open 10am–4.30pm summer and school holidays, other times by appt. The Beach Hut; 2 Beach Rd; 0437 242 535. **Riverside Anzac Park:** amazing children's playground, great picnic facilities and an interesting fountain. The park is named after a pine tree grown from a seed taken from Gallipoli; Beach Rd. **Fairway Park:** (also known as Dinosaur Park), next to a 60m giant water slide; open summer and school holidays; Beach Rd; **Shropshire Park:** barbecues, outdoor gym equipment and underfoot the path is inscribed with the Royal Australian Navy's 75-year history; Dial St. **Legion Park:** magnificent coastal setting; The Espl. **Tobruk Park:** includes a memorial wall; Hobbs Pde. **Shrine of Remembrance:** clock-tower memorial designed and built by European immigrants in 1953; Reibey St. **Ulverstone Lookout:** views over town; Upper Maud St. **Cradle Coast Farmers' Market:** the wharf; Sun. **Ulverstone Miniature Railway:** runs 1st and 3rd Sun each month Jan–Mar, 3rd Sun Apr–Dec; Maskells Rd; 0409 174 481; 2km E. **Goat Island Sanctuary:** cave and good fishing, but walking access to island at low tide only; 5km W. **Penguins:** view little penguins at dusk; Lillico Beach; 12km E. **Preston Falls:** easy walk to views; 19km S.

WARATAH
Population 235

Waratah is notable for its mining history and the picturesque waterfall in the centre of town. It was founded by tin miner James 'Philosopher' Smith in 1871 and soon became the site of the world's richest tin mine. The mine closed in 1947.

SEE & DO Museum: displays and artefacts of the area in the original courthouse. Provides brochures for a self-drive tour of town; Smith St. **Waratah Waterfall:** in the town centre; Smith St. **Philosopher Smith's Hut:** replica of 19th-century miner's hut; Smith St. **St James Anglican Church:** this 1880 church was the first in Tasmania to be lit by hydro-power; Smith St. **Lake Waratah:** barbecue area with rhododendron garden and walks to Waratah Falls; English St. **Kenworthy Stamper Mill:** working display of mining machinery; Smith St. **Tarkine Interpretation Centre:** information and displays about the takayna/Tarkine forests in the heritage Atheneum Hall; Smith St. **Savage River National Park:** the largest contiguous area of cool-temperate rainforest surviving in Australia. This is wild and remote country accessible only on foot. Contact Parks & Wildlife Service on 1300 135 513; 20km W. **Fishing:** excellent trout fishing in rivers and lakes in the area, including Talbots Lagoon; 20km E. **Old mines:** walks and drives to old mining sites; brochure from visitor centre. **Philosophers Falls:** pretty forest trail with marvellous fungi; 20km SW. **Whyte Lookout:** vistas of the takayna/Tarkine forests; 10km S. **Tarkine Trails:** guided multi-day treks into the takayna/Tarkine region; 1300 133 278.

WYNYARD
Population 5387

This small town at the mouth of the Inglis River between Burnie and Table Cape is located on a stunning stretch of coastline backed by rich and fertile farmland.

SEE & DO Table Cape Lookout; Rocky Cape National Park: *see* Top Attractions for both. **Gutteridge Gardens:** riverside gardens in the heart of town; Goldie St. **Nature walks:** include boardwalk along Inglis River; brochure at visitor centre. **Wonders of Wynyard:** art gallery and collection of vintage vehicles that include the equal-oldest Ford car in the world; 8 Exhibition Link; (03) 6443 8330. **Fossil Bluff:** scenic views from an unusual geological structure where the oldest marsupial fossil in Australia was found; 3km N. **Lobster Ponds:** volunteer-run sanctuary for the Giant Tasmanian Freshwater Lobster, which is the world's largest. Tearooms onsite; open 10am–3pm Thurs–Sun; 241 Robinhill Rd, Flowerdale; 0458 420 006; 6.5km NW. **Fishing:** Inglis and Flowerdale rivers provide excellent trout fishing; also good sea-fishing around Table Cape. **Scenic flights:** the best way to appreciate the patchwork colours of the fields in the area; bookings at Wynyard Airport (03) 6442 1111.

Midlands and North-East

Tasmania's Midlands region is the island's **historic heart**, and a journey along the Heritage Highway (aka the Midland Hwy) between Hobart and Launceston is a trip back in time, through picturesque **convict-built villages** and grand **Georgian architecture**. There's plenty of history in the north-eastern corner of the state too, if you don't get distracted by the delights of the **Tamar Valley wine region**, the many attractions of Launceston, Tasmania's **vibrant northern capital**, or the **magnificent beaches and warm welcome** you'll find on Flinders Island.

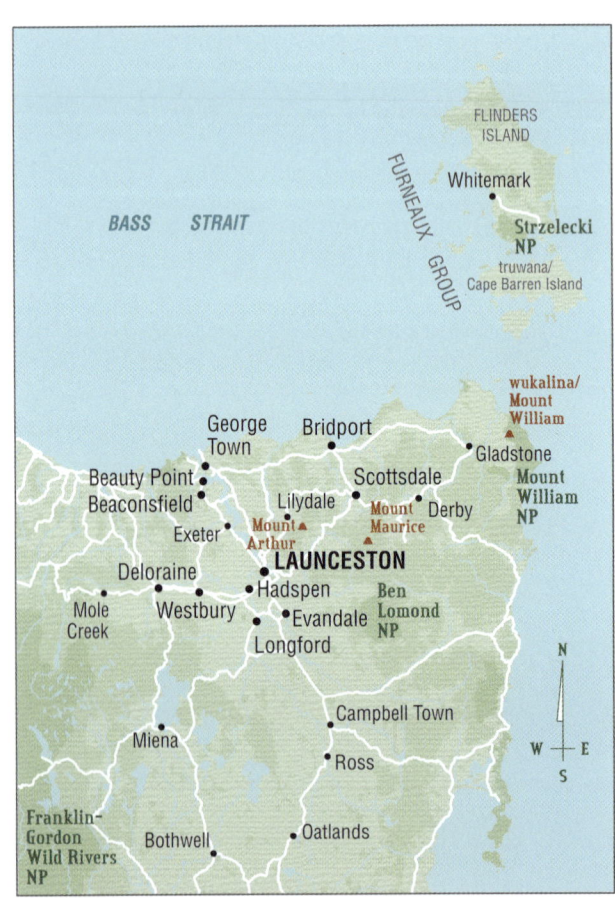

CHEAT SHEET

→ Allow around a week to tour the region, and at least two extra days if you want to explore Flinders Island.

→ Best time to visit: summer, when the weather is warm, although the gardens looks spectacular during spring and autumn.

→ Main towns: Campbell Town (see p.471) Deloraine (see p. 472), Launceston (see p. 474), Scottsdale (see p. 477).

→ The area is the Traditional Land of the palawa, including the lairmairrener, pyemmairrener, tommeginne and tyerrernotepanner Peoples. For a sober insight into the tragic consequences of European colonisation visit Wybalenna Historic Site on Flinders Island, where palawa People from across Tasmania were housed after being forcibly removed from their lands.

→ Don't miss: wine tasting in the Tamar Valley; Launceston's Cataract Gorge; touring the many grand historic houses; World Heritage-listed Woolmers Estate and Brickendon; Bridestowe Lavender Farm (at its most purple in Jan); Low Head; the convict-built town of Campbell Town.

Top: Brickendon Estate is a World Heritage Site **Opposite:** Eddystone Point Lighthouse, Mount William National Park

TOP ATTRACTIONS

BASS AND FLINDERS MARITIME MUSEUM: This museum in George Town (see p. 473) traces the many journeys of exploration of famous mariners, Bass and Flinders. Exhibits include several beautiful wooden replicas of historic boats, including a huon pine replica of Bass and Flinders sloop 'Norfolk' in which they circumnavigated Tasmania (then called Van Diemen's Land) in 1798, proving it was an island. Open 11am–3pm; 8 Elizabeth St, George Town; (03) 6382 3792.

BEACONSFIELD MINE AND HERITAGE CENTRE: Interactive displays and over 10,000 objects depict Beaconsfield's mining history, from its early days to the 2006 rescue of miners Todd Russell and Brant Webb. A 3D-holographic experience takes you through a labyrinth of mine tunnels and into the cage where the trapped miners spent 14 days 1km underground. Open 10am–4pm; West St, Beaconsfield; (03) 6383 1473.

BEN LOMOND NATIONAL PARK: Site of Tasmania's largest alpine area and premier ski field, this park has both downhill and cross-country skiing, with ski tows and ski hire. Ben Lomond Range is a plateau rising to over 1575m. The park also offers walking tracks and picnic areas in summer. Legges Tor, the second highest point in the state, has spectacular views. The area blooms with alpine wildflowers in summer. Contact Parks & Wildlife Service on 1300 135 513.

BOAG'S BREWERY: James Boag launched his brewing empire in 1881 near the banks of Launceston's North Esk River. Tours include a full circuit of the brewery from the brewhouse to the packaging line; start and finish at the 'James Boag Brewery Bar', which also houses a museum and a retail store. 39 William St, Launceston; (03) 6332 6300.

BRICKENDON: A World Heritage–listed convict site, this Georgian homestead in Longford (see p. 475) was built in 1824 and is still a working farm with an historic farm village; open Tues–Sun; 236 Wellington St, Longford; (03) 6391 1383.

BRIDESTOWE ESTATE LAVENDER FARM: One of the world's largest lavender oil producers, Bridestowe Estate's manicured lavender fields are at their best during Dec and Jan. There are tours, a lavender-inspired cafe and gift shop. 296 Gillespies Rd, Nabowla; (03) 6352 8182. The farm is 13km west of Scottsdale (see p. 477).

CALLINGTON MILL: Built in 1836, the old mill in Oatlands (see p. 475) was fully operational until 1892. After being battered by the elements and gutted by fire in the early 1900s, it was finally restored as part of Australia's bicentenary. In 2022, the mill became home to Callington Mill Distillery, producing a range of single-malt whiskies. 1 Mill La, Oatlands; 0482 509 019.

CATARACT GORGE: Spectacular day or night, 'the gorge' is a steep basalt chasm in the middle of Launceston (see p. 474), through which flows the South Esk River. A cliff-side path leads from historic Kings Bridge to manicured Victorian gardens, complete with preening peacocks and a restaurant. The world's longest single-span chairlift takes you to the First Basin lawns, cafes and an outdoor (and occasionally chilly) free swimming pool. Walking tracks lead further upstream to the Second Basin, and on to one of Australia's earliest hydro-electric developments, the 1895 Duck Reach Power Station. Off Trevallyn Rd, Trevallyn; (03) 6331 5915.

CLARENDON HOUSE: Just south of Evandale (see p. 472) is the stunning National Trust residence, Clarendon House. It was built in 1836 by James Cox, a wealthy grazier and merchant, and has been restored and furnished. Clarendon's high-ceilinged rooms, extensive formal gardens and range of connected buildings (dairy, bakehouse, gardener's cottage and stable) make it one of the most impressive Georgian houses in Australia. Its shepherd's cottage houses the **Australian Fly Fishing Museum** with a collection of fly-fishing memorabilia including heritage rods and flies. Open Sat–Sun 10am–3pm; 234 Clarendon Station Rd, Nile; (03) 6398 6220.

ENTALLY HOUSE: Thomas Reibey's original abode, built in 1819, is one of the most impressive heritage homes in the state. Entally has sprawling gardens, Regency furniture and other antiques, as well as a stunning riverside location on the South Esk River. The story of Thomas Reibey III is that he became premier after being fired as archdeacon of Launceston's Church of England. Reibey was prepared to fund construction of Hadspen's Church of the Good Shepherd, but withdrew his offer after a dispute with the bishop, who allegedly discovered Reibey's unorthodox sexual preferences and refused the 'tainted' money. As a result, the church only reached completion in 1961, more than 100 years later. Open Wed–Sat 10am–4pm; 782 Meander Valley Rd, Hadspen, (03) 6393 3200.

FRANKLIN HOUSE: This National Trust–listed Georgian home was built by convicts in 1838 for a Launceston brewer. It's furnished with period pieces and is surrounded by Victorian gardens and shady, 100-year-old trees. Open Mon–Fri 10am–4pm, Sat–Sun 12–4pm, reduced hours in winter; 413 Hobart Rd, Youngtown; (03) 6344 7824.

FURNEAUX MUSEUM: This museum on Flinders Island (see Whitemark, p. 474) has a wide range of memorabilia and houses displays on the short-tailed shearwater industry, the War Service Land Settlement and the nautical and natural histories of Flinders Island. Open Sat–Sun 1–4pm, Mon–Sun Jan–May; Settlement Point Rd, Emita; (03) 6359 8434.

MOLE CREEK KARST NATIONAL PARK: Set in the forests of the Western Tiers, this national park protects the Marakoopa and King Solomons caves, incredible caverns of calcite formations created by underground streams. **Marakoopa Cave** has a magnificent glow-worm display, while **King Solomons Cave** offers coloured stalagmites and stalactites and sparkling calcite crystals. Guided tours daily; (03) 6363 5182.

MOUNT WILLIAM NATIONAL PARK: This fairly remote park, created in 1973, protects Tasmania's Forester kangaroo and many bird species. The mountain is called wukalina/Mount William and stands at 216m. The view takes in the sandy beaches and coastal heath of the state's north-east corner and extends north to the Furneaux Islands and south to St Marys. With rolling hills, rugged headlands and pristine beaches this park offers swimming, fishing, diving and bushwalking. Georges Rocks and Eddystone Point are favoured diving spots, while Ansons Bay is well known for bream and Australian bass fishing. Walks vary in difficulty and are signposted. At Eddystone Point, at the southern end of the park, stands a historic, pink-granite lighthouse. Contact Parks & Wildlife Service on 1300 135 513.

NARAWNTAPU NATIONAL PARK: This coastal park is the best place in Tasmania to see large numbers of kangaroos and wallabies, and a popular spot for horseriding and waterskiing (conditions apply). Ranger-led walks are a highlight in summer. Access via Greens Beach or Badger Head or Bakers Beach rds; contact PWS Port Sorell (03) 6428 7920 or 1800 651 827.

PLATYPUS HOUSE: This is the only place in Australia where you can walk through an echidna room and get eye to eye with platypus as they swim and dive. There are platypus feeding ponds, an echidna garden and an interpretation centre. Open 10am–3.30pm; Inspection Head Wharf, 200 Flinders St, Beauty Point; (03) 6383 4884.

QUEEN VICTORIA MUSEUM AND ART GALLERY (QVMAG): This excellent regional museum is spread over two locations in Launceston (see p. 474). At Inveresk there are exhibits of First Nations and convict history, a display of the extinct Tasmanian tiger, a hands-on science education centre, a vast 1909 blacksmith shop and a planetarium. The Royal Park art gallery site has a superb collection of Tasmanian colonial paintings and the Guan Di Temple Chinese 'joss house'. Open 10am–4pm; 2 Wellington St, Royal Park, and 2 Invermay Rd, Inveresk; (03) 6323 3777.

ROSS FEMALE FACTORY SITE: Archaeologically the most intact female convict site in Australia, this operated as a probation station for female convicts and their babies in the 19th century. The women were trained as domestic help and hired out to landowners in the area. The Overseer's Cottage has a historic display and model. Off Bond St, Ross (see p. 476); contact Tasmanian Wool Centre for more information; (03) 6381 5466.

SEAHORSE WORLD: This centre in Beauty Point (see p. 471) is a seahorse breeding farm that supplies public aquariums around the world, and also researches endangered species to ensure their survival. Guided tours (45min) explore

Top: QVMAG in Launceston
Bottom: Kangaroos at Narawntapu National Park
Opposite: Woolmers Estate's Rose Garden

the life cycle of these secretive creatures, from when they are tiny newborns no bigger than a child's fingernail. There is a touch pool and craft centre. Open 9am–4.30pm; Shed 1A Inspection Head Wharf, 200 Flinders St, Beauty Point; (03) 6383 4111.

TAMAR VALLEY WINE REGION: The Tamar region produces standout cool-climate white wines. This region's most celebrated sparklings come from a cluster of makers located 20km to the west of Bridport around Pipers Brook. **Pipers Brook Vineyard** is one of the state's biggest names, and makes beautiful gewürztraminer and pinot noir. Its cellar also offers tastings of its Ninth Island label and Kreglinger sparklings. Pick up a self-drive map from the Launceston visitor centre (or download one) and meander through glorious valley scenery to architecturally acclaimed tasting rooms and tiny family-run outlets. Cellar doors worth visiting include **Dalrymple**, **Delamere**, **Bay of Fires** and **Tamar Ridge**. For masterpieces in sparkling, visit **Clover Hill**, whose picturesque cellar door is perfect for a picnic lunch, and **Jansz**, with its modern, architectural wine room featuring an interpretive centre.

TASMANIAN WOOL CENTRE: This attraction in the historic and picturesque town of Ross (*see* p. 476) houses a museum, wool exhibition and retail area – all illustrating the national importance of the wool industry. 48 Church St, Ross; (03) 6381 5466.

WOOLMERS ESTATE: A World Heritage–listed convict site, Woolmers was built c.1817 by the Archer family, who lived there for six generations. Tours of the house, the outbuildings, the gardens and the **Rose Garden** are conducted daily; Woolmers La, Longford; (03) 6391 2230.

WYBALENNA HISTORIC SITE: In 1831 Tasmania's palawa People, depleted to fewer than 160, from what some evidence indicates was between 40,000 and 70,000 people, were isolated on Flinders Island. Wybalenna ('black man's home') was set up there in 1834 to house those few survivors of Tasmania's pre-European population. Less than a third of the people held there survived the appalling living conditions. A lack of good food and water meant that by 1847, when the settlement was finally abandoned, evidence indicates an estimate of between 17 and 46 palawa People remained. The Wybalenna Historic Site at Settlement Point stands as a reminder of the doomed community. Located near Emita, it is one of the most important historic sites in Tasmania, and includes a National Trust–restored church and cemetery.

YARNS ARTWORK IN SILK: Created by more than 300 people and taking 10,000hrs to complete, Yarns is a 200m reflection of Tasmania's Great Western Tiers in four large panels corresponding to the passing seasons. Accompanied by an audio presentation and sound-and-light effects, the Yarns presentation operates every half hour; open 9.30am–4.30pm; 100 Emu Bay Rd, Deloraine; (03) 6362 5280.

OTHER ATTRACTIONS

BRIDPORT WILDFLOWER RESERVE: Best during Sept and Oct, this wildflower reserve spans 50ha of coastal heath and woodland. There is a 2.2km walking track that covers the length of the reserve and takes in scenic Adams Beach. Access via Main St, Bridport.

CITY PARK: This magnificent 5ha downtown park in Launceston (see p. 474) was once the gardens of the state governor's northern residence. The park features a raucous Japanese macaque monkey enclosure, the John Hart conservatory, a bandstand, a playground and lots of big shady trees; cnr Tamar and Brisbane sts, Launceston; (03) 6323 3000.

DELORAINE & DISTRICTS FOLK MUSEUM: Showcases the life of a country publican with exhibition gallery, garden, dairy, blacksmith's shop and family history room; open 9 am–5pm; 100 Emu Bay Rd, Deloraine; (03) 6362 5280.

DESIGN TASMANIA: Australia's only museum collection of contemporary wood design, along with beautifully designed ceramics and glass; open Tues–Sun 10am–4pm; cnr Brisbane and Tamar sts, Launceston; (03) 6331 5506.

FLOATING SAUNA LAKE DERBY: Enjoy a range of hot and cold therapies surrounded by nature in this very picturesque wood-fired Nordic sauna perched on a platform at Lake Derby, at the edge of the township of Derby (see p. 472); floatingsauna.com.au

HOLWELL GORGE: This fern-covered gorge has beautiful waterfalls. It's in the Dazzler Range to the west of Beaconsfield (see p. 471). There are basic picnic facilities at the eastern entrance and a 3hr return hiking track. For track conditions contact PWS Tamar Field Centre (03) 6336 5391; access is via Holwell or Greens Beach rds.

LIFFEY FALLS STATE RESERVE: Liffey Falls is surrounded by cool-temperate rainforest species of sassafras, myrtle and leatherwood. There is a 45min return nature walk from the picnic area through lush tree ferns, taking in smaller falls along the way. Contact Parks & Wildlife Service on 1300 135 513. The falls are 29km south of Deloraine (see p. 472).

LILYDALE FALLS: Situated within the temperate rainforest of Lilydale Park just north of Lilydale township (see p. 474), the waterfall is at the end of a pleasant 5min walk through ferns and eucalypts. A picnic area and playground are onsite, as well as two oak trees planted in 1937 from acorns picked near Windsor Castle in England to commemorate the coronation of King George VI.

LOW HEAD: This popular holiday retreat has safe swimming and surf beaches. The **Maritime Museum** is housed in Australia's oldest continuously used pilot station and has fascinating displays of memorabilia discovered in nearby shipwrecks. At kanamaluka/River Tamar's entrance stands the 12m high **Low Head Lighthouse**, built in 1888 and with distinctive red stripes on a white background, behind which lies a little penguin colony. Penguin-watching tours start around sunset; bookings on 0418 361 860 Low Head is 5km north of George Town.

NATIONAL AUTOMOBILE MUSEUM OF TASMANIA: More than 40 fully restored classic vehicles spanning 100 years of style and technical achievement; open 9am–5pm, reduced winter hours; cnr Willis and Cimitiere sts, Launceston; (03) 6334 8888.

RALPHS FALLS: A 20min return walk under a myrtle rainforest canopy arrives at Norms Lookout at the top of the falls. From here enjoy views of the Ringarooma Valley, Bass Strait and the Furneaux Islands. Picnic and barbecue facilities are available. The falls are 15km south-east of Ringarooma.

R STEPHENS TASMANIAN HONEY: At the home of Tasmania's unique aromatic honey, visitors can see clover and leatherwood honey being extracted and bottled. Tastings and sales are available. Open Mon–Fri; 25 Pioneer Dr, Mole Creek; (03) 6363 1170.

STRZELECKI NATIONAL PARK: The only national park on Flinders Island (see Whitemark, p. 477), featuring the Strzelecki Peaks and wetlands, heathland and lagoons. A 5hr return walk to the summit of the Strzelecki Peaks is steep, but rewards with excellent views of Franklin Sound and and the islands surrounding Flinders Island. Trousers Point, featuring magnificent rust-red boulders and clear waters is also in the park. Contact Parks & Wildlife Service on 1300 135 513.

Opposite top: Low Head Lighthouse Opposite bottom: Mountain biking in Derby

VISITOR INFORMATION

Launceston Travel and Information Centre,
68–72 Cameron St,
Launceston
1800 651 827
northerntasmania.com.au

Tamar Visitor Centre,
81 Main Rd, Exeter
1800 637 989
tamarvalley.com.au

Great Western Tiers Visitor Centre,
98–100 Emu Bay Rd,
Deloraine
(03) 6362 5280
greatwesterntiers.net.au

Flinders Island
visitflindersisland.com.au

KEY TOWNS

BEACONSFIELD
Population 1093

Now a modest apple-growing centre in Tasmania's north, Beaconsfield was once the wealthiest gold town in Tasmania. Gold was discovered here in 1847 with the first underground shaft sunk in 1879 on the rich Tasmania reef. The town is dominated by rush-era relics, including two massive Romanesque arches at the old pithead of the Tasmania Gold Mine. The town made headlines around the world during the dramatic rescue of two trapped miners in 2006; you can find out more about this at the Beaconsfield Mine and Heritage Centre.

SEE & DO **Beaconsfield Mine and Heritage Centre:** see Top Attractions. **Holwell Gorge:** see Other Attractions. **Beaconsfield Walk of Gold:** a self-guided 40min historical walk with stories of the town and its people; 1.8km round trip starting at the Heritage Centre; West St. **Gem and Stone Creations:** gallery and giftshop; 128 Weld St; (03) 6383 1514. **Auld Kirk:** a Gothic Revival–style, convict-built church (1843) on the banks of kanamaluka/ River Tamar at Sidmouth, with views to the spectacular A-frame Batman Bridge; 13km SE. **Wineries:** cellar-door tastings and sales to the east of town around Rowella, Kayena and Sidmouth. **Lavender House:** exhibition fields of 70 varieties of lavender, plus giftshop with 50 health and beauty products; 15km E.

BEAUTY POINT
Population 1231

Beauty Point is a riverside town and the base for the Australian Maritime College. It's also a good spot for fishing and yachting. The town's main attractions are the fascinating webbed and wriggling creatures at Seahorse World and Platypus House.

SEE & DO **Seahorse World; Platypus House; Narawntapu National Park:** see Top Attractions for all. **Sandy Beach:** safe swimming spot. **York Town monument:** site marks the first settlement in northern Tasmania (1804); 10km W. **Kelso and Greens Beach:** popular holiday towns to the north-west.

BRIDPORT
Population 1371

Bridport is a relaxed seaside holiday retreat and home to two world-class dune-based public links golf courses. There are sheltered beaches, excellent sea and freshwater fishing, and it's a hotspot for lovers of wildflowers.

SEE & DO **Tamar Valley Wine Region:** see Top Attractions. **Bridport Wildflower Reserve:** see Other Attractions. **Barnbougle Dunes:** links golf course; 425 Waterhouse Rd; (03) 6356 0094. **Barnbougle Lost Farm:** links golf course; Waterhouse Rd; (03) 6356 1124. **Waterhouse Protected Area:** offers 6700ha of coastal bush camping, rockpools, sand dunes and beaches. Access via the old goldmining village of Waterhouse; 26km E.

CAMPBELL TOWN
Population 823

Campbell Town is a historic town set on the Elizabeth River on the Midland Hwy and a lovely spot to browse antiques or break a journey between the north and south of Tassie. There are 35 convict-built heritage buildings here. This small town has been prominent in Tasmania's history: the first telephone call in the Southern Hemisphere was made from here to Launceston; the British Commonwealth's first agricultural show was held here in 1839, and the event is still held today; and it is the birthplace of Harold Gatty, the first person to fly around the world.

SEE & DO **Heritage Buildings:** of the 35 heritage buildings listed on the National Estate, the **Grange**, an old manor house built in the centre of town in 1840, is possibly the grandest. Others include the **Fox Hunter's Return**, **Campbell Town Inn** and **Red Bridge** – a three-arched structure built over the Elizabeth River by convicts in the 1830s. There is a map in Grange Park at the northern end of High St that lists the main historic buildings. **Heritage Highway Museum:** displays on local history; 75 High St; (03) 6381 1353. **Market:** Town Hall; 4th Sun each month. **Fishing:** Macquarie River (just west of town) and Lake Leake (30km E) are two good trout-fishing spots in the area.

DELORAINE
Population 2631

National Trust–classified Deloraine has become the artistic hub of northern Tasmania, hosting the largest craft fair in Australia each Nov. It is situated on the Meander River amid lovely rural scenery with the Great Western Tiers nearby, so its surroundings no doubt provide inspiration for the increasing number of artists who live in the area. Deloraine is Tasmania's largest inland town and a busy regional centre, yet it still retains a village atmosphere.

SEE & DO **Yarns Artwork in Silk:** see Top Attractions. **Folk Museum** and **Liffey Falls State Reserve:** see Other Attractions. **Galleries:** sales and exhibits of local artwork from paintings to furniture. Venues include Gallery 5 and Art as mania, both on Emu Bay Rd. **Deloraine Streetscape Sculptures:** 13 works of art in Deloraine's streets and parks forming part of the wider ranging Sculptures of the Great Western Tiers. Brochure at visitor centre. **Market:** Showgrounds, Lake Hwy; 1st Sat each month plus 3rd Sat Feb–May. **Exton:** tiny township full of antique shops and charming old cottages; 5km E. **41 Degrees South Tasmania:** salmon farm, wetlands and ginseng nursery, with tastings and cafe; 323 Montana Rd, Red Hills; (03) 6362 4130; 8km W. **Ashgrove Farm Cheeses:** sales and tastings of English-style cheeses; 6173 Bass Hwy, Elizabeth Town; (03) 6368 1105; 10km NW. **Quamby Bluff:** solitary mountain behind town, with 6hr return walking track to summit starting at Lake Hwy; 20km S. **Fishing:** excellent trout fishing in Meander River (north and south of town) and Mersey River (around 20km E). **Scenic drive:** through Central Highlands area via Golden Valley to yingina/Great Lake, one of the largest highland lakes in Australia. Check road conditions in winter with Parks & Wildlife Service; 1300 827 727.

DERBY
Population 109

Derby has truly been put on the map in the past few years as a popular and premier hub for world-class mountain-bike trails and the location of the highly Instagrammable Floating Sauna. The town was born when tin was discovered in 1874 and the 'Brothers Mine' opened two years later. The Cascade Dam was built and the mine prospered until 1929, when the dam flooded and swept through the town, killing 14 people. The mine closed and, although it eventually reopened, the town took a long time to recover. The charming streets still showcase old buildings and tin-mine memorabilia.

SEE & DO **Lake Derby Floating Sauna:** see Other Attractions. **Derby Schoolhouse:** a comprehensive museum with history displays, gemstones, minerals and tin-panning apparatus. Main St. **Gemstone fossicking:** Weld River in Moorina, where Tasmania's largest sapphire was discovered; Tasman Hwy; 8km NE. **Miners cemetery:** historic cemetery where early tin miners, including some Chinese, were buried; Moorina; 8km NE. **Fishing:** excellent trout fishing along Ringarooma River north of town.

EVANDALE
Population 1058

Just south of Launceston is this National Trust–classified town, with beautiful buildings of historical and architectural importance. Cyclists come for the annual Penny Farthing Championships, a race along the triangular circuit in the centre of the town.

SEE & DO **Ben Lomond National Park; Clarendon House:** see Top Attractions for both. **Heritage Walk:** Evandale is best appreciated with a copy of the brochure *Let's Talk About Evandale*, which lists over 35 historic buildings and sites in the town and many more in the district. Among them are **Blenheim** (1832), which was once a hotel, **St Andrews Uniting Church** (1840) with its classic belltower and Doric columns, and the former **Presbyterian Manse** (1840). Brochure available from visitor centre at 18 High St; (03) 6391 8128. **Miniature railway:** steam railway run by local enthusiasts; open Sun; Morven Park, Barclay St. **Market:** over 100 stalls; Falls Park, Russell St; Sun. **Symmons Plains International Raceway:** venue for national V8 Supercars meeting. A track is open for conditional public use; bookings on (03) 6398 2952; 10km S. **John Glover's grave:** burial site of prominent Tasmanian artist beside church designed by Glover; Deddington; 24km SE. **Trout fishing:** in North Esk and South Esk rivers.

EXETER
Population 1092

Exeter is a small rural town in the Tamar Valley, surrounded by scenic farmland and orchards. It lies just north of Launceston, in the centre of the Tamar Valley cool-climate wine country.

SEE & DO **Tamar Valley Wine Region:** see Top Attractions. **Bradys Lookout:** this scenic lookout was once the hideout of bushranger Matthew Brady, who used the high vantage point to find prospective victims on the road below. Today the site retains its magnificent view of the Tamar Valley and is an ideal picnic spot. 5km SE. **Paper Beach:** 5km return walking track to Supply River, where there are ruins of the first water-driven flour mill in Tasmania; 9km E. **Notley Fern Gorge:** 11ha wildlife and rainforest sanctuary with giant man-ferns and moss-covered forest. A 2hr return walk leads to Gowans Creek; Notley Hills; 11km SW. **Tamar Valley Wine Centre:** Let the wines come to you at this collective cellar door stocking tipples from more than 30 local vineyards; 49 Main Rd; (03) 6394 3223.

The town of Derby and surrounds has become a famed mountain-biking area

TOP EVENTS

- JAN Mona Foma music and arts festival (Launceston and Hobart); Tamar Valley Folk Festival (George Town); Triathlon and Barnbougle Polo (both Bridport); Picnic Day Races (Longford)
- FEB National Penny Farthing Championship (Evandale); Festivale (Launceston)
- MAR Glover Prize (landscape art, Evandale); Irish Festival with Maypole dancing (Westbury)
- APR Targa Tasmania (across the region); Colonial Fair (Richmond); V8 Supercars (Symmons Plains)
- MAY Agfest (Carrick)
- JUNE Agricultural Show (Campbell Town)
- AUG Scallop Fiesta (Bridport); Tamar Valley Peace Festival
- SEPT Junction Arts Festival (Launceston); Tamar Valley Writers Festival
- OCT North East Rivers Festival (Derby); Launceston Show
- NOV Tasmanian Craft Fair (Deloraine); Farmgate Festival (Tamar Valley); Festival of Roses (Longford)
- DEC Cycling Festival (Launceston)

TEMPERATURES

Jan: 12–25°C

July: 2–13°C

FLINDERS ISLAND
See Whitemark p. 477

GEORGE TOWN
Population 4408

George Town on the banks of kanamaluka/River Tamar is Australia's third-oldest settlement, after Sydney and Hobart. European settlement can be traced back to 1804 and the town abounds with historic buildings. It's also surrounded by beautiful coastal scenery and is a charming place to use as a base to explore the north coast.

SEE & DO **Bass and Flinders Maritime Museum Tamar Valley Wine Region:** see Top Attractions for both. **Low Head:** see Other Attractions. **The Grove:** this classic Georgian stone house (c. 1838) was the home of Mathew Friend, the port officer and magistrate of the settlement; 25 Cimitiere St. **York Cove:** scenic cove where George Town's centre was built, with mooring and pontoon facilities, and restaurants. **Self-guided Discovery Trail:** walking route through town; brochure from visitor centre. **George Town Watch House:** community history room and female factory display; Macquarie St. **Windmill Point Memorial:** honouring the optimism of William Paterson, who camped here after running his ship, *HMS Buffalo*, aground at York Cove. Ignoring the disaster, he ran up the flag, fired three shots in the air and played the national anthem. **Mount George Lookout:** scenic views of George Town, the north coast, and south to the Western Tiers. The lookout has a replica of a Tamar Valley semaphore mast used to relay messages in the 1800s; 1km E. **Fishing:** excellent fishing at Lake Lauriston and Curries River Dam; 13km E. **Lefroy:** old goldmining settlement, now a ghost town, with ruins of old buildings; 16km E. **Hillwood Berry Farm:** sales and pick-your-own patch, along with sampling of local fruit wines and liqueurs; 24km SE. **Beaches:** the area has many beautiful beaches including East Beach (facing Bass Strait and ideal for walking, swimming and surfing) and Lagoon Beach on kanamaluka/River Tamar (for family swimming). **Mountain biking:** New 80km network of trails on Mount George and the Tippogoree Hills; 2km E

GLADSTONE
Population 124

The north-eastern district surrounding Gladstone was once a thriving mining area, yielding both tin and gold. Today many of the once-substantial townships are ghost towns. Gladstone has survived, but its successful mining days have long since gone. It acts as a tiny service centre for surrounding dairy, sheep and cattle farms, as well as for visitors to Mount William National Park, and has the distinction of being Tasmania's most north-easterly town.

SEE & DO **Mount William National Park:** see Top Attractions. **Gladstone cemetery:** historic reminder of the miners, including many Chinese, who were drawn to the area; Carr St. **Little Blue Lake:** disused tin mine filled with brilliant blue water (coloured by pyrites) ; South Mount Cameron; 8km S. **Cube Rock:** large granite monolith on an outcrop, reached by 3hr return climb; South Mount Cameron; 8km S. **Beaches:** magnificent beaches to the north, including Petal Point; 25km N. **Geological formations:** impressive granite formations between Gladstone and South Mount Cameron. **Gem fossicking:** smoky quartz, topaz and amethyst can be found in the district; contact visitor centre for details.

HADSPEN
Population 2337

Just 8km from Launceston, today Hadspen is mostly a residential suburb – albeit one with an impressive main street lined with heritage buildings. Entally House, an 1819 heritage house, is also here.

SEE & DO **Entally House:** see Top Attractions. **Heritage buildings:** including the Red Feather Inn (c. 1844) and Hadspen Gaol (c. 1840). **Carrick:** neighbouring town with historical buildings. It hosts Agfest, one of Australia's biggest agricultural field days, in May; 10km SW.

HAMILTON
Population 241

Hamilton, an unspoilt National Trust–classified town about a half hour's drive from both Bothwell and New Norfolk, has avoided the commercialisation found in some parts of the state. Its buildings and tranquil lifestyle conjure up an image of 1830s Tasmania. It is situated in a valley on the Clyde River.

SEE & DO **Glen Clyde House:** convict-built c. 1840, this place now houses an award-winning craft gallery and tearooms; Grace St. **Heritage buildings:** many buildings of historical importance include the Old Schoolhouse (1856) and St Peter's Church (1837), which is notable for having just one door to prevent the once largely convict congregation from escaping. **Lake Meadowbank:** popular venue for picnics, boating, waterskiing and trout fishing; 10km NW.

★ LAUNCESTON
Population 80,943

Launceston is second in size to Hobart and may just be the perfect small Australian city. It has vibrant arts, food and wine scenes and gorgeous natural surrounds. Located in a natural basin at the head of kanamaluka/River Tamar, it is home to Australia's highest concentration of 19th-century buildings – a walk around the city's streets is like turning the pages of an architectural history textbook. While it presents an aura of elegant relaxation, it is also a busy tourist destination with lively student-filled pubs, modern marinas and manicured Victorian parks at every turn. The wide and picturesque kanamaluka/River Tamar is a prominent feature of Launceston, originating at the city from the convergence of two rivers. One of these cascades through the spectacular Cataract Gorge, which provides the city with a whitewater playground.

SEE & DO **Cataract Gorge; Queen Victoria Museum and Art Gallery; Boag's Brewery; Tamar Valley Wine Region; Franklin House:** see Top Attractions for all. **City Park, Design Tasmania; National Automobile Museum of Tasmania:** see Other Attractions for all. **Seaport:** a slick riverside complex at the head of kanamaluka/River Tamar, with restaurants, shops, marina and hotel; Seaport Blvd. **Launceston Tramway Museum:** pays homage to Launceston's early tramway system; open Tues–Sun 10am–4pm; 2 Invermay Rd; (03) 6334 8334. **Walking tours:** guided walking tours cover every interest from heritage and history to gourmet food tastings and ghosts. **Old Umbrella Shop:** picture-perfect 1860s shop, complete with creaky floorboards and housing a gift shop and information centre; open Mon–Fri 9am–5pm, Sat 9am–12pm; 60 George St; (03) 6331 9248. **Tamar River Cruises:** 50min boat jaunts around the city waterfront and Cataract Gorge, or 4-hour cruises downriver; open 8.30am–6pm; Home Point Pde; (03) 6334 9900. **Punchbowl Reserve:** extensive suburban glen full of outrageously colourful rhododendrons and native fauna; off Punchbowl Rd, Punchbowl; 5km SW. **Trevallyn Nature Recreation Area:** next to Cataract Gorge, this busy picnic spot has trail rides, hiking tracks and kayaking at Trevallyn Dam; Reatta Rd, Trevallyn; (03) 6777 2179; 6km W. **Treetops Adventure Tasmania:** segway tours, mountain-bike tracks, 1km tree-top zip-line and ropes course; open 9am–5pm; 66 Hollybank Rd, Underwood; (03) 6395 1390; 20km NW. **Tamar Island Wetlands:** urban wetlands reserve and birdlife haven, with a 2km boardwalk to Tamar Island, which has views up and down kanamaluka/River Tamar; West Tamar Hwy, Legana; (03) 6327 3964; 9km NW.

LILYDALE
Population 307

Once called Germantown, this small north-eastern township is known for the English style of its gardens. Yet the bushwalks through surrounding reserves and waterfalls are distinctly Australian, with native temperate rainforests lining the trails.

SEE & DO **Tamar Valley Wine Region:** see Top Attractions. **Lilydale Falls:** see Other Attractions. **Painted Poles:** scattered throughout the village centre are 15 hydro poles painted by professional and community artists to show the local history. **Lalla Flower Farm:** 12ha park reputed to have the best rhododendron display in Australia. Other species are also on display; Lalla; check website for open days; walkerrhododendron.com: 4km W. **Hollybank Forest Reserve:** 140ha forest reserve with Australia's first continuous cable tree-top tour, arboretum, picnic facilities and information centre with details on walking tracks; marked turn-off near Underwood; 5km S. **Mount Arthur:** 3hr return scenic walk to summit (1187m); 20km SE.

LONGFORD
Population 3711

Longford is classified as a historic town and serves the rich agricultural district just south of Launceston. The World Heritage-listed Woolmers Estate and Brickendon homestead and farm village are nearby. Longford was established when numerous settlers from Norfolk Island were given land grants in the area in 1813. Fittingly, the district became known as Norfolk Plains, while the settlement itself was called Latour.

SEE & DO **Woolmers estate; Brickendon:** see Top Attractions for both. **Historic Buildings:** These include the **Queen's Arms** (1835) in Wellington St, **Longford House** (1839) in Catherine St and the **Racecourse Hotel** (1840s) in Wellington St, which was originally built as a railway station, then used as a hospital and later a pub, and in which a patron was murdered after stealing and swallowing two gold sovereigns from local farmhands. The Racecourse Hotel is now a guesthouse and restaurant. Also on Wellington St is **Christ Church**, an 1839 sandstone building with outstanding stained-glass windows, early settler gravestones and a clock and bell presented by George VI. Path of History is the self-guided walk; brochure available from visitor centre; 52 Wellington St; (03) 6397 7303. **Walk:** track along the South Esk River. **The Village Green:** originally the site of the town market, now a picnic and barbecue spot; cnr Wellington and Archer sts. **Perth:** small town with historic buildings, including Eskleigh and Jolly Farmer Inn, and market on Sun mornings; 5km NE. **Tasmanian Honey Company:** tastings and sales of excellent range of honeys including leatherwood and flavoured varieties; 25A Main Rd, Perth; (03) 6398 2666; 5km NE. **Woodstock Lagoon Wildlife Sanctuary:** 150ha sanctuary for nesting waterfowl; 9km W.

MIENA
Population 127

Miena is on the shores of yingina/Great Lake on Tasmania's Central Plateau and has been popular with anglers since brown trout were released into the lake in 1870. The surrounding region, known as the Lake Country, can become very cold, with snow and road closures, even in summer.

SEE & DO **Fishing:** the 22km long yingina/Great Lake is the highest freshwater lake in Australia and, like most lakes in the area, offers excellent trout fishing. The Highland Dun mayflies that hatch in summer draw fly fishers from around the world. West of Liawenee (about 7km N) are more locations for fly fishing in isolated lakes and tarns of the Central Plateau Conservation Area (4WD recommended for several lakes, while some are accessible only to experienced bushwalkers). Lakes are closed during winter. Check licence conditions and seasons at ifs.tas.gov.au. **Pine Lake:** easy lakeside walk past ancient pencil pines; 25km N. **Waddamana Power Station Museum:** a fully intact hydro-electric power station; Main Rd, Waddamana; (03) 6259 6158; 17km S.

MOLE CREEK
Population 216

Mole Creek is named after the nearby creek that 'burrows' underground. Most visitors come to explore the limestone caves in Mole Creek Karst National Park. The unique honey from the leatherwood tree, which grows only in the west-coast rainforests of Tasmania, is also a drawcard. Each summer, apiarists transport hives to the nearby leatherwood forests.

SEE & DO **Mole Creek Karst National Park:** see Top Attractions. **R Stephens Tasmanian Honey:** see Other Attractions. **Mole Creek Tiger Bar:** local hotel with information and memorabilia on the Tasmanian tiger; Pioneer Dr. **Alum Cliffs Gorge:** 30min return walk; 3km NE. **Trowunna Wildlife Park:** see Tasmanian devils and other native fauna; 4km E. **Melita Honey Farm:** over 50 flavours of honey and an interactive bee display; open Sun–Fri; Chudleigh; 8km E. **Devils Gullet State Reserve:** World Heritage area with natural lookout on a 600m high cliff, reached by 30min return walking track; 40km SE. **Wild Cave Tours:** adventure tours to caves that are closed to the general public; bookings on (03) 6367 8142. **Walls of Jerusalem National Park:** accessible on foot only, from the end of the road that turns off around 15km W of Mole Creek and heads down to Lake Rowallan. With glacial lakes and dolerite peaks, it is a wonderland for self-sufficient and experienced bushwalkers.

OATLANDS
Population 562

The village of Oatlands has many graceful Georgian sandstone buildings, including the iconic and restored Callington Mill windmill. If you are approaching Oatlands from the north, look out for the topiary and striking metal sculptures by the roadside. The topiaries are a local tradition from the 1960s, while the recently created metal sculptures depict earlier times in the district. The village is on the shores of Lake Dulverton.

SEE & DO **Callington Mill:** see Top Attractions. **Lake Dulverton:** the lake is stocked with trout and onshore is a wildlife sanctuary protecting many bird species. Popular picnic spot; Espl. **Historic buildings:** Grab the 'Oatlands key' from one of several local businesses and gain entry to the convict-built Court House (1829), Gaoler's Residence (1836) and Commissariat (1827). **Convict-built mud walls:** 13km S on Jericho Rd. **Fishing:** excellent trout fishing in Lake Sorell and Lake Crescent; 29km NW.

ROSS
Population 291

Ross is a quaint and charming Midlands village, just off the highway and founded in 1812. Many 19th-century sandstone buildings adorn the main street and there are some interesting antique and bric-a-brac shops. The Ross Bridge spans the

Opposite: QVMAG in Launceston offers interactive experiences

Macquarie River and is a point of pride: one of the oldest and most beautiful bridges in Australia. The town's central junction reveals the different aspects of Ross's history and, perhaps, its potential; the four corners are known as Temptation (hotel), Recreation (town hall), Salvation (church) and Damnation (gaol).

SEE & DO **Tasmanian Wool Centre; Ross Female Factory Site:** *see* Top Attractions for both. **Heritage walk:** takes in 40 historic buildings in town, including Uniting Church (1885); booklet from Wool Centre. **Ross Bridge:** completed in 1836, the bridge was designed by colonial architect John Lee Archer and constructed by convicts, one of whom, Daniel Herbert, was given a pardon for his efforts. Herbert was responsible for 186 beautiful stone carvings along the side of the bridge, comprising images of animals, plants, Celtic gods and goddesses, and even the governor of the time, George Arthur. **Fishing:** there is world-class fly fishing for brown trout in Macquarie River and some of the state's best trout-fishing lakes (Sorell, Crescent, Tooms and Leake) are nearby.

SCOTTSDALE
Population 1979

Scottsdale is the major town in Tasmania's north-east, serving some of the richest agricultural and forestry country in the state. Indeed, as Government Surveyor James Scott observed in 1852, it has 'the best soil in the island'. A visitor to the town in 1868 noted with some surprise that the town had 'neither police station nor public house, but the people appear to get on harmoniously enough without them'. Present-day Scottsdale (now with both of those establishments) still retains a sense of harmony.

SEE & DO **Bridestowe Estate Lavender Farm:** *see* Top Attractions. **Barnbougle Dunes:** links golf courses; 425 Waterhouse Rd; (03) 6356 0094; 30km N. **Mount Stronach:** very popular 45min climb to views of the north-east; 4km S. **Cuckoo Falls:** uphill 2–3hr return walk to falls; Tonganah; 8km SE. **Springfield Forest Reserve:** popular picnic spot and 20min loop walk through Californian redwoods, English poplars, pines and native flora; 12km SW. **Sidling Range Lookout:** views of town and surrounding countryside; 16km W. **Mount Maurice Forest Reserve:** walks incorporating Ralph Falls; 30km S.

WESTBURY
Population 1666

Westbury's village green gives the town an English air. Just west of Launceston, the town was surveyed in 1823 and laid out in 1828, the assumption being that it would be the main stop between Hobart and the north-west coast. Originally planned as a city, it never grew beyond the charming country town it is today.

SEE & DO **The Village Green:** used for parades and fairs in the 1830s, the village green is still the focal point and fairground of Westbury – with one small difference: prisoners are no longer put in the stocks for all to see; King St. **White House:** this collection of buildings, enclosing a courtyard, was built in 1841. Later additions include a coach depot, a bakery and a flour mill; King St. **Pearn's Steam World:** said to be the largest collection of working steam traction engines in Australia; Bass Hwy. **Fishing:** good trout fishing at Four Springs Creek (15km NE) and Brushy Lagoon (15km NW).

WHITEMARK (FLINDERS ISLAND)
Population 308

Flinders Island in Bass Strait is the largest of the 52 islands in the Furneaux Group, once part of a land bridge that joined Tasmania to the mainland, although to get there today you'll need to fly from Hobart, Launceston or Melbourne, or catch the weekly barge from Bridport, Tasmania. It's a beautiful place, but with a tragic history; it was here, in a forced settlement at Wybalenna – now one of Tasmania's most important historic sites – that many palawa People died after 1834. The island has some of the country's most beautiful (if a little windswept) white sand beaches and a rugged mountainous interior. Whitemark is the island's largest town.

SEE & DO **Wybalenna Historic Site; Furneaux Museum:** see Top Attractions for both. **Strzelecki National Park:** see Other Attractions. **Bowman History Room:** displays of memorabilia show Whitemark since the 1920s; rear of E.M. Bowman & Co, 2 Patrick St. **Diving and snorkelling:** tours to shipwreck sites, limestone reefs and granite-boulder formations including Chalky Island Caves and Port Davies Reef; bookings on (03) 6359 8429. **Fishing tours:** from Port Davies to Prime Seal Island for pike and salmon, and Wybalenna Island for couta; bookings rockjawtours.com.au **Patriarchs Wildlife Sanctuary:** privately owned sanctuary with a vast range of birdlife and wallabies, which can be handfed; access via Lees Rd, Memana; 30km NE. **Logan Lagoon Wildlife Sanctuary:** houses a great diversity of birdlife in winter including the red-necked stint, common greenshank and eastern curlew; east of Lady Barron; 30km SE. **Mount Tanner:** lookout with stunning views of the northern end of the island and Marshall Bay; off West End Rd; Killiecrankie; 40km N. **Port Davies:** from the viewing platform see short-tailed shearwaters fly into their burrows at dusk. An enormous colony of these birds breed here between Sept and Apr and then set out on an annual migration to the Northern Hemisphere. West of Emita; 20km NW. **Fossicking:** Killiecrankie diamonds, a form of topaz released from decomposing granite, are found along the beach at Killiecrankie Bay and nearby Mines Creek; 43km NW. **Beachcombing:** rare paper-nautilus shells wash up along the island's western beaches.

Top: Wombat on Flinders Island
Opposite: Sunrise at The Dock on Flinders Island

Index

This index includes all towns, localities, roadhouses, national parks and islands shown in the text. The alphabetical order followed is that of 'word-by-word' – a space is considered to come before 'A' in the alphabet and punctuation marks are ignored. Names beginning with Mc are indexed as Mac and those beginning with St as Saint. The following abbreviations and contractions are used:

ACT – Australian Capital Territory
JBT – Jervis Bay Territory
NSW – New South Wales
NP – National Park
NT – Northern Territory
Qld – Queensland
SA – South Australia
Tas. – Tasmania
Vic. – Victoria
WA – Western Australia

90 Mile Straight WA 302
1000 Steps Walk (Kokoda Track Memorial Walk), Dandenong Ranges NP Vic. 118, 123

Abercrombie Caves NSW 74, 76
Abercrombie House, Bathurst NSW 74, 76
Abercrombie River NP NSW 15
Aberdeen NSW 35, 37, 41
Aberfeldy Vic. 133
Aboriginal art, culture and heritage
 Adventure Bay/karapati Tas. 453
 Albany WA 278
 Alice Springs NT 352, 353
 Arkaroola SA 250
 Armidale NSW 64
 Arnhem Land NT 337, 341
 Bairnsdale Vic. 141
 Barmah NP Vic. 181
 Barrington Tops NP NSW 43
 Bataluk Cultural Trail Vic. 141, 144
 Bathurst Island NT 333
 Biamanga NP NSW 85
 Bicheno Tas. 447
 Bladensburg NP Qld 427
 Blue Mountains NP NSW 13, 16
 Booderee NP NSW 83
 Boodjamulla (Lawn Hill) NP Qld 421
 Bouddi NP NSW 29
 Brewarrina NSW 107, 109
 Brisbane Water NP NSW 29
 Broome WA 325
 Bruny Island/lunawanna-allonnah Tas. 451, 453
 Budj Bim National Cultural Landscape Vic. 170, 173
 Buku-Larrnggay Mulka (Yirrkala) 337
 Bunjil's Shelter, Stawell Vic. 173, 179
 Burketown Qld 422
 Burleigh Heads Qld 374
 Cania Gorge NP Qld 393
 Cape York Qld 410, 412, 414, 415
 Carnarvon NP Qld 391
 Ceduna SA 259
 Chillagoe-Mungana Caves NP Qld 421
 Cobram Vic. 184
 Cooinda NT 338
 Cooktown Qld 414
 Coomee Nulunga Cultural Trail, Ulladulla NSW 85, 89
 Coorong NP SA 233
 Dampier WA 319
 Danggu Geikie Gorge NP WA 323
 Derby WA 326
 Dharug NP NSW 29
 Didthul (Pigeon House Mountain) NSW 85, 89
 Dubbo NSW 78
 Ewaninga Rock Carvings Conservation Reserve NT 351
 Fitzroy Crossing WA 326
 Flinders Group NP Qld 415
 Gab Titui Cultural Centre, Thursday Island Qld 409, 419
 Geelong Vic. 161
 Geraldton WA 314
 Glenbrook NSW 13, 16
 Goulburn River NP NSW 74
 Grampians NP Vic. 173
 Gulgong NSW 80
 Gunbalanya (Oenpelli) NT 338
 Gundabooka NP NSW 107
 Halls Creek WA 326
 Halls Gap Vic. 173, 178
 Hawker SA 251
 Hermannsburg NT 353
 High Country Vic. 191
 Hyden WA 292
 Ikara-Flinders Ranges NP SA 247
 Innamincka Regional Reserve SA 248
 Jabiru NT 240
 Judbarra-Gregory NP NT 343
 Kakadu NP NT 337, 339, 340
 Kalgoorlie-Boulder WA 305
 Karratha WA 320
 Katherine NT 333, 346
 Keep River NP NT 344
 Kempsey NSW 47
 Kojonup WA 283
 Kununurra WA 327
 Laura Qld 409, 410, 416
 Leura NSW 16
 Lockhart River Qld 414
 Maitland SA 230
 Melville Island NT 333
 Minjungbal Aboriginal Cultural Centre, Tweed Heads NSW 54–5
 Mission Beach Qld 417
 Mitchell River NP Vic. 142
 Mossman/Mossman Gorge Qld 410, 417
 Mount Augustus NP WA 310
 Mount Magnet WA 317
 Mount Yarrowyck Nature Reserve NSW 63
 Mungana Qld 422
 Mungo NP NSW 97
 Murramarang NP NSW 84
 Murujuga NP (Burrup Peninsula) WA 319
 Mutawintji NP NSW 108
 Namadgi NP ACT 22
 N'Dhala Gorge Nature Park NT 350
 Newman WA 320
 Nhulunbuy NT 337, 341
 Nitmiluk NP NT 343
 Noonamah NT 341
 Nooramunga Marine and Coastal Park Vic. 135
 Normanton Qld 423
 Northampton WA 317
 Nullarbor NP SA 257
 Nyinkka Nyunyu Art and Culture Centre, Tennant Creek NT 351
 Purnululu NP WA 324
 Rainbow Beach Qld 384
 Ravenshoe Qld 418
 rock art NT 339
 Rockhampton Qld 398
 Rocky Cape NP Tas. 462
 Roebourne WA 321
 Rutherglen Vic. 199
 St George Qld 380
 Split Rock and GuGu Yalangi rock-art sites Qld 410
 Springsure Qld 399
 Sturt NP NSW 108
 Tennant Creek NT 354
 Thursday Island Qld 409, 418
 Tiwi Islands NT 333
 Tower Hill Wildlife Reserve Vic. 167
 Tully Qld 419
 Uluru-Kata Tjuta NP NT 350
 Wagin WA 299
 Walga Rock WA 311
 Wallace Rockhole Aboriginal Community NT 354
 Wangaratta Vic. 199
 Warburton WA 306
 Watagans NP NSW 33
 Western Cape Cultural Centre – Achimbun, Weipa Qld 412, 419
 Wollemi NP NSW 14
 Wollombi NSW 38
 Wybalenna Historic Site, Flinders Island Tas. 469, 477
 Wyndham WA 327
 Yallingup WA 287
 Yanchep NP WA 290
 Yarrawarra Aboriginal Cultural Centre, Woolgoolga NSW 55
 Yengo NP NSW 30, 37
 Yeperenye (Emily and Jessie Gaps) Nature Park NT 350
 yidaki purchase in the NT 347
 Yirrkala NT 337
 Yulara NT 355
abseiling
 Bright Vic. 196
 Bunbury WA 280
 Cooma NSW 94
 Evans Crown Nature Reserve NSW 15
 Kalbarri NP WA 310
 Nymboida NSW 57
 Strathgordon Tas. 458
 Townsville Qld 407
Adaminaby NSW 92, 93
Adelaide Hills SA 204, 206, 214–19
Adelaide Hills wineries SA 204
Adelaide River NT 332, 337, 338, 339
Adelaide River Jumping Crocodile Cruises NT 337, 339
Adelaide River War Cemetery NT 338, 339
Adelaide SA 202–3
 daytrips from 204–5
Adelong NSW 92, 93
Adelong Falls Reserve and Gold Mill Ruins, Adelong NSW 92, 93
Adventure Bay/kaparati Tas. 440, 451, 452, 453
Agate Creek Qld 423
Age of Fishes Museum, Canowindra NSW 71, 77
Agnes Water Qld 393, 398

A.H. Doddridge Blacksmith Shop, Angaston SA 216, 217
Aileron Hotel Roadhouse NT 352
Aireys Inlet Vic. 168, 171
Airlie Beach Qld 402, 403, 404, 405
Alba Vic. 130
Albany WA 274, 275, 278, 279, 281, 294
Albury NSW 99, 100, 101, 103, 199
Aldgate SA 218
Aldinga SA 211
Aldinga Beach SA 205, 211
Alexandra Vic. 194, 197
Alexandra Headland Qld 385, 388
Alice Springs (Mparntwe) NT 349, 351, 352–3, 355
Alice Springs Desert Park NT 349, 352
Alice Springs Telegraph Station Historical Reserve NT 351, 352
All Saints Estate, Rutherglen Vic. 192
Allans Flat Vic. 199
Allora Qld 378, 379
Almaden Qld 422
Alpine NP Vic. 143, 144, 191, 195, 197
Alpine Way NSW 91, 94
Alstonville NSW 55, 56
Amamoor State Forest Qld 385
American River SA 212
Anakie Qld 392
Andamooka SA 250
Anderson Vic. 135
Angaston SA 216, 217
Anglers Rest Vic. 198
Anglesea Vic. 166, 168
Apollo Bay Vic. 165, 167, 168
Appin NSW 25
Araluen Cultural Precinct, Alice Springs NT 349, 352
Aramac Qld 428
Ararat Gallery TAMA, Ararat Vic. 173
Ararat Vic. 174, 175, 176, 177
Ardrossan SA 227, 229
Argyle Homestead Museum, Kununurra WA 324, 327
Ariah Park NSW 104
Arkaroola Ridgetop Tour, Arkaroola SA 247, 250
Arkaroola SA 247, 250
Arkaroola Wilderness Sanctuary SA 247
Arltunga Historical Reserve NT 353
Armidale NSW 62, 64, 65, 67
Arnhem Land NT 336, 337
Arno Bay SA 260
Arthurs Seat State Park, Dromana Vic. 129
Arve Forest Drive, Geeveston Tas. 452, 454
Ashbourne SA 212
Ashcombe Maze and Lavender Garden, Flinders Vic. 130, 131
Atherton Qld 411, 413, 415
Atherton Chinatown and Hou Wang Temple, Atherton Qld 411, 413
Atherton Tableland Qld 409, 413, 417, 418, 419
Auburn SA 221, 224

478

INDEX

Auburn River NP Qld 393, 398
Augusta WA 274, 275, 276, 278–9, 281
Augusta–Busselton Heritage Trail WA 279, 281
Australasian Golf Museum, Bothwell Tas. 452, 453
Australia Zoo, Beerwah Qld 287, 383
Australian Age of Dinosaurs Museum, Winton Qld 425, 435
Australian Alps Walking Track 199
Australian Arid Lands Botanic Garden, Port Augusta SA 249, 253
Australian Army Flying Museum, Oakey Qld 378, 380
Australian Axeman's Hall of Fame, Latrobe Tas. 461, 464
Australian Botanic Garden, Mount Annan NSW 19, 24
Australian Country Music Hall of Fame, Tamworth NSW 61, 67
Australian Kelpie Centre, Casterton Vic. 173, 176
Australian Motorlife Museum, Wollongong NSW 21, 27
Australian National Surf Museum, Torquay Vic. 165, 171
Australian Reptile Park, Somersby NSW 29, 31
Australian Rodeo Heritage Centre, Warwick Qld 378, 381
Australian Stockman's Hall of Fame and Outback Heritage Centre, Longreach Qld 425, 432
Australian Sugar Heritage Centre, Innisfail Qld 411, 417
Australian Workers Heritage Centre, Barcaldine Qld 425, 428
Australia's World Peace Bell, Cowra NSW 74, 78
Australind WA 276, 279
Aviation Museum, Temora NSW 98, 104
Avoca Tas. 448
Avoca Vic. 151, 152
Avon Valley WA 268, 296, 299
Avon Valley NP WA 289, 298
Avondale Discovery Farm, Beverley WA 290, 291
Ayr Qld 404, 405

Babbage Island WA 311
Babinda Qld 412, 413, 415
Bacchus Marsh Vic. 151
Back o' Bourke Exhibition Centre, Bourke NSW 108, 109
Badu Island Qld 419
Bagdad Tas. 476
Bago Bluff NP NSW 51
Baird Bay SA 262
Bairnsdale Vic. 141, 142, 143
Balaklava SA 222, 223
Balaklava Courthouse Gallery, Balaklava SA 222, 223
Balcanoona SA 249
Bald Rock NP NSW 61, 68
Balfour Track Tas. 465
Balgowan SA 230
Balingup WA 279, 281
Ball Bay Qld 403
Balladonia WA 302, 303
Ballan Vic. 151
Ballarat Vic. 119, 147, 148, 151-2, 157
Ballina NSW 54, 56, 57
Balmoral Vic. 177
Balnarring Vic. 131
Balranald NSW 100
Bamaga Qld 412
Bandilgnan (Windjana Gorge) NP WA 323, 326
Bangalow NSW 56
Banrock Station Wine & Wetland Centre, Barmera SA 233, 236
Baralaba Qld 394
Barcaldine Qld 425, 428
Bargara Qld 395
Barham NSW 99, 100
Barmah NP Vic. 181, 187

Barmedman NSW 105
Barmera SA 235, 236, 237
Barongarook Vic. 169
Barossa Farmers' Market SA 219
Barossa Museum, Tanunda SA 216
Barossa Valley SA 206, 214–19
Barossa Valley wineries SA 215, 216, 219
Barraba NSW 64, 69
Barranyi (North Island) NP NT 344, 345
Barren Grounds Nature Reserve, Barren Grounds NSW 21
Barren Junction NSW 69
Barrington Tops NP NSW 43, 47
Barron Gorge NP Qld 409, 416
Barrow Creek NT 353
Barung NT 345
Barwon Bluff Marine Sanctuary Vic. 161
Barwon Heads Vic. 118, 161, 163
Barwon Park, Winchelsea Vic. 160, 163
Bass and Flinders Maritime Museum, George Town Tas. 467, 473
Bass Coast Rail Trail Vic. 135, 139
Bass Highway Tas. 460, 461, 465
Bass Point Aquatic and Marine Reserve NSW 27
Bass Strait Maritime Centre, Devonport Tas. 461, 463
Bataluk Cultural Trail Vic. 141, 144
Batchelor NT 339–40
Batemans Bay NSW 85, 86
Bathurst NSW 74, 76, 79
Bathurst Island NT 333
Batlow NSW 93, 95
Battery Point Tas. 439
Baw Baw Alpine Resort Vic. 133
Baw Baw NP Vic. 133, 135
Bay of Fires Conservation Area, St Helens Tas. 445, 448, 449
Bay of Fires Lodge Walk Tas. 445
Beach Highway Qld 360
Beachmere Qld 367
Beachport Conservation Park SA 241, 243
Beachport SA 241, 242, 243
Beaconsfield Tas. 467, 470, 471
Beaconsfield Mine and Heritage Centre, Beaconsfield Tas. 467, 471
Beaudesert Qld 373, 375
Beaufort Vic. 152
Beaumaris Tas. 449
Beauty Point Tas. 468, 469, 471
Bedarra Island Qld 411, 417
Bedourie Qld 429
Beech Forest Vic. 169
Beechworth Vic. 191, 194, 197
Beechworth Gaol, Beechworth Vic. 191, 194
Beechworth Historic and Cultural Precinct, Beechworth Vic. 191, 194
Beechworth wine region Vic. 191, 194
Beechy Rail Trail Vic. 169
Beerenberg Strawberry Farm, Hahndorf SA 215, 218
Beerwah Qld 361, 383
Bega NSW 85, 86
Bega Cheese Heritage Centre, Bega NSW 85, 86
Belair NP SA 215, 218
Belgenny Farm, Camden NSW 21
Belgrave Vic. 118, 123
Bell Qld 380
Bellarine Peninsula Vic. 118, 121, 158–63
Bellarine Railway, Queenscliff Vic. 160, 162
Bellbrook NSW 48
Bellingen NSW 46, 49
Bells Beach Vic. 166, 171
Ben Lomond NP Tas. 448, 467, 472
Bena Vic. 135
Benalla Vic. 192, 193, 194–5, 197
Benalla Art Gallery, Benalla 192, 194
Benambra Vic. 198
Bendigo Vic. 147, 148, 151, 152

Bendigo Art Gallery, Bendigo Vic. 147, 152
Bendigo wine region Vic. 147
Beowa NP NSW 83, 87
Bermagui NSW 85, 86–7, 89
Berri SA 236
Berridale NSW 93
Berrigan NSW 102
Berrima NSW 21, 23
Berrima Courthouse, Berrima NSW 21, 23
Berry NSW 23, 25
Berry Springs Nature Park NT 333, 341
Bethany SA 219
Bethungra NSW 101
Beverley WA 290, 291
Biamanga NP NSW 85
Bibbulmun Track WA 268, 277, 279, 281, 282, 283, 286, 295
Bicentennial National Trail 369, 415
Bicheno Tas. 445, 446, 447, 449
Bicheno Penguin Tours, Bicheno Tas. 445, 447
Big Banana, Coffs Harbour NSW 43, 46
Big Bend, Swan Reach SA 233, 239
Big Bogan, Nyngan NSW 80
Big Croc, Wyndham WA 327
Big Desert Wilderness Park Vic. 187
Big Galah, Kimba SA 258, 261
Big Goanna, Crystal Brook SA 229
Big Golden Guitar Tourist Centre, Tamworth NSW 61, 67
Big Hole, The, Deua NP NSW 22
Big Lobster, Kingston S.E. SA 243
Big Mango, Bowen Qld 404
Big Merino, Goulburn NSW 19, 25
Big Orange, Harvey WA 283
Big Penguin, Penguin Tas. 460, 464
Big Pineapple, Woombye Qld 384, 388
Big Potato, Robertson NSW 26
Big Prawn, Ballina NSW 56
Big Rig, Roma Qld 377, 380
Big Strawberry, Koonoomoo Vic. 184
Big Trout, Adaminaby NSW 92, 93
Big Yellowbelly, Isisford Qld 432
Bigga NSW 25
Biggenden Qld 394
bilby 294, 425
Bilby Tours, Charleville Qld 425, 430
Biloela Qld 393, 394, 397
Bilpin NSW 29, 31
Binalong NSW 27
Binalong Bay Tas. 445, 449
Binda NSW 25
Bindarri NP NSW 45
Bingara NSW 64-5, 67
Binningup WA 279
Birchip Vic. 179
Bird Island SA 231
Birdland Animal Park, Batemans Bay NSW 85, 86
Birdsville Qld 255, 426, 428-9
Birdsville Track SA 252, 255, 428
birdwatching
 Albury NSW 100
 American River SA 212
 Aramac Qld 428
 Ardrossan SA 229
 Atherton Qld 413
 Avon Valley NP WA 289
 Ayr Qld 404
 Banrock Station Wine & Wetland Centre SA 233
 Barcaldine Qld 428
 Barmera SA 236
 Barraba NSW 64
 Barren Grounds Nature Reserve NSW 21
 Batchelor NT 340
 Bega NSW 86
 Benalla Vic. 195
 Berry Springs Nature Park NT 333
 Bicheno Tas. 445

Bingara NSW 64
Blackwood NP Qld 405
Bongil Bongil NP NSW 43
Boort Vic. 187
Bordertown SA 236
Bowen Qld 404
Brewarrina NSW 109
Bribie Island Qld 360, 365
Brindabella NP NSW 27
Broadwater NP NSW 57
Brook Islands Qld 405
Broome WA 325
Bruny Island/lunawanna-allonnah Tas. 453
Buderim Qld 386
Bundaberg Qld 394
Bunya Mountains NP Qld 365
Burketown Qld 422
Burnie Tas. 463
Burra SA 223
Burrowa–Pine Mountain NP Vic. 192
Burrum Coast NP Qld 393
Canunda NP SA 241
Cape Arid NP WA 303, 304
Cape Palmerston NP Qld 403
Cape Range NP WA 309
Cape York Qld 414
Capricornia Cays NP Qld 391
Carnarvon NP Qld 391
Casino NSW 57
Casterton Vic. 176
Childers Qld 393, 395
Clermont Qld 405
Cloncurry Qld 430
Clump Mountain NP Qld 417
Cobram Vic. 184
Cocklebiddy WA 302
Cocoparra NP NSW 98
Coffin Bay NP SA 257
Cohuna Vic. 184
Colac Vic. 168
Coles Bay Tas. 447
Coorong NP SA 233
Cootamundra NSW 101
Cowes Vic. 136
Crater Lakes NP Qld 411
Creswick Regional Park Vic. 149
Crowdy Bay NP NSW 43
Croydon Qld 423
Culgoa Floodplain NP Qld 381
Cunnamulla Qld 430
Currawinya NP Qld 425
Currie Tas. 463
Currimundi Lake Conservation Park Qld 385
Curtis Island NP and Conservation Park Qld 397
Cygnet Tas. 453
Daintree Qld 415
Dalby Qld 380
Deepwater NP Qld 393
Djiru NP Qld 417
Dorrigo NP NSW 44, 47
Dryandra Woodland National Park WA 289
Edenhope Vic. 178
Edithburgh SA 229
Elliott NT 346
Esperance WA 304
Eubenangee Swamp NP Qld 411
Eyre Bird Observatory WA 302
Flinders Vic. 131
Fogg Dam Conservation Reserve NT 332
Forbes NSW 79
Forest Den NP Qld 428
Gatton Qld 367
Goolwa SA 211
Goondiwindi Qld 380
Goose Island Conservation Park SA 231
Grampians NP Vic. 173
Granite Island Recreation Park SA 209
Great Sandy Strait Qld 392
Greater Bendigo NP Vic. 149
Greenough WA 315

479

Grenfell NSW 80
Griffiths Island Vic. 170
Gunbower Island Vic. 183
Gundabooka NP NSW 107
Hasties Swamp NP Qld 413
Hat Head NP NSW 45
Hattah–Kulkyne NP Vic. 183
Hay NSW 103
Heathcote–Graytown NP Vic. 149
Herberton Range NP Qld 412
Houtman Abrolhos Islands WA 311
Iluka Nature Reserve NSW 53
Ingham Qld 406
Innamincka Regional Reserve SA 247
Innisfail Qld 416
Inverell NSW 66
Inverloch Vic. 137
Jamberoo NSW 25
Jardine River NP Qld 412
Jurien Bay Marine Park WA 282
Kakadu NP NT 337
Kalbarri WA 315
Karumba Qld 423
Katanning WA 283
Kenilworth State Forest Qld 383
Kerang Vic. 186
K'gari (Fraser Island) Qld 392
Kimba SA 261
Kinchega NP NSW 107
Kingaroy Qld 368
Kings Billabong Wildlife Reserve Vic. 183
Kingston S.E. SA 243
Koondrook State Forest NSW 99
Kununurra WA 327
Kuranda Qld 416
Lady Elliot Island Qld 392
Laidley Qld 368
Lake Argyle WA 323
Lake Bindegolly NP Qld 431
Lake Boga Vic. 181
Lake Broadwater Conservation Park Qld 378
Lake Buloke Vic. 175
Lake Cargelligo NSW 80
Lake Hindmarsh Vic. 174
Lake Mulwala NSW 97
Launceston Tas. 474
Leeton NSW 104
Leeuwin–Naturaliste NP WA 274
Leschenault Inlet WA 276
Limmen NP NT 344
Lincoln NP SA 257
Little Desert NP Vic. 174
Livingstone NP NSW 105
Lizard Island NP Qld 410
Lochern NP Qld 427
Longford Tas. 475
McLeods Morass Wildlife Reserve Vic. 142
Macquarie Marshes NSW 74
Main Range NP Qld 371
Manjimup WA 284
Mapleton Falls NP Qld 385
Margaret River WA 284
Maroochydore Qld 387
Marramarra NP NSW 33
Maryborough Qld 397
Menindee NSW 111
Michaelmas Cay Qld 409
Millicent SA 243
Mimosa Rocks NP NSW 84
Minlaton SA 230
Mitchell Qld 433
Mogo State Forest NSW 84
Montague Island Nature Reserve NSW 84
Moogerah Peaks NP Qld 373
Moree NSW 67
Morgan SA 237
Moss Vale NSW 26
Mother of Ducks Lagoon, Guyra NSW 63
Mount Frankland NP WA 287
Mount Hypipamee NP Qld 412
Mount Isa Qld 434

Munghorn Gap Nature Reserve NSW 74
Murray Bridge SA 238
Murray River NP, Bulyong Island Section SA 239
Muttaburra Qld 434
Mutton Bird Island Vic. 169
Muttonbird Island Nature Reserve NSW 45
Naracoorte SA 244
Narrabri NSW 67
Narrogin WA 285
Newcastle Waters NT 346
Ngarkat Group of Conservation Parks SA 235
Nhill Vic. 179
Nhulunbuy NT 341
Nitmiluk NP NT 343
Nooramunga Marine and Coastal Park Vic. 135
Normanton Qld 423
Northcliffe WA 285
Nullarbor NP SA 258
Nuriootpa SA 219
Nuytsland Nature Reserve SA 302
Nyngan NSW 80
Oatlands Tas. 476
Ocean Grove Vic. 162
Onkaparinga River NP SA 210
Oyala Thumotang NP (CYPAL) Qld 419
Paddys Ranges State Park Vic. 150
Paluma Range NP Qld 403
Para Wirra Recreation Park SA 216
Paroo–Darling NP NSW 113
Penguin Island WA 277
Penguin Parade, Phillip Island Vic. 133
Penguin Tas. 464
Phillip Island Vic. 134
Pine Creek NT 341
Pinnaroo SA 238
Port Davies Tas. 477
Portland Vic. 170
Queenscliff Vic. 163
Ravensbourne NP Qld 378
Ravenshoe Qld 418
Richmond Range NP NSW 55
Rinyirru (Lakefield) NP (CYPAL) Qld 410
Riverland Biosphere Reserve SA 234
Robertson NSW 26
Rottnest Island WA 297
Russell River NP Qld 413
St Lawrence Qld 407
Shellharbour NSW 27
Shepparton Vic. 189
Sorell Tas. 448
South Stradbroke Island Qld 371
Southwood NP Qld 378
Streaky Bay SA 262
Strzelecki Regional Reserve SA 252
Sundown NP Qld 378
Swansea Tas. 449
Sweers Island Qld 422
Tamworth NSW 67
Taroom Qld 399
The Lakes NP Vic. 141
Thirlmere Lakes NP NSW 26
Tin Can Bay Qld 389
Toodyay WA 298
Toora Vic. 135
Townsville Qld 407
Tumby Bay SA 263
Two Peoples Bay Nature Reserve WA 278
Ulverstone Tas. 465
Undara Volcanic NP Qld 421
Upolo Cay Qld 409
Uralla NSW 68
Wagga Wagga NSW 105
Wagin WA 299
Waikerie SA 239
Warburton Vic. 127
Warren NSW 79
Wedderburn Vic. 156

Weddin Mountains NP NSW 73
Wee Waa NSW 69
Weeroona Island SA 231
Welford NP Qld 427
Wellington NSW 81
West Wyalong NSW 105
Whitemark Tas. 477
Wickepin WA 299
Willandra NP NSW 75
Willunga SA 213
Wilmington SA 254
Wingham NSW 55
Wudinna SA 263
Wyperfeld NP Vic. 183
Yalgorup NP WA 284
Yankalilla SA 213
Birdwood SA 204, 215, 216, 217–18, 219
Birregurra Vic. 165
Black Mountain (Kalkajalka) NP Qld 414
Blackall Qld 429
Blackbutt Qld 367, 369
Blackdown Tableland NP Qld 391, 394, 395
Blackheath NSW 13, 16, 17
Blackmans Bay Tas. 440, 455
Blackwater Qld 393, 394, 397
Blackwater International Coal Centre, Blackwater Qld 393, 394
Blackwood Vic. 151
Blackwood NP Qld 405
Blackwood Valley wine region WA 276, 279, 282
Bladensburg NP Qld 427, 435
Blairgowrie Vic. 131
Blayney NSW 76
Bligh Museum of Pacific Exploration, Bruny Island/lunawanna-allonnah Tas. 452, 453
Blinman SA 250
Blowering Dam, Kosciuszko NP NSW 92, 93
Blue Lake, Mount Gambier SA 241, 244
Blue Lake NP Qld 366
Blue Lotus Water Garden, Yarra Junction Vic. 124, 126
Blue Mountains NSW 4, 10, 12–17
Blue Mountains Botanic Gardens, Mount Tomah NSW 13
Blue Mountains Cultural Centre, Katoomba NSW 15
Blue Mountains NP NSW 13, 16
Blues Train, The, Queenscliff Vic. 159, 162
Blyth SA 224
Boag's Brewery, Launceston Tas. 467, 474
Boat Harbour Tas. 461, 462
Boat Mountain Conservation Park Qld 366, 369
boating and sailing
  Airlie Beach Qld 404
  Australind WA 279
  Baird Bay SA 262
  Barmera SA 236
  Barraba NSW 64
  Batemans Bay NSW 86
  Beachport Conservation Park SA 241
  Beauty Point Tas. 471
  Bega NSW 86
  Bethungra NSW 101
  Biloela Qld 394
  Boreen Point Qld 385
  Bournda NP NSW 85
  Bremer Bay WA 280
  Bribie Island Qld 360
  Brooklyn NSW 30
  Bunbury WA 280
  Byfield NP Qld 391
  Cardwell Qld 405
  Carnamah WA 291
  Ceduna SA 259
  Chaffey Dam NSW 63
  Chinchilla Qld 379
  Cleaverville Beach WA 320

Coffin Bay SA 259
Conningham Tas. 455
Coonamble NSW 77
Coorong NP SA 233
Copeton Dam State Recreation Area NSW 63
Crows Nest Qld 379
Cygnet Tas. 453
Dampier Archipelago WA 320
Daylesford Vic. 154
Dover Tas. 453
Dunolly Vic. 154
Echuca Vic. 184
Eildon Vic. 196
Esk Qld 367
Finley NSW 102
Freycinet NP Tas. 445
Geelong Vic. 161
Gippsland Lakes Vic. 141
Goolwa SA 211
Goulburn River NP 38
Great Sandy Strait Qld 392
Guilderton WA 299
Gunnedah NSW 65
Hamilton Island Qld 402
Hamilton Tas. 474
Hamilton Vic. 178
Harvey WA 283
Hopetoun WA 307
Huonville Tas. 454
Huskisson NSW 87
Innamincka SA 251
Inverell NSW 66
Judbarra–Gregory NP NT 343
Jurien Bay WA 292
Karratha WA 320
Karumba Qld 423
Katanning WA 283
Kerang Vic. 186
Kettering Tas. 454
Khancoban NSW 95
Kojonup WA 284
Lake Argyle WA 323
Lake Broadwater Conservation Park Qld 378
Lake Cargelligo NSW 80
Lake Eildon NP Vic. 193
Lake Hindmarsh Vic. 174
Lake Jindabyne NSW 91
Lake Kununurra WA 327
Lake Mulwala NSW 97
Lake Tinaroo Qld 412, 419
Lake Tyers Vic. 143
Lakes Entrance Vic. 143
Lancelin WA 299
Lithgow NSW 17
Lizard Island NP Qld 410
Mackay Qld 406
Maldon Vic. 156
Maleny Qld 387
Mallacoota Vic. 144
Manilla NSW 66
Mannum SA 237
Mansfield Vic. 197
Maryborough Qld 397
Metung Vic. 143
Milang SA 210
Mission Beach Qld 417
Moe Vic. 137
Monto Qld 398
Mooloolaba Qld 388
Moranbah Qld 406
Morgan SA 237
Mount Morgan Qld 398
Murgon Qld 369
Murray River NP, Bulyong Island Section SA 239
Myall Lakes NP NSW 44
Nambucca Heads NSW 49
Narooma NSW 88
Narrandera NSW 104
Nerang Qld 374
Newman WA 320
Noosa Heads Qld 388
Normanton Qld 423
Nowra NSW 88
Port Arthur Tas. 448

Port Augusta SA 253
Port Broughton SA 230
Port Kenny SA 262
Port Lincoln SA 261
Port Pirie SA 230
Port Stephens NSW 36
Port Vincent SA 231
Proserpine Qld 407
Richmond Tas. 476
Rinyirru (Lakefield) NP (CYPAL) Qld 410
St Helens Tas. 448
Sale Vic. 145
Sarina Qld 407
Shellharbour NSW 27
Smithton Tas. 465
Smoky Bay SA 259
South Cumberland Islands NP Qld 406
South Stradbroke Island Qld 371
South West Rocks NSW 44
Surfers Paradise Qld 375
Tallangatta Vic. 199
Taylors Beach Qld 406
Temora NSW 104
Texas Qld 381
Tin Can Bay Qld 389
Tooradin Vic. 137
Tweed Heads NSW 59
Wagin WA 299
Waikerie SA 239
Wallaga Lake NSW 85
Wallaroo SA 231
Warrnambool Vic. 171
Wee Waa NSW 69
Weipa Qld 419
Welshpool Vic. 139
Wentworth NSW 105
Whyalla SA 263
Wickepin WA 299
Wingham NSW 44, 51
Wollongong NSW 27
Woodburn NSW 57
Woy Woy NSW 33
Yarra Glen Vic. 127
Yarrawonga Vic. 189
Yeppoon Qld 399
Yuraygir NP NSW 54
Zeehan Tas. 459
Bodalla NSW 88
Bogong High Plains Vic. 195
Bolgart WA 296
Bollon Qld 381
Bombala NSW 84, 87, 89
Bonegilla NSW 100, 191, 199
Bonegilla Migrant Experience, Bonegilla NSW 191, 199
Bongil Bongil NP NSW 43, 51
Bonnie Doon Vic. 194
Bonorong Wildlife Sanctuary, Brighton Tas. 452, 455
Booderee Botanic Gardens, Jervis Bay JBT 83, 87
Booderee NP NSW 83, 87
Boodjamulla (Lawn Hill) NP Qld 421, 429, 434, 435
Bookham NSW 27
Booleroo Centre SA 252
Booligal NSW 98
Boonah Qld 361, 371, 373, 375
Boonoo Boonoo NP NSW 63, 68
Boorowa NSW 27
Boort Vic. 187
Booti Booti NP NSW 43, 47
Border Ranges NP NSW 53
Border Village WA 302, 304
Bordertown SA 236
Boreen Point Qld 385
Boreore Caves NSW 81
Borroloola NT 343, 345
Botanic Gardens and Bird World, Maleny Qld 385, 387
Bothwell Tas. 452, 453
Bouddi NP NSW 5, 29, 31
Boulia Qld 429
Bourke NSW 108, 109
Bournda NP NSW 85

Bowen Qld 404
Bowling Green Bay NP Qld 403, 407
Bowral NSW 19, 23, 25
Bowraville NSW 45
Boyanup WA 282
Boydtown NSW 85, 87
Boyne Island Qld 396
Boyup Brook WA 276, 279, 281
Bradman Museum & International Cricket Hall of Fame, Bowral NSW 19, 23
Bradman's Birthplace, Cootamundra NSW 98, 100
Braidwood NSW 21, 23–4
Braidwood Museum, Braidwood NSW 21
Brambuk – The National Park and Cultural Centre, Halls Gap Vic. 173, 178
Bramston Beach Qld 413
Bremer Bay WA 273, 279–80
Brewarrina NSW 109, 111
Brewarrina Fish Traps, Brewarrina NSW 107
Bribie Island Qld 360, 365, 367
Brickendon, Longford Tas. 467, 475
Bridestowe Estate Lavender Farm, Scottsdale Tas. 467, 476
Bridgetown WA 276, 280, 281
Bridgewater on Loddon Vic. 154
Bridport Tas. 469, 471, 473, 477
Bridport Wildflower Reserve, Bridport Tas. 470
Brierley Jigsaw Gallery, Bridgetown WA 276, 280
Brigalow Qld 397
Bright Vic. 192, 195–6, 197
Brighton Tas. 476
Brim Vic. 179
Brindabella NP NSW 27
daytrips from 360–1
Brisbane Qld 358–9
Brisbane and surrounds wine region Qld 372
Brisbane Hinterland Qld 360, 362, 364–8
Brisbane Ranges NP Vic. 151
Brisbane Valley Rail Trail Qld 367
Brisbane Water NP NSW 29, 31, 33
Broad Arrow WA 305
Broadbeach Qld 361, 371, 375
Broadford Vic. 155
Broadmarsh Tas. 476
Broadwater NP NSW 57
Broke NSW 41
Broken Hill NSW 108, 109–10, 111
Brook Islands Qld 405
Brooklyn NSW 30
Brookton WA 291
Broome WA 323, 324, 325, 327
Brooweena Qld 394
Broulee NSW 88
Bruce SA 254
Brunswick Heads NSW 53, 56
Brunswick Valley Historical Museum, Mullumbimby NSW 54, 58
Bruny Island/lunawanna-allonnah Tas. 440, 450, 451, 452, 453, 454
Bruny Island Cruises, Bruny Island/lunawanna-allonnah Tas. 451, 453
Bruthen Vic. 145
Buccaneer Archipelago WA 323, 325, 326
Buchan Vic. 141, 143
Buchan Caves Reserve, Buchan Vic. 141, 143
Buda Historic Home and Garden, Castlemaine Vic. 147, 153
Budderoo NP NSW 19, 25, 26
Buderim Qld 385, 386, 389
Buderim Forest Park Qld 385, 386
Budgewai Lake NSW 30
Budj Bim National Cultural Landscape Vic. 170, 173
Budj Bim NP Vic. 173
Bukalara Rocks NT 343

Buku-Larrnggay Mulka, Yirrkala NT 337, 341
Bulahdelah NSW 44, 46
Bulli Pass Scenic Reserve, Wollongong NSW 21
Bullocks Flat NSW 94, 95
Bunbury WA 273, 280, 281
Bundaberg Qld 391, 392, 393, 394–5, 397
Bundaberg Botanic Gardens, Bundaberg Qld 391, 394
Bundaberg Rum Distillery, Bundaberg Qld 393
Bundaleer Forest Reserve SA 222, 224
Bundanon NSW 83
Bundanoon NSW 24, 25, 88
Bundjalung NP NSW 53, 57
Bungendore NSW 19, 26
Bungle Bungle Range WA 324
Bungonia State Conservation Area, Bungonia NSW 21
Buninyong Vic. 152
Bunjil's Shelter, Stawell Vic. 173, 179
Bunurong Coastal Drive, Inverloch and Cape Paterson Vic. 133
Bunurong Marine NP Vic. 133, 139
Bunya Mountains NP Qld 365, 368
Burketown Qld 421, 422
Burleigh Heads Qld 372, 373–4, 375
Burleigh Heads NP Qld 374
Burnett Heads Qld 395
Burnie Tas. 461, 463
Burning Mountain NSW 39, 41
Burr Heritage Passport, Burra SA 221, 223
Burra SA 221, 223
Burrawang NSW 26
Burrowa–Pine Mountain NP Vic. 192, 196
Burrum Coast NP Qld 393, 395, 397
Burrum Heads Qld 397
bushwalking
  Abercrombie River NP NSW 15
  Albury NSW 100
  Alice Springs Telegraph Station Historical Reserve NT 351
  Alpine NP Vic. 144, 191
  Anglesea Vic. 168
  Apollo Bay Vic. 167
  Ararat Vic. 176
  Atherton Qld 413
  Augusta–Busselton Heritage Trail WA 279, 281
  Australian Alps Walking Track 199
  Avon Valley NP WA 289
  Bago Bluff NP NSW 51
  Balaklava SA 223
  Balfour Track Tas. 465
  Ballarat Vic. 152
  Balmoral Vic. 177
  Barren Grounds Nature Reserve NSW 21
  Barrington Tops NP NSW 43
  Barron Gorge NP Qld 409
  Bass Coast Rail Trail Vic. 135, 139
  Baw Baw NP Vic. 133
  Bedarra Island Qld 411
  Beechy Rail Trail Vic. 169
  Belair NP SA 215
  Bellingen NSW 46
  Ben Boyd NP NSW 83
  Ben Lomond NP Tas. 467
  Bermagui NSW 87
  Berry Springs Nature Park NT 341
  Bibbulmun Track WA 268, 277, 279, 281, 282, 283, 286, 295
  Bicentennial National Trail 368, 415
  Biggenden Qld 394
  Bindarri NP NSW 45
  Bingara NSW 64
  Birdwood SA 218
  Blackdown Tableland NP Qld 391
  Bladensburg NP Qld 427
  Blue Mountains NSW 4
  Blue Mountains NP NSW 13
  Boat Mountain Conservation Park Qld 366

Bombala NSW 87
Bongil Bongil NP NSW 43
Bonnie Doon Vic. 194
Booderee NP NSW 83
Boodjamulla (Lawn Hill) NP Qld 421
Boonoo Boonoo NP NSW 63
Border Ranges NP NSW 53
Bordertown SA 236
Bouddi NP NSW 29
Bournda NP NSW 85
Bowling Green Bay NP Qld 403
Bowral NSW 23
Bribie Island Qld 360, 365
Bridgetown WA 280
Brindabella NP NSW 27
Brisbane Ranges NP Vic. 151
Brisbane Water NP NSW 29
Broadwater NP NSW 57
Budderoo NP NSW 19
Budj Bim NP Vic. 173
Bulahdelah NSW 46
Bundjalung NP NSW 53
Bungonia State Conservation Area NSW 21
Bunya Mountains NP Qld 365
Burra SA 223
Burrowa–Pine Mountain NP Vic. 192
Butterly Gorge Nature Park NT 338
Cairns Qld 413
Camperdown–Timboon Rail Trail Vic. 167, 169
Cania Gorge NP Qld 393
Canunda NP SA 241
Cape Hillsborough NP Qld 403
Cape Le Grand NP WA 301
Carnarvon NP Qld 397
Castle Tower NP Qld 397
Cathedral Range State Park Vic. 124
Central Plateau Conservation Area Tas. 475
Clare SA 224
Cleland National Park SA 215
Clermont Qld 406
Clump Mountain NP Qld 417
Cockburn Ranges WA 323
Cocoparra NP NSW 98
Coffin Bay NP SA 257
Coffin Bay SA 259
Coffs Harbour NSW 46
Cohuna Vic. 184
Colac Vic. 169
Conimbla NP NSW 78
Conondale NP Qld 387
Coolah Tops NP NSW 33
Coopracambra NP Vic. 142
Coorong NP SA 233
Copeton Dam State Recreation Area NSW 63
Cradle Mountain–Lake St Clair NP Tas. 461
Crater Lakes NP Qld 411
Creswick Regional Park Vic. 149
Crookwell NSW 25
Crystal Brook SA 229
Curtis Island National Park and Conservation Park Qld 297
D'Aguilar NP Qld 365
Dalrymple NP Qld 403
Dandenong Ranges NP Vic. 123
Deep Creek National Park SA 209
Deloraine Tas. 471
Devonport Tas. 464
Dharug NP NSW 29
Dhilba Guuranda-Innes NP SA 227
Dinner Plain Vic. 195
Donald Vic. 177
Douglas–Apsley NP Tas. 446
Dover Tas. 453
Dryandra Woodland WA 289
Dularcha NP Qld 387
Dunk Island Qld 411
Dunkeld Vic. 178
Dwellingup WA 283
Edenhope Vic. 178
Elliston Coastal Trail SA 260
Elsey NP NT 343
Enfield State Park Vic. 149

481

Errinundra NP Vic. 142
Esperance WA 304
Evans Crown Nature Reserve NSW 15
Exeter Tas. 473
Expedition NP Qld 393
Fingal Tas. 448
Finke Gorge NP NT 349
Fitzroy Island Qld 409
Forrest Vic. 167
Franklin–Gordon Wild Rivers NP Tas. 458
Freycinet NP Tas. 445
Geegelup Heritage Trail WA 280
Gibraltar Range NP NSW 61
Gippsland Plains Rail Trail Vic. 144
Girringun NP Qld 401
Giru Qld 407
Glass House Mountains NP Qld 383
Glen Helen Gorge NT 349
Gloucester NP WA 273
Gold Coast hinterland Qld 361
Goldfields Track Vic. 153
Gordonvale Qld 415
Goulburn River NP NSW 38
Grampians NP Vic. 173
Great Ocean Walk Vic. 165
Great Otway NP Vic. 165
Great Sandy NP Qld 383
Great South West Walk Vic. 170, 171
Great Victorian Rail Trail Vic. 197
Great Walhalla Alpine Trail, Vic. 138
Greater Beedelup NP WA 276
Greater Bendigo NP Vic. 149
Gunbower Island NP 183
Guy Fawkes River NP NSW 47
Gympie Qld 386
Hanging Rock NSW 61
Hartz Mountains NP Tas. 452
Hat Head NP NSW 45
Hattah–Kulkyne NP Vic. 183
Heathcote NP NSW 27
Heathcote–Graytown NP Vic. 149
Hepburn Regional Park Vic. 149
Herberton Range NP Qld 412
Heysen Trail SA 213, 218, 222, 229, 250, 251
Hinchinbrook Island NP Qld 401
Holey Plains State Park Vic. 142
Hughenden Qld 431
Hume and Hovell Walking Track NSW 93
Ikara–Flinders Ranges NP SA 247
Iluka Nature Reserve NSW 53
Inverell NSW 66
John Forrest NP WA 289
Judbarra–Gregory NP NT 343
Kakadu NP NT 338
Kalamunda NP WA 295
Kalbarri/Kalbarri NP WA 310
Kalgoorlie–Boulder WA 305
Kanangra–Boyd NP NSW 14
Kara Kara NP Vic. 149
Karijini NP WA 319
Karlu Karlu–Devils Marbles Conservation Reserve NT 349
Katanning WA 283
Katanning–Piesse Heritage Trail WA 283
Keep River NP NT 344
Kenilworth State Forest Qld 383
Kennedy Range NP WA 311
Killarney Qld 380
Kimba SA 261
Kinglake NP Vic. 124
Kings Canyon NT 350, 351
Kingscote SA 212
Kingston S.E. SA 243
Kondalilla NP Qld 385
Kooyoora State Park Vic. 149
Kosciuszko NP NSW 91
Kwiambal NP NSW 63
Kyneton Vic. 155
Kyogle NSW 58
Lake Buloke Vic. 175
Lake Eildon NP Vic. 193
Lake Leschenaultia WA 295

Lakes Entrance Vic. 143
Lamington NP Qld 371
Larapinta Trail NT 350
Leeuwin–Naturaliste NP WA 274
Lerderderg State Park Vic. 150
Leschenault Inlet WA 276
Lilydale–Warburton Rail Trail Vic. 127
Lincoln NP SA 257
Litchfield NP NT 332
Little Desert NP Vic. 174
Long Island Qld 402
Longreach Qld 433
Lord Howe Island NSW 49
Lorne Vic. 169
Lower Glenelg NP Vic. 166
Macquarie Marshes NSW 74
Mahagony Walking Track Vic. 170
Main Range NP Qld 371
Maitland NSW 38
Malanda Qld 412
Mallacoota Vic. 144
Mansfield Vic. 197
Maria Island NP Tas. 445, 446
Mariala NP Qld 427
Marramarra NP NSW 33
Mary River NT 333
Marysville Vic. 126
Midge Point Qld 407
Miena Vic. 475
Millaa Millaa Qld 417
Millstream–Chichester NP WA 319
Mimosa Rocks NP NSW 84
Minlaton SA 230
Miriam Vale Qld 398
Mirima NP WA 324
Mission Beach Qld 417
Mogo State Forest NSW 84
Monga NP NSW 21
Monto Qld 398
Moorrinya NP Qld 431
Morton NP NSW 20
Mount Arapiles–Tooan State Park Vic. 174
Mount Archer NP Qld 393
Mount Barney NP Qld 372
Mount Buangor State Park Vic. 175
Mount Buffalo NP Vic. 192
Mount Field NP Tas. 441, 451
Mount Granya State Park Vic. 193
Mount Hotham Vic. 195
Mount Kaputar NP NSW 62
Mount Remarkable NP SA 247, 252
Mount Royal NP NSW 41
Mount Walsh NP Qld 393
Mount William NP Tas. 468
Mount Worth State Park Vic. 135
Munghorn Gap Nature Reserve NSW 74
Murray Bridge SA 238
Murray to Mountains Rail Trail Vic. 192, 195, 198
Murray–Sunset NP Vic. 181
Muttaburra Qld 434
Namadgi NP ACT 22
Nangar NP NSW 74
Nannup WA 285
Narrogin WA 295
N'Dhala Gorge Nature Park 350
Nerang NP and Nerang State Forest Qld 372
Newcastle NSW 40
Nightcap NP NSW 54
Nitmiluk NP NT 343
Noosa NP Qld 384
North Stradbroke/Minjerribah Qld 366
Northcliffe WA 285
Nuytsland Nature Reserve WA 302
Nymboida NSW 57
Old Beechy Rail Trail Vic. 169
Omeo Vic. 198
Onkaparinga River NP SA 210
Overland Track Tas. 461
Oxley Wild Rivers NP NSW 62
Oyala Thumotang NP (CYPAL) Qld 419

Para Wirra Recreation Park SA 216
Parnkalla Walking Trail SA 262
Peak Charles NP WA 307
Pemberton WA 286
Penguin Tas. 464
Pinjarra WA 286
Pinnaroo SA 238
Porongurup NP WA 275
Port Arthur Tas. 448
Port Campbell NP Vic. 167
Port Elliott SA 212
Port Fairy Vic. 170
Port Fairy–Warrnambool Rail Trail Vic. 170, 171
Port Lincoln SA 262
Port Welshpool Vic. 134
Pyrenees Ranges State Forest Vic. 150
Queanbeyan NSW 26
Quorn SA 253
Railway Reserves Heritage Trail WA 268
Ravensbourne NP Qld 378
Richmond NSW 31
Richmond Range NP NSW 55
Riverland Biosphere Reserve SA 234
Robertson NSW 26
Rosebery Tas. 459
Rottnest Island WA 297
Royal NP NSW 20
Ruby Gap Nature Park NT 350
Rylstone NSW 81
St Helens Tas. 449
Savage River NP Tas. 465
Seymour Vic. 188
Sheffield Tas. 464
Smithton Tas. 465
Snowy River NP Vic. 142
South Bruny NP Tas. 452
South Coast Track Tas. 452
Southport Tas. 454
Southwest NP Tas. 452
Springbrook NP Qld 371
Stanley Tas. 465
Stansbury SA 231
Stirling Range NP WA 275
Strathpine Qld 369
Streaky Bay SA 262
Strzelecki NP Tas. 470
Swan Reach SA 239
Swansea Tas. 449
Tamborine NP Qld 372
Tasman NP Tas. 446
Tasmanian Trail Tas. 453
Telowie Gorge Conservation Park SA 231
Terrick Terrick NP Vic. 183
Texas Qld 381
The Entrance NSW 32
The Lakes NP Vic. 141
Thorsborne Trail Qld 401
Thredbo NSW 95
Tjoritja/West MacDonnell NP NT 350
Tomaree NP NSW 36
Torndirrup NP WA 275
Trephina Gorge Nature Park NT 350
Tuart Forest NP WA 277
Tully Qld 419
Uluru–Kata Tjuṯa NP NT 350
Ulverstone Tas. 465
Umbrawarra Gorge Nature Park NT 338
Valley of the Giants WA 275
Wagga Wagga NSW 105
Wallaga Lake NSW 85
Walls of Jerusalem NP Tas. 475
Walpole WA 287
Waratah Tas. 465
Warburton Vic. 127
Warby–Ovens NP Vic. 193
Warren NP WA 277
Warrumbungle NP NSW 73
Watagans NP NSW 36
Watarrka NP NT 350

Wedderburn Vic. 156
Weddin Mountains NP NSW 73
Welshpool Vic. 139
Wentworth Falls NSW 13
West Cape Howe NP WA 278
Wet Tropics World Heritage Area Qld 417
Willunga SA 213
Wilsons Promontory NP Vic. 134
Wollemi NP NSW 14
Woodend Vic. 157
Wooroonooran NP Qld 410
Wyndham WA 327
Wyperfeld NP Vic. 183
Yangie Trail SA 258
Yankalilla SA 213
Yarra Glen Vic. 127
Yass NSW 27
Yengo NP NSW 37
Yuraygir NP NSW 54
Busselton WA 273, 281
Busselton Jetty WA 273, 281
Butler Memorial, Minlaton SA 228
Butterfly Gorge Nature Park NT 338
Buxton Qld 395
Byaduk Caves Vic. 175
Bybarra NSW 51
Byfield NP Qld 391, 399
Byron Bay NSW 56, 57
Byron Bay Wildlife Sanctuary, Ballina 54

Cabarlah Qld 381
Cable Beach WA 323, 325
Caboolture Qld 366, 367, 369
Caboolture Regional Art Gallery, Caboolture Qld 366, 367
Cabramatta NSW 4
Cabramurra NSW 91
Cadell SA 237–8
Caiguna WA 302, 303
Cairns Qld 363, 408, 409, 410, 412, 413, 415, 419
Cairns Aquarium, Cairns Qld 409, 413
Cairns Botanic Gardens, Cairns Qld 409, 413
Californian Redwoods, Apollo Bay Vic. 167
Callington Mill, Oatlands Tas. 467, 476
Calliope Qld 396, 397
Caloundra Qld 385, 386, 389
Camden NSW 21, 24
Cameron Corner NSW 107
Camooweal Qld 421, 427
Campania Tas. 476
Campbell Town Tas. 441, 471–2, 473
Campbelltown NSW 20, 21, 24–5
Campbelltown Arts Centre, Campbelltown NSW 21
Camperdown Vic. 168, 169
Camperdown–Timboon Rail Trail Vic. 167, 169
Canberra ACT 8–9
Canberra wine region NSW 19
Candelo NSW 86
Cania Gorge NP Qld 393, 398
Cann River Vic. 141, 143
canoeing
  Abercrombie River NP NSW 15
  Alpine NP Vic. 191
  Augusta WA 279
  Avon Valley NP WA 289
  Barmah NP Vic. 181
  Batchelor NT 340
  Baw Baw NP Vic. 133
  Bega NSW 86
  Bellingen NSW 48
  Berri SA 236
  Bethungra NSW 101
  Bongil Bongil NP NSW 43
  Boodjamulla (Lawn Hill) NP Qld 421
  Bordertown SA 236
  Boreen Point Qld 385
  Bungonia State Conservation Area NSW 21

INDEX

Burra SA 223
Cattai NP NSW 29
Cecil Plains Qld 380
Chiltern–Mount Pilot NP Vic. 193
Coffin Bay SA 259
Coffs Harbour NSW 47
Collie WA 281
Coorong NP SA 233
Croajingolong NP Vic. 141
Currawinya NP Qld 425–6
Currimundi Lake Conservation Park Qld 385
Deua NP NSW 22, 85
Dharug NP NSW 29
Diamantina NP Qld 427
Dunsborough WA 282
Esk Qld 367
Esperance WA 304
Eurimbula NP Qld 398
Franklin–Gordon Wild Rivers NP Tas. 458
Freycinet NP Tas. 445
Goondiwindi Qld 380
Gordonvale Qld 415
Guilderton WA 299
Gunbower Island Vic. 183
Guy Fawkes River NP NSW 47
Hattah–Kulkyne NP Vic. 183
Hay NSW 103
Hunter Wetlands Centre, Shortland NSW 37
Iluka Nature Reserve NSW 53
Judbarra–Gregory NP NT 343
Kalbarri NP WA 310
Kangaroo Valley NSW 84
Lake Argyle WA 323
Lake Leschenaultia WA 268, 295
Lake Mulwala NSW 97
Lithgow NSW 17
Lower Glenelg NP Vic. 166
Loxton SA 237
Marramarra NP NSW 33
Mooloolah River NP Qld 388
Mount Buffalo NP Vic. 192
Mount Isa Qld 434
Mundaring WA 295
Murray River NP, Bulyong Island Section SA 239
Myall Lakes NP NSW 44
Nannup WA 285
Narrandera NSW 104
Nitmiluk NP NT 343
Noosa River and the Everglades Qld 385
Nowra NSW 88
Nymboida NSW 57
Renmark SA 238
Riverland Biosphere Reserve SA 234
Russell River NP Qld 413
Stanthorpe Qld 381
Tennant Creek NT 354
Texas Qld 381
Thirlmere Lakes NP NSW 26
Walhalla Vic. 138
Walpole WA 287
Walwa Vic. 196
Warrabah NP NSW 63
Wellington NP WA 281
Willandra NP NSW 75
Yuraygir NP NSW 54
Canowindra NSW 77
Canunda NP SA 241, 243
Cape Arid NP WA 303, 304
Cape Bowling Green Qld 403
Cape Bridgewater Vic. 165, 170
Cape Byron NSW 53
Cape Conran Coastal Park Vic. 141
Cape Crawford NT 343
Cape Hillsborough NP Qld 403
Cape Hillsborough Qld 403
Cape Jaffa SA 243
Cape Jervis SA 212, 213, 250
Cape Le Grand NP WA 301, 304
Cape Leeuwin WA 274
Cape Leeuwin Lighthouse WA 276, 278
Cape Leveque WA 324
Cape Liptrap Vic. 136
Cape Melville NP (CYPAL) Qld 415
Cape Naturaliste WA 274, 281
Cape Otway Vic. 165
Cape Palmerston NP Qld 403, 407
Cape Paterson Vic. 133, 134, 139
Cape Range NP WA 309, 314
Cape Tribulation Qld 409, 415
Cape Upstart NP Qld 404–5
Cape Woolamai Vic. 135
Cape York Qld 409, 414
Capella Qld 395, 397
Capital Country NSW 18–27
Capricorn and K'gari (Fraser Island) Coast Qld 363, 390–9
Capricorn Caves Qld 399
Capricornia Cays NP Qld 391, 396
Captains Flat NSW 26
Caranbirini Conservation Park NT 343
Carboor Vic. 192
Carcoar NSW 71, 76
Cardwell Qld 401, 403, 405
Cardwell Bush Telegraph Heritage Centre, Cardwell Qld 403, 405
Carisbrook Vic. 156
Carlo Sandblow Qld 383
Carmila Qld 407
Carnaby Beetle and Butterfly Collection, Boyup Brook WA 276, 279
Carnamah WA 291
Carnarvon WA 309, 311, 312, 315
Carnarvon Heritage Precinct, Carnarvon WA 311
Carnarvon NP Qld 391–2, 395, 399, 433, 435
Carnarvon Space and Technology Museum, Carnarvon WA 309, 312
Carrara Qld 374, 375
Carrick Tas. 473
Carrieton SA 254
Casino NSW 56–7
Cassilis NSW 38
Casterton Vic. 173, 176, 177
Castle Tower NP Qld 396–7
Castlemaine Vic. 147, 148, 149, 152–3, 155
Castlemaine Art Museum, Castlemaine Vic. 149, 153
Castlemaine Diggings National Heritage Park, Castlemaine Vic. 149, 152, 153
Cataract Gorge, Launceston 467–8, 474
Cathcart NSW 87
Cathedral Range State Park Vic. 123
Cathedral Rock NP NSW 61, 65
Cattai NP NSW 29
Cave Gardens, Mount Gambier SA 241, 244
Cavendish Vic. 178
caves
 Abercrombie Caves NSW 74
 Borenore Caves NSW 81
 Bright Vic. 196
 Buchan Caves Reserve Vic. 141, 143
 Bungonia State Conservation Area NSW 21
 Byaduk Caves Vic. 175
 Camooweal Qld 427, 429
 Capricorn Caves Qld 399
 Chillagoe–Mungana Caves NP Qld 421, 422
 Cocklebiddy Caves WA 303
 Coonabarabran NSW 77
 Crystal Cave WA 290
 Crystal Caves Qld 413
 Cutta Cutta Caves Nature Park NT 344
 Deua NP NSW 85
 Drovers Cave NP WA 292
 Engelbrecht Cave SA 242
 Goulburn River NP NSW 38, 74
 Great Nowranie Cave Qld 427
 Gunns Plains Caves Tas. 461, 465
 Hastings Caves Tas. 451, 454
 Jenolan Caves NSW 14
 Jewel Cave WA 274
 Jingamia Cave WA 295
 King Solomons Cave Tas. 468
 Kooyoora State Park Vic. 149
 Lake Cave WA 274
 Leeuwin-Naturaliste NP WA 274
 Mammoth Cave WA 274
 Marakoopa Cave Tas. 468
 Mermaid's Cave NSW 16
 Mimbi Caves WA 326
 Mole Creek Karst NP Tas. 468, 475
 Moondyne Cave WA 274
 Mount Napier State Park Vic. 175
 Murrawijinie Caves SA 257
 Naracoorte Caves NP SA 242
 Newdegate Cave Tas. 451
 Ngilgi Cave WA 281, 287
 Princess Margaret Rose Caves Vic. 166
 Remarkable Cave Tas. 441, 446, 448
 Talia Caves SA 258
 Tantanoola Caves SA 243
 Tunnel Creek NP WA 323
 Wee Jasper NSW 22
 Wellington Caves NSW 73, 81
 Wiliyan-Ngurru NP Qld 427, 429
 Wombeyan Caves NSW 20
 Yallingup WA 287
 Yanchep NP WA 269, 290
 Yarrangobilly Caves NSW 91
Cecil Plains Qld 380
Cedars, The, Hahndorf SA 215, 218
Ceduna SA 229
Centennial Parklands, Glen Innes NSW 61, 65
Central Coast NSW 5, 10, 28–33
Central Deborah Gold Mine, Bendigo Vic. 147, 152
Central Greenough Historic Settlement, Greenough WA 311, 315
Central Plateau Conservation Area Tas. 475
Central Tilba NSW 83, 89
Central West NSW 11, 70–81
Central West Vic. 121, 172–9
Cervantes WA 289, 291
Cessnock NSW 35, 38
Chaffey Dam, Nundle NSW 63, 67
Chambers Pillar Historical Reserve (Itirkawara) NT 349
Channel Highway towns Tas. 440
Charity Island Tas. 453
Charleville Qld 425, 430
Charlotte Pass NSW 94
Charters Towers Qld 403, 404, 405
Cherbourg Qld 369
Cheshunt Vic. 192
Chewton Vic. 153
Childers Qld 393, 395, 397
Childers Vic. 139
Chillagoe Qld 415, 421, 422
Chillagoe–Mungana Caves NP Qld 421, 422
Chilli Beach Qld 414, 419
Chiltern Vic. 196
Chiltern–Mount Pilot NP Vic. 193, 196
Chinchilla Qld 378, 379
Chinchilla Historical Museum, Chinchilla Qld 378, 379
Chowilla Regional Reserve SA 234
Christies Beach SA 212
Church Hill State Heritage Area, Gawler SA 216, 218
Church of the Holy Cross, Morawa WA 311, 316
Churchill Island Vic. 136
City Park, Launceston Tas. 470, 473
Clairview Qld 407
Clare SA 221, 223–4
Clare Valley SA 206, 220–5
Clare Valley wine region SA 221, 223, 225
Clarence Town NSW 40
Clarendon House, Evandale Tas. 468, 472
Cleaverville WA 320, 321
Cleland National Park SA 215
Clermont Qld 405–6
Cleve SA 260
Cleveland Qld 366
Clifton Qld 379
Clifton Beach Qld 417
Cloncurry Qld 421, 426, 427, 430
Clump Mountain NP Qld 417
Clunes Vic. 153
Coal Creek Vic. 139
Coal Creek Community Park and Museum, Korumburra Vic. 133, 137
Coal Mines Historic Site, Port Arthur Tas. 445, 448
Coal River wine region Tas. 441, 476
Coalstoun Lakes NP Qld 394
Cobar NSW 108, 110, 111
Cobargo NSW 87
Cobb & Co. Museum, Toowoomba Qld 377, 381
Cobbitty NSW 24
Cobbold Gorge, Mount Surprise Qld 421
Cobram Vic. 184, 187
Cockburn Ranges WA 323
Cockle Creek Tas. 450, 451, 452, 454
Cockle Train, Goolwa Vic. 209, 211, 212, 218
Cocklebiddy WA 302, 303
Cocklebiddy Caves WA 303
Cocoparra NP NSW 98, 102
Coffin Bay SA 257, 258, 259
Coffin Bay NP SA 257, 259
Coffs Harbour NSW 43, 44, 45, 46–7, 49
Cohuna Vic. 184, 187
Colac Vic. 168–9, 171
Coldstream Vic. 127
Coleambally NSW 103
Colebrook Tas. 476
Coleraine Vic. 177
Coles Bay Tas. 447, 449
Coles Beach Tas. 461
Collie WA 277, 281
Collinsville Qld 405
Combo Waterhole Conservation Park Qld 425, 432
Comboyne NSW 51
Come-by-Chance NSW 112
Comet Qld 394
Condamine Qld 379, 380
Condobolin NSW 77
Conimbla NP NSW 78
Conningham Tas. 455
Conondale NP Qld 387
Convent Gallery, Daylesford Vic. 147, 154
Conway NP Qld 403, 404, 406
Coober Pedy SA 247, 248, 249, 250–1, 253, 306
Coober Pedy Opal Fields Golf Club, Coober Pedy SA 249, 251
Coober Pedy's Underground Churches, Coober Pedy SA 247, 251
Coobowie SA 229
Coo-Ee Heritage Centre NSW 79
Cooinda NT 338
Cooktown Botanic Gardens, Cooktown Qld 411, 414
Cooktown Museum, Cooktown Qld 409–10, 414
Cooktown Qld 410, 414, 415
Coolah Tops NP NSW 35
Coolangatta Qld 361, 374
Coolgardie WA 302, 303
Coolum Beach Qld 388
Cooma NSW 92, 94, 95
Cooma Cottage, Yass NSW 21, 27
Coombe Island Qld 411
Coomee Nulunga Cultural Trail, Ulladulla NSW 84, 89
Coominya Qld 367
Coonabarabran NSW 75, 77, 79
Coonamble NSW 77, 79
Coonawarra SA 241
Coonawarra wine region SA 241, 244

483

Coopracambra NP Vic. 142, 143
Coorabakh NP NSW 45, 50
Coorong NP SA 205, 233, 237, 243
Cooroy Qld 389
Cootamundra NSW 98, 100–1, 103
Copeton Dam State Recreation Area NSW 63
Coral Bay WA 310, 312–13
Coral Coast WA 271, 308–17
Corinna/kurina Tas. 457, 459
Cornwall Tas. 449
Corny Point SA 231
Corowa NSW 99, 103
Corrigin WA 290, 291
Corrigin Pioneer Museum, Corrigin WA 290, 291
Corroboree Rock Conservation Reserve NT 351, 352
Corryong Vic. 192, 196, 197
Cosmos Centre, Charleville Qld 425, 430
Cossack WA 319, 321
Cowangie Vic. 187
Cowell SA 258, 259–60
Cowes (Phillip Island) Vic. 136
Cowra Japanese Garden, Cowra NSW 71, 78
Cowra NSW 71, 74, 75, 77–8, 79
Cowra wine region NSW 71
Cracow Qld 399
Cradle Mountain Tas. 460, 461, 462
Cradle Mountain–Lake St Clair NP Tas. 461
Cradock SA 251
Craig's Hut Vic. 191
Cranbrook WA 275, 281
Cranky Rock Nature Reserve, Warialda NSW 63, 69
Crater Lakes, Camperdown Vic. 167
Crater Lakes NP Qld 411, 419
Cravensville Vic. 199
Crescent Head NSW 48, 49
Creswick Vic. 149, 153
Creswick Regional Park, Creswick Vic. 149, 153
Croajingolong NP Vic. 141, 143, 144
crocodiles, Top End 340
Crookwell NSW 25
Crowdy Bay NP NSW 43, 48
Crows Nest Qld 379
Crows Nest NP Qld 378, 379
Croydon Qld 422
Crystal Brook SA 229
Crystal Cave WA 290
Crystal Caves Qld 413
CSIRO Radio Telescope, Parkes NSW 71, 81
Cue WA 311, 313
Culburra NSW 88
Culcairn NSW 101
Culgoa Floodplain NP Qld 381
Culgoa NP NSW 109
Cummins SA 263
Cunderdin WA 292
Cunnamulla Qld 430–1
Currawinya NP Qld 425–6, 431
Currie Tas. 461, 463
Currimundi Lake Conservation Park Qld 385
Currumbin Wildlife Sanctuary, Currumbin Qld 371, 374
Curtis Island NP and Conservation Park Qld 397
Cutta Cutta Caves Nature Park NT 344
cycling and mountain-biking
 Alice Springs Telegraph Station Historical Reserve NT 351
 Alpine NP Vic. 191
 Angaston SA 217
 Bass Coast Rail Trail Vic. 135, 139
 Beechy Rail Trail Vic. 169
 Belair NP SA 215
 Bellingen NSW 46
 Bicentennial National Trail 369, 415
 Birdwood SA 218
 Blinman SA 249

Bombala NSW 87
Bonnie Doon Vic. 194
Bright Vic. 196
Brisbane Valley Rail Trail Qld 367
Camperdown–Timboon Rail Trail Vic. 169
Casterton Vic. 176
Castlemaine Vic. 153
Chiltern–Mount Pilot NP Vic. 193
Coolah Tops NP NSW 35
Crookwell NSW 25
Derby Tas. 472
Encounter Bikeway SA 209
Evandale Tas. 472
Forrest Vic. 167
French Island NP Vic. 129
Geelong Vic. 161
Gippsland Plains Rail Trail Vic. 144
Goldfields Track Vic. 153
Goolwa SA 209
Great Southern Rail Trail Vic. 135, 137
Great Victorian Rail Trail Vic. 197
Greater Bendigo NP Vic. 149
Kalbarri NP WA 310
Kwiambal NP NSW 63
Lake Argyle WA 323
Leschenault Inlet WA 276
Lilydale–Warburton Rail Trail Vic. 127
Magnetic Island/Yunbenun Qld 401
Mansfield Vic. 197
Mawson Trail SA 222, 249, 251
Mooloolah River NP Qld 388
Mornington Peninsula NP Vic. 129
Mount Buller Vic. 197
Mount Hotham Vic. 195
Mount Stirling Vic. 197
Munda Biddi Cycle Trail WA 268, 281, 285, 295
Murray to Mountains Rail Trail Vic. 192, 195, 198
Nerang NP and Nerang State Forest Qld 372
Northcliffe WA 286
Nuriootpa SA 219
Old Beechy Rail Trail Vic. 169
Port Fairy–Warrnambool Rail Trail Vic. 170, 171
Richmond Tas. 476
Rottnest Island WA 297
Royal NP NSW 20
Sale Vic. 145
Stansbury SA 231
Thredbo NSW 95
Uluru–Kata Tjuta NP NT 350
Wagga Wagga NSW 105
Walwa Vic. 196
Warburton Vic. 127
Wonthaggi Vic. 135
You Yangs Regional Park Vic. 160
Cygnet Tas. 441, 453, 455
CYP Museum, Maitland SA 228, 230

D'Aguilar NP Qld 365, 369
Daintree Qld 415
Daintree NP Qld 409, 415, 417
Dalby Qld 379–80
Dalgety NSW 93
Dalhousie Springs, Witjira NP SA 249
Dalmorton Tunnel NSW 63, 65
Dalrymple NP Qld 403, 405
Daly River NT 337, 341
Daly Waters NT 343, 345
Daly Waters Pub, Daly Waters NT 343, 345
Dampier WA 319, 320
Dampier Archipelago WA 320
Dampier Peninsula WA 324, 325
Dandenong Ranges Botanic Garden, Olinda Vic. 118, 123, 126
Dandenong Ranges NP Vic. 118, 123, 126
Danggali Conservation Park SA 234
Danggu Geikie Gorge NP WA 323, 326
D'Arenberg Cube, McLaren Vale SA 209, 212

Dargo Vic. 143
Darling Downs Qld 362, 376–81
Darling Downs Zoo, Clifton Qld 378, 379
Darling Ranges WA 268
Darlington Tas. 445
Dartmoor Vic. 166
Darwin NT 330–1
 daytrips from 332–3
Das Neumann Haus, Laidley Qld 366, 368
David Fleay Wildlife Park, Burleigh Heads Qld 372, 374
Davidson Whaling Station Historic Site, Kiah Inlet NSW 85
Davies Creek NP Qld 416
Day Dawn WA 313
Daydream Island Qld 402
Daylesford Vic. 119, 147, 149, 153–4
Deep Creek National Park SA 209, 213
Deepwater NSW 65
Deepwater NP Qld 393, 398
Deeral Qld 413
Delegate NSW 87
Deloraine Tas. 469, 470, 471, 472
Deloraine & districts Folk Museum, Deloraine Tas. 470, 472
Denham WA 309, 310, 313
Denial Bay SA 159
Deniliquin NSW 99, 101–2, 103
Denman NSW 35
Denmark WA 274, 275, 281, 282
D'Entrecasteaux Channel Tas. 440, 452, 453
D'Entrecasteaux NP WA 285, 286
Derby Tas. 470, 472, 473
Derby WA 323, 325–6, 327
Derghold State Park Vic. 175
Derrinallum Vic. 175
Derwent Valley Tas. 441, 455
Design Tasmania Centre and Shop, Launceston Tas. 470, 474
Deua NP NSW 22, 85, 88
Devils@Cradle, Cradle Mountain Tas. 462
Devonport Tas. 461, 462, 463–4
Devonport Regional Gallery, Devonport Tas. 462, 463
Dhamitjinya (East Woody Island) NT 341
Dharug NP NSW 29, 33
Dhilba Guuranda-Innes NP SA 227, 229, 231
Diamantina NP Qld 427, 429
didgeridoo see yidaki purchase in the NT 347
Didthul (Pigeon House Mountain) NSW 85, 89
Dimalurru (Tunnel Creek) NP WA 323, 326
Dimboola Vic. 177
Dinner Plain Vic. 195, 198
dinosaurs 435
Dirk Hartog Island WA 309, 313
diving
 Airlie Beach Qld 404
 Albany WA 278
 Aldinga Beach SA 211
 Batchelor NT 340
 Ben Boyd NP NSW 83
 Bicheno Tas. 447
 Bowen Qld 404
 Bremer Bay WA 280
 Broughton Island NSW 44
 Bunbury WA 280
 Bunurong Marine NP Vic. 133, 139
 Busselton Jetty WA 273
 Byron Bay NSW 56
 Cairns Qld 413
 Capricornia Cays NP Qld 391
 Cardwell Qld 405
 Coral Bay WA 312, 313
 Daydream Island Qld 402
 Dunsborough WA 282
 Eaglehawk Neck/tiralina Tas. 448
 Edithburgh SA 229

Ewens Ponds Conservation Park SA 241
Exmouth WA 314
Fitzroy Island Qld 409
Freycinet NP Tas. 445
Great Keppel Island Qld 392
Green Island Qld 409
Hamelin Bay Wreck Trail WA 274
Hamilton Island Qld 402
Hayman Island Qld 402
Heron Island Qld 391
HMAS Canberra Dive Site, Ocean Grove Vic. 160, 162
Houtman Abrolhos Islands WA 311
Huskisson WA 213
Jervis Bay Marine Park NSW 87
Jurien Bay WA 292
Lady Elliot Island Qld 392
Lord Howe Island NSW 49
Mackay Qld 406
Main Beach Qld 372
Montebello Islands WA 320
Mooloolaba Qld 388
MOUA (Museum of Underwater Art), Townsville Qld 407
Mount William NP Tas. 468
Mulgumpin (Moreton Island) Qld 361
Narooma NSW 88
Normanville SA 213
Orpheus Island NP Qld 402
Penguin Island WA 277
Piccaninnie Ponds Conservation Park SA 241, 242
Point Samson WA 321
Port Douglas Qld 418
Port Noarlunga Reef Underwater Trail SA 212
Port Victoria SA 228
Port Willunga SA 210
Rapid Bay SA 213
Rottnest Island WA 296
Shellharbour NSW 27
South West Rocks NSW 44
SS Yongala Wreck, Cape Bowling Green Qld 403
Stansbury SA 231
Tathra NSW 89
Townsville Qld 407
Tweed Heads NSW 59
Warrnambool Vic. 171
Whitemark Tas. 477
Whyalla SA 263
Yallingup WA 287
Yanchep WA 299
Yeppoon Qld 399
Djiru NP Qld 417
Doddridge, A.H., Blacksmith Shop, Angaston SA 216, 217
Dog on the Tuckerbox, Gundagai NSW 98, 102
Dolphin Discovery Centre, Bunbury WA 273, 280
Don Tas. 461
Don River Railway, Don Tas. 461, 463
Donald Vic. 177
Dongara–Denison WA 311, 313–14, 315
Donnybrook Qld 367
Donnybrook WA 282
Doo Town Tas. 448
Dooragan NP NSW 43
Dorrigo NSW 44, 47, 49
Dorrigo NP NSW 44, 47
Douglas–Apsley NP Tas. 446, 447
Dover Tas. 453
Drake NSW 68
Dromana Vic. 129, 130
Drovers Cave NP WA 282
Dryandra Woodland WA 289, 295
Drysdale Vic. 160, 161
Dubbo NSW 72, 74, 78
dugongs 309, 313
Dularcha NP Qld 387
Dunalley Tas. 447
Dunbogan NSW 48
Dundullimal Homestead, Dubbo NSW 74, 78

Dunera Museum, Hay NSW 98–9, 102
Dungog NSW 45
Dunk Island Qld 411
Dunkeld Vic. 177–8
Dunolly Vic. 154
Dunsborough WA 274, 282
Dunwich Qld 366
Dwellingup WA 276, 281, 282–3

Eagle Heights Qld 361, 375
Eagle Point Vic. 145
Eagle Rock Marine Sanctuary Vic. 168
Eaglehawk Vic. 152
Eaglehawk Vic. 152
Eaglehawk Neck/tiralina Tas. 446, 447–8
East Coast Tas. 442, 444–9
East Coast Natureworld, Bicheno Tas. 446, 447
East Coast wineries Tas. 447
East Gippsland Vic. 120, 140–5
Eastern Arnhem Land NT 341
Eastern View Vic. 166
Ebenezer NSW 30
Echuca Vic. 182, 184–5, 187
Eden NSW 84, 87, 89
Eden Valley wine region SA 215
Edenhope Vic. 177, 178
Edenvale, Pinjarra WA 276, 286
Edithburgh SA 229
Edogawa Commemorative Garden, Gosford NSW 30, 31
Eidsvold Qld 398
Eildon Vic. 196, 197
Eldorado Vic. 193, 199
Ella Bay NP Qld 416
Ellenborough Falls, Elands NSW 44, 51
Elliott Heads Qld 395
Elliott NT 346
Elliston SA 257, 258, 260
Elliston's Great Ocean Drive, Elliston SA 257, 260
Elmore Vic. 188
Elsey NP NT 343
Emerald Qld 392, 395, 397
Emerald Vic. 125, 127
Emmaville NSW 65
Emu Park Qld 399
Emu Valley Rhododendron Gardens, Burnie Tas. 461, 463
Encounter Bikeway, Goolwa and Victor Harbor SA 209, 211
Encounter Coast SA 205
Endeavour River NP Qld 414
Eneabba WA 291
Enfield Vic. 149
Enfield State Park, Enfield Vic. 149
Engelbrecht Cave SA 242, 244
Enormous Ellendale, Mundubbera Qld 398
Ensay Vic. 198
Entally House, Hadspen Tas. 468, 473
Erica Vic. 138
Erina NSW 31
Eromanga Qld 426, 435
Eromanga Natural History Museum, Eromanga Qld 426, 434, 435
Errinundra NP Vic. 142, 144
Esbank House Museum, Lithgow NSW 15
Esk Qld 367
Eskdale Vic. 199
Esperance WA 301, 303, 304, 305
Esperance Museum, Esperance WA 301, 304
Ettalong Beach NSW 33
Eubenangee Swamp NP Qld 411, 415
Eucla WA 301, 304
Eucla NP WA 302, 304
Eucla Telegraph Station Ruins, Eucla WA 301, 304
Eudunda SA 225
Eugowra NSW 78
Eulo Qld 426, 431
Eumundi Qld 383, 388, 389
Eungella Qld 401

Eungella NP Qld 401, 406
Eureka Centre, Ballarat Vic. 147, 151
Eureka Stockade, Ballarat Vic. 157
Eurimbula NP Qld 398
Euroa Vic. 185, 187
Eurobin Vic. 198
Eurobodalla Native Botanic Gardens, Batemans Bay NSW 85, 86
Eurobodalla NP NSW 88
Evandale Tas. 468, 472, 473
Evans Crown Nature Reserve, Oberon NSW 15
Evans Head NSW 57
Evercreech Forest Reserve, Fingal Tas. 446, 448
Ewaninga Rock Carvings Conservation Reserve NT 351, 352
Ewens Ponds Conservation Park SA 241–2, 244
Exeter NSW 24
Exeter Tas. 472
Exmouth WA 309, 314, 315
Expedition NP Qld 393, 399
Explorers Tree, Katoomba NSW 15
Exton Tas. 472
Eyre Bird Observatory WA 302, 303
Eyre Peninsula SA 207, 256–63

Fairhaven Vic. 166
Faith Island Tas. 453
Falls Creek Vic. 195, 197
Falmouth Tas. 449
Family Islands Qld 411, 417
Far West Coast Marine Park SA 257
Farm Shed Museum and Tourist Centre, Kadina SA 227, 230
Faulconbridge NSW 14
Federation Museum, Corowa NSW 99, 101
Fervale Qld 367
Fingal NSW 59
Fingal Tas. 446, 448, 449
Fingal Vic. 129, 130
Finke Gorge NP NT 349, 354
Finley NSW 102
Fish Creek Vic. 135
fishing
  Abercrombie River NP NSW 15
  Adaminaby NSW 93
  Airlie Beach Qld 404
  Albany WA 278
  Aldinga Beach SA 205
  Alexandra Vic. 194
  American River SA 212
  Anglers Rest Vic. 198
  Apollo Bay Vic. 168
  Aramac Qld 428
  Ararat Vic. 176
  Ardrossan SA 229
  Arno Bay SA 260
  Augusta WA 279
  Australind WA 279
  Ayr Qld 404
  Baird Bay SA 262
  Balgowan SA 230
  Ballarat Vic. 152
  Balmoral Vic. 177
  Balranald NSW 100
  Barcaldine Qld 428
  Bargara Qld 395
  Barham NSW 100
  Barmah NP Vic. 181
  Barmera SA 236
  Barraba NSW 64
  Barranyi (North Island) NP NT 344
  Batchelor NT 340
  Batemans Bay NSW 86
  Baw Baw NP Vic. 133
  Bay of Fires Conservation Area Tas. 445
  Beachmere Qld 367
  Beachport SA 243
  Beauty Point Tas. 471
  Bedarra Island Qld 411
  Bega NSW 86
  Bells Bay NSW 58
  Ben Boyd NP NSW 83

  Bermagui NSW 86
  Bicheno Tas. 447
  Biggenden Qld 394
  Biloela Qld 394
  Bingara NSW 64
  Bird Island SA 231
  Blackwater Qld 394
  Blowering Dam NSW 92
  Boat Harbour Tas. 462
  Bombala NSW 87
  Bongil Bongil NP NSW 43
  Boort Vic. 187
  Booti Booti NP NSW 43
  Bordertown SA 236
  Borroloola NT 345
  Bothwell Tas. 471
  Bouddi NP NSW 29
  Bournda NP NSW 85
  Bowen Qld 404, 405
  Boydtown NSW 85
  Boyne Island Qld 396
  Braidwood NSW 24
  Bremer Bay WA 279, 280
  Brewarrina NSW 109
  Bribie Island Qld 360, 365
  Bridgewater on Loddon Vic. 154
  Bridport Tas. 471
  Broadwater NP NSW 57
  Brooklyn NSW 30
  Broome WA 325
  Broughton Island NSW 44
  Bunbury WA 280
  Bundaberg Qld 395
  Bundjalung NP NSW 53
  Burnett Heads Qld 395
  Burnie Tas. 463
  Burrum Heads Qld 397
  Busselton Jetty WA 273, 281
  Buxton Qld 395
  Byfield NP Qld 391
  Byron Bay NSW 56
  Cairns Qld 413, 415
  Calliope Qld 396
  Caloundra Qld 386
  Campbell Town Tas. 472
  Canunda NP SA 241
  Cape Arid NP WA 303, 304
  Cape Jaffa SA 243
  Cape York Qld 414
  Cardwell Qld 405
  Carnarvon WA 312
  Casino NSW 57
  Casterton Vic. 176
  Ceduna SA 259
  Central Plateau Conservation Area Tas. 475
  Cervantes WA 291
  Charters Towers Qld 405
  Chiltern–Mount Pilot NP Vic. 193
  Chinchilla Qld 379
  Clairview Qld 407
  Cleaverville WA 320, 321
  Clermont Qld 406
  Cobram Vic. 184
  Cockburn Ranges WA 323
  Cocklebiddy WA 303
  Coffin Bay SA 259
  Coffs Harbour NSW 47
  Cohuna Vic. 184
  Coles Bay Tas. 447
  Condobolin NSW 77
  Cooktown Qld 414
  Coonamble NSW 77
  Copeton Dam State Recreation Area NSW 63
  Coral Bay WA 312, 313
  Corny Point SA 231
  Cowell SA 259, 260
  Cowes Vic. 136
  Cowra NSW 78
  Crater Lakes, Camperdown Vic. 167
  Crookwell NSW 25
  Crowdy Bay NP NSW 43
  Crows Nest Qld 379
  Croydon Qld 423
  Culburra NSW 88
  Currie Tas. 463

  Cygnet Tas. 453
  Daly River NT 337
  Dampier Archipelago WA 320
  Dampier Peninsula WA 324
  Deep Creek National Park SA 209
  Deepwater NSW 65
  Deloraine Tas. 471
  Denham WA 313
  Denial Bay SA 259
  Deniliquin NSW 101
  Denmark WA 282
  Derby Tas. 472
  Derrinallum Vic. 175
  Deua NP NSW 85
  Dharug NP NSW 29
  Dhilba Guuranda-Innes NP SA 227
  Diamantina NP Qld 427
  Donald Vic. 177
  Donnybrook Qld 367
  Drake NSW 68
  Dunsborough WA 282
  Eaglehawk Neck/tiralina Tas. 447
  Eden NSW 87
  Edenhope Vic. 178
  Edithburgh SA 229
  Eildon Vic. 196
  Elliott Head Qld 395
  Elliston SA 260
  Elsey NP NT 343
  Emerald Qld 395
  Emerald Vic. 125
  Ensay Vic. 198
  Esk Qld 367
  Eskdale Vic. 199
  Eulo Qld 431
  Eurimbula NP Qld 398
  Euroa Vic. 185
  Evandale Tas. 472
  Exmouth WA 314
  Falls Creek Vic. 195
  Falmouth Tas. 440
  Flinders Island SA 260
  Forbes NSW 79
  Forrest Vic. 167
  Forster–Tuncurry NSW 47
  Fowlers Bay SA 259
  Gayndah Qld 395
  Geelong Vic. 161
  George Town Tas. 473
  Geraldton WA 314
  Gerringong NSW 26
  Gin Gin Qld 396
  Gippsland Lakes Vic. 141
  Gladstone Qld 396
  Gloucester NP WA 273
  Goat Island Tas. 465
  Golden Beach Vic. 145
  Goolwa SA 211
  Goondiwindi Qld 380
  Grafton NSW 57
  Greenough WA 315
  Guilderton WA 299
  Gunnedah NSW 65
  Guy Fawkes River NP NSW 47
  Gympie 387
  Halls Creek WA 326
  Hamilton Island Qld 402
  Hamilton Tas. 473
  Hanging Rock NSW 61
  Harvey WA 283
  Hattah–Kulkyne NP Vic. 183
  Hawley Beach Tas. 464
  Hay NSW 103
  Hayman Island Qld 402
  Heathcote Vic. 154
  Hervey Bay Qld 397
  Hindmarsh Island SA 210
  Hopetoun Vic. 185
  Hopetoun WA 307
  Horsham Vic. 178
  Houtman Abrolhos Islands WA 311
  Huonville Tas. 454
  Iluka Nature Reserve NSW 53
  Imbil Qld 386
  Ingham Qld 406
  Innamincka SA 247, 251
  Innisfail Qld 415

485

Inverell NSW 66
Inverloch Vic. 137
Isisford Qld 432
Julia Creek Qld 432
Jurien Bay WA 292
Kalbarri NP WA 310
Kara Kara NP Vic. 149
Karratha WA 320
Karumba Qld 423
Kempsey NSW 48
Kerang Vic. 186
Kettering Tas. 454
Khancoban NSW 94, 95
Kiama NSW 26
King Ash Bay NT 344
Kingscote SA 212
Kingston Tas. 455
Kununurra WA 327
Kutini–Payamu NP Qld 419
Lady Musgrave Island Qld 395
Laidley Qld 368
Lake Argyle WA 323
Lake Boga Vic. 181
Lake Buloke Vic. 175
Lake Cania Qld 397, 398
Lake Cargelligo NSW 80
Lake Cathie NSW 50
Lake Eucumbene NSW 91
Lake Hindmarsh Vic. 174
Lake Jindabyne NSW 91
Lake Monduran Qld 396, 397
Lake Mulwala NSW 97
Lake Tinaroo Qld 412
Lake Tyers Vic. 143
Lakes Entrance Vic. 143
Lancelin WA 299
Leeton NSW 104
Lerderderg State Park Vic. 150
Leschenault Inlet WA 276
Limmen NP NT 344
Lithgow NSW 17
Lizard Island NP Qld 410
Loch Sport Vic. 145
Lombadina WA 324
Longreach Qld 433
Lorne Vic. 169
Lower Glenelg NP Vic. 166
Mackay Qld 406
Mackerel Islands WA 320
Macksville NSW 49
Main Beach Qld 372
Maldon Vic. 156
Maleny Qld 387
Mallacoota Vic. 144
Mandurah WA 269, 284
Manilla NSW 66
Manjimup WA 284
Manns Beach Vic. 139
Mansfield Vic. 197
Marlo Vic. 144
Maroochydore Qld 388
Mary River NT 333
Mary River NP NT 341
Maryborough Qld 397, 398
Marysville Vic. 126
Mathoura NSW 184, 185
Menindee NSW 111
Midge Point Qld 407
Miena Tas. 475
Milang SA 210
Miles Qld 380
Mitchell Qld 433
Moe Vic. 137
Montebello Islands WA 320
Monto Qld 398
Mooloolaba Qld 388
Moonta Bay SA 230
Moore Park Qld 395
Moranbah Qld 406
Mornington Vic. 131
Morwell Vic. 138
Mount Beauty Vic. 198
Mount Isa Qld 434
Mount Morgan Qld 398
Mount William NP Tas. 468
Mudgee NSW 80
Murgon Qld 369

Murray Bridge SA 238
Murray River NP, Bulyong Island Section SA 239
Muttaburra Qld 434
Myall Lakes NP NSW 44
Myrtleford Vic. 198
Nambucca Heads NSW 49
Nannup WA 285
Nariel Vic. 196
Narooma NSW 88
Narrandera NSW 104
Nathalia Vic. 185
Nerang Qld 374
Newcastle NSW 40
Noonamah NT 341
Nooramunga Marine and Coastal Park Vic. 135
Normanton Qld 423
Northampton WA 317
Northcliffe WA 285, 286
Nowra NSW 88
Nundle NSW 67
Nyngan NSW 80
Oatlands Tas. 476
Oberon NSW 17
Omeo Vic. 198
Onslow WA 320, 321
Orbost Vic. 144
Palm Cove Qld 417
Pambula NSW 88
Paradise Beach Vic. 145
Paynesville Vic. 145
Peaceful Bay WA 287
Pemberton WA 286
Pinjarra WA 286
Point Lonsdale Vic. 163
Point Samson WA 321
Port Albert Vic. 138
Port Bonython SA 258
Port Broughton SA 230
Port Campbell Vic. 169
Port Denison WA 313
Port Elliott SA 212
Port Germein SA 231
Port Gregory WA 317
Port Hedland WA 321
Port Kenny SA 262
Port Lincoln SA 261
Port MacDonnell SA 244
Port Macquarie NSW 49, 50
Port Neill SA 263
Port Pirie SA 230
Port Rickaby SA 230
Port Sorell Tas. 464
Port Stephens NSW 36
Port Victoria SA 231
Port Wakefield SA 222
Port Welshpool Vic. 134
Portland Vic. 170
Proserpine Qld 407
Queanbeyan NSW 26
Queenstown Tas. 459
Rainbow Beach Qld 384
Rapid Bay SA 213
Ravenshoe Qld 418
Rinyirru (Lakefield) NP (CYPAL) Qld 410
Riverland Biosphere Reserve SA 234
Robe SA 245
Robinvale Vic. 187
Rochester Vic. 188
Rockhampton Qld 398
Rockingham WA 286
Roma Qld 380
Rosebery Tas. 459
Ross Tas. 475
Rottnest Island WA 297
Rushworth Vic. 188
Rutherglen Vic. 199
Rylstone NSW 81
St George Qld 380
St Helens Tas. 448–9
Sale Vic. 145
Sarina Qld 407
Scamander Tas. 449
Scone NSW 41

Scotts Head NSW 49
Seal Rocks NSW 45
Seaspray Vic. 145
Sellicks Beach SA 211
Seven Emu Station NT 344
Seven Mile Beach NP NSW 22
Shellharbour NSW 27
Sheringa SA 261
Singleton NSW 41
Smithton Tas. 465
Smoky Bay SA 259
Southport Tas. 454
Southwest NP Tas. 452
Spalding SA 224
Stanley Tas. 465
Stansbury SA 231
Stanthorpe Qld 381
Strathpine Qld 369
Streaky Bay SA 262
Sultana Point SA 229
Swansea NSW 40
Swansea Tas. 446, 449
Sweers Island Qld 422
Swifts Creek Vic. 198
Tallangatta Vic. 199
Taree NSW 50
Taroom Qld 399
Tathra NSW 89
Taylors Beach Qld 406
Texas Qld 381
Thallon Qld 381
The Entrance NSW 30
Theodore Qld 399
Thredbo NSW 95
Tiaro Qld 398
Tin Can Bay Qld 389
Tocumwal NSW 104
Tomaree NP NSW 36
Tooradin Vic. 137
Toorbul Qld 367
Toowoomba Qld 381
Torquay Vic. 171
Tully Qld 419
Tumby Bay SA 263
Tweed Heads NSW 59
Ulladulla NSW 89
Ulverstone Tas. 465
Urunga NSW 51
Venus Bay SA 258
Victor Harbor SA 213
Wagga Wagga NSW 105
Waikerie SA 239
Walcha NSW 69
Walgett NSW 112
Walhalla Vic. 138
Walkers Point Qld 395
Wallaga Lake NSW 85
Wallaroo SA 231
Walpole WA 287
Wangaratta Vic. 199
Waratah Tas. 465
Warrabah NP NSW 63
Warren NSW 79
Warrnambool Vic. 171
Warwick Qld 381
Wee Jasper NSW 22
Weeroona Island SA 231
Weipa Qld 419
Wellington NSW 81
Welshpool Vic. 139
West Cape Howe NP WA 278
West Wyalong NSW 105
Westbury Tas. 477
Whitemark Tas. 477
Whyalla SA 263
Willandra NP NSW 75
William Bay NP WA 275
Windy Harbour WA 285
Wingham NSW 51
Wollongong NSW 27
Woodburn NSW 57
Woolgoolga NSW 59
Woy Woy NSW 33
Wycheproof Vic. 179
Wye River Vic. 169
Wynyard Tas. 465
Yallingup WA 287

Yamba NSW 59
Yanchep WA 299
Yanga NP NSW 100
Yankalilla SA 213
Yarra Glen Vic. 127
Yarram Vic. 139
Yarrawonga Vic. 189
Yass NSW 27
Yeppoon Qld 399
Yuraygir NP NSW 54
Zeehan Tas. 459
Fitzgerald River NP WA 273, 279, 280, 307
Fitzroy Crossing WA 323, 326, 327
Fitzroy Island Qld 409, 413
Five Rivers Lookout WA 324, 327
Flagstaff Hill Maritime Museum, Warrnambool Vic. 165, 171
Flaxton Qld 387
Fleet Arm Air Museum, Nowra NSW 83, 88
Fleurieu Peninsula SA 205, 206, 208–13
Fleurieu wine region SA 209, 213
Flinders Vic. 130, 131
Flinders Chase NP SA 209, 212
Flinders Discovery Centre, Hughenden Qld 426, 431
Flinders Group NP Qld 415
Flinders Island SA 260
Flinders Island Tas. 466, 468, 470, 471, 473, 477
Flinders Ranges SA 207, 246–55
Floating Sauna, Derby Tas. 470, 473
Flying High Bird Habitat, Apple Creek Qld 393, 395
Fogg Dam NT 338
Fogg Dam Conservation Reserve NT 332
Forbes NSW 78–9
Forest Den NP Qld 428
Forest Discovery Centre, Dwellingup WA 276, 282
Forests and Waterfall Drive, Otway Ranges Vic. 165, 168
Forrest Vic. 167
Forsayth Qld 421, 423
Forster–Tuncurry NSW 43, 47
Fort Scratchley, Newcastle NSW 35, 40
Fortescue Bay Tas. 446, 448
Forty Mile Scrub NP Qld 423
fossicking
  Agate Creek Qld 423
  Andamooka SA 250
  Barraba NSW 64, 69
  Bingara NSW 64, 65
  Bombala NSW 87
  Caloundra Qld 386
  Casino NSW 57
  Chinchilla Qld 379
  Clermont Qld 406
  Cloncurry Qld 430
  Coober Pedy SA 251
  Cranky Rock Nature Reserve NSW 63
  Creswick Regional Park Vic. 149
  Cue WA 313
  Derby Tas. 472
  Drake NSW 68
  Dunolly Vic. 154
  Emerald Qld 392, 395
  Gemtree Caravan Park NT 351
  Georgetown Qld 423
  Gladstone Tas. 473
  Gympie Qld 386
  Hanging Rock NSW 61
  Hughenden Qld 431
  Inglewood Vic. 154
  Inverell NSW 66, 69
  Kalgoorlie–Boulder WA 305–6
  Kilkivan Qld 369
  Lightning Ridge NSW 111
  Marysville Vic. 126
  Merriwa NSW 38
  Mimosa Rocks NP NSW 84
  Mount Surprise Qld 423

Murgon Qld 369
Muttaburra Qld 434
Nanango Qld 369
Norseman WA 307
Nundle NSW 67, 69
Opalton Qld 435
Ophir Goldfields NSW 74
Paddys Ranges State Park Vic. 150
Pine Creek NT 341
Ravensthorpe WA 307
Richmond Qld 426, 434
Rockhampton Qld 399
Sofala NSW 75
Sovereign Hill Vic. 148
Toompine Qld 434
Torrington NSW 63
Uralla NSW 68
Walgett NSW 112
Walhalla Vic. 138
Wangaratta Vic. 199
Wedderburn Vic. 156
White Cliffs NSW 113
Whitemark Tas. 477
Yackandandah Vic. 199
Yalgoo WA 317
Yowah Qld 431
fossils
　Age of Fishes Museum, Canowindra NSW 71
　Alice Springs NT 352
　Australian Age of Dinosaurs Museum, Winton Qld 425, 435
　Bathurst NSW 76
　Boodjamulla (Lawn Hill) NP Qld 421
　Chillagoe–Mungana Caves NP Qld 421
　Coonabarabran NSW 77
　Eromanga Qld 426, 435
　Gantheaume Point WA 325
　Gulgong NSW 80
　Hamelin Pool WA 309
　Hughenden Qld 426, 435
　Isisford Qld 432
　Kennedy Range NP WA 311
　Lark Quarry Conservation Park Qld 426, 435
　Leeuwin–Naturaliste NP WA 274
　Maria Island NP Tas. 445
　Muttaburra Qld 427, 434
　Naracoorte Caves NP SA 242
　Richmond Qld 426, 434, 435
　Riversleigh Fossil Fields Qld 434, 435
　Tathra NSW 89
　Wellington Caves NSW 73
　Winton Qld 425, 435
　Wynyard Tas. 465
　Yalgorup NP WA 284
Foster Vic. 135, 136, 137, 139
Fowlers Bay SA 259
François Peron NP WA 294, 311
Frank Hann NP WA 293
Frankland River wine region WA 281
Franklin Tas. 441, 454
Franklin–Gordon Wild Rivers NP Tas. 458
Franklin Harbour Historical Museum, Cowell SA 258, 260
Franklin House, Youngtown Tas. 468, 474
Fraser Coast 363
Frederickton NSW 48
Freeling SA 218
Fremantle WA 267, 269, 296
French Island NP Vic. 129
freshwater crocodiles 340
Freycinet NP Tas. 445, 447
Friday Island Qld 419
Fryerstown Vic. 149
Furneaux Museum, Emita Tas. 468, 477
Fyansford Vic. 161

Gab Titui Cultural Centre, Thursday Island Qld 409, 419
Gabo Island Vic. 144

Galaru (East Woody Beach) NT 341
Galley Museum, Queenstown Tas. 457, 459
Gantheaume Point WA 324, 325
Gapsted Vic. 198
Garden Island WA 287
Gardens of Stone NP NSW 13
Gariwerd/Grampians Vic. 121, 172–9
Gascoyne Junction WA 310
Gatton Qld 367, 369
Gawler SA 216, 218
Gawler Ranges NP SA 257, 263
Gayndah Qld 395, 397
Gayndah Historical Museum, Gayndah Qld 392, 395
Geegelup Heritage Trail WA 280
Geelong Vic. 118, 121, 158–63, 463
Geelong and the Bellarine wine region Vic. 159, 161
Geelong Art Gallery, Geelong Vic. 160, 161
Geelong Waterfront, Geelong Vic. 159, 161
Geeveston Tas. 451, 452, 453–4
Geeveston Visitor Centre, Geeveston Tas. 451, 454
Gelantipy Vic. 142
Gembrook Vic. 118, 123
Gemtree Caravan Park NT 351, 352
Geographe wine region WA 276, 280, 284
George Bass Coastal Walk Vic. 139
George Town Tas. 467, 473
Georgetown Qld 423
Geraldton WA 310, 314–15, 315
Gerringong NSW 26
Ghosts of Gold Heritage Trail, Charters Towers Qld 403, 405
Giant Barramundi, Normanton Qld 423
Gibb River Road WA 323, 326
Gibraltar Range NP NSW 61
Gilbert's potoroo 294
Gilgandra NSW 79
Gin Gin Qld 393, 395–6
Ginger Factory, Yandina Qld 384, 389
Gingin WA 290, 291–2
Gippsland Art Gallery, Sale Vic. 141, 145
Gippsland Gourmet Country Vic. 133, 139
Gippsland Heritage Park, Moe Vic. 135, 137
Gippsland Lakes Vic. 141, 143, 145
Gippsland Plains Rail Trail Vic. 144
Gippsland wine region Vic. 133
Gipsy Point Vic. 144
Girramay NP Qld 405
Girringun NP Qld 401, 405, 406
Giru Qld 407
Gisborne Vic. 157
Giwining (Flora River) Nature Park NT 344
Gladstone NSW 48
Gladstone Qld 396, 397
Gladstone SA 229
Gladstone Tas. 473
Glass House Mountains Qld 361, 387
Glass House Mountains NP Qld 383, 387
Glen Davis NSW 81
Glen Helen Gorge NT 349, 352
Glen Innes NSW 61, 62, 65, 67
Glenbrook NSW 13, 16
Glendambo SA 251, 259
Glengallan Homestead and Heritage Centre, Allora Qld 378, 379
Glenluce Vic. 149
Glenmorgan Qld 380
Glenrowan Vic. 193, 196–7
Glenrowan wine region Vic. 192, 196
gliding
　Balaklava SA 223
　Benalla Vic. 195
　Byron Bay NSW 56
　Gawler SA 218
　Kingaroy Qld 368

Leeton NSW 104
Locksley Vic. 185
Waikerie SA 239
Gloucester NSW 43, 47
Gloucester Island NP Qld 404
Gloucester NP WA 273, 286
Gnarojin Park, Narrogin WA 290, 295
Goat Island Tas. 465
Gold Coast Qld 361, 362, 370–1, 372, 373, 375
Gold Coast hinterland Qld 361, 362, 370–5
Golden Beach Vic. 145
Golden Dragon Museum, Bendigo Vic. 147, 152
Golden Gumboot, Tully Qld 419
Golden Pipeline Heritage Trail WA 292, 302
Golden Quest Discovery Trail WA 302, 305
Goldfields Vic. 121, 146–57
Goldfields WA 271, 300–7
Goldfields Exhibition Museum, Coolgardie WA 302, 303
Goldfields Track Vic. 153
Goldsborough Valley Qld 411–12, 415
golf
　Anglesea Vic. 168
　Barwon Heads Vic. 161
　Batchelor NT 340
　Bothwell Tas. 469, 471
　Bridport Tas. 471
　Caloundra Qld 386
　Cobram Vic. 184
　Coffs Harbour NSW 46
　Coober Pedy SA 249, 251
　Eucla WA 304
　Flinders Vic. 131
　French Island NP Vic. 129
　Greenvale Qld 405
　Kingston Tas. 455
　Lord Howe Island NSW 49
　Maroochydore Qld 388
　Moonah Links Golf Course, Fingal Vic. 129
　Mount Beauty Vic. 198
　Nerang Qld 374
　Nullarbor Links WA 304
　Port Macquarie NSW 50
　St Andrews Beach Vic. 131
　Sanctuary Cove Qld 374, 375
　Scottsdale Tas. 476
　Warburton Vic. 127
Good Night Scrub NP Qld 393, 395, 396
Goodna Qld 369
Googs Track SA 259
Goolwa SA 205, 209, 210, 211, 218
Goombungee Qld 379
Goomen Qld 369
Goomeri Qld 369
Goondiwindi Qld 379, 380
Goose Island Conservation Park SA 231
Gordon River Cruises, Strahan Tas. 457, 459
Gordonvale Qld 415
Gosford NSW 5, 30, 31
Gosford Regional Gallery, Gosford NSW 30, 31
Goulburn NSW 19, 25
Goulburn region Vic. 121, 180–9
Goulburn River NP NSW 38, 74, 80
Goulburn Weir Vic. 183
Grafton NSW 53, 57
Grafton Regional Gallery, Grafton NSW 53
Grampians NP Vic. 173, 178
Grampians wine region Vic. 174, 176
Grand Pacific Drive NSW 5
Granite Belt Qld 376, 377, 378, 381
Granite Belt wine region Qld 377, 381
Granite Island SA 205, 209, 212
Granite Island Recreation Park, Victor Harbor SA 209–10, 212
Gravity Discovery Centre, Gingin WA 290, 291

Great Alpine Road Vic. 192
Great Artesian Spa Complex, Mitchell Qld 427, 433
Great Barrier Reef Qld 408, 409, 410, 413, 417, 418
Great Cobar Museum, Cobar NSW 108, 110
Great Eastern Drive Tas. 445
Great Keppel Island Qld 392, 399
Great Nowranie Cave Qld 427
Great Ocean Drive WA 301, 304
Great Ocean Road Vic. 121, 164–71
Great Ocean Walk Vic. 165
Great Otway NP Vic. 165, 168, 169
Great Sandy NP Qld 383, 384, 385, 388
Great Sandy Strait Qld 392, 397
Great South West Walk Vic. 170, 171
Great Southern WA 270, 272–87
Great Southern Rail Trail Vic. 135, 137
Great Southern wine region WA 273–4, 285
Great Victorian Rail Trail Vic. 197
Great Walhalla Alpine Trail Vic. 135
Great Western Vic. 174
Greater Beedelup NP WA 276, 286
Greater Bendigo NP Vic. 149
Green Island Qld 409, 413, 417
Greenbushes WA 279
Greenough WA 311, 315
Greens Beach Tas. 471
Greenvale Qld 405
Greenwell Point NSW 88
Grenfell NSW 79–80
Griffith NSW 99, 102, 103
Griffiths Island Vic. 170
Grossman House, Maitland NSW 37, 38
Gugu Yalanji Rock-art Site, Laura 410, 416
Guilderton WA 299
Guildford WA 269
Gulaga NP NSW 85
Gulf Country NT 334, 342–7
Gulf Savannah Qld 363, 420–3
Gulf Station, Yarra Glen Vic. 124, 127
Gulflander (train) Qld 421, 422, 423
Gulgong NSW 71–2, 73, 79, 80
Gum San Chinese Heritage Centre, Ararat Vic. 174, 176
Gunbalanya (Oenpelli) NT 337, 338
Gunbower Island Vic. 183, 184
Gundabooka NP NSW 107, 108
Gundagai NSW 98, 99, 102
Gunnedah NSW 65, 67
Gunns Plains Tas. 462
Gunns Plains Caves Tas. 461, 465
Guthega NSW 91
Guy Fawkes River NP NSW 47
Guyra NSW 63, 65–6, 67
Gwalia WA 301, 302, 306
Gympie Qld 384, 385, 386–7, 389

Hadspen Tas. 468, 473
Hahndorf SA 205, 215, 217, 218–19
Halfway Across Australia Gem Shop and the Big Galah, Kimba SA 258, 261
Halifax Qld 406
Halls Creek WA 324, 326, 327
Halls Gap Vic. 173, 177, 178
Hamelin Bay WA 274
Hamelin Bay Wreck Trail WA 274
Hamelin Pool Stromatolites WA 286, 309, 313
Hamilton Tas. 441, 473
Hamilton Vic. 174, 175, 178
Hamilton Gallery, Hamilton Vic. 174, 178
Hamilton Botanic Gardens, Hamilton Vic. 175
Hamilton Island Qld 402
Hammond SA 254
hang-gliding and paragliding
　Avon Valley WA 268

Bright Vic. 195–6
Manilla NSW 66
Mount Buffalo NP Vic. 192
Mullumbimby NSW 58
North Tamborine Qld 375
Tumut NSW 95
West Cape Howe NP WA 278
Wollongong NSW 27
Hanging Rock NSW 61, 67
Hanging Rock Vic. 119, 148, 157
Hannans North Tourist Mine, Kalgoorlie WA 302, 305
Harcourt Vic. 153
Hard Hill Tourist Reserve, Wedderburn Vic. 148, 156
Hargraves NSW 80
Harrietville Vic. 195
Harrow Vic. 175, 177
Hartley NSW 13
Hartley's Crocodile Adventures, Cairns Qld 412, 417
Hartz Mountains NP Tas. 452, 453, 454
Harvey Dickson's Country Music Centre, Boyup Brook WA 276, 279
Harvey WA 281, 283
Hasties Swamp NP Qld 413
Hastings Tas. 451, 454
Hastings Vic. 131
Hastings Caves and Thermal Springs Tas. 451, 454
Hat Head NP NSW 44, 45
Hattah–Kulkyne NP Vic. 183, 185, 187
Hawker SA 251
Hawkesbury NSW 10, 28–33
Hawkesbury Regional Museum, Windsor NSW 30, 32
Hawkesbury River NSW 5
Hawley Beach Tas. 464
Hay NSW 98–9, 101, 102–3
Hayman Island Qld 402
Healesville Vic. 119, 123, 124, 125, 127
Healesville Sanctuary, Healesville Vic. 123, 125
Heartlands, The WA 271, 288–99
Heathcote Vic. 154
Heathcote–Graytown NP Vic. 149, 154
Heathcote NP NSW 27
Heathcote wine region Vic. 148, 154
Helenvale Qld 414
Helidon Qld 367
Henbury Meteorites Conservation Reserve NT 351
Henry Lawson Centre, Gulgong NSW 71–2, 80
Henry Parkes Centre, North Parkes NSW 72, 81
Henty NSW 101
Hepburn Regional Park, Hepburn Springs Vic. 149, 154
Hepburn Springs Vic. 148, 149, 153
Hepburn Springs Spas, Hepburn Springs Vic. 148, 154
Herberton Qld 412, 415
Herberton Mining Museum, Herberton Qld 412, 415
Herberton Range NP Qld 412, 415
Hermannsburg NT 353
Hermits Cave and Sir Dudley de Chair's Lookout, Griffith NSW 99, 102
Heron Island Qld 391, 396
Heronswood House and Garden, Dromana Vic. 130, 131
Hervey Bay Qld 395, 397
Heysen Trail SA 213, 218, 222, 229, 250, 251
Heywood Vic. 170
Hibiscus Coast Qld 403, 406
High Country Vic. 121, 190–9
Highfield Historic Site, Stanley Tas. 461
Highfields Qld 381
Hill End NSW 72
Hill End Historic Site, Hill End NSW 72, 76
Hillgrove NSW 64

Hillston NSW 80
Hinchinbrook Island Qld 401, 405
Hinchinbrook Island NP Qld 401
Hindmarsh Island SA 210
Historic and Folk Museum, Port Pirie SA 228
Historic Whaling Station, Albany WA 274, 278
HMAS *Canberra* Dive Site, Ocean Grove Vic. 160, 162
HMAS *Sydney II* Memorial, Geraldton WA 310, 314
Hobart Tas. 438–9, 441, 451, 453, 455, 473
daytrips from 440–1
Holbrook NSW 97, 103
Holey Plains State Park Vic. 142
Holiday Coast NSW 11, 42–51
Holwell Gorge, Beaconsfield Tas. 470, 471
Home Hill, Devonport Tas. 462, 463
Home Hill Qld 404, 405
Homebush Qld 406
Hook Island Qld 402
Hope Island Tas. 453
Hopetoun Vic. 185–6
Hopetoun WA 273, 307
Horn Island/Narupai Qld 419
horseriding
Alpine NP Vic. 191
Anglers Rest Vic. 198
Ararat Vic. 176
Baw Baw NP Vic. 133
Belair NP SA 215
Bellingen NSW 46
Bicentennial National Trail 369, 415
Bingara NSW 64
Birdwood SA 218
Blackheath NSW 16
Burra SA 223
Byron Bay NSW 56
Cape Tribulation Qld 415
Clunes Vic. 153
Coffs Harbour NSW 47
Cooma NSW 94
Dinner Plain Vic. 195
Echuca Vic. 184
Enfield State Park Vic. 149
Flinders Vic. 131
Kalbarri WA 316
Killarney Qld 380
Kingston Tas. 455
Kojonup WA 284
Kosciuszko NP NSW 93
Lilydale–Warburton Rail Trail Vic. 127
Mansfield Vic. 197
Miriam Vale Qld 398
Narawntapu NP Tas. 468
Nerang NP and Nerang State Forest Qld 372
Noosa Heads Qld 388
Omeo Vic. 198
Palm Cove Qld 417
Pinjarra WA 286
Port Douglas Qld 418
Scone NSW 41
Seymour Vic. 188
Warrnambool Vic. 171
Wilpena SA 254
Yarra Glen Vic. 127
Horsham Vic. 175, 177, 178
Horsham Regional Art Gallery, Horsham Vic. 175, 178
Hot Artesian Bore Baths, Lightning Ridge NSW 108
hot-air ballooning
Avon Valley WA 268
Benalla NT 195
Canowindra NSW 77
Carrara Qld 374
Cessnock NSW 38
Leeton NSW 104
Lyndoch SA 219
Mareeba Qld 416
Maroochydore Qld 388

Northam WA 296
Yarra Glen Vic. 127
HOTA (Home of the Arts), Surfers Paradise Qld 372, 375
Hotham Heights Vic. 143
Hotham Valley Tourist Railway, Pinjarra and Dwellingup WA 276, 282, 286
Houtman Abrolhos Islands WA 311, 314
Howard Springs Nature Park NT 341
Howden Tas. 455
Hub, The, Chillagoe Qld 421
Hughenden Qld 426, 431
Hume and Hovell Walking Track NSW 93
Hunter Valley and Coast NSW 5, 11, 34–41
Hunter Valley wine region NSW 5, 35, 38
Hunter Wetlands Centre, Shortland NSW 37, 40
Huon Valley Tas. 441, 452, 453, 454
Huon Valley wine region Tas. 441
Huonville Tas. 441, 452, 454, 455
Huskisson NSW 83, 87, 89
Hyams Beach NSW 83, 87
Hyden WA 290, 292, 293, 307

Idalia NP Qld 427
Ikara–Flinders Ranges NP SA 247, 249, 250, 251, 254
Ilbilbie Qld 403
Ilfracombe Qld 433
Illawarra NSW 10, 18–27
Illawarra Fly Tree Top Adventures, Knights Hill NSW 20, 26
Illawarra Light Railway Museum, Shellharbour NSW 20, 27
Iluka Nature Reserve, Iluka NSW 53, 57
Iluka NSW 53, 57
Imbil Qld 386
Ingham Qld 403, 405, 406
Inglewood Qld 381
Inglewood Vic. 154
Innamincka SA 247, 251–2, 253, 255
Innamincka Regional Reserve SA 247–8, 251
Inneston SA 227
Innisfail Qld 410, 411, 413, 415–16
Innot Hot Springs, Ravenshoe Qld 412, 418
Inskip Point Qld 389
Inverell NSW 62, 66, 67, 69
Inverloch Vic. 133, 137, 139
Ipswich Art Gallery, Ipswich Qld 365, 368
Ipswich Qld 365, 366, 367–8, 369
Iron Knob SA 263
Irwin District Museum, Dongara WA 311, 313
Isisford Qld 431–2
Isla Gorge NP Qld 393, 399
Israelite Bay WA 303
Iytwelepenty–Davenport Ranges NP NT 351

J Ward Museum, Ararat Vic. 175, 176
Jabiru NT 340
Jack Smith Scrub Regional Park, Murgon Qld 366, 369
Jamberoo Action Park, Jamberoo NSW 20, 25
Jamberoo NSW 20, 25
Jamestown SA 222, 224
Jamieson Vic. 144, 197
Jan Juc Vic. 166
Jardine River NP Qld 412, 419
Jasper Gorge NT 344
Jenolan Caves NSW 14
Jeparit Vic. 175, 178–9
Jerilderie NSW 103
Jervis Bay JBT 87, 89
Jervis Bay Marine Park NSW 87
Jervis Bay Maritime Museum, Huskisson NSW 83, 87

Jewel Cave WA 274
Jindabyne NSW 91, 93, 94
Jindera NSW 100
Jingamia Cave WA 294
John Flynn Place Museum and Art Gallery, Cloncurry Qld 426, 430
John Forrest NP WA 289
Jondaryan Qld 379
Jondaryan Woolshed, Oakey Qld 377, 380
Judbarra–Gregory NP NT 342, 343
Julia Creek Qld 432
Jundah Qld 432
Junee NSW 105
Jung Vic. 178
Jurien Bay WA 292, 293
Jurien Bay Marine Park WA 292

Kadina SA 227, 229–30
Kajabbi Qld 430
Kakadu NT 341
Kakadu NP NT 336, 337–8, 339, 340, 341
Kalamunda NP WA 295
Kalbar Qld 361, 373
Kalbarri WA 315–16
Kalbarri NP WA 310, 315
Kalgoorlie–Boulder WA 295, 301, 302, 303, 305
Kambalda WA 305
Kanangra–Boyd NP NSW 14
Kandos NSW 81
Kangaroo Island SA 206, 208–13
Kangaroo Island wines SA 210
Kangaroo Valley NSW 83–4, 88
Kanku–Breakawats Conservation Park SA 248, 251
Kapunda SA 222, 224–5
Kapunda Museum, Kapunda SA 222
Kara Kara NP Vic. 149, 156
Karijini NP WA 319, 321
Karlu Karlu–Devils Marbles Conservation Reserve NT 349, 355
Karoonda SA 238
Karratha WA 319, 320, 321
Karumba Qld 423
Kata Tjuṯa NT 350, 355
Katanning WA 283
Katanning-Piesse Heritage Trail WA 283
Kate's Berry Farm, Swansea Tas. 446, 449
Katherine NT 333, 344, 345, 346, 347
Katherine Hot Springs NT 344, 346
Katherine Museum 344
Kati Thanda–Lake Eyre NP SA 248, 249, 251, 252, 255
Katoomba NSW 4, 13, 14, 15, 16, 17
kayaking
Batchelor NT 340
Batemans Bay NSW 86
Bedarra Island Qld 411
Boreen Point Qld 385
Bright Vic. 196
Bunbury WA 280
Byron Bay NSW 56
Caloundra Qld 386
Cooma NSW 94
Coral Bay WA 313
Deniliquin NSW 101
Esk Qld 367
Exmouth WA 314
Forster-Tuncurry NSW 47
Gordonvale Qld 415
Kangaroo Valley NSW 84
Launceston Tas. 474
Laurieton NSW 48
Macquarie Marshes NSW 74
Mission Beach Qld 417
Nambucca Heads NSW 49
Noosa Heads Qld 388
Noosa River and the Everglades Qld 385
North Stradbroke/Minjerribah Qld 366
Nyngan NSW 80
Onkaparinga River NP SA 210

INDEX

Port Adelaide SA 205
Port Douglas Qld 418
Terrigal NSW 31
Tocumwal NSW 104
Walpole WA 287
Warrnambool Vic. 171
Keep River NP NT 344
Keiraville NSW 20
Keith SA 236–7
Kellerberrin WA 292
Kelso Tas. 471
Kempsey NSW 44, 47–8, 49
Kempton Tas. 476
Kendall NSW 48
Kendenup WA 285
Kenilworth Qld 361, 383, 389
Kenilworth State Forest Qld 383
Kennedy Range NP WA 311
Kennett River Vic. 169
Kenniff Courthouse, Mitchell Qld 427, 433
Keppel Bay Islands NP Qld 399
Kerang Vic. 186
Kettering Tas. 440, 451, 453, 454–5
K'gari (Fraser Island) Qld 390, 392, 397
Khancoban NSW 51, 91, 94–5
Kiah Inlet NSW 85
Kialla Vic. 189
Kiama NSW 20, 25–6
Kiama Blowhole, Kiama NSW 20, 25
Kilcoy Qld 360, 367
Kilcunda Vic. 134, 139
Kilkivan Qld 369
Killarney Qld 361, 371, 380
Killer Whale Museum, Eden NSW 84, 87
Kilmore Vic. 154–5
Kimba SA 258, 261
Kimberley, The WA 271, 322–7
Kinchega NP NSW 107, 111
King Ash Bay NT 344
King Island Tas. 460, 461, 463
King Island Dairy, Currie Tas. 461, 463
King Solomons Cave Tas. 468
King Valley wine region Vic. 192, 197
Kingaroy Qld 368, 369
Kinglake NP Vic. 124
Kings Billabong Wildlife Reserve Vic. 183, 186
Kings Canyon NT 350, 351
Kings Canyon Resort NT 351
Kings Creek Station NT 351
Kingscliff NSW 59
Kingscote (Kangaroo Island) SA 211–12
Kingston Tas. 440, 452, 455
Kingston S.E. SA 243
Knights Hill NSW 19
Koala Conservation Area, Rhyll Vic. 133, 136
Koala Hospital, Port Macquarie NSW 44, 49
Kojonup WA 283–4
Kokerbin Rock WA 292, 294
Kokynie WA 302, 306
Kolunga SA 229
Kondalilla NP Qld 385, 387
Koo Wee Rup Vic. 137
Koondrook Vic. 100, 186
Koondrook State Forest NSW 99, 100
Koonoomoo Vic. 184
Koonwarra Vic. 135
Koonya Tas. 449
Koorda WA 294
Kooyoora State Park Vic. 149, 156
Koppio Smithy Museum, Tumby Bay SA 257, 262
Koroit Vic. 171
Korumburra Vic. 133, 137, 139
Kosciuszko NP NSW 90, 91, 92, 93, 94, 95
Kronosaurus Korner, Richmond Qld 426, 434

Kroombit Tops NP Qld 394, 397
Krowathunkoolong Keeping Place, Bairnsdale Vic. 141
Kulin WA 293
kunanyi/Mount Wellington Tas. 439
Kunjarra/The Pebbles NT 354
Kununurra WA 323, 324, 325, 326–7
Kuranda Qld 409, 410, 416
Kuridala Qld 430
Kurrajong NSW 31
Kutini–Payamu NP Qld 419
Kwiambal NP NSW 63
Kwinana Beach WA 286
Kyabram Vic. 183
Kyabram Fauna Park, Kyabram Vic. 183
Kyalite NSW 100
Kyneton Vic. 155
Kynuna Qld 425, 432
Kyogle NSW 57–8

Labillardiere Peninsula Tas. 452
Lady Elliot Island Qld 392
Lady Julia Percy Island Vic. 170
Lady Musgrave Island Qld 395
Laggan NSW 25
Laidley Qld 366, 368, 369
Lake Argyle WA 323, 327
Lake Ballard WA 301
Lake Bindegolly NP Qld 431
Lake Boga Vic. 181, 187
Lake Broadwater Conservation Park Qld 378, 379
Lake Buloke Vic. 175, 177
Lake Cania Qld 397, 398
Lake Canobolas Reserve, Orange NSW 74, 81
Lake Cargelligo NSW 80
Lake Cathie NSW 50
Lake Cave WA 274
Lake Dartmouth Vic. 199
Lake Eildon NP Vic. 193, 196
Lake Eucumbene NSW 91, 93
Lake George NSW 19, 25
Lake Grace WA 293
Lake Guthridge Parklands, Sale Vic. 142, 145
Lake Hindmarsh Vic. 174, 178
Lake Illawarra NSW 27
Lake Jindabyne NSW 91
Lake King WA 293
Lake Kununurra WA 327
Lake Macquarie NSW 35
Lake Mountain Vic. 123
Lake Mulwala NSW 97, 104
Lake Munmorah NSW 30
Lake Tinaroo Qld 412, 419
Lake Torrens SA 250
Lake Tyers Vic. 143
Lakes Entrance Vic. 143, 145
Lameroo SA 238
Lamington NP Qld 361, 371, 374
Lancefield Vic. 157
Lancelin WA 293, 299
Landsborough Qld 361, 387
Lane Poole Reserve, Dwellingup WA 276
Langhorne Creek wine region SA 209, 210
Larapinta Trail NT 350
larapuna/Bay of Fires Tas. 445, 448, 449
Lark Quarry Conservation Park Qld 426, 435
Larrimah NT 345
Lascelles Vic. 179
Latrobe Tas. 461, 462, 463, 464
Launceston Tas. 441, 455, 463, 466, 467–8, 470, 471, 473, 477
Laura Qld 409, 410, 415, 416
Laura SA 229
Laurieton NSW 43, 48, 49
Lavandula Swiss Italian Farm, Daylesford Vic. 149, 154
Lavers Hill Vic. 165
Laverton WA 302, 306
Leeton NSW 103, 104

Leeuwin–Naturaliste NP WA 274, 278, 282, 285, 287
Lefroy Tas. 473
Lennox Head NSW 53
Leongatha Vic. 135, 137, 139
Leonora WA 302, 305, 306
Lerderderg State Park Vic. 150
Leschenault Inlet WA 276, 279
Lesmurdie Falls NP WA 295
Lesueur NP WA 292
Leura NSW 4, 13, 16–17
Leven Canyon, Loongana Tas. 462, 465
Leven River Cruises, Ulverstone Tas. 462, 465
Leyburn Qld 379
Licola Vic. 144
Liffey Falls State Reserve, Deloraine Tas. 470, 472
Light Pass SA 219
lighthouses
 Bunbury WA 280
 Cape Borda SA 212
 Cape Bruny Tas. 440, 453
 Cape Byron NSW 53
 Cape du Couedic SA 209
 Cape Jaffa SA 243
 Cape Leeuwin WA 274, 276, 278
 Cape Martin SA 243
 Cape Naturaliste WA 274, 281
 Cape Nelson Vic. 170
 Cape Northumberland SA 245
 Cape Otway Vic. 165
 Cape Schanck Vic. 129
 Cape Sorell Tas. 459
 Cape Wickham Tas. 463
 Clarence River NSW 59
 Corny Point SA 231
 Eddystone Point Tas. 468
 Gabo Island Vic. 144
 Green Cape NSW 85
 King Island Tas. 453
 Low Head Tas. 470
 Mersey Bluff Tas. 463
 Montague Island NSW 84
 Nelson Bay NSW 39
 Nora Head NSW 32
 Point Danger Qld 374
 Point Hicks Vic. 141
 Point Lonsdale Vic. 163
 Point Moore WA 314
 Smoky Cape NSW 44
 Split Point Vic. 168
 Sugarloaf Point NSW 45
 Tacking Point NSW 50
 Tweed Heads NSW 59
 Vlamingh Head WA 314
 Wadjemup WA 297
 West Cape SA 227
 Wilsons Promontory NP Vic. 134
 Wollongong NSW 27
Lightning Ridge NSW 108, 110–11
Lilydale Tas. 470, 474–5
Lilydale Falls, Lilydale Tas. 470, 474
Lilydale–Warburton Rail Trail Vic. 127
Limestone Coast SA 207, 240–5
Limmen Bight River Fishing Camp NT 344
Limmen NP NT 344
Lincoln NP SA 257, 261
Lind NP Vic. 142
Linda Tas. 459
Linden NSW 16
Line of Lode Miners Memorial and Visitor Centre, Broken Hill NSW 108, 109
Lismore NSW 57, 58
Litchfield NP NT 332, 336, 338, 339, 341
Lithgow NSW 15, 17
Littabella NP Qld 395
Little Desert NP Vic. 174, 177, 179
Little Dip Conservation Park SA 242, 245
Living Desert, Broken Hill NSW 108, 109

Livingstone NP NSW 105
Lizard Island NP Qld 410, 414
Lobethal SA 219
Loch Vic. 137
Loch Sport Vic. 141
Lochern NP Qld 427, 432
Lockhart NSW 105
Lockhart River Qld 414
Locksley Vic. 185
Loddon Valley wine region Vic. 154
Logans Beach Vic. 166, 171
Lombadina WA 324
Long Island Qld 402
Long Tunnel Extended Gold Mine, Walhalla Vic. 135, 138
Longford Tas. 469, 474, 475
Longreach Qld 425, 426, 432–3
Longwood Vic. 185
Loongana Tas. 462
Lord Howe Island NSW 48–9
Lorne Vic. 165, 169, 171
Lost City NT 343
Low Head Tas. 470, 473
Lower Glenelg NP Vic. 166
Lowood Qld 367
Loxton Historical Village, Loxton SA 233, 237
Lucinda Qld 401, 402, 406
Lucindale SA 244
Lucknow NSW 81
Lucky Bay SA 231
Lyndhurst SA 255
Lyndoch SA 216, 217, 219

Mac and Rose Chalmers Conservation Reserve NT 351
McCrossin's Mill, Uralla NSW 62, 68
Macedon Vic. 157
Macedon Ranges wine region Vic. 148, 157
Mackay Qld 405, 406
Mackerel Islands WA 320
McKinlay Qld 432
Macksville NSW 49
McLaren Vale SA 209, 211, 212
McLaren Vale wine region SA 209, 210, 212
Maclean NSW 54, 57
McLeods Morass Wildlife Reserve, Bairnsdale Vic. 142, 143
McLoughlins Beach Vic. 139
Macquarie Harbour Tas. 457, 459
Macquarie Marshes NSW 74, 77, 80
Macquarie Pass NP NSW 26
Madura WA 307
Maffra Vic. 144, 145
Maggie Beer's Farm Shop, Nuriootpa SA 216, 219
Magnetic Island/Yunbenun Qld 401, 405, 407
Magnetic Island/Yunbenun NP Qld 401
Mahagony Walking Track Vic. 170
Mail Run Tour, Coober Pedy SA 249, 251
Main Beach Qld 361, 372
Main Range NP Qld 371, 373, 380
Maitland Gaol, Maitland NSW 35, 38
Maitland NSW 35, 37, 38, 41
Maitland SA 228, 229, 230
Malanda Qld 412
Maldon Vic. 148, 155–6
Maleny Qld 361, 384, 385, 387, 389
Maleny–Blackall Range Tourist Drive Qld 385, 387
Mallacoota Vic. 141, 144, 145
Mallee Country Vic. 121, 180–9
Mallee Tourist and Heritage Centre, Pinnaroo SA 235, 238
Malmsbury Vic. 155
Mammoth Cave WA 274
Man from Snowy River Folk Museum, Corryong Vic. 192, 196
Mandurah WA 269, 276, 281, 284
Mandurang Vic. 152
Manilla NSW 66
Manjimup WA 277, 281, 284, 294

489

Manjimup wine region WA 274, 284
Manly NSW 5
Mann River Nature Reserve NSW 63, 65
Manns Beach Vic. 139
Mannum SA 205, 233, 237
Mannum Dock Museum, Mannum SA 233, 237
Mansfield Vic. 197
Mapleton Qld 385
Mapleton Falls NP Qld 385, 388
Mapoon Qld 419
Marakoopa Cave Tas. 468
Marble Arch, Deua NP 22
Marble Bar WA 320, 321
Marble Masterpiece, Gundagai NSW 99, 102
Marcoola Qld 388
Mareeba Qld 415, 416
Margaret River WA 274, 279, 281, 285
Margaret River wine region WA 274, 285
Margate Tas. 440, 455
Maria Island NP Tas. 445-6, 449
Maria Island/wukaluwikiwayna Tas. 444, 445, 449
Mariala NP Qld 427
Marine Discovery and Freshwater Centre, Queenscliff Vic. 159, 162
Marion Bay SA 231
Marion Bay Tas. 447
Maritime Discovery Centre, Portland Vic. 167, 170
Marla SA 253, 255
Marlo Vic. 144
Maroochydore Qld 387-8, 389
Marramarra NP NSW 33
Marree SA 248, 252, 253, 255
Martindale Hall, Mintaro SA 221, 225
Mary Cairncross Park, Maleny Qld 384, 387
Mary MacKillop Penola Centre, Penola SA 242, 244
Mary River NT 333
Mary River NP NT 351
Mary Valley Qld 361, 389
Mary Valley Heritage Railway, Gympie Qld 384, 386
Maryborough Qld 397-8
Maryborough Vic. 150, 156
Maryborough Railway Station, Maryborough Vic. 150, 156
Marysville Vic. 124, 125-6, 127
Maslin Beach SA 205, 211, 212
Mataranka NT 333, 344, 345, 346
Mataranka Homestead NT 344
Mathoura NSW 184
Mawbanna Tas. 465
Mawson Trail SA 222, 249, 251
Meckering WA 296
Medlow Bath NSW 4
Meekatharra WA 316
Meeniyan Vic. 137, 139
Melbourne Vic. 116-17, 463, 477
 daytrips from 118-19
Melrose SA 249, 252
Melrose National Trust Museum, Melrose SA 249, 252
Melton Vic. 151
Melville Island NT 333
Menangle NSW 25
Menindee NSW 111
Meningie SA 237
Menzies WA 301, 302, 306
Mereenia Loop NT 349-50
Merimbula NSW 84, 86, 87-8, 89
Merimbula Aquarium, Merimbula NSW 84, 88
Mermaid's Cave, Blackheath NSW 16
Meroogal, Nowra NSW 85, 88
Merredin WA 293-4
Merriwa NSW 38, 41
Metung Vic. 143, 145
Miami Qld 375
Mid-North SA 206, 220-5
Mid-West WA 271, 308-17

Middleton SA 212
Midge Point Qld 407
Midlands, The Tas. 441, 443, 466-77
Miena Tas. 475
Milang SA 210
Milawa Vic. 197
Mildura Vic. 182, 186, 187
Mildura Arts Centre and Rio Vista, Mildura Vic. 181, 186, 188
Miles Qld 379, 380
Millaa Millaa Qld 410, 417
Millicent Museum, Millicent SA 242, 243
Millicent SA 242, 243-4
Millmerran Qld 379, 381
Millstream-Chichester NP WA 319, 320, 321
Millstream Falls NP Qld 418
Millthorpe NSW 72, 76
Milparinka NSW 107
Milton NSW 89
Mimbi Caves WA 326
Mimosa Rocks NP NSW 84, 89
Minerva Hills NP Qld 399
Minjungbal Aboriginal Cultural Centre, Tweed Heads NSW 54-5
Minlaton SA 228, 230
Minnipa SA 263
Mintaro SA 221, 225
Mirani Qld 406
Mirboo North Vic. 137
Miriam Vale Qld 393, 398
Mirima NP WA 324, 327
Miss Traill's House, Bathurst NSW 74, 76
Mission Beach Qld 411, 415, 417
Mitchell Qld 427, 433
Mitchell River NP Vic. 142, 143
Mitchell River NP WA 324
Mitta Mitta Vic. 199
Mittagong NSW 23
Moama NSW 184
Moana Beach SA 212
Moe Vic. 133, 135, 137
Moggs Creek Vic. 166
Mogo NSW 84
Mogumber WA 296
Mole Creek Tas. 468, 470, 475
Mole Creek Karst NP Tas. 468, 475
Moliagul Vic. 154
Molong NSW 81
Mon Repos Conservation Park Qld 392, 394
MONA (Museum of Old and New Art), Hobart Tas. 451, 455, 473
Monarto Safari Park, Murray Bridge SA 235, 238
Monash SA 236
Monegeetta Vic. 157
Monga NP NSW 22, 24
Monkey Mia WA 310, 313
Montague Island NSW 84
Montague Island Nature Reserve NSW 84, 88
Montebello Islands WA 320
Montezuma Falls, Rosebery Tas. 457, 459
Monto Qld 393, 397, 398
Montville Qld 385, 387
Mooball NSW 59
Moogerah Peaks NP Qld 373
Mooloolaba Qld 384, 385, 388
Mooloolah River NP Qld 388
Moon Plain, Coober Pedy SA 248, 251
Moonah Links Golf Course, Fingal Vic. 129
Moonan Flat NSW 41
Moondyne Cave WA 274
Moonlit Sanctuary Wildlife Conservation Park, Pearcedale Vic. 130, 131
Moonta SA 227, 229, 230
Moonta Bay SA 230
Moonta Mines State Heritage Area, Moonta SA 227
Moora WA 294
Moore Qld 367

Moore Park Qld 395
Moore River NP WA 292
Mooroopna Vic. 189
Moorrinya NP Qld 431
Moranbah Qld 406
Morawa WA 311, 316
Moree NSW 62, 66-7
Moree Artesian Aquatic Centre, Moree NSW 62
Moreton Island/Mulgumpin Qld 361, 365-6
Morgan SA 234, 237
Mornington Vic. 130, 131
Mornington Peninsula Vic. 119, 128-31
Mornington Peninsula NP Vic. 129
Mornington Peninsula wine region Vic. 130
Morpeth NSW 36
Morton NP NSW 20, 26, 85
Moruya NSW 88, 89
Morwell Vic. 137-8
Morwell NP Vic. 135
Moss Vale NSW 25, 26
Mossman Qld 409, 417
Mossman Gorge Qld 409, 410
Mossman Gorge Centre, Mossman Qld 410, 417
Mother of Ducks Lagoon, Guyra NSW 63, 65
MOUA (Museum of Underwater Art), Townsville Qld 401, 407
Moulamein NSW 100
Mount Arapiles-Tooan State Park Vic. 174, 178
Mount Archer NP Qld 393
Mount Augustus NP WA 310, 314
Mount Barker SA 209, 218
Mount Barker WA 275, 281, 285
Mount Barney NP Qld 372
Mount Bauple NP Qld 398
Mount Baw Baw Vic. 135
Mount Beauty Vic. 197, 198, 199
Mount Benson wine region SA 242, 245
Mount Blue Cow NSW 91, 95
Mount Buangor State Park Vic. 175
Mount Buffalo NP Vic. 192, 195, 198
Mount Buller Vic. 195
Mount Bundy Station, Adelaide River NT 338, 339
Mount Burr SA 243
Mount Compass SA 213
Mount Coolum NP Qld 385, 387
Mount Donna Buang Vic. 124
Mount Dutton Bay Woolshed, Coffin Bay SA 258, 259
Mount Elephant Vic. 175
Mount Field NP Tas. 441, 451, 455
Mount Frankland NP WA 287
Mount Gambier SA 241, 242, 243, 244
Mount Gambier Visitor Centre, Mount Gambier SA 242, 243
Mount Garnet Qld 418
Mount Gibraltar NSW 23
Mount Glorious Qld 365
Mount Granya State Park Vic. 193
Mount Grenfell Historic Site, Cubba NSW 108
Mount Hotham Vic. 195
Mount Hypipamee NP Qld 412, 415
Mount Isa Qld 421, 426, 433-4
Mount Kaputar NP NSW 62, 65
Mount Kembla NSW 27
Mount Kosciuszko NSW 90, 91, 95
Mount Laura Homestead Museum, Whyalla SA 258, 263
Mount Lofty Botanic Gardens, Hahndorf SA 215, 218
Mount Macedon Vic. 119, 156
Mount Magnet (Warramboo Hill) WA 316-17
Mount Martha Vic. 131
Mount Morgan Qld 397, 398
Mount Napier State Park Vic. 175
Mount Panorama AND The National Motor Racing Museum NSW 72, 76
Mount Perry Qld 396

Mount Remarkable NP SA 248, 252
Mount Richmond NP Vic. 170
Mount Royal NP NSW 41
Mount Stirling Vic. 197
Mount Surprise Qld 421, 423
Mount Tamborine Qld 361, 375
Mount Tamborine wine region Qld 372, 375
Mount Tomah NSW 13
Mount Victoria NSW 17
Mount Walsh NP Qld 393, 394
Mount Whaleback Mine Tours, Newman WA 319, 320
Mount William NP Tas. 468, 473
Mount Wilson NSW 14
Mount Worth State Park Vic. 135
Mount Wudinna Recreation Reserve, Wuddina SA 258, 263
Mount Yarrowyck Nature Reserve NSW 63, 68
mountain-biking see cycling and mountain-biking
Moura Qld 397, 399
Mourilyan Qld 417
Moyarra Vic. 135
Mudgee NSW 76, 79, 80
Mudgee wine region NSW 72, 80
Mudgeeraba Qld 374
Mullewa WA 311, 315, 317
Mullumbimby NSW 54, 58
Mulwala NSW 104, 189
Munda Biddi Cycle Trail WA 268, 281, 285, 295
Mundaring WA 289, 291, 293, 295
Mundubbera Qld 398
Mundulla SA 236
Munga-Thirri NP Qld 429
Mungana Qld 422
Mungerannie Roadhouse SA 255
Munghorn Gap Nature Reserve NSW 74, 80
Mungo NP NSW 97
Murchison Vic. 188
Murgon Qld 366, 369
Murrabit Vic. 100, 186
Murramarang NP NSW 84
Murrawijinie Caves SA 257
Murray Art Museum Albury (MAMA), Albury NSW 99, 100
Murray Bridge SA 205, 235, 238
Murray Darling wine region Vic. 181
Murray region NSW 11, 96-105
Murray region SA 207, 232-9
Murray region Vic. 121, 180-9
Murray River NP, Bulyong Island section SA 239
Murray River NP, Katarapko section SA 233-4
Murray River towns SA 205
Murray-Sunset NP Vic. 181, 185, 187
Murray to Mountains Rail Trail Vic. 192, 195, 198
Murray Town SA 252
Murrayville Vic. 186-7
Murringo NSW 27
Murrumbateman NSW 19, 25
Murrumburrah NSW 101
Murrurundi NSW 39
Murtoa Vic. 174
Murujuga NP (Burrup Peninsula) WA 319, 320
Murwillumbah NSW 54, 57, 58-9
Museum of Art, Rockhampton, Qld 393
Museum of Geraldton WA 310, 314
Museum of the Goldfields, Kalgoorlie WA 301, 305
Museum of the Riverina, Wagga Wagga NSW 97, 105
Museum of Tropical Queensland, Townsville Qld 403, 407
Muswellbrook NSW 35, 39
Mutawinji NP NSW 108
Muttaburra Qld 427, 434
Muttaburrasaurus Interpretation Centre, Muttaburra Qld 427, 434
Mutton Bird Island Vic. 169

490

Muttonbird Island Nature Reserve NSW 45
Myall Lakes NP NSW 44, 46
Myalup WA 279
Myponga SA 213
Myrtleford Vic. 197, 198

Nagambie Vic. 187
Nagambie wine region Vic. 181–2, 187
Namadgi NP ACT 22
Nambour Qld 384, 388, 389
Nambucca Heads NSW 49
Nambung NP WA 289, 291
Nan Tien Temple, Wollongong NSW 22, 27
Nanango Qld 369
Nangar NP NSW 74, 78
Nannup WA 281, 285
Naracoopa Tas. 463
Naracoorte SA 244
Naracoorte Caves NP SA 242, 244
Narawntapu NP Tas. 464, 471
Nariel Vic. 196
Narooma NSW 85, 88, 89
Narrabri NSW 62, 65, 67
Narrandera NSW 103, 104
Narrogin WA 290, 291, 293, 295
Narromine NSW 78
Nathalia Vic. 185
National Automobile Museum of Tasmania, Launceston Tas. 470, 474
National Cartoon Gallery, Coffs Harbour NSW 44, 46
National Motor Museum, Birdwood SA 215, 217
National Wool Museum, Geelong Vic. 159, 161
Nattai NP NSW 23
N'Dhala Gorge Nature Park NT 350, 352
Nebo Qld 406
Ned Kelly country Vic. 197
Neerim South Vic. 139
Nelligen NSW 86
Nelson Vic. 171
Nelson Bay NSW 39
Nerang NP and Nerang State Forest Qld 372, 374
Nerang Qld 372, 374
Nerrigundah NSW 88
New England NSW 11, 60–9
New England NP NSW 61
New England Regional Art Museum, Armidale NSW 62, 64
New England wine region NSW 62, 68
New Italy NSW 55
New Norcia Museum and Art Gallery, WA 290
New Norcia WA 269, 295–6
New Norfolk Tas. 441, 451, 455
Newbridge NSW 76
Newcastle NSW 5, 35, 36, 39, 40, 41
Newcastle Museum, Honeysuckle NSW 36, 40
Newcastle Regional Art Gallery, Newcastle NSW 36, 40
Newcastle Waters NT 346
Newdegate Cave Tas. 451
Newdegate WA 293
Newhaven Vic. 136
Newman WA 319, 320, 321
Ngalba Bulal NP Qld 414–15
Ngarkat Group of Conservation Parks SA 235, 238
Ngilgi Cave WA 281, 287
Nhill Vic. 179
Nhulunbuy NT 337, 341
Nightcap NP NSW 54
Nimbin NSW 57, 59
Nindigully Qld 379, 380–1
Ninety Mile Beach Vic. 139, 141, 145
Ningaloo Marine Park WA 309, 310, 312, 314
Nitmiluk NP NT 333, 342, 343, 346
Nobbies Centre and Seal Rocks, Summerlands Vic. 134, 136

Nobby Qld 379
Nobby Beach Qld 375
Noojee Vic. 139
Noonamah NT 341
Noorama (sheep station) Qld 431
Nooramunga Marine and Coastal Park Vic. 135
Noorat Vic. 179
Noosa Heads Qld 360, 384, 385, 388–9
Noosa NP Qld 384, 388
Noosa River and the Everglades Qld 385, 388
Noosaville Qld 388
Norman Lindsay Gallery, Faulconbridge NSW 14
Normanton Qld 423
Normanville SA 213
Norseman WA 305, 307
North Bruny Tas. 440, 453
North Haven NSW 48
North Stradbroke/Minjerribah Qld 366
North, The Tas. 443, 466–77
North Tamborine Qld 361, 374–5
North-west Tas. 443, 460–5
North West Island Qld 391
North-West Shelf Gas Project Visitor Centre, Dampier WA 319, 320
Northam WA 289, 293, 296
Northampton WA 317
Northcliffe WA 277, 285–6
Northern beaches NSW 5
Nowra NSW 83, 84, 85, 88
NSW Rail Museum, Thirlmere NSW 20
Nullarbor SA 207, 256–63
Nullarbor WA 271, 300–7
Nullarbor NP SA 257–8
Nullarbor Roadhouse SA 257
Nullawil Vic. 179
numbats 294
Nundle NSW 63, 67, 69
Nundle Woollen Mill, Nundle NSW 63, 67
Nuriootpa SA 216, 219
Nyah Vic. 189
Nyamup WA 284
Nyinkka Nyunyu Art and Culture Centre, Tennant Creek NT 351, 354
Nymboida NSW 57
Nyngan NSW 80

Oakbank SA 219
Oakey Qld 377, 378, 380
Oatlands Tas. 441, 467, 475–6
Oberon NSW 15, 17
Ocean Beach, Strahan Tas. 458, 459
Ocean Grove Vic. 118, 160, 162
Old Beechy Rail Trail Vic. 169
Old Dubbo Gaol, Dubbo NSW 72
Old Hobart Town Model Village, Richmond Tas. 452, 455
Old Noarlunga SA 212
Old Telegraph Track Qld 414
Old Timers Mine, Coober Pedy SA 248, 251
Old Wentworth Gaol, Wentworth NSW 97, 105
Old Wool and Grain Store Museum, Beachport SA 241, 243
Olinda Vic. 118, 123, 126, 127
Olive Pink Botanic Gardens, Alice Springs NT 351, 352
Olivewood, Renmark SA 235, 238
Omeo Vic. 193, 197, 198
Onkaparinga River NP SA 210, 212
Onslow WA 320–1
Oodnadatta SA 249, 253, 255
Oodnadatta Track SA 248, 249, 252, 253
Opalton Qld 435
Ophir Goldfields NSW 74, 81
Ora Banda WA 305
Orange NSW 74, 76, 79, 80–1
Orange wine region NSW 72, 81
Orbost Vic. 143, 144–5
Orford Tas. 445, 449

Organ Pipes NP Vic. 151
Oriental Claims, Omeo Vic. 193, 198
Orpheus Island NP Qld 402, 406
O'Sullivan Beach SA 212
Otway Fly, Weeaproinah Vic. 166, 168
Otway Ranges Vic. 165, 166, 167
Otway Submarine, Holbrook NSW 97, 103
Our Lady of Mount Carmel Church, Mullewa WA 311, 317
Outback NSW 11, 106–13
Outback Qld 363, 424–35
Outback SA 207, 246–55
Outback at Isa, Mount Isa Qld 426, 434
Ouyen Vic. 187
Overland Corner SA 235
Overland Track Tas. 461
Oxley NSW 103
Oxley Vic. 197
Oxley Wild Rivers NP NSW 62
Oyala Thumotang NP (CYPAL) Qld 419

Paddlesteamer Cruises, Mildura, Swan Hill and Echuca Vic. 182, 186
Paddys Ranges State Park, Maryborough Vic. 150
Paddy's River Falls, Tumbarumba NSW 92, 95
Padthaway wine region SA 234, 236
Painted Desert SA 249, 253
Palm Beach NSW 5
Palm Beach Qld 374
Palm Cove Qld 415, 417
Palm Islands Qld 402, 406
Palms NP, The Qld 366, 369
Paluma Range NP Qld 403, 406
Pambula NSW 88
Para Wirra Recreation Park SA 216, 219
Parachilna SA 248, 250
parachuting see skydiving and parachuting
Paradise Beach Vic. 145
paragliding see hang-gliding and paragliding
Paringa SA 238
Parkes NSW 72, 73, 79, 81
Parnkalla Walking Trail, Port Lincoln SA 262
Paronella Park, Innisfail Qld 410, 417
Paroo–Darling NP NSW 113
Parr State Conservation Area NSW 30, 33
Parry Lagoons Nature Reserve WA 324, 327
Paskeville SA 229
Patchewollock Vic. 179, 185–6
Paterson NSW 38
Paul Wild Observatory (CSIRO Australia Telescope), Narrabri NSW 62, 67
Paynesville Vic. 141, 142, 145
PDR (Peninsula Development Road) Qld 414
Peaceful Bay WA 287
Peak Charles NP WA 307
Peak Hill NSW 77
Peak Range NP Qld 405
Pearcedale Vic. 130
Pearl Beach NSW 33
Pearl Luggers, Broome WA 324, 325
Peel wine region WA 276, 284
Peelwood NSW 25
Pella Vic. 179
Pemberton WA 273, 276, 277, 286
Pemberton wine region WA 274, 284, 286
Penguin Tas. 461, 464
Penguin Island SA 243
Penguin Island WA 277, 286
Penguin Parade, Summerlands Vic. 133, 136
Peninsula Hot Springs, Fingal Vic. 130
Penneshaw SA 212
Penola SA 242, 243, 244

Penong SA 258
Penong Windmill Museum, Penong SA 258
Penshurst Vic. 178
Peppermint Bay Tas. 452, 454
Peppin Heritage Centre, Deniliquin NSW 99, 101
Peregian Beach Qld 388
Perenjori WA 316
Perisher NSW 91, 94, 95
Perry Sandhills, Wentworth NSW 99, 105
Perth Tas. 475
Perth WA 266–7
daytrips from 268–9
Perth Hills wine region WA 289, 295
Peterborough SA 221, 225
Phillip Island Vic. 119, 120, 132–9
Phillip Island Grand Prix Circuit, Ventnor Vic. 134, 136
Piawaning WA 296
Piccaninnie Ponds Conservation Park SA 241–2, 244
Pichi Richi Railway, Quorn SA 248, 253
Picton NSW 26
Pieman River Cruise, Corinna/kuria Tas. 457, 459
Pilbara WA 271, 318–21
Pilliga Forest NSW 75
Pine Creek NT 338, 341
Pingelly WA 296
Pinjarra WA 276, 281, 286
Pink Roadhouse, Oodnadatta SA 253
Pinnaroo SA 235, 238
Pioneer Cottage, Buderim Qld 385, 386
Pioneer Museum, Northcliffe WA 277
Pioneer Park Museum, Griffith NSW 99, 102
Pioneer Village, Inverell NSW 62, 66
Pioneers Museum
Bega NSW 85, 86
Gulgong NSW 73
Pittsworth Qld 378
Pittsworth Pioneer Historical Village, Toowoomba Qld 378, 381
Platypus House, Beauty Point Tas. 468
Platypus Reserve, Bombala NSW 84, 87
Point Hicks Vic. 143
Point Labatt Conservation Park SA 258, 262
Point Leo Vic. 131
Point Lonsdale Vic. 162, 163
Point Lowly SA 258
Point Nepean Vic. 129
Point Samson WA 321
Pokolbin NSW 35, 39
Pomona Qld 389
Pontville Tas. 475
Pooncarie NSW 105
Poowong Vic. 137
Porcupine Gorge NP Qld 426, 431
Porongurup WA 274
Porongurup NP WA 275, 285
Port Adelaide SA 205
Port Albert Vic. 135, 138
Port Arthur Tas. 441, 445, 446, 447, 448
Port Arthur Historic Site, Port Arthur Tas. 446, 447, 448
Port Augusta SA 248, 249, 251, 253
Port Bonython SA 258
Port Broughton SA 229, 230
Port Campbell Vic. 167, 169
Port Campbell NP Vic. 167, 169
Port Davies Tas. 477
Port Denison WA 313
Port Douglas Qld 409, 415, 417–18
Port Elliot SA 205, 209, 212
Port Fairy Vic. 170, 171
Port Fairy–Warrnambool Rail Trail Vic. 170, 171
Port Germain SA 231
Port Gibbon SA 260

491

Port Gregory WA 317
Port Hedland WA 319, 321
Port Kembla NSW 27
Port Kenny SA 262
Port Lincoln SA 257, 259, 261–2
Port MacDonnell SA 241, 242, 244–5
Port MacDonnell Maritime Museum, Port MacDonnell SA 242, 244
Port Macquarie NSW 44, 47, 49–50
Port Macquarie Historical Society Museum, Port Macquarie NSW 44, 49
Port Neill SA 263
Port Noarlunga SA 212
Port Noarlunga Reef Underwater Trail SA 212
Port of Echuca Discovery Centre, Echuca Vic. 182, 184
Port of Morgan Museum, Morgan SA 234, 237
Port Pirie SA 227, 228, 229, 230–1
Port Rickaby SA 230
Port Sorell Tas. 463, 464
Port Stephens NSW 36, 39
Port Victoria SA 231
Port Vincent SA 229, 231
Port Wakefield SA 222
Port Welshpool Vic. 134, 135, 139
Port Willunga SA 205, 211, 212
Portarlington Vic. 118, 159, 163
Portland NSW 17
Portland Vic. 170–1
Portsea Vic. 129, 130, 131
Prairie Qld 431
Prairie Hotel, Parachilna SA 248
Princess Margaret Rose Caves Vic. 166
Princetown Vic. 165
Prisoner of War Camp Site, Cowra NSW 75, 78
Prom Country Cheese, Moyarra/Bena Vic. 135
Proserpine Qld 404, 406–7
Proston Qld 369
Pub with No Beer, Taylors Arm NSW 45, 46
Puffing Billy (train), Belgrave and Gembrook Vic. 118, 123, 125
Purnong SA 237
Purnululu NP WA 324, 327
Pyengana Tas. 446, 449
Pyramid Hill Vic. 187
Pyrenees Ranges State Forest Vic. 150, 151
Pyrenees wine region Vic. 148, 151

Q Train, The, Queenscliff Vic. 160, 162
Qantas Founders Museum, Longreach Qld 426, 432
Quambatook Vic. 187
Queanbeyan NSW 26
Queen Victoria Museum and Art Gallery, Launceston Tas. 468, 474
Queenscliff Vic. 118, 131, 159, 160, 162–3
Queensland Air Museum, Caloundra Qld 385, 386
Queensland Heritage Park Exhibition, Biloela Qld 393, 394
Queenstown Tas. 457, 458, 459
Quilpie Qld 427, 434
quokkas 294, 296
Quorn SA 248, 253

R Stephens Tasmanian Honey, Mole Creek Tas. 470, 475
Railton Tas. 464
Railway Reserves Heritage Trail WA 268
Rainbow Vic. 179
Rainbow Beach Qld 360, 383, 384, 389
Rainbow Valley Conservation Reserve NT 351, 352
rainforests
  Auburn River NP Qld 393
  Ayr Qld 404
  Barrington Tops NP NSW 43

Bindarri NP NSW 45
Bouddi NP NSW 29
Budderoo NP NSW 19
Buderim/Buderim Forest Park Qld 385, 386
Bundjalung NP NSW 53
Cape Tribulation Qld 409
Cape York Qld 414
Carnarvon NP Qld 391
Clump Mountain NP Qld 417
Cradle Mountain–Lake St Clair NP Tas. 461
Crater Lakes NP Qld 411
D'Aguilar NP Qld 365
Daintree NP Qld 409
Deepwater NP Qld 393
Dorrigo NP NSW 44, 47
Dunk Island Qld 411
Elsey NP NT 343
Errinundra NP Vic. 142
Eubenangee Swamp NP Qld 411
Franklin–Gordon Wild Rivers NP Tas. 458
Gibraltar Range NP NSW 61
Girringun NP Qld 401
Gloucester Island NP Qld 404
Gloucester NSW 47
Goldsborough Valley State Forest Qld 411
Good Night Scrub NP Qld 393
Gosford NSW 31
Great Sandy NP Qld 383
Hinchinbrook Island NP Qld 401
Iluka Nature Reserve NSW 53
Kenilworth State Forest Qld 383
Kondalilla NP Qld 385
Kuranda Qld 416
Kutini-Payamu NP Qld 419
Lamington NP Qld 371
Lennox Head NSW 53
Lilydale Tas. 470, 474
Lind NP Vic. 142
Lismore NSW 58
Main Range NP Qld 371
Mary Cairncross Park, Malany Qld 384
Mission Beach Qld 417
Mitchell River NP Vic. 142
Monga NP NSW 22
Morton NP NSW 20
Mount Hypipamee NP Qld 412
Mount Mee State Forest Qld 367
Mount Royal NP NSW 41
Nerang NP and Nerang State Forest Qld 372
New England NP 61
Ngalba Bulal NP Qld 414–15
Nightcap NP NSW 54
Noosa NP Qld 384
Oxley Wild Rivers NP NSW 62
Oyala Thumotang NP (CYPAL) Qld 419
Paluma Range NP Qld 403
Port Douglas Qld 417
Ravensbourne NP Qld 378
Ravenshoe Qld 418
Richmond Range NP NSW 55
Rosebery Tas. 459
Savage River NP Tas. 465
Springbrook NP Qld 361, 371–2
Springbrook NP Qld 371, 372
Susan Island NSW 55
Tamborine NP Qld 372
Tarra-Bulga NP Vic. 134
The Palms NP Qld 366
Toonumbar NP NSW 58
Tully/Tully Gorge NP Qld 410, 419
Washpool NP NSW 61
Watagans NP NSW 36
Werrikimbe NP NSW 45
Wingham NSW 44
Wooroonooran NP Qld 410
Wyong NSW 33
Wyrrabalong NP NSW 30
Yarra Ranges NP Vic. 124
Raleigh NSW 46
Ralphs Falls, Ringarooma Tas. 470

Ranelagh Tas. 441, 454
Rapid Bay SA 213
Rathdowney Qld 373
Ratho Farm, Bothwell Tas. 452, 453
Ravensbourne NP Qld 378, 379
Ravenshoe Qld 412, 415, 418
Ravensthorpe WA 305, 307
Ravenswood Qld 407
Rawson Vic. 138
Raymond Island Vic. 142, 145
Raymond Terrace NSW 37, 40
Recherche Archipelago WA 302
Red Centre NT 334, 348–55
Red Cliffs Vic. 186
Red Hill Vic. 130
Redhill SA 229
Reef Hills State Park Vic. 193, 194
Reef HQ Great Barrier Reef Aquarium, Townsville Qld 402, 407
Regional Tourism and Arts Centre, Port Pirie SA 227
Remarkable Cave Tas. 441, 446, 448
Renmark SA 235, 237, 238–9
Renner Springs NT 344
Rhyll Vic. 133
Richmond NSW 31
Richmond Qld 426, 434
Richmond Tas. 451, 455
Richmond Gaol Historic Site, Richmond Tas. 468, 476
Richmond Range NP NSW 55
Ringarooma Tas. 470
Rinyirru (Lakefield) NP (CYPAL) Qld 410, 416
River Murray International Dark Sky Reserve SA 235
Riverina NSW 11, 96–105
Riverina food and wine region NSW 98
Riverland Biosphere Reserve SA 234
Riverland wine region SA 234
Riversleigh Fossil Fields Qld 434, 435
Riverton SA 225
Robe SA 245
Robertson NSW 26
Robin Falls NT 338
Robinvale Vic. 187
Rochester Vic. 183, 187–8
Rochester Sports Museum, Rochester Vic. 183
rock climbing
  Border Ranges NP NSW 53
  Bright Vic. 196
  Burrowa-Pine Mountain NP Vic. 192
  Copeton Dam State Recreation Area NSW 63
  Evans Crown Nature Reserve NSW 15
  Freycinet NP Tas. 445
  Gardens of Stone NP NSW 13
  Glass House Mountains NP Qld 383
  Inverell NSW 66
  Kalbarri NP WA 310
  Kanangra-Boyd NP NSW 14
  Kimba SA 261
  Moogerah Peaks NP Qld 373
  Mount Arapiles-Tooan State Park Vic. 174, 178
  Mount Buffalo NP Vic. 192
  Nangar NP NSW 74
  Norseman WA 307
  Northcliffe WA 285
  Quorn SA 253
  Seymour Vic. 188
  Umbrawarra Gorge Nature Park NT 338
  Warrabah NP NSW 63
  Werribee Gorge State Park Vic. 150
Rockhampton Qld 393, 395, 397, 398–9
Rockhampton Botanic Gardens, Rockhampton Qld 392, 398
Rockingham WA 286–7
Rockley NSW 76
Rocky Cape NP Tas. 462
Rocky's Hall of Fame and Pioneers Museum, Barmera SA 235, 236

Roebourne WA 321
Roma Qld 377, 380, 391
Rosebery Tas. 457, 459
Rosebery Vic. 179
Rosebud Vic. 119, 131
Rosewood Qld 368
Roslyn NSW 25
Ross Female Factory Site, Ross Tas. 468–9, 475
Ross Tas. 441, 468–9, 475–6
Rossville Qld 414
Rottnest Island (Wadjemup) WA 269, 288, 289, 293, 294, 296–7
Rottnest Island Marine Reserve WA 297
Rowland Flat SA 216
Roxby Downs SA 253–4
Royal NP NSW 5, 20
Ruby Gap Nature Park NT 350, 352
Rubyvale Qld 392
Rupanyup Vic. 179
Rural Museum, Temora NSW 98, 104
Rushworth Vic. 182, 188
Rushworth State Forest Vic. 182
Russell River NP Qld 413
Ruston's Roses, Renmark SA 235, 238
Rutherglen Vic. 192, 195, 197, 199
Rutherglen wine region Vic. 192, 199
Rye Vic. 129, 131
Rylstone NSW 79, 81

sailboarding
  Clermont Qld 406
  Finley NSW 102
  Mulwala NSW 97
sailing *see* boating and sailing
St Albans NSW 5
St Andrews Beach Vic. 131
St Arnaud Vic. 152, 156
St Columba Falls, Pyengana Tas. 446, 448
St George Qld 380–1
St Helena Island Qld 366, 369
St Helens Tas. 445, 446, 447, 448–9
St Lawrence Qld 407
St Leonards Vic. 159
St Margaret Island Vic. 138
St Marys Tas. 449
Sale Vic. 141, 142, 145
Salmon Ponds, New Norfolk Tas. 452, 455
saltwater crocodiles 340
San Remo Vic. 134
Sanctuary Cove Qld 374, 375
Sandy Hollow NSW 39
Sandy Point Vic. 136
Sapphire Gemfields, Emerald Qld 392, 395
Sapphire Qld 392
Sarah Island Tas. 457, 459
Sarah Island Historic Site Tas. 457
Sarina Qld 403, 405, 407
Sarina Sugar Shed, Sarina Qld 403, 407
Saumarez Homestead, Armidale NSW 62, 64
Savage River NP Tas. 465
Savannah Way 342, 345
Savannahlander (train) Qld 421, 423
Sawtell NSW 49
Scamander Tas. 449
scenic flights
  Airlie Beach Qld 404
  Arkaroola SA 250
  Bicheno Tas. 447
  Blackwater Qld 393
  Borroloola NT 345
  Buccaneer Archipelago WA 323
  Coober Pedy SA 251
  Dirk Hartog Island WA 309
  Geraldton WA 314
  Great Barrier Reef Qld 409
  Hawker SA 251
  Hayman Island Qld 402
  Hervey Bay Qld 397
  Ikara–Flinders Ranges NP SA 247

492

Judbarra/Gregory NP NT 343
Kakadu NP NT 340
Kalgoorlie–Boulder WA 301
Kati Thanda–Lake Eyre NP SA 248, 249, 251, 252
Kings Creek Station NT 351
Kununurra WA 327
Lyndoch SA 219
Maroochydore Qld 388
Marree SA 252
Merimbula NSW 88
Mitchell River NP WA 324
Nhulunbuy NT 341
Nitmiluk NP NT 343
Parachilna SA 248
Purnululu NP WA 324
Surfers Paradise Qld 375
Taree NSW 50
Uluru NT 355
William Creek SA 249
Wolfe Creek Crater NP WA 324
Wynyard Tas. 465
Yeppoon Qld 399
Yulara NT 355
Scenic Railway and Skyrail, Kuranda and Cairns Qld 410, 413, 416
Scenic Rim Qld 361
Scenic World, Katoomba NSW 14
Scone NSW 35, 41
Scotts Head NSW 49
Scottsdale Tas. 467, 476
Sculptures in the Scrub, Coonabarabran NSW 75
Sea Cliff Bridge NSW 5
Sea Lake Vic. 179
Sea Life Sunshine Coast, Mooloolaba Qld 384, 388
Seaforth Qld 403
Seahorse World, Beauty Point Tas. 469, 471
Seal Bay Conservation Park SA 210, 212
Seal Rocks NSW 45
Seaspray Vic. 145
Secret Harbour WA 286
Sedan SA 235
Seisia Qld 418, 419
Sellicks Beach SA 211
Selwyn Snow Resort, Mount Selwyn NSW 91, 93
Seven Emu Station NT 344
Seven Mile Beach NP NSW 22, 25
Seventeen Seventy Qld 397
Seymour Vic. 187, 188, 197
Shackleton WA 294
Shannon NP WA 284, 286
Shark Bay WA 294, 313
Shark Bay World Heritage Area WA 309
Shear Outback, Hay NSW 99, 102
Shearwater Tas. 464
Sheep Hills Vic. 179
Sheffield Tas. 462, 463, 464
Shell Beach WA 310, 313
Shellharbour NSW 20, 25, 26–7
Shepparton Vic. 187, 188–9
Sheringa SA 261
shipwrecks
  Albany WA 278
  Aldinga Beach SA 211
  Apollo Bay Vic. 168
  Ayr Qld 404
  Barwon Bluff Marine Sanctuary Vic. 161
  Barwon Heads Vic. 161
  Beowa NP NSW 83
  Bouddi NP NSW 29
  Bunbury WA 280
  Coral Bay WA 313
  Cowell SA 260
  Currie Tas. 463
  Dunsborough WA 282
  Eaglehawk Neck/tiralina Tas. 448
  Edithburgh SA 229
  Flinders Island Tas. 477
  Great Otway NP Vic. 165
  Hamelin Bay Wreck Trail WA 274
  Houtman Abrolhos Islands WA 311
  K'gari (Fraser Island) Qld 392
  Kinchega NP NSW 107
  Kwinana Beach WA 286
  Lorne Vic. 169
  Main Beach Qld 372
  Montebello Islands WA 320
  Mulgumpin (Moreton Island) Qld 361
  Narooma NSW 88
  Normanville SA 213
  Ocean Grove Vic. 160
  Port Adelaide SA 205
  Port MacDonnell SA 245
  Port Victoria SA 228
  Port Willunga SA 210
  Rottnest Island WA 297
  Southern Ocean Shipwreck Trail SA 245
  SS Yongala Wreck, Cape Bowling Green Qld 403, 404
  Walpole WA 287
  Warrnambool Vic. 171
  Whitemark Tas. 477
  Woy Woy NSW 33
  Wyndham WA 327
  Yanchep WA 299
Shoalwater Bay Islands Marine Park WA 287
Shortland NSW 37
Shot Tower, Taroona Tas. 451, 455
Shute Harbour Qld 403, 404
Siding Spring Observatory, Coonabarabran NSW 75, 77
Silo Art Trail Vic. 179
Silvan Vic. 126
Silverton NSW 111
Simpson Desert Qld 428, 429
Singleton NSW 35, 41
Sir Henry Parkes School of Arts, Tenterfield NSW 62, 68
Sir Reginald Ansett Transport Museum, Hamilton Vic. 175, 178
Skenes Creek Vic. 165
Sketchley Cottage, Raymond Terrace NSW 37, 40
skiing
  Alpine NP Vic. 191
  Baw Baw NP Vic. 133
  Ben Lomond NP Tas. 467
  Charlotte Pass NSW 94
  Dinner Plain Vic. 195
  Falls Creek Vic. 195
  Guthega NSW 91
  Kosciuszko NP NSW 91
  Lake Mountain Vic. 123
  Mount Blue Cow NSW 91, 95
  Mount Buffalo NP Vic. 192
  Mount Buller Vic. 195
  Mount Field NP Tas. 441
  Mount Hotham Vic. 195
  Perisher NSW 91, 95
  Selwyn Snow Resort NSW 91
  Thredbo Ski Fields NSW 91, 95
skydiving and parachuting
  Airlie Beach Qld 404
  Avon Valley WA 268
  Byron Bay NSW 56
  Cessnock NSW 38
  Coffs Harbour NSW 47
  Esk Qld 367
  Locksley Vic. 185
  Mission Beach Qld 417
  Mullumbimby NSW 58
  Picton NSW 26
  Port Macquarie NSW 50
  Taree NSW 50
  Yarra Glen Vic. 127
Skypoint Observation Deck, Surfers Paradise Qld 371, 375
Smeaton Vic. 153
Smiggin Holes NSW 91
Smith Islands NP Qld 406
Smithton Tas. 463, 464–5
Smoky Bay SA 259
snorkelling
  Airlie Beach Qld 404
Bedarra Island Qld 411
Booderee NP NSW 83
Bouddi NP NSW 29
Brook Islands Qld 405
Bunbury WA 280
Bunurong Marine NP Vic. 133, 139
Busselton Jetty WA 273
Cape Range NP WA 309
Capricornia Cays NP Qld 391
Cardwell Qld 405
Carnarvon WA 312
Ceduna SA 259
Cervantes WA 291
Coral Bay WA 312, 313
Dampier Archipelago WA 320
Daydream Island Qld 402
Dunsborough WA 282
Ewens Ponds Conservation Park SA 241
Exmouth WA 314
Fitzroy Island Qld 409
Great Keppel Island Qld 392
Green Island Qld 409
Harvey WA 283
Hat Head NP NSW 45
Houtman Abrolhos Islands WA 311
Jurien Bay WA 292
Keppel Bay Islands NP Qld 399
Kingston Tas. 455
Lady Musgrave Island Qld 395
Lizard Island NP Qld 410
Lord Howe Island NSW 49
Mackay Qld 406
Magnetic Island Qld 401
Magnetic Island/Yunbenun Qld 401
Mimosa Rocks NP NSW 84
Mon Repos Conservation Park Qld 392
Montebello Islands WA 320
Mulgumpin (Moreton Island) Qld 361
Narooma NSW 88
Ningaloo Marine Park WA 310
Orpheus Island NP Qld 402
Penguin Island WA 277
Piccaninnie Ponds Conservation Park SA 241, 242
Point Samson WA 321
Port Noarlunga Reef Underwater Trail SA 212
Rockingham WA 286
Rottnest Island WA 269, 296, 297
Secret Harbour WA 286
Shellharbour NSW 27
Smith Islands NP Qld 406
Tomaree NP NSW 36
Tweed Heads NSW 59
Whitemark Tas. 477
Whyalla SA 263
William Bay NP WA 275
Windy Harbour WA 285
Yallingup WA 287
Yeppoon Qld 399
Snowtown SA 229
Snowy Hydro Discovery Centre, Cooma NSW 92, 94
Snowy Mountains NSW 11, 90–5
Snowy River NP Vic. 142
Snowy River Scenic Drive Vic. 142, 143
Snug Cove NSW 87
Sofala NSW 75, 76
Somersby NSW 29
Sorell Tas. 446, 448
Sorell Fruit Farm, Sorrell 446, 448
Sorrento Vic. 119, 129, 131
South Australian Whale Centre, Victor Harbor 210, 213
South Bruny NP Tas. 452, 453
South Bruny Tas. 440, 452, 453
South Burnett wine region Qld 366, 368, 369
South Coast NSW 11, 82–9
South Coast Track Tas. 452
South Cumberland Islands NP Qld 406
South-east Tas. 442, 450–5
South East Forest NP NSW 87
South Gippsland Vic. 120, 132–9
South Hedland WA 321
South Stradbroke Island Qld 371
South-west WA 270, 272–87
South West Rocks NSW 44, 47
South-west Wilderness Tas. 456
Southern beaches SA 205
Southern Cross WA 293, 298
Southern Highlands NSW 10, 18–27
Southern Highlands wine region NSW 20
Southern Ocean Shipwreck Trail SA 245
Southern Tasmanian wine region Tas. 448
Southport Qld 361
Southport Tas. 454
Southwest NP Tas. 452, 453
Southwood NP Qld 378
Sovereign Hill, Ballarat Vic. 119, 148, 151
Spa Country Vic. 119, 121, 146–57
Spalding SA 224
Spiky Bridge Tas., Swansea Tas. 446, 449
Split Rock Rock-art site, Laura Qld 410, 416
Springbrook NP Qld 361, 371–2, 374
Springsure Qld 391, 397, 399
Springwood NSW 15
SS Yongala Wreck, Cape Bowling Green Qld 403, 404
Staircase to the Moon
  Broome WA 324, 325
  Pilbara region WA 319
Stanley Tas. 460, 461, 462, 465
Stanley Vic. 194
Stansbury SA 231
Stanthorpe Qld 379, 381
Star of Greece, Port Willunga SA 210, 211
State Coal Mine, Wonthaggi Vic. 134, 139
Stawell Vic. 152, 173, 177, 179
Stawell Gift Hall of Fame Museum, Stawell Vic. 174, 179
Steamtown Heritage Rail Centre, Peterborough SA 221, 225
Steiglitz Vic. 162
Stirling SA 218
Stirling Range NP WA 275, 281
Stockport SA 218
Stokers Siding NSW 59
Stokes NP WA 304
Stonehenge NP 432
Stony Creek Vic. 135
Story House Museum, Yamba NSW 55, 59
Strahan Tas. 457, 458, 459
Stratford Vic. 144, 145
Strath Creek Vic. 155
Strathalbyn SA 211, 213, 218
Strathgordon Tas. 458
Strathpine Qld 361, 369
Streaky Bay SA 258, 262
Stroud NSW 49, 50
Strzelecki NP Tas. 470, 477
Strzelecki Regional Reserve SA 252
Strzelecki Track SA 251, 255
Stuart Town NSW 81
Stump-Jump Plough, Ardrossan SA 227, 229
Sturt, Charles 107, 109, 113
Sturt NP NSW 108, 112, 113
Suggan Buggan Vic. 143
Sultana Point SA 229
Summerland Farm, Alstonville NSW 55
Summerlands Vic. 133, 134
Sunbury wine region Vic. 148, 151
Sundown NP Qld 378
Sunshine Coast Qld 363, 382–9
Sunshine Coast hinterland Qld 361
Superpit Lookout, Kalgoorlie–Boulder WA 301, 305
Surat Qld 380
Surf Coast Vic. 121, 164–71

493

Surfers Paradise Qld 361, 371, 372, 373, 375

surfing
  Agnes Water Qld 398
  Alexandra Headland Qld 385, 388
  Anglesea Vic. 166, 168
  Bargara Qld 395
  Batemans Bay NSW 86
  Beaumaris Tas. 449
  Bells Beach Vic. 166
  Bermagui NSW 86
  Bicheno Tas. 447
  Bongil Bongil NP NSW 43
  Booti Booti NP NSW 43
  Bremer Bay WA 280
  Bribie Island Qld 365
  Broulee NSW 88
  Bruny Island/lunawanna-allonnah Tas. 453
  Bundjalung NP NSW 53
  Bunurong Marine NP Vic. 133
  Burleigh Heads Qld 373, 374
  Byron Bay NSW 56
  Cactus Beach SA 259
  Canunda NP SA 241
  Cape Woolamai Vic. 135
  Ceduna SA 259
  Cervantes WA 291
  Crescent Head NSW 48
  Culburra NSW 88
  Currie Tas. 463
  Denmark WA 282
  Eaglehawk Neck/Teralina Tas. 448
  Elliston SA 257
  Evans Head NSW 57
  Fairhaven Vic. 166
  George Town Tas. 473
  Geraldton WA 314
  Gerringong NSW 26
  Gladstone Qld 396
  Golden Beach Vic. 145
  Goolwa SA 211
  Greenough WA 315
  Harvey WA 283
  Hopetoun WA 307
  Houtman Abrolhos Islands WA 311
  Iluka NSW 57
  Jan Juc Vic. 166
  Jurien Bay WA 292
  Kempsey NSW 48
  Kiama NSW 26
  King Island Tas. 463
  Lennox Head NSW 53
  Lorne Vic. 169
  Low Head Tas. 470
  Macksville NSW 49
  Mallacoota Vic. 144
  Margaret River WA 285
  Marion Bay SA 231
  Miami Qld 375
  Mimosa Rocks NP NSW 84
  Mornington Peninsula NP Vic. 129
  Nambucca Heads NSW 49
  Newcastle NSW 40
  Nobby Beach Qld 375
  Noosa Heads 388
  Northampton WA 317
  Nowra NSW 88
  Ocean Grove Vic. 162
  Paradise Beach Vic. 145
  Point Leo Vic. 131
  Point Lonsdale Vic. 163
  Port Albert Vic. 138
  Port Elliot SA 212
  Port Macquarie NSW 49, 50
  Rainbow Beach Qld 384
  Robe SA 245
  Rottnest Island WA 297
  Scotts Head NSW 49
  Seaspray Vic. 145
  Secret Harbour WA 286
  Shellharbour NSW 27
  Smithton Tas. 465
  Southport Tas. 454
  Surf Coast Vic. 166
  Surfers Paradise Qld 375
  Swansea NSW 40
  Taree NSW 50
  Terrigal NSW 31
  Tomaree NP NSW 36
  Torquay Vic. 166, 171
  Tweed Heads NSW 59
  Ulladulla NSW 89
  Venus Bay SA 258
  Victor Harbor SA 213
  Wollongong NSW 27
  Woodside Beach Vic. 138
  Woolgoolga NSW 59
  Wye River Vic. 169
  Yallingup WA 287
  Yamba NSW 59
  Yorketown SA 231
  Yuraygir NP NSW 54

Susan Island NSW 55, 57
Sussex Inlet NSW 87
Sutton Forest NSW 23
Swan Hill Vic. 182, 189
Swan Hill Pioneer Settlement, Swan Hill Vic. 182, 189
Swan Hill wine region Vic. 182
Swan Reach SA 233, 235, 239
Swan Valley WA 269
Swan Valley wine region WA 269, 289, 295
Swansea NSW 40
Swansea Tas. 446, 449
Swansea Bark Mill and East Coast Museum, Swansea Tas. 446, 449
Sweers Island Qld 422, 434
Swifts Creek Vic. 198

swimming
  Abercrombie River NP NSW 15
  Airlie Beach Qld 404
  Albury NSW 100
  Aldinga Beach SA 211
  Anglesea Vic. 168
  Aramac Qld 428
  Augusta WA 279
  Australind WA 279
  Ayr Qld 404
  Babinda Qld 413
  Baird Bay SA 262
  Barmah NP Vic. 181
  Barmera SA 236
  Batchelor NT 340
  Batemans Bay NSW 86
  Bathurst NSW 76
  Beachport 241, 243
  Beauty Point Tas. 471
  Bedarra Island Qld 411
  Bega NSW 86
  Beowa NP NSW 83
  Bermagui NSW 86
  Berry Springs Nature Park NT 333
  Biloela Qld 394
  Binalong Bay Tas. 445
  Blackdown Tableland NP Qld 391
  Blackmans Bay Tas. 440
  Boat Harbour Tas. 462
  Bongil Bongil NP NSW 43
  Booderee NP NSW 83
  Boodjamulla (Lawn Hill) NP Qld 421
  Boonoo Boonoo NP NSW 63
  Booti Booti NP NSW 43
  Border Ranges NP NSW 53
  Bouddi NP NSW 29
  Bournda NP NSW 85
  Bowen Qld 405
  Bremer Bay WA 279
  Broadwater NP NSW 57
  Broulee NSW 88
  Bruny Island/lunawanna-allonnah Tas. 453
  Bunbury WA 280
  Bundjalung NP NSW 53
  Bunurong Marine and Coastal Park Vic. 139
  Burleigh Heads Qld 374
  Burnie Tas. 463
  Butterfly Gorge Nature Park NT 338
  Byron Bay NSW 56
  Cairns Qld 409, 413
  Caloundra Qld 386
  Cape Range NP WA 309
  Cardwell Qld 405
  Carnarvon WA 312
  Ceduna SA 259
  Cervantes WA 291
  Chaffey Dam NSW 63
  Christies Beach SA 212
  Cleaverville Beach WA 320
  Cobar NSW 110
  Cockburn Ranges WA 323
  Coffin Bay SA 259
  Collie WA 281
  Conningham Tas. 455
  Coobowie SA 229
  Coonamble NSW 77
  Copeton Dam State Recreation Area NSW 63
  Coral Bay WA 312
  Cowell SA 259, 260
  Cowes Vic. 136
  Cranbrook WA 281
  Crater Lakes, Camperdown Vic. 167
  Croydon Qld 423
  Culburra NSW 88
  Currimundi Lake Conservation Park Qld 385
  Dampier Archipelago WA 320
  Deua NP NSW 85
  Dharug NP NSW 29
  Douglas–Apsley NP Tas. 446
  Dover Tas. 453
  Dunolly Vic. 154
  Dunsborough WA 282
  Echuca Vic. 184
  Edithburgh SA 229
  Elliston SA 260
  Esk Qld 367
  Esperance WA 304
  Eungella NP 401
  Exmouth WA 314
  Forster–Tuncurry NSW 47
  Freycinet NP Tas. 445
  George Town Tas. 473
  Geraldton WA 314
  Gerringong NSW 26
  Giru Qld 407
  Gladstone Qld 396
  Gladstone Tas. 473
  Glenbrook NSW 13, 16
  Goolwa SA 211
  Goondiwindi Qld 380
  Gordonvale Qld 415
  Great Keppel Island Qld 392
  Greenough WA 315
  Guilderton WA 299
  Halls Creek WA 326
  Hamilton Vic. 178
  Harvey WA 283
  Hastings Tas. 451
  Hat Head NP NSW 45
  Hawley Beach Tas. 464
  Hay NSW 103
  Hervey Bay Qld 397
  Holey Plains State Park Vic. 142
  Hopetoun Vic. 185
  Hopetoun WA 307
  Howard Springs Nature Park NT 341
  Hughenden Qld 431
  Hyams Beach NSW 83
  Hyden WA 292
  Iluka 53, 57
  Ingham Qld 406
  Innamincka SA 255
  Innisfail Qld 415
  Inverell NSW 66
  Julia Creek Qld 432
  Jurien Bay WA 292
  Karijini NP WA 319
  Karratha WA 320
  Katanning WA 283
  Keppel Bay Islands NP Qld 399
  Kerang Vic. 186
  K'gari (Fraser Island) Qld 392
  Kiama NSW 26
  Kingscote SA 212
  Kingston Tas. 455
  Kwiambal NP NSW 63
  Lake Cargelligo NSW 80
  Lake Cathie NSW 50
  Lake Leschenaultia WA 268, 295
  Lake Mulwala NSW 97
  Lake Tyers Vic. 143
  Lancelin WA 299
  Laurieton NSW 48
  Laverton WA 306
  Lerderderg State Park Vic. 150
  Litchfield NP NT 332, 338
  Longreach Qld 433
  Low Head Tas. 470
  Lucinda Qld 406
  Mackay Qld 406
  Macksville NSW 49
  Magnetic Island/Yunbenun Qld 401
  Mallacoota Vic. 144
  Mandurah WA 269
  Manilla NSW 66
  Manjimup WA 284
  Mann River Nature Reserve NSW 63
  Marble Bar WA 320
  Mareeba Qld 416
  Margaret River WA 285
  Marion Bay Tas. 447
  Maroochydore Qld 387
  Maslin Beach SA 205, 211, 212
  Matarankа NT 344, 346
  Meekatharra WA 316
  Menindee NSW 111
  Midge Point Qld 407
  Millaa Millaa Qld 410
  Moana Beach SA 212
  Monto Qld 398
  Mooloolaba Qld 388
  Moonta Bay SA 230
  Mornington Peninsula NP Vic. 129
  Mount Beauty Vic. 198
  Mount Buffalo NP Vic. 192
  Mount Isa Qld 434
  Mount William NP Tas. 468
  Mundaring WA 295
  Murray Bridge SA 238
  Muttaburra Qld 434
  Nambucca Heads NSW 49
  Nannup WA 285
  Narrandera NSW 104
  Newcastle NSW 40
  Newman WA 320
  Ningaloo Marine Park WA 310
  Nitmiluk NP 343
  Noonamah NT 341
  Noosa Heads Qld 388
  Northampton WA 317
  Nowra NSW 84
  Ocean Grove Vic. 162
  Onslow WA 321
  Orford Tas. 445
  O'Sullivan Beach SA 212
  Palm Cove Qld 417
  Peaceful Bay WA 287
  Penguin Island WA 277
  Pine Creek NT 341
  Pink Lake WA 301
  Point Lonsdale Vic. 163
  Point Samson WA 321
  Port Albert Vic. 138
  Port Elliot SA 212
  Port Germein SA 231
  Port Gregory WA 317
  Port Hedland WA 321
  Port Kenny SA 262
  Port Lincoln SA 261
  Port Lowly Beach SA 258
  Port Macquarie NSW 50
  Port Pirie SA 230
  Port Rickaby SA 230
  Port Sorell Tas. 448
  Port Stephens NSW 36
  Port Victoria SA 231
  Port Vincent SA 231
  Port Wakefield SA 222
  Port Willunga SA 205, 212
  Portarlington Vic. 159
  Portsea Vic. 131
  Proserpine Qld 407
  Ravenshoe Qld 418

494

INDEX

Robe SA 245
Robinvale Vic. 187
Rockingham WA 286
Rosebud Vic. 131
Rottnest Island WA 269, 296, 297
Royal NP NSW 20
Rushworth Vic. 188
Sarina Qld 407
Scamander Tas. 449
Scotts Head NSW 49
Seven Mile Beach NP NSW 22
Shellharbour NSW 27
Smoky Bay SA 259
Southern Cross WA 297
Southport Tas. 454
Sultana Point SA 229
Swansea Tas. 449
Tallangatta Vic. 199
Tannum Sands Qld 396
Tathra NSW 89
Temora NSW 104
Tennant Creek NT 354
Terrigal NSW 31
Thallon Qld 381
The Lakes NP Vic. 141
Thirlmere Lakes NP NSW 26
Tin Can Bay Qld 389
Tinaburra Qld 419
Tocumwal NSW 104
Tomaree NP NSW 36
Torquay Vic. 171
Traralgon Vic. 138
Trephina Gorge Nature Park NT 350
Tully/Tully Gorge NP Qld 410, 419
Tweed Heads NSW 59
Twilight Cove WA 301
Ulladulla NSW 89
Umbrawarra Gorge Nature Park NT 338
Venus Bay SA 258
Wagin WA 299
Waikerie SA 239
Wallaga Lake NSW 85
Warrabah NP NSW 63
Warren NSW 79
Warrnambool Vic. 171
Warwick Qld 381
Watagans NP NSW 36
Wee Waa NSW 69
Wellington NP WA 281
West Cape Howe NP WA 278, 282
Whyalla SA 263
Wickepin WA 299
William Bay NP WA 275
Windy Harbour WA 285
Wingham NSW 51
Wollongong NSW 27
Wombeyan Caves NSW 20
Woodburn NSW 57
Woolgoolga NSW 59
Wooroonooran NP Qld 410
Woy Woy NSW 33
Wyndham WA 327
Yallingup WA 287
Yamba NSW 59
Yanchep WA 299
Yarrangobilly Caves NSW 91
Yeppoon Qld 399
Yuraygir NP NSW 54
Sydney NSW 2–3
daytrips from 4–5
Symmons Plains Tas. 473

Table Cape Lookout, Wynyard Tas. 462, 465
Tahune Forest Airwalk, Geeveston Tas. 452, 453, 454
Tailem Bend SA 238
takayna/Tarkine forests Tas. 460, 464, 465
Talaroo Hot Springs, Qld 421
Talbot Vic. 148
Talia Caves, Elliston SA 258
Tallangatta Vic. 199
Tamar Valley Tas. 473
Tamar Valley wine region Tas. 466, 469, 471, 473, 474

Tambo Qld 391, 434–5
Tamboon Vic. 141
Tamborine NP Qld 361, 372, 375
Tamborine Village Qld 361, 375
Tamrookum Qld 373
Tamworth NSW 61, 62, 67
Tanilba Bay NSW 37
Tanilba House, Tanilba Bay NSW 37, 40
Tannum Sands Qld 396
Tantanoola SA 243
Tantanoola Caves Conservation Park SA 243
Tanunda SA 216, 217
Taranna Tas. 441, 446
Taree NSW 45, 47, 50
Tarlee SA 225
Tarnagulla Vic. 154
Taronga Western Plains Zoo, Dubbo NSW 73, 78
Taroom Qld 393, 399
Taroona Tas. 440, 451, 455
Tarraville Vic. 138
Tarrawarra Museum of Art, Healesville Vic. 123, 125
Tarra–Bulga NP Vic. 134, 139
Tarrington Vic. 178
Tarkine Drive, Trowutta Tas. 462
Tasman Island Tas. 448
Tasman NP Tas. 446, 448
Tasman Peninsula/tukana Tas. 441, 446, 448
Tasmanian Arboretum, Devonport Tas. 462, 463
Tasmanian Devil Unzoo, Taranna Tas. 441, 446, 448
Tasmanian Trail Tas. 453
Tasmanian Wine Route Tas. 473
Tasmanian Wool Centra, Ross Tas. 469, 475
Tasmazia, Sheffield Tas. 462, 464
Tathra NSW 89
Tathra NP WA 291
Tatura Vic. 189
Tawonga Vic. 199
Taylors Arm NSW 45
Taylors Beach Qld 402, 406
Tea Tree Tas. 476
Telowie Gorge Conservation Park SA 231
Temora NSW 98, 104
Templin Qld 373
Tennant Creek NT 351, 354, 355
Tenterfield NSW 62, 63, 67, 68
Tenterfield Saddler, Tenterfield NSW 63, 68
Terang Vic. 179
Terowie SA 225
Terrick Terrick NP Vic. 183, 187
Terrigal NSW 5, 31
Territory Wildlife Park NT 333, 338
Tessellated Pavement, Eaglehawk Neck Tas. 446, 448
Tewantin Qld 383, 389
Texas Qld 379, 381
Thallon Qld 381
Thangool Qld 394
Thargomindah Qld 431
The Big Hole, Deua NP NSW 22
The Blues Train, Queenscliff Vic. 159, 162
The Cedars, Hahndorf SA 215, 218
The Channon NSW 59
The Dandenongs Vic. 118, 120, 122–7
The Entrance NSW 30, 31, 32
The Gap Qld 365
The Gums Qld 380
The Heartlands WA 271, 288–99
The House of Anvers Chocolate Factory, Latrobe Tas. 462, 463
The Hub, Chillagoe Qld 421
The Kimberley WA 271, 322–7
The Lakes NP Vic. 141
The Midlands Tas. 441, 443, 466–77
The North Tas. 443, 466–7
The Nut, Stanley Tas. 460, 462, 465
The Oaks NSW 24

The Palms NP Qld 366, 369
The Q Train, Queenscliff Vic. 160, 162
The Rock NSW 105
The Wildlife Habitat, Port Douglas Qld 412, 418
Theme Parks, Gold Coast Qld 372, 375
Theodore Qld 393, 399
Thevenard SA 259
Thirlmere Lakes NP NSW 26
Thirlmere NSW 20, 25
Thomson Bay WA 291, 296
Thorpdale Vic. 137
Thorsborne Trail Qld 401
Thredbo NSW 95
Thredbo Ski Fields NSW 91, 95
Thrushton NP Qld 381
Thursday Island/Waiben Qld 409, 415
Ti Tree NT 355
Tiaro Qld 399
Tibooburra NSW 111, 112, 113
Tidal River Vic. 134
Tilba Tilba NSW 83
Timber and Heritage Park, Manjimup WA 277
Timber Creek NT 344, 346
Timbertown, Wauchope NSW 44, 51
Timboon Vic. 167
Tin Can Bay Qld 389
Tinaburra Qld 419
Tinderbox Tas. 455
Tiwi Islands NT 333
Tjoritja/West MacDonnell NP NT 350
Tjuwaliyn (Douglas) Hot Springs Park NT 338
Tnorala (Gosse Bluff) Conservation Reserve NT 349
Tocumwal NSW 98, 104–5
Tocumwal Blowhole and The Rocks NSW 98, 104
Tolga Qld 413
Tom Price WA 321
Tomakin NSW 86
Tomaree NP NSW 36, 39
Toobeah Qld 380
Toodyay WA 293, 298
Toogoom Qld 397
Tooleybuc NSW 189
Tooma NSW 95
Toompine Qld 434
Toonumbar NP NSW 57
Toora Vic. 135
Tooradin Vic. 127
Toorale NP NSW 107
Toorbul Qld 367
Toowoomba Qld 377, 378, 381
Toowoomba's Parks and Gardens, Toowoomba Qld 377
Torndirrup NP WA 275, 278
Torquay Vic. 166, 171
Torrens Creek Qld 431
Torres Strait Qld 418–19
Torrington NSW 63, 65
Toukley NSW 32
Tourist Coalmine, Collie WA 277, 281
Tower Hill Wildlife Reserve Vic. 167, 171
Townsville Qld 401, 403, 404, 407
Towong Vic. 196
Toy Factory, Birdwood SA 216, 217
Traditional Owners/Lands
 Adelaide/Tarndanya area SA 202
 Adelaide Hills and Barossa Valley SA 215
 Adventure Bay/karapati Tas. 453
 Albury NSW 100
 Alice Springs (Mparntwe) NT 349, 352
 Ararat Vic. 176
 Arltunga Historical Reserve NT 353
 Arnhem Land NT 337, 341
 Ayr Qld 404
 Barrington Tops NP NSW 43
 Barron Gorge NP Qld 409
 Bay of Fires Conservation Area 445

Beaudesert Qld 373
Belair NP SA 215
Biamanga NP NSW 85
Bibbulmun Track WA 277
Big Desert Wilderness Park Vic. 187
Birdsville Qld 428
Blackdown Tableland NP Qld 391
Bladensburg NP Qld 427
Blowhole and the Rocks, Tocumwal NSW 98
Blue Mountains NP NSW 13
Bongil Bongil NP NSW 43
Booti Booti NP NSW 43
Borroloola NT 345
Brewarrina Fish Traps NSW 107, 109
Brisbane Hinterland 365
Brisbane/Meanjin Qld 358
Bruny Island/lunawanna-allonnah Tas. 451, 453
Budj Bim National Cultural Landscape Vic. 170, 173
Bunjil's Shelter, Stawell Vic. 173
Bunya Mountains NP Qld 365
Burketown Qld 422
Cairns Qld 409
Camden NSW 24
Camooweal Qld 429
Canberra ACT 8, 10
Cape York Qld 409
Capricorn and Fraser Coast Qld 391
Cattai NP NSW 29
Central West NSW 71
Chambers Pillar Historical Reserve (Itirkawara) NT 349
Clare Valley and Mid-North SA 220
Cobar NSW 110
Cooktown Qld 414
Coorabakh NP NSW 45
Coorong NP SA 233
Coral Coast and Mid-West WA 309
Corroboree Rock Conservation Reserve NT 351
Crowdy Bay NP NSW 43
Danggu Geikie Gorge NP WA 323
Darling Downs 377
Darwin/Garramilla NT 330
Didthul (Pigeon House Mountain) NSW 85, 89
Dimalurru (Tunnel Creek) NP WA 323
Dimboola Vic. 177
Dooragan NP NSW 43
Dubbo NSW 78
Dunkeld Vic. 177
East Coast Tas. 445
East Gippsland Vic. 141
Emerald Qld 395
Evans Crown Nature Reserve NSW 15
Evans Head NSW 57
Ewaninga Rock Carvings Conservation Reserve NT 351
Eyre Peninsula SA 257
Family Islands NP Qld 411
Fleurieu Peninsula Vic. 209
Flinders Ranges SA 247
Fogg Dam Conservation Reserve NT 332
Gariwerd/Grampians Vic. 172, 173
Gayndah Qld 395
Geelong, You Yangs and Bellarine Peninsula Vic. 159, 160, 161
Gladstone Qld 396
Glass House Mountains NP Qld 383
Gold Coast Qld 371
Goldfields and Spa Country Vic. 147
Goldsborough Valley State Forest Qld 411–12
Goulburn, Murray and Mallee regions Vic. 181
Granite Island SA 209
Great Ocean Road and Surf Coast Vic. 165
Great Sandy NP Qld 383
Gulf Country NT 343
Gulf Country Qld 421
Gundabooka NP NSW 107

495

Gympie Qld 386
Hat Head NP NSW 45
Hawkesbury NSW 29
Heartlands WA 289
Hermannsburg NT 353
High Country Vic. 191
Hobart/nipaluna 438
Holiday Coast NSW 43
Horsham Vic. 178
Hunter Valley NSW 35
Ikara–Flinders Ranges NP SA 247
Iytwelepenty–Davenport Ranges NP NT 351
Judbarra–Gregory NP NT 343
Kakadu NP NT 337
Karijini NP WA 319
Katherine NT 346
Keep River NP NT 344
K'gari (Fraser Island) Qld 391, 392
Kingston S. E. SA 243
Kunjarra/The Pebbles NT 354
Laverton WA 306
Limestone Coast SA 241
Lizard Island NP Qld 410
Maria Island NP Tas. 445
Meekatharra WA 316
Melbourne/Naarm area Vic. 116
Meningie SA 237
Merimbula NSW 88
Midlands and the north Tas. 467
Millaa Millaa Qld 417
Millstream–Chichester NP WA 319
Mimosa Rocks NP NSW 84
Mission Beach Qld 417
Mitchell Qld 433
Mitchell River NP WA 324
Montague Island Nature Reserve NSW 84
Moranbah Qld 406
Mornington Peninsula Vic. 129
Morton NP NSW 20
Morwell NP Vic. 135
Mossman Gorge Qld 410
Mount Augustus National Park WA 310
Mount Isa Qld 433
Mount Kaputar NP NSW 62
Mungo NP NSW 97
Murray region SA 233
Murray and Riverina NSW 97
Murray–Sunset NP Vic. 181
Mutawinji NP NSW 108
Myall Lakes NP NSW 44
Nambour Qld 388
New England NSW 61
Newcastle NSW 35
Nhulunbuy NT 341
Nimbin NSW 59
Nitmiluk NP 343, 346
Nooramunga Marine and Coastal Park Vic. 135
Normanton Qld 423
North-west Tas. 461
Northern South Australia 247
Nullarbor and Goldfields WA 301
Nullarbor SA 257
Nyinkka Nyunyu Art and Culture Centre, Tennant Creek NT 351
Outback NSW 107
Outback Qld 425
Paroo–Darling NP NSW 113
Perth/Boorloo WA 266
Phillip Island and South Gippsland Vic. 133
Pilbara WA 319
Pilliga Forest NSW 75
Pontville Tas. 476
Portland Vic. 170
Ravenshoe Qld 418
Raymond Island Vic. 142
Red Centre NT 349
Rinyirru (Lakefield) NP (CYPAL) Qld 410
Rockingham WA 286
Rottnest Island (Wadjemup) WA 269, 296
Snowy Mountains NSW 91

South Coast NSW 83
South-east Tas. 451
South-west WA 273
Southern Tablelands NSW 19
Sturt NP NSW 108
Sunshine Coast Qld 383
Sydney/Warrong area NSW 2, 10
The Kimberley WA 323
Tibooburra NSW 112
Tiwi Islands NT 333
Tjoritja/West MacDonnell NP NT 350
Tjuwaliyn (Douglas) Hot Springs Park NT 338
Tocumwal Blowhole and the Rocks NSW 98
Tomaree NP NSW 36
Toonumbar NP NSW 58
Toorale NP 107
Townsville Qld 407
Tropical North NSW 53
Tully Gorge NP Qld 410
Uluru NT 349, 350
Vulkathunha–Gammon Ranges NP SA 248-9
Wangaratta Vic. 199
Wardang Island SA 231
Warwick Qld 381
Watagans NP NSW 36
Weipa Qld 414
Werrikimbe NP NSW 45
Western Wilderness Tas. 457
Whitsunday Coast Qld 401
Wilsons Promontory NP Vic. 134
Windsor NSW 32
Wollemi NP NSW 14
Wollumbin NP NSW 53, 55
Wybalenna Historic Site, Flinders Island Tas. 469, 477
Wyperfeld NP Vic. 183
Wyrrabalong NP NSW 30
Yallock-Bulluk Marine and Coastal Park Vic. 134
Yarra Ranges Vic. 123
Yengo NP NSW 37
Yeperenye (Emily and Jessie Gaps) Nature Park NT 350
Yirrkala NT 337
Yorke Peninsula SA 227
You Yangs Regional Park Vic. 160
Traralgon Vic. 136, 138, 144
Tregole NP Qld 430
Trentham Vic. 150
Trephina Gorge Nature Park NT 350, 352
Trevallyn Tas. 468
Triabunna Tas. 449
Tropical North Coast NSW 11, 52-9
Tropical North Qld 408-19
Trowutta Tas. 462
Truganini Memorial, Bruny Island/lunawanna-allonnah 451, 453
Tuart Forest NP WA 277, 281
Tuena NSW 25
Tuggerah Lake NSW 30, 32, 33
Tully Falls NP Qld 410
Tully Gorge NP Qld 410, 419
Tully Qld 419
Tumbarumba NSW 92, 95
Tumby Bay SA 257, 262-3
Tumut NSW 95
Tuross Falls, Wadbilliga NP NSW 92
Tweed Heads NSW 54-5, 57, 59
Tweed Regional Art Gallery, Murwillumbah NSW 54, 59
Twelve Apostles Vic. 165, 167, 169
Two Peoples Bay Nature Reserve WA 278, 294
Two Wells SA 218
Tyabb Vic. 119, 131
Tynong Vic. 137

Ulan NSW 80
Ulladulla NSW 89
Ulmarra Village NSW 57
Ulupna Island Vic. 184
Uluru NT 349, 350, 355

Uluru–Kata Tjuta NP NT 306, 350
Ulverstone Tas. 460, 461, 462, 463, 465
Umagico Qld 414
Umbrawarra Gorge Nature Park NT 338
Umoona Opal Mine and Museum, Coober Pedy SA 248, 251
Umpherston Sinkhole, Mount Gambier SA 242, 244
Undara Volcanic NP Qld 421, 423
Unearthed Visitor Information Centre and Museum, Cloncurry Qld 427, 430
Ungarie NSW 105
Upper Ferntree Gully Vic. 125
Uralla NSW 62, 68-9
Urunga NSW 43, 50-1

Valla Beach NSW 49
Valley of the Giants WA 275, 277, 282
Vaughan Vic. 149
Ventnor Vic. 134
Venus Bay SA 258
Victor Harbor SA 205, 209, 211, 212-13, 218
Victoria Park Nature Reserve, Alstonville NSW 55
Victoria River Roadhouse NT 344
Victorian Goldfields Railway, Castlemaine Vic. 148
Vulkathunha–Gammon Ranges NP SA 248-9, 250

WA Museum Geraldton WA 310, 314
Wadbilliga NP NSW 92
Wadlata Outback Centre, Port Augusta SA 249, 251, 253
Wagga Wagga NSW 97, 98, 101, 103, 105
Wagga Wagga Art Gallery, Wagga Wagga NSW 98
Wagin WA 290, 293, 298-9
Wagin Historical Village, Wagin WA 290, 298
Wagonga Princess, Narooma NSW 85, 88
Waikerie SA 239
Walcha NSW 69
Waldegrave Island SA 160
Walga Rock WA 311, 313
Walgett NSW 112
Walhalla Vic. 133, 135, 138
Walkers Point Qld 395
Walkerville Vic. 136
Walla Walla NSW 101
Wallace Rockhole Aboriginal Community NT 354
Wallaga Lake, Bermagui NSW 85, 86
Wallaroo Heritage and Nautical Museum, Wallaroo SA 228
Wallaroo SA 228, 229, 230, 231
Wallingat NP NSW 43, 46
Wallington Vic. 162
Walls of Jerusalem NP Tas. 475
Walpole WA 275, 277, 287
Walpole–Nornalup NP WA 275, 287
Waltzing Matilda Centre, Winton Qld 426, 435
Walwa Vic. 196
Walyunga NP WA 269, 295
Wandiligong Vic. 193, 195, 197
Wandoan Qld 399
Wangaratta Vic. 192, 195, 197, 199
Waratah Tas. 465
Warburton Vic. 124, 126-7
Warburton WA 306
Warby–Ovens NP Vic. 193
Wardang Island SA 231
Warialda NSW 63, 69
Warrabah NP NSW 63, 66
Warracknabeal Vic. 179
Warradjan Aboriginal Cultural Centre, Cooinda NT 338
Warragul Vic. 134, 139
Warrawee Forest Reserve, Latrobe Tas. 462, 464

Warren NP WA 277, 286
Warren NSW 79
Warrnambool Vic. 165, 166, 171, 177
Warrumbungle NP NSW 73, 77
Warwick Qld 361, 378, 381
Washpool NP NSW 61
Watagans NP NSW 36, 38
Watarrka NP NT 350, 351
Waterfall Circuit, Millaa Millaa 410, 417
Waterhouse Tas. 471
Waterloo SA 225
waterskiing
  Barmera SA 236
  Batemans Bay NSW 86
  Boat Harbour Tas. 462
  Bremer Bay WA 280
  Ceduna SA 259
  Chinchilla Qld 379
  Clermont Qld 406
  Cohuna Vic. 184
  Collie WA 281
  Copeton Dam State Recreation Area NSW 63
  Cranbrook WA 281
  Crookwell NSW 25
  Croydon Qld 423
  Dunolly Vic. 154
  Echuca Vic. 184
  Ensay Vic. 198
  Freycinet NP Tas. 445
  Gladstone Qld 396
  Gladstone Tas. 473
  Hamilton Tas. 474
  Hay NSW 103
  Inverell NSW 66
  Jurien Bay WA 292
  Katanning WA 283
  Kojonup WA 284
  Lake Broadwater Conservation Park Qld 378
  Lake Cargelligo NSW 80
  Lake Eildon NP Vic. 193
  Lake Hindmarsh Vic. 174
  Lake Jindabyne NSW 91
  Lake Kununurra WA 327
  Lake Mulwala NSW 97
  Lake Tinaroo Qld 412
  Lithgow NSW 17
  Manilla NSW 66
  Mathoura NSW 185
  Menindee NSW 111
  Monto Qld 398
  Moranbah Qld 406
  Morwell Vic. 138
  Murray Bridge SA 238
  Nagambie Vic. 187
  Nambucca Heads NSW 49
  Narawntapu NP Tas. 468
  Narrabri NSW 67
  Narrandera NSW 104
  Nelson Vic. 171
  Nowra NSW 88
  Paynesville Vic. 145
  Port Lincoln SA 261
  Port Pirie SA 230
  Port Vincent SA 231
  Portland Vic. 170
  Proserpine Qld 407
  Richmond Qld 434
  Robe SA 245
  Robinvale Vic. 187
  Shellharbour NSW 27
  Stansbury SA 231
  Stanthorpe Qld 381
  Tallangatta Vic. 199
  Taroom Qld 399
  Townsville Qld 407
  Ulladulla NSW 89
  Wagin WA 299
  Waikerie SA 239
  Wallaga Lake NSW 85
  Wingham NSW 51
Watervale SA 224
Watheroo NP WA 294
Wauchope NSW 44, 45, 49, 51
Wauchope NT 349, 355

Wave Rock WA 290, 292
Wedderburn Vic. 148, 154, 156
Weddin Mountains NP NSW 73, 79
Wee Jasper NSW 22
Wee Waa NSW 69
Weeroona Island SA 231
Weethalle NSW 105
Weipa Qld 412, 415, 419
Welford NP Qld 427, 432
Wellington SA 238
Wellington Caves NSW 73, 81
Wellington NP WA 281
Wellington NSW 79, 81
Welshpool Vic. 139
Wentworth NSW 97, 99, 105
Wentworth Falls NSW 13
Werribee Vic. 119
Werribee Gorge State Park Vic. 150
Werribee Park and the Open Range Zoo, Werribee Vic. 119
Werrikimbe NP NSW 45
West Cape Howe NP WA 278, 282
West Coast Heritage Centre, Zeehan Tas. 457, 459
West Coast Visitor Information Centre, Strahan Tas. 458, 459
West Coast Wilderness Railway, Queenstown and Strahan Tas. 458, 459
West Gippsland Arts Centre, Warragul Vic. 134, 139
West Wyalong NSW 105
Westbury Tas. 473, 477
Western Cape Cultural Centre – Achimbun, Weipa Qld 412, 419
Western Plains Cultural Centre, Dubbo NSW 75, 78
Western Wilderness Tas. 442, 456-9
Wet Tropics World Heritage Area Qld 408, 409, 410, 411, 413, 414, 417
Wetlands and Y Water Discovery Centre, Yea Vic. 183, 189
whale-watching
 Airlie Beach Qld 404
 Albany WA 278
 Augusta WA 275, 278
 Ballina NSW 56
 Booderee NP NSW 83
 Bremer Bay WA 280
 Burleigh Heads NP Qld 374
 Byron Bay NSW 56
 Cape Byron NSW 53
 Cocklebiddy WA 303
 Coral Bay WA 313
 Dampier Archipelago WA 320
 Dampier Peninsula WA 324
 Denmark WA 282
 Dhilba Guuranda-Innes NP SA 227
 Dunsborough WA 282
 Eden NSW 87
 Esperance WA 304
 Exmouth WA 314
 Far West Coast Marine Park SA 257
 Fitzgerald River NP WA 273
 Great Ocean Drive WA 301
 Hat Head NP NSW 45
 Hayman Island Qld 402
 Hervey Bay Qld 397
 Iluka NSW 57
 Jervis Bay JBT 87
 Kalbarri NP WA 310
 K'gari (Fraser Island) Qld 392
 Lady Elliot Island Qld 392
 Leeuwin-Naturaliste NP WA 274
 Lennox Head NSW 53
 Logans Beach Vic. 166
 Lombadina WA 324
 Merimbula NSW 88
 Montague Island Nature Reserve NSW 84
 Narooma NSW 88
 Nelson Bay NSW 39
 Noosa Heads NP Qld 384
 Port Elliott SA 212
 Port Stephens NSW 36
 Portland Vic. 170
 Recherche Archipelago WA 302

Rottnest Island Marine Reserve WA 297
Sarina Qld 407
Seal Rocks NSW 45
Tweed Heads NSW 59
Venus Bay SA 258
Victor Harbor SA 210
Warrnambool Vic. 166, 171
Windy Harbour WA 285
Yallingup WA 287
Yamba NSW 59
Wheeler Island Qld 411
White Cliffs NSW 113
White Mountains NP Qld 431
Whitemark Tas. 468, 477
whitewater rafting
 Alpine NP Vic. 191
 Anglers Rest Vic. 198
 Avon Valley NP WA 268, 289
 Cairns Qld 413
 Chiltern-Mount Pilot NP Vic. 193
 Coffs Harbour NSW 47
 Ensay Vic. 198
 Franklin-Gordon Wild Rivers NP Tas. 458
 Kalbarri NP WA 310
 Mission Beach Qld 417
 Tahune Forest Reserve Tas. 452
 Townsville Qld 407
 Tully/Tully Gorge NP Qld 410, 419
 Wellington NP WA 281
 Wooroonooran NP Qld 410
Whitfield Vic. 192
Whitsunday Coast Qld 363, 400-7
Whitsunday Island Qld 402
Whitsunday Islands Qld 402
Whitsunday NP Qld 402
Whyalla SA 258, 263
Whyalla Maritime Museum, Whyalla SA 258, 263
Wiangaree NSW 57-8
Wickepin WA 299
Wickham WA 321
Wilcannia NSW 113
Wild Cattle Island Qld 396
wildflowers
 Aldinga Beach SA 211
 Alexandra Vic. 194
 Alpine NP Vic. 191
 Augusta WA 278
 Australind WA 279
 Avon Valley NP WA 289
 Avon Valley WA 268
 Baw Baw NP Vic. 133
 Ben Lomond NP Tas. 467
 Bibbulum Track WA 277
 Bicheno Tas. 447
 Boyup Brook WA 279
 Bribie Island Qld 360
 Bridport Tas. 469, 471
 Brisbane Ranges NP Vic. 151
 Brisbane Water NP NSW 29
 Bulahdelah NSW 46
 Burnie Tas. 463
 Cape Le Grand NP WA 301
 Cape Range NP WA 309
 Carnamah WA 291
 Cervantes WA 291
 Cocopara NP NSW 98
 Conimbla NP NSW 78
 Corrigin WA 291
 Cradle Mountain-Lake St Clair NP Tas. 461
 Cranbrook WA 281
 Cranky Rock Nature Reserve NSW 63
 Crows Nest Qld 379
 Donald Vic. 177
 Dunsborough WA 282
 Eneabba WA 291
 Enfield State Park Vic. 149
 Esperance WA 304
 Euroa Vic. 185
 Fitzgerald River NP WA 273, 279
 Frank Hann NP WA 293
 French Island NP Vic. 129
 Freycinet NP Tas. 445

Gascoyne Junction WA 310, 314
Gawler Ranges NP SA 257
Geraldton WA 314
Gilgandra NSW 79
Grampians NP Vic. 173
Hyden WA 292
Jurien Bay WA 292
Kalbarri/Kalbarri NP WA 310, 315, 316
Kattang Nature Reserve NSW 48
Keith SA 237
Kellerberrin WA 292
Kilmore Vic. 155
Kingston Tas. 455
Kojonup WA 284
Kulin WA 293
Lake Cargelligo NSW 80
Lake Grace WA 293
Lake King WA 293
Lake Mountain Vic. 123
Latrobe Tas. 464
Laurieton NSW 48
Laverton WA 306
Leeuwin-Naturaliste NP WA 287
Lerderderg State Park Vic. 150
Lesueur NP WA 292
Little Desert NP Vic. 174
Mansfield Vic. 197
Miles Qld 380
Moora WA 294
Moore River NP WA 292
Morwell NP Vic. 135
Mount Buffalo NP Vic. 192
Mount Granya State Park Vic. 193
Mount Magnet WA 317
Mount Richmond NP Vic. 170
Mullewa WA 317
Murray Bridge SA 238
Murray-Sunset NP Vic. 181
Murrurundi NSW 39
Nannup WA 285
Narrogin WA 295
Norseman WA 307
Northcliffe WA 285
Onkaparinga River NP SA 210
Pemberton WA 286
Pingelly WA 296
Pyramid Hill Vic. 187
Pyrenees Ranges State Forest Vic. 150
Rockingham WA 286
Rushworth State Forest Vic. 182, 188
Snowy Mountains NSW 90
South Bruny NP Tas. 452
Stawell Vic. 179
Stirling Range NP WA 275
Tathra NP WA 291
Torndirrup NP WA 275
Ulladulla NSW 89
Victor Harbor SA 213
Wagin WA 299
Walyunga NP WA 295
Warby-Ovens NP Vic. 193
Warialda NSW 69
Werrikimbe NP NSW 45
Wickepin WA 299
Wyperfeld NP Vic. 183
Yarram Vic. 139
York WA 299
Wildlife Habitat, The, Port Douglas Qld 412, 418
wildlife-watching
 Abercrombie River NP NSW 15
 Adelaide River NT 332, 337
 Alice Springs Desert Park NT 349
 Alice Springs NT 352
 Alice Springs Reptile Centre NT 352
 Alice Springs Telegraph Station Historical Reserve NT 351
 Amamoor State Forest Qld 385
 Apollo Bay Vic. 167, 168
 Atherton Qld 413
 Babinda Qld 413
 Baird Bay SA 262
 Bald Rock NP NSW 61
 Ballarat Vic. 152
 Ballina NSW 56

Barwon Heads Vic. 161
Batchelor NT 340
Bathurst NSW 76
Beauty Point Tas. 468, 469, 471
Bellingen NSW 46
Black Mountain (Kalkajaka) NP Qld 414
Bladensburg NP Qld 427
Bollon Qld 381
Boonoo Boonoo NP NSW 63
Bordertown SA 236
Bowling Green Bay NP Qld 403
Bribie Island Qld 360
Brighton Tas. 469
Broome WA 325
Bruny Island/lunawanna-allonnah Tas. 451
Bunbury WA 273, 280
Bundaberg Qld 394
Bunya Mountains NP Qld 365
Burketown Qld 422
Burleigh Heads Qld 374
Burnie Tas. 463
Burrowa-Pine Mountain NP Vic. 192
Burrum Coast NP Qld 393
Cairns Qld 412
Cape Bridgewater Vic. 165
Cape Byron NSW 53
Cape Range NP WA 309
Capricornia Cays NP Qld 391
Carnarvon NP Qld 391, 399
Carnarvon WA 312
Casterton Vic. 176
Ceduna SA 259
Charleville Qld 425
Cleland National Park SA 215
Cohuna Vic. 184
Conway NP Qld 403
Coolah Tops NP NSW 33
Coral Bay WA 313
Cowes Vic. 136
Cranky Rock Nature Reserve NSW 63
Crater Lakes NP Qld 411
Croajingolong NP Vic. 141
crocodiles NT 340
Crowdy Bay NP NSW 43
Crows Nest NP Qld 378
Culgoa NP NSW 109
Currumbin Wildlife Sanctuary Qld 371
Daintree Qld 415
Dalrymple NP Qld 403
David Fleay Wildlife Park, Burleigh Heads Qld 372
Denham WA 313
Derghold State Park Vic. 175
Deua NP NSW 22
Diamantina NP Qld 426
Dimalurru (Tunnel Creek) NP WA 323
Dooragan NP NSW 43
Dryandra Woodland WA 289
Dunsborough WA 282
East Coast Natureworld, Bicheno Tas. 446
Enfield State Park Vic. 149
Eungella NP 401
Exmouth WA 314
Flinders Chase NP SA 209
Flinders Island SA 260
Forster-Tuncurry NSW 47
François Peron NP WA 294
French Island NP Vic. 129
Freycinet NP Tas. 445
Geelong Vic. 162
George Town Tas. 473
Girringun NP Qld 401
Goose Island Conservation Park SA 231
Gosford NSW 5, 31
Goulburn River NP NSW 74
Great Otway NP Vic. 165
Great Sandy Strait Qld 392
Greater Bendigo NP Vic. 149
Gundabooka NP NSW 107
Gunnedah NSW 65

Gunns Plains Tas. 462
Hamilton Island Qld 402
Herberton Range NP Qld 412
Hervey Bay Qld 397
Hiskisson NSW 87
Idalia NP Qld 427
Ikara–Flinders Ranges NP SA 247
Ingham Qld 406
Jervis Bay JBT 97
Julia Creek Qld 432
Jurien Bay Marine Park WA 292
Kakadu NP 337
Kalbarri NP WA 310
Karijini NP WA 319
Karumba Qld 423
Kenilworth State Forest Qld 383
K'gari (Fraser Island) Qld 392
Koo Wee Rup Vic. 137
Koondrook State Forest NSW 99
Kununurra WA 327
Kuranda Qld 416
Kutini–Payamu NP Qld 419
Kwiambal NP NSW 63
Kyabram Fauna Park 183
Lady Elliot Island Qld 392
Lady Julia Percy Island Vic. 170
Lakes Entrance Vic. 143
Latrobe Tas. 462, 464
Lerderderg State Park Vic. 150
Lismore NSW 58
Little Desert NP Vic. 174
Lizard Island NP Qld 410
Lower Glenelg NP Vic. 166
Lyndoch SA 219
Mac and Rose Chalmers Conservation Reserve NT 351
Macksville NSW 49
Main Range NP Qld 371
Mandurah WA 269
Manjimup WA 284, 294
Mannum SA 237
Maria Island NP Tas. 445
Mariala NP Qld 427
Mary River NT 333
Minerva Hills NP Qld 399
Minlaton SA 230
Mole Creek Tas. 475
Mon Repos Conservation Park Qld 392
Monkey Mia WA 310, 313
Moorrinya NP Qld 431
Morgan SA 237
Morton NP NSW 20
Mount Buangor State Park Vic. 175
Mount Hypipamee NP Qld 412
Mount Kaputar NP NSW 62
Mount Yarrowyck Nature Reserve NSW 63
Mulgumpin (Moreton Island) Qld 361
Mundaring WA 295
Murramarang NP NSW 84
Murray River NP, Katarapko Section SA 234
Naracoorte Caves NP SA 242
Narawntapu NP Tas. 468
Nelson Bay NSW 39
Ngalba Bulal NP Qld 415
Ningaloo Marine Park WA 310
Nitmiluk NP NT 343
Noonamah NT 341
Normanton Qld 423
Northcliffe WA 286
Nymboida NSW 57
Ocean Grove Vic. 162
Orpheus Island NP Qld 402
Penguin Island SA 243
Phillip Island Vic. 119, 134
Pingelly WA 286
Platypus Reserve, Bombala NSW 84, 87
Point Labatt Conservation Park SA 258
Pontville Tas. 476
Port Bonython SA 258
Port Douglas Qld 412
Port Hedland WA 321

Port Kenny SA 262
Port Lincoln SA 262
Port Macquarie NSW 50
Port Stephens NSW 36
Portland Vic. 170
Proserpine Qld 407
Pyrenees Ranges State Forest Vic. 150
Queenscliff Vic. 163
Ravenshoe Qld 418
Raymond Island Vic. 142
Raymond Terrace NSW 40
Recherche Archipelago WA 302
Richmond Tas. 476
Rinyirru (Lakefield) NP (CYPAL) Qld 410
Rockingham WA 287
Rottnest Island Marine Reserve WA 297
Rottnest Island (Wadjemup) WA 269, 294, 296
Roxby Downs SA 254
Rushworth State Forest Vic. 182
Sarina Qld 407
Scotts Head NSW 49
Seal Bay Conservation Park SA 210
Shark Bay World Heritage Area WA 294
Sheffield Tas. 464
Sheringa SA 261
Sorrento Vic. 131
Southwood NP Qld 378
Sturt NP NSW 108
Susan Island NSW 55
Swan Reach SA 239
Telowie Gorge Conservation Park SA 231
Territory Wildlife Park NT 333, 338
Tin Can Bay Qld 389
Torndirrup NP WA 275
Tower Hill Wildlife Reserve Vic. 167
Tumby Bay SA 263
Tweed Heads NSW 59
Two Peoples Bay Nature Reserve WA 278, 294
Victoria Park Nature Reserve, Alstonville NSW 55
Waikerie SA 239
Wedderburn Vic. 156
Whitemark Tas. 477
Willandra NP NSW 75
Wingham NSW 44
Wycheproof Vic. 179
Yea Vic. 189
Yeppoon Qld 399
Yookamurra Sanctuary SA 235
Yungaburra Qld 419
Yuraygir NP NSW 54
Wildlife Wonders, Apollo Bay Vic. 167, 168
Wiliyan-Ngurru NP Qld 427, 429
Willandra NP NSW 75
William Bay NP WA 275, 282
William Creek SA 249, 255
William Ricketts Sanctuary, Olinda Vic. 118, 123, 126
Willie Creek Pearl Farm, Broome WA 324, 325
Willie Smith's Apple Shed, Huonville 452, 454
Willows Qld 392
Willunga SA 211, 213
Wilmington SA 254
Wilmot Tas. 464
Wilpena SA 247, 254
Wilpena Pound Resort SA 247, 254
Wilsons Promontory NP Vic. 134
Wimmera–Mallee Pioneer Museum, Jeparit Vic. 175, 178
Winchelsea Vic. 153, 160
Windorah Qld 429, 432
Windsor NSW 30, 31, 32
windsurfing
Australind WA 279
Beachport Conservation Park SA 241
Boreen Point Qld 385

Caloundra Qld 386
Cervantes WA 291
Crows Nest Qld 379
Geraldton WA 314
Hamilton Island Qld 402
Hopetoun WA 307
Houtman Abrolhos Islands WA 311
Inverloch Vic. 137
Jurien Bay WA 292
Lancelin WA 299
Milang SA 210
Narrabri NSW 67
Noosa Heads Qld 388
Port Gregory WA 317
Rockingham WA 286
Secret Harbour WA 286
Shellharbour NSW 27
South Stradbroke Island Qld 371
Tallangatta Vic. 199
Tennant Creek NT 354
Wickepin WA 299
Windy Harbour WA 285
Wine Food Farmgate Trail, Mornington Peninsula Vic. 130
Wineglass Bay Tas. 445, 447
wineries
Adelaide Hills wineries SA 204
Angaston SA 217
Bairnsdale Vic. 143
Balingup WA 279
Banrock Station Wine & Wetland Centre SA 233
Barossa Valley wine region SA 215, 216, 217
Barraba NSW 64
Beaconsfield Tas. 471
Beechworth wine region Vic. 191, 194
Bellingen NSW 46
Bendigo wine region Vic. 147, 152
Berridale NSW 93
Berrima NSW 23
Berry NSW 23
Birdwood SA 217
Blackwood Valley wine region WA 276, 279, 282
Bright Vic. 195
Brisbane and surrounds wine region Qld 372
Bulahdelah NSW 46
Bungendore NSW 19
Canberra wine region NSW 19
Canowindra NSW 77
Castlemaine Vic. 153
Clare Valley wine region SA 221, 223–4
Coal River wine region Tas. 441, 476
Colac Vic. 169
Coleraine Vic. 177
Coonabarabran NSW 77
Coonawarra wine region SA 241
Cootamundra NSW 101
Cowes Vic. 136
Cowra wine region NSW 71
Cranbrook WA 281
Crows Nest Qld 379
Cygnet Tas. 453
Denmark WA 282
Dubbo NSW 78
Dunalley Tas. 447
Dwellingup WA 283
East Coast wineries Tas. 447
Eden Valley wine region SA 215
Ensay Vic. 198
Exeter Tas. 473
Fleurieu wine region SA 209, 213
Forbes NSW 79
Frankland River wine region WA 281
Geelong and the Bellarine wine region Vic. 159, 161
Geographe wine region WA 276, 280, 284
George Town Tas. 473
Gippsland wine region Vic. 133
Gladstone Qld 396
Glenrowan wine region Vic. 192, 196

Goolwa SA 211
Gosford NSW 31
Grampians wine region Vic. 174, 176
Granite Belt wine region Qld 377
Great Southern wine region WA 273–4, 285
Great Western Vic. 174
Griffith NSW 102
Gulgong NSW 80
Gympie Qld 387
Hahndorf SA 205, 218
Harcourt Vic. 153
Harvey WA 283
Healesville Vic. 125
Heathcote wine region Vic. 148, 154
Hunter Valley wine region NSW 5, 35, 38
Huon Valley Tas. 441
Inverell NSW 66
Kangaroo Island wines SA 210
King Valley wine region Vic. 192, 197
Kyneton Vic. 155
Lakes Entrance Vic. 133
Langhorne Creek wine region SA 209, 210
Leeton NSW 104
Loddon Valley wine region Vic. 154
Loxton SA 237
Lyndoch SA 217, 219
Macedon Ranges wine region Vic. 148, 157
McLaren Vale wine region SA 209, 210, 212
Maitland SA 230
Mandurang Vic. 152
Manjimup wine region WA 274, 284
Mansfield Vic. 197
Mareeba Qld 416
Margaret River wine region WA 274, 285
Melrose SA 252
Milawa Vic. 197
Mintaro SA 225
Montville Qld 387
Mornington Peninsula wine region Vic. 130
Mount Beauty Vic. 198
Mount Benson wine region SA 242, 245
Mount Tamborine wine region Qld 372, 375
Mudgee region NSW 72, 80
Murchison Vic. 188
Murray Bridge SA 238
Murray Darling wine region Vic. 181
Muswellbrook NSW 39
Myrtleford Vic. 198
Nagambie wine region Vic. 181–2, 187
Nannup WA 285
New England wine region NSW 62, 68
North Tamborine Qld 375
Nuriootpa SA 219
Orange wine region NSW 72, 81
Oxley 197
Padthaway wine region SA 234, 236
Peel wine region WA 276, 284
Pemberton wine region WA 274, 284, 286
Perth Hills wine region WA 289, 295
Port Lincoln SA 262
Port Macquarie NSW 50
Port Sorell Tas. 448, 464
Port Stephens WA 39
Pyrenees wine region Vic. 148
Raleigh NSW 46
Ranelagh Tas. 441, 454
Red Hill Vic. 130
Renmark SA 238
Riverina food and wine region NSW 98
Riverland wine region SA 234
Robinvale Vic. 187
Rockingham WA 286
Rutherglen wine region Vic. 192

498

Rylstone NSW 81
St George Qld 380
Scone NSW 41
Seymour Vic. 188
Sheffield Tas. 464
Shellharbour NSW 27
South Burnett wine region Qld 366, 368, 369
Southern Highlands wine region NSW 20
Southern Tasmanian wine region Tas. 448
Sunbury wine region Vic. 148, 151
Sutton Forest NSW 23
Swan Hill wine region Vic. 182
Swan Valley wine region WA 269, 290, 295
Swansea Tas. 449
Tamar Valley wine region Tas. 466, 469, 471, 473, 474
Tanunda SA 216, 219
Tasmanian Wine Route, Tas. 473
Tocumwal NSW 104
Toodyay WA 298
Tumbarumba NSW 95
Wagga Wagga NSW 105
Warburton Vic. 127
Wauchope NSW 51
Wellington NSW 81
Wollombi NSW 38
Woodside SA 204
Wrattonbully wine region SA 244
Yackandandah Vic. 199
Yallingup WA 287
Yarra Valley wine region Vic. 124, 125, 127
Yea Vic. 189
Young NSW 27
Wingham NSW 44, 51
Wingham Museum, Wingham NSW 44
Wingham Brush, Wingham NSW 44, 51
Wing's Wildlife Park, Gunns Plains Tas. 462, 465
Winton Qld 425, 426, 431, 435
Winton Wetlands Vic. 192, 194
Wirrabara SA 252
Wisemans Ferry NSW 5, 29, 33
Witjira NP SA 249
Wittenoom WA 321
wildflowers, Wyndham WA 327
Wodonga Vic. 100, 197, 199
Wolfe Creek Crater NP WA 324
Wollemi NP NSW 14, 41, 81
Wollombi NSW 38
Wollongong NSW 5, 21, 22, 25, 27
Wollongong Botanic Garden, Keiraville NSW 20, 27
Wollumbin NP NSW 53, 55
Wombat State Forest Vic. 150, 151
Wombeyan Caves NSW 20, 25
Wondai Qld 369
Wonga Qld 417
Wonthaggi Vic. 134, 135, 139
Woodbridge Tas. 452
Woodburn NSW 57
Woodend Vic. 157
Woodford Qld 360, 367, 369
Woodgate Qld 393, 395
Woodside SA 204
Woodside Vic. 138
Woody Island WA 302
Woolgoolga NSW 55, 57, 59
Woolmers Estate, Longford Tas. 469, 475
Woombye Qld 384
Woomera SA 254
Woorim Qld 365
Wooroolin Qld 368
Wooroonooran NP Qld 410, 412, 413, 417
Wootton NSW 46
Workshops Rail Museum, Ipswich Qld 366, 368
Wowan Qld 398
Woy Woy NSW 33

Wrattonbully wine region SA 244
Wudinna SA 258, 263
Wyandra Qld 431
Wybalenna Historic Site, Emita Tas. 469, 477
Wycheproof Vic. 179
Wycliffe Well NT 351
Wye River Vic. 169
Wyndham WA 323, 324, 327
Wynyard Tas. 461, 462, 463, 465
Wyong NSW 33
Wyperfeld NP Vic. 183, 185
Wyrrabalong NP NSW 30, 32

Yackandandah Vic. 197, 199
Yalgoo WA 317
Yalgorup NP WA 284
Yallingup WA 287
Yallock–Bulluk Marine and Coastal Park Vic. 134
Yamba NSW 55, 57, 59
Yambuk Vic. 170
Yanchep WA 299
Yanchep NP WA 269, 290, 299
Yanco NSW 104
Yandilla Qld 381
Yandina Qld 384, 389
Yandoit Vic. 154
Yanga NP NSW 100
Yangie Trail SA 258, 259
Yankalilla SA 213
Yarns Artwork in Silk, Deloraine Tas. 469, 472
Yarra Glen Vic. 124, 127
Yarra Junction Vic. 124

Yarra Ranges NP Vic. 124
Yarra Valley Vic. 119, 120, 122–7
Yarra Valley wine region Vic. 124, 125, 127
Yarragon Vic. 135
Yarram Vic. 139
Yarraman Qld 369
Yarrawarra Aboriginal Cultural Centre, Corindi Beach NSW 55
Yarrawonga Vic. 104, 187, 189
Yarriabini NP NSW 49
Yarrongobilly Caves NSW 91
Yarta Purtli – Port Augusta Cultural Centre, Port Augusta SA 249, 253
Yass NSW 21, 27
Yea Wetlands Discovery Centre, Yea Vic. 183, 189
Yea Vic. 183, 189
Yengo NP NSW 30, 33, 37
Yeperenye (Emily and Jessie Gaps) Nature Park NT 350
Yeppoon Qld 391, 392, 397, 399
Yerranderie NSW 14, 24
yidaki purchase in the NT 347
Yirrkala NT 337, 341
Yookamurra Sanctuary, Sedan SA 235
York WA 293, 299
Yorke Peninsula SA 207, 226–31
Yorketown SA 231
You Yangs Regional Park Vic. 159, 160
Young Historical Museum, Young NSW 22, 27
Young NSW 21–2, 25, 27
Youngtown Tas. 468

Yowah Qld 431
Yulara NT 355
Yungaburra Qld 409, 415, 419
Yuraygir NP NSW 54, 59

Zeehan Tas. 457, 459
Zoodoo Zoo, Richmond Tas. 452, 455
zoos
 Batemans Bay NSW 85
 Beerwah Qld 361, 383
 Bundaberg Qld 394
 Cessnock NSW 38
 Clifton Qld 378
 Gosford NSW 5, 31
 Halls Gap Vic. 178
 Healesville Sanctuary Vic. 123, 125
 Merimbula NSW 88
 Mogo NSW 84
 Monarto Safari Park SA 235
 Moonlit Sanctuary Wildlife Conservation Park, Pearcedale Vic. 130
 Nelson Bay NSW 39
 Nowra NSW 88
 Port Macquarie NSW 50
 Richmond Tas. 441, 470
 Somersby NSW 29
 Strathpine Qld 369
 Taranna Tas. 441, 446
 Taronga Western Plains Zoo, Dubbo NSW 73
 Werribee Open Range Zoo, Werribee Vic. 119
 Wollongong NSW 27
 Woombye Qld 384

Photography credits

Cover: Jennifer Martin, iStock; **Endpapers:** Darren Tierney, iStock & JanelleLugge, iStock

Contents: ii TEQ (top), DNSW (bottom); iii: Shutterstock (top left), TA (top right & middle), Filippo Rivetti/DNSW (bottom); **Prelims:** iv TA; v TA (top & bottom), DNSW (middle); vii DNSW; viii Wayne Quilliam; ix TA (top & middle 2), Don Fuchs/DNSW (bottom); x Wayne Quilliam; xii TA; xiv cb_travel/Shutterstock; xv TA; xvi-xvii TA; xviii-xix TEQ. **NSW & ACT:** all DNSW, except: 4 Cessnock City Council/DNSW; 5 (2nd from top) Unsplash/Michael Io; 5 (2nd from bottom) Shutterstock; 8 Ramingining Artists; 9 (top) Willowtreehouse/Shutterstock, Alamy (middle), TA (bottom); 11 (top) Alexandra Adoncello/DNSW; 12 Joe Wigdhal Photography/DNSW; 15 (bottom) Tyson Mayr/DNSW; 23 (top) If & When Social Media Agency; 28 David Ross/Destination Central Coast/DNSW; 34 Nikki To/DNSW; 37 (top) Jarryd Salem; 38 Lee Nichols; 40 (top) Cessnock City Council; 41 (bottom) Australian Silo Art Trail; 45 (bottom) Northern Rivers Tropical NSW; 54 My Clarence Valley; 79 Australian Fossil and Mineral Museum; 86 Eurobodalla Coast Tourism; 92 & 94 (bottom) Don Fuchs/DNSW; 97 Tyson Mayr/DNSW. **Victoria:** all VV, except: 140-1 Jessica Shapiro, Destination Gippsland/VV; 158 Ross Hyde/Shutterstock; 159 Alice Barker; 162 Nicole Patience/Shutterstock; 163 K.A.Willis/Shutterstock; 172 Belinda VanZanen, Parks Victoria/VV; 178 Shutterstock; 182 & 185 Ewen Bell, Visit Swan Hill/VV; 190 Ride High Country/VV; 191 Andrew Railton, Mt Buller/VV. **SA:** all TA, except: 202 Andre Castellucci, SATC/TA; 203 (top) Stewart Bishop, TA; 205 (top) SATC; 208 Virgin Australia; 224 Steven Giles/Shutterstock; 226 myphotobank.com.au/Shutterstock; 227 & 231 Felipe da Costa Stahelin/Shutterstock; 230 Danita Delimont Alamy; 236 (bottom) Sean Heatley/Shutterstock; 240 Raphael Christinat, Shutterstock; 241 Groenewegphotography/Shutterstock; 244 (bottom) Robe; 252 Edward Haylan/Shutterstock. **WA:** all TA, except: 267 (top) Gordon Bell, Shutterstock; 269 Maneerat Shotiyanpitak/Shutterstock; 269 (bottom) Philip Schubert/Shutterstock; 276 (middle), 279 (bottom), 282 (top) Voyager Estate; 297 fritx16/Shutterstock; 298 David Dennis/Shutterstock; 302 electra/Shutterstock; 304 Hide's Edoventure/Shutterstock; 306 Annalucia/Shutterstock; 309 & 318 Jakub Maculewicz/Shutterstock; 310 (bottom) Australia's Coral Coast; 319 Chameleons Eye/Shutterstock; 320 (top) becauz gao/Shutterstock; 320 (bottom) Alamy; 325 Australian Pacific Touring; 327 Jacob Kinny,/Shutterstock. **NT:** all TA, except: 331 (top) Little Panda29/Shutterstock; 333 (top) Shutterstock; 333 (bottom 3) Liam Neal; 336 2021 Photography/Shutterstock; 337, 342 & 345 Sean Scott/TA; 338 (bottom) EA Given/Shutterstock; 343 Nick Brundle Photography/Shutterstock; 346 Josh Prostejovsky, Shutterstock; 355 P J Spooner/Shutterstock. **Queensland:** all TEQ, except: 367 (bottom) Rob D the Baker/Shutterstock; 368 jax10289/Shutterstock; 369 Roger Harrison, Shutterstock; 400 Melissa Findley/TEQ. **Tasmania:** all TA, except: 462 (top) Shujax10289/Shutterstock; 466 Tasmanian Walking Company/Great Walks of Australia/TA; 468 (bottom) Premier Travel Tasmania; 471 (bottom) Andrew Bain/Alamy.

Abbreviations

DNSW Destination New South Wales

NLA National Library of Australia

SATC South Australian Tourism Commission

TA Tourism Australia

TEQ Tourism and Events Queensland

VV Visit Victoria

TWA Tourism Western Australia

This fortieth edition published in 2023 by Hardie Grant Explore, an imprint of Hardie Grant Publishing.

Hardie Grant Explore (Melbourne)
Wurundjeri Country
Building 1, 658 Church Street
Richmond, Victoria 3121

Hardie Grant Explore (Sydney)
Gadigal Country
Level 7, 45 Jones Street
Ultimo, NSW 2007

www.hardiegrant.com/au/explore

All rights reserved. No part of this publication may be reproduced, stored in a retrieval system or transmitted in any form by any means, electronic, mechanical, photocopying, recording or otherwise, without the prior written permission of the publishers and copyright holders.

The moral rights of the author have been asserted.

Copyright concept, text, maps and design © Hardie Grant Publishing 2023

The maps in this publication incorporate data from the following sources:

© Commonwealth of Australia (Geoscience Australia), 2006. Geoscience Australia has not evaluated the data as altered and incorporated within this publication, and therefore gives no warranty regarding accuracy, completeness, currency or suitability for any particular purpose.

Incorporates or developed using [Roads Feb 2022, Hydrology Nov 2012] © Geoscape Australia for Copyright and Disclaimer Notice see geoscape.com.au/legal/data-copyright-and-disclaimer

Parks and reserves data which is owned by and copyright of the relevant state and territory government authorities. © Australian Capital Territory. www.ACTmapi.act.gov.au Creative Commons Attribution 4.0 International (CC BY 4.0) © State of New South Wales (Department of Planning, Industry and Environment) Creative Commons Attribution 4.0 International (CC BY 4.0) © State of New South Wales (Department of Primary Industries) Creative Commons Attribution 4.0 International (CC BY 4.0) © State of Victoria (Department of Environment, Land, Water and Planning) Creative Commons Attribution 4.0 international (CC BY 4.0) © State of South Australia (Department for Environment and Water) Creative Commons Attribution 4.0 Australia (CC BY 4.0) © State of Western Australia (Department of Biodiversity, Conservation and Attractions) Creative Commons Attribution 3.0 Australia (CC BY 3.0 AU) © Northern Territory Government of Australia (Department of Environment, Parks and Water Security) Creative Commons Attribution 4.0 International (CC BY 4.0) © The State of Queensland (Department of Environment and Science) Creative Commons Attribution 4.0 International (CC BY 4.0) © Commonwealth of Australia (Great Barrier Reef Marine Park Authority) Creative Commons Attribution 4.0 International (CC BY 4.0) © State of Tasmania (Department of Primary Industries, Parks, Water and Environment) Creative Commons Attribution 3.0 Australia (CC BY 3.0 AU)

Australian Bureau of Statistics (July 2022) Regional population, 2021 'Table 1. Estimated resident population, Statistical Areas Level 2 (ASGS2021), Australia, https://www.abs.gov.au/statistics/people, accessed 9 February 2023

A catalogue record for this book is available from the National Library of Australia

Hardie Grant acknowledges the Traditional Owners of the Country on which we work, the Wurundjeri People of the Kulin Nation and the Gadigal People of the Eora Nation, and recognises their continuing connection to the land, waters and culture. We pay our respects to their Elders past and present.

For all relevant publications, Hardie Grant Explore commissions a First Nations consultant to review relevant content and provide feedback to ensure suitable language and information is included in the final book. Hardie Grant Explore also includes traditional place names and acknowledges Traditional Owners, where possible, in both the text and mapping for their publications.

Traditional place names are included in *palawa kani*, the language of Tasmanian Aboriginal People, with thanks to the Tasmanian Aboriginal Centre.

Explore Australia 2024
ISBN 9781741178319

10 9 8 7 6 5 4 3 2 1

Full acknowledgements for individual contributions to previous editions of *Explore Australia* can be found in those publications. The publisher would like to thank the following individuals and organisations in the creation of this fortieth edition:

Publisher
Melissa Kayser

Project editor
Alice Barker

Writer
Andrew Bain

First Nations consultant
Jamil Tye, Yorta Yorta

Cartographer
Emily Maffei

Cover design
Akiko Chan

Typesetting
Megan Ellis

Colour reproduction by Megan Ellis and Splitting Image Colour Studio

Printed and bound in China by LEO Paper Products LTD.

MIX
Paper from responsible sources
FSC® C020056

The paper this book is printed on is certified against the Forest Stewardship Council® Standards and other sources. FSC® promotes environmentally responsible, socially beneficial and economically viable management of the world's forests.

Disclaimer: While every care is taken to ensure the accuracy of the data within this product, the owners of the data (including the state, territory and Commonwealth governments of Australia) do not make any representations or warranties about its accuracy, reliability, completeness or suitability for any particular purpose and, to the extent permitted by law, the owners of the data disclaim all responsibility and all liability (including without limitation, liability in negligence) for all expenses, losses, damages (including indirect or consequential damages) and costs which might be incurred as a result of the data being inaccurate or incomplete in any way and for any reason.

Publisher's Disclaimers: The publisher cannot accept responsibility for any errors or omissions. The representation on the maps of any road or track is not necessarily evidence of public right of way. The publisher cannot be held responsible for any injury, loss or damage incurred during travel. It is vital to research any proposed trip thoroughly and seek the advice of relevant state and travel organisations before you leave.

Publisher's Note: Every effort has been made to ensure that the information in this book is accurate at the time of going to press. The publisher welcomes information and suggestions for correction or improvement.

This fortieth edition published by Hardie Grant Publishing Pty Ltd, 2023
First published by George Phillip & O'Neil Pty Ltd, 1980
Second edition 1981
Third edition 1983
Reprinted 1984
Fourth edition 1985
Fifth edition 1986
Sixth edition published by Penguin Books Australia Ltd, 1987
Seventh edition 1988
Eighth edition 1989
Ninth edition 1990
Tenth edition 1991
Eleventh edition 1992
Twelfth edition 1993
Thirteenth edition 1994
Fourteenth edition 1995
Fifteenth edition 1996
Sixteenth edition 1997
Seventeenth edition 1998
Eighteenth edition 1999
Nineteenth edition 2000
Twentieth edition 2001
Twenty-first edition 2002
Twenty-second edition published by Explore Australia Publishing Pty Ltd, 2003
Twenty-third edition 2004
Twenty-fourth edition 2005
Twenty-fifth edition 2006
Twenty-sixth edition 2007
Twenty-seventh edition 2008
Twenty-eighth edition 2009
Twenty-ninth edition 2010
Thirtieth edition 2011
Thirty-first edition 2012
Thirty-second edition 2013
Thirty-third edition 2014
Thirty-fourth edition 2015
Thirty-fifth edition 2016
Thirty-sixth edition published by Hardie Grant Publishing Pty Ltd, 2018
Thirty-seventh edition 2019
Thirty-eighth edition 2021
Thirty-ninth edition 2022